All in One®

Recommended by **Teachers,** Trusted by **Toppers**

ECONOMICS

Class 11

EVERYTHING YOU NEED TO SCORE

- Simplified NCERT Theory
- Chapter Exercise
- All Types of Exam Pattern Questions
- CBQs; MCQs, A-R, Case Based
- Sample Question Papers

CBSE Exams 2026

Author
Maria Rashid

arihant
SUCCESS AND NOTHING LESS

arihant
SUCCESS AND NOTHING LESS

ARIHANT PRAKASHAN
(School Division Series)

卐 *ADMINISTRATIVE & PRODUCTION OFFICES*

Regd. Office

'Ramchhaya' 4577/15, Agarwal Road, Darya Ganj, New Delhi -110002
Tele: 011- 47630600, 43518550; Fax: 011- 23280316

卐 *Head Office*

Kalindi, TP Nagar, Meerut (UP) - 250002, Tel: 0121-7156203, 7156204

卐 *SALES & SUPPORT OFFICES*

Agra, Ahmedabad, Bengaluru, Bareilly, Chennai, Delhi, Guwahati, Hyderabad, Jaipur, Jhansi, Kolkata, Lucknow, Nagpur & Pune.

PO No : TXT-XX-XXXXXXX-X-XX

Published By Arihant Publications (India) Ltd.

For further information about the books published by Arihant, log on to www.arihantbooks.com or e-mail at info@arihantbooks.com

Follow us on

卐 *PRICE* ₹550.00

PRODUCTION TEAM

Publishing Managers
Mahendra Singh Rawat & Keshav Mohan

Cover Designer
Salman Shaikh

Inner Designer
Ankit Tyagi

Project Head
Saurabh Gupta

Page Layouting
Amit Bansal

Proof Reader
Apoorvi

Index *cum* Study Planner

One Book- Endless Features

to Help you Succeed

In this Chapter

At the start of each chapter, all the chapter topics have been listed, so that students may know what they are going to study.

02

CHAPTER

Collection of data refers to collecting the information about a situation/study or case on which statistical investigation is to be done.

YOUR STUDY GOALS

2.1 Sources of Data
2.2 Methods of Collecting Primary Data
2.3 Sources of Secondary Data
2.4 Census and Sample Surveys
2.5 Statistical Errors
2.6 Important Agencies of Secondary Data

YOUR PRACTICE GOAL

- Objective Type Questions (68 Qs ; MCQs, A-R, Statements, Matching, Concept Identification)
- Subjective Questions (22 SAs, 10 LAs)

Collection of Data

2.1 Sources of Data

Data is a tool which helps in reaching a suitable conclusion on any problem by providing information. Data is collected to understand, explain and analyse a problem to find cause behind it.

It can be collected from following sources

1. **Internal Sources of Data**
   It is the data collected from within an organisation using its own records and reports. e.g. Annual financial statements, operational reports, sales data, etc.
2. **External Sources of Data**
   It is the data collected from outside an organisation. e.g. Public records, industry reports, market surveys, data on medical tourists, etc. External sources can be further classified as primary and secondary data.

Solved Question 1 Represent the following marks scored by students of class XI in statistics in discrete frequency distribution

20	15	5	8	7	12	40	15	8	7	20
15	10	8	12	21	32	40	20	15	8	12

Sol. Discrete Frequency Distribution

Marks	Tally Marks	Frequency
5	|	01
7	||	02
8	||||	04
10	|	01
12	|||	03
15	||||	04
20	|||	03
21	|	01
32	|	01
40	||	02
	Total	22

Solved Examples

Solved Examples have been given in between the theory. These examples have been solved in step-by-step manner, so that students can learn the problem solving process completely.

Complete Theory in Each Chapter

Each chapter has Complete, Easy to Understand and Simplified theory covering latest syllabus and latest NCERT Textbook. Theory is developed in such a way that it is suitable for all types of learners.

2.1 Sources of Data

Data is a tool which helps in reaching a suitable conclusion on any problem by providing information. Data is collected to understand, explain and analyse a problem to find cause behind it.

It can be collected from following sources

1. **Internal Sources of Data**
   It is the data collected from within an organisation using its own records and reports. e.g. Annual financial statements, operational reports, sales data, etc.
2. **External Sources of Data**
   It is the data collected from outside an organisation. e.g. Public records, industry reports, market surveys, data on medical tourists, etc. External sources can be further classified as primary and secondary data.

Types of Data

Primary Data
Data collected directly by an investigator for the first time through methods such as personal interviews, questionnaires, telephonic interview or surveys.

Secondary Data
Data previously collected and processed by others, which is later used by investigators. This includes data from published sources (e.g. Government reports) and unpublished sources (e.g. Academic thesis).

One Book- Endless Features

to Help you Succeed

Boxed Matter

Information in the boxes is given to focus on important points related to the concepts.

Pilot Survey

It is a trial survey which helps to test the effectiveness of the questionnaire on a small group.

The pilot survey helps in

- Pre-testing of the questionnaire, so as to know the short-comings and drawbacks of the questions.
- Assessing the suitability of the questions, clarity of instructions, performance of enumerators and the cost and time involved in the actual survey.

Mind Map

A quick revision visual tool for the complete chapter.

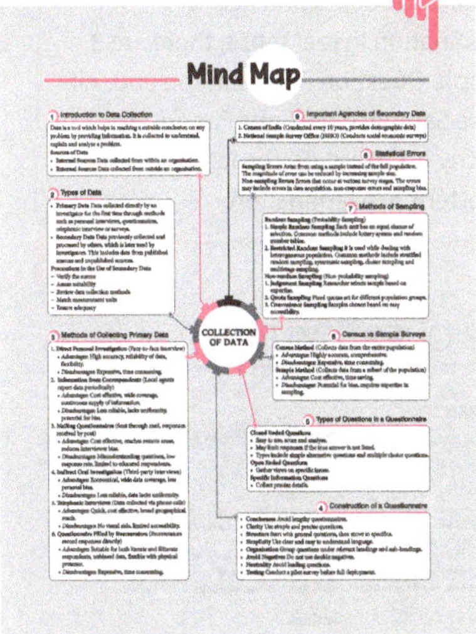

Exam Pattern Questions

To make students completely prepared for examination, Exam Pattern Questions are provided after theory. These questions cover all types of questions, like; MCQs, Case Based Questions, Assertion-Reason, SA & LA Type Questions. All the questions are fully explained helping students to understand, how to write the answers to get full marks in the exam.

EXAM PATTERN QUESTIONS

Objective Type Questions

Multiple Choice Questions (MCQs)

1. Which of the following is an example of internal sources of data?
   (a) Data from government publications
   (b) Data collected from medical tourists
   (c) Annual statement of a company's profit and loss
   (d) Reports of committees
2. Data that is collected for the first time by an investigator through personal interviews or questionnaires is known as ....
   (a) primary data (b) secondary data
   (c) internal data (d) statistical data
3. Identify the term that refers to the individual from whom statistical information is being collected.
   I. Respondents II. Variable
   III. Enumerators IV. Investigators
   Codes **Competency Based Que**
   (a) Only I (b) Both II and III
   (c) Only IV (d) All of these
7. In which situation is indirect oral investigation most suitable? **Competency Based Que**
   (a) When detailed information is required from a specific respondent
   (b) When the area of investigation is very large
   (c) When the investigator needs direct contact with the respondent
   (d) When respondents are highly educated
8. Which method allows for continuous and regular information collection over a large area?
   (a) Direct personal investigation
   (b) Telephonic interviews
   (c) Information from correspondents
   (d) Questionnaire filled by enumerators
9. Which method is most suitable for collecting data from a small and localised population?
   (a) Mailing questionnaires
   (b) Direct personal investigation
   (c) Telephonic interviews
   (d) Information from correspondents

Self Assessment Test

A Complete Test of Chapter in Exam Format

SELF ASSESSMENT TEST

Objective Type Questions

1. Industry reports are an example of ....
   (a) internal data (b) external data
   (c) personal data (d) None of these
2. Which of the following refers to the information about different variables collected for analysis?
   (a) Data (b) Respondents
   (c) Investigator (d) Enumerator
3. Which data collection method involves local agents collecting and reporting information periodically to an investigator, who processes it for analysis?
   (a) Direct observation
   (b) Census method
   (c) Sampling method
   (d) Information from correspondents
4. Which of the following is an advantage of the census method?
   (a) Results are not reliable
   (b) More chances of biasness at the time of collecting data
   (c) Data is collected for each and every item of the population
   (d) Cannot be applied in case of infinite population

Answers 1. (b) 2. (a) 3. (d) 4. (c) 5. (b) 6. (c) 7. (b) 8. (a)

Short Answer Type Questions

9. Differentiate between external and internal sources of data with examples.
10. Non-random sampling methods do not give every unit in the population an equal chance of being selected. Do you agree?
11. What are non-response errors? Explain with examples.
12. Define the following terms
    (i) Investigators (ii) Respondents
13. Explain the sources of secondary data with examples.
14. "Secondary data is collected, processed and tabulated by various national and state-level agencies." List and explain the two major national agencies for secondary data.

Long Answer Type Questions

15. Differentiate between census and sample method.
16. What are sampling and non-sampling errors? Explain

One Book- Endless Features

to Help you Succeed

Sample Project

Changing Consumer Awareness among Households

Relation Between Level of Education and Consumer Awareness

Name :
Class :
Roll No. :
Subject :
School :

Submitted by .... Submitted to ....

Project Work

487

Sample Question Papers

To make students practice of examination in real sense, there are 3 Sample Question Papers at the end. All these Sample Questions Papers are exactly prepared on the latest syllabus & pattern of examination.

Project Work

As per the latest syllabus, 20 marks have been kept for the project work. To make the students ready for this portion of the syllabus, a Sample Project Report has been given.

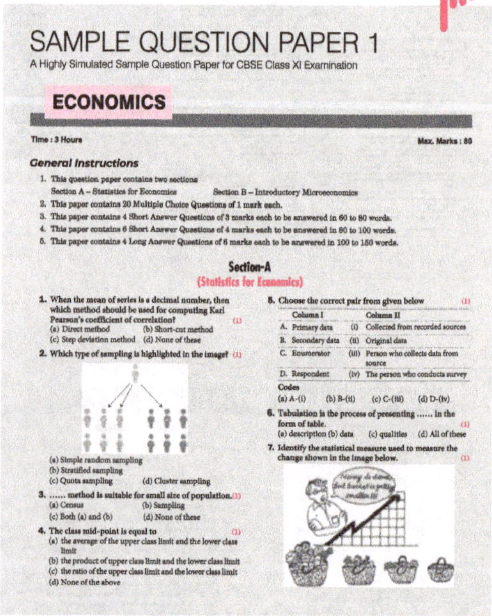

SAMPLE QUESTION PAPER 1

A Highly Simulated Sample Question Paper for CBSE Class XI Examination

ECONOMICS

Time : 3 Hours Max. Marks : 80

General Instructions

1. This question paper contains two sections
   Section A – Statistics for Economics Section B – Introductory Microeconomics
2. This paper contains 20 Multiple Choice Questions of 1 mark each.
3. This paper contains 4 Short Answer Questions of 3 marks each to be answered in 60 to 80 words.
4. This paper contains 6 Short Answer Questions of 4 marks each to be answered in 80 to 100 words.
5. This paper contains 4 Long Answer Questions of 6 marks each to be answered in 100 to 150 words.

Section-A
(Statistics for Economics)

1. When the mean of series is a decimal number, then which method should be used for computing Karl Pearson's coefficient of correlation? (1)
   (a) Direct method (b) Short-cut method
   (c) Step deviation method (d) None of these
2. Which type of sampling is highlighted in the image? (1)
   (a) Simple random sampling
   (b) Stratified sampling
   (c) Quota sampling (d) Cluster sampling
3. ...... method is suitable for small size of population. (1)
   (a) Census (b) Sampling
   (c) Both (a) and (b) (d) None of these
4. The class mid-point is equal to (1)
   (a) the average of the upper class limit and the lower class limit
   (b) the product of upper class limit and the lower class limit
   (c) the ratio of the upper class limit and the lower class limit
   (d) None of the above
5. Choose the correct pair from given below (1)

Column I	Column II
A. Primary data	(i) Collected from recorded sources
B. Secondary data	(ii) Original data
C. Enumerator	(iii) Person who collects data from source
D. Respondent	(iv) The person who conducts survey

Codes
(a) A-(i) (b) B-(ii) (c) C-(iii) (d) D-(iv)

6. Tabulation is the process of presenting ...... in the form of table. (1)
   (a) description (b) data (c) qualities (d) All of these
7. Identify the statistical measure used to measure the change shown in the image below. (1)

Latest Course Structure

Duration : 3 Hours		Max Marks : 80
Units		**Marks**
Part A : Statistics for Economics		
1.	Introduction	15
2.	Collection, Organisation and Presentation of Data	
3.	Statistical Tools and Interpretation	25
		40
Part B : Introductory Microeconomics		
1.	Introduction	4
2.	Consumer's Equilibrium and Demand	14
3.	Producer Behaviour and Supply	14
4.	Forms of Market and Price Determination Under Perfect Competition with Simple Applications	8
		40
Part C: Project Work		20
	Theory Paper (40+40 = 80 Marks)	

PART A
STATISTICS FOR ECONOMICS

In this course, the learners are expected to acquire skills in collection, organisation and presentation of quantitative and qualitative information pertaining to various simple economic aspects systematically. It also intends to provide some basic statistical tools to analyse, and interpret any economic information and draw appropriate inferences. In this process, the learners are also expected to understand the behaviour of various economic data.

Unit 1 Introduction

What is Economics?
Meaning, Scope, Functions and Importance of Statistics in Economics

Unit 2 Collection, Organisation and Presentation of Data

Collection of Data - Sources of Data - Primary and Secondary; How Basic Data is Collected with concept of Sampling, Methods of Collecting Data; Some Important Sources of Secondary Data: Census of India and National Sample Survey Organisation.

Organisation of Data: Meaning and Types of Variables; Frequency Distribution.

Presentation of Data: Tabular Presentation and Diagrammatic Presentation of Data:

(I) Geometric forms (bar diagrams and pie diagrams),
(ii) Frequency diagrams (histogram, polygon and ogive) and (iii) Arithmetic line graphs (time series graph).

Unit 3 Statistical Tools and Interpretation

(For all the numerical problems and solutions, the appropriate economic interpretation may be attempted. This means, the students need to solve the problems and provide interpretation for the results derived.)

Measures of Central Tendency- Arithmetic Mean, Median and Mode

Correlation - Meaning and Properties, Scatter Diagram; Measures of Correlation - Karl Pearson's Method (two variables ungrouped data) Spearman's Rank Correlation (Non-repeated ranks and Repeated ranks).
Introduction to Index Numbers - Meaning, Types - Wholesale Price Index, Consumer Price Index and Index of Industrial Production, Uses of Index Numbers; Inflation and Index Numbers, Simple Aggregative Method.

PART B

INTRODUCTORY MICROECONOMICS

UNIT 4 Introduction

Meaning of Microeconomics and Macroeconomics; Positive and Normative Economics

What is an Economy? Central Problems of an Economy: What, How and for Whom to Produce; Concepts of Production Possibility Frontier and Opportunity Cost.

UNIT 5 Consumer's Equilibrium and Demand

Consumer's Equilibrium - Meaning of Utility, Marginal Utility, Law of Diminishing Marginal Utility, Conditions of Consumer's Equilibrium Using Marginal Utility Analysis.

Indifference Curve Analysis of Consumer's Equilibrium-The Consumer's Budget (Budget Set and Budget Line), Preferences of the Consumer (Indifference Curve, Indifference Map) and Conditions of Consumer's Equilibrium.

Demand, Market Demand, Determinants of Demand, Demand Schedule, Demand Curve and Its Slope, Movement Along and Shifts in the Demand Curve; Price Elasticity of Demand-Factors Affecting Price Elasticity of Demand; Measurement of Price Elasticity of Demand - Percentage Change Method and Total Expenditure Method.

UNIT 6 Producer Behaviour and Supply

Meaning of Production Function – Short-Run and Long-Run

Total Product, Average Product and Marginal Product. Returns to a Factor

Cost: Short Run Costs - Total Cost, Total Fixed Cost, Total Variable Cost; Average Cost; Average Fixed Cost, Average Variable Cost and Marginal Cost-Meaning and Their Relationships.

Revenue - Total, Average and Marginal Revenue - Meaning and Their Relationship.

Producer's Equilibrium-Meaning and Its Conditions in Terms of Marginal Revenue-Marginal Cost. Supply, Market Supply, Determinants of Supply, Supply Schedule, Supply Curve and Its Slope, Movements Along and Shifts in Supply Curve, Price Elasticity of Supply; Measurement of Price Elasticity of Supply - Percentage-Change Method

UNIT 7 Perfect Competition - Price Determination and Simple Applications

Perfect Competition - Features; Determination of Market Equilibrium and Effects of Shifts in Demand and Supply. (Short Run Only)

Simple Applications of Demand and Supply: Price Ceiling, Price Floor.

PART C

Project in Economics

PART : A

STATISTICS FOR ECONOMICS

01
CHAPTER

Economics is the study of mankind in the ordinary business of life. *- Alfred Marshall*

Introduction to Economics and Statistics

▼ YOUR STUDY GOALS

▼ YOUR PRACTICE GOAL

- Objective Type Questions (60 Qs ; MCQs, A-R, Statements, Matching, Concept Identification)
- Subjective Questions (18 SAs, 8 LAs)
- Self Assessment Test (8 MCQs, 6 SAs, 3 LAs)

1.1 Meaning of Economics

Economics is the study of how people and society choose to employ scarce resources that could have alternative uses, in order to produce various commodities that satisfy their wants and to distribute them among various persons and groups in society.

Adam Smith referred economics as the 'science of wealth', focusing on how wealth is created, distributed and consumed within society.

Lionel Robbins viewed economics as "a science that examines human behaviour in relation to scarce resources that have alternative uses." This highlights the decision-making process, that individuals and societies go through when allocating limited resources to satisfy various needs and wants.

Core Focus Economics centers on how people and societies choose to allocate limited resources to satisfy unlimited wants. This leads to the study of **economic problems** arising from resource scarcity.

Budgeting at Home

A family with a limited monthly income has to decide how to allocate their money between essentials like food, rent, and utilities and non-essentials like entertainment and savings. This decision-making process reflects the core of economics i.e. managing resources (income) to satisfy various needs and wants.

Economic Problem

The economic problem arises due to the reasons specified below

Economic Problems
- Scarce resources
- Human wants are unlimited
- Resources have alternative uses

1. **Scarce Resources** Scarcity is the fundamental cause of all economic problems. It occurs when resources are insufficient to fulfill all human wants. Since resources are limited or scarce, people must decide which wants to satisfy.
2. **Unlimited Human Wants** Human wants are unlimited and recurring in nature. As soon as one want is satisfied, another emerges, creating a constant demand for resources.
3. **Alternative Uses of Resources** The resources available can be used in multiple ways, leading to the necessity of making choices. e.g. A farmer can choose to use land to grow different types of crops, each fulfilling different needs.

Important Terms Related to Economics

- **Consumer** One who buys goods or services to satisfy his own personal wants or those of his family.
- **Seller** One who sells goods with a view to earn profits.
- **Producer** One who produces goods (a farmer or a manufacturer) or services, is a producer.
- **Service Holder** One who is in a job, working for some other person and is getting paid for it, is a service holder or an employee.
- **Service Provider** One who provides some kind of services to others for a payment like doctors, lawyers, etc. is a service provider.
- **Employer** An employer is one who employs others and gives them wages.

Types of Activities

All human beings are engaged in some activity or the other in order to satisfy their wants and desires. e.g. Farmers are engaged in their field, workers are engaged in factories, professionals (like CA's or Doctors) are occupied with their profession, etc.

Depending on wants, all human activities can broadly be divided into two categories

Types of Activities

- **Economic**: Economic activities are actions taken with the primary goal of earning a livelihood. These activities include earning, spending, investing and distributing money. The are crucial for the functioning of the economy.

  Main Economic Activities
  - **Production** It is the process of converting raw materials into finished goods, such as manufacturing cars from steel and other components.
  - **Consumption** The act of satisfying needs and wants by using goods and services, like purchasing groceries or using public transportation.
  - **Distribution** It is the allocation of income among various factors of production, such as paying wages to workers or dividends to shareholders.

- **Non-economic**: Non-economic activities are actions that are not primarily aimed at earning money but are performed for personal satisfaction, social welfare or cultural reasons. These activities do not have a direct economic benefit.

  e.g. Volunteering at a charity, a parent teaching their child or someone pursuing a hobby like painting without the intention of selling their artwork.

Economic Activities

Production A farmer growing crops like wheat or rice is engaged in production, transforming raw resources into food products that can be sold in the market.

Consumption A family purchasing groceries for their daily meals is engaging in consumption, utilising their income to satisfy their basic needs.

Distribution A company distributing profits as dividends to shareholders after earning revenue from sales is an example of distribution in action.

1.2 Meaning of Statistics

Statistics refers to data and the methods of collecting data. So, it is basically used in two distinct senses; in plural sense and in singular sense.

Statistics in Plural Sense

In the plural sense, 'statistics' refers to a collection of numerical data gathered systematically with a specific purpose. According to **Yule and Kendall**, statistics consist of quantitative data influenced by various factors.

Statistics (Plural Sense)

A store tracks its monthly sales for different products, like the store sells 200 units of Product A and 150 units of Product B in a month. These numbers are collected systematically to analyse sales trends and make business decisions.

Quantitative and Qualitative Data

- **Quantitative Data** Data whose variables can be measured and expressed in numerical terms is referred to as quantitative data. e.g. Prices, income, height, weight, daily temperature, etc.
- **Qualitative Data** Data whose variables cannot be measured and expressed in numerical terms is referred to as qualitative data. e.g. Good, bad, intelligence, etc.

However, in context of statistics, only quantitative data is considered.

Statistics, when used in plural sense, must possess the following characteristics

- Aggregate of facts.
- Affected by multiplicity of causes.
- Collected for pre-determined purpose.
- Mutually relatable and comparable.
- Numerically expressed.
- Reasonable standard of accuracy.
- Collected in systematic manner.

Statistics in Singular Sense

In singular sense, statistics means statistical methods. It can be defined as the science of collection, organisation, presentation, analysing and interpretation of numerical data.

Studying statistics as a singular noun implies the knowledge of various stages of statistical study.

Stages	Description	Example
Collection of Data (C)	Gather all the relevant data about the problem.	Walmart collects data on daily sales of different products over a month. They gather information on quantities sold, prices and times of sales.
Organisation of Data (O)	Sort and arrange the data by editing, classifying and putting it into tables.	Walmart organises the sales data by sorting it into categories like product type, date and sales amount. They create spreadsheets and tables to manage and track this information efficiently.
Presentation of Data (P)	Show the data clearly using charts, graphs and tables.	Walmart uses graphs and charts to visually represent the sales data. For instance, they might use bar charts to show weekly sales for various products and line graphs to illustrate sales trends over time.

Stages	Description	Example
Analysis of Data (A)	Examine the data using techniques like averages and correlations to understand patterns.	Walmart analyses the data to identify patterns, such as which products are the best sellers and during which times of day sales peak. They calculate averages and look for correlations between sales and promotional periods.
Interpretation of Data (I)	Draw conclusions from the data analysis to make informed decisions.	Based on the analysis, Walmart decides which products should be restocked more frequently and which promotions are most effective. This information guides decisions on inventory management and marketing strategies.

Scope of Statistics

Statistics affects everybody and touches life at many points. It is an indispensable tool which facilitates the study of many subjects and helps in various operational activities.

Its scope is discussed below

Scope	Explanation
Statistics in Planning	• Statistics are very important for effective planning. By analysing historical data, planners can create frameworks to achieve future goals. • e.g. A city government uses past traffic data to plan new road construction and traffic management strategies.
Statistics in Business and Management	• Businesses rely on statistical data for decision-making in areas like marketing, production, finance, investment, etc. • e.g. A company analyses sales data to determine the best times for promotional campaigns.
Statistics in Industry	• Industries use statistics for quality control to ensure products meet standards. • e.g. A car manufacturer uses control charts to monitor production quality and detect defects.
Statistics in Economics	• Economic analysis heavily depends on statistical data to understand and forecast economic trends. • e.g. Economists use unemployment rates and GDP data to evaluate economic performance and guide policy decisions.
Statistics Use by the Government	• Governments use statistics to manage and plan public services and policies effectively. • e.g. A national census collects data on population size and distribution to allocate resources and plan infrastructure.

Nature of Statistics

The nature of statistics can be studied as both, i.e. as a science as well as an art.

As a Science

- Statistics is considered as science because it involves systematic knowledge and methods for studying relationships between variables to derive generalised results. It follows a structured approach similar to other sciences but differs in that it often deals with variables influenced by multiple factors, which are not always quantifiable.
- e.g. In medical research, statistical methods are used to understand the relationship between a drug and its effects, taking into account various factors like dosage, patient health and age.

As an Art

- Statistics is also seen as an art because it involves applying theoretical knowledge to address real life problems. It emphasises practical application, using data to solve specific issues and make informed decisions.
- e.g. In business, statistical techniques are applied to analyse customer preferences and optimise marketing strategies, tailoring solutions based on real world data.

Conclusion

Statistics integrates both scientific methods for understanding data relationships and artistic application for solving practical problems, making it a versatile tool in various fields.

Functions of Statistics

- It expresses facts relating to different phenomena in numbers.
- It enlarges an individual's knowledge, experience and power of reasoning.
- It compares the data relating to facts.
- It helps businesses in forecasting.
- It facilitates policy formulations.
- It presents complex data in a simple form so that it becomes easy to understand and comprehend.

Importance of Statistics in Economics

Importance of Statistics

- Understanding economic problems
- Working out cause and effect relationships
- Construction of economic theories or models
- Economic forecasting
- Formulation of policies
- Presenting facts in a definite form
- Condensing elaborative data into a concise form

1. **Understanding Economic Problems**
   - Statistics help economists identify and analyse economic issues like inflation and unemployment by providing data to understand their causes and to develop effective policies.
   - e.g. Analysing unemployment rates to identify trends and causes, and then formulating policies to reduce unemployment.
2. **Working Out Cause and Effect Relationships**
   - Economists use statistical methods to determine the relationships between different variables, verifying if and how one variable affects another.
   - e.g. Studying the relationship between income levels and consumer spending to understand how changes in income affect spending habits.
3. **Construction of Economic Theories or Models**
   - Statistical data helps in developing and testing economic theories by validating assumptions about relationships between variables.
   - e.g. Testing the assumption that higher education levels lead to higher income by analysing data on education and income levels.
4. **Economic Forecasting**
   - Statistics enable economists to predict future trends and changes by analysing current data, aiding in strategic planning and decision-making.
   - e.g. Forecasting future inflation rates based on current economic indicators to guide monetary policy.
5. **Formulation of Policies**
   - Statistical analysis assists in formulating economic policies by providing data on variables such as production and demand, which informs decisions on resource allocation.
   - e.g. Determining oil import levels by analysing data on domestic production and future demand.
6. **Presenting Facts in a Definite Form**
   - Statistics ensure that economic facts are presented clearly and accurately, reducing ambiguity and providing precise information.
   - e.g. Instead of saying 'average income is high,' stating 'average income is ₹ 7,500 per month' provides clear and specific information.
7. **Condensing Elaborative Data into a Concise Form**
   - Statistics summarise extensive data into manageable forms using tools like mean, median and mode, making it easier to understand and use.
   - e.g. Using per capita income to represent the average income of a population instead of listing individual incomes.

Limitations of Statistics

- Statistics is limited to the study of numerical facts only. It ignores qualitative aspect.
- It is the study of aggregates only. Individual items have no consequence in statistics.
- In the study of statistics, only homogeneous data is considered. Data of diverse qualities and kinds cannot be compared.

- Statistical results are true only on an average basis. They are not as exact as the laws of natural science.
- Without reference, statistical results may prove to be wrong.
- Statistics can be misused. Any person can misuse statistics to support a pre-drawn conclusions, etc.
- Statistics can be used by experts only, as its techniques are complicated in nature.

Statistical Methods are no Substitute for Common Sense

There is an interesting story to justify this point. It is said that a family of four persons (husband, wife and two children) once set out to cross a river. The father knew the average depth of the river. So, he calculated the average height of his family members. Since the average height of his family members was greater than the average depth of the river, he thought they could cross safely. Consequently, some members of the family (children) drowned while crossing the river.

Here, the fault does not lie with the statistical method of calculating averages, but with the misuse of average by the father. Thus, it is rightly said that statistical methods are no substitute for common sense.

1.3 Distrust of Statistics

It refers to a lack of confidence in statistical methods and statements. Despite the many benefits and uses of statistics, distrust persists regarding its usefulness, accuracy and reliability.

Causes of Distrust in Statistics

- Wrong application of statistical tools.
- Unreal assumptions.
- Incomplete knowledge of statistics.
- Ignorance of limitations of statistics.

Measures to Remove Distrust in Statistics

- Statistics should be used by experts only.
- The user should be impartial.
- Limitation of statistics should be taken care of, while using statistics.

Mind Map

INTRODUCTION TO ECONOMICS AND STATISTICS

1 Meaning of Economics

Economics is the study of how people and society choose to allocate limited resources to satisfy unlimited wants.

Economic Problem

- Scarcity of resources – Limited supply.
- Unlimited wants – Human desires never end.
- Alternative uses – Resources can be used in multiple ways.

Types of Activities

- **Economic Activities** Actions taken with the primary goal of earning a livelihood. These activities include earning, spending, investing and distributing money.
- **Non-economic Activities** Actions that are not primarily aimed at earning money but are performed for personal satisfaction, social welfare or cultural reasons.

2 Meaning of Statistics

- In plural sense, it is a collection of numerical data gathered systematically with a specific purpose.
- In singular sense, it can be defined as science of collection, organisation, presentation, analysis and interpretation of numerical data.

Stages of Statistical Study (COPAI Method)

- **Collection of Data** Gathering relevant data about problem.
- **Organisation of Data** Sorting and categorising data systematically.
- **Presentation of Data** Using charts, tables, graphs.
- **Analysis of Data** Finding patterns, relationships and trends.
- **Interpretation of Data** Drawing conclusions for decision-making.

3 Scope of Statistics

- **Statistics in Planning** Used in economic planning, development projects.
- **Statistics in Business and Management** Helps in market analysis, production, investment and finance.
- **Statistics in Industry** Used for quality control and efficiency improvement.
- **Statistics in Economics** Helps to analyse economic trends and forecast future conditions.
- **Statistics in Government Policies** Used for resource allocation, budgeting and policy-making.

4 Nature of Statistics

Statistics as a Science

- **Systematic and Logical Approach** Uses structured methods to study relationships between variables.
- **Generalised Results** Establishes patterns and trends based on data.
- **Influenced by Multiple Factors** Unlike physical sciences, it deals with variables that may not be fully quantifiable.

Statistics as an Art

- **Practical Application** Applies theoretical knowledge to solve real world problems.
- **Decision-making Tool** Helps businesses, governments and individuals make informed choices.

5 Importance of Statistics in Economics

- Understanding economic problems
- Establishing cause-and-effect relationships
- Formulating economic theories or models
- Economic forecasting, i.e. predicts future trends based on historical data
- Formulation of policies
- Presenting facts in a definite form
- Condensing elaborative data into a concise form

6 Limitations of Statistics

- Deals only with numerical data, i.e. cannot analyse qualitative factors like emotions, ethics or opinions.
- It focuses on aggregates and general trends, not exceptions.
- Homogeneous data is considered for comparisons.
- They are not as exact as the law of natural sciences.
- Incorrect use of statistical methods can lead to false conclusions.
- Complex techniques demand skilled interpretation.

7 Distrust of Statistics

Causes of Distrust

- Incomplete knowledge of statistics.
- Wrong application of statistical tools.
- Unrealistic assumptions.
- Ignorance of limitations of statistics.

Measures to Remove Distrust

- Use by experts only to ensure correct application and interpretation.
- Impartiality in analysis.
- Acknowledging limitations helps in making balanced judgements.

EXAM PATTERN QUESTIONS

Objective Type Questions

Multiple Choice Questions (MCQs)

1. **"Statistics ensure that economic facts are presented clearly and accurately, reducing ambiguity and providing precise information." How do statistics help in presenting economic facts?**

(a) By simplifying data into vague summaries.
(b) By reducing ambiguity and providing precise information.
(c) By eliminating the need for numerical data.
(d) By focusing only on qualitative analysis.

2. **"Statistics integrates both scientific methods for understanding data relationships and artistic application for solving practical problems, making it a versatile tool in various fields." In what way can statistics be considered a versatile tool?**

Competency Based Que

(a) It is limited to theoretical research
(b) It focuses only on data collection
(c) It avoids solving real-world problems
(d) It combines scientific methods with practical applications

3. **The primary focus of economics is to study how societies allocate ....**

(a) unlimited resources (b) scarce resources
(c) qualitative data (d) quantitative data

4. **The fundamental cause of all economic problems is ....**

(a) scarcity (b) unlimited resources
(c) limited wants (d) None of these

5. **Identify the type of economic problem from the given image.**

(a) Limited wants (b) Unlimited resources
(c) Scarcity of resources
(d) Alternative uses of resources

6. **Identify the type of activity from the given image.**

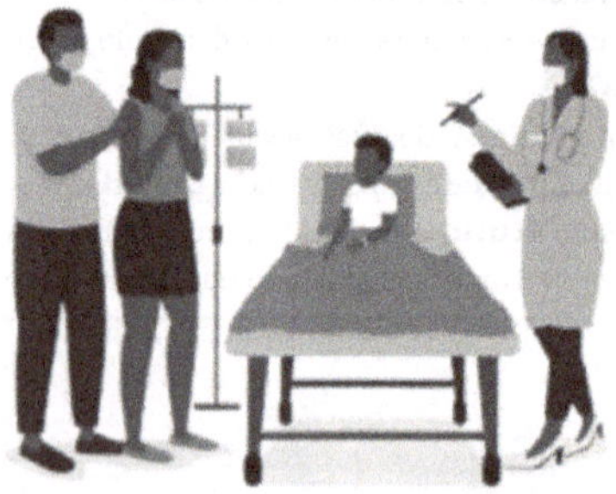

Doctor attending patient at her clinic

(a) Economic (b) Non-economic
(c) Financial (d) Managerial

7. **What is the term used for the process by which consumers satisfy their wants using goods and services?**

(a) Distribution (b) Consumption
(c) Production (d) Marketing

8. **Which of the following economic activity is highlighted in the below image?**

(a) Production (b) Consumption
(c) Analysis (d) Distribution

9. **Which of the following is an example of a non-economic activity?**

(a) A teacher teaching in a school
(b) A doctor treating patients in a hospital
(c) A person attending a social gathering
(d) A mechanic repairing cars in a garage

10. **Identify the type of activity from the given image.**

Mother teaching her child

(a) Economic
(b) Non-economic
(c) Both (a) and (b)
(d) None of the above

11. "Government uses economic data to revise GST rates."
– The Economic Times

The above headline reflects the use of statistics in …… .
Competency Based Que

(a) planning
(b) government policy formulation
(c) business management
(d) quality control

12. **Identify the stage of statistics that represents the collected and organised data through graphs, charts, etc.** **Competency Based Que**

I. Analysis of data
II. Presentation of data
III. Collection of data
IV. Reporting of data

Codes
(a) Only I (b) III and IV
(c) Only II (d) All of these

13. **Which of the following represents the data whose variables cannot be measured in numerical terms?**
(a) Quantitative data (b) Monetary data
(c) Financial data (d) Qualitative data

14. **Which of the following is not a characteristic of statistics in the plural sense?**
(a) Collection of numerical data
(b) Statistical methods
(c) Influenced by various factors
(d) Organised for a specific purpose

15. **The stage of statistical study that involves sorting and arranging data is ……… .**
(a) organisation of data (b) interpretation of data
(c) collection of data (d) analysis of data

16. **Which stage of statistical study process is highlighted in the given image?**

(a) Collection of data
(b) Organisation of data
(c) Presentation of data
(d) Analysis of data

17. "India's GDP growth rate analysed to predict future economic trends." – Business Standards

This headline highlights the role of statistics in
Competency Based Que

(a) understanding economic problems
(b) economic forecasting
(c) constructing economic theories
(d) presenting facts

18. **Identify the nature of statistics from the following alternatives.** **Competency Based Que**

I. Statistics is a science
II. Statistics is an art
III. Statistics is qualitative
IV. Statistics only focus on non-monetary data

Codes
(a) Both III and IV
(b) Only I
(c) Both I and II
(d) Only II

19. **The analysis of the relationship between average income and consumer spending is an example of determining a ……… and ……… relationship.**
Competency Based Que

(a) profit, loss
(b) cause, effect
(c) sales, revenue (d) None of these

20. **Which field heavily relies on statistical data for quality control?**
(a) Government (b) Business
(c) Economics (d) Industry

21. **Which of the following is a limitation of statistics?**
(a) It considers qualitative aspects
(b) It studies individual items
(c) It provides exact results like natural sciences
(d) It is limited to numerical facts only

22. **Statistical results are true only on a/an ……… basis.**
(a) average (b) total
(c) zero (d) maximum

23. **A retail company is analysing sales data to decide which products to promote. They rely on statistical results, but the team notices that these results only focus on averages, ignoring individual product performance.**

Why might relying solely on average sales data be problematic? **Competency Based Que**

(a) It might not consider the performance of each product
(b) It requires advanced statistical knowledge
(c) It could lead to incorrect predictions
(d) It overlooks numerical facts

24. **What is one of the causes of distrust in statistics?**
(a) Accurate application of statistical tools
(b) Clear understanding of statistics
(c) Ignorance of limitations
(d) Realistic assumptions

25. **Distrust in statistics can be caused by the .... application of statistical tools.**
(a) right (b) expert
(c) wrong (d) proper

26. **Identify the measures to remove distrust from statistics from the following alternatives.** Competency Based Que
I. Statistics should be used by experts
II. The user of statistics should be impartial
III. Limitations of statistics should be ignored
IV. Limitations of statistics should be taken care of while using it

Codes
(a) I and III (b) III and IV
(c) I, II and IV (d) Only III

Direction *Read the case study and answer the questions 27 to 30 on the basis of the same*

Walmart is analysing its monthly sales data to optimise its inventory management and marketing strategies. The company collects detailed data on the quantities sold, prices and times of sales and customer demographics for various products across different stores. This data is then organised into specific categories, such as product type, sales amount and location.

Walmart presents this data using bar charts and line graphs to visually capture sales trends and patterns. The analysis reveals that certain products, like snacks and beverages, sell significantly better during specific times of the day, particularly in the evening. This insight leads Walmart to adjust its restocking schedules, increase inventory for high demand periods and plan targeted promotions to maximise sales during peak times.

27. **Walmart uses data collection to gather information on which of the following?**
(a) Customer satisfaction
(b) Sales quantities, prices, times and customer demographics
(c) Employee performance
(d) Market trends

28. **How do the presentation of data using bar charts and line graphs helps Walmart?**
(a) Understand customer feedback
(b) Predict future sales trends
(c) Visually represent sales data
(d) Improve employee training

29. **Walmart collects data on sales quantities, prices and times of sales during the ...... stage of statistical study.**
(a) presentation of data (b) collection of data
(c) analysis of data (d) interpretation of data

30. **Walmart uses bar charts and line graphs in the .... stage.**
(a) collection of data (b) organisation of data
(c) presentation of data (d) analysis of data

Assertion-Reason

Direction (Q.No. 31 to 40) *Read the following Assertion (A) and Reason (R) and choose the correct alternative from the following*

Alternatives
(a) Both Assertion (A) and Reason (R) are true and Reason (R) is the correct explanation of Assertion (A)
(b) Both Assertion (A) and Reason (R) are true, but Reason (R) is not the correct explanation of Assertion (A)
(c) Assertion (A) is true, but Reason (R) is false
(d) Assertion (A) is false, but Reason (R) is true

31. **Assertion** (A) Economic problems arise due to the scarcity of resources and unlimited human wants.
Reason (R) Scarcity forces individuals and societies to make choices about which wants to satisfy.

32. **Assertion** (A) Adam Smith's definition of economics as the 'science of wealth' focuses on how wealth is created, distributed and consumed.
Reason (R) This perspective is outdated and does not consider the broader aspects of resource allocation and human behaviour.

33. **Assertion** (A) Production is an economic activity.
Reason (R) Production includes all those activities which are undertaken to produce goods and services for generation of income and satisfying human wants.

34. **Assertion** (A) Statistics can be used to formulate economic policies by analysing data on production and demand.
Reason (R) Statistical data helps in understanding economic problems and making informed decisions.

35. **Assertion** (A) Statistical results are always exact and reliable like the laws of natural science.
Reason (R) Statistics involves only the study of aggregates and ignores individual data.

36. **Assertion** (A) Statistics can be misused to support pre-drawn conclusions.
Reason (R) Statistical methods are complicated and require expertise to be used accurately.

37. **Assertion** (A) Qualitative data is essential for analysing numerical data in statistics.

Reason (R) Qualitative data describes characteristics and is not used in statistical analysis.

38. **Assertion** (A) In statistics, data must be homogeneous to ensure accurate comparisons.

Reason (R) Statistics ignore individual items and focus only on aggregated data.

39. **Assertion** (A) The scope of statistics includes its application in planning, business and government.

Reason (R) Statistics is used in various fields for decision-making and policy formulation.

40. **Assertion** (A) Distrust in statistics can be caused by the misuse of statistical methods.

Reason (R) Statistical techniques are complex and require expertise to apply correctly.

Two Statement Based MCQs

Direction (Q.No. 41 to 50) *Read the following statements carefully and choose the correct alternative*

Alternatives

(a) Statement I is correct and Statement II is incorrect
(b) Statement II is correct and Statement I is incorrect
(c) Both the statements are correct
(d) Both the statements are incorrect

41. **Statement I** Economics is the study of how scarce resources, with alternative uses, are employed to produce and distribute goods to satisfy societal needs and wants.

Statement II The core idea of economics understands how people and societies manage resource scarcity to address unlimited wants.

42. **Statement I** Scarcity of resources is the fundamental cause of economic problems.

Statement II Human wants are limited and do not create constant demand for resources.

43. **Statement I** The study of economics revolves around the use of unlimited resources.

Statement II Economic problem is the problem of choice.

44. **Statement I** Wealth definition of economics is biased towards money.

Statement II Donations to an NGO is an economic activity.

45. **Statement I** Economic activities are undertaken to earn money.

Statement II Economic activities are concerned with production, consumption and distribution of goods and services.

46. **Statement I** Statistics helps in understanding economic problems by analysing data related to inflation and unemployment.

Statement II Statistics is limited to qualitative data and does not include numerical analysis.

47. **Statement I** Statistics are limited to the study of aggregates and do not consider individual items.

Statement II Statistics include the study of individual items as well as aggregates.

48. **Statement I** In short, methods of statistics can be written as COPAI.

Statement II In singular sense, statistics relates to statistical methods.

49. **Statement I** Statistics have no importance in the field of business and management.

Statement II Economics is heavily dependent on quality control through statistics.

50. **Statement I** Distrust in statistics can be caused by unreal assumptions.

Statement II Distrust means lack of confidence in statistical methods.

Matching

51. Match the following

Column I		Column II	
A.	Resources	(i)	Unlimited
B.	Human wants	(ii)	Done for satisfaction
C.	Non-economic activities	(iii)	Done for money and earning
D.	Economic activities	(iv)	Limited

Codes

	A	B	C	D		A	B	C	D
(a)	(iii)	(iv)	(i)	(ii)	(b)	(iv)	(i)	(ii)	(iii)
(c)	(ii)	(iii)	(iv)	(i)	(d)	(iii)	(ii)	(i)	(iv)

52. Match the following

Column I		Column II	
A.	Consumer	(i)	One who is working for some other person.
B.	Producer	(ii)	One who produces goods or services.
C.	Service holder	(iii)	One who buys goods or services to satisfy needs and wants.
D.	Service provider	(iv)	One who provides some kind of service.

Codes

	A	B	C	D
(a)	(iii)	(iv)	(i)	(ii)
(b)	(iv)	(i)	(ii)	(iii)
(c)	(ii)	(iii)	(iv)	(i)
(d)	(iii)	(ii)	(i)	(iv)

53. Match the following

Column I	Column II
A. Collection of data	(i) Using statistical methods to study the data.
B. Organisation of data	(ii) Gathering of data from various sources.
C. Interpretation of data	(iii) Editing, classifying and tabulating data.
D. Analysis of data	(iv) Drawing conclusions from the data.

Codes

	A	B	C	D
(a)	(iii)	(iv)	(i)	(ii)
(b)	(iv)	(i)	(ii)	(iii)
(c)	(ii)	(iii)	(iv)	(i)
(d)	(iii)	(ii)	(i)	(iv)

54. Match the following

Column I	Column II
A. Singular sense	(i) Data collected in systematic manner.
B. Qualitative data	(ii) Expressed in numerical terms.
C. Plural sense	(iii) Statistical methods of study.
D. Quantitative data	(iv) Not measured in numbers.

Codes

	A	B	C	D
(a)	(iii)	(iv)	(i)	(ii)
(b)	(iv)	(i)	(ii)	(iii)
(c)	(ii)	(iii)	(iv)	(i)
(d)	(iii)	(ii)	(i)	(iv)

55. Match the following

Column I	Column II
A. Statistics in planning	(i) Welfare objectives and running of administration.
B. Statistics in economics	(ii) Formulation of framework to attain pre-determined objectives.
C. Statistics in business and management	(iii) Understanding economic problems.
D. Statistics for government	(iv) Decisions related to marketing, production, finance.

Codes

	A	B	C	D
(a)	(iii)	(iv)	(i)	(ii)
(b)	(iv)	(i)	(ii)	(iii)
(c)	(ii)	(iii)	(iv)	(i)
(d)	(iii)	(ii)	(i)	(iv)

Concept Identification

56. It refers to the fundamental economic problem of having unlimited wants and limited resources.

57. It refers to actions done to earn money or income.

58. This is the process of gathering all relevant data about a problem before analysing it.

59. It is the science of collecting, organising, presenting, analysing and interpreting numerical data.

60. This refers to the practice of using statistical results to make decisions about future actions, such as predicting economic trends.

Answers

1. (b) By reducing ambiguity and providing precise information.
2. (d) It combines scientific methods with practical applications
3. (b) scarce resources
4. (a) scarcity
5. (c) Scarcity of resources
6. (a) Economic
7. (b) Consumption
8. (d) Distribution
9. (c) A person attending a social gathering
10. (b) Non-economic
11. (b) The headline reflects the use of economic data in shaping and revising government policies, such as GST rates. It highlights how statistical information helps in policy formulation by providing data-driven insights for decision-making.
12. (c) Only II
13. (d) Qualitative data
14. (b) Statistical methods
15. (a) organisation of data
16. (a) Collection of data
17. (b) The headline indicates that the analysis of GDP growth rate is used to predict future economic trends. This reflects the role of statistics in economic forecasting, where current data is used to anticipate future economic conditions.
18. (c) Both I and II
19. (b) cause, effect
20. (d) Industry

21. (d) It is limited to numerical facts only
22. (a) average
23. (a) It might not consider the performance of each product
24. (c) Ignorance of limitations
25. (c) wrong
26. (c) I, II and IV
27. (b) Sales quantities, prices, times and customer demographics
28. (c) Visually represent sales data
29. (b) collection of data
30. (c) presentation of data
31. (a) Both Assertion (A) and Reason (R) are true and Reason (R) is the correct explanation of Assertion (A)
32. (c) Smith's definition may be considered narrow by modern standards, it is not inherently outdated; it provides a foundational perspective that is complemented by later developments in economics addressing broader aspects.
33. (a) Both Assertion (A) and Reason (R) are true and Reason (R) is the correct explanation of Assertion (A)
34. (a) Both Assertion (A) and Reason (R) are true and Reason (R) is the correct explanation of Assertion (A)
35. (d) Statistical results are not always exact and reliable in the same way as natural science laws due to their inherent limitations and reliance on data interpretation.
36. (b) Both Assertion (A) and Reason (R) are true, but Reason (R) is not the correct explanation of Assertion (A)
37. (d) Qualitative data, which describes characteristics, is not used in numerical statistical analysis, statistical analysis primarily deals with quantitative data.
38. (b) Both Assertion (A) and Reason (R) are true, but Reason (R) is not the correct explanation of Assertion (A)
39. (a) Both Assertion (A) and Reason (R) are true and Reason (R) is the correct explanation of Assertion (A)
40. (a) Both Assertion (A) and Reason (R) are true and Reason (R) is the correct explanation of Assertion (A)
41. (c) Both the statements are correct
42. (a) Human wants are unlimited and constantly evolving, which creates a continuous demand for resources, not a limited one.
43. (b) The study of economics revolves around the use of limited resources to meet unlimited wants. The economic problem involves making choices due to resource scarcity.
44. (a) Donations to an NGO are generally considered non-economic activities as they are done for personal satisfaction rather than earning money.
45. (c) Both the statements are correct
46. (a) Statistics include quantitative data i.e. numerical data.
47. (a) Statistics traditionally focus on aggregates and general trends rather than individual items.
48. (c) Both the statements are correct
49. (d) Statistics are crucial in business and management for making data-driven decisions. Also, while economics uses statistical methods for analysis, quality control is more related to industrial statistics rather than economic theory.
50. (c) Both the statements are correct
51. (b) (iv) (i) (ii) (iii)
52. (d) (iii) (ii) (i) (iv)
53. (c) (ii) (iii) (iv) (i)
54. (a) (iii) (iv) (i) (ii)
55. (c) (ii) (iii) (iv) (i)
56. Scarcity
57. Economic activity
58. Collection of data
59. Statistics
60. Economic forecasting

Subjective Questions

Short Answer Type Questions

1. Explain the concept of 'alternative uses of resources' with a real life example.

Ans. The concept of 'alternative uses of resources' refers to the idea that resources can be used in different ways to achieve various outcomes. Because resources are limited, choosing one use often means forgoing another.

e.g. A farmer has a plot of land that can either be used to grow wheat or corn.

If the farmer decides to plant wheat, the land cannot simultaneously be used to grow corn. The choice depends on factors like market demand, crop profitability and input costs.

The farmer must evaluate the potential returns from each crop and decide the best use of the land to maximise overall profitability. This scenario illustrates how resources (in this case, land) have alternative uses and the need for careful decision-making to allocate them efficiently.

2. **"Scarcity refers to the condition where resources are insufficient to meet all human wants." Explain why scarcity is considered the fundamental economic problem.** Competency Based Que

Ans. Scarcity is considered the fundamental economic problem because it arises from the fundamental mismatch between human wants and the limited availability of resources. Human wants are virtually limitless, as people continuously seek to improve their standard of living and fulfill new desires. However, resources such as time, money and raw materials are finite and cannot meet all these wants simultaneously.

3. **"You have unlimited wants and limited resources to satisfy them." Explain this statement by giving two examples.** NCERT; Competency Based Que

Ans Human wants are never ending, i.e. they can never be fully satisfied. As soon as one want is satisfied, another emerges. Wants of the people are unlimited and keep on multiplying and cannot be satisfied due to scarcity or limited resources.

For example,

(i) Suppose you have ₹ 25,000 and you want to purchase a computer and a LED TV. With cash of ₹ 25,000 only, you cannot buy both. You can either buy computer or LED TV.

(ii) A land is available. You can use it either for agriculture purpose or for industrial purpose. You can't use same land for both activities.

Thus, it can be concluded that scarcity is the root cause of all the problems.

4. **Differentiate between economic and non-economic activities.**

Ans. Difference between economic and non-economic activities are

Basis	Economic Activities	Non-economic Activities
Meaning	Economic activities are those which are performed to earn livelihood.	Non-economic activities are those which are performed out of love, sympathy, care, affection, self-satisfaction, patriotism, etc.
Purpose	To earn money.	To satisfy social and psychological needs.
Examples	A worker working in a factory, an entrepreneur performing entrepreneurial functions for production or trading of goods and services, etc.	A teacher teaching her son, a person going to temple for offering prayers, etc.

5. **"Economic activities are actions performed to earn income or money." Provide two examples of economic activities and explain why they are classified as such.** Competency Based Que

Ans. Two examples of economic activities are

(i) **Software Developer Creating Applications** This is an economic activity because the developer earns income by providing a valuable service through app creation, contributing to the economy.

(ii) **Farmer Growing Vegetables** This is an economic activity because the farmer produces goods for sale, generating income and supporting the food supply.

6. **Identify and explain the type of activity from the following image.** Competency Based Que

Ans. The given image highlights the economic activities. Economic activities are actions undertaken by individuals or organisations with the primary goal of earning income or money. These activities contribute to the economy by producing goods, providing services or engaging in transactions.

e.g. A retailer selling products in a store is an economic activity because it involves providing goods to consumers in exchange for money.

7. **"An activity can be economic activity in one situation and non-economic in another situation." Do you agree? Give an example to justify your answer.** Competency Based Que

Ans. Yes, I agree with the statement. Human activities are classified into economic and non-economic activities. Economic activities are those which are performed for some economic consideration, whereas non-economic activities are performed for psychological satisfaction and out of love, sympathy, patriotism, etc.

e.g. When a doctor treats a patient at a hospital or a clinic, he charges fee for that, thus it becomes an economic activity.

However, when the same doctor treats his son/daughter at home, it becomes a non-economic activity.

8. **A company is analysing its sales data and notices that the demand for a particular product has increased significantly during the summer months.**

The company is considering whether to increase production during this period or maintain current production levels. Based on the concept of scarcity and economic decision-making, explain how the company's decision to increase production during peak demand periods can help address the issue of scarcity and maximise profit. **Competency Based Que**

Ans. Scarcity refers to the limited availability of resources to meet unlimited wants. By increasing production during peak demand periods, the company can better align its supply with the high demand for the product, addressing the scarcity of the product in the market. This decision helps maximise profit by ensuring that the company can meet consumer needs and capitalise on higher sales volumes during peak periods.

It demonstrates effective economic decision-making by optimising resource allocation in response to market demand.

9. Identify the type of data shown in the image below and differentiate between the same. **Competency Based Que**

Rating - *** 250 gm

Ans. The above image shown indicates qualitative and quantitative data.

Difference between qualitative and quantitative data are as follows

Basis	Qualitative Data	Quantitative Data
Meaning	This refers to the data whose variables cannot be measured in numerical terms.	This refers to the data whose variables can be measured in numerical terms.
Examples	Honesty of individuals, intelligence of individuals, etc.	Price of commodities, heights, weights of individuals, etc.

10. " The government and policy makers use statistical data to formulate suitable policies of economic development." Illustrate with two examples. **NCERT; Competency Based Que**

Ans The examples which demonstrate that government and policy maker use statistical data to formulate suitable policies of economic development are given below

(i) The data on domestic production of oil and demand for oil will help the government in deciding how much it should import.

(ii) The data on consumption of wheat in past years and the rate of growth of population would help in determining the demand for future.

11. What is the importance of statistics in economics?

Ans. Statistics play a crucial role in economics by providing tools to analyse data, understand relationships and make informed decisions. It's importance in economics can be highlighted through following points

(i) It identifies economic problems like inflation and unemployment.

(ii) It determines cause-effect relationships between variables, such as income and spending.

(iii) It helps develop and test economic theories and models.

(iv) It forecasts future trends like inflation rates and consumer demand.

(v) It assists in formulating policies by analysing data on production and demand.

12. "Statistical methods are most dangerous tools in the hands of an inexpert." Which limitation of statistics does it indicate? **Competency Based Que**

Ans. It indicates that statistics can be used only by those persons who have special knowledge of statistical methods. Those who are ignorant about these methods cannot make sensible use of statistics, leading to dangerous consequences.

e.g. An inexpert person may assume that the average age of 20 persons represents the actual age of those 20 persons. However, this is not true. Out of those 20 persons, some of them will be aged below 20 years, some above 20 years and a few can be aged 20 years.

13. Identify and explain the scope of statistics highlighted in the given image. **Competency Based Que**

Source *Scope of statistics–Business and Management*

Ans. In business, statistics play a crucial role in decision-making and performance evaluation. By analysing sales data, market trends and customer preferences, etc. as shown in the image, businesses can make informed decisions and tailor their strategies to meet market demands.

Statistical methods help in assessing performance metrics, identifying areas for improvement and implementing effective strategies.

Additionally, statistics are essential for quality control and financial analysis. They help businesses monitor product quality, optimise operational processes and evaluate financial performance. By leveraging statistical tools, companies can enhance efficiency, reduce costs and improve overall management practices.

14. **" The subject matter of statistics could be studied through descriptive method or through inferential method."**

Elaborate with the help of an example.

Competency Based Que

Ans. Subject matter of statistics could be studied, both by descriptive method, as well as, inferential method.

In descriptive method, the data related to whole of the population is collected and analysed while in inferential method, the data is collected from a sample drawn from the population.

e.g. There are 225 employees working in ABC Publication. To find the average salary by descriptive method, data related to the salary of each of the 225 employees will be collected, added and the divided by 225 to find the average salary.

However, to find the average salary by inferential method, a sample of 50 or 60 employees will be drawn from the given population of 225 employees.

The data related to the salary of these employees will be collectively added and then divided to find the average salary.

The average so computed will be deemed to be the average salary of all the employees.

15. **"Statistics can be misused to support pre-drawn conclusions."**

What are some potential consequences of misusing statistical data in research or policy-making?

Competency Based Que

Ans. Misusing statistical data in research or policy-making can lead to several adverse consequences as follows

(i) It can result in inaccurate conclusions, as skewed or manipulated data may not reflect the true nature of the issues being studied.

This misrepresentation can misguide decision-making, leading to ineffective or harmful policies.

(ii) Misuse of statistics can erode public trust in both the data and the institutions that rely on it, undermining the credibility of research and policy. Additionally, it can lead to resource misallocation, where efforts and funds are directed based on incorrect or biased information, ultimately impacting the efficiency and effectiveness of interventions and solutions.

16. **DigiLocker was launched in 2016 as an initiative under MeitY, as part of the government's digital India programme to reduce the dependency on physical documents. So far, it was restricted only for personal use and documents like the Aadhaar card, Permanent Account Number (PAN), verification record, two-wheeler insurance policies, ration card and a vehicle's Registration Certificate (RC). Its popularity has grown among users. The total registered user base has grown from about 1.2 million in 2016 to a staggering 148 million presently, according to statistics published on the official website.**

In her speech on 1st February, Finance Minister Nirmala Sitharaman talked about the focus on simplifying the KYC processes. "A one-stop solution for reconciliation and updating of identity and address of individuals maintained by various government agencies, regulators and regulated entities will be established using DigiLocker service and Aadhaar as foundational identity," Sitharaman said.

Source *https://www.financialexpress.com/industry/govt-focuses-on-industry-value-added-services-in-digilocker-push/2979514/*

Based upon the above article, state how useful statistical data proves out to the government?

Competency Based Que

Ans. Government statistics are essential for a democratic government and they serve to advance businesses and the well-being of its citizens. Statistical agencies provide accurate, timely and credible information, which informs current and future policies. Respect and trust of data providers are fostered by maintaining confidentiality of their information.

Government statistics are collected through censuses, surveys, from administrative records as well as other sources. Defining practices of an effective statistical agency begin with a clear, well-accepted mission and a strong standing of independence.

17. **What are the key stages involved in statistical study?**

Ans. The key stages in statistical study are

(i) **Collection of Data**
Gathering relevant data from various sources.

(ii) **Organisation of Data**
Sorting and arranging data for analysis.

(iii) **Presentation of Data**
Displaying data using charts, graphs and tables.

(iv) **Analysis of Data**
Applying statistical methods to identify patterns and relationships.

(v) **Interpretation of Data**
Drawing conclusions and making decisions based on the analysis.

18. **What are the causes of distrust in statistics and how can it be removed?**

Ans. **Causes of Distrust in Statistics**

(i) Wrong application of statistical tools.
(ii) Unrealistic assumptions.
(iii) Incomplete knowledge of statistics.
(iv) Ignorance of statistical limitations.

Measures to Remove Distrust

(i) Statistics should be used by experts.
(ii) Users should remain impartial.
(iii) Limitations of statistics must be acknowledged.

Long Answer Type Questions

19. **Explain how human wants and the alternative uses of resources contribute to the economic problem of choice. Provide real life examples to support your explanation.**

Ans. Human wants are inherently unlimited and continuously evolving. As one want is satisfied, new wants emerge, perpetuating an endless cycle of desires. This endless nature of human wants creates a persistent demand for resources, which are limited and cannot fully satisfy all wants simultaneously. Furthermore, resources have alternative uses, which complicate the decision-making process.

For instance, consider a piece of land that a farmer can use either to cultivate food crops or non-food crops. The choice depends on factors such as current market prices, future demand and resource constraints.

Similarly, in urban areas, land that could be used for residential development might be repurposed for commercial or industrial use depending on economic priorities and potential benefits.

These two factors, i.e. the unlimited nature of human wants and the alternative uses of limited resources are central to the economic problem of choice. They require individuals and organisations to make decisions about how to best allocate their resources to meet the most urgent needs or achieve the highest benefits, given the constraints they face.

20. **"Local volunteer groups making a difference: non-economic contributions to community welfare."**

– The Hindu

Analyse the significance of non-economic activities, such as those performed by local volunteer groups, in enhancing community welfare. How do these activities contribute to the well-being of individuals and the overall social fabric of the community?

Competency Based Que

Ans. Local volunteer groups, as highlighted in the news headline, exemplify the impact of non-economic activities on community welfare.

These groups engage in various activities such as organising charity events, providing educational support and aiding in disaster relief, all of which are driven by the desire to improve community well-being rather than monetary gain.

The significance of such non-economic activities lies in their ability to foster a sense of solidarity and mutual support within the community. Volunteers contribute their time and skills to address local needs, creating a supportive environment that enhances the quality of life for individuals in the community. e.g. A volunteer led initiative providing free tutoring to underprivileged children not only helps in educational development but also empowers the children with opportunities they might otherwise lack.

Moreover, these non-economic activities strengthen the social fabric by promoting inclusivity, cooperation and shared values among community members. By engaging in acts of kindness and service, volunteers contribute to a more compassionate and connected society. Overall, non-economic activities play a pivotal role in building a resilient and cohesive community, underscoring their importance beyond economic considerations.

21. **"Statistical methods are no substitute for common sense." Comment with examples from your daily life.**

NCERT; Competency Based Que

Ans It is absolutely true that statistical methods are no substitute for common sense. Statistical data should not be believed blindly as they can be misinterpreted or misused.

The statistical data may involve personal bias or may be subjected to manipulations for one's own selfish motives.

Statistical data and methods are also subject to the errors committed by an investigator while surveying and collecting data. Thus, one should use his/her common sense while working with the statistical methods.

A classic example exhibiting this concept is of a statistician who wanted to cross a river with his family but did not know how to swim. He knew the average depth of the river to be 125 cm.

His height was 175 cm, that of his wife was 152 cm and his two children measured 120 cm and 90 cm respectively, in height.

He calculated the average height of his family and found it to be around 134 cm. He analysed that the average depth of the river was less than the average height of his family and concluded that they all could cross the river safely on foot.

This resulted in drowning of his children. This example proves that common sense must be used while applying statistical tools.

22. Describe the five key stages of a statistical study, providing a detailed explanation of each stage and its importance in the overall process. Use practical examples to illustrate how these stages contribute to making informed decisions based on data.

Ans. The five key stages of a statistical study are collection, organisation, presentation, analysis and interpretation of data, often abbreviated as COPAI. Each stage plays a crucial role in ensuring that data is effectively transformed into actionable insights.

(i) **Collection of Data**
This is the initial stage where relevant data is gathered. It involves identifying the data sources and determining the methods for data collection, such as surveys, experiments or secondary data sources.
e.g. A company might collect sales data from various regional offices to understand sales performance. Proper collection is essential to ensure that the data is relevant and comprehensive, laying the foundation for all subsequent stages.

(ii) **Organisation of Data**
Once collected, the data must be organised to make it manageable and meaningful. This involves sorting, editing and classifying the data into tables, categories or spreadsheets. e.g. the sales data from different regions might be organised into monthly reports by product category and sales figures. Organisation helps in preparing the data for effective analysis by ensuring that it is structured in a way that highlights key patterns and trends.

(iii) **Presentation of Data**
The organised data is then presented using visual tools such as charts, graphs and tables.
This stage is crucial for making the data understandable and accessible to stakeholders.
e.g. A company might use bar graphs to illustrate sales trends over the year or pie charts to show market share distribution among different products. Effective presentation helps in communicating findings clearly and supports better decision-making by providing a visual representation of the data.

(iv) **Analysis of Data**
In this stage, the data is analysed using statistical methods to identify patterns, relationships and insights. Techniques such as calculating averages, measuring dispersion and determining correlations are employed.
e.g. The company might analyse sales data to determine the average sales per month, identify seasonal trends and assess the correlation between advertising spend and sales performance.
Analysis transforms raw data into meaningful information by uncovering trends and insights that inform strategic decisions.

(v) **Interpretation of Data**
The final stage involves drawing conclusions based on the analysis and making decisions or recommendations. This step translates statistical findings into actionable insights.
e.g. After analysing the sales data, the company might conclude that certain products perform better during specific seasons and decide to adjust their marketing strategy accordingly. Interpretation ensures that the findings are applied effectively to solve problems or capitalise on opportunities.

23. A company, XYZ Ltd. is experiencing fluctuating sales figures for its product line. The management team decides to use statistical methods to understand the underlying reasons for these fluctuations and to develop strategies to stabilise and increase sales. They collect data on sales, marketing expenses, seasonal trends and customer feedback. The statistical analysis reveals a correlation between increased marketing expenses and higher sales, but the impact varies significantly with seasonal changes.

Analyse how the dual nature of statistics as a science and an art helps XYZ Ltd. in addressing its sales fluctuations.

Discuss the role of statistical science in analysing the data and the contribution of statistical art in applying the findings to improve sales strategies.

Competency Based Que

Ans. In addressing the sales fluctuations, XYZ Ltd. benefits from the dual nature of statistics.

As a science, statistics provides a systematic approach to analysing the collected data. The scientific method involves rigorous data collection, the use of statistical models to identify correlations and the analysis of trends.

For instance, the company uses statistical techniques to establish that there is a significant relationship between marketing expenses and sales, providing a quantitative basis for understanding the impact of marketing on sales performance.

As an art, statistics plays a crucial role in applying these scientific insights to develop practical strategies. The artistic aspect involves interpreting the data in the context of real life situations and making decisions based on statistical findings. e.g. The company may use the insights to create targeted marketing campaigns that align with seasonal trends, optimising their marketing spend to maximise sales.

This application requires creativity and judgement to translate the statistical analysis into actionable strategies, such as adjusting marketing budgets or launching promotions during peak seasons. By combining scientific analysis with artistic application, XYZ Ltd. can develop a more effective approach to stabilising and increasing sales, demonstrating the practical utility of statistics in solving business challenges.

24. "Government utilises historical data for strategic urban planning." – Business Today

How does the use of historical data and statistical methods contribute to effective urban planning, according to the headline? Provide an example of how these methods might be applied in real world planning scenarios. **Competency Based Que**

Ans. The headline highlights the crucial role of historical data and statistical methods in strategic urban planning. By analysing past data, planners can assess resource availability and determine whether growth targets are achievable. e.g. Historical data on population growth, infrastructure usage and economic activities can help urban planners forecast future needs for housing, transportation and public services.

This allows for the creation of realistic and sustainable development plans. For instance, if historical data shows a consistent increase in population density in certain areas, planners might use statistical models to predict future growth and design infrastructure projects to accommodate this increase, ensuring that urban development meets future demands efficiently.

25. Enumerate the limitations of statistics in detail.

Ans. The six limitations of statistics are explained below

(i) **Study of Numerical Facts Only**
Statistics is numerical statement of facts. Statistics is not appropriate for the study of qualitative aspects, like honesty, friendship, wisdom, etc. It can be used for measuring quantitative data only.

(ii) **Study of Aggregates Only**
Statistics is aggregate of facts. It does not study individuals units.

(iii) **Homogeneity of Data, an Essential Requirement**
The data must be homogeneous and uniform, otherwise the comparisons may not be possible.

(iv) **Results are True Only as an Average**
Most statistical findings are true only as an average. Hence, the conclusion are of approximate nature. So, statistics as a science is less exact as compared to natural sciences.

(v) **Without Reference, Results may Prove to be Wrong**
In order to understand the conclusions precisely, it is necessary that the circumstances and conditions under which these conclusions have been drawn are also studied, otherwise they may prove to be wrong.

(vi) **Can be Used Only by the Experts**
Statistics cannot/should not be used by inexperts. This will give rise to the distrust of statistics. Statistics is necessary but at the same time it is imperfect and should therefore be used by experts only.

26. A national economic survey was conducted to assess the standard of living across various regions. The survey collected detailed data on household incomes, expenditures and savings from thousands of households. The data included information on the income of every individual household, which was voluminous and complex to interpret.

(i) How can statistical methods be used to present economic facts in a more definite form, based on the case study provided? Illustrate with an example from the data collected

(ii) How can statistics be employed to condense elaborate data into a concise form for easier interpretation, using the information from the case study? Provide an example of how this might be done. **Competency Based Que**

Ans. (i) In the case study, presenting detailed income data for each household could be overwhelming and unclear. Statistical methods help in presenting economic facts in a more definite form such as rather than stating that the average income of households in a region is above the poverty line, which is vague, statistical analysis can present a precise figure.

e.g. If the data shows that the average monthly income of households in the region is \$3,500, this specific figure provides a clear and definite measure of economic well-being, removing ambiguity and aiding in more effective policy decisions.

(ii) Statistics can simplify and summarise extensive data, making it more accessible and easier to interpret. In the case study, instead of analysing individual household incomes, which would be cumbersome, statistical tools like mean, median and mode can condense the data into a more manageable form.
For instance, calculating the mean income across all surveyed households can provide a single representative figure, such as an average income of \$3,500 per month.

This concise summary allows policymakers and researchers to quickly understand the economic conditions without getting bogged down by the vast amount of raw data, facilitating more efficient decision-making and analysis.

SELF ASSESSMENT TEST

Objective Type Questions

1. What is the primary cause of economic problems?
   (a) Unlimited money supply
   (b) Scarcity of resources
   (c) Technological advancements
   (d) Increasing population
2. .... refers to actions performed without a direct economic benefit but for personal satisfaction or social welfare.
   (a) Economic activities
   (b) Productive activities
   (c) Non-economic activities
   (d) Service activities
3. Who defined economics as "a science that examines human behaviour in relation to scarce resources that have alternative uses"?
   (a) Adam Smith
   (b) Lionel Robbins
   (c) Alfred Marshall
   (d) John Maynard Keynes
4. Which of these is not a type of economic system?
   (a) Capitalism (b) Communism
   (c) Socialism (d) Democracy
5. .... describes the scope of statistics in industry.
   (a) Decision-making for marketing campaigns
   (b) Quality control of products
   (c) Analysis of unemployment rates
   (d) Allocation of government resources
6. Which of the following is not a measure to remove distrust from statistics?
   (a) User should be impartial
   (b) Used by experts only
   (c) Limitations to be taken care of
   (d) Unreal assumptions
7. Statistics summaries extensive data into .... forms.
   (a) complex (b) manageable
   (c) meaningless (d) qualitative
8. Why is statistics considered an art?
   (a) It only deals with numerical data
   (b) It applies theoretical knowledge to solve real life problems
   (c) It is used only in academic research
   (d) It eliminates the need for qualitative data analysis

Answers 1. (b) 2. (c) 3. (b) 4. (d) 5. (b) 6. (d) 7. (b) 8. (b)

Short Answer Type Questions

9. "Economics is the study of how people and society choose to employ scarce resources that could have alternative uses." Defend or Refute.
10. What are non-economic activities? Give examples to explain.
11. What is the scope of statistics in business and management?
12. Explain the following economic problems
    (i) Alternative uses of resources
    (ii) Unlimited human wants
13. "Statistics is considered both science and art." Do you agree?
14. What is distrust in statistics? Give its causes.

Long Answer Type Questions

15. A city has a limited amount of land. The local government must decide whether to use the land for building housing, parks or commercial areas. Allocating more land to housing will reduce the space available for parks and businesses, while more commercial development could limit housing options. The government needs to choose the best way to use the limited land to meet the city's needs.
    (i) What economic problem is highlighted in this case?
    (ii) What do we call the situation when there are not enough resources to satisfy all needs?
    (iii) Why does the government need to make a choice in this case?
16. Explain the concept of statistics in singular and plural sense briefly.
17. What is the importance of statistics in economics? Give examples for each importance.

02 CHAPTER

Collection of data refers to collecting the information about a situation/study or case on which statistical investigation is to be done.

YOUR STUDY GOALS

2.1 Sources of Data
2.2 Methods of Collecting Primary Data
2.3 Sources of Secondary Data
2.4 Census and Sample Surveys
2.5 Statistical Errors
2.6 Important Agencies of Secondary Data

YOUR PRACTICE GOAL

- Objective Type Questions (68 Qs ; MCQs, A-R, Statements, Matching, Concept Identification)
- Subjective Questions (22 SAs, 10 LAs)
- Self Assessment Test (8 MCQs, 6 SAs, 3 LAs)

Collection of Data

2.1 Sources of Data

Data is a tool which helps in reaching a suitable conclusion on any problem by providing information. Data is collected to understand, explain and analyse a problem to find cause behind it.

It can be collected from following sources

1. **Internal Sources of Data**
   It is the data collected from within an organisation using its own records and reports. e.g. Annual financial statements, operational reports, sales data, etc.
2. **External Sources of Data**
   It is the data collected from outside an organisation. e.g. Public records, industry reports, market surveys, data on medical tourists, etc. External sources can be further classified as primary and secondary data.

Types of Data

Primary Data
Data collected directly by an investigator for the first time through methods such as personal interviews, questionnaires, telephonic interview or surveys.

Secondary Data
Data previously collected and processed by others, which is later used by investigators. This includes data from published sources (e.g. Government reports) and unpublished sources (e.g. Academic thesis).

Primary Data

Apple Inc. conducts a survey to gather feedback on the user experience of their latest iPhone model directly from customers.

Secondary Data

Microsoft Corporation uses data from the US Census Bureau on technology adoption rates to inform their market strategies.

Important Terms related to Data Collection

1. **Data** It is the information about different variables collected for analysis.
2. **Variable** Elements that change, like annual foodgrain production or daily maximum temperature are called variables.
3. **Observation** Specific values of a variable collected during data collection are called observation.
4. **Statistical Investigation** It is the process of gathering information using statistical methods.
5. **Investigators** Individuals who conduct statistical investigations, are known as investigators.
6. **Enumerators** Assistants hired by investigators to collect data, are referred to as enumerators.
7. **Respondents** Individuals providing information during data collection are called respondents.
8. **Statistical Units** The units of observation or measurement for which data is collected, are called statistical units. e.g. Weight in kilograms or height in centimeters.

2.2 Methods of Collecting Primary Data

Method	Meaning	Suitability	Advantages	Disadvantages
Direct Personal Investigation (Personal Interview)	This method involves face-to-face interviews between the investigator and respondents to collect the required information.	When there is limited area, need for originality and accuracy of data, detailed information required, confidential data, direct contact with respondent is required.	High originality of data, uniformity, reliability of data, related information collection, flexibility in method.	Costly, time consuming, unsuitable for large areas, requires skilled investigators, prone to bias.
Information from Correspondents	Local agents or correspondents collect and report data periodically to the investigator, who then processes it for final analysis.	When regular information is needed, area of investigation is large, high accuracy is not required.	Extensive data wide coverage, continuous supply of information, cost effective, suitable for special investigations.	Data lacks uniformity, potential correspondent bias, time consuming, less reliable due to lack of direct contact.
Mailing Questionnaires	Data is gathered by sending questionnaires through mail, with responses returned by postage.	When there is very large area of investigation, literate respondents.	Cost effective, reaches remote areas, reduces interviewer bias, allows thoughtful responses, provides original data.	Possibility of misunderstanding questions, limited to educated respondents, low response rate, less reliable data, limited accuracy.
Indirect Oral Investigation	Data is gathered by interviewing third parties who are directly or indirectly concerned with the subject matter.	When there is large area of investigation, respondent's ignorance or illiteracy of respondent, complex investigations.	Cost effective, economical, less personal bias, useful for wide areas.	Less reliable, potential for personal prejudice, lack of uniformity, possible lack of respondent's interest.

Method	Meaning	Suitability	Advantages	Disadvantages
Telephonic Interviews	Data is collected by the investigator from respondents over the telephone.	Large area of investigation, respondents have phone access, quick and regular information required, no physical contact possible.	Cost effective, time efficient, broad geographical reach.	No visual aids, excludes those without phone access.
Questionnaire Filled by Enumerators	Enumerators visit respondents to ask questions and record answers on a questionnaire (schedule) themselves.	Wide area of investigation, physical contact possible, both literate and illiterate respondents, high accuracy needed.	Covers large area, unbiased data, flexible with physical presence, suitable for all literacy levels.	Expensive, time consuming, dependent on enumerator skills.

Real Life Examples

- **Direct Personal Investigation** A market researcher from *Nielsen India* conducts face-to-face interviews with consumers to gather feedback on new products.
- **Indirect Oral Investigation** *The Economic Times* interviews industry experts to gather insights on the impact of new taxation policies.
- **Information from Correspondents** *Times of India* uses correspondents across different states to collect regular reports on regional economic conditions.
- **Telephonic Interviews** *Myntra* surveys customers over the phone to gather opinions on their online shopping experience.
- **Mailing Questionnaire** *ICICI Bank* sends out questionnaires to its customers via mail to assess satisfaction with their banking services.
- **Questionnaire Filled by Enumerators** *National Sample Survey Office (NSSO)* deploys enumerators to fill out detailed surveys on rural employment conditions across India.

Construction of Questionnaire

A well-constructed questionnaire is essential for effective primary data collection. It serves as a structured tool to gather accurate and relevant information from respondents.

Here are key considerations for creating an effective questionnaire

1. **Conciseness** Ensure the questionnaire is not too lengthy.
2. **Clarity** Limit the number of questions to keep them clear and precise.
3. **Structure** Start with general questions and progress to more specific ones.
4. **Simplicity** Avoid confusing language and ensure questions are easy to answer quickly, correctly end clearly.
5. **Organisation** Group questions logically under relevant headings and sub-headings.
6. **Avoid Negatives** Do not use double negatives like 'wouldn't you' or 'don't you', etc.
7. **Neutrality** Prevent questions that lead to specific answers or imply alternatives.
8. **Relevance** Exclude personal questions that are irrelevant to the research.
9. **Testing** Test the questionnaire with a small sample to refine it before full deployment.

Pilot Survey

It is a trial survey which helps to test the effectiveness of the questionnaire on a small group.

The pilot survey helps in

- Pre-testing of the questionnaire, so as to know the short-comings and drawbacks of the questions.
- Assessing the suitability of the questions, clarity of instructions, performance of enumerators and the cost and time involved in the actual survey.

Types of Questions in a Questionnaire

In designing a questionnaire, choosing the right type of questions is crucial for obtaining useful data. Here are the primary types of questions used

1. **Closed Ended Questions**

   These are easy to use, score and analyse, but may limit responses, if true response is not present in alternatives. They can be of following types
   - **Simple Alternative Questions** This type of questions require a simple yes or no answer. e.g. "Do you own a car? Yes/No"
   - **Multiple Choice Questions** These questions offer two or more alternate answers for respondents to select from. e.g. "Which of the following best describes your employment status?"

     (a) Employed (b) Unemployed
     (c) Student (d) Retired

2. **Open Ended Questions**

   They ask about the views of respondents related to a specific problem or an issue.

   e.g. "What are your views on the deteriorating sex ratio in the country?"

3. **Specific Information Questions**

   These are designed to gather specific information from respondents. e.g. "Are you graduate?"

Sample Questionnaire

Questionnaire on Food Expenditure by Resident

(Put a tick against the most appropriate choice)

1. Name : ....
2. Age : 15-24 ☐ 25-34 ☐
   35-44 ☐ 45-54 ☐
   45-54 ☐ 55 and above ☐
3. Sex : Male ☐ Female ☐ Other ☐
4. Employment : Student ☐ Home maker ☐
   Self-employed ☐ Salaried ☐
   Seeking employment ☐
5. Monthly income
   Below ₹ 15,000 ☐ ₹ 15,000-₹ 25,000 ☐
   ₹ 25,000-₹ 35,000 ☐ ₹ 35,000 and above ☐
6. On an average, how many times you go out for dinner in a month?
   Zero ☐ 1-2 ☐ 2-5 ☐ More than 5 ☐
7. Do you prefer going out for dinner rather than making food at home?
   Yes ☐ No ☐
8. How much, on a average, you spend on food when you go out?
   ₹ 1,000-₹ 2,000 ☐ ₹ 2,000-₹ 5,000 ☐

2.3 Sources of Secondary Data

Secondary data are previously collected by others and are available from various sources. These sources are categorised into two main types

Sources of Secondary Data

Published

Readily available in various forms, such as
- Articles and reports from local, central and state governments.
- Publications by goverment organisations like NSSO and CSO.
- Reports from the Reserve Bank of India (RBI).
- Publications from international organisations such as IMF and World Bank.
- Magazines and journals.

Unpublished

Not readily available in printed form.
They can be
- Internal records maintained by private companies or businesses.
- Research papers and thesies from students and academic staff.

Precautions in the Use of Secondary Data

1. **Verify the Source** Check the credibility and capability of the organisation that collected the data.
2. **Assess Suitability** Ensure the data aligns with the objectives of your study.
3. **Review Data Collection Methods** Check the original method of data collection.
4. **Match Measurement Units** Confirm that units of measurement in initial collection are consistent with those used in your study.
5. **Ensure Adequacy** Use adequate data to avoid biases and ensure accurate conclusions.

2.4 Census and Sample Surveys

Survey is a method of collecting data. The most common instrument used in surveys is questionnaire. On the basis of area covered, there are two methods of survey

- Census method
- Sampling method

Census Method

The census method involves collecting data from every unit within a population, ensuring complete coverage.

The most common example of census method is the Census of India, conducted every ten years, where enumerators visit all households to gather detailed information on demographics, including household size, education and income. This method also collects vital statistics such as birth and death rates, literacy and life expectancy, which are published by the Registrar General of India.

Advantages and Disadvantages of Census Method

Advantages of Census Method	Disadvantages of Census Method
• The result collected by this method will be highly accurate and reliable. • There are less chances of biasness at the time of collection of data. • Data related to each and every item of the population is collected. • This method is suitable when different items of the population are not homogeneous.	• A lot of time, energy and money is required to collect the data. • This method cannot be applied in case of infinite population. • This method requires a large number of enumerators for collecting data. If the enumerators are not properly trained, then the data collected by them will not be accurate and reliable.

Sample Method

The sample method involves surveying a subset of the population rather than the entire group. A sample is chosen to represent the population and is used to infer characteristics of the whole.

e.g. To determine the average weight of 1,000 students, a sample of 50 students might be measured and their average weight would estimate the average weight for all students.

Advantages and Disadvantages of Sample Method

Advantages of Sample Method	Disadvantages of Sample Method
• This method is economical because only some units of the population are studied. • In this method, the process of investigation is not time consuming. • There is an administrative convenience in handling a limited number of items. • Less efforts are required as small portion of population is studied. • This method is more scientific, as the sample can be conveniently investigated from various angles.	• It is only a partial investigation of the universe. • It is not very easy to select a sample which would represent the characteristics of the entire population. • Sometimes area may be so diverse that it becomes difficult to frame a sample. • Sampling involves a set of technical procedures, which makes sampling a complex and difficult procedure. • Not possible, if the population is heterogeneous in nature.

> **Population**
>
> In statistics, *Population* or the *Universe* means totality of the items under study. Thus, the Population or the Universe is a group to which the results of the study are intended to apply. A population is always all the individuals/items who possess certain characteristics according to the purpose of the survey.

Essentials of Samples

A sample must possess the following essential characteristics so as to achieve right and unbiased conclusions

Essentials of Samples

- **Representative** The sample should accurately reflect the entire population, capturing its key characteristics.
- **Adequacy** The sample size must be adequate to reliably represent the population, ensuring that the findings are meaningful.
- **Independence** Sample units should be selected independently from each other to avoid bias and ensure that each unit contributes equally to the results.
- **Homogeneity** Samples should be chosen from a homogeneous group to prevent misleading results that arise from mixing diverse data.

Methods of Sampling

Broadly there are two methods of sampling

Methods of Sampling

- Random sampling
  - Simple random sampling
    - Lottery method
    - Table of random numbers
  - Restricted random sampling
    - Stratified random sampling
    - Systematic sampling
    - Cluster sampling
    - Multistage sampling
- Non-random sampling
  - Judgement/Purposive/Delibrate sampling
  - Quota sampling
  - Convenience sampling

I. Random Sampling

Random sampling is a method where individuals from the population are selected randomly, giving each unit an equal chance of being chosen. This approach is also known as 'probability sampling'.

There are two main types of random sampling, i.e.

1. **Simple Random Sampling** In simple random sampling, every item in the population has an equal chance of being selected. Common methods include
   - **Lottery Method** Each item is assigned a unique number written on identical piece of paper and placed in a bowl. Then, a random selection is made by drawing numbers from a bowl.
   - **Table of Random Numbers** For large population, random numbers are selected from pre-generated tables, like Tippett's Random Number Table, which provides a large set of random digits.

> **Exit Polls**
>
> Exit polls is a technique to predict the election results. In this technique, a random sample of voters, who exit from the polling booths are asked who they voted for.
>
> From the data of the sample of voters, the prediction is made as to which party will win the elections. It is to be noted that exit polls do not always predict correctly.

2. **Restricted Random Sampling** When dealing with heterogeneous populations, restricted random sampling is used. Common methods include
   - **Stratified Random Sampling** The population is divided into strata or groups based on specific characteristics. Samples are then randomly selected from each group. This method is useful for populations with diverse attributes. e.g. Comparing the marital status of males and females with similar education to find the likelihood of marriage among them.
   - **Systematic Sampling** Samples are selected by choosing every *n*th item from a list. e.g. From a list of 50,000 units, to form a sample of 50, selecting every 1000th item will give us the required sample.
   - **Cluster Sampling** The population is divided into clusters (some identified sub-divisions). Then a random selection of clusters is made and all items within these clusters are included in the sample. For instance, dividing an area into clusters and selecting a few for detailed study.
   - **Multistage Sampling** It is an extension of cluster sampling, involving multiple stages.
     - In first stage, population is divided into clusters and certain clusters are selected at random.
     - In second stage, first stage samples are sub-divided into clusters and from each cluster, samples are selected at random.

     In this way, the process continues till the best possible sample is selected.

II. Non-random Sampling

Non-random sampling methods do not give every unit in the population an equal chance of being selected. These methods rely on the investigator's judgement or convenience.

The main types of non-random sampling are

1. **Judgement/Purposive/Deliberate Sampling** The researcher selects specific units based on his/her expertise or judgement. This method can introduce personal bias but is useful for targeting particular groups or experts.
2. **Quota Sampling** The population is divided into sub-groups and fixed quotas are set for each sub-group. The investigator collects data from these pre-determined numbers of units in each sub-group to ensure diversity in the sample.
3. **Convenience Sampling** The researcher selects sample units based on his/her easy accessibility or proximity. This method is quick and convenient but may not be representative of the entire population.

Judgement/Purposive/ Deliberate Sampling

IIFL Finance (India) conducted a study on investment patterns among affluent investors in India. The company selected a sample of high net worth individuals from its own client base due to their targeted expertise and relevance to the study.

Quota Sampling

HDFC Bank conducted a survey on customer satisfaction and ensured they interviewed a fixed number of customers from different branches across various cities, such as Delhi, Mumbai and Bangalore, to achieve a balanced view of customer experience across different demographics.

2.5 Statistical Errors

Errors in statistics denote the difference between the true value and the estimated value. Symbolically,

$$\text{Error} = \text{True/Actual Value} - \text{Estimated Value}$$

They can be broadly classified into two types

1. Sampling Errors

These occur due to the variability between the sample estimate and the actual population parameter. They arise because a sample, rather than the entire population, is used for estimation. The magnitude of sampling errors can be reduced by increasing the sample size.

e.g. Take incomes of 5 farmers of Rajasthan. There income measurements are 500, 550, 600, 650 and 700. So,

$$\text{Average Income} = \frac{500 + 550 + 600 + 650 + 700}{5} = \frac{3,000}{5} = ₹\,600$$

Now, if we select a sample of two farmers having incomes as 500 and 600, then

$$\text{Sample Average} = \frac{500 + 600}{2} = \frac{1,100}{2} = ₹\,550$$

Here, the sampling error of the estimate = 600 (True Value) − 550 (Estimate) = ₹ 50

2. Non-sampling Errors

These are errors that occur during various stages of the survey process, including planning, data collection and analysis. Non-sampling errors are more challenging then sampling errors as they are difficult to minimise even with large samples

Error	Explanation
Errors in Data Acquisition	These are the mistakes that are made during data recording, such as incorrect entry of responses. e.g. During a customer satisfaction survey by Flipkart, a surveyor mistakenly recorded '20' instead of '200' for the number of items purchased, leading to incorrect analysis.
Non-response Errors	This error occurs when certain individuals from the sample are either unreachable or refuse to provide information, leading to incomplete data. e.g. In a health survey by the Indian Council of Medical Research (ICMR), several participants did not respond to questions about their health conditions, leading to incomplete data and potential biases.
Sampling Bias	It happens when the sampling method excludes certain segments of the population, causing the sample to not fully represent the population. e.g. HDFC Life Insurance conducted a survey on customer preferences but only sampled urban areas. This sampling bias excluded rural customers, leading to skewed results that do not represent the entire customer base.

2.6 Important Agencies of Secondary Data

Secondary data is collected, processed and tabulated by various national and state-level agencies. These agencies play a crucial role in gathering statistical information, which is used for analysis, planning and policy formulation.

Key national agencies include

1. Census of India

Conducted every ten years since 1881, with the most recent in 2011, the Census of India provides comprehensive demographic data, including population size, density, sex-ratio, literacy and migration.

The Office of Registrar General and Census Commissioner oversee this extensive data collection, which further informs economic and social policies.

2. National Sample Survey Organisation (NSSO)

Established in 1950 under the Ministry of Finance, the NSSO conducts nationwide surveys on socio-economic issues. It releases data through reports and its quarterly journal, Sarvekshana.

The NSSO's surveys cover a wide range of topics, including literacy, employment, public distribution systems and industrial activities. Data is collected periodically, with major surveys conducted every five years.

Mind Map

COLLECTION OF DATA

1 Introduction to Data Collection

Data is a tool which helps in reaching a suitable conclusion on any problem by providing information. It is collected to understand, explain and analyse a problem.

Sources of Data

- **Internal Sources** Data collected from within an organisation.
- **External Sources** Data collected from outside an organisation.

2 Types of Data

- **Primary Data** Data collected directly by an investigator for the first time through methods such as personal interviews, questionnaires, telephonic interview or surveys.
- **Secondary Data** Data previously collected and processed by others, which is later used by investigators. This includes data from published sources and unpublished sources.

Precautions in the Use of Secondary Data

– Verify the source
– Assess suitability
– Review data collection methods
– Match measurement units
– Ensure adequacy

3 Methods of Collecting Primary Data

1. **Direct Personal Investigation** (Face-to-face interview)
   - *Advantages*: High accuracy, reliability of data, flexibility.
   - *Disadvantages*: Expensive, time consuming.
2. **Information from Correspondents** (Local agents report data periodically)
   - *Advantages*: Cost effective, wide coverage, continuous supply of information.
   - *Disadvantages*: Less reliable, lacks uniformity, potential for bias.
3. **Mailing Questionnaires** (Sent through mail, responses received by post)
   - *Advantages*: Cost effective, reaches remote areas, reduces interviewer bias.
   - *Disadvantages*: Misunderstanding questions, low response rate, limited to educated respondents.
4. **Indirect Oral Investigation** (Third-party interviews)
   - *Advantages*: Economical, wide data coverage, less personal bias.
   - *Disadvantages*: Less reliable, data lacks uniformity.
5. **Telephonic Interviews** (Data collected via phone calls)
   - *Advantages*: Quick, cost effective, broad geographical reach.
   - *Disadvantages*: No visual aids, limited accessibility.
6. **Questionnaire Filled by Enumerators** (Enumerators record responses directly)
   - *Advantages*: Suitable for both literate and illiterate respondents, unbiased data, flexible with physical presence.
   - *Disadvantages*: Expensive, time consuming.

4 Construction of a Questionnaire

- **Conciseness** Avoid lengthy questionnaires.
- **Clarity** Use simple and precise questions.
- **Structure** Start with general questions, then move to specifics.
- **Simplicity** Use clear and easy to understand language.
- **Organisation** Group questions under relevant headings and sub-headings.
- **Avoid Negatives** Do not use double negatives.
- **Neutrality** Avoid leading questions.
- **Testing** Conduct a pilot survey before full deployment.

5 Types of Questions in a Questionnaire

Closed Ended Questions

- Easy to use, score and analyse.
- May limit responses if the true answer is not listed.
- Types include simple alternative questions and multiple choice questions.

Open Ended Questions

- Gather views on specific issues.

Specific Information Questions

- Collect precise details.

6 Census *vs* Sample Surveys

Census Method (Collects data from the entire population)

- *Advantages*: Highly accurate, comprehensive.
- *Disadvantages*: Expensive, time consuming.

Sample Method (Collects data from a subset of the population)

- *Advantages*: Cost effective, time saving.
- *Disadvantages*: Potential for bias, requires expertise in sampling.

7 Methods of Sampling

Random Sampling (Probability Sampling)

1. **Simple Random Sampling** Each unit has an equal chance of selection. Common methods include lottery system and random number tables.
2. **Restricted Random Sampling** It is used while dealing with heterogeneous population. Common methods include stratified random sampling, systematic sampling, cluster sampling and multistage sampling.

Non-random Sampling (Non-probability sampling)

1. **Judgement Sampling** Researcher selects sample based on expertise.
2. **Quota Sampling** Fixed quotas set for different population groups.
3. **Convenience Sampling** Samples chosen based on easy accessibility.

8 Statistical Errors

Sampling Errors Arise from using a sample instead of the full population. The magnitude of error can be reduced by increasing sample size.

Non-sampling Errors Errors that occur at various survey stages. The errors may include errors in data acquisition, non-response errors and sampling bias.

9 Important Agencies of Secondary Data

1. **Census of India** (Conducted every 10 years, provides demographic data)
2. **National Sample Survey Office** (NSSO) (Conducts social economic surveys)

EXAM PATTERN QUESTIONS

Objective Type Questions

Multiple Choice Questions (MCQs)

1. Which of the following is an example of internal sources of data?

(a) Data from government publications
(b) Data collected from medical tourists
(c) Annual statement of a company's profit and loss
(d) Reports of committees

2. Data that is collected for the first time by an investigator through personal interviews or questionnaires is known as ....

(a) primary data (b) secondary data
(c) internal data (d) statistical data

3. Identify the term that refers to the individual from whom statistical information is being collected.

I. Respondents **II. Variable**
III. Enumerators **IV. Investigators**

Codes Competency Based Que

(a) Only I (b) Both II and III
(c) Only IV (d) All of these

4. The values of variables, such as the maximum temperature of a city per day, are referred to as ....

(a) enumerators (b) investigators
(c) statistical units (d) observations

5. What is a common example of primary data?

(a) Census reports
(b) Market surveys conducted by a company
(c) Government publications
(d) Academic thesis

6. Which of the following statements is true about secondary data? Competency Based Que

I. It is originally collected by an investigator for the first time.
II. It is cheaper and can be collected from published or unpublished sources.
III. It requires a lot of manpower, money and time to collect.
IV. It is already collected by some other person.

Codes

(a) Only III (b) Only II
(c) Both II and IV (d) None of these

7. In which situation is indirect oral investigation most suitable? Competency Based Que

(a) When detailed information is required from a specific respondent
(b) When the area of investigation is very large
(c) When the investigator needs direct contact with the respondent
(d) When respondents are highly educated

8. Which method allows for continuous and regular information collection over a large area?

(a) Direct personal investigation
(b) Telephonic interviews
(c) Information from correspondents
(d) Questionnaire filled by enumerators

9. Which method is most suitable for collecting data from a small and localised population?

(a) Mailing questionnaires
(b) Direct personal investigation
(c) Telephonic interviews
(d) Information from correspondents

10. "Census 2024: Enumerators begin direct personal investigations across rural India."

What is a key advantage of using direct personal investigation for data collection in this context? Competency Based Que

(a) It is the most cost effective method
(b) It allows for the collection of detailed and accurate information
(c) It can cover a large geographical area quickly
(d) It eliminates the need for trained personnel

11. Which of the following method of collecting primary data is highlighted in the below image?

(a) Questionnaire by enumerators
(b) Personal interviews
(c) Telephonic interviews
(d) Information from correspondents

12. **In the .... method, data are collected by sending a set of questions through mail along with a covering letter, a self-addressed stamped envelope and assurances of confidentiality.**

(a) interview based (b) mailing questionnaire
(c) telephonic (d) observational

13. **When constructing a questionnaire, which of the following practices is recommended to ensure clarity and effectiveness?** **Competency Based Que**

(a) Using double negatives to make questions more precise
(b) Including a large number of questions to cover all possible aspects
(c) Ensuring questions move from general to specific to guide the respondent effectively
(d) Leading questions to direct the respondent towards a specific answer

14. **Identify the type of questionnaire question given in below image.**

On an average, how many times you go out for dinner in a month?
Zero ☐ 1-2 ☐ 2-5 ☐ More than 5 ☐

(a) Close ended MCQ
(b) Open ended question
(c) Information question
(d) Simple alternative question

15. **What type of question requires a simple 'Yes' or 'No' answer?**

(a) Open ended questions
(b) Specific information questions
(c) Multiple choice questions
(d) Simple alternative questions

16. **The pilot survey helps in which of the following?**

(a) Collecting large-scale data
(b) Ensuring uniformity in collected data
(c) Avoiding primary data collection
(d) Identifying shortcomings in the questionnaire

17. **Which of the following is an example of published secondary data?** **Competency Based Que**

(a) Research papers by students
(b) Reports of Reserve Bank of India (RBI)
(c) Records maintained by a private company
(d) Research papers of teachers

18. **A researcher wants to use a private company's internal records for a study. What crucial step the researcher must take to ensure that secondary data is reliable?**

I. Verify the company's financial health.
II. Ensure the method of data collection aligns with the study's requirement.
III. Check the company's employee list.
IV. Confirm that the company's records are published in journals. **Competency Based Que**

Codes
(a) Both I and II (b) Only II
(c) Only IV (d) All of these

19. **Unpublished secondary data are not readily available in .... form and can include records maintained by private companies or research papers.**

(a) digital (b) printed (c) electronic (d) audio

20. **Which of the following is not a precaution while using secondary data?**

(a) Verifying the source (b) Ensuring adequacy of data
(c) Ignoring measurement units
(d) Assessing data suitability

21. **Identify the source of secondary data from the following image.**

Europe and Central Asia
IBRD and IDA Lending by Sector/Fiscal 2014

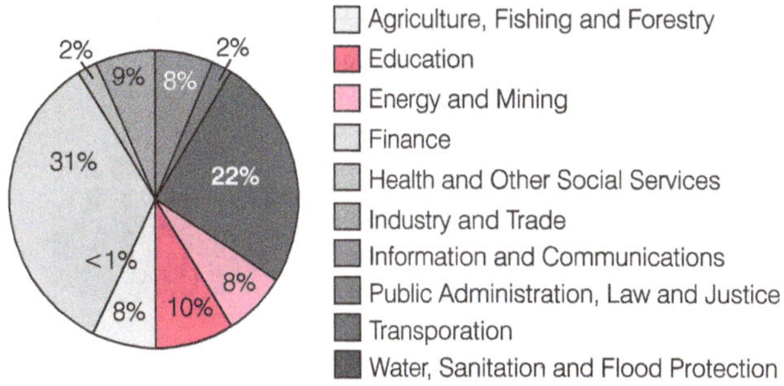

(a) Unpublished data (b) Published data
(c) Internal data (d) Primary data

22. **An investigator is reviewing a report published by the Reserve Bank of India (RBI) for a research study. To ensure the reliability of the secondary data, which precaution should the investigator primarily focus on?** **Competency Based Que**

(a) Confirming the data's suitability for the current study
(b) Checking the publication date of the report
(c) Ensuring the report includes recent news articles
(d) Verifying if the report has been cited in popular magazines

23. **In which sampling method, items are selected by taking every nth item from a complete list of available population?**

(a) Stratified random sampling
(b) Systematic sampling
(c) Cluster sampling (d) Multistage sampling

24. **Which sampling method involves assigning unique numbers to items and randomly drawing them from a bowl?**

(a) Stratified sampling (b) Lottery method
(c) Systematic sampling (d) Cluster sampling

25. **Which of the following statistical methods are shown in the image below?**

(a) Census (b) Sampling
(c) Proportion (d) None of these

26. **In .... sampling, the population is divided into different strata based on characteristics and samples are selected randomly from each stratum.**

(a) stratified random (b) systematic
(c) convenience (d) quota

27. **Which type of non-random sampling method is highlighted in the below image?**

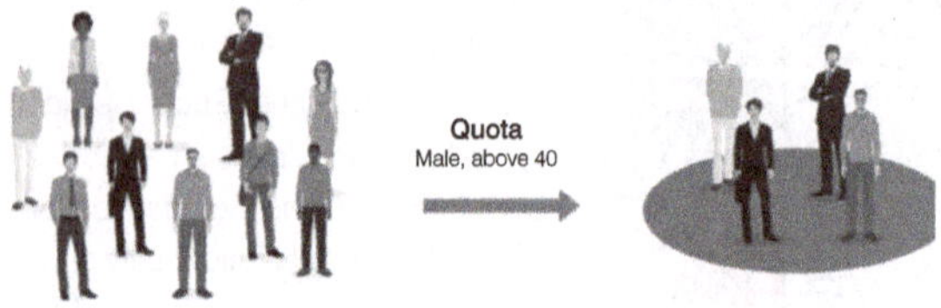

(a) Convenience sampling (b) Judgement
(c) Quota sampling (d) Multistage sampling

28. **......... sampling involves selecting sample units based on the investigator's convenience, rather than a random method.**

(a) Systematic (b) Cluster
(c) Convenience (d) Judgement

29. **Which of the following is a primary characteristic of sampling errors?** Competency Based Que

(a) They occur due to incorrect recording of responses
(b) They can be minimised by taking a larger sample
(c) They arise from non-response or sampling bias
(d) They are always easier to correct than non-sampling errors

30. **Non-sampling errors are considered more serious than sampling errors because ....**

(a) they are easier to measure and correct
(b) they can be minimised by increasing the sample size
(c) they arise from factors that are difficult to minimise, even with a large sample
(d) they only occur during data acquisition

31. **Which of the following is an example of a non-sampling error?** Competency Based Que

(a) The difference between the sample mean and the population mean
(b) The use of an inadequate sample size
(c) Errors in data acquisition, such as recording incorrect responses
(d) Sampling bias due to selecting an unrepresentative sample

32. **What occurs when certain segments of the population are excluded, leading to a sample that does not represent the entire population?**

(a) Sampling bias (b) Random sampling
(c) Cluster sampling (d) Systematic sampling

33. **Which organisation, established in 1950, conducts nationwide surveys on socio-economic issues and publishes its findings in the journal Sarvekshana?**

(a) Central Statistical Office (CSO)
(b) Reserve Bank of India (RBI)
(c) National Sample Survey Organisation (NSSO)
(d) Indian Council of Social Science Research (ICSSR)

34. **"Census of India 2024 : preparations underway for the first digital census."**

The recent headline indicates that the upcoming Census of India will be the first to use a digital approach. What is a primary function of the Census of India? Competency Based Que

(a) Conducting quarterly surveys on socio-economic issue
(b) Providing comprehensive demographic records of the population
(c) Publishing reports on retail prices of goods
(d) Estimating literacy rates and educational enrolment

Direction *Read the case study and answer the questions 35 to 38 on the basis of the same*

In an effort to enhance economic conditions in rural India, a comprehensive assessment was conducted using both primary and secondary data. The goal was to gather detailed information on income, employment and access to public services to guide policy decisions and development initiatives.

The study utilised various methods to collect data. Direct personal investigation involved face-to-face interviews with residents to collect detailed information about their income levels and employment status. Additionally, mailing questionnaires were sent to households to gather data on education, healthcare access and housing conditions.

To reach those who were difficult to contact in person, telephonic interviews were also conducted. These methods ensured a broad and detailed collection of data from a diverse population.

Alongside primary data collection, secondary data from established sources were used. The Census of India provided comprehensive demographic information, including population density and literacy rates, which was crucial for understanding broader trends. The National Sample Survey Organisation (NSSO) offered valuable insights into employment rates and public service usage, collected through periodic surveys.

The combined data from these sources helped identify key economic challenges in rural areas, such as gaps in education and healthcare.

The information was analysed to inform government policies aimed at improving infrastructure, education and healthcare services.

By using both primary and secondary data, the study provided a well-rounded view of rural economic conditions, facilitating targeted and effective development initiatives.

35. Which method was not used in the rural economic development assessment study?

(a) Direct personal investigation
(b) Mailing questionnaires
(c) Focus groups (d) Telephonic interviews

36. What was one of the sources of secondary data used in the study?

(a) National Sample Survey Organisation (NSSO)
(b) Local government reports
(c) Private sector surveys
(d) International development organisations

37. The study used .... to gather detailed information about residents' income levels and employment status.

38. Secondary data from the .... provided comprehensive demographic information, including population density and literacy rates.

Assertion-Reason

Direction (Q.No. 39 to 48) *Read the following Assertion (A) and Reason (R) and choose the correct alternative from the following*

Alternatives

(a) Both Assertion (A) and Reason (R) are true and Reason (R) is the correct explanation of Assertion (A)
(b) Both Assertion (A) and Reason (R) are true, but Reason (R) is not the correct explanation of Assertion (A)
(c) Assertion (A) is true, but Reason (R) is false
(d) Assertion (A) is false, but Reason (R) is true

39. Assertion (A) Primary data is more reliable than secondary data for specific research purposes.

Reason (R) Primary data is collected directly from the original sources for the first time.

40. Assertion (A) Secondary data can be used to save time and resources in research.

Reason (A) Secondary data is collected specifically for the current research study.

41. Assertion (A) Mailing questionnaires is a suitable method for collecting data from large, geographically dispersed populations.

Reason (R) Mailing questionnaires allow for direct interaction between the investigator and respondent.

42. Assertion (A) Direct personal investigation is ideal for collecting confidential and detailed information.

Reason (R) Direct personal investigation involves face-to-face interviews, which allow for flexibility and reliability in data collection.

43. Assertion (A) Published sources of secondary data are not easily accessible in various forms.

Reason (R) Records maintained by the central bank are examples of published sources.

44. Assertion (A) Unpublished sources of secondary data are often not readily available in printed form.

Reason (R) Research papers and records maintained by private companies for internal use are examples of unpublished sources of secondary data.

45. Assertion (A) Systematic sampling is a form of restricted random sampling.

Reason (R) Systematic sampling involves selecting every nth item from a list to form a sample.

46. Assertion (A) Cluster sampling can help in reducing the cost and effort of data collection.

Reason (R) In cluster sampling, samples are selected randomly from different strata of the population.

47. Assertion (A) Unrestricted random sampling is not useful in case of heterogeneous data.

Reason (R) Raw data collected by primary sources possesses similar as well as differentiated attributes.

48. Assertion (A) Quota sampling ensures that all sub-groups of a population are represented in the sample.

Reason (R) Quota sampling is a form of random sampling that provides equal chances of selection to all individuals in the population.

Two Statements Based MCQs

Direction (Q.No. 49 to 58) *Read the following statements carefully and choose the correct alternative*

Alternatives

(a) Statement I is correct and Statement II is incorrect
(b) Statement II is correct and Statement I is incorrect
(c) Both the statements are correct
(d) Both the statements are incorrect

49. **Statement I** Internal sources of data are data collected from outside an organisation.

Statement II External sources of data include data from public records and industry reports.

50. **Statement I** Secondary data is data collected for the first time for a specific research purpose.

Statement II Secondary data requires careful verification of its source and suitability.

51. **Statement I** Direct personal investigation ensures high originality and uniformity of data.

Statement II This method is suitable for large-scale surveys due to its cost effectiveness.

52. **Statement I** Information from correspondents is used for large areas requiring frequent updates.

Statement II Information from correspondents ensures high accuracy and uniformity.

53. **Statement I** Telephonic interviews can reach respondents quickly and are cost effective.

Statement II Telephonic interviews requires physical presence and is ideal for large areas.

54. **Statement I** Closed ended questions are more challenging to score and analyse compared to open ended questions.

Statement II Specific information questions are designed to gather detailed responses from respondents.

55. **Statement I** Questionnaire is the most common method of collecting statistical information.

Statement II Questionnaires should have limited, precise and clear questions.

56. **Statement I** Multistage sampling is an extension of cluster sampling.

Statement II In systematic sampling, every item in the population has an equal chance of being selected.

57. **Statement I** Cluster sampling should not be used if there are wide variations in the data present.

Statement II A good sample is the one which follows law of statistical rigidity.

58. **Statement I** Non-response errors are non-sampling errors.

Statement II A larger sample can reduce the magnitude of sampling error.

Matching

59. Match the following

Column I		Column II	
A.	Internal sources of data	(i)	Conducts statistical enquiry.
B.	External sources of data	(ii)	Gives the statistical information.
C.	Investigators	(iii)	Collected within the organisation.
D.	Respondents	(iv)	Collected from outside sources.

Codes

	A	B	C	D		A	B	C	D
(a)	(iii)	(iv)	(i)	(ii)	(b)	(iv)	(i)	(ii)	(iii)
(c)	(ii)	(iii)	(iv)	(i)	(d)	(iii)	(ii)	(i)	(iv)

60. Match the following

Column I		Column II	
A.	Data collected by interviewing third person.	(i)	Personal interview
B.	Data collected through mail.	(ii)	Indirect oral investigation
C.	Local agents appointed for enquiry.	(iii)	Mailing questionnaires
D.	Face-to-face enquiries.	(iv)	Information from correspondents

Codes

	A	B	C	D		A	B	C	D
(a)	(iii)	(iv)	(i)	(ii)	(b)	(iv)	(i)	(ii)	(iii)
(c)	(ii)	(iii)	(iv)	(i)	(d)	(iii)	(ii)	(i)	(iv)

61. Match the following

Column I		Column II	
A.	Sample	(i)	Totality of the items under study.
B.	Population	(ii)	Method of complete enumeration.
C.	Census	(iii)	Samples collected at random.
D.	Random sampling	(iv)	Part of population selected to represent the population.

Codes

	A	B	C	D		A	B	C	D
(a)	(iii)	(iv)	(i)	(ii)	(b)	(iv)	(i)	(ii)	(iii)
(c)	(ii)	(iii)	(iv)	(i)	(d)	(iii)	(ii)	(i)	(iv)

62. Match the following

Column I		Column II	
A.	Stratified random sampling	(i)	Depends upon whims and fantasies of the investigator.
B.	Cluster sampling	(ii)	Population divided into groups based on characteristics.
C.	Judgement sampling	(iii)	Population divided into identified sub-divisions.
D.	Convenience sampling	(iv)	Investigator selects samples consciously.

Codes

	A	B	C	D
(a)	(iii)	(iv)	(i)	(ii)
(b)	(iv)	(i)	(ii)	(iii)
(c)	(ii)	(iii)	(iv)	(i)
(d)	(iii)	(ii)	(i)	(iv)

63. Match the options of Column I with correct option in Column II

Column I		Column II	
A.	Data avaliable in published and unpublished form	(i)	Statistical error
B.	Sampling deliberately done by the investigator	(ii)	Direct interview
C.	Difference between estimated value and actual value of statistics	(iii)	Non-random sampling
D.	Highly elastic method	(iv)	Secondary source

Codes

	A	B	C	D		A	B	C	D
(a)	(i)	(ii)	(iii)	(iv)	(b)	(ii)	(iii)	(iv)	(i)
(c)	(iii)	(iv)	(i)	(ii)	(d)	(iv)	(iii)	(i)	(ii)

Concept Identification

64. Data collected from within an organisation using its own records and reports.

65. A method where local agents collect and report data to the investigator, suited for large areas needing regular updates.

66. A set of questions used to collect data from respondents.

67. The method of collecting data from every unit within a population to ensure comprehensive coverage.

68. Only a part of the population is surveyed to gather data, which is then used to estimate the characteristics of the whole population.

Answers

1. (c) Annual statement of a company's profit and loss
2. (a) primary data **3.** (a) Only I
4. (d) observations
5. (b) Market surveys conducted by a company
6. (c) Both II and IV
7. (b) When the area of investigation is very large
8. (c) Information from correspondents
9. (b) Direct personal investigation
10. (b) It allows for the collection of detailed and accurate information
11. (c) Telephonic interviews
12. (b) mailing questionnaire
13. (c) Ensuring questions move from general to specific to guide the respondent effectively
14. (a) Close ended MCQ
15. (d) Simple alternative questions
16. (d) Identifying shortcomings in the questionnaire
17. (b) Reports of Reserve Bank of India (RBI)
18. (b) Only II **19.** (b) printed
20. (c) Ignoring measurement units
21. (b) Published data
22. (a) Confirming the data's suitability for the current study
23. (b) Systematic sampling
24. (b) Lottery method **25.** (b) Sampling
26. (a) stratified random **27.** (c) Quota sampling
28. (c) Convenience
29. (b) They can be minimised by taking a larger sample
30. (c) they arise from factors that are difficult to minimise, even with a large sample
31. (c) Errors in data acquisition, such as recording incorrect responses
32. (a) Sampling bias

33. (c) National Sample Survey Organisation (NSSO)
34. (b) Providing comprehensive demographic records of the population
35. (c) Focus groups
36. (a) National Sample Survey Organisation (NSSO)
37. direct personal investigation
38. Census of India
39. (a) Both Assertion (A) and Reason (R) are true and Reason (R) is the correct explanation of Assertion (A)
40. (c) Secondary data indeed saves time and resources because it is already collected and available. However, secondary data is not collected specifically for the current research study but was originally gathered for other purposes.
41. (c) Mailing questionnaires is effective for large, dispersed populations as it reaches people remotely. However, mailing questionnaires does not involve direct interaction between the investigator and respondent.
42. (a) Both Assertion (A) and Reason (R) are true and Reason (R) is the correct explanation of Assertion (A)
43. (d) Published sources of secondary data are typically readily accessible in various forms like reports and journals.
44. (a) Both Assertion (A) and Reason (R) are true and Reason (R) is the correct explanation of Assertion (A)
45. (a) Both Assertion (A) and Reason (R) are true and Reason (R) is the correct explanation of Assertion (A)
46. (b) Both Assertion (A) and Reason (R) are true, but Reason (R) is not the correct explanation of Assertion (A)
47. (b) Both Assertion (A) and Reason (R) are true, but Reason (R) is not the correct explanation of Assertion (A)
48. (c) Quota sampling is not a form of random sampling; it is a non-random sampling technique where individuals are selected based on specific characteristics until the quotas are filled.
49. (b) Internal sources of data are data collected within an organisation, not from outside.
50. (b) Secondary data is data that has already been collected for a different purpose and requires careful verification for its relevance and accuracy in the new research context.
51. (a) This method is time-consuming, labour-intensive and expensive.
52. (a) The accuracy and uniformity of information depend on correspondent's reliability and expertise.
53. (a) Telephonic interviews are quick and cost effective but do not require physical presence and are not specifically ideal for large areas compared to methods like face-to-face interviews.
54. (b) Closed ended questions are generally easier to score and analyse than open ended questions. Specific information questions aim to gather detailed responses, which typically involves open ended questions.
55. (c) Both the statements are correct
56. (a) In systematic sampling, not every item has an equal chance of selection; instead, items are selected at regular intervals, which do not guarantee equal probability for every item.
57. (a) A good sample is the one which follows the principles of regularity and large numbers.
58. (c) Both the statements are correct
59. (a) (iii) (iv) (i) (ii)
60. (c) (ii) (iii) (iv) (i)
61. (b) (iv) (i) (ii) (iii)
62. (c) (ii) (iii) (iv) (i)
63. (d) (iv) (iii) (i) (ii)
64. Internal sources of data
65. Information from correspondents
66. Questionnaire
67. Census method
68. Sampling method

Subjective Questions

Short Answer Type Questions

1. Why is internal data considered particularly valuable for an organisation's strategic planning and decision-making processes? Competency Based Que

Ans. Internal data is invaluable for strategic planning as it provides insights directly from the organisation's operational and financial activities. It includes information such as sales figures, customer feedback and employee performance metrics, which are crucial for understanding internal strengths, weaknesses and areas for improvement.

This data helps organisations make informed decisions based on their unique context and performance history.

2. What is primary data?

Ans. Primary data is information collected directly from original sources through methods like surveys, interviews or experiments specifically for a research purpose.

This data is gathered firsthand and tailored to the study's needs, ensuring high relevance and accuracy. It provides fresh insights and detailed evidence directly related to the research questions.

3. What does secondary data refer to?

Ans. Secondary data refers to information that was collected by someone other than the researcher for a purpose other than the current study.

This data includes sources like published research papers, government reports and historical records. It is used to provide context, support findings or complement primary data by offering background information and trends.

4. Define the terms

(i) Enumerator **(ii) Investigator**

(iii) Respondent

Ans. (i) **Enumerator**

He is engaged by the investigator to help him in the collection of data. Often the enumerator is a trained person for field work.

(ii) **Investigator**

The person who conducts statistical investigation/ enquiry is referred to as investigator.

(iii) **Respondent**

The person from whom the statistical information is collected is referred to as respondent.

5. Differentiate between primary data and secondary data.

Ans. Difference between primary and secondary data

Basis	Primary Data	Secondary Data
Originality	They are original.	They are not original.
Time and Cost	The collection of primary data requires a lot of manpower, money and time.	This source is relatively cheaper.
Precautions	No precaution is required while using primary data.	It should be used with great care and caution.
Source	They are collected by some agency or person by using the various methods of data collection.	They are already collected and processed by some person or agency and are ready for use.

6. "A well-constructed questionnaire serves as a structured tool to gather accurate and relevant information from respondents." What are the key factors to consider when designing a questionnaire to ensure it gathers accurate and relevant data? Mention any six of them. Competency Based Que

Ans. Key considerations for creating an effective questionnaire (any six)

(i) **Conciseness**

Ensure the questionnaire is not too lengthy.

(ii) **Clarity**

Limit the number of questions to keep them clear and precise.

(iii) **Structure**

Start with general questions and progress to more specific ones.

(iv) **Simplicity**

Avoid confusing language and ensure questions are easy to answer.

(v) **Organisation**

Group questions logically under relevant headings.

(vi) **Avoid Negatives**

Steer clear of double negatives like wouldn't you or don't you.

(vii) **Neutrality**

Prevent questions that lead to specific answers or imply alternatives.

(viii) **Relevance**

Exclude personal questions that are irrelevant to the research.

(ix) **Testing**

Pilot the questionnaire with a small sample to refine it before full deployment.

7. Identify and explain the type of method of collecting primary data from the following image. Competency Based Que

Ans. The image depicts a direct personal investigation method. This method involves face-to-face interaction between the investigator and the respondent, as seen in the image where one person is conducting an interview with the other. It is effective for gathering detailed and accurate information as the investigator can ask follow-up questions and clarify responses immediately. This approach is often used when in-depth information is required and allows for personal engagement, which can enhance the quality of the data collected.

8. "Local correspondents provide live updates on flood damage across Himachal Pradesh." – Times of India

How does the role of local correspondents in providing live updates on flood damage illustrate the method of 'information from correspondents' in data collection? Competency Based Que

Ans. The headline highlights how local correspondents gather and transmit real time information about flood damage.

This method of data collection, 'information from correspondents,' involves local agents collecting data from specific regions and reporting it to central authorities or media outlets. By using correspondents who are on-site, the data collection process benefits from detailed localised insights and frequent updates, which enhance the accuracy and relevance of the information. This approach is particularly useful in covering large or diverse areas where direct contact by central investigators would be challenging.

9. What are the primary advantages of using questionnaires filled out by enumerators for data collection?

Ans. Advantages of using questionnairos are as follows (any four)

(i) **Direct Assistance**
Enumerators provide help to respondents, ensuring they understand and accurately complete the questions.

(ii) **Inclusive**
Effective for reaching respondents with varying literacy levels and those who may not be comfortable with written responses.

(iii) **Immediate Clarification**
Allows for on-the-spot clarification of ambiguities or misunderstandings.

(iv) **Higher Accuracy**
Reduces errors and omissions in responses through real time support.

(v) **Personal Interaction**
Builds rapport with respondents, which can enhance the quality of the data collected.

10. What is the difference between published and unpublished sources of data?

Ans. Following are the differences between published and unpublished data (any four)

Basis	Published Data	Unpublished Data
Meaning	Data available in public documents and publications.	Data not yet formally published, often found in internal reports or private documents.
Accessibility	Generally accessible to the public through libraries, websites and official publications.	Typically restricted to internal use within an organisation or accessed through special requests.
Formality	Official and often peer-reviewed or validated.	May lack formal review and validation.
Usage	Widely used for research, policy-making and general reference due to its availability.	Used within organisations for internal purposes or specific studies before public release.
Example	Government reports, academic journals, industry reports.	Company internal reports, draft research papers, private surveys.

11. A researcher is using secondary data from a government health report to study the impact of air pollution on respiratory diseases. Upon review, the researcher finds that the data was collected using different measurement units and methods from those used in their current study.

What precautions should the researcher take to ensure the secondary data is reliable and suitable for their study? Competency Based Que

Ans. To ensure the secondary data is reliable and suitable, the researcher should (any four)

(i) **Verify the Organisation's Credibility**
Check the reliability and capability of the organisation that collected the data.

(ii) **Assess Suitability**
Ensure the data aligns with the objectives of the current study.

(iii) **Review Data Collection Methods**
Understand the original method of data collection and compare it with the current study's requirements.

(iv) **Confirm Measurement Units**
Ensure that the units of measurement used in the original data are consistent with those used in the current study.

(v) **Use Adequate Data**
Ensure sufficient data is used to avoid biases and errors in conclusions.

12. "The census method involves collecting data from every unit within a population, ensuring complete coverage."

Define the census method and give the operational challenges associated with the census method.
Competency Based Que

Ans. The census method involves collecting data from every unit within a population to ensure complete and comprehensive coverage. It aims to provide a complete count and detailed information about all members of the population.

Operational Challenges

(i) **Resource Intensive**
Requires significant financial and human resources.

(ii) **Complexity**
Difficult to manage and coordinate data collection on a large-scale.

(iii) **Training Needs**
Demands extensive training for enumerators.

(iv) **Data Accuracy**
Ensuring accuracy across a large population is challenging.

(v) **Practicality Issues**
Impractical for very large or rapidly changing populations.

13. Give two examples of each sample, population and variable. NCERT

Ans. Two examples of sample, population and variable are

(i) In a study of average yield of wheat in Punjab, population would be all the farms growing wheat in Punjab. Sample would be number of farms out of the total, which are selected for the survey and variable would be the productivity of wheat.

(ii) In a study of population counting or census conducted by Government of India, population would be the census, sample would be the units taken from each group of population for further analysis and variable would be the individual units of population.

14. "In certain conditions, sampling becomes a necessity." Explain this statement. Competency Based Que

Ans. In certain specific conditions, use of census method is impossible or highly inappropriate. e.g. If one wants to check the quality of rice or wheat, it is impossible to check each and every grain.

Also, if one goes to purchase sweets, then the shopkeeper will give only a piece to taste. In these cases, the use of census method will be impossible. Sampling method in these cases, becomes a necessity. Also, census method is inappropriate if the population is infinite or there are limited resources and a fixed time frame. In these conditions, use of sampling method is inevitable.

15. Discuss how you would use the lottery method to select 3 students out of 10 in your class? NCERT; Competency Based Que

Ans. A representative (random) sample of 3 students can be taken out of 10 units through lottery method. The names of all the 10 students of the class are written on 10 separate pieces of paper of equal size and all the slips are folded in a similar manner. These slips are then mixed well and 3 slips are selected one by one to select three students.

16. Does the lottery method always give you a random sample? Explain. NCERT; Competency Based Que

Ans. Lottery method always gives a random sample if it is used in the proper manner without any bias.

If the slips are prepared properly and drawn out one by one, so that all the slips have equal chance of being selected in the sample, it will definitely give a random sample. But, if the slips are not made of identical size and identification is possible of the names or numbers on the slips, the selection will become biased.

Similarly, if the same name or number is written on more than one slip and if some name or number is missed then also the chances of selection of different units of population in the sample will not be equal.

In such cases even lottery method will not give a random sample.

17. An education researcher is studying the effectiveness of a new teaching method in a school. The researcher selects a group of students for the study.

Instead of randomly choosing students from the entire school, the researcher handpicks a few students based on their academic performance and their teacher's recommendations to ensure they represent different ability levels. The selected students are then asked to provide feedback on the new teaching method.

Which type of non-random sampling method is used by the researcher and how does it influence the selection of participants? Competency Based Que

Ans. The researcher in the case study uses judgement/ purposive/deliberate sampling. This method involves selecting participants based on the researcher's discretion, aiming to include individuals who are considered representative of specific characteristics relevant to the study.

It influences the selection by focusing on students identified as having diverse academic abilities, which may introduce personal bias but ensures targeted feedback.

18. Suppose there are 10 students in your class. You want to select three out of them. How many samples are possible? NCERT

Ans. In general, combinations are used to determine the number of ways one can select a sample of size n from a population of size N. The formula for the number of such combinations is $N!/(n!)(N-n)!$

where $N!$ (spoken 'N factorial') equals
$N(N-1)(N-2)\ldots[N-(N-1)]$
(e.g. $5! = (5)(4)(3)(2)(1) = 120$)

In this problem, our population size is $N = 10$ students, and our sample size is $n = 3$ students. Number of samples possible can be calculated as follows

$$\text{Number of samples} = 10!/(3!)(10-3)!$$

$$= 10!/(3)!(7)! = \frac{10 \times 9 \times 8 \times 7!}{3 \times 2 \times 1 \times 7!}$$

$= 120$ possible random samples

19. Which type of non-sampling error is depicted in the below image? Explain. Competency Based Que

Ans. The image depicts sampling bias.

Sampling bias occurs when the sample chosen for a study is not representative of the target population. In this case, the presenter only surveyed people who were present in the room and willing to participate in the survey. This self-selected group is likely to be biased towards people who enjoy surveys, as those who dislike surveys are less likely to attend such an event or participate in the survey.

As a result, the conclusion drawn from the survey, that people love responding to surveys, is flawed due to the biased sample.

20. Which of the following errors is more serious and why?
(i) Sampling error (ii) Non-sampling error NCERT

Ans. Non-sampling errors are more serious than sampling errors because a sampling error can be minimised by taking a large sample. But, it is difficult to minimise non-sampling error even by taking a large sample.

21. Describe the primary role of the Census of India and outline the types of data it collects about the population.

Ans. The Census of India, conducted every ten years, provides a comprehensive demographic record of the population.

It collects data on population size, density, sex-ratio, literacy rates, migration patterns and rural-urban distribution.

This information is crucial for analysing economic and social issues and for formulating policies and plans for national development.

22. What is the purpose of the National Sample Survey Organisation (NSSO) and how does it contribute to socio-economic research?

Ans. The NSSO, established in 1950, conducts nationwide surveys to gather data on socio-economic issues such as literacy, employment and public services utilisation.

It releases reports and a quarterly journal, Sarvekshana, providing periodic estimates and continuous surveys to address various socio-economic problems, aiding the Government of India in planning and policy-making.

Long Answer Type Questions

23. Discuss the indirect oral investigation method of primary data collection. Include its suitability, advantages and disadvantages.

Ans. Indirect oral investigation involves collecting data through interviews with third persons, known as witnesses, who are familiar with the subject matter of the enquiry but are not directly involved in it. This method is particularly suitable under the following conditions

(i) **Large Area of Investigation**
When the investigation covers a wide geographical area, making it impractical to reach all respondents directly.

(ii) **Respondent Limitations**
When the primary respondents are unable to provide accurate information due to ignorance, illiteracy or other constraints.

(iii) **Complex Investigations**
When the investigation requires expert knowledge or specialised information that only experts or informed individuals can provide.

Advantages of Indirect Oral Investigation

(i) **Cost Efficient**
This method is economical as it reduces the need for extensive direct data collection. It saves money, time and effort by relying on knowledgeable intermediaries rather than contacting each respondent individually.

(ii) **Wide Coverage**
It is beneficial for investigations that span large areas or involve numerous respondents, making it feasible to gather data indirectly from various locations.

(iii) **Reduced Personal Bias**
By collecting information from individuals who are well-versed in the subject matter, the method can minimise personal bias and provide a more objective view of the situation. The witnesses, being familiar with the context, can offer accurate and relevant information.

Disadvantages of Indirect Oral Investigation

(i) **Reliability Concerns**
Since data is collected from third parties rather than direct respondents, there is a risk that the information may not be entirely reliable. The accuracy of the data depends on the witness's ability to convey correct and complete information.

(ii) **Potential for Prejudice**
Despite the reduced personal bias, there is still a possibility of personal prejudice influencing the data collection process. Witnesses may have their own biases or interpretations of the information they provide.

(iii) **Lack of Uniformity**
The information gathered may lack uniformity due to variations in witnesses' perspectives and the manner in which they interpret and report the data.

(iv) **Disinterest from Respondents**
Witnesses may not be directly invested in the survey or the subject matter, which could lead to a lack of engagement or interest in providing detailed or accurate information.

24. **You want to do a research on the popularity of vegetable atta noodles among children. Design a suitable questionnaire for collecting this information.** **NCERT; Competency Based Que**

Ans. Questionnaire

Name...

Age.........................

Address...
....
....

Gender : Male ☐ Female ☐

(i) Do you eat noodles?
(a) Yes ☐ (b) No ☐

(ii) Do you like noodles more than other snacks?
(a) Yes ☐ (b) No ☐

(iii) How many packets of noodles do you consume in a month?
(a) Less than 2 packets ☐
(b) 2-5 packets ☐
(c) 5-8 packets ☐
(d) More than 8 packets ☐

(iv) Do you prefer atta noodles over maida noodles?
(a) Yes ☐ (b) No ☐

(v) Do you like vegetables in your noodles?
(a) Yes ☐ (b) No ☐

(vi) Do you think more vegetables should be added in vegetable atta noodles?
(a) Yes ☐ (b) No ☐

(vii) Which vegetables according to you should be added in vegetable atta noodles?
....
....

(viii) Do you think it should be spicier?
(a) Yes ☐ (b) No ☐

(xi) When do you prefer to have vegetable atta noodles?
(a) In breakfast ☐
(b) In lunch ☐
(c) As an evening snacks ☐
(d) In dinner ☐

(x) Do your parents also like vegetable atta noodles?
(a) Yes ☐ (b) No ☐

25. **ABC Electronics, a leading retailer of electronic gadgets, is planning to launch a new line of smart home devices. To ensure that the new products meet customer expectations and improve overall service, the company has decided to conduct a customer feedback survey.**

The survey is designed to gather information on customer satisfaction with existing products and services, preferences for new product features and suggestions for improvement.

Survey Questions

- **"Do you own any smart home devices? Yes/No"**
- **"Describe any recent issues you have experienced with our products or services and suggest improvements."**
- **"How often do you purchase electronics from ABC Electronics? (a) Monthly (b) Quarterly (c) Annually (d) Rarely"**

Identify and explain the types of questions included in the survey. Give examples. **Competency Based Que**

Ans. Following types of questions are included in the survey

(i) **Closed Ended Questions**
These are those that provide respondents with a set of pre-defined options to choose from. These questions are typically used to gather specific, quantifiable data that can be easily analysed.

Examples from Survey

"Do you own any smart home devices? Yes/No" is a simple yes/no question that aims to gather basic information about whether respondents currently own smart home devices.

This type of question is straightforward and easy to analyse, providing a clear measure of ownership.

"How often do you purchase electronics from ABC Electronics? (a) Monthly (b) Quarterly (c) Annually (d) Rarely" is a multiple choice question that seeks to categorise the frequency of purchases. It helps in understanding customer buying behaviour and can be analysed to identify patterns or trends in purchasing frequency.

(ii) **Open Ended Questions**
These allow respondents to provide detailed and personalised responses in their own words.

These questions are used to collect qualitative data and gain deeper insights into respondents' opinions, experiences and suggestions.

Examples from Survey

"Describe any recent issues you have experienced with our products or services and suggest improvements." This open ended question invites respondents to elaborate on any problems they have faced with ABC Electronics' products or services. It encourages them to provide detailed feedback and offer suggestions for improvement.

The responses can vary widely and provide rich, qualitative data that helps the company understand specific areas that need attention or enhancement.

26. **"An investigator should be careful while using secondary data." Discuss.** Competency Based Que

Ans. Secondary data should be used with great care and caution. While using secondary data, the investigator should specifically consider the following factors

(i) **Reliability of Data**
The first and foremost concern of the investigator should be that whether the secondary data is reliable or not.

In order to check the reliability of data, the investigator should enquire about

- the reliability, integrity and experience of the collecting organisation.
- the reliability of the source of information.
- the methods used for the collection and analysis of the data.

(ii) **Suitability of Data**
After satisfying himself as regards to the reliability of data, the investigator should check whether the data is suitable or not. For this, it is important that the investigator

- observes and compares the objectives, nature and scope of the given enquiry with the original enquiry.
- confirms that the various terms and units were clearly defined and were also uniform throughout the earlier investigation and these are relevant for the present enquiry also.
- takes into account the difference in time periods for the original enquiry and the investigation in hand.

(iii) **Adequacy of Data**
After satisfying himself about the reliability and suitability of data, the investigator should check whether data is adequate or not.

For this, he should

- check the area of study to which the data relates and
- also check the time period which the data covers.

27. **Explain the census method of data collection, detailing both its advantages and disadvantages.**

Ans. The census method of data collection involves gathering information from every unit within a population, ensuring that no individual or unit is left out.

This method is often used to obtain comprehensive demographic data and is exemplified by the Census of India, which is conducted every ten years.

Advantages of the Census Method

(i) **High Accuracy and Reliability**
The census method provides highly accurate and reliable results because it covers the entire population, eliminating sampling errors that might occur in other methods. e.g. The Census of India collects data from every household, which ensures that the demographic information, such as population size and distribution, is precise and comprehensive.

(ii) **Comprehensive Data Collection**
By including every unit in the population, the census method allows for detailed and extensive data collection.

This is particularly beneficial for studying heterogeneous populations where characteristics vary widely across different groups.

For instance, the Census of India gathers information on various factors, including education levels, income and employment status, providing a complete picture of the demographic landscape.

Disadvantages of the Census Method

(i) **Resource Intensive**
Conducting a census requires a significant amount of time, energy and financial resources. The process involves extensive planning, training of enumerators and data processing.

e.g. The Census of India, necessitates substantial funding and logistical coordination to manage the large-scale data collection and ensure accuracy.

(ii) **Logistical Challenges**
The census method can be impractical for very large or infinite populations due to the extensive logistical requirements.

Managing data collection across vast and diverse geographical areas can be challenging. For instance, conducting a census in a country with a large and dispersed population, like India, involves overcoming difficulties related to accessibility and coordination.

(iii) **Training and Data Quality Issues**
The effectiveness of the census depends on the training and performance of enumerators.

Inadequately trained enumerators may lead to errors in data collection, affecting the overall reliability of the results.

Proper training and supervision are crucial to minimise such issues and ensure the data collected is accurate and consistent.

28. **Do samples provide better results than surveys? Give reason for your answer.** NCERT; Competency Based Que

Or

Which of the following methods give better results and why?

(i) Census **(ii) Sample** NCERT

Ans. A survey, which includes every element of the population, is known as census or the method of complete enumeration. On the other hand, when a part of the population is studied and predictions are made about the population based on this part, it is called sampling.

In terms of accuracy of results, census is better as it studies all the units of population but this method is very time consuming, expensive and sometimes not feasible to use.

Hence, sampling is better due to following reasons

(i) **Economical**
Sampling involves study of a fraction of population and hence, the cost involved in sampling is relatively low. Census costs are high especially in case of large population with wide coverage in terms of area.

(ii) **Time Saving**
Huge amount of time is required to conduct a census survey, if the population size is large or spread over a wide area while sample studies do not take that much time to be conducted.

(iii) **Lesser Effort**
As only a part of the population is studied, it entails lesser effort on the part of the investigator than that required in census.

(iv) **Inappropriateness of Census**
In certain cases, when the population is infinite or exhaustible, census cannot be done and hence, sampling is the only choice.

e.g. One cannot burn all the units of coal available to know their calorific value, sample is the only means of testing it.

(v) **Considerable Accuracy**
Results from sampling may not be as accurate as in case of census, but the level of accuracy of these results can be established through statistical tests of significance and hence, can be applied in general to the whole population, if found significant.

29. **Differentiate between census survey and sample survey.**

Ans. Difference between census survey and sample survey are

Basis	Census Survey	Sample Survey
Coverage	The whole universe is taken for collection of data in census survey.	Only representative sample is taken for collection of data in sample survey.
Suitability	This method is suitable when the area under investigation is relatively small.	This method is suitable when the area under investigation is large.
Accuracy	Since, all items are studied under census survey, highest degree of accuracy is possible.	Since only representative samples are studied under sample survey, it is less accurate.
Time	Census survey is very time consuming as all items are studied.	Sample survey is less time consuming as only samples are studied.
Nature of Items	Census survey is suitable when items in the universe have diverse characteristics.	Sample survey is suitable when items in the universe are homogeneous.
Verification	Under census method the results of investion is generally not possible.	Under sampling method result can be verified by taking out another sample.

30. **Discuss the various types of non-sampling errors that can occur in a survey. How do these errors impact the accuracy and reliability of the survey results? Provide examples to illustrate each type of non-sampling error.**

Ans. Non-sampling errors are inaccuracies or biases in survey results that are not related to the sampling process. These errors can occur at any stage of the survey process, including planning, execution, data collection, processing and analysis.

Unlike sampling errors, which can be reduced by increasing the sample size, non-sampling errors are more challenging to manage and minimise.

Here are the main types of non-sampling errors

(i) **Errors in Data Acquisition**
These errors occur during the recording or entry of data, often due to mistakes made by investigators or enumerators. e.g. If an investigator mistakenly records '13' instead of '31' in a survey on income levels, this error can lead to inaccurate analysis and conclusions.

Such errors can distort the data and affect the overall reliability of the survey results. Accurate data acquisition is crucial to ensure that the information collected truly reflects the respondents' answers.

e.g. In a customer satisfaction survey, if a surveyor records '10' as the satisfaction rating for a customer who actually rated '50', the results will be skewed, leading to incorrect conclusions about customer satisfaction levels.

(ii) **Non-response Errors**
These errors occur when survey respondents are either unreachable or refuse to provide the required information. This can lead to incomplete data, which may not accurately represent the target population.

Non-response errors can arise from various factors, including reluctance to participate, lack of time or inability to contact the respondent. The absence of data from non-respondents can create biases if their characteristics differ significantly from those who did respond.

e.g. In a health survey, if a significant number of participants refuse to answer questions about sensitive health issues, the data collected may not fully capture the health conditions of the entire population, leading to incomplete and potentially biased results.

(iii) **Sampling Bias**
It occurs when the sampling plan excludes certain segments of the target population, leading to a sample that is not representative of the whole.

This bias can happen if the survey methodology or selection process systematically favours certain groups over others. Sampling bias can result in skewed data that does not accurately reflect the characteristics of the entire population.

e.g. If a survey on urban transportation preferences only includes respondents from metropolitan areas and excludes rural regions, the findings may not accurately represent the transportation needs and preferences of the entire population, including those in rural areas.

(iv) **Impact on Accuracy and Reliability**
Non-sampling errors can significantly affect the accuracy and reliability of survey results. They introduce inaccuracies and biases that can lead to incorrect conclusions and decisions based on the survey data. Ensuring rigorous survey design, thorough training for data collectors and careful data processing and analysis are essential to minimise non-sampling errors and enhance the validity of survey findings.

31. Write a brief note of national sample survey organisation and also state it's various objectives.

Ans. The NSSO was established in the year 1950 under the Ministry of Finance to conduct surveys and collect data on estimates of literacy, school enrolment, utilisation of educational services, employment, unemployment, manufacturing and service sector enterprises, morbidity, maternity, child care, utilisation of public distribution system, etc. and to publish the results of the surveys through reports and its quarterly journal 'Sarvekshana'.

The NSSO conducts continuous surveys on various problems in successive rounds quinquennially (every five years).

NSSO was formed with the following objectives in view

(i) To provide statistical information which helps the government to formulate various plans and policies.

(ii) To evolve suitable statistical techniques which help in the analysis of statistical data so that the solutions to various economic and administrative problems can be figured out and the future trends can be estimated.

(iii) To collect and publish data which can be used by various individuals and organisations to understand and resolve various economic problems.

(iv) To publish data which proves to be useful for those research workers who are engaged in research work in various socio-economic fields.

32. A company is preparing to launch a new consumer product and wants to gather initial feedback from potential customers to refine their marketing strategy and product features. Due to limited time and resources, the company decides to use non-random sampling methods to gather preliminary data.

The research team is considering three non-random sampling methods, i.e. judgement sampling, quota sampling and convenience sampling. They need to choose the most appropriate method for their objectives and explain their rationale.

Competency Based Que

(i) How could judgement sampling and quota sampling be employed? Discuss their advantages and disadvantages for the study.

(ii) How might convenience sampling be used? Explain its limitations.

Ans. (i) **Judgement Sampling**
In the market research study, judgement sampling could be employed by having the research team select specific individuals or groups based on their expertise or perceived relevance to the product. For instance, the team might choose industry experts, frequent users of similar products or individuals known for their strong opinions on consumer goods.

Advantages of judgement sampling are as follows

- **Expert Insight** Allows the collection of feedback from individuals who have a deep understanding of the market or the product category, providing valuable insights.

- **Relevance** Targets individuals who are believed to be most knowledgeable or influential regarding the product.

Disadvantages of judgement sampling are as follows

- **Bias** The selection process is subjective and may be influenced by the researcher's personal biases, leading to skewed results.
- **Limited Scope** May not capture a broad spectrum of opinions or preferences, limiting the generalisability of the findings.

Quota Sampling

In this method, the research team divides the population into different groups based on relevant characteristics (e.g. Age, gender, income level) and sets specific quotas for each group. e.g. They might set quotas for different age groups or income levels to ensure that the sample reflects these segments.

Advantages of quota sampling are as follows

- **Representation** Ensures that different segments of the population are represented in the sample, making the data more comprehensive.
- **Balanced Insights** Allows for the collection of data from diverse groups, which can provide a more nuanced understanding of market preferences.

Disadvantages of quota sampling are as follows

- **Resource Intensive** Requires careful planning and management to ensure that quotas are met, which can be time consuming and costly.
- **Potential for Bias** If the researcher does not accurately divide the population or if the quotas are not appropriately set, the sample may still be biased.

(ii) In the market research study, convenience sampling might involve selecting participants from locations or groups that are easily accessible to the research team.

e.g. The team might choose to gather feedback from people in a specific shopping mall or neighbourhood close to their office.

Limitations of convenience sampling are as follows

- **Bias and Non-representativeness**
  The sample may not accurately represent the broader population, leading to biased results that do not reflect the opinions of potential customers outside the convenient area.
- **Limited Generalisability**
  Findings may be skewed towards the characteristics of the easily accessible population, making it difficult to generalise the results to the entire market.

SELF ASSESSMENT TEST

Objective Type Questions

1. Industry reports are an example of ....
   (a) internal data (b) external data
   (c) personal data (d) None of these
2. Which of the following refers to the information about different variables collected for analysis?
   (a) Data (b) Respondents
   (c) Investigator (d) Enumerator
3. Which data collection method involves local agents collecting and reporting information periodically to an investigator, who processes it for analysis?
   (a) Direct observation
   (b) Census method
   (c) Sampling method
   (d) Information from correspondents
4. Which of the following is an advantage of the census method?
   (a) Results are not reliable
   (b) More chances of biasness at the time of collecting data
   (c) Data is collected for each and every item of the population
   (d) Cannot be applied in case of infinite population
5. .... method involves surveying a subset of the population rather than the entire group.
   (a) Census (b) Sample
   (c) Primary (d) Investigation
6. Which of the following refers to the totality of items under study?
   (a) Universe (b) Population
   (c) Both (a) and (b) (d) None of these
7. Which sampling method gives each unit of the population an equal chance of being selected?
   (a) Quota (b) Random
   (c) Non-random (d) Deliberate
8. Statistical errors are symbolically represented as ....
   (a) Error = True/Actual Value – Estimated Value
   (b) Error = False/Actual Value – Estimated Value
   (c) Error = True/Estimated Value – False Value
   (d) Error = True/False Value – Actual Value

Answers 1. (b) 2. (a) 3. (d) 4. (c) 5. (b) 6. (c) 7. (b) 8. (a)

Short Answer Type Questions

9. Differentiate between external and internal sources of data with examples.
10. Non-random sampling methods do not give every unit in the population an equal chance of being selected. Do you agree?
11. What are non-response errors? Explain with examples.
12. Define the following terms
    (i) Investigators (ii) Respondents
13. Explain the sources of secondary data with examples.
14. "Secondary data is collected, processed and tabulated by various national and state-level agencies." List and explain the two major national agencies for secondary data.

Long Answer Type Questions

15. Differentiate between census and sample method.
16. What are sampling and non-sampling errors? Explain briefly with examples.
17. A marketing firm is conducting a study to understand consumer preferences for a new energy drink. Due to limited resources and time, they opt for non-random sampling methods.
    The researcher decides to use judgement sampling to target fitness enthusiasts, quota sampling to ensure representation across age groups and convenience sampling to collect responses from a nearby gym. The firm aims to gain quick insights for refining their marketing strategy.
    (i) What type of sampling relies on the researcher's expertise or judgement to select specific units?
    (ii) How does quota sampling ensure diversity in the sample? Provide an example based on the case.
    (iii) Discuss the potential limitations of convenience sampling in the context of the study. Suggest one way to mitigate these limitations.

03

CHAPTER

Organisation of Data

It involves arranging raw data systematically for clarity and analysis. It covers classification, tabulation and graphical methods to simplify data for better understanding and decision-making.

YOUR STUDY GOALS

YOUR PRACTICE GOAL

- Objective Type Questions (60 Qs ; MCQs, A-R, Statements, Matching, Concept Identification)
- Subjective Questions (12 SAs, 6 LAs)
- 16 Numerical Questions
- Self Assessment Test (8 MCQs, 6 SAs, 2 LAs, 2 Numerical)

Data collected from primary and secondary sources, referred to as 'raw' or 'unclassified' data, is highly unorganised and challenging to manage. To facilitate understanding and mathematical analysis, raw data must be organised.

Organising data involves presenting it in a form that is easily understandable and suitable for further processing and interpretation.

3.1 Classification of Data

Classification is the process of arranging data into different groups or classes based on common characteristics or attributes. This process transforms raw data into an organised form.

According to **Conner**, "Classification is the process of arranging things in groups or classes according to their resemblances and affinities, and gives expression to the unity of attributes that may exist amongst a diversity of individuals."

Objectives of Classification

Objective	Explanation
Simplification	To simplify raw data by presenting it in a condensed, logical and comprehensible form.
Grouping	To group data based on similarities and dissimilarities.
Comparison	To facilitate comparison between different sets of data.
Presentation	To aid in the presentation of data in tabular and graphical forms.

Characteristics of an Ideal Classification

1. **Purpose Based** Classification should be aligned with the purpose of the study.
2. **Clarity** It should not cause confusion among those studying it.
3. **Comprehensive** Classification should include all items in the series.
4. **Flexibility** There should be flexibility to accommodate changes in data.
5. **Homogeneity** Similar items should be grouped together within a class.
6. **Consistency** A particular kind of investigation should use the same classification throughout the analysis.

Basis of Classification

Data can be classified on the basis of following four methods

Methods of Classification

- **Geographical/Spatial** Data classified as per geographical location or region.
- **Chronological** Data classified as per different time periods.
- **Qualitative** Data classified as per qualities or attributes
- **Quantitative** Data classified as per measurable characteristics

1. **Geographical/Spatial Classification** This type of classification is based on geographical or locational differences, such as countries, states or cities.

Agricultural Yield of Different Countries (in kg per hectare)

Country	Yield
China	269.2
India	123.7
Pakistan	257.5

Geographical/Spatial Classification

Population of India (in crores)

Year	Population
1971	54.8
1981	68.3
1991	84.4

Chronological/Temporal Classification

2. **Chronological/Temporal Classification** Chronological classification involves arranging data based on time differences.

   In the example given above, the variable 'population', is a time series as it represents values in different years.
3. **Qualitative Classification** Qualitative classification organises data based on qualities or attributes such as honesty, beauty, intelligence, etc.

   Qualitative classification can be of two types

Type	Explanation
Simple Classification	• When data is divided into two parts based on a single characteristic, it is referred to as simple classification. • e.g. Population divided by gender (male-female).
Manifold Classification	• When data is divided into more than two parts based on multiple characteristics, it is referred to as manifold classification. • e.g. Population first divided by gender (male-female) and then further divided by literacy (literate-illiterate).

4. **Quantitative Classification** This classification is based on quantifiable measurements like age, height, weight, sales or profits. It is also known as 'numerical classification'.

   The phenomenon being measured is called a variable, making this type of classification also known as 'classification by variables.'

   Classification of quantitative data often results in the formation of a frequency distribution.

Daily Earnings of 40 Departmental Stores
(in 000 rupees)

Daily Earning (in ₹)	Number of Stores
Upto 100	13
101-200	15
201-300	12

Quantitative Classification

3.2 Concept of Variable

A variable is a characteristic or phenomenon that can be measured and generally changes its value over time. It represents a quantity or attribute whose value varies and each specific value within its range is known as a **variate**.

e.g. 'Price' is a variable as it differs across commodities, 'Age' is a variable as it varies among individuals.

Types of Variables

Variables are broadly classified into two types

1. Discrete Variable

A discrete variable can take only specific integral values, meaning it only changes by finite jumps and does not take any fractional values. It moves from one value to another without assuming intermediate values.

e.g. The number of students in a class could be 1, 2, 4, 10, etc.

2. Continuous Variable

A continuous variable can take any value within a specified interval, including both integral and fractional values. It can assume an infinite number of values within a range, including proper and improper fractions.

e.g. Temperature of a city can be 20.5°C, 25.3°C, etc. height and weight of an individual can be 160.5 cm, 65.7 kg, etc.

3.3 Frequency Distribution

A frequency distribution is a method to classify raw data of a quantitative variable, showing how different values are distributed across various classes along with their corresponding frequencies. It facilitates easy understanding of data.

e.g. In a class of 25 students, if 5 students scored 80 marks, 7 scored 75 marks and 13 scored 90 marks, the frequencies are 5, 7 and 13, respectively.

Statistical Series

A statistical series is an arrangement of data in a systematic manner based on size, time period or other criteria. Frequency distribution is a type of statistical series.

Statistical series can be divided into two broad heads as mentioned below

On the Basis of Characteristics	On the Basis of Construction
Time series (Based on time periods)	**Individual series** (Based on individual items that take only integral values without frequency)
Spatial series (Based on geographical areas)	**Discrete series** (Based on ungrouped frequency distribution)
Condition series (Based on certain conditions)	**Continuous series** (Based on grouped frequency distribution)

Terms related to Frequency Distribution

Term	Explanation
Tally Marks	It is a simple tool used to count the number of times a variable appears in a distribution. It is represented by the symbol '|' for one value and '卌' for five values.
Frequency	It is the number of times a given value appears in a series.
Class Frequency	It is the number of values in a particular class.
Class Limits	These are two extreme ends of a class, with the lower value as the **lower class limit** and the higher value as the **upper class limit**. e.g. In the class interval 10-20, 10 is the lower class limit and 20 is the upper class limit.
Class Width (Class Interval)	It is the difference between the upper class limit and the lower class limit. Class Width = Upper Class Limit – Lower Class Limit
Class Mid-point	It is the middle value of a class, representing the class. It is calculated as the average of the upper and lower class limits. Class Mid-point = (Upper Class Limit + Lower Class Limit)/2
Class with Maximum Concentration of Data	The class with the highest frequency.
Class with Minimum Concentration of Data	The class with the lowest frequency.
Relative Frequency	It is the frequency of a group represented as a percentage of total frequency of the distribution. Relative Frequency = (Frequency of a Group / Frequency of Distribution) × 100

Individual Series

It refers to the series in which items are listed without any frequency as each item is different and unique. Individual series has two types

1. **Organised Individual Series** It is an orderly arrangement of raw data, i.e. these data are arranged either in the order of magnitude (increasing or decreasing order) or in serial number.
   e.g. Distribution of marks of students
   - Increasing order 5, 10, 15, 20, 25, 30
   - Decreasing order 30, 25, 20, 15, 10, 5
2. **Unorganised Individual Series** It is a presentation of raw data without any arrangement.
   e.g. Distribution of marks of students 20, 5, 10, 30, 15, 25.

3.4 Types of Frequency Distribution

It can be classified as

I. Discrete Frequency Distribution

A discrete frequency distribution organises data based on a discrete variable, which can only take specific integral values. The values jump from one specific value to another without taking any intermediate values. In this type of distribution, the discrete variable's values, along with their corresponding frequencies, are displayed in a table.

Discrete Frequency Distribution

Value	Tally Marks	Frequency
2	||	2
3	||||	4
4	||	2

Frequency Array

It is a special form of discrete frequency distribution in which the values are arranged in the order of magnitude (either increasing or decreasing).

Solved Question 1 Represent the following marks scored by students of class XI in statistics in discrete frequency distribution

20	15	5	8	7	12	40	15	8	7	20
15	10	8	12	21	32	40	20	15	8	12

Sol. **Discrete Frequency Distribution**

Marks	Tally Marks	Frequency
5	|	01
7	||	02
8	||||	04
10	|	01
12	|||	03
15	||||	04
20	|||	03
21	|	01
32	|	01
40	||	02
	Total	22

II. Continuous Frequency Distribution

A continuous frequency distribution organises data based on a continuous variable, which can take any value (integral or fractional) within specified limits. This distribution represents the continuous variable's class intervals (groups) and their respective class frequencies in a table format.

Continuous Frequency Distribution

Marks	Number of Students
0-10	2
10-20	5
20-30	10

Solved Question 2 Represent the following data using continuous frequency distribution of an interval of 10

8	10	12	16	18	24	28	31	38	49	50	53
58	56	39	43	48	44	41	49	55	59	63	69
61	74	29	27	22	34	39	32	44	78		

Sol. **Continuous Frequency Distribution of Marks Scored by Students**

Marks (Classes)	Tally Marks	Frequencies
0-10	|	01
10-20	||||	04
20-30	||||	05
30-40	~~||||~~ |	06
40-50	~~||||~~ ||	07
50-60	~~||||~~ |	06
60-70	|||	03
70-80	||	02
	Total	34

Type of Continuous Frequency Distribution

Different types of continuous frequency distributions are

Types of Continuous Frequency Distribution

- Exclusive frequency distribution
- Inclusive frequency distribution
- Cumulative frequency distribution
- Open ended frequency distribution
- Unequal class interval frequency distribution
- Mid-value frequency distribution

1. Exclusive Frequency Distribution

It is a frequency distribution where each class's upper limit becomes the lower limit of the next class.

Key Points

- **Classes** The classes are contiguous and do not overlap, maintaining continuity in the data.
- **Inclusion/Exclusion** Frequencies of upper class limits are excluded, while those of lower class limits are included.
- **Usage** Most suitable for continuous data where precision in class boundaries is essential.

Frequency Distribution of Income of 350 Employees of a Company

Income (₹)	Number of Employees
800-900	50
900-1000	100
1000-1100	200
Total	350

2. Inclusive Frequency Distribution

It is a frequency distribution where both the upper and lower limits of each class interval are included in the class.

Key Points

- **Classes** The upper limit of one class is included in the interval and does not become the lower limit of the next class.
- **Inclusion** Both class limits are part of the class interval.
- **Usage** Commonly used in cases where class intervals overlap slightly.

Frequency Distribution of Income of 350 Employees of a Company

Income (₹)	Number of Employees
800-899	50
900-999	100
1000-1099	200
Total	350

3. Cumulative Frequency Distribution

It is a frequency distribution where frequencies are accumulated successively, either from lowest to highest (increasing order) or from highest to lowest (decreasing order) values.

Types

(i) **More than Cumulative Frequency Distribution** Cumulative frequencies are added starting from the highest value down to the lowest value.

(ii) **Less than Cumulative Frequency Distribution** Cumulative frequencies are added starting from the lowest value-up to the highest value.

'More Than' Cumulative Frequency Distribution

Marks of Students	No. of Students
More than 0	50
More than 10	30
More than 20	18
More than 30	12
More than 40	06

'Less Than' Cumulative Frequency Distribution

Marks of Students	No. of Students
Less than 10	5
Less than 20	10
Less than 30	20
Less than 40	35
Less than 50	50

4. Open Ended Frequency Distribution

It is a frequency distribution where the extreme limits of the first and last classes are not specified (or missing).

Key Points

- **Class Limits** The lower limit of the first class is represented as 'less than' or 'below' and the upper limit of the last class is represented as 'more than' or 'above'.
- **Usage** Useful when data extends beyond known bounds or when exact limits are not available.

Open Ended Frequency Distribution

Marks of Students	No. of Students
Less than 10	10
10-15	05
15-20	15
More than 20	08

Open Ended Distribution into Continuous Distribution

Conversion

- If the given class intervals are uniform (except first and last class interval), then magnitude of first class interval and last class interval is assumed to be same as that of other classes.
- If the given class intervals are showing a uniform trend (except first and last class interval), then lower limit of first class and upper limit of last class is calculated by adjusting it with the trend.
  e.g. If width of 2nd class interval is 20, of 3rd class interval is 30, etc, it shows that width is rising by 10. Thus, assuming that width of first class will be 10, we can find out the lower limit of first class interval.
- If class intervals are of different width, then lower limit of the first class and upper limit of the last class cannot be determined.

5. Unequal Class Interval Frequency Distribution

It is a frequency distribution where the class intervals are not uniform and vary in size.

Key Points

- **Class Intervals** Some intervals may be wider or narrower than others, which can affect the representation and comparison of data.
- **Usage** Applied when data does not fit into equal intervals naturally or when certain ranges need more detailed analysis.

Unequal Class Interval Distribution

Marks of Students	No. of Students
0-5	10
5-10	05
10-20	06
20-40	04
40-45	05

6. Mid-value Frequency Distribution

It is a frequency distribution where mid-point or mid-value is given in place of class intervals.

Key Points

- **Class Mid-point** Calculated as the average of the upper and lower limits of each class.
- **Usage** Simplifies data representation by using mid-values instead of class intervals, which is helpful for certain types of analysis.

Mid-value Frequency Distribution

Mid-value	Frequency
5	04
15	06
25	05
35	10
45	02

Conversion of Mid-value Frequency Distribution into Continuous Distribution

- Calculate the difference between the two mid-values.
- After that, half of the difference is subtracted and added to each mid-value to find the lower and upper limit respectively of the class intervals.

Solved Question 3 **Represent the following information using continuous frequency distribution. Use suitable number of class.**

10	17	15	22	11	16	19	24	29	18
25	26	32	14	17	20	23	27	30	12
34	13	10	16	20	22	29	23	29	31
15	18	36	24	18	21	15	28	33	38

Sol. We need to decide suitable class interval.

Lowest item is 10 and largest item is 38.

Also, number of required class is 6 (assumed)

$$\therefore \text{Width of class} = \frac{\text{Lowest Item} - \text{Largest Item}}{\text{Number of Required Class}}$$

$$= \frac{38-10}{6} = 4.66 \text{ or } 5$$

Now, the data is given below in tabular form

X	Tally Marks	Frequency
10-15	𝍸 I	06
15-20	𝍸 𝍸 I	11
20-25	𝍸 𝍸	09
25-30	𝍸 II	07
30-35	𝍸	05
35-40	II	02
	Total	40

Solved Question 4 Convert the following inclusive distribution to exclusive frequency distribution

Height (In cms)	No. of Persons
113-121	20
122-130	10
131-139	5
140-148	3
149-157	6

Sol. For conversion of inclusive frequency distribution to exclusive frequency distribution, following steps should be followed

***Step* 1** Find out the difference between the upper limit of class interval and lower limit of next class interval, i.e. $122-121=1$.

***Step* 2** Half of the difference calculated in step 1 is to be added to the upper limit of each class interval and half of the difference is to be subtracted from the lower limit of each class interval i.e. 0.5 to be added to upper limit and 0.5 to be subtracted from lower limit.

The adjusted table is as follows

Height (In cms)	**No. of Persons**
112.5-121.5	20
121.5-130.5	10
130.5-139.5	5
139.5-148.5	3
148.5-157.5	6

Solved Question 5 Convert the following cumulative frequency distribution into normal exclusive series

Age (In years)	No. of Students
Above 5	50
Above 10	35
Above 15	20
Above 20	10
Above 25	5

Sol. Conversion of more than cumulative frequency distribution into normal frequency distribution is as follows

Age (In year)	**No. of Students**
5-10	$50-35=15$
10-15	$35-20=15$
15-20	$20-10=10$
20-25	$10-5=5$
25-30	5

Solved Question 6 Convert the following frequency distribution into a 'less than cumulative' and 'more than cumulative'

Marks	No. of Students
0-10	05
10-20	05
20-30	10
30-40	05
40-50	20

Sol. In order to convert the above series into cumulative frequency distribution, we will consider upper limits of the class for 'less than cumulative' and lower limits of the class for 'more than cumulative.' Thus, adjusted tables will be

(i) 'Less than' table

Less than Cumulative Frequency Distribution

Marks	No. of Students
Less than 10	05
Less than 20	$05+05=10$
Less than 30	$10+10=20$
Less than 40	$20+05=25$
Less than 50	$25+20=45$

(ii) 'More than' table

More than Cumulative Frequency Distribution

Marks	No. of Students
More than 0	$05+05+10+05+20=45$
More than 10	$05+10+05+20=40$
More than 20	$10+05+20=35$
More than 30	$05+20=25$
More than 40	20

Solved Question 7 Construct a frequency distribution from the following data by converting mid-value series into continuous series

Mid-value	Frequency
5	10
15	14
25	18
35	20
45	16

Sol. To convert mid-value series into continuous series, following steps are followed

(i) Difference between two mid-values $=15-5=10$

(ii) Half of the difference $=\frac{10}{2}=5$

It is reduced and added to each mid-value to determine lower limit and upper limit, as

Ist class interval $\rightarrow (5-5)-(5+5) \Rightarrow 0-10$

IInd class interval $\rightarrow (15-5)-(15+5) \Rightarrow 10-20$

IIIrd class interval $\rightarrow (25-5)-(25+5) \Rightarrow 20-30$

IVth class interval $\rightarrow (35-5)-(35+5) \Rightarrow 30-40$

Vth class interval $\rightarrow (45-5)-(45+5) \Rightarrow 40-50$

Now, frequency distribution will be shown as

Class Interval	Frequency
0-10	10
10-20	14
20-30	18
30-40	20
40-50	16

Some Specific Frequency Distributions

Some specific frequency distributions include univariate frequency distribution and bivariate frequency distribution

1. Univariate Frequency Distribution

It is a frequency distribution that classifies data based on a single variable.

Key Points

- **Description** Focuses on describing and analysing a single variable.
- **Also Known As** One-way frequency distribution.
- **Purpose** To summarise and display the distribution of values for one variable, making it easier to understand its pattern and frequency.
- **Example** Univariate frequency distribution showing marks of 10 students in Economics is given below

Marks in Economics	22	21	21	20	22	21	21	20	20	19

2. Bivariate Frequency Distribution

It is a frequency distribution that involves two variables, with their values grouped into various classes.

Key Points

- **Description** Examines the relationship between two variables by categorising their paired values.
- **Purpose** To determine and analyse the empirical relationship or correlation between two variables.
- **Example** Bivariate frequency distribution showing marks of 13 students in Accountancy and Economics is given below

Marks in Economics (Y) ↓	Marks in Accountancy (X) →				
	25	26	27	28	Total
19	I (1)	I (1)	I (1)	–	3
20	I (1)	II (2)	I (1)	–	4
21	–	I (1)	IIII (4)	I (1)	6
Total	2	4	6	1	13

Figures within brackets denote the frequency corresponding to each cell.

The above table reveals that there is 1 student who has scored 19 marks in Economics and 25 marks in Accountancy, 2 students have scored 26 marks in Accountancy and 20 marks in Economics and so on.

Components of Frequency Distribution

1. **Number of Classes** The number of distinct intervals or groups into which data is divided.

   How to Determine
   - ***Find the Range*** Calculate the difference between the largest and smallest values in the dataset.
     e.g. For data values 10, 31, 12, 15, 25, 30, 18, 13, 22 and 40, the range is 30 (40 – 10).
   - ***Calculate Number of Classes*** Divide the range by the chosen class interval.
     Number of Classes = Range/Class Interval

2. **Size of Class** (Class Interval) The width or size of each class interval in the frequency distribution.

   How to Determine
   - ***Calculate Class Interval*** Use the range and the number of classes to determine the size of each class.
   - ***Uniform or Unequal Intervals*** Classes are usually of equal size, but unequal intervals may be used if there are significant gaps in the data.
     Size of Class/Class Interval = Range/Number of Classes

3. **Determination of Class Limits** The boundaries of each class interval in the frequency distribution.

   How to Determine
   - ***Lower Limit*** Start with the minimum value or a value slightly less than the minimum.
   - ***Upper Limit*** Add the class interval size to the lower limit to get the upper limit.
   - ***Types of Limits*** Class limits can be inclusive, exclusive or open ended, depending on how data boundaries are defined.

4. **Determination of Frequency of Each Class** The number of observations within each class interval.

   How to Determine
   - ***Count Observations*** Use tally marks to count the frequency of values within each class.
   - ***Tally Marks*** A single tally (|) is used for each observation. After four tallies, the fifth is crossed over (~~||||~~) to form a group.
   - ***Calculate Frequency*** The number of tallies represents the frequency for each class.

Mind Map

ORGANISATION OF DATA

1 Classification of Data

It is the process of grouping data into different categories based on common characteristics.

Objectives

- Simplifies raw data.
- Group data based on similarities and dissimilarities.
- Facilitates comparison.
- Enhances clarity in presentation.

Characteristics of an Ideal Classification

Purpose based, clarity, comprehensive, flexibility, homogeneity and consistency.

2 Basis of Classification

- **Geographical/Spatial Classification** Based on location.
- **Chronological Classification** Based on time.
- **Qualitative Classification** Based on attributes. It includes simple classification and manifold classification.
- **Quantitative Classification** Based on measurable characteristics.

3 Concept of Variable

It is a characteristic that can be measured and generally changes its value over time.

Types of Variables

- **Discrete Variable** Takes only specific values (e.g. Number of students in a class).
- **Continuous Variable** Can take any value within a range (e.g. Height, temperature).

4 Frequency Distribution

It is a method to classify raw data based on how frequently different values occur.

Types of Statistical Series

- Time series (Based on time periods)
- Spatial series (Based on geographic regions)
- Condition series (Based on specific conditions)

5 Types of Frequency Distribution

Discrete Frequency Distribution

- It organises data based on a discrete variable, which can only take specific integral values.
- It includes tally marks and frequency counts.

Continuous Frequency Distribution

It organises data based on a continuous variable, which can take any value (integral or fractional) within specified limits.

Types of Continuous Frequency Distributions

- **Exclusive** Frequency distribution where each class's upper limit becomes the lower limit of the next class.
- **Inclusive** Frequency distribution where both the upper and lower limits of each class interval are included in the class.
- **Cumulative** It can be
  - More than cumulative (Adding frequencies starting from the highest value)
  - Less than cumulative (Adding frequencies starting from the lowest value)
- **Open Ended** Frequency distribution where the extreme limits of the first and last classes are not specified (or missing).
- **Unequal Class Interval** Frequency distribution where the class intervals are not uniform and vary in size.
- **Mid-value Frequency** Frequency distribution where mid-point or mid value is given in place of class intervals.

6 Some Specific Frequency Distributions

Univariate Frequency Distribution

- Organises data based on a single variable.
- Also known as one-way frequency distribution.
- Summarises and displays the distribution of values for one variable.

Bivariate Frequency Distribution

- Organises data based on two variables.
- Analyses the relationship between two variables.

7 Components of Frequency Distribution

Number of Classes

- Distinct intervals or groups in the data.
- *How to Determine*:
  - Find the range (Largest Value – Smallest Value).
  - Calculate the number of classes (Range/Class Interval)

Size of Class (Class Interval)

- The width or size of each class interval.
- *How to Determine:*
  Class Interval = Range/Number of Classes

Determination of Class Limits

- *Lower Limit*: Start with the minimum value or a value slightly less than the minimum.
- *Upper Limit*: Add the class interval size to the lower limit to get the upper limit.

Determination of Frequency of Each Class

- Number of observations within each class interval.
- *How to Determine*: Use tally marks to count observations.

EXAM PATTERN QUESTIONS

Objective Type Questions

Multiple Choice Questions (MCQs)

1. Which of the following is the process of arranging data into groups or categories for easier analysis?

(a) Classification (b) Statistical series
(c) Frequency distribution (d) Range

2. Identify the objective(s) of data classification from the following

I. To calculate the mean and median.
II. To simplify raw data and present it in a comprehensible form.
III. To create graphical representations of data.
IV. To perform complex statistical analyses.

Codes
(a) Only IV (b) Both I and II
(c) Both II and III (d) All of these

3. Classification that involves grouping data based on characteristics such as honesty or intelligence is called .... classification.

(a) quantitative (b) qualitative
(c) geographical (d) chronological

4. From 1991-92 to 2010-11, wheat production of a district Dumdum increased at an average annual growth rate of 3.2 percent.
NCERT (QR); Competency Based Que

(a) Time series classification (b) Spatial classification

5. "Qualitative classification can be further divided into simple and manifold classifications based on the number of characteristics."

Which classification type divides data into categories based multiple characteristics? Competency Based Que

(a) Simple classification (b) Manifold classification
(c) Numerical classification (d) Exclusive classification

6. The characteristic of an ideal classification that ensures it is aligned with the purpose of the study, is known as ....

(a) clarity (b) consistency
(c) purpose based (d) flexibility

7. Which of the following objectives of classification is shown in the image?

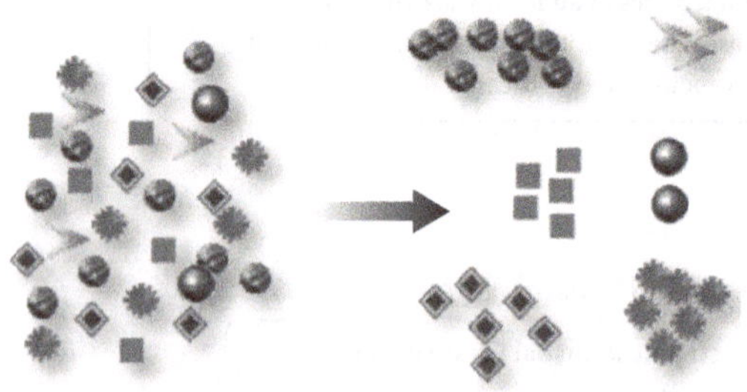

(a) Simplification of complex data
(b) Organisation on the basis of characteristics
(c) Facilitates comparison
(d) Both (a) and (b)

8. Which of the following is an example of a discrete variable? Competency Based Que

(a) Temperature of a city
(b) Height of an individual
(c) Number of students in a class
(d) Weight of an individual

9. Which of the following is not a feature of a continuous variable? Competency Based Que

(a) Can assume an infinite number of values within a range
(b) Can only take specific integral values
(c) Includes values such as fractions and decimals
(d) Can represent measurements like temperature and height

10. Which of the following represents continuous variables?

I. Number of cars in a parking lot.
II. Temperature of a city.
III. Height of an individual.
IV. Number of students in a class. Competency Based Que

Codes
(a) Only I
(b) Both II and III
(c) Both I and IV
(d) Only II

11. The following table provides information about a dataset and its parameters. Using the data, calculate the missing number of classes (denoted as '?').

Competency Based Que

Parameter	Value
Smallest Value	10
Largest Value	35
Class Interval	5
Range	?
Number of Classes	?

(a) 25, 5
(b) 20, 6
(c) 35, 7
(d) 30, 8

12. A statistical series that arranges data based on time periods is known as a .... series.

(a) spatial
(b) condition
(c) time
(d) discrete

13. Which type of statistical series is described by the statement "A frequency distribution where data is organised based on individual items that take only integral values without frequency"?

(a) Individual
(b) Discrete
(c) Continuous
(d) Spatial

14. Which term refers to the difference between the upper and lower class limits in a frequency distribution?

(a) Class mid-point
(b) Class frequency
(c) Class width
(d) Class limits

15. The following is an open ended frequency distribution table with some missing frequencies. Based on the data, calculate the missing value (denoted as '?').

Competency Based Que

Class Interval	Frequency
Below 20	12
20-40	18
40-60	25
60 and above	?
Total	70

(a) 10
(b) 15
(c) 12
(d) 20

16. If the class interval is 50-70 and the class mid-point is missing, find the mid-point. **Competency Based Que**

(a) 70
(b) 50
(c) 60
(d) 55

17. What type of classification is shown in the image below?

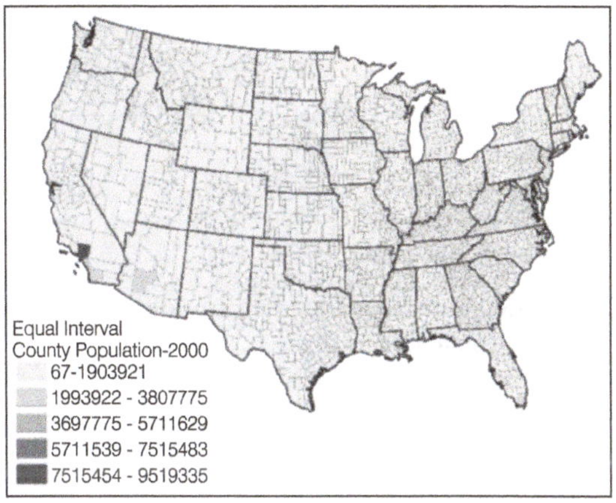

(a) Geographical classification
(b) Chronological classification
(c) Qualitative classification
(d) Quantitative classification

18. Which type of continuous frequency distribution series is given in the below image? **Competency Based Que**

Marks	Frequency
Below 10	4
10-15	2
15-20	6
20-25	3
25-30	8
30 and above	1
	N = 24

(a) Mid-value
(b) Close ended
(c) Spatial
(d) Open ended

19. A continuous series can be of which of the following types?

(a) Inclusive series
(b) Exclusive series
(c) Mid-value series
(d) Both (a) and (b)

20. In a frequency distribution, the total frequency is 200. If the frequency of a group is 50, what is the relative frequency of that group? **Competency Based Que**

(a) 20%
(b) 25%
(c) 30%
(d) 35%

21. Which type of frequency distribution is represented in the given image? **Competency Based Que**

Marks X	No. of Students
4	6
8	12
12	18

Marks X	No. of Students
16	15
20	9
	N = 60

(a) Discrete
(b) Continuous
(c) Both (a) and (b)
(d) None of the above

22. **In a mid-value frequency distribution, the class mid-point is calculated as the ……… of the upper and lower class limits.**

(a) sum (b) difference
(c) average (d) product

23. **The following figure represents ……… frequency distribution.** Competency Based Que

SAT Score	Frequency
450	1
550	1
600	1
640	3
670	1
710	1
720	1
730	1
780	1

(a) univariate (b) bivariate
(c) trivariate (d) None of these

24. **Identify the correct statement for bivariate frequency distribution.** Competency Based Que

I. A frequency distribution that involves two variables.
II. Variable values grouped into various classes.
III. A frequency distribution that classifies data based on a single variable.
IV. One-way frequency distribution.

Codes
(a) Both III and IV (b) Only III
(c) Both I and II (d) Only II

25. **The ……… in a frequency distribution can be calculated by dividing the range of the data by the class interval size.**

(a) size of each class interval
(b) number of classes
(c) frequency of each class
(d) class limits

26. **For a dataset with a range of 45 and a total of 9 classes, what is the size of each class interval?** Competency Based Que

(a) 4.5 (b) 5 (c) 5.5 (d) 6

27. **What do you add to the lower limit to calculate the upper limit in a frequency distribution?**

(a) Range (b) Frequency
(c) Class interval (d) Number of classes

Direction *Read the case study and answer the questions 28 to 31 on the basis of the same*

A city planner is tasked with analysing the population distribution across different urban and rural areas to determine how resources should be allocated for a new development project. The data collected includes population numbers for various districts over the past five years. The data has been organised into frequency distributions to make it easier to interpret and analyse.

The city planner has classified the population data into different classes based on geographical areas and time periods. The data is presented in the following way

Urban Areas		Rural Areas	
Class Interval	Frequency	Class Interval	Frequency
10,000-20,000	5	5,000-10,000	7
20,001-30,000	8	10,001-15,000	9
30,001-40,000	6	15,001-20,000	6
40,001-50,000	4		

28. **Which term best describes the range of values included in each class interval for both urban and rural areas?**

(a) Class limits (b) Class mid-point
(c) Class width (d) Class frequency

29. **For the rural areas frequency distribution, the total frequency for the class interval 10,001-15,000 is …… .**

30. **When calculating the total frequency for a given class interval, you would sum the frequencies of that interval. What is the correct method to find the total frequency for the class interval 10,000-20,000 in urban areas?**

(a) Add the frequencies of the class intervals 5,000-10,000, 10,001-15,000 and 15,001-20,000
(b) Add the frequencies of the intervals 10,000-20,000, 20,001-30,000, 30,001-40,000 and 40,001-50,000
(c) Add only the frequency of the class interval 10,000-20,000
(d) Add the frequencies of the class intervals 10,000-20,000 and 20,001-30,000

31. **In the urban areas frequency distribution, the class interval with the highest frequency is ……… .**

Assertion-Reason

Direction (Q.No. 32 to 41) *Read the following Assertion (A) and Reason (R) and choose the correct alternative from the following*

Alternatives

(a) Both Assertion (A) and Reason (R) are true and Reason (R) is the correct explanation of Assertion (A)

(b) Both Assertion (A) and Reason (R) are true, but Reason (R) is not the correct explanation of Assertion (A)

(c) Assertion (A) is true, but Reason (R) is false

(d) Assertion (A) is false, but Reason (R) is true

32. **Assertion** (A) Classification of data helps in organising raw data into a comprehensible form.

Reason (R) Organising data is only necessary for mathematical analysis and does not impact understanding.

33. **Assertion** (A) Qualitative classification is used to arrange data based on measurable quantities.

Reason (R) Qualitative classification focuses on attributes like honesty or beauty.

34. **Assertion** (A) Geographical classification is based on location.

Reason (R) Chronological classification arranges data according to time periods.

35. **Assertion** (A) Quantitative classification involves the arrangement of data based on attributes like beauty or intelligence.

Reason (R) Quantitative classification is also known as numerical classification and involves measurable data.

36. **Assertion** (A) Discrete variables do not assume fractional values.

Reason (R) Discrete variables change by finite jumps and only take specific integral values.

37. **Assertion** (A) Continuous variables can take on only specific integral values and do not include fractional values.

Reason (R) Continuous variables can assume an infinite number of values within a specified range, including fractional values.

38. **Assertion** (A) Cumulative frequency distributions are used to display the number of observations below or above a certain value in a dataset.

Reason (R) Cumulative frequency distributions can be classified into 'more than' and 'less than' types to represent different accumulation perspectives.

39. **Assertion** (A) The mid-value frequency distribution uses class mid-points to represent each class interval.

Reason (R) Class mid-points are calculated by averaging the upper and lower limits of each class.

40. **Assertion** (A) A bivariate frequency distribution is used to analyse the relationship between two variables by categorising their paired values.

Reason (R) Bivariate distribution is also known as a one-way frequency distribution and focuses on a single variable.

41. **Assertion** (A) To determine the frequency of each class in a frequency distribution, tally marks are used to count the number of observations in each class.

Reason (R) Tally marks are used because they simplify the process of counting observations, especially in datasets with large numbers of entries.

Two Statements Based MCQs

Direction (Q.No. 42 to 51) *Read the following statements carefully and choose the correct alternative*

Alternatives

(a) Statement I is correct and Statement II is incorrect

(b) Statement II is correct and Statement I is incorrect

(c) Both the statements are correct

(d) Both the statements are incorrect

42. **Statement I** Classification involves arranging data into different groups based on common characteristics or attributes.

Statement II Quantitative classification is concerned with organising data based on attributes like honesty or intelligence.

43. **Statement I** In simple classification, the data is divided into two parts based on a single characteristic.

Statement II In manifold classification, data is divided into more than two parts based on multiple characteristics.

44. **Statement I** Data is said to be homogeneous when there are different characteristics present in the universe.

Statement II Inclusive frequency distribution cannot be used for further mathematical calculation.

45. **Statement I** Temperature of a city is an example of continuous variables.

Statement II The number of students in a class is an example of discrete variables.

46. **Statement I** A discrete variable can take any value within a specified interval, including fractional values.

Statement II A continuous variable can take both integral and fractional values within a specified range.

47. **Statement I** Mid-point is calculated as the average of the upper and lower limits of each class.

Statement II Some intervals may be wider or narrower than others, which can affect the representation and comparison of data.

48. **Statement I** A frequency distribution table helps in condensing large datasets into meaningful patterns.

Statement II A cumulative frequency distribution provides a clear picture of data accumulation over different class intervals.

49. **Statement I** In a bivariate frequency distribution, data is grouped based on a single variable.

Statement II An inclusive frequency distribution includes both the upper and lower limits of each class interval.

50. **Statement I** In a frequency distribution, tally marks are used to record the number of observations for each class interval.

Statement II In a cumulative frequency distribution, frequencies are accumulated starting from the highest value down to the lowest value.

51. **Statement I** Unequal class intervals can be useful when there is a large variation in the range of values within a dataset.

Statement II Unequal class intervals are always preferable over equal class intervals, regardless of the data distribution.

Matching

52. Match the following

Column I		Column II
A. Arranging data into different groups or classes.	(i)	Qualitative
B. Data classified on measurable characteristics.	(ii)	Quantitative
C. Data classified on attributes.	(iii)	Classification
D. Data classified on the basis of time period.	(iv)	Temporal

Codes

	A	B	C	D
(a)	(iii)	(iv)	(i)	(ii)
(b)	(iv)	(i)	(ii)	(iii)
(c)	(ii)	(iii)	(iv)	(i)
(d)	(iii)	(ii)	(i)	(iv)

53. Match the following

Column I		Column II
A. Variable	(i)	Weight of individuals.
B. Variate	(ii)	Number of cars in a parking lot.
C. Continuous variable	(iii)	Characteristics that can be measured.
D. Discrete variable	(iv)	Each value within a range.

Codes

	A	B	C	D
(a)	(iii)	(iv)	(i)	(ii)
(b)	(iv)	(i)	(ii)	(iii)
(c)	(ii)	(iii)	(iv)	(i)
(d)	(iii)	(ii)	(i)	(iv)

54. Match the following

Column I		Column II
A. Data arranged in proper and systematic manner	(i)	Continuous series
B. Data arranged based on geographical are	(ii)	Statistical series
C. Ungrouped frequency distribution	(iii)	Spatial series
D. Grouped frequency distribution	(iv)	Discrete series

Codes

	A	B	C	D
(a)	(iii)	(iv)	(i)	(ii)
(b)	(iv)	(i)	(ii)	(iii)
(c)	(ii)	(iii)	(iv)	(i)
(d)	(iii)	(ii)	(i)	(iv)

55. Match the following

Column I		Column II
A. Frequency	(i)	The two extreme ends of a class.
B. Class limit	(ii)	The difference between the upper class limit and the lower class limit.
C. Class width	(iii)	Group represented as a percentage of the total frequency of the distribution.
D. Relative frequency	(iv)	The number of times a given value appears in a series.

Codes

	A	B	C	D
(a)	(iii)	(iv)	(i)	(ii)
(b)	(iv)	(i)	(ii)	(iii)
(c)	(ii)	(iii)	(iv)	(i)
(d)	(iii)	(ii)	(i)	(iv)

56. Match the following

Column I		Column II
A. Size of class	(i)	Range
B. Number of classes	(ii)	Lower Limit
C. Difference between largest and smallest value	(iii)	Range/Number of Classes
D. Minimum value of variables	(iv)	Range/Class Interval

Codes

	A	B	C	D		A	B	C	D
(a)	(iii)	(iv)	(i)	(ii)	(b)	(iv)	(i)	(ii)	(iii)
(c)	(ii)	(iii)	(iv)	(i)	(d)	(iii)	(ii)	(i)	(iv)

Concept Identification

57. The process of arranging data into different groups or classes based on common characteristics or attributes.

58. Classifying raw data into these intervals and displaying the frequencies of values in each interval.

59. Organising data based on such specific integral values and displaying their frequencies.

60. You are working with a frequency distribution where each class interval includes both the lower and upper limits. In this distribution, the upper limit of one class is part of the class interval and does not become the lower limit of the next class, allowing for some slight overlap between intervals.

Answers

1. (a) Classification
2. (c) Both II and III
3. (b) qualitative
4. (a) Time series classification
5. (b) Manifold classification
6. (c) purpose based
7. (d) Both (a) and (b)
8. (c) Number of students in a class
9. (b) Can only take specific integral values
10. (b) Both II and III
11. (a) Range = Largest Value – Smallest Value = 35 – 10 = 25
    Number of Classes = Range/Class Interval = 25/5 = 5
12. (c) time
13. (a) Individual
14. (c) Class width
15. (b) The total frequency is given as 70. The sum of known frequencies is 12 + 18 + 25 = 55.
    The missing frequency is calculated by subtracting the sum of known frequencies from the total 70 – 55 = 15
16. (c) Upper Class Limit + Lower Class Limit/2
    = 70 + 50 / 2 = 120 / 2 = 60
17. (a) Geographical classification
18. (d) Open ended
19. (d) Both (a) and (b)
20. (b) Frequency of the Group/Total Frequency × 100
    = 50/200 × 100 = 25%
21. (a) Discrete
22. (c) average
23. (a) univariate
24. (c) Both I and II
25. (b) number of classes
26. (b) Range/Number of Classes = 45/9 = 5
27. (c) Class interval
28. (c) Class width
29. 9
30. (c) Add only the frequency of the class interval 10,000-20,000
31. 20,001-30,000
32. (c) Organising data is crucial not just for mathematical analysis but also for enhancing understanding.
33. (d) Qualitative classification does not focus on measurable quantities; it focuses on attributes.
34. (b) Both Assertion (A) and Reason (R) are true, but Reason (R) is not the correct explanation of Assertion (A)
35. (d) Quantitative classification is based on measurable data, not attributes like beauty.
36. (a) Both Assertion (A) and Reason (R) are true and Reason (R) is the correct explanation of Assertion (A)
37. (d) Continuous variables can include fractional values, not just specific integral values.
38. (a) Both Assertion (A) and Reason (R) are true and Reason (R) is the correct explanation of Assertion (A)
39. (a) Both Assertion (A) and Reason (R) are true and Reason (R) is the correct explanation of Assertion (A)
40. (c) A bivariate frequency distribution examines the relationship between two variables, not a single variable.
41. (a) Both Assertion (A) and Reason (R) are true and Reason (R) the correct explanation of Assertion (A)
42. (a) Quantitative classification is based on numerical measurements, not on attributes like honesty.
43. (c) Both the statements are correct
44. (b) Data possessing different characteristics or attributes are said to the heterogeneous.
45. (c) Both the statements are correct
46. (b) A discrete variable can take only specific integral values, meaning it only changes by finite jumps and does not take any fractional values.
47. (c) Both the statements are correct
48. (c) Both the statements are correct
49. (b) A bivariate frequency distribution involves two variables, not one.

50. (a) Cumulative frequency distribution, the frequencies are accumulated starting from either the lowest value upward (in the case of 'less than' cumulative frequency) or the highest value downward.

51. (a) Equal class intervals are preferred when the data is evenly distributed, as they provide simpler and clearer analysis.

52. (d) (iii) (ii) (i) (iv)

53. (a) (iii) (iv) (i) (ii)

54. (c) (ii) (iii) (iv) (i)

55. (b) (iv) (i) (ii) (iii)

56. (a) (iii) (iv) (i) (ii)

57. Data classification

58. Frequency distribution

59. Discrete frequency distribution

60. Inclusive frequency distribution

Subjective Questions

Short Answer Type Questions

1. Do you agree that classified data is better than raw data? Why? NCERT; Competency Based Que

Ans. Yes, the raw data are very large and difficult to handle. It is difficult to draw meaningful conclusion from them as they do not yield to statistical methods easily. On the other hand, the classified data are comprehensible and concise.

It is easier to draw meaningful conclusion from them. Thus, classified data are better than raw data.

2. Conner stated, "Classification is the process of arranging things in groups or classes according to their resemblances and affinities." What does this process aim to achieve in data analysis? Competency Based Que

Ans. Conner's statement highlights that the process of classification aims to group similar items together based on their common attributes or resemblances. This process in data analysis seeks to express the unity of these attributes among diverse individuals or data points, transforming unorganised raw data into an organised and meaningful form. By classifying data, analysts can more easily identify relationships, patterns and trends, which facilitate a deeper understanding and more effective decision-making.

3. What type of classification is best suited for the data given in the following image?

State	Gender	Literate	Literate	Total Population
Uttar Pradesh	Male	40,000	10,000	50,000
Uttar Pradesh	Female	35,000	15,000	50,000
Kerala	Male	16,000	500	16,500
Kerala	Female	15,500	1,000	16,500
Maharashtra	Male	30,000	5,000	35,000
Maharashtra	Female	28,000	7,000	35,000

Ans. The data about literacy rates of men and women in different states can be classified using **manifold classification**. This method involves first categorising the population by gender (male and female) and then further dividing each gender category based on literacy status (literate and illiterate).

This type of classification helps in analysing the literacy rate differences not only between genders but also across different states.

(i) **First Level of Classification** (By Gender)
The population is divided into two groups male and female.

(ii) **Second Level of Classification** (By Literacy Status)
Within each gender group, the population is further classified based on literacy status literate and illiterate.

4. What is a variable? Distinguish between a discrete variable and a continuous variable. NCERT

Ans. A measurable characteristic which takes different values at different points of time and in different circumstances is called a variable.

The difference between discrete variable and continuous variable are

Basis	Discrete Variable	Continuous Variable
Meaning	A variable which can take only integral values is referred to as a discrete variable.	A variable which can take integral values as well as fractional values in a specified range is referred to as continuous variable.
Method of Data Collection	The data related to a discrete variable is collected by counting.	The data related to a continuous variable is collected by measurement.
Change in Value	Discrete variable can change only by integral values.	Continuous variable can change by integral values, as well as, fractional values.

5. Which of the following images represents the characteristics of discrete variable? **Competency Based Que**

Image 1

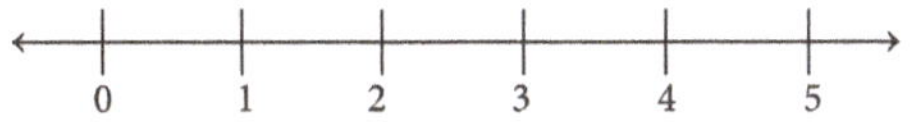

Image 2

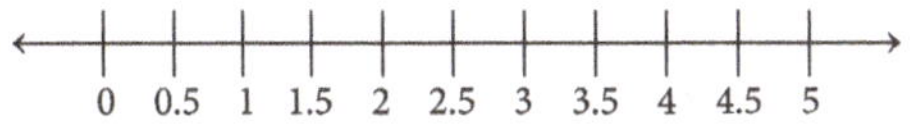

Ans. Image 1 shows discrete variables as it depicts only proper integral values. The image representing the characteristics of a discrete variable typically shows data that can only take specific, separate values without any intermediate values between them. Discrete variables are countable and examples include the number of students in a class, the number of cars in a parking lot or the number of goals scored in a match.

6. If the temperature of a city is recorded as 23.5°C, 24.8°C, 22.1°C and 25.3°C over four days, what type of variable does this data represent? **Competency Based Que**

Ans. The data represents a continuous variable. Continuous variables are those that can take any value within a specified range, including both whole numbers and fractions. In this example, the temperature of the city is measured with decimal precision, showing that it can take any value along the continuum within the range of possible temperatures.

Since temperatures can vary by small fractions, this data type reflects the characteristics of a continuous variable, which is capable of assuming an infinite number of possible values within a given interval.

7. "A discrete variable can take only specific integral values and does not take any fractional values." Do you agree? Give reason. **Competency Based Que**

Ans. Yes, I agree. A discrete variable is one that takes specific, countable values, with no intermediate values possible between these specific points.

e.g. Consider the number of students in a class. This value can be 1, 2, 3 and so forth, reflecting the countable nature of the data. You cannot have a non-integer number of students, such as 2.5 or 3.7. Thus, discrete variables are characterised by their ability to take on distinct, separate values, with no continuity between them, which is why they are limited to integral values only.

8. "The price of commodities is a variable because it differs across items." What type of variable does price represent and why? **Competency Based Que**

Ans. The price of commodities represents a continuous variable because it can take a wide range of values, including decimal or fractional amounts.

Prices are not limited to whole numbers; for instance, an item could be priced at $2.50, $3.99 or $4.25. This variability in price, where it can take on any value within a certain range, highlights its continuous nature.

In economic contexts, prices often fluctuate and they can be measured with precision down to the cent or even smaller units. This ability to assume a range of values, with no fixed steps between them, is a defining characteristic of a continuous variable.

9. What are the general guidelines for the construction of a frequency distribution?

Ans. The general guidelines for the construction of a frequency distribution are

(i) All class intervals should be of equal size.

(ii) The lower limit of the first class should either be 0 or multiple of 5.

(iii) We should avoid odd sized class interval.

(iv) Open ended classes should be avoided.

10. A researcher is analysing the income distribution of households in a city. The data collected includes household incomes ranging from ₹ 10,000 to ₹ 1,00,000. To capture the variability and distribution more accurately, the researcher decides to use a frequency distribution as follows

- **₹ 10,000-₹ 20,000**
- **₹ 20,000-₹ 35,000**
- **₹ 35,000-₹ 50,000**
- **₹ 50,000-₹ 70,000**
- **₹ 70,000-₹ 1,00,000**

In the given case study, what type of frequency distribution is being used and why was it chosen for analysing household incomes? **Competency Based Que**

Ans. The frequency distribution being used in the case study is an 'unequal class interval frequency distribution.' This type of distribution was chosen because it allows for varying class widths, which can be useful for capturing and analysing data where certain income ranges are more densely populated or require more detailed examination.

By using unequal intervals, the researcher can provide a more nuanced view of the income distribution, particularly in areas where income data is more concentrated or where specific income brackets are of greater interest.

11. If you have a dataset with variables for height and weight of individuals, which type of frequency distribution would be appropriate to analyse the relationship between these two variables?

Ans. To analyse the relationship between height and weight, a bivariate frequency distribution would be appropriate. This type of distribution allows you to examine how the values of height and weight vary together.

By grouping the data into classes for both height and weight, you can study how changes in one variable (e.g. Height) are associated with changes in the other variable (e.g. Weight), providing insights into their empirical relationship.

12. Class limits in a frequency distribution are always inclusive of the upper limit of one class and the lower limit of the next class. Do you agree with the statement? Give reason. Competency Based Que

Ans. No. I do not agree. In a frequency distribution with inclusive class limits, both the upper and lower limits of each class are included within that class interval. However, in an exclusive class interval distribution, the upper limit of one class is not included in that interval and becomes the lower limit of the next class.

Long Answer Type Questions

13. Explain the 'exclusive' and 'inclusive' methods used in classification of data. NCERT

Ans. Exclusive Method

In this method, the classes are formed in such a way that the upper class limit of one class becomes the lower class limit of the next class. Continuity of the data is maintained in this method.

Under this method, the upper class limit is excluded but the lower class limit of a class is included in the interval.

According to this method, an observation that is exactly equal to the upper class limit would not be included in that class but would be included in the next class.

On the other hand, if it is equal to the lower class limit then it would be included in that class.

e.g. If the class intervals are 0-5, 5-10, 10-15, 15-20 and so on, a value of 10 would be included in the class 10-15 and not in the class 5-10.

Inclusive Method

The inclusive method does not exclude the upper class limit in a class interval. It includes the upper limit in the class. Thus, both class limits are parts of the class interval. e.g. The class intervals of 0-5, 6-10, 11-15 and so on are inclusive.

14. Describe the different bases of classification for data, providing detailed explanations and examples for each type. Include how these classifications help in organising and analysing data.

Ans. Different basis of classification for data are as follows

(i) **Geographical/Spatial Classification**
Geographical or spatial classification involves organising data based on geographical or locational differences. This method is useful when data needs to be segmented according to specific locations or regions.
e.g. If a retail chain has data on sales across various states in India, the data can be classified into states like Maharashtra, Uttar Pradesh and Tamil Nadu to assess regional sales performance and tailor marketing strategies accordingly.

(ii) **Chronological/Temporal Classification**
Chronological or temporal classification organises data based on time periods, which helps in analysing trends and changes over time. This type of classification is essential for time series analysis, where data is arranged in a sequential order, typically over different years, months or days.
e.g. A dataset on annual population growth rates from 2000 to 2020 is a time series, where each year's population data is recorded and analysed to identify growth patterns and trends over two decades.

(iii) **Qualitative Classification**
Qualitative classification organises data based on non-numeric attributes or qualities. This method is useful for categorising data that is descriptive and not easily quantified.

- **Simple Classification** This involves dividing data into two parts based on a single characteristic. This type is straightforward and helps in basic comparative analysis.
e.g. Classifying a population by gender into male and female categories allows for the examination of gender distribution and related analyses.
- **Manifold Classification** This involves dividing data into multiple categories based on more than one characteristic. This method provides a more detailed view by considering multiple attributes.
e.g. A dataset might first classify the population by gender (male-female) and then further divide it by literacy status (literate-illiterate). This classification allows for a nuanced analysis of gender and education level, facilitating deeper insights into educational disparities across genders.

(iv) **Quantitative Classification**
Quantitative classification involves organising data based on measurable quantities. This method is crucial for statistical analysis and often results in the formation of a frequency distribution. It includes numerical attributes such as age, height, weight, sales or profits.
e.g. A company might classify its employees by age groups (20-30, 31-40, etc.) to analyse the distribution of ages within the workforce. This classification helps in understanding demographic trends and planning accordingly for age specific needs or policies.

Each type of classification serves to organise data in a manner that facilitates clearer analysis and interpretation, enabling more informed decision-making based on the structured data.

15. A teacher has collected the marks of students in a recent exam. The data from two different classes are as follows

Class A 85, 72, 91, 88, 79, 95

Class B 72, 88, 79, 85, 95, 91

For each class, classify the data as either 'organised individual series' or 'unorganised individual series' and explain why? **Competency Based Que**

Ans. **Class A**

The data (85, 72, 91, 88, 79, 95) can be classified as an unorganised individual series because the marks are presented in no specific order.

They are simply listed as they were collected, without any attempt to arrange them in increasing or decreasing order.

Class B

The data (72, 88, 79, 85, 95, 91) is also an unorganised individual series for the same reason. The marks are presented without any order or frequency count, making it an unordered list of individual marks.

Organising the data enhances clarity and facilitates more detailed statistical analysis, such as calculating measures of central tendency (mean, median) and dispersion (range, standard deviation).

It also aids in creating visual representations, like histograms or bar charts, to better communicate the performance distribution.

16. With the help of suitable example, explain conversion of an inclusive distribution into exclusive distribution.

Ans. In inclusive distribution, there is a gap or discontinuity between the upper class limit and lower class limit of the next class.

To maintain the continuity, the class intervals are adjusted and an exclusive distribution is obtained.

The adjustment is done with the help of following steps

Step 1 The difference between the lower limit of second class and upper class limit of first class is obtained.

Step 2 The difference obtained is divided by 2.

Step 3 Value obtained in *Step 2*, is subtracted from lower limit of all the classes and added to the upper limit of all the classes.

e.g. Consider the given distribution

Income of 350 Employees of a Company

Income (₹)	Number of Employees
800-899	50
900-999	100
1000-1099	200
Total	350

Sol.

Step 1 Difference between lower class limit of IInd group and upper class limit of Ist group is computed which is 1 (900-899).

Step 2 This difference is divided by 2 and we get 0.5 ($1/2 = 0.5$).

Step 3 0.5 will be subtracted from the lower class limit of each group and added to the upper class limit of each group.

The resulting distribution is given below

Income of 350 Employees of a Company
(Converted from inclusive distribution to exclusive distribution)

Income (₹)	Number of Employees
799.5-899.5	50
899.5-999.5	100
999.5-1099.5	200
Total	350

17. Distinguish between inclusive series and exclusive series.

Ans. Differences between inclusive series and exclusive series are

Basis	Inclusive Series	Exclusive Series
Meaning	In inclusive series, the upper class limit of one class does not become the lower class limit of the succeeding class.	In exclusive series, the upper class limit of one class becomes the lower class limit of the succeeding class.
Inclusion of Values	This series includes the values corresponding to the lower class limit, upper class limit and the values falling in the range of these limits.	This series includes the values corresponding to lower class limit, but not to upper class limit. Values falling in the range of lower class limit and one less than the upper class limit are also included.

Basis	Inclusive Series	Exclusive Series
Relevance in Statistical Computation	This series has no relevance for statistical computation.	This series has relevance for statistical computation.
Example	Group Frequency 0-9 5 10-19 10	Group Frequency 0-10 5 10-20 10

18. Explain the steps involved in determining the components of a frequency distribution, including the number of classes, size of each class interval, class limits and frequency of each class.

Ans. To determine the components of a frequency distribution, follow these steps

(i) **Number of Classes**

- **Find the Range**
  Calculate the difference between the largest and smallest values in the data set.
- **Determine Number of Classes**
  Divide the range by the chosen class interval. This gives an estimate of how many distinct intervals or groups are needed.

(ii) **Size of Class** (Class Interval)

- **Calculate Class Interval**
  Use the range and number of classes to determine the size of each class interval.
  Ensure that the intervals are of equal or suitable size for meaningful analysis.

(iii) **Determination of Class Limits**

- **Lower Limit**
  Start with the smallest value or a value slightly less than the smallest value in the dataset.
- **Upper Limit**
  Add the class interval size to the lower limit to define the upper boundary of the class interval. This creates clear boundaries for each class.

(iv) **Determination of Frequency of Each Class**

- **Count Observations**
  Use tally marks or other counting methods to record how many data points fall within each class interval.
- **Calculate Frequency**
  Sum the tallies to get the frequency for each class interval. This tells you how many observations fall into each group.

Numerical Questions

Numerical 1

Given the following data values 5, 12, 14, 19, 25, 27, 30, 32, 35, 40, 45. Calculate the number of classes required if you choose a class interval of 10.

Sol. Range Calculation

Largest Value = 45; Smallest Value = 5

Range = 45 − 5 = 40

Number of Classes

Class Interval = 10

Number of Classes = Range / Class Interval

Number of Classes = 40 / 10 = 4

So, 4 classes are required.

Numerical 2

For the following data set 8, 13, 15, 22, 24, 29, 31, 35, 40, 44, 50, determine the class interval size if you want to create 5 classes.

Sol. Range Calculation

Largest Value = 50; Smallest Value = 8

Range = 50 − 8 = 42

Class Interval Size

Number of Classes = 5

Class Interval Size = Range / Number of Classes

Class Interval Size = 42 / 5 $\approx$ 8.4

For practical purposes, round to the nearest whole number, so use a class interval size of 9.

Numerical 3

Using a class interval size of 7, determine the class limits for the following data set

4, 10, 15, 20, 25, 30, 36, 42, 47

Sol. Class Intervals

Start with the smallest value = 4

Class 1 Lower Limit = 4, Upper Limit = 4 + 7 − 1 = 10

Class 2 Lower Limit = 11, Upper Limit = 11 + 7 − 1 = 17

Class 3 Lower Limit = 18, Upper Limit = 18 + 7 − 1 = 24

Class 4 Lower Limit = 25, Upper Limit = 25 + 7 − 1 = 31

Class 5 Lower Limit = 32, Upper Limit = 32 + 7 − 1 = 38

Class 6 Lower Limit = 39, Upper Limit = 39 + 7 − 1 = 45

Class 7 Lower Limit = 46, Upper Limit = 46 + 7 − 1 = 52

Numerical 4

Create a frequency table for the following dataset 2, 3, 4, 4, 5, 6, 6, 6, 7, 8, 9, 9, 10, 10, 10, 10, 11. Use class intervals of 5.

Sol. **Range Calculation**

Largest Value = 11; Smallest Value = 2

Range = 11 − 2 = 9

Class Intervals

Class 1 1-5 **Class 2** 6-10

Class 3 11-15

Frequency Table

Class Interval	Frequency
1-5	5
6-10	11
11-15	1

Numerical 5

Given a dataset 12, 15, 18, 21, 25, 28, 30, 32, 34, 37. Create an open ended frequency distribution with the first class being less than 20 and the last class being more than 30.

Sol. **Class Intervals**

Class 1 Less than 20 (Frequency = 3)

Class 2 20-30 (Frequency = 4)

Class 3 More than 30 (Frequency = 3)

Frequency Table

Class Interval	Frequency
Less than 20	3
20-30	4
More than 30	3

Numerical 6

For the following class intervals 0-5, 6-10, 11-15, 16-20, determine the mid-points and create a frequency table with a provided frequency of 5, 10, 7 and 8 respectively.

Sol. **Class Mid-points Calculation**

Class 1 0-5 (Mid-point = (0 + 5) / 2 = 2.5)

Class 2 6-10 (Mid-point = (6 + 10) / 2 = 8)

Class 3 11-15 (Mid-point = (11 + 15) / 2 = 13)

Class 4 16-20 (Mid-point = (16 + 20) / 2 = 18)

Frequency Table

Class Interval	Mid-point	Frequency
0-5	2.5	5
6-10	8	10
11-15	13	7
16-20	18	8

Numerical 7

If the class marks (mid-points) in a grouped frequency distribution of weights (in kgs) of a group of students are 75, 84, 93, 102, 111, 120, 129.

Find out **Competency Based Que**

(i) Width of the class/size of the class interval.

(ii) The class limits assuming that weights are measured to the nearest kilograms.

(iii) The class boundaries.

Sol. (i) Width of the Class = Difference of Two Consecutive (Mid-values)

$= 84 - 75$ *or* $93 - 84 = 9$

(ii) The class limits are 71–79, 80–88, 89–97, 98–106, 107–115, 116–124, 125–133.

(iii) The class boundaries are

(a) $75 - \frac{9}{2}, 75 + \frac{9}{2}$ i.e. 70.5-79.5

(b) $84 - \frac{9}{2}, 84 + \frac{9}{2}$ i.e. 79.5-88.5

(c) $93 - \frac{9}{2}, 93 + \frac{9}{2}$ i.e. 88.5-97.5

(d) $102 - \frac{9}{2}, 102 + \frac{9}{2}$ i.e. 97.5-106.5

(e) $111 - \frac{9}{2}, 111 + \frac{9}{2}$ i.e. 106.5-115.5

(f) $120 - \frac{9}{2}, 120 + \frac{9}{2}$ i.e. 11.5 − 124.5

(g) $129 - \frac{9}{2}, 129 + \frac{9}{2}$ i.e. 124.5-133.5

Numerical 8

Prepare a frequency distribution by inclusive method taking class interval of 7 from the following data

28, 17, 15, 22, 29, 21, 23, 27, 18, 12, 7, 2, 9, 4, 1, 8, 3, 10, 5, 20, 16, 12, 8, 4, 33, 27, 21, 15, 3, 36, 27, 18, 9, 2, 4, 6, 32, 31, 29, 18, 14, 13, 15, 11, 9, 7, 1, 5, 37, 32, 28, 26, 24, 20, 19, 25, 19, 20, 6, 9 **NCERT**

Sol. As in the question, the lowest value is 1 and the highest is 37, we have to take a class interval of 7. The various class intervals of 7 on inclusive basis are given. With the help of tally bar, inclusive frequency distribution will be derived.

The frequency distribution by inclusive method of given data is shown below

Class Interval	Tally Bar	Frequency (f)
1–7	𝍸 𝍸 𝍸	15
8–14	𝍸 𝍸 II	12
15–21	𝍸 𝍸 𝍸	15

Class Interval	Tally Bar	Frequency (f)
22–28	卌 卌	10
29–35	卌 |	6
36–42	||	2
	Total	60

Numerical 9

Prepare a bivariate frequency distribution for the marks by 24 examinees in Statistics and Accountancy.

Marks		Marks	
Statistics	Accountancy	Statistics	Accountancy
22	16	23	16
23	16	25	17
23	18	23	17
23	16	22	17
23	16	27	16
24	17	27	16
23	16	26	18
25	19	28	19
22	16	25	19
23	18	24	16
24	18	23	17
24	17	24	19

Sol. The bivariate frequency array for the given data is shown below

Marks in Accountancy	Marks in Statistics							
	22	23	24	25	26	27	28	Total
16	||(2)	||||(5)	|(1)			||(2)		10
17	|(1)	||(2)	||(2)	|(1)				6
18		||(2)	|(1)		|(1)			4
19			|(1)	||(2)			|(1)	4
	3	9	5	3	1	2	1	24

Numerical 10

Convert the following inclusive class interval into exclusive class interval.

Inclusive Class Interval	Frequency
0-99	2
100-199	4
200-299	5
300-399	6
400-499	3
500-599	5
Total	25

Sol. The exclusive class interval table of given form is shown below

Exclusive Class Interval	Frequency (f)
0-99.5	2
99.5-199.5	4
199.5-299.5	5
299.5-399.5	6
399.5-499.5	3
499.5-599.5	5
Total	25

In this case as lower limit of first class is zero, hence 0.5 will not be subtracted from it.

Numerical 11

From the following data, relating to weights of 40 students in kg Competency Based Que

138, 164, 150, 131, 144, 125, 149, 157, 146, 148, 140, 147, 136, 148, 152, 144, 168, 126, 138, 176, 163, 119, 150, 165, 146, 173, 142, 147, 135, 153, 142, 135, 140, 135, 161, 145, 150, 156, 145, 128

(i) Obtain the range of weights of the students.

(ii) Divide the range into appropriate number of class interval and obtain the frequency distribution.

(iii) Find the number of students whose weight is
(a) less than 145 kg (b) more than 155 kg
(c) between 135 and 155 kg

Sol. (i) Range $= 176 - 119 = 57$

(ii) The frequency distribution by dividing into appropriate classes is shown below

Class Interval	Tally Bar	Frequency (f)
115-125	|	1
125-135	卌	4
135-145	卌 卌 ||	12
145-155	卌 卌 卌	14
155-165	||||	5
165-175	|||	3
175-185	|	1
	Total	40

(iii) Number of students whose weight is

(a) less than 145 kg $= 17\ (12 + 4 + 1)$

(b) more than 155 kg $= 9\ (5 + 3 + 1)$

(c) between 135 and 155 kg $= 26\ (12 + 14)$

Numerical 12

From the following data, prepare simple frequency distribution on the basis of equal class interval.

Marks	Number of Students
Less than 5	7
Less than 10	20
5-15	38
15 and above	55
20-25	20
25 and above	5
30 above	1

Sol. The simple frequency distribution table on the basis of equal class interval is shown below

Marks	Frequency (f)
0-5	7
5-10	13 [20 − 7]
10-15	25 [38 − 13]
15-20	30 [55 − 25]
20-25	20
25-30	4 [5 − 1]
30-35	1
Total	100

Numerical 13

Convert the following inclusive series into exclusive series.

Class Interval	1-5	6-10	11-15	16-20	21-25
Number of Workers	10	15	20	25	30

Sol. The exclusive series of the given inclusive series is shown below

Class Interval	Frequency (f)
0.5-5.5	10
5.5-10.5	15
10.5-15.5	20
15.5-20.5	25
20.5-25.5	30
Total	100

Numerical 14

Answer the questions based upon the tally bar given below

Class Interval	Tally Marks
150-200	||
200-250	|||
250-300	𝍸 |
300-350	𝍸
350-400	𝍸 ||
400-450	𝍸
450-500	|||

(i) Write the frequencies against each class and also calculate the mid-values from the given data.

(ii) From the table in part (i), derive 'less than cumulative frequency distribution'.

Competency Based Que

Sol. (i) Calculation of frequency and mid-values

Class Interval	Frequency	Mid-values
150-200	2	175
200-250	3	225
250-300	6	275
300-350	5	325
350-400	7	375
400-450	4	425
450-500	3	475

Mid-values = (L1 + L2)/2

(ii) Derivation of less than cumulative frequency distribution

Class Interval	Frequency
Lesss than 200	2
Lesss than 250	2 + 3 = 5
Lesss than 300	5 + 6 = 11
Lesss than 350	11 + 5 = 16
Lesss than 400	16 + 7 = 23
Lesss than 450	23 + 4 = 27
Lesss than 500	27 + 3 = 30

Numerical 15

Use the data in the given table that relate to monthly household expenditure (in ₹) on food of 50 households and

(i) obtain the range of monthly household expenditure on food.

(ii) divide the range into appropriate number of class intervals and obtain the frequency distribution of expenditure.

(iii) find the number of households whose monthly expenditure on food is

(a) less than ₹ 2,000

(b) more than ₹ 3,000

(c) between ₹ 1,500 and ₹ 2,500

NCERT; Competency Based Que

Monthly Household Expenditure (in ₹) on Food of 50 Households

1904	1559	3473	1735	2760
2041	1612	1753	1855	4439
5090	1085	1823	2346	1523
1211	1360	1110	2152	1183
1218	1315	1105	2628	2712
4248	1812	1264	1183	1171

Monthly Household Expenditure (in ₹) on Food of 50 Households

1007	1180	1953	1137	2048
2025	1583	1324	2621	3676
1397	1832	1962	2177	2575
1293	1365	1146	3222	1396

Sol. (i) Range = Largest Value − Smallest Value

Highest Value = 5090

Lowest Value = 1007

So, Range = 5090 − 1007 = 4083

(ii) **Frequency Distribution on Monthly Household Expenditure (in ₹) of 50 Households**

Class Interval	Tally Bar	Frequency
1000-1500	~~||||~~ ~~||||~~ ~~||||~~ ~~||||~~	20
1500-2000	~~||||~~ ~~||||~~ |||	13
2000-2500	~~||||~~ |	6
2500-3000	~~||||~~	5
3000-3500	||	2
3500-4000	|	1
4000-4500	||	2
4500-5000	—	0
5000-5500	|	1
	Total	50

(iii) (a) Number of households whose monthly expenditure on food is less than ₹ 2,000 = 20 + 13 = 33

(b) Number of households whose monthly expenditure on food is more than ₹ 3,000 = 2 + 1 + 2 + 0 + 1 = 6

(c) Number of households whose expenditure on food is between ₹ 1,500 and ₹ 2,500 = 13 + 6 = 19

Numerical 16

The following distribution shows the income of 50 households.

Monthly Income (in ₹)	Number of Households
2,000-4,000	6
4,000-6,000	8
6,000-8,000	12
8,000-10,000	14
10,000-12,000	10
Total	50

On the basis of the above distribution, answer the following questions **Competency Based Que**

(i) What will be the class frequency of the following groups?

(a) 4,000-6,000 (b) 8,000-10,000

(ii) What will be the upper and lower class limits of the following groups?

(a) 2,000-4,000 (b) 6,000-8,000

(iii) What will be the class interval for the group 4,000-6,000?

(iv) Find the class mid-point for the following groups.

(a) 8,000-10,000 (b) 10,000-12,000

(v) Find the relative frequency of the following groups.

(a) 6,000-8,000 (b) 10,000-12,000

(vi) Find the cumulative frequency of the following groups.

(a) 6,000-8,000 (b) 8,000-10,000

(vii) Which group has the highest concentration of data?

(viii) Which group has the lowest concentration of data?

(ix) What will be the frequency density of the group 4,000-6,000?

Sol. (i) (a) The class frequency of the group 4,000-6,000 is 8.

(b) The class frequency of the group 8,000-10,000 is 14.

(ii) (a) Upper class limit of the group 2,000-4,000 is 4,000.

Lower class limit of the group 2,000-4,000 is 2,000.

(b) Upper class limit of the group 6,000-8,000 is 8,000.

Lower class limit of the group 6,000-8,000 is 6,000.

(iii) Class Interval

$= \text{Upper Class Limit} - \text{Lower Class Limit}$

$= 6{,}000 - 4{,}000 = 2{,}000$

(iv) Class Mid-point

$$= \frac{\text{Upper Class Limit} + \text{Lower Class Limit}}{2}$$

(a) Class Mid-point (8,000-10,000)

$$= \frac{10{,}000 + 8{,}000}{2} = 9{,}000$$

(b) Class Mid-point (10,000-12,000)

$$= \frac{12{,}000 + 10{,}000}{2} = 11{,}000$$

(v) Relative Frequency $= \frac{\text{Frequency of Class}}{\text{Total Frequency}} \times 100$

(a) Relative Frequency (6,000-8,000)

$$= \frac{12}{50} \times 100 = 24\%$$

(b) Relative Frequency (10,000-12,000)

$$= \frac{10}{50} \times 100 = 20\%$$

(vi) (a) Cumulative frequency of group 6,000-8,000

$= 6 + 8 + 12 = 26$

(b) Cumulative frequency of group 8,000-10,000

$= 6 + 8 + 12 + 14 = 40$

(vii) Group 8,000-10,000 has the highest concentration of data.

(viii) Group 2,000-4,000 has the lowest concentration of data.

(ix) Frequency Density $= \frac{\text{Class Frequency}}{\text{Class Width}}$

$$= \frac{8}{2{,}000} = 0.004$$

SELF ASSESSMENT TEST

Objective Type Questions

1. Which of the following is a characteristic of ideal classification?
   (a) Ambiguity (b) Clarity
   (c) Inflexibility (d) Complexity
2. In a continuous frequency distribution, ... is displayed in a table.
   (a) individual values and their frequencies
   (b) only the class mid-points
   (c) only the total frequency
   (d) class intervals and their corresponding frequencies
3. Which of the following is not a type of frequency distribution?
   (a) Discrete frequency distribution
   (b) Continuous frequency distribution
   (c) Individual series frequency distribution
   (d) Mixed frequency distribution
4. What is the main difference between discrete and continuous frequency distribution?
   (a) Discrete distribution organises data into intervals, continuous does not
   (b) Continuous distribution organises data based on ungrouped frequency
   (c) Discrete distribution is based on specific values, continuous involves intervals
   (d) Continuous distribution excludes intermediate values, discrete does not
5. In .... type of classification, the data is arranged based on time periods.
   (a) chronological classification
   (b) quantitative classification
   (c) geographical classification
   (d) qualitative classification
6. In which of the following does the frequency of each class appear in increasing order?
   (a) Exclusive frequency distribution
   (b) Less than cumulative frequency distribution
   (c) Inclusive frequency distribution
   (d) More than cumulative frequency distribution
7. Which of the following statements is true?
   (a) In a cumulative frequency distribution, frequencies are counted for each individual value in the data set
   (b) A continuous frequency distribution uses distinct categories that do not overlap
   (c) An inclusive frequency distribution includes both the upper and lower limits in each class interval
   (d) A discrete frequency distribution organises data into continuous intervals to represent ranges of values.
8. In a frequency distribution, the class width is calculated by subtracting the .... of a class interval from the .... of the next class interval.
   (a) upper limit, lower limit
   (b) lower limit, lower limit
   (c) upper limit, upper limit
   (d) lower limit, upper limit

Answers 1. (b) 2. (d) 3. (d) 4. (c) 5. (a) 6. (b) 7. (c) 8. (a)

Short Answer Type Questions

9. What is the significance of cumulative frequency in a frequency distribution? Illustrate with an example.
10. "The class interval in a frequency distribution represents a range of values that are grouped together for analysis." Do you agree?
11. What are statistical series? Explain with example.
12. Define the following terms related to frequency distribution.
    (i) Class mid-point (ii) Class frequency
13. "A discrete frequency distribution organises data based on a discrete variable, which can only take specific integral values." What type of variable does a discrete frequency distribution handle and what characteristic does it have?
14. Differentiate between exclusive and inclusive frequency distribution series.

Long Answer Type Questions

15. Briefly explain the methods of classification.
16. In a research study, the age of participants, the number of students in a classroom and the height of individuals were recorded. The study found that
    - Age can vary continuously, ranging from 18 to 80 years with fractional values.
    - The number of students in a classroom is a fixed value and it can only take whole number values like 25, 30 or 35.

- The height of participants varies continuously and can be measured in fractional values, such as 170.5 cm, 175.8 cm, etc.
  (i) Identify the example of discrete variables from the above case.
  (ii) What do you understand by discrete and continuous variables?
  (iii) Describe the key differences between discrete and continuous variables and provide examples of each type in real life scenarios.

Numerical Questions

17. Convert the following inclusive series into exclusive series

Class Interval	Number of Workers
2-6	10
7-11	15
12-16	20
17-21	25
22-26	30

18. 20 families in an area spend the following monthly expenditure on food

115, 159, 196, 205, 223,
256, 271, 310, 129, 335,
241, 265, 298, 144, 135,
172, 173, 229, 220, 238

Find the number of families whose monthly expenditure on food is

(i) less than ₹ 250
(ii) more than ₹ 300
(iii) between ₹ 200 and ₹ 300

04

CHAPTER

Presentation of data means the data should be presented in such a way that the facts and figures are clearly understood and are capable of being analysed.

YOUR STUDY GOALS

YOUR PRACTICE GOAL

- Objective Type Questions (64 Qs ; MCQs, A-R, Statements, Matching, Concept Identification)
- Subjective Questions (20 SAs, 10 LAs)
- 25 Numerical Questions
- Self Assessment Test (8 MCQs, 4 SAs, 3 LAs, 10 Numerical)

Presentation of Data

4.1 Introduction

Presentation of data is important for conveying information clearly and effectively, allowing for accurate analysis and decision-making.

Proper data presentation transforms raw information into a format that is easy to interpret and understand.

The primary forms of presenting data include

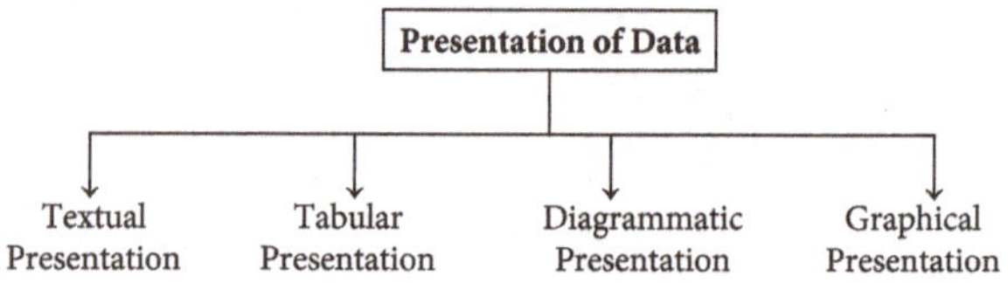

Textual or Descriptive Presentation of Data

This presentation involves conveying data through written paragraphs. It is generally used where data is not too large. e.g. It can report that despite a strike in Agra's cloth manufacturing sector, 60% of workers reported for duty and only 3 of 30 industries were completely shut down.

This type of presentation's main drawback is that readers need to go through the complete text to extract and understand the relevant data.

4.2 Tabular Presentation of Data

Tabular presentation involves arranging data systematically in rows (horizontally) and columns (vertically) in the form of a table. This process known as tabulation. The key **objectives** of tabulation are

1. **Simplification** Organises complex data in a structured (orderly) manner.
2. **Reference** Provides a consolidated format for future reference/use.
3. **Comparison** Facilitates easy comparison by presenting data at one place in an understandable manner.
4. **Space Utilisation** Makes efficient use of space by consolidating scattered data.
5. **Statistical Analysis** Supports further mathematical treatment and statistical analysis by centralising data.

Parts of a Table

Part	Explanation
Table Number	Table should be numbered for easy reference. It can be done by using integral (e.g. 1, 2) or subscribed numbers (e.g. 3.1).
Title of the Table	It is a concise description of the table's contents, including data nature, place, time, subject matter, etc. It should be short, clear and complete in all respects.
Head Note	It is the supplementary information explaining the table or its parts and provided in brackets below the title, such as units of measurement.
Column Heading or Caption	It describes the contents of a column and may have sub-heads for detailed classification.
Stubs or Row Headings	These are titles for rows that indicate the information contained in each row. The complete left column is referred to as stub column.
Body of the Table	It is the main section containing the data arranged according to column headings and row stubs. Each item in the body is referred to as a 'cell'.
Unit of Measurement	It specifies the measurement unit for data, included with the title or along with captions and stubs, if units vary.
Footnote	It provides additional explanation for specific data features, exception or special circumstances affecting the data.
Source Note	It provides the source of secondary data, including publication details, to ensure credibility and reference. It should be specified below the footnote.

Format of a Table

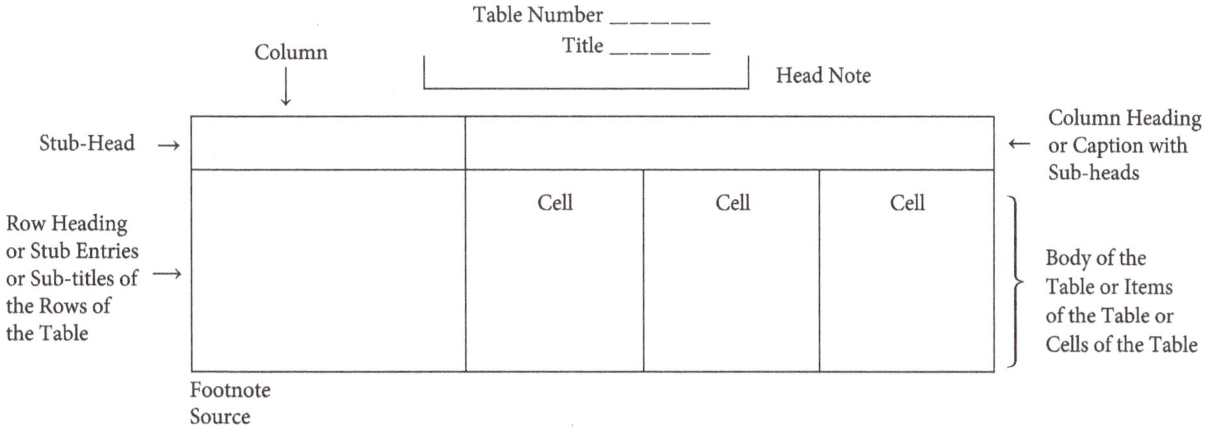

Essentials of a Good Table

- It should be comprised of an appropriate title which is self-explanatory along with a table number.
- Special emphasis should be given to data required to be compared by placing the data in head row or column and writing their titles in bold letters.
- The data required to be compared should be arranged closely to each other.
- The size of the table should be ideal keeping in mind the objectives and characteristics of data.
- A table should be simple, attractive and economical.
- Footnote should be given only when it is required and must bear any asterisk mark (*) corresponding to the concerned item.
- The table should be prepared in a systematic and logical manner.
- The table should be according to the object of statistical investigation.
- Table should provide clarity so that even a layman can draw inferences.
- Unit designations should be given at the top of the table below the title.

Table 4.1 Literacy Rate in Kerala
(in percentage)

Sex	Area		Total
	Urban	Rural	
Male	30.80	57.70	88.50
Female	63.32	30.03	93.35
Total	94.12	87.73	100

Source *Census of India 2001, provisional population total*

Note Figures are rounded to two decimal points

Types of Table

Statistical tables can be divided into different types based upon their methods of classification

Classification of Table

- Based on objectives
  - General purpose table
  - Special purpose table
- Based on nature of data
  - Original table
  - Derived table
- Based on extent of coverage
  - Simple table
  - Complex table

I. Based on Objective or Purpose

1. **General Purpose Table**
   - It displays raw data in detail and covers a wide range of information on the same subject without any analytical purpose.
   - Often used in government reports and is referred to as a 'reference table'.
2. **Special Purpose Table**
   - It provides data related to a specific inquiry, offering brief and concise information for data analysis results.
   - It is also known as a 'summary table,' it might show, for example, revenue figures for a firm over several years.

II. Based on Nature of Data

1. **Original Table**
   - It contains data in its initial (original) form as collected from primary sources, without any modifications or approximations.
   - It is also known as 'primary table' or 'classification table'.
2. **Derived Table**
   - It shows results derived from original data, such as percentages or averages.
   - It is also called 'derivative table'.

III. Based on Extent of Coverage

It is the most widely used form of table. It includes

1. **Simple Table**
   - It displays data related to a single variable i.e. it provides a univariate frequency distribution.
   - It is also known as 'one-way table' or 'first order table'.

Number of Students in Different Streams of Class XI

Sections	No. of Students
Science (Medical)	20
Science (Non-medical)	35
Commerce (with Maths)	25
Commerce (without Maths)	50
Humanities	40
Total	170

Simple Table

2. **Complex Table**

It shows data according to two or more characteristics, offering a multi-dimensional view.

It can be further divided as

(i) **Two-Way Table** (Double Table) It provides information on two inter-related features, such as students in different sections divided by gender.

Number of Students (Sex-wise) **in Different Sections of Class X**

Sections	No. of Students		Total
	Boys	Girls	
X-A	20	15	35
X-B	25	10	35
X-C	30	20	50
X-D	20	25	45
Total	95	70	165

Two-way Table

(ii) **Three-Way Table** (Treble Table) It displays three characteristics of data simultaneously, e.g. Adding transport mode to the two-way table of students and gender.

Number of Students (Sex-wise and on the Basis of use of Mode of Transportation) **in Different Sections of Class X**

Section	Boys			Girls			Total
	School Transport	Private Transport	Total	School Transport	Private Transport	Total	
X-A	5	15	20	10	5	15	35
X-B	20	5	25	5	5	10	35
X-C	15	15	30	15	5	20	50
X-D	5	15	20	15	10	25	45
Total	45	50	95	45	25	70	165

(iii) **Manifold Table** It presents data for more than three characteristics, encompassing a wide range of inter-related features related to a fact.

Number of Population (Area-wise, Gender-wise and Employment Type) **in Various States**

State	Rural Area				Urban Area				Total
	Male		Female		Male		Female		
	Employed	Unemployed	Employed	Unemployed	Employed	Unemp-loyed	Empl-oyed	Unemp-loyed	
Rajasthan	10	8	8	4	35	18	30	10	123
Haryana	15	7	7	3	40	17	35	15	139
Gujarat	12	4	13	7	44	20	40	12	152
Maharashtra	18	6	12	6	38	15	32	8	135
Total	55	25	40	20	157	70	137	45	549

4.3 Diagrammatic Presentation of Data

Diagrammatic presentation involves presenting data through diagrams, making complex information easier to understand and attractive. It can be done in two-ways

Types of Diagrams

- One-dimensional or bar diagrams (Simple, multiple, component, percentage and deviation)
- Two-dimensional or circular/ pie diagrams

Bar Diagram

A bar diagram presents data using bars or rectangles, where each bar represents a category or class of data. Key guidelines for creating bar diagrams are

1. **Uniform Breadth** All bars should have the same width.
2. **Variable Length** The length of each bar should correspond to the value of the data it represents.
3. **Orientation** Bars can be drawn horizontally or vertically, with vertical bars being the most common.
4. **Spacing** Bars should be equally spaced (equidistant) from each other.
5. **Base Line** Bars should start from a common baseline.
6. **Order** Arrange bars in ascending or descending order unless otherwise specified.

Types of Bar Diagram

Type	Explanation
Simple Bar Diagram	It represents a single set of numerical data with each bar showing a different item or value. It is suitable for depicting single variables like birth rate, weight of students, etc. Bars can be either horizontal or vertical. The main limitation is its focus on one data set at a time.
Multiple Bar Diagram	It displays two or more sets of data simultaneously, allowing for comparison between them. e.g. It can compare income and expenditure across different years. Bars are differentiated using different colours or shades to differentiate between data sets.
Component Bar Diagram	It shows a complete bar along with its sub-divisions into multiple components. Each component represents a part of the total value. To indicate different parts of the bar, these are shaded differently. It is also known as 'sub-divided or differential bar diagram'.
Percentage Bar Diagram	It represents different parts of the data as a percentage of a whole, with the total length of the bar equating to 100%. This type is useful for high magnitude values and employs different shades or colours to show percentage distribution.
Deviation Bar Diagram	It is used to compare net deviations in related variables with respect to time and location. Bars indicating positive and negative deviations are drawn both, above and below the baseline. It is suitable for variables with both positive and negative values, like temperature or savings.

Solved Question 1 The following hypothetical table gives data on birth rate in India according to census survey of different years. Present the information in the form of a simple vertical bar diagram.

Year	1951-60	1961-70	1971-80	1981-90	1991-2000	2001-2010
Birth Rate	45	35	30	28	24	20

Sol. A simple (vertical) bar diagram of given data is shown below

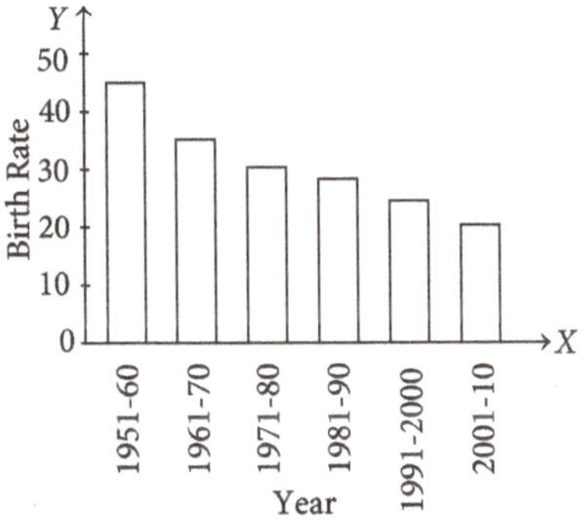

Solved Question 2 Present the following data in the form of horizontal bar diagram.

Students	M	N	O	P	Q	R
Marks Obtained	120	100	80	60	40	20

Sol. A horizontal bar diagram showing marks obtained by different students is given below

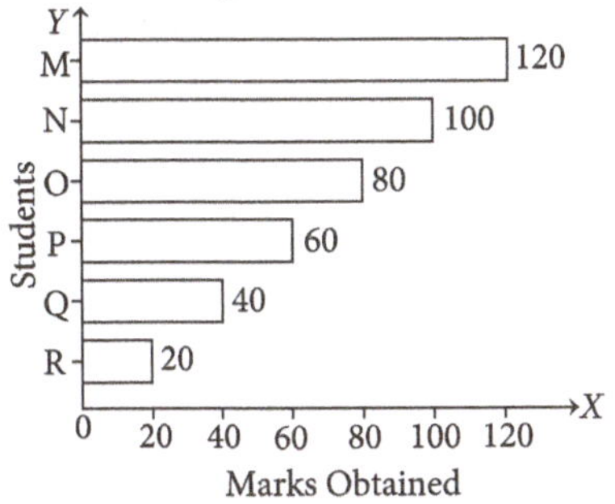

Solved Question 3 The following table shows birth and death rate in India according to the census reports between 1921-30 to 1991-2000. Present the data in the form of multiple bar diagram

Year	Birth Rate	Death Rate
1921-30	46	36
1931-40	45	31
1941-50	40	27
1951-60	42	23
1961-70	41	19
1971-80	37	15
1981-90	32.5	11.5
1991-2000	22.5	7.3

Sol. A multiple bar diagram showing birth rate and death rate in India (per thousand) (1921-30 to 1991-2000) is given below

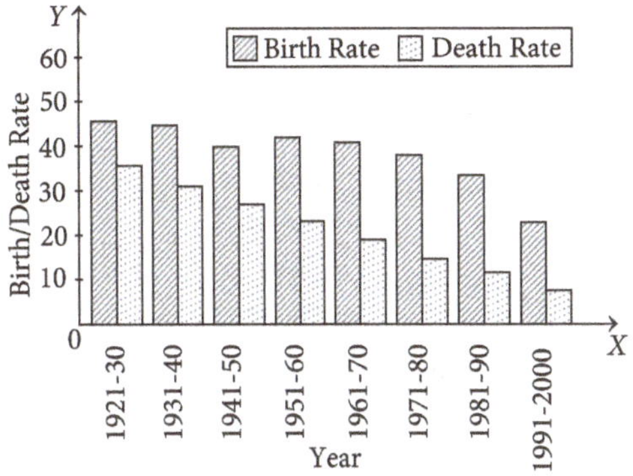

Note The above diagram has been drawn vertically. However, it can be drawn horizontally also.

Solved Question 4 Represent the following information related to number of students in a school using sub-divided or component bar graph.

Year	Science	Commerce	Humanities	Total
2020	15	30	20	65
2021	30	40	30	100
2022	40	60	30	130

Sol. A sub-divided bar graph of students in different streams over three years in a particular school is presented below

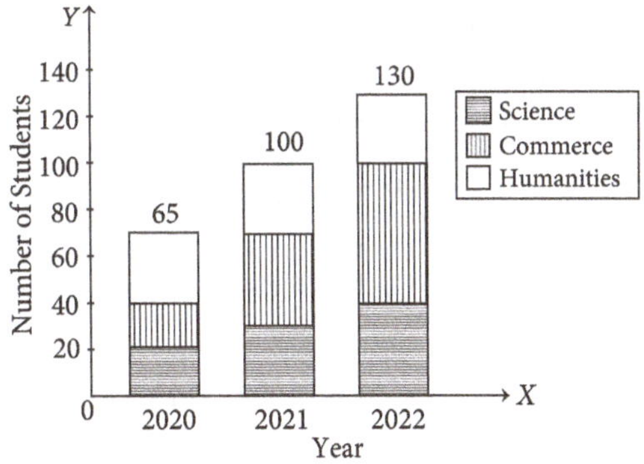

Solved Question 5 Net domestic product by industry of origin (at 2007–08 prices) is given for the years 2017–18 and 2019–20. Present this data in terms of percentage bar diagram.

Net Domestic Product by Industry of Origin
(at 2007-08 prices) **in 2017-18 and 2019-20** (₹ in crore)

Sector	Year (2017-18)	Year (2019-20)
Primary	6,65,751	6,71,674
Secondary	8,23,220	8,46,805
Tertiary	21,58,070	21,70,512
Total	36,47,041	36,88,991

Sol. The data is first reduced to percentage and then presented in terms of percentage bar diagram, as under

Sector	Year (2017-18)	Cumulative Percentage	Year (2019-20)	Cumulative Percentage
Primary	18.3	18.3	18.2	18.2
Secondary	22.6	40.9 (18.3 + 22.6)	23.0	41.2 (18.2 + 23)
Tertiary	59.1	100.00 (40.9 + 59.1)	58.8	100.0 (41.2 + 58.8)
Total	100.00		100.00	

Percentages are computed as under

Year 2017-18

Percentage share of primary sector

$$= \frac{6,65,751}{36,47,041} \times 100$$

$$= 18.25 \sim 18.3\%$$

Similarly, the percentages can be computed for different sectors in both the year.

Net Domestic Product by Industry of Origin in 2017-18 and 2019-20

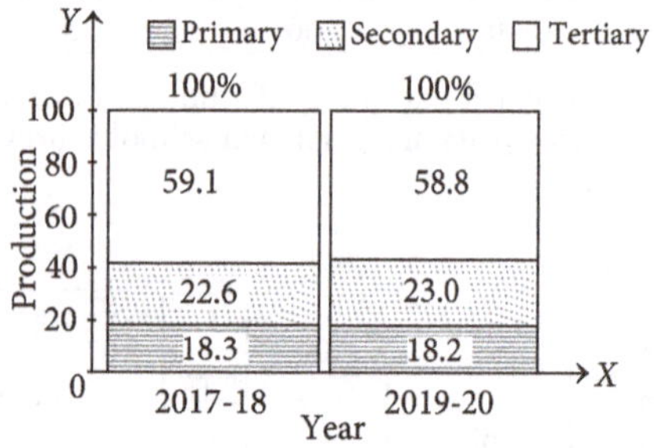

Solved Question 6 **Represent the following data by a deviation bar diagram.**

Year	2008	2009	2010	2011	2012	2013
Saving/Deficit (₹ in '000)	30	–20	10	15	–25	20

Sol. A deviation bar diagram of the given data is shown below

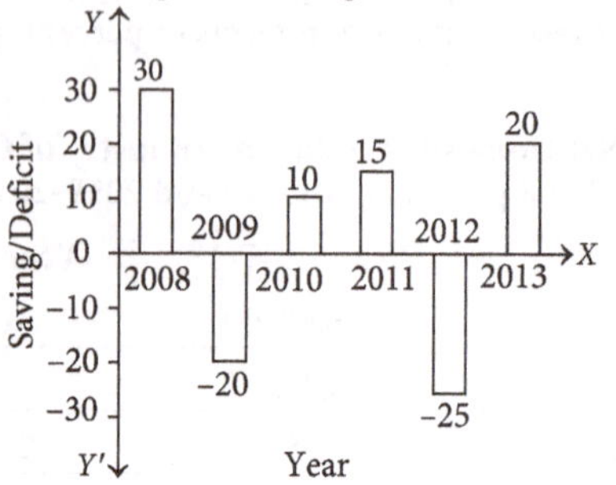

Pie or Circular Diagrams

A pie diagram, also known as a circular diagram, represents different values of a variable as segments of a circle. It is widely used to illustrate the proportion of various components within a whole.

Steps in the Construction of Pie Diagram

Step 1 Calculate the degree for each component using the formula

$$\left(\frac{\text{Value of Component}}{\text{Total Value}}\right) \times 360°$$

Step 2 Start by drawing the circle and its radius. Then, draw the sector representing the largest angle.

Step 3 Proceed to draw the other angles in descending order of their magnitude, moving clockwise.

Step 4 Use different colours or patterns for each segment to clearly differentiate them.

Solved Question 7 **The following data shows the number of cars manufactured by Maruti Ltd. Tata Motors and Hyundai in the year 2015-16. Represent it with the help of a pie diagram.**

Production of Cars (in ₹)

Maruti Limited	15,75,000
Tata Motors	7,25,000
Hyundai	5,50,000

Sol.

Name of the Company	Production	Angle (in degrees)
Maruti Limited	15,75,000	15,75,000/28,50,000 × 360° = 198.9 ~ 199°
Tata Motors	7,25,000	7,25,000/28,50,000 × 360° = 91.57 ~ 92°
Hyundai	5,50,000	5,50,000/28,50,000 × 360° = 69.47 ~ 69°
Total	28,50,000	360°

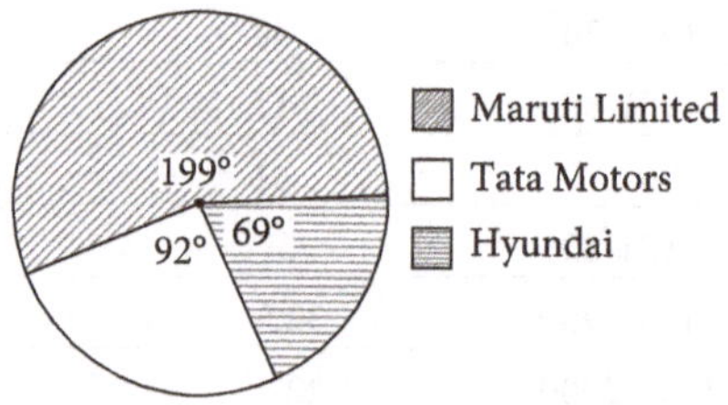

Advantages of Diagrammatic Presentation

- Data presented using diagrams are able to attract the attention of general public.
- Diagrams are easy to remember as compared to table with lots of information.
- Diagrams are capable of representing wide range of data in simple form.
- It has universal acceptability and facilitates comparison.
- It is easy to construct, thus saves time.

Disadvantages of Diagrammatic Presentation

- It has no use for experts as it does not give complete information of the statistical data.
- Diagram provides very limited and approximate information.
- It has limited use, i.e. can be used only for comparison purposes and not for further analysis.
- Diagrams are open to misuse, i.e. a wrong presentation of diagram may give a misleading result.

4.4 Graphical Presentation of Data

Graphical presentation involves presenting data with the help of graphs using visual elements such as points, lines, areas and geometric forms and symbols. Graphs can be broadly classified as

- Graphs of frequency distribution
- Graphs of time series

Graphs of Frequency Distribution

Frequency distribution graphs help in visualising how data is distributed among different classes. They are used to present the frequency of occurrences using class intervals, making it easier to analyse and interpret the data.

Graphs of Frequency Distribution

- Histogram
- Frequency polygon
- Frequency curve
- Cumulative frequency curve or ogive

Histogram

A histogram is a graphical representation of a continuous frequency distribution. It consists of adjacent rectangles where

- Rectangles touch each other, indicating continuous data.
- Base represents class intervals and the height corresponds to frequencies. The area of each rectangle reflects the frequency.
- Suitable for continuous data, not for discrete variables.

Construction of a histogram can be studied with respect to the conditions mentioned below

Condition	Steps
Equal Class Intervals	***Step* 1** Plot class intervals on the x-axis; width of each rectangle matches the interval size. ***Step* 2** Plot frequencies on the y-axis; height of each rectangle corresponds to the frequency.
Unequal Class Intervals	***Step* 1** Identify the smallest class interval width; use it as the standard width. ***Step* 2** Determine width of other class intervals and calculate adjustment factor using the formula $\text{Adjustment Factor} = \dfrac{\text{Width of Concerned Class}}{\text{Width of Lowest Class (Standard) Interval}}$ ***Step* 3** Adjust frequencies of other (non-standard) class intervals by dividing them by the adjustment factor $\text{Adjustment Frequency} = \dfrac{\text{Frequency of the Class}}{\text{Adjustment Factor}}$ ***Step* 4** Plot the histogram using adjusted frequencies for non-standard intervals and original frequencies for standard intervals.

Condition	Steps
Mid-points are Given	*Step* 1 Calculate the class interval width by finding the difference between consecutive mid-points and dividing it by 2. *Step* 2 Determine upper class limit by adding this value to mid-point and lower limit by subtracting this value from mid-point. *Step* 3 Construct the histogram in same manner as in case of equal class intervals.
Class Intervals are Inclusive	*Step* 1 Compute the difference between the upper limit of first class and the lower limit of the next class. *Step* 2 Divide this difference by 2 to get the adjustment value. *Step* 3 Convert inclusive intervals to exclusive intervals by subtracting the adjustment value from the lower limit and adding it to the upper limit. *Step* 4 Prepare the histogram using the exclusive class intervals.

Solved Question 8 Draw a histogram for the following distribution.

Wages (in ₹)	Number of Workers
0-5	4
5-10	10
10-15	14
15-20	22
20-25	32
25-30	15
30-35	3

Sol. A histogram for equal class interval is shown below

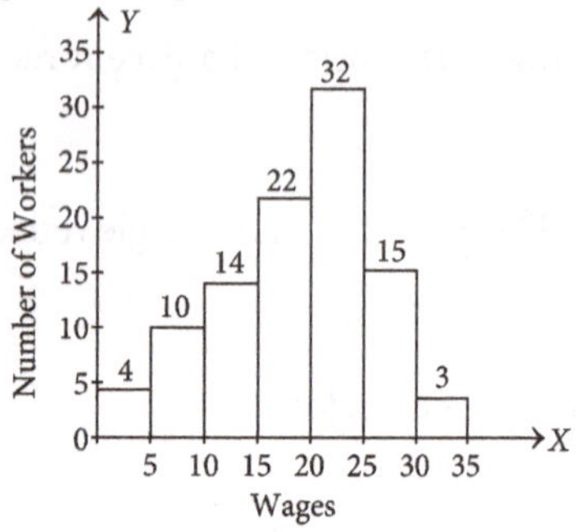

Solved Question 9 Construct the histogram for the following distribution.

Marks Obtained	Number of Students
0-10	6
10-20	10
20-30	26
30-40	22
40-60	10
60-90	9

Sol. **Adjustment of Frequencies**

Marks Obtained	Number of Students	Adjustment Factor	Adjusted Frequency
0-10	6	$10 \div 10 = 1$	$6 \div 1 = 6$
10-20	10	$10 \div 10 = 1$	$10 \div 1 = 10$
20-30	26	$10 \div 10 = 1$	$26 \div 1 = 26$
30-40	22	$10 \div 10 = 1$	$22 \div 1 = 22$
40-60	10	$20 \div 10 = 2$	$10 \div 2 = 5$
60-90	9	$30 \div 10 = 3$	$9 \div 3 = 3$

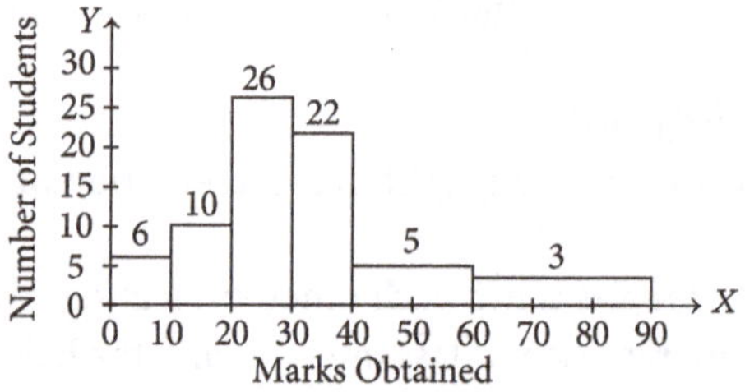

In the above histogram, it can be observed that the frequencies corresponding to classes with lowest class width are not affected.

Solved Question 10 Construct a histogram for the following frequency distribution.

Mid-points	Frequency
15	6
25	10
35	15
45	8
55	12
65	3
75	18

Sol. The distribution will take the following form

Classes	Frequency
10-20	6
20-30	10
30-40	15
40-50	8
50-60	12
60-70	3
70-80	18

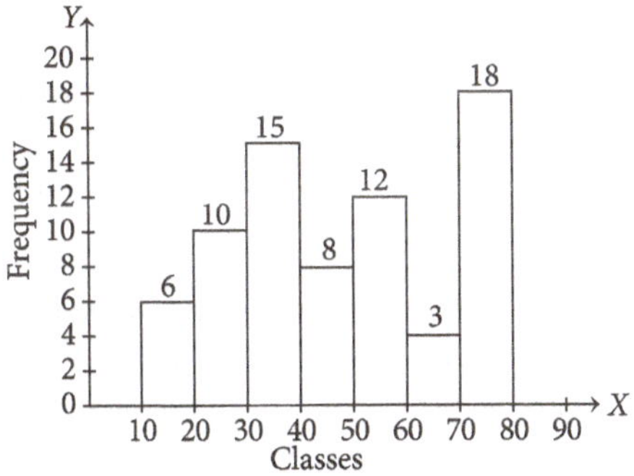

Solved Question 11 **Construct a histogram for the following frequency distribution.**

Marks Obtained	Number of Students
1-10	4
11-20	6
21-30	12
31-40	20
41-50	8
51-60	10

Sol. The distribution will take the following form

Marks Obtained	Number of Students
0.5-10.5	4
10.5-20.5	6
20.5-30.5	12
30.5-40.5	20
40.5-50.5	8
50.5-60.5	10

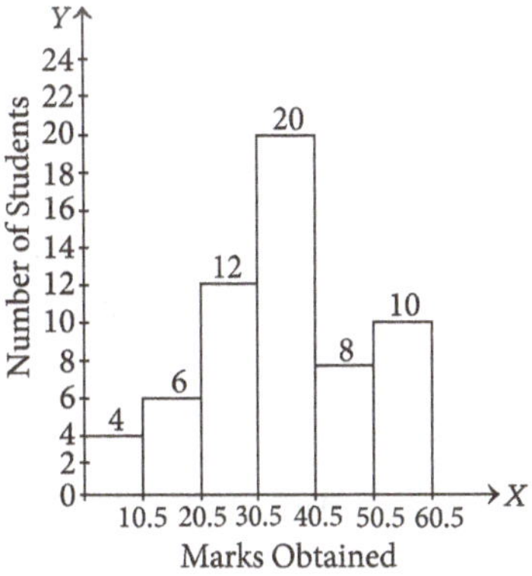

Note The difference of 0.5 is ignored while constructing the histogram. Therefore, the classes originate from 0.

Frequency Polygon

It is a graphical representation of a frequency distribution, in which the frequencies corresponding to different values are first plotted and then joined by straight lines.

A frequency polygon for a continuous frequency distribution can be drawn in two ways

- With the help of histogram.
- Without the help of histogram.

Steps for Constructing a Frequency Polygon

With the Help of a Histogram	Without the Help of a Histogram
***Step* 1** Draw the histogram for the given frequency distribution.	***Step* 1** Plot points corresponding to the mid-points of class intervals on the x-axis and their respective frequencies on the y-axis.
***Step* 2** Join the mid-points of the adjacent rectangles in the histogram with straight lines.	***Step* 2** Connect the plotted points with straight lines.
***Step* 3** Extend the end points of the polygon to meet the x-axis at hypothetical classes.	***Step* 3** Extend the end points of the polygon to meet the x-axis on the mid-points of hypothetical classes.

Solved Question 12 **Following table shows number of students of a college corresponding to different range of marks in Statistics. Make a frequency polygon with the help of histogram.**

Marks in Statistics	Number of Students
0-10	5
10-20	10
20-30	15
30-40	20
40-50	12
50-60	8
60-70	5

Sol. A frequency polygon with histogram is shown below

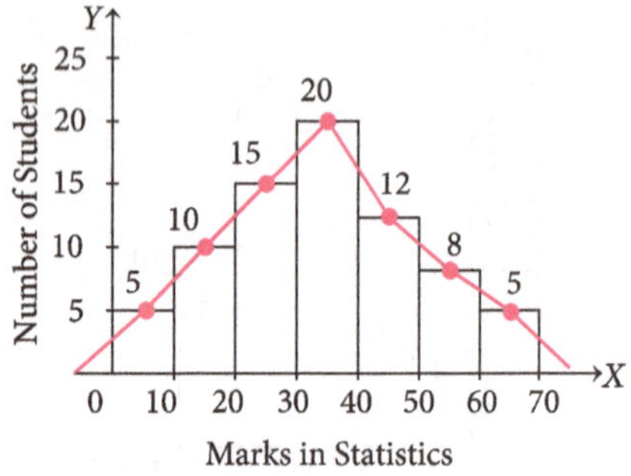

Note The end points of the polygon are extended to meet the mid-values of preceding class and succeeding class.

Solved Question 13 **Following table shows number of students of a college corresponding to different marks in Statistics. Make a frequency polygon without the help of histogram.**

Marks in Statistics (Mid-value)	Number of Students
5	5
15	10
25	15
35	20
45	12
55	8
65	5

Sol. The frequency polygon drawn without the help of histogram is illustrated below

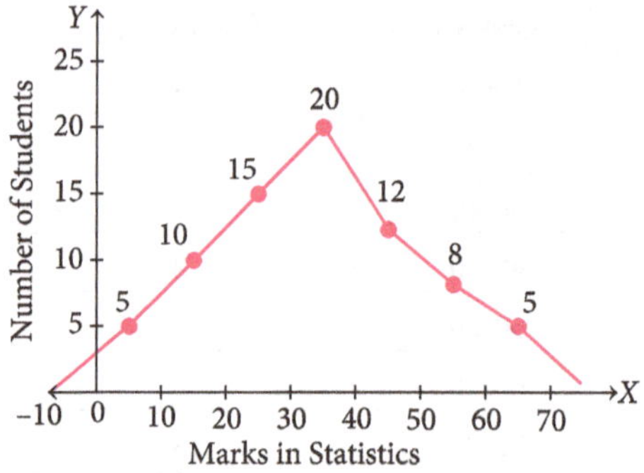

Frequency Curve

The frequency curve is obtained by drawing a smooth free hand curve passing through the mid-points of the histogram as closely as possible and extending it to meet the base line at hypothetical classes.

> ***Basic Difference between Frequency Polygon and Frequency Curve***
>
> Both frequency polygon and frequency curve are drawn by joining the mid-points of the rectangles of a histogram. But in case of frequency polygon, the points are joined using a foot rule, whereas in case of frequency curve, the points are joined free hand.

Solved Question 14 **Prepare a frequency curve of the following data.**

Class Interval	Frequency
0-10	6
10-20	10
20-30	16
30-40	12
40-50	8
50-60	4

Sol. A frequency curve of given data is shown below

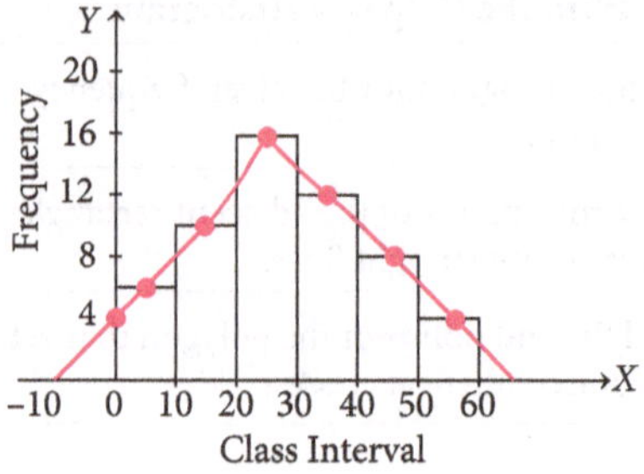

Cumulative Frequency Curve or Ogive

A cumulative frequency curve or ogive represents cumulative frequency distributions using graphs.

There are two primary types of ogives *viz.* less-than ogive and more-than ogive, each representing different cumulative frequency distributions.

Construction of Less-than Ogive	Construction of More-than Ogive
This type of ogive is based on a less-than cumulative frequency distribution, where the frequencies are cumulated and represented to the value corresponding to the upper limit of each class. **Steps for Construction of Less-than Ogive** ***Step 1*** Calculate cumulative frequencies by adding frequencies of all classes preceding a given class. Plot these values against the upper limit of each class, labelled as 'less-than'. ***Step 2*** Plot these cumulative frequencies on the y-axis against the upper class limits on the x-axis. ***Step 3*** Join the plotted points with a free hand smooth curve to create an upward sloping ogive.	This type of ogive is based on a more-than cumulative frequency distribution, where frequencies are cumulated for all classes succeeding each class interval. It represents the cumulative frequency starting from the lower limit of each class. **Steps for Construction of More-than Ogive** ***Step 1*** Calculate cumulative frequencies by adding all frequencies of classes succeeding each class. Plot these values against the lower limit of each class, labelled as 'more-than'. ***Step 2*** Plot these cumulative frequencies on the y-axis against the lower class limits on the x-axis. ***Step 3*** Join the plotted points with free hand smooth curve to create a downward sloping ogive.

Solved Question 15 **Construct 'less-than' ogive, on the basis of data given below.**

Marks	Number of Students
0-5	3
5-10	10
10-15	20
15-20	30
20-25	20
25-30	9
30-35	5
35-40	3

Sol. The data given above will first be converted into a less-than frequency distribution, as given below

Less-than Distribution

Marks	Number of Students
Less than 5	3
Less than 10	13 (10 + 3)
Less than 15	33 (13 + 20)
Less than 20	63 (33 + 30)
Less than 25	83 (63 + 20)
Less than 30	92 (83 + 9)
Less than 35	97 (92 + 5)
Less than 40	100 (97 + 3)

Less-than ogive is shown below

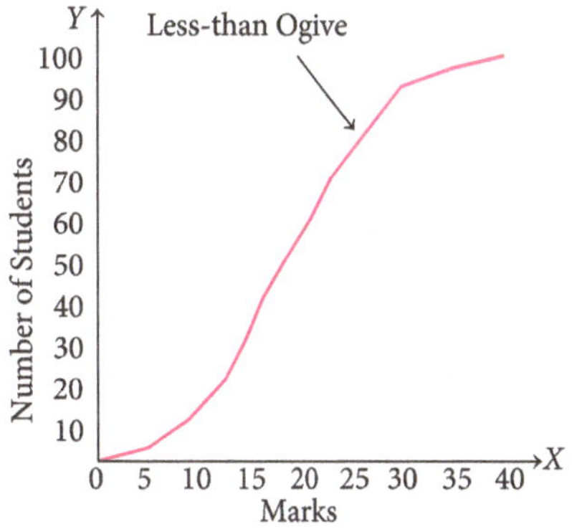

Solved Question 16 **Draw 'more-than' ogive, on the basis of data given below.**

Marks	Number of Students
0-5	3
5-10	10
10-15	20
15-20	30
20-25	20
25-30	9
30-35	5
35-40	3

Sol. The data given above will first be converted into a more-than frequency distribution, as given below

More-than Distribution

Marks	Number of Students
More than 0	100
More than 5	97 (100 – 3)
More than 10	87 (97 – 10)
More than 15	67 (87 – 20)
More than 20	37 (67 – 30)
More than 25	17 (37 – 20)
More than 30	8 (17 – 9)
More than 35	3 (8 – 5)

More-than ogive is shown below

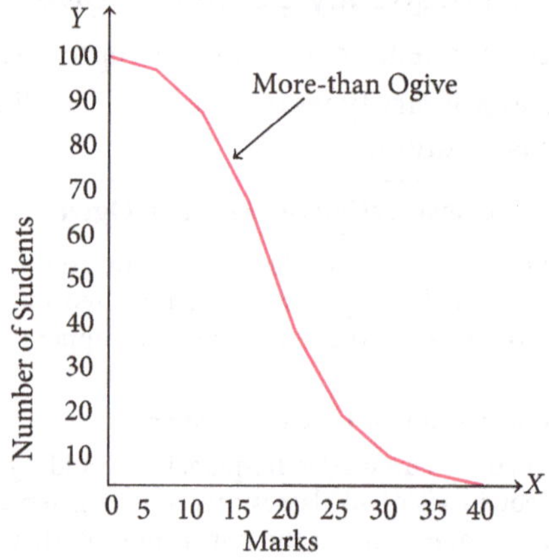

More-than and Less-than Ogives

Sometimes, to find the middle most value of the series (median), the more-than and less-than ogives are presented on the same graph.

The point of intersection of these curves, when extended to meet the x-axis, gives the middle most value of the series. The graph showing both (more-than and less-than) ogives is given aside.

In the given graph, the curves intersect at '*a*'. A perpendicular is dropped from '*a*', which meets the x-axis at point '*b*'. Then '*b*' is the middle most value. For the given distribution, the value of '*b*' is 17.8 or 18 approx.

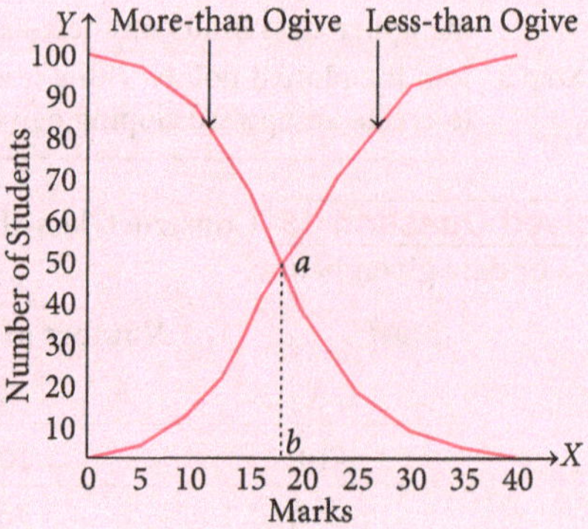

Graph of Time Series

Graphs of time series, also known as arithmetic line graphs or historigrams, are used to display variable's values with respect to the time of their occurrence. In this graph, time is plotted on the x-axis and the variable's values on the y-axis.

There are two main types

1. One Variable Graph

This graph shows the values of a single variable with respect to equal time intervals.

Steps for Construction of One Variable Graph

Step 1 Plot time intervals (e.g. Days, months) on the x-axis.

Step 2 Plot the corresponding values of the variable on the y-axis.

Step 3 Connect the plotted points with straight lines to create the time series graph.

Solved Question 17 **Plot the following data of annual profits of a firm on a time series graph.**

Year	Profit (in thousand ₹)
2008	50
2009	62
2010	65
2011	55
2012	70

Sol. The times series graph showing annual profits of a firm is given below

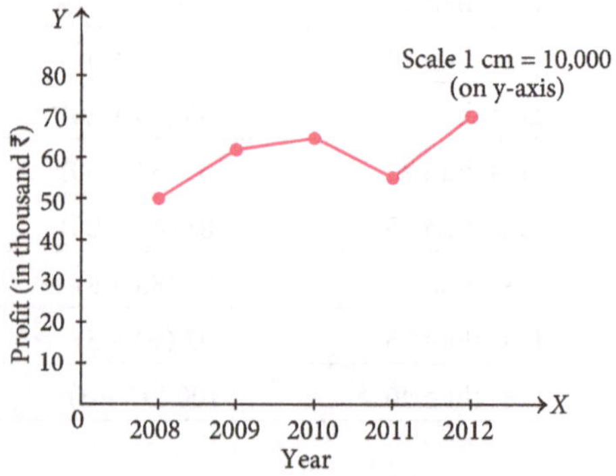

2. Two or More than Two Variable Graph

This graph displays the values of two or more variables over the same time period, allowing for comparisons. These are also called 'multiple time series graphs'.

Steps for Construction of More-than Two Variable Graph

Step 1 Plot time intervals on the x-axis.

Step 2 Plot the values of each variable on the y-axis.

Step 3 Connect the points for each variable with distinct lines (e.g. Solid line for one variable, dotted line for another) to differentiate between them.

Solved Question 18 **The following table gives data on the production of wheat and rice between 2008 and 2013. Make a two variable time series graph.**

Year	Wheat ('000 kg)	Rice ('000 kg)
2008	200	50
2009	250	100
2010	220	150
2011	300	90
2012	320	150
2013	330	200

Sol. The two variable graph with given data is shown below

Use of False Base Line

The scale of y-axis always begins from zero. However, the raw data sometimes start from a large value i.e. the gap between zero and smallest item of the series is high due to which the required curve may pulled up away from the point of origin.

To overcome such difficulty, we use 'false base line' to reduce the gap.

e.g. For data starting from 1,500 with minor variations in remaining values of variables, a false base line is introduced just below this value to minimise distortion.

Solved Question 19 **The following table shows the number of students, who have taken admission in a private school over different years. Use a appropriate diagram to present the data.**

Year	2010	2011	2012	2013	2014	2015	2016
No. of Students	200	210	250	300	330	400	450

Sol. The above data starts with a frequency of 200 and ends at 450. To cover up the gap between zero and 200, a false base line will be used in this situation as shown under

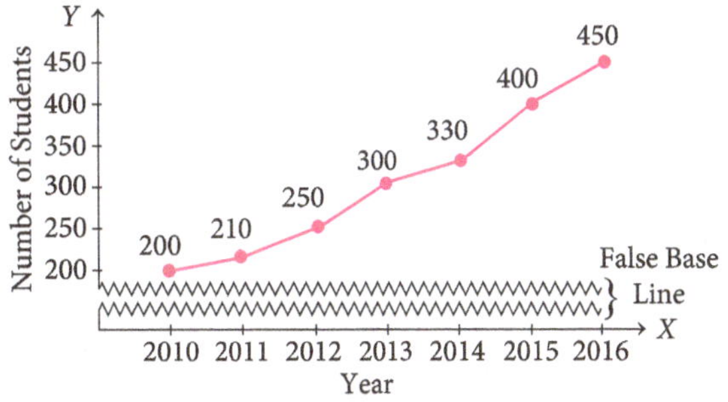

Advantages of Graphic Presentation

- Graphs are simple and attractive as compared to tabular or textual presentation.
- Graphs can be easily used to represent complex data in a simple form.
- Graphs facilitates comparison of different statistical data.
- Anyone can make use of graphs, i.e. one do not need to be an expert to make use of graphs.
- Graphs have universal utility as they help everyone to understand complex information.

Disadvantages of Graphic Presentation

- Graphic presentation is less useful for the experts, they are generally used to explain quantitative data to general public.
- They are subjective, i.e. varies from person to person.
- They represent approximate data, often lacking precise accuracy.
- They may represent misleading results as it is subject to misuse.

Mind Map

PRESENTATION OF DATA

1 Textual Presentation of Data

This presentation involves conveying data through written paragraphs. It is generally used where data is not too large.

2 Tabular Presentation of Data

It involves arranging data systematically in rows (horizontally) and columns (vertically) in the form of a table.

Parts of a Table

- Table number
- Title of the table
- Head note
- Column headings (Caption)
- Stubs (Row headings)
- Body of the table
- Unit of the measurement
- Footnote
- Source note

3 Types of Tables

1. **Based on Purpose**
- *General Purpose Table*: Provides a broad dataset without a specific analysis.
- *Special Purpose Table*: Focuses on a particular study or analysis.

2. **Based on Nature of Data**
- *Original Table*: Contains data in its original form.
- *Derived Table*: Contains calculated data like averages, percentages.

3. **Based on Extent of Coverage**
- *Simple Table*: Shows data of a single variable (univariate).
- *Complex Table*: Represents two or more characteristics. It includes
  – *Two-Way Table*: Data based on two characteristics (e.g. Students categorised by gender).
  – *Three-Way Table*: Data based on three characteristics (e.g. Gender-wise employment in urban/rural areas).
  – *Manifold Table*: Data categorised into four or more characteristics (e.g. Employment by state, gender, area and job type).

4 Diagrammatic Presentation of Data

It involves presenting data through diagrams, making complex information easier to understand and attractive.

5 Types of Diagrams

Bar Diagram It presents data using bars or rectangles, where each bar represents a category or class of data. It can be of following types

- **Simple Bar Diagram** Shows one set of data.
- **Multiple Bar Diagram** Compares two or more datasets side by side.
- **Component Bar Diagram** Represents sub-divisions within a complete bar.
- **Percentage Bar Diagram** Converts data into percentages (total = 100%).
- **Deviation Bar Diagram** Represents positive and negative values.

Pie Diagram (Circular Diagram) Represents data in a circle divided into proportional sectors.

Steps for Pie Diagram

– Convert values into angles using formula
  Angle = (Component Value/Total Value) × 360°
– Draw a circle and divide it into sectors.

6 Advantages and Disadvantages of Diagrammatic Presentation

Advantages

- Attracts attention
- Easy to remember
- Simplifies complex data
- Facilitates comparison
- Time saving

Disadvantages

- Lacks complete information
- Limited use
- Approximate representation
- Misleading possibility

7 Graphical Presentation of Data

It involves presenting data with the help of graphs using visual elements such as points, lines, areas and geometric forms and symbols. It can be classified as

Graphs of Frequency Distribution It includes

- *Histogram*: It consists of rectangles touching each other, showing continuous data.
- *Frequency Polygon*: Line graph joining mid-points of histogram rectangles.
- *Frequency Curve*: Smooth free hand curve connecting mid-points of histogram.
- *Ogive (Cumulative Frequency Curve)*: It includes
  – *Less-than Ogive*: Plots cumulative frequencies corresponding to upper class limits.
  – *More-than Ogive*: Plots cumulative frequencies from lower class limits.
  – *Intersection of Both Ogives*: Gives median value.

Graphs of Time Series It includes

- *One-variable Graph*: Shows variation of a single variable over time.
- *Two/multi variable Graphs*: Compares multiple variables over time.

8 Advantages and Disadvantages of Graphic Presentation

Advantages

- Simple and attractive
- Simplifies complex data
- Facilitates comparison
- Easy to use
- Universal utility

Disadvantages

- Less useful for experts
- Subjective interpretation
- Approximate data
- Can be misleading

EXAM PATTERN QUESTIONS

Objective Type Questions

Multiple Choice Questions (MCQs)

1. **Textual method of presentation of data is suitable when the quantity of data is**

(a) large (b) small
(c) Both (a) and (b) (d) None of these

2. **The main drawback of textual or descriptive presentation is that readers need to .... the entire text to extract and understand the relevant data.**

(a) analyse (b) skim
(c) go through (d) memorise

3. **Identify the correct type presentation of data from the following image.**

Presentation
There are 42,036 barangays in the Philippines. The largest barangay in terms of population size in Barangay 176 in Caloocan City with 247 thousand persons. It is followed by Commonwealth in Quezon City (198, 295) and Batasan Hills in Quezon City (161, 409). Twelve other barangays posted a population size of more than a hundered thousand persons.

(a) Tabular presentation
(b) Graphical presentation
(c) Diagrammatic presentation
(d) Textual presentation

4. **The .... of a table provides additional explanations for specific data features or exceptions.**

(a) body (b) footnote
(c) stub column (d) head note

5. **Which type of table is also known as a 'summary table'?**

(a) General purpose table
(b) Derived table
(c) Simple table
(d) Special purpose table

6. **"The title of a table should be clear and self-explanatory." Which characteristic of a good table does this statement describe?** **Competency Based Que**

(a) Relevance
(b) Clarity
(c) Appropriate title and number
(d) Effective comparison

7. **Which of the following is not an objective of tabular presentation?**

(a) Complexity (b) Simplification
(c) Comparison (d) Space utilisation

8. **Which type of table contains data in its initial form as collected from the primary sources?**

(a) Derived table (b) Original table
(c) Both (a) and (b) (d) None of these

9. **Identify the essentials of a good table from the following**

I. The table should be straightforward, attractive and cost effective.
II. The title should be complex and hard to understand.
III. Footnotes should be used sparingly and marked with an asterisk (*) corresponding to relevant items.
IV. Unit of measurement should not be stated in the table. **Competency Based Que**

Codes

(a) I and II (b) I and III
(c) II and IV (d) Only II

10. **Identify the type of table from the following image.**

Sections	Morning Shift			Night Shift			Total		
	Boys	Girls	Total	Boys	Girls	Total	Boys	Girls	Total
A	6	6	12	10	18	28	16	24	40
B	10	7	17	5	3	8	15	10	25
C	12	13	25	7	5	12	19	18	37
D	15	13	28	11	9	20	26	22	48
Total	43	39	82	30	35	68	76	74	150

(a) Three-way table
(b) Two-way table
(c) Manifold table
(d) Simple table

11. **Where should the 'source' be mentioned in the table?**

(a) At the beginning of the table
(b) At the end of the table
(c) Both (a) and (b)
(d) None of the above

12. "Government report utilises a general purpose table for detailed raw data display." What is the primary use of this type of table? **Competency Based Que**

(a) To present data for specific inquiries
(b) To display raw data in detail covering a wide range of information
(c) To summarise data related to a specific inquiry
(d) To show percentages or averages

13. Stubs are the ...... of the rows.

(a) parts (b) designations
(c) tool (d) All of these

14. Bar diagram is a **NCERT**

(a) one-dimensional diagram
(b) two-dimensional diagram
(c) diagram with no dimension
(d) None of the above

15. In a pie diagram, different values of a variable are represented as .... of a circle.

(a) lines (b) segments
(c) arcs (d) points

16. Identify the type of bar diagram given in the following image.

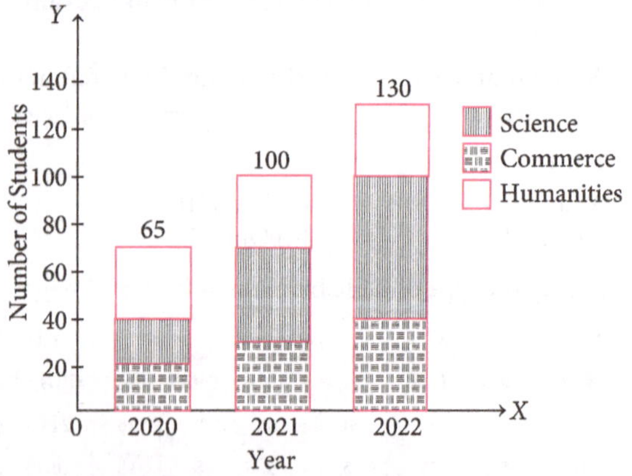

(a) Percentage bar diagram (b) Simple bar diagram
(c) Multiple bar diagram (d) Component bar diagram

17. Which of the following is a general guideline for creating bar diagrams?

(a) Bars can have varying widths based on the data
(b) Bars should overlap to show continuity
(c) Bar diagrams are always drawn horizontally
(d) The length of the bars represents the value of the data

18. "Company XYZ presents annual sales data using a chart to show market share distribution." What type of diagrammatic presentation is being utilised? **Competency Based Que**

(a) Simple bar diagram (b) Multiple bar diagram
(c) Pie or circular diagram (d) Histogram

19. Which of the following is/are the steps to construct a pie diagram? **Competency Based Que**

(i) Convert to degrees (ii) Shade segments
(iii) Add remaining angles
(iv) Draw the circle

Codes

(a) (i) and (ii) (b) (iii) and (iv)
(c) (i), (ii), (iii) and (iv) (d) (ii), (iii) and (iv)

20. 50 students were asked to choose their favourite sport and data below show the following results.

Sport	No. of Student
Cricket	12
Football	10
Hockey	11
Basketball	9
Tennis	8

What will be the degree of Hockey if this data is to be presented in a pie diagram? **Competency Based Que**

(a) 79.2° (b) 84.4° (c) 86.4° (d) 92.8°

21. What is the key difference between a frequency polygon and a frequency curve? **Competency Based Que**

(a) A frequency polygon is created using a histogram, but a frequency curve is not
(b) In a frequency polygon, points are joined with a foot rule, while in a frequency curve, points are joined free hand
(c) Frequency polygons are used for grouped data, while frequency curves are used for ungrouped data
(d) A frequency curve uses the lower limits of classes, while a frequency polygon uses the upper limits

22. Which graph of frequency distribution is represented in the given image?

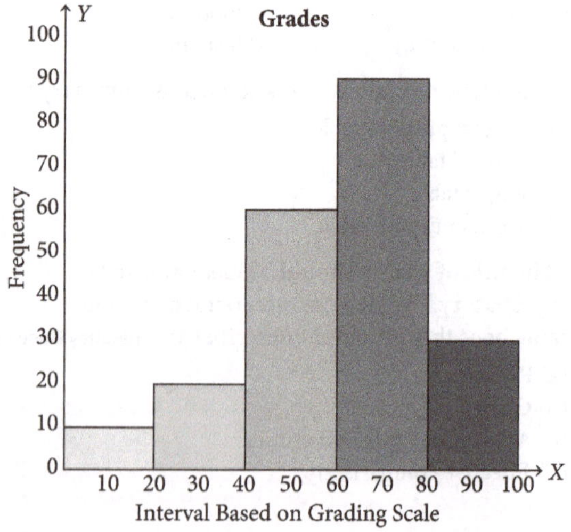

(a) Histogram
(b) Bar diagram
(c) Pie chart
(d) Time series graph

23. **Data represented through a histogram can help in finding graphically the** **NCERT**

(a) mean (b) mode
(c) median (d) All of these

24. **"A frequency polygon is similar to a histogram, but it uses points connected by lines." What does the frequency polygon emphasise?** **Competency Based Que**

(a) Proportions of a whole
(b) Cumulative frequency
(c) Trends over time
(d) Changes in frequency across intervals

25. **A frequency polygon is formed by connecting the mid-points of the top of the bars in a ....**

(a) pie chart
(b) histogram
(c) bar chart
(d) scatter diagram

26. **In the graph shown below, the frequency of the interval 40-50 is**

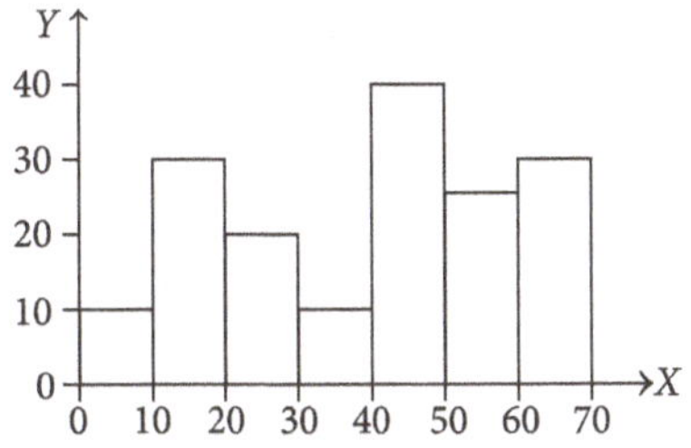

(a) 40 (b) 70 (c) 110 (d) 120

27. **Which type of ogive is created by joining points that are plotted with cumulative frequencies starting from the lower limit of each class?**

(a) Less-than ogive
(b) More-than ogive
(c) Combined ogive
(d) Frequency polygon

28. **What does a less-than ogive represent?**

I. The cumulative frequency starting from the lower limit of each class.
II. The cumulative frequency up to the upper limit of each class.
III. The average frequency of all classes.
IV. The median frequency distribution.

Codes **Competency Based Que**

(a) Only I (b) II and III
(c) Only II (d) II and IV

29. **Identify the type of time series graph given in the below image.**

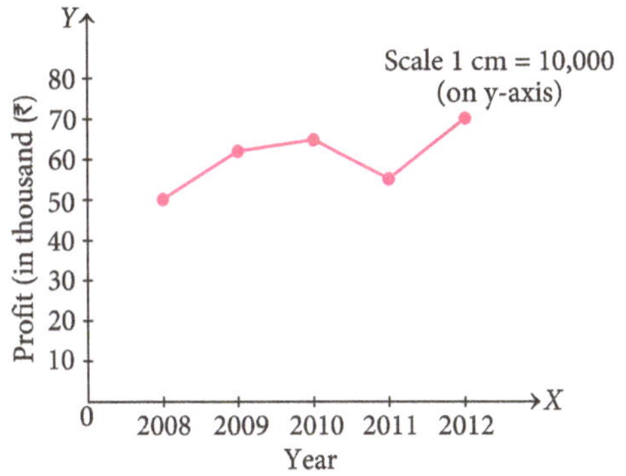

(a) One variable graph
(b) Two variable graph
(c) More than two variable graph
(d) None of the above

30. **Why is a false baseline used in graphs?**

(a) To start the y-axis scales from a value other than zero to minimise distortion for large initial values
(b) To make the graph visually appealing
(c) To adjust the x-axis scale for uneven intervals
(d) To ensure the graph always starts from zero

31. **In the context of graphical data representation, which term describes the line from which the height of bars or data points is measured?**

(a) Axis (b) Gridline (c) Data line (d) Base line

Direction *Read the case study and answer the questions 32 to 35 on the basis of the same*

XYZ Manufacturing Company tracked its monthly production output for the past year to analyse trends and improve efficiency.

Monthly Production Output Data

Month	Units Produced
January	5,000
February	5,200
March	5,600
April	4,800
May	5,700
June	5,300
July	6,000
August	5,400
September	5,800
October	5,900
November	6,100
December	5,500

32. **Which diagram is best suited for showing the monthly production trend at XYZ Manufacturing?**
(a) Pie chart (b) Component bar diagram
(c) Histogram (d) Line chart

33. **In which month was the production output lowest?**
(a) January (b) April
(c) November (d) December

34. **The .... diagram would be best for comparing production across different product categories in specific months.**

35. **According to data, the highest production is in the month of ....**

Assertion-Reason

Direction (Q.No. 36 to 44) *Read the following Assertion (A) and Reason (R) and choose the correct alternative from the following*

Alternatives

(a) Both Assertion (A) and Reason (R) are true and Reason (R) is the correct explanation of Assertion (A)
(b) Both Assertion (A) and Reason (R) are true, but Reason (R) is not the correct explanation of Assertion (A)
(c) Assertion (A) is true, but Reason (R) is false
(d) Assertion (A) is false, but Reason (R) is true

36. **Assertion** (A) Textual or descriptive presentation of data is ideal for smaller datasets requiring detailed explanations.

Reason (R) Textual presentation allows for easy comparison of data sets by summarising key points in a concise format.

37. **Assertion** (A) The main drawback of textual presentation is that readers need to go through the entire text to extract and understand the relevant data.

Reason (R) Textual presentation is also termed descriptive presentation of data.

38. **Assertion** (A) A derived table shows results derived from original data, such as percentages or averages.

Reason (R) An original table contains data in its initial form as collected from primary sources and is also known as a classification table.

39. **Assertion** (A) A general purpose table displays raw data in detail and covers a wide range of information.

Reason (R) A special purpose table provides data related to a specific inquiry and is known as a summary table.

40. **Assertion** (A) A manifold table displays three characteristics of data simultaneously.

Reason Two-way table provides information on two inter-related features.

41. **Assertion** (A) A component bar diagram divides a single bar into segments to illustrate different components of the total value.

Reason (R) A component bar diagram is used to represent multiple sets of data in a single bar.

42. **Assertion** (A) There are two primary types of ogives, i.e. the less-than ogive and the more-than ogive, each representing different cumulative frequency distributions.

Reason (R) Graphs of time series, also known as arithmetic line graphs or historigrams, are used to display how a variable's values change over time.

43. **Assertion** (A) False base lines are used in graphical presentations to minimise distortion when the y-axis starts from a high value.

Reason (R) By setting the false base line near the smallest data value, it reduces the gap and improves the clarity of data fluctuations.

44. **Assertion** (A) A histogram is used to display the distribution of a continuous frequency distribution by using adjacent rectangles.

Reason (R) The height of each rectangle in a histogram corresponds to the frequency, while the base represents the class intervals.

Two Statements Based MCQs

Direction (Q.No. 45 to 54) *Read the following statements carefully and choose the correct alternative*

Alternatives

(a) Statement I is correct and Statement II is incorrect
(b) Statement II is correct and Statement I is incorrect
(c) Both the statements are correct
(d) Both the statements are incorrect

45. **Statement I** Presentation of data is crucial for conveying information clearly and effectively.

Statement II Proper data presentation transforms raw information into a format that is easy to interpret and understand.

46. **Statement I** Source note is a compulsory part of an ideal table if matter is taken from any secondary source.

Statement II Profit and loss estimates of a given company for different years should be presented through general purpose table.

47. **Statement I** Footnotes cites the source of secondary data, including publication details, to ensure credibility and reference.

Statement II Stubs indicate the information contained in each row, with the complete left column referred to as the stub column.

48. **Statement I** General purpose table presents data related to a specific inquiry, offering brief and concise information for data analysis results.

Statement II Special purpose table displays raw data in detail and covers a wide range of information on the same subject without analytical intent.

49. **Statement I** The table should be appropriately sized based on the data's objectives and characteristics.

Statement II The table should be designed for clarity, allowing even a layman to draw inferences.

50. **Statement I** Simple bar diagrams display two or more sets of data simultaneously.

Statement II Percentage bar diagrams represent different parts of the data as percentages of a whole.

51. **Statement I** A pie diagram is also known as a circular diagram.

Statement II A pie diagram represents same values of a variable.

52. **Statement I** Diagrams are visually appealing and attract the attention of the general public.

Statement II Diagrams do not provide comprehensive details required for expert analysis.

53. **Statement I** Frequency polygon can only be constructed with the help of a histogram.

Statement II Frequency curve is a graphical representation of a frequency distribution, in which the frequencies corresponding to different values are first plotted and then joined by straight lines.

54. **Statement I** One variable graph shows the values of a single variable over equal time intervals.

Statement II Two or more variable graph displays the values of two or more variables over the same time period, allowing for comparisons.

Matching

55. Match the following

Column I	Column II
A. Diagrammatic presentation	(i) Describes data and trends through written descriptions and narratives.
B. Graphical presentation	(ii) Arranging data systematically in rows and columns to create a table.
C. Textual presentation	(iii) Visualising data through diagrams
D. Tabular presentation	(iv) Using visual elements such as points, lines, areas and geometric shapes to represent data.

Codes

	A	B	C	D
(a)	(iii)	(iv)	(i)	(ii)
(b)	(iv)	(i)	(ii)	(iii)
(c)	(ii)	(iii)	(iv)	(i)
(d)	(iii)	(ii)	(i)	(iv)

56. Match the following

Column I	Column II
A. Footnote	(i) Supplementary information explaining the table or its parts.
B. Source note	(ii) Cites the source of secondary data.
C. Head note	(iii) Provides additional explanations for specific data features.
D. Stubs	(iv) Titles for rows that indicate the information contained in each row.

Codes

	A	B	C	D
(a)	(iii)	(iv)	(i)	(ii)
(b)	(iv)	(i)	(ii)	(iii)
(c)	(ii)	(iii)	(iv)	(i)
(d)	(iii)	(ii)	(i)	(iv)

57. Match the options of Column I with their correct options in Column II

Column I	Column II
A. Frequency curve	(i) Two-dimensional
B. Frequency polygon	(ii) Measured mid-points
C. Histogram	(iii) One-dimensional
D. Bar graph	(iv) Smooth lines

Codes

	A	B	C	D
(a)	(iii)	(iv)	(ii)	(i)
(b)	(ii)	(iii)	(i)	(iv)
(c)	(i)	(iv)	(iii)	(ii)
(d)	(iv)	(ii)	(i)	(iii)

58. Match the following

	Column I		Column II
A.	Simple bar diagram	(i)	Used to compare net deviations in related variables.
B.	Multiple bar diagram	(ii)	Based on a single set of numerical data.
C.	Component bar diagram	(iii)	Shows two or more set of data simultaneously.
D.	Deviation bar diagram	(iv)	Shows a complete bar along with its sub-divisions.

Codes

	A	B	C	D
(a)	(iii)	(iv)	(i)	(ii)
(b)	(iv)	(i)	(ii)	(iii)
(c)	(ii)	(iii)	(iv)	(i)
(d)	(iii)	(ii)	(i)	(iv)

59. Match the following

	Column I		Column II
A.	Less-than ogive	(i)	Based on a more-than cumulative frequency distribution.
B.	More-than ogive	(ii)	Shows the values of a single variable over equal time intervals.
C.	One variable graph	(iii)	Displays the values of two or more variables over the same time period, allowing for comparisons.
D.	Two or more variable graph	(iv)	Based on a less-than cumulative frequency distribution

Codes

	A	B	C	D
(a)	(iii)	(iv)	(i)	(ii)
(b)	(iv)	(i)	(ii)	(iii)
(c)	(ii)	(iii)	(iv)	(i)
(d)	(iii)	(ii)	(i)	(iv)

Concept Identification

60. It involves a visual representation showing data along a single axis.

61. It involves a line graph representing the cumulative frequency or cumulative relative frequency of a dataset.

62. It refers to the range of values into which data is grouped for the purpose of creating a histogram or frequency distribution.

63. It involves plotting time intervals on the x-axis and the values of a variable on the y-axis to display how the variable's values change over time.

64. It involves setting the baseline closer to the smallest data value to minimise distortion when the y-axis starts from a large value.

Answers

1. (b) small **2.** (c) go through
3. (d) Textual presentation **4.** (b) footnote
5. (d) Special purpose table
6. (c) Appropriate title and number
7. (a) Complexity **8.** (b) Original table
9. (b) I and III **10.** (a) Three-way table
11. (b) At the end of the table
12. (b) To display raw data in detail covering a wide range of information
13. (b) designations
14. (a) one-dimensional diagram
15. (b) segments
16. (d) Component bar diagram
17. (d) The length of the bars represents the value of the data.
18. (c) Pie or circular diagram
19. (c) (i), (ii), (iii) and (iv)
20. (a) Degree of Hockey $= \frac{11}{50} \times 360° = 79.2°$
21. (b) In a frequency polygon, points are joined with a foot rule, while in a frequency curve, points are joined free hand
22. (a) Histogram **23.** (b) mode
24. (d) Changes in frequency across intervals
25. (b) histogram **26.** (a) 40
27. (b) More-than ogive **28.** (c) Only II
29. (a) One variable graph
30. (a) To start the y-axis scales from a value other than zero to minimise distortion for large initial values
31. (d) Base line **32.** (d) Line chart
33. (b) April **34.** component bar
35. November
36. (c) Textual presentation does not necessarily facilitate easy comparison of data sets; rather it provides detailed context.
37. (a) Both Assertion (A) and Reason (R) are true and Reason (R) is the correct explanation of Assertion (A)

38. (b) Both Assertion (A) and Reason (R) are true, but Reason (R) is not the correct explanation of Assertion (A)
39. (b) Both Assertion (A) and Reason (R) are true, but Reason (R) is not the correct explanation of Assertion (A)
40. (d) A manifold table presents data with more than three characteristics, encompassing a wide range of inter-related features.
41. (c) A component bar diagram does not represent multiple sets of data in a single bar. Instead, it shows different components of a single total value.
42. (b) Both Assertion (A) and Reason (R) are true, but Reason (R) is not the correct explanation of Assertion (A)
43. (a) Both Assertion (A) and Reason (R) are true and Reason (R) is the correct explanation of Assertion (A)
44. (a) Both Assertion (A) and Reason (R) are true and Reason (R) is the correct explanation of Assertion (A)
45. (c) Both the statements are correct
46. (a) A special purpose table should be used in the above situation as specific information is presented.
47. (b) Source note cites the source of secondary data, including publication details, to ensure credibility and reference.
48. (d) Special purpose table presents data related to a specific inquiry, offering brief and concise information for data analysis results.
General purpose table displays raw data in detail and covers a wide range of information on the same subject without analytical intent.
49. (c) Both the statements are correct
50. (b) Multiple bar diagrams display two or moer sets of data simultaneously.
51. (a) A pie diagram, also known as a circular diagram, represents different values of a variable as segments of a circle. It is widely used to illustrate the proportion of various components within a whole.
52. (c) Both the statements are correct
53. (d) Frequency polygon can be constructed with or without a histogram. The frequency curve is obtained by drawing a smooth free hand curve passing through the mid-points of the histogram as closely as possible.
54. (c) Both the statements are correct
55. (a) (iii) (iv) (i) (ii)
56. (d) (iii) (ii) (i) (iv)
57. (d) (iv) (ii) (i) (iii)
58. (c) (ii) (iii) (iv) (i)
59. (b) (iv) (i) (ii) (iii)
60. One-dimensional diagram
61. Ogive
62. Class interval
63. Graph of times series
64. False base line

Subjective Questions

Short Answer Type Questions

1. What is a key disadvantage of using textual or descriptive presentation for data reporting?

Ans. A key disadvantage of using textual or descriptive presentation is that readers must shift through the entire text to extract and understand the relevant data. This can be time consuming and may make it difficult for readers to quickly identify key insights or trends.

The detailed nature of the text requires readers to interpret and analyse the information within the narrative, potentially leading to delays in grasping the main points and making informed decisions.

2. In what scenario is textual or descriptive presentation most appropriate for conveying data?

Competency Based Que

Ans. Textual or descriptive presentation is most appropriate for conveying data when dealing with smaller datasets that require detailed explanations. This method is ideal for providing context and nuance, particularly when the data needs to be communicated with accompanying narrative to explain complex situations or specific nuances.

e.g. It is useful in reporting qualitative observations or explaining the impact of specific events, such as detailing the effects of a strike on an industry, where a simple numerical summary would not fully capture the situation's complexities.

3. What are the key objectives of tabulation in data presentation?

Ans. The key objectives of tabulation are simplification, reference, comparison, space utilisation and statistical analysis. It organises complex data systematically, provides a consolidated format for future reference, facilitates easy comparison, makes efficient use of space and supports further mathematical treatment and analysis.

4. What are the advantages and disadvantages of tabular presentation of data?

Ans. The advantages of tabular presentation are

(i) This method is the simplest form of data presentation. Data is easily understood, if tables are systematically prepared.

(ii) This method facilitates comparison of data by presenting the data properly in rows and columns.

(iii) This method highlights important characteristics of data. Accordingly, it becomes easy to draw inferences from it.

(iv) Arranging the data in rows and columns helps the investigator to detect various errors and omissions in the data collected.

The disadvantages of tabular presentation are

(i) Preparing tables require proper understanding of data, otherwise they will be misleading.

(ii) Tables are not very attractive as compared to diagrams.

5. A company wants to present its annual revenue data for the past five years in a way that allows for easy comparison and further analysis. They decide to use a table format. What type of table would be most suitable for presenting this data and why? Competency Based Que

Ans. A suitable type of table for presenting annual revenue data for easy comparison and further analysis would be a 'general purpose table' (also known as a reference table). This type of table displays detailed raw data over a range of years and allows for straightforward comparison and reference.

6. Identify the type of table given in the below image and explain its purpose. Competency Based Que

Number of Students (Sex-wise) **in Different Sections of Class X**

Sections	No. of Students		Total
	Boys	Girls	
X-A	20	15	35
X-B	25	10	35
X-C	30	20	50
X-D	20	25	45
Total	95	70	165

Ans. A two-way table, also known as a double table or contingency table, is a statistical table used to display data that involves two variables. It organises data into rows and columns, where each cell in the table represents the intersection of the two variables. The above table displays the numbers of students (gender wise) in sections of class X. By organising this data, the table allows for easy comparison between male and female students of the class.

7. Briefly explain any four factors which should be kept in mind while preparing a table.

Ans. The following factors should be kept in mind while preparing a table

(i) Headings should generally be written in the singular form. e.g. In the columns indicating goods, the word 'good' should be used.

(ii) Use of abbreviations should be avoided in the heading or sub-headings of the table.

(iii) Footnote should be given, only if needed.

(iv) Size of table should be in accordance with the size of the paper.

8. "A special purpose table provides data related to a specific inquiry and offers concise information for data analysis results."
What is the objective of a special purpose table in statistical data presentation? Competency Based Que

Ans. A special purpose table is designed to provide targeted, concise information for a specific inquiry or analysis, simplifying the process of interpreting data related to a particular question or aspect.

e.g. A special purpose table might summarise annual revenue figures for a company over several years, providing a clear and focused view of financial performance trends.

9. Distinguish between classification and tabulation of data.

Ans. Differences between classification and tabulation of data are

Basis	Classification	Tabulation
Meaning	Classification of data means that the data is arranged in different classes according to the presence or absence of certain attributes.	Tabulation of data means that the classified data is arranged in rows and columns, under suitable heads and sub-heads.
Sequence	Classification precedes the process of tabulation.	Data can be tabulated only after it has been classified.
Method or Process	Classification is a method which facilitates statistical analysis.	Tabulation is a process which facilitates the presentation of data by preparing table.
Tool	It is a tool which helps to organise data.	It is a tool which helps in the presentation of data.

10. "Diagrams are less accurate but more effective than tables in presenting the data." Comment. Competency Based Que

Ans. Diagrams lack accuracy as they show only approximate values. Small difference in values are not comprehensible in a diagram.

Yet, they are more effective than table in presenting the data because of the below mentioned reasons

(i) They are simple, attractive and capable of creating an impression.

(ii) They facilitate easy comparison.

11. A company wants to compare its sales and profit data across four quarters of the year. They want to visually present this comparison for better understanding.

Which type of bar diagram would be most appropriate for this purpose? **Competency Based Que**

Ans. A multiple bar diagram would be most appropriate for comparing sales and profit data across four quarters. This type of diagram displays two or more sets of data simultaneously, allowing for direct comparison between sales and profit for each quarter.

By using different colours or patterns for each dataset, viewers can easily analyse trends and relationships between the variables overtime.

12. What is component bar diagram used for?

Ans. A component bar diagram displays a complete bar along with its sub-divisions into multiple components, illustrating both the total and the individual parts of the data.

Each segment of the bar represents a different component of the whole value and the diagram is useful for showing the composition of the total value. e.g. It can depict total sales and break downs into various product categories, helping to visualise the contribution of each part to the overall total.

13. The image shows a circular diagram representing the percentage of students' favourite subjects. Which type of diagram is displayed in the image? **Competency Based Que**

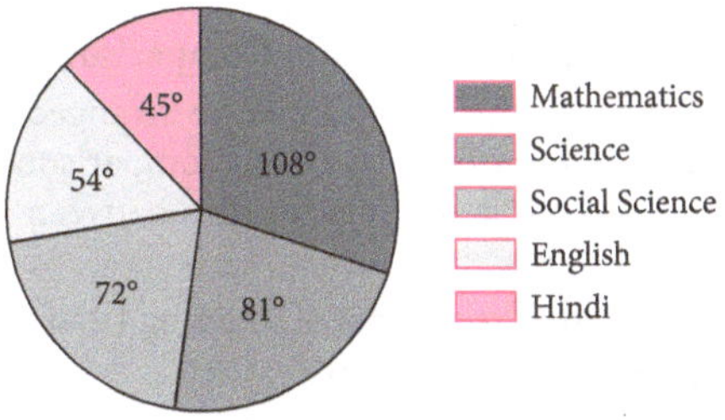

Ans. The diagram displayed in the image is a pie diagram. This type of diagram represents different components as segments of a circle, with each segment showing the proportion of each favourite subject among students.

The size of each segment reflects the percentage share of each subject, making it easy to visualise and compare the relative popularity of the subjects.

14. What kind of diagrams are more effective in representing the following?

(i) Components of cost in a factory.

(ii) Composition of population of Mumbai by religion.

(iii) Agriculture output of six states of India.

Ans. (i) Components of cost in a factory can be effectively presented with the help of 'component bar diagram'.

(ii) Composition of population of Mumbai by religion can be effectively presented with the help of 'percentage bar diagram'.

(iii) Agriculture output of six states can be effectively presented with the help of 'simple bar diagram'.

15. How does the procedure of drawing a histogram differ when class intervals are unequal in comparison to equal class intervals in a frequency table? **NCERT**

Ans. A histogram is a set of rectangles with bases as the intervals between class boundaries (along x-axis) and with areas proportionate to the class frequency.

When intervals are equal, all rectangles have the same base and area can conveniently be represented by the frequency of the interval.

But, when bases vary in their width, the heights of rectangles are to be adjusted to yield comparable measurements by dividing class frequency by width of the class interval instead of absolute frequency. This gives us the adjusted frequency for the purpose of comparison.

Thus, Adjusted Frequency

$$= \frac{\text{Width of the Lowest Class Interval} \times \text{Frequency of the Class}}{\text{Width of the Concerned Class Interval}}$$

16. A company tracks the monthly sales of three products over the past year. They want to compare how sales of each product have changed from month to month.

Which type of graph would be most suitable for displaying the sales data of multiple products over time and why? **Competency Based Que**

Ans. A graph of time series would be most suitable for displaying the sales data of multiple products over time. This type of graph plots the values of each product's sales against time intervals on the x-axis and their corresponding sales values on the y-axis, with distinct lines representing each product. This allows for easy comparison of sales trends and patterns across different products.

17. How is a histogram constructed when class intervals are equal? How does it differ from a frequency polygon?

Ans. While constructing a histogram which is based on a continuous frequency distribution with equal class intervals, the following steps should be followed

***Step* 1** On the x-axis, the class intervals are specified. The magnitude of class intervals will determine the width of the rectangle.

Step 2 On the y-axis, the frequencies are plotted, which determine the height of the rectangle.

Histogram presents a frequency distribution arranged in the form of adjacent rectangles, while frequency polygon is a graphical representation of a line joining the mid-values of the top of the frequency rectangles of histogram.

18. How can the use of a false base line in graphs impact the interpretation of data and when should it be used?

Ans. A false base line helps minimise distortion in graphs when the y-axis starts from a large value, making minor fluctuations more visible.

It should be used when it's important to accurately reflect small changes in data that might be obscured by a large starting point.

19. How is a frequency polygon constructed and what are its uses in data analysis?

Ans. A frequency polygon is created by plotting the mid-points of class intervals on the x-axis and their frequencies on the y-axis, then connecting these points with straight lines. The lines are extended to meet the x-axis at hypothetical class intervals on both ends.

Frequency polygons are useful for visualising the shape of data distributions, identifying trends and patterns and comparing multiple datasets by overlaying different polygons. They make it easier to understand the overall distribution and variations in the data.

20. Two methods of statistical presentation are shown below. Briefly explain the difference between the same. Competency Based Que

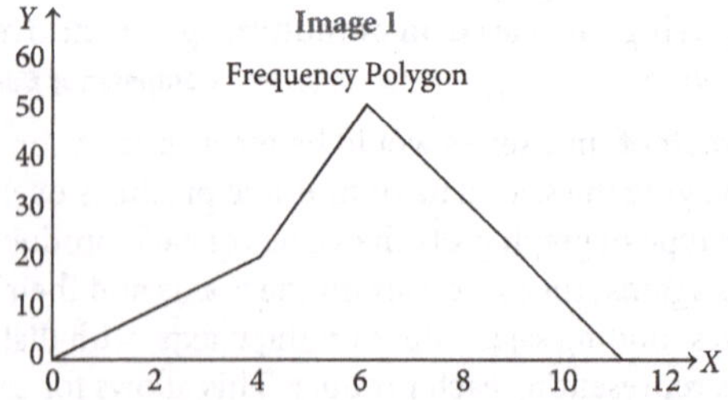

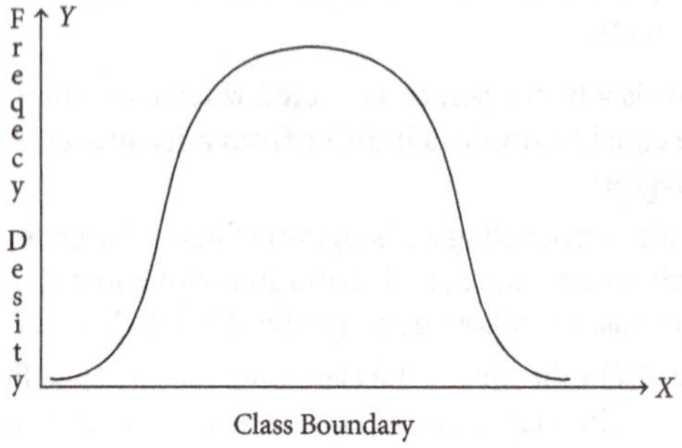

Ans. Image 1 represents frequency polygon and Image 2 indicates frequency curve.

The differences between frequency polygon and frequency curve are given below

Basis	Frequency Polygon	Frequency Curve
Meaning	Frequency polygon is a graphical representation of a frequency distribution in which frequencies are first plotted and then joined by straight lines with the help of a ruler.	Frequency curve is a graphical representation of a frequency distribution in which frequencies are first plotted and then joined by free hand.
Based on	A frequencies polygon for a continuous distribution can be made with the help of histogram.	A frequency curve is made with the help of frequency polygon.

Long Answer Type Questions

21. Briefly explain the guidelines for preparing a good table.

Ans. A good table is one which is able to convey the required information effectively. The guidelines for preparing a good table are stated below

(i) **Simple and Compact**

The table should be simple and compact, so that it should not create confusion in the mind of the user.

(ii) **Focus Attention on Main Comparisons**

The data in the table should be arranged so that it brings attention on the main comparisons and clearly exhibits the relationship between various related items.

For this, different fonts of lettering (italic, bold, capital letters, etc.) may be used.

(iii) **Complete and Self-explanatory**

A table should be complete and self-explanatory. It should contain all the essential parts of a table.

Also, in the preparation of table, use of abbreviations should be avoided. Only common abbreviations should be used.

(iv) **Attractive**

A table should be designed so that it is neither too long or narrow, nor too broad or short. If the data is very large, it should not be crowded in a single table, rather a number of different tables of reasonable size and shape should be prepared. All this helps in attractive presentation of data.

(v) **Accurate and Free from Errors**
The data contained in the table should be accurate and free from errors. For this, the entries in the table should be checked and re-checked.

(vi) **Classification According to a Specific Attribute**
The classification of data in a table should be according to a specific attribute.

22. Explain the different types of statistical tables based on their objectives, nature of data and extent of coverage.

Ans. Statistical tables are categorised based on their objectives, nature of data and extent of coverage, each serving distinct purposes in data presentation.

(i) **Based on Objective or Purpose**

- **General Purpose Table**
This table displays raw data in detail and covers a broad range of information on a single subject without analytical intent. It is often used in government reports to provide comprehensive data for reference.
For instance, a table showing annual population statistics across various regions without further analysis is a general purpose table.
- **Special Purpose Table**
This table offers concise information tailored to a specific inquiry, often summarising results for analysis. It might include, a table showing the revenue figures of a company over several years, providing a snapshot for financial analysis or decision-making.

(ii) **Based on Nature of Data**

- **Original Table**
This type contains data in its raw form, as collected from primary sources, without any modifications. It is also known as a primary or classification table. An example would be a table listing the raw survey responses from a customer satisfaction study.
- **Derived Table**
Derived from original data, this table displays results such as percentages or averages. It processes raw data to present summarised information.
e.g. A table showing the average monthly sales figures calculated from the original sales data is a derived table.

(iii) **Based on Extent of Coverage**

- **Simple Table**
This table presents data related to a single variable, providing a univariate frequency distribution. It is known as a one-way or first order table. An example would be a table showing the frequency distribution of student grades in a single subject.
- **Complex Table**
It shows data based on two or more characteristics, offering a multi-dimensional view. e.g.
(a) **Two-way Table** (Double Table) This table displays information on two inter-related features. An example is a table categorising students by section and gender.
(b) **Three-way Table** (Treble Table) This table includes three characteristics, such as a table showing students categorised by section, gender and sports participation.
(c) **Manifold Table** This table presents data with more than three characteristics, offering a detailed multi-dimensional view. An example would be a table showing students categorised by section, gender, sports participation and academic performance.

23. Discuss the different types of bar diagrams used in data presentation, highlighting their features and uses with examples.

Ans. Bar diagrams come in several types, each suited to different data presentation needs

(i) **Simple Bar Diagram**
Displays a single data set with bars of uniform width, showing values for each category. e.g. It can illustrate the number of students in each grade level.

(ii) **Multiple Bar Diagram**
Compares two or more data sets side by side using grouped bars. An example is comparing monthly income and expenditure.

(iii) **Component Bar Diagram**
Breaks down a total value into parts within a single bar. For instance, it could show a company's budget divided among departments.

(iv) **Percentage Bar Diagram**
Represents parts of a whole as percentages of the total bar length. This is useful for displaying the percentage distribution of student enrollments in various disciplines.

(v) **Deviation Bar Diagram**
Shows deviations from a baseline with bars extending above and below a central line, such as monthly temperature deviations from an average.

24. What kind of diagrams are more effective in representing the following?
(i) Monthly rainfall in a year.
(ii) Composition of the population of Delhi by religion.
(iii) Components of cost in a factory.
NCERT; Competency Based Que

Ans. (i) The monthly rainfall in a year can be best represented by a simple bar diagram as only one variable i.e. monthly rainfall is to be presented diagrammatically. The rainfall will be plotted on y-axis and the corresponding month will be plotted on the x-axis.

(ii) Composition of the population of Delhi by religion can be represented by a component bar diagram. A component bar diagram shows the bar and its sub-divisions into two or more components. Thus, the total population in different years can be sub-divided in terms of religion i.e. Hindus, Muslims, Sikhs and Christians and can be presented through a component bar diagram.

(iii) Different components of cost in a factory can most effectively be depicted through a pie chart.

The circle represents the total cost and various components of cost are shown by different segments of the circle.

25. A school has conducted a survey to determine the percentage of students favouring different extracurricular activities. The results are as follows 40% of students prefer sports, 30% prefer music, 20% prefer drama and 10% prefer art. The principal wants to present these findings in a visually appealing manner at the next school meeting. Explain how a pie diagram would be constructed to represent the survey results and discuss its advantages and disadvantages for presenting this data to the school community.

Competency Based Que

Ans. To construct a pie diagram for the survey results, follow these steps

(i) **Convert to Degrees**
Calculate the angle for each activity. e.g. For sports, the angle would be $40/100 \times 360 = 144$. Similarly, calculate for music (108°), drama (72°) and art (36°).

(ii) **Draw the Circle**
Begin by drawing a circle and dividing it into segments based on the calculated angles.

(iii) **Add Sectors**
Draw each sector according to the calculated angles, with the largest sector (sports) taking up the largest angle.

(iv) **Shade Segments**
Use different colours or patterns to distinguish between the activities.

Advantages of pie diagram are as follows

(i) **Visual Appeal**
The pie diagram provides a clear, visually engaging representation of the data, making it easier for the school community to grasp the proportions of each activity.

(ii) **Simplicity**
It simplifies the complex data into an easily understandable format, showing how each activity compares to the whole.

Disadvantages of pie diagram are as follows

(i) **Limited Detail**
It does not provide precise numerical details, only relative proportions, which may not be sufficient for detailed analysis.

(ii) **Misleading Interpretation**
If not carefully constructed, the diagram could mislead if similar-sized segments are hard to differentiate visually.

26. Describe the process of constructing a histogram for both equal and unequal class intervals and explain how to adjust the histogram when mid-points or inclusive intervals are given.

Ans. **Construction of a Histogram**

(i) **Equal Class Intervals**

- **Plot Class Intervals**
Begin by plotting the class intervals on the x-axis. Each rectangle's width corresponds to the interval size, which is consistent across the histogram.
- **Plot Frequencies**
On the y-axis, plot the frequencies for each interval. The height of each rectangle represents the frequency of the respective class interval.
- **Draw Rectangles**
Construct rectangles where the base represents the interval width and the height corresponds to the frequency. Ensure that the rectangles are adjacent, with no gaps between them, to signify continuous data.

(ii) **Unequal Class Intervals**

- **Identify Standard Width**
Determine the smallest class interval width and use it as the standard width for the rectangles.
- **Calculate Adjustment Factor**
Compute an adjustment factor using the formula to standardise widths.
- **Adjust Frequencies**
Modify the frequencies for non-standard intervals by dividing them by the adjustment factor to account for varying interval widths.
- **Draw Histogram**
Plot the histogram using the adjusted frequencies for intervals with non-standard widths and original frequencies for standard intervals. Ensure continuity by keeping the rectangles adjacent.

(iii) **When Mid-points are Given**

- **Calculate Interval Width**
  Find the class interval width by subtracting the mid-point of one interval from the mid-point of the next and dividing by 2.
- **Determine Class Limits**
  Use this interval width to adjust the mid-points to derive class limits by adding and subtracting the calculated value.
- **Construct Histogram**
  Plot the histogram based on these derived class intervals.

(iv) **When Class Intervals are Inclusive**

- **Compute Adjustment Value**
  Calculate the difference between the upper limit of one class and the lower limit of the next. Divide this difference by 2 to find the adjustment value.
- **Convert Intervals**
  Adjust inclusive intervals to exclusive intervals by subtracting the adjustment value from the lower limit and adding it to the upper limit.
- **Prepare Histogram**
  Construct the histogram using the adjusted exclusive class intervals.

27. Describe the construction process of less-than and more-than ogives. Explain the differences between these two types of cumulative frequency curves and their uses in data analysis.

Ans. **Construction of Ogives**

(i) **Less-than Ogive**

It shows cumulative frequency up to each class interval.

Steps to Construct Ogive

- Calculate cumulative frequencies by adding frequencies up to and including each class interval.
- Plot cumulative frequencies on the y-axis against the upper class limits on the x-axis.
- Connect the points with a smooth, upward sloping curve.

(ii) **More-than Ogive**

It displays cumulative frequency starting from each class interval and including all succeeding intervals.

Steps to Construct Ogive

- Calculate cumulative frequencies by adding frequencies for all classes above each interval.
- Plot these cumulative frequencies on the y-axis against the lower class limits on the x-axis.
- Connect the points with a smooth, downward sloping curve.

Differences and Uses of Less-than Ogive and More-than Ogive

(i) **Less-than Ogive**

- **Differences**
  Rises from left to right, showing how many observations are below each class interval.
- **Uses**
  Useful for finding percentiles and understanding the distribution up to a certain value.

(ii) **More-than Ogive**

- **Differences**
  Falls from left to right, showing how many observations are above each class interval.
- **Uses**
  Helps in determining the number of observations above a certain value and analysing higher percentiles.

28. Explain briefly the advantages and limitations of graphical presentation of data.

Ans. The following are the advantages of graphical presentation

(i) **Simple Form**
It presents the complex data in a simple or understandable form.

(ii) **Forecasting**
It is used for forecasting, interpolation and extrapolation. This helps to assess the future changes in the value of the variable.

(iii) **Study of Variations**
With the help of graphs, we can study the variations in the values of variables and can take corrective actions.

(iv) **Attractive**
Graphical presentation helps to present the data in an attractive manner which makes it interesting and impressive.

(v) **Easy Comparison**
Graphical presentation of data facilitates easy comparison between the values of the data.

(vi) **Universal Utility**
Graphical presentation is popularly used in journal, newspapers, board meeting, etc. to give the required information to the general users.

Graphical presentation of data suffers from the following limitations

(i) **Actual/Precise Values are not Disclosed**
Graphical presentation merely shows the tendency and fluctuations.
Actual and precise values are not disclosed through a graphical presentation, so it does not show precise values.

(ii) **Lead to Wrong Conclusions**
It may sometimes suggest wrong conclusions and give misleading information.

(iii) **Limited Information**
Graphical presentation can be used to depict only one or two characteristics. Because of this, only limited information can be presented through this presentation.

29. Explain how to construct graphs of time series for one variable and multiple variables. Additionally, describe the use and impact of a false base line in time series graphs.

Ans. Construction of Time Series Graphs

(i) **One Variable Graph**
It illustrates the changes in a single variable over equal time intervals.
Steps for Construction

- **Plot Time Intervals**
  Mark time intervals (e.g. Days, months) along the x-axis.
- **Plot Variable Values**
  Mark the values of the variable on the y-axis.
- **Connect Points**
  Draw straight lines connecting the plotted points to show the trend overtime.

(ii) **Two or More Variable Graph**
It compares the changes in multiple variables over the same time period.
Steps for Construction

- **Plot Time Intervals**
  Mark time intervals on the x-axis.
- **Plot Variable Values**
  Mark the values for each variable on the y-axis.
- **Connect Points**
  Use distinct lines (e.g. Solid, dashed) for each variable to illustrate their respective trends and facilitate comparison.

Use and Impact of False Base Line
A false base line is used when the y-axis starts from a large value, which can exaggerate or obscure data variations. It provides a clearer depiction of fluctuations by setting the baseline closer to the smallest value in the data set.

Steps for Implementation

- **Identify Smallest Value**
  Determine the smallest value in your dataset.
- **Set False Base Line**
  Position the false base line just below this smallest value to minimise the visual distortion caused by a large initial baseline.
- **Plot Data**
  Use this adjusted base line to plot the data, making the variations more noticeable and accurate.

Impact By using a false base line, you reduce the gap at the bottom of the graph, allowing for a more precise visualisation of minor fluctuations in the data, which might otherwise appear negligible or distorted due to the large scale of the y-axis.

30. The Indian Sugar Mills Association reported that, "sugar production during the first fortnight of December, 2001 was about 3,87,000 tonnes, as against 3,78,000 tonnes during the same fortnight last year (2000).

The off-take of sugar from factories during the first fortnight of December, 2001 was 2,83,000 tonnes for internal consumption and 41,000 tonnes for exports as against 1,54,000 tonnes for internal consumption and nil for exports during the same fortnight last season."

(i) Present the data in tabular form.

(ii) Suppose you were to present these data in diagrammatic form, which of the diagrams would you use and why?

(iii) Present these data diagrammatically.

NCERT; Competency Based Que

Ans. (i) Data in tabular form

Sugar Production in India

Month	Year	Total Production (tonnes)	Off-take for Internal Consumption (tonnes)	Off-take for Exports (tonnes)
December	2000	3,78,000	1,54,000	—
December	2001	3,87,000	2,83,000	41,000

(ii) The data can effectively be presented diagrammatically using the multiple bar diagram. This is because multiple bar diagrams are used for comparing two or more sets of data for different years or classes, etc.

(iii) Diagrammatic presentation of data

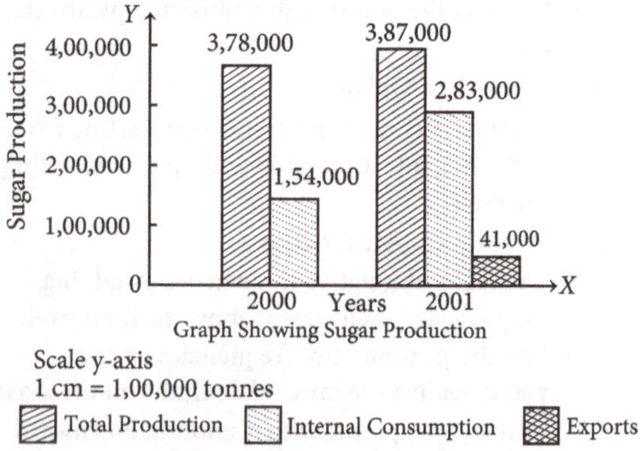

Graph Showing Sugar Production

Numerical Questions

Numerical 1

Prepare a blank table to show distribution of population according to age, sex and literacy for a particular year.

Sol. Distribution of population on the basis of age, sex and literacy in the year 2015 is tabulated below

Age	Sex				Total
	Male		Female		
	Literate	Illiterate	Literate	Illiterate	
3-18	—	—	—	—	
19-35	—	—	—	—	
36-60	—	—	—	—	
60 and above	—	—	—	—	

Numerical 2

There are 1,200 employees in a particular company. Of all the employees, one-fourth are women and one-tenth women are married. One-fifth of the men are married. Tabulate the given information.

Sol. **Distribution of Employees based upon Gender and Marital Status**

Marital Status	Men	Women	Total
Married	180	30	210
Unmarried	720	270	990
Total	900	300	1,200

Numerical 3

In 2019, out of a total of 2,000 applicants in a college, 1,200 were from commerce background. The number of girls was 750, out of which 330 were from science stream. In 2020, the total number of applicants were 3,500 of which 2,200 were boys. The number of students from science was 1,100 of which 610 were girls. Tabulate the given information.

Sol. **Distribution of Students in University Based upon Sex and Stream** (2019-2020)

Stream	2019			2020			Total		
	Boys	Girls	Total	Boys	Girls	Total	Boys	Girls	Total
Science	470	330	800	490	610	1,100	960	940	1,900
Commerce	780	420	1,200	1,710	690	2,400	2,490	1,110	3,600
Total	1,250	750	2,000	2,200	1,300	3,500	3,450	2,050	5,500

Numerical 4

In a trip, organised by a college, there were 80 people, each of whom paid ₹ 15.50 on an average.

There were 60 students, each of whom paid ₹ 16. Members of teaching staff were charged at a higher rate, the number of servants (all males) were 6 and they were not charged anything.

The number of females were 20% of the total and there was only one female staff member. Tabulate this information.

Sol. Total participants = 80

Number of students = 60

Number of servants = 6

∴ Number of teaching staff = 80 − (60 + 6) = 14

Number of female teaching staff = 1

∴Number of male teaching staff = 14 − 1 = 13

Total number of females = 80 × 20% = 16

Number of female students = 16 − 1 = 15

Total contribution = 80 × 15.50 = ₹ 1,240

Contribution from students = 60 × 16 = ₹ 960

Contribution from teaching staff = 1,240 − 960 = ₹ 280

∴ Contribution per head in teaching staff

$$= \frac{280}{14} = ₹\ 20$$

Now, this information can be tabulated as below

Participants	Sex		Total	Contribution Per Head	Total Contribution
	Males	Females			
Students	45	15	60	16	960
Teaching Staff	13	1	14	20	280
Servants	6	—	6	—	—
Total	64	16	80	15.50	1,240

Numerical 5

In 2019, out of total of 700 employees of a factory, 475 employees were skilled. The number of women employed was 450 of which 175 were unskilled. In 2020, the number of skilled employees decreased to 360 of which 120 were men.

On the other hand, the number of unskilled employees fell down to 190 of which 80 were women. Tabulate the above information.

Sol. **Table 4.2 Distribution of Employees based upon Gender and Training**

Year	Number of Employees						Grand Total		
	Men			Women					
	Skilled	Unskilled	Total	Skilled	Unskilled	Total	Skilled	Unskilled	Total
2019	200	50	250	275	175	450	475	225	700
2020	120	110	230	240	80	320	360	190	550
Total	320	160	480	515	255	770	835	415	1,250

Numerical 6

Present the following information in a suitable tabular form

(i) In 2020, out of total 2,000 workers in a factory, 1,550 were members of a trade union. The number of women workers employees was 250, out of which 200 did not belong to any trade union.

(ii) In 2022, the number of union workers was 1,725 of which 1,600 were men. The number of non-union workers was 380, among which 155 were women.

Sol. The information given in the question can be summarised as follows

(i) **Year 2020**

Total no. of workers in the factory = 2,000

Total no. of trade union workers = 1,550

Total no. of non-trade union workers = (2,000 – 1,550) = 450

Total no. of women worker = 250

Total no. of non-trade union women worker = 200

Total no. of trade union women worker = (250 – 200) = 50

Total no. of trade union men worker = (1,550 – 50) = 1,500

Total no. of non-trade union men worker = (450 – 200) = 250

Total no. of men workers = 1,500 + 250 = 1,750

(ii) **Year 2022**

Total no. of trade union workers = 1,725

Total no. of trade union men worker = 1,600

Total no. of non-trade union women worker = (1,725 – 1,600) = 125

Total no. of non-trade union workers = 380

Total no. of non-trade union women worker = 155

Total no. of non-trade union men worker = (380 – 155) = 225

Total no. of workers in the factory = 1,725 + 380 = 2,105

Total no. of men workers = 1,600 + 225 = 1,825

Total no. of women workers = 125 + 155 = 280

Distribution of Workers in a Factory
(according to member of trade union and gender)

Year	Trade Union			Non-trade Union			Total		
	Male	Female	Total	Male	Female	Total	Male	Female	Total
2020	1,500	50	1,550	250	200	450	1,750	250	2,000
2022	1,600	125	1,725	225	155	380	1,825	280	2,105
Total	3,100	175	3,275	475	355	830	3,575	530	4,105

Numerical 7

Rice yield per hectare is given below. Show the data diagrammatically.

Year	Yield per Hectare (in kg)
1999-2000	668
2000-2001	1,013
2001-2002	1,123
2002-2003	1,235
2003-2004	1,336
2004-2005	1,552
2005-2006	1,482

Sol. The above data can be presented with the help of a simple bar diagram, since only one variable is to be presented. The figure is drawn below

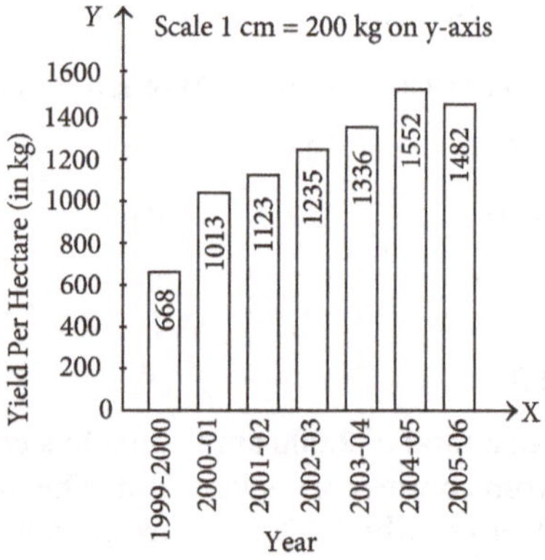

Numerical 8

Represent the following data by an appropriate bar diagram.

Import and Export of India

Year	Import in Current Price (₹ in thousand crore)	Export in Current Price (₹ in thousand crore)
2002-03	139	119
2003-04	154	130
2004-05	176	142
2005-06	149	119

Sol. The above table shows data related to two variables, therefore it is represented with the help of multiple bar diagram.

The bar diagram showing import and export of India is given below

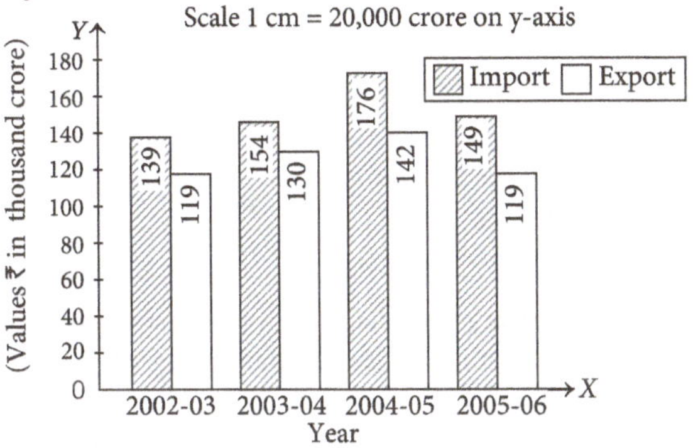

Numerical 9

Represent the following data by an appropriate bar diagram.

Index Numbers of Agricultural Production
(base 1991-92 = 100 and figures to the nearest of unit value)

Year	Foodgrains		
	Rice	Wheat	Pulses
1999-2000	149	157	141
2000-01	162	170	131
2001-02	165	187	139
2002-03	155	176	121
2003-04	164	197	140
2004-05	166	189	127
2005-06	173	201	145

Sol. The above table shows data related to three variables, therefore it is represented through a multiple bar diagram. The bar diagram showing index number of agricultural production is given below

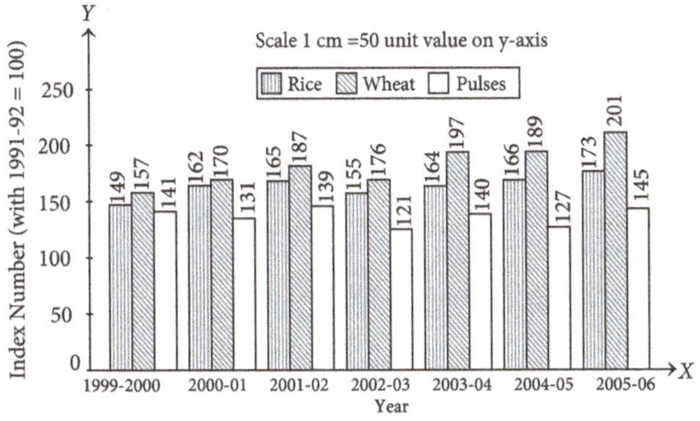

Numerical 10

Subsidies on food, fertilisers, export promotion and others given by the government are shown in the table below (in crores).

Represent the data diagrammatically.

Year	Food	Fertilisers	Export Promotion	Others	Total
2006-07	2,000	1,897	788	891	5,576
2007-08	2,200	2,210	960	909	6,279
2008-09	2,300	3,000	1,091	925	7,316

Sol. The data shows the sub-division of subsidy in different components. Therefore, it is represented through a sub-divided bar diagram.

The diagrammatic representation of the given data is shown below

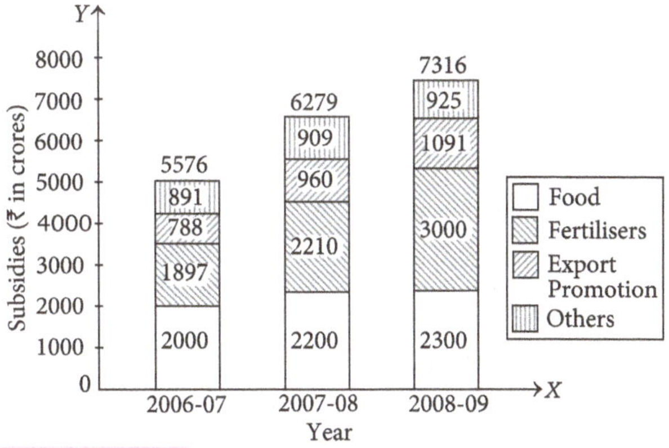

Numerical 11

Present the following data by a percentage sub-divided bar diagram.

Subject	Number of Students (in'000)	
	2011-12	2012-13
Statistics	25	30
Economics	40	42
History	35	28

Sol. First, we prepare a percentage table.

Percentage Table

Subject	2011-12		2012-13	
	Number of Students (in'000)	Percent	Number of Students (in'000)	Percent
Statistics	25	25	30	30
Economics	40	40	42	42
History	35	35	28	28
Total	100	100	100	100

Now, we draw bars of equal length (100%) corresponding to each year. Then, each bar is divided according to percentage of different years.

A percentage sub-divided bar diagram of given data is shown below

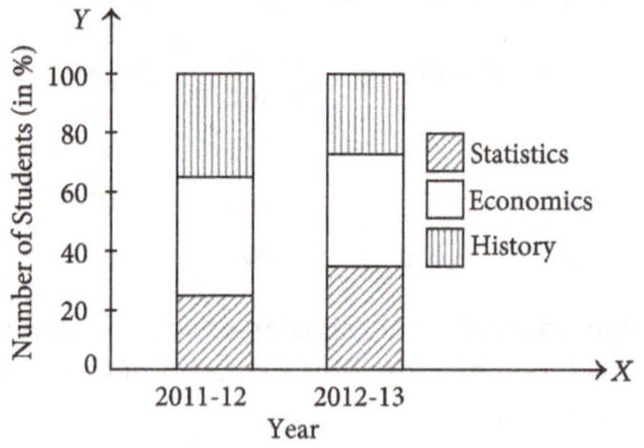

Numerical 12

The minimum temperature of Shimla in the last week of December is given below

Date	Temperature
25th December	3°C
26th December	−1°C
27th December	−2°C
28th December	2°C
29th December	4°C
30th December	−3°C
31st December	−4°C

Represent the above data with the help of suitable diagram.

Sol. The temperature is positive, as well as, negative. So, this data can be presented with the help of sub-divided bar diagram.

The diagrammatic representation of the given data is shown below

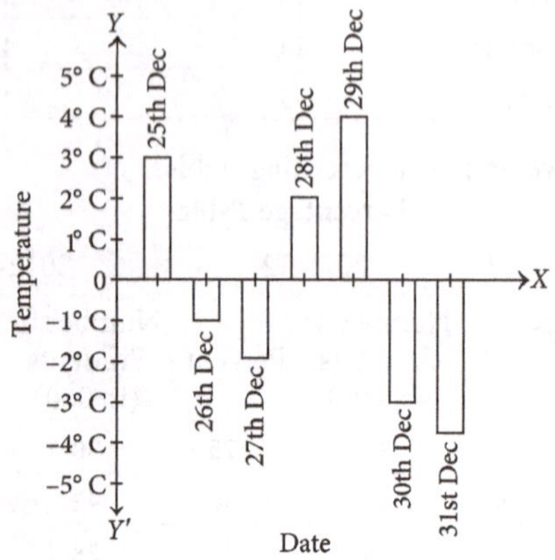

Numerical 13

Construct a pie diagram to represent the cost of construction of a house in Delhi.

Items	Expenditure (in %)
Labour	25
Bricks	15
Cement	20
Steel	15
Timber	10
Supervision	15

Sol. For constructing a pie diagram, it is necessary to convert the percentage into angles of different degree. This conversion is shown below

Items	Expenditure (in %)	Expenditure in Degree
Labour	25	$\frac{25}{100}\times 360° = 90°$
Bricks	15	$\frac{15}{100}\times 360° = 54°$
Cement	20	$\frac{20}{100}\times 360° = 72°$
Steel	15	$\frac{15}{100}\times 360° = 54°$
Timber	10	$\frac{10}{100}\times 360° = 36°$
Supervision	15	$\frac{15}{100}\times 360° = 54°$
Total	100	360°

A pie diagram to show cost of construction of a house in Delhi is given below

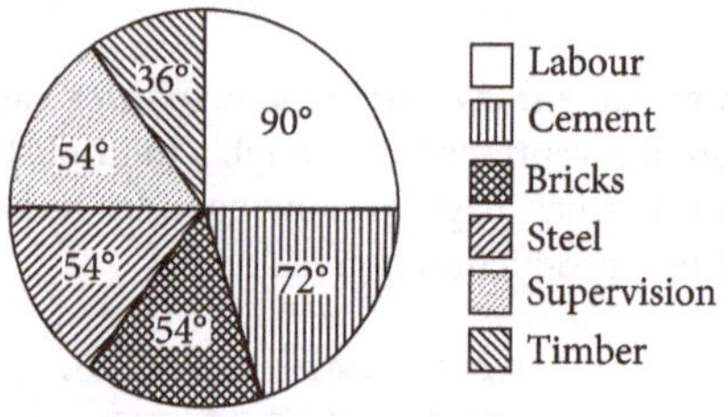

Numerical 14

Draw a pie diagram from the following data

Mode of Transport	School Bus	Van	Metro	Public Bus	Private Cars
No. of Students	220	400	180	100	300

Sol. **Calculation of Degree**

Mode of Transport	No. of Students	Degree
School Bus	220	$(220/1,200) \times 360° = 66°$
Van	400	$(400/1,200) \times 360° = 120°$
Metro	180	$(180/1,200) \times 360° = 54°$
Public Bus	100	$(100/1,200) \times 360° = 30°$
Private Car	300	$(300/1,200) \times 360° = 90°$
Total	1,200	360°

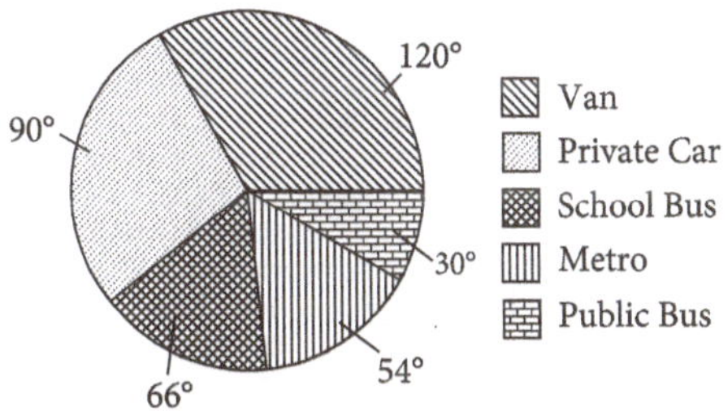

Numerical 15

Direction of export is shown in the following table. Prepare a pie diagram to show the percentage distribution of export.

Country	Export (in %)
USA	25
Japan	15
UK	30
China	20
Others	10

Sol. For constructing a pie diagram, it is necessary to convert the percentage into angles of different degree. This conversion is shown below

Country	Percentage of Export	Degree of Angles
USA	25	$\frac{25}{100} \times 360° = 90°$
Japan	15	$\frac{15}{100} \times 360° = 54°$
UK	30	$\frac{30}{100} \times 360° = 108°$
China	20	$\frac{20}{100} \times 360° = 72°$
Others	10	$\frac{10}{100} \times 360° = 36°$
Total	100	360°

A pie diagram to show percentage distribution export is given below

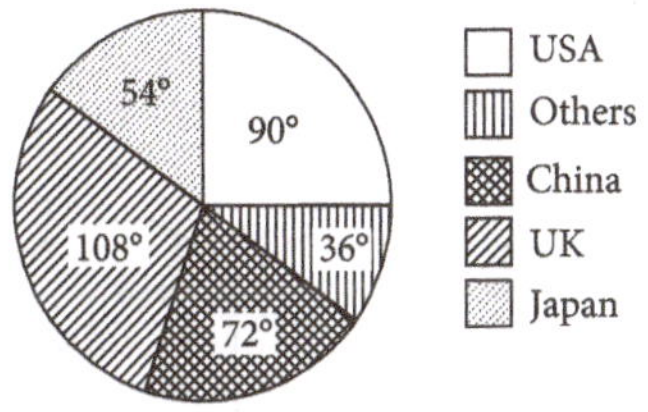

Numerical 16

Present the data given in the table below with the help of a histogram.

Marks	Frequency
0-10	4
10-20	10
20-30	16
30-40	22
40-50	20
50-60	18
60-70	8
70-80	2

Sol. A histogram showing given data is given below

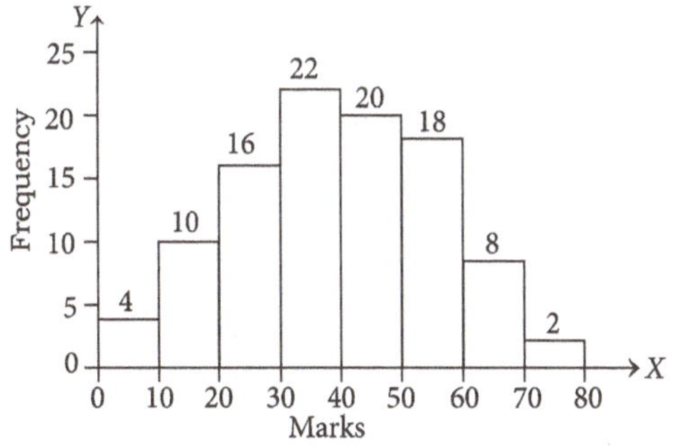

Numerical 17

Construct a frequency polygon with histogram for the following data.

Class Interval	Frequency
0-10	4
10-20	6
20-30	7
30-40	14
40-50	16
50-60	14
60-70	8
70-80	6
80-90	5

Sol. A frequency polygon with histogram using the given data is shown below

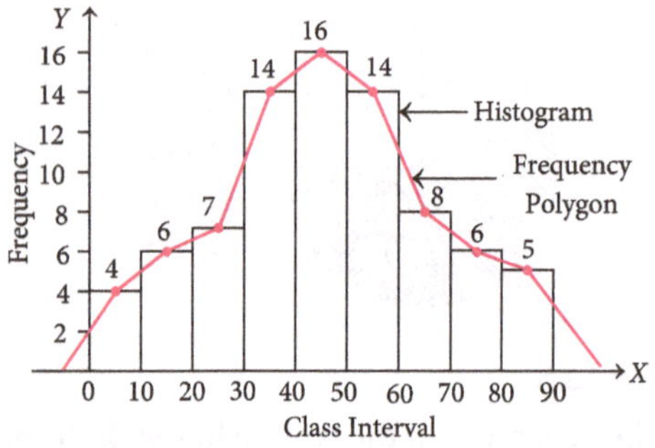

Numerical 18

Present the following data in the form of histogram.

Weekly Wages (in ₹)	Number of Workers
10-15	7
15-20	10
20-25	27
25-30	15
30-40	12
40-60	12
60-80	8

Sol. As per the question, unequal distribution of weekly wages are given. Before plotting histogram, first of all we should adjust the frequency.

Frequency distribution of given data with adjusted frequencies is shown below

Weekly Wages (in ₹)	Number of Workers	Adjusted Frequency
10-15	7	$\frac{5}{5} \times 7 = 7$
15-20	10	$\frac{5}{5} \times 10 = 10$
20-25	27	$\frac{5}{5} \times 27 = 27$
25-30	15	$\frac{5}{5} \times 15 = 15$
30-40	12	$\frac{5}{10} \times 12 = 6$
40-60	12	$\frac{5}{20} \times 12 = 3$
60-80	8	$\frac{5}{20} \times 8 = 2$

A histogram in case of unequal class intervals is shown below

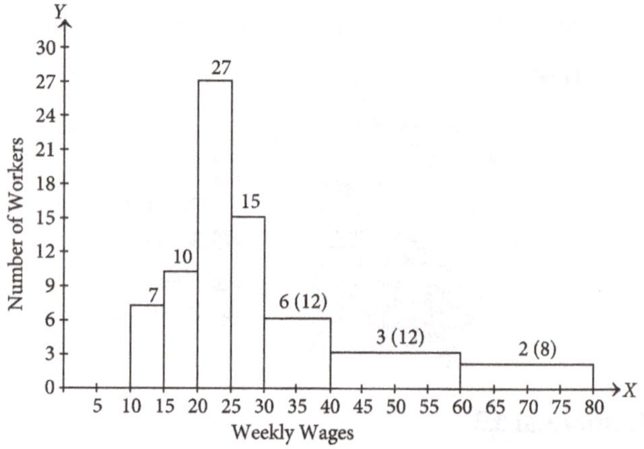

Note
- Adjusted Frequency = $\frac{\text{Minimum Interval} \times \text{Class Frequency}}{\text{Class Interval}}$
- Figures in bracket show actual frequency.

Numerical 19

Draw the 'less-than' and 'more-than' ogive from the data given below

Weekly Wages (in ₹)	Number of Workers
0-20	10
20-40	20
40-60	40
60-80	20
80-100	10

Sol. For less-than and more-than ogives we will have to prepare less-than and more-than frequency distributions.

Less-than Distribution		More-than Distribution	
Weekly Wages (in ₹)	Number of Workers	Weekly Wages (in ₹)	Number of Workers
Less than 20	10	More than 0	100
Less than 40	30	More than 20	90
Less than 60	70	More than 40	70
Less than 80	90	More than 60	30
Less than 100	100	More than 80	10

The 'less-than' and 'more-than' ogives of the given data are shown below

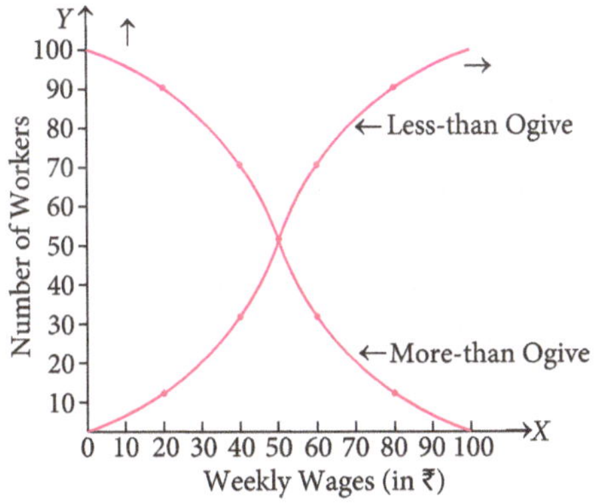

Numerical 20

Given below is the data related to company's net profit and loss over past 5 years. Represent the following data using a suitable diagram

Year	2016	2017	2018	2019	2020
Net Profit/Loss (in ₹)	200	350	400	180	–200

Sol. As there are both positive and negative values, deviation bar graph will be best fit in this case.

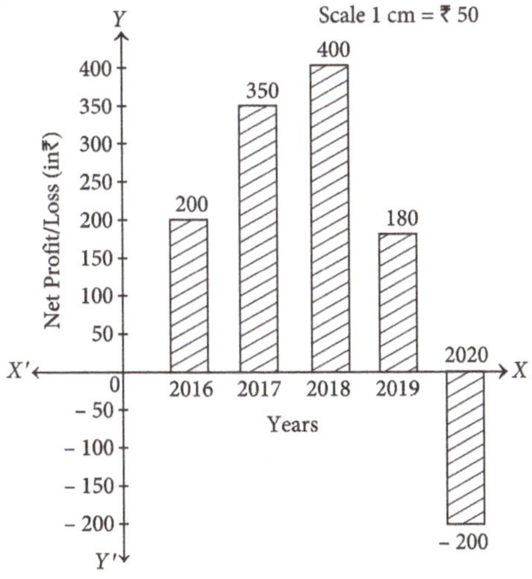

Numerical 21

Represent the following data using a suitable diagram

Marks	0-5	5-10	10-20	20-40	40-45	45-50
No. of Students	03	04	08	08	06	02

Sol. As the data is continuous, histogram will be used. Also, the distribution is unequal, thus we first need to apply the adjustment factor.

Marks	0-5	5-10	10-20	20-40	40-45	45-50
No. of Students	03	04	08	08	06	02
Adjusted Frequency	03	04	08 ÷ 02 = 04	08 ÷ 04 = 02	06	02

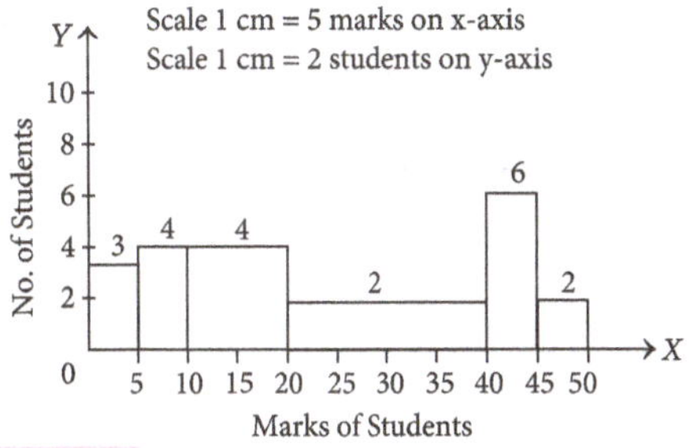

Numerical 22

Represent the following data using a frequency polygon (without histogram).

Marks	0-10	10-20	20-30	30-40	40-50
No. of Students	4	2	6	10	8

Sol. In order to construct a frequency polygon without histogram, we need to find the mid-values.

Marks	0-10	10-20	20-30	30-40	40-50
Mid-values	5	15	25	35	45
Frequency	4	2	6	10	8

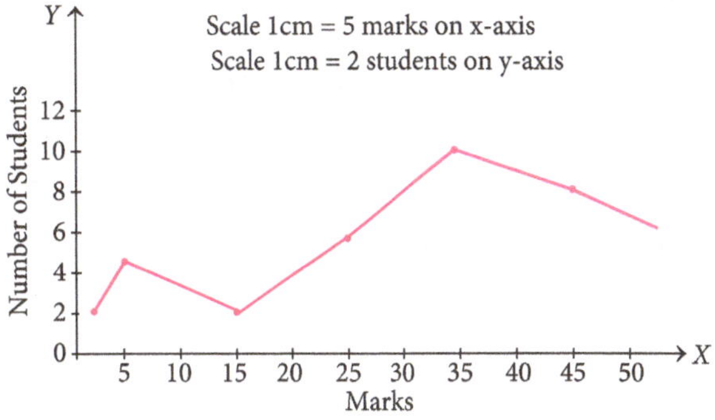

Numerical 23

Show the annual profit figures of a firm with the help of a time series graph.

Year	Profit (in ₹ '000)
2006	60
2007	72
2008	75
2009	65
2010	80
2011	95

Sol. As per the question, year 2006 to 2011 and their respective profits are given. Before plotting the graph, a false base line should be prepared in order to make profit scale equal.

A time series graph of given annual profit figures is shown below

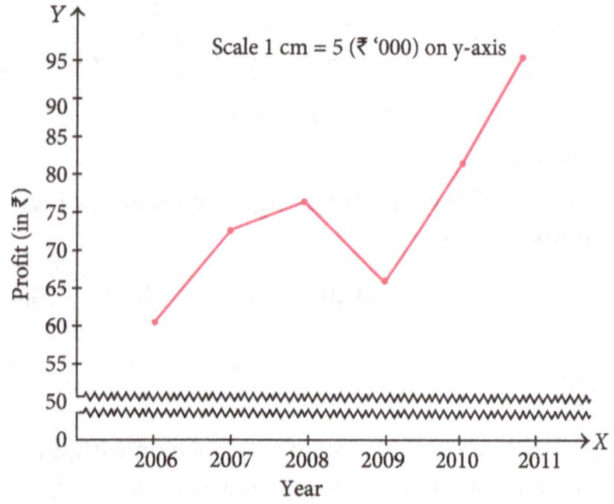

Numerical 24

Represent the following information through a time series graph.

Year	2005	2006	2007	2008	2009	2010	2011
Export (₹ in crore)	300	320	400	350	360	250	340
Import (₹ in crore)	450	300	280	375	330	450	325

Sol. Graph showing exports and imports from year 2005 to 2011 is given below

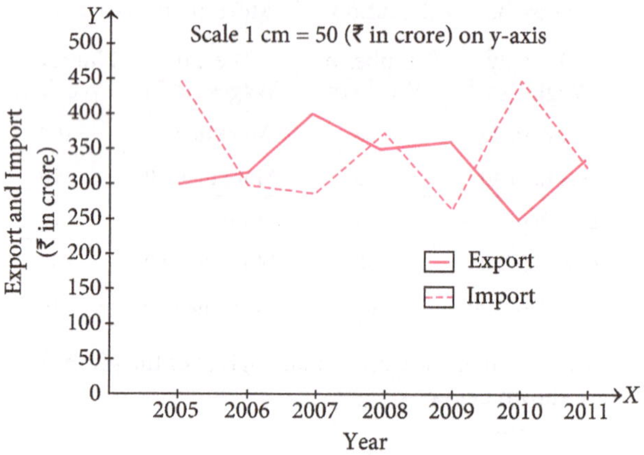

Numerical 25

The following table shows the estimated sectoral real growth rates (percentage change over the previous year) in GDP at factor cost. **NCERT**

Year	Agriculture and Allied Sectors	Industry	Services
1994-95	5.0	9.2	7.0
1995-96	−0.9	11.8	10.3
1996-97	9.6	6.0	7.1
1997-98	−1.9	5.9	9.0
1998-99	7.2	4.0	8.3
1999-2000	0.8	6.9	8.2

Represent the data as multiple time series graphs.

Sol. Graph showing estimated real growth rates in agriculture sector, industry and services sector is given

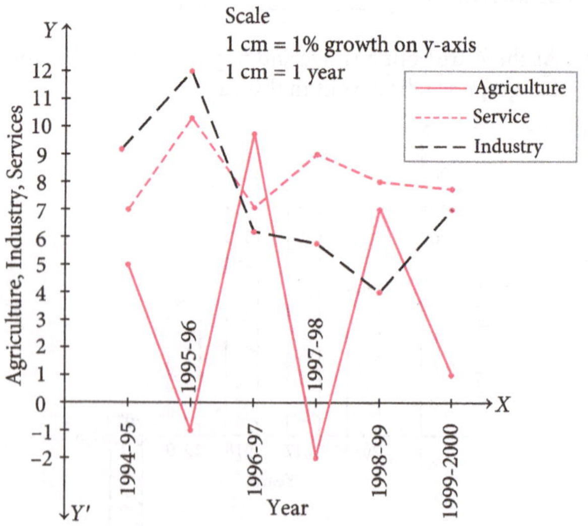

SELF ASSESSMENT TEST

Objective Type Questions

1. What is the main objective of tabular presentation of data?
   (a) To make data more complex
   (b) To simplify and organise data systematically
   (c) To highlight textual descriptions
   (d) To avoid data comparison

2. Which part of a table is referred to as the main section containing the data?
   (a) Body of the table (b) Stub column
   (c) Head note (d) Caption

3. What is a manifold table used for?
   (a) Presenting data for a single characteristic
   (b) Displaying two inter-related features
   (c) Showing three characteristics simultaneously
   (d) Presenting data for more-than three characteristics

4. What is the primary objective of diagrammatic presentation of data?
   (a) To provide detailed and complete information for experts
   (b) To make complex information simple and attractive
   (c) To eliminate the need for numerical data
   (d) To replace all forms of data analysis

5. ……… is the main feature of a deviation bar diagram.
   (a) Bars represent data in percentages
   (b) Bars are divided into components
   (c) Bars indicate positive and negative deviations from a baseline
   (d) Bars are always drawn horizontally

6. In a less-than ogive, frequencies are plotted against ……… values.
   (a) mid-points of class intervals
   (b) lower limits of class intervals
   (c) upper limits of class intervals
   (d) cumulative frequencies

7. In a frequency polygon, how are the points joined?
   (a) Using straight lines
   (b) Using rectangles
   (c) Using dotted lines
   (d) Using free-hand curves

8. Which of the following graphs uses both less-than and more-than ogives?
   (a) Time series graph (b) Histogram
   (c) Comparison graph (d) Median graph

Answers 1. (b) 2. (a) 3. (d) 4. (b) 5. (c) 6. (c) 7. (a) 8. (d)

Short Answer Type Questions

9. List and explain any three objectives of tabulation of data.

10. "Diagrammatic presentation makes complex information easier to understand and attractive." Do you agree? Give reasons.

11. What is a frequency polygon?

12. How is one variable graph constructed? Give steps with an example.

Long Answer Type Questions

13. Describe the procedure of drawing a histogram when class interval are equal and unequal.

14. What are bar diagrams? Explain the different types of bar diagrams.

15. What is a pie diagram? Give the steps in the construction of a pie diagram.

Numerical Questions

16. Percentage distribution of exports of India is given below. Construct a pie diagram using this data.

Commodity Group	Agriculture	Minerals	Manufactured Goods	Petroleum Products	Others	Total
Export (in %)	18	12	50	14	6	100

17. Draw a pie diagram to represent the following information of expenditure.

Items of Expenditure	Food	Education	Housing	Miscellaneous
Total Expenditure (in %)	60	20	05	15

18. Represent the following data with the help of multiple bar diagram.

Year	2009	2010	2011	2012
Export (₹ in crore)	73	80	85	80
Import (₹ in crore)	70	72	75	75

19. Rearrange the following blank table with a view to make it more intelligible.

Sex	Brahmin		Rajput		Vaish		Harijan	
	Literate	Illiterate	Literate	Illiterate	Literate	Illiterate	Literate	Illiterate
Males	...	...	...	...	...	...	...	...
Females	...	...	...	...	...	...	...	...

20. Draw a frequency polygon using mid-values from the following table.

Marks	0-10	10-20	20-30	30-40	40-50	50-60
Number of Students	5	12	15	22	14	4

21. Represent the following data by a graph using false base line.

Year	2001	2002	2003	2004	2005	2006	2007	2008	2009	2010
Sales (in ₹ '000)	25	28	30	26	21	35	30	23	16	38

22. From the following distribution, construct the 'less-than ogive'.

Capital (in lakhs)	10-20	20-30	30-40	40-50	50-60
Number of Companies	7	11	15	7	23

23. Draw the histogram of daily earnings of 70 workers in a factory which are given below.

Daily Earnings (in ₹)	60-70	70-80	80-90	90-100	100-110
Number of Workers	5	10	30	15	5

24. The following data are the sale figures of LEDs of Firm A, during 2010 to 2013.

Year	2010	2011	2012	2013
Sale (in thousand units)	2,155	2,201	2,250	2,190

Plot the data on time series graph.

25. Make a frequency curve of the following data.

Age (in year)	0-10	10-20	20-30	30-40	40-50	50-60	60-70
Number of Residents	150	300	500	800	500	400	100

05

CHAPTER

> An average is a single value within the range of data that is used to represent all the values in the series. Since an average is somewhere within the range of the data, it is also called a measure of central value.
>
> *—Croxton and Cowden*

YOUR STUDY GOALS

YOUR PRACTICE GOAL

- Objective Type Questions (55 Qs ; MCQs, A-R, Statements, Matching, Concept Identification)
- Subjective Questions (10 SAs, 8 LAs)
- 20 Numerical Questions
- Self Assessment Test (8 MCQs, 4 SAs, 2 LAs, 6 Numerical)

Measures of Central Tendency : Arithmetic Mean

5.1 Meaning of Central Tendency

Central tendency refers to a statistical technique where a single value represents an entire dataset, often termed as 'average' or 'measure of location'. This value is central because most observations fall closer than to any other value.

Objectives and Functions of Central Tendency

- It simplifies data presentation by reducing a large dataset to a single, comprehensible figure.
- It facilitates comparison across different datasets.
- It assists in decision-making by providing a benchmark figure for policy-makers.
- It helps in establishing the relationship between variables.
- It enables further mathematical analysis of data.

Requisites of a Good Average

It should be

- clearly or rigidly defined.
- based on all data points in the series.
- least affected by changes in data contained in a series.
- capable of further mathematical treatment.
- least affected by extreme values.
- certain and reliable in nature.

Types of Central Tendency

Following are the types of central tendency described below

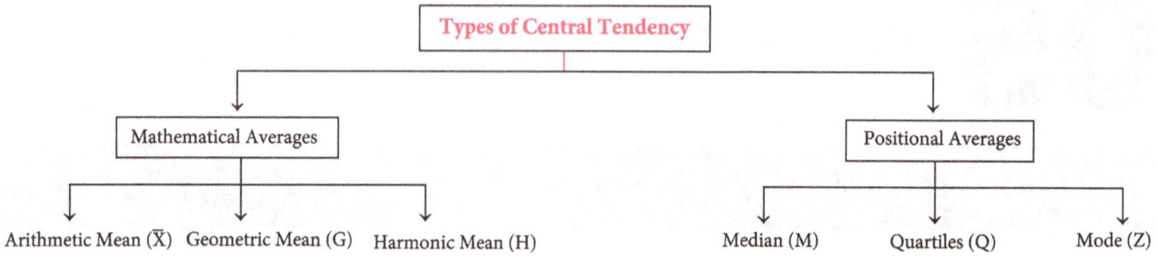

In the present chapter, we will discuss about arithmetic mean.

5.2 Arithmetic Mean

This is the most widely used measure of central tendency, representing the average value of a dataset. It is calculated by summing all the values in a dataset and dividing by the number of observations. It is commonly referred to as the 'mean' or 'average' and is usually denoted by ($\bar{X}$).

Types of Arithmetic Mean

1. **Simple Arithmetic Mean** It treats all items in a series with equal importance.
2. **Weighted Arithmetic Mean** It assigns different weights to items based on their relative importance, making it more relevant for data where some items are more significant than others.

Calculation of Simple Arithmetic Mean

Arithmetic mean can be computed for individual, discrete and continuous series.

Arithmetic Mean for Individual Series

It is also known as **ungrouped data**, where each item appears separately as an individual unit.

The arithmetic mean for this series can be computed by the following methods

1. Direct Method

Arithmetic mean by direct method is calculated by taking sum of all observations in a series and dividing it by the total number of observations.

$$\text{Arithmetic Mean } (\bar{X}) = \frac{\Sigma X}{n}$$

Here, $\Sigma X = \text{Sum of all observations} = X_1 + X_2 + X_3 \ldots\ldots\ldots X_n$

$n = \text{Number of observations or terms}$

Solved Question 1 **Calculate arithmetic mean from the data showing marks of students in a class in an Economics test 30, 40, 45, 68, 48.**

Sol. $\text{Arithmetic Mean } (\bar{X}) = \frac{\Sigma X}{n} \text{ or } \frac{X_1 + X_2 + X_3 + \ldots + X_n}{n} \Rightarrow \bar{X} = \frac{30 + 40 + 45 + 68 + 48}{5} = \frac{231}{5}$

$\Rightarrow \quad \bar{X} = 46.2$

The average marks of students in Economics test is 46.2.

2. Assumed Mean Method

When dealing with a large number of observations, calculating the arithmetic mean using direct method is difficult. So, to save time, the assumed mean method can be used. This method involves the following steps

Step 1 Select a specific value from the dataset and assume it as the assumed mean (A). Assumed mean can also be a number that is not present in the series.

Step 2 Determine the deviation of each observation (X) from the assumed mean using the formula $dx = X - A$.

Step 3 Find the sum of all deviations to find the total deviation (Σdx).

Step 4 Use the following formula to compute the arithmetic mean

$$\overline{X} = A + \frac{\Sigma dx}{n}$$

Here, $\overline{X}$ = Arithmetic mean, A = Assumed mean, Σdx = Sum of deviations of A from individual observations, i.e. $\Sigma(X - A)$, n = Number of observations.

Note Step deviation method is usually not applicable in case of individual series as there is no common factor present.

Solved Question 2 **Calculate the arithmetic mean of marks of 6 students by assumed mean or short-cut method. Marks obtained (X)**

50, 54, 56, 58, 59, 60

Sol. Let, assumed mean $A = 54$

Then we have the following table

Calculation of Arithmetic Mean

S.No.	Marks Obtained (X)	$dx(X - A)$ $A = 54$	
1	50	−4	−4
2	54 = A	0	
3	56	+2	+17
4	58	+4	
5	59	+5	
6	60	+6	
$n = 6$		$\Sigma dx = +13$	

Now, $n = 6$, $\Sigma dx = +13$, $A = 54$

Then, $\overline{X} = A + \frac{\Sigma dx}{n} = 54 + \frac{13}{6}$

$= 54 + 2.17 = 56.17$

Hence, required arithmetic mean = 56.17

Arithmetic Mean for Discrete Series

In a discrete series, items are represented alongwith their respective frequencies. It is referred to as **grouped data**. The arithmetic mean in this series can be calculated using following methods

Direct Method	Assumed Mean Method (or Short-cut Method)	Step Deviation Method
Step 1 Multiply each observation (X) by its frequency (f) to get the product fX, then find the sum products as ΣfX. ***Step 2*** Calculate the sum of frequencies and denote it as Σf. ***Step 3*** Compute the arithmetic mean ($\overline{X}$) using the formula $\overline{X} = \frac{\Sigma fX}{\Sigma f}$ Here, ΣfX = Sum of the product of observations and corresponding frequencies Σf = Sum of frequencies	***Step 1*** Choose an assumed mean (A) from the observations (X) (preferably the mid-value). ***Step 2*** Calculate the deviation of variable X from the assumed mean as $dx = X - A$. ***Step 3*** Multiply these deviations by their corresponding frequencies and sum them up to get Σfdx. ***Step 4*** Calculate the arithmetic mean ($\overline{X}$) using the formula $\overline{X} = A + \frac{\Sigma fdx}{\Sigma f}$ Here, A = Assumed mean Σf = Sum of frequencies Σfdx = Sum of the products of frequency and deviation from assumed mean	It is a simplified version of assumed mean method. It is used where difference in size of items is equal or where deviations are divisible by a common factor. Steps to be followed here are ***Step 1 & 2*** Same as in the case of assumed mean method. ***Step 3*** Divide the deviation (dx) by a common factor (c) to get $d'x = \frac{dx}{c}$ ***Step 4*** Multiply each step deviation by its frequency to compute $fd'x$. ***Step 5*** Sum up the product of step deviations and frequencies $\Sigma fd'x$. ***Step 6*** Calculate the arithmetic mean ($\overline{X}$) using the formula $\overline{X} = A + \frac{\Sigma fd'x}{\Sigma f} \times c$ Here, $\Sigma fd'x$ = Sum of product of step deviations with frequency c = Common factor; A = Assumed mean Σf = Sum of frequencies

Solved Question 3 **Calculate mean farm size of cultivating households in a village from the following data**

Farm Size (in acre)	Number of Cultivating Households
64	8
63	18
62	12
61	9
60	7
59	6

Sol. **Calculation of Arithmetic Mean**

Farm Size (in acre) (X)	Number of Cultivating Households (f)	fX
64	8	512
63	18	1,134
62	12	744
61	9	549
60	7	420
59	6	354
	$\Sigma f = 60$	$\Sigma fX = 3{,}713$

$$\therefore \quad \overline{X} = \frac{\Sigma fX}{\Sigma f} = \frac{3{,}713}{60} = 61.88 \text{ acre}$$

Solved Question 4 **Calculate arithmetic mean by assumed mean or short-cut method from the data given in previous example.**

Sol. Let Assumed mean $(A) = 62$

Calculation of Arithmetic Mean

Farm Size (in acre) (X)	Number of Cultivating Households (f)	dx (X − A) (A = 62)	fdx	
64	8	+2	+16	+34
63	18	+1	+18	
62 = A	12	0	0	
61	9	−1	−9	−41
60	7	−2	−14	
59	6	−3	−18	
	$\Sigma f = 60$		$\Sigma fdx = -7$	

$$\text{Now, } \overline{X} = A + \frac{\Sigma fdx}{\Sigma f} = 62 + \frac{(-7)}{60} = 62 + (-0.12) = 61.88 \text{ acre}$$

Solved Question 5 **Wage rate of 19 workers is given below**

Wages (in ₹)	Number of Workers
10	4
15	5
20	3
25	2
30	5

Calculate arithmetic mean using step deviation method.

Sol. Let the assumed mean $(A) = 20$ and common factor $(c) = 5$

Calculation of Arithmetic Mean

Wages (in ₹) (X)	Number of Workers (f)	dx (X−A) (A = 20)	$d'x\left(\frac{dx}{c}\right)$ c = 5	Product of Step Deviation and Frequency (i.e. fd′x)	
10	4	−10	−2	−8	−13
15	5	−5	−1	−5	
20 = A	3	0	0	0	+12
25	2	5	+1	+2	
30	5	10	+2	+10	
	$\Sigma f = 19$			$\Sigma fd'x = -1$	

Here, $A = 20$, $c = 5$, $\Sigma f = 19$, $\Sigma fd'x = -1$

On putting these values in the formula, we get

$$\overline{X} = A + \frac{\Sigma fd'x}{\Sigma f} \times c = 20 + \left(\frac{-1}{19}\right) \times 5$$

$$= 20 + (-0.26)$$

$$= 19.74$$

Hence, required arithmetic mean $(\overline{X}) = 19.74$

Arithmetic Mean for Continuous Series

In continuous series data, values are organised into different class intervals alongwith their corresponding frequencies. To calculate the arithmetic mean for such data, mid-points of these intervals are used in place of the intervals themselves.

This approach simplifies the calculation, making it similar to that used for discrete data, regardless of whether the class intervals are exclusive, inclusive or of varying sizes.

The arithmetic mean in this series can be calculated using following methods

Direct Method	Assumed Mean Method (or Short-Cut Method)	Step Deviation Method
Step 1 Compute the mid-value of each class interval using the formula Mid-value $(m) = \dfrac{\text{Lower Limit} + \text{Upper Limit}}{2}$ ***Step 2*** Multiply each mid-value (m) by its corresponding frequency (f) to get fm. ***Step 3*** Calculate the sum of these products (Σfm) and the sum of frequencies (Σf). ***Step 4*** Compute the arithmetic mean $(\overline{X})$ using the formula $\overline{X} = \dfrac{\Sigma fm}{\Sigma f}$ Here, Σfm = Sum of product of mid-value and frequencies Σf = Sum of frequencies	***Step 1*** Determine the mid-value (m) of each class interval and choose an assumed mean (A) from these mid-values. ***Step 2*** Compute the deviation of each mid-value from the assumed mean i.e. $dm = m - A$. ***Step 3*** Multiply each deviation by its corresponding frequency and sum these products Σfdm. ***Step 4*** Calculate the arithmetic mean $(\overline{X})$ using the formula $\overline{X} = A + \dfrac{\Sigma fdm}{\Sigma f}$ Here, A = Assumed mean Σfdm = Sum of product of frequency and deviations of mid-values from assumed mean Σf = Sum of frequencies or sum of observations	***Step 1*** Compute the mid-values (m) and choose an assumed mean (A), similar to the assumed mean method. ***Step 2*** Determine a common factor (c) for the class intervals. ***Step 3*** Calculate step deviations i.e. $d'm = \dfrac{m - A}{c}$ ***Step 4*** Multiply each step deviation by its frequency to get $fd'm$ and find their sum $\Sigma fd'm$ and also sum of frequencies as Σf. ***Step 5*** Calculate the arithmetic mean $(\overline{X})$ using the formula $\overline{X} = A + \dfrac{\Sigma fd'm}{\Sigma f} \times c$ Here, A = Assumed mean $\Sigma fd'm$ = Sum product of frequency and step deviations of mid-values from assumed mean c = Common factor or width of class interval Σf = Sum of frequencies

Solved Question 6 **From the following data calculate arithmetic mean by direct method.**

Marks	10-20	20-30	30-40	40-50	50-60	60-70	70-80
Number of Students	2	7	10	15	20	16	6

Sol. **Calculation of Arithmetic Mean**

Marks	Number of Students (f)	Mid-value (m)	fm
10-20	2	15	30
20-30	7	25	175
30-40	10	35	350
40-50	15	45	675
50-60	20	55	1,100
60-70	16	65	1,040
70-80	6	75	450
	$\Sigma f = 76$		$\Sigma fm = 3{,}820$

Now, $\overline{X} = \dfrac{\Sigma fm}{\Sigma f} \Rightarrow \overline{X} = \dfrac{3{,}820}{76} = 50.26$

Hence, required arithmetic mean $= 50.26$

Solved Question 7 **Calculate arithmetic mean by assumed mean method from the data given in previous example.**

Sol. Let assumed mean $(A) = 45$

Calculation of Arithmetic Mean

Marks	Number of Students (f)	Mid-value (m)	$dm\,(m - A)$ $A = 45$	fdm	
10-20	2	15	−30	−60	
20-30	7	25	−20	−140	−300
30-40	10	35	−10	−100	
40-50	15	$45 = A$	0	0	
50-60	20	55	+10	+200	
60-70	16	65	+20	+320	+700
70-80	6	75	+30	+180	
	$\Sigma f = 76$			$\Sigma fdm = +400$	

Now, $\overline{X} = A + \frac{\Sigma fdm}{\Sigma f} = 45 + \frac{400}{76}$

$= 45 + 5.26 = 50.26$

Solved Question 8 **Calculate mean marks of the following students using step deviation method.**

Marks	Number of Students
0-10	5
10-20	12
20-30	15
30-40	25
40-50	8
50-60	3
60-70	2

Sol. Let assumed mean $(A) = 35$ and width of class intervals $(c) = 10$

Calculation of Arithmetic Mean

Marks	Number of Students (f)	Mid-value (m)	$dm\,(m-A)$ $A=35$	$d'm\left(\frac{dm}{c}\right)$ $(c=10)$	$fd'm$	
0-10	5	5	−30	−3	−15	
10-20	12	15	−20	−2	−24	−54
20-30	15	25	−10	−1	−15	
30-40	25	$35 = A$	0	0	0	
40-50	8	45	10	1	+8	
50-60	3	55	20	2	+6	+20
60-70	2	65	30	3	+6	
	$\Sigma f = 70$				$\Sigma fd'm = -34$	

Now, $\overline{X} = A + \frac{\Sigma fd'm}{\Sigma f} \times c \Rightarrow \overline{X} = 35 + \frac{(-34)}{70} \times 10$

$\Rightarrow \quad \overline{X} = 35 + (-4.86) = 30.14$

Hence, required arithmetic mean $= 30.14$

5.3 Certain Specific Conditions of Mean

Certain specific conditions related to Arithmetic Mean (A.M.) are discussed below

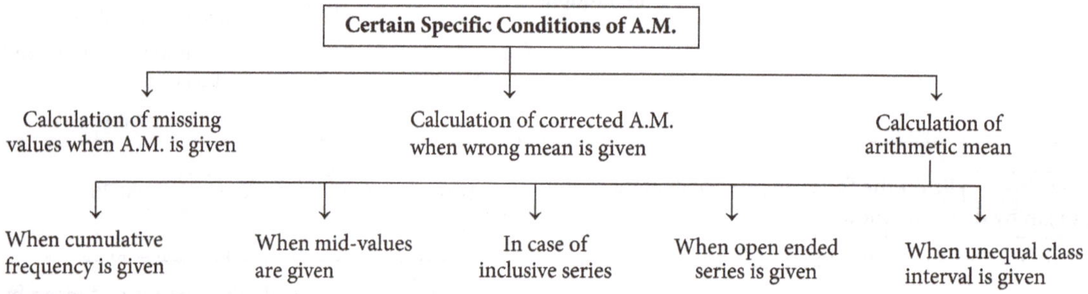

Calculation of Missing Values when Arithmetic Mean is Given

When the arithmetic mean of a dataset is given but one value is missing, the missing value can be determined using the formula for the mean. Rearranging the mean formula helps to solve for the missing value. This is done by multiplying the mean by the total number of observations (including the missing one) and then subtracting the sum of the known values.

Solved Question 9 **Suppose mean of a series of 5 items is 60. Four values are 10, 25, 30 and 35 respectively. Find the missing 5th value of the series.**

Sol. Let 5th value be X_5

Given, $X_1 = 10,\ X_2 = 25,\ X_3 = 30,\ X_4 = 35,\ X_5 = ?$,

$\overline{X} = 60, n = 5$

Now, $\overline{X} = \frac{X_1 + X_2 + X_3 + X_4 + X_5}{n}$

$\Rightarrow \quad 60 = \frac{10 + 25 + 30 + 35 + X_5}{5}$

or $\quad 60 = \frac{100 + X_5}{5}$

$\Rightarrow \quad 60 \times 5 = 100 + X_5$

$\Rightarrow \quad 300 = 100 + X_5$

$\Rightarrow \quad X_5 = 300 - 100 = 200$

Thus, value of the 5th item $= 200$

Calculation of Corrected Arithmetic Mean when Wrong Mean is Given

Sometimes, in the calculation of arithmetic mean, some wrong items or values may be taken for calculation.

Accordingly, the mean so computed will also be wrong. Such mean value can be corrected with the help of following formula

$$\overline{X} = \frac{\Sigma X(\text{Wrong}) + (\text{Correct Value}) - (\text{Incorrect Value})}{n}$$

Here, Wrong Mean = Initially calculated mean, Correct Value = Accurate value that should have been included, Incorrect Value = Erroneous value and n = Number of observations. This adjustment aligns the mean with the corrected data.

Solved Question 10 **Mean marks obtained by 100 students are estimated to be 40. Later on it is found that one value was read as 83 instead of 53. Find out the 'corrected' mean.**

Sol. Given, $\overline{X} = 40$, $n = 100$

Now, $\overline{X} = \frac{\Sigma X}{n} \Rightarrow 40 = \frac{\Sigma X}{100}$

$\Rightarrow \Sigma X \text{ (wrong)} = 40 \times 100 = 4{,}000$

Also given, correct value = 53, incorrect value = 83

$\therefore$ Correct $\overline{X}$

$$= \frac{\Sigma X(\text{Wrong}) + (\text{Correct value}) - (\text{Incorrect value})}{n}$$

$$= \frac{4{,}000 + 53 - 83}{100} = \frac{3{,}970}{100} = 39.70$$

Thus, corrected mean = 39.70

Solved Question 11 **The average age of a class having 30 students is 15 years. When the age of the class teacher is added to the total sum of ages of students, average of whole class rose up by 0.5 years.**
Calculate the age of the teacher.

Sol. Total number of students = 30

Average age = 15

$\therefore$ Sum total of ages of all the students = $30 \times 15 = 450$

Total number of students and class teacher = 31

New Average age = 15.5

$\therefore$ Sum total of age of all the students including class teacher = $31 \times 15.5 = 480.5$

$\therefore$ Age of class teacher = $480.5 - 450$

= 30.5 years

Calculation of Arithmetic Mean in Certain Situations

Situation	Explanation
When Cumulative Frequency is Given	If cumulative frequency is given, then the series will be converted into simple frequency series and after that the arithmetic mean will be calculated, by using either of the methods discussed above. The cumulative frequencies series can be 'less-than' or 'more-than'.
When Mid-values are Given	When mid-values (or class marks) of class intervals are provided, calculate the arithmetic mean using these mid-values directly. This simplifies the process because there is no need to compute mid-points from class limits. Just multiply each mid-value by its corresponding frequency, sum these products and divide by the total frequency to get the mean.
In Case of Inclusive Series	For continuous data with inclusive class intervals, there is no need to convert them to exclusive intervals. The mid-values used for calculations are unaffected by whether intervals are inclusive or exclusive. Use the mid-values directly to calculate the mean, as the calculations will yield accurate results without conversion.
When Open Ended Series is Given	In open ended series where the extreme class limits are missing, estimate the mean by assuming the missing limits based on the pattern of the other class intervals. This involves using reasonable assumptions about the class limits to complete the data and then calculating the mean.
When Unequal Class Interval is Given	When dealing with unequal class intervals, calculate the mean by finding the mid-values of each interval. Despite the intervals being unequal, the arithmetic mean can be computed using standard methods once mid-values and frequencies are determined. No special adjustments are necessary for the varying interval sizes.

Solved Question 12 **Calculate arithmetic mean with the help of following data using step deviation method.**

Marks (Less than)	10	20	30	40	50	60
Number of Students	3	10	20	25	28	30

Sol. First of all, convert the less than cumulative frequency series into an ordinary series and then calculate the value of arithmetic mean.

Calculation of Arithmetic Mean

Marks	Frequency (f)	Mid-value (m)	$dm = m - A$ ($A = 25$)	$d'm = \frac{dm}{c}$ ($c = 10$)	$fd'm$	
0-10	3	5	−20	−2	−6	
10-20	10−3 = 7	15	−10	−1	−7	−13
20-30	20−10 = 10	25 = A	0	0	0	
30-40	25−20 = 5	35	+10	+1	+5	
40-50	28−25 = 3	45	+20	+2	+6	17
50-60	30−28 = 2	55	+30	+3	+6	
	$\Sigma f = 30$				$\Sigma fd'm = +4$	

Now, $\overline{X} = A + \frac{\Sigma fd'm}{\Sigma f} \times c = 25 + \frac{4}{30} \times 10$

$= 25 + 1.33 = 26.33$

Hence, required arithmetic mean = 26.33

Solved Question 13 **Calculate arithmetic mean with the help of following data using step deviation method.**

Marks (More than)	0	10	20	30	40	50
Number of Students	30	27	20	10	5	2

Sol. First of all, convert the more-than cumulative frequency series into ordinary one and then calculate the value of arithmetic mean.

Marks	Frequency (f)	Mid-value (m)	$dm = m - A$ ($A = 25$)	$d'm = dm/c$ ($c = 10$)	$fd'm$	
0-10	30 − 27 = 3	5	−20	−2	−6	−13
10-20	27 − 20 = 7	15	−10	−1	−7	
20-30	20 − 10 = 10	25 = A	0	0	0	
30-40	10 − 5 = 5	35	10	1	+5	
40-50	5 − 2 = 3	45	20	2	+6	+17
50-60	2	55	30	3	+6	
	$\Sigma f = 30$				$\Sigma fd'm = +4$	

Now, $\overline{X} = A + \frac{\Sigma fd'm}{\Sigma f} \times c = 25 + \frac{4}{30} \times 10 = 25 + 1.33 = 26.33$

Solved Question 14 **Following table gives marks in Statistics of the students of class XI. Find out mean marks using direct method.**

Mid-value	5	10	15	20	25	30
Number of Students	5	7	9	10	8	6

Sol. In this series, mid-values are given. The calculation of arithmetic mean involves the same procedure as in the case of exclusive series.

Calculation of Arithmetic Mean

Mid-value (m)	Number of Students (f)	fm
5	5	25
10	7	70
15	9	135
20	10	200
25	8	200
30	6	180
	$\Sigma f = 45$	$\Sigma fm = 810$

$$\overline{X} = \frac{\Sigma fm}{\Sigma f} = \frac{810}{45} = 18$$

Hence, required arithmetic mean = 18 marks

Solved Question 15 **Calculate arithmetic mean from the following data using step deviation method.**

Size	10-19	20-29	30-39	40-49	50-59
Frequency	10	8	6	4	2

Sol. Here given series is inclusive

Let assumed mean, $(A) = 24.5$ and $c = 10$

Calculation of Arithmetic Mean

Class Interval	Frequency (f)	Mid-value (m)	$d = m - A$ ($A = 24.5$)	$d'm = dm/c$ ($c = 10$)	$fd'm$	
10-19	10	14.5	−10	−1	−10	−10
20-29	8	24.5	0	0	0	
30-39	6	34.5	+10	+1	+6	
40-49	4	44.5	+20	+2	+8	+20
50-59	2	54.5	+30	+3	+6	
	$\Sigma f = 30$				$\Sigma fd'm = +10$	

Now, $\overline{X} = A + \frac{\Sigma fd'm}{\Sigma f} \times c = 24.5 + \frac{10}{30} \times 10$

$\Rightarrow \quad = 24.5 + \frac{100}{30} = 24.5 + 3.33 = 27.83$

Hence, required arithmetic mean = 27.83

Solved Question 16 Calculate arithmetic mean from the following data

Wages (in ₹)	Less than 100	100-200	200-300	300-400	Above 500
No. of Workers	06	15	12	05	04

Sol. In the above situation, as the class interval is uniform, i.e. 100, so we will consider the same interval for extreme values.

Calculation of Arithmetic Mean

Wages (in ₹)	No. of Workers (f)	Mid-value (m)	fm
0-100	06	50	300
100-200	15	150	2,250
200-300	12	250	3,000
300-400	05	350	1,750
400-500	04	450	1,800
	$\Sigma f = 42$		$\Sigma fm = 9{,}100$

$$\overline{X} = \frac{\Sigma fm}{f} = \frac{9{,}100}{42} = 216.67$$

Solved Question 17 Calculate arithmetic mean from the following data

Marks	0-10	10-30	30-40	40-70	70-80
No. of Students	08	12	30	06	04

Sol. **Calculation of Arithmetic Mean**

Marks	No. of Students (f)	Mid-value (m)	fm
0-10	08	05	40
10-30	12	20	240
30-40	30	35	1,050
40-70	06	55	330
70-80	04	75	300
	$\Sigma f = 60$		$\Sigma fm = 1{,}960$

$$\overline{X} = \frac{\Sigma fm}{\Sigma f} = \frac{1{,}960}{60} = 32.67$$

5.4 Calculation of Weighted Arithmetic Mean

The weighted arithmetic mean is used when items in a dataset do not have equal importance. Unlike the simple arithmetic mean, which treats each item with the same significance, the weighted arithmetic mean assigns different weights to items based on their importance or relevance.

This method is particularly useful when some data points are more influential than others in determining the average.

Following steps are used to calculate weighted arithmetic mean

Step 1 Determine the significance of each item in the dataset and assign weights accordingly. Each weight represents the relative importance of an item and is denoted by 'W'.

Step 2 For each item (X), multiply it by its corresponding weight (W) to get the weighted value and find their sum i.e. ΣXW.

Step 3 Divide the total weighted sum ΣXW by the total sum of weights ΣW, to get required weighted mean, i.e.

$$\overline{X}w = \frac{\Sigma XW}{\Sigma W}$$

where, $\overline{X}w$ = Weighted arithmetic mean

ΣW = Sum of weights

ΣWX = Sum of product of items and weights

Solved Question 18 Find out the weighted arithmetic mean from the following data

Books	Price per Book	Number Sold
Statistics (S)	20	40
Physics (P)	30	25
Economics (E)	15	12
Commerce (C)	25	13
Chemistry (Ch)	25	10

Sol. **Calculation of Weighted Arithmetic Mean**

Books	Price per Book (X)	Number Sold (W)	XW
S	20	40	800
P	30	25	750
E	15	12	180
C	25	13	325
Ch	25	10	250
		$\Sigma W = 100$	$\Sigma XW = 2{,}305$

Now, $\overline{X}w = \frac{\Sigma XW}{\Sigma W} = \frac{2{,}305}{100} = 23.05$

Hence, required weighted arithmetic mean = 23.05

5.5 Combined Arithmetic Mean

If the mean of two or more groups and the number of items of each group are given, then combined mean of all the series can be calculated with the help of following formula

$$\text{Combined mean } (\overline{X}_{1,2,3,\ldots,n}) = \frac{n_1 \cdot \overline{X}_1 + n_2 \cdot \overline{X}_2 + n_3 \cdot \overline{X}_3 + \ldots n_n \overline{X}_n}{n_1 + n_2 + n_3 \ldots n}$$

Here, $\overline{X}_{1,2,3\ldots n}$ = Combined arithmetic mean of n series
$\overline{X}_1$ = Arithmetic mean of series 1 ; $\overline{X}_2$ = Arithmetic mean of series 2 ; $\overline{X}_3$ = Arithmetic mean of series 3;
$\overline{X}_n$ = Arithmetic mean of series n ; n_1 = Number of items in series 1; n_2 = Number of items in series 2 ;
n_3 = Number of items in series 3 ; n_n = Number of items in series n.

Solved Question 19 **If 8 students average 100 kg in weight and 12 students average 90 kg, find the combined arithmetic mean of all the 20 students.**

Sol. Here, $n_1 = 8,\ \overline{X}_1 = 100,\ n_2 = 12,\ \overline{X}_2 = 90$

Then $\overline{X}_{1,2} = \dfrac{n_1\overline{X}_1 + n_2\overline{X}_2}{n_1 + n_2}$

$$= \frac{8 \times 100 + 12 \times 90}{8 + 12} = \frac{800 + 1{,}080}{20} = \frac{1{,}880}{20} = 94$$

Hence, combined arithmetic mean = 94 kg

Solved Question 20 **In a certain town, there are three factories A, B and C with number of workers being 100, 80 and 200 respectively with average wages being ₹ 500, ₹ 800 and ₹ 600 respectively. Find the combined mean of the factories taken together.**

Sol. Given

Factories	No. of Workers (n)	Mean ($\overline{X}$)
A	100	500
B	80	800
C	200	600

$$\text{Combined Mean } \overline{X}_{A,B,C} = \frac{n_A \cdot \overline{X}_A + n_B \cdot \overline{X}_B + n_C \cdot \overline{X}_C}{n_A + n_B + n_C}$$

$$= \frac{(100 \times 500) + (80 \times 800) + (200 \times 600)}{100 + 80 + 200}$$

$$= \frac{50{,}000 + 64{,}000 + 1{,}20{,}000}{380} = \frac{2{,}34{,}000}{380} = 615.78$$

5.6 Properties of Arithmetic Mean

- The sum of deviations of the observations from their arithmetic mean is always zero.
- The sum of the squares of deviations of the items from their mean is minimum.
- If the arithmetic mean and the number of items of two or more than two related groups are given, then one can calculate combined mean.
- If each observation of a series is increased or decreased by a constant number or value, then the mean of the series will also increase or decrease by that number or value.
- If all the items in a series are multiplied or divided by a constant number or value, then mean of these items also gets multiplied or divided by that number or value.

Merits of Arithmetic Mean

- It is easy to calculate and understand.
- It is rigidly defined and based on all items in the series.
- It is least affected by sample fluctuations.
- It is capable of further algebraic treatment.
- It is suitable for comparison across different datasets.
- It provides a single value that summarises the entire dataset.

Demerits of Arithmetic Mean

- It is sensitive to extreme values (outliers).
- It cannot be calculated for open ended series.
- It provides only a summary measure and may not fully represent the data.
- It is not applicable to qualitative data.
- It cannot be determined graphically.
- Sometimes it gives impractical results, such as fractional counts.

Mind Map

MEASURES OF CENTRAL TENDENCY: ARITHMETIC MEAN

1 Meaning of Central Tendency

It is a statistical technique where a single value represents an entire dataset, often termed as 'average' or 'measure of location'.

Objectives and Functions
- Simplifies large datasets
- Facilitates comparison across datasets
- Helps in decision-making
- Enables further mathematical analysis

Requisites of a Good Average
- Clearly defined
- Based on all data points
- Not heavily affected by extreme values
- Can be used for further calculation

2 Arithmetic Mean

This is the most widely used measure of central tendency representing the average value of a dataset. It is denoted as $\overline{X}$.

Types of Arithmetic Mean
- Simple arithmetic mean (equal importance to all values)
- Weighted arithmetic mean (assign different weights based on relative importance)

3 Arithmetic Mean for Individual Series

It is also known as ungrouped data. In this series, arithmetic mean can be computed by following methods
- **Direct Method**

  Arithmetic Mean $(\overline{X}) = \frac{\Sigma X}{n}$
- **Assumed Mean Method**

  $X = A + \frac{\Sigma dx}{n}$

4 Arithmetic Mean for Discrete Series

Items are represented along with their respective frequencies. It is referred to as grouped data. Following methods can be used
- **Direct Method** $\overline{X} = \frac{\Sigma fX}{\Sigma f}$
- **Assumed Mean Method** $\overline{X} = A + \frac{\Sigma fdx}{\Sigma f}$
- **Step Deviation Method** $\overline{X} = A + \frac{\Sigma fd'x}{\Sigma f} \times c$

5 Arithmetic Mean for Continuous Series

Values are organised into different class intervals along with their corresponding frequencies. For calculation, mid-points of these intervals are used in place of the intervals themselves. Following methods can be used
- **Direct Method** $\overline{X} = \frac{\Sigma fm}{\Sigma f}$
- **Assumed Mean Method** $\overline{X} = A + \frac{\Sigma fdm}{\Sigma f}$
- **Step Deviation Method** $\overline{X} = A + \frac{\Sigma fd'm}{\Sigma f} \times c$

6 Special Cases in Arithmetic Mean

Calculation of Missing Values
- When arithmetic mean is given but one value is missing.
- Formula

  Missing Value = (Mean × Total Observation) – Sum of known Values

Corrected Arithmetic Mean when Wrong Mean is Given
- It is used when incorrect data affects the mean.
- Formula

$$\overline{X} = \frac{\Sigma X(\text{Wrong}) + (\text{Correct Value}) - (\text{Incorrect Value})}{n}$$

When Cumulative Frequency is Given
- Convert to a simple frequency series before calculation.

When Mid-values are Given
- Directly use mid-values to find the mean.

In Case of Inclusive Series
- No need to convert inclusive intervals to exclusive.

When Open Ended Series is Given
- Assume missing class limits based on the pattern of other intervals.

When Unequal Class Intervals are Given
- Calculate mean using mid-values without any special adjustments.

7 Calculation of Weighted Arithmetic Mean

It is used when items have different importance.
Following formula is used

$$\overline{X}_w = \frac{\Sigma XW}{\Sigma W}$$

Combined Arithmetic Mean

It is used to calculate combined mean of two or more groups, using following formula

$$X_{1,2,3,\ldots n} = \frac{n_1\overline{X}_1 + n_2\overline{X}_2 + \ldots + n_n\overline{X}_n}{n_1 + n_2 + \ldots + n_n}$$

8 Properties of Arithmetic Mean

- Sum of deviations from mean is always zero.
- Sum of squared deviations is minimum.
- Affects the mean if values are changed by a constant.
- Mean changes proportionally, if values are multiplied or divided by a constant.
- Combined mean can be calculated for multiple groups.

9 Merits and Demerits of Arithmetic Mean

Merits
- Easy to calculate and understand.
- Rigidly defined and based on all values.
- Least affected by sample fluctuations.
- Suitable for algebraic treatment and comparisons.
- Provides a single representative value.

Demerits
- Affected by extreme values (outliers).
- Cannot be calculated for open ended series.
- May not fully represent the dataset.
- Not applicable to qualitative data.
- Cannot be determined graphically.
- May give impractical fractional results.

EXAM PATTERN QUESTIONS

Objective Type Questions

Multiple Choice Questions (MCQs)

1. Which of the following is not an objective of central tendency?

(a) Simplifies data presentation
(b) Facilitates comparison across datasets
(c) Identifies outliers in the dataset
(d) Assists in decision-making for policy-makers

2. Central tendency helps in .... by providing a benchmark figure for policy-makers.

(a) comparison (b) decision-making
(c) summarisation (d) data collection

3. Which measure of central tendency is highlighted in the below image?

$$\tilde{X}$$

(a) Mode (b) Quartile (c) Median (d) Mean

4. According to Croxton and Cowden, what is an average?

(a) A value that minimises the effects of extreme values
(b) A single figure that summarises the range of data
(c) A single value within a data range that represents all values
(d) A measure of dispersion in a dataset

5. Based upon the image given below, what will be the average number of pizzas?

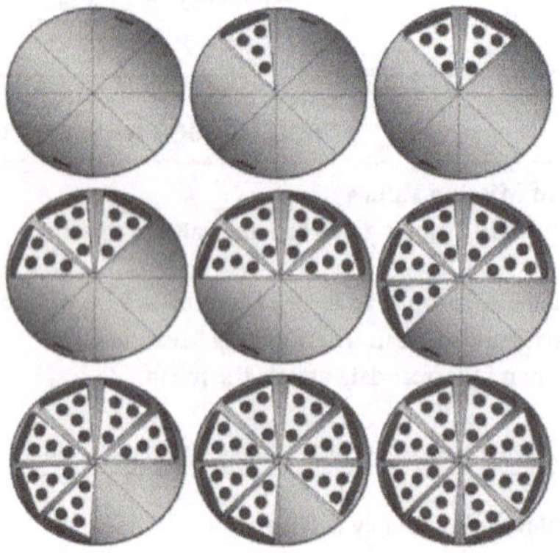

(a) 3.6 (b) 4
(c) 4.6 (d) Can't be determined

6. Identify the correct difference between simple and weighted arithmetic mean.

I. The simple arithmetic mean uses a larger dataset.
II. The weighted arithmetic mean assigns different weights to items.
III. The simple arithmetic mean is always higher in value.
IV. The weighted arithmetic mean is only used in financial data. **Competency Based Que**

Codes
(a) I and II (b) Only II
(c) III and IV (d) Only I

7. In .... arithmetic mean, all values are assumed to be equally important.

(a) simple (b) weighted
(c) combined (d) None of these

8. If the assumed mean (A) is 10 and one of the observations (X) is 14, what is the deviation (dx)? **Competency Based Que**

(a) 4 (b) 2
(c) -4 (d) -2

9. The arithmetic mean using the direct method is calculated by summing all observations in a series and dividing by the ....

(a) sum of deviations
(b) total number of observations
(c) assumed mean (d) highest observation

10. Find the missing figures and choose the correct alternative. **Competency Based Que**

Marks	No. of Students (f)	M	fm
10-20	8	15	...
20-30	9	...	225
30-40	...	35	350
40-50	12	45	...

(a) 120, 20, 11, 540 (b) 120, 25, 10, 540
(c) 80, 20, 10, 500 (d) 150, 30, 11, 480

11. Identify the component that is not needed to calculate the corrected Arithmetic Mean (A.M.) when the wrong mean is given.

I. Wrong mean
II. Number of observations (n)
III. Median of the data
IV. Correct value **Competency Based Que**

Codes
(a) Only III (b) II and IV
(c) I and II (d) Only I

12. **Which of the following measures are indicated by the dark line in the image given below?**

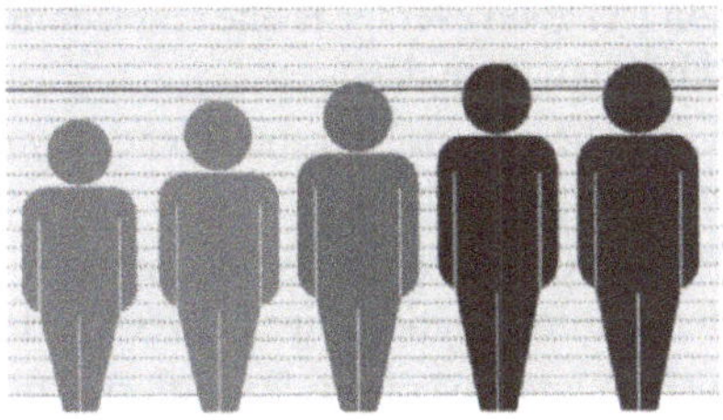

(a) Arithmetic mean (b) Average
(c) Positional average (d) Both (a) and (b)

13. **Look at the following table and identify the type of class intervals used to calculate the mean.**
Competency Based Que

Class Interval	Frequency
0-10	5
10-20	8
20-50	10
50-100	7

(a) Inclusive series (b) Unequal class
(c) Equal class (d) Continuous series

14. **For the class interval 30-40, what is the mid-value?**
Competency Based Que

(a) 35 (b) 28
(c) 30 (d) 32

15. **The weighted arithmetic mean assigns different .... to items based on their importance or relevance.**

(a) frequencies (b) categories
(c) weights (d) ranges

16. **What is the weighted sum of the following data?**
Competency Based Que

Item	Weight
2	3
4	1

(a) 20 (b) 40 (c) 15 (d) 10

17. **Unlike the simple arithmetic mean, which treats each item with the same ...., the weighted arithmetic mean accounts for varying levels of significance among items.**

(a) value (b) weight
(c) importance (d) frequency

18. **If you have the means and number of items for two groups, what is the correct approach to find the combined mean of these groups?**
Competency Based Que

(a) Add the number of items from both groups and find the average of their means
(b) Multiply each group's mean by its number of items, then combine these totals
(c) Simply take the average of the two means
(d) Add the means of both groups and then divide by the total number of items

19. **If there are two groups with mean 10 and 15 and number of items is 6 each, combined mean will be**
Competency Based Que

(a) 12.5 (b) 25
(c) 20 (d) 30

20. **Which property of mean is highlighted in the below table?**
Competency Based Que

Observation	Deviation from Mean
5	−2
7	0
3	2
Total	0

(a) The sum of deviations from the arithmetic mean is always zero
(b) Minimising sum of squared deviations
(c) Effect of adding or subtracting a constant
(d) None of the above

21. **The arithmetic mean is least affected by sample fluctuations and provides a single value that summarises the entire dataset, but it is ....**

(a) sensitive to extreme values
(b) suitable for qualitative data
(c) capable of graphical determination
(d) rigidly defined and based on all items of the series

Direction *Read the case study and answer the questions 22 to 25 on the basis of the same*

In a recent research project, a statistical analysis was performed on the average scores of students across different subjects, the mean income of households in different neighbourhoods and the weighted average of various investment returns.

The study aimed to provide insights into the central tendency of these datasets to help policy-makers and educators make informed decisions.

Scenario

1. **Student Scores** The average scores of students in Mathematics, Science, and English were analysed. The scores were recorded as follows
   (a) **Mathematics** Mean score = 75, Number of students = 30
   (b) **Science** Mean score = 80, Number of students = 25
   (c) **English** Mean score = 70, Number of students = 20
2. **Household Income** The average income of households in three different neighbourhoods was reported
   (a) **Neighbourhood A** Mean income = ₹ 50,000
   (b) **Neighbourhood B** Mean income = ₹ 60,000
   Neighbourhood C Mean income = ₹ 55,000
3. **Investment Returns** The weighted average returns of investments in three sectors were analysed
   (a) **Sector X** Return = 10%, Weight = 40%
   (b) **Sector Y** Return = 8%, Weight = 35%
   (c) **Sector Z** Return = 12%, Weight = 25%

22. **The combined mean score is ....**

23. **In the given research project, what is the primary purpose of analysing the average scores of students across different subjects?**
(a) To determine the range of scores for each subject
(b) To assess the central tendency of the scores to understand overall student performance
(c) To identify the highest and lowest scores in each subject
(d) To compare the variance in scores among subjects.

24. **If you have the mean income of households in neighbourhoods A, B and C and the number of households in each neighbourhood is 50, 60 and 40 respectively, the combined mean income is ....**

25. **Why is the weighted average return important when analysing investment returns across different sectors?**
(a) It shows the average return without considering the sector's importance
(b) It accounts for the varying significance of each sector by incorporating their respective weights
(c) It provides the maximum return achievable from the investments
(d) It determines the least risk associated with each sector

Assertion-Reason

Direction (Q.No. 26 to 35) *Read the following Assertion (A) and Reason (R) and choose the correct alternative from the following*

Alternatives
(a) Both Assertion (A) and Reason (R) are true and Reason (R) is the correct explanation of Assertion (A)
(b) Both Assertion (A) and Reason (R) are true, but Reason (R) is not the correct explanation of Assertion (A)
(c) Assertion (A) is true, but Reason (R) is false
(d) Assertion (A) is false, but Reason (R) is true

26. **Assertion** (A) Central tendency simplifies data presentation by reducing large datasets to a single, comprehensible figure.
Reason (R) The measure of central tendency is used to describe data distribution and helps in understanding relationships between variables.

27. **Assertion** (A) good average is one that is minimally affected by changes in data.
Reason (R) The measure of central tendency can only be used for qualitative data.

28. **Assertion** (A) Central tendency measures are not useful for understanding relationships between variables.
Reason (R) A good average is least affected by extreme values.

29. **Assertion** (A) Arithmetic mean reduces the sampling fluctuations in both symmetric and asymmetric distribution.
Reason (R) Arithmetic mean is a representative of the whole set of observations.

30. **Assertion** (A) The simple arithmetic mean assigns different weights to items based on their importance.
Reason (R) The simple arithmetic mean treats all items in a series with equal importance.

31. **Assertion** (A) The assumed mean method simplifies the calculation process by using assumed mean and calculating deviations from it.
Reason (R) The assumed mean method is particularly useful for large datasets where calculating the arithmetic mean directly is time consuming.

32. **Assertion** (A) The calculation of arithmetic mean for an open ended series involves assuming missing class limits.
Reason (R) This assumption helps in estimating the mean when class limits are not provided.

33. **Assertion** (A) The weighted arithmetic mean is primarily used in educational assessments to average test scores.
Reason (R) The weighted arithmetic mean is more useful when some data points are more influential than others in determining the average.

34. **Assertion** (A) The arithmetic mean is sensitive to extreme values.
Reason (R) The arithmetic mean is calculated by summing all values and dividing by the total number of values, so any extreme value (very high or very low) disproportionately affects the overall result.

35. **Assertion** (A) The combined mean of several groups can be calculated using the means and sample sizes of the groups.
Reason (R) Adding or subtracting a constant value from each observation will shift the mean by that constant.

Two Statements Based MCQs

Direction (Q.No. 36 to 45) *Read the following statements carefully and choose the correct alternative*

Alternatives

(a) Statement I is correct and Statement II is incorrect
(b) Statement II is correct and Statement I is incorrect
(c) Both the statements are correct
(d) Both the statements are incorrect

36. **Statement I** The objective of central tendency is to assist in understanding relationships between variables.

Statement II Central tendency reduces large datasets to multiple figures for easier comprehension.

37. **Statement I** Central tendency is useful for mathematical analysis of data.

Statement II A good average should not be capable of further mathematical manipulation.

38. **Statement I** According to Croxton and Cowden, an average is a single value within a data range that represents all values in the series.

Statement II Clark and Sekkade describe the average as a single figure that summarises all data points.

39. **Statement I** No adjustment is required for calculation of mean in case of mid-value series.

Statement II In order to combine mean of two different series, we simply need to add the average values of two series.

40. **Statement I** The simple arithmetic mean considers all items in a dataset with equal importance.

Statement II The arithmetic mean is calculated by summing all values and dividing by the number of observations.

41. **Statement I** The arithmetic mean for a discrete series can only be calculated using the direct method.

Statement II The assumed mean method and step deviation method are also valid methods for calculating the arithmetic mean for a discrete series.

42. **Statement I** The formula to determine the missing value is derived from multiplying the arithmetic mean by the total number of observations and then subtracting the sum of the known values.

Statement II If one value is missing, the total number of observations should be the number of known values plus one.

43. **Statement I** Arithmetic mean is rigidly defined.

Statement II Assumed mean should always be selected from a given series.

44. **Statement I** The sum of deviations from the arithmetic mean is always positive.

Statement II The arithmetic mean is not applicable to quantitative data.

45. **Statement I** If the mean of two or more groups and the number of items of each group are given, then combined mean of all the series can be calculated.

Statement II The combined arithmetic mean is calculated by considering the weighted average of the means of the individual groups, where the weights are the sample sizes of each group.

Matching

46. Match the following measures of central tendency with their correct symbols

Column I		Column II	
A.	Mean	(i)	Z
B.	Median	(ii)	M
C.	Mode	(iii)	$(\overline{X})$
D.	Quartiles	(iv)	Q

Codes

	A	B	C	D		A	B	C	D
(a)	(iii)	(iv)	(i)	(ii)	(b)	(iv)	(i)	(ii)	(iii)
(c)	(ii)	(iii)	(iv)	(i)	(d)	(iii)	(ii)	(i)	(iv)

47. Match the options of Column I with correct options in Column II

Column I		Column II	
A.	Arithmetic mean	(i)	Assign different importance for different items of series
B.	Combined mean	(ii)	Based upon all items
C.	Corrected mean	(iii)	Gives composite mean
D.	Weighted mean	(iv)	Rectified actual mean

Codes

	A	B	C	D		A	B	C	D
(a)	(ii)	(iv)	(i)	(iii)	(b)	(ii)	(iii)	(iv)	(i)
(c)	(i)	(ii)	(iii)	(iv)	(d)	(iv)	(iii)	(i)	(ii)

48. Match the following

Column I		Column II	
A.	Individual series	(i)	Items classified into class intervals and frequencies
B.	Discrete series	(ii)	Class intervals overlapping their boundaries

Column I		Column II
C. Continuous series	(iii)	Items listed separately
D. Inclusive series	(iv)	Items represented along with frequencies

Codes

	A	B	C	D
(a)	(iii)	(iv)	(i)	(ii)
(b)	(iv)	(i)	(ii)	(iii)
(c)	(ii)	(iii)	(iv)	(i)
(d)	(iii)	(ii)	(i)	(iv)

49. Match the following

Column I		Column II
A. Direct method	(i)	Calculates mean using weighted values for different importance.
B. Assumed mean method	(ii)	Computes mean by summing values and dividing by total count.
C. Step deviation method	(iii)	Uses a guessed mean to simplify deviation calculations.
D. Weighted average method	(iv)	Uses a base value for easier deviation calculations in multiples.

Codes

	A	B	C	D		A	B	C	D
(a)	(iii)	(iv)	(i)	(ii)	(b)	(iv)	(i)	(ii)	(iii)
(c)	(ii)	(iii)	(iv)	(i)	(d)	(iii)	(ii)	(i)	(iv)

50. Match the following

Column I		Column II
A. Deviations	(i)	Σf
B. Sum of frequencies	(ii)	(Lower Limit + Upper Limit)/2
C. Mid-value	(iii)	(m – A)
D. Deviation of mid-value	(iv)	(X – A)

Codes

	A	B	C	D		A	B	C	D
(a)	(iii)	(iv)	(i)	(ii)	(b)	(iv)	(i)	(ii)	(iii)
(c)	(ii)	(iii)	(iv)	(i)	(d)	(iii)	(ii)	(iv)	(i)

Concept Identification

51. It refers to a statistical measure representing a single value to summarise an entire dataset, often termed as the 'average.'

52. It involves calculating the average value of a dataset by summing all values and dividing by the total number of values.

53. This concept is used to compute the arithmetic mean of class intervals by using mid-values.

54. The mean is calculated by summing weighted values of items based on their relative importance.

55. It that involves calculating the mean of multiple groups by considering their sizes and individual means.

Answers

1. (c) Identifies outliers in the dataset
2. (b) decision-making
3. (d) Mean
4. (c) A single value within a data range that represents all values
5. (b) 4
6. (b) Only II
7. (a) simple
8. (a) $dx = X - A = 14 - 10 = 4$
9. (b) total number of observations
10. (b) $fm = f \times m = 8 \times 15 = 120$
    $m = fm/f = 225/9 = 25$
    $(f) = fm/m = 350/35 = 10$
    $fm = f \times m = 12 \times 45 = 540$
11. (a) Only III
12. (d) Both (a) and (b)
13. (b) Unequal class
14. (a) $\dfrac{\text{Lower Limit} + \text{Upper Limit}}{2} = \dfrac{30+40}{2} = \dfrac{70}{2} = 35$
15. (c) weights
16. (d) Weighted Sum = $(2 \times 3) + (4 \times 1) = 6 + 4 = 10$
17. (c) importance
18. (b) Multiply each group's mean by its number of items, then combine these totals
19. (a) $\overline{X}_{1,2} = \dfrac{n_1.\overline{X}_1 - n_2.\overline{X}_2}{n_1 + n_2} = \dfrac{(10 \times 6) + (15 \times 6)}{6+6}$
    $= \dfrac{60+90}{12} = \dfrac{150}{12} = 12.5$
20. (a) The sum of deviations from the arithmetic mean is always zero
21. (a) sensitive to extreme values
22. $(75 \times 30) + (80 \times 25) + (70 \times 20)/30 + 25 + 20$
    $= 5,650/75 = 75.33$
23. (b) To assess the central tendency of the scores to understand overall student performance
24. $(50,000 \times 50) + (60,000 \times 60) + (55,000 \times 40)/50 + 60 + 40 = 55,333.33$
25. (b) It accounts for the varying significance of each sector by incorporating their respective weights

26. (a) Both Assertion (A) and Reason (R) are true and Reason (R) is the correct explanation of Assertion (A)
27. (c) A good average should be minimally affected by changes in data, but central tendency measures can be used for both qualitative and quantitative data, not just qualitative.
28. (d) Central tendency measures are useful for understanding relationships between variables, but it is true that a good average should be least affected by extreme values.
29. (a) Both Assertion (A) and Reason (R) are true and Reason (R) is the correct explanation of Assertion (A)
30. (d) The simple arithmetic mean treats all items equally, while the weighted arithmetic mean assigns different weights to items based on their importance.
31. (a) Both Assertion (A) and Reason (R) are true and Reason (R) is the correct explanation of Assertion (A)
32. (a) Both Assertion (A) and Reason (R) are true and Reason (R) is the correct explanation of Assertion (A)
33. (a) Both Assertion (A) and Reason (R) are true and Reason (R) is the correct explanation of Assertion (A)
34. (a) Both Assertion (A) and Reason (R) are true and Reason (R) is the correct explanation of Assertion (A)
35. (b) Both Assertion (A) and Reason (R) are true, but Reason (R) is not the correct explanation of Assertion (A)
36. (a) Central tendency helps to understand relationships between variables, but it simplifies data by reducing to a single figure, not multiple figures
37. (a) Central tendency does enable further mathematical analysis, while a good average should be capable of further mathematical manipulation
38. (c) Both the statements are correct
39. (a) In order to combine the mean of two different series, we need to add the product of sum total of all the items with their frequencies of the series and then divide by total number of terms.
40. (c) Both the statements are correct
41. (b) The arithmetic mean for a discrete series can be calculated using multiple methods, including the direct method, assumed mean method, and step deviation method.
42. (c) Both the statements are correct
43. (a) Assumed mean can also be a number which is not present in the series.
44. (d) The sum of deviations from the arithmetic mean is always zero, not positive. The arithmetic mean is applicable to quantitative data, not qualitative data.
45. (c) Both the statements are correct
46. (d) (iii) (ii) (i) (iv)
47. (b) (ii) (iii) (iv) (i)
48. (a) (iii) (iv) (i) (ii)
49. (c) (ii) (iii) (iv) (i)
50. (b) (iv) (i) (ii) (iii)
51. Central tendency
52. Arithmetic mean
53. Assumed mean method
54. Weighted arithmetic mean
55. Combined arithmetic mean

Subjective Questions

Short Answer Type Questions

1. "Central tendency is a statistical technique where a single value represents an entire dataset." Do you agree? Competency Based Que

Ans. Yes. Central tendency is a fundamental concept in statistics designed to describe the center of a data distribution. It provides a single value that represents the entire dataset, summarising the overall pattern of the data.

This central value, such as the mean, median or mode, helps in understanding the general trend and distribution of the data points, making it easier to interpret and compare datasets.

2. A company is comparing sales performance across different months using central tendency measures. They find that the average sales for January, February and March are 500, 600 and 700 units, respectively. Which central tendency measure might they use to summarise these monthly sales figures and why? Competency Based Que

Ans. The company might use the arithmetic mean to summarise the monthly sales figures. To calculate the arithmetic mean, they would add the sales figures for January, February and March, and then divide by the number of months. Specifically, they would calculate the mean as follows $(500 + 600 + 700)/3 = 600$ units.

This mean provides a single average value that represents the overall sales performance across the three months.

3. What do you understand by change in origin and change in scale?

Ans. **Change in origin** is a condition in which all values of a series are increased or decreased by constant value. e.g. Three values are given as 3, 5 and 7. Now, each value is increased by 2. So, this represents change in origin.

Change in scale is a condition when all values of a series are multiplied or divided by a constant value. e.g. Three values are given as 3, 5 and 7. Now, each value is multiplied by 5. So, this represents change in scale.

4. Identify and explain the measure of central tendency given in the below image. Competency Based Que

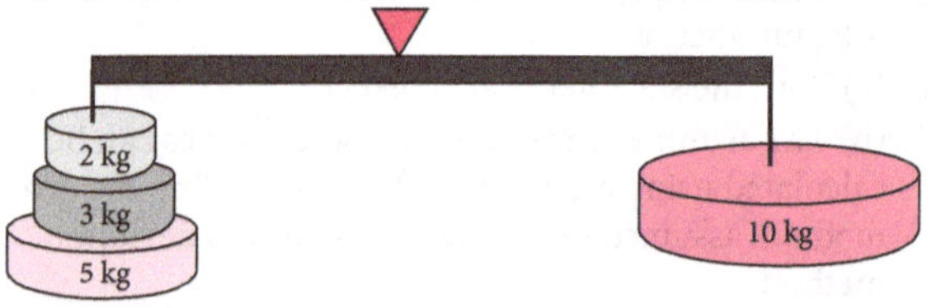

Ans. The measure of central tendency represented in the image is the arithmetic mean (or simply, the mean).

In the image, the total weight on both sides of the balance is equal, indicating that the average or mean weight is being illustrated. The left side shows a single weight of 10 kg, while the right side shows three weights that sum up to 10 kg (5 kg + 3 kg + 2 kg). This visual representation suggests that the mean weight on both sides of the balance is 10 kg. This balance is symbolic of the mean as a central value that equalises the total distribution of weights (or data points) across a dataset.

5. Which average would be suitable in the following cases?

(i) Average production in a factory per shift.

(ii) Average wages in an industrial concern.

(iii) When the sum of absolute deviations from average is least. NCERT; Competency Based Que

Ans. (i) **Arithmetic Mean**

The average production in a factory per shift is best calculated by arithmetic mean as it will capture all types of fluctuations in production during the shifts.

(ii) **Arithmetic Mean**

It gives a fair idea of average wage bill taking into account all the workers.

(iiii) **Arithmetic Mean**

The algebraic sum of the deviations of values about arithmetic mean is zero. Hence, when the sum of absolute deviations from average is the least, then mean could be used to calculate the average.

6. List the steps to calculate arithmetic mean for discrete series by using the direct method.

Ans. Following are the steps to calculate arithmetic mean for discrete series using direct method

Step 1 Multiply each observation (X) by its frequency (f) to get the product fX, then find the sum ΣfX.

Step 2 Calculate the sum of frequencies Σf.

Step 3 Compute the arithmetic mean ($\overline{X}$) using the formula

$$\overline{X} = \frac{\Sigma fX}{\Sigma f}$$

Here,

ΣfX = Sum of the product of observations and corresponding frequencies

Σf = Sum of frequencies

7. "The sum of deviations from the arithmetic mean is always zero." Do you agree? Competency Based Que

Ans. Yes, I agree. The statement is true.

The sum of deviations from the arithmetic mean is always zero. This property arises from the definition of the arithmetic mean, which is the point where the total deviations from the mean balance out.

Mathematically, if ($\overline{X}$) represents the arithmetic mean of a dataset, then the sum of the deviations ($X_i - \overline{X}$) for all individual data points X_i in the set is zero $\Sigma(X_i - x) = 0$

This is because the mean is calculated as the balance point where the sum of the positive deviations equals the sum of the negative deviations, ensuring that their sum is zero.

8. How is the combined mean of two or more groups calculated when the mean and the number of items in each group are known?

Ans. Following steps are followed to calculate combined mean

Step 1 The combined mean of two or more groups is calculated by first multiplying the mean of each group by the number of items in that group to obtain the total sum for each group.

Step 2 These sums are then added together to get the total sum for all groups.

Step 3 Finally, the combined mean is found by dividing this total sum by the total number of items across all groups.

This method ensures that the combined mean reflects the overall average of all groups, taking into account the size and mean of each individual group.

9. State some special properties of the arithmetic mean.

Ans. Some special properties of the arithmetic mean are

(i) The sum of deviations of the observations from their arithmetic mean is always zero.

(ii) The product of arithmetic mean and the number of values on which the mean is based, is equal to the sum of all given values.

Symbolically,

$$n\bar{x} = \Sigma X \qquad \left[\because \bar{x} = \frac{\Sigma X}{n}\right]$$

(iii) It is affected both by change in origin and change in scale.

(iv) The sum of the squares of the deviation of a set of values is minimum when taken from mean.

10. What are the merits of using arithmetic mean?

Ans. The merits of using arithmetic mean are as follows

(i) It is easy to calculate and understand.

(ii) It is rigidly defined and based on all items of the series.

(iii) It is least affected by sample fluctuations.

(iv) It is capable of further algebraic treatment.

(v) It is suitable for comparison across different datasets.

(vi) It provides a single value that summarises the entire dataset.

Long Answer Type Questions

11. Explain the concept of central tendency and discuss the significance of arithmetic mean as a measure of central tendency.

Ans. Central tendency refers to the statistical measure that identifies a single value as representative of an entire dataset, focusing on the center of the distribution. It summarises the data into one central point, often referred to as the average.

Arithmetic mean is one of the most commonly used measures of central tendency. It is calculated by summing all the values in a dataset and dividing by the number of observations. The significance of the arithmetic mean lies in its simplicity and its ability to consider all data points in the series, making it a reliable measure for comparing datasets.

It is widely used in various fields such as economics, finance and social sciences to understand the general trend of data and make informed decisions.

12. Enumerate the main objectives for computing an average.

Ans. The main objectives of computing an average are given below

(i) Average is a single simple expression, in which the net result of a complex group or a vast data is represented.

(ii) Average presents the concise picture of a group by a single value, so it is very convenient to compare the different homogeneous groups by their average.

(iii) Average helps in the formulation of economic policy. e.g. For the removal of poverty from India, our government should take into account per capita income, average productivity of labour, etc. which are examples of average.

(iv) Average is the basis of statistical analysis. The knowledge of average marks secured by the students in different subjects, can help to analyse the subjects in which the students are weak.

(v) Average helps to obtain an idea about the whole population on the basis of sample drawn from the population. The average of the sample is deemed to be the average of the population.

(vi) Average helps in computation of various other statistical measures such as dispersion, correlation, etc.

13. Critically evaluate the statement "The arithmetic mean provides a true representation of a dataset."

Competency Based Que

Ans. The arithmetic mean provides a true representation of a dataset under certain conditions. It is effective when the dataset is symmetrically distributed, meaning that the values are evenly spread around the mean. In such cases, the arithmetic mean accurately reflects the central tendency of the data.

However, the arithmetic mean may not provide a true representation in cases where the dataset is skewed or contains outliers. In such situations, the mean can be distorted by extreme values, leading to a result that does not accurately reflect the typical value of the dataset. e.g. In income data where a few individuals earn significantly more than others, the arithmetic mean may overestimate the general income level.

Moreover, the arithmetic mean is not applicable to ordinal or qualitative data, which further limits its representation of diverse datasets. While it is a useful measure in many scenarios, reliance solely on the arithmetic mean without considering the data's distribution can lead to misleading conclusions.

14. Why is the assumed mean method preferred over the direct method in certain situations? Discuss with an example.

Ans. The assumed mean method is preferred for its efficiency in handling large datasets. Instead of performing extensive calculations directly, which can be time consuming and prone to errors, this method uses a chosen assumed mean to simplify the process. By calculating deviations from this assumed mean, it streamlines the arithmetic mean calculation, making it more manageable and less error-prone.

e.g. Consider a dataset with 1,000 values, where calculating the arithmetic mean directly is complex. Suppose you assume the mean to be 50. You then calculate the deviations of each value from this assumed mean, sum these deviations, and adjust to find the accurate mean.

This method reduces the number of calculations needed and simplifies the process of finding the arithmetic mean, especially when dealing with large volumes of data.

15. Explain how the arithmetic mean is calculated for an inclusive series and why conversion to exclusive intervals is not necessary?

Ans. In an inclusive series, class intervals overlap with their upper and lower limits, but this does not affect the calculation of the arithmetic mean. To find the mean, you use the mid-values of these intervals directly.

The mid-value is calculated by averaging the lower and upper limits of each interval. Multiply each mid-value by its corresponding frequency, sum these products and divide by the total frequency to obtain the mean.

Conversion to exclusive intervals is not necessary because the arithmetic mean remains accurate with mid-values from inclusive intervals. This method simplifies calculations and avoids the need for additional adjustments.

16. Explain the concept of the weighted arithmetic mean and describe the steps involved in its calculation.

Ans. The weighted arithmetic mean is a statistical measure used when different items in a dataset have varying levels of importance or significance. Unlike the simple arithmetic mean, which assumes all data points contribute equally to the average, the weighted arithmetic mean considers the varying degrees of importance by assigning weights to each item.

This method is particularly useful in situations where some data points are more influential than others, providing a more accurate reflection of the average when items have different levels of relevance.

To calculate the weighted arithmetic mean, follow these steps

Step 1 Determine the significance of each item in the dataset and assign weights accordingly. Each weight represents the relative importance of an item and is denoted by W.

Step 2 For each item X, multiply it by its corresponding weight W to get the weighted value. Sum these weighted values across all items to obtain ΣXW.

Step 3 Divide the total weighted sum ΣXW by the total sum of weights ΣW.

This gives the weighted arithmetic mean, which accounts for the varying significance of different items.

$$\overline{X}w = \frac{\Sigma XW}{\Sigma W}$$

where,

$\overline{X}w$ = Weighted arithmetic mean

ΣW = Sum of weights

ΣWX = Sum of product of items and weights

17. "The arithmetic mean gets distorted by extreme values in the series and that the value of arithmetic mean may not be a figure in the series at all." Write the limitations of mean with the help of above statement.

Competency Based Que

Ans. The limitations of mean are

(i) The mean value may sometimes be that value which does not be the figure in the series at all.

(ii) Arithmetic mean sometimes offers illogical conclusions.

(iii) The main defect of arithmetic mean is that it gets distorted by extreme values of the series.

(iv) It cannot be determined by inspection.

(v) It is not suitable for qualitative characteristics such as honesty, beauty, etc.

(vi) In skewed distributions, arithmetic mean is not a suitable measure.

18. A research team is analysing the average number of hours students spend on social media daily. The data is presented as a cumulative frequency distribution.

(i) How can the arithmetic mean be calculated in this scenario?

(ii) What are the specific considerations when working with cumulative frequencies?

Competency Based Que

Ans. (i) To calculate the arithmetic mean from a cumulative frequency distribution, follow these steps

- **Convert Cumulative Frequencies to Simple Frequencies**
  Compute the frequency for each class interval by subtracting the cumulative frequency of the previous class interval from the cumulative frequency of the current class interval. This gives the frequency for each class.
- **Calculate Mid-points**
  Determine the mid-point of each class interval. The mid-point (or class mark) is calculated as the average of the upper and lower boundaries of each class interval.

- **Compute Weighted Sum**
  Multiply each mid-point by its corresponding frequency to obtain the weighted values. Then sum these weighted values.
- **Calculate Total Frequency**
  Sum all the frequencies to get the total number of observations.
- **Compute the Arithmetic Mean**
  Divide the total weighted sum (sum of mid-point multiplied by frequency) by the total number of observations. This gives the arithmetic mean.

(ii) When working with cumulative frequencies, consider the following

- **Conversion to Simple Frequencies**
  Cumulative frequencies provide the total count up to each class interval.
  To perform calculations, you need to convert these to simple frequencies, which represent the count for each specific class interval.
- **Mid-point Calculation**
  Accurate calculation of mid-points is crucial. Each class interval's mid-point should be used in calculations, as it represents the central value of that interval.
- **Handling Intervals**
  Ensure correct handling of intervals, especially if they are open ended or have unequal class widths. This might affect the accuracy of the mean if not addressed properly.
- **Accuracy in Summation**
  Ensure accurate summation of frequencies and weighted values. Errors in these steps can lead to incorrect results.
- **Interpreting Results**
  The final arithmetic mean obtained from cumulative frequencies will be an estimate based on class intervals and their mid-points. Ensure that this estimate is interpreted with an understanding of the data's grouping and potential variations within intervals.

Numerical Questions

Numerical 1

For the dataset 8, 14, 10, 6 and 12, calculate the arithmetic mean.

Sol. Arithmetic Mean $= \dfrac{\text{Sum of All Observations}}{\text{Number of Observations}}$

$$= \frac{(8+14+10+6+12)}{5} = \frac{50}{5} = 10$$

Numerical 2

Compute the arithmetic mean for the following dataset using the direct method.
$X = (3, 7, 10)$ and their frequencies $f = (2, 5, 3)$.

Sol. $X = \dfrac{\Sigma(X_1 \times f_1)}{\Sigma f_1} = \dfrac{(3\times 2)+(7\times 5)+(10\times 3)}{2+5+3}$

$$X = \frac{6+35+30}{10} = \frac{71}{10} = 7.1$$

Numerical 3

If mean of a distribution is ₹ 700 and sum of all the observations is ₹ 6,300, then find the number of observations.

Sol. Mean $= \dfrac{\text{Sum of all the Observations}}{\text{Number of Observations}}$

$$\Rightarrow \quad 700 = \frac{6{,}300}{n} \quad \Rightarrow \quad n = \frac{6{,}300}{700} = 9$$

So, number of observations are 9.

Numerical 4

The following table gives the daily income of ten workers in a factory. Find the arithmetic mean. NCERT

Workers	A	B	C	D	E	F	G	H	I	J
Daily Income (in ₹)	120	150	180	200	250	300	220	350	370	260

Sol. **Calculation of Arithmetic Mean**

Workers	Daily Income (in ₹) (X)
A	120
B	150
C	180
D	200
E	250
F	300
G	220
H	350
I	370
J	260
Total	$\Sigma X = 2{,}400$

$n = 10$

$$\Rightarrow \quad \overline{X} = \frac{\Sigma X}{n} = \frac{2,400}{10} = 240$$

Arithmetic mean = ₹ 240

Numerical 5

Following information pertains to the daily income of 150 families. Calculate the arithmetic mean. NCERT

Income (in ₹)	Number of Families
More than 75	150
More than 85	140
More than 95	115
More than 105	95
More than 115	70
More than 125	60
More than 135	40
More than 145	25

Hint As per the question, cumulative frequencies are given. First of all, they will be changed into exclusive class interval and thereafter, we will calculate arithmetic mean by step deviation method.

Sol. **Calculation of Arithmetic Mean Using Step Deviation Method**

Income (in ₹)	Number of Families (f)	Mid-value (m)	dm $(m-A)$ $(A=110)$	$d'm = \frac{dm}{c}$ $(c=10)$	$fd'm$	
75-85	10	80	−30	−3	−30	−100
85-95	25	90	−20	−2	−50	
95-105	20	100	−10	−1	−20	
105-115	25	110	0	0	0	
115-125	10	120	+10	+1	+10	+195
125-135	20	130	+20	+2	+40	
135-145	15	140	+30	+3	+45	
145-155	25	150	+40	+4	+100	
	$\Sigma f = 150$				$\Sigma fd'm = +95$	

$$\overline{X} = A + \frac{\Sigma fd'm}{\Sigma f} \times c = 110 + \frac{95}{150} \times 10$$

$$= 110 + 6.33 = ₹\, 116.33$$

$$\therefore \quad \overline{X} = ₹\, 116.33$$

Numerical 6

Prove that the algebraic sum of deviations of a given set of observations from their mean is zero. Give an example also.

Sol. Sum of Deviations $= \Sigma(X - \overline{X})$

$$= \Sigma X - \Sigma \overline{X} = \Sigma X - n\overline{X} \quad [\because \Sigma \overline{X} = n\overline{X}]$$

$$= n\overline{X} - n\overline{X} = 0$$

$$\left[\text{as } \overline{X} = \frac{\Sigma X}{n} \Rightarrow \Sigma X = n\overline{X}\right]$$ Hence proved.

In order to show this, we take an example

X	$dx\ (X-\overline{X})\ \overline{X}=6$
2	−4
4	−2
6	0
8	+2
10	+4
$\Sigma X = 30,\ n = 5$	$\Sigma dx = 0$

$$\overline{X} = \frac{\Sigma X}{n} = \frac{30}{5} = 6$$

This shows that the sum of deviations of the values of the variables from their arithmetic mean is equal to zero.

Numerical 7

Find unknown frequency in the table given below

X	Frequency (f)
5	5
10	7
15	?
20	10
25	8
30	6
	$\Sigma f = 50$

Sol. To find unknown frequency, subtract the sum of known frequencies from sum of total frequencies.

$$\Sigma f = 50$$

$\because$ Sum of known frequency $= 5 + 7 + 10 + 8 + 6 = 36$

$\therefore$ Unknown Frequency = Total Frequency − Sum of Known Frequencies

$$= 50 - 36 = 14$$

Numerical 8

For a dataset with class intervals 1-3, 4-7 and 8-10 with frequencies 4, 6 and 3, respectively, compute the arithmetic mean using mid-values.

Sol. Mid-values = 2, 5.5, 9

Weighted Sum = (2 × 4) + (5.5 × 6) + (9 × 3)
= 8 + 33 + 27 = 68

Sum of Frequencies = 4 + 6 + 3 = 13

$$\text{Mean} = \frac{68}{13} = 5.23$$

Numerical 9

The annual salaries of four men were ₹ 5,000, ₹ 6,000, ₹ 6,500 and ₹ 30,000.

(i) Find the arithmetic mean of their salaries.

(ii) Does this average represent their salaries? Which property of arithmetic mean is reflected here?

Sol. (i) $\text{Arithmetic mean} = \frac{5{,}000 + 6{,}000 + 6{,}500 + 30{,}000}{4}$

$$\therefore \quad \overline{X} = \frac{\Sigma X}{n} = \frac{47{,}500}{4} = ₹\ 11{,}875$$

(ii) This mean does not represent the series because it is very high than the actual salary of three persons of the group of four persons and substantially less than the salary of the fourth person. The property of arithmetic mean reflected is that it is affected by extreme values.

Numerical 10

Find out the missing item X of the following distribution, where arithmetic mean $(\overline{X})$ is 11.37.

X	5	7	x	11	13	16	20
Frequency	2	4	29	54	11	8	4

Sol. **Calculation of Missing Item**

X	Frequency (f)	fX
5	2	10
7	4	28
x	29	$29x$
11	54	594
13	11	143
16	8	128
20	4	80
	$\Sigma f = 112$	$\Sigma fX = 983 + 29x$

$$\therefore \quad \overline{X} = \frac{\Sigma fX}{\Sigma f} \Rightarrow 11.37 = \frac{983 + 29x}{112}$$

$$\Rightarrow \quad 1{,}273.44 = 983 + 29x \Rightarrow 29x = 290.44$$

$$\Rightarrow \quad x = 10.01 \cong 10$$

Hence, the missing value is 10.

Numerical 11

Following are the marks obtained by 100 students in Economics. Calculate the average marks by using assumed mean method (take 35 as assumed mean).

Marks	0-10	10-20	20-30	30-40	40-50	50-60
Number of Students	5	10	25	30	20	10

Sol. **Calculation of Average Marks by Assumed Mean Method**

Class Interval	Frequency (f)	Mid-value (m)	$dm(m-A)$ ($A=35$)	fdm	
0-10	5	5	−30	−150	− 600
10-20	10	15	−20	−200	
20-30	25	25	−10	−250	
30-40	30	35	0	0	
40-50	20	45	+10	+200	+ 400
50-60	10	55	+20	+200	
	$\Sigma f = 100$			$\Sigma fdm = -200$	

$$\overline{X} = A + \frac{\Sigma fdm}{\Sigma f} = 35 + \frac{(-200)}{100} = 33$$

Numerical 12

Calculate arithmetic mean from the data given below by short-cut method.

Marks	1-9	10-19	20-29	30-39	40-49
Number of Students	05	04	06	10	05

Sol. **Calculation of Arithmetic Mean by Short-cut Method**

Marks	Frequency (f)	Mid-value (m)	d ($A = 14.5$)	fd	
1-9	05	5	− 9.5	− 47.5	
10-19	04	$14.5 = A$	0	0	
20-29	06	24.5	10	60	410
30-39	10	34.5	20	200	
40-49	05	44.5	30	150	
	$\Sigma f = 30$			$\Sigma fd = 362.5$	

$$\overline{X} = A + \frac{\Sigma fd}{\Sigma f} = 14.5 + \frac{362.5}{30} = 14.5 + 12.08 = 26.58$$

Numerical 13

Find out the arithmetic mean using the step deviation method.

Items	Frequency
More than 0	28
More than 10	24
More than 20	14
More than 30	4

Hint In the above problem, cumulative frequencies are given. Firstly, it will be changed into exclusive class interval and thereafter, we will calculate arithmetic mean using the step deviation method.

Sol. **Calculation of Arithmetic Mean by Step Deviation Method**

Items	Mid-value (m)	Frequency (f)	$dm\,(m-A)$ $(A=15)$	$d'm\left(\frac{dm}{c}\right)$ $(c=10)$	$fd'm$
0-10	5	$28-24=4$	-10	-1	-4
10-20	15	$24-14=10$	0	0	0
20-30	25	$14-4=10$	$+10$	$+1$	$+10$
30-40	35	4	$+20$	$+2$	$+8$
		$\Sigma f=28$			$\Sigma fd'm=+14$

$$\therefore \quad \overline{X}=A+\frac{\Sigma fd'm}{\Sigma f}\times c=15+\frac{14}{28}\times 10=15+5$$

$$\Rightarrow \quad \overline{X}=20$$

Numerical 14

Calculate the weighted mean of the following distribution.

Items	12	29	14	41
Weight	6	4	5	2

Sol. **Calculation of Weighted Mean**

X	W	XW
12	6	72
29	4	116
14	5	70
41	2	82
	$\Sigma W=17$	$\Sigma XW=340$

$$\overline{X}_W=\frac{\Sigma XW}{\Sigma W}=\frac{340}{17}=20$$

Thus, $\overline{X}_W=20$

Numerical 15

The calculated mean is 40; but it was found that one value was wrongly recorded as 35 instead of 45. Find the corrected arithmetic mean.

Sol. Original Mean = 40; Incorrect Value = 35

Correct Value = 45

Corrected Mean Calculation

Sum with Incorrect Value = $40\times n=40n$

Corrected Sum = $40n-35+45=40n+10$

Corrected Mean = $40n+10/n=40+(10/n)$

For $n=10$

Corrected Mean = $40+(10/10)=41$

Numerical 16

The mean of the given distribution is ₹ 425. Find the missing frequency.

Wages (₹)	Number of Workers
100-200	12
200-300	8
300-400	20
400-500	32
500-600	x
600-700	8
700-800	5

Sol. **Calculation of Missing Frequency**

Wages (₹)	Number of Workers (f)	Mid-value (m)	fm
100-200	12	150	1,800
200-300	8	250	2,000
300-400	20	350	7,000
400-500	32	450	1,4400
500-600	x	550	$550x$
600-700	8	650	5,200
700-800	5	750	3,750
	$\Sigma f=85+x$		$\Sigma fm=34{,}150+550x$

We know that, $\overline{X}=\frac{\Sigma fm}{\Sigma f}$

$$\Rightarrow \quad 425=\frac{34{,}150+550x}{85+x}$$

$$\Rightarrow \quad 425\,(85+x)=34{,}150+550x$$

$$36{,}125+425x=34{,}150+550x$$

$$\Rightarrow \quad 36{,}125-34{,}150=550x-425x$$

$$1{,}975=125x$$

$$\Rightarrow \quad \frac{1{,}975}{125}=x=15.8 \text{ or } 16$$

Hence, missing frequency is 16.

Numerical 17

The mean of 200 items was 50. Later, it was discovered that two items were misread as 92 and 8 instead of 192 and 88. Find the correct mean.

Sol. Incorrect $\overline{X} = 50$, $\Sigma X = \overline{X} \times n$ $\left[\because \overline{X} = \frac{\Sigma X}{n}\right]$

$\therefore$ Incorrect $\Sigma X = 200 \times 50 = 10{,}000$

Correct Mean

$$= \frac{\text{Incorrect } \Sigma X - \text{Sum of Incorrect Values} + \text{Sum of Correct Values}}{n}$$

$$= \frac{10{,}000 - (92 + 8) + (192 + 88)}{200} = \frac{10{,}000 - 100 + 280}{200}$$

$$= \frac{10{,}180}{200} = 50.9$$

$\therefore$ Correct mean $= 50.9$

Numerical 18

There are two factories employing 100 and 80 men, respectively. If the arithmetic mean of their monthly salaries are ₹ 575 and ₹ 625, then find the arithmetic mean of the salaries of both the factories together.

Sol. Given, $n_1 = 100, \overline{X}_1 = 575, n_2 = 80, \overline{X}_2 = 625$

Now, Combined Mean $(\overline{X}_{1,2}) = \frac{n_1\overline{X}_1 + n_2\overline{X}_2}{n_1 + n_2}$

$$\Rightarrow \quad \overline{X}_{1,2} = \frac{575 \times 100 + 625 \times 80}{100 + 80} = \frac{57{,}500 + 50{,}000}{180}$$

$$= \frac{1{,}07{,}500}{180} = 597.2$$

$\therefore \overline{X}_{1,2} = 597.2$

Numerical 19

Average daily wages of 50 workers of a factory was ₹ 200. Each worker is given a raise of ₹ 20. What is the new average daily wages? Which property of arithmetic mean does the above example point to?

Sol. Increase in wages of each worker = ₹ 20

Total increase in wages = 50 × 20 = ₹ 1,000

Total wages before increase in wages = 50 × 200 = ₹ 10,000

Total wages after increase in wages

= 10,000 + 1,000 = ₹ 11,000

New average wage $= \frac{\Sigma X}{n} = \frac{11{,}000}{50} =$ ₹ 220

Thus, mean wage has increased by ₹ 20.

The property of arithmetic mean which is brought forward by the above example is that arithmetic mean is affected by change in origin.

Numerical 20

The following shows the distribution of persons according to different income groups

Income (in ₹ 1,000)	0-8	8-16	16-24	24-32	32-40	40-48
No. of Persons	8	7	16	24	15	7

(i) Find the average income of the persons by short-cut method.

(ii) If all the numbers in the above series are increased by 5, how will be the arithmetic mean impacted?

Sol. (i) Short-cut method to calculate average income

Class	f_i	x_i $A = 28$	$d_i = (x_i - A)/c$ $c = 8$	$f_i d_i$ $(c = 5)$
0-8	8	4	−3	−24
8-16	7	12	−2	−14
16-24	16	20	−1	−16
24-32	24	28	0	0
32-40	15	36	1	15
40-48	7	44	2	14
Total	$n = 77$			−25

$$\overline{X} = A + \frac{\sum_{i=1}^{n} f_i d_i}{n} \times c = 28 + \frac{-25}{77} \times 8 = 25.40$$

(ii) If all the numbers of a given series are increased by a fixed number, arithmetic mean also gets increased by the same constant number.

As, in the above case all the numbers are increased by a constant number 5, therefore, the mean will also get increased by 5 and the new mean will be 30.40.

SELF ASSESSMENT TEST

Objective Type Questions

1. Central tendency represents a dataset using a single value, often referred to as the ....
   (a) sum
   (b) average
   (c) deviation
   (d) frequency

2. In the step deviation method, what does *c* represent?
   (a) Mid-point
   (b) Frequency
   (c) Mean value
   (d) Common factor

3. When is the assumed mean method preferred?
   (a) When observations are minimal
   (b) When the mean is unknown
   (c) When observations are large in number
   (d) When deviations are zero

4. Which of the following is not a requisite of a good average?
   (a) Clearly defined
   (b) Affected by extreme values
   (c) Based on all data points
   (d) Capable of further mathematical treatment

5. The arithmetic mean is calculated by dividing the sum of all observations by the .... of observations.
   (a) number
   (b) frequency
   (c) mean
   (d) total

6. For open ended series, missing limits are assumed based on the .... of other intervals.
   (a) pattern (b) range
   (c) frequency (d) total

7. Which of the following statements about arithmetic mean is correct?
   (a) Arithmetic mean is always greater than the highest observation in the dataset
   (b) Arithmetic mean cannot be calculated for a continuous series
   (c) Arithmetic mean is equal to the frequency of the most common observation
   (d) Arithmetic mean is affected by extreme values in the dataset

8. Which of the following is the most widely used measure of central tendency?
   (a) Median
   (b) Mode
   (c) Arithmetic mean
   (d) Geometric mean

Answers 1. (b) 2. (d) 3. (c) 4. (b) 5. (a) 6. (a) 7. (d) 8. (c)

Short Answer Type Questions

9. How is the weighted average mean calculated?
10. What is central tendency? Explain.
11. Define the following terms
    (i) Simple arithmetic mean
    (ii) Weighted arithmetic mean
12. Why sum of deviations is zero when taken from mean?

Long Answer Type Questions

13. A teacher conducted a math test in a class of 10 students. The test scores (out of 50) were distributed unevenly. While most students scored between 35 and 45, a few scored significantly higher and one student scored the lowest marks in the class.

    The teacher analysed the central tendency measures to summarise the class performance.
    (i) What does the term 'central tendency' refer to in the context of analysing student scores?
    (ii) In a dataset where most students score similarly, but a few scores are significantly different, which measure of central tendency best represents the performance of the majority of the students? Justify your answer.

14. Explain the methods of calculating mean in a discrete series.

Numerical Questions

15. Average income of 50 families is ₹ 3,000.

Of these, average income of 12 families is ₹ 1,800. Find out the average income of the remaining families.

Ans. $\overline{X}$ = ₹ 3378.95

16. Calculate the mean from the following data

Class Interval	10-20	10-30	10-40	10-50	10-60
Frequency	5	17	31	41	49

Ans. $\overline{X} = 35.08$

17. Find out arithmetic mean from the following distribution by step deviation method

Items	10-8	8-6	6-4	4-2	2-0
Frequency	10	8	6	4	2

Ans. $\overline{X} = 6.33$

18. The following table shows wages of the workers. Calculate the average wage of the workers.

Wages (in ₹)	10-19	20-29	30-39	40-49	50-59
Number of Workers	8	9	12	11	6

Ans. $\overline{X}$ = ₹ 34.07

Hint The given inclusive distribution should be converted into an exclusive distribution.

19. In the following frequency distribution, if the arithmetic mean is 45.6, then find out missing frequency.

Class Interval	10-20	20-30	30-40	40-50	50-60	60-70	70-80
Frequency	5	6	7	?	4	3	9

Ans. Missing frequency = 16

Hint Use direct method.

20. Calculate the weighted mean of the following data

Items	96	102	104	124	148	164
Weight	5	6	3	7	12	9

Ans. $\overline{X}_W = 131.52$

06

CHAPTER

Mean is not capable of measuring qualitative characteristics of a given distribution, thus, other measures of central tendency are used for this purpose, which are known as positional averages.

Measures of Central Tendency : Median and Mode

YOUR STUDY GOALS

6.1 Median

6.2 Certain Specific Conditions for Median

6.3 Quartiles

6.4 Mode

6.5 Certain Specific Cases of Mode

YOUR PRACTICE GOAL

- Objective Type Questions (60 Qs ; MCQs, A-R, Statements, Matching, Concept Identification)
- Subjective Questions (9 SAs, 6 LAs)
- 22 Numerical Questions
- Self Assessment Test (6 MCQs, 4 SAs, 2 LAs, 10 Numerical)

Positional averages are based on a specific position or value within a dataset and can evaluate both quantitative as well as qualitative characteristics of a variable.

Positional averages can be classified as

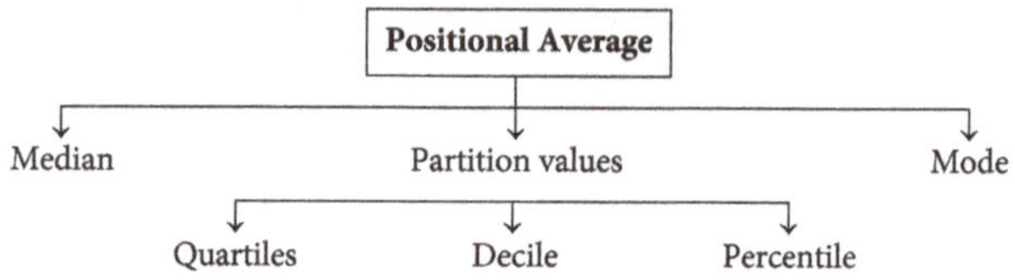

6.1 Median

The median is the value that divides a distribution into two equal parts, with one half of the data values being greater than median value and the other half being lesser. It represents the 'middle value' when data is arranged in order of magnitude (ascending or descending order).

Mean vs Median

The mean is the average of all numbers in a set, but it can be affected by really high or low numbers. The median is the middle number when all numbers are ordered, so it is not affected by extreme values. The mean is good for balanced data, while the median works better when there are outliers.

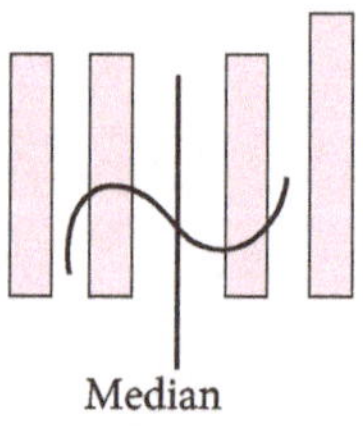

Calculation of Median

Calculation of median in individual, discrete and continuous series is discussed as follows

In an Individual Series

Step 1 Arrange all values in ascending or descending order.

Step 2 Find the total number of items (n).

Step 3 If n is odd, then calculate the median using the formula

$$\text{Median } (M) = \text{Size of} \left(\frac{N+1}{2}\right) \text{th Item}$$

Step 4 And if n is an even number, then the following formula can be used

$$M = \frac{\left(\frac{N}{2}\right)\text{th Item} + \text{Size of}\left(\frac{N}{2}+1\right)\text{th Item}}{2}$$

In a Discrete Series

In a discrete series, frequencies accompany each value and the median is calculated using following steps

Step 1 Arrange the data in order of magnitude and denote values as X and frequencies as f.

Step 2 Calculate cumulative frequencies (cf).

Step 3 Use the formula to find median position

$$\text{Median } (M) = \left(\frac{N+1}{2}\right) \text{th Item}$$

where, N = Sum of frequencies

Step 4 Locate the median position through cumulative frequency and the corresponding value at this position is the median.

In Continuous Series

In case of continuous series, median cannot be located straightforward. In this case, median lies in between lower and upper limit of a class interval. Following steps are followed in this case

Step 1 First of all, arrange the data in ascending or descending order.

Step 2 Calculate the cumulative frequencies.

Step 3 Find the value of ($N/2$)th item and then by inspecting cumulative frequencies (cf), find out the cumulative frequency which is either equal to or just greater than it. The class interval corresponding to this value is called **median class.**

Step 4 Now, apply the following formula to determine the actual median value

$$\text{Median } (M) = l_1 + \frac{\frac{N}{2} - cf}{f} \times c$$

where,

l_1 = Lower limit of the median class ; cf = Cumulative frequency of the class preceding the median class

f = Frequency of the median class ; c = Magnitude of the median class interval

N = Sum of frequencies (Σf)

Solved Question 1 ***(When number is odd)*** **Calculate median from the following data**

20, 25, 30, 15, 17, 35, 26, 18, 40, 45, 50

Sol. First of all, arrange the values in ascending or descending order and put serial numbers accordingly.

Calculation of Median

S.No.	Values
1	15
2	17
3	18
4	20
5	25
6	26
7	30
8	35
9	40
10	45
11	50
$n = 11$	

Here, number of items, i.e. $n = 11$ which is odd.

$$\therefore \text{Median } (M) = \text{Size of} \left(\frac{N+1}{2}\right) \text{th item}$$

$$= \text{Size of} \left(\frac{11+1}{2}\right) \text{th item}$$

$$= \text{Size of} \left(\frac{12}{2}\right) \text{th item}$$

$$= \text{Size of 6th item}$$

6th item is 26. So, median = 26

Solved Question 2 *(When number is even)* **Calculate median from the following data**

8, 12, 15, 22, 35, 42, 45, 58

Sol. The values are already in ascending order. The data is represented as below

Calculation of Median

S.No.	1	2	3	4	5	6	7	8
Values	8	12	15	22	35	42	45	58

Here, number of items, i.e. $n = 8$ which is even.

∴ Median

$$= \frac{\text{Size of}\left(\frac{N}{2}\right)\text{th item} + \text{Size of}\left(\frac{N}{2}+1\right)\text{th item}}{2}$$

$$= \frac{\text{Size of}\left(\frac{8}{2}\right)\text{th item} + \text{Size of}\left(\frac{8}{2}+1\right)\text{th item}}{2}$$

$$= \frac{\text{Size of 4th item} + \text{Size of 5th item}}{2}$$

$$= \frac{22+35}{2} = 28.5 \Rightarrow \text{Median} = 28.5$$

Solved Question 3 **Compute the median from the following data**

Marks	40	41	42	43	44	45	46	47
Number of Students	2	3	7	8	10	12	14	16

Sol. **Calculation of Median**

Marks (X)	Number of Students (f)	Cumulative Frequency (cf)
40	2	2
41	3	5
42	7	12
43	8	20
44	10	30
45	12	42
46	14	56
47	16	72
	$N = \Sigma f = 72$	

Here, n = Sum of frequency = 72

$$\text{Position of Median} = \left(\frac{N+1}{2}\right)\text{th item}$$

$$= \left(\frac{72+1}{2}\right)\text{th item} = 36.5\text{th item}$$

The cumulative frequency just greater than 36.5 is 42 and the marks corresponding to this cumulative frequency is 45. Therefore, required median is 45.

Solved Question 4 **Compute median from the following data**

Marks	No. of Students
5	2
10	3
15	1
20	4
25	5
30	3
35	3

Sol. Calculation of median in discrete series

X	f	cf
5	2	2
10	3	5
15	1	6
20	4	10
25	5	15
30	3	18
35	3	21
	$N = 21$	

$$\text{Median} = \left(\frac{N+1}{2}\right)\text{th term}$$

$$M = \left(\frac{21+1}{2}\right)\text{th term} = \left(\frac{22}{2}\right)\text{th term} = 11\text{th term}$$

Median = 25

Solved Question 5 **From the following table, find out the value of median**

Marks	0-10	10-20	20-30	30-40	40-50	50-60
Number of Students	5	10	15	10	6	4

Sol. **Calculation of Median**

Marks (X)	Number of Students (f)	Cumulative Frequency (cf)
0–10	5	5
10–20	10	15
20–30	15	30
30–40	10	40
40–50	6	46
50–60	4	50
	$N = \Sigma f = 50$	

Here, $N = 50$

$\therefore$ Median class (m) = Size of $\left(\frac{N}{2}\right)$th item

$= \left(\frac{50}{2}\right)$th item = 25th item

The cf just greater than 25 is 30 and its corresponding class is 20-30. So, median class is 20-30.

$\therefore \quad l_1 = 20, \; cf = 15, \; f = 15$

and $\quad c = 10 \; (30 - 20)$

Now, Median $(M) = l_1 + \dfrac{\frac{N}{2} - cf}{f} \times c$

$\Rightarrow \quad M = 20 + \dfrac{\frac{50}{2} - 15}{15} \times 10$

$= 20 + \dfrac{10 \times 10}{15} = 20 + 6.67$

$\Rightarrow \quad M = 26.67$ marks

6.2 Certain Specific Conditions for Median

Calculation of median in certain specific conditions is discussed below

Condition	Explanation
In a Cumulative Frequency Distribution	When cumulative frequency distribution is given, convert it into a simple frequency distribution to calculate the median. Following steps are to be followed ***Step 1*** Identify if the cumulative frequency series is 'less-than' or 'more-than'. ***Step 2*** Convert this cumulative series into a simple frequency distribution. ***Step 3*** Follow the steps discussed for calculating the median in a continuous series.
In a Mid-value Series	For series where mid-values are provided, convert these into an exclusive series before calculating the median. Following steps are followed ***Step 1*** Calculate the difference between two consecutive mid-values. ***Step 2*** Divide this difference by 2 and add as well as subtract the result to adjust each mid-value to find the lower and upper limits. ***Step 3*** Follow the continuous series method to determine the median.
In an Inclusive Series	When inclusive series is given, convert it to an exclusive series by adjusting class limits. Following steps are followed to calculate median ***Step 1*** Compute the difference between the lower class limit of the second class and the upper class limit of the first class. ***Step 2*** Divide this difference by 2. Then, subtract and add a result to the lower and upper class limits to find exclusive class limits. ***Step 3*** Calculate the median using the same method as in continuous series.
When Unequal Class Intervals are Given	When class intervals are unequal, no adjustment is needed to make them equal. The calculation can proceed by adjusting the frequencies, if needed. The median is calculated similarly to continuous series. ***Step 1*** Use the existing class intervals and frequencies. ***Step 2*** Apply the continuous series method to find the median.
In an Open Ended Class Interval	For open ended intervals where limits are missing, there is no requirement to find the missing limits and complete the class interval. Proceed with the calculation of median in same way as in continuous series, ignoring the missing limits. Median is considered as the best average of open ended continuous series because the extreme values will not affect median and the average will be representative of the series.
Calculation of Missing Frequency When Median is Given	When the dataset has missing frequencies but the median is known, use it to determine the missing values. Utilise the given median to solve for the missing frequency or frequencies based on the median's position.

Solved Question 6 Calculate median from the following data

Wages (in ₹)	Number of Workers
Less than 5	4
Less than 10	10
Less than 15	20
Less than 20	30
Less than 25	55
Less than 30	79
Less than 35	99
Less than 40	100

Sol. **Calculation of Median**

Wages (in ₹) X	Number of Workers (f)	Cumulative Frequency (cf)
0-5	4	4
5-10	6	10
10-15	10	20
15-20	10	30
20-25	25	55
25-30	24	79
30-35	20	99
35-40	1	100
	$N=\Sigma f=100$	

Here, $N=100$

$\therefore m=\text{Size of}\left(\frac{N}{2}\right)\text{th item}=\left(\frac{100}{2}\right)\text{th item}=50\text{th item}$

cf just greater than 50 is 55 and the corresponding class is 20-25, hence, median class is 20-25.

Now $l_1=20,\ cf=30,\ f=25,\ c=5$

$$\therefore \quad M=l_1+\frac{\frac{N}{2}-cf}{f}\times c$$

$$=20+\left(\frac{50-30}{25}\right)\times 5=20+4=24$$

Hence, required median $=24$

Solved Question 7 Calculate median from the following data

Wages (in ₹)	Number of Workers
More than 100	200
More than 150	180
More than 200	150
More than 250	70
More than 300	10

Sol. **Calculation of Median**

Wages (in ₹)	No. of Workers (f)	Cumulative Frequency (cf)
100-150	20 (200 − 180)	20
150-200	30 (180 − 150)	20 + 30 = 50
200-250	80 (150 − 70)	50 + 80 = 130
250-300	60 (70 − 10)	130 + 60 = 190
300-350	10	190 + 10 = 200
	$N=\Sigma f=200$	

$\text{Median class}=\left(\frac{N}{2}\right)\text{th term}=\left(\frac{200}{2}\right)\text{th}=100\text{th term}$

cf just greater than 100 is 130 and the corresponding class is 200-250, hence, class is 200-250.

Now, $l_1=200,\ \frac{N}{2}=100,\ cf=50,\ f=80,\ c=50$

$$\therefore \quad M=l_1+\frac{\frac{N}{2}-cf}{f}\times c=200+\left(\frac{100-50}{80}\right)\times 50$$

$$=200+\left(\frac{50\times 50}{80}\right)$$

$$=200+31.25=231.25$$

Hence, required median $=231.25$

Solved Question 8 Compute median from following data

Marks (Mid-value)	5	15	25	35	45
No. of Students	10	12	8	11	9

Sol. First, we will find class interval using mid-value.

Difference between two consecutive mid- values $(15-5=10)$.

Now, this difference is divided by 2 and the result (5) is subtracted and added to the mid-value to find lower and upper limits respectively.

Calculation of Median

Marks (X)	Number of Students (f)	Cumulative Frequency (cf)
0-10	10	10
10-20	12	22
20-30	8	30
30-40	11	41
40-50	9	50
	$N=\Sigma f=50$	

Here, $N = 50$

$\therefore \quad m = \text{Size of} \left(\frac{N}{2}\right) \text{th item} = \left(\frac{50}{2}\right) \text{th item} = 25\text{th item}$

cf just greater than 25 is 30 and the corresponding class is 20-30, hence median class is 20-30.

$\therefore \quad l_1 = 20, \quad cf = 22, \quad f = 8, \quad c = 10$

Now, $M = l_1 + \frac{\frac{N}{2} - cf}{f} \times c = 20 + \left(\frac{25-22}{8}\right) \times 10$

$= 20 + \frac{30}{8} = 20 + 3.75 = 23.75$

Hence, required median marks = 23.75

Solved Question 9 **Calculate median wages from the following data**

Daily Wages (in ₹)	50-59	60-69	70-79	80-89	90-99
Number of Workers	15	40	50	60	45

Sol. First of all, the given inclusive series will be converted into an exclusive series.

Calculation of Median

Daily Wages (in ₹) (X)	Frequency (f)	Cumulative Frequency (cf)
49.5-59.5	15	15
59.5-69.5	40	55
69.5-79.5	50	105
79.5-89.5	60	165
89.5-99.5	45	210
	$N = \Sigma f = 210$	

Here, $N = 210$

$\therefore m = \text{Size of} \left(\frac{N}{2}\right) \text{th item} = \left(\frac{210}{2}\right) \text{th item} = 105\text{th item}$

cf is equal to 105 and it lies in the group 69.5-79.5.

Hence, median class is 69.5-79.5.

$\therefore \quad l_1 = 69.5, \quad cf = 55, \quad f = 50, \quad c = 10$

Now, $M = l_1 + \frac{\frac{N}{2} - cf}{f} \times c = 69.5 + \left(\frac{105-55}{50}\right) \times 10$

$= 69.5 + 10 = 79.5$

Hence, required median wages = ₹ 79.5

Solved Question 10 **Calculate the median of the following distribution of data**

Class Interval	0-10	10-30	30-60	60-80	80-90
Frequency	5	15	25	8	3

Sol. **Calculation of Median**

Class Interval (X)	Frequency (f)	Cumulative Frequency (cf)
0-10	5	5
10-30	15	20
30-60	25	45
60-80	8	53
80-90	3	56
	$N = \Sigma f = 56$	

Here, $N = 56$

$\therefore \quad M = \text{Size of} \left(\frac{N}{2}\right) \text{th item} = \left(\frac{56}{2}\right) \text{th item} = 28\text{th item}$

cf just greater than 28 is 45 and the corresponding group is 30-60, hence median class is 30-60.

$\therefore \quad l_1 = 30, \quad cf = 20, \quad f = 25, \quad c = 30\,(60-30)$

Now, $M = l_1 + \frac{N/2 - cf}{f} \times c = 30 + \frac{240}{25} = 30 + 9.6 = 39.6$

Hence, required median = 39.6

Solved Question 11 **Find the median size of profits earned by some companies.**

Profit (₹ 000's)	Less than 100	100-200	200-300	300-400	400 and above
Number of Companies	40	80	50	20	10

Sol. **Calculation of Median**

Profit (₹ 000's) (X)	Number of Companies (f)	Cumulative Frequency (cf)
Less than 100	40	40
100-200	80	120
200-300	50	170
300-400	20	190
400 and above	10	200
	$N = \Sigma f = 200$	

Here, $N = 200$

$\therefore \quad m = \text{Size of} \left(\frac{N}{2}\right) = \left(\frac{200}{2}\right) \text{th item} = 100\text{th item}$

cf just greater than 100 is 120 and the corresponding group is 100-200, hence median class is 100-200.

$\therefore l_1 = 100, \quad cf = 40, \quad f = 80, \quad c = 100$

Now, $M = l_1 + \frac{N/2 - cf}{f} \times c$

$= 100 + \left(\frac{100-40}{80}\right) \times 100 = 100 + 75 = 175$

Hence, required median profit = ₹ 1,75,000

Solved Question 12 **Given the following data on monthly wages of 1,000 workers, frequencies of two class intervals are missing. Locate these if the median of the series is 56.**

Wages (in ₹ 000's)	20-30	30-40	40-50	50-60	60-70	70-80
Number of Workers	60	60	?	200	?	285

Sol. Let f_1 and f_2 be the frequencies of the class 40-50 and 60-70 respectively

Given, $N = \Sigma f = 1{,}000$

Calculation of Missing Frequencies

Wages (in ₹) (X)	Number of Workers (f)	Cumulative Frequency (cf)
20-30	60	60
30-40	60	120
40-50	f_1	$120 + f_1$
50-60	200	$320 + f_1$
60-70	f_2	$320 + f_1 + f_2$
70-80	285	$605 + f_1 + f_2$
	$N = \Sigma f = 1{,}000$	

Here, $N = 1{,}000$

$\therefore m = \text{Size of} \left(\frac{N}{2}\right) \text{th item} = \left(\frac{1{,}000}{2}\right) \text{th item} = 500 \text{th item}$

Here, f_1 and f_2 are unknown, so we cannot find the cf equal or just greater than 500 but median = 56 is given and it lies in the interval 50-60, so median class is 50-60.

$\therefore \quad l_1 = 50, \quad cf = 120 + f_1, \; f = 200, \quad c = 10$

Now, $M = l_1 + \dfrac{\frac{N}{2} - cf}{f} \times c$

$\Rightarrow \quad 56 = 50 + \left(\dfrac{500 - 120 - f_1}{200}\right) \times 10$

$\Rightarrow \quad 56 = 50 + \left(\dfrac{380 - f_1}{20}\right)$

$\Rightarrow \quad 56 - 50 = \dfrac{380 - f_1}{20} \Rightarrow 6 = \dfrac{380 - f_1}{20}$

$\Rightarrow 380 - f_1 = 6 \times 20$

$\Rightarrow \quad f_1 = 380 - 120 = 260$

Also sum of frequencies = 1,000 (given)

$\Rightarrow \quad 60 + 60 + f_1 + 200 + f_2 + 285 = 1{,}000$

$\Rightarrow \quad 605 + f_1 + f_2 = 1{,}000$

$\Rightarrow \quad f_1 + f_2 = 1{,}000 - 605$

$260 + f_2 = 395$

$\therefore \quad f_2 = 395 - 260 = 135$

$\because \quad f_1 = 260$

Hence, frequency of 40-50 class = 260 ; frequency of 60-70 class = 135.

Location of Median by Graph

Median can be located graphically by three different methods

Using Both 'More-than' and 'Less-than' Ogives	Using Only 'Less-than' Ogive	Using Only 'More-than' Ogive
Steps 1. Convert the frequency distribution into a 'less-than' ogive and plot it. 2. Convert the frequency distribution into a 'more-than' ogive and plot it. 3. Plot both ogive curves on the same graph. 4. From the point of intersection, a parallel line to y-axis is drawn. The point at which this line meets the x-axis, is the median.	***Steps*** 1. Convert the frequency distribution into a 'less-than' distribution and plot it on a graph. 2. Find $n/2$, and draw a horizontal line from y-axis, on less than ogive from $n/2$. 3. From this point, draw a perpendicular on x-axis. Corresponding point on x-axis will be median.	***Steps*** 1. Convert the frequency distribution into a 'more-than' cumulative frequency distribution and plot it. 2. Calculate $n/2$ and draw a horizontal line from y-axis on 'more than' ogive from $n/2$. 3. From this point, drawn a perpendicular on x-axis. Corresponding point on x-axis will be the median.

Solved Question 13 **From the given series, find the value of median graphically with the help of**

(i) More than and less than ogives (ii) Less than ogive (iii) More than ogive

Wages (in ₹)	0-5	5-10	10-15	15-20	20-25	25-30	30-35	35-40
Number of Workers	4	6	10	10	25	24	20	1

Sol. Calculation of median by graphical method.

Converting the given distribution into 'less than' and 'more than' cumulative distributions.

Wages	Number of Workers	Wages	Number of Workers
Less than 5	4	More than 0	100
Less than 10	10	More than 5	96
Less than 15	20	More than 10	90
Less than 20	30	More than 15	80
Less than 25	55	More than 20	70
Less than 30	79	More than 25	45
Less than 35	99	More than 30	21
Less than 40	100	More than 35	1

(i) Finding median with the help of 'less-than' and 'more-than' ogives.

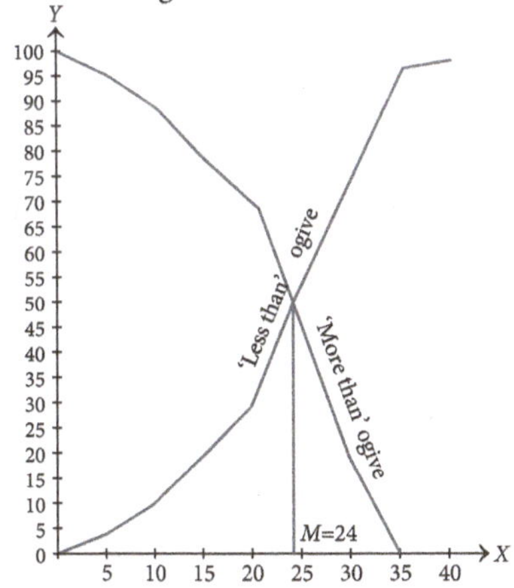

(ii) Finding median with the help of 'less than' ogive
M = Size of $(n/2)$th item = Size of $(100/2)$th item
= Size of 50th item

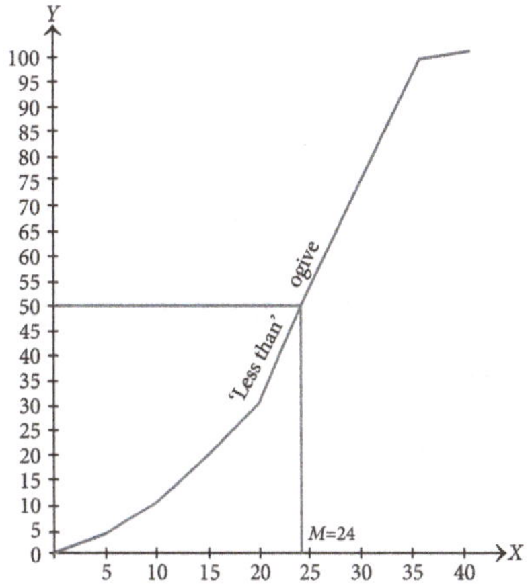

(iii) Finding median with the help of 'more than' ogive
M = 50 th item

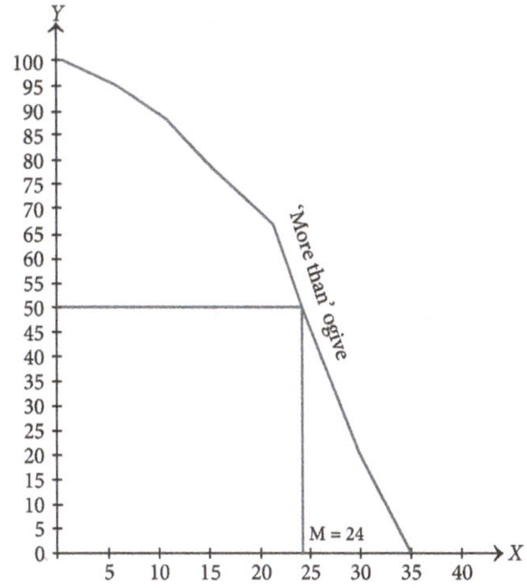

Properties of Median

- The sum of absolute deviations from the median is the smallest compared to other measures.
- Median is unaffected by extreme values, as it is based upon middle 50% of data.

Merits of Median

- Easy to calculate and understand.
- Provides a definite value and can be graphically located with ogive curves.
- Not influenced by extreme values.
- Useful for qualitative data also.
- Can be calculated even with incomplete series.

Demerits of Median

- Not based on all data items.
- Can be affected by changes in sampling.
- Not capable of further mathematical treatment.
- Requires data to be arranged for calculation.
- Does not facilitate comparison as it only reflects the central value of the dataset.

6.3 Quartiles

Quartiles are positional averages that divide a dataset into four equal parts, each containing an equal number of observations. They are also known as partitional averages. There are three key quartiles

1. **First Quartile** (Q_1) It is also known as the lower quartile. 25% of the items in the dataset are below Q_1 and 75% are above it.
2. **Second Quartile** (Q_2) This is the same as the median. 50% of the items are below Q_2 and 50% are above it.
3. **Third Quartile** (Q_3) It is also known as the upper quartile. 75% of the items are below Q_3 and 25% are above it.

We can understand the quartiles using the number scale given below

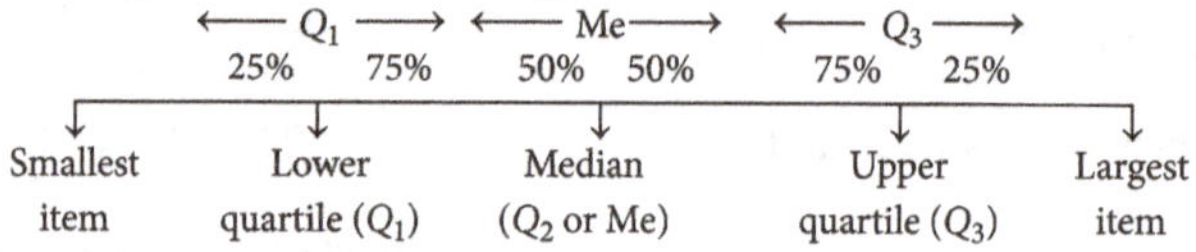

Other Positional Averages : Deciles and Percentiles

Deciles distribute the series into ten equal parts and is generally expressed as *D*. Accordingly, we have nine deciles $D_1, D_2, D_3, \ldots, D_9$ of a series.

Percentiles divide the series into hundred equal parts and is generally expressed as *P*. There are 99 percentiles in a series denoted by $P_1, P_2, P_3, \ldots, P_{99}$.

Also remember, $M = Q_2 = D_5 = P_{50} \Rightarrow Q_1 = P_{25}$ and $Q_3 = P_{75}$

Calculation of Quartiles

Calculation of quartiles in individual, discrete and continuous series is discussed below

In Individual Series

Step 1 Arrange the data in ascending order.

Step 2 Use the following quartile formulae to find Q_1, Q_2 (median) and Q_3.

$$Q_1 = \text{Size of} \left(\frac{N+1}{4}\right) \text{th item} \qquad Q_3 = \text{Size of } 3\left(\frac{N+1}{4}\right) \text{th item}$$

$$Q_2 = \text{Size of } 2\left(\frac{N+1}{4}\right) \text{th item } \textit{or} \text{ Size of } \frac{(N+1)}{2} \text{ th item (same as median)}$$

In Discrete Series

Step 1 Ensure the data is arranged in ascending order.

Step 2 Calculate cumulative frequencies.

Step 3 Apply the same quartile formulae as given in individual series.

Note If on division, the result is a decimal number, then following formula should be applied to find quartiles = Size of Integral Number + Decimal Part [size of next number – size of integral number].

In Continuous Series

Step 1 Convert the series into an exclusive format if needed (e.g. From inclusive or mid-values) and arrange them in ascending order.

Step 2 Determine quartile positions using. q_1 number $= \left(\frac{N}{4}\right)$th item, q_2 number $= 2\left(\frac{N}{4}\right)$th item, q_3 number $= 3\left(\frac{N}{4}\right)$th item

Step 3 Locate the quartile groups and use interpolation to calculate Q_1, Q_2 and Q_3

$$Q_1 = l_1 + \frac{\left(\frac{N}{4}\right) - cf}{f} \times c; \qquad Q_2 = l_1 + \frac{2\left(\frac{N}{4}\right) - cf}{f} \times c; \qquad Q_3 = l_1 + \frac{3\left(\frac{N}{4}\right) - cf}{f} \times c$$

where, l_1 = Lower limit of class group ; c = Width of the class group

cf = Cumulative frequency of the class preceding the class group and

f = Frequency of class group ; $N = \Sigma f$ = Sum of frequencies

Solved Question 14 Calculate Q_1, Q_2 and Q_3, with the help of following data

1, 2, 3, 4, 6, 8, 9, 10, 11, 13, 15, 17, 19, 20, 21, 22, 23, 24, 25

Sol. The data is already in ascending order. It can be presented as follows

Calculation of Quartiles

S.No.	Items (X)
1	1
2	2
3	3
4	4
5	6
6	8
7	9
8	10
9	11
10	13
11	15
12	17
13	19
14	20
15	21
16	22
17	23
18	24
19	25
$n=19$	

Here, n = number of item = 19

(i) $Q_1 = \text{Size of}\left(\frac{N+1}{4}\right)\text{th item} = \text{Size of}\left(\frac{19+1}{4}\right)\text{th item}$

$= \text{Size of 5th item} = 6$

$\therefore \quad Q_1 = 6$

(ii) $Q_2 = \text{Size of}\frac{2(N+1)}{4}\text{th item} = \text{Size of}\frac{2(19+1)}{4}\text{th item}$

$= \text{Size of 10th item} = 13$

$\therefore Q_2 = 13$

(iii) $Q_3 = \text{Size of}\frac{3(N+1)}{4}\text{ th item} = \text{Size of}\frac{3(19+1)}{4}\text{ th item}$

$= \text{Size of}\left(\frac{60}{4}\right)\text{th item} = \text{Size of 15th item} = 21$

$\therefore Q_3 = 21$

Solved Question 15 Calculate Q_1 and Q_3 with the help of following data

X	10	15	20	25	30	35	40	45	50	55	60	65	70
f	4	6	5	7	12	5	8	9	12	10	7	8	6

Sol. **Calculation of Q_1 and Q_3**

X	Frequency (f)	Cumulative Frequency (cf)
10	4	4
15	6	10
20	5	15
25	7	22
30	12	34
35	5	39
40	8	47
45	9	56
50	12	68
55	10	78
60	7	85
65	8	93
70	6	99
	$N=99$	

Here, $N = \Sigma f = 99$

(i) $Q_1 = \text{Size of}\left(\frac{N+1}{4}\right)\text{th item} = \text{Size of}\left(\frac{99+1}{4}\right)\text{th item}$

$= \text{Size of 25th item, it lies in } cf \text{ 34.}$

Hence, $Q = 30$

(ii) $Q_3 = \text{Size of } 3\left(\frac{N+1}{4}\right)\text{th item} = \text{Size of } 3\left(\frac{99+1}{4}\right)\text{th item}$

$= \text{Size of 75th item, it lies in } cf \text{ 78.}$

Hence, $Q_3 = 55$

Note The value of X is already in ascending order, therefore, the series is not rearranged.

Solved Question 16 Calculate Q_1 and Q_3 from the following data

Marks	0-5	5-10	10-15	15-20	20-25	25-30	30-35	35-40
Number of Students	4	6	8	12	12	8	6	4

Sol. **Calculation of Q_1 and Q_3**

Marks (X)	Number of Students (f)	Cumulative Frequency (cf)
0–5	4	4
5–10	6	10
10–15	8	18
15–20	12	30
20–25	12	42
25–30	8	50
30–35	6	56
35–40	4	60
	$N=60$	

(i) $q_1 = \text{Size of}\left(\frac{N}{4}\right)\text{th item} = \text{Size of}\left(\frac{60}{4}\right)\text{th item}$

$= \text{Size of 15th item. It lies in 10-15 group}$

$$\therefore \quad Q_1 = l_1 + \frac{\frac{N}{4} - cf}{f} \times c$$

$$= 10 + \frac{\frac{60}{4} - 10}{8} \times 5$$

$$= 10 + \frac{5 \times 5}{8} = 10 + 3.125$$

$$\Rightarrow \quad Q_1 = 13.125$$

(ii) $q_3 = \text{Size of } 3\left(\frac{N}{4}\right)\text{th item}$

$= \text{Size of } 3\left(\frac{60}{4}\right)\text{th item}$

$= \text{Size of 45th item. It lies in 25-30 group}$

$$\therefore \; Q_3 = l_1 + \frac{3\left(\frac{N}{4}\right) - cf}{f} \times c = 25 + \frac{3\left(\frac{60}{4}\right) - 42}{8} \times 5$$

$$= 25 + \frac{3 \times 5}{8} = 25 + \frac{15}{8} = 25 + 1.875$$

$$\Rightarrow Q_3 = 26.875$$

Points to be Remembered While Computing Quartiles

- The properties, merits and limitations of quartiles are the same as that of the median.
- While calculating quartiles, the series should be arranged in ascending order only, otherwise the value of Q_1 and Q_3 will get interchanged.
- For the computation of quartiles, inclusive frequency distribution is required to be converted into exclusive frequency distribution.
- If mid-values are given, then exclusive frequency distribution should be formed before computing quartiles.
- Unequal class intervals need not be converted into equal class intervals.
- In case of open ended series, quartile is calculated in the same way as median. Class intervals of the quartile class are considered.

6.4 Mode

The mode is the value that appears most frequently in a dataset i.e. it represents that value which is repeated maximum number of times in the distribution. It can be denoted by 'Z'.

Classification Based on Number of Modes

- **No-modal Series** No mode if no value appears more frequently than others. e.g. 4, 4, 5, 5, 6, 6.
- **Uni-modal Series** It has one mode, which is the value that appears most frequently. e.g. 3, 4, 5, 3, 7, 3 (mode is 3).
- **Bi-modal Series** It has two modes, each appearing with highest frequency. e.g. 3, 4, 3, 5, 10, 4 (modes are 3 and 4).
- **Multi-modal Series** It has more than two modes, with several values appearing with the highest frequency. e.g. 3, 4, 5, 3, 5, 4, 10, 8, 6, 7 (modes are 3, 4 and 5).

Calculation of Mode

Calculation of mode in individual, discrete and continuous series is discussed below

Calculation of Mode in Individual Series

By Observing Data	By Conversion of Data into a Discrete Series
Step 1 Arrange the data in ascending or descending order. ***Step 2*** Identify the value that appears most frequently. This value is the mode.	***Step 1*** Convert the individual series into a discrete series by listing each value and counting its frequency. ***Step 2*** Find the value with the highest frequency. This value is the mode.

Solved Question 17 **From the heights of 15 students, calculate the value of mode.**
Height (in inches) 50 50 66 70 66 66 70 66 60 67 70 67 50 60 65

Sol. By arranging the series in an ascending order, we get 50, 50, 50, 60, 60, 65, 66, 66, 66, 66, 67, 67, 70, 70, 70.

By observation, height of 66 inches occurs most frequently, i.e. three times, therefore the modal height (M_o) is 66 inches.

Solved Question 18 **Calculate the value of mode from the following data**

Wages 30 40 35 40 45 40 36 25 32 40 40 46 47 25 35

Sol.

Calculation of Mode

Wages	Number of Times
30	1
40	5
35	2
45	1
36	1
25	2
32	1
46	1
47	1

Here, mode is 40 because it occurs the maximum number of times.

Calculation of Mode in Discrete Series

In a discrete series, mode can be calculated in the following two ways

1. By Inspection Method

In this method, the value corresponding to the highest frequency is the mode.

2. By Grouping Method

In certain cases, the items concentrate around more than one value, so it becomes difficult to observe the modal value. In such cases, the grouping method is used.

Following steps are followed in this method

Step 1 Create a grouping table with columns for values, frequencies and various frequency totals. Format of a grouping table given aside

Step 2 Record the given frequencies in the first column and mark the highest frequency.

Step 3 Add two frequencies, starting from the top, record totals in the second column and mark the highest total.

Grouping Table

Size of Items	Frequency (f)					
	I	II	III	IV	V	VI

Step 4 Repeat the addition process, starting from second frequency and record totals in third column. Mark the highest total.

Step 5 Add three frequencies, starting from top, record these in fourth column and mark the highest total.

Step 6 Repeat the addition process (three frequencies), starting from second frequency, record these in fifth column and mark the highest total.

Step 7 Repeat the addition process (three frequencies), starting from third frequency, record these in fifth column and mark the highest total.

Step 8 Prepare an *analysis table*. While preparing this table, put column numbers on the left hand side and the various values of (x) on the right hand side.

The highest total of frequencies marked in each column is now entered in the analysis table against the concerned values of X or item. We use tick mark (✓) in the relevant box to show these entries. Format of an analysis table is given aside

Column Number	Values of X						
	–	–	–	–	–	–	–
I							
II							
Total							

Step 9 At the end, we find total number of tick marks for each value of X. The value of X having maximum tick marks is called mode of the given series.

Solved Question 19 Find mode from the following data

Marks	100	200	300	400	500
Number of Students	20	30	15	10	5

Sol. **Calculation of Mode**

Marks	100	200	300	400	500
Number of Students (f)	20	30	15	10	5

By inspection, we observe that the highest frequency is 30. The value corresponding to this frequency is 200.

∴ Modal marks = 200

Solved Question 20 Find out mode of the following series

Size	8	9	10	11	12	13	14	15
Frequency	5	6	8	7	9	8	9	6

Sol. Two items 12 and 14 have the highest frequency of 9. So, grouping of frequencies is essential.

Grouping Table

Size (X)	Frequency (f) I	II	III	IV	V	VI
8	5	11		19		
9	6		14		21	
10	8	15				**24**
11	7		16	**24**		
12	**9**	**17**			**26**	
13	8		17			23
14	**9**	15				
15	6					

Now, prepare analysis table.

Analysis Table

Column No.	**8**	**9**	**10**	**11**	**12**	**13**	**14**	**15**
I					✓		✓	
II					✓	✓		
III						✓	✓	
IV				✓	✓	✓		
V					✓	✓	✓	
VI			✓	✓	✓			
Total	—	—	1	2	5	4	3	—

The size (x) = 12 has maximum number of tick marks (5 times). So, mode = 12.

Tick (✓) marks have been put on the following basis

- In column 1, the maximum frequency 9 corresponds to two values *viz.* 12 and 14. So, a tick mark is put before these values.
- In column 2, the maximum total of 17 is obtained by adding frequencies 9 and 8. These frequencies correspond to values 12 and 13.
  Hence, a tick mark is put before these values in column 2 of the analysis table. In the same way, tick marks can be put in subsequent columns.

Calculation of Mode in Continuous Series

By Inspection Method

Step 1 Identify the modal class, which is the class with the highest frequency.

Step 2 Use the following formula to calculate the exact value of the mode within this class

$$\text{Mode}(M_o) = l_1 + \frac{f_1 - f_0}{2f_1 - f_0 - f_2} \times c$$

where,

l_1 = Lower limit of modal class

f_1 = Frequency of the modal class

f_0 = Frequency of the class preceding the modal class

f_2 = Frequency of class succeeding the modal class

c = Class interval of the modal class

By Grouping Method

Step 1 Determine the modal class with the highest frequency using the grouping method. (Same as in discrete series)

Step 2 Calculate the exact value of the mode using the provided formula

$$M_o = l_1 + \frac{f_1 - f_0}{2f_1 - f_0 - f_2} \times c$$

where,

l_1 = Lower limit of modal class

f_1 = Frequency of the modal class

f_0 = Frequency of the class preceding the modal class

f_2 = Frequency of class succeeding the modal class

c = Class interval of the modal class

Solved Question 21 Calculate mode from the following data

Marks	0–10	10–20	20–30	30–40	40–50	50–60
Number of Students	4	10	20	35	15	6

Sol. By observation, the modal class is 30-40, since it has maximum frequency 35.

Now, $l_1 = 30, \quad f_1 = 35$

$f_2 = 15, \quad f_0 = 20$

$c = 10$

$$\therefore \quad \text{Mode } (M_o) = l_1 + \frac{f_1 - f_0}{2f_1 - f_0 - f_2} \times c$$

$$= 30 + \frac{35 - 20}{2 \times 35 - 20 - 15} \times 10$$

$$= 30 + \frac{15 \times 10}{35}$$

$$= 30 + \frac{150}{35} = 30 + 4.28$$

$\therefore$ Mode $(M_o) = 34.28$ marks

Solved Question 22 From the following data, determine mode

Size	10–15	15–20	20–25	25–30	30–35	35–40	40–45	45–50
Frequency	4	10	25	15	23	22	12	3

Sol. By inspection, the modal class is not clear. Although, class interval 20–25 has the highest frequency (25), yet greatest concentration of items is around class interval 30–35 (with frequency of 23). Hence, we will prepare a grouping table and then analysis table to determine the modal class.

Grouping Table

Size (X)	Frequency (f) I	II	III	IV	V	VI
10–15	4	14		39		
15–20	10		35		50	
20–25	**25**	40				63
25–30	15		**38**	60		
30–35	23	**45**			57	
35–40	22		34			37
40–45	12	15				
45–50	3					

Analysis Table

Column Number	10-15	15-20	20-25	25-30	30-35	35-40	40-45	45-50
I			✓					
II					✓	✓		
III				✓	✓			
IV				✓	✓	✓		
V					✓	✓	✓	
VI			✓	✓	✓			
Total	–	–	2	3	5	3	1	–

It is clear from the analysis table that modal class is 30-35 and frequency of this class is 23.

Now, Mode $(M_o) = l_1 + \frac{f_1 - f_0}{2f_1 - f_0 - f_2} \times c$

$\therefore \quad l_1 = 30, \; f_1 = 23, \; f_0 = 15, \; f_2 = 22, \; c = 5$

$$M_o = 30 + \frac{23 - 15}{2 \times 23 - 15 - 22} \times 5 = 30 + \frac{8}{9} \times 5 = 34.44$$

6.5 Certain Specific Cases of Mode

Different types of numerical based on certain specific conditions are discussed below

Certain Specific Cases of Mode

Calculation of mode
- In inclusive class intervals
- When mid-values are given
- In cumulative series
- In unequal class intervals
- In open ended series

Computation of missing frequencies when mode is given

Mode Calculation in Inclusive Class Intervals	Mode Calculation When Mid-values are Given
Step 1 Convert the inclusive class intervals into exclusive class intervals. ***Step 2*** Apply the formula for calculating mode as you would in an exclusive class interval series.	***Step 1*** Convert the mid-values into class intervals. ***Step 2*** Calculate the mode using the formula designed for class intervals.

Mode Calculation in Cumulative Series	Mode Calculation in Unequal Class Intervals
Step 1 Convert the cumulative frequency distribution (less-than or more-than type) into a simple frequency distribution. ***Step 2*** Calculate the mode from the simple frequency distribution.	***Step 1*** Convert the unequal class intervals into equal class intervals. Adjust the frequencies accordingly. ***Step 2*** Calculate the mode from the adjusted distribution.

Mode Calculation in Open Ended Series

For calculation of mode in open ended series, there is no special adjustment needed for missing extreme limits to complete the class intervals. Follow the normal method for calculating the mode.

Computation of Missing Frequencies When Mode is Given

Use the given mode to calculate the missing frequency or frequencies by applying appropriate methods or formulae based on the data provided.

Solved Question 23 **Calculate mode in the following distribution**

Marks	30-39	40-49	50-59	60-69	70-79	80-89
Number of Students	12	30	24	20	12	2

Sol. Here, inclusive class interval will be converted to exclusive class interval and thereafter mode will be determined.

Marks	Number of Students (f)
29.5-39.5	12
39.5-49.5	30
49.5-59.5	24
59.5-69.5	20
69.5-79.5	12
79.5-89.5	2

By inspection, the modal class is not clear. Although, class interval 49.5–59.5 has the highest frequency 30, yet greatest concentration of items is around class interval 59.5–69.5 (with frequency of 24). Therefore, we will find mode by the method of grouping.

Grouping Table

Size (X)	Frequency (f) I	II	III	IV	V	VI
29.5–39.5	12	42		66		
39.5–49.5	**30**		54		74	
49.5–59.5	24	44				56
59.5–69.5	20		32	34		
69.5–79.5	12	14				
79.5–89.5	2					

Analysis Table

Column Number	Frequency (f) 29.5–39.5	39.5–49.5	49.5–59.5	59.5–69.5	69.5–79.5	79.5–89.5
I		✓				
II			✓	✓		
III		✓	✓			
IV	✓	✓	✓			
V		✓	✓	✓		
VI			✓	✓	✓	
Total	1	4	5	3	1	

From the analysis table, the modal class is 49.5 – 59.5. The frequency of this group is 24. So,

$$\text{Mode } (M_o) = l_1 + \frac{f_1 - f_0}{2f_1 - f_0 - f_2} \times c$$

But in this case, $f_1(24)$ is less than $f_0(30)$. It means $(f_1 - f_0)$ will be negative and because of this modal value will lie outside the group.

In such cases, mode is calculated by the following formula,

$$M_o = l_1 + \frac{f_2}{f_0 + f_2} \times c$$

$$\Rightarrow \quad M_o = 49.5 + \frac{20}{30+20} \times 10 = 49.5 + 0.4 \times 10$$

$$\Rightarrow \quad M_o = 49.5 + 4$$

$$\Rightarrow \quad M_o = 53.5$$

Solved Question 24 Calculate the mode from the following data

Marks (Mid-value)	5	10	15	20	25	30	35	40	45
Number of Students	7	13	19	24	32	28	17	8	6

Sol. Here, the mid-values are given, so we need to convert it into continuous series and we get the following table

Marks	Number of Students (f)
2.5–7.5	7
7.5–12.5	13
12.5–17.5	19
17.5–22.5	24
22.5–27.5	32
27.5–32.5	28
32.5–37.5	17
37.5–42.5	8
42.5–47.5	6

By inspection, we observe that the modal class is 22.5–27.5 as it has the highest frequency 32.

$\therefore \; l_1 = 22.5, \quad f_1 = 32, \quad f_0 = 24, \quad f_2 = 28, \quad c = 5$

$$\text{Now, Mode } (M_o) = l_1 + \frac{f_1 - f_0}{2f_1 - f_0 - f_2} \times c$$

$$= 22.5 + \frac{32 - 24}{2 \times 32 - 24 - 28} \times 5$$

$$= 22.5 + \frac{8}{64 - 52} \times 5 = 22.5 + \frac{8}{12} \times 5$$

$$= 22.5 + \frac{40}{12} = 22.5 + 3.33$$

$$\Rightarrow \quad M_o = 25.83$$

Solved Question 25 Calculate mode from the following data

Marks	Less than 10	Less than 20	Less than 30	Less than 40	Less than 50
Number of Students	10	30	60	80	90

Sol. Here, cumulative frequencies are given, so we first convert it into simple frequencies.

Marks	0–10	10–20	20–30	30–40	40–50
Number of Students (f)	10	20	30	20	10

By inspection, we observe that the modal class is 20–30 as it has the highest frequency (30).

$\therefore \; l_1 = 20, \quad f_1 = 30, \quad f_0 = 20, \quad f_2 = 20$ and $\quad c = 10$

$$\text{Now, Mode } M_o = l_1 + \frac{f_1 - f_0}{2f_1 - f_0 - f_2} \times c$$

$$= 20 + \frac{30 - 20}{2 \times 30 - 20 - 20} \times 10$$

$$= 20 + \frac{10}{60 - 40} \times 10 = 20 + \frac{10 \times 10}{20}$$

$$= 20 + \frac{100}{20} = 20 + 5$$

$\Rightarrow$ Hence, Mode $(M_o) = 25$

Solved Question 26 Calculate mode from the following distribution

Wages in ₹ (More than)	500	1,000	1,500	2,000	2,500	3,000
No. of Workers	60	48	30	18	10	4

Sol. **Calculation of Mode**

Wages	Frequency (f)
500-1000	$60 - 48 = 12$
1000-1500	$48 - 30 = 18$
1500-2000	$30 - 18 = 12$
2000-2500	$18 - 10 = 8$
2500-3000	$10 - 4 = 6$
3000-3500	4

By observation method, 1000-1500 is the modal class.

$\therefore \; l_1 = 1000, \quad f_1 = 18, \quad f_0 = 12, \quad f_2 = 12, \quad c = 500$

$$\text{Now, Mode } (Z) = l_1 + \frac{f_1 - f_0}{2f_1 - f_2 - f_0} \times c$$

$$= 1{,}000 + \left(\frac{18 - 12}{2 \times 18 - 12 - 12}\right) \times 500$$

$$= 1{,}000 + \left(\frac{6}{36 - 24}\right) \times 500$$

$$= 1{,}000 + \frac{6}{12} \times 500 = 1{,}000 + 250 = 1{,}250$$

Solved Question 27 **Find out mode from the following data**

Size	0-4	4-6	6-10	10-15	15-20	20-30	30-35	35-40
Frequency	2	4	3	5	2	20	6	8

Sol. Groups are rearranged in the following manner

Size	0-10	10-20	20-30	30-40
Frequency (f)	9 [2 + 4 + 3]	7 [5 + 2]	20	14 [6 + 8]

By inspection, mode lies in class 20–30.

$\therefore$ $l_1 = 20$, $f_1 = 20$, $f_0 = 7$, $f_2 = 14$, $c = 10$

$$\therefore \quad \text{Mode } (M_o) = l_1 + \frac{f_1 - f_0}{2f_1 - f_0 - f_2} \times c$$

$$= 20 + \frac{20 - 7}{2 \times 20 - 7 - 14} \times 10$$

$$= 20 + \frac{13}{19} \times 10 = 20 + 6.84$$

$$M_o = 26.84$$

Solved Question 28 **Calculate mode from following data**

Marks	No. of Student
Below 20	04
20-30	06
30-40	18
40-50	05
50-60	03
60-70	02
Above 70	10

Sol.

Calculation of Mode

Marks	Frequency (f)
Below 20	04
20-30	06
30-40	18
40-50	05
50-60	03
60-70	02
Above 70	10

By observation method, modal class is 30-40.

$\therefore$ $l_1 = 30$, $f_1 = 18$, $f_0 = 06$, $f_2 = 05$, $c = 10$

$$Z = l_1 + \frac{f_1 - f_0}{2f_1 - f_0 - f_2} \times c$$

$$= 30 + \frac{18 - 06}{(2 \times 18) - 06 - 05} \times 10$$

$$= 30 + \frac{12}{36 - 11} \times 10 = 30 + \frac{12 \times 10}{25}$$

$$= 30 + 4.8 = 34.8$$

Solved Question 29 **Determine the missing frequencies when mode is 36 and total frequency is 30.**

Class Interval	10-20	20-30	30-40	40-50	50-60
Frequency (f)	—	5	12	—	2

Sol. Let the missing frequencies be x and y.

Given, $n = \Sigma f = 30$

Calculation of Missing Frequencies

Class Interval	Frequency (f)
10-20	x
20-30	5
30-40	12
40-50	y
50-60	2
	$n = 30$

As the value of mode is 36, so the modal class is 30-40.

$$\therefore \quad \text{Mode, } (M_0) = l_1 + \frac{f_1 - f_0}{2f_1 - f_0 - f_2} \times c$$

$$\Rightarrow \quad 36 = 30 + \frac{12 - 5}{24 - 5 - y} \times 10$$

$$\Rightarrow \quad 6 = \frac{7}{19 - y} \times 10$$

$$\Rightarrow \quad 6(19 - y) = 70 \Rightarrow 114 - 6y = 70$$

$$\Rightarrow \quad 6y = 44$$

$$\Rightarrow \quad y = \frac{44}{6} = 7.33 = 7$$

[as the frequencies cannot be in fractions]

Also, given sum of frequencies = 30

$$x + 5 + 12 + y + 2 = 30$$

$$\therefore\Rightarrow \quad x + 5 + 12 + 7 + 2 = 30 \qquad [\because y = 7]$$

$$\therefore \quad x = 4$$

Thus, the two missing frequencies are 4 and 7.

Mode by Graphical Method

To locate the mode of a continuous series graphically, follow these steps

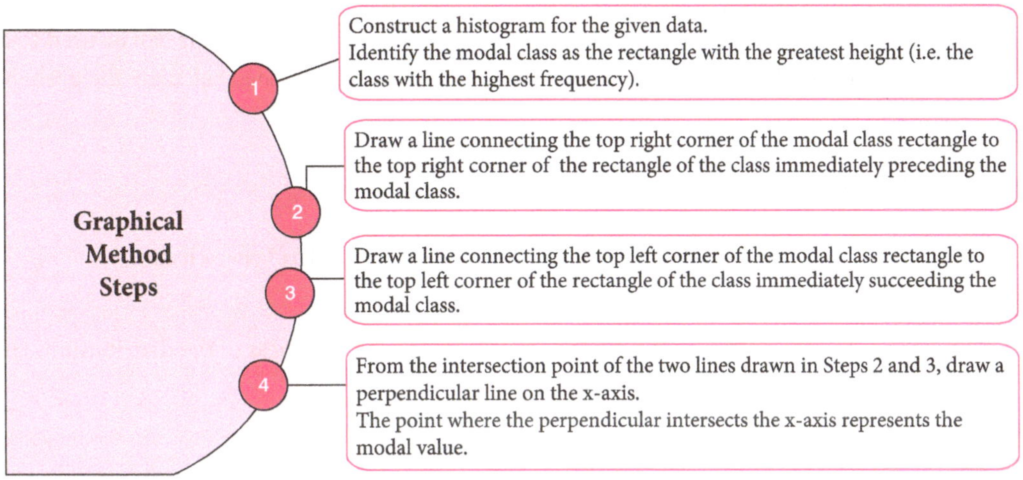

Solved Question 30 **Calculate the value of mode graphically from the following data**

Marks	0-5	5-10	10-15	15-20	20-25	25-30
Number of Students	6	10	20	12	8	4

Sol.

Calculation of Mode

Marks	Number of Students (f)
0-5	6
5-10	10
10-15	20
15-20	12
20-25	8
25-30	4

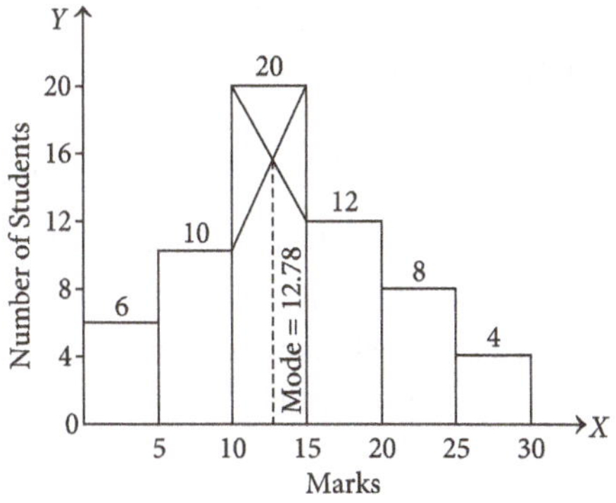

The histogram of given data is drawn. Maximum of height of rectangle is 20 which represents group 10-15. So, 10–15 is the modal class. From the graph, it is clear that required mode of given data is 12.78.

Merits of Mode

- Easy to calculate as less mathematical calculations are required.
- Not affected by changes in extreme values.
- Can be calculated graphically.
- Can be used for both qualitative and quantitative data.
- Best representative of data.

Demerits of Mode

- Not rigidly defined.
- Not based on all items of the series.
- Not capable of further algebraic treatment.
- Affected by changes in sampling values.

Empirical Relationship between Mean, Median and Mode

The following empirical relationship is observed between mean, median and mode
Mode $(M_0) = 3$ Median $(M) - 2$ Mean $(\overline{X})$
In case, in a series, the mode is ill-defined, i.e. cannot be calculated, then the above formula can be used to compute mode. e.g. If the arithmetic mean of a distribution is 24.5 and the median is 30.6, then calculate the probable value of mode.

Sol. We know that,

$$\text{Mode} = 3\ \text{Median} - 2\ \text{Mean}$$

$$M_o = 3 \times 30.6 - 2 \times 24.5 = 91.8 - 49 = 42.8$$

Note Modal value calculated by the empirical relation and that by the usual method may differ from each other.

Relationship between Mean, Median and Mode

The relationship between the mean, median, and mode varies based on the skewness of the distribution. Here's a summary of their relationships in different types of distributions

1. Symmetrical Distribution

- **Mean = Median = Mode**
- In a perfectly symmetrical distribution, all three measures of central tendency coincide, as the data is equally distributed on both sides of the center.

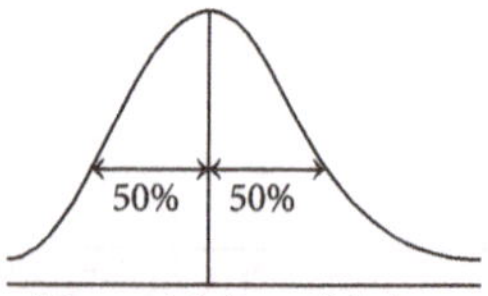

Mean = Median = Mode

2. Negatively Skewed Distribution

- **Mode > Median > Mean**
- In a negatively skewed distribution, where the tail is longer on the left side, the mode is greater than the median, which in turn is greater than the mean. This indicates that the majority of the data is concentrated on the left side.

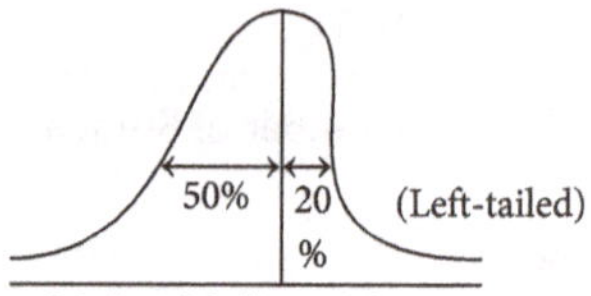

Mode > Median > Mean

3. Positively Skewed Distribution

- **Mean > Median > Mode**
- In a positively skewed distribution, where the tail is longer on the right side, the mean is greater than the median, which is greater than the mode. This indicates that the majority of the data is concentrated on the right side.

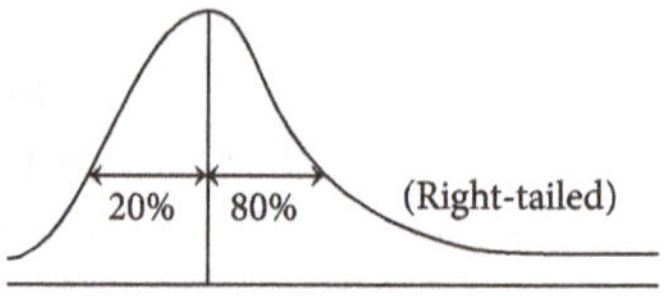

Mean > Median > Mode

Comparison among Mean, Median and Mode

- Mean and median are certain values but not the mode. It is not so precise and accurate.
- It is difficult to calculate mode as compared to mean and median.
- Mean is based on all the items in the series but median and mode are not based on all the items in the series.
- Algebraic treatment is possible with the help of mean. Median and mode are not useful for algebraic treatment.
- Mode is not affected by extremely small values. Median is slightly affected by extreme values, mean is affected by extreme values to a great extent.
- Median and mode can be computed graphically but not mean.

Mind Map

MEASURES OF CENTRAL TENDENCY: MEDIAN AND MODE

1 Median

- It is the middle value that divides the dataset into two equal halves when arranged in order.
- It is considered better than mean when data has extreme values.
- **Formula**
  – When n is odd,
  $$\text{Median} = \left(\frac{n+1}{2}\right)^{th} \text{ item}$$
  – When n is even,
  $$\text{Median} = \frac{\left(\frac{n}{2}\right)^{th} + \left(\frac{n}{2}+1\right)^{th}}{2} \text{ item}$$

Calculation in Different Series

- **Individual Series** Arrange data, apply formula.
- **Discrete Series** Use cumulative frequency to find median position.
- **Continuous Series** Use median class and apply following formula
$$\text{Median } (M) = l_1 + \frac{\frac{N}{2} - cf}{f} \times c$$

2 Special Cases of Median

- Cumulative frequency given (Convert into simple frequency first)
- Mid-values given (Convert to class intervals before calculation)
- Inclusive class intervals (Convert to exclusive format)
- Open-ended class intervals (Use normal median formula)
- Unequal class intervals (No need to adjust class intervals)
- Missing frequency given (Use the median formula to find missing values)

3 Location of Median by Graph

Median can be determined graphically using ogives

Using Both 'More-than' and 'Less-than' Ogives

- Convert frequency distribution into less-than and more-than ogives and plot both curves on the same graph.
- Draw a vertical line from the intersection point to the x-axis.
- The point on x-axis is the median.

Using Only 'Less-than' Ogive

- Convert data into a less-than cumulative frequency distribution and plot the ogive on a graph.
- Find $N/2$ on the y-axis and draw a horizontal line.
- Drop a perpendicular line to the x-axis is median.

Using Only 'More-than' Ogive

- Convert data into a more-than cumulative frequency distribution and plot the ogive on a graph.
- Find $N/2$ on the y-axis and draw a horizontal line.
- Drop a perpendicular line to the x-axis is median.

4 Quartiles

- Q_1 *(First Quartile)*: Lower 25% of data.
- Q_2 *(Median)*: Middle 50% of data.
- Q_3 *(Third Quartile)*: Upper 75% of data.

Formula for continuous series

for
$$Q_1 = l_1 + \frac{\left(\frac{N}{4}\right) - cf}{f} \times c; \quad Q_2 = l_1 + \frac{2\left(\frac{N}{4}\right) - cf}{f} \times c; \quad Q_3 = l_1 + \frac{3\left(\frac{N}{4}\right) - cf}{f} \times c$$

5 Mode

It is the most frequently occurring value in a dataset and denoted as Z.

Classification of Data based on Mode

- No-modal series (No mode exists)
- Uni-modal series (Single mode)
- Bi-modal series (Two modes)
- Multi-modal series (More than two modes)

Calculation in Different Series

1. **Individual Series**
   - Value that appears most frequently.
2. **Discrete Series**
   - Inspection Method – Find the highest frequency.
   - Grouping Method – Used if data is concentrated around multiple values.
3. **Continuous Series**
   - Use modal class and apply formula
$$M_0 = l_1 + \frac{f_1 - f_0}{2f_1 - f_0 - f_2} \times c$$

6 Special Cases of Mode

- Inclusive class intervals (Convert to exclusive first)
- Mid-values given (Convert to class intervals before calculation)
- Unequal class intervals (Adjust frequencies accordingly)
- Open-ended class intervals (No need for missing limits)
- Missing frequency given (Use mode formula to determine unknown values)

Graphical Method for Mode

Using histogram

- Identify the tallest bar (modal class).
- Draw two lines connecting the top corners of modal and adjacent bars.
- The intersection point on the x-axis gives the mode.

7 Empirical Relationship Between Mean, Median and Mode

Mode (M_o) = 3 Median (M) – 2 Mean ($\bar{X}$)

It is used when mode is difficult to determine or ill defined.

Different Cases in Distribution

- Symmetrical distribution (Mean = Median = Mode).
- Negatively skewed (Mode > Median > Mean).
- Positively skewed (Mean > Median > Mode).

EXAM PATTERN QUESTIONS

Objective Type Questions

Multiple Choice Questions (MCQs)

1. **In addition to the arithmetic mean, ... are used to evaluate qualitative aspects of a distribution by focusing on specific positions within a dataset.**

(a) measures of dispersion (b) positional averages
(c) standard deviations (d) frequencies

2. **Which of the following best describes the median?**

I. The value that divides a dataset into two equal halves, with half of the data points being greater and half being lesser.
II. The value calculated by adding the highest and lowest numbers in a dataset and dividing by two.
III. The most frequently occurring value in a dataset.
IV. The average of all numbers in a dataset, which can be skewed by extreme values.

Codes **Competency Based Que**

(a) II and III (b) I and II
(c) Only I (d) Only IV

3. **Identify the measure of central tendency highlighted in the image given below.**

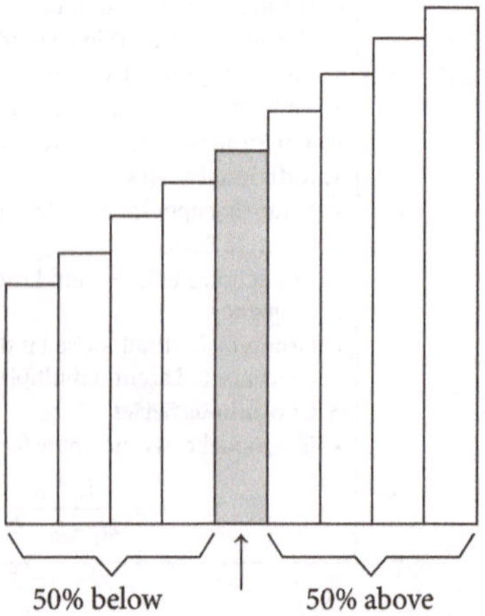

(a) Mathematical average (b) Median
(c) Mode (d) Both (a) and (b)

4. **In what scenario is the median preferred over the mean?** **Competency Based Que**

(a) When data is balanced and does not contain outliers
(b) When the dataset is highly skewed by extreme values or outliers
(c) When calculating the average of all numbers in the dataset
(d) When the dataset has a normal distribution

5. **Viaan wants to get an accurate picture of household salary in his neighbourhood. The salaries for people in his neighbourhood are ₹ 87,000, ₹ 94,000, ₹ 1,03,000, ₹ 97,000 and ₹ 55,000. Which measure of central tendency will most accurately describe the data?** **Competency Based Que**

(a) Median (b) Mode
(c) Both (a) and (b) (d) Neither (a) nor (b)

6. **In a discrete series with the following frequencies 4, 6, 8, 7 and 5, where the values are 10, 20, 30, 40 and 50 respectively, what is the median value?** **Competency Based Que**

(a) 20 (b) 50
(c) 40 (d) 30

7. **If the data are arranged in ascending order, then the value of items to the left of the median will be**

(a) less than the median value
(b) more than the median value
(c) either less than or more than the median value
(d) None of the above

8. **When calculating the median from an inclusive series, first convert the series into an .... series.**

(a) cumulative (b) open ended
(c) exclusive (d) mid-value

9. **Given the following cumulative frequencies Less-than 5 : 4, less-than 10 : 9, less-than 15 : 16. What is the median?** **Competency Based Que**

(a) 9 (b) 5
(c) 10 (d) 20

10. **While computing median in a continuous series, the following formula is used,**

$$M = l_1 + \frac{N/2 - cf}{f} \times c$$

In the given formula, l_1 represents

(a) lower limit of the median class
(b) upper limit of the median class
(c) class interval of the median class
(d) None of the above

11. Which quartile is also known as the median?

(a) First quartile (Q_1) (b) Second quartile (Q_2)
(c) Third quartile (Q_3) (d) None of these

12. Which quartile is highlighted by number 4 in the below image?

2 2 (4) 5 5 (5) 8 9 (9) 9 12

(a) First quartile (Q_1)
(b) Second quartile (Q_2)
(c) Third quartile (Q_3)
(d) None of the above

13. What does the third quartile (Q_3) represent in a dataset? **Competency Based Que**

I. 25% of the items are below Q_3 and 75% are above it.
II. 50% of the items are below Q_3 and 50% are above it.
III. 75% of the items are below Q_3 and 25% are above it.
IV. The median value of the dataset.

Codes

(a) I and II (b) I and IV
(c) I, II and III (d) Only III

14. To calculate quartiles in a discrete series, the data should first be ...., then cumulative frequencies are calculated and finally, quartile formulae are applied.

(a) sorted in descending order
(b) sorted in ascending order
(c) randomised
(d) converted into continuous series

15. Identify the quartile that is calculated by using the formula given in the following image.

$$= 2\left(\frac{N}{4}\right)\text{th item}$$

(a) Q_1 (b) Q_2
(c) Q_3 (d) Q_4

16. The value of deciles divides the total number of observations into .... equal parts.

(a) 100 (b) 10
(c) 2 (d) None of these

17. Which type of series has no mode?

(a) No-modal series (b) Uni-modal series
(c) Multi-modal series (d) Bi-modal series

18. A series with more than two values where each appear with the highest frequency is called a .... series.

(a) no-modal series (b) uni-modal series
(c) multi-modal series (d) bi-modal series

19. Identify the mode from the image given below.

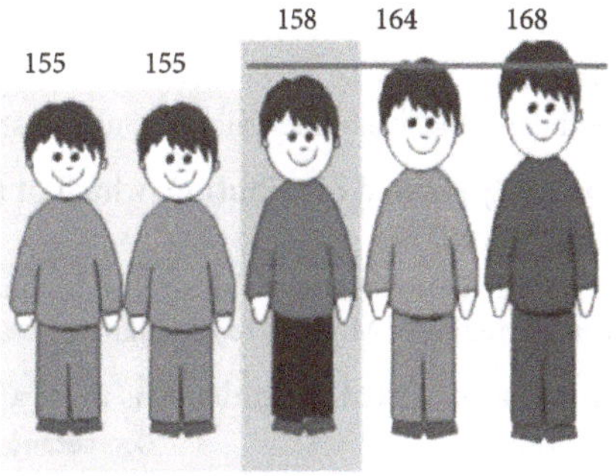

(a) Boy with height 158
(b) Boy with height 168
(c) Boy with height 155
(d) Boy with height 164

20. Dataset 7, 8, 7, 10, 12, 7, 15. What is the mode of the dataset? **Competency Based Que**

(a) 7 (b) 8
(c) 10 (d) 12

21. Which of the following steps are involved in the grouping method for calculating the mode in a discrete series?

I. Create a grouping table with columns for values, frequencies and frequency totals.
II. Identify the value with the highest frequency directly from the data.
III. Record the given frequencies in the first column and mark the highest frequency.
IV. Prepare an analysis table to summarise which values have the highest totals of frequencies.
V. Add frequencies in pairs, starting from the top and record these totals in the second column.

Codes **Competency Based Que**

(a) I and II (b) I, III, IV and V
(c) I and III (d) II and IV

22. Mode = 3 Median − 2 ....

(a) Quartile (b) Mean (c) GM (d) HM

23. Which type of distribution is highlighted in the below image?

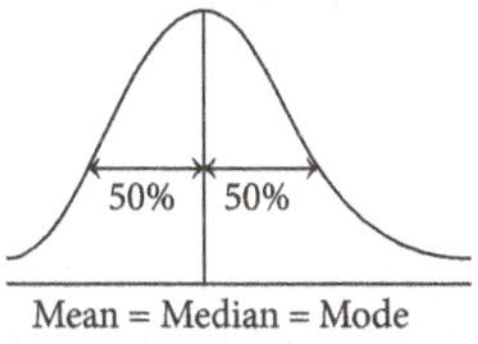

(a) Symmetric (b) Negatively skewed
(c) Positively skewed (d) Asymmetric

24. When calculating the mode for a distribution with unequal class intervals, the first step is to ....

(a) convert the unequal class intervals into equal class intervals
(b) calculate the cumulative frequencies
(c) adjust the frequencies accordingly
(d) use the original class intervals without adjustment

25. **In a positively skewed distribution, which of the following is true?**
(a) Mean < Median < Mode (b) Mean = Median = Mode
(c) Mean > Median > Mode (d) Median > Mean > Mode

26. **Which measure of central tendency is most affected by extreme values?** **Competency Based Que**
(a) Mean (b) Median
(c) Mode (d) All are equally affected

Direction *Read the case study and answer the questions 27 to 30 on the basis of the same*

A retail company has analysed its monthly sales data for the past year. The sales figures (in thousands) for twelve months are as follows 50, 52, 54, 60, 61, 65, 70, 75, 78, 80, 85 and 90. The company wants to understand the central tendency of their sales data to make better strategic decisions. They are particularly interested in the median and mode of the sales figures, as well as how the mean compares to these measures. Additionally, they have noticed that some months had significantly higher or lower sales compared to others, which might affect their analysis.

27. **What is the median sales figure for the company based on the data provided?**
(a) 60.35 (b) 67.5 (c) 70.5 (d) 75

28. **What is the mode of the sales data for the company?**
(a) 54 (b) 60
(c) 70 (d) There is no mode

29. **The median sales figure is found by arranging the sales data in .... and selecting the middle value.**

30. **If the company wants to reduce the impact of months with significantly higher or lower sales on their analysis, they should use the .... as the measure of central tendency.**

Assertion-Reason

Direction (Q.No. 31 to 40) *Read the following Assertion (A) and Reason (R) and choose the correct alternative from the following*

Alternatives
(a) Both Assertion (A) and Reason (R) are true and Reason (R) is the correct explanation of Assertion (A)
(b) Both Assertion (A) and Reason (R) are true, but Reason (R) is not the correct explanation of Assertion (A)
(c) Assertion (A) is true, but Reason (R) is false
(d) Assertion (A) is false, but Reason (R) is true

31. **Assertion** (A) Median is a positional average which is located at the mid-point of a given distribution.
Reason (R) Calculation of median depends upon its arrangement in either increasing order or decreasing order.

32. **Assertion** (A) The median divides a dataset into two equal parts, with half of the data points being greater and the other half being lesser.
Reason (R) The median is calculated by averaging the highest and lowest values in a dataset.

33. **Assertion** (A) For a continuous series with unequal class intervals, the median is calculated similarly to continuous series without needing adjustments for the class intervals.
Reason (R) The median is unaffected by extreme values and reflects the middle point of the dataset.

34. **Assertion** (A) In a cumulative frequency distribution, converting it into a simple frequency distribution is necessary before calculating the median.
Reason (R) Cumulative frequencies alone do not allow for direct calculation of the median.

35. **Assertion** (A) The properties, merits and limitations of quartiles are the same as that of the median.
Reason (R) For the computation of quartiles, inclusive frequency distribution is required to be converted into exclusive frequency distribution.

36. **Assertion** (A) First quartile is also known as the lower quartile.
Reason (R) The first quartile represents the value below which 25% of the data falls.

37. **Assertion** (A) In a multi-modal series, each mode appears with equal frequency, which distinguishes it from other types of modal series.
Reason (R) A multi-modal series has more than two modes, with several values appearing with the highest frequency.

38. **Assertion** (A) In a negatively skewed distribution, the mode is greater than the median, which is greater than the mean.
Reason (R) In a negatively skewed distribution, the tail on the left side is longer, causing the mean to be less than the median and mode.

39. **Assertion** (A) The relationship between mean, median and mode can be expressed as Mean − Mode = 3 (Mean − Median) for moderately skewed data.
Reason (R) The empirical relationship holds only for distributions where the skewness is neither extreme nor perfectly symmetric.

40. **Assertion** (A) Mode is the measure of central tendency used to measure mostly the qualitative data.

Reason (R) Arithmetic mean and median are not useful in case of qualitative data.

Two Statements Based MCQs

Direction (Q.No. 41 to 50) *Read the following statements carefully and choose the correct alternative*

Alternatives

(a) Statement I is correct and Statement II is incorrect
(b) Statement II is correct and Statement I is incorrect
(c) Both the statements are correct
(d) Both the statements are incorrect

41. **Statement I** Median can be located graphically in a cumulative distribution without converting it to normal frequency distribution.

Statement II If a series is arranged in descending order, quartile values will be interchanged.

42. **Statement I** The median is the middle number when all numbers are ordered, so it is not affected by extreme values.

Statement II In case of continuous series, median can be located straightforward.

43. **Statement I** Median cannot be used for both qualitative and quantitative data.

Statement II Median is based on all data points.

44. **Statement I** 25% of the items in the dataset are below Q_2 and 75% are above it.

Statement II 75% of the items are below Q_3 and 25% are above it.

45. **Statement I** For calculating quartiles in individual series, data is arranged in ascending order.

Statement II Unequal class intervals should be converted into equal class intervals to calculate quartiles.

46. **Statement I** Quartiles help to understand the distribution of data by highlighting key points that divide the data into equal segments.

Statement II Quartiles are positional averages.

47. **Statement I** Mode is undefined in case of open ended frequency distribution.

Statement II Median is equal to quartile second and decile fifth.

48. **Statement I** Mode is the value which has the greatest frequency density in its immediate neighbourhood.

Statement II Mode can be denoted by Z.

49. **Statement I** No-modal series has more than two modes, with several values appearing with the highest frequency.

Statement II Multi-modal series has two modes, each appearing with the highest frequency.

50. **Statement I** Algebraic treatment is possible with the help of mean.

Statement II Median and mode are not useful for algebraic treatment.

Matching

51. Match the following

Column I		Column II	
A.	Median	(i)	Divide data into four equal parts.
B.	Mode	(ii)	Distribute series into ten equal parts.
C.	Quartile	(iii)	Middle element when data set is arranged in order of magnitude.
D.	Decile	(iv)	The value that appears most frequently in a dataset.

Codes

	A	B	C	D
(a)	(iii)	(iv)	(i)	(ii)
(b)	(iv)	(i)	(ii)	(iii)
(c)	(ii)	(iii)	(iv)	(i)
(d)	(iii)	(ii)	(i)	(iv)

52. Match the following

Column I		Column II	
A.	Frequency of the modal class	(i)	i
B.	Number of items in series	(ii)	f_1
C.	Cumulative frequency of class	(iii)	N
D.	Quartile class	(iv)	cf

Codes

	A	B	C	D
(a)	(iii)	(iv)	(i)	(ii)
(b)	(iv)	(i)	(ii)	(iii)
(c)	(ii)	(iii)	(iv)	(i)
(d)	(iii)	(ii)	(i)	(iv)

53. Match the following

Column I	Column II
A. Percentiles	(i) 25% of the items in the dataset are below Q_1 and 75% are above it.
B. First quartile	(ii) 50% of the items are below Q_2 and 50% are above it.
C. Second quartile	(iii) 75% of the items are below Q_3 and 25% are above it.
D. Third quartile	(iv) Series divided into 100 equal parts

Codes

	A	B	C	D		A	B	C	D
(a)	(iii)	(iv)	(i)	(ii)	(b)	(iv)	(i)	(ii)	(iii)
(c)	(ii)	(iii)	(iv)	(i)	(d)	(iii)	(ii)	(i)	(iv)

54. Match the following

Column I	Column II
A. No-modal series	(i) Has more than two modes
B. Uni-modal series	(ii) Has two modes
C. Multi-modal series	(iii) No mode
D. Bi-modal series	(iv) Has one mode

Codes

	A	B	C	D		A	B	C	D
(a)	(iii)	(iv)	(i)	(ii)	(b)	(iv)	(i)	(ii)	(iii)
(c)	(ii)	(iii)	(iv)	(i)	(d)	(iii)	(ii)	(i)	(iv)

55. Match the options of Column I with correct options in Column II

Column I	Column II
A. A series with two modal values	(i) Mean > Median > Mode
B. Left tailed distribution	(ii) Decile
C. Right tailed distribution	(iii) Bi-modal
D. Partition value	(iv) Mode > Median > Mean

Codes

	A	B	C	D		A	B	C	D
(a)	(iii)	(iv)	(i)	(ii)	(b)	(i)	(ii)	(iii)	(iv)
(c)	(ii)	(iii)	(iv)	(i)	(d)	(iv)	(i)	(iii)	(ii)

Concept Identification

56. It identifies the value that divides a dataset into two equal halves, with one half of the data points being greater and the other half being lesser.

57. It divides a dataset into four equal parts, each containing 25% of the data.

58. It measures the most frequent value in a dataset.

59. It is used to graphically represent the cumulative frequency distribution.

60. It concept divides a dataset into ten equal parts.

Answers

1. (b) positional averages
2. (c) Only I
3. (b) Median
4. (b) When the dataset is highly skewed by extreme values or outliers
5. (a) Median
6. (d) N = 4 + 6 + 8 + 7 + 5 = 30; Median position = N + 1/2 = 30 + 1/2 = 15.5

   Cumulative frequencies 4 (for 10), 10 (for 20), 18 (for 30), 25 (for 40), 30 (for 50)

   The median falls in the cumulative frequency interval that includes the 15.5th position.

   This falls into the cumulative frequency of 18 (corresponding to the value 30).
7. (a) less than the median value
8. (c) exclusive
9. (a) 9
10. (a) lower limit of the median class
11. (b) Second quartlie (Q_2)
12. (a) First quartlie (Q_1)
13. (d) Only III
14. (b) Sorted in ascending order
15. (b) Q_2
16. (b) 10
17. (a) No-modal series
18. (c) multi-modal series
19. (c) Boy with height 155
20. (a) The mode is the value that appears most frequently in a dataset. The number 7 appears 3 times.
21. (b) I, III, IV and V
22. (b) Mean
23. (a) Symmetric

24. (a) convert the unequal class intervals into equal class intervals

25. (c) Mean > Median > Mode

26. (a) Mean

27. (b) To find the median, first arrange the sales data in ascending order 50, 52, 54, 60, 61, 65, 70, 75, 78, 80, 85, 90. Since there are 12 data points (an even number), the median is the average of the 6th and 7th values in the ordered list. These values are 65 and 70.

Median = 65 + 70/2 = 67.5

28. (d) The mode is the value that appears most frequently in a dataset. In this dataset, each sales figure appears only once. Therefore, there is no value that repeats, so there is no mode.

29. ascending order **30.** median

31. (b) Both Assertion (A) and Reason (R) are true, but Reason (R) is not the correct explanation of Assertion (A)

32. (c) The mean is calculated by averaging the highest and lowest values in a dataset.

33. (a) Both Assertion (A) and Reason (R) are true and Reason (R) is the correct explanation of Assertion (A)

34. (a) Both Assertion (A) and Reason (R) are true and Reason (R) is the correct explanation of Assertion (A)

35. (b) Both Assertion (A) and Reason (R) are true, but Reason (R) is not the correct explanation of Assertion (A)

36. (a) Both Assertion (A) and Reason (R) are true and Reason (R) is the correct explanation of Assertion (A)

37. (a) Both Assertion (A) and Reason (R) are true and Reason (R) is the correct explanation of Assertion (A)

38. (a) Both Assertion (A) and Reason (R) are true and Reason (R) is the correct explanation of Assertion (A)

39. (a) Both Assertion (A) and Reason (R) are true and Reason (R) is the correct explanation of Assertion (A)

40. (c) Arithmetic mean may not apply to qualitative data, the median can still be meaningful for certain ordinal qualitative data.

41. (c) Both the statements are correct

42. (a) In case of continuous series, median cannot be located straightforward. In this case, median lies in between lower and upper limit of a class interval.

43. (d) The median can be used for both qualitative and quantitative data. The median is not based on all data points, it only considers the middle value(s) in an ordered dataset.

44. (b) First quartile (Q_1) is also known as the lower quartile. 25% of the items in the dataset are below Q_1 and 75% are above it.

45. (a) Unequal class intervals do not need to be converted into equal class intervals to calculate quartiles. Quartiles can be calculated directly from the given class intervals using the continuous series method.

46. (c) Both the statements are correct

47. (b) Mode is based upon middle 50% data, so it is unaffected by extreme values.

48. (c) Both the statements are correct

49. (d) Multi-modal series has more than two modes, with several values appearing with the highest frequency. Two-modal series two modes, each appearing with the highest frequency.

50. (c) Both the statements are correct

51. (a) (iii) (iv) (i) (ii) **52.** (c) (ii) (iii) (iv) (i)

53. (b) (iv) (i) (ii) (iii) **54.** (a) (iii) (iv) (i) (ii)

55. (a) (iii) (iv) (i) (ii)

56. Median

57. Quartile **58.** Mode

59. Ogive **60.** Decile

Subjective Questions

Short Answer Type Questions

1. "Median has definite and certain value." Explain any three merits of median with the help of given statement. Competency Based Que

Ans. Merits of median are (any three)

(i) It is easy to calculate and simple to understand.

(ii) It is well-defined, so it possesses the qualities of good average.

(iii) We can determine median graphically with the help of ogives.

(iv) In case of open ended classification, it is specially useful because only the position is to be ascertained.

(v) It is useful for studying social phenomena, like wage, distribution of wealth, skill, etc.

(vi) It is a positional value and not a calculated value.

2. Which of the following measure of central tendency is depicted by number 4 in the below image? Explain. Competency Based Que

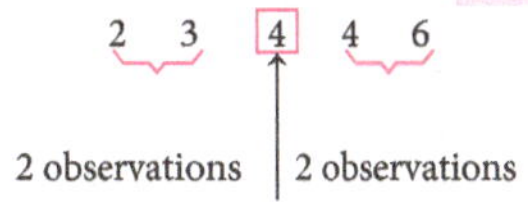

Ans. In the dataset 2, 3, 4, 4, 6, the number 4 represents the median, which is the middle value when the numbers are arranged in ascending order. The median divides the dataset into two equal halves, with half of the values being less than or equal to 4, and the other half being greater than or equal to 4.

For an odd number of data points, the median is simply the value located at the middle position and in this case, 4 is that middle value. Thus, the median provides a central point around which the dataset is evenly distributed.

3. How is median measured for a discrete series?

Ans. In a discrete series, frequencies accompany each value and the median is found using cumulative frequencies.

Step 1 Arrange the data in order and denote values as X and frequencies as f.

Step 2 Calculate cumulative frequencies (cf).

Step 3 Use the formula where, N = Sum of frequency

$$\text{Median } (M) = \left(\frac{N+1}{2}\right)\text{th item}$$

where, N = Sum of frequency

Step 4 Locate the median position through cumulative frequency and the corresponding value is the median.

4. Identify and explain the measure of central tendency highlight below. Competency Based Que

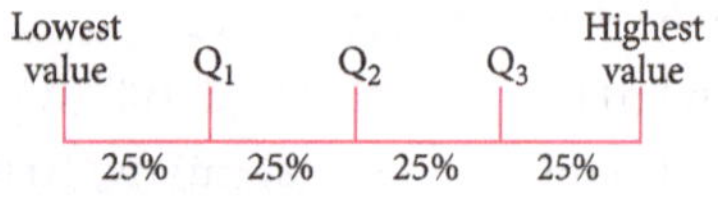

Ans. The image highlights the quartiles of a dataset. Specifically, it shows the division of data into four equal parts, with each quartile representing 25% of the data. The key points identified are

(i) Q_1 (First Quartile)

This is the value below which 25% of the data falls.

(ii) Q_2 (Second Quartile)

Also known as the median, this is the value below which 50% of the data falls.

(iii) Q_3 (Third Quartile)

This is the value below which 75% of the data falls.

5. How do deciles and percentiles differ in their approach to dividing a dataset?

Ans.

Basis	Deciles	Percentiles
Division of Dataset	Divides the dataset into 10 equal parts.	Divides the dataset into 100 equal parts.
Intervals	Each decile represents 10% of the data	Each percentile represents 1% of the data.
Notation	Noted as $D_1, D_2, ..., D_9$.	Noted as $P_1, P_2, ..., P_{99}$.
Common Applications	Used for broader analysis, such as income distribution.	Used for detailed analysis, such as educational assessments or investment returns.

6. "Mode is the best representative value of all items of the series because it is that value which occurs most frequently in the series." State any four advantages of mode in the context of above statement. Competency Based Que

Ans. Mode is the best representative value of all items of the series because

(i) It is easy to calculate and can be easily understood. It can be located by inspection only.

(ii) It is not affected by the extreme values in a series.

(iii) It can be calculated even in case of open ended classes.

(iv) Mode helps in describing the qualitative aspects of phenomenon.

7. Identify and explain if the below image depicts positively or negatively skewed data. Competency Based Que

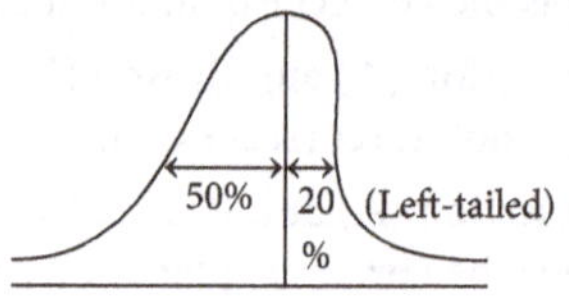

Ans. The image shows negatively skewed distribution, where

(i) Mode > Median > Mean

(ii) In a negatively skewed distribution, where the tail is longer on the left side, the mode is greater than the median, which in turn is greater than the mean. This indicates that the majority of the data is concentrated on the left side.

8. List the merits and demerits of using mode.

Ans. Merits of using mode are

(i) It is easy to calculate as less mathematical calculations are required.

(ii) It is not affected by changes and extreme values.

(iii) It can be calculated graphically.

(iv) It can be used for both qualitative and quantitative data.

(v) It is the best representation of data.

Demerits of using mode are

(i) It is not rigidly defined.

(ii) It is not based on all items of the series.

(iii) It is not capable of further algebraic treatment.

(iv) It is affected by changes in sampling values.

(v) It sometimes become indeterminate.

9. Which average would be suitable in the following cases? NCERT

(i) **Average size of readymade garments.**
(ii) **Average intelligence of students in a class.**
(iii) **In case of open ended frequency distribution.**

Ans. (i) **Mode**

Average size of readymade garments should be the size for which demand is the maximum. Hence, the modal value should be taken as the average size to be produced.

(ii) **Median**

Median will be the best measure for calculating the average intelligence of students in a class as it is the best measure for qualitative characteristics.

(iii) **Median**

It is the most suitable measure for open ended frequency distribution.

Long Answer Type Questions

10. Explain the steps involved in calculating the median for individual, discrete and continuous series.

Ans. (i) **Calculation of Median in an Individual Series**

The median in an individual series is the middle value when data is arranged in order.

Step 1 Arrange all values in ascending or descending order.

Step 2 Find the total number of items (n).

Step 3 If n is odd, calculate the median using the formula

$$\text{Median } (M) = \text{Size of} \left(\frac{N+1}{2}\right) \text{the item}$$

Step 4 And if n is an even number, then the following formula can be used

$$M = \frac{\left(\frac{N}{2}\right)\text{th item} + \text{Size of} \left(\frac{N}{2}+1\right)\text{th item}}{2}$$

(ii) **Calculation of Median in Discrete Series**

In a discrete series, frequencies accompany each value and the median is found using cumulative frequencies.

Step 1 Arrange the data in order and denote values as X and frequencies as f.

Step 2 Calculate cumulative frequencies (cf).

Step 3 Use the formula

$$\text{Median } (M) = \left(\frac{N+1}{2}\right) \text{th item}$$

where, N = Sum of frequencies

Step 4 Locate the median position through cumulative frequency, and the corresponding value is the median.

(iii) **Calculation of Median in Continuous Series**

In case of continuous series, median cannot be located straightforward. In this case, median lies in between lower and upper limit of a class interval.

Step 1 First of all, arrange the data in ascending or descending order.

Step 2 Calculate the cumulative frequencies.

Step 3 Find the value of (N/2) th item and then by inspecting cumulative frequencies (cf) find out the cumulative frequency which is either equal to or just greater than it. The class interval corresponding to this value is called median class.

Step 4 Now, apply the following formula to determine the actual median value

$$\text{Median } (M) = l_1 + \frac{\frac{N}{2} - cf}{f} \times c$$

where,

l_1 = Lower limit of the median class
cf = Cumulative frequency of the class preceding the median class
f = Frequency of the median class
c = Magnitude of the median class interval
N = Sum of frequencies (Σf)

11. "Median can be located graphically by three different methods." Do you agree? If yes, explain the methods. Competency Based Que

Ans. Yes, I agree. Median can be located graphically using three methods which are as follows

(i) **Using Both 'More-than' and 'Less-than' Ogives**

This method involves plotting both 'more-than' and 'less-than' ogive curves on the same graph.

Steps

1. Convert the frequency distribution into a 'less-than' ogive and plot it.
2. Convert the frequency distribution into a 'more-than' ogive and plot it.
3. Plot both ogive curves on the same graph.
4. Draw a horizontal line at the point where the cumulative frequency reaches 50% of the total. The intersection of this line with the x-axis on either ogive will give the median.

(ii) **Using Only 'Less-than' Ogive**

This method uses only the 'less-than' ogive for locating the median.

Steps

1. Convert the frequency distribution into a 'less-than' distribution and plot it on a graph.

2. Find $n/2$ and draw a horizontal line from y-axis, on less-than ogive from $n/2$.
3. From this point, draw a perpendicular on x-axis. Corresponding point on x-axis will be median.

(iii) **Using Only 'More-than' Ogive**

This method uses only the 'more-than' ogive for locating the median.

Steps

1. Convert the frequency distribution into a 'more than' cumulative frequency distribution and plot it.
2. Calculate $n/2$ where n is the total number of observations.
3. Draw a horizontal line at the point where the cumulative frequency is $n/2$. The intersection of this line with the x-axis on the 'more than' ogive will give the median.

12. Is it necessary to convert inclusive class intervals while calculating median? Give reason to support your answer. Competency Based Que

Ans. Yes, converting inclusive class intervals to exclusive intervals is often necessary when calculating the median, especially in continuous data series. Inclusive intervals include both the lower and upper boundaries, which can cause overlap and ambiguity in determining the median class.

To avoid this, we convert the intervals to exclusive ones, where each class includes the lower limit but excludes the upper limit. This conversion helps in accurately identifying the median class, ensuring that there is no overlap between classes, which simplifies the calculation process.

e.g. Converting an inclusive interval of 10-20 to an exclusive interval might result in 9.5-19.5. This adjustment eliminates any confusion about which interval contains the median, allowing for a clear and precise calculation.

13. Explain the different types of modal series and provide examples for each type.

Ans. Modal series are categorised based on the number of modes or the most frequently occurring values, present in a dataset. The classification includes

(i) **No-modal series**

In a no-modal series, there is no mode because no value appears more frequently than others. The data is evenly distributed and no particular value stands out.

e.g. Consider the dataset 4, 4, 5, 5, 6, 6. Each value appears exactly twice, so there is no mode.

(ii) **Uni-modal Series**

A uni-modal series has one mode, meaning only one value appears with the highest frequency.

e.g. In the dataset 3, 4, 5, 3, 7, 3, the mode is 3 because it appears more frequently than any other value.

(iii) **Bi-modal Series**

A bi-modal series has two modes, with two distinct values each occurring with the highest frequency.

e.g. In the dataset 3, 4, 3, 5, 10, 4, the modes are 3 and 4, as both appear twice.

(iv) **Multi-modal Series**

A multi-modal series has more than two modes, with several values appearing with the same highest frequency.

e.g. Consider the dataset 3, 4, 5, 3, 5, 4, 10, 8, 6, 7. Here, the modes are 3, 4 and 5, as each of these values appears twice.

14. Answer the following

(i) Explain the process of calculating the mode in cumulative series.

(ii) How do you compute missing frequencies when the mode is given?

Ans. (i) **Calculating the Mode in Cumulative Series**

To calculate the mode in a cumulative series, follow these steps

- **Convert Cumulative Frequency Distribution**
  Begin by converting the cumulative frequency distribution (whether less than or more than type) into a simple frequency distribution. This involves subtracting successive cumulative frequencies to obtain individual class frequencies.
- **Calculate the Mode**
  Once the simple frequency distribution is calculated, apply the usual formula for calculating the mode in a frequency distribution. This allows you to determine the modal value based on the highest frequency in the distribution.

(ii) **Computing Missing Frequencies When Mode is Given**

When the mode is provided and we need to find missing frequencies, follow these steps

- **Use the Given Mode**
  Start by utilising the mode value and its corresponding class interval. Set-up an equation using the mode formula, which relates the mode to the frequencies of the modal class and adjacent classes.
- **Solve for Missing Frequencies**
  Rearrange the equation to solve for the missing frequency or frequencies.

This often involves simple algebraic manipulation based on the relationship between the mode and the surrounding frequencies. Adjust the equation accordingly to find the unknown values.

15. Explain the relationship between mean, median and mode in different types of distributions.

Ans. The relationship between mean, median and mode varies based on the skewness of the distribution

(i) **Symmetrical Distribution**

In a perfectly symmetrical distribution, the mean, median and mode coincide. This happens because the data is evenly distributed on both sides of the center, making all three measures equal.

Thus, we have Mean = Median = Mode

(ii) **Negatively Skewed Distribution**

In a negatively skewed distribution, where the left tail is longer, the majority of the data is concentrated on the left side. The mode is the highest value, followed by the median, with the mean being the smallest value.

Therefore Mode > Median > Mean

(iii) **Positively Skewed Distribution**

In a positively skewed distribution, where the right tail is longer, the mean is the highest value, followed by the median, with the mode being the smallest value.

This indicates that the data is concentrated on the right side Mean > Median > Mode

Numerical Questions

Numerical 1

Given the dataset 3, 5, 7, 9, 11. Find the median.

Sol. Arrange the data in ascending order 3, 5, 7, 9, 11.

Since there are 5 data points (odd number), the median is the middle value.

Median = 7

Numerical 2

Consider the following data with frequencies.

Value	4	6	8	10
Frequency	3	5	7	2

Find the median.

Sol. Calculate the total number of observations

$3 + 5 + 7 + 2 = 17$

Median position = (17 + 1)/2 = 9th

Cumulative frequencies

- Up to 4: 3
- Up to 6: 3 + 5 = 8
- Up to 8: 8 + 7 = 15 (median falls in this class)

Median = 8

Numerical 3

For the dataset 10, 20, 30, 40, 50, 60, 70, calculate Q_1.

Sol. Arrange the data in ascending order 10, 20, 30, 40, 50, 60, 70.

Number of data points (n) = 7

Q_1 is the value at the n + 1/4 th position

= (7 + 1)/4 th position

$Q_1 = 20$

Numerical 4

Given the dataset 2, 4, 4, 6, 8, 10. Determine the mode.

Sol. Arrange the data in ascending order 2, 4, 4, 6, 8, 10.

The value that appears most frequently is 4.

Mode = 4

Numerical 5

Calculate the median of the following frequency distribution

Salary (in ₹)	40	45	48	50	55	60
Number of Labourers	5	7	6	10	5	8

Sol. **Calculation of Median**

Salary (in ₹)	Number of Labourers (f)	Cumulative Frequency (cf)
40	5	5
45	7	12
48	6	18
50	10	28
55	5	33
60	8	41
	$\Sigma f = 41$	

$$\therefore \text{Median} = \text{Size of} \left(\frac{N+1}{2}\right) \text{th item}$$

$$= \text{Size of} \left(\frac{41+1}{2}\right) \text{th item} = \text{Size of 21st item}$$

21st item will correspond to the cumulative frequency of 28.

Value of salary corresponding to this value is 50.

Therefore, $M = 50$.

Numerical 6

Find out the median of the data given below by arranging them in ascending order.

X	160	150	152	161	156
Frequency	5	8	6	3	7

Sol. On arranging the data in ascending order, we get

Calculation of Median

X	Frequency (f)	Cumulative Frequency (cf)
150	8	8
152	6	14
156	7	21
160	5	26
161	3	29
	$\Sigma f = 29$	

$\therefore \; M = \text{Size of}\left(\frac{N+1}{2}\right)\text{th item}$

$= \text{Size of}\left(\frac{29+1}{2}\right)\text{th item} = \text{Size of 15th item}$

and 15th item lies in cf 21, hence $M = 156$

Numerical 7

Calculate median from the following data

Marks	No. of Students
More than 10	500
More than 20	450
More than 30	320
More than 40	200
More than 50	150
More than 60	80
More than 70	30

Sol. **Calculation of Median**

Marks	Frequency (f)	Cumulative Frequency (cf)
10-20	50 (500 − 450)	50
20-30	130 (450 − 320)	50 + 130 = 180
30-40	120 (320 − 200)	180 + 120 = 300
40-50	50 (200 − 150)	300 + 50 = 350
50-60	70 (150 − 80)	350 + 70 = 420
60-70	50 (80 − 30)	420 + 50 = 470
70-80	30	470 + 30 = 500
	$\Sigma f = 500$	

$$\text{Median Class} = \left(\frac{N}{2}\right)\text{th term} = \left(\frac{500}{2}\right)\text{th} = 250 \text{ th term}$$

$$\therefore \; l_1 = 30, \frac{N}{2} = 250, \quad cf = 180, \quad f = 120, \quad c = 10$$

$$M = l_1 + \left(\frac{N/2 - cf}{f}\right) \times c = 30 + \left(\frac{250 - 180}{120}\right) \times 10$$

$$= 30 + \frac{70 \times 10}{120} = 30 + 5.83 = 35.83$$

Numerical 8

Recast the following cumulative table into the form of an ordinary frequency distribution and determine value of the median.

Number of Days Absent	Number of Students
Less than 5	29
Less than 10	224
Less than 15	465
Less than 20	582
Less than 25	634
Less than 30	644
Less than 35	650
Less than 40	653
Less than 45	655

Sol. **Calculation of Median**

Class Interval	Frequency (f)	Cumulative Frequency (cf)
0-5	29	29
5-10	224-29 = 195	224
10-15	465-224 = 241	465
15-20	582-465 = 117	582
20-25	634-582 = 52	634
25-30	644-634 = 10	644
30-35	650-644 = 6	650
35-40	653-650 = 3	653
40-45	655-653 = 2	655
	$N = \Sigma f = 655$	

$$\therefore \text{Median number } (m) = \text{Size of}\left(\frac{N}{2}\right)\text{th item}$$

$$= \left(\frac{655}{2}\right)\text{th item} = 327.5\text{th item}$$

cf just greater than 327.5 is 465 and the corresponding class interval is 10-15. So, 10-15 is the median class.

$\therefore \quad l_1 = 10, cf = 224, f = 241, c = 5$

Now, $M = l_1 + \frac{\frac{N}{2} - cf}{f} \times c$

$= 10 + \frac{327.5 - 224}{241} \times 5$

$= 10 + \frac{103.5}{241} \times 5 = 10 + 2.15 = 12.15$

Hence, required median $(M) = 12.15$

Numerical 9

If the arithmetic mean of the data given below is 28, find
(i) the missing frequency
(ii) the median of the series **NCERT**

Profit Per Retail Shop (in ₹)	0-10	10-20	20-30	30-40	40-50	50-60
Number of Retail Shops	12	18	27	—	17	6

Sol. (i) Let the missing frequency be f_1.

Arithmetic Mean = 28 (given)

Calculation of Missing Frequency

Profit Per Retail Shop (in ₹)	Number of Retail Shops (f)	Mid-value (m)	fm
0-10	12	5	60
10-20	18	15	270
20-30	27	25	675
30-40	f_1	35	$35f_1$
40-50	17	45	765
50-60	6	55	330
	$\Sigma f = 80 + f_1$		$\Sigma fm = 2{,}100 + 35f_1$

$\overline{X} = \frac{\Sigma fm}{\Sigma f}$

or $\quad 28 = \frac{2{,}100 + 35f_1}{80 + f_1}$

or $\quad 2{,}240 + 28f_1 = 2{,}100 + 35f_1$

or $\quad 2{,}240 - 2{,}100 = 35f_1 - 28f_1$

or $\quad 140 = 7f_1$

$f_1 = 20$

Hence, the missing frequency is 20.

(ii) **Calculation of Median**

Groups	Frequency	Cumulative Frequency
0-10	12	12
10-20	18	30
20-30	27	57
30-40	20	77
40-50	17	94
50-60	6	100
	$\Sigma f = 100$	

$\Sigma f = N = 100$

So, the Median class (m) = Size of $\left(\frac{N}{2}\right)$th item

= 50 th item

50th item lies in the 57th cumulative frequency and the corresponding class is 20-30.

Median $= l_1 + \frac{\frac{N}{2} - cf}{f} \times c = 20 + \frac{\frac{100}{2} - 30}{27} \times 10$

$= 20 + \frac{50 - 30}{27} \times 10$

$= 20 + \frac{20}{27} \times 10 = 27.4$

Numerical 10

The size of land holdings of 380 families in a village is given below. Find the median size of land holdings. **NCERT**

Size of Land holdings (in acre)	Less than 100	100–200	200–300	300–400	400 and above
Number of Families	40	89	148	64	39

Sol. **Calculation of Median**

Size of Landholdings (in acre)	Number of Families (f)	Cumulative Frequency (cf)
0–100	40	40
100–200	89	129
200–300	148	277
300–400	64	341
400–500	39	380
	$N = \Sigma f = 380$	

Median number (m) = size of $\left(\frac{N}{2}\right)$th item

$=\left(\frac{380}{2}\right)$th item = 190th item; 190th item lies in the 277th cf and the corresponding class is 200–300.

$\therefore \quad l_1 = 200,\ cf = 129,\ f = 148,\ c = 100$

$$\text{Now, Median } (M) = l_1 + \frac{\frac{N}{2} - cf}{f} \times c$$

$$= 200 + \frac{190-129}{148} \times 100 = 200 + \frac{61}{148} \times 100$$

$$= 200 + 41.22 = 241.22 \text{ acres}$$

Numerical 11

The wages of 8 workers expressed in rupees are 42, 45, 49, 38, 56, 54, 55 and 47. Find median and quartile wages.

Sol. On arranging the given wages in ascending order, we get 38, 42, 45, 47, 49, 54, 55, 56.

The total number of observations is 8 which is even, therefore

$$\text{Median} = \text{Size of}\left(\frac{N+1}{2}\right)\text{th item}$$

$$= \text{Size of}\left(\frac{8+1}{2}\right)\text{th item} = \text{Size of 4.5 th item}$$

$$M = \frac{\text{4th item} + \text{5th item}}{2} = \frac{47+49}{2} = \frac{96}{2} = 48$$

$\therefore \quad M = 48$

Calculation of Quartiles

$$Q_1 = \left(\frac{N+1}{4}\right)\text{th term} = \left(\frac{8+1}{4}\right)\text{th term} = 2.25\text{ th term}$$

$$= \text{2nd term} + 0.25(\text{3rd} - \text{2nd})\text{ term}$$

$$= 42 + 0.25(45 - 42) = 42 + (0.25 \times 3) = 42.75$$

$$Q_3 = 3\left(\frac{N+1}{4}\right)\text{th term} = 3\left(\frac{8+1}{4}\right)\text{th term} = 6.75\text{ th term}$$

$$= \text{6th term} + 0.75\,(\text{7th} - \text{6 th})\text{ term}$$

$$= 54 + 0.75(55 - 54)$$

$$= 54 + (0.75 \times 1) = 54.75$$

Numerical 12

Calculate Q_1 and Q_3 from the following data

Marks	Number of Students
10	4
20	10
30	20
40	8
50	6
60	3

Sol. **Calculation of Q_1 and Q_3**

Marks	Number of Students (f)	Cumulative Frequency (cf)
10	4	4
20	10	14
30	20	34
40	8	42
50	6	48
60	3	51
	$N = \Sigma f = 51$	

Now, $\quad Q_1 = \text{Size of}\left(\frac{N+1}{4}\right)\text{th item}$

$$= \text{Size of}\left(\frac{51+1}{4}\right)\text{th item}$$

$= \text{Size of 13th item and it lies in } cf \text{ 14,}$

hence $\quad Q_1 = 20$ marks

and $\quad Q_3 = \text{Size of } 3\left(\frac{N+1}{4}\right)\text{th item}$

$$= \text{Size of } 3\frac{(51+1)}{4}\text{ th item}$$

$= \text{Size of 39th item and it lies in } cf \text{ 42,}$

hence $\quad Q_3 = 40$ marks

Numerical 13

Find the missing frequency of the group 20-30, if it is given that $M = 28$.

Class Interval	0–10	10–20	20–30	30–40	40–50
Frequency	5	8	f	16	6

Sol. **Calculation of Missing Frequency**

Class Interval	Frequency (f)	Cumulative Frequency (cf)
0–10	5	5
10–20	8	13
20–30	f	$13 + f$
30–40	16	$29 + f$
40–50	6	$35 + f$
	$N = \Sigma f = 35 + f$	

Given, Median = 28. So it lies in the class interval 20-30.

$$\text{Now, } M = l_1 + \frac{\frac{N}{2} - cf}{f} \times h$$

$$\Rightarrow \quad 28 = 20 + \frac{\frac{35+f}{2} - 13}{f} \times 10$$

$$\Rightarrow \quad 8 = \frac{\frac{35+f}{2} - 13}{f} \times 10$$

$$\Rightarrow \quad 8f = \left(\frac{35+f}{2} - 13\right) \times 10$$

$$\Rightarrow \quad 8f = \left(\frac{35+f-26}{2}\right) \times 10$$

$$\Rightarrow \quad 16f = 350 + 10f - 260$$

$$\Rightarrow \quad 6f = 90$$

$$\therefore \quad f = \frac{90}{6} = 15$$

Thus, the missing frequency is 15.

Numerical 14

The Covid-19 pandemic, also known as coronavirus pandemic, is an ongoing pandemic of coronavirus disease caused by the transmission of severe acute respiratory syndrome coronavirus 2 (SARS-CoV-2) among humans. The following tables shows the age distribution of case admitted during a day in two different hospitals.

Age (in years)	5-15	15-25	25-45	35-45	45-55	55-65
No. of Cases	6	11	21	23	14	5

Compute median from the following data.

Sol. Computation of median from the data above

Age (in years) (X)	5-15	15-25	25-45	35-45	45-55	55-65
No. of Cases (f)	6	11	21	23	14	5
Cumulative Frequency	6	17	38	61	75	80

Median Class $= (N/2)$th term

$= (80/2)$th term $=$ 40th term $= 35\text{-}45$

Median $= l_1 + (N/2 - cf)/f \times c$

Median $= 35 + (40 - 38)/23 \times 5$

Median $= 35 + (10/23) = 35 + 0.43$

Median $= 35.43$

Numerical 15

Compute mode from the following data

Score	Frequency
0–10	10
10–20	20
20–30	18
30–40	32
40–50	21

Sol. By observation method, it is clear that the modal value lies in the group of 30-40 because it has the highest frequency.

$\therefore \quad l_1 = 30, \quad f_0 = 18, \quad f_1 = 32, \quad f_2 = 21, \quad c = 10$

$$\text{Now, Mode} = l_1 + \frac{f_1 - f_0}{2f_1 - f_0 - f_2} \times c$$

$$= 30 + \frac{32 - 18}{2 \times 32 - 18 - 21} \times 10$$

$$= 30 + \frac{14}{25} \times 10 = 30 + 5.6 = 35.6$$

Hence, the modal value is 35.6 score.

Numerical 16

The following table shows the distribution of 105 families according to their expenditure per week. Number of families corresponding to the expenditure groups ₹ 10-20 and ₹ 30-40 are missing from the table. The median and mode for the distribution are ₹ 25 and ₹ 24, respectively. Calculate the missing frequencies.

Expenditure (in ₹)	0–10	10–20	20–30	30–40	40–50
Number of Families	14	?	27	?	15

Sol. Let us suppose that the frequencies of groups ₹ 10–20 and ₹ 30–40 are f_1 and f_2, respectively. We can write the table in the following manner

Expenditure (X)	Number of Families (n)	Cumulative Frequency (cf)
0–10	14	14
10–20	f_1	$14 + f_1$
20–30	27	$41 + f_1$
30–40	f_2	$41 + f_1 + f_2$
40–50	15	$56 + f_1 + f_2$
	$N = 56 + f_1 + f_2$	

Since, Median = 25 (given)

So, median lies in the class interval 20–30.

Then, $l_1 = 20, \quad f = 27,$

$cf = 14 + f_1, \quad c = 10$

$$\therefore \quad \text{Median } (M) = l_1 + \frac{\frac{N}{2} - cf}{f} \times c$$

$$\Rightarrow \quad 25 = 20 + \frac{\frac{56 + f_1 + f_2}{2} - (14 + f_1)}{27} \times 10$$

$$\Rightarrow \quad \frac{27(25-20)}{10} = \frac{56 + f_1 + f_2}{2} - (14 + f_1)$$

$$\Rightarrow \quad \frac{2 \times 27 \times 5}{10} = 56 + f_1 + f_2 - 28 - 2f_1$$

$$\Rightarrow \quad 27 = 28 + f_2 - f_1$$

$$\Rightarrow \quad f_1 - f_2 = 1 \quad \text{...(i)}$$

Also, Mode = 24 (given)

So, mode lies in the class interval 20–30.

Then, $l_1 = 20, \quad f_1 = 27, \quad f_0 = f_1, \quad f_2 = f_2, \quad c = 10$

$$\therefore \text{Mode } (M_o) = l_1 + \frac{f_1 - f_0}{2f_1 - f_0 - f_2} \times c$$

$$\Rightarrow \quad 24 = 20 + \frac{27 - f_1}{54 - f_1 - f_2} \times 10$$

$$\Rightarrow \quad 4 = \frac{27 - f_1}{54 - f_1 - f_2} \times 10$$

$$\Rightarrow \quad 4(54 - f_1 - f_2) = 10(27 - f_1)$$

$$\Rightarrow \quad 216 - 4f_1 - 4f_2 = 270 - 10f_1$$

$$\Rightarrow \quad 6f_1 - 4f_2 = 54$$

$$\Rightarrow \quad 3f_1 - 2f_2 = 27 \quad \text{...(ii)}$$

Now, we have two equations

$$f_1 - f_2 = 1 \quad \text{...(i)}$$

and $$3f_1 - 2f_2 = 27 \quad \text{...(ii)}$$

On multiplying eq. (i) by 2 and subtracting eq. (ii) from it, we get

$$2f_1 - 2f_2 = 2$$
$$3f_1 - 2f_2 = 27$$
$$- \quad + \quad -$$
$$-f_1 = -25$$

$$\Rightarrow \quad f_1 = 25$$

On putting the value of f_1 in eq. (i), we get

$$\Rightarrow \quad f_2 = 25 - 1$$

$$\Rightarrow \quad f_2 = 24$$

Hence, the number of families in the groups ₹ (10–20) and ₹ (30–40) are 25 and 24, respectively.

Numerical 17

In a Vidyalaya, there are two sections A and B. 39 students are there in section A and in section B, there are 41 students.

A periodic test was conducted to assess the performance of students, thereafter analysing and planning the teaching learning process accordingly. The marks obtained out of 40 are given below in the table

Marks Obtained By the Students	Number of Students
Less than 5	3
Less than 10	12
Less than 15	22
Less than 20	35
Less than 25	42
Less than 30	60
Less than 35	71
Less than 40	80

(i) How many students have obtained more than or equal to 35 marks?

(ii) Arrange the given data in class interval and find the mode of the marks obtained.

Sol. (i) Conversion of cumulative frequency distribution into normal frequency distribution

Marks Obtained by the Students	Number of Students	Marks	Frequency
Less than 5	3	0-5	3
Less than 10	12	5-10	$12 - 3 = 9$
Less than 15	22	10-15	$22 - 12 = 10$
Less than 20	35	15-20	$35 - 22 = 13$
Less than 25	42	20-25	$42 - 35 = 7$
Less than 30	60	25-30	$60 - 42 = 18$
Less than 35	71	30-35	$71 - 60 = 11$
Less than 40	80	35-40	$80 - 71 = 9$

The students who have obtained more than or equal to 35 marks are 9.

(ii) Calculation of mode from the following data

Marks	Frequency
0-5	3
5-10	$12 - 3 = 9$
10-15	$22 - 12 = 10$
15-20	$35 - 22 = 13$
20-25	42 35 = 7
25-30	$60 - 42 = 18$
30-35	$71 - 60 = 11$
35-40	$80 - 71 = 9$

$$\text{Mode } (M_0) = l_1 + \frac{f_1 - f_0}{2f_1 - f_0 - f_2} \times c$$

By observation method modal class is 25-30.

So, $l_1 = 25$, $f_1 = 18$, $f_0 = 7$, $f_2 = 11$

$$M_0 = 25 + \frac{18-7}{36-7-11} \times 5 = 25 + \frac{11}{18} \times 5$$

$$M_0 = 25 + \frac{55}{18} = 25 + 3.05 = 28.05$$

Numerical 18

Calculate Q_1 and Q_3 from the following table

Wages (in ₹)	Number of Workers
0–5	4
5–10	6
10–15	3
15–20	8
20–25	12
25–30	7

Sol. **Calculation of Q_1 and Q_3**

Wages	Number of Workers (f)	Cumulative Frequency (cf)
0–5	4	4
5–10	6	10
10–15	3	13
15–20	8	21
20–25	12	33
25–30	7	40
	$N = \Sigma f = 40$	

∴ First quartile number

$$(q_1) = \text{Size of } \left(\frac{N}{4}\right) \text{th item}$$

$$= \left(\frac{40}{4}\right) \text{th item} = 10\text{th item}$$

10th item will correspond to the class 5–10.

So, $l_1 = 5$, $cf = 4$, $f = 6$, $c = 5$

$$\text{Now, } q_1 = l_1 + \frac{\frac{N}{4} - cf}{f} \times c = 5 + \frac{10-4}{6} \times 5$$

$$= 5 + \frac{6 \times 5}{6} = 5 + \frac{30}{6} = 5 + 5$$

$$\Rightarrow \quad q_1 = 10$$

Third quartile number

$$(q_3) = \text{Size of} \left(\frac{3N}{4}\right) \text{th item}$$

$$= \left(\frac{3 \times 40}{4}\right) \text{th item} = 30\text{th item}$$

30th item will correspond to the class 20–25.

So, $l_1 = 20$, $cf = 21$, $f = 12$, $c = 5$

$$\text{Now, } Q_3 = l_1 + \frac{\frac{3N}{4} - cf}{f} \times c$$

$$= 20 + \frac{30-21}{12} \times 5$$

$$= 20 + \frac{45}{12} = 20 + 3.75$$

$$\Rightarrow \quad Q_3 = 23.75$$

Numerical 19

following series relates to the daily income of workers employed in a firm. Compute **NCERT**

(i) Highest income of lowest 50% workers.

(ii) Minimum income earned by top 25% workers.

(iii) Maximum income earned by lowest 25% workers.

Daily Income (in ₹)	Number of Workers
10-14	5
15-19	10
20-24	15
25-29	20
30-34	10
35-39	5

Note In the above question,inclusive class intervals are given, so, firstly we convert them into exclusive class intervals. Thereafter, we will calculate the required quartiles.

Sol. **Calculation of Quartiles**

Daily Income	Exclusive Group	Number of Workers (f)	Cumulative Frequency (cf)
10-14	9.5-14.5	5	5
15-19	14.5-19.5	10	15
20-24	19.5-24.5	15	30
25-29	24.5-29.5	20	50
30-34	29.5-34.5	10	60
35-39	34.5-39.5	5	65
		$N = \Sigma f = 65$	

(i) To find the highest income of lowest 50% workers, we calculate second quartile, i.e. median (M)

$$m = \text{Size of} \left(\frac{N}{2}\right) \text{th item} = \left(\frac{65}{2}\right) \text{th item}$$

$= 32.5$ th item

32.5th item lies in class 24.5–29.5

$$M = l_1 + \frac{\frac{N}{2} - cf}{f} \times c$$

$$= 24.5 + \frac{32.5 - 30}{20} \times 5$$

$$= 24.5 + \frac{2.5}{20} \times 5 = 24.5 + 0.6$$

$$\Rightarrow \quad M = 25.1$$

(ii) To find the minimum income earned by the top 25% workers, we calculate upper quartile (Q_3).

$$\therefore \quad Q_3 = \text{Size of } 3\left(\frac{N}{4}\right) \text{th item}$$

$$= \left(\frac{3 \times 65}{4}\right) \text{th item} = 48.75\text{th item}$$

48.75 th item lies in class interval 24.5-29.5

$$\therefore \quad Q_3 = l_1 + \frac{\frac{3}{4}N - cf}{f} \times c$$

$$= 24.5 + \frac{48.75 - 30}{20} \times 5$$

$$= 24.5 + \frac{18.75 \times 5}{20} = 24.5 + 4.7$$

$$\Rightarrow Q_3 = 29.2$$

(iii) To find the maximum income earned by lowest 25% workers, we calculate lower quartile (Q_1)

$$\therefore \; Q_1 = \text{Size of} \left(\frac{N}{4}\right) \text{th item}$$

$$= \left(\frac{65}{4}\right) \text{th item}$$

$= 16.25$th item

16.25th item lies in class interval 19.5–24.5

$$Q_1 = l_1 + \frac{\frac{N}{4} - cf}{f} \times c$$

$$= 19.5 + \frac{16.25 - 15}{15} \times 5$$

$$= 19.5 + \frac{1.25 \times 5}{15} = 19.5 + 0.42$$

$$\Rightarrow \quad Q_1 = 19.92$$

Numerical 20

Find mode of the given class interval.

X	120–130	130–140	140–150	150–160	160–170
f	8	2	20	12	8

Sol. Calculation of Mode

By observation method 140–150 is modal class so,

$f_1 = 20, f_0 = 2, \; f_2 = 12, \; c = 10, \; l_1 = 140$

$$\text{Mode } (Z) = l_1 + \frac{f_1 - f_0}{2f_1 - f_0 - f_2} \times c$$

$$= 140 + \frac{20 - 2}{(2 \times 20) - 2 - 12} \times 10$$

$$= 140 + \frac{18}{40 - 14} \times 10$$

$$= 140 + \frac{18}{26} \times 10$$

$$= 140 + 6.92 = 146.92$$

Numerical 21

The following table gives production yield in kg per hectare of wheat of 150 farms in a village. Calculate the mean, median and mode values.

Production Yield (kg per hectare)	Number of Farms
50-53	3
53-56	8
56-59	14
59-62	30
62-65	36
65-68	28
68-71	16
71-74	10
74-77	5

Sol.

Production (X)	No. of Farms (f)	Mid-value (m)	fm	cf
50-53	3	51.5	154.5	3
53-56	8	54.5	43.6	11
56-59	14	57.5	805.0	25

Production (X)	No. of Farms (f)	Mid-value (m)	fm	cf
59-62	30	60.5	1815.0	55
62-65	36	63.5	2286.0	91
65-68	28	66.5	1862.0	119
68-71	16	69.5	1112.0	135
71-74	10	72.5	725.0	145
74-77	5	75.5	377.5	150
	$\Sigma f = 150$		$\Sigma fm = 9573$	

$$\text{Mean } (\overline{X}) = \frac{\Sigma fm}{\Sigma f} = \frac{9573}{150} = 63.82$$

$$\text{Median} = \left(\frac{N}{2}\right)\text{th term}$$

$$= \left(\frac{150}{2}\right)\text{th term} = 75\text{th term}$$

$$\text{Median} = l_1 + \left(\frac{\frac{N}{2} - cf}{f}\right) \times c$$

$$= 62 + \left(\frac{75-55}{36}\right) \times 3$$

$$= 62 + \frac{20 \times 3}{36} = 63.67$$

$$\text{Mode } (Z) = 3 \text{ Median} - 2 \text{ Mean}$$

$$= 3\,(63.67) - 2\,(63.82) = 191.01 - 127.64$$

$$= 63.37$$

Numerical 22

Locate the mode graphically.

Marks	0–10	10–20	20–30	30–40	40–50	50–60	60–70
Number of Students	5	10	20	25	20	10	5

Sol. Firstly, we draw the histogram of the given data. Here, maximum height of rectangle is 25. So, modal class is 30-40

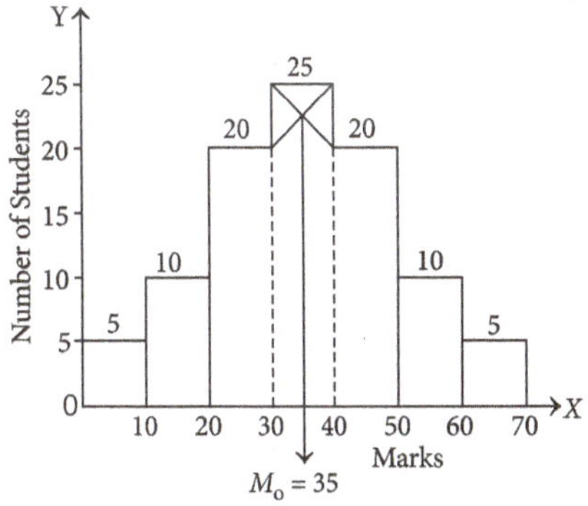

It is clear from the histogram that the value of mode is 35.

SELF ASSESSMENT TEST

Objective Type Questions

1. The properties, merits and limitations of quartiles are the same as that of the ....
   (a) median (b) mode
   (c) mean (d) None of these
2. Why is the median considered the best measure of central tendency for an open ended continuous series?
   (a) Because it is affected by extreme values, making it more accurate
   (b) Because it represents the arithmetic mean of the series
   (c) Because it is not affected by extreme values and is representative of the series
   (d) Because it requires finding missing limits to complete the intervals
3. Which of the following steps is not involved in finding the median using a 'less-than' ogive?
   (a) Convert the frequency distribution into a 'less-than' cumulative distribution and plot it
   (b) Calculate the arithmetic mean of the data to find the median
   (c) Find n/2 and draw a horizontal line from the y-axis to intersect the ogive
   (d) Draw a perpendicular line from the intersection point to the x-axis to determine the median
4. Quartiles are positional averages that divide a dataset into .... equal parts, each containing an equal number of observations.
   (a) three (b) two
   (c) five (d) four
5. What is a uni-modal series?
   (a) A series with no mode
   (b) A series with more-than one mode
   (c) A series with exactly one mode, which is the value that appears most frequently
   (d) A series where all values have the same frequency
6. Which of the following statements is true regarding the comparison among mean, median and mode?
   (a) Mean is based on all items in the series, while median and mode are not
   (b) Mode is precise and accurate, unlike mean and median
   (c) Median and mode are unaffected by extreme values, while mean is also unaffected
   (d) Mean can be computed graphically, while median and mode cannot

Answers 1. (a) 2. (c) 3. (b) 4. (d) 5. (c) 6. (a)

Short Answer Type Questions

7. "For calculation of mode in open ended series, there is no special adjustment needed for missing extreme limits to complete the class intervals." Do you agree? Give reasons.
8. What are the steps of calculating median by using only 'less than ogive'?
9. Define the following terms
   (i) Quartile
   (ii) Decile
10. Classify the mode on the basis of number of modes. Give example for each.

Long Answer Type Questions

11. Explain the relationship between mean, median and mode with diagrams.
12. A company is analysing the monthly sales data of its representatives. They notice that the sales figures tend to concentrate around multiple values, making it challenging to identify the mode directly. To resolve this, they decide to use the grouping method to determine the mode accurately.
    (i) Why is the grouping method used in identifying the mode of a dataset?
    (ii) What are the key steps involved in creating the grouping table during the grouping method?
    (iii) How the analysis table is prepared and how is the mode determined from it in the grouping method?

Numerical Questions

13. Calculate Q_1 and Q_3 from the following data

Wages (in ₹)	0–5	5–10	10–15	15–20	20–25	25–30
Number of Workers	4	6	3	8	12	7

Ans. $Q_1 = 10, Q_3 = 23.75$

14. Find the median from the following data

Mid-value	37.5	42.5	47.5	52.5	57.5
Number of Students	30	20	15	13	22

Ans. Median = 45

Hint Exclusive frequency distribution should first be derived.

15. Calculate the values of lower quartile and upper quartile from the following data

Class Interval (Less than)	10	20	30	40	50
Frequency	22	60	106	141	161

Ans. $Q_1 = 14.80, Q_3 = 34.21$

16. Find the median and quartiles from the following data

Size	11–15	16–20	21–25	26–30	31–35	36–40	41–45	46–50
Frequency	7	10	13	26	35	22	11	5

Ans. $M = 31.71, Q_1 = 25.93, Q_3 = 36.81$

Hint The given inclusive distribution should be converted into an exclusive distribution.

17. Mean marks obtained by a student in his five subjects are 15. In English, he secures 8 marks, in Economics 12, in Mathematics 18 and in Commerce 9. Find out the marks he secured in Statistics.

Ans. Marks in Statistics = 28 marks

Hint Marks in Statistics $= (5 \times 15) - (8 + 12 + 18 + 9)$

18. Calculate mode of the following series using the graphic technique. Counter check the modal value by computing it arithmetically.

Wages	0–10	10–20	20–30	30–40	40–50
Number of Workers	28	46	54	42	30

Ans. $M_0 = 24$

19. Find out mode from the following series, using grouping method

Marks	10–19	20–29	30–39	40–49	50–59	60–69	70–79	80–89	90–99
Number of Students	29	87	181	247	263	133	40	9	2

Ans. $M_0 = 50.59$

20. From the following data, calculate the value of mode

Salary (in ₹)	2000	2100	2400	2900	3100	3300
Number of Workers	3	5	10	19	8	4

Ans. $M_0 = 2900$

21. Find out mode value from the following data

Mid-value	15	25	35	45	55	65	75	85
Frequency	5	8	12	16	28	15	3	2

Ans. $M_0 = 54.8$

22. Calculate mode of the following series

X	Below 5	5–10	10–15	15–20	20–25	25–30	30–35	35–40	Above 40
Frequency	20	24	32	28	20	16	34	10	8

Ans. $M_0 = 13.33$

07

CHAPTER

Measures of Correlation

> Whenever some definite connection exists between the two or more groups, classes or series or data, there is said to be a correlation. —*Boddington*

YOUR STUDY GOALS

YOUR PRACTICE GOAL

- Objective Type Questions (60 Qs ; MCQs, A-R, Statements, Matching, Concept Identification)
- Subjective Questions (18 SAs, 6 LAs)
- 16 Numerical Questions
- Self Assessment Test (5 MCQs, 4 SAs, 9 Numerical)

7.1 Meaning of Correlation

Correlation is a statistical concept used to study and measure the direction and strength of the relationship between two variables. When two variables change together, they are said to be correlated. For instance, as summer temperature rises, both the number of visitors to hill stations and ice-cream sales tend to increase. This indicates a correlation between rising temperature, increased hill station visitors and higher ice-cream sales.

Correlation and Causation

While correlation indicates that two variables change together, it does not necessarily mean that change in one is the cause of changes in the other. There are different types of relationships that can exist

1. **Direct Causation** One variable (A) directly influences another (B). e.g. A fall in mobile prices can lead to a rise in their demand.
2. **Reverse Causation** The second variable (B) influences the first (A). e.g. Increased demand for mobile phones can cause their prices to rise.
3. **Common Cause** Both variables (A and B) are influenced by a third factor. e.g. The increase in the sale of woollen clothes and electric heaters during winter is due to lower temperature, depicting no direct relationship between the two items.

4. **Cyclic Causation** Variables influence each other in a cyclical pattern (i.e. A causes B, B causes A). e.g. As national income rises, aggregate demand increases and this increased demand further boost national income.
5. **Indirect Causation** One variable (A) causes another variable (C) which further causes variable (B). e.g. The popularity of cricket (A) increases the interest of youngsters (C) in the sport, affecting other sports (B) indirectly.
6. **Spurious Correlation** There is no relationship between the variables and their correlation is purely coincidental. e.g. The correlation between ice-cream consumption and exam scores is coincidental and not meaningful.

Importance of Correlation

- It helps in measuring the extent of relationship between two or more variables.
- It facilitates decision-making in real world scenarios.
- It reduces uncertainty as predictions based on correlation are likely to be more reliable.
- It facilitates understanding economic behaviour and helps in locating the importance of critical concepts.

Types of Correlation

Types of correlation can be classified as

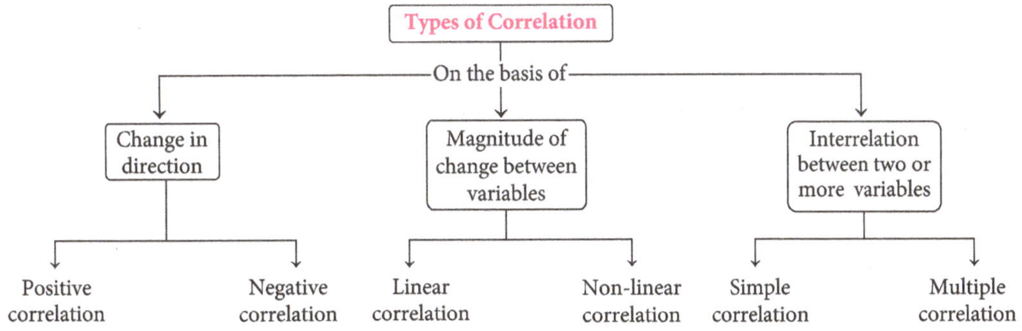

On the Basis of Change in Direction

1. **Positive Correlation** It occurs when two related variables move in the same direction i.e. when one variable increases, the other also increases and *vice-versa*. e.g.
   - As the price of a commodity rises, the supply of that commodity often increases.
   - Ice-cream sales typically rise with high temperature in daytime.
2. **Negative Correlation** It occurs when two variables move in opposite directions i.e. when one variable increases, the other decreases and *vice-versa*. e.g.
   - The growing popularity of television has led to a decrease in revenue for the film industry.
   - Sales of woollen garments tend to fall as temperature rises.

Positive Correlation

Increase in Both Variables		Decrease in Both Variables	
A	B	A	B
30	75	50	145
35	100	42	120
38	110	36	104
42	120	30	75

Negative Correlation

Increase in One Variable (A) causing Decrease in Other Variable (B)		Decrease in One Variable (A) causing Increase in Other Variable (B)	
A	B	A	B
25	55	80	50
30	45	70	70
35	35	60	90
40	25	50	110

On the Basis of Magnitude of Change between Variables

1. **Linear Correlation** It describes a situation where the change in one variable has a constant ratio to the change in another variable. This relationship is represented by a straight line on a graph.

   e.g. If the price of a product increases, the quantity supplied might increase in a consistent proportion.

2. **Non-linear Correlation** It occurs when the change in one variable does not have a constant ratio to the change in another variable. This relationship is represented by a curve on a graph rather than a straight line.

   e.g. The relationship between advertising expenditure and sales might initially show rapid increase but eventually level-off.

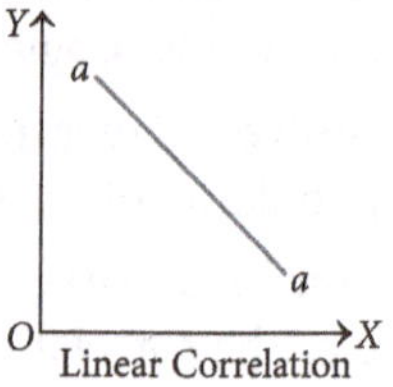

Linear Correlation

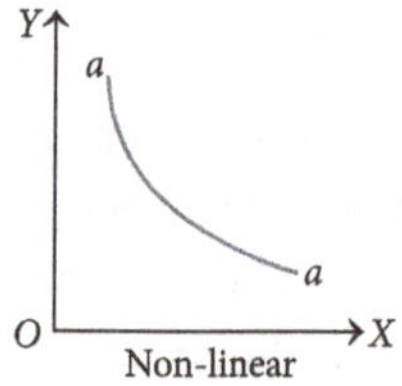

Non-linear Correlation

On the Basis of Inter-relation between Two or More Variables

1. **Simple Correlation** It involves the study of the relationship between two variables only.

   e.g. The relationship between the price of a good and its demand.

2. **Multiple Correlation** It involves the study of the relationship among three or more variables simultaneously.

   e.g. The production of food crops depends on multiple factors such as rainfall, use of fertilisers and other variables.

Degrees of Correlation

Degree of Correlation	Positive Correlation	Negative Correlation
Perfect Correlation	+1	−1
Very High Degree of Correlation	+ 0.9	− 0.9
Fairly High Degree of Correlation	Between + 0.75 and + 0.9	Between − 0.75 and − 0.9
Moderate Degree of Correlation	Between + 0.25 and + 0.75	Between − 0.25 and − 0.75
Low Degree of Correlation	Between 0 and + 0.25	Between 0 and − 0.25
No Correlation	0	0

7.2 Methods of Computing Correlation

Different methods of computing correlation are

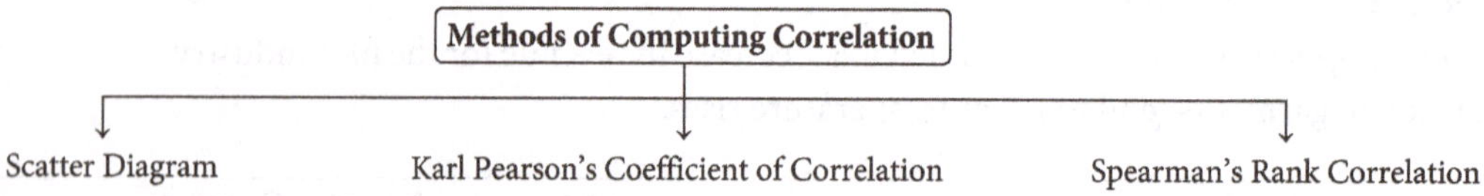

Scatter Diagram

A scatter diagram is a graphical method used to show the relationship between two variables. It provides a visual representation of the direction and degree of correlation between the variables, without involving numerical calculations.

To construct a Scatter Diagram

- Place the independent variable on the x-axis (horizontal axis).
- Place the dependent variable on the y-axis (vertical axis).
- Plot their values as a dot on the graph.
- The pattern formed by the dots (or scatter points) indicates the type of correlation between the variables.

Various Degrees of Correlation Depicted by Scatter Diagram

1. **Positive Correlation** Points are clustered around an upward sloping line indicating the movement of variables in same direction, i.e. as the independent variable increases, the dependent variable also increases and *vice-versa*.

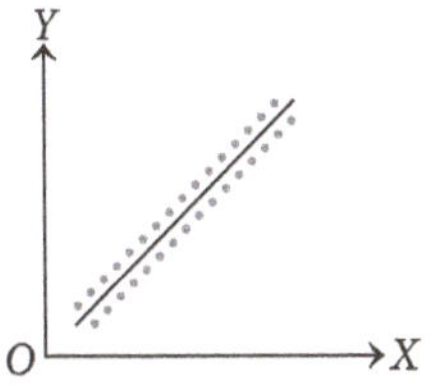

Positive Correlation

2. **Negative Correlation** Points are clustered around a downward sloping line indicating that variables move in opposite direction, i.e. as the independent variable increases, the dependent variable decreases and *vice-versa*.

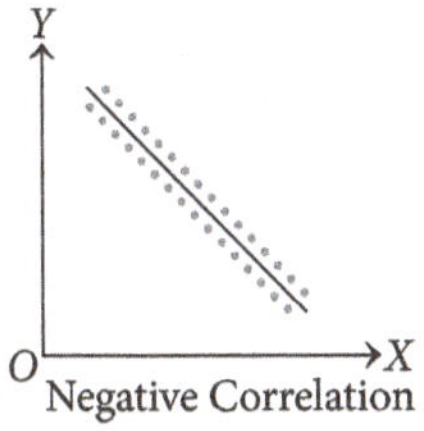

Negative Correlation

3. **No Correlation** Points are scattered randomly without any noticeable pattern, indicating no clear relationship between the variables.

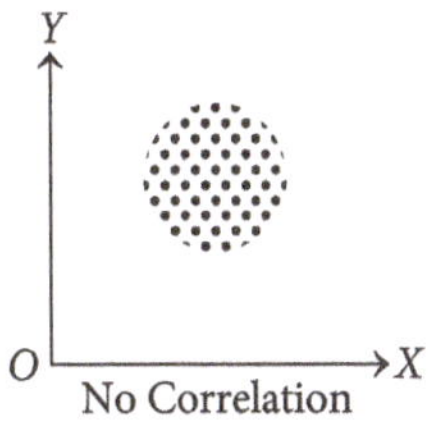

No Correlation

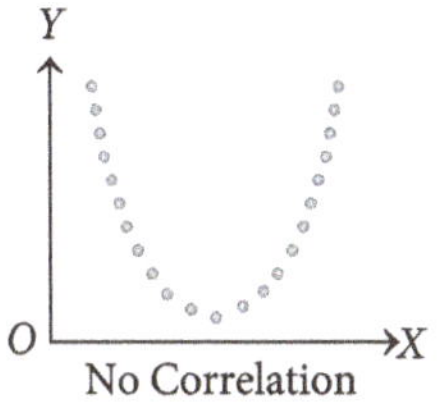

No Correlation

4. **Perfect Positive Correlation** Points lie exactly on an upward sloping line, showing a perfect positive correlation ($r = 1$).

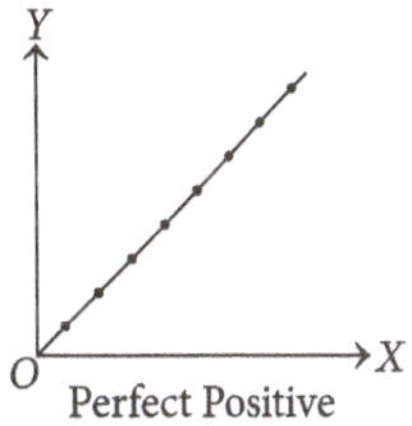

Perfect Positive Correlation

5. **Perfect Negative Correlation** Points lie exactly on a downward sloping line, showing a perfect negative correlation ($r = -1$).

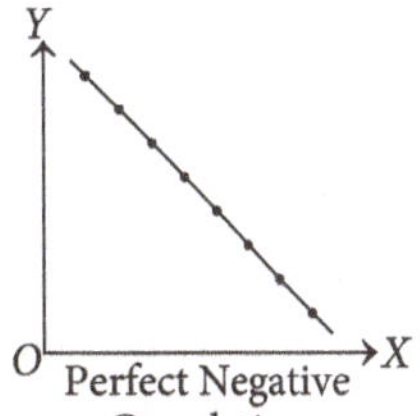

Perfect Negative Correlation

Points to be Remembered while Interpreting a Scatter Diagram

- If the scatter points are widely dispersed around the line, the correlation is low.
- Correlation is said to be linear if the scatter points lie on a straight line.
- If the points move from left to right upwards, the correlation is said to be positive, whereas the movement of points from left to right downwards, it indicates a negative correlation.
- Points falling close to each other in a straight line indicate high degree of correlation.
- If plotted points show no trend at all, then it shows absence of correlation or no correlation between the two variables.

Solved Question 1 **Following are the heights and weights of 10 students of class XI**

Height (in inches) X	**Weight** (in kgs) Y
62	50
72	65
68	63
58	50
65	54
70	60
66	61
63	55
60	54
70	65

Draw a scatter diagram and indicate whether the correlation is positive or negative.

Sol. The scatter diagram of the above data is shown below

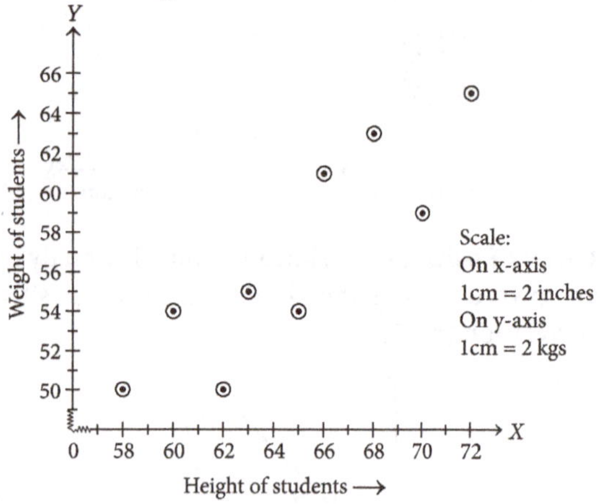

Since the points are dense, i.e. close to each other, we may expect a high degree of correlation between the series of heights and weights. Further, since the points reveal an upward trend starting from left bottom and going up towards the right top, the correlation is positive.
Hence, we may expect a fairly high degree of positive correlation between height and weight of the students of class XI.

Merits of Scatter Diagram

- It is a simple method as it does not involve any mathematical calculation.
- It is easy to understand and interpret.
- It is not affected by extreme values.

Demerits of Scatter Diagram

- It is a non-mathematical method, thus, cannot be fully relied upon.
- It only gives rough idea about the inter-relation between variables.
- It cannot be used in case of large distributions.

Karl Pearson's Coefficient of Correlation

The scatter diagram method indicates the direction of correlation but does not give an exact value of magnitude.

To address this limitation, British statistician, **Karl Pearson**, developed a mathematical method known as the **correlation coefficient**.

The correlation coefficient, denoted as r_{xy}, quantifies the strength and direction of the linear relationship between two variables, x and y.

Pearson's correlation coefficient is calculated as the ratio of the covariance between x and y to the product of their standard deviations.

Symbolically,

$$\text{Correlation Coefficient } (r) = \frac{Cov(x, y)}{\sigma_x \times \sigma_y}$$

$$or \quad = \frac{\Sigma x \cdot y}{n \cdot \sigma_x \cdot \sigma_y}$$

where

$Cov(x, y) =$ Covariance between x and y

and is computed as, $\frac{\Sigma xy}{n}$

where

$\Sigma x = \Sigma(X - \bar{X})$ and $\Sigma y = \Sigma(Y - \bar{Y})$

$n =$ Number of observations,

$\sigma_x =$ Standard deviation of x,

$\sigma_y =$ Standard deviation of y

This method is applicable only when the deviations of the variables are calculated from their actual mean and not from an assumed mean.

Unlike the scatter diagram, Pearson's correlation coefficient provides an exact numerical value that ranges from **−1 to +1.**

- **+1** indicates a perfect positive linear relationship.
- **−1** indicates a perfect negative linear relationship.
- **0** indicates no linear relationship between the variables.

Covariance

It is a statistical representation of the degree to which two variables vary together. In other words, it is a number reflecting the degree to which two variables vary together. Covariance of two variables (say x and y) is denoted *as* $= Cov(x, y)$.

Methods of Calculating Karl Pearson's Coefficient of Correlation

There are three methods to calculate coefficient of correlation by Karl Pearson's method, which are as follows

Actual Mean Method

Step 1 Compute the mean values of the X and Y series.

Step 2 Calculate deviations of each observation in the X and Y series from their respective means and denote them as x and y.

Step 3 Square these deviations and sum them to find Σx^2 and Σy^2.

Step 4 Multiply the corresponding deviations of the X and Y series to obtain xy and sum these products to find Σxy.

Step 5 Calculate the standard deviations of both series using following formulae

$$\sigma_x = \sqrt{\frac{\Sigma x^2}{n}}$$

$$\sigma_y = \sqrt{\frac{\Sigma y^2}{n}}$$

Step 6 Use the following formula to find the correlation coefficient.

$$r = \frac{\Sigma xy}{n \cdot \sigma_x \cdot \sigma_y}$$

where symbols have the same meaning as discussed.

Alternately, the following formula can also be applied,

$$r = \frac{\Sigma xy}{\sqrt{\Sigma x^2 \times \Sigma y^2}}$$

Short-cut Method

The short-cut method simplifies calculations when means are in fractions. It uses assumed mean instead of actual mean. Following steps are taken

Step 1 Take any convenient whole numbers as the assumed means of X and Y series respectively.

Step 2 Take the deviations of X series from the assumed mean, so as to get dx and obtain their total i.e. Σdx.

Step 3 Take the deviations of Y series from the assumed mean, so as to get dy and obtain their total i.e. Σdy.

Step 4 Square dx and obtain their total, i.e. Σdx^2.

Step 5 Square dy and obtain their total, i.e. Σdy^2.

Step 6 Multiply the corresponding deviations of X and Y series and add these products to get $\Sigma dx.dy$.

Step 7 Substitute the above values in the given formula to get the value of coefficient of correlation (r).

$$r = \frac{\Sigma dx \cdot dy - \frac{\Sigma dx \times \Sigma dy}{n}}{\sqrt{\Sigma dx^2 - \frac{(\Sigma dx)^2}{n}} \times \sqrt{\Sigma dy^2 - \frac{(\Sigma dy)^2}{n}}}$$

or

$$= \frac{\Sigma dx \cdot dy \cdot n - (\Sigma dx)(\Sigma dy)}{\sqrt{\Sigma dx^2 \cdot n - (\Sigma dx)^2} \times \sqrt{\Sigma dy^2 \cdot n - (\Sigma dy)^2}}$$

where symbols have the same meaning as discussed.

Step Deviation Method

This method is used when the values are large and divisible by a common factor. It involves the following steps

Steps 1 to 3 Same as in the short-cut method.

Step 4 Divide dx and dy by some common factor as

$$dx' = \frac{dx}{c_1} \text{ and } dy' = \frac{dy}{c_2},$$

here c_1 is the common factor for x and c_2 is the common factor for y. dx' and dy' are step deviations.

Step 5 Sum the step deviations to get $\Sigma dx'$ and $\Sigma dy'$.

Step 6 Multiply the step deviations and sum these products to get $\Sigma dx' dy'$.

Step 7 Square the step deviations and sum them to find out Σdx^2 and $\Sigma dx'^{-2}$.

Step 8 Use the following formula to calculate the correlation coefficient.

$$r = \frac{\Sigma dx'dy' - \frac{\Sigma dx' \times \Sigma dy'}{n}}{\sqrt{\left[\Sigma dx'^2 - \frac{\Sigma dx'^2}{n}\right]} \times \sqrt{\left[\Sigma dy'^2 - \frac{\Sigma dy'^2}{n}\right]}}$$

where symbols have the same meaning as discussed.

Solved Question 2 **Compute Karl Pearson's coefficient of correlation from the following data by direct method**

X	10	12	11	13	12	14	9	12	14	13
Y	7	9	12	9	13	8	10	12	7	13

Sol. **Calculation of Coefficient of Correlation**

X	$x(X-\overline{X})$ $\overline{X}=12$	Square of Deviation (x^2)	Y	$y(Y-\overline{Y})$ $\overline{Y}=10$	Square of Deviation (y^2)	xy
10	−2	4	7	−3	9	6
12	0	0	9	−1	1	0
11	−1	1	12	2	4	−2
13	1	1	9	−1	1	−1
12	0	0	13	3	9	0
14	2	4	8	−2	4	−4
9	−3	9	10	0	0	0
12	0	0	12	2	4	0
14	2	4	7	−3	9	−6
13	1	1	13	3	9	3
$\Sigma X=120$	$\Sigma x=0$	$\Sigma x^2=24$	$\Sigma Y=100$	$\Sigma y=0$	$\Sigma y^2=50$	$\Sigma xy=-4$

Here, $n = 10$

Mean of X series $(\bar{X}) = \frac{\Sigma X}{n} = \frac{120}{10} = 12$

Mean of Y series $(\bar{Y}) = \frac{\Sigma Y}{n} = \frac{100}{10} = 10$

Standard deviation of X series,

$$(\sigma_x) = \sqrt{\frac{\Sigma x^2}{n}} = \sqrt{\frac{24}{10}} = \sqrt{2.4} = 1.55$$

Standard deviation of Y series,

$$(\sigma_y) = \sqrt{\frac{\Sigma y^2}{n}} = \sqrt{\frac{50}{10}} = \sqrt{5} = 2.24$$

$\because$ Karl Pearson's coefficient of correlation,

$$r = \frac{\Sigma xy}{n \cdot \sigma_x \cdot \sigma_y} = \frac{-4}{10 \times 1.55 \times 2.24}$$

$$\therefore \quad = \frac{-4}{34.72} = -0.115$$

There is low degree of negative correlation between X and Y.

Solved Question 3 **If the covariance between two variables X and Y is 8.4 and variance of Y series is 9.4 and variance of X series is 12.4, calculate coefficient of correlation.**

Sol. Coefficient of correlation $(r) = \frac{Cov(x, y)}{\sigma_x \cdot \sigma_y}$

Now, $\quad Cov(x, y) = \frac{\Sigma xy}{n} = 8.4$

Variance of $X = \sigma_x^2 = 12.4$

$\therefore \quad \sigma_x = 3.52$

Variance of $Y = \sigma_y^2 = 9.4$

$\therefore \quad \sigma_y = 3.06$

Putting values in formula,

$$r = \frac{\Sigma xy}{n \cdot \sigma_x \cdot \sigma_y} = 8.4 \times \frac{1}{3.52} \times \frac{1}{3.06}$$

$$= \frac{8.4}{10.77} \Rightarrow 0.77 \text{ (High degree of positive correlation)}$$

Solved Question 4 **Calculate Karl Pearson's coefficient of correlation between the following two series by short-cut method**

X	24	27	28	28	29	30	32	33	35	35	40
Y	18	20	22	25	22	28	28	30	27	30	22

Sol. **Calculation of Coefficient of Correlation**

X	dx (X − A) A = 32	dx^2	Y	dy(Y − A) A = 25	dy^2	dxdy
24	−8	64	18	−7	49	56
27	−5	25	20	−5	25	25
28	−4	16	22	−3	9	12
28	−4	16	25	0	0	0
29	−3	9	22	−3	9	9
30	−2	4	28	3	9	−6
32	0	0	28	3	9	0
33	1	1	30	5	25	5
35	3	9	27	2	4	6
35	3	9	30	5	25	15
40	8	64	22	−3	9	−24
$n = 11$	$\Sigma dx = -11$	$\Sigma dx^2 = 217$		$\Sigma dy = -3$	$\Sigma dy^2 = 173$	$\Sigma dx\,dy = 98$

$$r = \frac{n\Sigma dxdy - (\Sigma dx)(\Sigma dy)}{\sqrt{\Sigma dx^2 \cdot n - (\Sigma dx)^2} \times \sqrt{\Sigma dy^2 \cdot n - (\Sigma dy)^2}}$$

$$= \frac{11 \times 98 - (-11)(-3)}{\sqrt{217 \times 11 - (-11)^2} \times \sqrt{173 \times 11 - (-3)^2}}$$

$$= \frac{1078 - 33}{\sqrt{2387 - 121} \times \sqrt{1903 - 9}}$$

$$= \frac{1045}{\sqrt{2266} \times \sqrt{1894}} = \frac{1045}{47.6 \times 43.52} = 0.505 \text{ (approx)}$$

It shows medium degree of positive correlation between X and Y series.

Solved Question 5 **Calculate coefficient of correlation from the following information.**

(i) Sum of deviation of X values from assumed mean is 6.

(ii) Sum of deviation of Y values from assumed mean is 5.

(iii) Sum of square of deviation of X values from assumed mean is 35.

(iv) Sum of square of deviation of Y values from assumed mean is 40.

(v) Sum of products of deviations of X and Y values from their respective assumed mean is 40.

(vi) Number of items are 10.

Sol. Coefficient of Correlation

$$(r) = \frac{n \cdot \Sigma dx \cdot dy - (\Sigma dx)(\Sigma dy)}{\sqrt{n \cdot \Sigma dx^2 - (\Sigma dx)^2} \times \sqrt{n \cdot \Sigma dy^2 - (\Sigma dy)^2}}$$

According to question,

$\Sigma dx = 6, \quad \Sigma dy = 5, \quad \Sigma dx^2 = 35,$

$\Sigma dy^2 = 40, \quad \Sigma dx \cdot dy = 40, \quad n = 10$

$$\therefore r = \frac{(10 \times 40) - (6 \times 5)}{\sqrt{[10(35) - (6)^2][10(40) - (5)^2]}}$$

$$= \frac{400 - 30}{\sqrt{(350 - 36)(400 - 25)}} = \frac{370}{\sqrt{314 \times 375}}$$

$$= \frac{370}{\sqrt{117750}} = \frac{370}{343.14} = 1.078 \text{ (Positive correlation)}$$

Solved Question 6 **Calculate coefficient of correlation between the price and quantity demanded.**

Price (in ₹)	5	10	15	20	25
Demand (in kg)	40	35	30	25	20

Sol.

Calculation of Coefficient of Correlation

X	$dx(X-A)$ $A=15$	$dx'\left(\frac{dx}{c_1}\right)$ $c_1=5$	dx'^2	Y	$dy(Y-A)$ $A=30$	$dy'\left(\frac{dy}{c_2}\right)$ $c_2=5$	dy'^2	$dx'dy'$
5	–10	–2	4	40	10	2	4	–4
10	–5	–1	1	35	5	1	1	–1
15	0	0	0	30	0	0	0	0
20	5	1	1	25	–5	–1	1	–1
25	10	2	4	20	–10	–2	4	–4
$n=5$		$\Sigma dx'=0$	$\Sigma dx'^2=10$			$\Sigma dy'=0$	$\Sigma dy'^2=10$	$\Sigma dx'dy'=-10$

$$\text{Coefficient of Correlation } (r) = \frac{\Sigma dx'dy' - \frac{\Sigma dx' \times \Sigma dy'}{n}}{\sqrt{\left[\Sigma dx'^2 - \frac{(\Sigma dx')^2}{n}\right]} \times \sqrt{\left[\Sigma dy'^2 - \frac{(\Sigma dy')^2}{n}\right]}} = \frac{-10 - \frac{0}{5}}{\sqrt{10 - \frac{0}{5}} \times \sqrt{10 - \frac{0}{5}}} = \frac{-10}{\sqrt{10} \times \sqrt{10}} = \frac{-10}{10}$$

$$\therefore \qquad r = -1$$

This is a situation of perfectly negative correlation between price and quantity demanded.

Merits of Karl Pearson's Coefficient of Correlation

- It is one of the most useful methods as it is based upon all the items in the series.
- It helps in knowing the degree as well as direction of correlation.

Demerits of Karl Pearson's Coefficient of Correlation

- It is affected by change in extreme values.
- It is a difficult and time consuming method.
- It is applicable only in the case of linear relationship between two variables.

Spearman's Rank Correlation

Spearman's rank correlation is a statistical method, developed by Charles Edward Spearman, particularly useful for analysing relationships between variables that cannot be measured quantitatively, such as qualitative traits like beauty, honesty, intelligence, etc. Instead of using exact numerical values, this method ranks the data, making it more meaningful for such characteristics.

The rank correlation coefficient, denoted as r_k, is calculated using the formula

$$r_k = 1 - \frac{6\Sigma D^2}{n^3 - n}$$

Where, r_k = Coefficient of rank correlation ; ΣD^2 = Sum of the square of the difference between ranks
n = Number of pairs

Calculation of Spearman's Rank Correlation Coefficient

It can be studied under two conditions

Calculation of Spearman's Rank Correlation

- When ranks are given
- When ranks are not given

1. When Ranks are Given

When ranks are given, there can be two possible conditions

When Ranks are Not Repeated	When Ranks are Repeated
Step 1 Denote the ranks of the first series as R_1 and the ranks of the second series as R_2. **Step 2** Compute the difference between the corresponding ranks, $D = R_1 - R_2$. **Step 3** Find the square of each difference and sum these values to obtain ΣD^2. **Step 4** Apply the following formula to find correlation coefficient $r_k = 1 - \frac{6\Sigma D^2}{n^3 - n}$ Here, r_k = Coefficient of rank correlation n = Number of pairs ΣD^2 = Sum of total squared rank differences between R_1 and R_2	Repetition of ranks implies that two or more contestants are given a similar rank by a judge. e.g. Judge 1 can give 3rd rank to contestants M, Y and Z. When ranks are repeated, a correction factor $\frac{m(m^2-1)}{12}$ is applied. Following steps are followed **Steps 1 to 3** are same as discussed in case 'When ranks are not repeated.' **Step 4** Apply the given formula $r_k = 1 - \frac{6\left[\Sigma D^2 + \frac{1}{12}(m^3 - m) + \frac{1}{12}(m^3 - m) + \ldots\right]}{n^3 - n}$ where, ΣD^2 = Sum of squared differences m = Number of times a rank is repeated n = Number of pairs **Note** Students should remember that the correlation factor should be added for each repetition of rank in either of the series.

Solved Question 7 In a dance competition, two judges accorded following ranks to the 10 participants.

Judge X	Judge Y
9	1
3	10
4	2
2	8
8	3
7	9
6	4
5	6
10	5
1	7

Calculate coefficient of rank correlation.

Sol. **Calculation of Rank Correlation**

Judge X (R_1)	Judge Y (R_2)	$D(R_1 - R_2)$	D^2
9	1	8	64
3	10	−7	49
4	2	2	4
2	8	−6	36
8	3	5	25
7	9	−2	4
6	4	2	4
5	6	−1	1
10	5	5	25
1	7	−6	36
Total			$\Sigma D^2 = 248$

Here, $n = 10$, $\Sigma D^2 = 248$

$\because \; r_k = 1 - \frac{6\Sigma D^2}{n^3 - n} \Rightarrow r_k = 1 - \frac{6 \times 248}{(10)^3 - 10} = 1 - \frac{1{,}488}{990}$

$= 1 - 1.503 \Rightarrow r_k = -0.503$

There is a moderate degree of negative correlation between the opinions of Judge X and Judge Y.

Solved Question 8 Five competitors in a beauty contest are ranked by three judges in the following order

Rank by Judge A	Rank by Judge B	Rank by Judge C
1	2	1
2	4	3
3	1	5
4	5	2
5	3	4

Using rank correlation coefficient, determine which pair of judges has a common perception of beauty.

Sol. **Calculation of Rank Correlation**

R_1	R_2	R_3	$D_{1,2}$ $(R_1 - R_2)$	$D_{2,3}$ $(R_2 - R_3)$	$D_{1,3}$ $(R_1 - R_3)$	$D^2_{1,2}$	$D^2_{2,3}$	$D^2_{1,3}$
1	2	1	–1	1	0	1	1	0
2	4	3	–2	1	–1	4	1	1
3	1	5	2	–4	–2	4	16	4
4	5	2	–1	3	2	1	9	4
5	3	4	2	–1	1	4	1	1
						$\Sigma D^2_{1,2} = 14$	$\Sigma D^2_{2,3} = 28$	$\Sigma D^2_{1,3} = 10$

Here, $n = 5$, $\Sigma D^2_{1,2} = 14$, $\Sigma D^2_{2,3} = 28$, $\Sigma D^2_{1,3} = 10$

Applying the formula,

Correlation coefficient of Judge A and Judge B $(r_{k_{1,2}}) = 1 - \frac{6\Sigma D^2_{1,2}}{n^3 - n} = 1 - \frac{6 \times 14}{(5)^3 - 5} = 1 - \frac{84}{120} = 1 - 0.7 = 0.3$

Correlation coefficient of Judge B and Judge C $(r_{k_{2,3}}) = 1 - \frac{6\Sigma D^2_{2,3}}{n^3 - n} = 1 - \frac{6 \times 28}{(5)^3 - 5} = 1 - \frac{168}{120} = 1 - 1.4 = -0.4$

Correlation coefficient of Judge A and Judge C $(r_{k_{1,3}}) = 1 - \frac{6\Sigma D^2_{1,3}}{n^3 - n} = 1 - \frac{6 \times 10}{(5)^3 - 5} = 1 - \frac{60}{120} = 1 - 0.5 = +0.5$

Since, the coefficient of rank correlation is positive and highest for judges A and C, we conclude that they have similar perception of beauty. Judges B and C have very different perceptions.

Solved Question 9 **The following ranks were given to 11 students, based on their overall annual performance by two teachers.**

Roll no. of Student	Rank given by Teacher T	Rank given by Teacher L
1	6	1
2	3	2
3	8.5	9.5
4	10	4
5	1.5	5
6	8.5	3
7	5	8
8	1.5	7
9	7	9.5
10	4	11
11	11	6

Find the rank correlation.

Sol. **Calculation of Rank Correlation**

Rank given by Teacher T	Rank given by Teacher L	Difference in Ranks (D)	D^2
6	1	5	25
3	2	1	1
8.5	9.5	–1	1
10	4	6	36
1.5	5	–3.5	12.25
8.5	3	5.5	30.25
5	8	–3	9
1.5	7	–5.5	30.25
7	9.5	–2.5	6.25
4	11	–7	49
11	6	5	25
$n = 11$			$\Sigma D^2 = 225$

$$\rho = r_k = 1 - \frac{6\left[\Sigma D^2 + \frac{1}{12}(m^3 - m) + \frac{1}{12}(m^3 - m) + \frac{1}{12}(m^3 - m)\right]}{n^3 - n}$$

$$= 1 - \frac{6\left[225 + \frac{1}{12}(2^3 - 2) + \frac{1}{12}(2^3 - 2) + \frac{1}{12}(2^3 - 2)\right]}{11^3 - 11}$$

$$= 1 - \frac{6\,[225 + 0.5 + 0.5 + 0.5]}{1331 - 11} = 1 - \frac{6\,[226.5]}{1320}$$

$$= 1 - 1.0295 = -0.0295$$

There is low degree of negative correlation in the given by the two teachers.

Note The correlation factor has been added three times because three ranks are repeated, viz.
- Rank 8.5 is repeated two times in 1st series.
- Rank 1.5 is repeated two times in 1st series.
- Rank 9.5 is repeated two times in the 2nd series.

2. When Ranks are Not Given

When ranks are not given, they must be assigned before calculating the rank correlation coefficient.

There are two scenarios to consider

When Ranks Assigned are Not Repeated	When Ranks Assigned are Repeated
If all the values in a series are distinct, the ranks assigned will be unique and not repeated. To compute the rank correlation coefficient, following steps are followed ***Step 1*** Assign the ranks to the given values. ***Step 2*** Ranks can be assigned in two ways • **Option 1** Assign the highest value the 1st rank and subsequent lower values receive subsequent ranks. The lowest value gets the last rank. • **Option 2** Assign the highest value the last rank, and subsequent lower values receive earlier ranks. The lowest value gets the 1st rank. Ensure that the ranking order in the first series is consistently followed in the second series. ***Step 3*** Follow steps 1, 2, 3 and 4 as discussed in case 'When ranks are given and they are not repeated'.	If some values in the series are repeated, the ranks will also be repeated. Following steps will be followed ***Step 1*** Assign ranks to given values. Following points should be remembered • When values are equal, assign them the average of the ranks they would have occupied. e.g. If two items would both be ranked 7th due to equal values, they should each receive a rank of 7.5 (i.e. the average of 7th and 8th ranks). • After assigning average ranks to repeated values, continue ranking the next values as if these was no repetition. e.g. If two items are ranked 7.5, the next value should receive the 9th rank in the series. ***Step 2*** Follow steps 1 to 4 given in case 'When ranks are given and there is repetition in ranks'.

Solved Question 10 Calculate the coefficient of rank correlation of the following data

X	87	22	33	75	37
Y	29	63	52	46	48

Sol. **Calculation of Rank Correlation**

X	R_1	Y	R_2	$D(R_1-R_2)$	D^2
87	1	29	5	−4	16
22	5	63	1	4	16
33	4	52	2	2	4
75	2	46	4	−2	4
37	3	48	3	0	0
					$\Sigma D^2 = 40$

Here, $n = 5$, $\Sigma D^2 = 40 \Rightarrow r_k = 1 - \frac{6\Sigma D^2}{n^3 - n} = 1 - \frac{6 \times 40}{5^3 - 5}$

$$= 1 - \frac{240}{125 - 5} = 1 - \frac{240}{120}$$

$$= 1 - 2 = -1$$

$\therefore \quad r_k = -1$

It shows a perfect negative correlation between X and Y series.

Solved Question 11 Calculate the coefficient of correlation from the following data by the Spearman's rank correlation method

X	20	11	24	18	20	22
Y	24	9	20	22	9	21

Sol. **Calculation of Rank Correlation**

X	R_1	Y	R_2	$D(R_1-R_2)$	D^2
20	3.5	24	1	2.5	6.25
11	6	9	5.5	0.5	0.25
24	1	20	4	−3.0	9.00
18	5	22	2	3.0	9.00
20	3.5	9	5.5	−2.0	4.00
22	2	21	3	−1.0	1.00
					$\Sigma D^2 = 29.50$

Here, $n = 6$, $\Sigma D^2 = 29.50$

$m_1 = 2$, $m_2 = 2$

$$r_k = 1 - \frac{6\left[\Sigma D^2 + \frac{1}{12}(m_1^3 - m_1) + \frac{1}{12}(m_2^3 - m_2)\right]}{n^3 - n} = 1 - \frac{6\left[29.50 + \frac{1}{12}(2^3 - 2) + \frac{1}{12}(2^3 - 2)\right]}{6^3 - 6}$$

$$= 1 - \frac{6\left[29.50 + \frac{1}{12}(6) + \frac{1}{12}(6)\right]}{216 - 6} = 1 - \frac{6\left[29.50 + \frac{1}{2} + \frac{1}{2}\right]}{210} = 1 - \frac{6 \times 30.50}{210} = 1 - \frac{183}{210} = 1 - 0.87$$

$\therefore\ r_k = 0.13$

There is low degree of positive correlation between series X and series Y.

Merits of Spearman's Rank Correlation

- It is easy to calculate and understand.
- It can be used in case of qualitative data.
- It can be used even when the actual data is not provided and only ranks are given.

Demerits of Spearman's Rank Correlation

- It cannot be used for finding out correlation in a bivariate frequency distribution.
- It is difficult to use in case of large frequency distribution.
- This method lacks precision as compared to Karl Pearson's method

7.3 Properties of Correlation Coefficient

- Correlation coefficient (r) has no unit. It is a pure number. It means units of measurement are not part of r.
- A negative value of r indicates an inverse relation. A change in one variable is associated with change in the other variable in the opposite direction.
- If r is positive, the two variables move in the same direction.
- If $r = 0$, the two variables are uncorrelated or they are not linearly correlated.
- If $r = 1$ or $r = -1$, the correlation is perfect. The relation between variables is exact.
- A high value of r indicates strong linear relationship. Its value is said to be high when it is close to + 1 or –1.
- A low value of r indicates a weak linear relation. Its value is said to be low when it is close to zero.
- The value of the correlation coefficient lies between –1 and +1, i.e. $-1 \leq r \leq 1$.
- The value of r is unaffected by the change in origin or scale.

Mind Map

MEASURES OF CORRELATION

1 Meaning of Correlation

It is a statistical concept used to study and measure the direction and strength of the relationship between two variables.

Correlation *vs* Causation

- *Direct Causation*: One variable directly affects another.
- *Reverse Causation*: The effected variable influences the cause variable.
- *Common Cause*: Both variables are influenced by a third factor.
- *Cyclic Causation*: A causes B and B causes A in a cycle.
- *Indirect Causation*: A affects C, which then affects B.
- *Spurious Correlation*: No actual relationship; just coincidental.

2 Types of Correlation

Based on Direction of Change

- *Positive Correlation*: Both variables move in the same direction.
- *Negative Correlation*: Variables move in opposite directions.

Based on Magnitude of Change

- *Linear Correlation*: Proportional change, represented by a straight line graph.
- *Non-linear Correlation*: Varying proportional change, forming a curve.

Based on Number of Variables

- *Simple Correlation*: Relationship between two variables.
- *Multiple Correlation*: Relationship among three or more variables.

3 Degrees of Correlation

- **Perfect Correlation** (+1 or − 1) A change in one variable results in a perfectly proportional change in the other.
- **High Correlation** (±0.75 to ±0.9) A strong relationship exists between variables, meaning changes in one variable significantly impact the other.
- **Moderate Correlation** (±0.25 to ±0.75) A noticeable but weaker relationship; some external factors may also influence the variables.
- **Low Correlation** (0 to ±0.25) A weak relationship where changes in one variable have little impact on the other.
- **No Correlation** (0) No relationship exists between the variables.

4 Scatter Diagram

The scatter diagram is a graphical method used to visually represent the relationship between two variables. It helps to identify the direction and strength of correlation by plotting data points on a graph.

Interpretation of Scatter Diagrams

- *Positive Correlation*: Points follow an upward trend, meaning both variables increase together.
- *Negative Correlation*: Points follow a downward trend, meaning one variable increases while the other decreases.
- *No Correlation*: Points are scattered randomly, indicating no clear relationship between the variables.
- *Perfect Positive Correlation*: Points lie exactly on an upward sloping line.
- *Perfect Negative Correlation*: Points lie exactly on a downward sloping line.

5 Karl Pearson's Coefficient of Correlation

- It is developed by Karl Pearson to measure the strength and direction of a linear relationship.
- It provides an exact numerical value between −1 and +1.

Interpretation

- +1 indicates perfect positive correlation
- −1 indicates perfect negative correlation
- 0 indicates correlation

Methods

- **Actual Mean Method**

$$r = \frac{\Sigma xy}{\sqrt{\Sigma x^2 \times \Sigma y^2}}$$

- **Short-cut Method**

$$r = \frac{\Sigma dx \cdot dy - \frac{\Sigma dx \times \Sigma dy}{n}}{\sqrt{\Sigma dx^2 - \frac{(\Sigma dx)^2}{n}} \times \sqrt{\Sigma dy^2 - \frac{(\Sigma dy)^2}{n}}}$$

$$= \frac{\Sigma dx \cdot dy \cdot n - (\Sigma dx)(\Sigma dy)}{\sqrt{\Sigma dx^2 \cdot n - (\Sigma dx)^2} \times \sqrt{\Sigma dy^2 \cdot n - (\Sigma dy)^2}}$$

- **Step Deviation Method**

$$r = \frac{\Sigma dx'dy' - \frac{\Sigma dx' \times \Sigma dy'}{n}}{\sqrt{\left[\Sigma dx'^2 - \frac{\Sigma dx'^2}{n}\right]}\sqrt{\left[\Sigma dy'^2 - \frac{\Sigma dy'^2}{n}\right]}}$$

6 Spearman's Rank Correlation

- It is developed by Charles Edward Spearman.
- It measures correlation for qualitative variables (e.g. Beauty, intelligence).
- It ranks data instead of using exact numerical values.
- **Formula**

$$r_k = 1 - \frac{6\Sigma D^2}{n^3 - n}$$

- **Calculation Methods**
  - *When Ranks Not Repeated*: Direct calculation using differences in ranks.

$$r_k = 1 - \frac{6\Sigma D^2}{n^3 - n}$$

  - *When Ranks Repeated*: Uses a correction factor $\frac{m(m^2 - 1)}{12}$ for repeated ranks

$$r_k = 1 - \frac{6\left[\Sigma D^2 + \frac{1}{12}(m^3 - m) + \frac{1}{2}(m^3 - m) + ...\right]}{n^3 - n}$$

7 Properties of Correlation Coefficient

- Unit free measure, i.e. r has no unit; it is a pure number.
- Direction of relationship can be positive or negative.
- The strength of correlation varies from perfect ($r = \pm 1$), to strong (r close to 1), weak (r close to 0) and none ($r = 0$).
- It ranges between −1 and +1.
- Independence from scale, i.e. unaffected by changes in origin or scale.

EXAM PATTERN QUESTIONS

Objective Type Questions

Multiple Choice Questions (MCQs)

1. Which of the following techniques deals with the association between two or more variables?
(a) Index number (b) Correlation
(c) Dispersion (d) None of these

2. Correlation is a statistical concept used to measure the .... and .... of the relationship between two variables.
(a) duration, magnitude (b) direction, strength
(c) quantity, type (d) rate, frequency

3. The arrow between the ice-cream cone and sunburn indicates which of the following?

(a) Causation (b) Correlation
(c) Both (a) and (b) (d) Neither (a) nor (b)

4. Which of the following is correct about spurious correlation? **Competency Based Que**

I. Spurious correlation indicates a genuine relationship between variables.
II. Spurious correlation occurs when two variables move in opposite directions.
III. Spurious correlation describes a cyclical pattern between variables.
IV. Spurious correlation is when the correlation between variables is due to chance.

Codes
(a) I and II (b) III and IV
(c) Only IV (d) Only II

5. Which of the following describes a relationship where the change in one variable has a constant ratio to the change in another variable?
(a) Non-linear correlation (b) Simple correlation
(c) Linear correlation (d) Multiple correlations

6. The given diagram represents

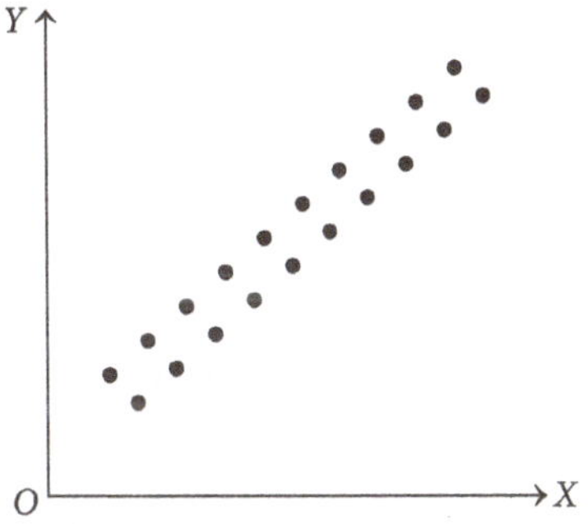

(a) perfect positive correlation
(b) high degree of positive correlation
(c) moderate degree of positive correlation
(d) low degree of positive correlation

7. Which type of causation occurs when both variables are affected by a third factor?
(a) Common cause
(b) Direct causation
(c) Reverse causation (d) Spurious correlation

8. Under .... causation, one variable affects another through a third variable.
(a) direct (b) reverse
(c) common cause (d) indirect

9. Of the following three measures, which type can measure any type of relationship? **NCERT**
(a) Karl Pearson's coefficient of correlation
(b) Spearman's rank correlation
(c) Scatter diagram

10. If a scatter diagram shows a perfect positive correlation, what is the correlation coefficient (r)? **Competency Based Que**
(a) 0
(b) 1
(c) –1
(d) 0.5

11. In a scatter diagram, which axis is used to plot the independent variable?
(a) The y-axis (vertical axis)
(b) The z-axis
(c) The x-axis (horizontal axis)
(d) The diagonal axis

12. **Which type of correlation is highlighted in the below image?**

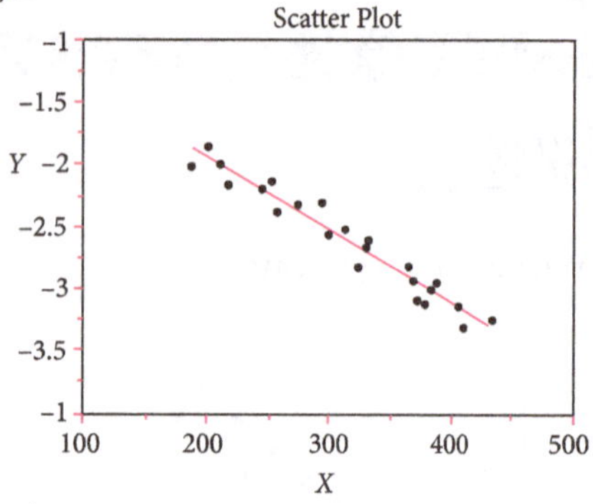

(a) Perfect positive (b) Perfect negative
(c) Positive (d) No correlation

13. **If the scatter points are widely dispersed around the line, the correlation is** Competency Based Que

(a) high (b) low
(c) moderate (d) None of these

14. **If r_{xy} is positive, the relation between X and Y is of the type** NCERT; Competency Based Que

(a) when Y increases, X increases
(b) when Y decreases, X increases
(c) when Y increases, X does not change

15. **Which value of Karl Pearson's coefficient of correlation indicates a perfect negative linear relationship?**

(a) +1 (b) −1
(c) 0 (d) 0.5

16. **If the correlation coefficient (r) between two variables is 0, what does this indicate?**

I. No linear relationship
II. Perfect positive correlation
III. Strong linear relationship
IV. Perfect negative correlation Competency Based Que

Codes

(a) Only I (b) II and III
(c) Only III (d) I, II, III and IV

17. **What does the following image indicate?**

$$r = \frac{\Sigma xy}{\sqrt{\Sigma x^2 \times \Sigma y^2}}$$

(a) Modified version of Spearman's formula
(b) Modified version of rank correlation formula
(c) Modified version of Karl Pearson's formula
(d) Modified version of positive correlation formula

18. **Karl Pearson's coefficient of correlation is calculated as the ratio of the covariance between x and y to the product of their ....**

(a) means (b) variances
(c) sum (d) standard deviations

19. **If precisely measured data are available, the simple correlation coefficient is** NCERT; Competency Based Que

(a) more accurate than rank correlation coefficient
(b) less accurate than rank correlation coefficient
(c) as accurate as the rank correlation coefficient

20. **When the mean of series is a decimal number, then which method should be used for computing Karl Pearson's coefficient of correlation?**

(a) Direct method (b) Short-cut method
(c) Step deviation method (d) None of these

21. **If Spearman's rank correlation coefficient (r_k) is +1, what does it indicate?**

(a) Perfect positive correlation
(b) No relationship between the variables
(c) Perfect negative correlation
(d) Weak positive correlation

22. **When ranks are repeated, the correction factor is applied to .... to obtain the Spearman's rank correlation coefficient.**

(a) $\Sigma dxdy$ (b) Σx^2
(c) Σdy^2 (d) ΣD^2

23. **Identify the correct statement about rank correlation.**

I. Spearman's rank correlation can be used even when the actual data is not given and only ranks are provided.
II. When calculating Spearman's rank correlation, if ranks are repeated, a correction factor must be applied.
III. Spearman's rank correlation coefficient ranges between −1 and +1, where −1 indicates a perfect negative correlation and +1 indicates a perfect positive correlation.
IV. Spearman's rank correlation is denoted as d.

Codes Competency Based Que

(a) I, II and III (b) II, III and IV
(c) I and III (d) II and IV

24. **Rank correlation is a superior method of analysis in case of .... distributions such as those relating to virtue, wisdom or ignorance.**

(a) quantitative (b) qualitative
(c) data (d) None of these

25. **What is the purpose of applying a correction factor in Spearman's rank correlation?**

(a) To adjust for any deviations from the mean
(b) To correct for repeated ranks
(c) To calculate the covariance between two variables
(d) To account for outliers in the data

26. **A high value of r indicates .... linear relation.**

(a) weak (b) neutral (c) strong (d) zero

Direction *Read the case study and answer the questions 27 to 30 on the basis of the same*

Alex owns a popular ice cream shop in a bustling city. Each summer, he meticulously records the daily temperature and the number of ice-creams sold to understand the relationship between these two variables. This year, he decided to use the data to improve his marketing strategies. Alex collected data over a period of 30 days, noting that on hotter days, his shop experienced a noticeable increase in sales.

After analysing his data, Alex plotted it on a scatter diagram. The points showed an upward trend: as the temperature increased, so did the number of ice-creams sold. Curious about the strength and direction of this relationship, Alex calculated the correlation coefficient to quantify the linear relationship between temperature and sales.

To gain a deeper insight, Alex used the Pearson correlation coefficient and found that it was close to +1. This high positive value indicated a strong linear relationship between temperature and ice-cream sales. Alex also noted that this correlation was unaffected by changes in scale or origin, reaffirming the strength of the relationship.

Based on his findings, Alex is confident that a targeted marketing campaign during hotter days would be beneficial for his business. He plans to use this insight to optimise his promotions and stock inventory more efficiently.

27. **What does a correlation coefficient close to +1 indicate in the context of Alex's analysis?**

(a) No relationship between temperature and ice-cream sales
(b) A perfect negative linear relationship between temperature and ice-cream sales
(c) A strong positive linear relationship between temperature and ice-cream sales
(d) A weak positive relationship between temperature and ice-cream sales

28. **Which of the following properties of the correlation coefficient is demonstrated by Alex's finding that the coefficient is unaffected by changes in scale or origin?**

(a) Correlation coefficient is a unit less measure
(b) Correlation coefficient measures the direction of the relationship
(c) Correlation coefficient only applies to linear relationships
(d) Correlation coefficient can be negative or zero

29. **The value of the correlation coefficient is not affected by changes in .... and ...., ensuring that the strength of the linear relationship remains constant.**

30. **In analysing the relationship between temperature and ice-cream sales, if Alex observed a correlation coefficient of −0.85, this would indicate a .... linear relationship, meaning as the temperature increases, ice-cream sales would ....**

Assertion-Reason

Direction (Q.No. 31 to 40) *Read the following Assertion (A) and Reason (R) and choose the correct alternative from the following*

Alternatives

(a) Both Assertion (A) and Reason (R) are true and Reason (R) is the correct explanation of Assertion (A)
(b) Both Assertion (A) and Reason (R) are true, but Reason (R) is not the correct explanation of Assertion (A)
(c) Assertion (A) is true, but Reason (R) is false
(d) Assertion (A) is false, but Reason (R) is true

31. **Assertion** (A) Correlation analysis facilitates understanding of economic behaviour.

Reason (R) Correlation facilitates the decision-making in the business world.

32. **Assertion** (A) Direct causation is when two variables change together due to a common third factor.

Reason (R) The rise in mobile phone prices leading to increased demand for them is an example of direct causation.

33. **Assertion** (A) Positive correlation occurs when two related variables move in the same direction.

Reason (R) In positive correlation, when one variable increases, the other also increases and *vice-versa.*

34. **Assertion** (A) A scatter diagram is a graphical method used to show the relationship between two variables.

Reason (R) A scatter diagram is a non-mathematical method, thus, cannot be fully relied upon.

35. **Assertion** (A) When points lie exactly on a downward sloping line, it indicates perfect negative correlation.

Reason (R) Perfect negative correlation is denoted by $r = +1$.

36. **Assertion** (A) Karl Pearson's coefficient of correlation is ideal measure of correlation.

Reason (R) Karl Pearson's method is based upon arithmetic mean and standard deviation.

37. **Assertion** (A) +1 indicates a perfect positive linear relationship.

Reason (R) 0 indicates no linear relationship between the variables.

38. **Assertion** (A) The short-cut method involves calculating the correlation coefficient using the actual mean values.

Reason (R) The short-cut method simplifies calculations when means are in fractions.

39. **Assertion** (A) When ranks are not provided for a set of data, they must be assigned before calculating the rank correlation coefficient.

Reason (R) If all the values in a series are distinct, the ranks assigned will be unique and not repeated.

40. **Assertion** (A) A negative value of r indicates an inverse relation.

Reason (R) A change in one variable is associated with change in the other variable in the opposite direction.

Two Statements Based MCQs

Direction (Q.No. 41 to 50) *Read the following statements carefully and choose the correct alternative*

Alternatives

(a) Statement I is correct and Statement II is incorrect
(b) Statement II is correct and Statement I is incorrect
(c) Both the statements are correct
(d) Both the statements are incorrect

41. **Statement I** Both variables (A and B) are affected by a third factor in cyclic causation.

Statement II One variable (A) affects another variable (B) through a third variable (C) when there is direct causation.

42. **Statement I** Negative correlation ranges from minus infinity to zero.

Statement II In case of multiple correlation, there are more than one independent variables.

43. **Statement I** The independent variable is placed on the y-axis in a scatter diagram.

Statement II The pattern formed by the dots (or scatter points) indicates the type of correlation between the variables.

44. **Statement I** Scatter diagram is a simple method as it does not involve any mathematical calculation.

Statement II A scatter diagram cannot be used in case of large distributions.

45. **Statement I** The correlation coefficient is denoted as r_k.

Statement II British statistician, Karl Pearson developed a mathematical method known as the correlation coefficient.

46. **Statement I** Coefficient of correlation is independent of unit of measurement.

Statement II Correlation is independent of both change in scale as well as origin.

47. **Statement I** Pearson's correlation coefficient is calculated as the ratio of the covariance between x and y to the product of their standard deviations.

Statement II Pearson's correlation coefficient only identifies the degree of correlation, not the direction.

48. **Statement I** Spearman's rank correlation is a statistical method developed by Charles Edward Spearman in 1904.

Statement II The rank correlation coefficient is denoted as r_k.

49. **Statement I** When ranks are provided for two series of data, Spearman's rank correlation coefficient can be used to measure only the strength of relationship between ranks.

Statement II The difference between the corresponding ranks is computed as $D = R_1 - R_2$.

50. **Statement I** If some values in the series are same, the ranks will not need to be repeated.

Statement II Rank correlation can be used for finding out correlation in a bivariate frequency distribution.

Matching

51. Match the following

Column I		Column II	
A.	Direct causation	(i)	The second variable (B) influences the first (A).
B.	Reverse causation	(ii)	Both variables (A and B) are affected by a third factor.
C.	Common cause	(iii)	There is no real relationship between the variables and their correlation is due to chance.
D.	Spurious correlation	(iv)	One variable (A) directly influences another (B).

Codes

	A	B	C	D		A	B	C	D
(a)	(iii)	(iv)	(i)	(ii)	(b)	(iv)	(i)	(ii)	(iii)
(c)	(ii)	(iii)	(iv)	(i)	(d)	(iii)	(ii)	(i)	(iv)

52. Match the following

Column I	Column II
A. Positive correlation	(i) Involves the study of the relationship between two variables.
B. Negative correlation	(ii) Describes a situation where the change in one variable has a constant ratio to the change in another variable.
C. Simple correlation	(iii) Occurs when two related variables move in the same direction.
D. Linear correlation	(iv) Occurs when two variables move in opposite directions.

Codes

	A	B	C	D		A	B	C	D
(a)	(iii)	(iv)	(i)	(ii)	(b)	(iv)	(i)	(ii)	(iii)
(c)	(ii)	(iii)	(iv)	(i)	(d)	(iii)	(ii)	(i)	(iv)

53. Match the following

Column I	Column II
A. Independent variable	(i) Points lie exactly on an upward sloping line
B. Dependent variable	(ii) *x*-axis (horizontal axis)
C. No correlation	(iii) *y*-axis (vertical axis)
D. Perfect positive correlation	(iv) Points are scattered randomly without any discernible pattern

Codes

	A	B	C	D		A	B	C	D
(a)	(iii)	(iv)	(i)	(ii)	(b)	(iv)	(i)	(ii)	(iii)
(c)	(ii)	(iii)	(iv)	(i)	(d)	(iii)	(ii)	(i)	(iv)

54. Match the following

Column I	Column II
A. Σdx	(i) Karl Pearson's coefficient of correlation
B. r_{xy}	(ii) Spearman's rank correlation
C. r_k	(iii) Number of pair of observations
D. N	(iv) Sum of deviations of X series

Codes

	A	B	C	D		A	B	C	D
(a)	(iii)	(iv)	(i)	(ii)	(b)	(iv)	(i)	(ii)	(iii)
(c)	(ii)	(iii)	(iv)	(i)	(d)	(iii)	(ii)	(i)	(iv)

55. Match the options of Column I with correct options in Column II

Column I	Column II
A. Perfect positive correlation	(i) Between 0 to 1
B. Negative correlation	(ii) $r_{xy} = 0$
C. Uncorrelated	(iii) $r_{xy} = 1$
D. Positive correlation	(iv) $-1 \le r_{xy} < 0$

Codes

	A	B	C	D		A	B	C	D
(a)	(i)	(ii)	(iii)	(iv)	(b)	(iv)	(i)	(ii)	(iii)
(c)	(iii)	(iv)	(ii)	(i)	(d)	(ii)	(iii)	(iv)	(i)

Concept Identification

56. It describes a statistical measure that indicates the extent to which two variables move together.

57. It is a relationship between two variables that can be graphically represented with a straight line.

58. It involves a measure of the degree to which two variables vary together, indicating the direction of their relationship but not the strength.

59. It involves a graphical method to show the relationship between two variables, providing a visual representation without numerical calculations.

60. It describes data points that are significantly higher or lower than the majority of other values, potentially affecting correlation measures.

Answers

1. (b) Correlation
2. (b) direction, strength
3. (b) Correlation
4. (c) Only IV
5. (c) Linear correlation
6. (b) high degree of positive correlation
7. (a) Common cause
8. (d) indirect
9. (c) Scatter diagram
10. (b) 1
11. (c) The x-axis (horizontal axis)
12. (b) Perfect negative
13. (b) low
14. (a) when Y increases, X increases
15. (b) −1
16. (a) Only I
17. (c) Modified version of Karl Pearson's formula
18. (d) standard deviations
19. (a) more accurate than rank correlation coefficient
20. (b) Short-cut method
21. (a) Perfect positive correlation
22. (d) ΣD^2
23. (a) I, II and III
24. (b) qualitative
25. (b) To correct for repeated ranks
26. (c) strong
27. (c) A strong positive linear relationship between temperature and ice-cream sales
28. (a) Correlation coefficient is a unit less measure
29. scale, origin
30. strong negative, decrease
31. (b) Both Assertion (A) and Reason (R) are true, but Reason (R) is not the correct explanation of Assertion (A)
32. (d) Direct causation involves one variable directly influencing another without intermediaries.
33. (a) Both Assertion (A) and Reason (R) are true and Reason (R) is the correct explanation of Assertion (A)
34. (b) Both Assertion (A) and Reason (R) are true, but Reason (R) is not the correct explanation of Assertion (A)
35. (c) Points lie exactly on a downward sloping line, showing a perfect negative correlation ($r = -1$).
36. (a) Both Assertion (A) and Reason (R) are true and Reason (R) is the correct explanation of Assertion (A)
37. (b) Both Assertion (A) and Reason (R) are true, but Reason (R) is not the correct explanation of Assertion (A)
38. (d) The actual mean method involves calculating the correction coefficient using the actual mean values.
39. (b) Both Assertion (A) and Reason (R) are true, but Reason (R) is not the correct explanation of Assertion (A)
40. (a) Both Assertion (A) and Reason (R) are true and Reason (R) is the correct explanation of Assertion (A)
41. (d) Both variables (A and B) are affected by a third factor in common cause. One variable (A) affects another variable (B) through a third variable (C) when there is indirect causation.
42. (b) Negative correlation ranges from −1 to 0.
43. (b) The independent variable is placed on the x-axis in a scatter diagram.
44. (c) Both the statements are correct
45. (b) The correlation coefficient, denoted as r_{xy}, quantifies the strength and direction of the linear relationship between two variables, x and y.
46. (c) Both the statements are correct
47. (a) Correlation coefficient helps in knowing the degree as well as direction of correlation.
48. (c) Both the statements are correct
49. (b) When ranks are provided for two series of data, Spearman's rank correlation coefficient can be used to measure the strength and direction of the relationship between the two variables.
50. (d) If some values in series are same, the ranks will need to be repeated. Rank correlation cannot be used for finding out correlation in a bivariate frequency distribution.
51. (b) (iv) (i) (ii) (iii)
52. (a) (iii) (iv) (i) (ii)
53. (c) (ii) (iii) (iv) (i)
54. (b) (iv) (i) (ii) (iii)
55. (c) (iii) (iv) (ii) (i)
56. Correlation
57. Linear relationship
58. Covariance
59. Scatter diagram or plot
60. Outliers

Subjective Questions

Short Answer Type Questions

1. What is the key difference between correlation and causation?

Ans. Correlation refers to a statistical relationship between two variables where they change together, either in the same or opposite directions. However, correlation does not imply that one variable causes the change in the other.

Causation, on the other hand, implies a direct cause and effect relationship, where changes in one variable directly result in changes in the other.

2. "Correlation between two variables always indicates that one variable causes the other to change." Do you agree? Give reason. Competency Based Que

Ans. No, I do not agree. While correlation shows that two variables tend to move together, it does not necessarily mean that one variable causes the other to change. Correlation can occur due to direct causation, reverse causation, a common cause or even by chance (spurious correlation).

e.g. The correlation between ice-cream sales and drowning incidents in summer is not due to one causing the other but due to a common cause—warmer weather.

3. During the summer, an ice-cream company noticed that as temperature increased, their sales also increased. Identify the type of correlation present between temperature and ice-cream sales. Competency Based Que

Ans. The correlation present here is positive correlation. This occurs because both variables i.e. temperature and ice-cream sales, move in the same direction. As temperatures rise, more people buy ice-cream to cool off, leading to increased sales.

This is a common example of how two related variables can change together.

4. Which type of causation is highlighted in the given image? Competency Based Que

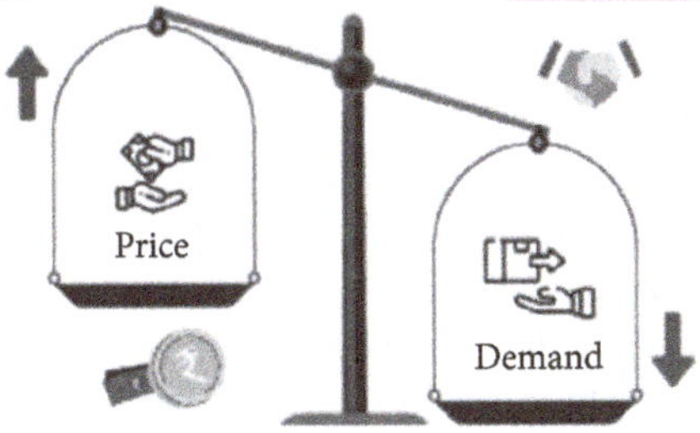

Ans. The image depicts direct causation. As the price increases, the demand drops, which is a direct cause and effect relationship. In this case, the increase in price (cause) directly leads to a decrease in demand (effect), following the law of demand in economics where higher prices typically result in lower demand for a product.

5. "A study shows that as the use of fertilisers increases, the production of food crops also increases, but this relationship is not consistent." Identify and explain the type of correlation. Competency Based Que

Ans. The type of correlation highlighted here is non-linear correlation. In this case, the relationship between fertiliser use and crop production does not follow a straight line, meaning the increase in crop production does not occur at a constant rate relative to the increase in fertiliser use. Initially, more fertiliser might significantly boost crop production, but after a certain point, the increase in production might slow down, showing a curved line when plotted on a graph.

6. Does zero correlation mean independence? NCERT

Ans. No, zero correlation does not mean independence. If there is zero correlation, it means the two variables are not correlated and there is no linear relation between them. However, other types of relation may be there and they may not be independent.

7. Which type of correlation is depicted by the given scatter plot? Competency Based Que

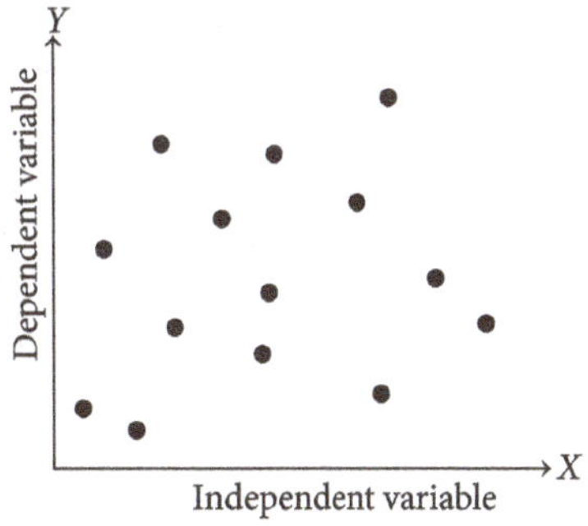

Ans. The correlation type depicted here is no correlation. A scatter plot that shows no correlation is characterised by points that are scattered randomly across the graph, without forming any discernible pattern, line or curve.

In this type of scatter plot, the points do not cluster around a line or curve in any direction, meaning there is no clear relationship between the two variables being plotted.

8. A scatter diagram shows points lying exactly on a downward sloping line. Which type of correlation does this depict and what does it signify about the relationship between the variables?

Ans. This scatter diagram depicts a perfect negative correlation, signified by points lying exactly on a downward sloping line. This indicates a very strong inverse relationship between the two variables, meaning that as one variable increases, the other decreases consistently in a proportional manner. This type of correlation has a correlation coefficient of –1.

9. Draw three hypothetical scatter diagrams showing the following value of r

(i) $r=-1$ **(ii) $r=+1$**
(iii) $r=0$

Ans.

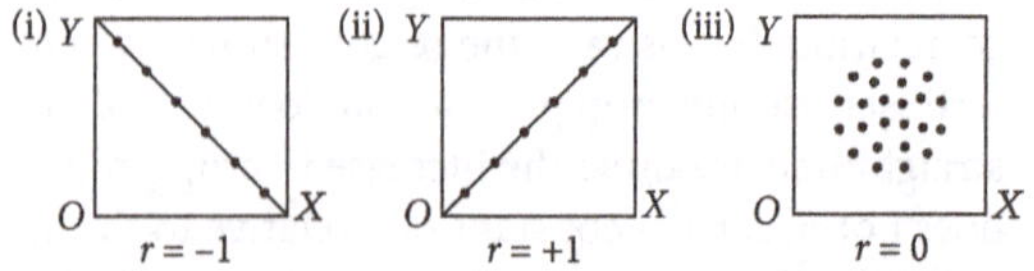

10. A scatter diagram is used to analyse the relationship between the number of hours studied and exam scores of a group of students. The points on the scatter diagram form a dense cluster around an upward sloping line. What can be inferred from this pattern? Competency Based Que

Ans. The dense cluster of points around an upward sloping line in the scatter diagram suggests a positive correlation between the number of hours studied and exam scores. This implies that, generally, as students study more hours, their exam scores tend to increase. The closeness of the points to the line indicates a strong positive relationship, meaning the correlation is likely to be significant.

11. What does a scatter diagram usually represent and how is it used in correlation analysis?

Ans. A scatter diagram usually represents the relationship between two variables by plotting data points on a graph. The independent variable is placed on the x-axis, while the dependent variable is placed on the y-axis.

By examining the pattern of the plotted points, one can determine the direction and strength of the correlation between the two variables.

If the points cluster around a line, it indicates a strong correlation, while a random scatter indicates little to no correlation.

12. Give the merits of using scatter diagram.

Ans. Following are the merits of scatter diagram

(i) It is a simple method as it does not involve any mathematical calculation.

(ii) It is easy to understand and interpret.

(iii) It is not affected by extreme values.

13. Can 'r' lie outside the –1 and 1 range depending on the type of data? NCERT

Ans. No, the value of the correlation coefficient lies between minus one and plus one, i.e. $-1 \le r \le 1$. If the value of 'r' is outside this range in any type of data, it indicates error in calculation.

14. "Karl Pearson's coefficient of correlation is only applicable when deviations of variables are calculated from an assumed mean." Do you agree? Give reason. Competency Based Que

Ans. No, I don't agree. Karl Pearson's coefficient of correlation is applicable only when the deviations of variables are calculated from their actual mean, not from an assumed mean.

The actual mean method provides a more accurate calculation of the correlation coefficient.

15. Give the demerits of Karl Pearson's coefficient of correlation.

Ans. Following are the demerits of Karl Pearson's coefficient of correlation

(i) It is affected by change in extreme values.

(ii) It is a difficult and time consuming method.

(iii) It is applicable only in case of linear relationship between two variables.

16. Why does rank correlation coefficient differ from Pearsonian correlation coefficient? NCERT

Ans. Rank correlation coefficient differs from Pearsonian correlation coefficient in the following ways

(i) Rank correlation coefficient is preferred to measure the correlation between qualitative variables as these variables cannot be measured precisely.

(ii) The rank correlation coefficient uses ranks instead of the full set of observations that leads to some loss of information.

(iii) If extreme values are present in the data, then the rank correlation coefficient is more precise and reliable.

17. What are the properties of Spearman's rank correlation?

Ans. The properties of Spearman's rank correlation are

(i) Spearman's rank correlation also lies between + 1 and – 1.

(ii) It is not affected by either change in scale or change in origin.

(iii) It can be calculated even when the data is not known.

18. **In a study on student preferences for different teaching methods, the data show that some students have the same preference rankings. How should these ranks be handled when calculating Spearman's rank correlation coefficient?** **Competency Based Que**

Ans. For repeated ranks, each group of tied ranks should be assigned the average of the ranks they would have occupied. e.g. If two students both have the 5th rank, they should each receive a rank of 5.5. After assigning these average ranks, proceed with the standard steps to calculate the correlation coefficient, including applying a correction factor for any repeated ranks.

Long Answer Type Questions

19. Does correlation imply causation? **NCERT**

Ans. No, correlation measures do not imply causation. Correlation measures covariation and not causation.

Correlation does not imply cause and effect relation. The knowledge of correlation only gives us an idea of the direction and intensity of change in a variable when the correlated variable changes.

The presence of correlation between two variables x and y simply means that when the value of one variable is found to change in one direction, the value of the other variable is found to change either in the same direction (i.e. positive change) or in the opposite direction (i.e. negative change), in a definite way.

However, it does not mean that y changes because of change in x. For any two correlated events x and y, the following relationships are possible

(i) x causes y.

(ii) y causes x.

(iii) x and y are consequence of a common cause but do not cause each other.

(iv) x causes y and y causes x.

(v) x causes z which causes y.

(vi) There is no connection between x and y and correlation between them is merely by chance.

20. **Consider the examples given below**

(i) As price falls, demand for product 'A' increases.

(ii) Effect of adequate irrigation facilities, fertilisers and pesticides on per hectare productivity of wheat.

On the basis of above examples, explain the main difference between simple correlation and multiple correlation. **Competency Based Que**

Ans. The first example involves only two variables, *viz.* price and demand. Therefore, it relates to simple correlation.

The second example involves more than two variables, i.e. how the productivity of wheat is affected by use of irrigation facilities, fertilisers and pesticides. Therefore, it relates to multiple correlation.

The main difference between simple correlation and multiple correlation is

Simple Correlation	Multiple Correlation
When the relationship between only two variables is studied, it is called simple correlation.	When the relationship among three or more than three variables is studied simultaneously, it is called multiple correlation.

21. **List and explain the type of correlations depicted by scatter diagrams.**

Ans. Types of correlation depicted by scatter diagrams

(i) **Positive Correlation**

Points are clustered around an upward sloping line. As the independent variable increases, the dependent variable also increases.

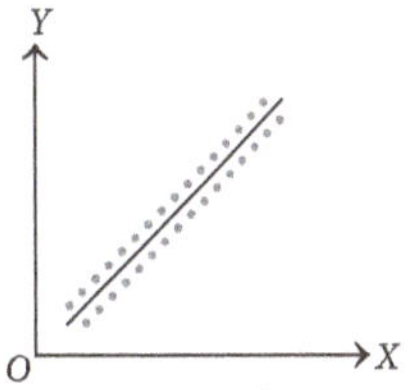

Positive Correlation

(ii) **Negative Correlation**

Points are clustered around a downward sloping line. As the independent variable increases, the dependent variable decreases.

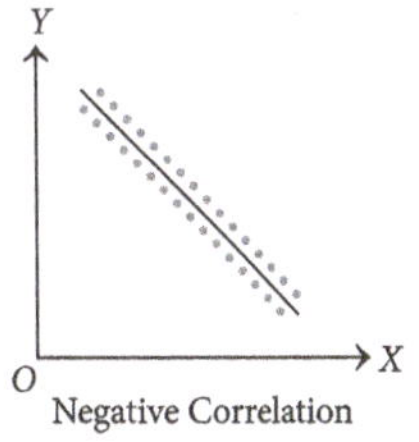

Negative Correlation

(iii) **No Correlation**

Points are scattered randomly without any discernible pattern, indicating no clear relationship between the variables.

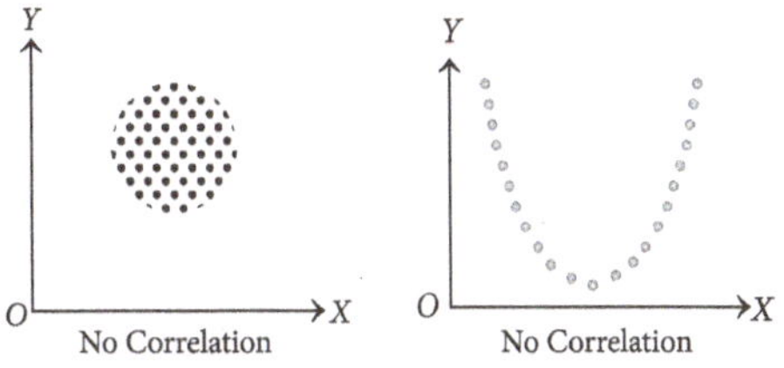

(iv) **Perfect Positive Correlation**
Points lie exactly on an upward sloping line, showing a perfect positive correlation ($r = 1$).

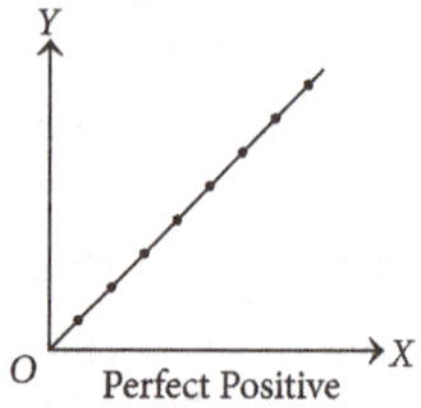

Perfect Positive Correlation

(v) **Perfect Negative Correlation**
Points lie exactly on a downward sloping line, showing a perfect negative correlation ($r = -1$).

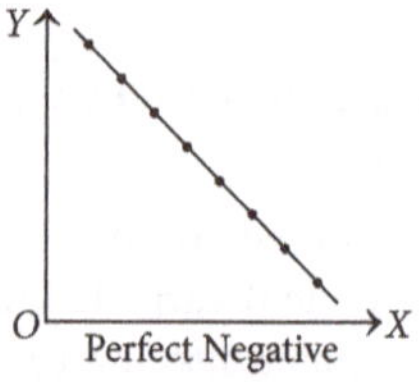

Perfect Negative Correlation

22. How can correlation coefficient be calculated using the short-cut method?

Ans. The short-cut method simplifies calculations when means are in fractions. It uses assumed mean instead of actual mean

Step 1 Take any convenient whole numbers as the assumed means of X and Y series respectively.

Step 2 Take the deviations of X series from the assumed mean, so as to get dx and obtain their total i.e. Σdx.

Step 3 Take the deviations of Y series from the assumed mean, so as to get dy and obtain their total i.e. Σdy.

Step 4 Square dx and obtain their total, i.e. Σdx^2.

Step 5 Square dy and obtain their total, i.e. Σdy^2.

Step 6 Multiply the corresponding deviations of X and Y series and add these products to get $\Sigma dxdy$.

Step 7 Substitute the above values in the given formula to get the value of coefficient of correlation (r).

$$r = \frac{\Sigma dxdy - \dfrac{\Sigma dx \times \Sigma dy}{n}}{\sqrt{\Sigma dx^2 - \dfrac{(\Sigma dx)^2}{n}} \times \sqrt{\Sigma dy^2 - \dfrac{(\Sigma dy)^2}{n}}}$$

or

$$= \frac{\Sigma dxdy \cdot n - (\Sigma dx)(\Sigma dy)}{\sqrt{\Sigma dx^2 \cdot n - (\Sigma dx)^2} \times \sqrt{\Sigma dy^2 \cdot n - (\Sigma dy)^2}}$$

23. When is rank correlation more precise than simple correlation coefficient? NCERT

Ans. Rank correlation is more precise than simple correlation coefficient in the following situations

(i) **When the Measurements of the Variables are Suspect**
If exact measurement of a quantifiable variable cannot be taken, then rank correlation should be preferred.
e.g. In a remote village, where measuring rods or weighing scales are not available, height and weight of people cannot be measured precisely but the people can be easily ranked in terms of height and weight.

(ii) **When Data is Qualitative**
It is difficult to quantify qualities such as fairness, honesty, etc. Ranking may be a better alternative for quantification of qualities.

(iii) **When Data has Extreme Values**
Sometimes the correlation coefficient between two variables with extreme values may be quite different from the coefficient without the extreme values.
Under these circumstances, rank correlation provides a better alternative to simple correlation.

24. Company XYZ is analysing the relationship between employee training hours and their productivity scores.

(i) Based on a scatter diagram plotted with training hours on the x-axis and productivity scores on the y-axis, the points show a clear upward trend.
What type of correlation is depicted by this scatter diagram and what does it suggest about the relationship between employee training hours and productivity?

(ii) If Company XYZ calculates a Pearson correlation coefficient of +0.85 between training hours and productivity scores, what does this coefficient indicate about the strength and direction of the relationship between these two variables?

Competency Based Que

Ans. (i) The scatter diagram with training hours on the x-axis and productivity scores on the y-axis shows a clear upward trend. This pattern indicates a positive correlation between employee training hours and productivity scores. Positive correlation means that as one variable increases, the other variable also tends to increase.
In this case, when training hours increase, productivity scores rise as well. This implies that investing more time in employee training is likely to enhance their productivity.

The upward trend suggests that the relationship might be linear, where the changes in training hours lead to proportional changes in productivity.

However, the actual strength and consistency of this relationship would need to be quantified.

(ii) A Pearson correlation coefficient of +0.85 suggests a strong positive linear relationship between training hours and productivity scores. The coefficient, ranging between −1 and +1, quantifies the strength and direction of the linear relationship. A value close to +1, such as +0.85, means a very strong positive relationship, implying that higher training hours are consistently associated with higher productivity scores.

With a coefficient of +0.85, the relationship is not only strong but also relatively reliable, i.e. the variation in productivity scores can be largely explained by the variation in training hours.

This result suggests that training hours account for a significant portion of the changes in productivity and implementing or expanding training programmes could lead to measurable productivity improvements.

Numerical Questions

Numerical 1

Draw a scatter diagram and indicate the nature of correlation.

X	10	20	30	40	50	60	70	80
Y	5	10	15	20	25	30	35	40

Sol. Now, we plot the points on a graph paper which is shown below

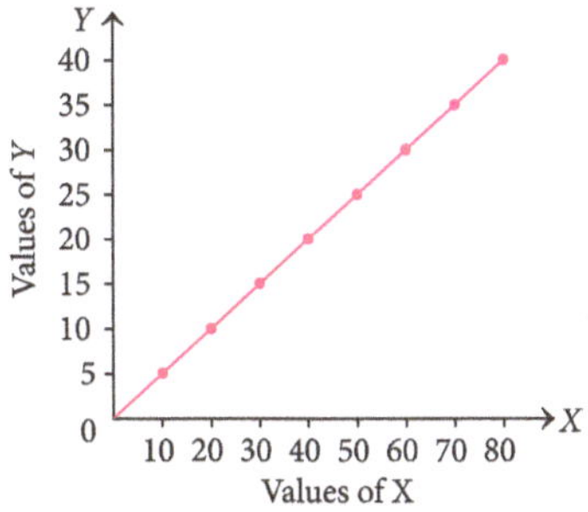

The diagram indicates that there is perfect positive correlation between the values of the two variables *X* and *Y*.

Numerical 2

Draw a scatter diagram and interpret whether the correlation is positive or negative.

X	4	5	6	7	8	9	10	11	12	13	14	15
Y	78	72	66	60	54	48	42	36	30	24	18	12

Sol. The pair of points are

(4, 78), (5, 72), (6, 66), (7, 60), (8, 54), (9, 48), (10, 42), (11, 36), (12, 30), (13, 24), (14, 18) and (15, 12).

Now, we plot the points on a graph paper, which is shown below

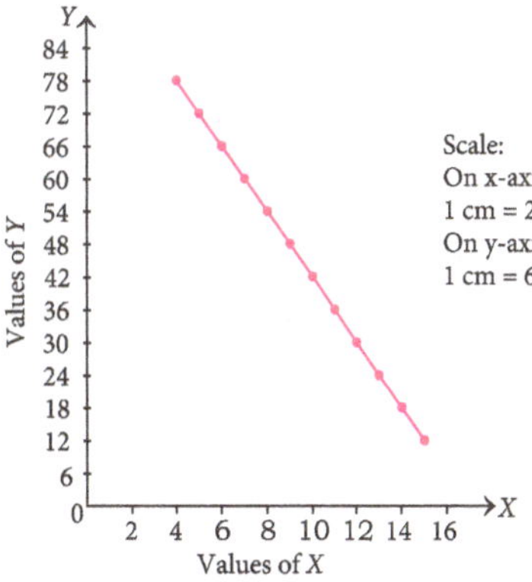

The diagram indicates that there is perfect negative correlation between the values of the two variables *X* and *Y*.

Numerical 3

Draw a scatter diagram of the following data and interpret to find the nature of correlation.

X	2	3	5	6	8	9
Y	6	5	7	8	12	11

Sol. The pair of points are (2, 6), (3, 5), (5, 7), (6, 8), (8, 12) and (9, 11). Now, we plot the points on a graph paper, which is shown below

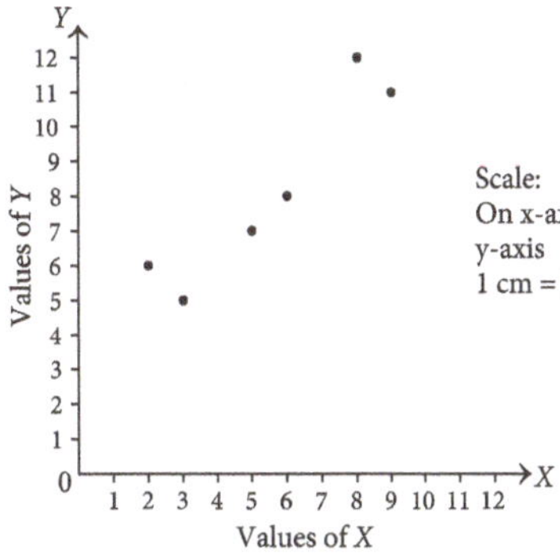

The diagram indicates that there is high degree of positive correlation because the plotted points are near to each other and the trend of the points is upward.

Numerical 4

Calculate the coefficient of correlation from the following data

$$\Sigma xy = 4{,}880, \quad \sigma_x = 28.70, \quad \sigma_y = 18.02, \quad n = 10$$

Sol. Given that

$$\Sigma xy = 4{,}880, \quad \sigma_x = 28.70, \quad \sigma_y = 18.02, \quad n = 10$$

$$r = \frac{\Sigma xy}{n \cdot \sigma_x \cdot \sigma_y} = \frac{4{,}880}{10 \times 28.70 \times 18.02} = \frac{4{,}880}{5171.74} = 0.94$$

Numerical 5

Compute Karl Pearson's coefficient of correlation by direct method and interpret the result.

Marks in Mathematics	15	18	21	24	27
Marks in Accountancy	25	25	27	31	32

Sol. Let X and Y denote marks in Mathematics and Accountancy respectively.

Calculation of Coefficient of Correlation

X	$x(X-\bar{X})$, $\bar{X}=21$	x^2	Y	$y(Y-\bar{Y})$ $\bar{Y}=28$	y^2	xy
15	−6	36	25	−3	9	18
18	−3	9	25	−3	9	9
21	0	0	27	−1	1	0
24	3	9	31	3	9	9
27	6	36	32	4	16	24
$\Sigma X = 105$		$\Sigma x^2 = 90$	$\Sigma Y = 140$		$\Sigma y^2 = 44$	$\Sigma xy = 60$

Here, $\Sigma X = 105$, $\Sigma Y = 140$, $\Sigma xy = 60$, $\Sigma x^2 = 90$, $\Sigma y^2 = 44$

$$\bar{X} = \frac{\Sigma X}{n} = \frac{105}{5} = 21; \quad \bar{Y} = \frac{\Sigma Y}{n} = \frac{140}{5} = 28$$

$$r = \frac{\Sigma xy}{\sqrt{\Sigma x^2 \times \Sigma y^2}} = \frac{60}{\sqrt{90 \times 44}} = \frac{60}{\sqrt{3{,}960}}$$

$$= \frac{60}{62.928} = 0.95$$

It indicates that there is high degree of positive correlation between marks in Mathematics and Accountancy.

Numerical 6

Calculate the correlation coefficient between X and Y and comment on their relationship. **NCERT**

X	1	3	4	5	7	8
Y	2	6	8	10	14	16

Sol. **Calculation of Correlation Coefficient**

X	Y	XY	X^2	Y^2
1	2	2	1	4
3	6	18	9	36
4	8	32	16	64
5	10	50	25	100
7	14	98	49	196
8	16	128	64	256
$\Sigma X = 28$	$\Sigma Y = 56$	$\Sigma XY = 328$	$\Sigma X^2 = 164$	$\Sigma Y^2 = 656$

Here, $n = 6$, $\Sigma XY = 328$, $\Sigma X^2 = 164$, $\Sigma Y^2 = 656$

$$\therefore \quad r = \frac{\Sigma XY}{\sqrt{\Sigma X^2 \times \Sigma Y^2}} = \frac{328}{\sqrt{164 \times 656}} = \frac{328}{328} = 1$$

As the correlation coefficient between the two variables is + 1, so the two variables are perfectly positively correlated.

Numerical 7

Calculate coefficient of correlation between age group and rate of mortality from the following data

Age Group	0-20	20-40	40-60	60-80	80-100
Rate of Mortality	350	280	540	760	900

Hint Since, class interval are given for age, so mid-value should be used for the calculation of r.

Sol. **Calculation of Coefficient of Correlation**

Age Group	Mid-value (X)	$dx(X-A)$ $A=50$	$dx'\left(\frac{dx}{c_1}\right)$ $c_1=20$	dx'^2	Rate of Mortality (Y)	$dy(Y-A)$ $A=540$	$dy'\left(\frac{dx}{c_2}\right)$ $c_2=10$	dy'^2	$dx'dy'$
0-20	10	−40	−2	4	350	−190	−19	361	38
20-40	30	−20	−1	1	280	−260	−26	676	26
40-60	50	0	0	0	540	0	0	0	0
60-80	70	20	1	1	760	220	+22	484	22
80-100	90	40	2	4	900	360	+36	1296	72
			$\Sigma dx'=0$	$\Sigma dx'^2=10$			$\Sigma dy'=13$	$\Sigma dy'^2=2817$	$\Sigma dx'\,dy'=158$

Here, $n=5$, $\Sigma dx'=0$, $\Sigma dx'^2=10$, $\Sigma dy'=13$, $\Sigma dy'^2=2817$, $\Sigma dx'dy'=158$

Now,

$$r=\frac{\Sigma dx'dy'-\frac{\Sigma dx'\times\Sigma dy'}{n}}{\sqrt{\Sigma dx'^2-\frac{(\Sigma dx')^2}{n}}\times\sqrt{\Sigma dy'^2-\frac{(\Sigma dy')^2}{n}}}=\frac{158-\frac{0\times 13}{5}}{\sqrt{10-\frac{(0)^2}{5}}\times\sqrt{2817-\frac{(13)^2}{5}}}$$

$$=\frac{158}{\sqrt{10-0}\times\sqrt{2817-\frac{169}{5}}}=\frac{158}{\sqrt{10}\times\sqrt{2817-33.8}}=\frac{158}{\sqrt{10}\times\sqrt{2783.2}}=\frac{158}{3.16\times 52.8}=\frac{158}{166.8}=+0.95$$

There is high degree of positive correlation between age group and rate of mortality.

Numerical 8

From the data given below, calculate Karl Pearson's coefficient of correlation between density of population and death rate by step deviation method.

Region	Area (in sq km)	Population	Death
A	200	40,000	480
B	150	75,000	1,200
C	120	72,000	1,080
D	80	20,000	280

Hint First of all, we shall compute density of population, i.e. population per sq km and death rate per 1,000.

$$\text{Density of Population}=\frac{\text{Population}}{\text{Area}};\quad \text{Death Rate}=\frac{\text{Number of Deaths}}{\text{Population}}\times 1{,}000$$

Sol. **Calculation of Coefficient of Correlation**

Region	Density (X)	$dx(X-A)$ $A=500$	$dx'\left(\frac{dx}{c_1}\right)$ $c_1=50$	dx'^2	Death Rate (Y)	$dy(Y-A)$ $A=16$	$dy'\left(\frac{dy}{c_2}\right)$ $c_2=1$	dy'^2	$dx'dy'$
A	200	−300	−6	36	12	−4	−4	16	24
B	500	0	0	0	16	0	0	0	0
C	600	100	2	4	15	−1	−1	1	−2
D	250	−250	−5	25	14	−2	−2	4	10
			$\Sigma dx'=-9$	$\Sigma dx'^2=65$			$\Sigma dy'=-7$	$\Sigma dy'^2=21$	$\Sigma dx'dy'=32$

Here, $dx'=-9$, $\Sigma dx'^2=65$, $\Sigma dy'=-7$, $\Sigma dy'^2=21$, $\Sigma dx'dy'=32$

$$\therefore \quad r = \frac{\Sigma dx'dy' - \frac{\Sigma dx' \times \Sigma dy'}{n}}{\sqrt{\Sigma dx'^2 - \frac{(\Sigma dx')^2}{n}} \times \sqrt{\Sigma dy'^2 - \frac{(\Sigma dy')^2}{n}}}$$

$$= \frac{32 - \frac{(-9 \times -7)}{4}}{\sqrt{65 - \frac{(-9)^2}{4}} \times \sqrt{21 - \frac{(-7)^2}{4}}}$$

$$= \frac{32 - 15.75}{\sqrt{65 - 20.25} \times \sqrt{21 - 12.25}}$$

$$= \frac{16.25}{\sqrt{44.75} \times \sqrt{8.75}} = \frac{16.25}{6.69 \times 2.96} = \frac{16.25}{19.80} = 0.82$$

There is high degree of positive correlation between density of population and death rate.

Numerical 9

Compute coefficient of correlation from the following data

	X Series	Y Series
Mean	15	28
Sum of Squares of Deviation from Mean	144	225

Sum of products of deviation of X and Y series from their respective mean is 20. Number of pairs of observations is 10.

Sol. Given, $\Sigma x^2 = 144, \quad \Sigma y^2 = 225, \quad \Sigma xy = 20, \; n = 10$

$$r = \frac{\Sigma xy}{\sqrt{\Sigma x^2 \times \Sigma y^2}} = \frac{20}{\sqrt{144 \times 225}} = \frac{20}{\sqrt{32400}} = \frac{20}{180} = +0.11$$

Numerical 10

Find the rank correlation from the following data

X	18	12	32	45	90	17	26	31
Y	10	12	15	8	7	21	32	45

Sol. **Calculation of Rank Correlation**

X	R_1	Y	R_2	$D\,(R_1 - R_2)$	D^2
18	3	10	3	0	0
12	1	12	4	−3	9
32	6	15	5	1	1
45	7	8	2	5	25
90	8	7	1	7	49
17	2	21	6	−4	16
26	4	32	7	−3	9
31	5	45	8	−3	9
					$\Sigma D^2 = 118$

$$\text{Coefficient of Rank Correlation } (r_k) = 1 - \frac{6\Sigma D^2}{n^3 - n}$$

$$= 1 - \frac{6 \times 118}{(8)^3 - 8} = 1 - \frac{708}{504}$$

$$= 1 - 1.404 = -0.404 \text{ (Negative correlation)}$$

Numerical 11

The coefficient of rank correlation of marks obtained by 15 students in two subjects is 0.6. It was later discovered that difference in ranks obtained by one student was taken as 4 instead of 7. Find the correlation.

Sol. Given in question,

Coefficient of rank correlation $(r_k) = 0.6, \quad n = 15$

Now, $\quad r_k = 1 - \frac{6\Sigma D^2}{n^3 - n} = 0.6 = 1 - \frac{6\Sigma D^2}{(15)^3 - 15}$

$$0.4 = \frac{6\Sigma D^2}{3{,}360} \Rightarrow \Sigma D^2 = \frac{1{,}344}{6} = 224$$

Correct $\Sigma D^2 = 224 - (4)^2 + (7)^2 = 224 - 16 + 49 = 257$

Corrected $r_k = 1 - \frac{6\Sigma D^2}{n^3 - n} = 1 - \frac{6 \times 257}{3{,}360}$

$= 1 - 0.46 = 0.54$ (Positive correlation)

Numerical 12

Consider the following data with ranks assigned to two variables.

Item	Rank in Series 1 (R_1)	Rank in Series 2 (R_2)
A	1	3
B	2	1
C	3	4
D	4	2
E	5	5

Calculate the Spearman rank correlation coefficient (ρ) between series 1 and series 2.

Sol. **Represent the Ranks**

The ranks are already given as follows

Series 1 (R_1) 1, 2, 3, 4, 5; **Series 2** (R_2) 3, 1, 4, 2, 5

Calculate Differences (D)

Compute the difference between corresponding ranks

$D_1 = R_1 - R_2 = 1 - 3 = -2$; $\quad D_2 = R_1 - R_2 = 2 - 1 = 1$

$D_3 = R_1 - R_2 = 3 - 4 = -1$; $\quad D_4 = R_1 - R_2 = 4 - 2 = 2$

$D_5 = R_1 - R_2 = 5 - 5 = 0$

Square the Differences (D^2)

Find the square of each difference

$D_1^2 = (-2)^2 = 4$; $D_2^2 = (1)^2 = 1$

$D_3^2 = (-1)^2 = 1$; $D_4^2 = (2)^2 = 4$

$D_5^2 = (0)^2 = 0$

Sum these squared differences

$\Sigma D^2 = 4 + 1 + 1 + 4 + 0 = 10$

Apply the Formula

The formula for Spearman's rank correlation coefficient (ρ) is

$$\rho = 1 - \frac{6\Sigma D^2}{n(n^2 - 1)}$$

Here, n is the number of items. For this problem, $n = 5$

Plugging in the values

$$\rho = 1 - \frac{6 \times 10}{5(5^2 - 1)} = 1 - \frac{60}{5 \times 24}$$

$$= 1 - \frac{60}{120} = 1 - 0.5$$

The Spearman rank correlation coefficient (ρ) between Series 1 and Series 2 is 0.5, indicating a moderate positive correlation between the two series.

Numerical 13

The ranking of ten students in two subjects *A* and *B* are as below

A	3	5	8	4	7	10	2	1	6	9
B	6	4	9	8	1	2	3	10	5	7

What is the coefficient of rank correlation?

Sol. **Calculation of Rank Correlation**

R_1	R_2	$D(R_1 - R_2)$	D^2
3	6	-3	9
5	4	1	1
8	9	-1	1
4	8	-4	16
7	1	6	36
10	2	8	64
2	3	-1	1
1	10	-9	81
6	5	1	1
9	7	2	4
			$\Sigma D^2 = 214$

Here, $n = 10$ and $\Sigma D^2 = 214$

$$\therefore \quad r_k = 1 - \frac{6\Sigma D^2}{n^3 - n} = 1 - \frac{6 \times 214}{10^3 - 10} = 1 - \frac{1284}{990} = -0.297$$

There is low degree of negative correlation between A and B subjects.

Numerical 14

In a poem recitation competition, ten participants were recorded following marks by two different judges *X* and *Y*.

X	15	17	14	13	11	12	16	18	10	9
Y	15	12	4	6	7	9	3	10	2	5

Calculate the coefficient of rank correlation.

Sol. **Calculation of Rank Correlation**

X	R_1	Y	R_2	$D(R_1 - R_2)$	D^2
15	4	15	1	3	9
17	2	12	2	0	0
14	5	4	8	-3	9
13	6	6	6	0	0
11	8	7	5	3	9
12	7	9	4	3	9
16	3	3	9	-6	36
18	1	10	3	-2	4
10	9	2	10	-1	1
9	10	5	7	3	9
					$\Sigma D^2 = 86$

Here, $n = 10$, $\Sigma D^2 = 86$

$$r_k = 1 - \frac{6\Sigma D^2}{n^3 - n} = 1 - \frac{6 \times 86}{(10)^3 - 10}$$

$$= 1 - \frac{516}{990} = 1 - 0.52 = 0.48$$

It indicates that there is moderate degree of positive correlation between *X* and *Y* series.

Numerical 15

Calculate the correlation coefficient between the height of fathers in inches (*X*) and their sons (*Y*) **NCERT**

X	65	66	57	67	68	69	70	72
Y	67	56	65	68	72	72	69	71

Sol. **Calculation of Coefficient of Correlation**

X	$x(X-\bar{X})$ $\bar{X}=66.75$	x^2	Y	$y(Y-\bar{Y})$ $\bar{Y}=67.5$	y^2	xy
65	−1.75	3.0625	67	−0.5	0.25	0.875
66	−0.75	0.5625	56	−11.5	132.25	8.625
57	−9.75	95.0625	65	−2.5	6.25	24.375
67	0.25	0.0625	68	0.5	0.25	0.125
68	1.25	1.5625	72	4.5	20.25	5.625
69	2.25	5.0625	72	4.5	20.25	10.125
70	3.25	10.5625	69	1.5	2.25	4.875
72	5.25	27.5625	71	3.5	12.25	18.375
$\Sigma X=534$		$\Sigma x^2=143.5$	$\Sigma Y=540$		$\Sigma y^2=194$	$\Sigma xy=73$

Here, $n=8$, $\Sigma X=534$, $\Sigma x^2=143.5$, $\Sigma Y=540$, $\Sigma y^2=194$, $\Sigma xy=73$

Now, $\bar{X}=\frac{\Sigma X}{n}=\frac{534}{8}=66.75$; $\bar{Y}=\frac{\Sigma Y}{n}=\frac{540}{8}=67.5$

$$r=\frac{\Sigma xy}{\sqrt{\Sigma x^2\times\Sigma y^2}}=\frac{73}{\sqrt{143.5\times194}}=\frac{73}{\sqrt{27839}}=\frac{73}{166.85}=0.438$$

It indicates that there is low degree of positive correlation between height of fathers and sons.

Numerical 16

Find out rank difference correlation of X and Y.

X	80	78	75	75	58	67	60	59
Y	12	13	14	14	14	16	15	17

Sol. **Calculation of Rank Correlation**

X	R_1	Y	R_2	$D(R_1-R_2)$	D^2
80	1	12	8	-7	49
78	2	13	7	-5	25
75	3.5	14	5	-1.5	2.25
75	3.5	14	5	-1.5	2.25
58	8	14	5	3	9
67	5	16	2	3	9
60	6	15	3	3	9
59	7	17	1	6	36
					$\Sigma D^2=141.50$

Here, $n=8, \Sigma D^2=141.50, m_1=2$ and $m_2=3$

$$\therefore\quad r_k=1-\frac{6\left[\Sigma D^2+\frac{1}{12}(m_1^3-m_1)+\frac{1}{12}(m_2^3-m_2)\right]}{n^3-n}=1-\frac{6\left[141.50+\frac{1}{12}(2^3-2)+\frac{1}{12}(3^3-3)\right]}{8^3-8}$$

$$=1-\frac{6\left[141.50+\frac{6}{12}+\frac{24}{12}\right]}{512-8}=1-\frac{6\,(141.50+0.50+2)}{504}=1-\frac{6\times144}{504}=1-\frac{864}{504}=1-1.714=-0.714$$

It indicates that there is moderate degree of negative correlation.

SELF ASSESSMENT TEST

Objective Type Questions

1. What is the term used to describe a situation where two variables influence each other in a continuous loop (e.g. A causes B and B causes A)?
   (a) Linear causation
   (b) Uni-directional influence
   (c) Random correlation
   (d) Cyclic causation

2. No correlation is indicated by ....
   (a) +1
   (b) –1
   (c) 0
   (d) 0.9

3. When is correlation said to be linear?
   (a) When the scatter points lie on or near a straight line
   (b) When the scatter points are evenly distributed across the graph
   (c) When the scatter points form a circular pattern
   (d) When the scatter points form a zig-zag pattern

4. Pearson's correlation coefficient is calculated as the .... of the covariance between x and y to the product of their standard deviations.
   (a) sum (b) product
   (c) ratio
   (d) difference

5. Which of the following is a merit of Spearman's rank correlation?
   (a) It is difficult to use in the case of large frequency distributions
   (b) It can be used even when the actual data is not given and only ranks are available
   (c) It lacks precision compared to Karl Pearson's method
   (d) It cannot be used for bivariate frequency distribution

Answers 1. (d) 2. (c) 3.(a) 4. (c) 5. (b)

Short Answer Type Questions

6. What is the importance of correlation? List any three.

7. "If the scatter points are widely dispersed around the line, the correlation is low." Do you agree? Give reasons.

8. Define the following
   (i) Correlation (ii) Causation

9. Explain the various degrees of correlation that can be depicted by a scatter diagram.

Numerical Questions

10. Using assumed mean in Karl Pearson's formula, calculate correlation coefficient using following data

X	78	89	97	69	59	79	68	61
Y	125	137	156	112	107	106	123	108

Ans. $r = +0.85$

11. Calculate coefficient of correlation with the help of following data by using step deviation method

Price Index	120	150	190	220	230
Money Supply (₹ in crore)	1,800	2,000	2,500	2,700	3,000

Ans. $r = 0.99$

12. Given below is the percentage of marks secured by 5 students in Economics and Statistics.

Students	A	B	C	D	E
Marks in Economics	60	48	49	50	55
Marks in Statistics	85	60	55	65	75

Calculate the coefficient of rank correlation.

Ans. $r = 0.90$

13. Compute Karl Pearson's coefficient of correlation from the following data

X	Y
10	7
12	9
11	12
13	9
12	13
14	8
9	10
12	12
14	7
13	13

Ans. $r = -0.115$

14. Ten students got the following percentage of marks in Accountancy and English

Accountancy	1	2	3	4	5	6	7	8	9
English	3	2	1	5	6	4	7	8	6

Calculate the coefficient of rank correlation.

Ans. $r = +0.85$

15. From the following data, compute the coefficient of correlation between X and Y

Particulars	X	Y
Number of Items	15	15
Arithmetic Mean	25	18
Sum of Square of Deviation from Mean	136	138

Summation or product of deviations of X and Y series from their respective arithmetic mean is 122.

Ans. $r = +0.89$

16. Calculate the coefficient of correlation between the age of husband and wife.

Age of Husband (in years)	21	22	28	32	35	36
Age of Wife (in years)	18	20	25	30	31	32

Ans. $r = +0.993$

17. In a fancy dress competition, two judges accorded following ranks to the 10 participants

Judge A	1	2	3	4	5	6	7	8	9	10
Judge B	10	6	5	4	7	9	8	2	1	3

Calculate the coefficient of rank correlation.

Ans. $r = -0.6$

18. Calculate correlation of the following data using Karl Pearson's method.

Series A	112	114	108	124	145	150	119	125	147	150
Series B	200	190	214	187	170	170	210	190	180	181

Ans. $r = -0.85$

08

CHAPTER

An index number is a statistical measure designed to show changes in a variable or group of related variables with respect to time, geographic location or other characteristics. —*Spiegel*

YOUR STUDY GOALS

YOUR PRACTICE GOAL

- Objective Type Questions (60 Qs ; MCQs, A-R, Statements, Matching, Concept Identification)
- Subjective Questions (20 SAs, 8 LAs)
- 19 Numerical Questions
- Self Assessment Test (5 MCQs, 4 SAs, 1 LA, 10 Numerical)

Index Numbers

8.1 Concept of Index Numbers

An index number is a statistical tool used to measure changes in the magnitude of a group of related variables, such as price and quantity of goods and services over two different time periods.

It is a unit-free measure, expressed as a ratio between a current period and a base period. This ratio is often presented as a percentage. Index numbers are applied to measure various economic variables, such as

- Prices of commodities (e.g. Wheat, gold, consumer goods, cereals, etc).
- Trade volumes, production level in industries and agriculture, exports or imports, firm's sale or profit and so on.
- National income, stock prices, wage structure, bank deposits, cost of living, etc.

Mathematically,

$$\text{Index Number for Period } N = \left[\frac{\text{Value of Variable under consideration in Period } N}{\text{Value of Variable under consideration in Base Period}}\right] \times 100$$

Features of Index Numbers

1. **Special Averages** Unlike arithmetic mean, median or mode, index numbers can compare two different series having different units of measurement.
2. **Expressed in Percentage** Index numbers express changes as percentages which are independent of measurement units, making comparison between different variables or periods easier.

3. **Measures Changes Over Time or Place** They help compare changes over period of time, locations or other contexts.
4. **Helps to Measure Changes that are not Directly Measurable** Index numbers helps to study the changes in the effects of such factors which are not capable of direct measurement.

Issues in Construction of Index Numbers

Issue	Description	Examples
Selection of Averages	Among different types of averages, arithmetic mean and geometric mean is used most often. Making choice between these two averages is used also a difficult task as they are calculated by different methods.	If the prices of goods A, B and C are ₹ 10, ₹ 15 and ₹ 20, the arithmetic mean price is ₹ 15. The geometric mean, however, would give a slightly different average, better reflecting proportional changes.
Determination and Definition of Purpose	Clearly defining the purpose and scope of desired index number helps in choosing the right method to construct an index number.	If the goal is to track inflation, an index like the Consumer Price Index (CPI) would be suitable as it measures changes in the prices of consumer goods.
Selection of Sources of Data	Choosing reliable and accurate data from either primary or secondary sources is essential. It should be selected depending on the extent of coverage, accuracy, nature, objective, etc.	To calculate a price index for agricultural products, data can be sourced directly from farmers (primary) or government reports (secondary).
Selection of Base Year	The base year is the reference point for comparison in index numbers. It should be a normal year free from major economic disruptions like elections, war or natural calamities. The base year value is always taken as 100.	If 2015 is chosen as the base year, prices in that year are set at 100 and subsequent years' prices are compared against it.
Selection of Items/ Commodities	The items included in the index number should be relevant and standardised, i.e. easy to be described, recognised and understood. Number of commodities should be neither too large or too small.	For a food price index, common items like rice, milk and bread would be included, representing the typical diet of the population.
Selection of the Price	Different types of prices of commodities (e.g. Wholesale price, retail price) can lead to variations in the index. Also, the sources of price collection makes it difficult to rely upon.	A retail price index might show higher values than a wholesale price index because retail prices include a markup.
Selection of Weighing Methods	Weights are assigned to items based on their importance or quantity in the index. It depends upon the purpose of index number.	In a consumer price index, housing might be given more weight than entertainment because people spend more on housing.
Selection of the Formula	The formula used to calculate the index affects the final value and interpretation. It should be decided based on the purpose of study and the data available.	Laspeyre's formula might be used if you want to give more importance to base year quantities, while Paasche's formula focuses on current year quantities.

Base Period

A base period is the reference date from which an index number is calculated. Different index numbers have different base years.

e.g. 2011-2012 is the base year for the consumer price index. Base period can be updated to remain relevant to the changing times. If we assume the base period to be 2011-12 and index number in 2021-22 is 250, then it suggests that

- Price has increased by 150% on an average between 2011-12 and 2021-22 or
- Same basket of goods in 2021-22 costs 2.5 times as much as in 2011-12.

Advantages/Uses of Index Numbers

Following are the advantages or uses of index numbers

Advantages of Index Numbers
- Barometer of Economic Progress
- Importance for the Government
- Throws Light on Economic Condition
- Wage Fixation and Policy-making
- Importance for Producer
- Tool for Addressing Income Inequality

1. **Barometer of Economic Progress** Index numbers act as a barometer, measuring the value of money and assessing economic progress over time. By comparing the value of money across different years, one can easily determine whether a country is progressing (when the value rises) or regressing (when the value falls).
2. **Importance for the Government** Changes in the value of money directly affect the public, prompting the government to adjust its fiscal and monetary policies based on the results provided by index numbers.
3. **Throws Light on Economic Condition** Index numbers are very useful for comparing the economic conditions of specific group of people across different time periods, offering valuable insights into their well-being.
4. **Wage Fixation and Policy-making** The cost of living index guides the government and executives in setting and revising wages. Index numbers help to ensure that wages align with changes in living costs.
5. **Importance for Producer** The price index number helps producers to decide on production levels. A rising price level suggests higher profit margins, encouraging increased production.
6. **Tool for Addressing Income Inequality** The wholesale price index can highlight regional disparities, aiding in the implementation of measures to distribute wealth more evenly and reduce income inequality.

Types of Index Numbers

Index numbers can be broadly classified into the following categories

Types of Index Numbers
- **Price Index Numbers**: These index numbers measure the general changes in prices between the current year and the base year.
  - **Wholesale Price Index** (WPI) Measures changes in wholesale prices of goods.
  - **Retail/Consumer Price Index** (CPI) Measures changes in retail prices that consumers pay for goods and services.
- **Quantity Index Numbers**: These index numbers measure changes in the quantity of goods produced during the periods under review.
- **Value Index Numbers**: These index numbers compare the total value of the period under study with that of the base period, focusing on changes in the total value of production, profits, sales, etc.

8.2 Methods of Constructing Price Index Numbers

Following are the main methods of constructing an price index number

Methods of Constructing Price Index Number
- Simple Index Number
  - Simple Aggregative Method
  - Simple Average of Price Relative Method
- Weighted Index Number
  - Weighted Average of Price Relative Method
  - Weighted Aggregative Method

I. Simple Index Numbers

Simple index numbers assign equal weightage to all items under consideration, treating all goods and services with equal importance. There are two primary methods for constructing simple index numbers

Simple Aggregative Method	Simple Average of Price Relatives Method
This method calculates the index by calculating the sum total of prices of goods and services in the current year as a percentage of the sum total of prices in the base year. ***Step* 1** Find the sum of prices of all goods and services under consideration for the current year (denoted as Σp_1). ***Step* 2** Find the sum of prices of all goods and services under consideration for the base year (denoted as Σp_0). ***Step* 3** Apply the given formula $P_{01} = \frac{\Sigma p_1}{\Sigma p_0} \times 100$ where symbols have their usual meaning and P_{01} = Price index of current year	This method calculates the index by taking the average of price relatives, which is the percentage ratio between the price of a commodity in the current year and its price in the base year. ***Step* 1** Compute the price relative for each item using the following formula Price Relative $(I) = \frac{p_1}{p_0} \times 100$ ***Step* 2** Sum up all the price relatives (denoted as ΣI). ***Step* 3** Find the index number as the average of the price relatives using following formula $P_{01} = \frac{\Sigma I}{n}$ where, ΣI = Sum of price relatives and n = Number of items

Solved Question 1 With the help of the following data, calculate index number for 2020 taking 2015 as base year.

Commodity	Price in 2015 (in ₹)	Price in 2020 (in ₹)
A	100	145
B	90	130
C	145	200
D	180	275
E	85	150

Sol. **Calculation of Index Number by Simple Aggregative Method**

Commodity	Price in 2015 (p_0)	Price in 2020 (p_1)
A	100	145
B	90	130
C	145	200
D	180	275
E	85	150
	$\Sigma p_0 = 600$	$\Sigma p_1 = 900$

$$P_{01} = \frac{\Sigma p_1}{\Sigma p_0} \times 100 = \frac{900}{600} \times 100 = 150$$

It means that there is a net increase of 50% in the price of commodities in 2020 as compared to the price of 2015.

Solved Question 2 Construct index number by simple average of price relative method for 2020 taking the price of 2015 as base from the data given below

Commodity	Price (in ₹)	
	2015	2020
A	30	45
B	40	50
C	60	72
D	80	88
E	10	13

Sol. **Construction of Index Number Using Simple Average of Price Relative Method**

Commodity	Price (in ₹)		Price Relative
	2015 (p_0)	2020 (p_1)	$= \left(\frac{p_1}{p_0} \times 100\right)$
A	30	45	$\frac{45}{30} \times 100 = 150$
B	40	50	$\frac{50}{40} \times 100 = 125$
C	60	72	$\frac{72}{60} \times 100 = 120$
D	80	88	$\frac{88}{80} \times 100 = 110$
E	10	13	$\frac{13}{10} \times 100 = 130$
$n = 5$			$\Sigma I = 635$

$$P_{01} = \frac{\Sigma I}{n} = \frac{635}{5} = 127$$

It means that prices in year 2020 has increased by 27% as compared to the year 2015.

II. Weighted Index Numbers

Weighted index numbers assign different weights to different items in the series, depending upon their relative importance. There are two methods of constructing weighted index number

1. Weighted Average of Price Relative Method

This method calculates the index as a weighted arithmetic mean of price relatives. The steps to be followed while computing this index number are given below

Step 1 Compute price relatives for each item using the following formula

$$\text{Price Relative}(I) = \frac{p_1}{p_0} \times 100$$

Step 2 Multiply each price relative by its respective weight to find *IW*.

Step 3 Sum the weighted price relatives (ΣIW).

Step 4 Sum the weights (ΣW).

Step 5 Calculate the index using the formula

$$P_{01} = \frac{\Sigma IW}{\Sigma W}$$

where symbols have the same meaning as defined above.

Solved Question 3 **From the following data, construct a weighted index number for 2020 with 2010 as base year.**

Commodity	Weight	Price (in ₹)	
		2010	2020
Wheat	15	10	15
Rice	10	8	16
Pulses	5	5	10
Milk	4	2	4
Oil	6	4	6
Sugar	7	3	6
Salt	3	1	2

Sol. **Construction of Weighted Index Number**

Commodity	Weight (W)	Price (in ₹)		Price Relative $(I) = (p_1/p_0 \times 100)$	IW
		2010 (p_0)	2020 (p_1)		
Wheat	15	10	15	150	2,250
Rice	10	8	16	200	2,000
Pulses	5	5	10	200	1,000
Milk	4	2	4	200	800
Oil	6	4	6	150	900
Sugar	7	3	6	200	1,400
Salt	3	1	2	200	600
	$\Sigma W = 50$				$\Sigma IW = 8{,}950$

$$\text{Weighted Index Number} = \frac{\Sigma IW}{\Sigma W} = \frac{8{,}950}{50} = 179$$

It means that prices in the current year has increased by 79% as compared to base year.

2. Weighted Aggregative Method

This method involves assigning weights to various items and computing the weighted aggregate of prices. There are many methods to construct weighted aggregative index number.

Three of them are as follows

Laspeyre's Method	Paasche's Method	Fisher's Index Method
It uses the base year's quantity (q_0) as the weight. ***Step 1*** Multiply current year price of commodities with base year quantity and sum the products ($\Sigma p_1 q_0$). ***Step 2*** Multiply base year price of commodities with base year quantity and sum the products ($\Sigma p_0 q_0$). ***Step 3*** Calculate Laspeyre's index using the following formula $P_{01} = \frac{\Sigma p_1 q_0}{\Sigma p_0 q_0} \times 100$	In this method, quantity consumed in current year (q_1) is taken as weight. ***Step 1*** Multiply current year price of commodities with current year quantities and sum the products ($\Sigma p_1 q_1$). ***Step 2*** Multiply base year price of commodities with current year quantities and sum the products ($\Sigma p_0 q_1$). ***Step 3*** Calculate Paasche's index using the following formula $P_{01} = \frac{\Sigma p_1 q_1}{\Sigma p_0 q_1} \times 100$	Introduced by Professor Irving Fisher, this method combines the techniques of Laspeyre's method and Paasche's method. Fisher used both base year as well as current year quantities (q_0, q_1) as weight. ***Step 1*** Multiply base year quantities with both base and current year prices and then sum the products ($\Sigma p_0 q_0$ and $\Sigma p_1 q_0$). ***Step 2*** Multiply current year quantities with both base and current year prices and then sum the products ($\Sigma p_0 q_1$ and $\Sigma p_1 q_1$). ***Step 3*** Apply the Fisher's index following formula to compute the index $P_{01} = \sqrt{\frac{\Sigma p_1 q_0}{\Sigma p_0 q_0} \times \frac{\Sigma p_1 q_1}{\Sigma p_0 q_1}} \times 100$

Fisher's Ideal Index

Fisher's method is considered as ideal method of index number due to the following reasons
- This formula is geometric mean of Laspeyre's method and Paasche's method.
- It considers both base year and current year quantities as weight, so it avoids any kind of biasness.
- It also satisfies time reversal test and factor reversal test of statistics.

Solved Question 4 Construct index number of price from the data given below by applying
(i) Laspeyre's method (ii) Paasche's method (iii) Fisher's method

Commodity	Base Year		Current Year	
	Price (in ₹)	Quantity	Price (in ₹)	Quantity
A	2	40	3	20
B	1.5	30	2.5	40
C	1	50	1.5	30
D	2.5	20	2	80

Sol. **Construction of Price Index Number**

Commodity	Base Year		Current Year		p_1q_0	p_0q_0	p_1q_1	p_0q_1
	Price (p_0)	Quantity (q_0)	Price (p_1)	Quantity (q_1)				
A	2	40	3	20	120	80	60	40
B	1.5	30	2.5	40	75	45	100	60
C	1	50	1.5	30	75	50	45	30
D	2.5	20	2	80	40	50	160	200
					Σp_1q_0 =310	Σp_0q_0 = 225	Σp_1q_1 =365	Σp_0q_1 =330

(i) **Laspeyre's Method**

$$P_{01} = \frac{\Sigma p_1q_0}{\Sigma p_0q_0} \times 100 = \frac{310}{225} \times 100 = 137.8$$

(ii) **Paasche's Method**

$$P_{01} = \frac{\Sigma p_1q_1}{\Sigma p_0q_1} \times 100 = \frac{365}{330} \times 100 = 110.6$$

(iii) **Fisher's Method**

$$P_{01} = \sqrt{\frac{\Sigma p_1q_0}{\Sigma p_0q_0} \times \frac{\Sigma p_1q_1}{\Sigma p_0q_1}} \times 100 = \sqrt{\frac{310}{225} \times \frac{365}{330}} \times 100 = \sqrt{1.378 \times 1.106} \times 100 = 1.23 \times 100 = 123$$

8.3 Consumer Price Index (CPI)

CPI measures the average change in prices of goods and services paid by specific consumer classes in the current year compared to a base year. It serves as an indicator of inflation in a country.

CPI is also known as
- Cost of living index number
- Retail price index number
- Price of living index number

Different CPI for Different Consumers

Different consumer groups have different consumption patterns. So, there are different CPI based on consumption patterns of different consumers, which are as follows
- CPI for Industrial Workers (CPI-IW) [*Base year is considered as 2001*].
- CPI for Agricultural Labour (CPI-AL) and Rural Labour (CPI-RL) [*Base year is considered as 1986-87*].
- CPI for Rural, Urban and Combined Sectors [*Base year is considered as 2011-12*].

Construction of Consumer Price Index (CPI)

Following steps are involved in construction of CPI

***Step* 1** **Deciding the Scope and Coverage of Index Number** Determine the class of people (e.g. Industrial workers, rural labourers) for whom the index number is to be constructed. Also, clearly define the coverage, specifying whether the index is for a rural, urban, city or town population.

***Step* 2** **Family Budget Enquiry** Conduct a family budget enquiry by randomly selecting samples from the target group (i.e. class of people selected). This survey should be conducted during a normal year, ensuring economic stability to accurately reflect typical consumption patterns.

CPI can be broadly categorised into five major groups

• Food • Clothing • Fuel and lighting • House rent • Miscellaneous

***Step* 3** **Collecting Price Quotations** Collecting retail prices is challenging due to price variations in different locations. There is no one formula for collecting the prices, however following broad principles may be followed

- Retail prices should reflect actual prices charged from consumers.
- Discount allowed and interest rate for payment must be considered.
- Prices should be linked to a fixed list of items alongwith quality specifications.
- During price control periods, both controlled and illegal prices charged openly, should be considered.

Methods of Construction of Consumer Price Index (CPI)

There are two primary methods used for constructing the Consumer Price Index (CPI)

Aggregative Expenditure Method	Family Budget Method
This method is similar to Laspeyre's method for constructing a weighted index. The CPI is calculated using following formula $\text{CPI} = \frac{\Sigma p_1 q_0}{\Sigma p_0 q_0} \times 100$ Here, $\Sigma p_1 q_0$ = Aggregate expenditure in the current year (Sum of product of current year price with base year quantity) $\Sigma p_0 q_0$ = Aggregate expenditure in the base year (Sum of product of base year price with base year quantity)	This method involves studying the family budgets of a large sample of people, for whom the CPI is being constructed. Then, the aggregate expenditure of an average family on various commodities is estimated. These values constitute the weights. CPI is computed in the same manner as weighted average of price relative method. Following formula is applied to compute CPI $\text{CPI} = \frac{\Sigma IW}{\Sigma W}$ Here, ΣIW = Sum of products of price relative with weights ΣW = Sum of weights

Solved Question 5 **Find the consumer price index or cost of living index number for the current year from the following data by aggregative expenditure method.**

Commodity	Base Year		Current Year	
	Price	Quantity	Price	Quantity
A	2	12	4	5
B	5	12	6	10
C	4	20	5	15
D	3	10	3	10

Sol.

Construction of Consumer Price Index Number

Commodity	Base Year		Current Year		$p_1 q_0$	$p_0 q_0$
	Price (p_0)	Quantity (q_0)	Price (p_1)	Quantity (q_1)		
A	2	12	4	5	48	24
B	5	12	6	10	72	60
C	4	20	5	15	100	80
D	3	10	3	10	30	30
					$\Sigma p_1 q_0 = 250$	$\Sigma p_0 q_0 = 194$

$$\text{CPI} = \frac{\Sigma p_1 q_0}{\Sigma p_0 q_0} \times 100 = \frac{250}{194} \times 100 = 128.87$$

Solved Question 6 **Construct the consumer price index number for 2011 on the basis of the following data using family budget method.**

Items	Price in 2000 (₹)	Price in 2011 (₹)	Weight
Food	200	280	30
Rent	100	200	20
Clothing	150	120	20
Fuel and Lighting	50	100	10
Miscellaneous	100	200	20

Sol. **Construction of Consumer Price Index Number for 2011**

[Base year 2000 = 100 (Family Budget Method)]

Items	Weight (W)	Price in 2000 (p_0)	Price in 2011 (p_1)	$I = \frac{p_1}{p_0} \times 100$	IW
Food	30	200	280	140	4,200
Rent	20	100	200	200	4,000
Clothing	20	150	120	80	1,600
Fuel and Lighting	10	50	100	200	2,000
Miscellaneous	20	100	200	200	4,000
	$\Sigma W = 100$				$\Sigma IW = 15{,}800$

Consumer Price Index Number for 2011

$$= \frac{\Sigma IW}{\Sigma W} = \frac{15{,}800}{100} = 158$$

Weights in CPI

Weights are assigned to different categories of consumption goods based on the relative importance of each item in the average family budget.

Government agencies often use standard weights, for computing CPI, which are tabulated below

The Group of Items in CPI for Industrial Workers and their Weightage

Major Group	Weight in %
Food and Beverages	45.86
Pan, Tobacco and Intoxicants	2.38
Fuel and Light	6.84
Housing	10.07
Clothing and Footwear	6.53
Miscellaneous Group	28.32
General	100.00

Source *Economic Survey, 2014-15 Government of India.*

Use of Consumer Price Index (CPI)

- CPI helps in wage negotiations, formulation of wage policies, pricing policies for goods and services, etc.
- CPI is used by government departments to regulate Dearness Allowances (DA) periodically to reflect changes in the cost of living.
- The purchasing power of money is inversely related to the CPI.

  Mathematically,

  $$\text{Purchasing Power of Money} = \frac{1}{\text{CPI}} \times 100$$

  e.g. If CPI is 120, therefore, purchasing power will be $\frac{1}{120} \times 100 = 0.83$, i.e. purchasing power of a rupee in this case is 71 paise as compared to the base year.
- CPI helps in measuring real wages in the economy, which are calculated as

  $$\text{Real Wages} = \frac{\text{Nominal Wages/Money Wages}}{\text{CPI}} \times 100$$
- CPI assists in analysing the market for specific types of goods or services, providing insights into economic trends.

Solved Question 7 **During a period of time, the cost of living index goes up from 120 to 150 and the wages during the same period increased from ₹ 100 to ₹ 120. Has the workers really gained due to this increase?**

Sol. With increase in cost of living index from 120 to 150, the wages of the workers should be increased to $\frac{100 \times 150}{120}$

$= ₹\ 125.$

But, the wages have gone up to ₹ 120 only. Hence, the workers have not gained.

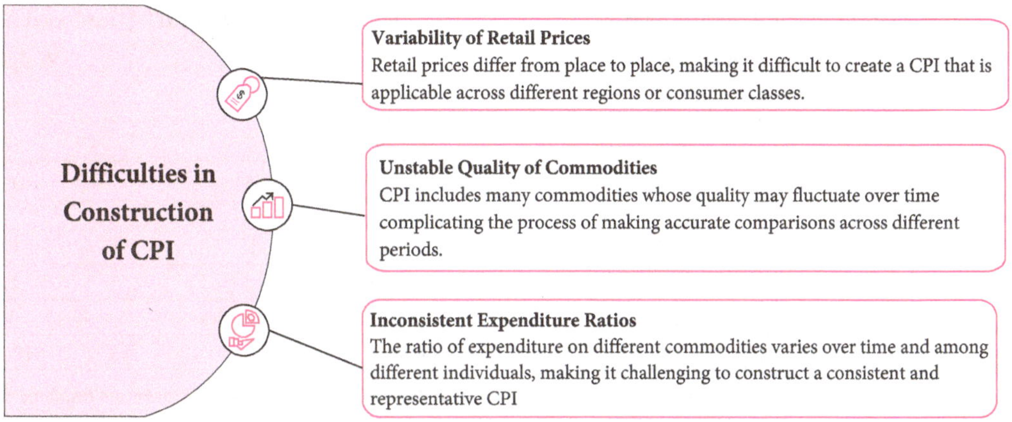

8.4 Wholesale Price Index (WPI)

The Wholesale Price Index (WPI) measures changes in the general price level of the country. This price index is calculated on the basis of commodities traded at wholesale rates, such as oil, sugar, wheat, rice, etc. Unlike the Consumer Price Index (CPI), WPI excludes the service sector and is calculated weekly for the entire country, using 2011-12 as the base year.

The methods for computing wholesale price index are same as discussed in consumer price index.

Commodity Groups for Wholesale Price Index

1. **Primary Articles**

   It includes 117 commodities (like food articles, non-food articles and minerals, etc.) with a total weightage of 22.62%.

2. **Fuel and Power**

   It comprises 16 items (like coal, petroleum products, electricity, etc.) with a total weightage of 13.15%.

The Categories in WPI and their Weightage

Category	Weight in %
Primary Articles	22.62
Fuel and Power	13.15
Manufactured Products	64.23
All Commodities 'Headline Inflation'	100.00
'WPI Food Index'	24.23

Source *Ministry of Statistics and Programme Implementation, 2016-17*

3. **Manufactured Products**

   It consists of 564 commodities (like food products, beverages, textiles, metal products, etc.) with a total weightage of 64.23%.

Uses of Wholesale Price Index (WPI)

- WPI serves as a key indicator of overall inflation in the economy.
- It helps in forecasting the demand and supply of commodities.
- WPI helps in setting and adjusting the wage rates of workers.
- WPI is used to eliminate the effect of price changes when calculating aggregates like national income.

8.5 Index of Industrial Production (IIP)

The Index of Industrial Production (IIP) measures changes in the level of industrial production or output in the country compared to level of production in base year. It includes the production data from both the public and private sectors and reflects the general level of industrial activity in the country.

Composition of IIP

The current series of IIP has a base year of 2011-12 and it comprises number of items. These items can be classified in following two ways

1. **Sector-wise Composition** IIP items are categorised into three sectors *viz.* mining, manufacturing and electricity.

Broad Industrial Grouping and their Weights

Sector	Weight (%)
Mining	14.4
Manufacturing	77.6
Electricity	8.00
General Index	100.00

Source *Ministry of Statistics and Programme Implementation, 2016-17*

2. **Use-wise Composition** Items are classified into categories such as basic goods, capital goods, intermediate goods, consumer goods, etc.

Weightage Pattern of IIP (Use-based Groups)

Group	Weight (%)
Primary	34.1
Capital Goods	8.2
Intermediate Goods	17.2
Infrastructure/ Construction Goods	12.3
Consumer Durables	12.8
Consumer Non-durables	15.3
General Index	100.00

Source *Ministry of Statistics and Programme Implementation, 2016-17*

Computation of IIP

Following steps are followed to compute industrial production index

Step 1 Calculate quantity relative with the help of the following formula

$$\text{Quantity Relative (QR)} = \frac{q_1}{q_0} \times 100$$

Here, q_1 = Current year's production and q_0 = Base year's production

Step 2 Multiply the quantity relative with the assigned weight and sum up the products to get ΣQRW.

Step 3 Add the weights of all items to obtain ΣW.

Step 4 Calculate IIP using the formula $\boxed{\text{IIP} = \frac{\Sigma QRW}{\Sigma W}}$

where variables have the same meaning as discussed above.

Solved Question 8 **Construct index number of industrial production from the following data**

Industry	Output		Weight
	Base Year	Current Year	
Manufacturing Production	120	250	85
Electrical Products	200	400	5
Mining	65	90	10

Sol. **Construction of Industrial Production Index Number**

Industry	Output		Quantity Relative (QR) $\left(\frac{q_1}{q_0} \times 100\right)$	Weight (W)	QRW
	Base Year (q_0)	Current Year (q_1)			
Manufacturing Production	120	250	$\frac{250}{120} \times 100 = 208.33$	85	17708.05
Electrical Products	200	400	$\frac{400}{200} \times 100 = 200$	5	1000
Mining	65	90	$\frac{90}{65} \times 100 = 138.46$	10	1384.6
				$\Sigma W = 100$	$\Sigma QRW = 20092.65$

$$\text{Index Number of Industrial Production } (\text{IIP}_{01}) = \frac{\Sigma QRW}{\Sigma W} = \frac{20092.65}{100} = 200.92 \text{ (approx)}$$

Other Important Index Numbers

Sensex	**Human Development Index** (HDI)
• Sensex stands for the Bombay Stock Exchange (BSE) sensitive index, using 1978-79 as its base year. It serves as the benchmark index for the Indian stock market, comprising 30 prominent and financially sound companies in the economy. • **Interpretation** — **Rising Sensex** Indicates improved market performance, better earnings expectations and growing investor confidence in the economy's health. — **Falling Sensex** Suggests a decline in stock prices of most companies within the sensex, reflecting lower investor confidence.	• The Human Development Index (HDI) is an index used to evaluate the level of development in different countries. Prepared by the United Nations (UN), it incorporates three key components — Per capita income (Measured in $ PPP). — Gross enrollment ratio and years of schooling. — Life expectancy at birth. • Countries are ranked on a scale of 0 to 1 based on their HDI value, with higher values indicating better development levels.

Use of Index Numbers in Economics

- Consumer Price Index (CPI) is helpful in wage negotiation, formulation of income policy, price policy, rent control, taxation and general economic policy formulation.
- CPI is used in calculating the purchasing power of money and real wage.
- Wholesale Price Index (WPI) is used to estimate the effect of changes in prices on aggregates such as national income, capital formation, etc.
- Index of Industrial Production (IIP) provides a quantitative figure about the change in production in the industrial sector.
- Agricultural production index provides a ready reckoner of the performance of the agricultural sector.
- Sensex is a useful guide for investors in the stock market. A rising sensex indicates optimism about the future performance of the economy and an appropriate time for investment.

Limitations of Index Numbers

- It only provides relative changes and does not show actual change in variables.
- It does not consider qualitative changes.
- It is affected by extreme values and manipulation of the results is possible.
- Index numbers are based on selected items and not all items, thus, these are correct only on an average.
- It is not rigidly defined; different methods are used for different purposes which gives different results.

Inflation and Index Number

Inflation refers to a situation characterised by a sustained increase in the general price level.

A minor or irregular price rise does not constitute inflation.

Wholesale Price Index (WPI) is most commonly accepted measure of inflation, due to following attributes

- WPI is the most widely used price index as an indicator of rate of inflation in the economy.
- It serves as a general index indicating price movements in the economy.
- WPI is available on a weekly basis with a shortest time lag of 2 weeks.

However, in recent times, CPI is increasingly being referred to as a measure of inflation.

Mind Map

INDEX NUMBERS

1 Concept of Index Numbers

It measures changes in a variable or group of variables over two different time periods.

Mathematically, Index Number = $\frac{\text{Value in Current Period}}{\text{Value in Base Period}} \times 100$

Features

- **Special Averages** Measures changes across different series and units.
- **Expressed in Percentage** Expressed as percentages for easy comparison.
- **Tracks Variations** Analyses changes over time, place or context.
- **Helps to Measure Changes not Directly Measurable** Captures trends in factors not directly measurable.

2 Issues in Constructing Index Numbers

- **Selection of Averages** Choosing the appropriate type of average (arithmetic mean, geometric mean).
- **Determination and Definition of Purpose** Defining the purpose and scope of desired index number.
- **Selection of Sources of Data** Use reliable primary or secondary sources based on accuracy and coverage.
- **Selection of Base Year** Selecting a reliable and stable base year.
- **Selection of Items/Commodities** Items included in the index number should be relevant and standardised.
- **Selection of the Price** Different price types and sources affect index accuracy.
- **Selection of Weighing Methods** Assigning proper weights based on importance
- **Selection of the Formula** Choosing the most suitable formula for calculation.

3 Uses of Index Numbers

- Barometer of economic progress
- Helps government to adjust fiscal and monetary policies
- Throws light on economic condition
- Helps in wage fixation and policy-making
- Assists producers in setting output levels
- Identifies regional disparities for fair wealth distribution

4 Types of Index Numbers

- **Price Index Numbers** Measures price fluctuations. It can be Wholesale Price Index (WPI) and Consumer Price Index (CPI).
- **Quantity Index Numbers** Tracks production changes.
- **Value Index Numbers** Assesses changes in total value.

5 Simple Index Numbers

They assign equal weightage to all items under consideration, creating all goods and services with equal importance.

Methods of Calculation

- **Simple Aggregative Method**
  Compares total prices of current and base year. $\Rightarrow P_{01} = \frac{\Sigma P_1}{\Sigma P_0} \times 100$
- **Simple Average of price Relative Method**
  Computes average percentage change in prices. $\Rightarrow P_{01} = \frac{\Sigma I}{n}$

6 Weighted Index Numbers

They assign different weights to different items in the series, depending upon their relative importance.

Methods of Calculation

- **Weighted Average of Price Relatives Method**

$$P_{01} = \frac{\Sigma IW}{\Sigma W}$$

- **Weighted Aggregative Method**

Laspeyre's Method	Uses base year quantity as weight.	$P_{01} = \frac{\Sigma p_1 q_0}{\Sigma p_0 q_0} \times 100$
Paasche's Method	Uses current year quantity as weight.	$P_{01} = \frac{\Sigma p_1 q_1}{\Sigma p_0 q_1} \times 100$
Fisher's Ideal Method	Combines Laspeyre's and Paasche's methods using a geometric mean.	$P_{01} = \sqrt{\frac{\Sigma p_1 q_0}{\Sigma p_0 q_0} \times \frac{\Sigma p_1 q_1}{\Sigma p_0 q_1}} \times 100$

7 Consumer Price Index (CPI)

- It measures average price changes in price of goods and services for specific consumer groups and indicates inflation.
- It also known as cost of living index, retail price index and price of living index.
- Major categories include food, clothing, fuel and lighting, house rent, miscellaneous.

Methods of Calculation

- **Aggregative Expenditure Method**
  Weighted index using base year quantities.

$$\text{CPI} = \frac{\Sigma p_1 q_0}{\Sigma p_0 q_0} \times 100$$

- **Family Budget Method** Uses household expenditure patterns as weights.

$$\text{CPI} = \frac{\Sigma IW}{\Sigma W}$$

8 Wholesale Price Index (WPI)

It measures price changes of wholesale goods, excluding services. The base year is considered 2011-12 and calculated weekly.

Commodity Groups

- *Primary Articles*: 22.62 % (Food, non-food, minerals, etc.)
- *Fuel and Power*: 13.15 % (Coal, petroleum, electricity, etc.)
- *Manufactured Products:* 64.32 % (Food, beverage, textiles, metals, etc.)

Uses of WPI

- Key indicator of inflation
- Helps forecast demand and supply
- Assists in wage adjustments
- Eliminates price effect in national income calculations

9 Index of Industrial Production (IIP)

It measures changes in industrial production levels compared to production level in base year.

Composition

- Sector-wise (Mining, manufacturing, electricity)
- Use-wise (Capital goods, consumer goods, infrastructure, etc)
- **Formula**

$$\text{IIP} = \frac{\Sigma QRW}{\Sigma W}$$

EXAM PATTERN QUESTIONS

Objective Type Questions

Multiple Choice Questions (MCQs)

1. Index numbers are expressed in ...., making it easier to compare changes between different variables or time periods.

(a) percentages (b) whole numbers
(c) averages (d) units

2. Which of the following devices is used for measuring differences in the magnitude of a group of related variables?

(a) Arithmetic mean (b) Index number
(c) Correlation (d) Mode

3. Which of the following is not a feature of index numbers? **Competency Based Que**

I. They are expressed in percentages.
II. They measure changes over time or place.
III. They only apply to economic variables.
IV. They use special averages to compare different series.

Codes

(a) I and II (b) Only III
(c) II and IV (d) Only IV

4. Complete the blank boxes from the given below.

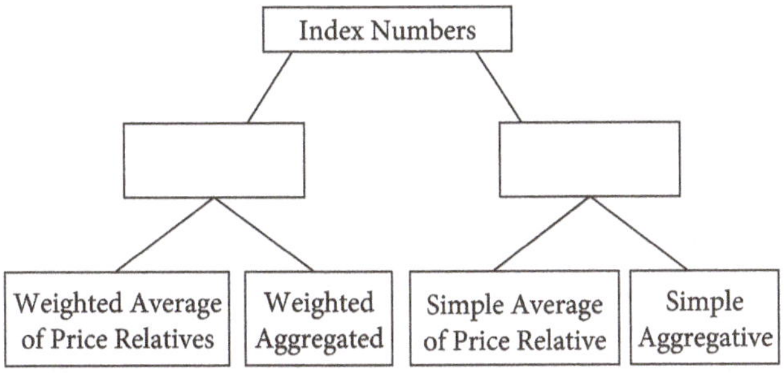

(a) Unweighted, Weighted
(b) Weighted, Unweighted
(c) Weighted, Weighted
(d) Unweighted, Unweighted

5. If the sum of prices of all goods in the current year is ₹ 200 and in the base year is ₹ 100, what is the simple aggregative index number? **Competency Based Que**

(a) 100 (b) 150
(c) 200 (d) 300

6. If a commodity's price in the base year is ₹ 50 and in the current year is ₹ 75, what is the price relative for this commodity? **Competency Based Que**

(a) 100% (b) 125% (c) 175% (d) 150%

7. An index number which accounts for the relative importance of the items is known as **NCERT**

(a) weighted index (b) simple aggregative index
(c) simple average of relatives

8. Which advantage of index numbers is highlighted in the below image?

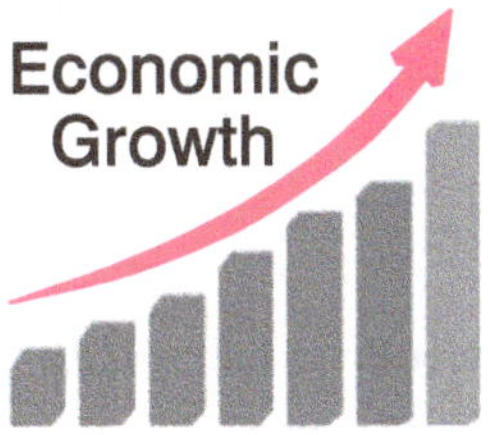

(a) Government value
(b) Wage fixation
(c) Barometer of economic progress
(d) None of the above

9. In Laspeyre's index number, the weight pertains to

(a) base year quantities (b) current year
(c) Both (a) and (b) (d) None of these

10. What is another name for the Consumer Price Index (CPI)?

(a) Producer price index (b) Retail price index
(c) Export price index (d) Wholesale price index

11. What does the image given below indicates related to value of money?

(a) Increase in CPI leads to fall in the purchasing power of money
(b) Decrease in CPI leads to fall in the purchasing power of money
(c) Increase in CPI leads to rise in the purchasing power of money
(d) Decrease in CPI leads to rise in the purchasing power of money

12. **Consumer price index number for the year 1957 was 313 with 1940 as the base year, the average monthly wages in 1957 of the workers in a factory was ₹ 160. Their real wage is** Competency Based Que

(a) 48.40 (b) 51.12
(c) 40.30 (d) None of these

13. **The Consumer Price Index (CPI) is inversely related to the .... of money.**

(a) value (b) purchasing power
(c) cost (d) weight

14. **If the base year CPI is 100 and the current year CPI is 150, what is the purchasing power of money in the current year?** Competency Based Que

(a) 50% (b) 66.67%
(c) 75% (d) 80%

15. **The Consumer Price Index (CPI) for urban sectors uses the base year ....**

(a) 2011-12 (b) 1986-87
(c) 2001-02 (d) 2015-16

16. **The item having the highest weight in consumer price index for industrial workers is** NCERT

(a) food
(b) housing
(c) clothing

17. **If the base year WPI is 100 and the current year WPI is 130, by what percentage have the wholesale prices increased?** Competency Based Que

(a) 20% (b) 25% (c) 30% (d) 35%

18. **Which of the following is excluded from the Wholesale Price Index (WPI)?**

(a) Manufactured products (b) Fuel and power
(c) Primary articles (d) Services

19. **The Wholesale Price Index (WPI) gives the highest weightage to ....**

(a) manufactured products (b) fuel and power
(c) primary articles (d) services

20. **Cost of living index numbers are also used to find real wage by the process of**

(a) base shifting (b) splicing of index number
(c) deflating of index number (d) None of these

21. **Index of industrial production is a .... of quantitative relative.**

(a) simple average (b) weighted average
(c) Both (a) and (b) (d) None of these

22. **Identify the components of index of industrial production.** Competency Based Que

I. Mining **II. Manufacturing**
III. Agriculture **IV. Electricity**

Codes
(a) Only III (b) I, II and III
(c) I, II and IV (d) III and IV

23. **If the Index of Industrial Production (IIP) for the base year is 250 and the current year IIP is 150, what is the percentage increase in industrial production?** Competency Based Que

(a) 20% (b) 25% (c) 40% (d) 35%

24. **............ is the benchmark index for the Indian stock market.**

(a) Price index (b) Agricultural index
(c) Sensex (d) None of these

25. **Movements in prices will appear to be more or less significant, according to the year chosen for the prices of items selected. It is important, therefore, to select a year when prices were relatively stable and so years during periods either of severe inflation or deflation should be avoided.**

Which of the following problems of index number is indicated in the given extract? Competency Based Que

(a) Problem of choice of weight
(b) Problem of choice of base year
(c) Problem of choice of commodity
(d) None of the above

26. **In general, inflation is calculated by using** NCERT

(a) wholesale price index (b) consumer price index
(c) producer's price index

Direction *Read the case study and answer the questions 27 to 30 on the basis of the same*

ABC Industries is analysing its production performance and inflation impact on its costs. The management decided to use various index numbers to evaluate the economic trends and the effectiveness of their strategies. They used the Index of Industrial Production (IIP) to assess their production changes and the Consumer Price Index (CPI) to understand inflation's effect on their cost of production.

In the base year (2011-12), the IIP was set at 200 and in the current year, it is 240. The CPI for the base year was 150 and in the current year, it has increased to 180.

27. **The percentage change in IIP is ....**

28. **Which index number measures changes in the level of industrial production in the country?**

(a) Consumer Price Index (CPI)
(b) Wholesale Price Index (WPI)
(c) Index of Industrial Production (IIP)
(d) Sensex

29. **The percentage change in CPI is ....**

30. **What does the Consumer Price Index (CPI) primarily measure?**

(a) Changes in stock market prices
(b) Changes in industrial production
(c) Changes in prices of goods and services paid by consumers
(d) Changes in wholesale commodity prices

Assertion-Reason

Direction (Q.No. 31to 40) *Read the following Assertion (A) and Reason (R) and choose the correct alternative from the following*

Alternatives

(a) Both Assertion (A) and Reason (R) are true and Reason (R) is the correct explanation of Assertion (A)
(b) Both Assertion (A) and Reason (R) are true, but Reason (R) is not the correct explanation of Assertion (A)
(c) Assertion (A) is true, but Reason (R) is false
(d) Assertion (A) is false, but Reason (R) is true

31. **Assertion** (A) Index numbers are the 'barometer of economic activity'.

Reason (R) Index number are devices for measuring difference in the magnitude of related variables.

32. **Assertion** (A) Unlike arithmetic mean or median, index numbers can compare different series with different units of measurement.

Reason (R) The formula used to calculate the index does not affect the final value and interpretation.

33. **Assertion** (A) The base period associated with index number is a period of time that is used for comparison.

Reason (R) The base year should be a normal year and greater than current year.

34. **Assertion** (A) CPI measures the average change in prices of goods and services paid by specific consumer classes in the current year compared to a base year.

Reason (R) CPI serves as an indicator of inflation in a country.

35. **Assertion** (A) CPI for Industrial Workers (CPI-IW) uses the base year 2001.

Reason (R) CPI for Agricultural Labour (CPI-AL) and Rural Labour (CPI-RL) use the base year 1986-87.

36. **Assertion** (A) The purchasing power of money is positively related to the CPI.

Reason (R) The Consumer Price Index (CPI) is used to adjust wage policies and Dearness Allowances (DA) to reflect changes in the cost of living.

37. **Assertion** (A) The Wholesale Price Index (WPI) measures changes in the general price level of commodities.

Reason (R) Unlike the Consumer Price Index (CPI), WPI excludes the service sector and is calculated weekly for the entire country.

38. **Assertion** (A) WPI serves as a key indicator of overall inflation in the economy.

Reason (R) WPI cannot predict the demand and supply of commodities.

39. **Assertion** (A) IIP items are categorised into three sectors *viz.* mining, manufacturing and electricity.

Reason (R) Items in the IIP are assigned weights based on their significance in the overall industrial production.

40. **Assertion** (A) The Sensex is a benchmark index of the Bombay Stock Exchange (BSE).

Reason (R) The Sensex helps investors gauge the overall performance of the stock market and serves as a barometer for the Indian economy.

Two Statements Based MCQs

Direction (Q. No. 41 to 50) *Read the following statements carefully and choose the correct alternative*

Alternatives

(a) Statement I is correct and Statement II is incorrect
(b) Statement II is correct and Statement I is incorrect
(c) Both the statements are correct
(d) Both the statements are incorrect

41. **Statement I** Index numbers are crucial for comparing the economic conditions of specific groups of people across different time periods.

Statement II A base period is the reference date from which an index number is calculated.

42. **Statement I** Simple aggregative methods are influenced by the magnitude of the price.

Statement II Index number measure changes which are not directly measurable.

43. **Statement I** Laspeyre's method uses the current year's quantity as the weight.

Statement II Paasche's method uses the base year's quantity as the weight.

44. **Statement I** Consumer price index is calculated by the formula of Paasche's index number.

Statement II Index is used for forecasting as well.

45. **Statement I** CPI helps in measuring real wages in the economy.

Statement II CPI assists in analysing the market for specific types of goods or services, providing insights into economic trends.

46. **Statement I** The wholesale price index includes the manufacturing and service sector.

Statement II WPI helps in setting and adjusting workers' wage rates.

47. **Statement I** IIP includes the production data from both the public and private sectors and reflects the general level of industrial activity.

Statement II The Index of Industrial Production (IIP) measures changes in the level of industrial production or output in the country compared to the base year, 2000-2001.

48. **Statement I** Rising sensex indicates improves market performance.

Statement II Falling sensex indicates a decline in stock prices of most companies within the sensex.

49. **Statement I** Per capita income indicates the overall health conditions.

Statement II Life expectancy at birth is measured in terms of Purchasing Power Parity (PPP).

50. **Statement I** WPI is the most commonly accepted measure of inflation.

Statement II WPI is available on a weekly basis with a shortest time lag of two weeks.

Matching

51. Match the following

Column I	Column II
A. Sensex	(i) A statistical measure used to represent changes in a variable or a group of variables over time.
B. Index number	(ii) An index that accounts for the relative importance of different items by assigning weights.
C. Weighted index number	(iii) Statistical measures that summarise central tendencies.
D. Averages	(iv) A stock market index that tracks the performance of the 30 largest and most actively traded stocks on the Bombay Stock Exchange (BSE) in India.

Codes

	A	B	C	D
(a)	(iii)	(iv)	(i)	(ii)
(b)	(iv)	(i)	(ii)	(iii)
(c)	(ii)	(iii)	(iv)	(i)
(d)	(iii)	(ii)	(i)	(iv)

52. Match the following

Column I	Column II
A. Price index numbers	(i) Comparison of total value of period under study.
B. Quantity index numbers	(ii) Reference date of calculation of index number.
C. Value index numbers	(iii) Track general changes in prices.
D. Base period	(iv) Measure changes in quantity of goods.

Codes

	A	B	C	D
(a)	(iii)	(iv)	(i)	(ii)
(b)	(iv)	(i)	(ii)	(iii)
(c)	(ii)	(iii)	(iv)	(i)
(d)	(iii)	(ii)	(i)	(iv)

53. Match the following

Column I	Column II
A. P_1	(i) Base year quantity
B. P_0	(ii) Price of current year
C. P_{01}	(iii) Price of base year
D. Q_0	(iv) Price index of current year

Codes

	A	B	C	D
(a)	(iii)	(iv)	(i)	(ii)
(b)	(iv)	(i)	(ii)	(iii)
(c)	(ii)	(iii)	(iv)	(i)
(d)	(iii)	(ii)	(i)	(iv)

54. Match the following

Column I	Column II
A. CPI for rural, urban and combined sectors	(i) Base year 2001
B. CPI for Agricultural Labour (CPI-AL) and Rural Labour (CPI-RL)	(ii) Base year 1986-87
C. CPI for Industrial Workers (CPI-IW)	(iii) Base year 2011-12

Codes

	A	B	C
(a)	(i)	(ii)	(iii)
(b)	(iii)	(i)	(ii)
(c)	(ii)	(iii)	(i)
(d)	(iii)	(ii)	(i)

55. Match the options of Column I with correct options in Column II

Column I	Column II
A. Simple aggregative method	(i) $\left(\frac{\Sigma IW}{\Sigma W}\right)$
B. Paasche's index number	(ii) $\left(\frac{\Sigma p_1 q_0}{\Sigma p_0 q_0}\right) \times 100$
C. Laspeyre's index number	(iii) $\left(\frac{\Sigma p_1}{\Sigma p_0}\right) \times 100$
D. Family budget method	(iv) $\left(\frac{\Sigma p_1 q_1}{\Sigma p_0 q_1}\right) \times 100$

Codes

	A	B	C	D		A	B	C	D
(a)	(i)	(ii)	(iii)	(iv)	(b)	(ii)	(i)	(iv)	(iii)
(c)	(iii)	(iv)	(ii)	(i)	(d)	(iv)	(i)	(iii)	(ii)

Concept Identification

56. It represents changes in the price level of goods and services purchased by consumers over time.

57. This concept uses both base year and current year quantities as weights to calculate an index.

58. It is used to measure economic progress and includes components like health, education, and income.

59. It calculates the index number as the sum of current year prices as a percentage of the sum of base year prices.

60. It refers to the reference point or time period used for comparison when calculating index numbers.

Answers

1. (a) percentages

2. (b) Index number

3. (b) Only III

4. (b) Weighted, Unweighted

5. (c) Simple Aggregative Index Number

$$= \frac{\Sigma p_1}{\Sigma p_0} \times 100 = \frac{200}{100} \times 100 = 200$$

6. (d) Price Relative $= \frac{p_1}{p_0} \times 100 = \frac{75}{50} \times 100 = 150\%$

7. (a) weighted index

8. (c) Barometer of economic progress

9. (a) base year quantities

10. (b) Retail price index

11. (a) Increase in CPI leads to fall in the purchasing power of money

12. (b) Price index number = 313

Average wage = ₹ 160

$\because$ Price Index $= \frac{p_1}{p_0} \times 100$

$\Rightarrow \quad 313 = \frac{160}{p_0} \times 100$

$\Rightarrow \quad p_0 = \frac{160 \times 100}{313} = 51.12$

13. (b) purchasing power

14. (b) Since purchasing power is inversely related, purchasing power in current year will be

$$= \frac{100}{150} = 0.6667 \text{ or } 66.67\%.$$

15. (a) 2011-12

16. (a) food

17. (c) The percentage increase is calculated as

$$\frac{(130 - 100)}{100} \times 100 = 30$$

18. (d) Services

19. (a) manufactured products

20. (c) deflating of index number

21. (b) weighted average

22. (c) I, II and IV

23. (c) Percentage Increase = Current Year IIP – Base Year IIP/Base Year IIP × 100

$$= \frac{250 - 150}{250} \times 100 = 40\%$$

24. (c) Sensex

25. (b) Problem of choice of base year

26. (a) wholesale price index

27. Percentage Change = Current Year IIP – Base Year IIP/Base Year IIP × 100

$$= \frac{240 - 200}{200} \times 100 = 20\%$$

28. (c) Index of Industrial Production (IIP)

29. Percentage Change = Current Year CPI – Base Year CPI/Base Year CPI × 100

$$= \frac{180 - 150}{150} \times 100 = 20\%$$

30. (c) Changes in prices of goods and services paid by consumers

31. (b) Both Assertion (A) and Reason (R) are true, but Reason (R) is not the correct explanation of Assertion (A)

32. (c) The formula used to calculate the index affects the final value and interpretation.

33. (c) While the base year should be a 'normal year', it cannot be greater than the current year.

34. (a) Both Assertion (A) and Reason (R) are true and Reason (R) is the correct explanation of Assertion (A)

35. (b) Both Assertion (A) and Reason (R) are true, but Reason (R) is not the correct explanation of Assertion (A)

36. (d) The purchasing power of money is inversely related to the CPI and CPI helps in measuring real wages and analysing market trends for specific goods or services.

37. (b) Both Assertion (A) and Reason (R) are true, but Reason (R) is not the correct explanation of Assertion (A)

38. (c) Wholesale price index aids in predicting the demand and supply of commodities.

39. (b) Both Assertion (A) and Reason (R) are true, but Reason (R) is not the correct explanation of Assertion (A)

40. (a) Both the Assertion (A) and Reason (R) are true and Reason (R) is the correct explanation of Assertion (A)

41. (c) Both the statements are correct

42. (c) Both the statements are correct

43. (d) Paasche's method uses the current year's quantity as the weight. Laspeyre's method uses the base year's quantity as the weight.

44. (b) CPI is calculated using Laspeyre's index number.

45. (c) Both the statements are correct.

46. (b) Unlike the Consumer Price Index (CPI), WPI excludes the service sector and is calculated weekly for the entire country, using 2011-12 as the base year.

47. (a) The Index of Industrial Production (IIP) measures changes in the level of industrial production or output in the country compared to the base year, 2011-12.

48. (c) Both the statements are correct

49. (d) The overall health condition is indicated by the life expectancy at birth and the per capita income is measured in terms of PPP.

50. (c) Both the statements are correct

51. (b) (iv) (i) (ii) (iii)

52. (a) (iii) (iv) (i) (ii)

53. (c) (ii) (iii) (iv) (i)

54. (d) (iii) (ii) (i)

55. (c) (iii) (iv) (ii) (i)

56. Consumer Price Index (CPI)

57. Fisher's index method

58. Human Development Index (HDI)

59. Simple aggregative method

60. Base period

Subjective Questions

Short Answer Type Questions

1. What is an index number?

Ans. An index number is a statistical measure used to represent changes in a variable or a group of variables over time. It compares the current period to a base period, usually expressed as a percentage, to show the relative change in magnitude. It helps in analysing trends by providing a unit-free measure of change.

2. What are the desirable properties of the base period?

Or **"While selecting base period certain factors should be considered." Discuss.** NCERT; Competency Based Que

Ans. Base period should have the following properties

(i) The base year should be a normal year in which extraordinary events such as earthquake, flood, war, elections, etc. should not have occurred.

(ii) The period should not be too far in the past as comparison cannot be done with such a base year because policies, economic and social conditions change with time.

(iii) Base period should be updated periodically.

Thus, we can conclude that while selecting base period, certain factors should be considered.

3. What issues can arise during the construction of index numbers?

Ans. Issues in constructing index numbers include

(i) The choice of average used (e.g. Arithmetic vs geometric mean) can affect data representation.

(ii) Defining the purpose clearly to select appropriate methods and data sources.

(iii) Choosing reliable and accurate data sources are crucial for valid results.

(iv) Selecting a base year that represents normal economic conditions.

(v) The relevance and representation of items or commodities included in the index.

(vi) Different types of prices (wholesale vs retail) can lead to variations.

(vii) Deciding on the appropriate weighing methods and formulas to use.

4. What is the difference between a price index and a quantity index? NCERT

Ans. The differences between a price index and a quantity index are as follows

(i) Price index numbers measure and allow for comparison of the prices of certain goods while quantity index numbers measure the changes in the physical volume of production, construction or employment.

(ii) Price index numbers are more widely used as compared to quantity index numbers.

5. How are simple index numbers constructed?

Ans. Simple index numbers can be constructed using

(i) **Simple Aggregative Method**
Sum the prices of goods in the current year and base year, then compare the current year's total to the base year's total.

(ii) **Simple Average of Price Relatives Method**
Compute the price relative for each item (current price vs base price), then average these price relatives to get the index.

6. How does Paasche's method differ from Laspeyre's method? Competency Based Que

Ans. Paasche's method uses current year quantities as weights, making it more reflective of present consumption and market conditions. It involves multiplying current year prices by current year quantities, summing the products and comparing this to the sum of base year prices multiplied by current year quantities. While it adapts well to changes in consumption patterns, it is more complex as it requires current data, which may not always be readily available.

Laspeyre's method on the other hand, uses base year quantities as weights, focusing on historical consumption patterns. It multiplies current year prices by base year quantities, summing the products and comparing this to the sum of base year prices multiplied by base year quantities. This method is simpler and better suited for long-term comparisons but may overstate price increases as it does not account for shifts in consumption behaviour over time.

7. Is the change in any price reflected in a price index number? NCERT; Competency Based Que

Ans. No, the change in any price is not reflected in a price index number.

Price index numbers measure and permit comparison of the prices of certain goods included in the basket being used to compare prices in the base period with prices in the current period.

Moreover, an equal rise in the price of an item with large weight and that of an item with low weight will have different implications for overall change in price index.

8. How is the Consumer Price Index (CPI) constructed?

Ans. The CPI is constructed by

(i) Deciding the scope and coverage, including the class of people for whom the index is to be created.

(ii) Conducting a family budget survey to gather data on typical consumption patterns.

(iii) Collecting price quotations for a fixed list of items and adjusting for discounts and interest rates.

9. Why is it essential to have different CPI for different categories of consumers? NCERT; Competency Based Que

Ans. It is essential to have different CPI for different categories of consumers as in each category, consumption baskets contain many dissimilar items. In India, three CPIs are constructed

(i) CPI for industrial workers.

(ii) CPI for Agricultural Labour (CPI-AL) and Consumer Price Index for Rural Labour (CPI-RL).

(iii) CPI for rural, urban and combined sectors.

10. What are the primary categories included in the Consumer Price Index (CPI)?

Ans. The CPI is broadly categorised into five major groups

(i) **Food**
Includes expenditures on essential food items like grains, vegetables, fruits and beverages.

(ii) **Clothing**
Covers costs related to clothing, footwear and other apparel.

(iii) **Fuel and Lighting**
Accounts for energy expenses, such as electricity, gas and other fuels.

(iv) **House Rent**
Represents rental expenses or imputed rent for owned homes.

(v) **Miscellaneous**
Includes healthcare, education, transportation, entertainment and other services.

11. What is the Wholesale Price Index (WPI)? Which commodity groups are included in the WPI?

Ans. The Wholesale Price Index (WPI) measures changes in the general price level of commodities traded at wholesale rates.

Unlike the CPI, it excludes the service sector and is calculated weekly, with a base year of 2011-12.

The WPI includes three main commodity groups

(i) Primary articles (22.62% weight).

(ii) Fuel and power (13.15% weight).

(iii) Manufactured products (64.23% weight).

12. How is the Index of Industrial Production (IIP) computed?

Ans. For computation of IIP, following steps are required to be followed

Step 1 Calculate quantity relative with the help of the following formula

$$\text{Quantity Relative } (QR) = \frac{q_1}{q_0} \times 100$$

Here, q_1 = Current year's production and

q_0 = Base year's production

Step 2 Multiply the quantity relative by the assigned weight and sum up the products to get ΣQRW.

Step 3 Add the weights of all items to obtain ΣW.

Step 4 Calculate IIP using following formula

$$\text{IIP} = \frac{\Sigma QRW}{\Sigma W}$$

where, variables have the same meaning as discussed above.

13. Which type of index number is most appropriate in the case shown below? Also briefly explain the steps involved in its construction. Competency Based Que

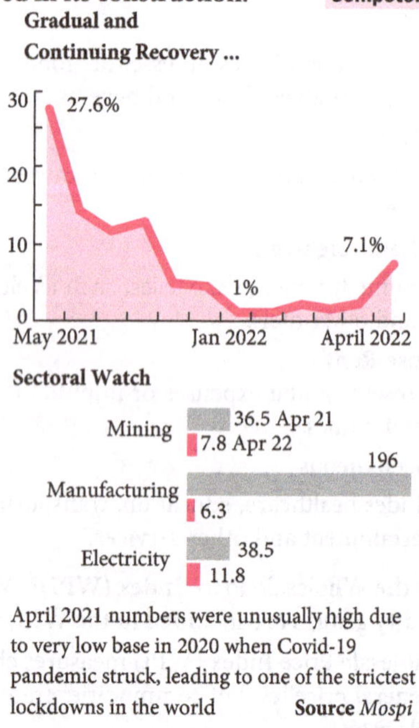

Ans. The Index of Industrial Production (IIP) is the most suitable index for the given case. The IIP measures the volume of industrial output, specifically focusing on manufacturing, mining and electricity.

This aligns directly with the data presented in the image, which shows the performance of these sectors.

By comparing current production levels to a base year, the IIP provides a clear assessment of growth or decline, as evident in the image's comparison to April 2021.

Additionally, the IIP's breakdown by industry allows for a detailed analysis of specific sectors' contributions to the overall economic recovery, reflected in the image's focus on mining, manufacturing and electricity.

14. "Simple index numbers are different from weighted index numbers."
Do you agree? Give reason. Competency Based Que

Ans. Yes, I agree. Simple index numbers treat all items equally and do not account for their relative importance.

They are calculated using either the simple aggregative method or the simple average of price relatives method.

In contrast, weighted index numbers assign different weights to items based on their importance.

This approach is used in methods like the weighted average of price relative method and weighted aggregative method, where weights reflect the relative significance of each item, providing a more accurate measure of overall changes.

15. Read the following table carefully and give your comments. NCERT; Competency Based Que

Index of Industrial Production Base 1993-94

Industry	Weight (in %)	1996-97	2003-04
General Index	100	130.8	189.0
Mining and Quarrying	10.73	118.2	146.9
Manufacturing	79.58	133.6	196.6
Electricity	10.69	122.0	172.6

Ans. The following conclusions can be made by analysing the table

(i) Manufacturing industry has the highest weight of 79.58% in Index of Industrial Production (IIP) while mining and quarrying and electricity industries account for 10.73% and 10.69%, respectively.

(ii) Manufacturing industry has registered the highest growth among all industrial sectors in both the years 1996-97 and 2003-04.

(iii) Mining and quarrying has registered the lowest growth rate in both the years.

(iv) The general index shows that industrial production increased by 30.8% in 1996-97 as compared to 1993-94 and by 89% in 2003-04.

16. How is inflation related to index numbers?

Ans. Inflation refers to the sustained increase in the general price level over time. Index numbers, such as the CPI and WPI, measure inflation by comparing current prices to a base period, reflecting changes in the cost of living and overall price levels.

17. What are the limitations of index numbers?

Ans. Following are the limitations of index numbers

(i) It only provides relative changes and does not show actual change in variables.

(ii) It does not consider qualitative changes.

(iii) It is affected by extreme values and manipulation of the results is possible.

(iv) Index numbers are based on selected items and not all items, thus, these are correct only on an average.

(v) It is not rigidly defined; different methods are used for different purposes which gives different results.

18. Why is the CPI increasingly referred to as a measure of inflation?

Ans. The CPI is increasingly used as a measure of inflation because it directly reflects changes in the cost of living for consumers by tracking price changes in goods and services they commonly purchase. This makes it a relevant and timely indicator of inflationary trends in the economy.

19. "Index numbers measures the changes in the variables under study." Name some of the variables in which the changes are studied. Competency Based Que

Ans. Some of the variables in which changes are studied with the help of index numbers are

(i) Prices of commodities like wheat, gold, steel, consumer goods, cereals, etc.

(ii) Volume of trade, factory production, industrial and agriculture production, exports or imports, prices of stocks or shares, sales and profits of a firm, etc.

(iii) National income of a country, wage structure of workers in various sectors, cost of living of persons of a particular community, class or profession, etc.

20. Write any three uses of index number especially in economics.

Ans. Uses of index number are

(i) Index numbers are helpful in measuring the purchasing power, i.e. value of the money.

(ii) These numbers are used to measure level of economic activities like import, export, production, population, etc.

(iii) These numbers are helpful in evaluating economic policy. e.g. Index number helps in knowing the effect of export policy on export.

Long Answer Type Questions

21. Why do we need an index number? NCERT

Ans. Index numbers are needed because of the various advantages which pertain to the use of index numbers. These advantages are

(i) **Barometer of Economic Progress**
Index numbers are a barometer for measuring the value of money and assessing the level of economic progress.

(ii) **Importance for the Government**
The government adopts suitable monetary and fiscal policies according to the changes in index numbers.

(iii) **Throws Light on Economic Condition**
Index numbers are very helpful in comparing the economic condition of a particular group of people across two time periods.

(iv) **Fixation of Wages and Policy-making**
Index numbers such as CPI and WPI help the government and executives for the fixation and revision of wages.

(v) **Importance for the Producer**
Price index number helps the producers to decide whether they should expand or contract the level of production.

(vi) **Measure to Remove Inequality of Income**
Index numbers like WPI indicate about regional disparity.
This helps government to take different measures to ensure that inequalities in income are checked.

22. What do you understand by absolute change, relative change and net change?

Ans. **Absolute change** is the actual difference between the price of a good/service in current year as compared to base year.

e.g. The price of sugar in 2010 was ₹ 15 per kg and in 2016 is ₹ 42 per kg. So, absolute change in price is ₹ 27 per kg (42-15).

Relative change is the percentage increase or decrease between the price of a good/service in current year as compared to base year. In case of the example discussed above, the relative change in the price of sugar will be 180%, which is computed with the help of given formula,

$$\text{Relative Change} = \frac{\text{Change in Price}}{\text{Price in Base Year}} \times 100$$

$$= \frac{27}{15} \times 100 = 180\%$$

Net change is the average of the percentage change in the prices of goods or services in the current year as compared to a base year.

e.g. Price of sugar increases by 180% and price of oil increases by 40%. So, on an whole, the net change in prices is 110% $\left[\frac{180+40}{2}\right]$.

23. List the advantages/uses of index number.

Ans. Advantages/Uses of index numbers are as follows

(i) **Barometer of Economic Progress**
Index numbers act as a barometer, measuring the value of money and assessing economic progress over time. By comparing the value of money across different years, one can easily determine whether a country is progressing (when the value rises) or regressing (when the value falls).

(ii) **Importance for the Government**
Changes in the value of money directly affect the public, prompting the government to adjust its fiscal and monetary policies based on the results provided by index numbers.

(iii) **Insight into Economic Conditions**
Index numbers are crucial for comparing the economic conditions of specific groups of people across different time periods, offering valuable insights into their well-being.

(iv) **Wage Fixation and Policy-making**
Index numbers, particularly the cost of living index, guide the government and executives in setting and revising wages. They help ensure that wages align with changes in living costs.

(v) **Importance for Producers**
The price index number helps producers decide on production levels. A rising price level suggests higher profit margins, encouraging increased production.

(vi) **Tool for Addressing Income Inequality**
The wholesale price index can highlight regional disparities, aiding in the implementation of measures to distribute wealth more evenly and reduce income inequality.

24. Explain briefly the process of data collection for Consumer Price Index (CPI).

Ans. Primary data is collected every month to compute rural and urban CPI in the following ways

(i) For CPI (rural), two villages are selected from each district. Presently, data is collected from 1181 villages. Number of items for price data collection is identified through the market survey and it is around 225. Price data is collected from selected shops in the villages every month by the department of posts.

(ii) For CPI (urban), data is collected from all cities, having a population of more than 9 lakhs. Presently, total number of selected cities is 310. Number of items for price data collection is identified through the market survey and it is around 250. Each selected market is visited every month for price data collection from shops and outlets.

(iii) 4.75 lakh price data records collected from rural and urban areas are uploaded per month to the web portal of National Informatics Centre, which is the formal data collection arm of NSSO (National Sample Survey Organisation).

25. Discuss the construction and purpose of the Consumer Price Index (CPI).

Ans. CPI measures the average change in prices of goods and services paid by specific consumer classes in the current year compared to a base year. It serves as an indicator of inflation in a country.

Methods of Construction of Consumer Price Index (CPI)

There are two primary methods used for constructing the Consumer Price Index (CPI)

(i) **Aggregative Expenditure Method**
This method is similar to Laspeyre's method for constructing a weighted index. The CPI is calculated by taking the aggregate expenditure in the current year and comparing it with the aggregate expenditure in the base year.

$$\text{CPI} = \frac{\Sigma p_1 q_0}{\Sigma p_0 q_0} \times 100$$

Here,
$\Sigma p_1 q_0$ = Aggregate expenditure in the current year (Sum of product of current year price with base year quantity)
$\Sigma p_0 q_0$ = Aggregate expenditure in the base year (Sum of product of base year price with base year quantity)

(ii) **Family Budget Method**
This method involves studying the family budgets of a large sample of people for whom the CPI is being constructed. The CPI is computed by estimating the aggregate expenditure of an average family on various commodities, which serves as the weights.

$$\text{CPI} = \frac{\Sigma IW}{\Sigma W}$$

Here, ΣIW = Sum of products of price relative with weights
ΣW = Sum of weights

The **purpose of CPI** is to reflect changes in the cost of living, guide wage negotiations, adjust policies for cost of living changes and analyse economic trends. It provides valuable insights into inflation and purchasing power.

26. Explain the various steps involved in the construction of index number on industrial production.

Ans. Following are the steps involved in the construction of index number on industrial production

(i) **Classification of Industries**

Major industries are grouped under the following heads

- Mining
- Manufacturing
- Electricity

(ii) **Choice of the Base Year**

The base year should be the year of economic stability. It should not be at much distance from the current year.

(iii) **Data Related to Industrial Production**

The data relating to the production of different industries are collected.

(iv) **Assigning Weights**

Weights are assigned on the basis of the relative importance of different industries. The weights are based on the values of net output of different industries, capital invested and their contribution to national income.

(v) **Formula**

Index number on industrial production is calculated by using the following formula

$$\text{Index Number} = \frac{\Sigma\left[\frac{q_1}{q_0}\times 100\right]W}{\Sigma W}$$

Here, q_1 = Current year's quantity

q_0 = Base year's quantity

W = Weights

27. What is the purpose of sensex and human development index?

Ans. Sensex

(i) It stands for the Bombay Stock Exchange (BSE) sensitive index, using 1978-79 as its base year. It serves as the benchmark index for the Indian stock market, comprising 30 prominent and financially stable companies.

(ii) **Interpretation**

- **Rising Sensex**

  Indicates improved market performance, better earnings expectations and growing investor confidence in the economy's health.

- **Falling Sensex**

  Suggests a decline in stock prices of most companies within the sensex, reflecting lower investor confidence.

Human Development Index (HDI)

(i) The Human Development Index (HDI) is an index used to evaluate the level of development in different countries.

Prepared by the United Nations (UN), it incorporates three key components

- **Per Capita Income**

  Measured in terms of Purchasing Power Parity (PPP) in US dollars.

- **Gross Enrollment Ratio and Years of Schooling**

  Reflecting the education level.

- **Life Expectancy at Birth**

  Indicating the overall health conditions.

(ii) Countries are ranked on a scale of 0 to 1 based on their HDI value, with higher values indicating better development levels.

28. An economic research firm is tasked with evaluating the effectiveness of different index numbers in analysing economic conditions overtime. The firm is comparing three types of index numbers *viz.* simple index numbers, weighted index numbers and the Consumer Price Index (CPI). **Competency Based Que**

(i) Discuss the advantages and disadvantages of using simple index numbers compared to weighted index numbers for evaluating changes in consumer prices.

(ii) Explain how the Consumer Price Index (CPI) is constructed and why it might be preferred over other index numbers for analysing inflation trends in a country.

Ans. (i) **Simple Index Numbers**

Advantages

- Simple index numbers are easy to calculate as they do not require weights or detailed data inputs.
- They treat all items equally, making it straightforward to compare price or quantity changes over time.

Disadvantages

- Simple index numbers do not account for the varying importance of different items, which can result in less realistic representations of economic changes.
- Equal treatment of all items may distort the significance of changes in major goods or services.

Weighted Index Numbers

Advantages

- Weighted index numbers reflect the relative importance of items, ensuring that significant goods or services have a proportionate impact on the index.
- They are better suited for comprehensive economic analysis and provide a more accurate representation of price or quantity changes.

Disadvantages

- Weighted index numbers are more complex to calculate as they require detailed data on weights, quantities and prices.
- The results may be misleading if the weights used are outdated or incorrect, reducing the reliability of the index.

(ii) **Construction of CPI**

The Consumer Price Index (CPI) is constructed by selecting a fixed basket of goods and services that represents the consumption patterns of households. Family budget surveys are conducted to determine the relative importance of each item in the basket, and weights are assigned accordingly. Retail prices for these goods and services are collected from various regions at regular intervals to track changes in the overall cost of the basket over time.

Preference for CPI

The CPI is preferred for analysing inflation because it effectively reflects changes in the cost of living for different consumer groups.

It provides valuable insights into price trends at the consumer level, making it a critical tool for policy-makers to adjust wages, pensions and other financial policies to mitigate the impact of inflation on the population.

Numerical Questions

Numerical 1

Using the simple aggregative method, calculate the index number for the given data.

	A	B	C	D
p_1	15	22	20	27
p_0	10	20	18	25

Sol. **Construction of Index Number**

Commodity	p_0 (Base Year)	p_1 (Current Year)
A	10	15
B	20	22
C	18	20
D	25	27
	$\Sigma p_0 = 73$	$\Sigma p_1 = 84$

$$P_{01} = \frac{\Sigma p_1}{\Sigma p_0} \times 100 = \frac{84}{73} \times 100 = 115.07$$

Numerical 2

Construct index number of 2015 from the given data by the simple aggregative method and the simple average of relative method.

Commodity	A	B	C	D	E	F
Price in 2015 (₹)	10	18	16	14	12	17
Price in 2010 (₹)	8	15	12	10	8	12.5

Sol. **Construction of Index Number**

Commodity	Price in 2010 (₹) (p_0)	Price in 2015 (₹) (p_1)	$I\left(\frac{p_1}{p_0} \times 100\right)$
A	8	10	125
B	15	18	120
C	12	16	133.3
D	10	14	140
E	8	12	150
F	12.5	17	136
$n=6$	$\Sigma p_0 = 65.5$	$\Sigma p_1 = 87$	$\Sigma I = 804.3$

Simple Aggregative Method

$$P_{01} = \frac{\Sigma p_1}{\Sigma p_0} \times 100 = \frac{87}{65.5} \times 100 = 132.8$$

Simple Average of Relative Method

$$P_{01} = \frac{\Sigma I}{n} = \frac{804.3}{6} = 134.05$$

Numerical 3

Construct the index number by simple average of price relative method and by simple aggregative method.

Commodity	A	B	C	D	E
Price in 2014 (₹)	16	40	35	5.25	2
Price in 2015 (₹)	20	60	50	6.25	1.5

Sol. **Construction of Index Number**

Commodity	Price in 2014 (₹) (p_0)	Price in 2015 (₹) (p_1)	$I\left(\frac{p_1}{p_0} \times 100\right)$
A	16	20	125
B	40	60	150
C	35	50	142.9
D	5.25	6.25	119.05
E	2	1.50	75
$n=5$	$\Sigma p_0 = 98.25$	$\Sigma p_1 = 137.75$	$\Sigma I = 611.95$

Simple Average of Price Relative Method

$$P_{01} = \frac{\Sigma I}{n} = \frac{611.95}{5} = 122.39$$

Simple Aggregative Method

$$P_{01} = \frac{\Sigma p_1}{\Sigma p_0} \times 100 = \frac{137.75}{98.25} \times 100 = 140.20$$

Numerical 4

In the weighted average of price relatives method, the price relative for item A is 120 and for item B is 130. The weights for items A and B are 3 and 2, respectively. Calculate the weighted index number.

Sol. Weighted Index Number

$$= \frac{\Sigma\,(\text{Price Relative} \times \text{Weight})}{\Sigma\ \text{Weights}}$$

$$= \frac{(120 \times 3) + (130 \times 2)}{3 + 2} = \frac{360 + 260}{5}$$

$$= \frac{620}{5} = 124$$

Numerical 5

Using Laspeyre's method, if the base year prices and quantities of item X are 10 and 5 units and current year prices and quantities are 12 and 6 units, calculate the Laspeyre's index.

Sol. Laspeyre's Index

$$= \frac{\text{Sum of (Current Year Prices} \times \text{Base Year Quantities)}}{\text{Sum of (Base Year Prices} \times \text{Base Year Quantities)}} \times 100$$

$$= \frac{(12 \times 5)}{(10 \times 5)} \times 100 = \frac{60}{50} \times 100 = 120$$

Numerical 6

Calculate the weighted average of price relative index for 2016 on the basis of 2012 from the following data

Commodity	W	p_0 2012	p_1 2016
A	10	15	20
B	8	10	12
C	6	5	8
D	6	10	13
E	4	4	5

Sol. **Construction of Weighted Index Number**

Commodity	W	Price in (₹) (p_0) 2012	Price in (₹) (p_1) 2016	$I\left(\frac{p_1}{p_0} \times 100\right)$	IW
A	10	15	20	133.33	1,333
B	8	10	12	120.00	960
C	6	5	8	160.00	960
D	6	10	13	130.00	780
E	4	4	5	125.00	500
	ΣW =34				ΣIW =4,533

$$P_{01} = \frac{\Sigma IW}{\Sigma W} = \frac{4{,}533}{34} = 133.3$$

Numerical 7

Construct index number of price for the year price of 2016 from the following data by

(i) Laspeyre's method (ii) Paasche's method

(iii) Fisher's method

Commodity	2008		2016	
	Price	Quantity	Price	Quantity
A	10	30	12	35
B	9	10	11	15
C	8	15	10	20
D	6	20	7	25

Sol. **Construction of Price Index Number**

Commodity	2008 (Base Year)		2016 (Current Year)		p_0q_0	p_0q_1	p_1q_0	p_1q_1
	p_0	q_0	p_1	q_1				
A	10	30	12	35	300	350	360	420
B	9	10	11	15	90	135	110	165
C	8	15	10	20	120	160	150	200
D	6	20	7	25	120	150	140	175
					Σp_0q_0 =630	Σp_0q_1 =795	Σp_1q_0 =760	Σp_1q_1 =960

(i) **Laspeyre's Method**

$$P_{01} = \frac{\Sigma p_1 q_0}{\Sigma p_0 q_0} \times 100 = \frac{760}{630} \times 100 = 120.63$$

(ii) **Paasche's Method**

$$P_{01} = \frac{\Sigma p_1 q_1}{\Sigma p_0 q_1} \times 100 = \frac{960}{795} \times 100 = 120.75$$

(iii) **Fisher's Method**

$$P_{01} = \sqrt{\frac{\Sigma p_1 q_0}{\Sigma p_0 q_0} \times \frac{\Sigma p_1 q_1}{\Sigma p_0 q_1}} \times 100 = \sqrt{\frac{760}{630} \times \frac{960}{795}} \times 100$$

$$= \sqrt{1.206 \times 1.207} \times 100$$

$$= \sqrt{1.455} \times 100 = 1.2065 \times 100 = 120.65$$

Numerical 8

The monthly per capita expenditure incurred by workers for an industrial centre during 1980 and 2005 on the following items are given below. The weights of these items are 75, 10, 5, 6 and 4, respectively. Prepare a weighted index number for cost of living for 2005 with 1980 as base. NCERT

Item	Price in 1980	Price in 2005
Food	100	200
Clothing	20	25
Fuel and Lighting	15	20
House Rent	30	40
Miscellaneous	35	65

Sol. **Construction of Consumer Price Index**

Item	W	Price in 1980 (₹) (p_0)	Price in 2005 (₹) (p_1)	I $\left(\frac{p_1}{p_0} \times 100\right)$	IW
Food	75	100	200	200.00	15,000
Clothing	10	20	25	125.00	1,250
Fuel and Lighting	5	15	20	133.33	666.65
House Rent	6	30	40	133.33	799.98
Miscella-neous	4	35	65	185.71	742.84
	$\Sigma W = 100$				$\Sigma IW = 18{,}459.47$

$$\text{CPI} = \frac{\Sigma IW}{\Sigma W} = \frac{18{,}459.47}{100} = 184.59 = 185 \text{ (approx)}$$

Numerical 9

If the salary of a person in the base year is ₹ 4,000 per annum and the current year salary is ₹ 6,000, by how much should his salary be raised to maintain the same standard of living, if the CPI is 400? NCERT

Sol. Base year salary = ₹ 4,000, Base year index = 100 (assumption), Current year index = 400

Salary required in the current year to maintain the same standard of living of base year

$$= \text{Base Year Salary} \times \frac{\text{CPI of Current Year}}{\text{CPI of Base Year}}$$

$$= 4{,}000 \times \frac{400}{100}$$

$$= ₹\ 16{,}000$$

Current year salary = ₹ 6,000

The increase in current salary required

$$= 16{,}000 - 6{,}000$$

$$= ₹\ 10{,}000$$

Numerical 10

An enquiry into the budgets of the middle class families in a certain city gave the following information

Expenses on Items	Fuel 10%	Clothing 20%	Rent 15%	Food 35%	Miscellaneous 20%
Price in 2004 (₹)	250	750	300	1,500	400
Price in 1995 (₹)	200	500	200	1,400	250

What is the cost of living index during the year 2004 as compared with 1995? NCERT

Sol. **Construction of Consumer Price Index**

Item	W (%)	Price in 1995 (₹) (p_0)	Price in 2004 (₹) (p_1)	$I\left(\frac{p_1}{p_0} \times 100\right)$	IW
Food	35	1,400	1,500	107.14	3,750 (approx)
Fuel	10	200	250	125.00	1,250
Clothing	20	500	750	150.00	3,000
Rent	15	200	300	150.00	2,250
Miscella-neous	20	250	400	160.00	3,200
	$\Sigma W = 100$				$\Sigma IW = 13{,}450$

$$\text{CPI} = \frac{\Sigma IW}{\Sigma W} = \frac{13{,}450}{100} = 134.5$$

This result indicates that the CPI in the year 2004 has increased by 34.5% as compared to the year 1995.

Numerical 11

The price quotation of different commodities for 2014 and 2015 are given below. Calculate the index number for 2015 with 2014 as base year by using

(i) Simple average of price relative **(ii) Weighted average of price relative**

Commodity	Unit	Weight	Price (₹) 2014	Price (₹) 2015
A	kg	5	2.00	4.50
B	quintal	7	2.50	3.20
C	dozen	6	3.00	3.50
D	kg	2	1.00	1.80

Sol.

Construction of Weighted Index Number

Commodity	Weight (W)	Price in 2014 (p_0)	Price in 2015 (p_1)	$I\left(\frac{p_1}{p_0}\times 100\right)$	IW
A	5	2.00	4.50	$\frac{4.50}{2.0}\times 100 = 225$	1,125.00
B	7	2.50	3.20	$\frac{3.20}{2.50}\times 100 = 128$	896.00
C	6	3.00	3.50	$\frac{3.50}{3.00}\times 100 = 116.67$	700.02
D	2	1.00	1.80	$\frac{1.80}{1.00}\times 100 = 180$	360.00
$n = 4$	$\Sigma W = 20$			$\Sigma I = 649.67$	$\Sigma IW = 3{,}081.02$

(i) Simple Average of Price Relative Method $P_{01} = \frac{\Sigma I}{n} = \frac{649.67}{4} = 162.42$

(ii) Weighted Average of Price Relative Method $P_{01} = \frac{\Sigma IW}{\Sigma W} = \frac{3{,}081.02}{20} = 154.051$

Numerical 12

Calculate the cost of living index number using family budget method.

Commodity	Wheat	Rice	Pulses	Ghee	Sugar	Oil	Fuel	Clothes
Units Consumed in Base Year	200	50	56	20	40	50	60	40
Price in ₹ (Base Year)	1.0	3.0	4.0	20.0	2.5	10.0	2.0	15.0
Price in ₹ (Current Year)	1.2	3.5	5.0	30.0	5.0	15.5	2.5	18.0

Sol.

Construction of Cost of Living Index Number

Commodity	Unit Consumed in Base Year (p_0)	Price in Base Year (₹) (p_0)	Price in Current Year (₹) (p_1)	$I\left(\frac{p_1}{p_0}\times 100\right)$	$W(p_0 q_0)$	IW
Wheat	200	1.0	1.2	120.00	200	24,000
Rice	50	3.0	3.5	116.67	150	17,500.5
Pulses	56	4.0	5.0	125.00	224	28,000
Ghee	20	20.0	30.0	150.00	400	60,000
Sugar	40	2.5	5.0	200.00	100	20,000
Oil	50	10.0	15.5	155.00	500	77,500
Fuel	60	2.0	2.5	125.00	120	15,000
Clothes	40	15.0	18.0	120.00	600	72,000
					$\Sigma W = 2{,}294$	$\Sigma IW = 3{,}14{,}000.5$

$$\text{CPI} = \frac{\Sigma IW}{\Sigma W} = \frac{3,14,000.5}{2,294} = 136.88$$

This result indicates that CPI in the current year has increased by 36.88% as compared to the base period.

Numerical 13

Given the following data

Year	1995-96	1996-97	1997-98	1998-99	1999-2000	2000-01	2001-02	2002-03
WPI (1993-94)	121.6	127.2	132.8	140.7	145.7	155.7	161.3	166.8

Calculate the inflation rate and interpret the result.

Sol. Rate of Inflation $= \frac{X_t - X_{t-1}}{X_{t-1}} \times 100$

Inflation rate for different years are calculated as

Year 1996-97 $= \frac{127.2 - 121.6}{121.6} \times 100 = 4.6\%$

Year 1997-98 $= \frac{132.8 - 127.2}{127.2} \times 100 = 4.40\%$

Year 1998-99 $= \frac{140.7 - 132.8}{132.8} \times 100 = 5.94\%$

Year 1999-2000 $= \frac{145.7 - 140.7}{140.7} \times 100 = 3.55\%$

Year 2000-01 $= \frac{155.7 - 145.7}{145.7} \times 100 = 6.86\%$

Year 2001-02 $= \frac{161.3 - 155.7}{155.7} \times 100 = 3.59\%$

Year 2002-03 $= \frac{166.8 - 161.3}{161.3} \times 100 = 3.40\%$

There are many ups and downs in the rate of inflation based on WPI.

Numerical 14

A department store sells stereo systems, television sets and radios. The percentage distribution of the total sales volume (in ₹) is estimated as 30% stereos, 50% televisions and 20% radios. The price of one stereo, one television and one radio in 2009 was ₹ 20,000, ₹ 15,000 and ₹ 500 respectively, while their respective price in 2012 were ₹ 25,000, ₹ 20,000 and ₹ 800. A weighted price index for 2012 with base 2009 is to be computed.

(i) Which index number formula is appropriate? Why?

(ii) Compute the index.

Sol. (i) Here, weighted average of price relative method is appropriate because the relative importance or contribution of various products, i.e. stereo systems, televisions and radios, to the total sales volume is to be considered.

(ii) **Construction of Weighted Index Number**

Product	Weight (W)	Price in 2009 (₹) (p_0)	Price in 2012 (₹) (p_1)	$I\left(\frac{p_1}{p_0} \times 100\right)$	IW
Stereo	30	20,000	25,000	$\frac{25,000}{20,000} \times 100 = 125$	3,750
Television	50	15,000	20,000	$\frac{20,000}{15,000} \times 100 = 133.3$	6,665
Radio	20	500	800	$\frac{800}{500} \times 100 = 160$	3,200
	$\Sigma W = 100$				$\Sigma IW = 13,615$

Hence, the weighted price index for 2012 with base 2009, is given by $P_{01} = \frac{\Sigma IW}{\Sigma W} = \frac{13,615}{100} = 136.15$

Numerical 15

In the WPI calculation, if the weights for two commodities are 40% and 60%, and their price relatives are 110 and 120 respectively, calculate the weighted WPI.

Sol. Weighted WPI $= (\text{Price Relative}_1 \times \text{Weight}_1) + (\text{Price Relative}_2 \times \text{Weight}_2)$

$= (110 \times 0.4) + (120 \times 0.6) = 44 + 72 = 116$

Numerical 16

For the index of industrial production, if the quantity produced in the base year is 1,000 units and in the current year is 1,200 units, and the weight is 50, calculate the IIP.

Sol. $\text{IIP} = \frac{\text{Quantity in Current Year}}{\text{Quantity in Base Year}} \times 100 = \frac{1,200}{1,000} \times 100 = 120$

Numerical 17

A price index of two items of A and B is being estimated. If two items are assigned weights of 64 and 36 respectively, then the price index becomes 279. Similarly, if they are assigned weights of 50 each, then the price index turns out to be 265. Determine the individual price index number of items A and B.

Sol. There are two situations in the given conditions. Let I_1 be the index for the first item and I_2 be the index for the second item.

First Situation

$$279 = \frac{64I_1 + 36I_2}{64 + 36} \quad \left[\because P_{01} = \frac{I_1W_1 + I_2W_2}{W_1 + W_2}\right] \quad \ldots\text{(i)}$$

Second Situation $$265 = \frac{50I_1 + 50I_2}{50 + 50} \quad \ldots\text{(ii)}$$

From equation (i), $64I_1 + 36I_2 = 27,900$

$\Rightarrow \quad 16I_1 + 9I_2 = 6,975 \quad \ldots\text{(iii)}$

From equation (ii), $I_1 + I_2 = 530 \quad \ldots\text{(iv)}$

On solving equation (iii) and equation (iv), we get

$$I_1 = 315, I_2 = 215$$

Numerical 18

The monthly expenditure (₹) of a family on some important items and the Goods and Services Tax (GST) rates applicable to these items is as follows **NCERT**

Item	Monthly Expense (₹)	GST Rate %
Cereals	1,500	0
Eggs	250	0
Fish, meat	250	0
Medicines	50	5
Biogas	50	5
Transport	100	5
Butter	50	12
Babool	10	12
Tomato ketchup	40	12
Biscuits	75	18
Cakes, pastries	25	18
Branded garments	100	18
Vacuum cleaner, car	1,000	28

Calculate the average tax rate as far as this family is concerned.

Sol.

Category	Expenditure Weight (W)	GST Rate (X)	WX
Category 1	2,000	0	0
Category 2	200	0.05	10
Category 3	100	0.12	12
Category 4	200	0.18	36
Category 5	1,000	0.28	280
	$\Sigma W = 3,500$		$\Sigma WX = 338$

Note Goods with 0% tax rates are combined together and goods with 5% tax are combined together and so on. Also, tax rates are in percentage to 5% is taken as 0.05 and so on.

Average tax rate $= \frac{338}{3,500} \times 100 = 9.66\%$

Average tax $= 0.966$

Numerical 19

Given the following data

Year	CPI of Industrial Worker (1982 =100)	CPI of Agricultural Labourer (1986-87 = 100)	WPI (1993-94 = 100)
1995-96	313	234	121.6
1996-97	342	256	127.2
1997-98	366	264	132.8
1998-99	414	293	140.7
1999-2000	428	306	145.3
2000-01	444	306	155.7
2001-02	463	309	161.3
2002-03	482	319	166.8
2003-04	500	331	175.9

Source *Economic Survey, 2004-2005, Government of India*

(i) Comment on the relative values of the index numbers.

(ii) Are they comparable? **NCERT**

Sol. (i) **Inflation Using CPI of Industrial Workers**

Year	CPI of Industrial Workers (1982 = 100)	Inflation Rate (in %) $\left(\frac{X_t - X_{t-1}}{X_{t-1}} \times 100\right)$
1995-96	313	—
1996-97	342	$\frac{342 - 313}{313} \times 100 = 9.26\%$
1997-98	366	$\frac{366 - 342}{342} \times 100 = 7.02\%$

Year	CPI of Industrial Workers (1982 = 100)	Inflation Rate (in %) $\left(\frac{X_t - X_{t-1}}{X_{t-1}} \times 100\right)$
1998-99	414	$\frac{414 - 366}{366} \times 100 = 13.11\%$
1999-2000	428	$\frac{428 - 414}{414} \times 100 = 3.38\%$
2000-01	444	$\frac{444 - 428}{428} \times 100 = 3.74\%$
2001-02	463	$\frac{463 - 444}{444} \times 100 = 4.28\%$
2002-03	482	$\frac{482 - 463}{463} \times 100 = 4.10\%$
2003-04	500	$\frac{500 - 482}{482} \times 100 = 3.73\%$

Inflation Using CPI of Non-manual Employees

Year	**CPI of Non-manual Employee** (1986 = 100)	**Inflation Rate** (in %) $\left(\frac{X_t - X_{t-1}}{X_{t-1}} \times 100\right)$
1995-96	257	—
1996-97	283	$\frac{283 - 257}{257} \times 100 = 10.12\%$
1997-98	302	$\frac{302 - 283}{283} \times 100 = 6.71\%$
1998-99	337	$\frac{337 - 302}{302} \times 100 = 11.59\%$
1999-2000	352	$\frac{352 - 337}{337} \times 100 = 4.45\%$
2000-01	352	$\frac{352 - 352}{352} \times 100 = 0\%$
2001-02	390	$\frac{390 - 352}{352} \times 100 = 10.80\%$
2002-03	405	$\frac{405 - 390}{390} \times 100 = 3.85\%$
2003–04	420	$\frac{420 - 405}{405} \times 100 = 3.70\%$

Inflation Using CPI of Agricultural Labourers

Year	CPI of Agricultural Labourer (1986-87=100)	Inflation Rate (in %) $\left(\frac{X_t - X_{t-1}}{X_{t-1}} \times 100\right)$
1995-96	234	—
1996-97	256	$\frac{256 - 234}{234} \times 100 = 9.40\%$
1997-98	264	$\frac{264 - 256}{256} \times 100 = 3.13\%$
1998-99	293	$\frac{293 - 264}{264} \times 100 = 10.98\%$
1999-2000	306	$\frac{306 - 293}{293} \times 100 = 4.44\%$
2000-01	306	$\frac{306 - 306}{306} \times 100 = 0\%$
2001-02	309	$\frac{309 - 306}{306} \times 100 = 0.98\%$
2002-03	319	$\frac{319 - 309}{309} \times 100 = 3.24\%$
2003-04	331	$\frac{331 - 319}{319} \times 100 = 3.76\%$

Inflation Using WPI

Year	**WPI** (1993-94 = 100)	**Inflation Rate** (in %) $\left(\frac{X_t - X_{t-1}}{X_{t-1}} \times 100\right)$
1995-96	121.6	—
1996-97	127.2	$\frac{127.2 - 121.6}{121.6} \times 100 = 4.61\%$
1997-98	132.8	$\frac{132.8 - 127.2}{127.2} \times 100 = 4.40\%$
1998-99	140.7	$\frac{140.7 - 132.8}{132.8} \times 100 = 5.94\%$
1999-2000	145.3	$\frac{145.3 - 140.7}{140.7} \times 100 = 3.27\%$
2000-01	155.7	$\frac{155.7 - 145.3}{145.3} \times 100 = 7.15\%$
2001-02	161.3	$\frac{161.3 - 155.7}{155.7} \times 100 = 3.60\%$
2002-03	166.8	$\frac{166.8 - 161.3}{161.3} \times 100 = 3.41\%$
2003-04	175.9	$\frac{175.9 - 166.8}{166.8} \times 100 = 5.45\%$

The relative value of index number implies the percentage change in the value of the index number of a year, as compared to the previous year. The rate of inflation represents the relative value of the index number. The relative value of all the four index numbers show no fix trend.

(ii) No, the index numbers are not comparable because of the following reasons

- Base periods for CPI of industrial workers, urban non-manual workers, agricultural labourers and WPI are different.
- Commodities and their weightage in different index numbers may be different.

SELF ASSESSMENT TEST

Objective Type Questions

1. "An index number is a unit-free measure, expressed as a ratio between a current period and a base period."

   What is an index number primarily used for?

   (a) To measure changes in the magnitude of unrelated variables over multiple time periods
   (b) To analyse the relationship between different goods and services in a single time period
   (c) To measure changes in the magnitude of a group of related variables, such as price and quantity of goods and services, over two different time periods
   (d) To calculate the total value of goods and services in an economy

2. What is the primary consideration when selecting items for an index number?

   (a) The items must include every possible commodity, regardless of relevance
   (b) The items should be relevant, standardised and represent a typical diet or consumption pattern
   (c) The items must only include luxurious goods to reflect economic trends
   (d) The number of commodities must always be as large as possible to ensure accuracy

3. A .... is the reference date from which an index number is calculated.

   (a) base period (b) index number
   (c) CPI (d) wholesale number

4. Which index number measure changes in the quantity of goods produced during the periods under review?

   (a) Price index numbers
   (b) Value index numbers
   (c) Ratio index numbers
   (d) Quantity index numbers

5. Which of the following statements about the commodity groups in the Wholesale Price Index (WPI) is correct?

   (a) The 'primary articles' group includes 564 commodities with a total weightage of 64.23%
   (b) 'Fuel and power' comprises 16 items like coal, petroleum products and electricity, with a total weightage of 13.15%
   (c) 'Manufactured products' consist of 117 commodities and have a total weightage of 22.62%
   (d) All commodity groups in WPI are given equal weightage

Answers 1. (c) 2. (b) 3.(a) 4. (d) 5. (b)

Short Answer Type Questions

6. What is a base period? Give example.
7. "Fisher's method is considered as an ideal method of calculating index numbers." Why? Give reasons
8. Define the following

   (i) Consumer price index (ii) Wholesale price index
9. Explain Human Development Index (HDI) with example.

Long Answer Type Question

10. Mr. Arjun is an economics student preparing for a major presentation on the uses of index numbers in economics. To make his presentation comprehensive, he decides to explore the Consumer Price Index (CPI), Wholesale Price Index (WPI), Index of Industrial Production (IIP), agricultural production index and the sensex.

    While exploring these indices, Arjun learns that the CPI has multiple applications, WPI, on the other hand, is critical for analysing how price changes affect the economy's aggregates like national income and capital formation. He also discovers that the IIP and agricultural production index measure industrial and agricultural performance, respectively. Lastly, the sensex, which reflects investor sentiment, can provide valuable insights into whether it is a good time to invest in the stock market.

    (i) What is one key use of the Consumer Price Index (CPI)?
    (ii) How are the Wholesale Price Index (WPI) and the Index of Industrial Production (IIP) helpful in economic analysis?
    (iii) Discuss how a rising Sensex can influence investor decisions and how it relates to the future performance of the economy?

Numerical Questions

11. The monthly wage income of a worker increases from ₹ 3,500 in 2000-01 to ₹ 5,500 in 2006-07. Consumer price index during this period also rises from 100 to 200. Calculate real money wage of the worker.

Ans. ₹ 2,750

Hint Real Wage

$$= \frac{\text{Wage in Current Year} \times \text{CPI of Current Year}}{\text{CPI of Base Year}}$$

12. Compute index number for 1996 taking 1985 as the base year, using simple aggregative method.

Commodity	A	B	C	D	E
Price in 1980	80	60	50	40	20
Price in 1993	100	80	70	50	10

Ans. ₹ 124

13. Construct index of industrial production on the basis of following information

Goods	Quantity (Million Tonne)		Weight
	Base Year (q_0)	Current Year (q_1)	
Mining	50	60	10
Manufacturedg oods	120	200	80
Electricity	200	300	10

Ans. 160.33

14. Following are the price of commodities in the years 2001 and 2005. Calculate the price index using price relative method.

Commodity	Price in 2001	Price in 2005
A	45	55
B	60	70
C	20	30
D	50	75
E	85	90
F	120	130

Ans. Index number = 125.51

15. The following table contains information from the raw material purchase records of a small factory for the years 2000 and 2005

Commodity	Year 2000		Year 2005	
	Price (₹/unit) (p_0)	Total Value	Price (₹/unit) (p_1)	Total Value
A	5	50	6	72
B	7	84	10	80
C	10	80	12	96
D	4	20	5	30
E	8	56	8	64

Calculate Fisher's ideal index number.

Ans. Fisher's ideal index number = 121.49

Hint Quantity will be computed by dividing total value by price per unit.

16. Construct cost of index number for 2006 on the basis of 1994 from the following data using family budget method.

Article	Quantity (in kg)	Price (in ₹)	
		1994	2006
A	10	20	30
B	7	21	28
C	5	20	25
D	2	10	12
E	2	6	8

Ans. Consumer price index number = 137.11

Hint Quantity given is taken as weights.

17. Construct the index of industrial production from the following data.

Industry	Output (in tonne)		Weight
	2002	2005	
Mining	120	180	25
Electrical Products	200	290	45
Manufactured Goods	150	220	30

Ans. Index of industrial production = 146.75

18. Calculate weighted average of price relative index number of price for 2003 on the basis of 1999 from the following data.

Commodity	Quantity in 1999	Price in 1999 (in ₹)	Price in 2003 (in ₹)
A	20	20	35
B	12	15	18
C	8	10	11
D	4	5	5
E	6	4	5

Ans. Index number = 139.4

19. Compute Paasche's and Laspeyre's index number from the following data.

Commodity	Base Year		Current Year	
	Quantity	Price	Quantity	Price
A	40	4	35	3
B	15	3	20	4
C	20	6	15	5
D	30	5	25	2

Ans. Paasche's index = 74.70; Laspeyre's index = 71.58

20. Price quotations of four different articles for 1951 and 1965 are given below. With 1951 as the base year, find the price index number for 1965, using

(i) Simple average of relative (ii) Weighted average of relative

Group	Weight	1965	1951
A	5	4.50	2.00
B	7	3.20	2.50
C	6	4.50	3.00
D	2	1.80	1.00

Ans. (i) 170.75 (ii) 164.05

PART : B

INTRODUCTORY MICROECONOMICS

01

CHAPTER

This chapter introduces the study of economics, focusing on the challenges of meeting unlimited human needs with limited resources. It emphasises the concept of scarcity and need for making choices among alternative uses of resources.

Economics, Economy and its Central Problems

▼ **YOUR STUDY GOALS**

1.1 Introduction to Economics
1.2 Economy
1.3 Central Problems of an Economy
1.4 Production Possibility Frontier (PPF)

▼ **YOUR PRACTICE GOAL**

- Objective Type Questions (60 Qs ; MCQs, A-R, Statements, Matching, Concept Identification)
- Subjective Questions (24 SAs, 6 LAs)
- 5 Numerical Questions
- Self Assessment Test (8 MCQs, 6 SAs, 2 LAs 2 Numericals)

1.1 Introduction to Economics

Economics is concerned with the study of economic issues or problems that arise because of the fact that our needs are unlimited but the resources which satisfy these needs are scarce, i.e. limited. Also, the resources have alternative uses, i.e. one resource can be put to multiple uses.

Thus, economics is about making choices in the backdrop of scarcity.

e.g. Coal is an important source of energy in India. However, it's supply is limited, as it is a natural resource with multiple uses. This is one of the most relevant cases of scarcity of resource with alternative uses.

Scarcity

Scarcity refers to the situation where the supply of a good or service is less than the demand for it. This fundamental concept drives economic problems and decisions.

Scarcity leads to higher prices, as seen in case of diamonds and natural resources like petroleum and oil. Effective management of these scarce resources is crucial to ensuring their availability for future generations.

Scarce Resource

Oil is a finite natural resource with limited reserves. The scarcity of oil demonstrates the economic concept of limited resources, i.e. when a resource is not abundant enough to meet the total demand, it impacts its price, availability and the decisions made by consumers and policy-makers.

Nature of Economics

Economics is a science as well as an art. As a science, the nature of economics can be studied with respect to the following two concepts

Economics as a Positive Science	Economics as a Normative Science
• This aspect focuses on objective analysis of economic issues related to past, present and future using factor and figures. • It deals with cause and effect relationships and describes economic phenomena as they are (i.e. 'what was', 'what is' and 'what will be') without making value judgements. • For instance, positive economics would study facts like the presence of unemployment or rising urban poverty in India.	• This perspective involves evaluating economic events from a moral and ethical standpoint. • It addresses what should be done (i.e. 'what ought to be') and makes value judgements about economic policies. • For instance, normative economics deals with statements like the government should implement policies to reduce unemployment or address migrant labour issues.

Subject Matter of Economics

Economics is broadly divided into two main branches

1. Microeconomics

Microeconomics focuses on economic issues at the level of an individual like individual person, individual firm, individual industry, etc. These are also termed as microeconomic variables. It examines how prices for goods and services, as well as factors of production are determined.

Key Theories of Microeconomics

- Theory of consumer behaviour
- Theory of producer behaviour
- Theory of price determination

Tools of microeconomics are demand and supply analysis.

Focus microeconomics is concerned with price determination at an individual firm or industry level, often referred to as the theory of price.

Pricing of Vegetables – Microeconomic Example

- When the supply of vegetables like tomatoes is low due to seasonal factors, local markets may increase their prices.
- Conversely, if the supply is abundant, prices might drop.
- This pricing decision is based on the demand and supply for tomatoes in that particular market, illustrating microeconomic principles.

Introduction of GST – Macroeconomics Example

- GST unified India's tax system, replacing multiple indirect taxes.
- It impacted the entire economy by simplifying taxation, improving government revenue and boosting economic growth, showcasing macroeconomic reform on a national scale.

2. Macroeconomics

Macroeconomics deals with the behaviour of the economy as a whole, studying aggregate concepts such as national income, full employment, aggregate consumption, etc. These are also termed as macroeconomic variables.

Key Theories of Macroeconomics

- Theory of equilibrium level of output and employment
- Theory of inflationary and deflationary gap in the economy
- Theory of multiplier
- Study of government budget, exchange rate and Balance of Payments (BoP)

Tools of macroeconomics are aggregate demand and aggregate supply analysis.

Focus Macroeconomics deals with the overall income determination in the economy, known as the theory of income determination.

In essence, microeconomics deals with individual and market level economic issues, while macroeconomics addresses broader economic aggregates and policies.

Interdependence

Microeconomics and Macroeconomics

Microeconomics and macroeconomics are interdependent. This can be understood with the help of following examples

- In microeconomics, law of demand came into existence through the behavioural analysis of group of individuals.
- General price level prevailing in the economy influence the price of a commodity.
- In macroeconomics, national income of a country is the sum total of income of individuals in a country.
- Aggregate demand is determined by the combined demand of individual households of the economy.

1.2 Economy

An economy is a system by which people earn their living to satisfy their needs and wants through the process of production, consumption, investment and exchange.

These core economic activities are

Activities	Description	Example
Production	The creation of utility, transforming inputs (raw materials, ideas) into goods or services.	A factory in India manufactures smartphones using raw materials and labour.
Consumption	The process of using up goods or services to satisfy human wants.	A family uses electricity in their home for daily activities.
Investment	The process of adding to the existing stock of capital for future income generation.	A company buys new machinery to increase future production capacity.
Exchange	The process of transferring ownership of goods or services from seller to buyer for a consideration.	A shop owner sells clothes to a customer in exchange for money.

Types of Economy

1. **Market Economy** In this economy, goods and resources are bought and sold freely in the market, means of production are privately owned and economic activities are guided by self-interest and profit motive. It is also known as capitalist or free economy.
2. **Centrally Planned Economy** In this economy, all economic decisions are made by the government or by an authorised central authority with a focus on social welfare.

3. **Mixed Economy** In this economy, both private and public sectors coexist, with economic decisions aimed at profit maximisation and social welfare under centralised planning.

Economy Types

- **Market Economy** In the US, businesses set their own prices for products based on supply and demand.
- **Centrally Planned Economy** In North Korea, the government controls production and pricing of all goods and services.
- **Mixed Economy** In India, both private businesses and government-owned enterprises operate together, with government regulation guiding key industries.

Economic and Non-economic Activities

- **Economic Activities** They refer to the activities which are related to the use of available scarce resources in order to earn livelihood. e.g. Production, consumption, investment and exchange.
- **Non-economic Activities** They refer to the activities which are related with maximising social welfares or which are undertaken to satisfy social, religious and cultural aspects. These are done for self-satisfaction, care, affection, etc. e.g. Prime Minister Relief Funds, Awas Yojana by Central Government, etc.

Economic Problem

An economic problem arises because it is impossible to produce enough goods to meet everyone's needs due to the scarcity of resources and their alternative uses. This creates the need to make choices about how to allocate scarce resources effectively to satisfy unlimited human wants.

Causes of Economic Problem

It arises due to the following reasons

Cause	Explanation
Human Wants are Unlimited	Human wants are unlimited. Fulfillment of one want leads to the surfacement of another want.
Economic Resources are Limited	Economic resources are limited in supply in relation to their demand. No economy can be self-sufficient in everything. Scarcity is a universal phenomenon, which continues indefinitely. It is the cause of economic problem for every country in the world.
Resources have Alternative Uses	The resources are not only scarce in supply but they also have alternative uses. e.g. Land can be used to produce wheat or rice or build a hospital or a school. A choice between the alternative uses of land has to be made. This problem of choice leads to the economic/central problems.

1.3 Central Problems of an Economy

Central problems of an economy are the problems of fuller and efficient utilisation of resources to satisfy maximum number of wants with given resources.

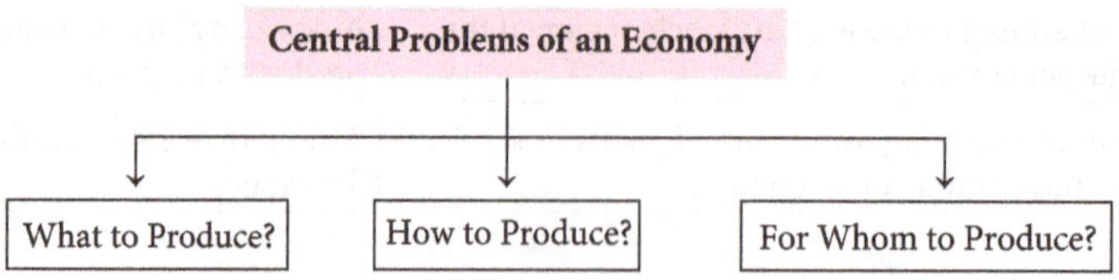

1. What to Produce?

An economy has millions of commodities to produce. It has to decide which goods and services to be produced and what should be its sufficient quantity. Thus, the problem of 'what to produce' has two dimensions i.e. **types of goods to be produced and quantity of goods to be produced.**

e.g. An economy has to decide whether to produce luxury goods or inferior goods, capital goods or consumer goods, war goods or peace goods, etc. After deciding the goods to be produced, the economy has to decide how much quantity of the decided goods to be produced.

2. How to Produce?

The problem of 'how to produce' is a problem relating to the choice of technique of production. There are two types of techniques of production, which are as follows

(i) **Labour Intensive Technique** In this technique, labour is required more than capital.

(ii) **Capital Intensive Technique** In this technique, capital is required more than labour.

e.g. In agriculture, farmers in India can choose between using manual labour to harvest crops (labour-intensive) or using machines like tractors and harvesters (capital-intensive) to improve efficiency.

3. For Whom to Produce?

This problem is related to the distribution of goods and services among the people, i.e. to select the category of people who will ultimately consume the goods produced in the economy.

Each economy has to decide whether to produce goods for rich or for the poor. If the economy produces goods for poor, then the profit of the producers would remain low, implying low GDP growth. If economy produces goods for rich people, then this will increase inequality in society.

e.g. Luxury car manufacturers like Mercedes or BMW often target affluent customers, while affordable car brands like Maruti Suzuki focus on middle-class buyers, affecting income distribution and inequality.

Note Modern economists have identified two more central economic problems, i.e. 'fuller and efficient utilisation of resources' and 'growth of resources'.

Opportunity Cost

Opportunity cost refers to the value of the next best alternative that is foregone in order to produce or obtain one commodity. Since resources are limited, it is impossible to increase the production of all goods simultaneously, making opportunity cost a critical concept in decision-making.

It highlights the trade-offs involved in choosing one option over another, making it an essential part of economic analysis. Due to its significance, opportunity cost is often called **economic cost**.

e.g. A farmer can produce 10,000 quintals of wheat on a plot of land. With the same resources, he can also produce 7,000 quintals of rice. In this case, the opportunity cost of producing 10,000 quintals of wheat is 7,000 quintals of rice.

1.4 Production Possibility Frontier (PPF)

A **Production Possibility Frontier** (PPF) is a curve that illustrates the different combinations (alternative production possibilities) of two goods that can be produced using available resources and technology. It demonstrates the trade-offs in production when resources are limited.

The PPF is also referred to as the Production Possibility Curve (PPC) or transformation curve or production boundary. It serves as a key tool for addressing central economic problems, such as what and how to produce.

The table that shows alternative production possibilities of two goods is called **production possibility schedule**.

Assumptions of PPF

- The resources available are fixed.
- The technology remains unchanged.
- The resources are fully employed.
- The resources are not equally efficient in production of all the goods. So, if resources are transferred from the production of one good to another, the marginal opportunity cost increases.

The concept of PPF can be understood with the help of following schedule and graph

Production Possibility Schedule of Wheat and Pulses

Production Possibilities	Wheat (in lakh quintal)	Pulses (in lakh quintal)	MOC
A	0	15	—
B	1	14	1:1
C	2	12	2:1
D	3	9	3:1
E	4	5	4:1
F	5	0	5:1

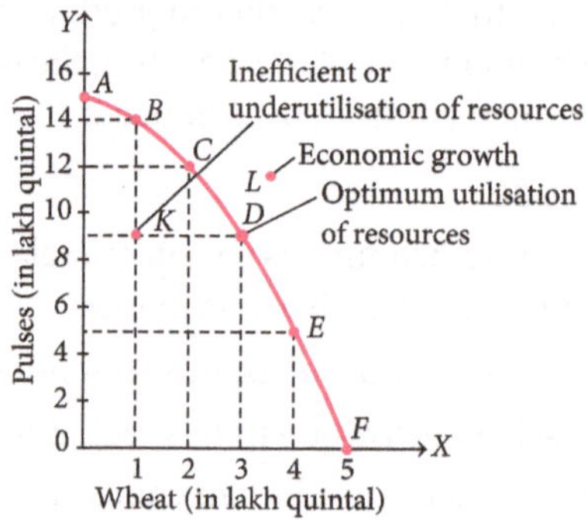

Observations

- With given resources and techniques of production, various combinations of wheat and pulses that can be produced, are A, B, C, D, E and F.
- An economy has to choose out of these various alternative production possibilities.
- In the above figure, point K (inside PPF) represents under utilisation of resources, i.e. showing unemployment. This point is **attainable** combination of output.
- Point L (outside PPF) represents over utilisation of resources, i.e. showing over employment, this point is **unattainable** unless there is a growth of resources.

Properties of Production Possibility Frontier (PPF)

1. **Downward Slope of PPF** The PPF slopes downward from left to right because to produce more of one good, the production of the other must decrease, reflecting an inverse relationship.
2. **PPF Concave to Origin** The PPF is concave to the origin. This shape indicates that the marginal opportunity cost increases as production shifts from one good to another.

***Marginal Opportunity Cost** (MOC) **or Marginal Rate of Transformation** (MRT)*

The marginal opportunity cost is the rate at which the quantity of output of one commodity is sacrificed to produce one more unit of the other commodity. Thus, MOC is calculated in terms of the loss of output of Y for every additional unit of X produced, when resources are shifted from Y to X.

$$MOC = \frac{\text{Unit of One Good Sacrificed}}{\text{More Units of Other Good Produced}} = \frac{\Delta Y}{\Delta X} \quad \text{or} \quad MOC = \frac{\text{Loss in Good Y}}{\text{Gain in Good X}}$$

Shape of PPF

The shape of PPF depends on marginal rate of transformation, as stated below

MRT is Rising	MRT is Constant	MRT is Falling
PPF will be concave to the origin which is always the case. 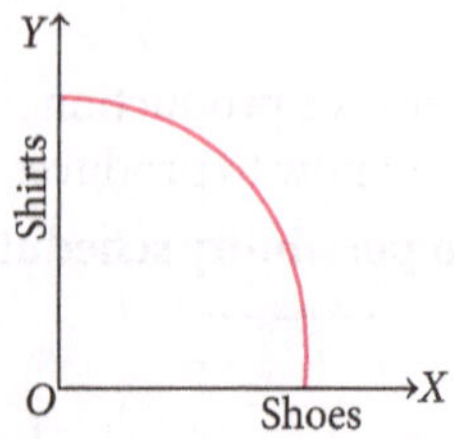 Rising MRT means that the economy is willing to sacrifice more and more units of the other good in order to produce each additional unit of first good. MRT rises as resources are not equally efficient in production of all goods.	PPF will be a straight line. 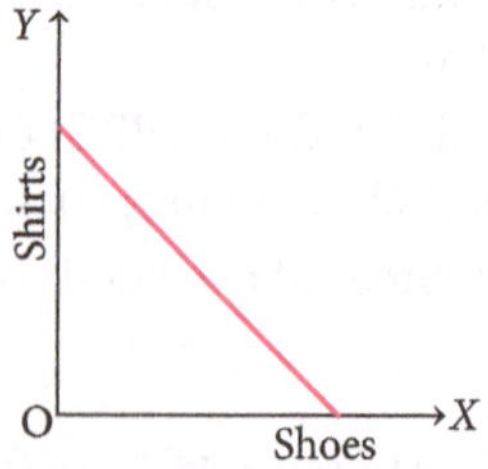 Constant MRT means economy needs to sacrifice equal quantity of other good for each additional unit of first good. This happens when resources are equally efficient.	PPF will be convex to the origin which is the best shape. 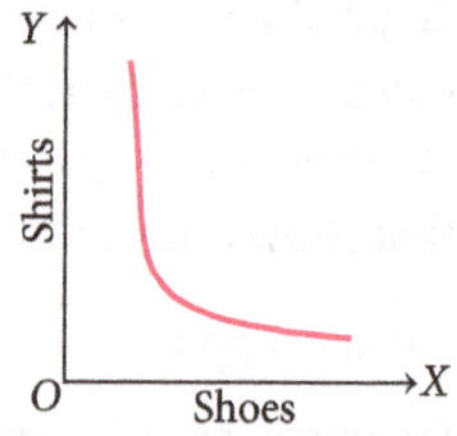 Decreasing MRT means economy needs to sacrifice lesser and lesser units of other good in order to produce each additional unit of first good. This happens when resources are inefficiently employed.

Shift of the Production Possibility Frontier

The Production Possibility Frontier (PPF) shifts based on changes in resources or technology. It can shift either rightward or leftward

1. **Rightward Shift in PPF**
    - Indicates an increase in resources or an improvement in production technology.
    - Represents the economy's enhanced ability to produce more goods.
2. **Leftward Shift in PPF**
    - Reflects a decrease in resources or a degradation in production technology.
    - Shows a reduction in the economy's production capacity.

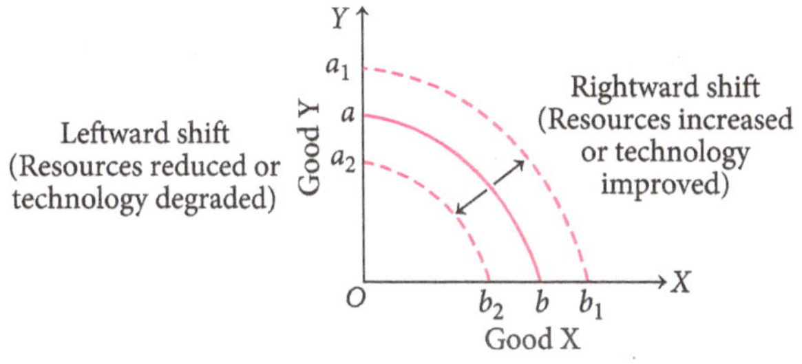

Rotation in Production Possibility Frontier

The Production Possibility Frontier (PPF) can exhibit rotation based on changes affecting one good while keeping the other constant

Outward Rotation of PPF	Inward Rotation of PPF
PPF will rotate outward under the following two conditions • Improvement in technology in favour of one commodity (Keeping the technology of the other commodity constant). • Growth of resources for the production of one commodity (Keeping the resources of the other commodity constant). 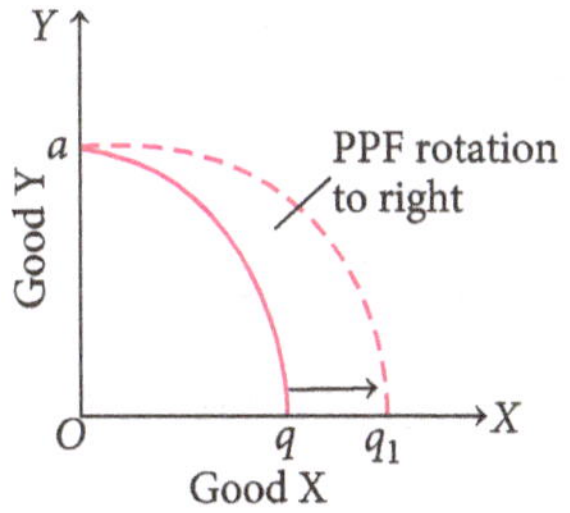 When the technologies are efficient or there is a growth of resources for a commodity *X*, PPF rotates from *aq* to aq_1, as this will raise the productivity of *X*. 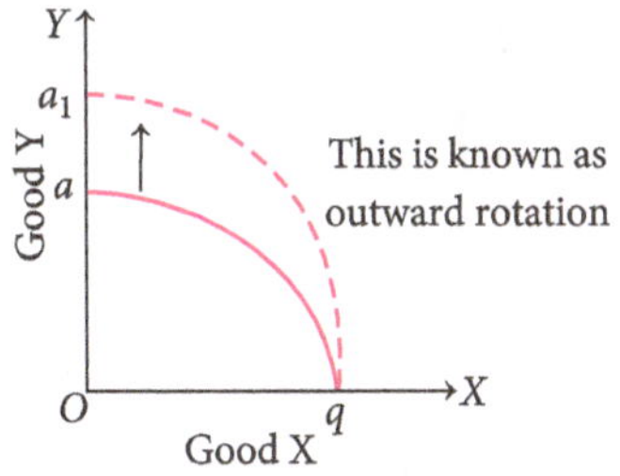 When the technologies are efficient or there is a growth of resources for a commodity *Y*, PPF rotates from *aq* to a_1q, as this will raise the productivity of *Y*.	PPF will rotate inward under the following two conditions • Degradation of technology of one commodity (Keeping the technology of the other commodity constant). • Fall in resources for the production of one commodity (Keeping the resources of the other commodity constant). 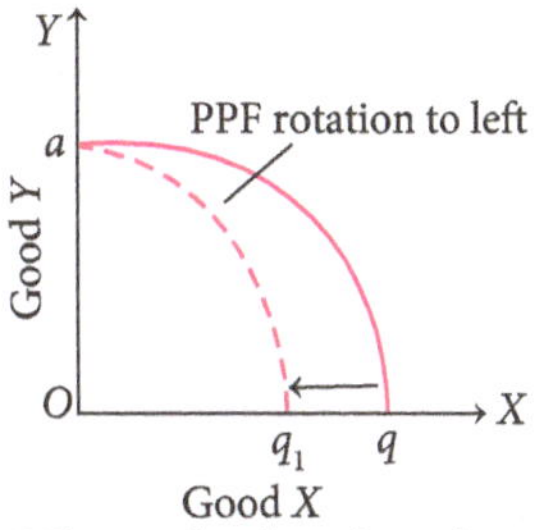 When technology degrades or there is a fall in resources for commodity *X*, PPF rotates from *aq* to aq_1 as this will reduce the production of '*X*'. 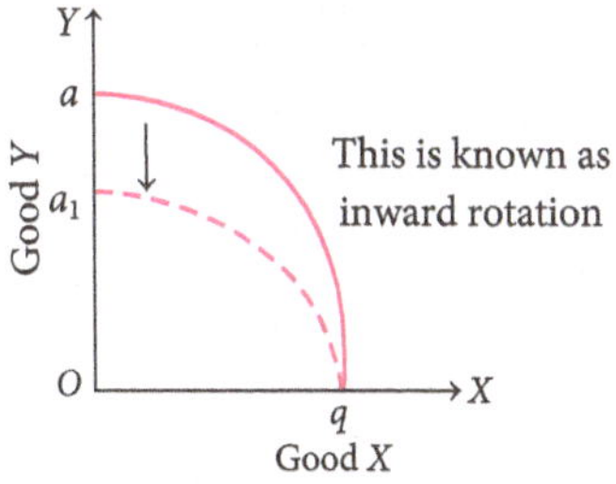 When technology degrades or there is a fall in resources for commodity *Y*, PPF rotates from *aq* to a_1q, as this will reduce the production of '*Y*'.

Mind Map

ECONOMICS, ECONOMY AND ITS CENTRAL PROBLEMS

1 Introduction to Economics

Economics studies how limited resources can be used to satisfy unlimited human wants.

Scarcity It refers to the situation where the supply of a good or service is less than the demand for it.

Nature of Economics

- **Positive Science** Describes economic phenomena as they are.
- **Normative Science** Evaluates economic policies based on moral and ethical grounds.

2 Branches of Economics

Microeconomics

- It studies individual level analysis.
- Theories of microeconomics include theory of consumer behaviour, theory of producer behaviour and theory of price determination.

Macroeconomics

- It studies economy as a whole.
- Theories of macroeconomics include theory of equilibrium level of output and employment, theory of inflationary and deflationary gap in the economy, theory of multiplier and study of government budget, exchange rate and Balance of Payments (BoP).

3 Economy

It is a system by which people earn their living to satisfy their needs and wants through the process of production, consumption, investment and exchange.

Types of Economy

- Market economy (Capitalist economy)
- Centrally planned economy (Command economy)
- Mixed economy

4 Economic Problem

It arises due to scarcity of resources and their alternative uses, requiring choices in allocation.

Causes

- Unlimited human wants
- Limited economic resources
- Alternative uses of resources

5 Central Problems of an Economy

- **What to Produce?** Deciding which goods and services to produce.
- **How to Produce?** Deciding which technique to be used, i.e. labour-intensive technique or capital-intensive technique.
- **For Whom to Produce?** Deciding about distribution of goods among different categories of people.

6 Opportunity Cost

- It is the value of the next best alternative foregone when making a choice.
- It highlights the trade-offs involved in choosing one option over another, making it an essential part of economic analysis. Due to its significance, opportunity cost is often called economic cost.

7 Production Possibility Frontier (PPF)

- It is a curve showing different combinations of two goods that can be produced using available resources and technology.
- It is also called Production Possibility Curve (PPC), Transformation Curve or Production Boundary.

Production Possibility Schedule A table showing alternative production possibilities of two goods.

Assumptions of PPF

- Fixed resources
- Unchanged technology
- Full employment of resources
- Resources are not equally efficient, leading to increasing marginal opportunity cost.

Properties of PPF

- Downward slope of PPF
- Concave to origin

8 Shape of Production Possibility Frontier (PPF)

Concave to Origin (Rising MRT)

- *Reason*: Resources are not equally efficient in producing all goods.
- *Effect*: Economy sacrifices more units of the other good as production shifts.

Convex to Origin (Falling MRT)

- *Reason*: Economy sacrifices lesser and lesser units of the other good.
- *Effect*: Happens when resources are inefficiently employed.

Straight Line (Constant MRT)

- *Reason*: Resources are equally efficient in producing both goods.
- *Effect*: Equal trade-off between the two goods.

9 Shifts and Rotations of PPF

Shift of PPF

- **Rightward Shift** Increase in resources or improved technology and higher production capacity.
- **Leftward Shift** Decrease in resources or degraded technology and lower production capacity.

Rotation of PPF

- **Outward Rotation** Increase in resources or improved technology for one good (other remains constant) and higher production of that good.
- **Inward Rotation** Decrease in resources or degraded technology for one good (other remains constant) and lower production of that good.

EXAM PATTERN QUESTIONS

Objective Type Questions

Multiple Choice Questions (MCQs)

1. What is the primary concern of economics?

(a) Managing unlimited resources
(b) Satisfying unlimited needs with limited resources
(c) Increasing prices of goods
(d) Reducing government intervention

2. Economics as a ……… science involves evaluating economic events from a moral and ethical standpoint.

(a) normative (b) positive
(c) descriptive (d) statistical

3. "An energy crisis is looming over a vast swathe of land from the Northern states to Southern India as low coal supplies across the majority of thermal power plants have set-off blackouts in several urban and rural areas where domestic demand for electricity has spiked manifold because of an unusually early and record-shattering heat wave and dry weather."

Which economic concept is demonstrated by the recent energy crisis in India, where limited coal supplies have led to blackouts despite high demand for electricity? **Competency Based Que**

(a) Inflation
(b) Scarcity
(c) Monetary policy
(d) Trade deficit

4. Identify the tools commonly used in microeconomics.

I. Aggregate analysis
II. Theory of the multiplier
III. Demand and supply analysis
IV. Study of government budget **Competency Based Que**

Codes

(a) Only II (b) III and IV
(c) I, II, III and IV (d) Only III

5. ……… focuses on the economy as a whole, studying aggregate concepts such as national income and full employment.

(a) Microeconomics
(b) Macroeconomics
(c) Development economics
(d) Behavioural economics

6. What does positive economics focus on?

(a) Moral evaluations of economic policies
(b) Objective analysis of economic issues
(c) Value judgements about economic decisions
(d) Predictions about future economic trends

7. Scarcity is a situation when demand for good is **NCERT (QR)**

(a) equal to supply (b) less than supply
(c) more than supply (d) None of these

8. Which of the following questions is/are the part of normative economics?

(a) What are the causes of unemployment?
(b) Why prices are rising?
(c) Was demonetisation justified?
(d) All of the above

9. Identify the positive economics out of the two images given below.

Image 1

Image 2

(a) Image 1 (b) Image 2
(c) Both Images 1 and 2
(d) Neither image 1 nor image 2

10. Which of the following best describes 'production' in economic terms?

(a) Transforming inputs into goods or services
(b) Buying and selling goods for money
(c) Investing in new machinery for future use
(d) Using goods or services to satisfy human wants

11. Which type of economy is highlighted in the below image?

(a) Market (b) Centrally planned
(c) Mixed (d) Traditional

12. **"An economic problem arises due to the scarcity of resources which leads to the need for making choices."**

Based on the statement, which of the following best describes an economic problem? Competency Based Que

(a) Excess supply of goods leading to price drops
(b) High levels of investment in technology
(c) Increasing government intervention in the economy
(d) Unlimited human wants versus limited resources

13. **Identify the type of economy in which the government makes all economic decisions.**

I. Market economy
II. Mixed economy
III. Centrally planned economy
IV. Traditional economy Competency Based Que

Codes
(a) I and II (b) III and IV
(c) Only III (d) Only I

14. **.............. is the problem which is concerned with the distribution of national income among those who have helped to produce it.**

(a) How to produce? (b) What to produce?
(c) Why to produce? (d) For whom to produce?

15. **If on a piece of land, a farmer can produce either 1,000 kg rice or 1,500 kg pulses with given resources, then find the opportunity cost of producing pulses.** Competency Based Que

(a) 1,500 kg pulses (b) 1,000 kg rice
(c) 1,000 kg pulses (d) 1.5 kg rice

16. **Problem of resource allocation deals with** NCERT (QR)

(a) How to produce? (b) From whom to produce?
(c) What to produce? (d) All of these

17. **Which of the following is not a central economic problem?**

(a) What to produce?
(b) How to produce?
(c) For whom to produce?
(d) How to achieve economic growth?

18. **"During the Covid-19 pandemic, many factories shifted from producing regular goods to essential items like masks and sanitisers."**

What central economic problem does this statement illustrate? Competency Based Que

(a) How to produce?
(b) What to produce?
(c) For whom to produce? (d) Investment decisions

19. **The value of the next best alternative forgone when a choice is made is referred to as ....**

(a) marginal cost
(b) economic rent
(c) fixed cost
(d) opportunity cost

20. **Observe the image given below and identify the cause of the problems shown below**

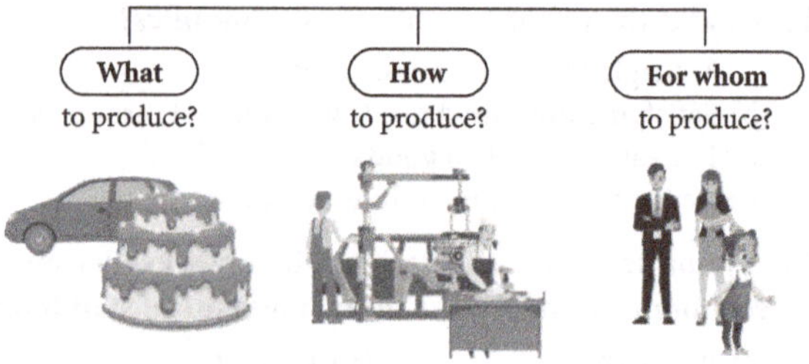

(a) Scarcity of resources
(b) Unlimited human wants
(c) Alternative use of resources
(d) All of the above

21. **"Climate change is impacting India's agricultural sector which employs 40 per cent of its labour, according to a report collated by Climate Trends, a research based consulting and capacity-building initiative that aims to bring greater focus on issues."**

Source *https://www.deccanherald.com/science/climate-change-threatens-indias-agricultural-sector-report-finds-2795608*

Which of the following best describes the impact of climate change on India's agricultural sector as it relates to the Production Possibility Frontier (PPF)? Competency Based Que

(a) Rightward shift in PPF due to increased agricultural efficiency
(b) Leftward shift in PPF due to decreased agricultural output
(c) Outward rotation of PPF due to improved technology in farming
(d) Inward rotation of PPF due to an increase in available resources

22. **What will be the impact of the coronavirus pandemic on the transformation curve of a given country?** Competency Based Que

(a) Downward movement on PPC
(b) Leftward shift in PPC
(c) Production possibility will come down, keeping PPC unchanged
(d) No change in PPC

23. **What trade-off is depicted between goods in the given PPF?**

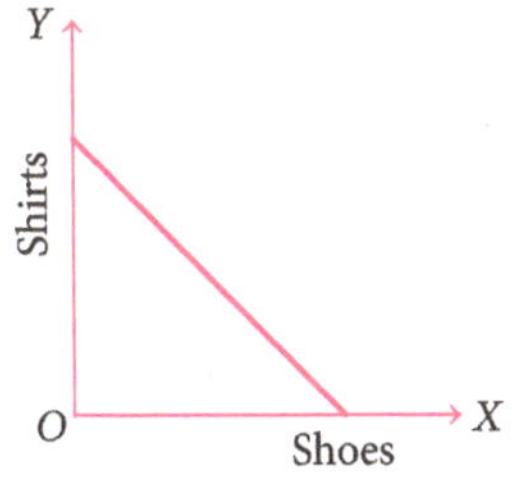

(a) Resources are equally efficient in production
(b) Resources are being used inefficiently
(c) Resources are not equally efficient
(d) None of the above

24. **"The Production Possibility Frontier (PPF) can exhibit a rightward shift based on improvements in technology or an increase in resources."**

According to this statement, which situation would result in a rightward shift of the PPF?

Competency Based Que

(a) Decline in technology for one good
(b) Increase in resources for one good
(c) Decrease in the production capacity of all goods
(d) Reduction in the efficiency of production

25. **When there is use of outdated technology in the production, then the production possibility curve will**

(a) shift to right (b) shift to left
(c) become straight line (d) remain same

26. **When the Marginal Rate of Transformation (MRT) is rising, the PPF is .... to the origin.**

(a) concave (b) convex
(c) not related (d) None of these

Direction *Read the case study and answer the questions 27 to 30 on the basis of the same*

Rivertown is a small, historically agricultural town that has recently faced significant economic changes. Traditionally, Rivertown's economy relied heavily on farming, specifically wheat and pulses. The town's Production Possibility Frontier (PPF) used to reflect a stable balance between these two commodities.

However, recent technological advancements and increased demand for manufactured goods have brought about a shift in the town's economic focus.

The local government of Rivertown decided to invest in new machinery and technology for the production of wheat. This decision was driven by the rising demand for wheat due to its use in various processed foods and biofuels. Consequently, the town also saw an increase in investment from private firms interested in setting up manufacturing units for wheat based products.

With the introduction of advanced farming technology, Rivertown experienced a noticeable rightward shift in its PPF for wheat production.

The improved machinery allowed the town to produce more wheat efficiently. However, the focus on wheat also meant that fewer resources were allocated to pulse cultivation. As a result, the town faced a decrease in pulse production, which was reflected in a leftward rotation of the PPF for pulses.

The changes brought about a new set of economic problems and opportunities. While wheat production flourished, the decline in pulses led to higher prices for pulses in the local market. This imbalance created new challenges for the town, including managing the trade-offs between producing more wheat and maintaining pulse supplies.

27. **The rightward shift in Rivertown's Production Possibility Frontier (PPF) for wheat production was primarily due to ....**

28. **Which of the following best describes the economic trade-off Rivertown faces due to its shift in focus towards wheat production?**

(a) Decreased employment opportunities
(b) Reduced production of pulses
(c) Higher prices for manufactured goods
(d) Increased investment in agriculture

29. **The leftward rotation of Rivertown's PPF for pulses resulted from ....**

30. **What economic problem does Rivertown experience as a result of the decreased pulse production?**

(a) Increased unemployment
(b) Overproduction of wheat
(c) Higher prices for pulses (d) Excess supply of pulses

Assertion-Reason

Direction (Q.No. 31 to 40) *Read the following Assertion (A) and Reason (R) and choose the correct alternative from the following*

Alternatives

(a) Both Assertion (A) and Reason (R) are true and Reason (R) is the correct explanation of Assertion (A)
(b) Both Assertion (A) and Reason (R) are true, but Reason (R) is not the correct explanation of Assertion (A)
(c) Assertion (A) is true, but Reason (R) is false
(d) Assertion (A) is false, but Reason (R) is true

31. **Assertion** (A) Economics explores how to manage limited resources to satisfy unlimited needs.

Reason (R) Macroeconomics focuses on individual economic units such as firms and markets.

32. **Assertion** (A) Scarcity in economics refers to having unlimited resources to meet unlimited wants.

Reason (R) Scarcity necessitates making choices about how to allocate resources effectively.

33. **Assertion** (A) Economics as a positive science focuses on objective analysis of economic issues based on factual data.

Reason (R) Positive economics would study facts like the presence of unemployment or rising urban poverty in India.

34. **Assertion** (A) Microeconomics focuses on the study of individual economic units, such as firms and markets.

Reason (R) Microeconomics examines aggregate concepts like national income and overall consumption.

35. **Assertion** (A) In a market economy, decisions about production and consumption are guided by self-interest and profit motive.

Reason (R) A market economy typically involves government control over production and distribution to ensure social welfare.

36. **Assertion** (A) Opportunity cost refers to the value of the next best alternative that is foregone when a choice is made.

Reason (R) Opportunity cost is not relevant in the decision-making process as resources are abundant.

37. **Assertion** (A) In a centrally planned economy, the government controls all economic activities and decisions.

Reason (R) The centralised control allows the government to focus on achieving social welfare goals and addressing inequalities in wealth distribution.

38. **Assertion** (A) A rightward shift of the PPF represents an increase in resources or an improvement in production technology.

Reason (R) A rightward shift of the PPF indicates a reduction in the economy's production capacity.

39. **Assertion** (A) PPC is convex to the origin means we need to sacrifice less and less for production of more units of other good.

Reason (R) MOC increases when resources are not equally efficient in production of all the goods.

40. **Assertion** (A) A straight line production possibility frontier is a representative of substitute goods.

Reason (R) When the economy is willing to sacrifice equal quantities of both goods, PPC is straight line.

Two Statements Based MCQs

Direction (Q.No. 41 to 50) *Read the following statements carefully and choose the correct alternative*

Alternatives

(a) Statement I is correct and Statement II is incorrect
(b) Statement II is correct and Statement I is incorrect
(c) Both the statements are correct
(d) Both the statements are incorrect

41. **Statement I** Microeconomics only deal with the individuals so, their is no aggregation.

Statement II Normative statement is based upon 'value judgement'.

42. **Statement I** Scarcity in economics refers to the situation where the supply of a good is less than its demand.

Statement II Scarcity only affects luxury goods and has no impact on essential resources like water or energy.

43. **Statement I** Microeconomics studies the overall performance of the economy, including national income and aggregate consumption.

Statement II Macroeconomics focuses on individual decision-making and market structures.

44. **Statement I** In microeconomics, the law of demand comes into play, stating that, all else being equal, as the price of a good decreases, the quantity demanded increases and *vice-versa.*

Statement II In macroeconomics, national income of a country is the sum total of income of individuals in a country.

45. **Statement I** Resources are unlimited compared to their demand.

Statement II An economic problem arises because it is impossible to produce enough goods to meet everyone's needs due to the scarcity of resources.

46. **Statement I** Production is the creation of utility, transforming inputs (raw materials, ideas) into goods or services.

Statement II Consumption is the process of using up goods or services to satisfy human wants.

47. **Statement I** Opportunity cost cannot be included while calculating accounting cost.

Statement II Outflow of foreign exchange is an indication of inefficient allocation of resources.

48. **Statement I** The PPF shows the maximum feasible output combinations of two goods that can be produced.

Statement II A point inside the PPF represents a level of production that is unattainable with current resources.

49. **Statement I** The PPF is concave to the origin due to increasing marginal opportunity cost as production shifts between goods.

Statement II If the MRT is constant, the PPF will be a downward sloping straight line.

50. **Statement I** The PPF can shift leftward if there is an improvement in production technology.

Statement II A concave PPF indicates that the opportunity cost of producing one good increases as more of it is produced.

Matching

51. Match the following

Column I	Column II
A. Economics	(i) The study of individual and business decision-making in markets.
B. Economy	(ii) The study of the economy as a whole, including national and global economic trends.
C. Microeconomics	(iii) The study of economic issues and problems.
D. Macroeconomics	(iv) A system for producing, distributing and consuming goods and services.

Codes

	A	B	C	D		A	B	C	D
(a)	(iii)	(iv)	(i)	(ii)	(b)	(iv)	(i)	(ii)	(iii)
(c)	(ii)	(iii)	(iv)	(i)	(d)	(iii)	(ii)	(i)	(iv)

52. Match the following

Column I	Column II
A. Scarcity	(i) An economic system where supply and demand determine prices and production.
B. Mixed economy	(ii) The limited availability of resources relative to unlimited wants.
C. Centrally planned economy	(iii) An economic system combining private and public sector elements.
D. Market economy	(iv) An economy where the government controls and directs all economic activities.

Codes

	A	B	C	D		A	B	C	D
(a)	(iii)	(iv)	(i)	(ii)	(b)	(iv)	(i)	(ii)	(iii)
(c)	(ii)	(iii)	(iv)	(i)	(d)	(iii)	(ii)	(i)	(iv)

53. Match the following

Column I	Column II
A. Production	(i) A company buys new machinery to increase future production capacity.
B. Consumption	(ii) A family uses electricity in their home for daily activities.
C. Investment	(iii) A factory in India manufactures smartphones using raw materials and labour.
D. Exchange	(iv) A shop owner sells clothes to a customer in exchange for money.

Codes

	A	B	C	D		A	B	C	D
(a)	(iii)	(iv)	(i)	(ii)	(b)	(iv)	(i)	(ii)	(iii)
(c)	(ii)	(iii)	(iv)	(i)	(d)	(iii)	(ii)	(i)	(iv)

54. Match the following

Column I	Column II
A. Economic problem	(i) Types of goods to be produced and quantity of goods to be produced.
B. What to produce?	(ii) Choosing the technique of production.
C. How to produce?	(iii) The distribution of goods and services among the people.
D. For whom to produce?	(iv) It is impossible to produce enough goods to meet everyone's needs.

Codes

	A	B	C	D		A	B	C	D
(a)	(iii)	(iv)	(i)	(ii)	(b)	(iv)	(i)	(ii)	(iii)
(c)	(ii)	(iii)	(iv)	(i)	(d)	(iii)	(ii)	(i)	(iv)

55. Match the following

Column I	Column II
A. Opportunity cost	(i) Reflects the trade-off between producing different goods.
B. Production possibility curve	(ii) The value of the next best alternative that is foregone.
C. Marginal opportunity cost	(iii) A curve that illustrates the different combinations of two goods.
D. Shape of PPF	(iv) The rate at which the quantity of output of one commodity is sacrificed to produce one more unit of the other commodity.

Codes

	A	B	C	D		A	B	C	D
(a)	(iii)	(iv)	(i)	(ii)	(b)	(iv)	(i)	(ii)	(iii)
(c)	(ii)	(iii)	(iv)	(i)	(d)	(iii)	(ii)	(i)	(iv)

Concept Identification

56. It represents the value of the next best alternative forgone when making a decision.

57. It describes the economic system where supply and demand determine prices and production without central planning.

58. It involves evaluating economic events from a moral and ethical stand point, making value judgements about policies.

59. It explains the shape of the PPF when the marginal opportunity cost is increasing as production shifts from one good to another.

60. The economy sacrifices an equal amount of one good to produce an additional unit of another, represented by a straight line PPF.

Answers

1. (b) Satisfying unlimited needs with limited resources
2. (a) normative
3. (b) Scarcity
4. (d) Only III
5. (b) Macroeconomics
6. (b) Objective analysis of economic issues
7. (c) more than supply
8. (c) Was demonetisation justified?
9. (a) Image 1
10. (a) Transforming inputs into goods or services
11. (c) Mixed
12. (d) Unlimited human wants versus limited resources
13. (c) Only III
14. (d) For whom to produce?
15. (b) Opportunity cost of producing 1,500 kg pulses is production of 1,000 kg rice sacrificed.
16. (d) All of these
17. (d) How to achieve economic growth?
18. (b) What to produce?
19. (d) opportunity cost
20. (d) All of the above
21. (b) Leftward shift in PPF due to decreased agricultural output
22. (b) Due to the pandemic, there is decrease in human resources, leading to fall in production capacity of an economy.
23. (a) Resources are equally efficient in production
24. (b) Increase in resources for one good
25. (b) When the resources are destroyed or there is a use of outdated technology, then production of an economy goes down and as a result production possibility curve will shift to left.
26. (a) concave
27. improved farming technology
28. (b) Reduced production of pulses
29. increased focus on wheat production
30. (c) Higher prices for pulses
31. (c) Macroeconomics focuses on aggregate concepts like national income and inflation, while microeconomics focuses on individual economic units such as firms and markets.
32. (d) Scarcity refers to the situation where resources are limited relative to unlimited wants, not unlimited resources.
33. (a) Both Assertion (A) and Reason (R) are true and Reason (R) is the correct explanation of Assertion (A)
34. (c) Macroeconomics examines aggregate concepts.
35. (c) In a market economy, decisions are guided by self-interest and profit motive. However, government control is more characteristic of a centrally planned economy, not a market economy.
36. (c) Opportunity cost is relevant precisely because resources are limited, not abundant.
37. (a) Both Assertion (A) and Reason (R) are true and Reason (R) is the correct explanation of Assertion (A)
38. (c) A rightward shift of the PPF actually indicates an increase in the economy's production capacity, not a reduction.
39. (b) Both Assertion (A) and Reason (R) are true, but Reason (R) is not the correct explanation of Assertion (A)
40. (a) Both Assertion (A) and Reason (R) are true and Reason (R) is the correct explanation of Assertion (A)
41. (b) While microeconomics primarily focuses on individual units such as households, firms and specific markets, it does involve some level of aggregation.
42. (a) Scarcity affects all resources, not just luxury goods and is a fundamental economic problem impacting both essential and non-essential resources.
43. (d) Microeconomics deals with individual units and market structures, while macroeconomics studies the overall economy, including national income and aggregate consumption.

44. (c) Both the statements are correct
45. (b) Resources are limited compared to their demand, creating scarcity, which is a global phenomenon.
46. (c) Both the statements are correct
47. (a) The outflow of foreign exchange is not necessarily an indication of inefficient allocation of resources. It can be a result of various factors.
48. (a) The point inside the PPF indicates underutilisation of resources, not unattainability.
49. (c) Both the statements are correct
50. (b) A leftward shift of the PPF indicates a decrease in resources or technology, not an improvement.
51. (a) (iii) (iv) (i) (ii)
52. (c) (ii) (iii) (iv) (i)
53. (d) (iii) (ii) (i) (iv)
54. (b) (iv) (i) (ii) (iii)
55. (c) (ii) (iii) (iv) (i)
56. Opportunity cost
57. Market economy
58. Normative economics
59. PPF is concave to origin
60. Constant Marginal Rate of Transformation (MRT)

Subjective Questions

Short Answer Type Questions

1. What is the core issue of economics and why does it arise?

Ans. The core issue of economics is scarcity, which arises because resources are finite while human wants are boundless. This means that there are not enough resources to meet all the needs and desires of individuals and societies, forcing us to make choices about how to allocate these limited resources effectively.

2. Why do scarce goods like diamonds and petroleum often command higher prices in the market and how does this reflect the economic principle of demand and supply? **Competency Based Que**

Ans. Scarce goods like diamonds and petrol command higher prices because their limited supply relative to high demand increases their value.

According to the economic principle of demand and supply, when the availability of a good is restricted and demand remains high, prices rise to balance the market. This reflects the premium placed on scarce resources and the willingness of consumers to pay more for them.

3. Identify the type of economics from the given image and explain it. **Competency Based Que**

Ans. The picture depicts normative economics because it depicts a group of people engaged in conversation about economic policies. This implies that they are expressing their opinions, beliefs or preferences regarding economic issues. These opinions are subjective, as they are based on individual values and perspectives.

Normative economics addresses what should be done and makes value judgements about economic policies.

4. "Microeconomics focuses on individual economic units, such as individuals, firms, industries and markets."

What are the key areas of focus in microeconomics and how does it analyse these individual economic units? **Competency Based Que**

Ans. Microeconomics focuses on the behaviour and decisions of individual economic units such as consumers, firms, industries and markets.

It analyses how these units interact within the market to determine prices, demand and supply. e.g Microeconomics studies how a firm sets its prices based on production costs and consumer demand or how individual consumer preferences influence market demand for goods and services.

5. What do you understand by positive economic analysis? **NCERT**

Ans. Positive economic analysis is confined to cause and effect relationship.

In other words, it states 'what is.' It relates to what the facts are, were or will be about various economic phenomena in the economics.

e.g. It deals with the analysis of questions like what are the causes of unemployment.

6. "Economics is a science as well as art." In what ways can economics be characterised as both a science and an art and what does this dual nature entail? Competency Based Que

Ans. Economics is considered a science because it involves the objective study of economic phenomena through factual data and empirical analysis. It uses scientific methods to understand cause and effect relationships within the economy.

Simultaneously, economics is an art because it requires making subjective judgements and recommendations about economic policies based on ethical and normative considerations.

This dual nature means that while economics relies on rigorous analysis, it also involves interpretation and decision-making that reflect moral values and societal goals.

7. "Microeconomics deals with individual and market level economic issues, while macroeconomics addresses broader economic aggregates and policies." Do you agree? Give reasons. Competency Based Que

Ans. Yes, I agree with the statement. Microeconomics focuses on individual and market level issues, such as consumer behaviour, pricing and supply demand dynamics in specific markets. In contrast, macroeconomics addresses broader economic aggregates like national income, inflation, unemployment and government policies. Both fields are interconnected, as individual decisions studied in microeconomics collectively influence the broader trends analysed in macroeconomics.

8. What is the difference between normative and positive science?

Ans. Differences between positive science and normative science are

Basis	Positive Science	Normative Science
Meaning	It looks at facts as 'they are', i.e. based upon actual data/facts.	It looks at facts as 'they should be', i.e. not based upon actual data.
Verification	These facts can be verified using empirical evidences.	These statements cannot be verified as they are not based upon true events.
Value Judgement	It does not pass any value judgement.	It passes value judgement.
Example	Poverty in India has declined significantly since independence.	India should make policies to remove poverty completely.

9. Give three examples of micro variables and macro variables.

Ans. Examples of micro variables are
(i) Consumer's demand for a good.
(ii) Market price of a commodity.
(iii) Firm's output (supply).

Examples of macro variables are
(i) Aggregate demand in the economy.
(ii) General price level in the economy.
(iii) Aggregate supply in the economy.

10. Distinguish between a centrally planned economy and a market economy. NCERT

Ans. Differences between planned and market economy are

Basis	Planned Economy	Market Economy
Meaning	It is that economy in which course of economic activities is decided by some central authority or by the government.	It is that economy in which economic activities are fully dependent on the role of market forces.
Right to Produce	Producers are not free to produce. Only a central authority decides the full variety of goods and services that people can consume.	Producers are free to produce the highly demanded goods in order to maximise their profits.
Aim	Social welfare is the prime consideration.	Self-interest is the prime consideration.

11. "An economic problem arises because it is impossible to produce enough goods to meet everyone's needs due to the scarcity of resources."

Why does scarcity of resources lead to economic problems, and how does it affect decision-making in an economy? Competency Based Que

Ans. Scarcity of resources leads to economic problems because resources are limited, while human wants are unlimited. This forces economies to make difficult choices about how to allocate these scarce resources to meet the most pressing needs.

As a result, decisions must be made regarding what goods to produce, how to produce them and for whom they should be produced. Without scarcity, there would be no need for such trade-offs, but because it exists, every choice comes with an opportunity cost, making resource management crucial.

12. **Identify the central problem given below and explain the same briefly.** Competency Based Que

Ans. Central problem highlighted in the image is 'what to produce'. An economy has millions of commodities to produce.

It has to decide which goods and services to be produced that should be in sufficient quantity, as all the goods cannot be produced due to scarcity of resources.

e.g. An economy has to decide whether to produce luxury goods or inferior goods, capital goods or consumer goods.

This problem has two dimensions

(i) Types of goods to be produced.

(ii) Quantity of goods to be produced.

13. **What is a market economy and how does it operate?**

Ans. A market economy is an economic system where goods and resources are bought and sold freely, guided by self-interest and profit motives.

Private ownership prevails, and prices are determined by the forces of demand and supply without significant government intervention.

14. **"In a centrally planned economy, all economic decisions are made by the government or central authority with a focus on social welfare."**

How does a centrally planned economy differ from a market economy in terms of decision-making and resource allocation? Competency Based Que

Ans. In a centrally planned economy, the government or central authority makes all key economic decisions, including what to produce, how to produce and for whom to produce, with a focus on achieving social welfare and reducing inequality.

Resources are allocated based on government plans rather than market demand. In contrast, a market economy relies on the forces of demand and supply to guide decision-making and resource allocation. Private individuals and firms make economic decisions based on profit motives and prices serve as signals for resource allocation.

As a result, a market economy tends to be more dynamic, while a centrally planned economy prioritises equitable distribution.

15. **"Human desires are endless, fulfilling one leads to the emergence of another."**

How do unlimited human wants contribute to the central economic problem of scarcity and what role does it play in shaping economic choices? Competency Based Que

Ans. Unlimited human wants contribute to the central economic problem of scarcity because resources are limited and cannot meet the endless desires of individuals. As soon as one want is satisfied, another emerges, creating a constant demand for goods and services.

This continuous cycle of new wants forces economies to make difficult decisions about how to allocate their finite resources.

The need to prioritise which wants to satisfy and which to defer plays a central role in shaping economic choices, driving the allocation of resources toward the most urgent needs or the most profitable options.

16. **Explain how scarcity and choice go together?**

Ans. Resources are not only scarce, but also have alternative uses. Land can be used for producing wheat or for constructing warehouses. Hence, the problem of choice is the essence of an economic problem. However, if resources were not scarce, one could have everything at any time and there would be no problem of choice.

17. **What is the role of investment in economic activities?**

Ans. Investment plays a crucial role in economic activities by adding to the stock of capital, such as machinery or infrastructure, to generate future income. It is a forward-looking activity that helps enhance production capacity and long-term economic growth.

18. **"Opportunity cost refers to the value of the next best alternative that is foregone in order to produce or obtain another commodity."**

Why opportunity cost is considered a critical concept in economic decision-making and how does it influence the allocation of resources? Competency Based Que

Ans. Opportunity cost is critical in economic decision-making because it reflects the trade-offs involved in choosing one option over another.

Since resources are scarce, choosing to allocate them to one use means forgoing their use in another, potentially beneficial, way.

This concept helps individuals, businesses and governments prioritise their choices, ensuring that resources are allocated in a manner that maximises overall benefit. Opportunity cost forces decision-makers to consider the value of alternatives, leading to more efficient resource utilisation.

19. **What is opportunity cost? Explain with the help of a numerical example.**

Ans. Opportunity cost for a commodity is the amount of other commodity that has been foregone in order to produce additional unit of the first.

e.g. If a person 'A' is working in a bank and gets a job offer of a journalist. A as a bank executive, gets ₹ 40,000 and as journalist would get ₹ 45,000. In this case, the opportunity cost of being a journalist is ₹ 40,000, which is the second best opportunity.

20. **What is a production possibility frontier?** NCERT

Ans. It refers to a graphical representation of all the possible combinations of two products that can be produced with the given resources and technology, where all the resources are fully and efficiently utilised.

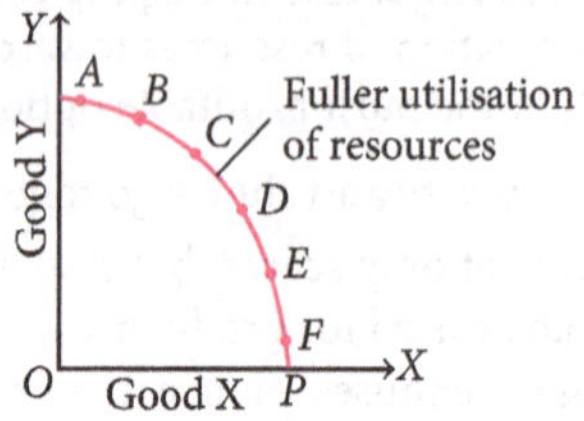

21. **How does the PPF help in addressing central economic problems?**

Ans. The PPF helps in addressing central economic problems by illustrating the trade-offs an economy faces in allocating its limited resources. It helps answer questions about what goods to produce, how much of each to produce and the opportunity costs associated with these decisions.

22. **Gulf countries have acquired more capital goods by selling oil to various countries. What would be its impact on production possibility curve?** Competency Based Que

Ans. It is an example of increase or growth of resources.

It results in rightward shift of production possibility curve as it shows higher level of output of both the given goods.

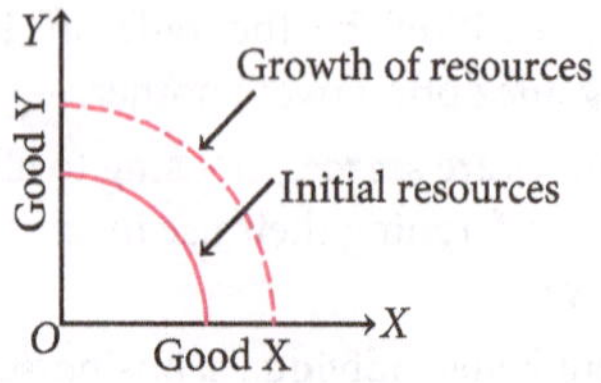

23. **"The PPF slopes downward from left to right, illustrating the trade-off between the production of two goods."**

How does the downward slope of the PPF demonstrate the concept of trade-offs in production? Competency Based Que

Ans. The downward slope of the PPF demonstrates that producing more of one good requires producing less of another due to limited resources. This trade-off reflects the need to allocate resources efficiently and make decisions about which goods to prioritise, as resources cannot produce unlimited amounts of both goods simultaneously.

24. **"The concave shape of the PPF indicates that the marginal opportunity cost increases as production shifts from one good to another."**

Why does the concave shape of the PPF indicate increasing marginal opportunity costs and how does it affect production decisions? Competency Based Que

Ans. The concave shape of the PPF indicates that as more resources are allocated to producing one good, the economy must sacrifice increasingly larger amounts of the other good. This occurs because resources are not equally suited for producing all goods, leading to rising marginal opportunity costs.

As a result, economies must carefully consider how much of each good to produce to minimise these trade-offs.

Long Answer Type Questions

25. **Discuss the subject matter of economics.** NCERT

Ans. Economics is concerned with the study of economic problems at the level of an economy as a whole, on one side and on the other, it is concerned with the study of an individual too.

The subject matter of economics is studied under two broad branches *viz* microeconomics and macroeconomics.

Vital theories or studies of microeconomics are

(i) Theory of consumer behaviour.
(ii) Theory of producer behaviour.
(iii) Theory of price.

Vital theories or studies of macroeconomics are

(i) Theory related to equilibrium level of output and employment.
(ii) Theory related to inflationary and deflationary gap in the economy.
(iii) Theory of multiplier.
(iv) Study of government budget.
(v) Study of exchange rate and Balance of Payments (BoP).

26. Distinguish between microeconomics and macroeconomics. NCERT

Ans. Differences between microeconomics and macroeconomics are

Basis	Microeconomics	Macroeconomics
Meaning	It is that branch of economics which studies individual economic variables like demand, supply, price, etc.	It is that branch of economics which studies aggregate economic variables like aggregate demand, aggregate supply, price level, etc.
Area of Study	It deals with determination of price and output in individual market.	It deals with determination of general price level and national output of the country.
Scope	It has a narrow scope, i.e. an individual person, an individual market, etc.	It has a very wide scope, i.e. a country as a whole.
Degree of Aggregation	Minor degree of aggregation in case of market demand or market supply, etc.	Major degree of aggregation, as it deals with economy as a whole.
Parameter	The basic parameter of microeconomics is price, i.e. consumers and producers take economic decisions on the basis of price.	The basic parameter of macroeconomics is income, i.e. economic decisions relating to consumption, saving, investment, etc. are on the basis of national income.

27. "Economics as a positive science deals with cause and effect relationships and describes economic phenomena as they are, without making value judgements."

How does positive economics approach the analysis of economic issues and why does it avoid making value judgements? Competency Based Que

Ans. Positive economics takes an objective approach to studying economic issues by focusing solely on the facts and data available. It emphasises the analysis of cause and effect relationships, aiming to describe and explain economic phenomena as they exist in the real world.

e.g. It might explore why unemployment rates are rising or how changes in inflation impact consumer spending, without offering opinions or recommendations on what policies should be enacted.

The key reason positive economics avoids making value judgements is that its goal is to provide a neutral, unbiased understanding of economic activities. It does not delve into whether certain economic outcomes are good or bad, fair or unfair.

Instead, it leaves the ethical and policy-related interpretations to normative economics, which explicitly deals with what should be done to address economic issues based on moral, ethical or societal goals.

28. Discuss the central problems of an economy. NCERT

Ans. We know that resources are limited in relation to the unlimited wants, so it is important to economise their use and utilise them in the most efficient manner.

It leads to following central problems, that are faced by every economy

(i) **What to Produce?**

There are limited resources and thus producers cannot produce all the goods in an economy.

So, every economy has this problem that what to produce and in what quantity.

It has two dimensions

- Kinds of goods to be produced.
- Quantity of goods to be produced.

(ii) **How to Produce?**

This problem refers to the selection of technique to be used for production of goods and services.

There are various techniques available to produce goods

- Labour intensive technique.
- Capital intensive technique.

Thus, it is difficult to allocate the resources efficiently and effectively.

(iii) **For Whom to Produce?**

Due to lack of resources in every economy, all the wants of the people cannot be satisfied.

So, there is problem to select the category of people who consume the goods. Whether to produce goods for rich section or poor section of society or more for rich and less for poor section.

Thus, every economy faces the problem of allocating the scarce resources to the production of different possible goods and services and distribution of these among the individuals with in the economy. The allocation of scarce resources and the distribution of the final goods and services are the central problems of any economy.

29. Explain the rotations in a PPF.

Ans. The Production Possibility Frontier (PPF) can exhibit rotation based on changes affecting one good while keeping the other constant

(i) **Outward Rotation**

- Advances in technology for one good (while technology for the other remains unchanged).
- Increase in resources dedicated to one good (with resources for the other remaining unchanged).

- Results in increased production capacity for the improved good.

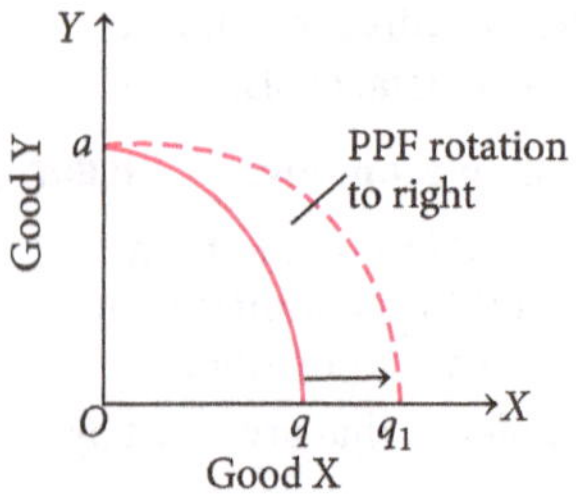

When the technologies are efficient or there is a growth of resources for a commodity *X*, PPF rotates from *aq* to aq_1, as this will raise the productivity of *X*.

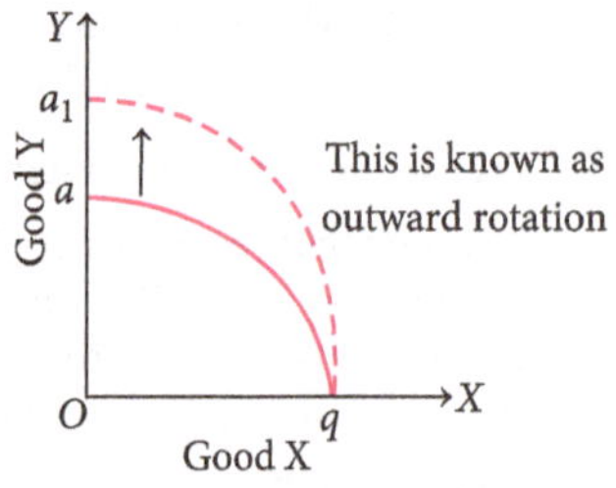

When the technologies are efficient or there is a growth of resources for a commodity *Y*, PPF rotates from *aq* to a_1q, as this will raise the productivity of *Y*.

(ii) **Inward Rotation**

- Decline in technology for one good (while technology for the other remains unchanged).
- Decrease in resources for one good (with resources for the other remaining unchanged).
- Leads to a decreased production capacity for the affected good.

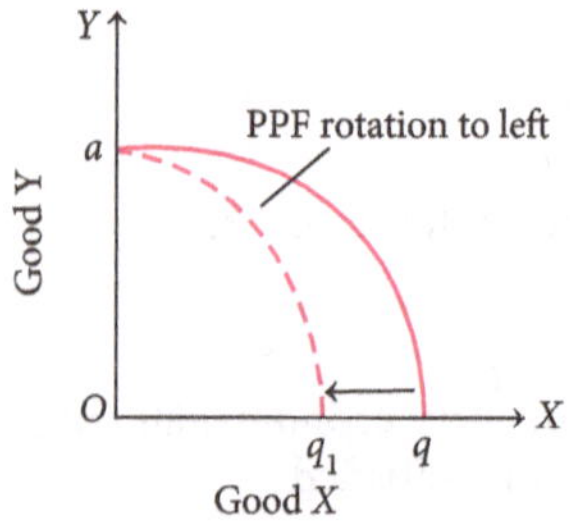

When technology degrades or there is a fall in resources for commodity *X*, PPF rotates from *aq* to aq_1 as this will reduce the production of '*X*'.

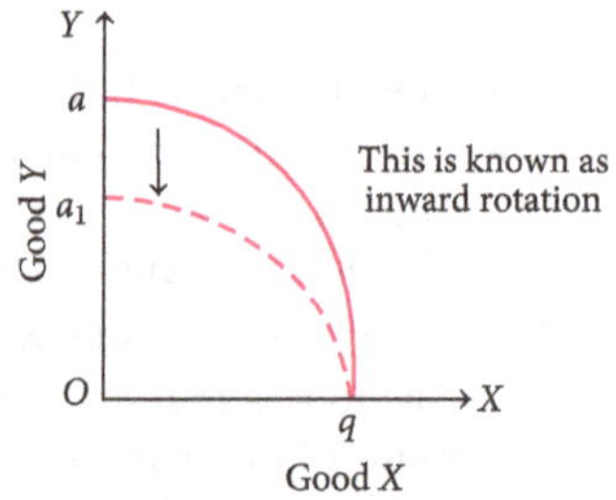

When technology degrades or there is a fall in resources for commodity *Y*, PPF rotates from *aq* to a_1q, as this will reduce the production of '*Y*'.

30. **Each economy has scarce resources and will have possibility of being exhausted gradually after a continuous use.**

Growth of resources, therefore, become a basic problem of the economy.

It can achieve this objective through technological advancement. Underdeveloped countries like India, Pakistan, Thailand, etc. have remained poor because of poor growth of their resources.

Besides fuller utilisation of resources, these countries should try to raise their productive capacities by exploring further availability of natural resources and discovering better techniques for their use.

Moreover, full use of productive capacity is also indispensable for the growth of the economy. Economic theory is classified into micro and macro theory. Microeconomic theory deals with the allocation of resources in the market economy.

In this theory, decisions regarding 'what', 'how' and 'for whom' to produce are decided on the basis of price mechanism. Goods are freely bought and sold in the market economy on an agreed price. Macroeconomic theory deals with the fuller and efficient use of resources.

It also deals with the growth of resources and problems relating to saving, investment, inflation, unemployment, etc. Development economics deals with the problem of growth of resources. **Competency Based Que**

(i) **Explain the interrelation between microeconomics and macroeconomics.**

(ii) **What is allocation of resources and why do we need to allocate various resources for production?**

Ans. (i) Microeconomic analysis offers insights into such disparate efforts as making business decisions or formulating public policies. Macroeconomics is more abstruse. It describes relationship among aggregates so big as to be hard to apprehend, such as national income, savings and the overall price level.

The field is conventionally divided into the study of national economic growth in the long-run, the analysis of short-run departures from equilibrium and the formulation of policies to stabilise the national economy, i.e. to minimise fluctuations in growth and prices. Those policies can include spending and taxing actions by the government or monetary policy actions by the central bank.

(ii) The problem in which an economy has to assign the scarce available resources in a way that the maximum wants of the society are fulfilled is known as the allocation of resources.

The need to allocate the resources arises because of the limited availability of resources and unlimited wants of society. Therefore, the basic aim behind the allocation of resources is to economise the use of available resources and utilise them in the best possible efficient manner.

Simply put, an economy has to allocate the resources and choose from different options of goods (What to produce) choose from different production techniques (How to produce) and decide the end consumer of the goods (For whom to produce).

Numerical Questions

Numerical 1

Calculate Marginal Opportunity Cost (MOC) from the following schedule

Shirts (in millions)	0	1	2	3	4	5
Cars (in thousands)	200	190	170	140	100	50

Sol.

Shirts (in millions)	**Cars** (in thousands)	**MOC** $\left[\frac{\text{Loss (of cars)}}{\text{Gain (of shirts)}}\right]$
0	200	—
1	190	10:1 = 10
2	170	20:1 = 20
3	140	30:1 = 30
4	100	40:1 = 40
5	50	50:1 = 50

Hint MOC when 4 million shirts are produced

$$= \frac{140 - 100}{4 - 3} = \frac{40}{1}$$

$$\therefore \quad MOC = 40$$

Numerical 2

An economy produces two goods, i.e. Barley and Jowar and the following table summarises its production possibilities. Calculate the marginal opportunity cost of Barley at various combinations.

Barley	100	80	55	25	10	0
Jowar	0	25	50	75	85	87

Sol. Marginal Opportunity Cost (MOC) of Barley

$$= \frac{\text{Units of Barley Sacrified}}{\text{More Units of Jowar Produced}}$$

Barley (Y)	**Jowar** (X)	**MOC**
100	0	—
80	25	$\frac{100-80}{25-0} = \frac{20}{25} = 0.8$
55	50	$\frac{80-55}{50-25} = \frac{25}{25} = 1$
25	75	$\frac{55-25}{75-50} = \frac{30}{25} = 1.2$
10	85	$\frac{25-10}{85-75} = \frac{15}{10} = 1.5$
0	87	$\frac{10-0}{87-85} = \frac{10}{2} = 5$

The curve will be downward sloping and concave to the origin, as MOC is rising.

Numerical 3

With the same amount of resources, a farmer can feed the following combinations of goats and cows

Options	**Goats**	**Cows**
I	188	64
II	170	70

With the given options, what is the opportunity cost of the farmer feeding one cow?

Sol. The opportunity cost of the farmer feeding one cow will be equal to the number of goats which cannot be fed because of feeding a cow.

Here, to increase the number of cows to be fed from 64 to 70, i.e. 6, the number of goats which are fed reduced from 188 to 170, i.e. 18.

Thus, the opportunity cost of the farmer feeding 1 cow $= \left[\frac{18}{6} = 3\right]$ goats.

Numerical 4

A farmer in Country X can produce either 100 units of corn or 50 units of wheat using the same amount of resources. If the farmer decides to produce 80 units of corn, what is the opportunity cost of producing these 80 units of corn in terms of wheat?

Sol. To find the opportunity cost, calculate the number of wheat units that could have been produced instead of the 80 units of corn. The opportunity cost of producing 100 units of corn is 50 units of wheat. Therefore, the opportunity cost of producing 80 units of corn is

Opportunity Cost

$$= \frac{\text{50 Units of Wheat}}{\text{100 Units of Corn}} \times \text{80 Units of Corn} = \text{40 units of Wheat}$$

Numerical 5

Calculate marginal rate of transformation in each of the following cases and comment on the shape of production possibility frontier

(i)

Wheat (in kg)	100	90	70	40	0
Rice (in kg)	0	1	2	3	4

(ii)

Guns (in units)	0	1	2	3	4
Butter (in units)	100	60	30	10	0

(iii)

Bread (in kg)	10	20	30	40	50	60
Biscuits (in kg)	200	160	120	80	40	00

Sol. (i)

Wheat (in kg) (Y)	**Rice** (in kg) (X)	**MRT** ($\Delta Y/\Delta X$)
100	0	—
90	1	$(90-100)/(1-0)=10:1$
70	2	$(70-90)/(2-1)=20:1$
40	3	$(40-70)/(3-2)=30:1$
00	4	$(00-40)/(4-3)=40:1$

Note MRT is considered in absolute terms only.

As in the above case MRT is increasing, PPF will be concave to the origin.

(ii)

Guns (in units) (X)	**Butter** (in units) (Y)	**MRT** ($\Delta Y/\Delta X$)
0	100	—
1	60	$(60-100)/(1-0)=40:1$
2	30	$(30-60)/(2-1)=30:1$
3	10	$(10-30)/(3-2)=20:1$
4	00	$(00-10)/(4-3)=10:1$

Note MRT is considered in absolute terms only.

As in the above case MRT is decreasing, PPF will be convex to the origin.

(iii)

Bread (in kg) (X)	**Biscuits** (in kg) (Y)	**MRT** ($\Delta Y/\Delta X$)
10	200	—
20	160	$(160-200)/(20-10)=4:1$
30	120	$(120-160)/(30-20)=4:1$
40	80	$(80-120)/(40-30)=4:1$
50	40	$(40-80)/(50-40)=4:1$
60	00	$(00-40)/(60-50)=4:1$

Note MRT is considered in absolute terms only.

As in the above case MRT is constant, PPF will be a straight line.

SELF ASSESSMENT TEST

Objective Type Questions

1. Which of the following is a key characteristic of scarcity?
   (a) Unlimited supply of resources
   (b) Unlimited wants and limited resources
   (c) Absence of alternative uses for resources
   (d) Surplus production of goods

2. .... primarily causes higher prices in the case of scarcity.
   (a) Demand exceeding supply
   (b) Excessive government regulation
   (c) Overproduction of goods
   (d) Technological inefficiencies

3. What is the core activity of an economy related to transforming inputs into goods or services?
   (a) Consumption (b) Production
   (c) Exchange (d) Investment

4. Non-economic activities are primarily undertaken to maximise .... welfare.
   (a) personal (b) financial
   (c) social (d) economic

5. Which type of economy combines both private and public sectors with government regulation guiding key industries?
   (a) Market economy
   (b) Centrally planned economy
   (c) Mixed economy
   (d) Free economy

6. The PPF curve demonstrates the .... in production when resources are limited.
   (a) trade-offs (b) abundance
   (c) unlimited supply (d) surplus

7. What is Marginal Opportunity Cost (MOC)?
   (a) Gain in Good Y per unit of Good X sacrificed
   (b) Loss in Good Y per unit of Good X gained
   (c) Total cost of production for all goods
   (d) Cost of technology improvement

8. Which of the following represents the problem of 'what to produce'?
   (a) Choosing between manual labour and machines
   (b) Allocating resources efficiently
   (c) Distributing goods among different income groups
   (d) Deciding whether to produce luxury or essential goods

Answers 1. (b) 2. (a) 3. (b) 4. (c) 5. (c) 6. (a) 7. (b) 8. (d)

Short Answer Type Questions

9. What are scarce resources? Explain with an example.

10. "The process of transferring ownership of goods or services from seller to buyer for a consideration." Which economic activity is highlighted in the given statement? Explain.

11. What is a production possibility schedule?

12. Define the following
    (i) Microeconomics (ii) Macroeconomics

13. "The resources are not only scarce in supply but they also have alternative uses." Do you agree? Give reasons.

14. What are the assumptions of the Production Possibility Frontier (PPF)?

Long Answer Type Questions

15. What are the key differences between a market economy, a centrally planned economy and a mixed economy?

16. Explain how changes in resources or technology can cause shifts in the Production Possibility Frontier (PPF)?

Numerical Questions

17. A country is deciding how to allocate its resources between producing wheat and rice. The following table shows the production possibilities

Production Possibility	Wheat (in quintals)	Rice (in quintals)
A	50	0
B	40	20
C	30	40
D	20	60
E	10	80

Calculate the Marginal Opportunity Cost (MOC) of producing rice when moving from possibility A to possibility B and from B to C.

18. Calculate marginal rate of transformation in the following case and comment on the shape of production possibility frontier.

Pizza (in units)	0	1	2	3	4
Soft Drink (in units)	120	110	90	60	20

02

CHAPTER

A consumer is an individual who uses goods and services to satisfy his/her wants. A rational consumer aims to maximise satisfaction (or utility) by wisely allocating his income across various goods and services.

Consumer's Equilibrium

(Utility Analysis and Indifference Curve Analysis)

YOUR STUDY GOALS

2.1 Concept of Utility
2.2 Cardinal Utility Concepts
2.3 Consumer's Equilibrium
2.4 Ordinal Utility Analysis: Indifference Curve (IC)

YOUR PRACTICE GOAL

- Objective Type Questions (60 Qs ; MCQs, A-R, Statements, Matching, Concept Identification)
- Subjective Questions (22 SAs, 10 LAs)
- 10 Numerical Questions
- Self Assessment Test (8 MCQs, 5 SAs, 2 LAs, 5 Numericals)

2.1 Concept of Utility

The utility refers to the amount of satisfaction that a consumer derives from consuming a commodity and is measured in **utils.**

There are two main approaches to measure utility

1. **Cardinal Utility Approach** Introduced by Professor **Alfred Marshall,** this approach suggests that utility can be measured in exact numerical units, such as 1, 2, 3, etc.
2. **Ordinal Utility Approach** Proposed by Professors **Allen and Hicks,** this approach argues that utility cannot be measured in numbers, rather a consumer can rank his/her preference from a set of most preferred to least preferred bundles.

In both approaches, the goal of the consumer is to maximise utility with the given income.

Cardinal Utility
A consumer gets 20 utils from eating apples and 15 utils from oranges, showing a numerical difference in satisfaction.

Ordinal Utility
A consumer prefers pizza over pasta and pasta over sandwiches, ranking choices without exact numbers.

2.2 Cardinal Utility Concepts

Cardinal utility has two concepts

1. Total Utility (TU)

It refers to the overall (total) satisfaction a consumer gets from consuming a specific quantity of a commodity. It is the sum total of marginal utilities obtained from each unit consumed.

Mathematically,

$$TU = MU_1 + MU_2 + \ldots + MU_n \ \ or \ \ = \Sigma MU$$

e.g. If a consumer gets 30, 20 and 15 utils from consuming 3 ice-creams then, the total utility will be 30 + 20 + 15 = 65 utils.

2. Marginal Utility (MU)

It is the satisfaction derived from consuming an additional unit of a commodity. Mathematically, it is calculated as

$$MU_{nth} = TU_n - TU_{n-1} \quad or \quad MU = \frac{\Delta TU}{\Delta Q}$$

Here, MU = Marginal Utility; TU_n = Total Utility from n units; TU_{n-1} = Total Utility from $(n-1)$ units
ΔQ = Change in Quantity; ΔTU = Change in Total Utility

e.g. If consuming a second ice-cream increases total utility from 30 utils to 50 utils, the marginal utility of the 2nd ice-cream is (50 – 30) = 20 utils.

Relationship between TU and MU

Schedule and diagram given below illustrates the relationship between TU and MU

Quantity (Q)	**Total Utility** (TU)	**Marginal Utility** (MU)
0	0	—
1	5	5
2	9	4
3	12	3
4	14	2
5	15	1
6	15	0
7	14	–1
8	12	–2

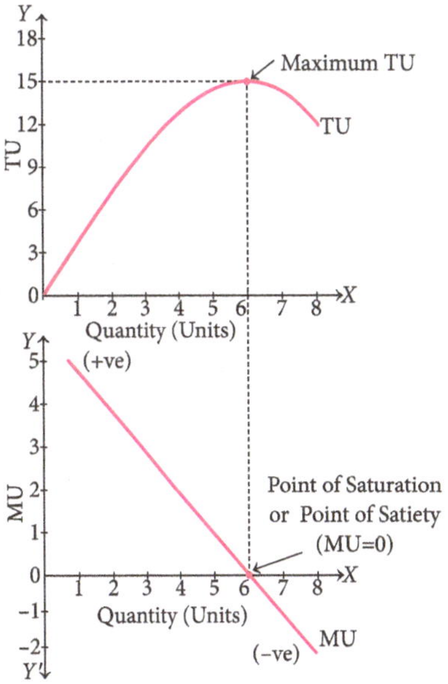

Observations

- When MU is diminishing but remains positive (+ve), i.e. till 5th unit, TU tends to increase at a diminishing rate.
- When MU becomes zero, i.e. at 6th unit, TU reaches its maximum point. This point is known as point of saturation or point of satiety.
- When MU becomes negative (–ve), i.e. from 7th unit onwards, TU starts to fall.

The above relationship between TU and MU is due to the operation of law of diminishing marginal utility.

Solved Question 1 Ajay is a consumer and his total utility schedule is given below

Units	0	1	2	3	4	5
TU	0	30	56	80	102	122

You are required to derive Ajay's marginal utility schedule.

Sol.

Units	TU	MU $(TU_n - TU_{n-1})$
0	0	0
1	30	$30 - 0 = 30$
2	56	$56 - 30 = 26$
3	80	$80 - 56 = 24$
4	102	$102 - 80 = 22$
5	122	$122 - 102 = 20$

Solved Question 2 Amit is a consumer and his marginal utility schedule is given below

Units	1	2	3	4	5	6
MU	32	30	26	20	12	2

You are required to derive Amit's total utility schedule.

Sol.

Units	MU	TU $(TU = \Sigma MU)$
1	32	32
2	30	$32 + 30 = 62$
3	26	$62 + 26 = 88$
4	20	$88 + 20 = 108$
5	12	$108 + 12 = 120$
6	2	$120 + 2 = 122$

Law of Diminishing Marginal Utility (DMU)

This law states that as a consumer consumes more units of a commodity continuously, the satisfaction (marginal utility) derived from each additional unit goes on diminishing.

Initially, total utility increases at a diminishing rate, reaches its maximum point and then starts to fall.

This psychological law, given by **Prof. Gossen**, is also known as *Gossen's First Law of Consumption* or *Fundamental Law of Satisfaction* or *Fundamental Psychological Law.*

Assumptions of the Law of DMU

- Utility is measurable in numerical units called 'utils'.
- Consumer is a rational consumer.
- Standard and identical units of a good must be consumed.
- Marginal utility of money is assumed to be constant.
- Quality of a commodity is assumed to be uniform.
- Consumption should be continuous.
- Price of the commodity remains constant.
- Income of the consumer doesn't change.

Exceptions to the Law of DMU

The law of DMU does not hold good for

- Money and expensive metals such as gold, silver, etc.
- Reading
- Listening to music
- Acquiring knowledge

Law of Equi-marginal Utility

This law states that to maximise satisfaction, consumers should allocate their income on two goods such that the ratio of marginal utility of a commodity to its price becomes equal to the ratio of marginal utility of another commodity to its price.

i.e. $$\frac{MU_X}{P_X} = \frac{MU_Y}{P_Y}$$

where, MU_X = Marginal Utility of Good X; MU_Y = Marginal Utility of Good Y

P_X = Price of Good X; P_Y = Price of Good Y

Also known as the second psychological law of consumption, this law emphasises optimal allocation of resources for maximum satisfaction.

Assumptions

Law of Equi-marginal Utility

- Fixed income of the consumer.
- Substitute goods are available in market.
- Utility is measurable in cardinal units.
- Constant prices of the goods.
- The law of diminishing marginal utility operates.

2.3 Consumer's Equilibrium

It refers to a situation where a consumer maximises satisfaction from purchasing a commodity within his/her given income, with no intention to change his/her current spending. This state of rest occurs when the consumer achieves maximum utility with the resources available.

Conditions of Consumer's Equilibrium (Marginal Utility Analysis)

These conditions can be studied under two cases as discussed below

1. In Case of Single Commodity

In the case of a single commodity, a consumer reaches equilibrium when he/she buys the quantity of a good that provides maximum satisfaction. Three factors influence this decision

- Price of the commodity.
- Marginal utility of the commodity (MU_X).
- Marginal utility of money (MU_M).

Marginal Utility of Money (MU_M)

It is the money worth of 'utils'. Util is an arbitary unit of utility. In order to convert 'utils' in money value, MU_M is used. When 'utils' are divided by MU_M, it gets converted into utility in monetary terms.

Mathematically,

$$\frac{MU_X \text{ (Units)}}{MU_M} = MU_X \text{ (in rupees)}$$

e.g. If $MU_M = 1$; ₹ 1 = 1 util; if $MU_M = 2$; ₹ 1 = 2 utils and so on.

In case of a single commodity, consumers attain equilibrium when

(i) $\frac{MU_X}{P_X} = MU_M$ *or* $\frac{MU_X}{MU_M} = P_X$

It implies that in state of equilibrium, ratio of marginal utility of X to the marginal utility of money is equal to price of commodity.

(ii) $MU_X = P_X$

It implies that in state of equilibrium, marginal utility derived from the consumption of a commodity is equal to its price, when $MU_M = 1$.

The following schedule and graph will help in a better understanding of the above concept

Units Consumed	MU_X (Utils)	MU_X in terms of ₹ $\left(\frac{MU_X}{2}\right)$	Price	Gain/ Loss
1	10	5	3	2
2	8	4	3	1
3	6	3	3	0
4	4	2	3	–1
5	2	1	3	–2
6	0	0	3	–3

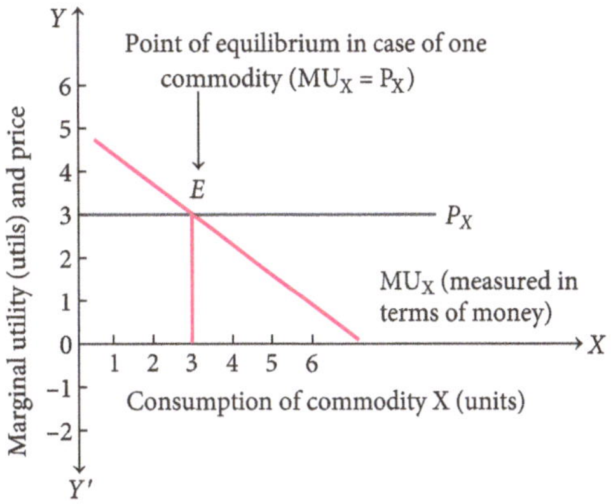

Consumer's equilibrium : One commodity case
(Curve is based on hypothetical data)

Assumption It is assumed that MU of a rupee is 2 utils, i.e. ₹ 1 = 2 utils and price of good X is ₹ 3 per unit.

Observations

- MU_X curve is downward sloping curve showing that marginal utility falls as consumption of commodity X increases, due to operation of law of DMU.
- P_X is a horizontal straight line as price of a commodity is fixed as ₹ 3 per unit.
- It is clear that consumer is at equilibrium when he is consuming 3 units, because here

$$\frac{MU_X}{MU_M} = P_X \quad or \quad \frac{6}{2} = 3 \quad or \quad 3 = 3$$

Solved Question 3 **Find consumer's equilibrium from the data given below, if price of the good is ₹ 10 per unit and marginal utility of money is 2.**

Units Consumed	TU (in utils)
1	50
2	90
3	120
4	140
5	150
6	150
7	140
8	120

Sol. Calculation of consumer's equilibrium under one commodity case with P_X = ₹ 10

Condition of equilibrium $\Rightarrow \frac{MU_X}{MU_M} = P_X$

Q	TU (Utils)	MU_X (Utils)	MU_X (₹) = MU (Utils/MU_M = 2)	P_X
1	50	50	50/2 = 25	10
2	90	90 − 50 = 40	40/2 = 20	10
3	120	120 − 90 = 30	30/2 = 15	10
4	140	140 − 120 = 20	20/2 = 10	10
5	150	150 − 140 = 10	10/2 = 5	10
6	150	150 − 150 = 0	0/2 = 0	10
7	140	140 − 150 = − 10	− 10/2 = − 5	10
8	120	120 − 140 = − 20	− 20/2 = − 10	10

The condition of consumer's equilibrium is satisfied when consumer consumes 4 units of the good as both MU_X (in ₹) is equal to price.

2. In Case of Two Commodities

In case of two commodities, consumer attains equilibrium, when

(i) $\frac{MU_X}{P_X} = \frac{MU_Y}{P_Y} = MU_M$

It implies that in state of equilibrium, utility per rupee obtained by consumer from consuming good X or good Y with the ratio of respective prices of good should be equal to marginal utility of money. This condition is based on **law of equi-marginal utility.**

(ii) $\frac{MU_X}{P_X} = \frac{MU_Y}{P_Y}$ (When P_X is not equal to P_Y)

It implies that in state of equilibrium, utility per rupee from good X must be equal to utility per rupee from good Y, when $MU_M = 1$.

The above condition can also be written as,

$$\frac{MU_X}{MU_Y} = \frac{P_X}{P_Y}$$

It implies that in state of equilibrium, ratio of marginal utilities of two commodities is equal to the ratio of their prices.

(iii) $MU_X = MU_Y$, when $MU_M = 1$ and $P_X = P_Y$. (Assumption : $P_X = P_Y$ = ₹ 1 per unit)

(iv) Total expenditure on good X and good Y is equal to consumer income, i.e. $P_X . Q_X + P_Y . Q_Y = M$ and marginal utility must fall with rise in units of consumption.

The following schedule and graph will help in a better understanding of the above concept

Units of 'X'	MU_X	P_X	MU_X in terms of ₹ $\left(\frac{MU_X}{P_X}\right)$	Units of 'Y'	MU_Y	P_Y	MU_Y in terms of ₹ $\left(\frac{MU_Y}{P_Y}\right)$
1	100	10	10	1	24	2	12
2	80	10	8	2	22	2	11
3	60	10	6	3	20	2	10
4	40	10	4	4	18	2	9
5	20	10	2	5	16	2	8

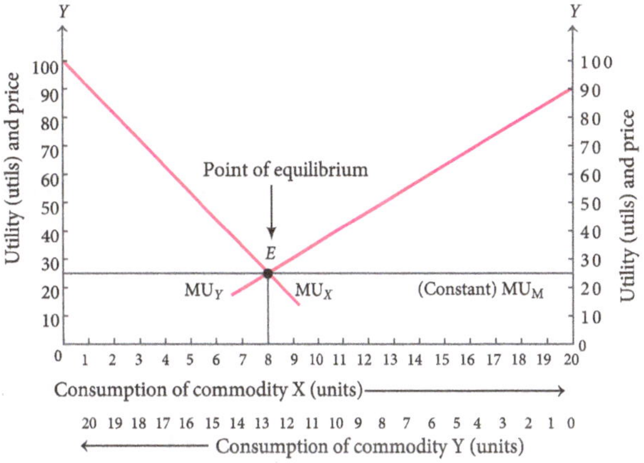

Consumer's equilibrium : Two commodities case
(Curve is based on hypothetical data)

Observations

- $\frac{MU_X}{P_X} = \frac{MU_Y}{P_Y}$, when consumer is consuming 1 unit of good X and 3 units of goods Y or 2 units of good X and 5 units of good Y.
- Now, assuming that his money income is ₹ 30. So, for first combination, he pays $1 \times 10 + 3 \times 2 =$ ₹ 16, which is less than his money income, therefore he is not in equilibrium.
- For the second combination, he pays $2 \times 10 + 5 \times 2 =$ ₹ 30, which is equal to his money income. Also, at this level, total utility is maximum. Therefore, equilibrium is struck when he consumes 2 units of X and 5 units of Y.

Equilibrium equation for '*n*' number of commodities

$$\frac{MU_1}{P_1} = \frac{MU_2}{P_2} = \frac{MU_3}{P_3} = \ldots = \frac{MU_{nth}}{P_{nth}} = MU_M$$

Solved Question 4 **Find consumer's equilibrium from the following data given below, when price of both goods are ₹ 5 per unit and marginal utility of money is 1. Consumer has a income of ₹ 45.**

Units Consumed	MU_X (Utils)	MU_Y (Utils)
1	50	40
2	40	35
3	30	30
4	20	25
5	10	20
6	00	15
7	−10	10
8	−20	05

Sol. Calculation of consumer's equilibrium under two commodity case.

Condition of equilibrium $= \frac{MU_X}{P_X} = \frac{MU_Y}{P_Y} = MU_M$;

When $MU_M = 1$ and $P_X = P_Y$

$\therefore \quad MU_X = MU_Y$ ...(i)

and $\quad P_X \cdot Q_X + P_Y \cdot Q_Y = M$ ...(ii)

Q	MU_X (Utils/MU_M)	MU_Y (Utils/MU_M)
1	50	40
2	40	35
3	30	30
4	20	25
5	10	20
6	00	15
7	−10	10
8	−20	05

Note $MU_M = 1$; $\therefore$ MU_X (Utils) $= MU_X$(₹); $P_x = P_y = 5$

First condition of equilibrium is satisfied under following cases

(x, y) = (2, 1), (3, 3), (4, 5), (5, 7). However, the second condition is satisfied at (4, 5), i.e., $P_x \cdot Q_x + P_y \cdot Q_y = M$ or $(5 \times 4) + (5 \times 5) = 45$.

So, consumer will be in equilibrium by consuming 4 units of good X and 5 units of good Y.

2.4 Ordinal Utility Analysis: Indifference Curve (IC)

An indifference curve is the graphical representation, which represents all those combinations of two commodities, which give same level of satisfaction to a consumer.

In other words, indifference curve is the locus of all the bundles of two goods, which gives consumer equal level of satisfaction, i.e. he is indifferent between the bundles.

The concept can be highlight through following schedule and graph

Combination	Good X	Good Y
a	1	6
b	2	4
c	3	2
d	4	1

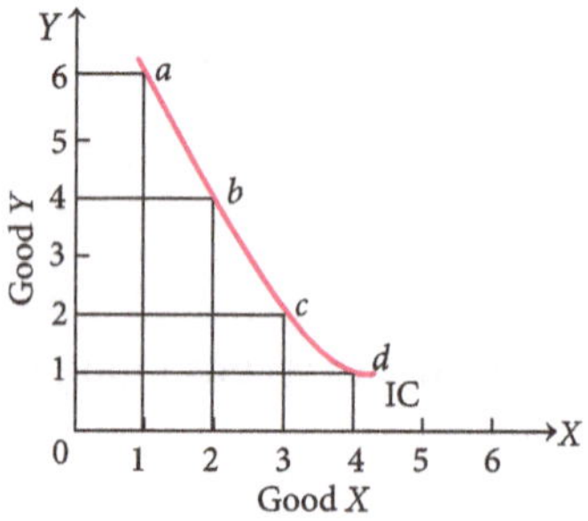

In the given indifference curve, level of satisfaction of the consumer at point *a* is same as at point *b*, *c* or *d*. These combinations together are known as indifference set.

Assumptions of the Indifference Curve

- IC is drawn for two commodities.
- Consumer is a rational consumer.
- Prices of the commodity are constant.
- Income of consumer remains constant.
- Ordinal method of utility, i.e. consumer can rank his preferences on the basis of his satisfaction.
- An ideal IC is always convex.

Monotonic Preferences

Consumer's behaviour is governed by monotonic preferences. It means that a rational consumer always prefers more of a commodity over less units, as it offers him a higher level of satisfaction.

Consumer's preferences are assumed to be such that between any two bundles (x_1, x_2) and (y_1, y_2), if (x_1, x_2) has more of at least one of the goods and no less of the other good compared to (y_1, y_2), then the consumer prefers (x_1, x_2) to (y_1, y_2).

Indifference Map

It refers to a set or family of indifference curves representing consumer preferences corresponding to different income levels of the consumer.

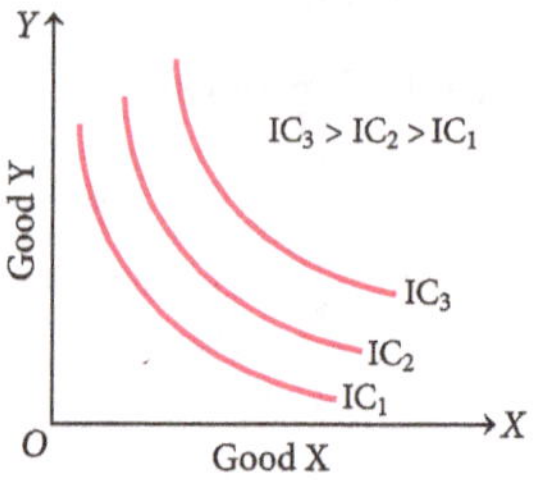

In graph, IC_1 shows the lowest level of satisfaction, while IC_2 shows the satisfaction level more than that of IC_1 and IC_3 shows the highest level of satisfaction.

Marginal Rate of Substitution (MRS)

MRS refers to the rate at which a consumer is willing to sacrifice one good in order to gain additional unit of the other good. Slope of indifference curve is known as Marginal Rate of Substitution (MRS).

It is mathematically calculated as

$$MRS = \frac{\Delta Y}{\Delta X} = \frac{\text{Loss in Units of Good Y}}{\text{Gain in Units of Good X}}$$

Solved Question 5 Calculate marginal rate of substitution from the following data.

Good X	Good Y
1	40
2	31
3	24
4	19
5	15
6	12
7	10

Sol. **Calculation of MRS**

Good X	Good Y	MRS
1	40	—
2	31	9 : 1
3	24	7 : 1
4	19	5 : 1
5	15	4 : 1
6	12	3 : 1
7	10	2 : 1

Features/ Properties of IC

- Indifference curve slope downwards from left to the right or is negatively sloped, as consumption of both goods cannot be increased at once.
- Indifference curve is convex to the origin, due to diminishing marginal rate of substitution.
- Two indifference curves can never touch or intersect each other.
- A higher indifference curve represents a higher level of satisfaction.
- It is often assumed that a consumer buys a combination of two goods. Hence, an indifference curve touches neither x-axis nor y-axis.

Consumer's Budget

It represents the financial resources available to a consumer, which determine the quantity and combination of goods he/she can purchase at given prices. There are two aspects of consumer's budget as discussed below

Budget Set

It refers to all possible combinations of two goods that a consumer can afford given their income and the prevailing market prices. Equation of budget set is

$$P_X Q_X + P_Y Q_Y \leq M$$

where, P_X = Price of Good X; P_Y = Price of Good Y; Q_X = Quantity of good X; Q_Y = Quantity of Good Y; M = Money income

Budget Set

A consumer is having ₹ 60 to spend on good X and good Y. Price of good X is ₹ 2 per unit and price of good Y is ₹ 1 per unit. The attainable budget set of two goods X and Y for a consumer will be

Units of Good X	0	10	20	30
Units of Good Y	60	40	20	0

Budget Line

It is a graphical representation of various combinations of two goods that a consumer can buy with his/her given income and the prevailing prices of goods. Each point on the budget line represents a combination where the total expenditure equals the consumer's income.

Mathematically,

$$\text{Equation of budget line, } M = P_X Q_X + P_Y Q_Y$$

Here, M = Given money income

P_X and P_Y = Per unit price of Goods X and Y

Q_X and Q_Y = Quantity of Goods X and Y

It is assumed here that consumer spends all of his money income.

In the given figure, the budget line drawn is based on the budget set schedule given above

Accordingly, maximum 30 units of Good X are purchased when entire budget is spent on Good X and maximum 60 units of Good Y can be purchased when entire budget is spent on Good Y.

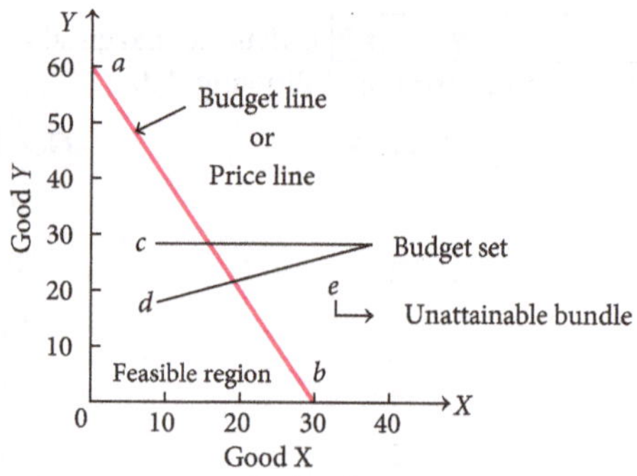

Budget line

Slope of the Budget Line

The slope indicates the rate at which one good can be exchanged for another. It is known as the 'price ratio' or 'market rate of exchange'.

Mathematically, Slope of Budget Line $= \dfrac{\Delta Y}{\Delta X}$ *or* $\dfrac{P_X}{P_Y}$, i.e. the ratio of prices of two commodities, also known as market rate of exchange.

Properties of Budget Line

- Budget line is drawn for two commodities.
- Price of both goods is assumed to be constant.
- Consumer's income is fixed.
- Consumer is rational who spends his entire income on both goods.
- Slope of budget line is constant slope, i.e. it is linear curve. Budget line always slopes downwards.

Why Budget Line Slopes Downwards?

Budget line always slopes downward as consumer has a fixed income and he is assumed to spend his entire income on the consumption of two goods. Thus, consumption of one good can only be increased by reducing consumption of the other good. e.g. If a consumer is consuming 5 units of Good X and 10 units of Good Y by spending his entire income, additional units of Good X can be consumed only by sacrificing units of Good Y.

Shift in Budget Line

Budget line may shift under two situations

Change in Income of the Consumer

Keeping price of both goods constant, a rise in income of the consumer shifts the budget line rightwards, while fall in income causes a leftward shift in the budget line. This is known as shift in budget line.

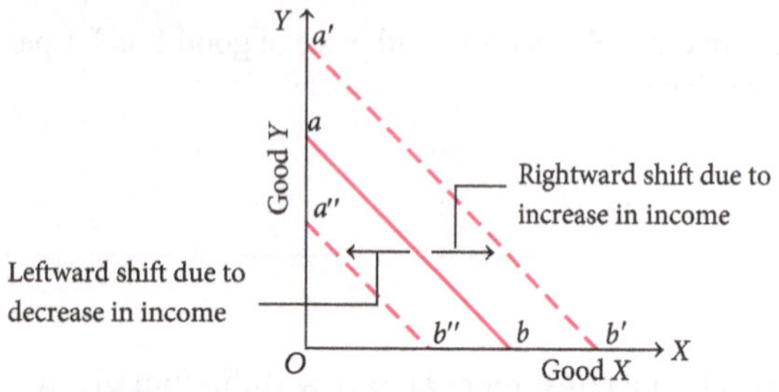

Effect of change in income on budget line

Change in Price of Commodities

Change in price of one good will rotate the budget line. Fall in price causes outward rotation due to rise in purchasing power and *vice-versa*.

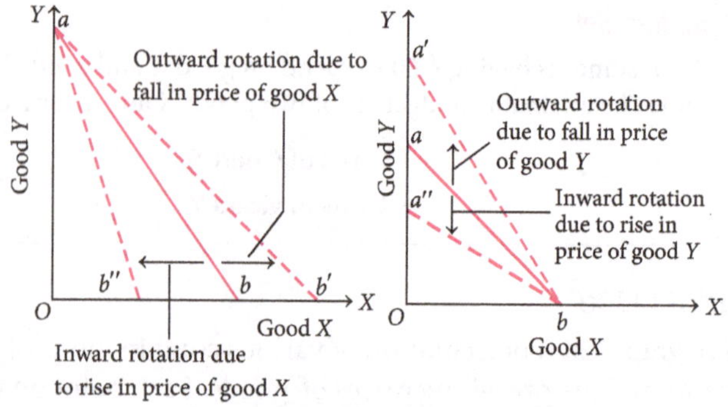

Effect of change in price of one good

If price of both the goods falls simultaneously, then there will be an outward/rightward shift in the budget line and *vice-versa*. (Similar to change in income).

Conditions of Consumer's Equilibrium using Indifference Curve Analysis

In indifference curve analysis, a consumer achieves equilibrium when he strikes a balance between what he wishes to buy and what he can buy. This equilibrium is determined by the following conditions

1. The slope of the indifference curve must be equal to the slope of the budget line.

   It can be expressed as, $MRS_{XY} = \frac{P_X}{P_Y}$.

   Here, MRS_{XY} = Marginal Rate of Substitution between Good X and Good Y and

   $\frac{P_X}{P_Y}$ = Price ratio between Good X and Good Y or slope of budget line.

2. The indifference curve must be convex to the origin at the point of equilibrium. This ensures that the MRS is diminishing. In the given diagram, BL = Budget Line.

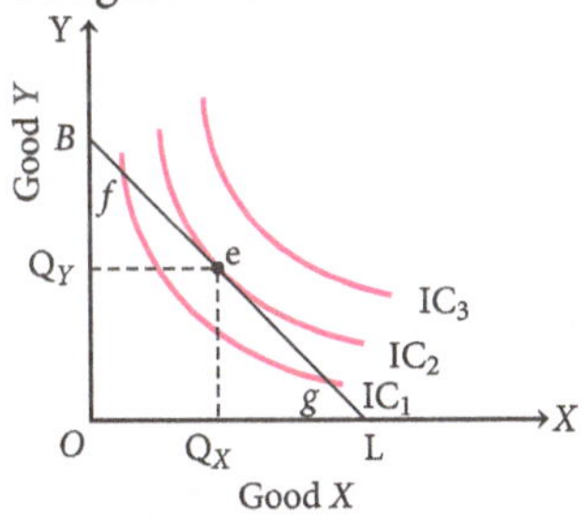

IC_1, IC_2, IC_3 = Set of Indifference Curves or Indifference Map

Observations

- Consumer is in equilibrium at point '*e*'. At this point, BL is tangent to IC_2, signifying $MRS_{XY} = P_X / P_Y$.
- Consumer will not be in equilibrium at point *f* and *g* because they belong to lower IC i.e. IC_1.
- Indifference curve, IC_3 represent highest possible satisfaction. However, consumer cannot afford IC_3 as it is beyond his income level.

Mind Map

CONSUMER'S EQUILIBRIUM

1 Concept of Utility

It refers to the amount of satisfaction that a consumer derives from consuming a commodity and is measured in utils.

Approaches to Utility Measurement

- **Cardinal Utility** (by Alfred Marshall) Utility can be measured in numerical terms.
- **Ordinal Utility** (by Allen and Hicks) Consumers rank preferences instead of assigning numerical values.

2 Cardinal Utility Concepts

- **Total Utility** (TU) It is the total satisfaction that consumer gets from consuming all units.
  $$TU = \sum MU$$
- **Marginal Utility** (MU) It is the additional satisfaction from consuming one more unit.
  $$MU = \Delta TU/\Delta Q$$
- **TU and MU Relationship**
  - TU increases at a decreasing rate when MU is positive.
  - TU reaches its maximum when MU is equal to zero (Point of saturation).
  - TU declines when MU is negative.

3 Law of Diminishing Marginal Utility (DMU)

- It states that as a consumer consumes more of a commodity continuously, the satisfaction (marginal utility) derived from each additional unit goes on diminishing.
- It is given by Prof. Gossen (Gossen's First Law of Consumption).
- MU curve slopes downward due to decreasing MU.

4 Law of Equi-Marginal Utility

- This law states that to maximise satisfaction, consumers should allocate their income on two goods such that the ratio of marginal utility of a commodity to its price becomes equal to the ratio of marginal utility of another commodity to its price.
- Mathematical Condition
  $$MU_x / P_x = MU_y / P_y$$
  (Utility per rupee spent must be equal for both goods)

5 Consumer's Equilibrium

It is a situation where a consumer maximises satisfaction from purchasing a commodity within his/her given income, with no intention to change his/her current spending.

Conditions of Consumer's Equilibrium (Marginal Utility Analysis)

Case 1 Single Commodity

- $MU_x/P_x = MU_M$ (Marginal Utility of Money)
- $MU_x = P_x$

Case 2 Two Commodities

- $MU_x/P_x = MU_y / P_y = MU_M$
- Equilibrium when prices differ
  $$MU_x/P_x = MU_y/P_y$$
- Total expenditure on both goods equals the consumer's income
  $$P_x.Q_x + P_y.Q_y = M$$

6 Ordinal Utility Analysis: Indifference Curve (IC)

Indifference Curve (IC) shows different combinations of two goods that provide the same level of satisfaction.

Properties of Indifference Curves

- Negatively sloped (More of one good → Less of another).
- Convex to origin (Diminishing MRS).
- ICs never intersect.
- Higher IC = Higher satisfaction.

Indifference Map It is a set of ICs representing consumer preferences corresponding to different income levels of consumer.

Marginal Rate of Substitution (MRS) It is a rate at which a consumer sacrifices one good for another.

$$MRS = \Delta Y / \Delta X$$

7 Consumer's Budget

It represents the financial resources available to a consumer, determining the quantity and combination of goods he/she can buy at given prices.

Two Aspects

- **Budget Set** It represents all possible combinations of two goods that a consumer can afford given their income and the prevailing market prices.
  $$P_x.X_x + P_y.X_y \le M$$
- **Budget Line** It is a graphical representation of various combinations of two goods that a consumer can buy with given income and the prevailing market prices.
  $$P_XQ_X + P_YQ_Y = M$$

8 Shift in Budget Line

Change in Income of the Consumer

- Increase in Income– Rightward Shift
- Decrease in Income– Leftward Shift

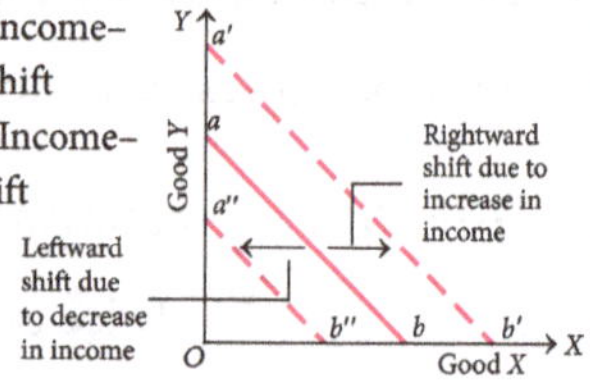

Change in Price of the Commodities

- Price of One Good Decreases – Outward Rotation
- Price of One Good Increases – Inward Rotation

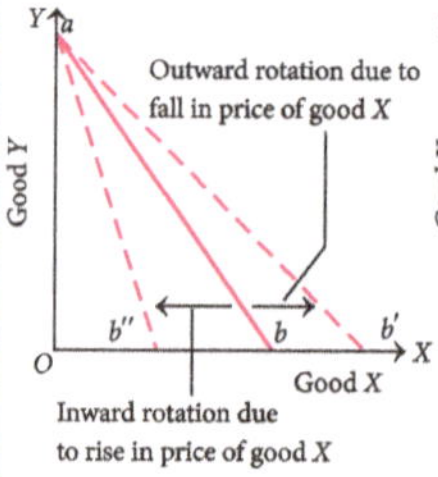

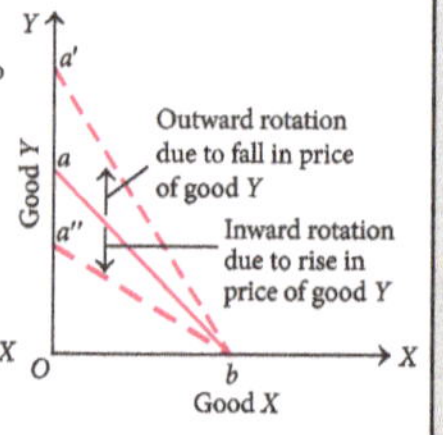

9 Consumer's Equilibrium (IC Approach)

- Slope of IC = Slope of Budget Line
  $$MRS_{xy} = P_x/P_y$$
- IC must be convex to origin (ensuring diminishing MRS).

Equilibrium Point Budget line is tangent to the highest IC.

EXAM PATTERN QUESTIONS

Objective Type Questions

Multiple Choice Questions (MCQs)

1. What is the main goal of a rational consumer according to the concept of utility?

(a) To minimise utility
(b) To maximise income
(c) To maximise satisfaction
(d) To increase prices

2. The law of diminishing marginal utility was proposed by Prof ....

(a) Marshall (b) Hicks
(c) Allen (d) Gossen

3. Identify the point at which marginal utility becomes zero. **Competency Based Que**

I. Equilibrium II. Satiety
III. Maximum utility IV. Minimum utility

Codes

(a) I and II (b) Only II
(c) III and IV (d) Only I

4. Which of the following law is demonstrated in the following image?

(a) Consumers equilibrium
(b) Law of equi-marginal utility
(c) Law of diminishing marginal utility
(d) Consumer budget

5. "Demand for gold surges despite rising prices and falling marginal utility."

Source *https://economictimes.indiatimes.com/demand-for-gold-surges-despite-rising-prices/articleshow/2987369.cms?from=mdr*

This headline suggests that the law of diminishing marginal utility **Competency Based Que**

(a) does not apply to goods like gold
(b) applies to all goods equally
(c) does not affect consumer demand at all
(d) leads to an increase in total utility

6. "When marginal utility becomes zero, total utility reaches its maximum point."

The relationship between marginal utility and total utility indicates that once marginal utility becomes zero, further consumption of the commodity will .... **Competency Based Que**

(a) increase total utility (b) decrease total utility
(c) leave total utility unchanged
(d) double the marginal utility

7. Identify the law in the statement below. **Competency Based Que**

"A consumer with a given income allocates his expenditure among commodities, so that last rupee spent on each brings equal marginal utility."

(a) Law of diminishing marginal utility
(b) Law of equi-marginal utility
(c) Law of diminishing MRS
(d) None of the above

8. Find the missing figures and choose the correct alternative. **Competency Based Que**

Units	TU	MU
1	60	...
2	...	52
3	160	...
4	...	44

(a) 0, 52, 160, 44 (b) 60, 112, 48, 204
(c) 112, 60, 48, 204 (d) 0, 60, 48, 44

9. Which of the following is not an assumption of the law of diminishing marginal utility?
(a) Time gap between consumption is significant
(b) Utility is measurable
(c) Consumer's income remains constant
(d) Identical units of the commodity are consumed

10. Utility approach is ....
(a) cardinal
(b) ordinal
(c) Both cardinal and ordinal
(d) None of the above

11. An indifference curve represents combinations of two goods that provide .... level of satisfaction.
(a) different (b) maximum
(c) equal (d) minimal

12. In case of single commodity, a consumer is at equilibrium point, marginal utility derived from consumption of commodities is 12, find the price of that commodity (when $MU_M = 1$). **Competency Based Que**
(a) ₹ 1 (b) ₹ 2 (c) ₹ 12 (d) ₹ 10

13. When is consumer equilibrium achieved with two commodities, if the prices of both goods are same?
(a) Marginal utility of one good is greater than the other
(b) Marginal utility of both goods is equal
(c) Marginal utility of one good is zero
(d) Marginal utility of both goods is negative

14. According to indifference curve approach, at the point of equilibrium **NCERT (QR)**
(a) Slope of indifference curve is not equal to slope of price line
(b) Slope of indifference curve < Slope of price line
(c) Slope of indifference curve = Slope of price line
(d) Slope of indifference curve > Slope of price line

15. "Spiraling prices of essentials, fuel strain household budgets across India."
Source https://www.business-standard.com/article/economy-policy/spiralling-prices-of-essentials-fuel-strain-household-budgets-across-india-122041200380_1.html
This headline relates to which aspect of consumer equilibrium? **Competency Based Que**
(a) Law of diminishing marginal utility
(b) Marginal rate of substitution
(c) Impact of changing prices on consumer's equilibrium
(d) Increase in total utility

16. Which of the following statements is true for an indifference curve? **Competency Based Que**
I. Indifference curves cannot intersect.
II. A higher indifference curve represents a lower level of satisfaction.
III. Indifference curves are convex to the origin.
IV. Indifference curves are positively sloped.

Codes
(a) I and III
(b) II and IV
(c) I, II, III and IV (d) None of the above

17. In case of $MU_X/P_X > MU_Y/P_Y$ **NCERT (QR)**
(a) consumer will shift some expenditure from Y to X
(b) consumer will shift some expenditure from X to Y
(c) consumer will spend less on both X and Y
(d) consumer will spend more on both X and Y

18. "In the case of two commodities, a consumer reaches equilibrium when the ratio of marginal utilities equals the ratio of prices."
Which concept is highlighted in the above statement? **Competency Based Que**
(a) Law of diminishing marginal utility
(b) Law of total utility
(c) Law of equi-marginal utility
(d) Law of constant utility

19. Observe the image given below and choose the most suitable option.

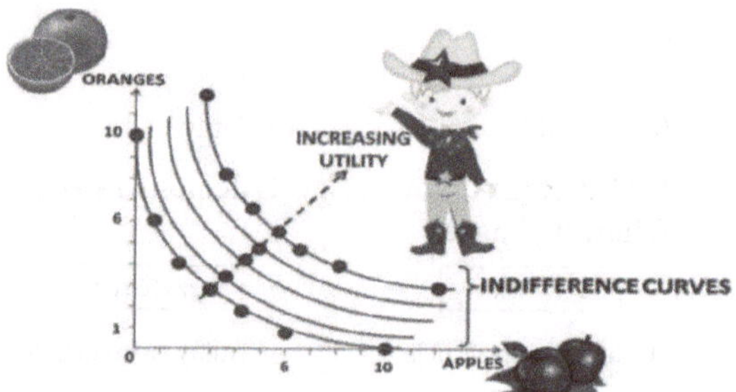

(a) Marshall's utility approach (b) Indifference map
(c) Concave indifference curves (d) None of these

20. Look at the image given below and identify the correct statement based upon the same. 25 utils of satisfaction from eating a bowl of ice cream while someone else would only get 5 utils of satisfaction.

(a) Utility is subjective in nature
(b) Utility is depending on urgency of wants
(c) Utility is cardinally measured
(d) Both (a) and (b)

21. ………… is the set of all possible combination of two goods which a consumer can afford, at his given income. **NCERT (QR)**

(a) Budget line (b) Indifference curve
(c) Diminishing marginal rate of substitution
(d) Marginal rate of substitution

22. "In equilibrium, the rate at which the consumer is willing to substitute one good for another must match the rate at which the market allows them to make this substitution."

This statement describes ……… . **Competency Based Que**

(a) convexity of indifference curve
(b) consumer's equilibrium condition
(c) slope of budget line
(d) law of diminishing marginal utility

23. Which of the following leads to a rightward shift in the budget line?

(a) Increase in the price of one good
(b) Decrease in consumer's income
(c) Fall in the price of one good
(d) Decrease in prices of both goods

24. If the income of Mr Viaan increases, then his budget line of two Goods X and Y will

(a) shift rightward (b) shift inward
(c) no change (d) positively sloped

25. A consumer is willing to give up 4 units of Good Y to gain 2 additional units of Good X. What is the Marginal Rate of Substitution (MRS)? **Competency Based Que**

(a) 1 (b) 2 (c) 0.5 (d) 4

26. If price of X commodity (P_X) is ₹ 6 and slope of budget line is 1.5, then find price of Y commodity (P_Y).

(a) ₹ 6 (b) ₹ 4 (c) ₹ 9 (d) ₹ 1.5

Direction *Read the case study and answer the questions 27 to 30 on the basis of the same*

Rahul, a college student, loves to eat burgers and fries. He has a fixed weekly budget of ₹ 500 to spend on food. The price of one burger is ₹ 100 and the price of a portion of fries is ₹ 50. Rahul is a rational consumer who aims to maximise his satisfaction while staying within his budget. He also experiences diminishing satisfaction with each additional burger or fries he consumes.

Rahul's task is to allocate his ₹ 500 between burgers and fries in such a way that he gets the most enjoyment out of his meals. After consuming his third burger and second portion of fries, Rahul notices that the additional enjoyment he gets from eating more burgers is starting to decrease. He finds that consuming an additional burger would give him less satisfaction than an extra portion of fries. This leads him to think about how he can distribute his budget wisely to maximise his utility from both items.

He calculates the Marginal Utility (MU) for each burger and portion of fries and compares it to the price of each. After some thought, Rahul decides that his ideal consumption will be 3 burgers and 4 portions of fries, as this combination provides him with the maximum satisfaction according to the law of equi-marginal utility.

27. According to the law of equi-marginal utility, Rahul achieves equilibrium when the marginal utility per rupee for both burgers and fries is …………… .

28. Why does Rahul decide to buy more portions of fries instead of another burger after consuming three burgers?

(a) The price of fries is lower
(b) The marginal utility of another burger is greater than the marginal utility of fries
(c) The marginal utility of another burger is lower than the marginal utility of fries
(d) Rahul prefers fries over burgers

29. When Rahul consumes his fourth burger, he notices that the marginal utility of the fourth burger is …………… compared to the marginal utility he gets from the additional portion of fries.

30. If Rahul had spent his money on an additional burger instead of fries, which of the following would likely be true about his total satisfaction?

(a) His total satisfaction would increase at a higher rate
(b) His total satisfaction would not change
(c) His total satisfaction would increase, but at a diminishing rate
(d) His total satisfaction would decrease

Assertion-Reason

Direction (Q.No. 31 to 40) *Read the following Assertion (A) and Reason (R) and choose the correct alternative from the following*

Alternatives

(a) Both Assertion (A) and Reason (R) are true and Reason (R) is the correct explanation of Assertion (A)
(b) Both Assertion (A) and Reason (R) are true, but Reason (R) is not the correct explanation of Assertion (A)
(c) Assertion (A) is true, but Reason (R) is false
(d) Assertion (A) is false, but Reason (R) is true

31. Assertion (A) Different persons derive different levels of utility from consumption of similar types of commodities.

Reason (R) The want satisfying power of any commodity is known as its utility, which is measured in 'utils' under cardinal approach.

32. **Assertion** (A) Consumer's utility is the point of 'satiety' where he attains maximum gain with given resources.

Reason (R) A rational consumer always prefers consumption of more units of goods as compared to less units.

33. **Assertion** (A) Total utility is the overall satisfaction a consumer gets from consuming a specific quantity of a commodity.

Reason (R) Marginal utility is the additional satisfaction gained from consuming one more unit of a commodity.

34. **Assertion** (A) When marginal utility becomes zero, total utility is at its minimum point.

Reason (R) When marginal utility is negative, total utility starts to fall.

35. **Assertion** (A) In case of a single commodity, a consumer reaches equilibrium when they buy the quantity of a good that provides maximum satisfaction.

Reason (R) Equilibrium ensures the consumer is getting maximum satisfaction from their available resources without overspending.

36. **Assertion** (A) Consumer's equilibrium with two commodities occurs when a consumer maximises satisfaction from purchasing both goods within their given income, ensuring that no changes in expenditure would increase satisfaction.

Reason (R) Consumer's equilibrium is achieved when the ratio of marginal utility to price is equal for both goods, ensuring optimal allocation of income for maximum satisfaction.

37. **Assertion** (A) An indifference curve represents a graphical tool used in ordinal utility analysis to illustrate different combinations of two commodities that provide the same level of satisfaction to a consumer.

Reason (R) Indifference map refers to a set or family of indifference curves representing consumer preferences corresponding to different income levels of the consumer.

38. **Assertion** (A) The budget set refers to all possible combinations of one good that a consumer can afford given his/her income and the prevailing market prices.

Reason (R) Budget set defines the range of options available to the consumer within his/her financial constraints.

39. **Assertion** (A) When a consumer's income increases while price remain constant, the budget line shifts rightwards.

Reason (R) This shift indicates that the consumer can now afford to purchase more of both goods.

40. **Assertion** (A) In indifference curve analysis, a consumer achieves equilibrium when his/her preferences align with his/her budget constraints.

Reason (R) The slope of the indifference curve must be equal to the slope of the budget line.

Two Statements Based MCQs

Direction (Q.No. 41 to 50) *Read the following statements carefully and choose the correct alternative*

Alternatives

(a) Statement I is correct and Statement II is incorrect
(b) Statement II is correct and Statement I is incorrect
(c) Both the statements are correct
(d) Both the statements are incorrect

41. **Statement I** Ordinal utility approach suggests that utility can be measured in exact numerical terms.

Statement II Cardinal utility approach argues that utility cannot be quantified in numbers.

42. **Statement I** Total utility is the sum of marginal utilities from each unit consumed.

Statement II Total utility is the additional satisfaction gained from consuming one extra unit of a commodity.

43. **Statement I** Total utility increases at a diminishing rate, reaches a maximum point and then starts to decline.

Statement II Utility is measurable in numerical units called 'utils.'

44. **Statement I** Law of diminishing utility doesn't hold true in absence of continuous consumption.

Statement II A consumer consumes one good and is in equilibrium. He will get more utility when the price of the good falls.

45. **Statement I** The consumer achieves equilibrium when the utility obtained per rupee spent on each commodity is equal to the marginal utility of money.

Statement II The ratio of the marginal utilities of the two commodities should equal the ratio of their prices.

46. **Statement I** An indifference curve assumes that the income of the consumer is not fixed.

Statement II Each point on the indifference curve represents a combination of two goods that gives the consumer equal satisfaction.

47. **Statement I** Indifference map is a set of indifference curves representing different levels of satisfaction.

Statement II Total utility initially increases at an increasing rate.

48. **Statement I** The indifference curve must be convex to the origin at the point of equilibrium.

Statement II At equilibrium, the rate at which the consumer is willing to substitute one good for another (MRS) must match the rate at which the market allows them to make this substitution (price ratio).

49. **Statement I** If the prices of both goods decrease, the budget line shifts leftward.

Statement II If the prices of both goods increase, the budget line shifts rightward.

50. **Statement I** When the price of one good changes, the budget line rotates around the intercept of the other good.

Statement II When a consumer's income increases while prices remain constant, the budget line shifts rightwards.

Matching

51. Match the following

Column I	Column II
A. Utility	(i) Utility expressed through ranking preferences, without assigning exact numerical values.
B. Cardinal utility	(ii) A measurable concept of utility where satisfaction is expressed in numerical terms (e.g. Utils).
C. Ordinal utility	(iii) The satisfaction or pleasure derived from consuming goods and services.
D. Marginal utility	(iv) The additional satisfaction from consuming one more unit of a good.

Codes

	A	B	C	D
(a)	(iii)	(iv)	(i)	(ii)
(b)	(iv)	(i)	(ii)	(iii)
(c)	(ii)	(iii)	(iv)	(i)
(d)	(iii)	(ii)	(i)	(iv)

52. Match the following

Column I	Column II
A. Positive MU	(i) TU starts to fall.
B. Negative MU	(ii) TU reaches at its maximum point.
C. MU is zero	(iii) The sum of marginal utilities from each unit consumed.
D. Total utility	(iv) TU tends to increase at a diminishing rate.

Codes

	A	B	C	D		A	B	C	D
(a)	(ii)	(iii)	(iv)	(i)	(b)	(iv)	(i)	(ii)	(iii)
(c)	(ii)	(iii)	(iv)	(i)	(d)	(iii)	(ii)	(i)	(iv)

53. Match the following

Column I	Column II
A. Law of diminishing marginal utility	(i) The trade-off rate between two goods for equal satisfaction.
B. Law of equi-marginal utility	(ii) Extra satisfaction from spending one more unit of money.
C. Marginal rate of substitution	(iii) Satisfaction decreases as more units of a good are consumed.
D. Marginal utility of money	(iv) Maximising satisfaction by equalising utility per dollar across all goods.

Codes

	A	B	C	D		A	B	C	D
(a)	(iii)	(iv)	(i)	(ii)	(b)	(iv)	(i)	(ii)	(iii)
(c)	(ii)	(iii)	(iv)	(i)	(d)	(iii)	(ii)	(i)	(iv)

54. Match the following

Column I	Column II
A. Consumer's equilibrium	(i) The financial resources available to a consumer.
B. Indifference curve	(ii) Consumer maximises satisfaction from purchasing a commodity within their given income
C. Indifference map	(iii) A graphical tool used in ordinal utility analysis
D. Consumer's budget	(iv) A set or family of indifference curves

Codes

	A	B	C	D		A	B	C	D
(a)	(iii)	(iv)	(i)	(ii)	(b)	(iv)	(i)	(ii)	(iii)
(c)	(ii)	(iii)	(iv)	(i)	(d)	(iii)	(ii)	(i)	(iv)

55. Match the following

Column I	Column II
A. Equal utility per rupee	(i) $MU_X = MU_Y$
B. Total expenditure equals income	(ii) $\frac{MU_X}{MU_Y} = \frac{P_X}{P_Y}$
C. Equal marginal utilities when prices are equal	(iii) $\frac{MU_X}{P_X} = \frac{MU_Y}{P_Y} = MU_M$
D. Equal utility per rupee for different prices	(iv) $P_X \cdot Q_X + P_Y \cdot Q_Y \leq M$

Codes

	A	B	C	D		A	B	C	D
(a)	(iii)	(iv)	(i)	(ii)	(b)	(iv)	(i)	(ii)	(iii)
(c)	(ii)	(iii)	(iv)	(i)	(d)	(iii)	(ii)	(i)	(iv)

Concept Identification

56. It refers to the overall satisfaction a consumer gets from consuming a specific quantity of a commodity.

57. It describes the additional satisfaction gained from consuming one more unit of a commodity.

58. It describes the condition where the marginal utility of a good is equal to its price and the consumer has no incentive to alter their consumption.

59. It describes the situation where the slope of the indifference curve matches the slope of the budget line, ensuring the consumer's satisfaction is maximised.

60. It explains why total utility initially increases at a diminishing rate, reaches a maximum and then starts to decline as more units are consumed.

Answers

1. (c) To maximise satisfaction
2. (d) Gossen
3. (b) Only II
4. (c) Law of diminishing marginal utility
5. (a) does not apply to goods like gold
6. (b) decrease total utility
7. (b) Law of equi-marginal utility
8. (b) $TU = \Sigma MU, MU = TU_n - TU_{n-1}$
9. (a) Time gap between consumption is significant
10. (c) Both cardinal and ordinal
11. (c) equal
12. (c) If $MU_M = 1$, then consumer equilibrium will be $MU_X = P_X = 12 =$ ₹ 12
13. (b) Marginal utility of both goods is equal
14. (c) Slope of indifference curve = Slope of price line
15. (c) Impact of changing prices on consumer's equilibrium
16. (a) I and III
17. (a) consumer will shift some expenditure from Y to X
18. (c) Law of equi-marginal utility
19. (b) Indifference map
20. (a) Utility is subjective in nature
21. (a) Budget line
22. (b) consumer's equilibrium condition
23. (d) Decrease in prices of both goods
24. (a) Due to increase in income, purchasing power of the consumer will increase, as a result his budget line will shift rightward, keeping prices of two goods constant.
25. (b) 2
26. (b) Slope of budget line $= \frac{P_X}{P_Y}$
27. equal
28. (c) The marginal utility of another burger is lower than the marginal utility of fries
29. lower
30. (c) His total satisfaction would increase, but at a diminishing rate
31. (b) Both Assertion (A) and Reason (R) are true, but Reason (R) is not the correct explanation of Assertion (A)
32. (c) The point of satiety refers to the stage where the marginal utility becomes zero, meaning no additional satisfaction is gained from consuming more.
33. (b) Both Assertion (A) and Reason (R) are true, but Reason (R) is not the correct explanation of Assertion (A)
34. (d) When MU becomes zero, TU reaches at its maximum point. This point is known as point of saturation or point of satiety.
35. (a) Both Assertion (A) and Reason (R) are true and Reason (R) is the correct explanation of Assertion (A)
36. (a) Both Assertion (A) and Reason (R) are true and Reason (R) is the correct explanation of Assertion (A)
37. (b) Both Assertion (A) and Reason (R) are true, but Reason (R) is not the correct explanation of Assertion (A)
38. (d) The budget set refers to all possible combinations of two goods that a consumer can afford given his/her income and the prevailing market prices.

39. (a) Both Assertion (A) and Reason (R) are true and Reason (R) is the correct explanation of Assertion (A)
40. (b) Both Assertion (A) and Reason (R) are true, but Reason (R) is not the correct explanation of Assertion (A)
41. (d) Ordinal utility approach argues that utility cannot be quantified in numbers. Cardinal utility approach suggests that utility can be measured in exact numerical terms.
42. (a) Marginal utility is the additional satisfaction gained from consuming one extra unit of a commodity. It is calculated by the change in total utility due to a change in the quantity consumed.
43. (c) Both the statements are correct
44. (c) Both the statements are correct
45. (c) Both the statements are correct
46. (b) Statement II is correct and Statement I is incorrect
47. (a) Statement I is correct and Statement II is incorrect
48. (c) Both the statements are correct
49. (d) If the prices of both goods decrease, the budget line shifts outward/rightward, reflecting an overall increase in purchasing power. If the prices of both goods increase, the budget line shifts inward/leftward, reflecting a decrease in purchasing power.
50. (c) Both the statements are correct
51. (d) (iii) (ii) (i) (iv)
52. (b) (iv) (i) (ii) (iii)
53. (a) (iii) (iv) (i) (ii)
54. (c) (ii) (iii) (iv) (i)
55. (a) (iii) (iv) (i) (ii)
56. Total utility
57. Marginal utility
58. Consumer's equilibrium (Single commodity)
59. Equality of slopes (Consumer's equilibrium using indifference curve analysis)
60. Law of diminishing marginal utility

Subjective Questions

Short Answer Type Questions

1. What is the definition of utility in economics?

Ans. Utility in economics is defined as the satisfaction or pleasure that a consumer derives from consuming goods and services. It represents the value or benefit that the consumer receives, which motivates their purchasing decisions.

Utility helps in understanding consumer behaviour and decision-making processes in the context of maximising satisfaction with available resources.

2. What is the difference between cardinal utility and ordinal utility?

Ans. Differences between cardinal and ordinal utility are

Basis	Cardinal Utility	Ordinal Utility
Concept	It refers to the measurement of utility in terms of numbers as 1, 2, 3, etc.	It refers to the measurement of utility in terms of psychological satisfaction on consuming one good in comparison to other.
Example	A basket of oranges offers 10 utils of utility to a consumer.	A pizza offers greater satisfaction to a consumer than a chapatti.
Propounded By	Professor Alfred Marshall.	Professor Allen and Hicks.

3. What do you mean by law of equi-marginal utility?

Ans. The law of equi-marginal utility states that to achieve maximum satisfaction, a consumer should allocate their income between different goods so that the ratio of the marginal utility of each good to its price is the same across all goods. This means that the marginal utility per dollar spent is equal for each good, optimising the overall satisfaction derived from the consumer's budget.

4. Explain the meaning of diminishing marginal rate of substitution with the help of a numerical example.

Ans. Marginal rate of substitution refers to the rate at which the consumer is willing to sacrifice one good to obtain one more unit of the other good.

$$MRS_{XY} = \frac{\text{Quantity of the Good Sacrificed}}{\text{Quantity of the Good Obtained}} \text{ or } \frac{\Delta Y}{\Delta X}$$

e.g.

Combination	Good X	Good Y	Marginal Rate of Substitution (MRS)
A	1	8	–
B	2	4	4Y : 1X
C	3	2	2Y : 1X
D	4	1	1Y : 1X

∴ The above table shows that the consumer is willing to sacrifice less unit of Y to obtain additional unit of X.

5. List two assumptions of the law of Diminishing Marginal Utility (DMU).

Ans. Assumptions of the law of DMU are

(i) Utility is assumed to be measurable in numerical units called 'utils,' allowing for quantification of satisfaction.

(ii) The consumer is rational and seeks to maximise their utility, making choices that enhance their overall satisfaction given their budget constraints.

6. "A consumer continues to consume additional units of a good until their marginal utility becomes zero."

Explain how this behaviour impacts the total utility curve and why the consumers stops consuming at this point, even though they still have the option to consume more. Competency Based Que

Ans. When marginal utility becomes zero, the total utility curve reaches its peak, indicating maximum satisfaction. The consumer stops consuming because additional units would result in negative marginal utility, decreasing total satisfaction. This is the point of satiety or saturation.

7. What does the law of equi-marginal utility emphasise in consumer behaviour? Competency Based Que

Ans. The law of equi-marginal utility emphasises the optimal allocation of a consumer's resources to maximise satisfaction. It states that a consumer should allocate their income so that the marginal utility per dollar spent is equal across all goods consumed, ensuring that resources are distributed in a way that maximises overall utility.

8. What price a consumer is ready to pay for a commodity in state of equilibrium?

Ans. In a state of equilibrium, the price that a consumer is ready to pay, is exactly equal to the price prevailing in the market. Because in a state of equilibrium, money worth of marginal utility, that the consumer gets, is exactly equal to the market price, he has to pay.

9. How is consumer's equilibrium achieved in terms of marginal utility and price? Competency Based Que

Ans. Consumer's equilibrium is achieved when the consumer allocates their budget such that the marginal utility per dollar spent on each good is equal. This is expressed as $MU_X/P_X = MU_Y/P_Y$.

At this point, the consumer has maximised their satisfaction because they are getting the same level of additional satisfaction for each dollar spent on different goods.

10. Observe the image given below carefully and identify the characteristics of indifference curve shown. Also explain the same briefly. Competency Based Que

Ans. Higher indifference curve represents higher level of satisfaction. In other words, any combination that lie on a higher indifference curve, i.e. away from origin, represents higher level of satisfaction.

The underlying assumption here is the assumption of monotonic preference which represents that a consumer will prefer a combination which contains more of at least one good and no less of the other good.

11. What do you understand by consumer's equilibrium?

Ans. Consumer's equilibrium occurs when a consumer allocates their income in such a way that maximises their overall satisfaction or utility. This happens when the marginal utility per dollar spent on each good is equal across all goods consumed, meaning $MU_X/P_X = MU_Y/P_Y$.

At this point, the consumer has optimised their consumption given their budget constraint and any reallocation of spending would not increase their total satisfaction.

12. How is equilibrium of the consumer affected in case, when MU_M is rising and P_X is constant?

Ans. Equilibrium is struck, when $\frac{MU_X}{P_X} = MU_M$

If MU_X rises and P_X is constant, the consumer will find his equilibrium only when consumption of commodity X is decreased. The above equation can be re-written as $MU_X = P_X \times MU_M$. As P_X is constant and MU_M is rising, hence MU_X must, also rise for the consumer to be in equilibrium, hence consumption of good X must fall.

13. Why is an ideal indifference curve convex to the origin, and what does this convexity signify about the consumer's willingness to substitute between two goods? Competency Based Que

Ans. An ideal indifference curve is convex to the origin due to the assumption of diminishing marginal rate of substitution.

This convexity indicates that as a consumer moves along the curve and consumes more of one good while giving up some of another, he/she is willing to give up progressively less of the first good to gain additional units of the second good. This reflects the decreasing marginal rate of substitution, meaning that the consumer values each additional unit of the good he/she is acquiring less as compared to the good he/she is giving up.

14. If a consumer has monotonic preferences, can she be indifferent between the bundles (10, 8) and (8, 6)? **NCERT**

Ans. The bundle (10, 8) should be strictly preferred instead of bundle (8, 6) because bundle (10, 8) has more of both the goods. So, a consumer having monotonic preferences will not be indifferent across these two bundles.

15. What is marginal rate of substitution?

Ans. MRS refers to the rate at which a consumer is willing to sacrifice one good in order to gain additional unit of the other good. Slope of indifference curve is known as Marginal Rate of Substitution (MRS). It is mathematically calculated as

$$MRS = \frac{\Delta Y}{\Delta X} = \frac{\text{Loss in Units of Goods Y}}{\text{Gain in Units of Good X}}$$

16. How does the budget line change, if the consumer's income increases to ₹ 40 but the price remains unchanged? **NCERT**

Ans. If consumer's income increases to ₹ 40, then consumer can buy more of both the goods.

It will shift the budget line upward right from *AB* to A_1B_1, but new budget line will be parallel to the old budget line, as there is no change in slope of budget line.

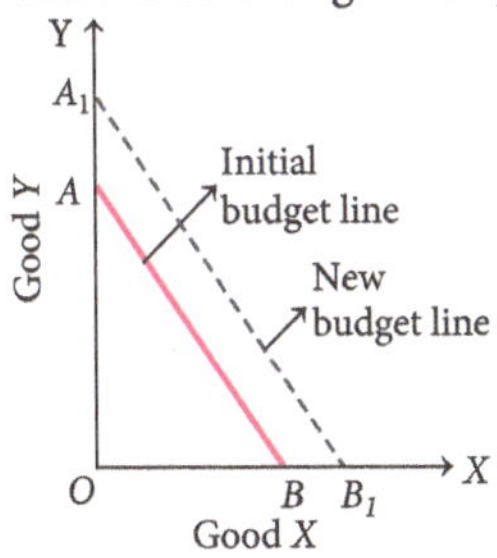

17. "The budget line rotates outward when the price of one good falls." What does this situation indicate? **Competency Based Que**

Ans. If the price of one good falls, the budget line rotates outward from the intercept of the other good. This indicates that the consumers can now afford to purchase more of the good whose price has decreased, increasing their purchasing power for that good while keeping the budget constraint in mind.

18. What are the assumptions of law of diminishing marginal utility?

Ans. The law of diminishing marginal utility states that as a consumer consumes more units of a commodity, the satisfaction (marginal utility) derived from each additional unit decreases.

Assumptions of the law of DMU are

(i) Standard and identical units of a commodity must be consumed.
(ii) Utility is measurable in numerical units called 'utils.'
(iii) The consumer is rational and seeks to maximise utility.
(iv) The marginal utility of money remains constant.
(v) Continuous consumption without significant time gaps.
(vi) The quality of the commodity remains uniform.
(vii) The price of the commodity is constant.
(viii) The income of the consumer remains unchanged.

19. What does the below image represent? Explain. **Competency Based Que**

Ans. The given image represents a the concept of consumer budget. Consumer's budget represents the financial resources available to a consumer, which determine the quantity and combination of goods they can purchase at given prices.

In the image, the consumer is thinking on how much money to spend on which goods.

20. What do you mean by the budget set of the consumer? **NCERT**

Ans. It refers to the set of attainable combinations of two goods that the consumer can afford to buy with his/her income at the prevailing market prices. The equation of budget set is given as, $P_X \cdot Q_X + P_Y \cdot Q_Y \leq M$.

21. How does the budget line change, if the price of good Y decreases by a rupee but the price of good X and consumer income remain unchanged? **NCERT**

Ans. If price of good Y decreases, consumer can buy more of good Y. The budget line *AB* will pivot at *B* and rotate upwards to A_1B. The movement of the budget line from *AB* to A_1B indicates an increase in the consumption of good Y.

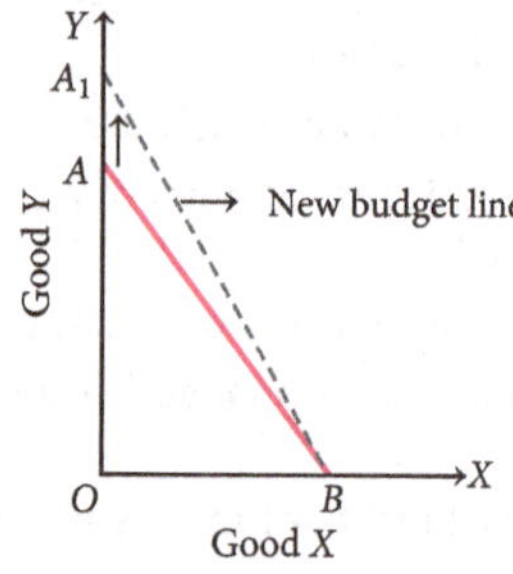

22. What do you mean by 'monotonic preferences'? NCERT

Ans. It means that a rational consumer always prefers more unit of atleast one commodity with no less units of the other or more units of both commodities, as it offers him a higher level of satisfaction.

Long Answer Type Questions

23. Explain the law of equi-marginal utility.

Ans. The law of equi-marginal utility states that to maximise satisfaction, consumers should allocate their income between two goods such that the ratio of marginal utility to price is the same for both goods. Mathematically, it is expressed as

i.e. $$\frac{MU_X}{P_X} = \frac{MU_Y}{P_Y}$$

where, MU_X = Marginal Utility of Good X
MU_Y = Marginal Utility of Good Y
P_X = Price of Good X
P_Y = Price of Good Y

This means the consumers will continue reallocating their income until the utility per unit of money spent is equal for both goods.

Also known as the Second Psychological Law of Consumption, this law emphasises optimal allocation of resources for maximum satisfaction.

Assumptions of the law of equi-marginal utility are

(i) **Fixed Income of the Consumer**
The consumer has a limited and fixed income to spend on goods.

(ii) **Substitute Goods Available in the Market**
There are at least two or more goods available that the consumers can choose from and allocate their income to.

(iii) **Utility is Measurable in Cardinal Units**
The satisfaction (utility) derived from consuming goods can be quantified in numerical terms.

(iv) **Constant Prices of the Goods**
The prices of the goods remain constant during the decision-making process.

(v) **The Law of Diminishing Marginal Utility Operates**
The marginal utility of good decreases as its consumption increases.

24. What is the relationship between total utility and marginal utility? Give example.

Ans. Relationship between TU and MU is as follows

The schedule and diagram given below illustrates the relationship between TU and MU

Quantity (Q)	Total Utility (TU)	Marginal Utility (MU)
0	0	—
1	5	5
2	9	4
3	12	3
4	14	2
5	15	1
6	15	0
7	14	–1
8	12	–2

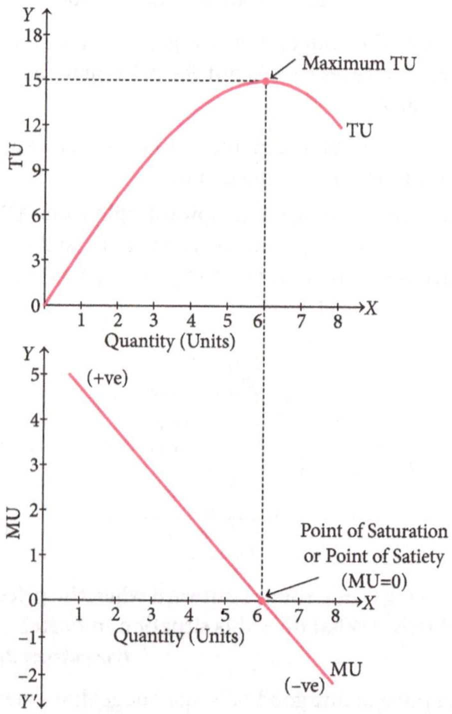

From the given schedule and curve, we observe that by consuming successive units of a particular commodity, the total utility initially increases at a decreasing rate, reaches its maximum and eventually falls.

Relationship between total utility and marginal utility can be understood from the following points

(i) When MU is diminishing but remains positive (+ve), i.e. till 5th unit, TU tends to increase at a diminishing rate.

(ii) When MU becomes zero, i.e. at 6th unit, TU reaches at its maximum point. This point is known as point of saturation or point of satiety.

(iii) When MU becomes negative (–ve), i.e. from 7th unit onwards, TU starts to fall.

The above relationship between TU and MU is due to the operation of law of diminishing marginal utility.

25. How a consumer will reach to the equilibrium point, if market rate of exchange is not equal to MRS? Competency Based Que

Ans. Market rate of exchange refers to the price ratio, while Marginal Rate of Substitution (MRS) is the rate at which a consumer is willing to exchange one commodity for the other.

If, $\frac{P_X}{P_Y}$ is not equal to MRS, then two cases arise which are given below

(i) **When MRS > $\frac{P_X}{P_Y}$**

In this case, consumer will buy more of good X than of good Y, as he is getting more worth of good X, paying price of X, hence satisfaction from X (MU_X) will fall and MU_Y will rise, till the time, MRS $=\frac{P_X}{P_Y}$.

(ii) **When MRS < $\frac{P_X}{P_Y}$**

In this case, consumer will consume more of good Y than of good X, as he is now getting more worth buying good Y, paying price P_Y, as a result, MU_Y will fall and MU_X will rise till the time, MRS $=\frac{P_X}{P_Y}$.

26. What are the properties of an indifference curve? Also, list the assumptions of indifference curve.

Ans. Properties of indifference curve are given below

(i) Indifference curve slope downwards from left to the right or is negatively sloped, as consumption of both the goods cannot be increased at once.

(ii) Indifference curve is convex to the origin, due to diminishing marginal rate of substitution.

(iii) Two indifference curves can never touch or intersect each other.

(iv) A higher indifference curve represents a higher level of satisfaction.

(v) It is often assumed that a consumer buys a combination of two goods. Hence, an indifference curve touches neither x-axis nor y-axis.

Assumptions of indifference curve are

(i) **Two Commodities**
The analysis considers only two goods at a time.

(ii) **Rational Consumer**
The consumer is assumed to be rational, meaning they make choices to maximise their satisfaction based on their preferences.

(iii) **Constant Prices**
The prices of the commodities are assumed to be constant.

(iv) **Constant Income**
The consumer's income is fixed.

(v) **Ordinal Utility**
The consumer can rank their preferences for different combinations of goods based on satisfaction.

(vi) **Convexity**
An ideal indifference curve is convex to the origin, reflecting the assumption of diminishing marginal rate of substitution, which means the consumer is willing to give up less of one good for additional units of another as they move along the curve.

27. "The Marginal Rate of Substitution (MRS) refers to the rate at which a consumer is willing to sacrifice one good in order to gain an additional unit of the other good."

What does the Marginal Rate of Substitution (MRS) measure and how does it help in understanding consumer preferences? Competency Based Que

Ans. The Marginal Rate of Substitution (MRS) measures how much of one good a consumer is willing to give up obtaining one more unit of another good while maintaining the same level of satisfaction.

It helps in understanding consumer preferences by indicating the trade-off rate between two goods that the consumer is willing to make, reflecting their relative valuation of the goods.

It also reflects the diminishing willingness of consumers to trade one good for another as they consume more of one good and less of the other. This diminishing MRS is a result of the law of diminishing marginal utility, which states that as the quantity of one good increases, the additional satisfaction derived from consuming each additional unit decreases. The concept is graphically represented by the convex shape of an indifference curve, which illustrates that consumers are less willing to give up large quantities of one good as they gain more of the other.

This behaviour helps explain consumer decision-making and the balancing of preferences when resources are limited.

28. Explain the conditions of consumer's equilibrium with the help of indifference curve analysis.

Ans. According to indifference curve analysis, consumer is in equilibrium at a point, where the slope of indifference curve is equal to the slope of budget line or price line.

The condition of the consumer's equilibrium can be written as, $MRS_{XY} = \frac{P_X}{P_Y}$.

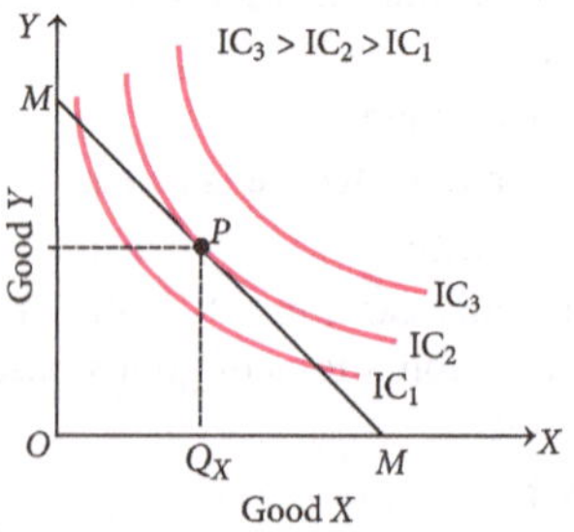

At the point of equilibrium, indifference curve is convex to the origin. It implies that at the point of equilibrium, MRS must be diminishing. In given diagram, *P* is the equilibrium point at which budget line touches the higher Indifference Curve IC_2 within the consumer budget and IC_3 is not an affordable curve.

29. A consumer consumes only two goods. Explain consumer's equilibrium with the help of utility analysis.

Competency Based Que

Ans. In case of two commodities, consumer attains equilibrium, when

(i) $\frac{MU_X}{P_X} = \frac{MU_Y}{P_Y}$

It implies that in state of equilibrium, utility per rupee from good X must be equal to utility per rupee from good Y. The above condition can also be written as

$$\frac{MU_X}{MU_Y} = \frac{P_X}{P_Y}.$$

It implies that in state of equilibrium, ratio of Marginal utilities of two commodities is equal to the ratio of their prices.

(ii) $\frac{MU_X}{P_X} = \frac{MU_Y}{P_Y} = MU_M$

It implies that in state of equilibrium, utility per rupee obtained by the consumer from good X or good Y should be equal to marginal utility of money. (Assumption $P_X = P_Y =$ ₹ 1 per unit)

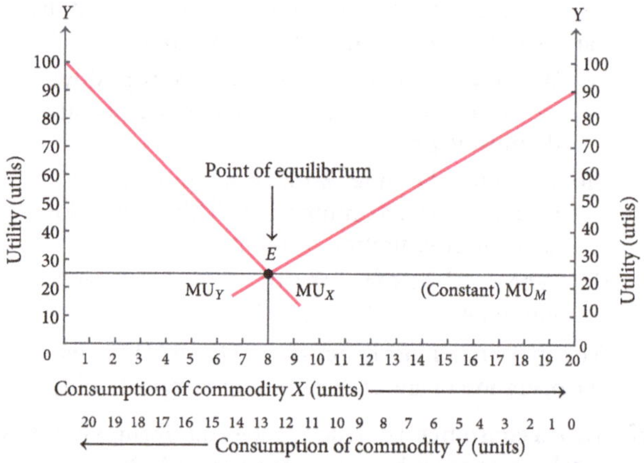

Consumer's equilibrium: Two commodities case

(Curve is based on hypothetical data)

30. Briefly describe the conditions of shift in a budget line.

Ans. Shift in the budget line occurs due to changes in a consumer's income or the prices of goods, affecting the combinations of goods a consumer can afford.

It is explained as follows

(i) **Change in Income**

- **Increase in Income** When a consumer's income increases while prices remain constant, the budget line shifts rightwards. This shift indicates that the consumer can now afford to purchase more of both goods.
- **Decrease in Income** Conversely, a decrease in income shifts the budget line leftwards, reflecting a reduction in purchasing power and the ability to buy fewer goods.

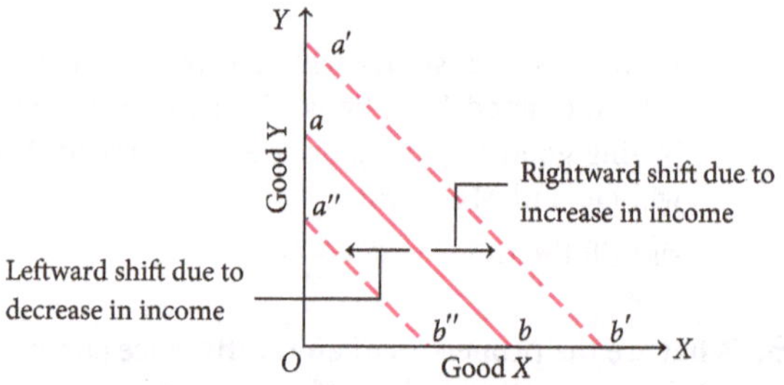

Effect of change in income on budget line

(ii) **Change in Price of Commodities**

- **Price Change of One Good** If the price of one good falls, the budget line rotates outward, indicating an increase in purchasing power for that good while if the price of one good rises, the budget line rotates inward, indicating reduced purchasing power for that good.

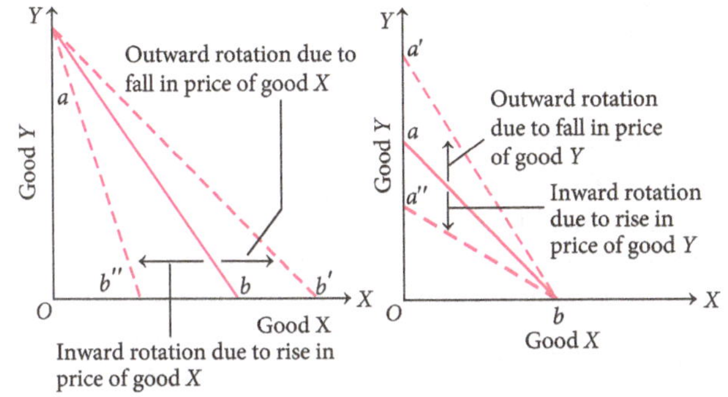

Effect of Change in price of one good

- **Simultaneous Change in Prices** If the prices of both goods decrease, the budget line shifts outward/rightward, reflecting an overall increase in purchasing power while if the prices of both goods increase, the budget line shifts inward/leftward, reflecting a decrease in purchasing power.

31. **A consumer wants to consume two goods. The prices of the two goods are ₹ 4 and ₹ 5 respectively. The consumer's income is ₹ 20.**

(i) Write down the equation of the budget line.

(ii) How much of Good 1 can the consumer consume, if she spends her entire income on that good?

(iii) How much of Good 2 can she consume, if she spends her entire income on that good?

(iv) What is the slope of the budget line?

NCERT; Competency Based Que

Ans. (i) Let the Good 1 be X and Good 2 be Y. Now, we are given,

$$P_X = ₹\ 4; \quad P_Y = ₹\ 5$$

Consumer's income (M) = ₹ 20

Equation of budget line is

$$P_X \cdot X + P_Y \cdot Y = M$$

$$\Rightarrow \quad 4X + 5Y = 20$$

(ii) If consumed quantity of good Y = 0.

Then, budget equation becomes, $P_X X + P_Y 0 = M$

$$\Rightarrow \quad 4X + 0 = 20$$

$$\Rightarrow \quad X = \frac{20}{4} = 5 \text{ units}$$

(iii) If consumed quantity of good X = 0.

Then, budget equation becomes, $P_X 0 + P_Y Y = M$

$$\Rightarrow \quad 0 + 5Y = 20$$

$$\Rightarrow \quad Y = \frac{20}{5} = 4 \text{ units}$$

(iv) Slope of budget line $= \frac{P_X}{P_Y} = \frac{4}{5} = 0.8$

32. **Suppose a consumer wants to consume two goods which are available only in integer units. The two goods are equally priced at ₹ 10 and the consumer's income is ₹ 40.**

(i) Write down all the bundles that are available to the consumer.

(ii) Among the bundles that are available to the consumer, identify those which cost her exactly ₹ 40. **NCERT; Competency Based Que**

Ans. (i) Given, price of both the goods = ₹ 10

Income of consumer = ₹ 40

The bundles are available to the consumer

First option is (0, 0), (0, 1), (0, 2), (0, 3), (0, 4).

Second option is (1, 0), (1, 1), (1, 2), (1, 3).

Third option is (2, 0), (2, 1), (2, 2).

Fourth option is (3, 0), (3, 1).

Fifth option is (4, 0).

(ii) The exact cost is ₹ 40, the bundles are (0, 4), (1, 3), (2, 2), (3, 1) and (4, 0).

Explanation

- First bundle is (0, 4).
  Cost $= 0 \times 10 + 4 \times 10 =$ ₹ 40
- Second bundle is (1, 3).
  Cost $= 1 \times 10 + 3 \times 10 =$ ₹ 40
- Third bundle is (2, 2).
  Cost $= 2 \times 10 + 2 \times 10 =$ ₹ 40
- Fourth bundle is (3, 1).
  Cost $= 3 \times 10 + 1 \times 10 =$ ₹ 40
- Fifth bundle is (4, 0).
  Cost $= 4 \times 10 + 0 \times 10 =$ ₹ 40

Numerical Questions

Numerical 1

Suppose a consumer can afford to buy 6 units of Good 1 and 8 units of Good 2, if she spends her entire income. The prices of two goods are ₹ 6 and ₹ 8 respectively. How much is the consumer's income? **NCERT**

Sol. The consumer's income will be equal to the money obtained from budget line equation.

Given, Price of good 1 = ₹ 6, Price of good 2 = ₹ 8

Good 1 = 6 units, Good 2 = 8 units,

$M = P_1X + P_2Y = 6 \times 6 + 8 \times 8 = 36 + 64 = 100$

∴ Consumer's income = ₹ 100

Numerical 2

If a consumer's total utility from consuming 3 units of a good is 45 utils and the total utility from consuming 2 units is 30 utils, what is the marginal utility of the 3rd unit?

Sol. Marginal Utility (MU) = Total utility of 3 units − Total Utility of 2 units

MU = 45 utils − 30 utils = 15 utils

Numerical 3

The total utility schedule of individual A is given below. Derive his marginal utility schedule.

Units Consumed	0	1	2	3	4	5
Total Utility	0	16	29	41	52	62

Sol.

Units Consumed	0	1	2	3	4	5
Total Utility (TU)	0	16	29	41	52	62
Marginal Utility ($MU_{nth} = TU_n - TU_{n-1}$)	—	16	13	12	11	10

Numerical 4

Calculate total utility from the following marginal utility schedule

Units Consumed	0	1	2	3	4	5	6	7
Marginal Utility	—	10	8	6	4	2	0	−2

Sol.

Units Consumed	0	1	2	3	4	5	6	7
Marginal Utility (MU)	—	10	8	6	4	2	0	−2
Total Utility (TU)	0	10	18	24	28	30	30	28

Numerical 5

The cost of an ice-cream is ₹ 20. Akanksha who likes ice-cream, has already consumed 4 ice-creams. Her marginal utility is 4 of one rupee. Should she consume more ice-cream or should she stop the consumption?

Sol. A consumer attains equilibrium, when $\frac{MU_X}{MU_M} = P_X$

Substituting the given values, we get $\frac{MU_X}{4} = 20$ implying that, in a state of equilibrium, Akanksha's MU_X must be equal to 80 utils. If having consumed 4 ice-creams, Akanksha's $MU_X = 80$ utils, then she must stop consuming more.

However, if $MU_X > 80$, she should have consumed more ice creams till MU_X reduces to 80 and in terms of its money, worth is equal to P_X (where, $P_X = 20$).

Numerical 6

A consumer is deciding between two goods. The marginal utility of good X is 50 utils and its price is $5. The marginal utility of good Y is 30 utils and its price is $3. Which good provides a higher utility per dollar spent?

Sol. Utility per dollar for good X = 50 utils / $5 = 10 utils per dollar.

Utility per dollar for good Y = 30 utils / $3 = 10 utils per dollar.

Both goods provide the same utility per dollar spent.

Numerical 7

Find consumer's equilibrium from the following data, when $P_X = P_Y = 3$ and $MU_M = 1$ and consumer's income is ₹ 12.

Units	MU_X	MU_Y
1	100	70
2	80	50
3	70	30
4	60	10
5	50	00

Sol.

Units	MU_X (₹)	MU_Y (₹)
1	100	70
2	80	50
3	70	30
4	60	10
5	50	00

Conditions of equilibrium

(i) $MU_X = MU_Y$ (when $P_X = P_Y$ and $MU_M = 1$)

(ii) $P_X \cdot Q_Y + P_Y \cdot Q_Y = M$

First condition of equilibrium is satisfied at (X, Y) = (3, 1) and (5, 2), however the second condition is satisfied at $(3 \times 3) + (3 \times 1) = 12$

So, equilibrium is at the point where 3 units of good X and 2 units of Y are consumed.

Numerical 8

Calculate marginal rate of substitution from the following data and comment on the shape of indifference curve

X	1	2	3	4	5	6
Y	100	80	62	46	32	20

Sol. Calculation of marginal rate of substitution

X	1	2	3	4	5	6
Y	100	80	62	46	32	20
MRS ($\Delta Y / \Delta X$)	—	20 : 1	18 : 1	16 : 1	14 : 1	12 : 1

Thus, based on the above calculation, the shape of indifference curve will be convex to the orign.

Numerical 9

A consumer's total utility from consuming 4 units of a commodity is 80 utils, and their total utility from consuming 5 units is 90 utils. What is the marginal utility of the 5th unit?

Sol. Marginal Utility (MU) = Total Utility of 5 units – Total Utility of 4 units

MU = 90 utils – 80 utils = 10 utils

Numerical 10

A consumer consumes two goods X and Y, price of good X and good Y are ₹ 5 and ₹ 2 respectively. If MRS_{XY} of a certain unit of consumption is 10, is the consumer in equilibrium? What will be his reaction?

Sol. Conditions of consumer equilibrium (using ordinal approach)

(i) $MRS_{XY} = P_X / P_Y$ (ii) MRS must be diminishing

According to question,

$$MRS_{XY} > P_X / P_Y \Rightarrow 10 > \frac{5}{2}$$

Thus, the consumer is not in equilibrium.

In this case, he will consume more of Good X and less of Good Y to reach to the point of equilibrium.

SELF ASSESSMENT TEST

Objective Type Questions

1. Which of the following statements best describes the cardinal utility approach?
   (a) Utility can be ranked in order of preference without assigning exact numerical values.
   (b) Utility can be measured in exact numerical units, such as 1, 2, 3, etc.
   (c) Utility cannot be measured or compared in any form.
   (d) Utility is only qualitative and cannot be ranked.
2. What is the point called when Total Utility (TU) reaches its maximum?
   (a) Point of saturation
   (b) Point of increasing utility
   (c) Point of negative utility
   (d) Point of diminishing returns
3. According to the Law of diminishing marginal utility, what happens when a consumer consumes more units of a commodity?
   (a) Marginal utility increases with each additional unit consumed
   (b) Marginal utility remains constant with each additional unit consumed
   (c) Marginal utility diminishes with each additional unit consumed
   (d) Total utility starts to decrease immediately
4. If the marginal utility of money (MU_M) is 2, ……… utils are equivalent to 4 rupees.
   (a) 2 utils (b) 4 utils
   (c) 8 utils (d) 1 util
5. In the context of indifference curves, what does it mean if a consumer is indifferent between two bundles?
   (a) The two bundles provide different levels of satisfaction.
   (b) The two bundles provide the same level of satisfaction.
   (c) The consumer prefers one bundle over the other.
   (d) The consumer experiences diminishing marginal utility from both bundles.
6. According to the principle of monotonic preferences, if a consumer is given two bundles (X_1 and X_2), how would the consumer react if X_1 contains more of at least one good and no less of the other?
   (a) The consumer would be indifferent between the two bundles.
   (b) The consumer would prefer bundle X_2 over X_1.
   (c) The consumer would choose X_1 only if the total number of goods in it is less than in X_2.
   (d) The consumer would prefer bundle X_1 over X_2.
7. The equation of the budget set can be expressed as ……… .
   (a) $P_1X_1 + P_2X_2 = I$
   (b) $P_1X_1 + P_2X_2 \leq I$
   (c) $P_1X_1 + P_2X_2 > I$
   (d) $P_1X_1 + P_2X_2 = 0$
8. If a consumer's income decreases, what happens to the budget line?
   (a) It rotates outward
   (b) It shifts rightward
   (c) It shifts leftward
   (d) It rotates inward

Answers 1. (b) 2. (a) 3. (c) 4. (c) 5. (b) 6. (d) 7. (b) 8. (c)

Short Answer Type Questions

9. Explain cardinal and ordinal utility approach with examples.
10. "Consumer's behaviour is governed by monotonic preferences." Do you agree? Give reasons.
11. What is an indifference curve? Explain with diagram.
12. Define the following
    (i) Consumer's budget
    (ii) Consumer's equilibrium
13. Why budget line slopes downwards? Explain.

Long Answer Type Questions

14. "The theory of indifference curve depends on level of income." Justify.
15. In case, a consumer consumes two goods, explain his equilibrium with the help of utility approach.

Numerical Questions

16. The amount of good X is given with its TU. Calculate its MU.

Amount of Good X	1	2	3	4	5
Total Utility	8	16	22	26	28

17. Complete the following table

Amount Consumed	1	2	3	4	5
Total Utility	50	90	...	140	150
Marginal Utility	50	...	30	...	...

18. The following is the utility schedule of a person

Amount Consumed	1	2	3	4	5	6
Marginal Utility	6	5	4	3	2	1

Suppose, that the commodity is sold for ₹ 3. How many units of the commodity, the person will purchase so that his TU is maximum?

19. Find the consumer's equilibrium when he spends his income on two goods X and Y. Price of X is ₹ 1 and that of Y is ₹ 2, MU_X and MU_Y schedules is as follows

MU_X	P_X	MU_Y	P_Y
10	1	22	2
9	1	20	2
8	1	16	2
7	1	12	2

20. Given, P_X = ₹ 5 and P_Y = ₹ 10, find consumer's equilibrium from the following values of MU_X and MU_Y

MU_X	MU_Y
100	160
80	150
60	120
50	110

03

CHAPTER

Demand represents the willingness and ability of consumers to purchase goods or services at various prices.

Demand and Price Elasticity of Demand

YOUR STUDY GOALS

YOUR PRACTICE GOAL

- Objective Type Questions (72 Qs ; MCQs, A-R, Statements, Matching, Concept Identification)
- Subjective Questions (25 SAs, 15 LAs)
- 24 Numerical Questions
- Self Assessment Test (8 MCQs, 5 SAs, 2 LAs, 4 Numerical)

3.1 Demand

Demand is the quantity of a commodity that a consumer is willing and able to buy at various possible prices during a given period of time. e.g. A consumer demands 5 kg of sugar in a month at ₹ 40 per kg.

Demand is different from a desire as desire is merely a wish while demand reflects both willingness and the ability to buy.

Demand is majorly comprised of four components

1. **Willingness to Buy** The desire to purchase.
2. **Price** The cost of the good.
3. **Ability to Buy** The financial capacity to make the purchase.
4. **Time Period** The duration over which demand is measured.

Demand for a commodity can be studied with respect to an individual or market as specified below

1. **Individual Demand** The quantity of a good demanded by one person during a given period of time.
2. **Market Demand** The total quantity demanded by all consumers in a market over a given period of time.

Quantity Demanded It refers to specific quantity of a commodity demanded at specific price.

Determinants of Individual Demand

Determinants are also known as factors which affect demand of a commodity.

Determinant	Description	Examples
Price of the Commodity (P)	As price decreases, demand increases and *vice-versa*. Thus, demand of normal commodity is inversely related to its price.	A fall in the price of smartphones in India leads to higher sales.
Income of Consumers (Y)	More income leads to more demand for normal goods. In contrast, demand for inferior goods decreases with increase in income. Thus, demand of normal goods is directly related to income of consumer.	• **Normal Goods** A family in India may switch to better quality grains as their income rises. • **Inferior Goods** A family might stop buying toned milk and shift to full cream milk as their earnings increase.
Price of Related Goods (P)	There are two types of related goods • **Substitute Goods** These are goods that can be consumed in place of each other. When the price of one good increases, consumers switch to its substitute, increasing demand for substitute good. • **Complementary Goods** These goods are consumed together. If the price of one rises, demand for the other falls because both are needed for consumption.	• **Substitute Goods** If coke's price rises, demand for pepsi will rise. • **Complementary Goods** If petrol prices go up, demand for petrol cars will decrease.
Taste and Preferences of Consumers (T)	These are influenced by fashion, climate, etc. Favourable tastes and preferences increase the demand for goods and *vice-versa*.	In summers, demand for cotton clothes increases in India.
Expectations about Future Price of Good (E)	If consumers expect prices to rise in future, they buy more now and *vice-versa*.	If consumer expects future rise in price of wheat, he/she may purchase more quantity now.

Determinants of Market Demand

Alongwith the determinants of individual demand, market demand is also influenced by following factors

Determinant	Description	Examples
Distribution of Income (D_y)	When income is distributed equally, demand increases across society. While unequal distribution reduces overall demand.	In Kerala, equal income distribution leads to steady demand for basic goods, unlike areas with large income gaps.
Size of Population (N)	A larger population leads to higher demand for goods and services and *vice-versa*.	India's large population creates high demand for essentials like housing, especially in cities like Mumbai.
Composition of Population (P_c)	If the majority of the population is young, demand for gadgets and fashion will rise, while an older population increases demand for healthcare services.	Bengaluru's young population drives demand for gadgets, while Dehradun's older population increases demand for healthcare services.

Normal and Inferior Goods

- **Normal Goods** These are the goods for which the demand is directly related to consumers' income. Other things remaining constant, demand for these goods increases in response to an increase in consumer's income and *vice-versa*.
- **Inferior Goods** These are the goods for which the demand is inversely related to consumers' income. Other things remaining constant, demand for these goods decreases in response to increase in income and *vice-versa*.

Demand Function

The functional relationship between the demand for a commodity and the factors affecting demand is termed as demand function.

Demand function can be further classified as

Individual Demand Function	Market Demand Function
It refers to the functional relationship between individual demand and its determinants. Mathematically, it is shown as $D_X = f(P_x, P_r, Y, T, E)$ Here, D_X = Demand for commodity X f = Functional relationship P_x = Price of given commodity X P_r = Price of related goods Y = Consumer's income T = Consumer's taste and preference E = Consumer's expectations about future price	It refers to the functional relationship between market demand and its determinants. Mathematically, it is shown as $D_X = f(P_x, P_r, Y, T, E, N, D_y, P_c)$ Here, D_X = Market demand for commodity X f = Functional relationship P_X = Own price of the commodity X P_r = Price of related goods ; Y = Income of the consumers T = Taste and preference of consumers E = Expectations of consumers about future price N = Population size ; D_y = Distribution of income P_c = Composition of population

Demand Schedule

Demand schedule is referred to as tabular presentation which shows various quantities of a commodity demanded at different prices, during a given period of time.

It is of two types, which are as follows

1. Individual Demand Schedule

It refers to the demand schedule of an individual buyer. It shows different quantities of a commodity which an individual buyer can buy at different possible prices of that commodity at a given point of time.

Price of Rice (₹)	Quantity Demanded of Rice (in kgs)
5	2
4	3
3	5
2	8

The given table shows different quantities of rice to be brought by a consumer at different prices, at a given point of time.

2. Market Demand Schedule

It refers to the demand schedule for a commodity by all the consumers in the market. It shows different quantities of a commodity which all the consumers intend to buy at different possible prices of that commodity at a given point of time.

Price of Ice-cream (₹)	A's Demand (1)	B's Demand (2)	Market Demand (1+2=3)
1	.4	5	4 + 5 = 9
2	3	4	3 + 4 = 7
3	2	3	2 + 3 = 5
4	1	2	1 + 2 = 3

The inverse relationship between own price of the commodity and its quantity demanded holds good for both, individual demand schedule and market demand schedule.

Demand Curve

Demand curve is a graphical representation of demand schedule. Like demand schedule, it is also of two types

1. Individual Demand Curve

It shows demand for a commodity by a person at different prices at a given point of time or we can say, it is a graphical representation of an individual demand schedule.

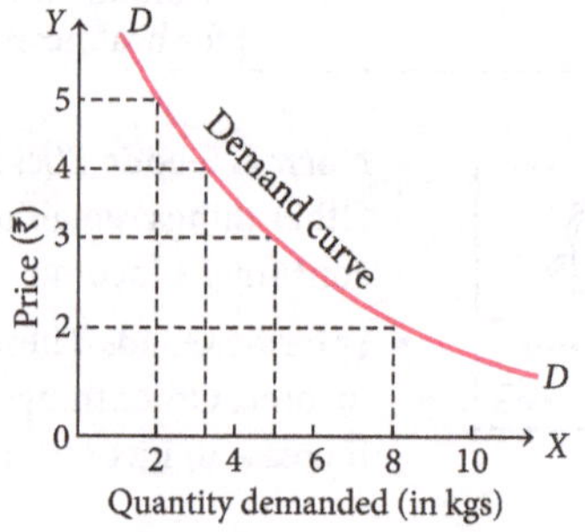

Individual demand curve

In this figure, demand curve slopes downward from left to right. It shows inverse relationship between price and quantity demanded. Therefore, it is said that demand curve is **negatively sloped.**

2. Market Demand Curve

It shows demand for a commodity made by all the persons in the market at different possible prices at a given point of time or we can say, it is a graphical representation of market demand schedule.

Market demand curve has a negative slope and it is flatter, while individual demand curve is steeper.

$D_X D_X$ is the individual demand curve of A.

$D_Y D_Y$ is the individual demand curve of B.

$D_M D_M$ is the market demand curve.

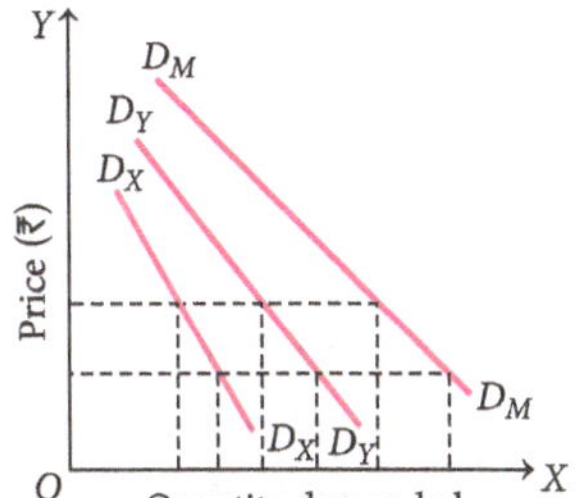

Market demand curve

Slope of Demand Curve

Slope of demand curve measures the rate at which demand changes with respect to its price. It is equal to $\frac{\Delta P}{\Delta Q}$. For 'a' unit increase in the price of the good, the demand falls by '*b*' units.

It is shown in the diagram given aside

A linear demand curve can be written as

$$q = a - bp$$

where, p = Price

a = Intercept that demand curve makes with horizontal or quantity axis

b = Slope of demand curve

q = Quantity

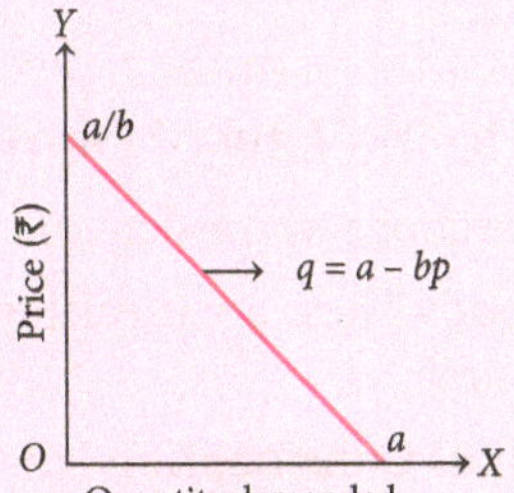

Linear demand curve

3.2 Law of Demand

The law of demand states that other factors remaining constant, the quantity demanded for a commodity expands with fall in its price and contracts with rise in its price. It shows inverse relationship between price of commodity and its quantity demanded.

This law can be explained using following schedule and curve

Demand Schedule

Price (₹)	**Quantity Demanded** (units)
10	50
8	60
6	70
4	80
2	90

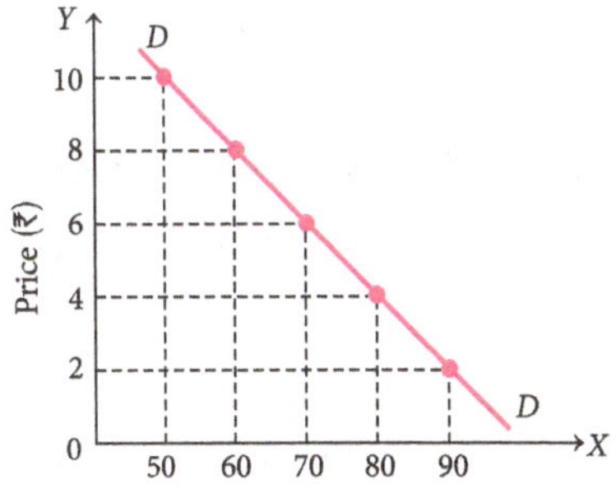

Demand curve

The above schedule and curve clearly depict that demand of the commodity expands with fall in its price and contracts with rise in its price.

Assumptions of the Law of Demand

Law of demand holds true when other factors remain constant. Here 'other factors' cover following assumptions

- Consumer's taste and preference do not change.
- Prices of substitute and complementary goods do not change.
- The distribution of income remains constant.
- Consumer income remains unchanged.
- Consumers do not anticipate future price changes.
- There is no change in population.

Causes for Downward Sloping of Demand Curve

- **Law of Diminishing Marginal Utility** As consumers consume more, the satisfaction (utility) from each additional unit decreases. So, for every additional unit, they are willing to pay less.
- **Income Effect** A fall in price increases real income of consumer, enabling consumers to buy more.
- **Substitution Effect** It occurs when consumers switch from a more expensive good to a cheaper alternative, maintaining their utility. (e.g. CNG over petrol)
- **Size of Consumer Group** Fall in price of commodity attracts new buyers, hence quantity demanded rises and *vice-versa.*
- **Multiple Uses** Many goods (like milk) have various uses. If price of such goods reduces, their demand will increase and *vice-versa.*

Exceptions to the Law of Demand

These are those goods whose demand do not increase with fall in price or *vice-versa*. These exceptions are

1. **Giffen Goods** These are special type of highly inferior goods whose demand increases with increase in their prices and *vice-versa.*
2. **Conspicuous Consumption** Law of demand does not apply to costly items like diamond, as demand for these goods persists despite higher prices.
3. **Necessities** This law also does not hold true for essential items like medicines or salt, as these goods maintain constant demand regardless of price changes.
4. **Ignorance** Consumers, who are unaware of competitive prices of commodity, may purchase goods at higher price. Thus, such ignorance also makes this law ineffective.
5. **Future Expectations regarding Change in Price** If consumers expect prices of goods to drop further in future, they will delay purchases, thereby defying the law of demand.
6. **Conspicuous Necessities** Items like automobiles and TVs, have become necessities of modern life. Thus, these goods are bought despite their price increase.

3.3 Movement along the Demand Curve (Change in Quantity Demanded)

Moving from one point to other on the same demand curve is called movement along a demand curve. It is caused by a change in quantity demanded of a good in response to change in its own price, other factors remaining constant. Movement along a demand curve can take the following forms

1. **Extension in Demand** It refers to rise in quantity demanded due to fall in the price of goods, keeping other factors constant. It is indicated by downward movement along the same demand curve.
2. **Contraction in Demand** It refers to fall in quantity demanded due to rise in the price of goods, keeping other factors constant. It is indicated by an upward movement on the same demand curve.

An imaginary tabular and graphical presentation of extension and contraction in demand

Price (₹)	Quantity Demanded (units)	Description
1	500	
2	400	↓ Contraction
3	300	
4	200	↑ Extension
5	100	

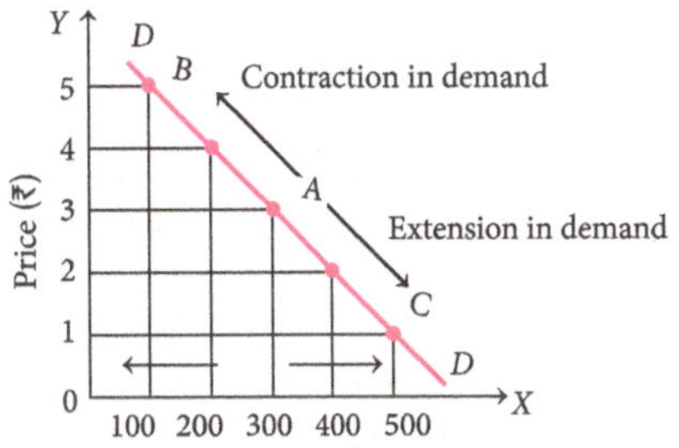

Curve showing extension and contraction of demand

3.4 Shift in Demand Curve (Change in Demand)

A shift in the demand curve occurs due to change in factors other than own price of the good.

Shift in demand curve can take the following forms

1. **Increase in Demand** It refers to rise in demand of a commodity and is indicated by a forward or rightward shift (left to right) of the demand curve (from A to B in graph)

   The following schedule and figure illustrates this situation

Price (₹)	Quantity (units)
20	10
20	15

   It is clear from the above schedule, that at the same price of ₹ 20, demand has increased from 10 to 15 units.

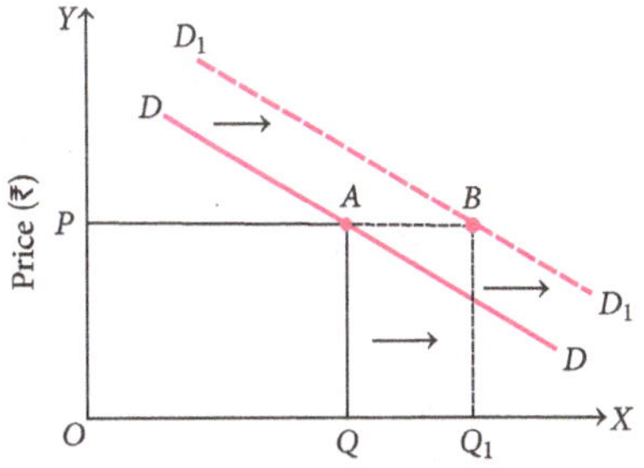

Shift in demand curve : Increase in demand

Causes for Increase in Demand

- Increase in consumer's income for normal goods.
- Increase in prices of substitute goods.
- Favourable shift in taste and preference.
- Decrease in consumer's income for inferior goods.
- Fall in price of complementary goods.
- Future expectations regarding rise in price of goods.

2. **Decrease in Demand** It refers to fall in demand of a commodity and is indicated by a backward or leftward shift (right to left) of the demand curve (from B to A in graph)

   The following schedule and figure illustrates this situation

Price (₹)	Quantity (units)
20	15
20	10

   It is clear from the above schedule, that at the same price of ₹ 20, demand has decreased from 15 to 10 units.

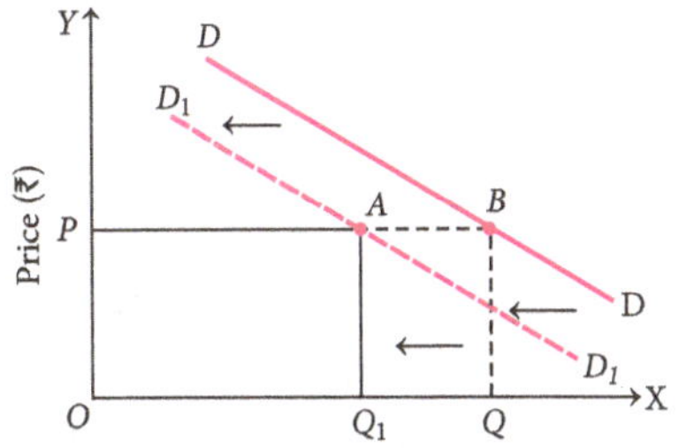

Shift in demand curve : Decrease in demand

Causes for Decrease in Demand

- Decrease in consumer's income for normal goods.
- Decrease in price of substitute goods.
- Unfavourable shift in taste and preference.
- Increase in consumer's income for inferior goods.
- Increase in price of complementary goods.
- Future expectations regarding fall in price of goods.

Cross Price Effects : Change in Demand Due to Change in Prices of Related Goods

Quantity of a good can increase or decrease with rise or fall in the price of related goods depending on their nature, i.e. whether goods are substitute or complementary to each other. The effect of change in price of a related good on the demand of other good is called **cross price effect**.

<table>
<tr><th>Substitute Goods</th><th>Complementary Goods</th></tr>
<tr><td>When the price of one good increases, the demand for its substitute also increases, depicting direct relation between the two.
e.g. Rise in price of Pepsi will make consumers switch to Coke, thus shifting its demand curve to the right (from D to D_1).
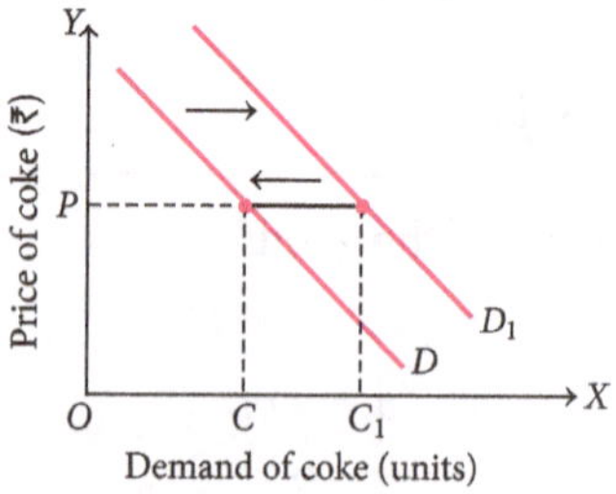

Substitute goods</td><td>When the price of one good increases, the demand for its complementary good decreases, depicting inverse relation between the two.
e.g. With the rise in price of petrol, the demand for petrol cars will decrease, shifting the demand curve to the left (from D to D_1).
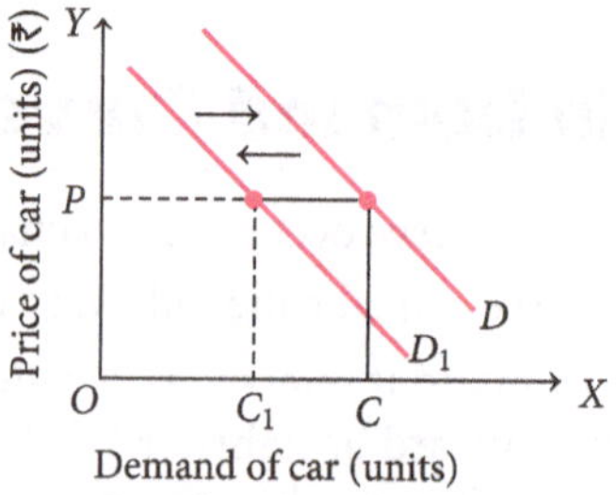

Complementary goods</td></tr>
</table>

Change in Demand Due to Change in Income

<table>
<tr><th>Normal Goods</th><th>Inferior Goods</th></tr>
<tr><td>When consumer's income increases, keeping other factors constant, the demand for normal goods will rise, shifting the demand curve to the right (from D to D_1 in graph below) and vice-versa.
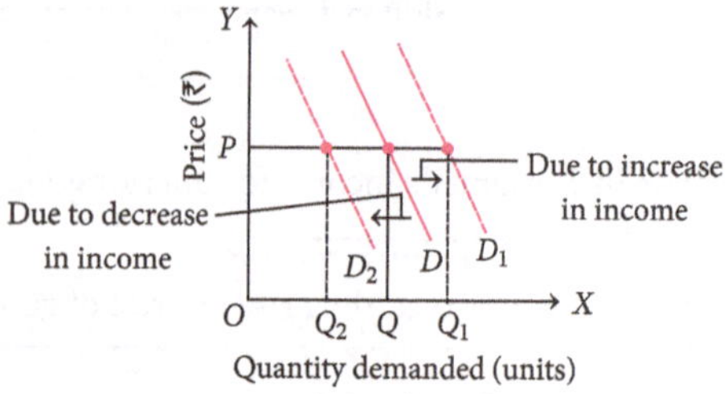

Normal goods</td><td>An increase in consumer's income leads to a decrease in demand for inferior goods, shifting the demand curve to the left (from D to D_1 in graph below) and vice-versa.
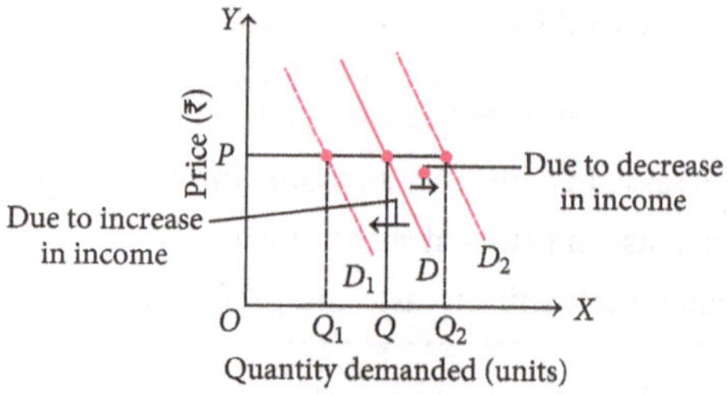

Inferior goods</td></tr>
</table>

3.5 Elasticity of Demand

It refers to the degree of responsiveness of demand due to changes in its determinants, such as price, consumer's income, prices of related goods, etc. There are three main types of elasticity of demand

1. **Price Elasticity of Demand** Measures how quantity demanded of a commodity changes in response to a change in its own price.
2. **Income Elasticity of Demand** Measures how quantity demanded of a commodity changes due to change in consumer's income.
3. **Cross Elasticity of Demand** Measures how quantity demanded of one good change due to change in the price of a related good.

Price Elasticity of Demand (E_d)

It is calculated as the percentage change in quantity demanded for the commodity divided by the percentage change in its price. It is a pure number and does not depend on the units in which price and quantity are measured.

Measurement of Price Elasticity of Demand

It can be calculated using following methods

- Percentage or proportionate method
- Total expenditure or total outlay method
- Geometric method

Note Geometric method is beyond the scope of the syllabus.

Percentage or Proportionate Method

It is the most common approach to measure price elasticity of demand. It calculates elasticity by the ratio of the percentage change in quantity demanded to the percentage change in own price of commodity.

$$E_p \text{ or } E_d = (-)\frac{\text{Percentage Change in Quantity Demanded}}{\text{Percentage Change in Price}}$$

Percentage Change in Quantity Demanded $= \frac{\Delta Q}{Q} \times 100$; Percentage Change in its Price $= \frac{\Delta P}{P} \times 100$

The formula of proportionate method can mathematically be presented as under

$$E_p \text{ or } E_d = (-)\frac{\Delta Q}{\Delta P} \times \frac{P}{Q}$$

where, Q = Actual quantity; ΔQ = Change in quantity; P = Actual price; ΔP = Change in price

Note E_p or E_d is a negative number because price and quantity demanded are inversely related. In numericals, the minus sign is dropped from the numbers for simplicity and all percentage changes are treated as positive.

Solved Question 1 **Due to a 10% fall in the price of a commodity, its quantity demanded rises from 400 units to 450 units. Calculate its price elasticity of demand.**

Sol. Percentage Change in Quantity Demanded $= \frac{\Delta Q}{Q} \times 100$

$$= \frac{(450 - 400)}{400} \times 100 = \frac{50}{400} \times 100 = 12.5\%$$

$$E_d = \frac{(-)\text{ Percentage Change in Quantity Demanded}}{\text{Percentage Change in Price}}$$

$$= \frac{12.5}{(-)\ 10} = 1.25$$

$\therefore$ Price Elasticity of Demand (E_d) $= (-)\ 1.25$ (more than unity)

Solved Question 2 **A consumer demands 20 units of a good at a price of ₹ 5 per unit. When price of the good falls by ₹ 1 per unit, demand increases by 50 units.**

Calculate elasticity of demand by proportionate method.

Sol. Original Quantity (Q) = 20

Change in Quantity (ΔQ) = 50

Original Price (P) = 5

Change in Price (ΔP) = −1

$$E_d = (-)\frac{\Delta Q}{\Delta P} \times \frac{P}{Q} = (-)\frac{50}{-1} \times \frac{5}{20}$$

$$= \frac{25}{2} = 12.5$$

Total Expenditure or Total Outlay Method

It assesses price elasticity by comparing total expenditure on a commodity before and after the price change. It categorises demand elasticity into three situations

1. **Elasticity of Demand will be Greater than Unity** ($E_d > 1$) When total expenditure increases with fall in price and decreases with rise in price, elasticity will be greater than 1.

2. **Elasticity of Demand will be Equal to One** ($E_d = 1$) When total expenditure remains unchanged in response to change in price of the commodity, elasticity will be equal to 1.
3. **Elasticity of Demand will be Less than Unity** ($E_d < 1$) When total expenditure decreases with fall in price and increases with rise in price, elasticity will be less than 1.

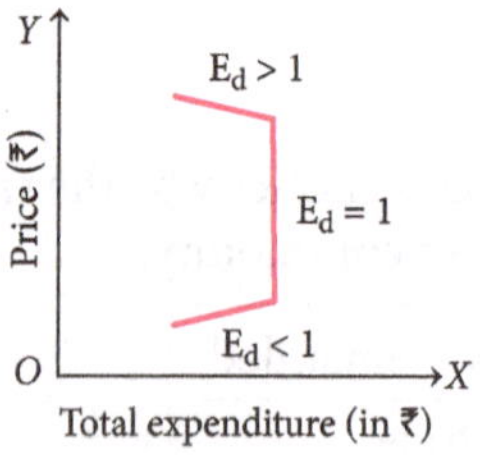

Total expenditure method

Solved Question 3 **Price of a commodity is ₹ 10 per unit, quantity demanded at this price is 100 units. If price rises by ₹ 2 per unit, quantity falls by 20 units.**

What will be the price elasticity of demand by total expenditure method?

Sol. At price ₹ 10, quantity is 100 units

Thus, Total Expenditure = Price × Quantity

= 10 × 100

= ₹ 1,000

When price rises by ₹ 2, quantity falls by 20 units

∴ New total expenditure = New Price × New Quantity

= 12 × 80

= ₹ 960

As price and total expenditure are changing in opposite direction, price elasticity of demand will be more than unity i.e. elastic demand.

Degrees of Price Elasticity of Demand

1. **Perfectly Elastic Demand** ($E_d = \infty$) In this, a slight change in price will cause an infinite change in demand. Thus, small rise in price will result in zero demand of commodity.

   In this case, demand curve is horizontal, i.e. parallel to x-axis.

Price (₹)	Quantity (units)
5	10
5	20
5	30

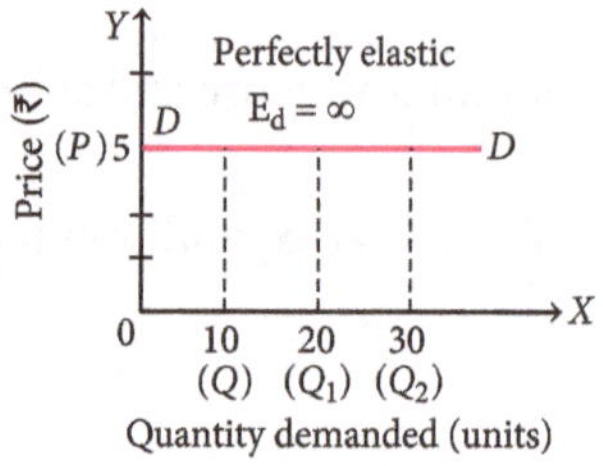

2. **Unitary Elastic Demand** ($E_d = 1$) In this, the change in quantity demanded equals the percentage change in its price. Here, the demand curve forms a rectangular hyperbola shape as the total area under such curve remains constant.

Price (₹)	Quantity (units)
5	100
4	120

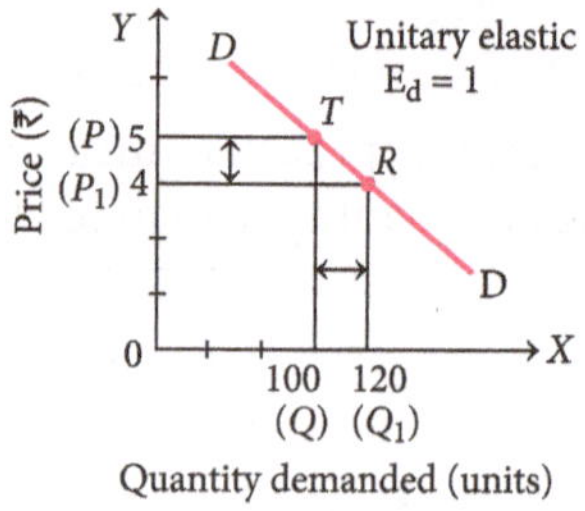

3. **Less than Unitary Elastic Demand** ($E_d < 1$) In this, the percentage change in quantity demanded is less than the percentage change in its price, resulting in a steeper demand curve.

Price (₹)	Quantity (units)
5	100
4	105

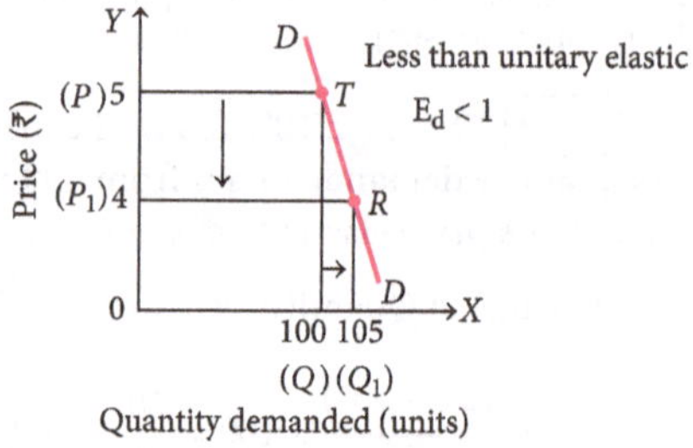

4. **Perfectly Inelastic Demand** ($E_d = 0$) Here, change in price causes no change in quantity demanded. In this case, the demand curve is vertical, i.e. parallel to y-axis.

Price (₹)	Quantity (units)
5	100
4	100
3	100

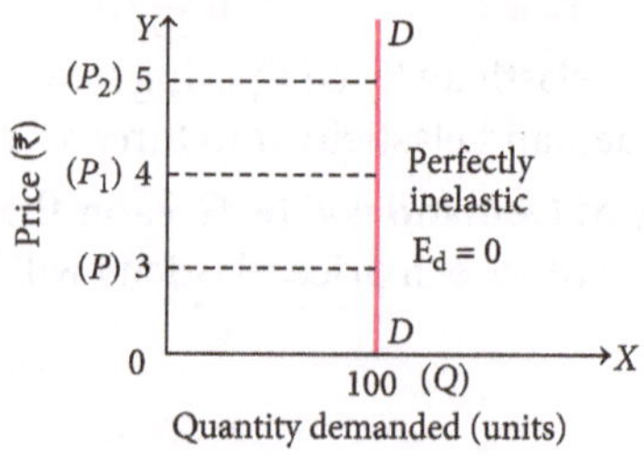

5. **More than Unitary Elastic Demand** ($E_d > 1$) In this, the percentage change in quantity demanded is more than that of percentage change in price, leading to a flatter demand curve.

Price (₹)	Quantity (units)
5	100
4	140

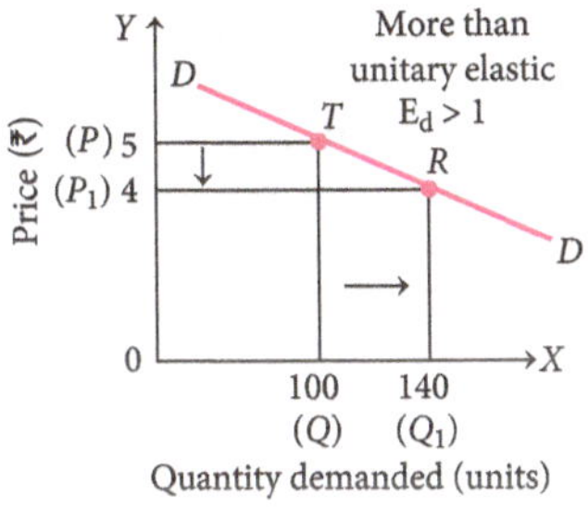

Relation between Slope of Demand Curve and Elasticity of Demand

Slope of demand curve and price elasticity of demand are inversely proportional. This can be expressed as

$$E_p^d = (-)\frac{\Delta Q}{\Delta P} \times \frac{P}{Q} \quad or \quad E_p^d = (-)\frac{1}{\Delta P / \Delta Q} \times \frac{P}{Q}$$

$$or \quad E_p^d = (-)\frac{1}{\text{Slope of Demand Curve}} \times \frac{P}{Q}$$

∴ When slope of demand curve is higher, elasticity of demand will be low and *vice-versa*.

Factors affecting Price Elasticity of Demand

1. **Nature of the Commodity** Necessities like food items and prestige goods have an inelastic demand, while luxuries and comforts have elastic demand.
2. **Availability of Substitutes** Commodities with close substitutes have elastic demand. e.g. If the price of coke rises, consumers will switch to pepsi.
3. **Postponement of Consumption** Goods whose consumption can be postponed for sometime, have elastic demand, such as televisions, whereas it is inelastic demand for necessities like medicines.
4. **Different Uses of the Commodity** Goods with multiple uses, have elastic demand, like milk, steel, etc. while commodity having only one use has inelastic demand like salt.
5. **Time Period** Longer duration of period will lead to greater elasticity of demand as consumers can adjust their demand in long-run.
6. **Habits** If consumers are habituated of some commodities, the demand for such commodities will usually be inelastic, e.g. Alcohol.
7. **Proportion of Income Spent on Goods** Items that take up a small portion of income (like toothpaste, matchbox, etc.) have inelastic demand, while larger expenses (like clothing) usually exhibit elastic demand.

Mind Map

DEMAND AND PRICE ELASTICITY OF DEMAND

1 Demand

It is the quantity of a commodity that consumers are willing and able to purchase at various prices during a given period.

Components of Demand

- Willingness to buy
- Price
- Ability to buy
- Time period

2 Individual Demand

It is a demand by an individual consumer.

Determinants of Individual Demand

- Price of the commodity
- Income of consumers
- Price of related goods
- Taste and preferences of consumers
- Expectations about future price of good

Individual Demand Function It is a functional relationship between individual demand and its determinant. $D_x = f(P_x, P_r, Y, T, E)$

3 Market Demand

It is a aggregate demand by all consumers in a market.

Determinants of Market Demand

- Distribution of income
- Size of population
- Composition of population

Market Demand Function It is a functional relationship between market demand and its determinants. $D_x = f(P_x, P_r, Y, T, E, N, D_y, P_c)$

4 Demand Schedule and Curve

Demand Schedule It is a tabular representation showing different quantities of a commodity demanded at various prices over a given period. It can be classified into individual demand schedule (for a single buyer) and market demand schedule (for all consumers in a market).

Demand Curve It is a graphical representation of the demand schedule. It can be classified into individual demand curve and market demand curve.

5 Law of Demand

It states that other things remaining constant, the quantity demanded of a commodity falls when its price rises and *vice-versa*.

Exceptions to the Law of Demand These are the cases where demand does not follow the usual inverse price-demand relationship. These are

- **Giffen Goods** Inferior goods with rising demand as price increases.
- **Conspicuous Consumption** Luxury goods remain in demand despite high prices.
- **Necessities** Essential goods have constant demand regardless of price.
- **Ignorance** Consumers unaware of better prices may buy at higher costs.
- **Future Expectations** If prices are expected to drop, consumers delay purchases.
- **Conspicuous Necessities** Modern essentials are bought despite price hikes.

6 Movement and Shift in Demand Curve

Movement along the Demand Curve

Change in quantity demanded or movement occurs when demand of a good changes due to a change in its own price, keeping other factors constant.

- **Extension** Demand rises as price falls.
- **Contraction** Demand falls as price rises.

Shift in the Demand Curve

Change in demand or shift takes place when demand changes due to factors other than price, like income or preferences.

- **Increase in Demand** Rightward shift.
- **Decrease in Demand** Leftward shift.

7 Elasticity of Demand

It is the degree of responsiveness of demand due to changes in its determinants.

Types

- **Price Elasticity of Demand** Change in quantity demanded due to change in price.
- **Income Elasticity of Demand** Change in quantity demanded due to change in consumer's income.
- **Cross Elasticity of Demand** Change in quantity demanded of one good due to change in price of another good.

8 Price Elasticity of Demand

It can be calculated using following methods

- **Percentage or Proportionate Method** It calculates elasticity by the ratio of the percentage change in quantity demanded to the percentage change in own price of commodity.
- **Total Expenditure** (Outlay) **Method** It calculates price elasticity of demand by comparing total expenditure before and after a price change.

9 Degrees of Price Elasticity of Demand

- **Perfectly Elastic Demand** ($E_d = \infty$) Demand changes infinitely with any price change (horizontal demand curve).
- **More than Unitary Elastic Demand** ($E_d > 1$) A price change is less than a change in quantity demanded.
- **Unitary Elastic Demand** ($E_d = 1$) Percentage change in price equals the percentage change in quantity demanded.
- **Less than Unitary Elastic Demand** ($E_d < 1$) Change in demand is less than the change in price.
- **Perfectly Inelastic Demand** ($E_d = 0$) Quantity demanded remains constant, regardless of price changes (vertical demand curve).

EXAM PATTERN QUESTIONS

Objective Type Questions

Multiple Choice Questions (MCQs)

1. Demand of a commodity depends upon ....

(a) price (b) income
(c) price of related good (d) All of these

2. What is the key difference between demand and desire?

(a) Demand is a wish, while desire includes the ability to buy
(b) Desire is a wish, while demand reflects willingness and ability to buy
(c) Desire is measurable, while demand is not
(d) Demand is unlimited, while desire is restricted

3. Which of the following best describes market demand?

(a) Demand by individual consumers for a good
(b) Total demand for a good from all consumers in the market
(c) Demand by the government for goods
(d) Demand influenced by advertisements

4. Which of the following does not affect demand?

(a) The consumer's willingness to buy
(b) The price of the commodity
(c) The ability of the consumer to buy
(d) The production cost of the good

5. "Gold, silver rebound on strong festive demand." What does the 'strong festive demand' for gold and silver indicate in terms of price elasticity? Competency Based Que

(a) Demand for gold and silver is perfectly elastic during festivals
(b) Demand for gold and silver is inelastic due to cultural significance
(c) Demand for gold and silver becomes unitary elastic
(d) Demand for gold and silver is highly sensitive to price changes

6. Identify the determinant of individual demand highlighted in the below image.

(a) Income of consumers (Y)
(b) Taste and preferences (T)
(c) Price of related goods (P)
(d) Expectations about future prices (E)

7. Comment on the nature of goods, if the demand of one good increases due to decrease in the price of another good. NCERT (QR); Competency Based Que

(a) Substitute goods
(b) Complementary goods
(c) Inferior goods
(d) Giffen goods

8. Which of the following is an example of complementary goods?

(a) Petrol and petrol cars
(b) Full-cream milk and toned milk
(c) Smartphones and laptops
(d) Coke and Pepsi

9. What is the impact of consumers expecting future price increases?

(a) They postpone purchases
(b) They buy more now
(c) They wait for discounts
(d) They reduce overall demand

10. Which of the following best describes normal goods?

(a) Goods whose demand is unaffected by income changes
(b) Goods whose demand decreases with rising income
(c) Goods whose demand increases with rising income
(d) Goods with no relationship to income levels

11. Which of the following is an example of an inferior good?

(a) Branded clothing (b) Luxury cars
(c) Public transport (d) Organic food

12. What is the key difference between normal goods and inferior goods?

(a) Normal goods are cheaper, while inferior goods are expensive
(b) Demand for normal goods increases with income, while demand for inferior goods decreases with income
(c) Demand for both normal and inferior goods increases with income
(d) Normal goods are necessities, while inferior goods are luxuries

13. Quantity of goods and services that people are willing to buy for a particular price and at a particular point of time is called NCERT (QR)
(a) quantity supplied (b) budget line
(c) quantity demanded (d) law of demand

14. Which of the following is a characteristic of the slope of the demand curve? Competency Based Que
I. It measures the rate at which demand changes with respect to its price.
II. It remains constant regardless of price changes.
III. It is always positive.
IV. It has no relation to demand.
Codes
(a) I and II (b) Only I (c) Only III (d) I and IV

15. Which type of demand curve is shown in the given image?

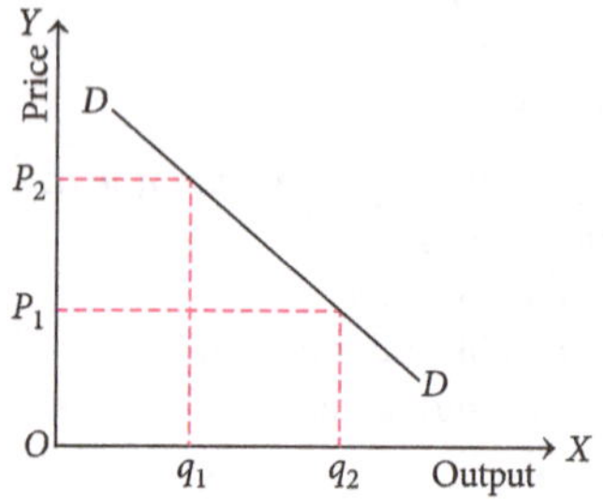

(a) Market (b) Individual
(c) Sloping (d) Upward

16. Which of the following explains the downward slope of the demand curve?
(a) Increase in the size of the consumer group due to a price fall
(b) Substitution effect driving consumers to more expensive options
(c) Ignorance of competitive pricing
(d) Conspicuous consumption of luxury goods

17. What is the behaviour of demand for giffen goods?
(a) Demand decreases as prices increase
(b) Demand remains constant regardless of price changes
(c) Demand increases as prices increase
(d) Demand decreases with an increase in substitutes

18. When the quantity demanded decreases in response to an increase in consumer income, the good is known as
(a) inferior goods (b) normal goods NCERT (QR)
(c) giffen goods (d) None of these

19. If the price of any complementary good rises, then ....
(a) demand curve shifts to left
(b) demand curve shifts to right
(c) demand curve moves downward
(d) demand curve moves upward

20. What will be the impact on demand curve of inferior goods, if consumer's income increase?
(a) Demand curve shifts to the right
(b) Demand curve shifts to the left
(c) Downward movement along demand curve
(d) Upward movement along demand curve

21. If the market demand schedule is derived from individual demand schedules, what does the horizontal summation of quantities at each price level represent? Competency Based Que
(a) The average price at which goods are demanded
(b) The total market demand for the commodity at that price
(c) The quantity demanded by the consumer with the highest demand
(d) The cumulative price of all individual demands

22. Observe the demand curve given below and identify the slope of the curve.

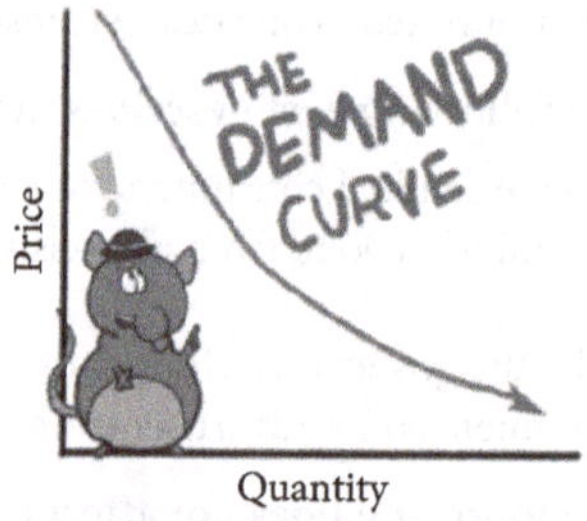

(a) Linear demand curve with decreasing slope
(b) Non-linear demand curve with decreasing slope
(c) Linear demand curve with constant slope
(d) Non-linear demand curve with decreasing slope

23. The union government will not hesitate to import coal or impose Section 11 of the Electricity Act (Emergency Law), if needed, to meet the country's rising power demand, Power Minister RK Singh said on 1st February in an interaction with reporters in New Delhi.
How this move is expected to impact the demand for electricity in India? Competency Based Que
(a) Demand curve will shift to the right
(b) Demand curve will shift to the left
(c) Downward movement along demand curve
(d) Upward movement along demand curve

24. "The demand for essential items like medicines or salt maintains constant demand regardless of price changes."
What type of goods does this statement refer to? Competency Based Que
(a) Giffen goods
(b) Luxury goods
(c) Inferior goods
(d) Necessities

25. **"Lifestyle inflation beats essential."**

Source *https://timesofindia.indiatimes.com/city/mumbai/lifestyle-inflation-outstrips-price-rise-in-essential-commodities-since-fy18-mumbai-news/articleshow/107806149.cms*

What could be a likely impact of rising prices on the demand for essential goods? **Competency Based Que**

(a) Demand will increase
(b) Demand will remain unchanged
(c) Demand will decrease
(d) Demand will fluctuate wildly

26. **Which of the following are the assumptions of the law of demand?** **Competency Based Que**

I. Consumer preferences do not change.
II. Consumer income remains changed.
III. The distribution of income remains constant.
IV. The size and demographics of the population vary.

Codes

(a) I and III (b) I, II, III and IV
(c) I and IV (d) II, II and IV

27. **The price of a commodity increases from ₹ 20 to ₹ 25, causing the quantity demanded to decrease from 100 units to 80 units. The price elasticity of demand (E_d) is ....** **Competency Based Que**

(a) 0.8 (b) 1.0 (c) 1.2 (d) 1.5

28. **What shape does the demand curve take under unitary elastic demand?**

(a) Straight line sloping downward
(b) Perfectly vertical line
(c) Perfectly horizontal line (d) Rectangular hyperbola

29. **When is elasticity of demand less than unity ($E_d < 1$)?**

(a) When totals expenditure increases with a fall in price
(b) When totals expenditure decreases with a fall in price and increases with a rise in price
(c) When total expenditure remains constant with a change in price
(d) When demand curve is a rectangular hyperbola

30. **Which type of commodity typically has inelastic demand?**

(a) Luxuries and comforts
(b) Necessities like food and medicines
(c) Goods with multiple uses
(d) Substitutable goods

31. **How does the availability of substitutes affect price elasticity of demand?**

(a) It decreases elasticity
(b) It makes demand perfectly inelastic
(c) It increases elasticity as consumers can easily switch to alternatives
(d) It has no effect on elasticity

32. **If the price of a product decreases from ₹ 30 to ₹ 25 and the quantity demanded increases from 50 to 70 units, what happens to the total expenditure on the product?** **Competency Based Que**

(a) Decreases (b) Remains the same
(c) Increases (d) Cannot be determined

33. **The image given below indicates which of the following types of elasticity of demand?**

(a) Elastic demand (b) Inelastic demand
(c) Perfectly inelastic demand
(d) None of the above

34. **A 10% increase in the price of a luxury car leads to a 30% decrease in the quantity demanded. What is the price elasticity of demand for this luxury car?** **Competency Based Que**

(a) 0.33 (b) 1.0 (c) 1.5 (d) 3.0

35. **If a product has a price elasticity of demand of 0.5, how is the demand for this product classified?** **Competency Based Que**

(a) Perfectly elastic (b) Unitary elastic
(c) Inelastic (d) Elastic

36. **A company notices that when it increases the price of its product from ₹ 40 to ₹ 50, the quantity demanded drops from 200 units to 150 units. Calculate the price elasticity of demand.** **Competency Based Que**

(a) 0.5 (b) 1.0 (c) 1.5 (d) 2.0

37. **Which factor affecting price elasticity of demand is given in the below image?**

(a) Postponement of consumption
(b) Availability of substitutes
(c) Time period
(d) Different uses of the commodity

38. **Price elasticity of demand is .... in number because price and quantity demanded are inversely related.**
(a) positive (b) negative
(c) constant (d) prime

Direction *Read the case study and answer the questions 39 to 42 on the basis of the same*

XYZ Electronics, a prominent smartphone manufacturer in India, introduced two models : Smartphone A, a budget friendly option, and Smartphone B, a premium model. To boost sales, XYZ Electronics reduced the price of Smartphone A while maintaining the price of Smartphone B.

Smartphone A : After the price drop, demand surged, showcasing elastic demand. This indicates that consumers were sensitive to the lower price and increased their purchases accordingly.

Smartphone B : In contrast, the demand for Smartphone B remained stable despite no price change, indicating inelastic demand. This suggests that its niche market values quality over price.

This scenario illustrates how understanding elasticity of demand is crucial for effective pricing strategies. The price reduction for Smartphone A successfully attracted price-sensitive consumers, while the stable demand for Smartphone B highlighted consumer loyalty to premium products.

39. **What type of demand is characterised by a significant change in quantity demanded due to a price change?**
(a) Inelastic
(b) Elastic
(c) Perfectly elastic
(d) Perfectly inelastic

40. **The .... effect states that as the price of a good decreases, the quantity demanded increases significantly, indicating elastic demand.**

41. **If a product has inelastic demand, which of the following statements is true?**
(a) Demand will drastically change with price changes
(b) Consumers will continue to buy it regardless of price changes
(c) There are many substitutes available
(d) Consumers are highly sensitive to price changes

42. **Goods that are considered necessities usually exhibit .... demand, meaning their quantity demanded does not change significantly with price fluctuations.**

Assertion-Reason

Direction (Q. No. 43 to 52) *Read the following Assertion (A) and Reason (R) and choose the correct alternative from the following*

Alternatives
(a) Both Assertion (A) and Reason (R) are true and Reason (R) is the correct explanation of Assertion (A)
(b) Both Assertion (A) and Reason (R) are true, but Reason (R) is not the correct explanation of Assertion (A)
(c) Assertion (A) is true, but Reason (R) is false
(d) Assertion (A) is false, but Reason (R) is true

43. **Assertion** (A) Demand is the quantity of a good that a consumer is willing and able to buy at various possible prices during a specific period.
Reason (R) Demand is different from a simple desire because it reflects both willingness and the ability to buy.

44. **Assertion** (A) When income is distributed equally, demand increases across society.
Reason (R) A larger population in India leads to higher demand for goods and services.

45. **Assertion** (A) Market demand schedule is obtained by horizontally summation of individual demand schedules.
Reason (R) Market demand schedule is a graphical representation of demand schedule.

46. **Assertion** (A) Demand curve shows the inverse relation between own price of a good and its quantity demanded.
Reason (R) Law of diminishing marginal utility advocates that consumer gets lesser satisfaction for each additional units consumed.

47. **Assertion** (A) If consumers expect prices to drop further, they rush purchases.
Reason (R) The law of demand operates under the assumption that 'other factors remain constant'.

48. **Assertion** (A) Extension in demand is indicated by downward movement along the same demand curve.
Reason (R) Contraction in demand is indicated by an upward movement on the same demand curve.

49. **Assertion** (A) If the price of one good increases, the demand for its complementary good decreases.
Reason (R) Complementary goods are those that are used together, so an increase in the price of one reduces the quantity demanded of both.

50. **Assertion** (A) A commodity which can be put to several use, is price inelastic.
Reason (R) As price falls, number of buyers increase in the market.

51. **Assertion** (A) Price elasticity measures how quantity demanded changes in response to a change in the price of the same commodity.

Reason (R) Price elasticity of demand for a commodity is calculated as the percentage change in quantity demanded for the commodity divided by the percentage change in its price.

52. **Assertion** (A) Perfectly elastic demand curve forms a rectangular hyperbola.

Reason (R) In perfectly inelastic demand, price do not affect the quantity demanded.

Two Statements Based MCQs

Direction (Q. No. 53 to 62) *Read the following statements carefully and choose the correct alternative*

Alternatives

(a) Statement I is correct and Statement II is incorrect
(b) Statement II is correct and Statement I is incorrect
(c) Both the statements are correct
(d) Both the statements are incorrect

53. **Statement I** Market demand is the quantity of a good demanded by one person.

Statement II Individual demand is the total quantity demanded by all consumers in a market.

54. **Statement I** Market demand curve is vertical summation of individual demand curves.

Statement II Slope of demand curve and elasticity of demand are inversely related.

55. **Statement I** Change in price of a given commodity leads to movement along the demand curve.

Statement II If the consumers expects price to fall in future, demand at present also falls.

56. **Statement I** The law of demand states that there is a positive relationship between the price of the commodity and its quantity demanded.

Statement II As consumers buy more, the satisfaction from each additional unit decreases, so they are willing to pay less.

57. **Statement I** Essential items like medicines or salt maintain constant demand regardless of price changes.

Statement II Luxury goods like diamonds defy the law as demand persists despite higher prices.

58. **Statement I** A fall in demand indicated by a leftward shift of the demand curve.

Statement II A fall in demand indicated by a rightward shift of the demand curve.

59. **Statement I** The effect of change in price of a related good on the demand of other good is called cross price effect.

Statement II When consumer income increases, the demand for normal goods rises, shifting the demand curve to the right.

60. **Statement I** Cross elasticity measures how quantity demanded changes with a change in consumer income.

Statement II Income elasticity measures the change in quantity demanded of one good in response to a change in the price of a related good.

61. **Statement I** Percentage or proportionate method is the most common approach to measure price elasticity.

Statement II Percentage or proportionate method assesses price elasticity based on changes in total expenditure (or total outlay) before and after a price change.

62. **Statement I** Goods with multiple uses, like milk (used for cheese, butter, etc.) have elastic demand.

Statement II Items that take up a small portion of income (like toothpaste) have inelastic demand.

Matching

63. Match the following

Column I	Column II
A. Individual demand	(i) Specific amount of a product consumers are willing to buy at a given price.
B. Market demand	(ii) Mathematical representation of the relationship between demand and its determinants.
C. Quantity demanded	(iii) Demand from a single consumer for a specific product.
D. Demand function	(iv) Total demand from all consumers for a product in the market.

Codes

	A	B	C	D		A	B	C	D
(a)	(iii)	(iv)	(i)	(ii)	(b)	(iv)	(i)	(ii)	(iii)
(c)	(ii)	(iii)	(iv)	(i)	(d)	(iii)	(ii)	(i)	(iv)

64. Match the following

Column I	Column II
A. Income of consumer	(i) N
B. Price of related goods	(ii) P_r
C. Population size	(iii) Y
D. Distribution of income	(iv) D_y

Codes

	A	B	C	D		A	B	C	D
(a)	(iii)	(iv)	(i)	(ii)	(b)	(iv)	(i)	(ii)	(iii)
(c)	(ii)	(iii)	(iv)	(i)	(d)	(iii)	(ii)	(i)	(iv)

65. Match the following

Column I	Column II
A. Demand extension	(i) Upward movement along the demand curve.
B. Demand contraction	(ii) Rightward shift to the demand curve.
C. Increase in demand	(iii) Leftward shift to the demand curve.
D. Decrease in demand	(iv) Downward movement along the demand curve.

Codes

	A	B	C	D		A	B	C	D
(a)	(iii)	(iv)	(i)	(ii)	(b)	(iv)	(i)	(ii)	(iii)
(c)	(ii)	(iii)	(iv)	(i)	(d)	(iii)	(ii)	(i)	(iv)

66. Match the following

Column I	Column II
A. $E_d > 1$	(i) Unitary elastic demand
B. $E_d = 1$	(ii) Inelastic demand
C. $E_d < 1$	(iii) Perfectly elastic demand
D. $E_d = \infty$	(iv) Elastic demand

Codes

	A	B	C	D		A	B	C	D
(a)	(iii)	(iv)	(i)	(ii)	(b)	(iv)	(i)	(ii)	(iii)
(c)	(ii)	(iii)	(iv)	(i)	(d)	(iii)	(ii)	(i)	(iv)

67. Match the following

Column I	Column II
A. Less than unitary elastic demand	(i) Rectangular hyperbola
B. Perfectly inelastic demand	(ii) Steeper demand curve
C. More than unitary elastic demand	(iii) Vertical demand curve
D. Unitary elastic demand	(iv) Flatter demand curve

Codes

	A	B	C	D
(a)	(iii)	(iv)	(i)	(ii)
(b)	(iv)	(i)	(ii)	(iii)
(c)	(ii)	(iii)	(iv)	(i)
(d)	(iii)	(ii)	(i)	(iv)

Concept Identification

68. It describes the specific quantity of a good that consumers are willing to purchase at a particular price.

69. The concept that captures the assumption of constant factors when analysing the law of demand.

70. This concept illustrates the inverse relationship between price and quantity demanded.

71. It explains the relationship between price changes and the quantity demanded for a specific good.

72. It explains how demand for one good changes in response to price changes in a related good.

Answers

1. (d) All of these
2. (b) Desire is a wish, while demand reflects willingness and ability to buy
3. (b) Total demand for a good from all consumers in the market
4. (d) The production cost of the good
5. (b) Demand for gold and silver is inelastic due to cultural significance
6. (c) Price of related goods (P)
7. (a) Substitute goods
8. (a) Petrol and petrol cars
9. (b) They buy more now
10. (c) Goods whose demand increases with rising income
11. (c) Public transport
12. (b) Demand for normal goods increases with income, while demand for inferior goods decreases with income
13. (c) quantity demanded
14. (b) Only I
15. (a) Market
16. (a) Increase in the size of the consumer group due to a price fall
17. (c) Demand increases as prices increase
18. (a) inferior goods
19. (a) demand curve shifts to left
20. (b) Demand curve shifts to left
21. (b) The total market demand for the commodity at that price
22. (b) Non-linear demand curve with decreasing slope
23. (a) Demand curve will shift to the right

24. (d) Necessities
25. (c) Demand will decrease
26. (a) I and III
27. (a) Percentage Change in Quantity Demanded

$$= \frac{(80-100)}{100} \times 100 = 20\%$$

Percentage Change in Price $= \frac{(25-20)}{20} \times 100 = 25\%$

Percentage Elasticity of demand

$$E_d = \frac{-20\%}{25\%} = -0.8 \text{ (absolute value is 0.8).}$$

28. (d) Rectangular hyperbola
29. (b) When totals expenditure decreases with a fall in price and increases with a rise in price
30. (b) Necessities like food and medicines
31. (c) It increases elasticity as consumers can easily switch to alternatives
32. (c) Initial Total Expenditure = Price × Quantity

$$= 30 \times 50 = ₹\ 1{,}500$$

New Total Expenditure = 25 × 70 = ₹ 1,750

Total expenditure increases from ₹ 1,500 to ₹ 1,750.

33. (a) Elastic demand
34. (d) Price Elasticity of Demand $= \frac{30\%}{10\%} = 3.0$
35. (c) Since $E_d < 1$, the demand is classified as inelastic.
36. (b) Percentage Change in Quantity Demanded

$$= \frac{(150-200)}{200} \times 100 = -25\%$$

Percentage Change in Price $= \frac{(50-40)}{40} \times 100 = 25\%$

Percentage Elasticity of Demand

$$E_d = \frac{-25\%}{25\%} = -1 \text{ (absolute value is 1)}$$

37. (d) Different uses of the commodity
38. (b) negative
39. (b) Elastic
40. price
41. (b) Consumers will continue to buy it regardless of price changes
42. inelastic
43. (b) Both Assertion (A) and Reason (R) are true, but Reason (R) is not the correct explanation of Assertion (A)
44. (b) Both Assertion (A) and Reason (R) are true, but Reason (R) is not the correct explanation of Assertion (A)
45. (c) Demand curve is a graphical representation of demand schedule.
46. (a) Both Assertion (A) and Reason (R) are true and Reason (R) is the correct explanation of Assertion (A)
47. (d) If consumers expect prices to drop further, they delay purchases.
48. (b) Both Assertion (A) and Reason (R) are true, but Reason (R) is not the correct explanation of Assertion (A)
49. (a) Both Assertion (A) and Reason (R) are true and Reason (R) is the correct explanation of Assertion (A)
50. (d) A commodity that can be put to several uses is generally considered to have elastic demand rather than inelastic demand.
51. (a) Both Assertion (A) and Reason (R) are true and Reason (R) is the correct explanation of Assertion (A)
52. (d) Unitary elastic demand curve forms a rectangular hyperbola.
53. (d) Individual demand is the quantity of a good demanded by one person. Market demand is the total quantity demanded by all consumers in a market.
54. (b) Statement II is correct and Statement I is incorrect
55. (c) Both the statements are correct
56. (b) Law of demand states that there is an inverse relationship between the price of the commodity and its quantity demanded.
57. (c) Both the statements are correct
58. (a) A rise in demand indicated by a rightward shift of the demand curve.
59. (c) Both the statements are correct
60. (d) Cross elasticity measures the change in quantity demanded of one good in response to a change in the price of a related good. Income elasticity measures how quantity demanded changes with a change in consumer income.
61. (a) The total expenditure method assesses price elasticity based on changes in total expenditure (or total outlay) before and after a price change.
62. (c) Both the statements are correct
63. (a) (iii) (iv) (i) (ii)
64. (d) (iii) (ii) (i) (iv)
65. (b) (iv) (i) (ii) (iii)
66. (b) (iv) (i) (ii) (iii)
67. (c) (ii) (iii) (iv) (i)
68. Quantity demanded
69. Ceteris Paribus
70. Law of demand
71. Price elasticity of demand
72. Cross price elasticity of demand

Subjective Questions

Short Answer Type Questions

1. What does demand reflect in the context of consumer behaviour?

Ans. Demand reflects a consumer's willingness and ability to purchase a good or service at various prices within a specific time frame. Unlike mere desire, which indicates an interest in a product, demand considers both the financial capacity and the intent to buy. This dual aspect ensures that demand is a more accurate representation of consumer behaviour, providing insights into market dynamics and influencing pricing and production decisions.

2. Suppose there are two consumers in the market for a good and their demand functions are as follows
$d_1(p) = 20 - p$ for any price less than or equal to 20 and $d_1(p) = 0$ at any price greater than 20.
$d_2(p) = 30 - 2p$ for any price less than or equal to 15 and $d_1(p) = 0$ at any price greater than 15.
Find out is the market demand function.

NCERT; Competency Based Que

Ans. In the given demand functions, both the consumers do not want to demand the goods for any price above ₹ 15. Both of them demand only at a price less than or equal to ₹ 15.

Therefore, market demand will be

$$d(p) = d_1(p) + d_2(p)$$
$$d(p) = 20 - p + 30 - 2p$$
$$d(p) = 50 - 3p \ (P \leq 15)$$

For any price less than or equal to 15 and market demand (p) = 0 at any price greater than 15.

3. How does the price of a commodity influence demand?

Ans. The price of a commodity inversely affects demand, as indicated by the law of demand. When prices decrease, consumers are generally more willing to purchase larger quantities, leading to increased demand.

Conversely, when prices rise, the quantity demanded typically falls as consumers may seek alternatives or reduce consumption. This relationship highlights the importance of pricing strategies in business and helps in forecasting consumer behaviour in response to market changes.

4. Identify the changes that will take place in the demand curve due to the factors shown in the image below. Explain the changes in demand in general.

Competency Based Que

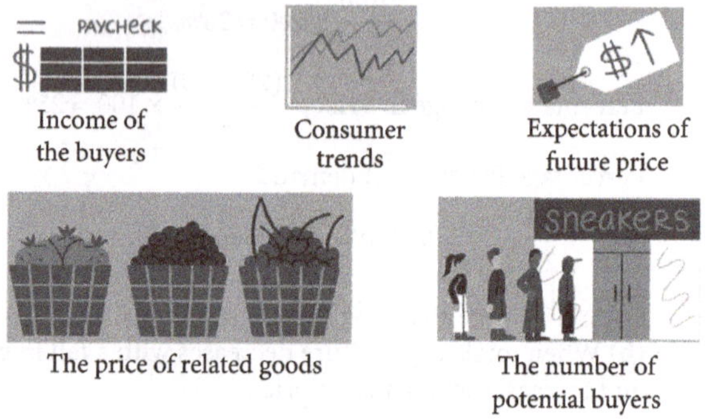

Ans. The above factors will lead to shift in demand curve.

A demand curve shift refers to fundamental changes in the balance of supply and demand that alter the quantity demanded at the same price.

(i) Shift of the demand curve to the right indicates an increase in demand at the same price because a factor, such as consumer trend or taste, has risen for it.

(ii) A shift to the left displays a decrease in demand at the same price because another factor, such as number of buyers, has slumped.

5. "No good is 'normal' or 'inferior', it depends on consumer to consumer." Do you agree? Justify.

Competency Based Que

Ans. Yes, the above statement is correct that, we cannot categorise goods as normal or inferior. It varies from one person to another, depending upon the level of income of consumer. A single good (say toned milk) may be a normal good for a person with low income while it may be an inferior good for other person with high income.

6. List and explain the determinants of market demand with examples.

Ans. Determinants of market demand are

(i) **Distribution of Income** (D_Y)
When income is distributed equally, demand increases across society. Unequal income distribution reduces overall demand. e.g. In Kerala, equal income distribution leads to steady demand for basic goods, unlike areas with large income gaps.

(ii) **Size of Population** (N)
A larger population leads to higher demand for goods and services. e.g. India's large population creates high demand for essentials like housing, especially in cities like Mumbai.

(iii) **Composition of Population** (P_C)
The demographic composition of the population affects demand.

Younger populations drive demand for gadgets and fashion, while older populations increase demand for healthcare. e.g. Bengaluru's young population drives gadget demand, whereas Dehradun's older population increases demand for healthcare services.

7. **"If consumers expect prices to rise, they buy more now." Do you agree? Give reason.** **Competency Based Que**

Ans. Yes, I agree with the statement. This phenomenon is rooted in the concept of consumer behaviour and expectations. When consumers anticipate an increase in prices for certain goods or services, they tend to purchase more of those items before the anticipated price hike occurs.

This behaviour is especially evident during events like sales or seasonal promotions, where consumers believe prices will rise after the event. As a result, this can lead to increased current demand and temporary shortages in the market, impacting overall supply and demand dynamics.

8. **Distinguish between individual demand and market demand with the help of a schedule.**

Ans. Demand by an individual is the demand of a commodity at different price level at a particular period of time by an individual. An individual demand schedule is as follows

Individual Demand Schedule

Price of Ice-cream (₹)	Quantity Demanded by 'A' (units)
1	4
2	3
3	2
4	1

Whereas, market demand is the sum of individual's demand at different price level at a particular period of time by different people.

A market demand schedule is as follows

Market Demand Schedule

Price of Ice-cream (₹)	A's Demand (1)	B's Demand (2)	Market Demand (1+2 =3)
1	4	5	4 + 5 = 9
2	3	4	3 + 4 = 7
3	2	3	2 + 3 = 5
4	1	2	1 + 2 = 3

9. **How does an increase in the price of one good affects the demand for its substitute?** **Competency Based Que**

Ans. An increase in the price of one good typically leads to a higher demand for its substitute.

This occurs because consumers seek alternatives to minimise their expenses. e.g. If the price of butter rises, consumers might opt for margarine instead. This shift in demand reflects the relationship between substitute goods, where the price increase of one directly impacts the consumption patterns of the other.

10. **Draw a demand curve with unitary price elasticity. Give explanation.**

Ans.

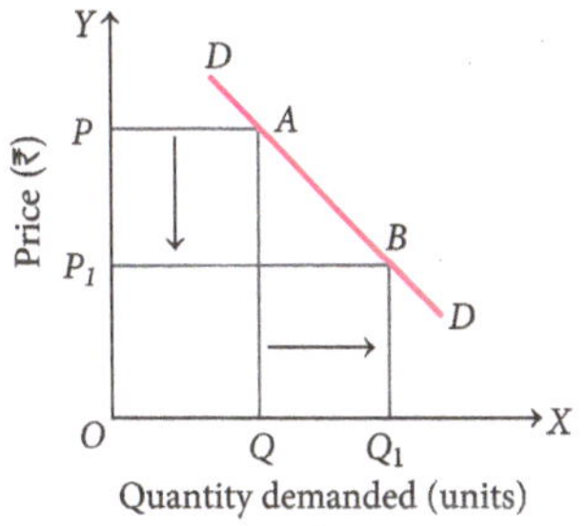

$E_d = 1$ at all points

Elasticity of demand is unitary on any point on the demand curve, if percentage change in quantity demanded is equal to the percentage change in price. A unit elastic demand curve extends towards x and y-axis in an uniform manner, without touching them.

11. **"Diminishing marginal utility suggests that as consumers buy more, the satisfaction from each additional unit decreases." How does this affect demand?** **Competency Based Que**

Ans. This affects demand because as satisfaction decreases with each additional unit purchased, consumers are less willing to pay high prices for further units. Consequently, they will only buy more if the price falls, illustrating the downward slope of the demand curve.

12. **Explain the meaning of change in quantity demanded. How does it affect demand curve?**

Ans. Change in quantity demanded means change in demand due to change in own price of the commodity, keeping other factors constant. This results at more being demanded at reduced price (extension in demand) and less being demanded at increased price (contraction in demand).

Change in quantity demanded causes a movement along the same demand curve. Extension in demand causes rightward movement, whereas, contraction in demand causes leftward movement.

13. **"Giffen goods may see increased demand when prices rise." Can you explain this exception to the law of demand?** **Competency Based Que**

Ans. Giffen goods are an exception to the law of demand, which states that quantity demanded decreases as price increases.

For giffen goods, demand increases even when prices rise because they are typically inferior goods and higher prices reduce the consumer's purchasing power, making it difficult to afford better substitutes. As a result, consumers may buy more of the Giffen good, despite its higher price, to meet their basic needs.

14. List the assumptions of the law of demand.

Ans. The law of demand operates under the assumption that 'other factors remain constant' (ceteris paribus). These assumptions are

(i) Consumer tastes and preferences does not change.
(ii) Consumer's income remains unchanged.
(iii) Prices of substitutes and complements stay the same.
(iv) Consumers do not anticipate future price changes.
(v) The distribution of income remains constant.
(vi) The size and demographics of the population do not vary.

15. Distinguish between causes of increase in demand and decrease in demand.

Ans. Differences between causes of increase and decrease in demand

Causes	Increase in Demand (Rightward shift in demand)	Decrease in Demand (Leftward shift in demand)
Income of Consumer	Increase in the income of the consumers in case of normal goods.	Decrease in the income of the consumers in case of normal goods.
Price of Substitute Goods	Increase in the price of substitute goods.	Decrease in the price of substitute goods.
Price of Complementary Goods	Fall in the price of complementary goods.	Rise in the price of complementary goods.
Taste and Preferences	Changes in tastes and preferences in favour of the commodity.	Changes in tastes and preferences against the commodity.

16. "When the price of a complementary good rises, the demand for the associated good decreases." Illustrate this relationship with an example. Competency Based Que

Ans. This relationship exists because complementary goods are consumed together. When the price of one good rises, the overall cost of using both goods increases, reducing the demand for both. e.g. If the price of petrol increases, owning and using petrol cars becomes more expensive, leading to a decrease in demand for petrol cars.

This results in a leftward shift in the demand curve for petrol cars, reflecting lower demand at each price level.

17. What is the difference between movement along the demand curve and a shift in the demand curve?

Ans. Difference between movement along the demand curve and shift in the demand curve is as follows

Basis	Movement along the Demand Curve	Shift in the Demand Curve
Cause	Due to changes in the price of the good itself.	Due to changes in factors other than the price of the good (e.g. income, preferences, prices of related goods).
Effect on Demand	Results in a change in quantity demanded.	Results in a change in overall demand.
Curve Behaviour	Movement occurs along the same demand curve (upward or downward).	The entire demand curve shifts left (decrease) or right (increase).
Example	If the price of apples drops, consumers buy more apples, moving downward along the curve.	If consumers' income increases, they may buy more apples at all price levels, shifting the demand curve to the right.

18. What is cross price effect?

Ans. The quantity of a good that the consumer chooses can increase or decrease with the rise or fall in the price of related goods depending on whether the goods are substitute or complementary to each other. The effect of change in price of a related good on the demand of other good is called cross price effect.

19. Which type of price elasticity is depicted in the given image? Explain. Competency Based Que

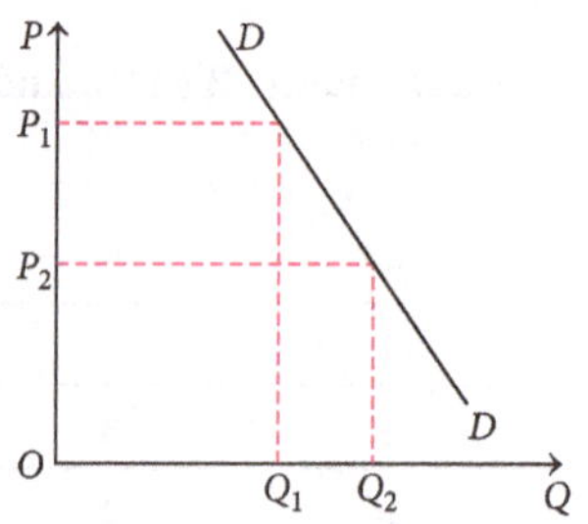

Ans. Inelastic demand is depicted in the given image. An inelastic demand curve illustrates a situation where the quantity demanded of a good or service changes very little in response to a change in its price.

This means that consumers are relatively insensitive to price fluctuations for these goods. The demand curve is steep, indicating that even significant price changes result in only minor changes in quantity demanded.

20. Suppose there was a 4% derease in the price of a good and as a result, the expenditure on the good increased by 2%. What can you say about the elesticity of demand? NCERT; Competency Based Que

Ans. The expenditure increases with a decrease in the price of good, this is the opposite change. Thus, the elasticity of demand is more than unit elastic, i.e. ($E_d > 1$)

21. Suppose the price elasticity of demand for a good is – 0.2. How will the expenditure on the good be affected if there is a 10% increase in the price of the good? NCERT; Competency Based Que

Ans. Total expenditure will rise if there is a 10% rise in the price of goods, since its demand is inelastic, i.e. $E_d = -0.2$.

22. "Necessities like food tend to have inelastic demand." Do you agree? Give reason. Competency Based Que

Ans. Yes, I agree. Necessities such as food generally exhibit inelastic demand because they are essential for survival. Even if prices rise, consumers will still purchase similar quantities because they need food to live. e.g. Staple foods like rice and bread see less fluctuation in demand despite price changes, highlighting the inelastic nature of essential goods.

23. "Goods that take up a small portion of income generally have inelastic demand." Do you agree? Give reason. Competency Based Que

Ans. Yes, I agree. Goods that take up a small portion of income, like toothpaste or salt, typically exhibit inelastic demand. This means that even if the price of these items increases, the quantity demanded does not change significantly because consumers view them as necessities that do not substantially impact their budgets.

24. Explain any two factors that affect the price elasticity of demand.

Ans. Two factors that affect price elasticity of demand are as follows

(i) **Availability of Substitutes**
The demand for commodities having close substitutes is very elastic because if there is an increase in the price of a commodity, people will start using substitute commodities.

(ii) **Proportion of Income Spent on the Goods**
Items such as thread, needle will have an inelastic demand as consumers spend a small proportion of their income on such items.
On the other hand, goods on which the consumers spend a large proportion of their income (clothes, food items, etc.) tend to have elastic demand.

25. How own price elasticity of demand is different from income elasticity of demand?

Ans. Price elasticity of demand is a quantitative relationship between change in quantity demanded due to change in price.
On the other hand, income elasticity of demand is a quantitative instrument which measures the responsiveness of change in demand due to change in income of the consumer, it is calculated as

$$E_y = \frac{\text{Percentage Change in Demand}}{\text{Percentage Change in Income}}$$

Where, E_y = Income Elasticity of Demand.

Long Answer Type Questions

26. List and explain the determinants of individual demand.

Ans. Determinants of individual demand are

(i) **Price of the Commodity** (P)
As the price of a commodity decreases, demand increases and *vice-versa*. e.g. A fall in smartphone prices in India leads to higher sales.

(ii) **Income of Consumers** (Y)
Demand for normal goods increases as income rises, while demand for inferior goods decreases. e.g. Families may switch to higher quality grains as their income rises.

(iii) **Price of Related Goods** (G)
The demand for substitute good increases when the price of its counterpart rises and the demand for complementary goods decreases when the price of the related good rises.

(iv) **Taste and Preferences** (T)
Consumer preferences, influenced by factors like fashion, climate and advertisements, affect demand. e.g. Cotton clothes see higher demand in summer.

(v) **Expectations about Future Prices** (E)
When consumers expect prices to rise, they tend to buy more immediately.
e.g. Gold demand spikes during festivals due to price expectations.

27. Explain with the help of diagrams, the effect of the following changes on the demand for a commodity

(i) A fall in the price of substitute goods.

(ii) A fall in the income of its buyer.

Ans. (i) Demand for a commodity will decrease when there is a fall in the price of substitute goods, implying that demand curve would shift backward. Less will be purchased at the same price. Demand for commodity falls from *OQ* to OQ_1.

So, fall in the price of tea will cause demand for coffee to fall. This situation is described in below figure.

The given figure illustrates this situation

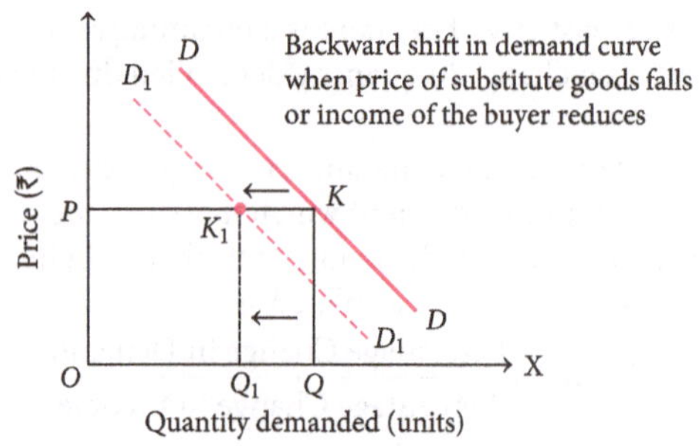

(ii) Demand for a commodity will decrease when there is a fall in the income of the consumer (assuming that the commodity demanded is a normal good). This would imply a backward shift in demand curve. Less will be purchased at the same price. Demand for commodity falls from OQ to OQ_1.

So, decrease in consumer's income will cause his demand for pure ghee to fall. This situation is described in above figure.

28. Explain the concept of the demand function. Also, differentiate between individual demand function and market demand function.

Ans. The demand function represents the relationship between the quantity demanded for a commodity and the various factors that influence this demand.

It highlights how demand varies in response to changes in price, consumer preferences, income and other determinants.

Difference between individual demand function and market demand function is as follows

Basis	Individual Demand Function	Market Demand Function
Definition	Refers to the demand for a commodity by a single consumer.	Refers to the aggregate demand for a commodity by all consumers in the market.
Mathematical Expression	$D_x = f(P_x, P_r, Y, T, E)$	$D_x = f(P_x, P_r, Y, T, E, N, D_y, P_c)$
Factors Considered	Considers price, related goods, income, preferences, and expectations.	Includes all factors of individual demand along with population size, income distribution, and population composition.
Scope	Narrow, focusing on an individual's consumption behaviour.	Broad, encompassing the collective behaviour of all consumers in the market.

29. Distinguish between change in demand and change in quantity demanded.

Ans. Differences between change in demand and change in quantity demanded are

Basis	Change in Demand	Change in Quantity Demanded
Factors	This is caused by change in determinants, other than own price of the commodity.	This is caused by change in own price of the commodity, other factors remaining constant.
Effect	This happens when at the same price, more or less is being demanded.	This happens when at a lower price, more is being demanded or at a higher price, less is being demanded.
Change in Curve	Diagrammatically, this is shown as a forward or backward shift in demand curve.	Diagrammatically, this is shown as a downward or an upward movement on the same demand curve.
Graph	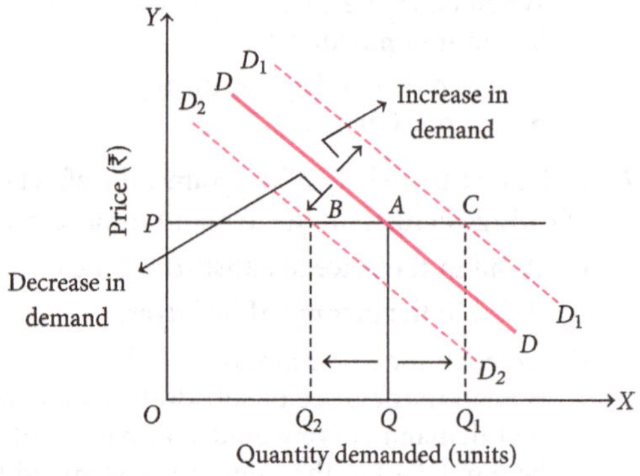	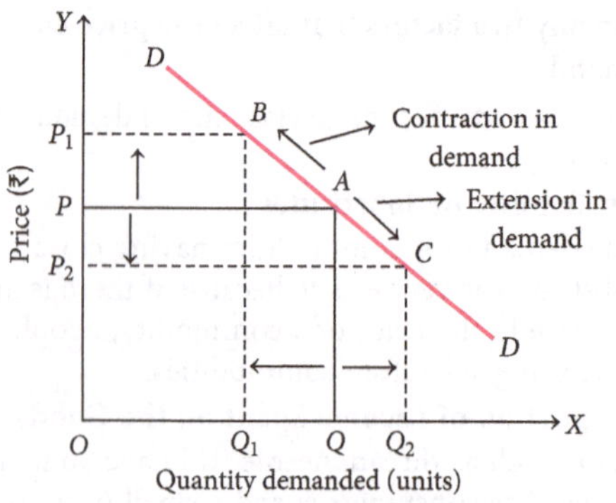

30. "The demand curve represents the relationship between the price of a commodity and the quantity demanded and its slope indicates the responsiveness of demand to price changes." Discuss the importance of the demand curve in economic analysis and how its slope informs decision-making for businesses and policy-makers. Competency Based Que

Ans. The demand curve is essential in economic analysis as it visually represents the inverse relationship between price and quantity demanded, reflecting the law of demand. Its slope indicates price elasticity a steep slope signifies inelastic demand, meaning consumers are less responsive to price changes, while a flatter slope indicates elastic demand, where consumers react significantly to price fluctuations.

For businesses, understanding the slope helps in pricing strategies to optimise sales and revenue. Policy-makers use the demand curve to anticipate the effects of taxes or subsidies on consumer behaviour. Overall, the demand curve is crucial for making informed decisions that affect market dynamics and consumer welfare.

31. "The law of demand asserts that the quantity demanded for a commodity expands with a fall in its price and contracts with a rise in its price."

Discuss how this principle applies to various market scenarios and the implications it has for consumer behaviour. Competency Based Que

Ans. The law of demand illustrates an essential economic principle as the price of a commodity decreases, consumers are likely to purchase more of it and conversely, when the price increases, the quantity demanded tends to decrease. This behaviour can be explained through the concepts of diminishing marginal utility, where the additional satisfaction derived from consuming each extra unit declines as more units are consumed.

For instance, if the price of a popular snack decreases, consumers may buy larger quantities, enjoying the increased utility. Conversely, if prices rise, consumers may reduce their purchases or seek substitutes. This principle has significant implications for businesses and policy-makers, as it helps predict consumer behaviour in response to price changes, guiding pricing strategies and taxation policies.

32. Explain the causes of a rightward shift in demand curve of a commodity of an individual consumer.

Ans. Causes of a rightward shift in demand curve of a commodity are as follows

(i) **Fall in Income in Case of Inferior Goods**
When income of the consumer decreases, he will increase the consumption of inferior goods, e.g. A person increases the consumption of dalda refined when his income falls.

(ii) **Rise in Income in Case of Normal Goods**
When income of the consumer increases, he will increase the consumption of normal goods, e.g. A person increases the consumption of pure ghee when his income increases.

(iii) **Rise in Price of Substitute Goods**
In case of such goods, increase in the price of one causes increase in the demand of other, e.g. Tea and coffee. If the price of the tea rises, then demand for coffee rises.

(iv) **Fall in Price of Complementary Goods**
In case of such goods, decrease in the price of one causes increase in the demand of other, e.g. Car and petrol. If the price of the petrol falls, consumer will demand more cars.

33. Explain the movement along the demand curve briefly.

Ans. Moving from one point to other on the same demand curve is called movement along a demand curve. A movement along the demand curve is caused by a change in quantity demanded of a good in response to change in its own price, other factors remaining constant. Movement along a demand curve can take the following forms

(i) **Extension in Demand**
It refers to rise in quantity demanded due to fall in the price of goods, keeping other factors constant. It is indicated by downward movement along the same demand curve.

(ii) **Contraction in Demand**
It refers to fall in quantity demanded due to rise in the price of goods, keeping other factors constant. It is indicated by an upward movement on the same demand curve.

An imaginary tabular and graphical presentation of extension and contraction in demand

Price (₹)	Quantity Demanded (units)	Description
1	500	
2	400	↓ Contraction
3	300	
4	200	↑ Extension
5	100	

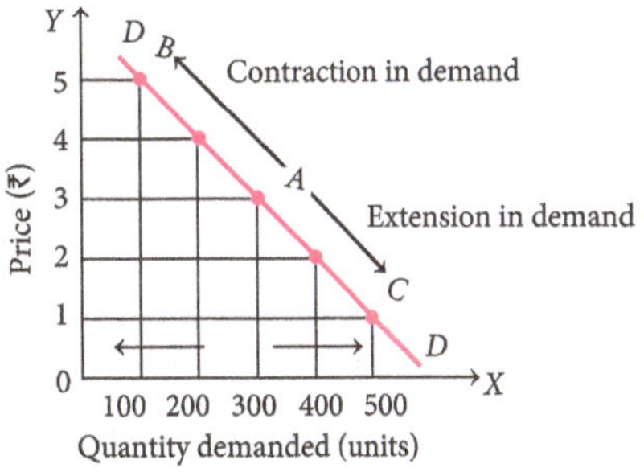

Curve showing extension and contraction of demand

34. Explain the change in demand of a good on account of change in prices of related goods.

Or **How is demand for a commodity affected by the rise in price of related goods? Explain with the help of diagram.** Competency Based Que

Or **Explain how the demand for a good is affected by the price of its related goods? Give examples.**

Ans. Related goods are of two types

(i) **Substitute Goods**

When price of the substitute good increases, demand curve for good X shifts to the right, implying demand increases from OQ to OQ_1 even when price of good X continues to be constant and *vice-versa.* e.g. An increase in the price of coffee will result in an increase in demand of its substitute good, i.e. tea.

(ii) **Complementary Goods**

When price of the complementary good increases, demand curve for good X shifts to the left, implying demand decreases from OQ to OQ even when price of good X continues to be OP (constant) and *vice-versa.* e.g. An increase in price of petrol will result in decrease in demand of its complementary good, i.e. car.

Following figure illustrates the effect of change in price of the related goods

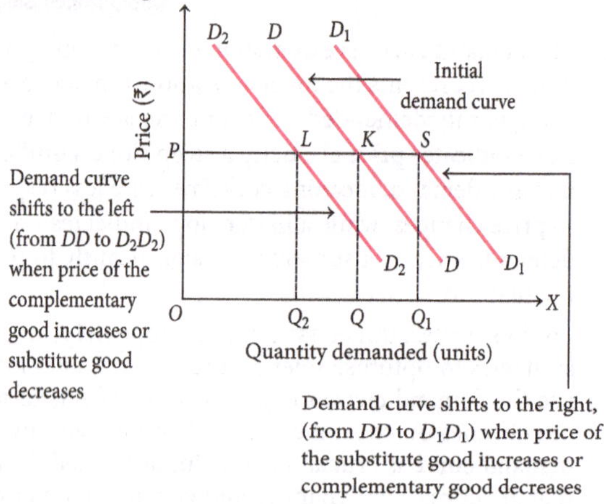

35. Distinguish between decrease in demand and decrease in quantity demanded.

Ans. Differences between decrease in demand and decrease in quantity demanded are

Basis	Decrease in Demand	Decrease in Quantity Demanded
Meaning	It is defined as fall in demand at the same price of the commodity.	It is defined as fall in quantity demanded due to rise in price of the commodity.
Direction	In this, there is a leftward shift in the demand curve.	In this, the consumer moves upward on the same demand curve.
Graphs	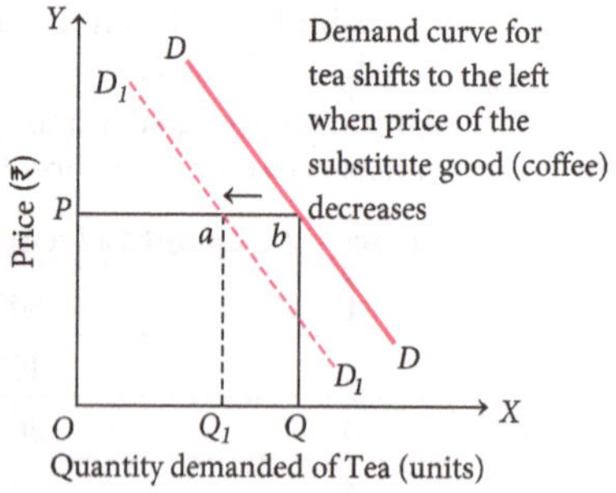	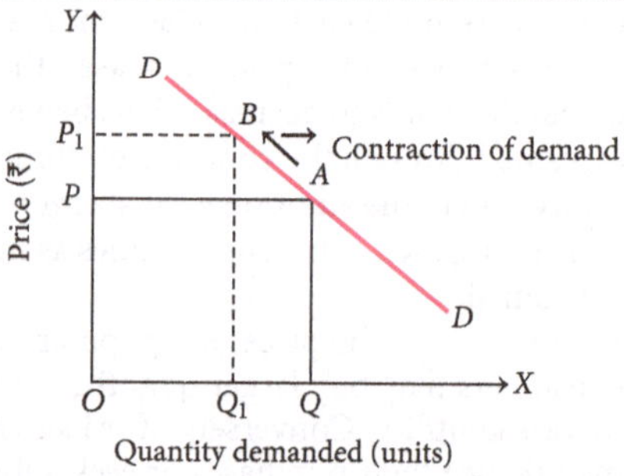
Reasons	It is due to (i) Fall in consumer's income in case of normal goods. (ii) Fall in the price of substitute goods. (iii) Rise in the price of complementary goods. (iv) Unfavourable changes in consumer's taste for this good.	It is due to rise in the price of the commodity only.
Change in Demand Curve	It signifies shift of a demand curve.	It signifies movement along a demand curve.

36. "Elasticity of demand measures the responsiveness of demand to changes in its determinants." Discuss the various types of elasticity of demand and how each type is calculated. Competency Based Que

Ans. Elasticity of demand is a crucial concept in economics that gauges how sensitive the quantity demanded of a good is to changes in various factors.

There are three primary types

(i) **Price elasticity of demand** assesses how the quantity demanded changes in response to price fluctuations of the same commodity. It is calculated by taking the percentage change in quantity demanded divided by the percentage change in price. If E_d is greater than one, demand is considered elastic; if less than one, inelastic; and if equal to one, unitary elastic.

(ii) **Income elasticity of demand** measures how quantity demanded changes in response to changes in consumer income. It is calculated by dividing the percentage change in quantity demanded by the percentage change in income. Normal goods exhibit a positive income elasticity, while inferior goods show a negative income elasticity.

(iii) **Cross elasticity of demand** evaluates how the quantity demanded of one good changes when the price of a related good changes. It is calculated similarly to the other elasticities, focusing on the relationship between two goods substitutes will have positive cross elasticity, while complements will have negative cross elasticity.

37. Explain the total expenditure method of assessing the price elasticity of demand.

Ans. Total Expenditure or Total Outlay Method

It assesses price elasticity based on changes in total expenditure (or total outlay) before and after a price change. It categorises demand elasticity into three situations

(i) **Elastic Demand** ($E_d > 1$)
Total expenditure increases when prices decrease and decreases when prices increase. e.g. If fashion apparel prices fall, total expenditure rises due to higher demand.

(ii) **Unitary Elastic Demand** ($E_d = 1$)
Total expenditure remains unchanged with price changes. For instance, if bus fares increase but commuter numbers stay the same, total expenditure stays stable.

(iii) **Inelastic Demand** ($E_d < 1$)
Total expenditure decreases when prices decrease and increases when prices increase. e.g. A price drop in medicines may not significantly boost sales, as consumers tend to buy a consistent amount.

38. "Various factors affect the price elasticity of demand, including the nature of the commodity and the availability of substitutes." Discuss how these factors influence demand elasticity. **Competency Based Que**

Ans. Factors that influence demand elasticity are

(i) **Nature of the Commodity**
Necessities like food have inelastic demand, while luxuries have elastic demand. e.g. Basic groceries are less sensitive to price changes, but luxury cars are more sensitive.

(ii) **Availability of Substitutes**
Commodities with close substitutes have elastic demand. If the price of Coke rises, consumers may switch to Pepsi.

(iii) **Postponement of Consumption**
Elastic demand is found in goods whose consumption can be delayed, such as televisions, whereas inelastic demand is seen in necessities like medicines.

(iv) **Different Uses of the Commodity**
Goods with multiple uses, like milk (used for cheese, butter, etc.), have elastic demand. In contrast, salt has inelastic demand due to its singular use.

(v) **Time Period**
Demand elasticity increases over time. Consumers can adjust their habits and switch products more easily in the long-run.

(vi) **Habits**
Goods that consumers are accustomed to, such as alcohol or cigarettes, tend to have inelastic demand because of established habits.

(vii) **Proportion of Income Spent**
Items that take up a small portion of income (like toothpaste) have inelastic demand, while larger expenses (like clothing) usually exhibit elastic demand.

39. What are the different degrees of price elasticity of demand?

Ans. Following are the degrees of price elasticity of demand

(i) **Perfectly Elastic Demand** ($E_d = \infty$)

Slight increase in price results in zero demand i.e. a small change in price leads to an infinite change in demand. In this case, demand curve is horizontal, i.e. parallel to x-axis.

Price (₹)	**Quantity** (units)
5	10
5	20
5	30

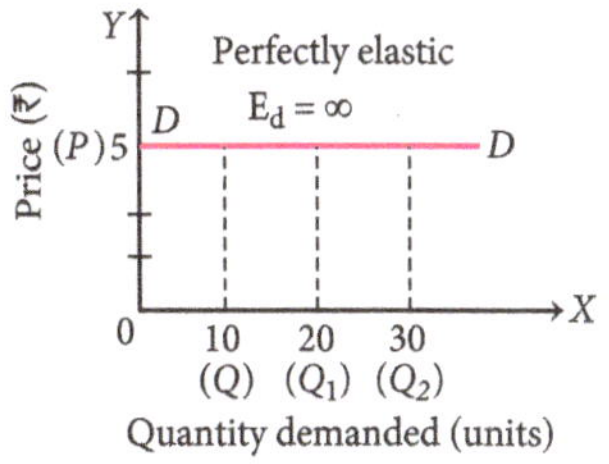

(ii) **Unitary Elastic Demand** ($E_d = 1$)
The percentage change in quantity demanded equals the percentage change in price. The demand curve forms a rectangular hyperbola, maintaining constant total expenditure.

Price (₹)	**Quantity** (units)
5	100
4	120

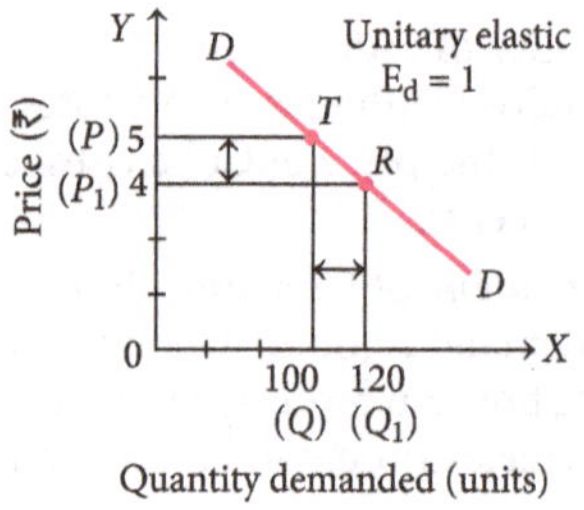

(iii) **Less than Unitary Elastic Demand** ($E_d < 1$)
The percentage change in quantity demanded is less than the percentage change in price, resulting in a steeper demand curve.

Price (₹)	**Quantity (units)**
5	100
4	105

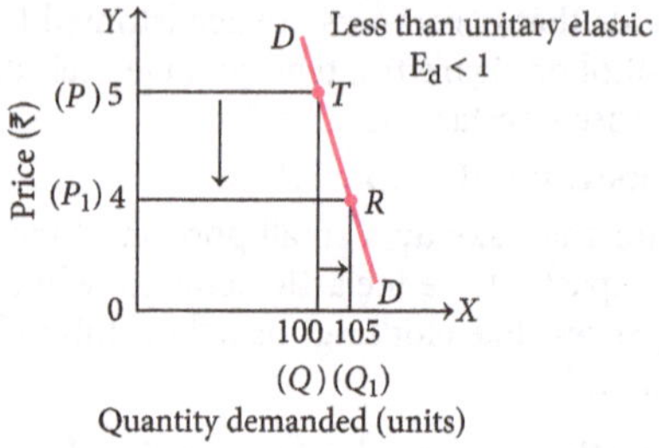

(iv) **Perfectly Inelastic Demand** ($E_d = 0$)
Changes in price do not affect the quantity demanded. The demand curve is vertical, indicating that demand remains constant regardless of price changes.

Price (₹)	**Quantity (units)**
5	100
4	100
3	100

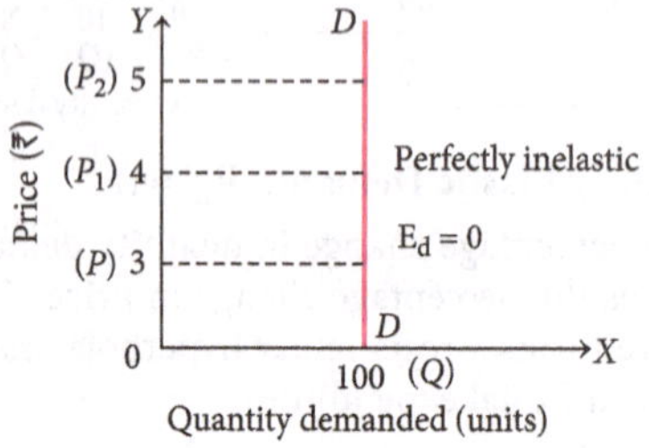

(v) **More than Unitary Elastic Demand** ($E_d > 1$)
The percentage change in quantity demanded exceeds the percentage change in price, leading to a flatter demand curve.

Price (₹)	**Quantity (units)**
5	100
4	140

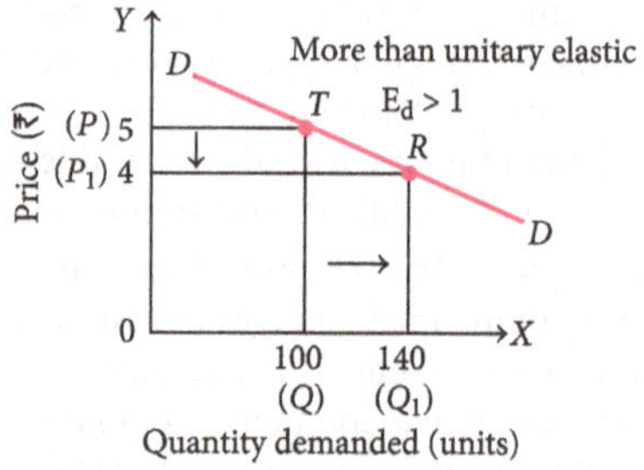

40. **In India, the demand for smartphones has seen significant fluctuations due to various determinants, including changes in consumer income, prices of substitute goods and evolving consumer preferences. For instance, when the price of a popular smartphone brand decreases from ₹ 40,000 to ₹ 30,000, many consumers perceive this as an opportunity to upgrade, leading to an increase in quantity demanded.**

Conversely, when a competing brand introduces a similar smartphone at a lower price, the demand for the original brand may decline as consumers shift to the more affordable option.

Additionally, during festive seasons, consumer income often increases, further driving up demand for higher end smartphones. Companies must analyse these factors closely to anticipate market demand and adjust their production and marketing strategies accordingly.

Competency Based Que

(i) **What happens to the demand for a smartphone when its price decreases?**
(ii) **How does the introduction of a competing brand at a lower price affect the demand for an existing smartphone brand?**
(iii) **Discuss the impact of consumer income and festive seasons on the demand for smartphones in India. Provide examples to support your answer.**

Ans. (i) The demand for a smartphone increases when its price decreases.
(ii) The introduction of a competing brand at a lower price may decrease the demand for the existing smartphone brand as consumers may shift to the more affordable option.
(iii) Consumer income significantly impacts the demand for smartphones. During festive seasons, when consumer income often increases, many people are willing to spend more on higher end smartphones.
e.g. If a family's income rises during Diwali, they might choose to purchase a premium smartphone model that they previously deemed too expensive. This increase in income leads to a rightward shift in the demand curve for smartphones, reflecting a higher quantity demanded at various price levels.

Numerical Questions

Numerical 1

Suppose there are 20 consumers for a good and they have identical demand functions

$d(p) = 10 - 3p$ for any price less than or equal to $\frac{10}{3}$ and

$d_1(p) = 0$ at any price greater than $\frac{10}{3}$. What is the market demand function? **NCERT**

Sol. In the given demand function, if the consumers demand only when price is either less than or equal to $\frac{10}{3}$, then market demand will be

Market demand

$$d(p) = 20\,[d(p)]$$
$$d(p) = 20\,(10 - 3p)$$
$$d(p) = 200 - 60 \qquad p\left(P \le \frac{10}{3}\right)$$

For any price less than or equal to $\frac{10}{3}$ and market $(p) = 0$ at any price greater than $\frac{10}{3}$.

Numerical 2

Consider a market where there are just two consumers and suppose their demands for the good are given as follows

P	d_1	d_2
1	9	24
2	8	20
3	7	18
4	6	16
5	5	14
6	4	12

Calculate the market demand for the good. **NCERT**

Sol.

Price (₹)	Demand (d_1)	Demand (d_2)	Market Demand ($d_1 + d_2$)
1	9	24	33
2	8	20	28
3	7	18	25
4	6	16	22
5	5	14	19
6	4	12	16

Numerical 3

Calculate market demand from the following information

Price (₹)	Demand (d_X)	Demand (d_Y)	Market demand
1	7	16	...
2	6	14	...
3	5	12	...
4	4	8	...

Sol.

Price (₹)	Demand (d_X)	Demand (d_Y)	Market demand ($d_X + d_Y$)
1	7	16	**23**
2	6	14	**20**
3	5	12	**17**
4	4	8	**12**

Numerical 4

Quantity demanded of a commodity rises by 6 units, when its price falls by ₹ 1 per unit. Its price elasticity of demand is (–) 1. If the price before the change was ₹ 20 per unit, calculate quantity demanded at this price.

Sol. Given, $P = ₹\,20$; $\Delta P = (-)\,₹\,1$, $Q = ?$, $\Delta Q = 6$ units

$E_d = (-)\,1$

Price Elasticity of Demand $(E_d) = \frac{P}{Q} \times \frac{\Delta Q}{\Delta P}$

$$(-)\,1 = \frac{20}{Q} \times \frac{6}{(-)\,1}$$

$$(-)\,1 = \frac{120}{(-)\,Q} \Rightarrow Q = 120$$

∴ Quantity demanded before change in price = 120 units

Numerical 5

Price elasticity of demand of a good is (–) 0.75. Calculate the percentage fall in its price that will result in 15% rise in its demand.

Sol. $E_d = \frac{\text{Percentage Change in Quantity Demanded}}{\text{Percentage Change in Price}}$

$$0.75 = \frac{15}{\text{Percentage Change in Price}}$$

Percentage Change (Fall) in Price $= \frac{15}{0.75} = 20\%$

Numerical 6

Consider the demand for a good. At price ₹ 4, the demand for the good is 25 units. Suppose price of good increases to ₹ 5 and as a result, the demand for the good falls to 20 units. Calculate the price elasticity. NCERT

Sol. $P_0 = 4, \quad q_0 = 25, \quad P_1 = 5, \quad q_1 = 20, \quad \Delta P = 1, \ \Delta q = -5$

$$E_d = -\left(\frac{\Delta q}{\Delta p} \times \frac{P_0}{q_0}\right) = \frac{5}{1} \times \frac{4}{25} = 0.8$$

Numerical 7

Consider the demand curve D(p) = 10−3p. What is the elasticity at price $\frac{5}{3}$? NCERT

Sol. Given, Demand curve D (p) = 10 − 3p

$a = 10, \ b = -3, \ \text{Price (p)} = \frac{5}{3}$

$$E_d = -\frac{bp}{a - bp} = \frac{-3 \times \frac{5}{3}}{10 - 3 \times \frac{5}{3}} = \frac{-5}{5} = -1 \text{ (Unitary elastic)}$$

Numerical 8

When price of a good falls by 10%, its quantity demanded rises from 40 units to 50 units. Calculate price elasticity of demand by percentage method.

Sol. Given, $\Delta Q = Q_1 - Q = 50 - 40 = 10, \ Q = 40, \ Q_1 = 50$

Percentage Change in Quantity Demanded

$$= \frac{\Delta Q}{Q} \times 100 = \frac{10}{40} \times 100 = 25\%$$

Percentage change in price (given) = 10%

$$E_d = \frac{\text{Percentage Change in Quantity Demanded}}{\text{Percentage Change in Price}}$$

$$= \frac{25}{10} = 2.5$$

Price elasticity of demand (E_d) = 2.5 (more than unitary elastic)

Numerical 9

When the price of a commodity falls by 20%, its demand rises from 400 units to 500 units. Calculate its price elasticity of demand.

Sol. Given, Q = 400 units, $Q_1 = 500$ units

Percentage Change in Quantity Demanded

$\Delta Q = Q_1 - Q = 500 - 400 = 100$

∴Percentage change in quantity demanded

$$= \frac{\Delta Q}{Q} \times 100 = \frac{100}{400} \times 100 = 25\%$$

$$E_d = \frac{\text{Percentage Change in Quantity Demanded}}{\text{Percentage Change in Price}}$$

$E_d = \frac{25}{20}; \ E_d = 1.25$ (more than unitary elastic)

Numerical 10

The price elasticity of demand for a good is (−) 0.4. If its price increases by 5%, by what percentage will its demand fall? Calculate.

Sol. $E_d = \frac{\text{Percentage Change in Quantity Demanded}}{\text{Percentage Change in Price}}$

$$0.4 = \frac{\text{Percentage Change in Quantity Demanded}}{5}$$

Percentage Change in Quantity Demanded

$= 0.4 \times 5 = 2$

∴ Demand falls by 2%.

Numerical 11

5% fall in the price of a good raises its demand from 300 units to 318 units. Calculate its price elasticity of demand.

Sol. Given, Q = 300 units, $Q_1 = 318$ units

$$\text{Percentage Change in Quantity Demanded} = \frac{\Delta Q}{Q} \times 100$$

$$\Delta Q = Q_1 - Q = 318 - 300 = 18$$

∴ Percentage change in quantity demanded

$$= \frac{18}{300} \times 100 = 6\%$$

$$E_d = \frac{\text{Percentage Change in Quantity Demanded}}{\text{Percentage Change in Price}}$$

$E_d = \frac{6}{5} = 1.2$ (more than unitary elastic)

Numerical 12

Calculate price elasticity of demand by percentage method.

Price per Unit (₹)	Quantity Demanded (units)
0	10
1	5

Sol. Given, $P = 0, \quad P_1 = 1$

$\Delta P = P_1 - P = 1 - 0 = 1$

$Q = 10, \ Q_1 = 5$

$\Delta Q = Q_1 - Q = 5 - 10 = -5$

$$\text{Price Elasticity of Demand } (E_d) = \frac{P}{Q} \times \frac{\Delta Q}{\Delta P}$$

$= \frac{0}{10} \times \frac{-5}{1} = \frac{0}{2} = 0$ (perfectly inelastic demand)

Numerical 13

A 5% rise in price of a good leads to 5% fall in its demand. A consumer buys 100 units of a good when price is ₹ 5 per unit. At what price will he buy 120 units? Calculate.

Sol. $E_d = \frac{\text{Percentage Change in Quantity Demanded}}{\text{Percentage Change in Price}} = \frac{5}{5} = 1$

Here, $P = ₹\,5$, per unit $P_1 = ?$

$\Delta P = P_1 - P = P_1 - 5$

$Q = 100$ units, $Q_1 = 120$ units

$\Delta Q = Q_1 - Q = 120 - 100 = 20$ units

$E_d = (-)\frac{P}{Q} \times \frac{\Delta Q}{\Delta P}$

$1 = (-)\frac{5}{100} \times \frac{20}{P_1 - 5} \Rightarrow 1 = \frac{-1}{P_1 - 5}$

$P_1 - 5 = -1 \Rightarrow P_1 = -1 + 5 \Rightarrow P_1 = 4$

$\therefore$ He will buy 120 units at a price of ₹ 4 per unit.

Numerical 14

Price elasticity of demand of a good is (–) 1. At a given price, the consumer buys 60 units of the good. How many units will he buy if the price falls by 10%?

Sol. Given, $E_d = (-)1$

Percentage change in price = 10%, Q = 60 units

$E_d = \frac{\text{Percentage Change in Quantity Demanded}}{\text{Percentage Change in Price}}$

$(-)1 = \frac{\text{Percentage Change in Quantity Demanded}}{-10}$

Percentage change in quantity demanded = 10%

So, $Q = 60$ units, $Q_1 = ?$

$Q_1 = Q + \Delta Q = Q + (10\% \text{ of } Q)$

$= 60 + \left(60 \times \frac{10}{100}\right) = 66$ units

Numerical 15

When price of a good is ₹ 13 per unit, the consumer buys 11 units of that good. When price rises to ₹ 15 per unit, the consumer continues to buy 11 units. Calculate price elasticity of demand.

Sol. Given, $P = ₹\,13, P_1 = ₹\,15$

$\Delta P = P_1 - P = 15 - 13 = ₹\,2$

$Q = 11$ units, $Q_1 = 11$ units

$\Delta Q = Q_1 - Q = 11 - 11 = 0,$

$E_d = (-)\frac{P}{Q} \times \frac{\Delta Q}{\Delta P} = (-)\frac{13}{11} \times \frac{0}{2} = 0$

$\therefore$ $E_d = 0$ (perfectly inelastic demand)

Numerical 16

On the basis of the following schedule, calculate price elasticity of demand by percentage method.

Price per Unit (₹)	Total Expenditure (₹)
10	180
9	162

Sol.

Price (P) (₹)	Total Expenditure (TE) (₹)	Quantity Demanded (TE/P) (units)
10	180	(180 ÷ 10) 18
9	162	(162 ÷ 9) 18

$\Delta P = 9 - 10 = -1,\ \Delta Q = 18 - 18 = 0$

Percentage Change in Quantity Demanded

$= \frac{\Delta Q}{Q} \times 100 = \frac{0}{18} \times 100 = 0$

Percentage Change in Price $= \frac{\Delta P}{P} \times 100 = \frac{1}{100} \times 100 = ₹\,10$

$E_d = \frac{\text{Percentage Change in Quantity Demanded}}{\text{Percentage Change in Price}} = \frac{0}{10} = 0$

$E_d = 0$ (perfectly inelastic demand)

Numerical 17

A 5% fall in price of a good leads to 10% rise in its demand. A consumer buys 40 units of a good at a price of ₹ 10 per unit. How many units will he buy at a price of ₹ 12 per unit?

Sol. $E_d = \frac{\text{Percentage Change in Quantity Demanded}}{\text{Percentage Change in Price}} = \frac{10}{5} = 2$

Here, $P = ₹\,10$ per unit, $P_1 = ₹\,12$ per unit

$\Delta P = P_1 - P = 12 - 10 = ₹\,2$ per unit

$Q = 40$ units, $Q_1 = ?$

$\Delta Q = Q_1 - Q = Q_1 - 40$

$E_d = (-)\frac{P}{Q} \times \frac{\Delta Q}{\Delta P} \Rightarrow 2 = (-)\frac{10}{40} \times \frac{(Q_1 - 40)}{2}$

$2 = \frac{-Q_1 + 40}{8} \Rightarrow 16 = -Q_1 + 40$

$Q_1 = 40 - 16 = 24$ units

$\therefore$ He will buy 24 units.

Numerical 18

Price elasticity of demand of a good is (–) 2. The consumer buys a certain quantity of this good at a price of ₹ 8 per unit. When the price falls, he buys 50% more quantity. What is the new price?

Sol. Given, $E_d = (-)2,\ P = ₹\,8,\ P_1 = ?$

Percentage change in quantity demanded = 50%

$E_d = \frac{\text{Percentage Change in Quantity Demanded}}{\text{Percentage Change in Price}}$

$(-)2 = \frac{50}{\text{Percentage Change in Price}}$

Percentage change in price $= (-)\frac{50}{2} = (-)\,25\%$

So, $P_1 = P + \Delta P = P - (25\% \text{ of actual price})$

$= 8 - \left(8 \times \frac{25}{100}\right)$

$= 8 - 2 = ₹\,6$ per unit

Numerical 19

Price elasticity of demand of a good is (–) 3. If the price rises from ₹ 10 per unit to ₹ 12 per unit, what is the percentage change in demand?

Sol. Given, $P = 10$, $P_1 = 12$, $\Delta P = 12$

$$\Delta P = 12 - 10 = ₹\ 2$$

$$\text{Percentage Change in Price} = \frac{\Delta P}{P} \times 100 = \frac{2}{10} \times 100 = 20\%$$

Given, $E_d = (-)\ 3$

$$E_d = \frac{\text{Percentage Change in Quantity Demanded}}{\text{Percentage Change in Price}}$$

$$(-)\ 3 = \frac{\text{Percentage Change in Quantity Demanded}}{20}$$

$$-60 = \text{Percentage change in quantity demanded}$$

∴ Percentage change in quantity demanded = 60%

Numerical 20

The price elasticity of a commodity is (–) 1.5. When its price falls by ₹ 1 per unit, its quantity demanded rises by 3 units. If the quantity demanded before the price change was 30 units, what was the price at this demand? Calculate.

Sol. Given, $\Delta P = (-)\ ₹\ 1$ per unit, $P = ?$

$E_d = (-)\ 1.5$, $\Delta Q = 3$ units, $Q = 30$ units

$$E_d = \frac{\Delta Q}{\Delta P} \times \frac{P}{Q} \Rightarrow (-)\ 1.5 = \frac{3}{1} \times \frac{P}{30}$$

$$P = \frac{30 \times 1.5}{3} = ₹\ 15$$

∴ Price before change was ₹ 15.

Numerical 21

When price of a good is ₹ 12 per unit, the consumer buys 24 units of that good. When price rises to ₹ 14 per unit, the consumer buys 20 units. Calculate price elasticity of demand.

Sol. Given, $P = ₹\ 12$, $P_1 = ₹\ 14$

$\Delta P = P_1 - P = 14 - 12 = ₹\ 2$

$Q = 24$ units, $Q_1 = 20$ units

$\Delta Q = Q_1 - Q = 20 - 24 = (-)\ 4$ units

$$E_d = (-)\frac{\Delta Q}{\Delta P} \times \frac{P}{Q} = (-)\frac{-4}{2} \times \frac{12}{24} = 1$$

Price elasticity of demand $(E_d) = 1$ (Unitary elastic demand)

Numerical 22

A consumer buys 80 units of a good at a price of ₹ 5 per unit. Suppose price elasticity of demand is (–) 2. At what price will he buy 64 units?

Sol. Given, $P = ₹\ 5$, $P_1 = ?$, $Q = 80$ units, $Q_1 = 64$ units

$\Delta Q = Q_1 - Q = 64 - 80 = (-)\ 16$ units

$$E_d = (-)\ 2,\ E_d = \frac{P}{Q} \times \frac{\Delta Q}{\Delta P}$$

$$(-)\ 2 = \frac{5}{80} \times \frac{(-)16}{\Delta P};\ \Delta P = \frac{1}{2} = 0.5$$

∴ New price $(P_1) = P + \Delta P = 5 + 0.5 = ₹\ 5.5$

Numerical 23

Suppose the price elasticity of demand for a good is −0.2. If there is a 5% increase in the price of the good, by what percentage will the demand for the good go down? **NCERT**

Sol. Given,

Change in price (increase) = 5%

Elasticity of Demand $(E_d) = -0.2$

$$E_d = \frac{\%\ \text{Change in Quantity Demanded}}{\%\ \text{Change in Price}}$$

$$(-)\ 0.2 = \frac{\%\ \text{Change in quantity demanded}}{5}$$

% Change in quantity demanded = −1 % (decrease)

Numerical 24

A consumer buys 10 units of a commodity at a price of ₹ 10 per unit. He incurs an expenditure of ₹ 200 on buying 20 units. Calculate price elasticity of demand by percentage method. Comment on the shape of demand curve based on this information.

Sol.

Price (₹) (P)	Quantity Demanded (units) (Q)	Total Expenditure (₹) (P × Q)
10	10	100
10	20	200

$$\text{Total Expenditure} = \text{Price }(P_1) \times \text{Quantity }(Q_1)$$

$$200 = \text{Price }(P_1) \times 20$$

$$200 \div 20 = \text{Price }(P_1)$$

$$\text{Price }(P_1) = ₹\ 10 \text{ per unit}$$

$$\Delta P = 10 - 10 = 0$$

$$\Delta Q = 20 - 10 = 10$$

Percentage Change in Quantity Demanded

$$= \frac{\Delta Q}{Q} \times 100 = \frac{10}{10} \times 100 = 100\%$$

Percentage Change in Price

$$= \frac{\Delta P}{P} \times 100 = \frac{0}{10} \times 100 = 0\%$$

$$E_d = \frac{\text{Percentage Change in Quantity Demanded}}{\text{Percentage Change in Price}}$$

$$= \frac{100}{0} = \infty \quad or \quad E_d = \infty$$

Elasticity of demand is perfectly elastic. Therefore, demand curve is a straight line parallel to x-axis.

SELF ASSESSMENT TEST

Objective Type Questions

1. Demand for complementary goods .... when the price of one good increases.
   (a) increases (b) decreases
   (c) remains constant (d) doubles

2. What does the law of demand state?
   (a) Demand decreases with a rise in price, keeping other factors constant
   (b) Demand increases with a rise in price, keeping other factors constant
   (c) Demand remains unchanged with changes in price
   (d) Demand and price are directly related

3. Which of the following is a cause for a downward sloping demand curve?
   (a) Law of diminishing marginal utility
   (b) Law of increasing marginal utility
   (c) Constant income effect
   (d) Increase in population size

4. The demand curve generally has a .... slope.
   (a) upward (b) flat
   (c) downward (d) steep

5. What kind of relationship exists between the price of complementary goods and demand?
   (a) Direct relationship (b) No relationship
   (c) Inverse relationship (d) Proportional relationship

6. If total expenditure increases as price decreases, what type of elasticity exists?
   (a) Inelastic demand (b) Unit elastic demand
   (c) Perfectly inelastic demand (d) Elastic demand

7. Which goods exhibit an increase in demand despite an increase in price?
   (a) Normal goods (b) Inferior goods
   (c) Giffen goods (d) Complementary goods

8. Elasticity of demand is measured as the percentage change in quantity demanded divided by the percentage change in ....
   (a) time (b) price (c) income (d) supply

Answers 1. (b) 2. (a) 3. (a) 4. (c) 5. (c) 6. (d) 7. (c) 8. (b)

Short Answer Type Questions

9. List and explain the major components of demand.

10. "These goods are consumed together. If the price of one rises, demand for the other falls because both are needed for consumption."

    Which goods are highlighted in the above statement? Explain with example.

11. What are the determinants of market demand?

12. Define the following
    (i) Normal goods
    (ii) Inferior goods

13. Explain the law of demand with a diagram.

Long Answer Type Questions

14. Explain price elasticity of demand. List and explain the different degrees of price elasticity of demand.

15. Explain the determinants of price elasticity of demand.

Numerical Questions

16. The quantity demanded of a commodity at a price of ₹ 10 per unit is 40 units. Its price elasticity of demand is (–) 2. Its price falls by ₹ 2 per unit. Calculate its quantity demanded at the new price.

Ans. 44 units

17. Price of a good rises by 10%. As a result, demand falls by 4%. Find out price elasticity of demand. Is the demand elastic or inelasitc?

Ans. $E_d = 0.4$ (elastic)

18. When price of good falls from ₹ 5 to ₹ 3 per unit, its demand increases by 40%. Calculate its price elasticity of demand.

Ans. $E_d = 1$

19. A consumer buys 80 units of a good at a price of ₹ 5 per unit. Suppose price elasticity of demand is (–) 2. At what price will he buy 64 units?

Ans. ₹ 5.50

04

CHAPTER

Production function represents the relationship between the quantity of inputs and the quantity of outputs produced.

YOUR STUDY GOALS

YOUR PRACTICE GOAL

- Objective Type Questions (60 Qs ; MCQs, A-R, Statements, Matching, Concept Identification)
- Subjective Questions (20 SAs, 8 LAs)
- 10 Numerical Questions
- Self Assessment Test (8 MCQs, 4 SAs, 2 LAs, 3 Numerical)

Production Function

4.1 Production

Production is the process of transforming various inputs like labour, machines, land, raw materials, etc. into output. By combining these inputs in different proportions, firms produce goods and services.

Factors of Production

The inputs that firms use to produce goods are called factors of production. These factors can be categorised into two main types

1. Factor Inputs

These are the traditional resources that directly contribute to production. There are four primary types of factor inputs

- Land
- Labour
- Capital
- Entrepreneur

These factors can be further categorised as

(i) **Fixed Factors** These are inputs that cannot be changed in the short-run to change production level. e.g. Land and machinery. Since these factors take time to adjust, they are considered constant in short-run.

(ii) **Variable Factors** These are inputs that can be easily changed in both the short-run and long-run. Variable factors, like labour and raw materials, vary directly with the level of production. When output increases or decreases, variable factors adjust accordingly.

2. Non-factor Inputs

These refer to supplementary resources used in the production process. They include items like power, water, tools and other equipment.

Concept of Time Period in Production

The concept of time plays a vital role in how firms adjust their production. There are three main time periods to consider

1. **Market Period** (Very short period) In this period, producers cannot change any factor of production to change their level of output.
2. **Short Period** Only variable factors can be changed in this period, while fixed factors remain constant, allowing limited changes in production.
3. **Long Period** All factors of production can be changed in this period as all factors are variable in long-run. Here, production can change significantly.

4.2 Production Function

A production function represents the functional relationship between the inputs used and output produced.

It shows the maximum quantity of output that can be produced using given quantities of inputs, assuming the efficient use of these inputs. The production function depends on technology, i.e. when technology improves, the output for the same input combination also increases.

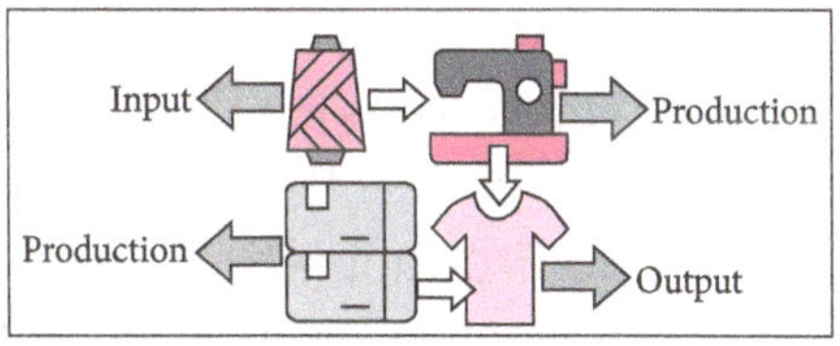

The production function can be expressed as

$$Q_X = f\ (L, K)$$

Here, Q_X = Production of commodity X ; L = Labour ; K = Capital

Here, it is assumed that only two factors of production are used for production, i.e. labour and capital. e.g. A firm manufactures helmets with the help of two factors of production, i.e. labour and capital. Thus, its production function can be written as

$$Q_{Helmets} = f(L, K)$$

Here, production function represents maximum number of helmets that can be produced with the given capital and labour. Thus, if production function of this firm is expressed as $1{,}000 = f(20\ L, 5\ K)$, then it will represent that 20 units of labour and 5 units of capital can produce 1,000 helmets.

Types of Production Function

Production function can be following two types

1. **Short-run** In the short-run, production is increased by adjusting only the variable inputs (such as labour), while the fixed inputs (such as capital) remain constant. This is also known as **variable proportion type production function** and is explained by the law of variable proportions.
2. **Long-run** In the long-run, all factor inputs (labour and capital) are variable and can be increased to increase the production in same proportion.

Mathematically, these functions can be expressed as

- **Short-run Production Function**

$$Q_X = f(L, \overline{K})$$

Here, Q_X = Output of commodity X; L = Labour ; f = Functional relation ; $\overline{K}$ = Capital

In the above case, labour is a variable factor and capital is a fixed factor.

- **Long-run Production Function**

$$Q_X = f(L, K)$$

Here, Q_X = Output of commodity X; L = Labour ; f = Functional relation; K = Capital

In the above case, all factors are variable.

4.3 Concept of Product

Product refers to the quantity of goods produced by a firm or industry during a given period of time. The key concepts related to the product are Total Product (TP), Average Product (AP) and Marginal Product (MP).

1. Total Product (TP)

It is the total output produced by all units of labour, in combination with other factors of production in a given period of time. It is also known as **total physical product** of variable input. It is calculated as

$$TP = \Sigma MP$$
or $$TP = TP_1 + TP_2 + \ldots + TP_n$$
or $$TP = AP \times L$$

Here, AP = Average Product ; L = Units of Variable Factor (Labour)
MP = Marginal Product

The shape of TP curve is initially steep from the origin, then begins to get flatten and eventually declines after reaching its maximum point.

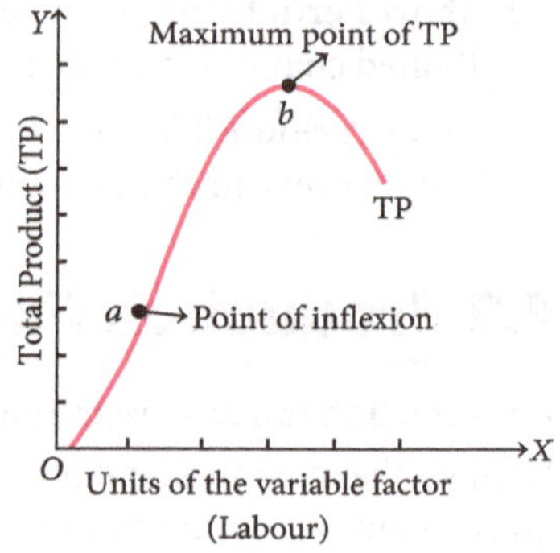

General shape of TP curve

2. Average Product (AP)

It represents the output per unit of a variable input (like labour). It is calculated by dividing the total product by the number of variable input units. It is also referred to as **average physical product**. Mathematically, it is calculated as

$$AP = TP/L$$

As Labour (L) is taken as variable factor.
The average product curve is hump shaped or inverted 'U' shaped.

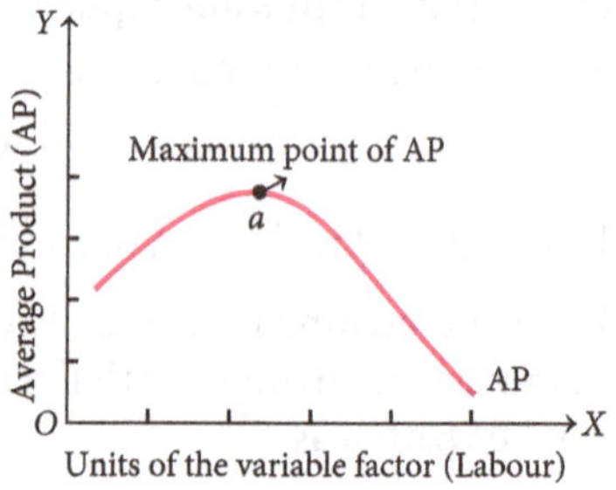

General shape of AP curve

3. Marginal Product (MP)

It measures the additional output generated when one more unit of a variable input (like labour) is added, keeping other inputs unchanged. It represents the change in total production as a result of a unit change in input of a variable factor.
It is also referred to as **marginal physical product.** It is calculated as

$$MP = TP_n - TP_{n-1} \text{ or } MP = \frac{\Delta TP}{\Delta L}$$

Here, MP = Marginal Product ; ΔTP = Change in Total Product
ΔL = Change in units of variable factor (Labour)
TP_n = Total product when 'n' units of variable factor are employed
TP_{n-1} = Total product when '$n-1$' units of variable factor are employed

The marginal product curve is generally inverted 'U' shaped.

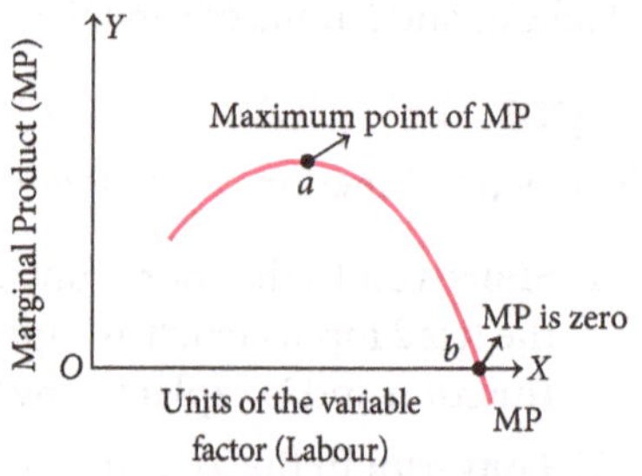

General shape of MP curve

Solved Question 1 **Calculate TP and MP, when AP and L is given.**

Units of Labour (L)	Average Product (AP)
1	50
2	60
3	70
4	80
5	90

Sol.

L	AP	$TP = AP \times L$	$MP_{nth} = TP_n - TP_{n-1}$
1	50	50	50
2	60	120	70
3	70	210	90
4	80	320	110
5	90	450	130

Solved Question 2 Calculate Total Product (TP) and Average Product (AP) from the following data

Units of Labour (L)	**Marginal Product** (MP)
1	10
2	12
3	10
4	8
5	−4

Sol.

L	MP	TP (ΣMP)	AP (TP / L)
1	10	10	10
2	20	10 + 12 = 22	11
3	10	22 + 10 = 32	10.67
4	8	32 + 8 = 40	10
5	−4	40 + (−4) = 36	7.2

4.4 Returns to a Factor: Law of Variable Proportion

This law describes how production changes in the short-run when the quantity of a variable factor is increased while keeping a fixed factor constant.

It states that as more and more units of a variable factor are employed with fixed factors, total product increases at an increasing rate in the beginning, then increases at a diminishing rate, reaches its maximum and finally starts falling.

According to this law, TP and MP changes in three stages, which are as follows

- ***Stage I*** TP increases at increasing rate and MP also increases.
- ***Stage II*** TP increases at decreasing rate and MP starts falling but remains positive.
- ***Stage III*** TP decreases and MP becomes negative.

Assumptions of Law

- Technique of production does not change.
- All units of variable factor are equally efficient.
- Factors of production are not perfect substitute of each other after a certain limit.
- There must be some inputs whose quantity is kept fixed. Because of this, the ratio between the fixed factor and variable factor changes.

Explanation of the Law

This law may be explained with the help of following schedule and diagram (based on hypothetical data)

Units of Land	Units of Labour	Total Product	Marginal Product	Stage
1	1	2	2	I = Increasing returns
1	2	5	3	
1	3	9	4	
1	4	12	3	II = Diminishing returns
1	5	14	2	
1	6	15	1	
1	7	15	0	III = Negative returns
1	8	14	−1	

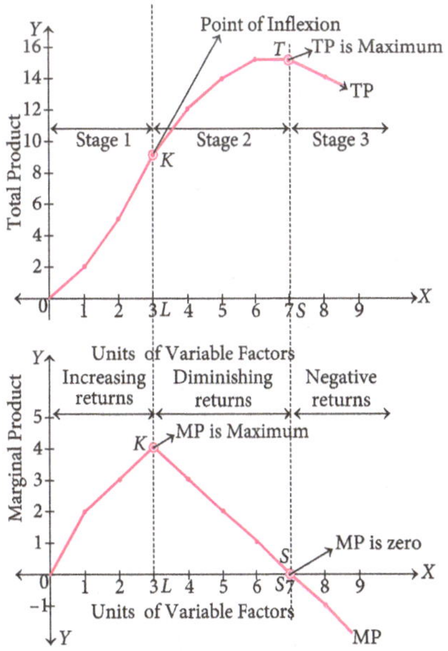

Law of variable proportion

Observations

- MP rises till 3rd unit of labour employed. In this stage, TP increases at an increasing rate. This stage is called stage of **increasing returns to factors**.
- With the use of 4th unit of labour, MP starts decreasing but remains positive and TP increases at decreasing rate. This stage is called stage of **diminishing returns to factors**.
- At 7th unit of variable factor, decreasing MP reduces to zero, TP is maximum and constant.
- At 8th unit of variable factor, when MP is negative, TP starts declining. This stage is called stage of **negative returns to factor**.

Stages of Law of Variable Proportion

The production process experiences three distinct stages i.e. increasing returns, diminishing returns and negative returns to a factor.

1. Stage of Increasing Returns to Factor

In this stage, MP is increasing and because of this TP is increasing at an increasing rate (*O* to *K* on TP curve).

In this stage, increasing returns to a variable factor is obtained because greater use of the variable factors makes it possible to utilise fixed indivisible factors fully and to introduce a greater degree of division of labour.

2. Stage of Diminishing Returns To Factor

In this stage, MP is decreasing but remains positive and because of this TP is increasing at a decreasing rate [K (*point of inflexion*) to T on TP curve].

In this stage, diminishing returns to a factor is obtained because in this stage, the proportion between the variable factor such as labour has less fixed factors to work upon.

> **Point to Inflexion**
> It is a point from where slope of TP curve changes. Upto this point, TP has been increasing at the increasing rate. From this point onwards, TP increases but only at a diminishing rate.

3. Stage of Negative Returns to Factor

In this stage, TP starts declining because MP becomes negative (beyond T on TP curve). In this stage, the variable factors become too much relative to fixed factors, disturbing the production process due to which there is a fall in total product.

Causes of Stages of Returns

Causes of increasing returns, diminishing returns and negative returns to a factor are as follows

Increasing Returns to a Factor	Diminishing Returns to Factor	Negative Returns to Factor
• **Fuller Utilisation of the Fixed Factor** In the initial stages, fixed factor remains underutilised. Its fuller utilisation is possible by adding additional units of the variable factor to total output and the marginal product of the variable factor tends to increase. • **Increased Efficiency of the Variable Factor** Additional application of the variable factor causes process based division of labour that creates high degree of specialisation of the factors. Accordingly, marginal productivity of the factor tends to rise. • **Better Coordination between the Factors** As long as fixed factor remains underutilised, additional application of the variable factor tends to improve. As a result, total output increases at an increasing rate.	• **Fixity of the Factor** It is the principal cause behind the law of diminishing returns. As more and more units of the variable factor is combined with the fixed factor, the latter gets excessively utilised, leading to decrease in its productivity. • **Imperfect Factor Substitutability** Factors of production are imperfect substitutes of each other. e.g. More and more of labour cannot be continuously used in place of additional capital. Accordingly, diminishing returns to the variable factor become inevitable. • **Poor Coordination between the Factors** Continuous increasing application of the variable factor alongwith fixed factors beyond a point, crosses the limit of ideal factor ratio. This results in poor coordination between the fixed and variable factors.	• **Limitation of Fixed Factor** The fixed factor can be optimally used only upto a certain level. • **Decrease in Efficiency of Variable Factor** As the variable factor is increased, its efficiency tends to fall. • **Poor Coordination between the Fixed and the Variable Factors** As the variable factor is increased, it leads to a lack of coordination between the fixed and the variable factors leading to a fall in total product.

Operation Stage for a Producer

A rational producer will choose to operate in the **2nd stage** of the law of variable proportion. In this stage, the total product is maximised and the marginal product of each additional unit of variable factor remains positive. Here's how the different stages impact production

- In 1st stage, use of every additional unit of variable factor will give more and more output, resulting in an increase in marginal product. Thus, producer will increase its production with more units of variable factor to earn more profits.
- In 3rd stage, marginal product of each additional unit of variable factor becomes negative, indicating technical inefficiency. Consequently, producers will avoid operating in this stage.

Postponement of the Law

The law of variable proportions can be postponed under two conditions

- When there is improvement in technology used in the process of production, so that greater output is achieved with the same inputs.
- When some substitute of the fixed factor is discovered, so that the constraint of fixity of the factor is removed.

Law of Diminishing Marginal Product (Law of Variable Proportion in Terms of MP)

This law states that with the increase in a variable factor, keeping all other factors constant, the marginal product of the variable factor diminishes after a certain level of production and eventually becomes negative. This law was given by classical economists and related to agriculture.

This law may be explained with the help of an imaginary schedule and diagram

Land (acre)	**Labour** (units)	**Total Product** (quantity)	**Marginal Product** (quantity)
5	1	50	50
5	2	120	70
5	3	200	80
5	4	280	80
5	5	350	70
5	6	400	50
5	7	430	30
5	8	440	10
5	9	440	0
5	10	430	−10
5	11	410	−20

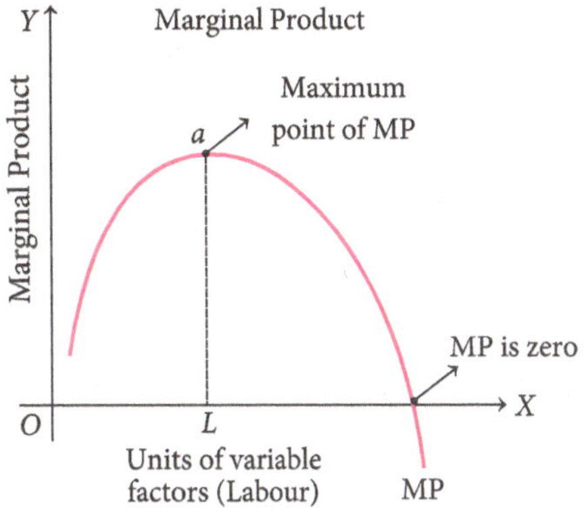

Marginal Product Curve

Note Law of diminishing marginal product operates in the second stage of law of variable proportion.

In this schedule, law of diminishing marginal product is shown from 5th unit of labour onwards.

In the diagram, after point '*a*' on MP curve, marginal product diminishes continuously, showing the law of diminishing marginal product, i.e. with the employment of 5th labour, diminishing returns operates.

4.5 Relationship between TP, AP and MP Curves

The relationship between product curves can be understood with the help of following graph

From the given curves, following **observations** are made on the relationship between TP and MP

- When TP increases at an increasing rate, MP also increases.
- When TP increases at a diminishing rate, MP declines but remains positive.
- When TP reaches its maximum, MP becomes zero.
- When TP begins to decline, MP becomes negative.

From the given curves, following **observations** are made on the relationship between AP and MP

- AP increases so long as MP > AP.
- AP is at its maximum when AP = MP.
- AP decreases when MP < AP.
- MP may be zero or negative, but AP continues to be positive.
- AP increases, even when MP falls but MP should lie above AP.

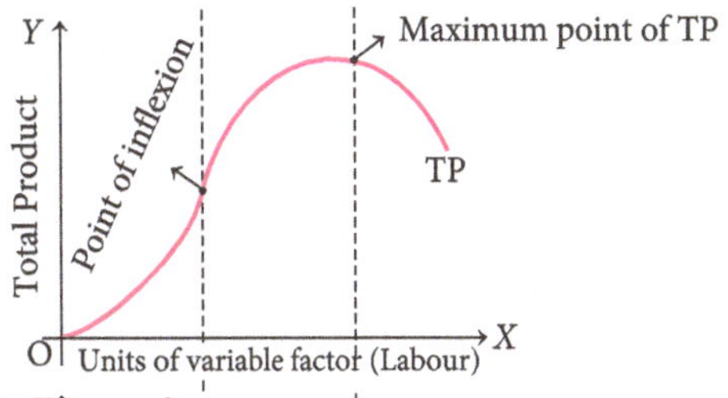

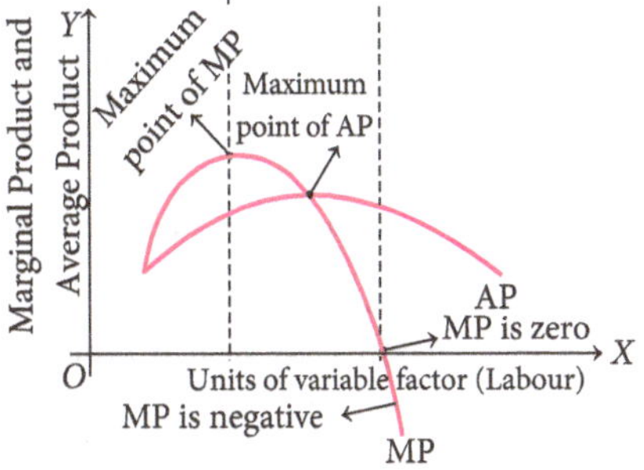

Mind Map

PRODUCTION FUNCTION

1 Production

Production is the process of transforming various inputs like labour, land, capital, raw materials, etc. into output.

Factors of Production

These are the inputs used by firms to produce goods. They are classified into

- **Factor Inputs** These are direct resources in production which include land, labour, capital and entrepreneur. These factors can be further categorised as
  - **Fixed Factors** They cannot change in the short-run (e.g. Land, machinery).
  - **Variable Factors** They can be adjusted in both short and long-run (e.g. Labour, raw materials).
- **Non-factor Inputs** These are supplementary resources like power, water and tools that aid production.

2 Concept of Time Period in Production

- **Market Period** (Very Short Period) In this period, firms cannot adjust any factor of production.
- **Short Period** Firms can modify only variable factors, while fixed factors remain unchanged.
- **Long Period** All factors of production are variable, enabling firms to scale production significantly by adjusting both labour and capital.

3 Production Function

It is the functional relationship between inputs (labour, capital) and output, assuming efficient use of resources.

Formula: $Q_X = f(L, K)$

Types of Production Function

- **Short-run Production Function** Only variable inputs can be adjusted, while fixed inputs remain constant. It is explained by the law of variable proportions.

$$Q_X = f(L, K)$$

- **Long-run Production Function** All inputs are variable, allowing proportional changes in production.

$$Q_X = f(L, K)$$

4 Concept of Product

It is the quantity of goods produced by a firm/industry in a given period of time.

Types

- **Total Product** (TP) It is the total output produced using variable input (labour), in combination with other factors of production in a given period of time. It is also known as total physical product of variable input.

$$TP = \Sigma MP \text{ or } TP = AP \times L$$

- **Average Product** (AP) It is the output per unit of variable input. It is also referred to as average physical product.

$$AP = TP / L$$

- **Marginal Product** (MP) It is the additional output generated by adding one more unit of variable input. It is also referred to as marginal physical product.

$$MP = TP_n - TP_{n-1} \text{ or}$$
$$MP = \Delta TP / \Delta L$$

5 Return to a Factor– Law of Variable Proportion

It states that as more and more units of a variable factor are employed with fixed factors, total product increases at an increasing rate in the beginning, then increases at a diminishing rate, reaches its maximum and finally starts falling.

According to this law, TP and MP changes in three stages, which are as follows

- ***Stage I*** TP increases at increasing rate and MP also increases.
- ***Stage II*** TP increases at decreasing rate and MP starts falling but remains positive.
- ***Stage III*** TP decreases and MP becomes negative.

Postponement of Law

- When there is improvement in technology used in the process of production, so that greater output is achieved with the same inputs.
- When some substitute of the fixed factor is discovered, so that the constraint of fixity of the factor is removed.

6 Law of Diminishing Marginal Product (Law of Variable Proportion in Terms of MP)

It states that as more units of a variable factor are added to fixed factors, MP starts decreasing after a certain level of production and eventually becomes negative.

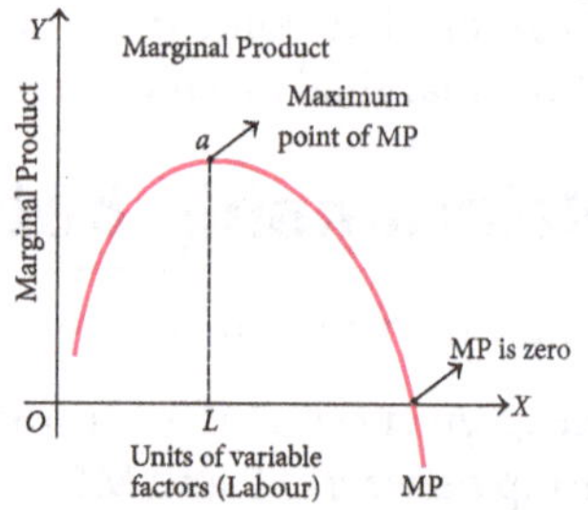

7 Relationship Between TP, AP and MP Curves

Total Product (TP) **and Marginal Product** (MP)

- TP ↑ at increasing rate → MP ↑
- TP ↑ at diminishing rate → MP ↓ (but positive)
- TP max → MP = 0
- TP ↓ → MP negative

Average Product (AP) **and Marginal Product** (MP)

- MP > AP → AP ↑
- AP max → MP = AP
- MP < AP → AP ↓
- MP can be 0 or negative, but AP stays positive
- AP can rise even if MP falls (if MP > AP)

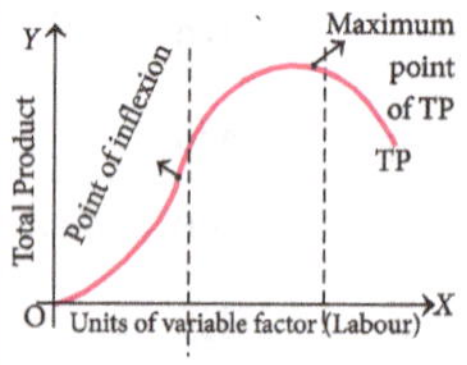

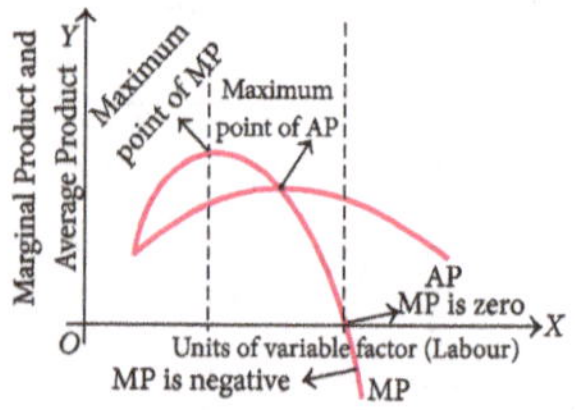

EXAM PATTERN QUESTIONS

Objective Type Questions

Multiple Choice Questions (MCQs)

1. What is 'production' in economics?

(a) Creation/Addition to the value of output
(b) Production of foodgrains
(c) Creation of services
(d) Manufacturing of goods

2. Production contribution of human who works is called .... **NCERT (QR)**

(a) machine (b) capital (c) labour (d) land

3. Which of the following is not considered a factor of production? **Competency Based Que**

I. Land II. Labour
III. Capital IV. Power

Codes

(a) I and III (b) Only III (c) Only II (d) Only IV

4. "Challenge of creating a skilled workforce: The Indian government has undertaken a range of impactful measures to create a vibrant and conducive jobs ecosystem in the country."

Source *https://www.newindianexpress.com/opinions/2024/May/29/challenge-of-creating-a-skilled-workforce*

What is workforce classified as in the factors of production? **Competency Based Que**

(a) Non-factor input (b) Fixed factor
(c) Capital (d) Factor input

5. "Non-factor inputs include items like tools, power, etc. that are necessary for production but are not considered traditional factors."

Which of the following is an example of a non-factor input? **Competency Based Que**

(a) Land (b) Entrepreneur
(c) Water (d) Capital

6. In which time period, all factors of production become variable and factors of production change with the change in level of production?

(a) Long period (b) Market period
(c) Short period (d) All of these

7. Which of the following is correct?

(a) Fixed factors are easily changed in the short-run
(b) Variable factors remain constant in the short-run
(c) The production function shows the maximum output for given inputs
(d) Non-factor inputs are the only inputs used in production

8. Observe the factors of production given below and identify the factor that is not available in long-run.

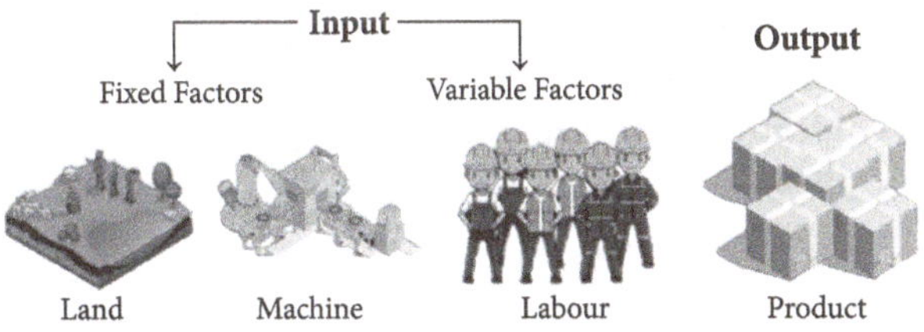

(a) Fixed factors (b) Variable factors
(c) Both (a) and (b) (d) None of these

9. What does the image given below indicates?

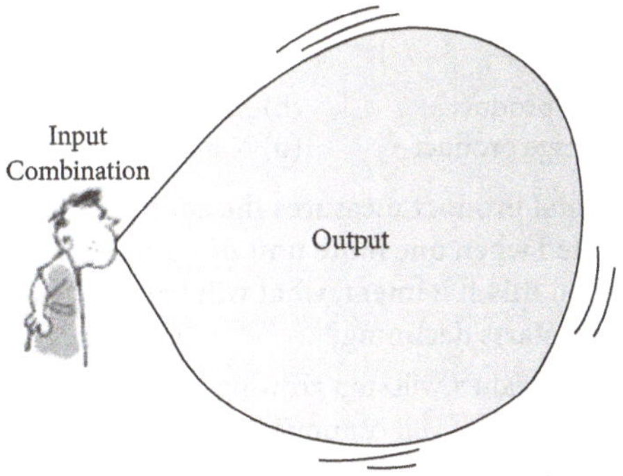

(a) Production (b) Production function
(c) Output projection (d) None of these

10. If the production function is represented as $Q_x = 3L + 2K$, what will be the output when 4 units of labour and 3 units of capital are employed? **Competency Based Que**

(a) 2 (b) 14
(c) 18 (d) 20

11. If the total product of 5 labours is 50 units of output and total product of 6 labours is 66 units of output, find Average Product (AP) of 6th unit of labour. **Competency Based Que**

(a) 10 units of output (b) 11 units of output
(c) 50 units of output (d) 16 units of output

12. **If the Average Product (AP) of a labour is 30 units of outputs, then find total product of 2 labours.** Competency Based Que

(a) 10 units of output (b) 15 units of output
(c) 30 units of output (d) 60 units of output

13. **Find the missing figures and choose the correct alternative** Competency Based Que

Units of Labour	TP	AP
1	16	...
2	...	20
3	60	...
4	...	18

(a) 16, 20, 60, 18 (b) 16, 40, 60, 18
(c) 16, 40, 20, 72 (d) 16, 20, 72, 40

14. **Identify the type of product curve given in the below image.**

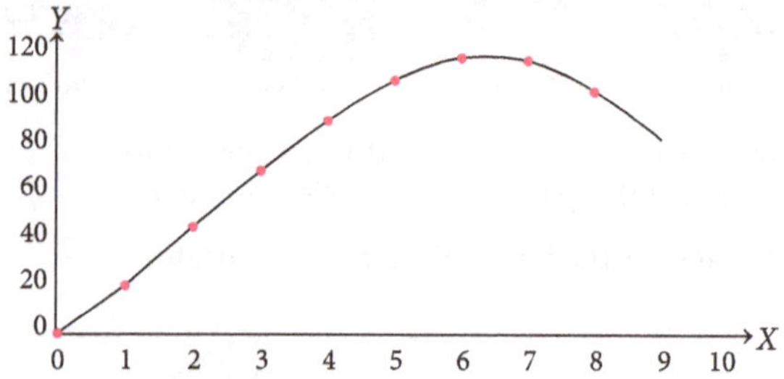

(a) Total product (b) Marginal product
(c) Average product (d) None of these

15. **"Marginal product measures the additional output generated when one more unit of input is added." Based on this statement, what will happen if marginal product starts declining?** Competency Based Que

(a) Total product will stop growing
(b) Total product will continue increasing but at a diminishing rate
(c) Total product will decrease
(d) Average product will remain constant

16. **If a firm hires 10 units of labour and produces 500 units of output, what is the average product?**

(a) 5 (b) 10 (c) 50 (d) 500

17. **Arrange the following in the correct sequence of a firm's production stages.** Competency Based Que

(i) **Marginal product declines**
(ii) **Marginal product is zero**
(iii) **Marginal product increases**
(iv) **Marginal product becomes negative**

Codes
(a) (iii), (i), (ii), (iv) (b) (i), (iii), (ii), (iv)
(c) (iii), (iv),(ii), (i) (d) (iv), (i), (ii), (iii)

18. **Which of the following is correct regarding marginal product?** Competency Based Que

I. **Marginal product measures total output produced.**
II. **Marginal product remains constant as more input is added.**
III. **Marginal product represents the output per unit of labour.**
IV. **Marginal product is the additional output from one more unit of input.**

Codes
(a) I and IV (b) Only IV
(c) III and IV (d) I and II

19. **Law of variable proportion is valid when ....**

(a) atleast one input is fixed and all other inputs are kept variable
(b) all factors are kept constant
(c) all inputs are varied in the same proportion
(d) None of the above

20. **In the first stage of law of variable proportions, total product increases at an ....**

(a) decreasing rate (b) increasing rate
(c) constant rate (d) Both (a) and (b)

21. **Which of the following stages does the graph represent where the marginal product is negative?**

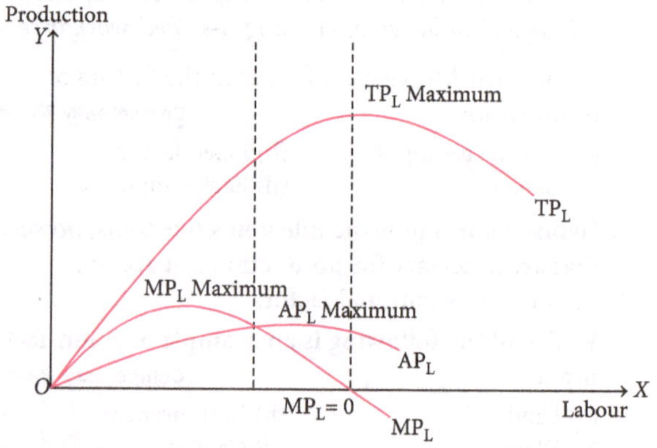

(a) Stage I (Increasing returns)
(b) Stage II (Diminishing returns)
(c) Stage III (Negative returns)
(d) None of the above

22. **The chart indicates that as labour is increased, marginal product starts to decrease. Which law is demonstrated here?**

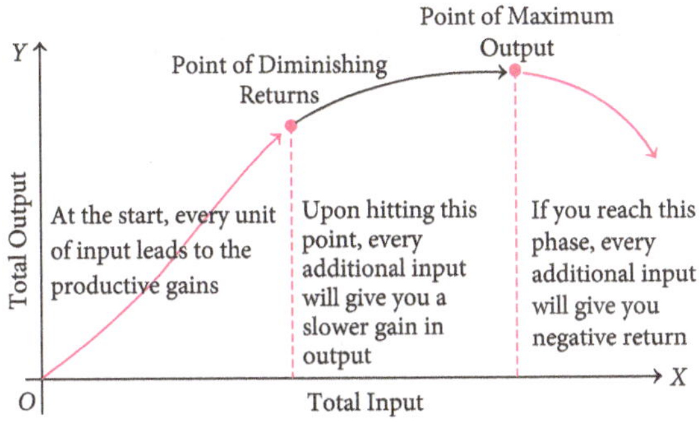

(a) Law of increasing returns
(b) Law of diminishing marginal product
(c) Law of negative returns
(d) Law of proportional returns

23. **"Can automation pull us through the global labour shortages?"**

Source *https://www.weforum.org/agenda/2023/01/how-automation-will-pull-us-through-the-labour-shortage-davos23/*

Based on the law of variable proportions, what impact could automation have on labour's marginal product in manufacturing? **Competency Based Que**

(a) Increase it in the short-run
(b) Decrease it immediately
(c) Keep it constant (d) Make it negative

24. **At the point of inflexion, the marginal product is ....**

(a) increasing (b) decreasing
(c) maximum (d) negative

25. **"MP rises till the 3rd unit of labour is employed." In which stage of the law of variable proportions does MP rise?** **Competency Based Que**

(a) Second (b) Third
(c) Forth (d) First

26. **Which of the following statements is correct?**

I. **MP may be negative, but AP continues to be positive.**
II. **When TP is maximum, MP is zero.**
III. **MP is always greater than AP.**
IV. **When MP is greater than AP, AP increases.**

Codes **Competency Based Que**

(a) I, II, III, IV (b) I, II, III
(c) I, II, IV (d) II, III, IV

Direction *Read the case study and answer the questions 27 to 30 on the basis of the same*

Ravi is a small-scale farmer who owns 10 acres of land. Over the years, he used a fixed amount of machinery and tools to grow crops. To increase his production, Ravi decided to hire more workers (labour) to help manage the farm. Initially, adding labour resulted in a significant increase in the total output of crops. However, as he continued to hire more workers, the increase in output began to slow down.

Despite having more labourers, the farm's output was increasing at a diminishing rate because the fixed resources, such as land and machinery, could not keep pace with the growing number of workers. Eventually, when Ravi hired even more labour, the farm became overcrowded and the total product started to decline. Workers began to get in each other's way and the marginal product of each additional worker fell, even becoming negative. Ravi realised that simply adding more labour was not the solution to increasing production.

27. **According to the law of variable proportions, what is the behaviour of the marginal product when Ravi experienced an increase in total output at a diminishing rate?**

(a) Marginal product increases
(b) Marginal product decreases but remains positive
(c) Marginal product is zero
(d) Marginal product becomes negative

28. **In which stage of production did Ravi's total product begin to decline while adding more labourers?**

(a) Stage I–Increasing returns
(b) Stage II–Diminishing returns
(c) Stage III–Negative returns
(d) Stage IV–Constant returns

29. **When Ravi's total product increased at a decreasing rate, it marked the stage of .... returns to a factor.**

30. **The law of variable proportions assumes that the .... factor remains constant while the .... factor increases.**

Assertion-Reason

Direction (Q.No. 31 to 40) *Read the following Assertion (A) and Reason (R) and choose the correct alternative from the following*

Alternatives

(a) Both Assertion (A) and Reason (R) are true and Reason (R) is the correct explanation of Assertion (A)
(b) Both Assertion (A) and Reason (R) are true, but Reason (R) is not the correct explanation of Assertion (A)
(c) Assertion (A) is true, but Reason (R) is false
(d) Assertion (A) is false, but Reason (R) is true

31. **Assertion** (A) Factor inputs are the traditional resources that directly contribute to production.

Reason (R) The inputs that firms use to produce goods are called factors of production.

32. **Assertion** (A) Short-run is a time period where production cannot be changed.

Reason (R) All factors of production are fixed in very short-run.

33. **Assertion** (A) The production function shows the minimum quantity of output that can be produced using given quantities of inputs.

Reason (R) The production function depends on technology.

34. **Assertion** (A) In the long-run, all factors of production are variable.

Reason (R) In the long-run, firms can adjust their scale of production to achieve the desired level of output.

35. **Assertion** (A) Average physical product initially increases and eventually fall which makes it inverse 'U' shaped.

Reason (R) In initial phases of product, both fixed and variable factors are highly efficient.

36. **Assertion** (A) Marginal product shows the change in total product due to the employment of an extra unit of input.

Reason (R) Average product measures the additional output generated when one more unit of a variable input (like labour) is added.

37. **Assertion** (A) The law of variable proportion describes how production changes in the short-run.

Reason (R) The law explains the behaviour of Total Product (TP) and Marginal Product (MP) in three distinct stages as more units of the variable factor are employed.

38. **Assertion** (A) In increasing returns, TP increases at a diminishing rate.

Reason (R) When there are negative returns, TP starts to fall.

39. **Assertion** (A) When TP increases at an increasing rate, MP also increases.

Reason (R) When TP begins to decline, MP becomes negative.

40. **Assertion** (A) For operation of law of variable proportion, state of technology should be constant.

Reason (R) Change in technology makes production process inconsistent.

Two Statements Based MCQs

Direction (Q.No. 41 to 50) *Read the following statements carefully and choose the correct alternative*

Alternatives

(a) Statement I is correct and Statement II is incorrect
(b) Statement II is correct and Statement I is incorrect
(c) Both the statements are correct
(d) Both the statements are incorrect

41. **Statement I** Factor inputs include land, labour, entrepreneur and capital.

Statement II Non-factor inputs refer to supplementary resources used in the production process.

42. **Statement I** Variable factors are inputs that cannot be altered in the short-run.

Statement II Fixed factors are inputs that can be easily changed in both the short run and the long-run.

43. **Statement I** The distinction between short-run and long-run is based on a calendar period.

Statement II Short or long-run is a functional concept that depends on production.

44. **Statement I** Product refers to the quantity of goods produced by a firm or industry over a specific period.

Statement II The key concepts related to the product are Total Product (TP), Average Product (AP) and Marginal Product (MP).

45. **Statement I** Total product is also known as total physical product.

Statement II Total product is the minimum output produced by all units of labour, in combination with other factors of production, during a given period.

46. **Statement I** Average product represents the output per unit of a variable input.

Statement II Average product is calculated by dividing the total product by the number of variable input units.

47. **Statement I** Law of variable proportions becomes inconsistent when there is a technological advancement.

Statement II In case of diminishing returns to factor, marginal product increases and marginal cost decreases.

48. **Statement I** The proportion of variable factor to the fixed factor changes as more variable inputs are used.

Statement II The law of variable proportion assumes that there is no fixed factor.

49. **Statement I** A rational producer will choose to operate in the second stage of the law of variable proportion.

Statement II In the first stage, the use of every additional unit of the variable factor increases output, resulting in a rise in marginal product.

50. **Statement I** There is no production function in market period.

Statement II Law of variable proportion only holds in the field of production.

Matching

51. Match the following

Column I	Column II
A. Factor inputs	(i) Land and machinery
B. Non-factor inputs	(ii) Raw materials
C. Fixed factors	(iii) Land, labour
D. Variable factors	(iv) Power, water

Codes

	A	B	C	D		A	B	C	D
(a)	(iii)	(iv)	(i)	(ii)	(b)	(iv)	(i)	(ii)	(iii)
(c)	(ii)	(iii)	(iv)	(i)	(d)	(iii)	(ii)	(i)	(iv)

52. Match the following **NCERT (QR)**

Column I	Column II
A. Total product	(i) Fixed factor
B. Short-run	(ii) Total product/Total labour
C. Average product	(iii) Sum of total output produced
D. Marginal product	(iv) Change in output/ Change in input

Codes

	A	B	C	D		A	B	C	D
(a)	(iii)	(i)	(ii)	(iv)	(b)	(i)	(ii)	(iii)	(iv)
(c)	(iv)	(iii)	(ii)	(i)	(d)	(ii)	(iv)	(i)	(iii)

53. Match the options of Column I with correct options in Column II

Column I	Column II
A. Labour	(i) All factors are variable
B. Long-run	(ii) Not present in long-run
C. Fixed factors	(iii) Variable factor
D. Average product	(iv) Output per unit of variable factor

Codes

	A	B	C	D		A	B	C	D
(a)	(i)	(ii)	(iii)	(iv)	(b)	(ii)	(iii)	(iv)	(i)
(c)	(iii)	(i)	(ii)	(iv)	(d)	(iv)	(i)	(ii)	(iii)

54. Match the following

Column I	Column II
A. Increasing returns	(i) Slope of TP curve changes
B. Diminishing returns	(ii) TP increases at an increasing rate
C. Negative returns	(iii) TP increases at a decreasing rate
D. Point of inflexion	(iv) TP starts to fall

Codes

	A	B	C	D
(a)	(iii)	(iv)	(i)	(ii)
(b)	(iv)	(i)	(ii)	(iii)
(c)	(ii)	(iii)	(iv)	(i)
(d)	(iii)	(ii)	(i)	(iv)

55. Match the following

Column I	Column II
A. AP = MP	(i) AP increases
B. MP < AP	(ii) AP decreases
C. MP > AP	(iii) AP is at its maximum
D. TP begins to decline	(iv) MP becomes negative

Codes

	A	B	C	D		A	B	C	D
(a)	(iii)	(iv)	(i)	(ii)	(b)	(iv)	(i)	(ii)	(iii)
(c)	(ii)	(iii)	(iv)	(i)	(d)	(iii)	(ii)	(i)	(iv)

Concept Identification

56. It refers to the maximum output produced from given quantities of inputs.

57. It explains the point where marginal product begins to decline after initially increasing.

58. It explains the stage where total product continues to rise but at a decreasing rate while marginal product remains positive.

59. It refers to the behaviour of total and marginal products as more units of a variable factor are used while keeping fixed factors constant.

60. It states that with the increase in a variable factor, the marginal product will eventually start to decline.

Answers

1. (a) Creation/Addition to the value of output
2. (c) labour
3. (d) Only IV
4. (d) Factor input
5. (c) Water
6. (a) Long period is a time period when producer changes both fixed and variable factors of production to change the level of production. There is no difference between fixed and variable factors in the long-run.
7. (c) The production function shows the maximum output for given inputs
8. (a) Fixed factors
9. (b) Production function
10. (c) Substitute L = 4 and K = 3 into the production function $Q_x = 3(4) + 2(3) = 18$
11. (b) Average Product (AP) is total product per unit employment of a labour.

    i.e. $AP = \frac{TP}{L} = \frac{66}{6} = 11$ units of output
12. (d) Total Product (TP) is the sum total of output produced by all units of labour.

    $TP = AP \times L$ where, AP = Average Product

    $TP = 30 \times 2 = 60$ units

    L = Number of Labour
13. (c) $TP = AP \times L$, $AP = TP/L$
14. (a) Total product
15. (b) Total product will continue increasing but at a diminishing rate
16. (c) AP = TP/L = 500/10 = 50
17. (a) (iii), (i), (ii), (iv)
18. (b) Only IV
19. (a) atleast one input is fixed and all other inputs are kept variable
20. (b) increasing rate
21. (c) Stage III (Negative returns)
22. (b) Law of diminishing marginal product
23. (a) In the short-run, this can increase the marginal product of labour, as workers become more productive with the help of machines. However, this effect may not last indefinitely.
24. (c) maximum
25. (d) First
26. (c) I, II, IV
27. (b) Marginal product decreases but remains positive
28. (c) Stage III–Negative returns
29. diminishing
30. fixed, variable
31. (a) Both Assertion (A) and Reason (R) are true and Reason (R) is the correct explanation of Assertion (A)
32. (c) In short-run, only variable factors can be changed, while fixed factors remain constant, allowing limited changes in production.
33. (d) The production function shows the maximum quantity of output that can be produced using given quantities of inputs.
34. (a) Both Assertion (A) and Reason (R) are true and Reason (R) is the correct explanation of Assertion (A)
35. (a) Both Assertion (A) and Reason (R) are true and Reason (R) is the correct explanation of Assertion (A)
36. (c) Marginal product measures the additional output generated when one more unit of a variable input (like labour) is added
37. (a) Both Assertion (A) and Reason (R) are true and Reason (R) is the correct explanation of Assertion (A)
38. (d) TP increases at an increasing rate in stage I–increasing returns.
39. (b) Both Assertion (A) and Reason (R) are true, but Reason (R) is not the correct explanation of Assertion (A)
40. (b) Both Assertion (A) and Reason (R) are true, but Reason (R) is not the correct explanation of Assertion (A)
41. (c) Both the statements are correct
42. (d) Variable factors are the inputs that can be easily changed in both the short-run and the long-run. Fixed factors cannot be altered in the short-run.
43. (b) The distinction between short-run and long-run is neither based on a calendar period nor based on a fixed time span.
44. (c) Both the statements are correct
45. (a) Total product is the total output produced by all units of labour, in combination with other factors of production, during a given period.
46. (c) Both the statements are correct
47. (a) In case of diminishing returns, MP falls and MC increases.
48. (a) The law of variable proportion assumes that there is at least one fixed factor and the variable factor cannot fully substitute it.
49. (c) Both the statements are correct
50. (c) Both the statements are correct
51. (a) (iii) (iv) (i) (ii)
52. (a) (iii) (i) (ii) (iv)
53. (c) (iii) (i) (ii) (iv)
54. (c) (ii) (iii) (iv) (i)
55. (d) (iii) (ii) (i) (iv)
56. Production function
57. Inflexion point
58. Stage of diminishing returns
59. Law of variable proportion
60. Law of diminishing marginal product

Subjective Questions

Short Answer Type Questions

1. Explain the concept of a production function. **NCERT**

Ans. It is the technological knowledge that determines the maximum levels of output that can be produced using different combinations of inputs. If the technology improves, the maximum levels of output obtainable for different input combinations increase. Then we have a new production function.

e.g. A firm produces a product (Y) by using two inputs X_1 and X_2. Then production function can be expressed as $q_y = f(X_1.X_2)$

2. Explain the concepts of the short-run and the long-run. **NCERT**

Ans. **Short-run**

Short-run refers to a period in which output can be changed by changing only variable factors. In the short-run, fixed inputs like land, building, plant and machinery, etc. cannot be changed. It means, production can be raised by increasing only variable factors, but till the extent of fixed factors.

Long-run

Long-run refers to a period in which output can be changed by changing all factors of production. In the long-run, firm can change its factory size, techniques of production, purchase new plant and machinery, patents, etc.

3. Production of gift packs one week before Diwali falls in which period?

Ans. Production of gift packs during Diwali season will fall under short period, as the period of Diwali is of one week. So in this period, only variable factors like material, labour, etc. can be increased. Fixed factors like new plant and machinery cannot be increased. Hence, production period relates to due short period.

4. "In the market period, producers cannot change any factors of production to alter output."

What does this statement imply about the flexibility of production in the market period? **Competency Based Que**

Ans. This statement implies that during the market period, producers have no flexibility to alter production levels. Since none of the factors of production can be changed, producers cannot respond to shifts in demand by adjusting output.

This period is very short and production remains fixed because it takes time to modify factors like labour or capital to increase or decrease production.

5. What are the two types of factor inputs used in production?

Ans. The two types of factor inputs are fixed factors and variable factors. Fixed factors, such as land and machinery, cannot be easily changed in the short-run, meaning they remain constant regardless of production changes.

Variable factors, like labour and raw materials, can be adjusted in both the short-run and long-run, allowing producers to change their input levels as output requirements shift.

6. Which concept is depicted in the below image? Explain. **Competency Based Que**

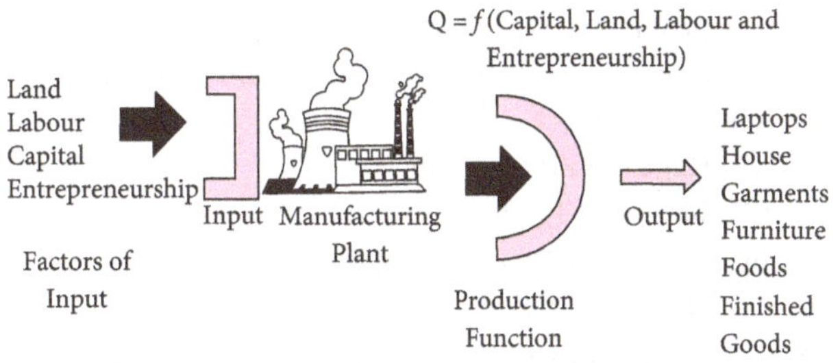

Ans. The image depicts production function. A production function is a mathematical representation that shows the relationship between the quantities of inputs used in production (like labour, capital and raw materials) and the maximum quantity of output that can be produced from those inputs.

7. State giving reasons, whether the following statements are true or false **Competency Based Que**

(i) Increase in total product always indicates that there are increasing returns to a factor.

(ii) When there are diminishing returns to a factor, marginal and total product both fall?

Ans. (i) False, it is not necessary because in the stage of diminishing returns to a factor, total product also increases but at a diminishing rate.

(ii) False, in the case of diminishing returns to a factor, only marginal product tends to fall. Total product tends to increase at a diminishing rate.

8. Identify the curve given below and briefly explain the underlying law associated with same. Competency Based Que

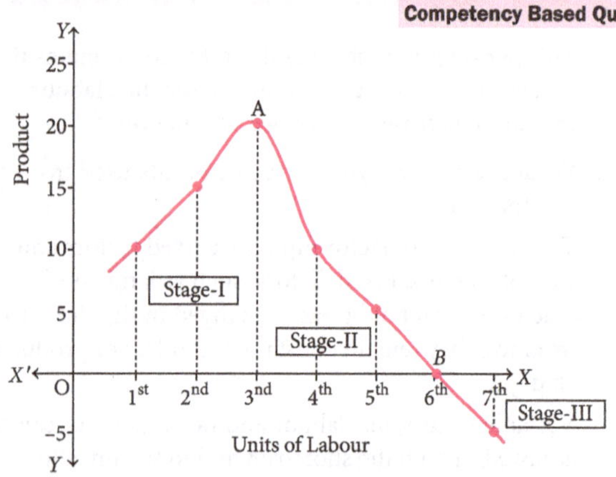

Ans. The curve shown above is marginal product and the underlying law is law of variable proportion.

The law states that if we keep all other factors constant and increase the units of a variable factor, then the marginal physical product initially increases, then decreases and finally becomes negative. Therefore, it has three stages

(i) **Stage I** MPP increasing

(ii) **Stage II** MPP decreasing but remaining positive

(iii) **Stage III** MPP continuing to decrease and becoming negative

9. "Average product can never be zero while marginal product can be." Comment. Competency Based Que

Ans. MP can become zero when production does not increase with increase in the number of variable factor. On the other hand, AP can never be zero as it is calculated on the basis of TP and variable units of input.

Both TP and variable units cannot be zero which makes it impossible for AP to be zero. Hence, it is clear that MP can be zero, but AP will never be zero.

10. What is the difference between total product and marginal product?

Ans. Differences between total production and marginal product are

Basis	Total Product	Marginal Product
Meaning	The total output produced by all units of the input.	The additional output produced by one more unit of input.
Calculation	Sum of all outputs from all units of input.	Change in total product when one more unit of input is added.
Behaviour	Increases as more inputs are employed until it reach a maximum.	Initially increases, then decreases due to diminishing returns.
Usefulness	Measures total production capacity of a firm.	Measures productivity of each additional unit of input.

11. State giving reasons, whether the following statements are true or false. Competency Based Que

(i) When there are diminishing returns to a factor, total product always decreases?

(ii) Total product will increase only when marginal product increases.

Ans. (i) False, in a situation of diminishing returns to a factor, marginal product tends to fall, which implies that total product should be increasing though at a diminishing rate.

(ii) False, total product will also increase when marginal product decreases. In that case, total product increases at a diminishing rate.

12. What does it mean when the marginal product becomes negative?

Ans. When the Marginal Product (MP) becomes negative, it means that adding more units of a variable input, such as labour, actually reduces the total output instead of increasing it. This situation arises due to excessive use of the variable input relative to the fixed inputs, leading to inefficiencies and overuse of resources like land or machinery.

13. "It shows the change in total product due to the employment of an extra unit of input."

Which concept does this statement describe and how is it calculated? Competency Based Que

Ans. This statement describes the concept of marginal product, which is calculated by determining the change in total product when one additional unit of a variable input, like labour, is employed.

Marginal product helps firms understand how each additional worker or unit of input contributes to overall production. Initially, this may lead to an increase in output, but as more inputs are added, diminishing returns may set in, reducing the effectiveness of each additional unit.

14. What is the total product of an input? NCERT

Ans. Total product is the sum total of output produced by all the units of labour along with all other factors of production.

$$TP = AP \times L$$

Here, TP = Total Product
AP = Average Product
L = Units of variable factor

15. What is the average product of an input? NCERT

Ans. Average product is per unit production of the variable factor.

$$AP = TP/L$$

Here, AP = Average Product
TP = Total Product
L = Units of variable factor

16. What is the law of variable proportions? NCERT

Ans. It states that as more and more units of a variable factor are employed with fixed factors, total product increases at an increasing rate in the beginning, then increases at a diminishing rate and finally starts falling.

17. "Fixed cost of input is ignored in the study of the law of increasing return." Do you agree? Give reason. Competency Based Que

Ans. No, it is not correct. In fact, fixed cost plays an important role in deriving increasing returns from variable inputs. A firm can leverage its fixed cost to derive better returns due to improved productivity of resources.

e.g. Rent is paid every month for the factory space which is fixed cost. By employing more labours, the production can be maximised and returns of paying rent as fixed cost can be increased. Hence, fixed cost is not ignored in the analysis of law of increasing returns to variable factor.

18. What is meant by returns to a factor? State the law of diminishing returns to a factor.

Ans. Returns to a Factor

It refers to the behaviour of output when only one variable factor of production is increased in short-run and fixed factors remain constant.

Law of Diminishing Returns to a Factor

It refers to a situation in which total output increases at a diminishing rate when more and more variable factor is combined with the fixed factor of production. In this situation, marginal product of the variable factor must be diminishing.

19. "A rational producer will choose to operate in the second stage of the law of variable proportion." Why does a rational producer prefer to operate in the stage mentioned in the statement above? Competency Based Que

Ans. A rational producer prefers to operate in the second stage of the law of variable proportion because, in this stage, the total product is maximised while the marginal product of each additional unit of the variable factor remains positive.

This stage indicates that the producer is utilising resources efficiently, as output continues to increase, although at a decreasing rate.

Operating in this stage allows the producer to achieve the highest level of productivity without encountering the inefficiencies and diminishing returns associated with the third stage, where marginal product becomes negative and total product begins to decline.

20. Explain the relationship between MP and TP of an input. NCERT

Ans. Relationship between MP and TP is stated below

(i) When MP increases, TP increases at an increasing rate.
(ii) When MP decreases, TP increases at a diminishing rate.
(iii) When MP = 0, TP is maximum.
(iv) When MP is negative, TP declines.

Long Answer Type Questions

21. Explain the production process and its significance in the economy. What are the different types of inputs involved in production?

Ans. The production process transforms inputs into outputs, creating goods and services essential for the economy. It plays a critical role in meeting consumer demands, driving economic growth, and generating employment.

There are two main types of inputs involved in production

(i) **Factor Inputs**
These are the primary resources directly contributing to production
- **Land** Natural resources used in production.
- **Labour** Human effort and skills.
- **Capital** Machinery and tools.
- **Entrepreneurship** Individuals who organise and manage production.

(ii) **Non-factor Inputs**
These are supplementary resources, such as raw materials and power, not classified as traditional production factors but necessary for production processes.

22. "In the short-run, only variable factors can be changed while fixed factors remain constant."
Discuss how this limitation impacts production decisions. Competency Based Que

Ans. In the short-run, the inability to change fixed factors such as capital and land while only variable factors like labour and raw materials can be adjusted significantly impacts production decisions.

This constraint forces producers to optimise the use of their variable inputs to enhance output. Since fixed factors remain constant, producers must carefully manage how many variable inputs to employ to maximise production efficiency and minimise costs.

If too many variable inputs are added without sufficient fixed capacity, it may lead to diminishing marginal returns, where each additional unit of input contributes less to total output.

Additionally, this limitation requires producers to make strategic decisions based on existing fixed resources. For example, they may focus on training labour to improve productivity or enhancing the efficiency of variable inputs. It also means that in times of increased demand, producers may face challenges in scaling up quickly due to fixed constraints. As a result, businesses must plan for both short-term operational efficiency and long-term investment in fixed assets to remain competitive in the market.

23. A local bakery produces various types of bread using different amounts of flour, yeast and water. Over the past month, the bakery has been experimenting with its production process to increase output. The owner notices that as more flour is added to the dough, the total quantity of bread produced increases.

However, they also realise that while the output rises with each additional batch of dough made, the amount of bread produced per batch starts to decrease after a certain point. This observation leads the owner to analyse their production strategy more closely.

Competency Based Que

(i) What are the key distinctions between total product, average product and marginal product?

(ii) How do these different types of products influence production decisions in the bakery?

Ans. (i) Total Product (TP) is the overall quantity of output produced with a specific combination of inputs during a given period. Average Product (AP) represents the output produced per unit of a variable input, calculated by dividing TP by the number of variable input units used.

Marginal Product (MP) measures the additional output generated by adding one more unit of a variable input while keeping other inputs constant.

(ii) In the context of the bakery, understanding these distinctions is crucial for production decisions.

TP helps the owner gauge the overall effectiveness of the production process, while AP indicates how efficiently each unit of input contributes to output.

MP is particularly important, as it highlights the changes in output as more flour is added.

If MP begins to decline, it signals diminishing returns, prompting the owner to reassess the optimal mix of inputs to maximise efficiency and output without overextending resources.

24. The development of production function is very important especially in the agricultural sector, because agricultural production depends significantly upon climatic or environmental factors or both. In developing countries, application of new and improved farming techniques (such as irrigation, fertiliser usage, seed of new varieties) has been lacking.

As a result, agricultural crop yield may be more susceptible to climatic factors. Therefore, the undetermined and stochastic events in nature may significantly change the crop production that results in unreliable crop forecasts.

Thus, it is important to develop forecasting techniques that depend upon the most reliable and objective variables. Based upon the above case, explain any four causes of law of variable proportion.

Competency Based Que

Ans. Causes for the operation of the law of variable proportion are as follows

(i) Firstly, in the short-term duration, it is difficult to change all factors of production. In such cases, we maintain only one variable factor while others remain fixed.

(ii) All other factors when combined optimally can generate the maximum output.

There can be increased marginal production if the units of a variable factor are increased prior to the point of optimum combination, as the factor proportion becomes more suitable leading to much better utilisation of the fixed factors.

(iii) During the initial stages, it has been observed that the total product tends to improve in value at an increasing rate if the producer puts in more units of a variable factor in comparison to the fixed factors.

(iv) Subsequently, beyond the point of optimum combination, if the producer still continues the use of more units of the variable factor, then it counteracts and the factor proportion becomes inefficient. This causes the marginal product of that variable factor to declining.

25. Explain the different stages of the law of variable proportion.

Ans. The production process experiences three distinct stages, i.e. increasing returns, diminishing returns and negative returns to a factor.

For explanation, refer to topic 'Stages of law of variable proportion' on page 338.

26. What criteria does a rational producer use to decide on the optimal stage of operation? Discuss how this choice impacts production efficiency.

Ans. A rational producer decides on the optimal stage of operation based on the relationship between Total Product (TP) and Marginal Product (MP).

The key criteria include

(i) **Marginal Product Analysis**
A rational producer aims to maximise profits by operating where the marginal product is positive but decreasing. In Stage II of the law of variable proportions, the TP increases at a diminishing rate and the MP is still positive. This stage balances increased output while avoiding inefficiencies that arise in Stage III, where MP becomes negative.

(ii) **Cost Considerations**
Producers also consider the cost of additional variable inputs. The choice of operation stage involves weighing the additional costs against the benefits derived from increased production. The optimal stage is one where the additional revenue generated from the output exceeds the costs incurred.

Impact on Production Efficiency

Choosing the optimal stage enhances production efficiency by ensuring that resources are utilised effectively. Operating in Stage II allows for maximum output with positive returns, contributing to higher profitability without incurring losses from overuse of inputs.

When producers remain in the efficient operational stage, they can respond better to market demands, adjust production levels and maintain a competitive edge while avoiding wastefulness associated with negative returns.

27. Briefly explain the relationship between TP, AP and MP curves.

Ans. The relationship between product curves can be understood with the help of following graph

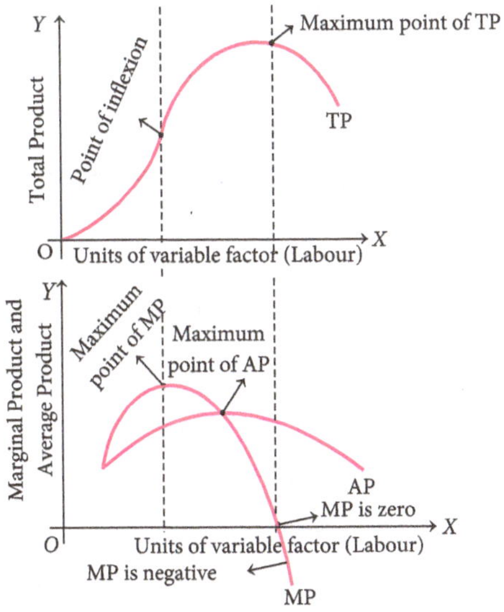

(i) From the above curves, following observations are made on the relationship between TP and MP
- When TP increases at an increasing rate, MP also increases.
- When TP increases at a diminishing rate, MP declines but remains positive.
- When TP reaches its maximum, MP becomes zero.
- When TP begins to decline, MP becomes negative.

(ii) From the given curves, following observations are made on the relationship between AP and MP
- AP increases so long as MP > AP.
- AP is at its maximum when AP = MP. AP decreases when MP < AP.
- MP may be zero or negative, but AP continues to be positive.
- AP increases, even when MP falls but MP should lie above AP.

28. ABC Manufacturing is a company specialising in the production of electronic components. The company uses a combination of fixed and variable factors of production to meet market demand. Fixed factors include the manufacturing plant and machinery, while variable factors consist of labour and raw materials. ABC Manufacturing operates in a competitive market where efficiency and output are critical for maintaining profitability.

In the first stage of production, ABC Manufacturing increases the labour force to utilise the available machinery more efficiently. As the number of workers increases, the total output rises at an increasing rate.

However, as the company continues to hire more workers, it enters the second stage of production, where the marginal product begins to decline. The fixed machinery becomes a bottleneck, limiting the effectiveness of the additional labour.

In the third stage of production, the company faces overcrowding and inefficiencies. With too many workers using the same machinery, the marginal product becomes negative, leading to a decrease in total output.

Recognising this, ABC Manufacturing decides to optimise its production process by investing in additional machinery to relieve the bottleneck and enhance overall efficiency. **Competency Based Que**

(i) What are the fixed and variable factors of production at ABC Manufacturing?

(ii) Explain the implications of the bottleneck created by fixed factors in the second stage of production for ABC Manufacturing's output.

(iii) **Analyse how ABC Manufacturing's decision to invest in additional machinery can improve production efficiency. Discuss the potential benefits and challenges associated with this decision.**

Ans. (i) • **Fixed Factors of Production**

The manufacturing plant and machinery.

• **Variable Factors of Production**

Labour and raw materials.

(ii) The bottleneck created by fixed factors in the second stage of production limits the effectiveness of additional labour. As more workers are hired, the machinery becomes overloaded, leading to diminishing returns. This means that while total output may still increase, the rate of increase slows down, causing the marginal product of labour to decline.

Consequently, ABC Manufacturing may not achieve optimal production levels, affecting overall efficiency and profitability.

(iii) Investing in additional machinery can significantly improve production efficiency at ABC Manufacturing by alleviating the bottleneck caused by fixed factors. With more machinery available, the company can better utilise its labour force, leading to an increase in both total output and marginal product. This investment can also allow for a more flexible production process, enabling the company to respond quickly to changes in market demand.

However, this decision comes with challenges, such as the initial capital investment and potential training needs for workers to operate the new machinery effectively. There may also be a period of adjustment during which the production process is optimised.

Nevertheless, if managed well, the benefits of increased efficiency and output can outweigh these challenges, positioning ABC Manufacturing more competitively in the market.

Numerical Questions

Numerical 1

Let the production function of a firm be $Q = 5, L^{1/2}K^{1/2}$. Find out the maximum possible output that the firm can produce with 100 units of L and 100 units of K. NCERT

Sol. Given, $Q = 5$; $L = 100$ units ; $K = 100$ units

$\because$ $Q_x = f(X_1 \cdot X_2)$ (Production function equation)

After putting values

$$Q_x = 5 \cdot 100^{1/2} \cdot 100^{1/2} = 5\sqrt{100} \cdot \sqrt{100} = 500$$

$\therefore$Maximum output = 500 units

Numerical 2

If productivity of labour is 50 units and a firm has 5 workers. Calculate its total productivity.

Sol. Average Product = 50 units; Number of workers = 5

Total Product = AP × Number of Workers

$= 50 \times 5 = 250$ units

Numerical 3

Let the production function of a firm be $Q = 2L^2K^2$. Find out the maximum possible output that the firm can produce with 5 units of L and 2 units of K.

What is the maximum possible output that the firm can produce with zero unit of L and 10 units of K? NCERT

Sol. Given, $Q = 2L^2K^2$; L = 5 units ; K = 2 units

$\because$ $Q_x = f(X_1.X_2)$

After putting given values

$$Q = 2\,(5)^2 \cdot (2)^2 = 200 \text{ units}$$

Maximum possible output with 0 unit of L and 10 units of K

Again putting new values in equation

$$Q = 2\,(0)^2 \cdot (10)^2 = 0 \text{ units}$$

Numerical 4

Find out the maximum possible output for a firm with zero unit of L and 10 units of K when its production function is $Q = 5L + 2K$. NCERT

Sol. Given $Q = 5L + 2K$; L = 0 units ; K = 10 units

After putting values in equation

$$Q = 5(0) + 2\,(10) = 20 \text{ units}$$

$\therefore$ The maximum output = 20 units

Numerical 5

From the following information about a firm, calculate average product and marginal product.

Labour	10	20	30	40	50
Total Product	100	220	360	460	500

Sol.

Units of Labour (L)	Total Product (TP)	Average Product (TP/L)	Marginal Product $(TP_n - TP_{n-1})$
10	100	10	—
20	220	11	120
30	360	12	140
40	460	11.5	100
50	500	10	40

Numerical 6

Marginal Physical Product (MPP) of a factory is 20, 25, 18, 0 and – 10 and its levels of variable factor are 1, 2, 3, 4 and 5 respectively. Calculate its TPP and APP.

Sol.

Units of Labour/ Variable Factor (L)	Marginal Physical Product (MPP)	Total Physical Product (TPP) $= \Sigma$ MPP	Average Physical Product (TPP/L)
1	20	20	20
2	25	45	22.5
3	18	63	21
4	0	63	15.75
5	–10	53	10.6

Numerical 7

The following table gives the Total Product (TP) schedule of labour. Find the corresponding Average Product (AP) and Marginal Product (MP) schedules of labour. NCERT

Units of Labour (L)	0	1	2	3	4	5
Total Product (TP)	0	15	35	50	40	38

Sol.

Labour (L)	TP	AP = TP/L	$MP_{nth} = TP_n - TP_{n-1}$
0	0	—	—
1	15	15.00	15 – 0 = 15
2	35	17.50	35 – 15 = 20
3	50	16.67	50 – 35 = 15
4	40	10.00	40 – 50 = – 10
5	38	7.60	38 – 40 = – 2

Numerical 8

The following table gives the Average Product (AP) schedule of labour. Find the Total Product (TP) and Marginal Product (MP) schedules. It is given that the total product is zero at zero level of labour employment. NCERT

Labour (L)	1	2	3	4	5	6
Average Product (AP)	2	3	4	4.25	4	3.5

Sol.

Units of Labour (L)	Average Product (AP)	Total Product (TP = AP × L)	Marginal Product ($MP_{nth} = TP_n - TP_{n-1}$)
1	2.00	2	—
2	3.00	6	6 – 2 = 4
3	4.00	12	12 – 6 = 6
4	4.25	17	17 – 12 = 5
5	4.00	20	20 – 17 = 3
6	3.50	21	21 – 20 = 1

Numerical 9

Identify different phases of the law of variable proportion from the following schedule. Give reasons.

Variable Inputs (units)	Total Product (TP) (units)	Marginal Product (MP) (units)
1	4	4
2	9	5
3	13	4
4	15	2
5	15	0
6	12	– 3

Sol.

Variable Inputs (units)	TP (units)	MP (units)	Stages of Law of Variable Proportion	
1	4	4	Stage I	TP is increasing at an increasing rate and MP is also increasing.
2	9	5		
3	13	4	Stage II	TP is increasing at a diminishing rate and MP starts declining.
4	15	2		
5	15	0	Stage III	MP becomes negative and TP falls.
6	12	-3		

Numerical 10

The following table gives the marginal product schedule of labour. It is also given that total product of labour is zero at zero level of employment. Calculate the total and average product schedules of labour. NCERT

L	1	2	3	4	5	6
MP_L	3	5	7	5	3	1

Sol.

Labour (L)	MP of Labour (units)	TP (units)	AP (units) $\left(\frac{TP}{L}\right)$
1	3	3	3
2	5	3 + 5 = 8	4
3	7	8 + 7 = 15	5
4	5	15 + 5 = 20	5
5	3	20 + 3 = 23	4.60
6	1	23 + 1 = 24	4

SELF ASSESSMENT TEST

Objective Type Questions

1. Which of the following is not a factor input?
   (a) Labour (b) Land
   (c) Raw materials (d) Tools

2. What is the relationship between input and output in the production process called?
   (a) Production function (b) Marginal cost
   (c) Utility function (d) Demand function

3. The shape of the marginal product curve is generally ....
   (a) U shaped
   (b) inverted U shaped
   (c) V-shaped
   (d) linear

4. Which stage of the law of variable proportion represents technical inefficiency?
   (a) Increasing returns (b) Diminishing returns
   (c) Negative returns (d) Constant returns

5. In the short-run, production is adjusted by changing .... inputs.
   (a) fixed (b) variable
   (c) constant (d) average

6. What does 'point of inflexion' in the total product curve represent?
   (a) Maximum point of marginal product
   (b) Maximum point of average product
   (c) Change from increasing to diminishing returns
   (d) Beginning of negative returns

7. The .... curve represents the output per unit of variable input.
   (a) marginal product (b) average product
   (c) total product (d) utility

8. Which of the following statements is correct?
   (a) The total product curve declines in the first stage of production
   (b) Marginal product becomes zero when total product is at its maximum
   (c) Average product becomes negative when marginal product becomes negative
   (d) In the short run, all factors of production are variable

Answers 1. (d) 2. (a) 3.(b) 4. (c) 5. (b) 6. (c) 7. (b) 8. (b)

Short Answer Type Questions

9. "All factors of production can be changed in the long period as all factors are variable in long-run." Support or refute the given statement with reasons.

10. What is marginal product? Explain with example.

11. Define the following
    (i) Production function (ii) Point of inflexion

12. Explain the relationship between TPP and MPP.

Long Answer Type Questions

13. Explain law of variable proportion using appropriate schedule and diagram.

14. Fixed factors are ignored in the study of law of increasing returns. Do you agree?

Numerical Questions

15. 4 units of labour produces 100 units of output and 5 units of labour produces 120 units of output. Calculate MPP of the labour.

    Complete the following table

Units of Labour	Average Product (units)	Marginal Product (units)
1	8	—
2	10	...
3	...	10
4	9	...
5	...	4
6	7	...

Ans. AP = 10, 8; MP = 12, 6, 2

16. Calculate total product and marginal product of a firm, if its average product is as under.

Labour	1	2	3	4	5	6
Average Product	10	12	14	12	10	8

Ans. TP = 10, 24, 42, 48, 50, 48
MP = –, 14, 18, 6, 2, –2

17. Identify the different phases of the law of variable proportions from the following schedule. Give reasons for your answer.

Units of Variable Input	1	2	3	4	5
TP (units)	4	9	13	15	12

05

CHAPTER

The concept of cost is central to understanding how resources are utilised and valued in any business activity. It helps in evaluating expenses, making informed decisions and optimising profitability.

YOUR STUDY GOALS

YOUR PRACTICE GOAL

- Objective Type Questions (60 Qs ; MCQs, A-R, Statements, Matching, Concept Identification)
- Subjective Questions (20 SAs, 8 LAs)
- 14 Numerical Questions
- Self Assessment Test (8 MCQs, 4 SAs, 6 Numerical)

Concept of Cost

5.1 Cost

Cost refers to the monetary and non-monetary expenditure incurred by a producer on factor as well as non-factor inputs to produce a certain amount of output of a commodity.

The cost of production can also be classified as

1. **Implicit Cost** This is the estimated cost of self-owned and self-employed resources, like rent on the producer's own land or interest on their own capital. This is also referred to as non-accounting cost and is measured in terms of opportunity cost. It is called implicit as producers do not make payments to others for such kind of cost.
2. **Explicit Cost** This cost includes actual cash payments made to outsiders for hiring their services and goods, such as wages, raw material costs, rent, interest, etc.
3. **Opportunity Cost** The cost of next best alternative forgone. It is considered essential as it forms the basis of concept of cost.

Note The sum total of explicit and implicit costs is known as **economic cost**.

Implicit Cost

A farmer using his own land for cultivation doesn't pay rent, but the implicit cost is the rent he could earn if he rented the land to someone else.

Explicit Cost

A bakery owner pays for flour, sugar, electricity and wages. These payments are explicit costs because they involve actual cash outflows to external suppliers and employees.

Cost Function

A cost function represents the functional relationship between output and cost of production.

Cost function is given as

$$C = f(Q)$$

Here, C = Cost; Q = Units of output; f = Functional relationship

It depends on factors like the quantum of goods produced, prices of factors of production and government taxation policies.

5.2 Short-run Costs

In the short-run, there is a combination of fixed and variable factors. Thus, short-run cost can be classified into two parts i.e. fixed cost and variable cost. These costs are classified as follows

Fixed Cost (FC) **or Total Fixed Cost** (TFC)

- It is the sum total of expenditure incurred by the producer on the purchase or hiring of fixed factors of production.
- It is also called **supplementary cost** or **overhead cost** or **indirect cost**. e.g. Rent, insurance premium, salaries of the permanent employees, etc.
- This cost cannot be changed in short-run. The firm has to bear this cost even at the zero level of output.
- Explanation using schedule and diagram

Units of Output	Fixed Cost (₹)
0	10
1	10
2	10
3	10
4	10
5	10

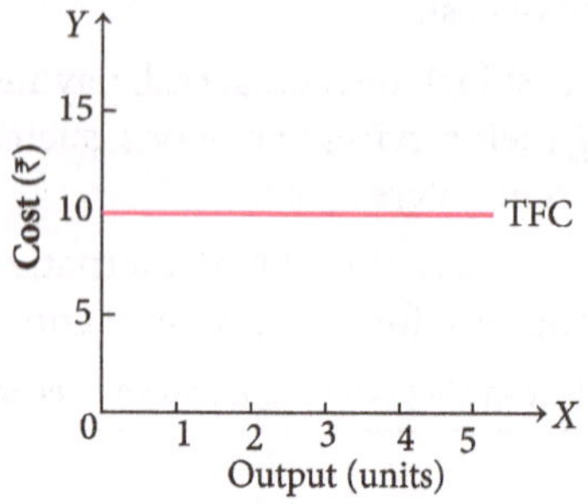

Fixed cost curve

In the above graph, total fixed cost curve is a horizontal straight line parallel to x-axis, indicating that total fixed cost is constant at all levels of output.

Variable Cost (VC) **or Total Variable Cost** (TVC)

- This is the total cost incurred by firm on hiring variable factors of production. It varies directly with the quantity of output produced.
- It is also called **prime cost** or **direct cost**. e.g. Wages of labour, cost of raw materials, fuel, electricity, etc.
- This cost increases with increase in output and *vice-versa*. Thus, at zero level of output, this cost becomes zero.
- Explanation using schedule and diagram

Units of Output	Variable Cost (₹)
0	0
1	10
2	18
3	24
4	28
5	34

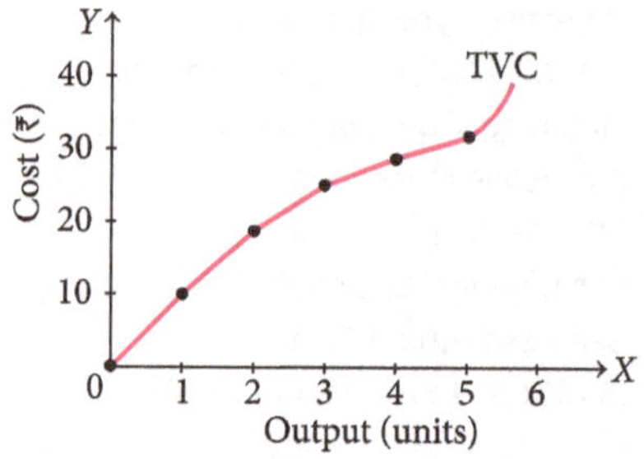

Variable cost curve

In the above graph, total variable cost curve initially increases at a diminishing rate and eventually increases at an increasing rate due to law of variable proportions. Thus, TVC curve is an inversely 'S' shaped curve.

Total Cost (TC)

It is defined as the aggregate of all costs of production at a given level of output. TC is derived by the sum total of TFC and TVC, i.e. TC = TFC + TVC. Since, TFC remains same at all levels of output, the change in TC is entirely due to TVC.

Explanation of total cost using schedule and diagram

Output (units)	**Fixed Cost** (₹)	**Variable Cost** (₹)	**Total Cost** (₹)
0	10	0	10
1	10	10	20
2	10	18	28
3	10	24	34
4	10	28	38
5	10	32	42
6	10	40	50

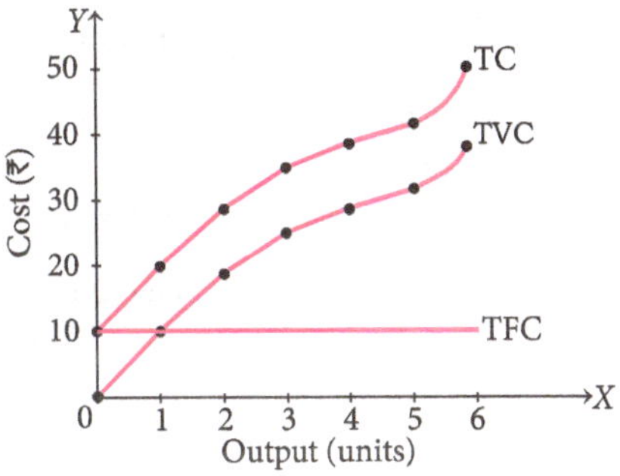

Total cost curve is parallel to total variable cost curve as TFC remains constant at all levels. Because of this, the difference between TC and TVC curves is the same at all levels. Thus, total cost curve is also inversely 'S' shaped curve.

Average Cost (AC)

It is the cost per unit of output produced. It is also called **unit cost of production or Average Total Cost** (ATC). It is obtained by dividing the total cost by the total number of units produced.

Symbolically, $\text{Average Cost (AC)} = \dfrac{\text{Total Cost (TC)}}{\text{Number of Units Produced (Q)}}$

Explanation of average cost using schedule and diagram

Output	**Total Cost** (TC)	**Average Cost** (AC)
0	10	—
1	20	$20 \div 1 = 20$
2	28	$28 \div 2 = 14$
3	34	$34 \div 3 = 11.33$
4	38	$38 \div 4 = 9.5$
5	42	$42 \div 5 = 8.4$
6	50	$50 \div 6 = 8.33$
7	60	$60 \div 7 = 8.57$
8	72	$72 \div 8 = 9$

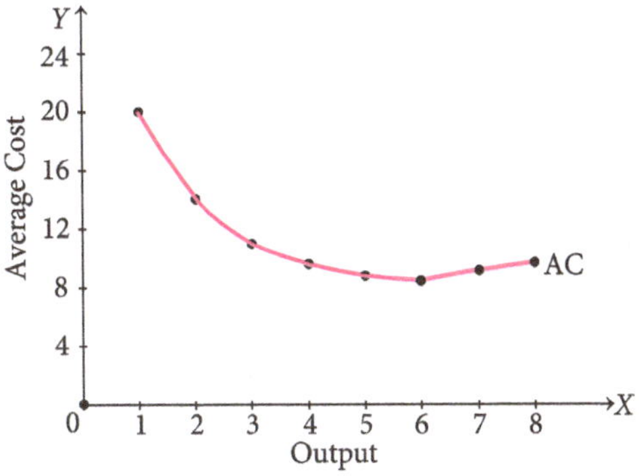

It can be seen from the above schedule and graph, that, AC is derived from TC by dividing with output. Till output level 6, AC is falling and from output 7, it starts to increase, which makes it 'U' shaped.

Average cost comprises of two components namely, Average Fixed Cost (AFC) and Average Variable Cost (AVC). Thus, it can also be computed using formula

$$AC = AFC + AVC$$

The above said components are explained as follows

Average Fixed Cost (AFC)

- It is defined as the fixed cost of producing per unit of the commodity.
- It is obtained by dividing TFC by the level of output, i.e.

$$\text{AFC} = \frac{\text{TFC}}{\text{Number of Units Produced (Q)}}$$

- AFC falls with increase in output as TFC remains same at all levels of output.
- Explanation using schedule and diagram

Output	Total Fixed Cost (TFC)	Average Fixed Cost (AFC)
0	60	—
1	60	60 ÷ 1 = 60
2	60	60 ÷ 2 = 30
3	60	60 ÷ 3 = 20
4	60	60 ÷ 4 = 15
5	60	60 ÷ 5 = 12
6	60	60 ÷ 6 = 10
7	60	60 ÷ 7 = 8.5
8	60	60 ÷ 8 = 7.5

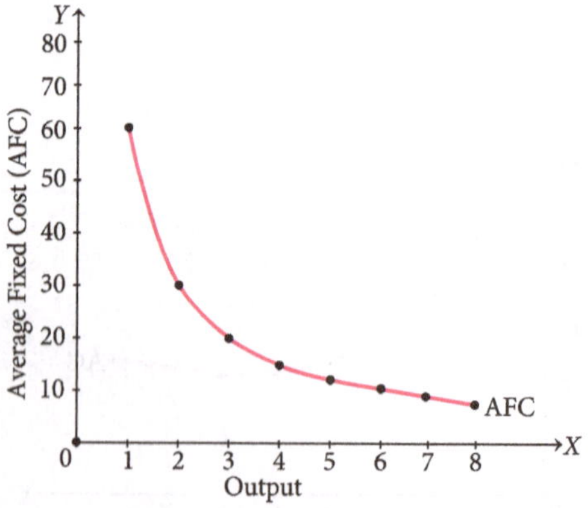

It can be seen from the above schedule and graph that AFC falls continuously with rise in the level of output. This makes AFC a rectangular hyperbola shaped curve as the area of each rectangle under AFC curve is same. Also, AFC can never be zero as it is derived from TFC and fixed costs can never be zero, that is why AFC never touches either x-axis or y-axis.

Average Variable Cost (AVC)

- It is defined as the variable cost of producing per unit of the commodity.
- It is obtained by dividing TVC by the level of output, i.e.

$$\text{AVC} = \frac{\text{TVC}}{\text{Number of Units Produced (Q)}}$$

- AVC initially falls with rise in output and once the output reaches its optimum level, AVC starts rising.
- Explanation using schedule and diagram

Output	Total Variable Cost (TVC)	Average Variable Cost (AVC)
0	0	—
1	10	10 ÷ 1 = 10
2	18	18 ÷ 2 = 9
3	24	24 ÷ 3 = 8
4	28	28 ÷ 4 = 7
5	34	34 ÷ 5 = 6.8
6	42	42 ÷ 6 = 7
7	56	56 ÷ 7 = 8
8	72	72 ÷ 8 = 9

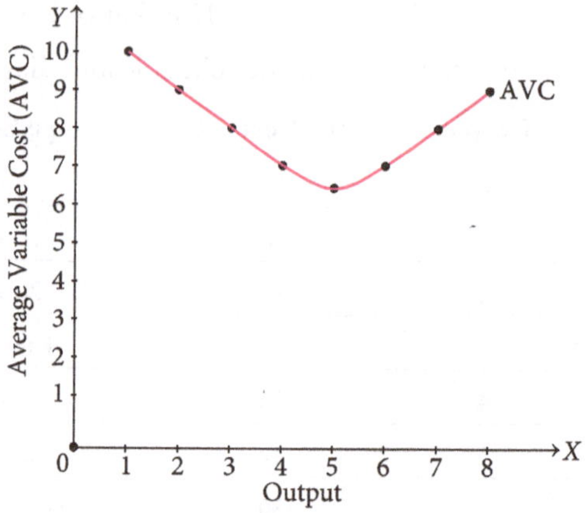

It is shown in the above schedule and graph that AVC is also 'U' shaped, i.e. it initially decreases (till output level 5) and eventually increases (from output level 6).

AVC curve is 'U' shaped due to law of variable proportions. It shows that AVC initially falls due to increasing returns to a factor, reaches to its minimum level and then start rising due to diminishing returns to a factor.

Important Points related to AC, AVC and AFC

- AC curve always lie above the AVC curve, as AC includes both AVC and AFC at all levels of output.
- AVC reaches its minimum point at a level of output lower than that of AC. It is so because, AC continues to fall due to falling AFC, when AVC is at its minimum point.
- With increase in output, the gap between AC and AVC curves reduces but they never intersect each other because AFC can never be zero.

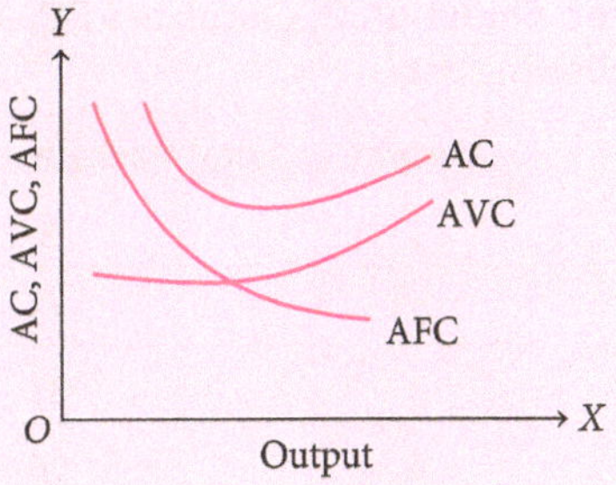

Marginal Cost (MC)

It is defined as addition made to total variable cost or total cost when one more unit of output is produced. It can be calculated as

$$MC_n = TC_n - TC_{n-1} \text{ or } \frac{\Delta TC}{\Delta Q} \text{ or } TVC_n - TVC_{n-1}$$

Here,

MC_n = Marginal Cost of nth unit of output
TC_n = Total Cost of n units of output
TC_{n-1} = Total Cost of $n-1$ units of output
ΔTC = Change in Total Cost
ΔQ = Change in Quantity
TVC_n = Total Variable Cost of n units of output
TVC_{n-1} = Total Variable Cost of $n-1$ units of output

Explanation of marginal cost using schedule and diagram

Output	Total Variable Cost (TVC)	Marginal Cost (MC)
0	0	—
1	10	10 − 0 = 10
2	18	18 − 10 = 8
3	24	24 − 18 = 6
4	28	28 − 24 = 4
5	34	34 − 28 = 6
6	42	42 − 34 = 8
7	56	56 − 42 = 14
8	72	72 − 56 = 16

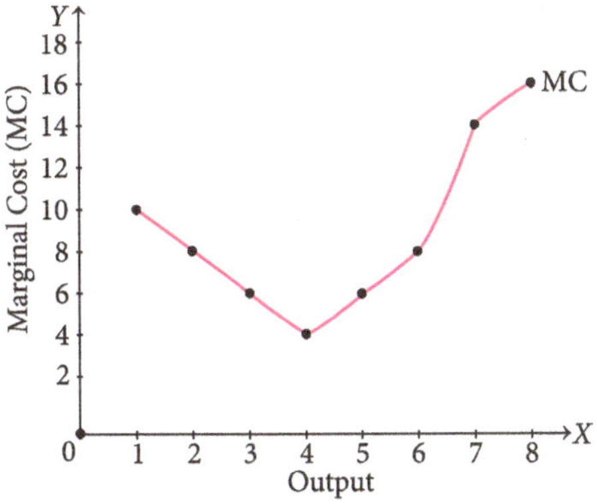

As shown in the above schedule and graph, MC curve is also 'U' shaped and derived from TVC. Initially, it decreases (till output level 4) and eventually increases (from output level 5), this make MC curve 'U' shaped.

MC curve as 'U' shaped indicates that marginal cost falls initially due to law of increasing returns to factor and ultimately, it rises due to law of decreasing returns.

It should be remembered that MC is the addition to the variable cost as fixed cost remains constant.

Solved Question 1 **Calculate total variable cost, total fixed cost and marginal cost from the following data**

Output	Total Cost (TC)
0	10
1	18
2	25
3	31
4	36
5	42
6	49
7	57
8	66

Sol.

Output	TC	TFC	TVC (TC − TFC)	MC ($TVC_n - TVC_{n-1}$)
0	10	10	0	—
1	18	10	8	8
2	25	10	15	7
3	31	10	21	6
4	36	10	26	5
5	42	10	32	6
6	49	10	39	7
7	57	10	47	8
8	66	10	56	9

Solved Question 2 Calculate AFC, AVC and AC from the following data

Output	Total Variable Cost (TVC)
1	8
2	15
3	31
4	36
5	42
6	49
7	56

Total cost at zero level of output is 10.

Sol.

Output	TFC	TVC	TC	AFC	AVC	AC
1	10	8	18	10	8	18
2	10	15	25	5	7.5	12.5
3	10	31	41	3.3	10.33	13.66
4	10	36	46	2.5	9	11.5
5	10	42	52	2	8.4	10.4
6	10	49	59	1.66	8.16	9.83
7	10	56	66	1.42	8	9.42

Hint At zero level of output TC = TFC.

Formula used

TC = TFC + TVC

$$AFC = \frac{TFC}{Q}; \quad AVC = \frac{TVC}{Q}; \quad AC = \frac{TC}{Q}$$

Solved Question 3 Complete the following table

Output (units)	Average Fixed Cost (AFC) (₹)	Average Variable Cost (AVC) (₹)	Marginal Cost (MC) (₹)	Total Cost (TC) (₹)	Average Cost (AC) (₹)
1	...	...	18	...	...
2	36	16	14	...	...
3	24	...	...	120	...
4	18	18	...	...	...

Sol.

Output (Q) (units)	TFC (₹)	AFC (₹)	AVC (₹)	MC (₹)	TC (₹)	AC (₹)	TVC (₹)
1	72	**72**	**18**	18	**90**	**90**	18
2	72	36	16	14	**104**	**52**	32
3	72	24	16	**16**	120	**40**	48
4	72	18	18	**24**	**144**	**36**	72

Formulae used

$$TC = TFC + TVC; \quad TVC = AVC \times Q$$

$$AVC = TVC/Q \quad or \quad AC - AFC$$

$$MC_{nth} = TVC_n - TVC_{n-1}$$

$$AFC = \frac{TFC}{Q}, \quad TFC = AFC \times Q$$

Solved Question 4 Complete the following table

Output (units)	Total Cost (TC) (₹)	Average Fixed Cost (AFC) (₹)	Average Variable Cost (AVC) (₹)	Marginal Cost (MC) (₹)
0	36	—	—	—
1	...	...	...	18
2	...	...	...	14
3	...	...	16	...
4	...	...	...	24

Sol.

Output (Q) (units)	TC (₹)	TFC (₹)	AFC (₹)	AVC (₹)	MC (₹)	TVC (₹)
0	36	36	—	—	—	0
1	**54**	36	**36**	**18**	18	18
2	**68**	36	**18**	**16**	14	32
3	**84**	36	**12**	16	**16**	48
4	**108**	36	**9**	**18**	24	72

Formulae used

$$TC = TFC + TVC$$

$$TVC = AVC \times Q$$

$$AVC = TVC/Q \quad or \quad AC - AFC$$

$$MC_{nth} = TVC_n - TVC_{n-1}$$

$$AFC = \frac{TFC}{Q}$$

TFC = First value of TC at zero level of output

Solved Question 5 Complete the following table

Output (units)	Total Cost (TC) (₹)	Average Variable Cost (AVC) (₹)	Marginal Cost (MC) (₹)
1	90	...	30
2	...	27	...
3	...	...	27
4	180	30	...

Sol.

Output (Q) (units)	TFC (₹)	TC (₹) (TFC+ TVC)	TVC (₹) (AVC × Q)	AVC (₹) (TVC / Q)	MC (₹) ($TVC_n - TVC_{n-1}$)
1	60	90	30	**30**	30
2	60	**114**	54	27	**24**
3	60	**141**	81	**27**	27
4	60	180	120	30	**39**

5.3 Relation between Cost Curves

There exists a close relationship between the various costs, which can be studied under following sub-heads

1. Relationship between Average Cost (AC) and Marginal Cost (MC)

- Both AC and MC are 'U' shaped.
- When AC falls, MC is less than AC.
- When AC rises, MC is greater than AC.
- When AC is constant and minimum, MC is equal to AC.
- MC is always to the left of AC and cuts AC from its lowest point.

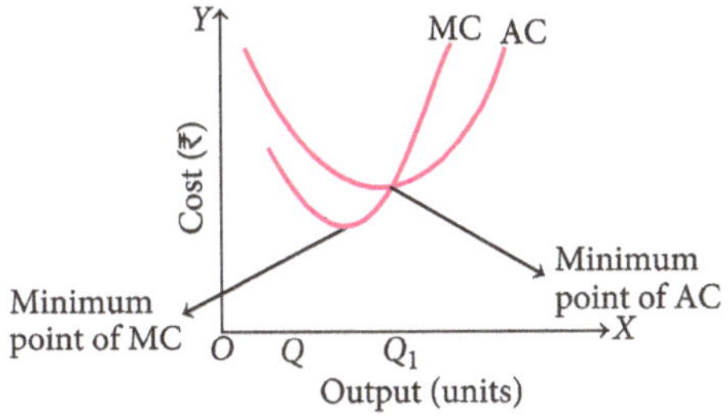

Relationship between AC and MC

2. Relationship between Marginal Cost (MC) and Average Variable Cost (AVC)

- Both AVC and MC curves are 'U' shaped.
- When AVC is falling, AVC is greater than MC.
- When AVC is constant and minimum, AVC is equal to MC.
- When AVC is rising, AVC is less than MC.
- MC curve cuts AVC curve at its lowest point.
- Both AVC and MC curves starts from same point.

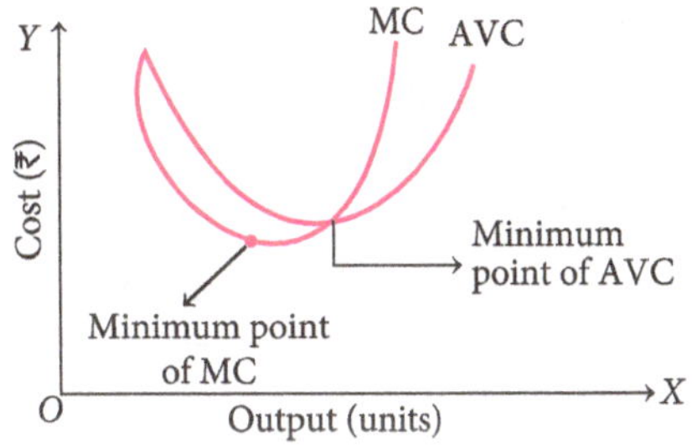

Relationship between MC and AVC

3. Relationship between Average Cost (AC) and Average Variable Cost (AVC)

- Both AC and AVC are 'U' shaped, i.e. they intially decrease, reaches their minimum and eventually increases.
- The vertical gap between AC and AVC narrows down with increase in level of output as AFC decreases with higher output.
- AC and AVC never coincides or intersects each other as AFC can never be zero.
- Minimum point of AVC lies to the left of minimum point of AC .

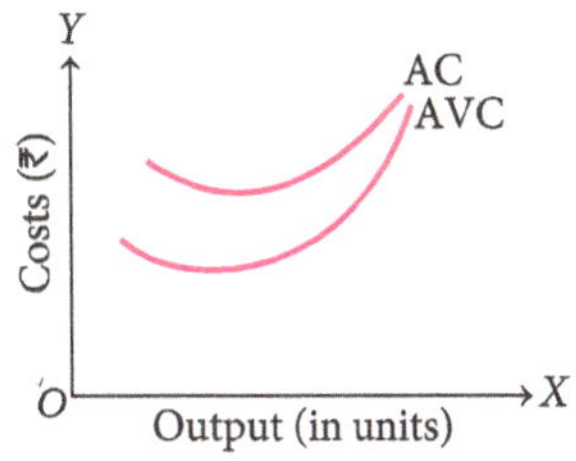

Relationship between AC and AVC

4. Relationship between AC, AVC And MC

- All the three cost curves i.e AC, AVC and MC are 'U' shaped.
- AVC and MC starts from the same point, while AC lies above AVC and MC.
- As long as MC is below AC and AVC (i.e. MC< AC and MC< AVC), both AC and AVC falls.
- MC is equal to AC and AVC at their respective minimum points, i.e. at point *d* and *c*.
- When MC is above AC and AVC (i.e. MC > AC and MC > AVC), both AC and AVC rises.

- The vertical gap between AC and AVC falls with rise in level of output as the gap represents AFC which decreases with increase in output.

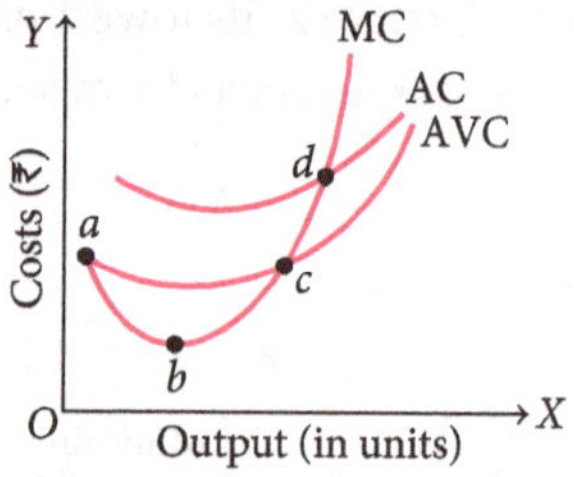

Relationship between AC, AVC and MC

In graph,
a = Starting point of AVC and MC
b = Minimum point of MC
c = Minimum point of AVC
d = Minimum point of AC

5. Relationship between Total Cost (TC) and Marginal Cost (MC)

- MC is estimated as the difference between TC of two successive units of output, i.e. MC is the slope of TC.

Thus, $MC_{nth} = TC_n - TC_{n-1}$

- When MC is diminishing, TC increases at a diminishing rate.
- When MC reaches its lowest point, TC stop increasing at a decreasing rate, it represents the point of inflexion of TC curve.
- When MC is rising , TC increases at an increasing rate.
- The area under MC represents TVC.

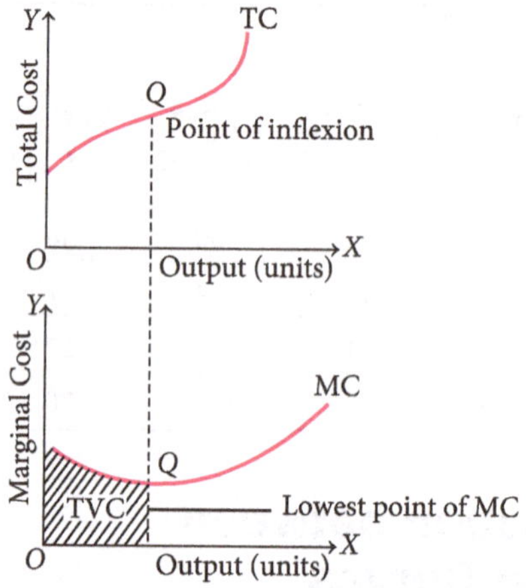

Relationship between TC and MC

Mind Map

CONCEPT OF COST

1 Cost

Cost refers to the monetary and non-monetary expenditure incurred by a producer on factor as well as non-factor inputs to produce a certain amount of output of a commodity.
The cost of production can also be classified as

- **Implicit Cost** It is the cost of self-owned resources (e.g. Land, capital). It is also called non-accounting cost and measured in terms of opportunity cost.
- **Explicit Cost** It includes actual payments to outsiders for hiring their services and goods.
- **Opportunity Cost** It is the value of next best alternative forgone.

Economic Cost = Explicit Cost + Implicit Cost

- **Cost Function** It is the functional relationship between output and cost of production. Cost function is given as

$$C = f(Q)$$

2 Short-run Costs

It is the combination of fixed and variable factors.

Fixed Cost (FC)/**Total Fixed Cost** (TFC)

- It is the cost of fixed factors of production.
- It is also called supplementary cost, overhead cost or indirect cost.
- e.g. Rent, insurance, permanent employee salaries.
- It remains constant in the short-run (incurred even at zero output).
- Total fixed cost curve is a horizontal straight line parallel to the x-axis.

Variable Cost (VC)/**Total Variable Cost** (TVC)

- It is the cost of variable factors of production.
- It is also called prime cost or direct cost.
- e.g. Wages, raw material cost, fuel, electricity.
- It varies directly with output (zero when output is zero).
- TVC curve is an inversely 'S' shaped curve.

3 Total Cost (TC)

- It is the aggregate of all production costs at a given output level. It comprises of two components, i.e. Total Fixed Cost (TFC) and Total Variable Cost (TVC).
- Formula: TC = TFC + TVC
- TFC remains constant, so changes in TC are due to TVC.
- TC curve is parallel to TVC curve and it is also inversely 'S'-shaped curve.

4 Average Cost (AC)

- It is the cost per unit of output produced. It comprises of two components, i.e. Average Fixed Cost (AFC) and Average Variable Cost (AVC).
- Formula: AC = TC/Output *or* AC = AFC + AVC

Average Fixed Cost (AFC) It is the fixed cost of producing per unit of the commodity.

AFC = TFC/Output

Average Variable Cost (AVC) It is the variable cost of producing per unit of the commodity.

AVC = TVC/Output

5 Marginal Cost (MC)

- It is the additional cost incurred when one more unit of output is produced.
- Formula: $MC = TC_n - TC_{n-1}$ *or* $MC = TVC_n - TVC_{n-1}$ *or* $MC = \Delta TC/\Delta Q$
- MC is derived from TC or TVC (TFC remains constant).
- MC curve falls initially, reaches a minimum and then rises due to diminishing returns.
- MC curve intersects AVC and AC curves at their lowest points.

6 Relationship between Average Cost (AC) and Marginal Cost (MC)

- Both AC and MC are U-shaped.
- When AC falls, MC < AC.
- When AC rises, MC > AC.
- When AC is constant and at its minimum, MC = AC.
- MC is always to the left of AC and cuts AC at its lowest point.

7 Relationship between Marginal Cost (MC) and Average Variable Cost (AVC)

- When AVC falls, MC < AVC.
- When AVC is constant and at its minimum, MC = AVC.
- When AVC rises, MC > AVC.
- Both AVC and MC curves are U-shaped.

8 Relationship between Average Cost (AC) and Average Variable Cost (AVC)

- Both AC and AVC are U-shaped (fall initially, reach a minimum, then rise).
- The gap between AC and AVC decreases as output increases (due to AFC decreasing).
- AC and AVC never intersect because AFC can never be positive.
- The minimum point of AVC lies to the left of the minimum point of AC.

9 Relationship between AC, AVC and MC

- All three curves (AC, AVC, MC) are U-shaped.
- AVC and MC start from the same point, while AC lies above AVC and MC.
- When MC < AC and AVC, both AC and AVC falls.
- MC = AC and AVC at their respective minimum points.
- When MC > AC and AVC, both AC and AVC rises.

10 Relationship between Total Cost (TC) and Marginal Cost (MC)

- MC = Change in TC (Slope of TC curve).
- When MC diminishes, TC increases at a diminishing rate.
- When MC reaches its lowest point, TC stops increasing at a decreasing rate (point of inflexion).
- When MC is rising, TC increases at an increasing rate.
- Area under MC represents TVC.

EXAM PATTERN QUESTIONS

Objective Type Questions

Multiple Choice Questions (MCQs)

1. What does the term 'cost' in economics refer to?

(a) Monetary expenditure only
(b) Non-monetary expenditure only
(c) Total monetary and non-monetary expenditure
(d) Total factor expenditure only

2. Cost function explains the relationship between

(a) income and expenditure
(b) input and output
(c) fixed cost and variable cost
(d) output and cost of production

3. **Gold prices hit a more than four week low on Monday, as the US dollar firmed after stronger than expected jobs data fanned concerns that the federal reserve might keep hiking interest rates.**

Source *https://economictimes.indiatimes.com/markets/commodities/news/gold-hits-over-4-week-low-as-dollar-edges-higher/articleshow/97633098.cms*

Which of the following costs is indicated in the above article? **Competency Based Que**

(a) Explicit cost (b) Implicit cost
(c) Opportunity cost (d) None of these

4. **Which of the following costs is highlighted in the given image?**

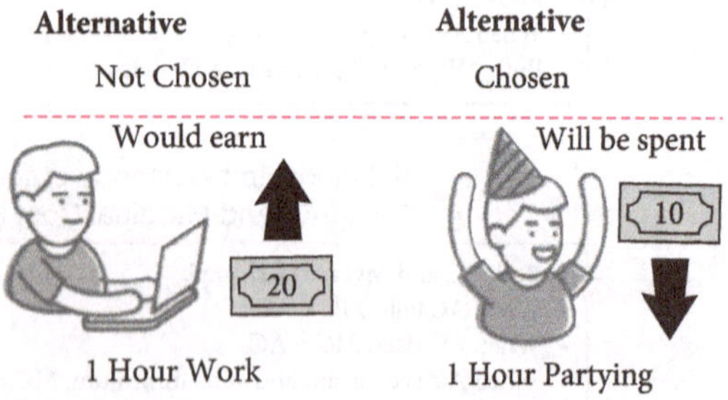

(a) Implicit cost (b) Explicit cost
(c) Total cost (d) Opportunity cost

5. **Arrange the following cost components in increasing order of flexibility.** **Competency Based Que**

(i) Marginal cost **(ii) Fixed cost**
(iii) Variable cost

Codes

(a) (ii), (iii), (i) (b) (ii), (i), (iii)
(c) (iii), (ii), (i) (d) (i), (iii), (ii)

6. **If TFC = ₹ 100 and TC = ₹ 300 when output is 10 units, TVC is ....**

(a) ₹ 500 (b) ₹ 400
(c) ₹ 600 (d) ₹ 200

7. **For 15 units of output, TVC is ₹ 450 and AFC is ₹ 10. What is the TC?**

(a) ₹ 600 (b) ₹ 800
(c) ₹ 650 (d) ₹ 700

8. **Observe the image given below and identify the implicit cost.**

Purchase of machinery for production   Rent of own building

(a) Purchase of machinery for production
(b) Rent of own building
(c) Both (a) and (b)
(d) Neither (a) nor (b)

9. **Identify the variable cost from the following.**

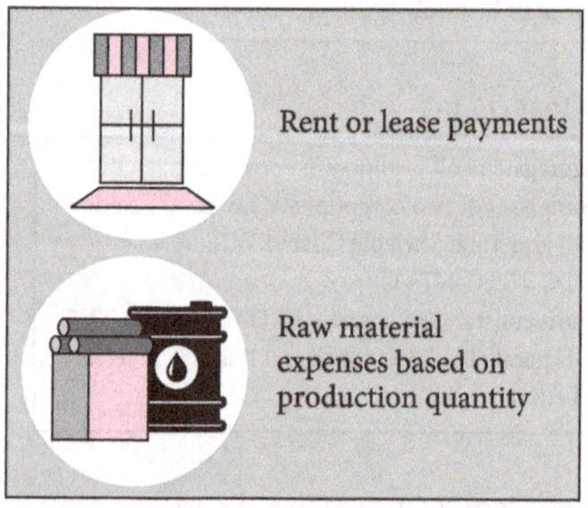

(a) Rent or lease payments
(b) Raw material expenses based on production quantity
(c) Both (a) and (b)
(d) None of the above

10. **Which statement is incorrect about Marginal Cost (MC)?**

(a) MC is derived from total cost
(b) MC affects fixed cost
(c) MC only impacts variable cost
(d) MC can be calculated as the addition to TVC

11. "The MC curve is U shaped." This indicates

I. marginal cost remains constant.
II. marginal cost initially falls and then rises.
III. marginal cost is always decreasing.
IV. marginal cost does not change with output.

Codes **Competency Based Que**

(a) I and II (b) Only III
(c) III and IV (d) Only II

12. Find the missing figures and choose the correct alternative. **Competency Based Que**

Output (Q)	TVC	AVC
1	25	...
2	...	15
3	48	...
4	...	18

(a) 25, 30, 16, 72 (b) 25, 30, 48, 72
(c) 25, 35, 16, 72 (d) 25, 45, 16, 72

13. "Income tax slab changes budget 2024 highlights: decoding changes in income tax slabs, standard deduction, capital gains tax, NPS in Budget 2024."

Source *https://economictimes.indiatimes.com/wealth/tax/income-tax-budget-2024-live-updates-income-tax-slab-changes-standard-deduction-new-income-tax-regime-announcements-finance-minister-nirmala-sitharaman-latest-news-23-july-2024/liveblog/111941622.cms?from=mdr*

How might changes in income tax slabs affect a producer's cost of production? **Competency Based Que**

(a) By increasing fixed costs through higher corporate taxes
(b) By decreasing variable costs through lower material prices
(c) By having no impact on the overall cost structure of production
(d) By increasing implicit costs due to higher opportunity costs

14. Which of the following is included in the computation of average cost? **Competency Based Que**

I. Total costs
II. Variable costs
III. Number of units produced
IV. Opportunity cost

Codes

(a) I and IV (b) II and III
(c) I and III (d) III and IV

15. The law of diminishing returns being at the level of output where **NCERT (QR)**

(a) MC at its minimum (b) AVC at its minimum
(c) AFC at its minimum (d) TC at its minimum

16. A manufacturing firm analyses its cost structures as it increases production from 10 to 50 units. The firm's management observes the relationships between Average Cost (AC), Average Fixed Cost (AFC) and Average Variable Cost (AVC) to make informed decisions about pricing and production levels.

Based on the firm's observations, which of the following statements is true regarding the relationship between AC, AFC and AVC? **Competency Based Que**

(a) The AC curve will always lie below the AVC curve as production increases
(b) AVC reaches its minimum point at the same output level as AC, indicating the efficiency of resource utilisation
(c) As production increases, the gap between the AC and AVC curves reduces, but they will never intersect due to the presence of fixed costs
(d) The AC will continue to rise even when AVC is at its minimum because fixed costs increase with output

17. When output is 6 units, TFC is ₹ 60 and TVC is ₹ 240. The AVC is .... **Competency Based Que**

(a) ₹ 40 (b) ₹ 45
(c) ₹ 50 (d) ₹ 55

18. If MC for producing the 5th unit is ₹ 20 and the TC for 4 units is ₹ 100, then TC for 5 units is .... **Competency Based Que**

(a) ₹ 200 (b) ₹ 150 (c) ₹ 120 (d) ₹ 100

19. Short-run supply curve of the firm is ....

(a) rising portion of MC curve
(b) rising portion of MC curve which lies above AVC curve
(c) rising portion of MC curve which lies above AFC curve
(d) entire MC curve

20. Which cost curve is given in the below image?

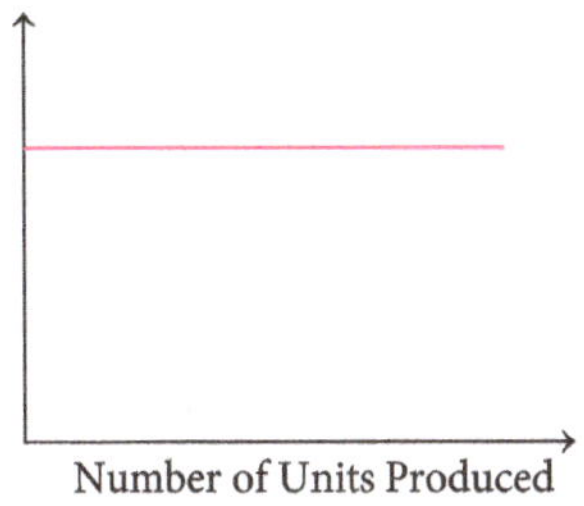

(a) Variable cost (b) Total fixed cost
(c) Marginal cost (d) Average cost

21. Area under MC curve is ....
(a) total cost
(b) total fixed cost
(c) total variable cost
(d) None of the above

22. When average cost curve is rising, then marginal cost ....
(a) must be decreasing (b) must be constant
(c) must be rising (d) Any of these

23. Identify the correct statement. Competency Based Que
(i) Both AC and AVC curves are U shaped.
(ii) MC cuts AVC at its maximum point.
(iii) The gap between AC and AVC narrows as output increases.
(iv) MC is always greater than AC at higher output levels.

Codes
(a) II and IV (b) I and II
(c) I, II, III and IV (d) I and III

24. Which of the following relationship is depicted in the below image?

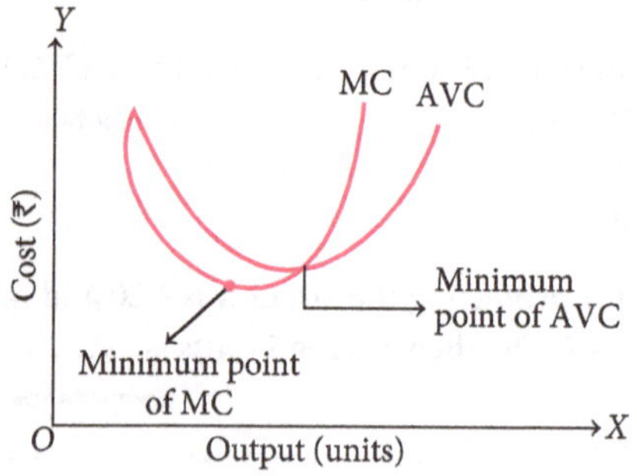

(a) MC curve cuts the AVC curve at its lowest point
(b) MC curve cuts the AVC curve at its highest point
(c) MC curve does not cut AVC curve
(d) When AVC is falling, MC is more than AVC

25. "The AC curve always lies above the AVC curve, as AC includes both AVC and AFC at all levels of output."
Which of the following accurately describes the relationship between Average Cost (AC) and Average Variable Cost (AVC)? Competency Based Que
(a) AC includes only variable costs
(b) AC is always lower than AVC
(c) AC is always greater than AVC at all levels of output
(d) AC and AVC curves intersect at some output levels

26. Which of the following best explains why the Average Fixed Cost (AFC) curve always declines as output increases? Competency Based Que
(a) Fixed costs decrease with an increase in output
(b) Variable costs remain constant with increasing output
(c) Fixed costs are spread over a larger number of units as output increases
(d) Marginal cost decreases as output increases

Direction *Read the case study and answer the questions 27 to 30 on the basis of the same*

XYZ Manufacturing is a company that produces custom furniture. The management team at XYZ has been analysing their production costs to improve profitability and efficiency. They categorised their costs into explicit and implicit costs, identified fixed and variable costs and examined the relationships between average cost, marginal cost and total cost.

In the last quarter, XYZ Manufacturing faced an increase in demand, leading to an increase in production from 500 to 800 units.

During the analysis, the team discovered that the Average Fixed Cost (AFC) was decreasing as output increased, while the Average Variable Cost (AVC) was initially decreasing but started to rise after reaching the optimal production level. They noted that the Marginal Cost (MC) decreased initially, reflecting increased efficiency, before beginning to rise due to the law of diminishing returns.

XYZ Manufacturing aims to maintain its competitive edge by carefully managing its cost structure, ensuring that they understand the implications of production levels on their costs.

The management is keen to utilise these insights to make informed decisions about scaling production further and optimising their operational efficiency.

27. The Total Cost (TC) of producing 800 units at XYZ Manufacturing can be calculated using the formula TC = ... + ...

28. What happens to the Average Variable Cost (AVC) as production initially increases at XYZ Manufacturing?
(a) AVC rises immediately
(b) AVC falls initially and then rises
(c) AVC remains constant
(d) AVC becomes irrelevant

29. When the Marginal Cost (MC) is below the Average Cost (AC), what effect does this have on the AC?
(a) AC increases (b) AC remains unchanged
(c) AC becomes zero (d) AC decreases

30. As output increases, the Average Fixed Cost (AFC) .... because fixed costs are spread over a larger number of units.

Assertion-Reason

Direction (Q.No. 31 to 40) *Read the following Assertion (A) and Reason (R) and choose the correct alternative from the following*

Alternatives

(a) Both Assertion (A) and Reason (R) are true and Reason (R) is the correct explanation of Assertion (A)
(b) Both Assertion (A) and Reason (R) are true, but Reason (R) is not the correct explanation of Assertion (A)
(c) Assertion (A) is true, but Reason (R) is false
(d) Assertion (A) is false, but Reason (R) is true

31. **Assertion** (A) The total of explicit and implicit costs is known as economic cost.

Reason (R) A cost function represents the relationship between the level of output and the cost of production.

32. **Assertion** (A) In the short-run, a producer faces only variable costs.

Reason (R) Variable costs fluctuate directly with the quantity of output produced.

33. **Assertion** (A) Total variable cost initially increases at a diminishing rate and eventually at an increasing rate.

Reason (R) In the initial phase of variable proportions, factors of production are highly efficient.

34. **Assertion** (A) As the output increases, AFC decreases because the fixed cost is spread over more units of production.

Reason (R) AFC can be zero as it is derived from TFC.

35. **Assertion** (A) Rate of change in marginal cost is higher than rate of change in average cost.

Reason (R) When average cost rises, marginal cost is above average cost.

36. **Assertion** (A) With increase in output, the gap between AC and AVC curves increases.

Reason (R) AVC reaches its minimum point at a level of output lower than that of AC.

37. **Assertion** (A) Both AC and MC are U shaped.

Reason (R) MC equals AC when AC is at its minimum point.

38. **Assertion** (A) When MC reaches its lowest point, TC stops increasing at a diminishing rate, marking the point of inflexion on the TC curve.

Reason (R) The area under the MC curve represents the average variable cost.

39. **Assertion** (A) MC equals AC and AVC at their respective maximum points.

Reason (R) AVC and MC start from the same point, while AC is always above AVC and MC.

40. **Assertion** (A) Marginal cost curve is inversely related to marginal product curve.

Reason (R) When variable factors are highly efficient, each unit add less to cost and more to output.

Two Statements Based MCQs

Direction (Q.No. 41 to 50) *Read the following statements carefully and choose the correct alternative*

Alternatives

(a) Statement I is correct and Statement II is incorrect
(b) Statement II is correct and Statement I is incorrect
(c) Both the statements are correct
(d) Both the statements are incorrect

41. **Statement I** Implicit cost is the estimated cost of self-owned and self-employed resources.

Statement II Implicit costs are non-accounting costs, often imputed based on market value.

42. **Statement I** Opportunity cost is the cost of the next best alternative that is forgone.

Statement II Opportunity costs are irrelevant in the computation of economic costs.

43. **Statement I** Fixed costs refer to expenditures on fixed factors of production that change with the level of output.

Statement II Variable costs do not fluctuate directly with the quantity of output produced.

44. **Statement I** Since fixed cost remain unchanged, any change in total cost is due to changes in variable costs.

Statement II Total cost refers to the cost per unit of output produced.

45. **Statement I** AVC curve is 'U' shaped due to law of variable proportions.

Statement II AVC initially falls due to increasing returns to a factor, reaches to its minimum level and then start rising due to diminishing returns to a factor.

46. **Statement I** Average cost always moves faster than marginal cost.

Statement II Average fixed cost is rectangular hyperbola shaped, which means with increase in output it tends to zero.

47. **Statement I** Both AC and AVC are V shaped, initially decreasing and eventually increasing.

Statement II The minimum point of AVC lies to the left of the minimum point of AC.

48. **Statement I** When MC is above AC and AVC, both AC and AVC rise.

Statement II All three cost curves i.e. AC, AVC and MC are U shaped.

49. **Statement I** When AC is falling, MC is more than AC.

Statement II When AC is rising, MC is lesser than AC.

50. **Statement I** Total fixed cost curve is horizontal line parallel to x-axis.

Statement II Average variable cost falls when it is greater than marginal cost.

Matching

51. Match the following

Column I		Column II
A. Implicit cost	(i)	Indirect costs, like overheads that support production.
B. Explicit cost	(ii)	The opportunity cost of using resources owned by the firm.
C. Prime costs	(iii)	The direct payment made to others for resources or services.
D. Supplementary costs	(iv)	The direct costs of materials and labour involved in production.

Codes

	A	B	C	D		A	B	C	D
(a)	(iii)	(iv)	(i)	(ii)	(b)	(iv)	(i)	(ii)	(iii)
(c)	(ii)	(iii)	(iv)	(i)	(d)	(iii)	(ii)	(i)	(iv)

52. Match the following

Column I		Column II
A. Fixed cost	(i)	AFC + AVC
B. Variable cost	(ii)	$TC_n - TC_{n-1}$
C. Average cost	(iii)	Salaries of permanent staff
D. Marginal cost	(iv)	Raw material costs

Codes

	A	B	C	D		A	B	C	D
(a)	(iii)	(iv)	(i)	(ii)	(b)	(iv)	(i)	(ii)	(iii)
(c)	(ii)	(iii)	(iv)	(i)	(d)	(iii)	(ii)	(i)	(iv)

53. Match the following

Column I		Column II
A. AC curve	(i)	MC > AC
B. AC is falling	(ii)	MC < AC
C. AC is rising	(iii)	U shaped
D. MC = AC	(iv)	AC at minimum point

Codes

	A	B	C	D		A	B	C	D
(a)	(iii)	(iv)	(i)	(ii)	(b)	(iv)	(i)	(ii)	(iii)
(c)	(ii)	(iii)	(iv)	(i)	(d)	(iii)	(ii)	(i)	(iv)

54. Match the following

Column I		Column II
A. AVC	(i)	TFC/Number of units produced
B. AFC	(ii)	AFC + AVC
C. AC	(iii)	TFC + TVC
D. TC	(iv)	TVC/Number of units produced

Codes

	A	B	C	D		A	B	C	D
(a)	(iii)	(iv)	(i)	(ii)	(b)	(iv)	(i)	(ii)	(iii)
(c)	(ii)	(iii)	(iv)	(i)	(d)	(iii)	(ii)	(i)	(iv)

55. Match the options of Column I with correct options in Column II

Column I		Column II
A. $\Sigma MC + TFC$	(i)	$Q = 0$
B. $TVC_n - TVC_{n-1}$	(ii)	TC
C. $(AC \times Q) - (AVC \times Q)$	(iii)	MC
D. $TC = TFC$	(iv)	TFC

Codes

	A	B	C	D
(a)	(i)	(ii)	(iii)	(iv)
(b)	(ii)	(iii)	(iv)	(i)
(c)	(iii)	(iv)	(i)	(ii)
(d)	(iv)	(i)	(ii)	(iii)

Concept Identification

56. It refers to the total monetary and non-monetary expenditure incurred to produce goods or services.

57. It describes the direct payment made to others for resources or services in production.

58. It indicates the fixed cost per unit of output that decreases as production increases.

59. It illustrates how costs change with different levels of output in production.

60. It encompasses both fixed and variable costs at a given level of output.

Answers

1. (c) Total monetary and non-monetary expenditure
2. (d) output and cost of production
3. (d) None of these
4. (d) Opportunity cost
5. (a) Fixed cost is least flexible as it remains constant regardless of production level. Variable cost is more flexible as it changes in proportion to output. Marginal cost is most flexible since it reflects the additional cost of producing one more unit, making it highly responsive to changes in production.
6. (d) TC = TFC + TVC $\Rightarrow$ 300 = 100 + TVC
   TVC = 300 − 100 = ₹ 200
7. (a) TFC = AFC × Output = 10 × 15 = ₹ 150
   Now, TC = 150 + 450 = ₹ 600
8. (b) Rent of own building
9. (b) Raw material expenses based on production quantity
10. (b) MC affects fixed cost
11. (d) Only II
12. (a) TVC = AVC × Q, AVC = TVC/Q
13. (a) By increasing fixed costs through higher corporate taxes
14. (c) I and III
15. (a) MC at its minimum
16. (c) As production increases, the gap between the AC and AVC curves reduces, but they will never intersect due to the presence of fixed costs
17. (a) AVC = TVC/Output = 240/6 = 40
18. (c) TC for 5 units = TC for 4 units + MC
    = 100 + 20 = ₹ 120
19. (b) rising portion of MC curve which lies above AVC curve
20. (b) Total fixed cost
21. (c) total variable cost
22. (c) must be rising
23. (d) I and III
24. (a) MC curve cuts the AVC curve at its lowest point
25. (c) AC is always greater than AVC at all levels of output
26. (c) Fixed costs are spread over a larger number of units as output increases
27. TFC, TVC
28. (b) AVC falls initially and then rises
29. (d) When Marginal Cost (MC) is below Average Cost (AC), the AC decreases. This is because producing an additional unit at a lower cost pulls the average down.
30. decreases
31. (b) Both Assertion (A) and Reason (R) are true, but Reason (R) is not the correct explanation of Assertion (A)
32. (d) In the short-run, a producer faces both fixed and variable costs, as some factors of production are fixed while others can vary.
33. (a) Both Assertion (A) and Reason (R) are true and Reason (R) is the correct explanation of Assertion (A)
34. (c) AFC can never be zero as it is derived from TFC and fixed costs can never be zero that is why AFC never touches either x-axis or y-axis.
35. (b) Both Assertion (A) and Reason (R) are true, but Reason (R) is not the correct explanation of Assertion (A)
36. (d) With increase in output, the gap between AC and AVC curves reduces but they never intersect each other.
37. (b) Both Assertion (A) and Reason (R) are true, but Reason (R) is not the correct explanation of Assertion (A)
38. (c) The area under the MC curve represents the Total Variable Cost (TVC).
39. (d) MC equals AC and AVC at their respective minimum points.
40. (a) Both Assertion (A) and Reason (R) are true and Reason (R) is the correct explanation of Assertion (A)
41. (c) Both the statements are correct
42. (a) Opportunity costs are the cost of the next best alternative that is forgone when resources are used for the current production. It is crucial as it forms the basis of understanding economic cost.
43. (d) Fixed costs refer to expenditures on fixed factors of production that do not change with the level of output. Variable costs fluctuate directly with the quantity of output produced.
44. (a) Average cost refers to the cost per unit of output produced.
45. (c) Both the statements are correct
46. (d) MC moves faster than AC. AFC can never be zero as TFC is always positive.
47. (b) Both AC and AVC are U shaped, initially decreasing and eventually increasing.
48. (c) Both the statements are correct
49. (d) When AC is falling, MC is less than AC. When AC is rising, MC is greater than AC.
50. (c) Both the statements are correct
51. (c) (ii) (iii) (iv) (i)
52. (a) (iii) (iv) (i) (ii)
53. (d) (iii) (ii) (i) (iv)
54. (b) (iv) (i) (ii) (iii)
55. (b) (ii) (iii) (iv) (i)
56. Cost
57. Explicit cost
58. Average Fixed Cost (AFC)
59. Cost function
60. Total cost

Subjective Questions

Short Answer Type Questions

1. A producer borrows money and opens a shop. The shop premises is owned by him. Identify implicit cost and explicit cost from this information. Explain. Competency Based Que

Ans. In the above example, interest paid on borrowed money will be explicit cost, whereas, the imputed rent of the shop premises is implicit cost.

Explicit Cost
These are those cash payments, which firms make to outsiders for their services and goods. e.g. Wages, payment for raw material, rent, interest, etc.

Implicit Cost
These are the costs of self-owned and self-employed resources. e.g. Entrepreneur may utilise his own building for factory use, interest on self-capital, etc.

2. If a firm's variable cost increases while the fixed cost remains constant, how will it impact the total cost? Competency Based Que

Ans. The total cost will increase as variable costs rise with production levels. Fixed costs remain constant, so any change in total cost is due to changes in variable costs, which are dependent on output. This highlights the impact of production volume on total cost.

3. Identify the type of cost depicted in the given image. Competency Based Que

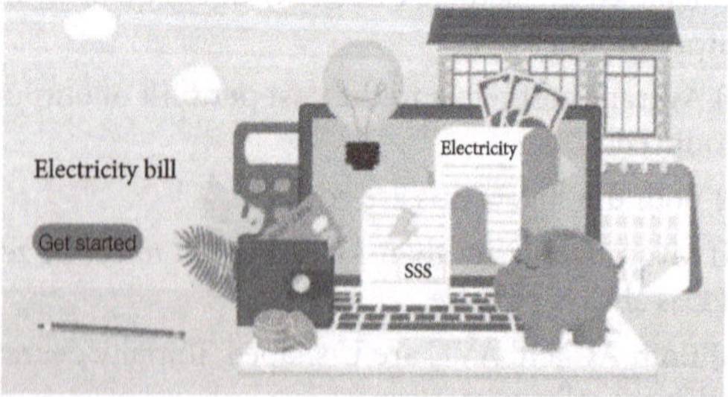

Ans. The type of cost depicted in an electricity bill is classified as an explicit cost. These are actual payments made to external parties for services and goods. In this case, the electricity bill represents a direct payment made to the utility company for the electricity consumed. This payment is a cash outflow and is easily measurable, as it reflects the cost incurred for a specific service used in the production process or in daily operations.

4. Briefly explain the concept of the cost function. NCERT

Ans. A cost function shows the functional relationship between output and cost of production.

$$C = f(Q)$$

Where, C = Cost
f = Functional relationship
Q = Units of output

5. "At the initial stages of production, TVC increases at a diminishing rate." Justify. Competency Based Que

Ans. Yes, the above statement is correct that at the initial stages, TVC increases at a diminishing rate. This is due to the applicability of law of variable proportions'.

In the first stage of this law, with every additional unit of variable factor employed, total product increases at an increasing rate. Because of this total variable cost increases at a diminishing rate.

6. A firm decides to increase its scale of production by expanding its factory and hiring more workers. How would this decision impact the long-run cost curves, particularly the Average Cost (AC) curve and what role do economies of scale play in this context?

Ans. In the long-run, when a firm increases its scale of production, all factors of production become variable. If the firm experiences economies of scale, the Average Cost (AC) curve will shift downward due to a reduction in per-unit costs as output increases.

This occurs because larger-scale operations often lead to operational efficiencies, better utilisation of resources and lower input costs. However, if diseconomies of scale set in, the AC curve may rise due to inefficiencies or challenges in managing a larger scale of operations. Thus, the decision's impact on costs depends on whether the firm achieves economies or diseconomies of scale.

7. Differentiate between fixed cost and variable cost.

Ans. Differences between fixed cost and variable cost are

Basis	Fixed Cost	Variable Cost
Meaning	It is incurred on fixed factors of production. It does not change with change in quantity of output.	It is incurred on variable factors of production. It changes with change in quantity of output.
Output	It remains the same whether output is zero or maximum.	It is zero when output is zero. It increases with increase in output and decreases with decrease in output.
Examples	Rent of building, licence fee, etc.	Cost of raw material, wages of casual labour, etc.

8. "Marginal cost is the additional cost incurred when one more unit of output is produced." Do you agree? Give reason. Competency Based Que

Ans. Yes. Marginal Cost (MC) is the additional cost associated with producing one more unit of output. It reflects the change in total cost that results from increasing production by a single unit and is important for understanding production efficiency.

As firms analyse marginal costs, they can make informed decisions about scaling production, managing resources and optimising profit margins.

9. "The expenditure incurred to produce goods or services is known as cost." What is the significance of understanding the concept of cost in production? Competency Based Que

Ans. Understanding the concept of cost is crucial for producers as it helps them determine pricing strategies, analyse profitability and make informed decisions regarding resource allocation. It allows businesses to identify areas where they can minimise expenses, thereby improving their overall financial performance.

10. "Prime costs are the direct costs of materials and labour involved in production." In what way do prime costs affect the pricing strategy of a product? Competency Based Que

Ans. Prime costs directly impact the pricing strategy of a product as they constitute the essential expenses required to manufacture goods.

Understanding these costs helps businesses establish a minimum price point to cover expenses while ensuring a profit margin. If prime costs are too high relative to the market price, it may prompt a revaluation of production methods or sourcing strategies.

11. What does the average fixed cost curve look like? Why does it look so? NCERT

Ans. AFC curve is downward sloping to right. As the output increases, the average fixed cost gets decreased, i.e. AFC falls. It is rectangular hyperbola shaped. It looks so, because TFC is constant at all levels of output. So, the area below AFC curve is the same at different output levels.

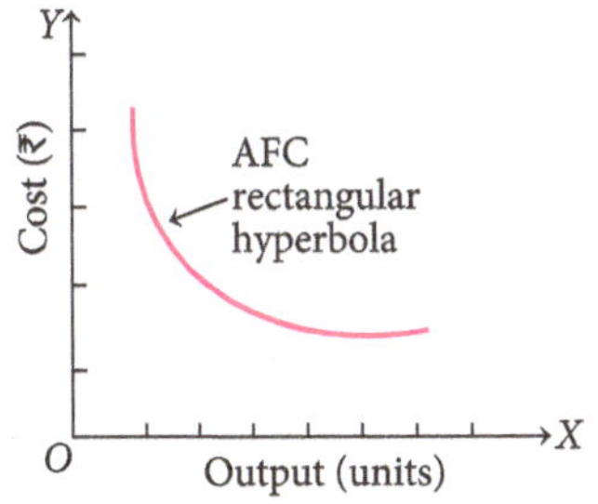

12. Why is the short-run marginal cost curve U shaped? NCERT

Ans. Short-run marginal cost curve is U shaped because of the law of variable proportions.

In the short-run, as the employment of variable factor increases (fixed factor being constant) in the initial stage MC decreases owing to increasing return but finally tends to rise in accordance with the law of variable proportion. Hence, the U shape of MC.

13. "The cost of producing one unit of output is referred to as the unit cost of production." Why is it critical for manufacturers to monitor unit costs regularly? Competency Based Que

Ans. Monitoring unit costs is critical for manufacturers because it directly influences pricing, profitability and competitiveness in the market. Regular analysis of unit costs allows businesses to identify trends, assess production efficiency and make timely adjustments to operations that can lead to cost reductions and improved financial outcomes.

14. Giving reasons, state whenever the following statements are true or false. Competency Based Que

(i) Average product will increase only when marginal product increases.

(ii) With increase in level of output, average fixed cost goes on falling till reaches zero.

(iii) Under diminishing returns to factor, total product continues to increase till marginal product reaches zero.

Ans. (i) False, average product can rise even when marginal product falls, but lies above AP.

(ii) False, because as output increases, average fixed cost falls but can never be zero. Average fixed cost must remain positive even when it is falling continuously with rise in output.

(iii) True, total product declines only when marginal product is negative.

15. Differentiate between average cost and marginal cost.

Ans. Differences between average cost and marginal cost are

Basis	Average Cost	Marginal Cost
Meaning	It is the per unit cost of output.	It is the change in total cost when more and more additional unit of a commodity is produced.
Formula	$AC = TC/Q$	$MC_{nth} = TC_n - TC_{n-1}$ or $\Delta TC/\Delta Q$
Example	Production of 10 units is ₹ 70, then AC = 70 ÷ 10 = ₹ 7.	For producing, 4 units of a commodity costs ₹ 170 and 5th unit costs ₹ 200. Then, MC = 200 − 170 = ₹ 30.

16. (i) What are cost curves?

(ii) What relationship is depicted in the below image?

Competency Based Que

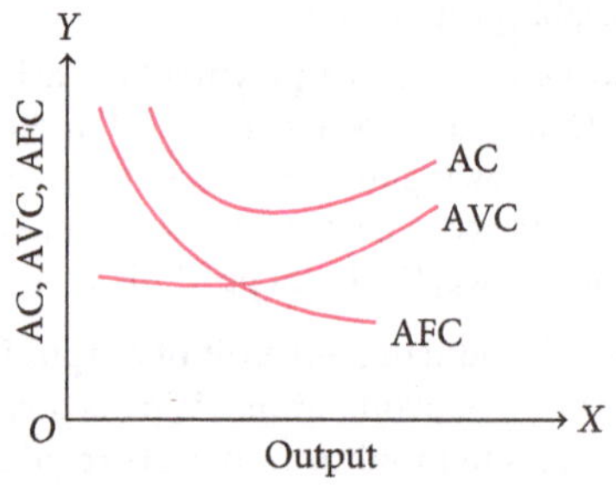

Ans. (i) Cost curves are graphical representations that illustrate the relationship between the quantity of output produced and the associated costs of production.

They are essential tools in economics and managerial accounting for analysing how cost changes as production levels vary.

(ii) The image depicts the relationship between AC, AVC and AFC

- AC curve always lie above the AVC curve, as AC includes both AVC and AFC at all levels of output.
- AVC reaches its minimum point at a level of output lower than that of AC. It is so because; AC continues to fall due to falling AFC, when AVC is at its minimum point.
- With increase in output, the gap between AC and AVC curves reduces but they never intersect each other.

17. "AC is more consistent than MC." Discuss.

Competency Based Que

Ans. AC is more consistent because it is not directly affected by the law of variable proportion.

On the other hand, MC is directly affected by law of variable proportion due to which it is narrow 'U' shaped curve whereas, AC curve is wide 'U' shaped curve.

18. Why AFC curve is a rectangular hyperbola?

Ans. Average Fixed Cost (AFC) is derived from TFC, which remains constant for all levels of output whether output is zero or 100. Hence, AFC is per unit TFC. Because of this, the area under AFC remains constant for all levels of output. As a result, AFC curve is rectangular hyperbola.

19. "The minimum point of AVC lies to the left of the minimum point of AC." Do you agree? Give reason.

Competency Based Que

Ans. Yes, "The minimum point of Average Variable Cost (AVC) lies to the left of the minimum point of Average Cost (AC)" is accurate.

This occurs because AVC, which reflects the variable costs per unit of output, reaches its minimum before AC, as AC includes both variable and fixed costs.

Graphically, as production increases, Average Fixed Costs (AFC) decrease, allowing AC to continue falling even after AVC has hit its minimum. Thus, the minimum AVC occurs at a lower output level than the minimum AC, illustrating the relationship between variable and fixed costs in production.

20. "The area under the MC curve represents the Total Variable Cost (TVC)." Why understanding the relationship between marginal cost and total variable cost crucial for effective cost management in production?

Competency Based Que

Ans. Understanding the relationship between Marginal Cost (MC) and Total Variable Cost (TVC) is essential for effective cost management because it guides managers in making informed production and pricing decisions. The area under the MC curve represents the TVC, showing how total variable costs increase with each additional unit produced.

By analysing this relationship, managers can identify the optimal production level where marginal costs align with marginal revenue, maximising profits and minimising waste. This insight aids in strategic planning, resource allocation and overall cost control.

Long Answer Type Questions

21. What are the total fixed cost, total variable cost and total cost of a firm? How are they related?

NCERT

Ans. (i) **Total Fixed Cost**

The cost which does not change with the change in output. Even when output is zero. In other words, fixed costs are the sum total expenditure on the purchase or hiring of fixed factors of production.

(ii) **Total Variable Cost**

The cost which change with the change in output. In other words, variable costs are the expenditure incurred on the use of variable factors of production.

(iii) **Total Cost**

Total cost is the sum total of total fixed cost and total variable cost at various level of output.

Relationship among TFC, TVC and TC

Relationship between TFC, TVC and TC can be understood with the help of the following points, schedule and graph below

- TC is the sum total of TFC and TVC.
- TFC is constant at all levels of output.
- TVC increases as output increases.
- TC is parallel to TVC.

Cost Schedule Table

Output (units)	**TFC**	**TVC**	**TC = TFC + TVC**
0	15	0	15 + 0 = 15
1	15	5	15 + 5 = 20
2	15	12	15 + 12 = 27
3	15	20	15 + 20 = 35
4	15	28	15 + 28 = 43
5	15	35	15 + 35 = 50
6	15	42	15 + 42 = 57

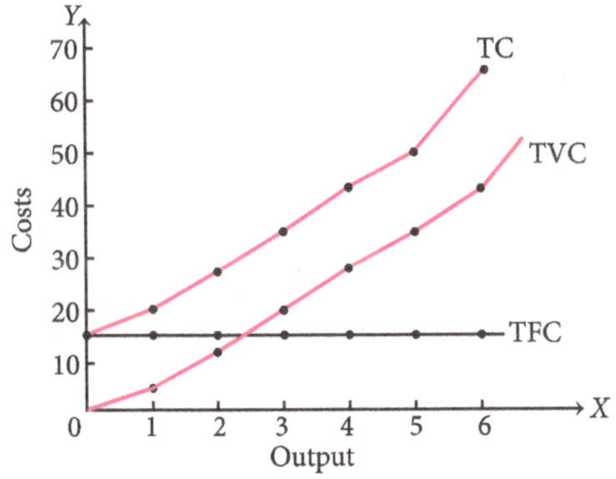

22. **What are the average fixed cost, average variable cost and average cost of a firm? How are they related?** **NCERT**

Ans. (i) **Average Fixed Cost** (AFC)

It refers to the per unit fixed cost of production.

Calculated as $AFC = \frac{TFC}{Q}$

where, TFC = Total Fixed Cost
Q = Quantity of Output

(ii) **Average Variable Cost** (AVC)

It refers to the per unit variable cost of production.

Calculated as $AVC = \frac{TVC}{Q}$

where TVC = Total Variable Cost
Q = Quantity of Output

(iii) **Average Cost** (AC)

It refers to the per unit total cost of production.

Calculated as $AC = \frac{TC}{Q}$

where, TC = Total Cost
Q = Quantity of Output

Relation of AFC, AVC and AC

Relationship between AFC, AVC and AC is as follows

- AC is sum total of AFC and AVC.
- AC and AVC can never be equal for any level of output.
- AFC is never zero as TFC is fixed at all levels of output.
- AFC must fall because TFC is constant.
- The curves of AC and AVC never intersect.

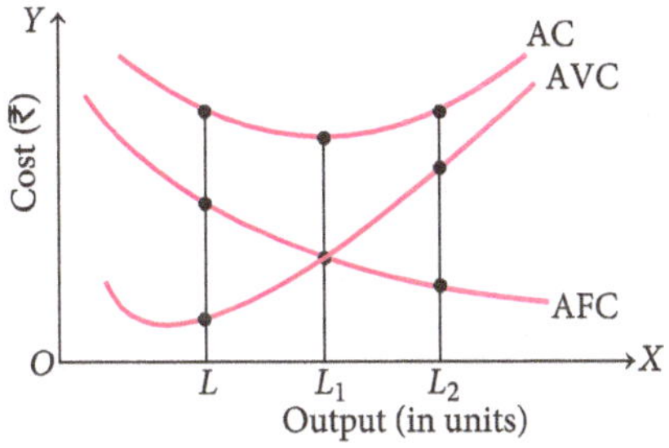

23. **"When AVC is decreasing, it indicates that producing additional units lowers the average cost per unit."**

What does this suggest about the relationship between AVC and MC during this phase of production? **Competency Based Que**

Ans. When Average Variable Cost (AVC) is decreasing, it suggests that the Marginal Cost (MC) of producing additional units is less than the AVC.

This relationship implies that each additional unit produced is adding a smaller cost than the average cost of the previous units, resulting in a reduction in the overall average cost per unit. As more units are produced efficiently, the benefits of spreading fixed costs over a larger output and achieving economies of scale come into play.

Consequently, this scenario indicates that the firm is likely operating at an efficient production level, where the cost of production is optimised and profit margins can potentially increase.

24. **How does the relationship between Total Cost (TC) and Marginal Cost (MC) affect a firm's decision-making process regarding output levels? Provide example to illustrate your answer.**

Ans. The relationship between Total Cost (TC) and Marginal Cost (MC) significantly influences a firm's output decisions.

When a firm considers increasing production, it evaluates the additional cost of producing one more unit, represented by MC. If the MC is less than the price at which the product can be sold, the firm can increase profits by producing more.

For instance, if a toy manufacturer finds that the cost of producing an additional toy is \$10, but it can sell it for \$15, it will likely increase production to capitalise on this profit margin.

Conversely, if the MC exceeds the price (say it costs \$20 to make an additional toy but only sells for \$15), the firm may decide to reduce production to avoid losses.

This relationship also helps firms identify optimal production levels. When the MC curve intersects the TC curve, it indicates the point at which producing more units will no longer be beneficial.

e.g. If a car manufacturer experiences a rising MC due to inefficiencies as production scales up, it may signal a need to reconsider its production strategy. Ultimately, understanding the interaction between TC and MC aids firms in maximising their profits while ensuring they do not overextend themselves in production.

25. Based upon the image given below, explain the relationship between the cost curves given.

Competency Based Que

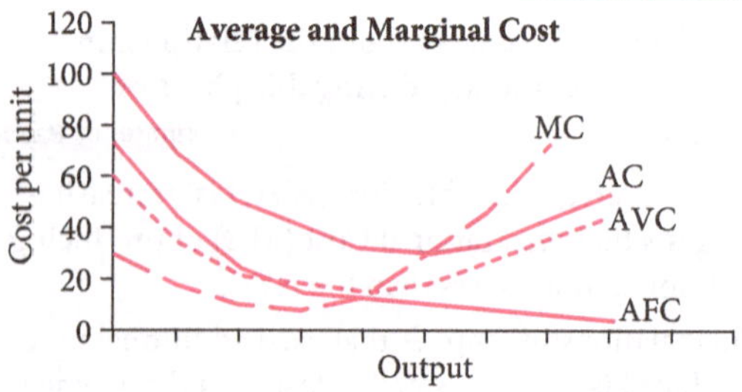

Ans. Relationship between MC, AC, AVC and AFC is as follows

(i) In the beginning, both AVC and AFC curves fall. Hence, the AC curve falls as well.

(ii) AVC curve starts rising, but the AFC curve is still falling. Hence, the ATC curve continues to fall.
This is because, during this phase, the fall in the AFC curve is greater than the rise in the AVC curve.

(iii) As the output rises further, the AVC curve rises sharply. This offsets the fall in the AFC curve. Hence, the AC curve falls initially and then rises.

(iv) If the average cost falls due to an increase in the output, the marginal cost is less than the average cost.

(v) If the average cost rises due to an increase in the output, the marginal cost is more than the average cost.

(vi) Marginal cost is equal to the average cost when the average cost is minimum. It can be seen in the given figure that the MC curve cuts the AC curve at its minimum or optimum point.

26. "MC equals AVC at the minimum point of AVC curve." Why is this intersection significant for determining the optimal level of production efficiency?

Competency Based Que

Ans. The intersection of Marginal Cost (MC) and Average Variable Cost (AVC) at the minimum point of the AVC curve is significant for determining optimal production efficiency for several reasons.

First, when MC equals AVC, it indicates that producing one more unit does not increase the average variable cost; this is a critical point in production where efficiency is maximised. At this level of output, the firm is utilising its resources effectively, as any additional production will not raise the average cost per unit, allowing the firm to maximise its profitability.

Moreover, this intersection serves as a crucial indicator for decision-making. When firms are operating at this point, they can be confident that they are not over-extending their resources.

If production continues beyond this intersection, MC will begin to rise above AVC, leading to increasing average costs. Consequently, firms need to monitor this relationship closely, as operating at or near this optimal point allows for better pricing strategies and enhanced competitiveness in the market. Thus, understanding the significance of this intersection aids in strategic planning, ensuring that firms can maintain or enhance their production efficiency while optimising their cost structures.

27. Explain the relationship between AC and MC curve, and MC and AVC curve.

Ans. Relationship between Average Cost (AC) **and Marginal Cost** (MC)

(i) Both AC and MC are U shaped.

(ii) When AC is falling, MC is less than AC.

(iii) When AC is rising, MC is greater than AC.

(iv) MC equals AC when AC is at its minimum point and constant.

(v) MC curve cuts the AC curve from its lowest point and is always to the left of AC.

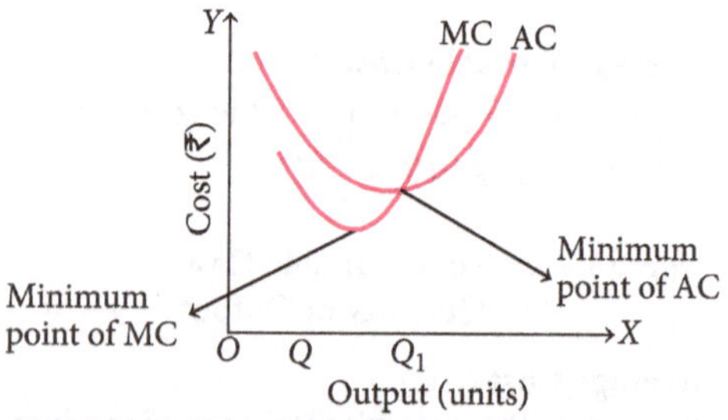

Diagrammatic representation of relationship between AC and MC

Relationship between Marginal Cost (MC) **and Average Variable Cost** (AVC)

(i) Both AVC and MC are U shaped and start from the same point.

(ii) When AVC is falling, MC is less than AVC.

(iii) When AVC is constant and minimum, MC equals AVC.

(iv) When AVC is rising, MC is greater than AVC.

(v) MC curve cuts the AVC curve at its lowest point.

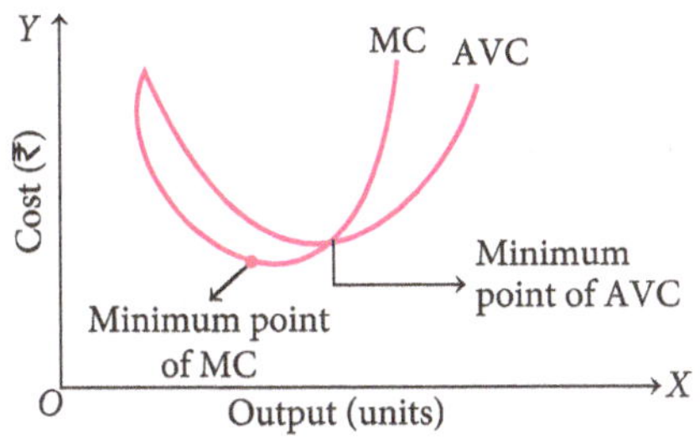

Diagrammatic representation of relationship between MC and AVC

28. XYZ Manufacturing, a mid-sized producer of electronic components, faced pressure to enhance production efficiency and control costs. The company focused on its variable costs, which included raw materials, labour and utilities. Analysing the Average Variable Cost (AVC) and Marginal Cost (MC) curves revealed that AVC decreased at lower output levels due to economies of scale. However, as production expanded beyond a certain point, MC began to rise, surpassing AVC, indicating diminishing returns on additional units produced. In response, XYZ Manufacturing implemented strategies to optimise production. They invested in advanced machinery to improve efficiency and adopted a just in time inventory system, which reduced storage costs and waste.

These initiatives allowed the company to increase production capacity while controlling costs. As a result, XYZ Manufacturing observed improved profitability and maintained a competitive edge by effectively managing its cost structure and making informed decisions based on the relationships between Total Cost (TC), Average Cost (AC) and Marginal Cost (MC).

(i) What does it mean when the Marginal Cost (MC) surpasses Average Variable Cost (AVC) in XYZ Manufacturing's production process?

(ii) How does understanding the relationship between Total Cost (TC) and Average Cost (AC) help XYZ Manufacturing in its decision-making process?

(iii) Discuss the implications of AVC decreasing initially and then increasing as production rises for cost management at XYZ Manufacturing. How do these changes affect overall production strategy? **Competency Based Que**

Ans. (i) It indicates diminishing returns on production, suggesting that producing additional units increases average costs.

(ii) Understanding this relationship enables XYZ Manufacturing to determine the optimal level of production where AC is minimised, ensuring maximum cost efficiency.

(iii) The initial decrease in AVC indicates improved efficiency and cost effectiveness at lower output levels, allowing the company to capitalise on economies of scale.

However, once AVC begins to rise, it signals that production is becoming less efficient, which prompts the company to reassess its production strategy.

This knowledge helps XYZ Manufacturing to optimise output levels, make necessary adjustments to avoid overproduction and implement cost control measures to sustain profitability.

Numerical Questions

Numerical 1

XYZ Manufacturing currently produces 1,000 electronic components. The Total Fixed Cost (TFC) is \$ 5,000 and the Total Variable Cost (TVC) at this production level is \$ 15,000. Calculate the Average Cost (AC) per unit produced.

Sol. Total Cost (TC) = TFC + TVC

TC = 5,000 + 15,000 = ₹ 20,000

$$\text{Average Cost (AC)} = \frac{\text{TC}}{\text{Total units produced}}$$

$$\text{AC} = \frac{20,000}{1,000} = ₹\ 20 \text{ per unit}$$

Numerical 2

A lawyer who is currently working at a corporate law firm is thinking about starting their own legal practice. After establishing their private law practice, the lawyer expects to earn around ₹ 8,00,000 per year. This lawyer may require office space and an assistant to function.

According to the lawyer, the cost of renting an office space may be ₹ 3,00,000 per year, while the cost of hiring an assistant could be around ₹ 2,40,000 per year. What is the explicit cost of the lawyer?

Sol. Explicit Costs = Office Rental + Assistant's Salary

Explicit Costs = 3,00,000 + 2,40,000 = ₹ 5,40,000

Numerical 3

Rishi started a business by investing ₹ 5 lakh. ₹ 4 lakh was borrowed from a bank at 10% p.a. interest. He hired a manager to look after his business and paid him ₹ 30,000 per month as salary. Rishi used his own land for start-up, which has a market price of ₹ 5,000 per month, if taken on rent. Calculate implicit cost and explicit cost per annum in this case.

Sol. Explicit Cost = Interest on Loan + Salary of Manager
= (10% of 4,00,000) + (30,000 × 12)
= 40,000 + 3,60,000 = ₹ 4,00,000

Implicit Cost = Interest on Self-supplied Sum + Imputed Value of Owner's Land
= (10% of 1,00,000) + (5,000 × 12)
= 10,000 + 60,000 = ₹ 70,000

Numerical 4

Complete the following table

Output (Q) (units)	Total Variable Cost (TVC) (₹)	Average Variable Cost (AVC) (₹)	Marginal Cost (MC) (₹)
1	10	...	...
2	...	8	6
3	27	...	...
4	...	10	13

Sol.

Output (Q) (units)	**TVC** (₹) (AVC× Q)	**AVC** (₹) (TVC/Q)	**MC** (₹) ($TVC_n - TVC_{n-1}$)
1	10	**10**	**10**
2	**16**	8	6
3	27	**9**	**11**
4	**40**	10	13

Numerical 5

Complete the following table

Output (units)	Total Variable Cost (TVC) (₹)	Average Variable Cost (AVC) (₹)	Marginal Cost (MC) (₹)
1	...	12	...
2	20	...	...
3	...	10	10
4	40	...	...

Sol.

Output (Q) (units)	**TVC** (₹) (AVC×Q)	**AVC** (₹) (TVC/Q)	**MC** (₹) ($TVC_n - TVC_{n-1}$)
1	**12**	12	**12**
2	20	**10**	**8**
3	**30**	10	10
4	40	**10**	**10**

Numerical 6

Calculate total cost and average variable cost of a firm at each given level of output from its cost schedule given below

Output (units)	1	2	3	4	5	6
Average Fixed Cost (AFC) (₹)	60	30	20	15	12	10
Marginal Cost (MC) (₹)	32	30	28	30	35	43

Sol.

Output (Q) (units)	**AFC** (₹)	**TFC** (₹)	**MC** (₹)	**TVC** (₹)	**AVC** (₹)	**TC** (₹)
1	60	60	32	32	32	92
2	30	60	30	62	31	122
3	20	60	28	90	30	150
4	15	60	30	120	30	180
5	12	60	35	155	31	215
6	10	60	43	198	33	258

Formulae used

$TC = TFC + TVC$; $TVC = AVC \times Q$; $AVC = TVC/Q$ *or* $AC - AFC$

$MC = TVC_n - TVC_{n-1}$; $AFC = \frac{TFC}{Q}$; $TFC = AFC \times Q$

Numercial 7

Calculate total variable cost and total cost from the following cost schedule of a firm whose fixed costs are ₹ 10.

Output (units)	1	2	3	4
Marginal Cost (MC) (₹)	6	5	4	6

Sol.

Output (Q) (units)	**TFC** (₹)	**MC** (₹)	**TVC** (₹) (ΣMC)	**TC** (₹) (TFC + TVC)
1	10	6	6	16
2	10	5	11	21
3	10	4	15	25
4	10	6	21	31

Numerical 8

Calculate total variable cost and marginal cost from the following cost schedule of a firm, whose total fixed costs are ₹ 12.

Output (units)	1	2	3	4
Total Cost (TC) (₹)	20	26	31	38

Sol.

Output (Q) (units)	**TC** (₹)	**TFC** (₹)	**TVC** (₹) (TC − TFC)	**MC** (₹) ($TVC_n - TVC_{n-1}$)
1	20	12	8	8
2	26	12	14	6
3	31	12	19	5
4	38	12	26	7

Numerical 9

Complete the following table

Output (units)	Average Fixed Cost (AFC) (₹)	Marginal Cost (MC) (₹)	Total Cost (TC) (₹)
1	...	...	72
2	...	10	82
3	20	8	...
4	...	...	99
5	12	10	...

Sol.

Output (Q) (units)	Total Fixed Cost (TFC) (₹) (AFC × Q)	Average Fixed Cost (AFC) (₹) (TFC/Q)	Marginal Cost (MC) (₹) ($TC_n - TC_{n-1}$)	Total Cost (TC) (₹)
1	60	**60**	**12**	72
2	60	**30**	10	82
3	60	20	8	**90**
4	60	**15**	**9**	99
5	60	12	10	**109**

Numerical 10

Complete the following table

Output (units)	Marginal Cost (MC) (₹)	Average Variable Cost (AVC) (₹)	Average Fixed Cost (AFC) (₹)	Average Cost (AC) (₹)
1	...	...	...	140
2	...	45	...	...
3	45	...	30	...
4	...	48	22.5	...
5	...	52	18	...

Sol.

Output (Q) (units)	MC (₹) ($TVC_n - TVC_{n-1}$)	AVC (₹) (TVC/Q)	AFC (₹) (TFC/Q)	AC (₹) (AFC + AVC)	TVC (₹) (AVC×Q)	TFC (₹) AFC×Q
1	**50**	**50**	**90**	140	50	90
2	**40**	45	**45**	**90**	90	90
3	45	**45**	30	**75**	135	90
4	**57**	48	22.5	**70.5**	192	90
5	**68**	52	18	**70**	260	90

Numerical 11

Complete the following table

Output (units)	Average Variable Cost (AVC) (₹)	Total Cost (TC) (₹)	Marginal Cost (MC) (₹)
1	...	60	20
2	18	...	...
3	...	...	18
4	20	120	...
5	22	...	...

Sol.

Output (Q) (units)	AVC (₹) (TVC/Q)	TVC (₹) (AVC×Q) *or* (TC − TFC)	TC (₹) (TFC+TVC)	TFC (₹) (TC − TVC)	MC (₹) ($TVC_n - TVC_{n-1}$)
1	**20**	20	60	40	20
2	18	36	**76**	40	**16**
3	**18**	54	**94**	40	18
4	20	80	120	40	**26**
5	22	110	**150**	40	**30**

Numerical 12

The following table shows the total cost schedule of a firm. What is the total fixed cost schedule of this firm? Calculate the TVC, AFC, AVC, SAC and SMC schedules of the firm. **NCERT**

Q	0	1	2	3	4	5	6
TC	10	30	45	55	70	90	120

Sol.

Q (units)	TC (₹)	TFC (₹)	TVC (TC − TFC)	SAC $\left(\frac{TC}{Q}\right)$	SMC ($TC_n - TC_{n-1}$)	AFC $\left(\frac{TFC}{Q}\right)$	AVC $\left(\frac{TVC}{Q}\right)$
0	10	10	0	–	–	–	–
1	30	10	20	30 / 1 = 30	30 − 10 = 20	10	20
2	45	10	35	45 / 2 = 22.5	45 − 30 = 15	5	17.50
3	55	10	45	18.33	55 − 45 = 10	3.33	15
4	70	10	60	17.50	15	2.50	15
5	90	10	80	18	20	2	16
6	120	10	110	20	30	1.67	18.33

Here, Q = Output in Units; TC = Total Cost
TFC = Total Factor Cost (Fixed) ; TVC = Total Variable Cost
SAC = Short-run Average Cost or AC; SMC = Short-run Marginal Cost or MC
AFC = Average Factor Cost (Fixed); AVC = Average Variable Cost

Numerical 13

The following table gives the total cost schedule of a firm. It is also given that the average fixed cost at 4 units of output is ₹ 5. Find the TVC, TFC, AVC, AFC, SAC and SMC schedules of the firm for the corresponding values of output. NCERT

Q	1	2	3	4	5	6
TC	50	65	75	95	130	185

Sol.

Q (units)	TC (₹)	TFC (U×S)	TVC (TC – TFC)	SAC $\left(\frac{TC}{Q}\right)$	SMC $(TC_n - TC_{n-1})$	AFC $\left(\frac{TFC}{Q}\right)$	AVC $\left(\frac{TVC}{Q}\right)$
1	50	20	30	50	30	20	30
2	65	20	45	32.5	15	10	22.50
3	75	20	55	25	10	6.67	18.33
4	95	20	75	23.75	20	5	18.75
5	130	20	110	26.0	35	4	22
6	185	20	165	30.83	55	3.33	27.50

Numerical 14

A firm's SMC schedule is shown in the following table. The total fixed cost of the firm is ₹ 100. Find the TVC, TC, AVC and SAC schedules of the firm. NCERT Modified

Q	0	1	2	3	4	5	6
MC	–	500	300	200	300	500	800

Sol.

Q (units)	MC (₹)	TFC (₹)	TVC(ΣMC)	TC(FC+VC)	AVC $\left(\frac{TVC}{Q}\right)$	SAC $\left(\frac{TC}{Q}\right)$
0	–	100	0	100	–	–
1	500	100	500	600	500	600
2	300	100	500 + 300 = 800	900	400	450
3	200	100	800 + 200 = 1,000	1,100	333.33	366.67
4	300	100	1,000 + 300 = 1,300	1,400	325	350
5	500	100	1,300 + 500 = 1,800	1,900	360	380
6	800	100	1,800 + 800 = 2,600	2,700	433.33	450

SELF ASSESSMENT TEST

Objective Type Questions

1. What is another name for fixed cost?
   (a) Prime cost (b) Overhead cost
   (c) Opportunity cost (d) Direct cost
2. What is the formula for Average Cost (AC)?
   (a) AC = AFC + AVC (b) AC = TVC ÷ Q
   (c) AC = FC ÷ Q (d) AC = MC × Q
3. The sum of implicit and explicit costs is known as ....
   (a) total cost (b) opportunity cost
   (c) accounting cost (d) economic cost
4. What is the shape of the Total Fixed Cost (TFC) curve?
   (a) 'U' shaped (b) Upward sloping
   (c) Horizontal straight line (d) Downward sloping
5. Which cost curve starts at the same point as the Average Variable Cost (AVC)?
   (a) Marginal Cost (MC) (b) Fixed Cost (FC)
   (c) Average Cost (AC) (d) Total Cost (TC)
6. The Average Fixed Cost (AFC) curve is shaped as a ....
   (a) straight line (b) 'U' shaped curve
   (c) rectangular hyperbola (d) downward sloping line
7. The .... is the point at which Marginal Cost (MC) equals Average Cost (AC).
   (a) break-even point (b) minimum point of AC
   (c) maximum point of AC (d) inflection point of AC
8. What happens when Marginal Cost (MC) is greater than Average Cost (AC)?
   (a) AC increases (b) MC equals AC
   (c) AC remains constant (d) AC decreases

Answers 1. (b) 2. (a) 3. (d) 4. (c) 5. (a) 6. (c) 7. (b) 8. (a)

Short Answer Type Questions

9. "With increase in output, the gap between AC and AVC curves reduces but they never intersect each other." Do you agree? Give reasons.
10. Explain the relationship between Average Cost (AC) and Marginal Cost (MC).
11. Define the following
    (i) Implicit costs (ii) Explicit costs
12. What are short-run costs? Mention its classifications.

Numerical Questions

13. From the data given below, calculate marginal cost.

Output (units)	1	2	3	4	5	6
AVC (₹)	60	40	30	26.25	28	35

14. Calculate MC and AVC at each level of output.

Output (units)	0	1	2	3	4
TC (₹)	100	160	212	280	356

15. Complete the following table

Output (units)	Total Variable Cost (₹)	Average Variable Cost (₹)	Marginal Cost (₹)
1	10	...	...
...	...	8	6
3	27	...	...
...	...	10	13

16. Given below is the cost schedule of the firm. Its total fixed cost is ₹ 120. Find TC, TVC, AFC, AVC, MC.

Output (units)	1	2	3
ATC (₹)	160	96	80

17. A firm's average fixed cost, when it produces 2 units is ₹ 30. Its average total cost schedule is given below. Find TC, TVC, AFC, AVC, MC.

Output (units)	1	2	3
ATC (₹)	80	48	40

18. Complete the following table. Find TC and MC.

Output (units)	Price (₹)	Marginal Revenue (₹)	Total Revenue (₹)
1	...	16	...
2	12	...	24
3	...	6	...
4	7	...	28

06

CHAPTER

Revenue is the total monetary value that a firm earns through the sale of its goods or services. It plays a crucial role in assessing a firm's financial health and decision-making processes.

▼ YOUR STUDY GOALS

▼ YOUR PRACTICE GOAL

- Objective Type Questions (60 Qs ; MCQs, A-R, Statements, Matching, Concept Identification)
- Subjective Questions (15 SAs, 7 LAs)
- 14 Numerical Questions
- Self Assessment Test (6 MCQs, 4 SAs, 6 Numerical)

Concept of Revenue

6.1 Meaning of Revenue

Revenue refers to the money received by a firm from the sale of its products. It is the total sales' receipts, distinct from profit concept, which forms part of revenue concept. Revenue consists of both cost recovery and profit, i.e.

$$\text{Revenue} = \text{Cost} + \text{Profit}$$

Concept of Revenue

Concept of revenue has three variants, *viz.* Total Revenue (TR), Average Revenue (AR) and Marginal Revenue (MR). These are discussed below

1. Total Revenue (TR)

It is defined as the total receipts to the firm from the sale of a given quantity of a commodity. It can be calculated by multiplying the units of sales with the price of a commodity. Also, it is sum of total marginal revenue, i.e.

$$TR = P \times Q \quad or \quad \Sigma MR$$

Where, $TR =$ Total Revenue

$P =$ Price

$Q =$ Quantity

$MR =$ Marginal Revenue

2. Average Revenue (AR)

It is revenue per unit of output sold. It can be obtained by dividing total revenue by the quantity sold. In other words, it is the per unit revenue received from the sale of one unit of a commodity. It can be calculated as

$$AR = \frac{TR}{Q}$$

Where, AR = Average Revenue
TR = Total Revenue
Q = Quantity

Average Revenue (AR) and Price are Same

It should be noted that Average Revenue (AR) is equal to Price (P).

As we know, $AR = \frac{TR}{Q}$ ...(i)

$TR = P \times Q$ ...(ii)

(Here, P = Price, Q = Quantity or output sold)

Thus, $AR = \frac{P \times Q}{Q}$ [from equation (i) and (ii)]

Hence, it is proved, AR Price.

3. Marginal Revenue (MR)

It is the addition to total revenue by the sale of an additional unit of the commodity. It is the change in total revenue on account of the sale of an additional unit of output. It can be calculated as

$$MR = TR_n - TR_{n-1} \quad or \quad \frac{\Delta TR}{\Delta Q}$$

Where, MR = Marginal Revenue
TR_{n-1} = Total Revenue from $(n-1)$ units
TR_n = Total Revenue from n units
ΔTR = Change in Total Revenue
ΔQ = Change in Quantity

TR and MR

A car dealer sells 10 cars in a month. The Total Revenue (TR) from selling 10 cars is ₹ 1,00,00,000. If selling an 11th car increases the TR to ₹ 1,10,00,000, the Marginal Revenue (MR) from selling additional car is 1,10,00,000 – 1,00,00,000 = ₹ 10,00,000. Thus, the dealer earns ₹ 10,00,000 extra by selling one more car.

Solved Question 1 Calculate AR and MR from the following data

Q	0	1	2	3	4	5	6	7	8
TR	0	10	20	30	40	50	60	70	80

Sol.

Q	TR	AR	MR
0	0	—	—
1	10	10	10
2	20	10	10
3	30	10	10
4	40	10	10
5	50	10	10
6	60	10	10
7	70	10	10
8	80	10	10

Solved Question 2 Compute TR and MR from following data

Q	1	2	3	4	5	6	7
AR	10	9	8	7	6	5	4

Sol.

Q	AR	TR ($AR \times Q$)	MR ($TR_n - TR_{n-1}$)
1	10	10	10
2	9	18	8
3	8	24	6
4	7	28	4
5	6	30	2
6	5	30	0
7	4	28	−2

6.2 Relationship between Revenue Concepts

Understanding the relationship between revenue concepts requires knowledge of different market forms, primarily perfect competition and imperfect competition

1. **Perfect Competition** In this market form, the price remains constant, i.e. sellers can sell any quantity but only at a given price.
2. **Imperfect Competition** In this market, price falls as the output rises, i.e. seller should lower the price to sell additional units.

Relationship between Revenue Curves under Perfect Competition (When Price Remains Constant)

- MR is merely an addition to TR from selling one more unit.
- In case, price is constant, MR should also be constant and equal to AR, forming a horizontal straight line parallel to the x-axis.

- TR increases at a constant rate as each additional unit sold adds the same amount to revenue (due to constant MR). As a result, TR curve is a positively sloped straight line starting from the origin.
- In perfect competition, Price = AR = MR. Also, the area under the MR curve equals TR. In graph, TR at OC level of output = OS × OT = Area under price line (or MR).

Output	Price/AR (₹)	TR	MR
1	4	4	4
2	4	8	4
3	4	12	4
4	4	16	4
5	4	20	4

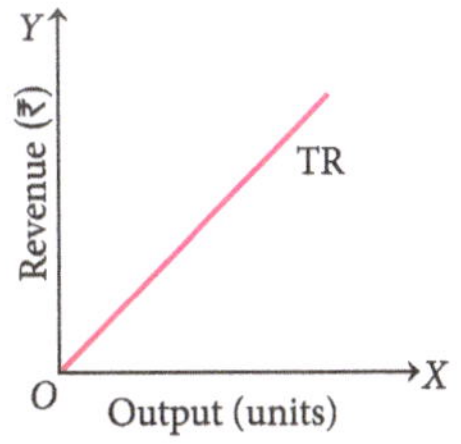

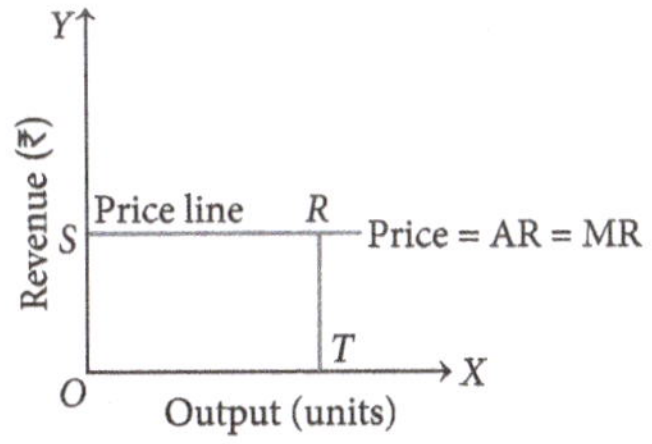

Relationship between Revenue Curves under Imperfect Competition

(When Price Falls with Rise in Output)

From the curves below, following relationship is derived between TR and MR (at falling price)

- TR increases at diminishing rate, when MR is diminishing but remains positive.
- TR is maximum and constant, when MR is zero.
- TR decreases, when MR becomes negative.

Output	Price	TR	AR $\left(\frac{TR}{Q}\right)$	MR
0	20	0	—	—
1	19	19	19	19
2	18	36	18	17
3	17	51	17	15
4	16	64	16	13
5	15	75	15	11
6	14	84	14	9
7	13	91	13	7
8	12	96	12	5
9	11	99	11	3
10	10	100	10	1
11	9	99	9	–1

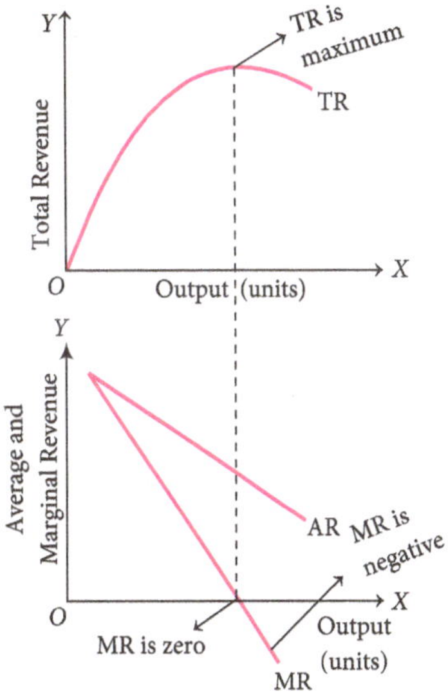

From the above curves, following relationship is derived between AR and MR

- When AR is diminishing, MR falls faster than AR, i.e. MR < AR. As a result, both AR and MR curves slope downward from left to right and MR curve is below AR curve.
- MR can be negative, but AR cannot.
- Slope of MR is twice of slope of AR.

Relation between MR and Price Elasticity of Demand

- When MR has positive value, then price elasticity of demand is more than one.
- When MR has negative value, price elasticity of demand becomes less than unity.
- Price elasticity of demand is unity, when value of MR is zero.

$$MR = AR\left(1 - \frac{1}{e}\right) \quad or \quad MR = P\left(1 - \frac{1}{e}\right)$$

Here, e = Elasticity of Demand

General Relationship between Revenue Concepts

- When TR increases at an increasing rate, both MR and AR rise.
- When TR increases at a diminishing rate, MR falls but remains positive and AR first increases to its maximum point, then starts falling.
- When TR is constant and maximum, MR is zero.
- When TR falls, MR becomes negative, while AR falls but remains positive.
- MR equals AR at the maximum point of AR.

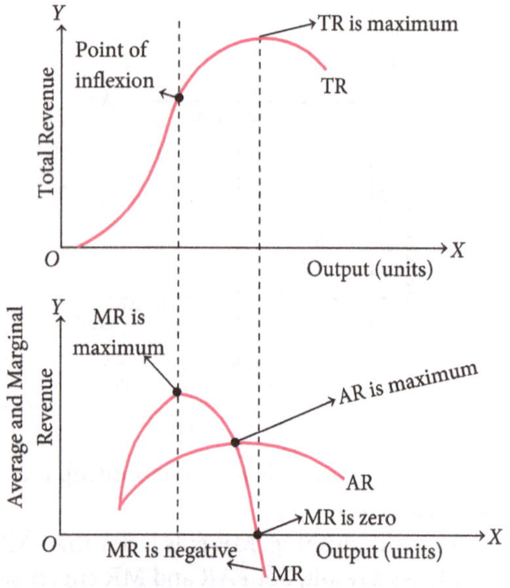

6.3 Firm's Revenue Curve in Different Markets

The shape and behaviour of a firm's revenue curves depends on the market structure in which it operates. Broadly, markets can be classified into perfect competition and imperfect competition, with the later including monopoly, monopolistic competition and oligopoly.

Revenue Curves under Perfect Competition

- A firm in a perfectly competitive market is a price taker, i.e. it has no control over the market price. It has to accept the prevailing price in the market.
- The firm can sell any quantity of output at the market price but cannot charge more or less than the prevailing price.
- In this market form, Average Revenue (AR) remains constant at all levels of output and equals the market price.
- In this market form, Marginal Revenue (MR) is also constant and equal to AR.
- As a result, both AR and MR curves are horizontally parallel to the x-axis, reflecting perfectly elastic nature.

Explanation of revenue curves under perfect competition using schedule and graph

Firm's Revenue Status when Price is Fixed (P = ₹ 6)
(an imaginary schedule)

Output/ Sales (Units) (Q)	Average Revenue = Price (₹) AR (P) = TR / Q	Total Revenue (₹) TR = AR × Q	Marginal Revenue (₹) MR_{nth} $= TR_n - TR_{n-1}$
1	6	6	6
2	6	12	6
3	6	18	6
4	6	24	6

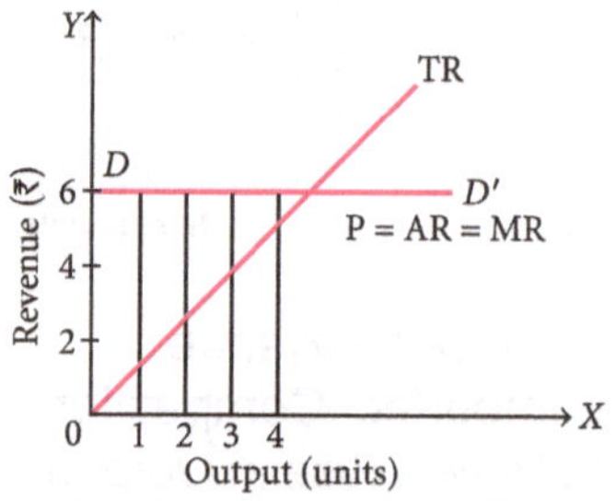

Firm's revenue curves under perfect competition

Revenue Curves under Imperfect Competition

It can be studied under various heads which are as follows

1. Revenue Curves under Monopoly

- In a monopoly, the firm is a price-maker and can influence the price by adjusting its output.
- To sell more of commodity, the firm has to lower the price. This implies an inverse relationship between price and quantity demanded.
- In this market form, Total Revenue (TR) initially increases at a diminishing rate, reaches its maximum and becomes constant and then starts to decline.
- In this market form, AR and MR curves are downward sloping and negatively sloped, reflecting inelastic demand due to the absence of close substitutes.

Explanation of revenue curve under monopoly using schedule and graph

Firm's Revenue Status, when Price is set by the Producer to Sell more and more Units of Output (an imaginary schedule)

Output/ Sales (units)(Q)	Average Revenue = Price (₹) AR (P) = TR / Q	Total Revenue (₹) TR = AR× Q	Marginal Revenue (₹) $MR_{nth} = TR_n - TR_{n-1}$
1	9	9	9
2	8	16	7
3	7	21	5
4	6	24	3

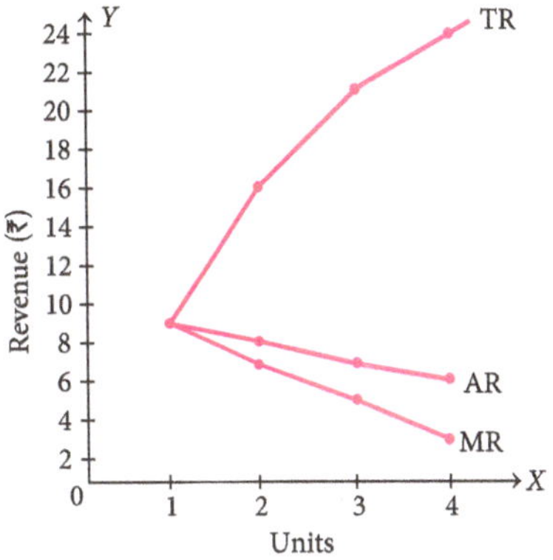

2. Revenue Curves under Monopolistic Competition

- Similar to monopoly, AR and MR curves under monopolistic competition are downward sloping and negatively sloped.
- However, these curves are more elastic than in monopoly because of the availability of close substitutes.
- The presence of product differentiation gives firms some pricing power, but not as much as in monopoly.

Explanation of revenue curve under monopolistic competition using schedule and graph

Firm's Revenue Status, when Producers have Partial Control over Price (an imaginary schedule)

Output/ Sales (units) (Q)	Average Revenue = Price (₹) AR (P) = TR /Q	Total Revenue (₹) TR= AR× Q	Marginal Revenue (₹) $MR_{nth} = TR_n - TR_{n-1}$
1	9	9	9
2	8.5	17	8
3	8	24	7
4	7.5	30	6

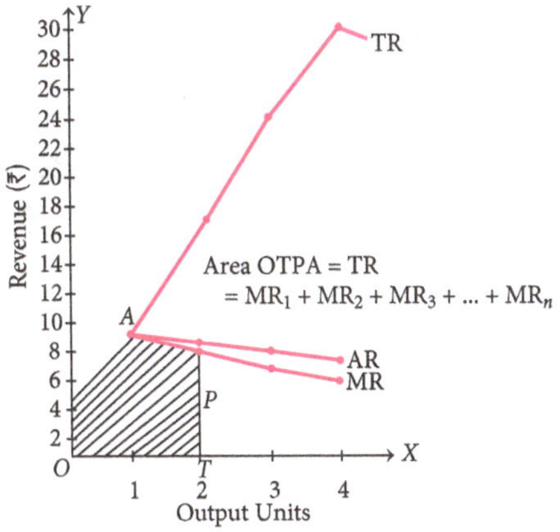

3. Revenue Curves under Oligopoly

- In oligopoly, there is a high level of interdependence between firms, so the behaviour of one firm impacts the others.
- As a result, the demand curve is not well defined in an oligopolistic market.

Comparison of Revenue Curves (Demand Curves)

- Firm's demand curve is perfectly elastic under perfect competition, it is relatively less elastic under monopoly and more elastic under monopolistic competition.
- D_P is demand curve under perfect competition. It is perfectly elastic.
- D_M is demand curve under monopoly. It is relatively less elastic.
- D_{MC} is demand curve under monopolistic competition. It is relatively more elastic.

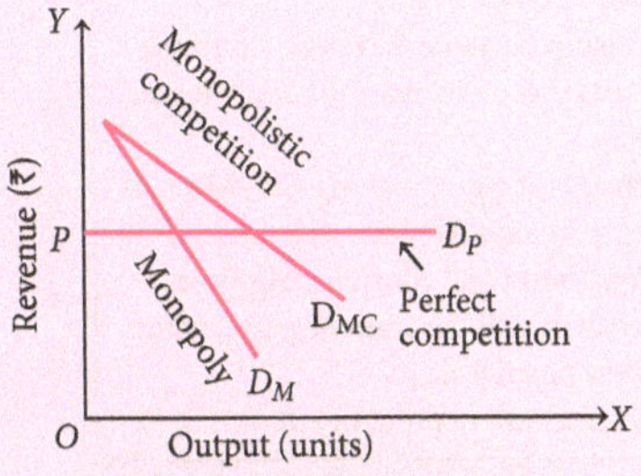

Firm's average revenue curve in different market situations

Mind Map

CONCEPT OF REVENUE

1 Meaning of Revenue

It refers to the money received by a firm from the sale of its products. It is the total sales' receipts, distinct from profit concept, which forms part of revenue concept. Revenue consists of both cost recovery and profit .

Revenue = Cost + Profit

2 Types of Revenue

(i) **Total Revenue** (TR)
- It is the total income a firm receives from selling a given quantity of a commodity.
- Formula: $TR = P \times Q$ *or* $TR = \sum MR$

(ii) **Average Revenue** (AR)
- It is the revenue per unit of output sold.
- Formula: $AR = TR/Q$

(iii) **Marginal Revenue** (MR)
- It is the additional revenue earned from selling one extra unit of a commodity.
- Formula: $MR = TR_n - TR_{n-1}$ *or* $MR = \Delta TR/\Delta Q$

3 Relationship between Revenue Curves

Under Perfect Competition
- Total revenue increases at a constant rate (straight line upward) and area under MR curve.
- Marginal revenue is constant and equal to AR (horizontal line).
- Average revenue is same as price and MR.

Under Imperfect Competition
- TR increases at a diminishing rate, when MR is diminishing but positive.
- TR is maximum and constant, when MR = 0.
- TR decreases, when MR becomes negative.
- When AR is diminishing, MR falls faster than AR.
- MR can be negative, but AR remains positive.
- Slope of MR is twice that of AR.

General Relationship between Revenue Concepts
- When TR increases at an increasing rate, MR and AR also increase.
- When TR increases at a diminishing rate, MR falls but remains positive and AR first rises then falls.
- When TR is maximum and constant, MR is zero.
- When TR decreases, MR becomes negative, while AR falls but stays positive.
- MR = AR at the maximum point of AR.

4 Revenue Curve under Perfect Competition

- A firm is a price taker and has to accept the price prevailing in market.
- A firm can sell any quantity of output at market price.
- AR remains constant at all levels of output and equals market price.
- MR is also constant and equal to AR.
- Both AR and MR curves are horizontally parallel to x-axis.

5 Revenue Curves under Monopoly

- A firm is price-maker and can influence the price by adjusting its output.
- There is an inverse relationship between price and quantity demanded.
- TR initially increases at diminishing rate, reaches its maximum, becomes constant and then starts to decline.
- AR and MR curves are downward sloping and negatively sloped.

6 Revenue Curves under Monopolistic Competition

- AR and MR curves are downward sloping and negatively sloped.
- These curves are more elastic than in monopoly because of the availability of close substitutes.
- The presence of product differentiation gives firms some pricing power, but not as much as in monopoly.

7 Revenue Curves under Oligopoly

- There is a high level of interdependence between firms, so the behaviour of one firm impacts the others.
- As a result, the demand curve is not well defined in an oligopolistic market.

EXAM PATTERN QUESTIONS

Objective Type Questions

Multiple Choice Questions (MCQs)

1. Which of the following is distinct from revenue?

(a) Profit (b) Total revenue
(c) Average revenue (d) Marginal revenue

2. If AR is ₹ 40 per unit from the sale of 3 goods and it is ₹ 30 per unit from the sale of 4 goods, find the marginal revenue of 4th unit of goods. **Competency Based Que**

(a) ₹ 10 (b) ₹ 30 (c) ₹ 40 (d) 0

3. "Revenue is the total sales receipts received by a firm." Which concept of revenue is this statement referring to? **Competency Based Que**

(a) Marginal revenue (b) Average revenue
(c) Total revenue (d) None of these

4. Identify the correct formula for calculating average revenue.

(a) TR/Q (b) TR/P
(c) Q × TR (d) P × TR

5. Arrange the following in terms of calculation sequence for TR. **Competency Based Que**

(i) Identify the price per unit.
(ii) Multiply the price by the quantity.
(iii) Count the total units sold.

Codes

(a) (i), (ii), (iii) (b) (iii), (i), (ii)
(c) (ii), (iii), (i) (d) (iii), (ii), (i)

6. When the firm is producing 3 tonnes of sugar, it receives total revenue of ₹ 24. Raising production to 4 tonnes, increases total revenue to ₹ 28. Thus, marginal revenue is .... **Competency Based Que**

(a) ₹ 4 (b) ₹ 8
(c) ₹ 28 (d) ₹ 52

7. A firm sells 10 units at ₹ 50 per unit. What is its Total Revenue (TR)?

(a) ₹ 450 (b) ₹ 500
(c) ₹ 550 (d) ₹ 600

8. A firm's total revenue increases from ₹ 200 to ₹ 240 when it sells one additional unit. What is its Marginal Revenue (MR) from the additional unit? **Competency Based Que**

(a) ₹ 20 (b) ₹ 30 (c) ₹ 40 (d) ₹ 50

9. Which of the following types of revenue is indicated in the image given?

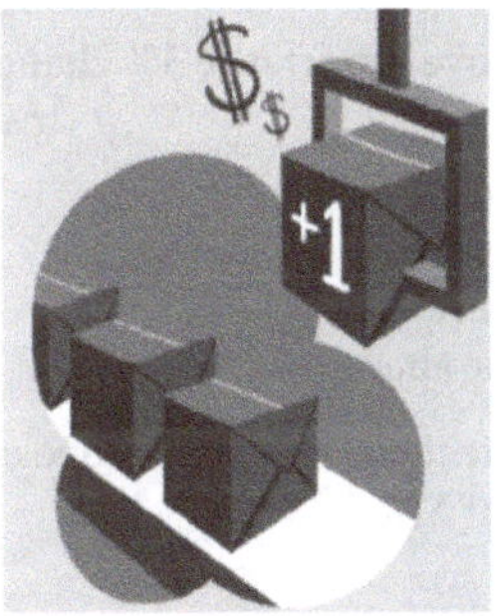

(a) Total revenue (b) Average revenue
(c) Marginal revenue (d) None of these

10. Find the missing figures and choose the correct alternative **Competency Based Que**

Output (Q)	Price	TR
5	24	...
6	...	90
7	12	...
8	...	80

(a) 10, 84, 15, 120 (b) 24, 90, 12, 80
(c) 120, 15, 10, 84 (d) 120, 15, 84, 10

11. Which of the following type of competitive market is depicted in the given image?

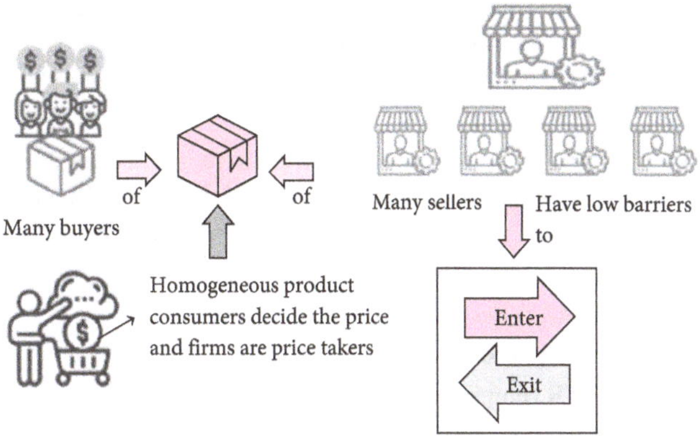

(a) Imperfect (b) Perfect
(c) Stable (d) Production

12. **UPS reported a 3 percent decline in Q_4 2022 revenue at \$ 27 billion on 3 percent increase in domestic package revenue and 8 percent drop in international package revenue. Consolidated operating profit was \$ 3.2 billion, down 17.9 percent compared to the fourth quarter of 2021 and down 3.3 percent on an adjusted basis.**

Source *https //www.stattimes.com/logistics/ups-to-plan-conservatively-pivot-quickly-in-2023-ceo-carol-tome-1347759*

As per the above report, the 3% change in revenue is on account of **Competency Based Que**

(a) total revenue
(b) average revenue
(c) marginal revenue
(d) None of the above

13. **Under imperfect competition, slope of AR is generally ...... of slope of MR.**

(a) half
(b) twice
(c) equal
(d) one-third

14. **"India's growth is competitive in dynamic market, says Unilever CFO."**

Source *https://www.business-standard.com/companies/news/india-continues-to-grow-in-value-rural-volumes-positive-unilever-123072500779_1.html*

How does competitive growth in a dynamic market, such as India, influence the concepts of revenue for firms operating there? **Competency Based Que**

(a) Firms can only focus on increasing total revenue without considering average or marginal revenue
(b) Increased competition may lead firms to lower prices, affecting both Average Revenue (AR) and Marginal Revenue (MR)
(c) Firms will always experience an increase in average revenue regardless of market conditions
(d) Marginal revenue becomes irrelevant in a competitive market

15. **If a firm in an imperfectly competitive market has TR increasing at a diminishing rate, which of the following is true?** **Competency Based Que**

I. MR is positive and constant.
II. MR is decreasing but still positive.
III. MR becomes zero.
IV. TR remains constant.

Codes

(a) I and II (b) III and IV
(c) I, II, III and IV (d) Only II

16. **Identify the market form from the image given below.**

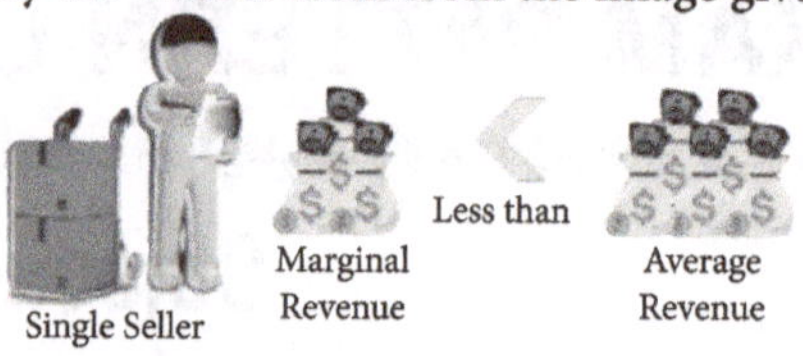

(a) Perfect competition (b) Imperfect competition
(c) Both (a) and (b) (d) Neither (a) nor (b)

17. **A firm operating under imperfect competition sees its total revenue rise but at a diminishing rate. The MR is decreasing but remains positive.**

What can be inferred about the Average Revenue (AR) behaviour? **Competency Based Que**

(a) AR is increasing (b) AR is constant
(c) AR is decreasing (d) AR is irrelevant

18. **Identify the correct statement.**

(a) In perfect competition, the marginal revenue curve is above the average revenue curve
(b) Marginal revenue can be negative
(c) Average revenue is always lower than total revenue
(d) Total revenue increases at a rising rate when marginal revenue decreases

19. **Identify the type of market highlighted in the given image.**

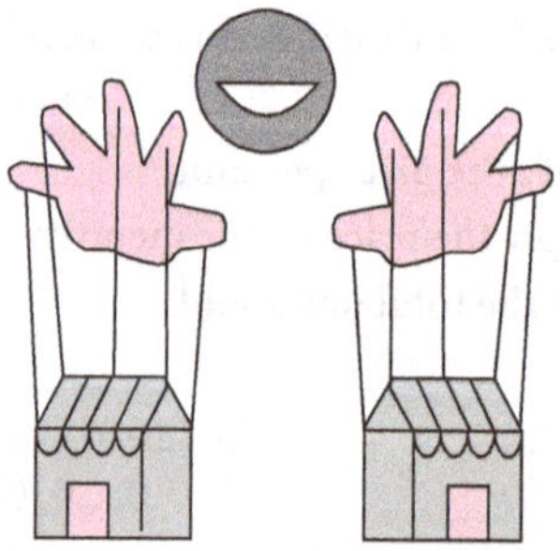

(a) Oligopoly (b) Monopolist
(c) Monopoly (d) Perfect

20. **In monopoly and monopolistic competitions, AR and MR curve are downward sloping because the firms can sell more by**

(a) increasing the price (b) lowering the price
(c) keep in price constant (d) All of these

21. **A monopolistic firm notices that as it increases output from 5 to 6 units, its average revenue decreases from ₹ 30 to ₹ 25. What can be inferred about the demand curve?** **Competency Based Que**

(a) It is downward sloping
(b) It is horizontal
(c) It is perfectly inelastic
(d) It is perfectly elastic

22. **Identify the correct statement about monopoly.**

I. MR is always greater than AR.
II. TR initially increases at a diminishing rate.
III. AR and MR are downward sloping.
IV. The firm can influence the market price.

Codes **Competency Based Que**

(a) I, II and III (b) II, III and IV
(c) Only IV (d) I and III

23. **Arrange the following steps in the correct sequence to calculate Marginal Revenue (MR) under imperfect competition.** **Competency Based Que**

(i) Determine the Total Revenue (TR) for 'n' units of output.
(ii) Subtract the Total Revenue (TR) of '$n-1$' units from the TR of 'n' units.
(iii) Identify the quantity change (ΔQ) between 'n' and '$n-1$' units.
(iv) Divide the change in Total Revenue (ΔTR) by the change in Quantity (ΔQ).

Codes

(a) (i), (iii), (iv), (ii) (b) (i), (ii), (iv), (iii)
(c) (iii), (i), (ii), (iv) (d) (i), (ii), (iii), (iv)

24. **The below image depicts the revenue curve under .... competition.**

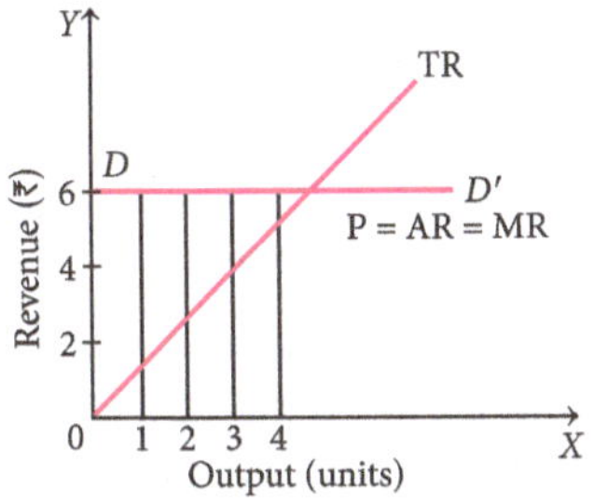

(a) imperfect (b) oligopoly
(c) monopoly (d) perfect

25. **In perfect competition,**

(a) AR = MR (b) AR = P
(c) TR is positively sloped straight line from origin
(d) All of the above

26. **Under which market are the market revenue or demand curves not clearly defined?**

(a) Oligopoly (b) Monopoly
(c) Monopolist (d) Perfect

Direction *Read the case study and answer the questions 27 to 30 on the basis of the same*

ABC Electronics operates in various market structures, focusing on electronic gadgets. The company sells products in three distinct markets: perfect competition, monopolistic competition and monopoly.

ABC sells basic electronic components like resistors in a perfectly competitive market, where many firms offer identical products. The company cannot influence the price, which is determined by the market. Here, Total Revenue (TR), Average Revenue (AR) and Marginal Revenue (MR) are constant and equal to the market price. ABC offers smartphones that compete with similar products.

In monopolistic market, the company has some pricing control. As it sells more smartphones, it must lower the price to attract customers, resulting in downward sloping AR and MR curves. TR increases at a diminishing rate.

ABC holds a monopoly on a patented electronic device with no close substitutes. As the sole seller, it can influence the price by adjusting output. Initially, TR increases, but it may decline when MR becomes negative, with both AR and MR curves being downward sloping.

Understanding revenue concepts across these market structures enables ABC Electronics to strategise pricing and output effectively, maximising revenue and adapting to market changes.

27. **In a perfectly competitive market, the Average Revenue (AR) remains constant and is equal to the ....**

28. **What happens to the Marginal Revenue (MR) in monopolistic competition as output increases?**

(a) MR remains constant (b) MR increases
(c) MR decreases (d) MR becomes negative

29. **In a monopoly, the Total Revenue (TR) initially increases but may start to decline when .... becomes negative.**

30. **In a monopoly, the firm's demand curve is**

(a) downward sloping (b) horizontal
(c) perfectly elastic (d) vertical

Assertion-Reason

Direction (Q.No. 31 to 40) *Read the following Assertion (A) and Reason (R) and choose the correct alternative from the following*

Alternatives

(a) Both Assertion (A) and Reason (R) are true and Reason (R) is the correct explanation of Assertion (A)
(b) Both Assertion (A) and Reason (R) are true, but Reason (R) is not the correct explanation of Assertion (A)
(c) Assertion (A) is true, but Reason (R) is false
(d) Assertion (A) is false, but Reason (R) is true

31. **Assertion** (A) A monopolist can never achieve positive total revenue when marginal revenue is zero.

Reason (R) Positive total revenue requires marginal revenue to be positive.

32. **Assertion** (A) Average revenue is the revenue earned per unit of output sold.

Reason (R) Average revenue is calculated by multiplying the price of the product (P) by the quantity sold (Q).

33. **Assertion** (A) Marginal revenue and price are the same in an imperfect market.

Reason (R) Marginal revenue is the additional revenue earned by selling one more unit of output.

34. **Assertion** (A) Total revenue is the total income a firm earns from selling a given quantity of a product.

Reason (R) Revenue of a firm includes its sales or money receipts.

35. **Assertion** (A) A producer always prefers producing above the mid-point of AR curve.

Reason (R) Above the mid-point of downward sloping demand curve, elasticity of demand is greater than one.

36. **Assertion** (A) In imperfect competition, the price remains constant, i.e. sellers can sell any quantity but only at a fixed price.

Reason (R) In imperfect competition, price decreases as the output increases, so sellers should lower the price to sell additional units.

37. **Assertion** (A) When MR has positive value, the price elasticity of demand is more than one.

Reason (R) Price elasticity of demand is in unity, when the value of MR is zero.

38. **Assertion** (A) The shape and behaviour of a firm's revenue curves vary based on the market structure it operates in.

Reason (R) A firm in a perfectly competitive market is a price maker.

39. **Assertion** (A) Charging lower price for additional units ensures higher revenue.

Reason (R) As price falls, demand for goods by consumers increases.

40. **Assertion** (A) In monopolistic competition, the AR curve is more elastic than in monopoly.

Reason (R) The presence of close substitutes in monopolistic competition increases consumers' sensitivity to price changes.

Two Statements Based MCQs

Direction (Q.No. 41 to 50) *Read the following statements carefully and choose the correct alternative*

Alternatives

(a) Statement I is correct and Statement II is incorrect
(b) Statement II is correct and Statement I is incorrect
(c) Both the statements are correct
(d) Both the statements are incorrect

41. **Statement I** The concept of revenue is same as the concept of profit.

Statement II Revenue is equal to the sum of cost and profit.

42. **Statement I** Average Revenue (AR) decreases as Total Revenue (TR) increases indefinitely.

Statement II Marginal Revenue (MR) remains constant regardless of the number of units sold.

43. **Statement I** Average Revenue (AR) is the revenue earned per unit of output sold.

Statement II Marginal Revenue (MR) is always greater than Total Revenue (TR).

44. **Statement I** Average revenue and price are one or the same thing.

Statement II When total revenue is constant, average revenue falls.

45. **Statement I** When Average Revenue (AR) decreases, Marginal Revenue (MR) falls faster and is always below AR.

Statement II The Marginal Revenue (MR) curve slopes downward under imperfect competition as price falls with increased output.

46. **Statement I** In perfect competition, Price = AR = MR.

Statement II In imperfect competition, when Marginal Revenue (MR) is zero, Total Revenue (TR) is at its maximum.

47. **Statement I** When Total Revenue (TR) falls, Marginal Revenue (MR) remains positive.

Statement II Average Revenue (AR) can be negative while Marginal Revenue (MR) remains positive.

48. **Statement I** When marginal revenue becomes zero, average revenue is maximum.

Statement II At the mid-point of average revenue curve under imperfect competition, elasticity of demand is unity.

49. **Statement I** Under monopoly, the Average Revenue (AR) curve is horizontal, like in perfect competition.

Statement II In a monopoly, Total Revenue (TR) initially rises, reaches a maximum and then starts to decline as Marginal Revenue (MR) becomes negative.

50. **Statement I** In an oligopoly, the demand curve is not clearly defined due to the interdependence of firms and strategic behaviour.

Statement II In a monopoly, the firm is a price maker and must lower prices to sell additional units.

Matching

51. Match the following

Column I		Column II	
A.	Revenue	(i)	The total expenditure incurred by a firm.
B.	Revenue curve	(ii)	A graphical representation of a firm's revenue at different output levels.
C.	Cost	(iii)	Income earned by a firm from selling goods or services.
D.	Profit	(iv)	The financial gain a firm makes.

Codes

	A	B	C	D
(a)	(iii)	(iv)	(i)	(ii)
(b)	(iv)	(i)	(ii)	(iii)
(c)	(ii)	(iii)	(iv)	(i)
(d)	(iii)	(ii)	(i)	(iv)

52. Match the following

Column I		Column II	
A.	Total revenue	(i)	$TR_n - TR_{n-1}$
B.	Marginal revenue	(ii)	TR/Q
C.	Average revenue	(iii)	$P \times Q$

Codes

	A	B	C		A	B	C
(a)	(iii)	(i)	(ii)	(b)	(i)	(iii)	(ii)
(c)	(ii)	(iii)	(i)	(d)	(iii)	(ii)	(i)

53. Match the following

Column I		Column II	
A.	Perfect competition	(i)	Firms control prices, differentiated products.
B.	Imperfect competition	(ii)	Few large firms dominate the market.
C.	Oligopoly	(iii)	One seller controls price and supply.
D.	Monopoly	(iv)	Many firms, identical products, no price control.

Codes

	A	B	C	D		A	B	C	D
(a)	(iii)	(iv)	(i)	(ii)	(b)	(iv)	(i)	(ii)	(iii)
(c)	(ii)	(iii)	(iv)	(i)	(d)	(iii)	(ii)	(i)	(iv)

54. Match the following

Column I		Column II	
A.	Perfectly elastic demand	(i)	Complex revenue curves, with no clear shape.
B.	Inelastic demand	(ii)	Horizontal AR and MR curves.
C.	Elastic curves	(iii)	Downward sloping AR and MR curves.
D.	Oligopoly	(iv)	Availability of substitutes.

Codes

	A	B	C	D		A	B	C	D
(a)	(iii)	(iv)	(i)	(ii)	(b)	(iv)	(i)	(ii)	(iii)
(c)	(ii)	(iii)	(iv)	(i)	(d)	(iii)	(ii)	(i)	(iv)

55. Match the options of Column I with the correct options in Column II

Column I		Column II	
A.	Monopoly	(i)	Relative inelastic demand curve
B.	Monopolistic	(ii)	Perfectly elastic demand
C.	Perfect competition	(iii)	Maximum total revenue
D.	Zero marginal revenue	(iv)	Relative elastic demand curve

Codes

	A	B	C	D		A	B	C	D
(a)	(i)	(ii)	(iii)	(iv)	(b)	(ii)	(iii)	(iv)	(i)
(c)	(i)	(iv)	(ii)	(iii)	(d)	(iv)	(i)	(ii)	(iii)

Concept Identification

56. It refers to the income earned by a firm from selling goods or services.

57. It describes the revenue earned per unit of output sold.

58. It explains a market structure where many firms sell identical products and no single firm can influence the market price.

59. It reflects the behaviour of revenue curves under imperfect competition, including monopoly and monopolistic competition.

60. It involves a market structure characterised by a few large firms that dominate the market and may collude on prices.

Answers

1. (a) Profit
2. (d) Total revenue from 3 goods sold,

$$TR_3 = AR \times Q = 40 \times 3 = ₹\,120$$

Total revenue from 4 goods sold,

$$TR_4 = AR \times Q = 30 \times 4 = ₹\,120$$

Marginal Revenue $(MR_4) = TR_4 - TR_3 = 120 - 120 = 0$

3. (c) Total revenue
4. (a) TR/Q
5. (b) (iii), (i), (ii)
6. (a) ₹ 4
7. (b) $TR = 50 \times 10 = ₹\,500$
8. (c) $MR = \frac{\Delta TR}{\Delta Q} = \frac{40}{1} = ₹\,40$
9. (c) Marginal revenue
10. (d) Price = TR/Q, TR = Price × Q
11. (b) Perfect
12. (a) total revenue
13. (b) In imperfect competition, a firm can sell more by lowering the price of its commodity therefore, both Marginal Revenue (MR) and Average Revenue (AR) is downward negatively sloped and slope of AR is twice of slope of MR. In other words, MR falls twice faster than AR.
14. (b) Increased competition may lead firms to lower prices, affecting both Average Revenue (AR) and Marginal Revenue (MR)
15. (d) Only II
16. (b) Imperfect competition
17. (c) AR is decreasing
18. (b) Marginal revenue can be negative
19. (c) Monopoly
20. (b) AR and MR curves are downward sloping because firms can earn more revenue by selling their output at lower prices.
21. (a) A decrease in AR with an increase in output indicates a downward sloping demand curve.
22. (b) II, III and IV
23. (d) (i), (ii), (iii), (iv)
24. (d) perfect
25. (d) All of the above
26. (a) Oligopoly
27. market price
28. (c) MR decreases
29. Marginal Revenue (MR)
30. (a) downward sloping
31. (d) A monopolist can have positive TR even when MR = 0 because TR depends on the price and quantity already sold, not just the change in revenue.
32. (c) Average revenue is calculated by dividing Total Revenue (TR) by the quantity sold (Q).
33. (d) Marginal revenue and price are not the same. Average revenue and price are the same.
34. (b) Both Assertion (A) and Reason (R) are true, but Reason (R) is not the correct explanation of Assertion (A)
35. (a) Both Assertion (A) and Reason (R) are true and Reason (R) is the correct explanation of Assertion (A)
36. (d) In perfect competition, the price remains constant, i.e. sellers can sell any quantity but only at a fixed price.
37. (b) Both Assertion (A) and Reason (R) are true, but Reason (R) is not the correct explanation of Assertion (A)
38. (c) A firm in a perfectly competitive market is a price taker, i.e. it has no control over the market price.
39. (a) Both Assertion (A) and Reason (R) are true and Reason (R) is the correct explanation of Assertion (A)
40. (a) Both Assertion (A) and Reason (R) are true and Reason (R) is the correct explanation of Assertion (A)
41. (b) Revenue is the total income from sales, while profit is the remaining amount after subtracting costs from revenue.
42. (d) AR depends on the price and number of units sold, it can remain constant or even increase if TR increases at a steady rate. MR often changes with the quantity sold.
43. (a) MR is the additional revenue from selling one more unit and it can never exceed the total accumulated TR.
44. (c) Both the statements are correct
45. (c) Both the statements are correct
46. (c) Both the statements are correct
47. (d) When TR falls, MR becomes negative, reflecting a losss in revenue from selling more units. AR can never be negative; it's always positive or zero since it represents revenue per unit.
48. (b) When MR falls to zero, AR also falls but remains positive.
49. (b) In monopoly, AR is downward sloping as the firm have to lower the price to sell more units.
50. (c) Both the statements are correct
51. (d) (iii) (ii) (i) (iv)
52. (a) (iii) (i) (ii)
53. (b) (iv) (i) (ii) (iii)
54. (c) (ii) (iii) (iv) (i)
55. (c) (i) (iv) (ii) (iii)
56. Revenue
57. Average Revenue (AR)
58. Perfect competition
59. Downward sloping revenue curve
60. Oligopoly

Subjective Questions

Short Answer Type Questions

1. How are the total revenue of a firm, market price and quantity sold by the firm related to each other? NCERT

Ans. Total revenue is considered as total money receipts of a producer on account of the sale of his total output. It is obtained by multiplying the per unit price of commodity with the quantity of output sold.

TR = Price × Quantity *or* P × Q

2. What is the price line? NCERT

Ans. Price line or firm's demand curve is same as the firm's AR curve, because AR means price and demand curve shows the relationship between price and quantity demanded of firm's output.

3. "Average revenue curve represents law of demand." Comment. Competency Based Que

Ans. Average revenue is determined by dividing total revenue by the quantity sold which indicates price of the commodity. Hence, average revenue curve shows the relationship between price of a commodity and quantity demanded.

It is downward sloping curve because to increase its sales, firms have to lower their prices. So, it possesses all the characteristics of the demand curve. Therefore, we can say that average revenue curve represents law of demand.

4. "Marginal Revenue (MR) is the additional revenue earned by selling one more unit of output." Do you agree? Give reason. Competency Based Que

Ans. Yes. Marginal Revenue (MR) is defined as the additional revenue generated from the sale of one more unit of a product. It is a crucial concept in economics as it helps firms make decisions about production levels.

Specifically, MR is calculated as the change in Total Revenue (TR) divided by the change in quantity sold, indicating how revenue changes as sales increase.

5. What will be the effect of the following changes in total revenue on marginal revenue? Competency Based Que

(i) Total revenue increases at a decreasing rate.
(ii) Total revenue increases at a constant rate.

Ans. (i) Total revenue increases at a decreasing rate, when marginal revenue falls but remains positive.

(ii) Total revenue increases at a constant rate, when marginal revenue is constant and equal to average revenue.

6. Which type of market competition is depicted in the given image? Competency Based Que

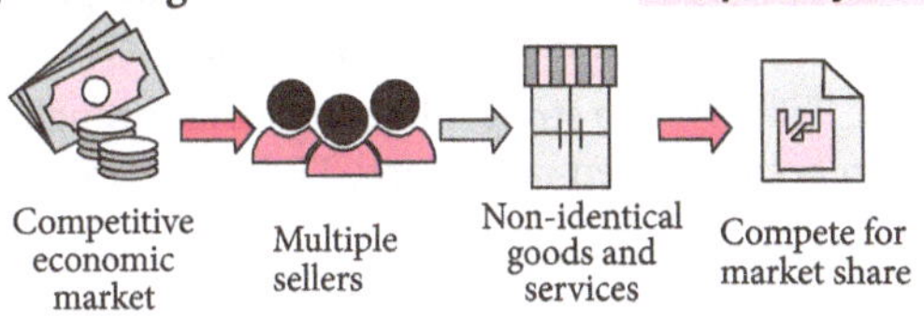

Ans. The image likely depicts an imperfect competition market structure, which may include forms such as monopoly, monopolistic competition or oligopoly. In imperfect competition, firms have some degree of control over their prices due to product differentiation or limited competition, unlike in perfect competition where firms are price takers.

7. Explain the relationship between Marginal Revenue (MR) and Average Revenue (AR).

Ans. Relationship between marginal revenue and average revenue is stated below

(i) When AR is constant, MR = AR.
(ii) When AR is diminishing, AR > MR.
(iii) When AR is rising, AR < MR.
(iv) MR can be negative, but not AR.

8. What is the relation between market price and marginal revenue of a price taking firm? NCERT

Ans. For a price taking firm, market price is equal to marginal revenue because firm can sell more quantity of commodity at the same price. As a result, that revenue earned from every additional unit (MR) is equal to price or Average Revenue (AR).

9. Draw a single diagram of the average revenue and marginal revenue curves of a firm which can sell any quantity of the good at a given price. Explain.

Ans. In a perfectly competitive market form, a uniform price prevails in the market, which is decided by the market forces of demand and supply.

Sellers can sell any number of units at that price. Uniform price results in constant AR and MR. Therefore, in this market form, price = AR = MR.

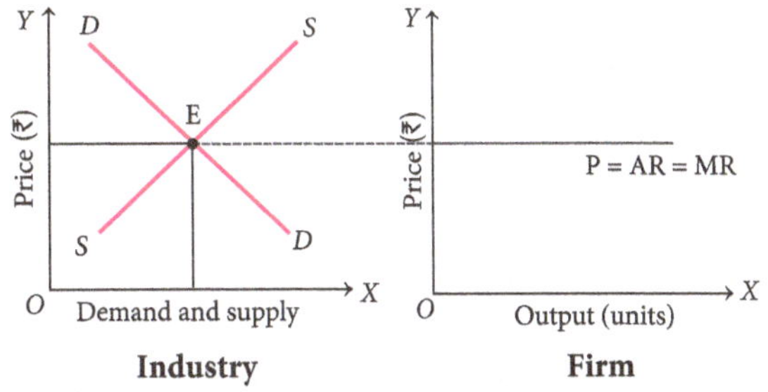

10. **Why the total revenue curve of a competitive firm faces a straight line passing through origin?**

Ans. A competitive firm sells its output at the uniform price. The price or AR is constant and MR is also constant which is equal to AR. The total revenue is the sum total of MR corresponding to different levels of output. Since, MR is constant, TR increases at a constant rate.

Thus, TR curve is a straight line. It passes through the origin because when sale is zero, TR is also zero.

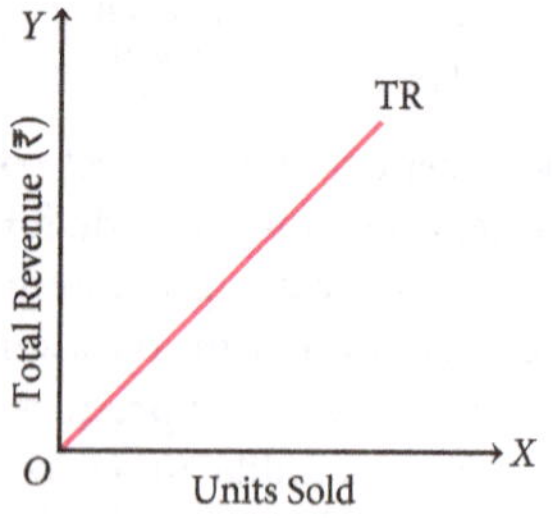

11. **"The slope of the marginal revenue curve is twice that of the average revenue curve."**

Why is the slope relationship between marginal revenue and average revenue important for understanding revenue dynamics? **Competency Based Que**

Ans. The relationship between the slopes of the Marginal Revenue (MR) and Average Revenue (AR) curves is crucial because it illustrates how changes in output affect revenue. A steeper slope for MR indicates that it falls more rapidly than AR, which suggests diminishing returns on additional output. This informs firms about the potential need to adjust pricing strategies as they scale production, particularly in imperfect competition, where the demand curve is downward sloping.

12. **Explain the relationship between price elasticity of demand and marginal revenue with the help of a diagram.**

Ans. There is a close relationship between E_d and MR

(i) When MR is positive, $E_d > 1$.

(ii) When MR is zero, $E_d = 1$.

(iii) When MR is negative, $E_d < 1$.

The above relationship is illustrated with the help of adjoining diagram $MR = AR\left(1 - \frac{1}{e}\right)$ or $P\left(1 - \frac{1}{e}\right)$

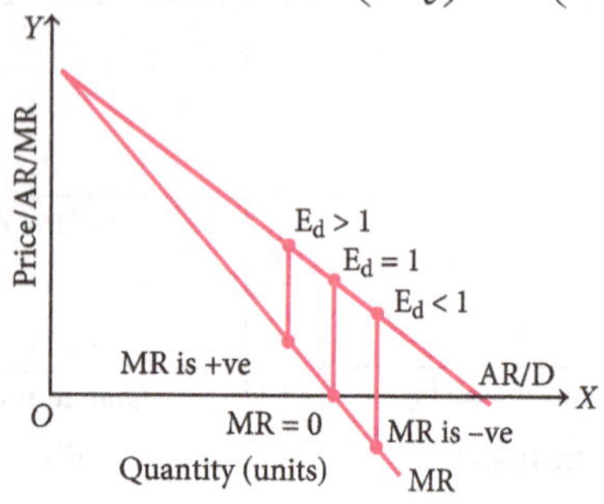

13. **State giving reasons, whether the following statements are true or false** **Competency Based Que**

(i) When total revenue is constant, average revenue will also be constant.

(ii) When marginal revenue falls to zero, average revenue becomes maximum.

(iii) Marginal revenue is always the price at which the last unit of the commodity is sold.

(iv) When marginal revenue is positive and constant, average revenue and total revenue will both increase at constant rate.

Ans. (i) False, when total revenue is constant, average revenue will be diminishing.

(ii) False, when marginal revenue is zero, average revenue will be diminishing.

(iii) False, marginal revenue can never be the price at which the last unit of the commodity sold. It simply refers to additional revenue, when an additional unit of output is sold.

(iv) False, because when marginal revenue is positive and constant, total revenue increases at constant rate but average revenue tends to be equal to marginal revenue.

14. **Why is the total revenue curve of a price taking firm an upward sloping straight line? Why does the curve pass through the origin?** **NCERT**

Ans. At zero level of sales, total revenue is zero. Therefore, total revenue curve starts from origin. As sales increase, total revenue also increases. The total revenue curve is an upward sloping straight line through the origin at a constant rate because the price of commodity remains constant for each level of output for a price taking firm (perfect competition).

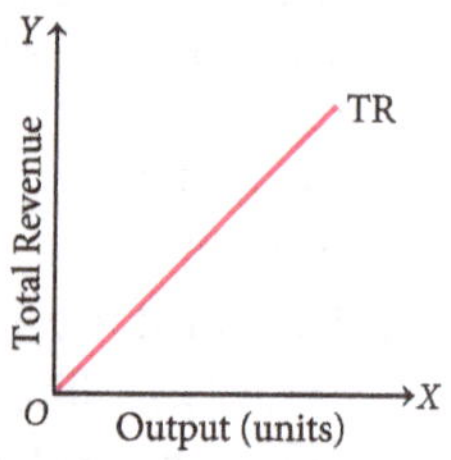

15. **Draw average revenue and marginal revenue curves under monopolistic competition.**

Ans. Under monopolistic competition, average and marginal revenue curves are different and downward sloping. It means that if the seller intends to sell more units of the commodity, he will have to lower the price.

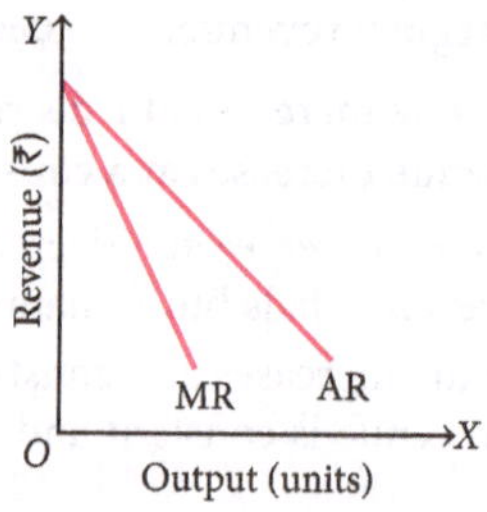

Long Answer Type Questions

16. Explain the concept of revenue and its significance for a firm.

Ans. Revenue is the total income a firm generates from selling its goods or services over a specific period.

It is a key component of a firm's financial performance and represents the funds available for covering production costs, generating profit and reinvesting in the business.

Revenue is broadly categorised into Total Revenue (TR), Average Revenue (AR) and Marginal Revenue (MR), each reflecting different aspects of income generation.

Significance of revenue is as follows

(i) **Cost Coverage**
It provides funds to cover fixed and variable costs.

(ii) **Profit Generation**
It forms the basis for calculating profits after expenses.

(iii) **Market Insight**
It helps in analysing consumer demand and market trends.

(iv) **Pricing Decisions**
It aids in setting optimal prices for goods and services.

(v) **Investment Planning**
It serves as a primary source for funding business growth and expansion initiatives.

17. Discuss the differences between Total Revenue (TR), Average Revenue (AR) and Marginal Revenue (MR).

Ans. Differences between Total Revenue (TR), Average Revenue (AR) and Marginal Revenue (MR)

Basis	**Total Revenue** (TR)	**Average Revenue** (AR)	**Marginal Revenue** (MR)
Definition	The total income earned by a firm from selling a specific quantity of goods.	Revenue earned per unit of output sold.	Additional revenue earned by selling one more unit of output.
Formula	TR = Price (P) × Quantity (Q)	AR = TR/Q	MR = Change in TR/Change in Quantity ($\Delta TR/\Delta Q$)
Nature	Represents the overall income at a specific output level.	Represents revenue per unit sold and equals price in perfect competition.	Reflects the contribution of each additional unit to total revenue.
Relationship	Increases with output; at a diminishing rate under imperfect competition.	Typically decreases with output under imperfect competition.	Declines faster than AR under imperfect competition and can become negative.
Purpose	Helps evaluate total income at different production levels.	Indicates per unit revenue for pricing strategies.	Helps determine the impact of selling an additional unit on overall revenue.

18. Evaluate the importance of understanding revenue curves for business decision-making.

Ans. Understanding revenue curves is crucial for business decision-making, as they provide insights into how changes in pricing, output levels and market conditions affect a firm's revenue.

By analysing the relationships between Total Revenue (TR), Average Revenue (AR) and Marginal Revenue (MR), firms can make informed decisions about pricing strategies, product offerings and market entry or exit.

e.g. Knowing the point at which MR equals zero can guide firms in determining the optimal output level to maximise profits. Additionally, recognising the impact of market structure—whether perfect or imperfect competition—enables firms to adapt their strategies in response to competitive pressures.

Overall, a clear understanding of revenue curves helps firms optimise their operations, enhance profitability and maintain a competitive edge.

19. Analyse the revenue relationship in a perfectly competitive market and answer the following Competency Based Que

(i) Explain the characteristics of Average Revenue (AR) and Marginal Revenue (MR) in a perfectly competitive market.

(ii) Discuss the implications of the revenue relations- hip on Total Revenue (TR) in a perfectly competitive market.

Ans. (i) In a perfectly competitive market, Average Revenue (AR) and Marginal Revenue (MR) are constant and equal to the market price. Since firms are price takers, they cannot influence the price and must accept the prevailing market rate. This results in both AR and MR being represented by horizontal lines parallel to the x-axis, indicating perfectly elastic demand.

As the firm sells additional units, the revenue gained from each unit sold remains the same, demonstrating that any increase in output does not affect the price at which goods are sold.

(ii) The relationship between AR and MR in a perfectly competitive market has significant implications for Total Revenue (TR).

Since TR is calculated by multiplying the quantity sold (Q) by the market price (P) and both AR and MR are constant at this price, TR increases linearly as output increases. Each additional unit sold contributes the same amount to TR, resulting in a positively sloped TR curve that rises at a constant rate.

This predictable revenue growth allows firms to plan and make informed production decisions, reinforcing the notion that market conditions are crucial in determining revenue outcomes in such a competitive environment.

20. Discuss how revenue curves behave under imperfect competition, highlighting the differences across monopoly, monopolistic competition and oligopoly?

Ans. Under imperfect competition, revenue curves differ due to the firms' ability to influence prices

(i) **Monopoly**

A monopolistic firm is a price maker and faces a downward sloping demand curve. To increase sales, it must lower the price, leading to diminishing Total Revenue (TR) as output increases. Both Average Revenue (AR) and Marginal Revenue (MR) curves are also downward sloping, with MR falling faster than AR due to the price reduction necessary for selling additional units.

(ii) **Monopolistic Competition**

Firms sell differentiated products, allowing for some pricing power. However, the presence of close substitutes keeps demand relatively elastic. As a result, AR and MR curves are downward sloping but are less steep than in monopoly. Firms must lower prices to sell additional units, but they have more flexibility than monopolists due to product differentiation.

(iii) **Oligopoly**

In an oligopolistic market, firms are interdependent and their pricing and output decisions affect one another. The demand curve can be ambiguous because of strategic behaviour, such as collusion or price wars.

Revenue curves in oligopoly are complex and do not follow a predictable pattern due to the interplay of pricing strategies among the few dominant firms.

21. How does interdependence among firms in an oligopolistic market influence pricing strategies and revenue outcomes? **Competency Based Que**

Ans. Interdependence among firms in an oligopolistic market influences pricing strategies and revenue outcomes in several key ways

(i) **Strategic Pricing**

Firms monitor competitors closely. If one firm lowers prices, others may follow, leading to price wars and reduced profits. Conversely, a price increase by one firm may not be matched, risking market share loss.

(ii) **Collusion**

Firms may collude to set prices or output levels, leading to higher prices and revenues, but this can be illegal and risky.

(iii) **Kinked Demand Curve**

This concept suggests that prices remain stable because firms believe raising prices will not be matched, while lowering prices will lead to matching cuts by competitors, resulting in reduced revenues.

(iv) **Non-price Competition**

Firms may compete through advertising and product differentiation instead of price, affecting market share and revenue.

22. ABC Corporation operates in a market characterised by monopolistic competition, where it sells differentiated products such as flavoured beverages. The company faces downward sloping Average Revenue (AR) and Marginal Revenue (MR) curves. Additionally, ABC Corporation is considering expanding its product line by introducing a new flavour to attract more customers.

Despite a strong brand presence, ABC Corporation must carefully assess its pricing strategy to maximise revenue. The firm has observed that when it lowers prices, sales volumes increase, but the revenue generated from additional sales is diminishing.

Furthermore, the company has been keeping an eye on competitors who are also introducing new flavours, making the market increasingly competitive. This situation emphasises the importance of understanding the relationship between pricing, revenue curves and market structure. **Competency Based Que**

(i) What type of market structure does ABC Corporation operate in and what characterises it?

(ii) Explain how the downward sloping AR and MR curves affect ABC Corporation's pricing strategy?

(iii) Analyse the implications of introducing a new flavour on ABC Corporation's revenue. Consider the potential effects on demand elasticity, market competition and pricing strategy.

Ans. (i) ABC Corporation operates in a monopolistic competition market structure, characterised by many firms selling differentiated products, allowing some pricing power but also facing competition from similar products.

(ii) The downward sloping AR and MR curves indicate that ABC Corporation must lower its price to sell additional units. This means that while lowering prices can increase sales volume, the additional revenue gained from selling those extra units will diminish. As a result, the firm must find a balance between attracting customers through lower prices and ensuring that the revenue generated remains profitable.

(iii) Introducing a new flavour can significantly impact ABC Corporation's revenue in several ways

- **Demand Elasticity**
  If the new flavour successfully differentiates itself from existing products, it may attract price sensitive consumers, increasing demand. However, if the new flavour is perceived as similar to competitors' offerings, demand elasticity may be higher, meaning consumers might easily switch brands based on price changes.
- **Market Competition**
  As competitors are also likely to respond by introducing their flavours or adjusting their pricing strategies, this can lead to increased competition, potentially driving prices down across the market. ABC Corporation must anticipate these reactions to maintain its market share.
- **Pricing Strategy**
  The firm may consider an introductory pricing strategy to entice customers to try the new flavour. However, it must ensure that the lower prices do not lead to unsustainable revenue loss. A careful analysis of the MR curve will be crucial to determine the optimal price point that maximises revenue without compromising profitability.

Numerical Questions

Numerical 1

Complete the following table

Output (units)	Price (₹)	Total Revenue (₹)	Marginal Revenue (₹)
4	9	36	—
5	...	...	4
6	...	42	...
7	6	...	...
8	...	40	...

Sol.

Output (Q) (units)	Price (P) (₹) $\left(\frac{TR}{Q}\right)$	Total Revenue (TR) (₹) (P×Q)	Marginal Revenue (MR) (₹) $(TR_n - TR_{n-1})$
4	9	36	—
5	**8**	**40**	4
6	**7**	42	**2**
7	6	**42**	**0**
8	**5**	40	**– 2**

Numerical 2

Complete the following table

Output (units)	Total Revenue (₹)	Marginal Revenue (₹)	Average Revenue (₹)
1	...	...	8
2	...	4	...
3	15	...	...
4	8	...	2

Sol.

Output (Q) (units)	Total Revenue (TR) (₹) (AR×Q)	Marginal Revenue (MR) (₹) $(TR_n - TR_{n-1})$	Average Revenue (AR) (₹) (TR/Q)
1	**8**	**8**	8
2	**12**	4	**6**
3	15	**3**	**5**
4	8	**–7**	2

Numerical 3

Complete the following table

Price (₹)	Output (units)	Total Revenue (₹)	Marginal Revenue (₹)
...	1	6	...
4	2	...	2
...	3	6	...
1	4	...	– 2

Sol.

Price (P) (₹) (TR/Q)	Output (Q) (units)	Total Revenue (TR) (₹) (P×Q)	Marginal Revenue (MR) (₹) ($TR_n - TR_{n-1}$)
6	1	6	**6**
4	2	**8**	2
2	3	6	**– 2**
1	4	**4**	– 2

Numerical 4

Complete the following table

Price (₹)	Output (units)	Total Revenue (₹)	Marginal Revenue (₹)
10	1	...	...
...	2	14	...
...	3	...	1
...	4	12	...

Sol.

Price (P)(AR) (₹) (TR/Q)	Output (Q) (units)	Total Revenue (TR) (₹) (P×Q)	Marginal Revenue (MR) (₹) ($TR_n - TR_{n-1}$)
10	1	**10**	**10**
7	2	14	**4**
5	3	**15**	1
3	4	12	**– 3**

Numerical 5

Complete the following table

Price (₹)	Output (units)	Total Revenue (₹)	Marginal Revenue (₹)
7	...	7	...
...	2	10	...
...	3	...	–1
1	...	...	–5

Sol.

Price (P) (AR) (₹) (TR/Q)	Output (Q) (units) (TR/P)	Total Revenue (TR) (₹) (P×Q)	Marginal Revenue (MR) (₹) ($TR_n - TR_{n-1}$)
7	**1**	7	**7**
5	2	10	**3**
3	3	**9**	– 1
1	**4**	**4**	– 5

Numerical 6

Producer can sell more of a good only by lowering price. Prepare total revenue and marginal revenue schedule. Take four output levels.

Sol.

Output (Q) (units)	Price (P) (₹)	Total Revenue (TR) (₹) (P × Q)	Marginal Revenue (MR) (₹) ($TR_n - TR_{n-1}$)
1	10	10	10
2	8	16	6
3	7	21	5
4	6	24	3

Numerical 7

Complete the following table

Output (units)	Price (₹)	Total Revenue (₹)	Marginal Revenue (₹)
1	7	...	...
2	6	...	...
3	4	...	...
4	2	...	...

Sol.

Output (Q) (units)	Price (P) (₹)	Total Revenue (TR) (₹) (P×Q)	Marginal Revenue (MR) (₹) ($TR_n - TR_{n-1}$)
1	7	**7**	**7**
2	6	**12**	**5**
3	4	**12**	**0**
4	2	**8**	**– 4**

Numerical 8

Complete the following table

Output (units)	Total Revenue (₹)	Marginal Revenue (₹)	Average Revenue (₹)
1	14	...	...
2	24	...	...
3	24	...	...
4	16	...	...

Sol.

Output (Q) (units)	Total Revenue (TR) (₹)	Marginal Revenue (MR) (₹)($TR_n - TR_{n-1}$)	Average Revenue (AR) (₹) (TR/Q)
1	14	**14**	**14**
2	24	**10**	**12**
3	24	**0**	**8**
4	16	**– 8**	**4**

Numerical 9

Complete the following table

Output (units)	Marginal Revenue (₹)	Total Revenue (₹)	Average Revenue (₹)
1	10	...	...
2	8	...	...
3	0	...	...
4	– 2	...	...

Sol.

Output (Q) (units)	Marginal Revenue (MR) (₹)	Total Revenue (TR) (₹) (ΣMR *or* $MR_1 + MR_2 + ... + MR_n$)	Average Revenue (AR) (₹) (TR/Q)
1	10	**10**	**10**
2	8	**18**	**9**
3	0	**18**	**6**
4	–2	**16**	**4**

Numerical 10

From the following schedule, calculate TR, AR and MR.

Price (P) (₹)	6	7	8
Units sold (Q)	5	4	3

Sol.

Price (P) (₹)	Units Sold (Q)	Total Revenue (TR) (₹) (P × Q)	Average Revenue (AR) (₹) (P)	Marginal Revenue (MR)(₹) ($TR_n - TR_{n-1}$)
6	5	30	6	—
7	4	28	7	– 2
8	3	24	8	– 4

Numerical 11

A firm can sell as many units of a good as it wants to sell at a given price. Prepare a schedule showing total revenue, average revenue and marginal revenue of such a firm.

Sol. $TR = AR \times Q$, $MR_{nth} = TR_n - TR_{n-1}$

Output/Sales (units) (Q)	Average Revenue = Price (₹)	Total Revenue (₹) (AR × Q)	Marginal Revenue (₹) ($TR_n - TR_{n-1}$)
1	5	5	5
2	5	10	5
3	5	15	5
4	5	20	5

Numerical 12

A producer can sell more of a good at the same price. Prepare a total revenue and marginal revenue schedule.

Sol. Schedule of Total Revenue and Marginal Revenue

Output (Q) (units)	Price (P) (₹)	TR (₹) (Q×P)	MR (₹) ($MR_n = TR_n - TR_{n-1}$)
1	12	12	12
2	12	24	12
3	12	36	12
4	12	48	12

Numerical 13

Compute the total revenue, marginal revenue and average revenue schedules in the following table. Market price of each unit of the good is ₹ 10. NCERT

Quantity Sold (Units)	TR (₹)	MR (₹)	AR (₹)
0	...	...	...
1	...	...	...
2	...	...	...
3	...	...	...
4	...	...	...
5	...	...	...
6	...	...	...

Sol.

Quantity Sold (units)	Price (P) (₹)	TR (P×Q) (₹)	AR $\left(\frac{TR}{Q}\right)$(₹)	MR $(TR_n - TR_{n-1})$ (₹)
0	10	0	10	0
1	10	10	10	10
2	10	20	10	10
3	10	30	10	10
4	10	40	10	10
5	10	50	10	10
6	10	60	10	10

Numerical 14

A firm in a perfectly competitive market sells its product at a constant market price of ₹ 10 per unit. The firm sells 50 units in the first week and then decides to increase production to 70 units in the second week.

Calculate the following

(i) **Total Revenue (TR) for the firm in both weeks.**

(ii) **Average Revenue (AR) for both weeks.**

(iii) **Marginal Revenue (MR) when the firm increases its output from 50 to 70 units.**

Sol. (i) **Total Revenue** (TR)

- **Week 1**

$$TR_1 = \text{Price} \times \text{Quantity} = 10 \times 50 = ₹\ 500$$

- **Week 2**

$$TR_2 = \text{Price} \times \text{Quantity} = 10 \times 70 = ₹\ 700$$

(ii) **Average Revenue** (AR)

In a perfectly competitive market. AR is equal to the market price

- **Week 1**

$$AR_1 = \frac{TR_1}{\text{Quantity}} = \frac{500}{50} = ₹\ 10$$

- **Week 2**

$$AR_2 = \frac{TR_2}{\text{Quantity}} = \frac{700}{70} = ₹\ 10$$

(iii) **Marginal Revenue** (MR)

MR is the change in TR from selling one aditional unit

$$MR = \frac{TR_2 - TR_1}{\text{Change in Quantity}} = \frac{700-500}{70-50} = \frac{200}{20} = ₹\ 10$$

Therefore,

- Total revenue in Week 1: ₹ 500
- Total revenue in Week 2: ₹ 700
- Average revenue in Week 1: ₹ 10
- Average revenue in Week 2: ₹ 10
- Marginal revenue for increase from 50 to 70 units: ₹ 10

SELF ASSESSMENT TEST

Objective Type Questions

1. What does Marginal Revenue (MR) represent?
   (a) Additional revenue earned from selling one more unit
   (b) Average revenue per unit sold
   (c) Total revenue minus total cost
   (d) Total revenue from all units sold

2. What does the kinked demand curve explain?
   (a) Perfect competition pricing strategies
   (b) Maximum revenue under monopoly
   (c) TR and AR relationship under monopolistic competition
   (d) Price stability in oligopolistic markets

3. Average Revenue (AR) is also equal to .... in perfect competition.
   (a) total cost (b) price
   (c) marginal cost (d) fixed cost

4. The area under the MR curve is equal to ....
   (a) AR (b) TR
   (c) price (d) quantity

5. Under monopolistic competition, AR is more elastic because
   (a) close substitutes are available
   (b) prices remain constant
   (c) TR increases at a constant rate
   (d) marginal cost is zero

6. AR and MR curves under monopolistic competition are ....
   (a) horizontal
   (b) vertical
   (c) downward sloping
   (d) upward sloping

Answers 1. (a) 2. (d) 3. (b) 4. (b) 5. (a) 6. (c)

Short Answer Type Questions

7. What is total revenue? How is it calculated?

8. "MR is merely an addition to TR from selling one more unit." Support or refute this statement with reasons.

9. Define the following
   (i) Monopoly (ii) Oligopoly

10. What is the relationship between revenue curves under perfect competition?

Numerical Questions

11. In the given table, AR and output is given, calculate TR and MR.

AR	Output
80	1
60	2
40	3
20	4

12. Complete the following table

Output (units)	Price (₹)	Total Revenue (₹)	Marginal Revenue (₹)
4	9	36	...
5	...	...	4
6	...	42	...
7	6	...	...
8	...	40	...

13. Complete the following table

Q	1	2	3	4	5	6	7
TR	10	...	...	25	...	...	...
MR	...	6	...	...	3	...	1
AR	...	...	7	...	...	5	...

14. Complete the following table

Price (₹)	Output (units)	Total Revenue (₹)	Marginal Revenue (₹)
...	1	6	...
4	2	...	2
...	3	6	− 3
1	4	...	− 2

15. From the table given below, calculate total revenue, average revenue and marginal revenue.

Price (₹)	4	5	6
Units Sold	3	2	1

16. A perfectly competitive firm faces market price equals to ₹ 15. Derive its total revenue schedule for the range of output from zero to 10 units.

07

CHAPTER

Producer's Equilibrium

Producer aims to maximise its satisfaction in terms of profit. So, producer's equilibrium focuses on how a producer determines the optimal output level to maximise profit.

YOUR STUDY GOALS

7.1 Introduction

7.2 Concept of Producer's Equilibrium

- Conditions of Producer's Equilibrium
- Break-even Point
- Shut Down Point

YOUR PRACTICE GOAL

- Objective Type Questions (58 Qs ; MCQs, A-R, Statements, Matching, Concept Identification)
- Subjective Questions (10 SAs, 5 LAs)
- 10 Numerical Questions
- Self Assessment Test (8 MCQs, 4 SAs, 1 LA, 2 Numerical)

7.1 Introduction

To understand the concept of producer's equilibrium, let us first understand the meaning of producer and profit

- A producer is someone who produces goods and supplies them in the market with the goal of earning profit.
- Profit is the difference between the revenue generated from selling goods and the cost incurred in producing them. It can be calculated as

$$\pi = TR - TC$$

Here, π = Profit, TR = Total Revenue, TC = Total Cost

But it should be kept in mind that a firm may not always earn profit. At times, firms may suffer a loss. This occurs when cost exceeds revenue of a firm.

There is another situation which may arise when firm earns exactly as much as the cost, i.e. revenue is equal to cost, this is known as **normal profit** or **break-even point**.

So, there are three possible scenarios

- Revenue > Cost = Super normal profit or abnormal profit.
- Revenue < Cost = Super normal loss or abnormal loss.
- Revenue = Cost = Normal profit or break-even point.

Profit

Amul makes a profit when it spends ₹ 30 to process a liter of milk and sells it for ₹ 45, earning ₹ 15 profit per liter.

7.2 Concept of Producer's Equilibrium

A producer is said to be in equilibrium when he produces that level of output at which his profits are maximum or losses are minimised, with the given input and has no tendency to change from that level of output.

So, producer's equilibrium can be referred to as the situation of profit maximisation or cost minimisation.

At equilibrium, a firm or a producer will have no inclination to either expand or contract his production level beyond this point as both the conditions would result in earning lesser profits than before.

Assumptions for Producer's Equilibrium

- Producer's behaviour is rational.
- Producer's behaviour is consistent, i.e. it does not change frequently.
- There are two factors; machine and labour taken into consideration for determining producer's equilibrium.

Conditions of Producer's Equilibrium (When Price Remains Constant)

The equilibrium of the firm can be analysed with the help of marginal curves, i.e. MR and MC curves.

Under perfect competition, as price remains constant, additional revenue (marginal revenue) becomes equal to average revenue i.e. price. It means, AR curve is same as MR curve.

The **equilibrium conditions** are as follows

- MR = MC *or* AR = MR = MC.
- MC should exceed MR after the equality *or* MC should cut MR from below.

Here, MR is a horizontal line, thus its slope is equal to zero. Hence, the second condition becomes, Slope of MC > 0.

The second condition means that MC is greater than MR, after the output level where MR = MC.

In other words, MC curve must be rising at the point of equilibrium or MC curve must cut MR curve from below.

Under *MR and MC approach*, a producer is in equilibrium, where

- MR = MC, also AR = MR, hence, AR = MR = MC.
- MC should be rising after MC = MR output level.

Explanation of Concept using following Graph and Example

In the diagram, OL_2 is the output level and OP is the price charged by the firm at the state of equilibrium.

As shown in the diagram, first condition of equilibrium is fulfilled at two points i.e. N and Q. However, the second condition of equilibrium is satisfied only at point Q.

At output level OL_1, MC is equal to MR but post that MC is diminishing, which indicates that profit levels are not maximum, so being a rational producer, he will continue the production till output level OL_2.

At this OL_2 level, producer's equilibrium will be determined at point Q because at this point, the following two conditions are satisfied

- MC = MR and
- MC is greater than MR after MC = MR output level

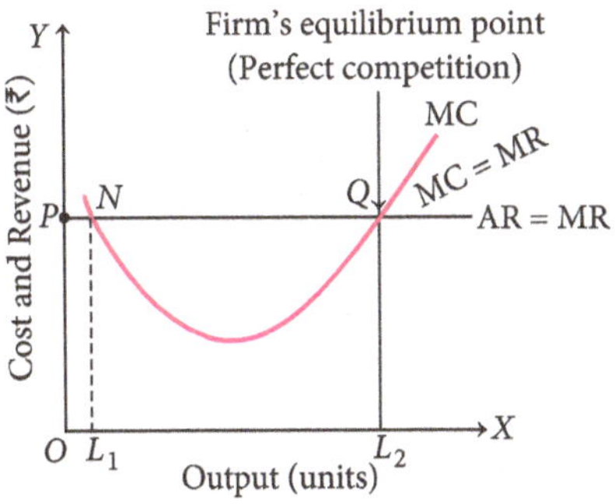

Producer's equilibrium in terms of MR and MC approach

Solved Question 1 In the following table, find out the level of output, at which the producer will be in equilibrium. Give reason for your answer.

Output (units)	Marginal Revenue (₹)	Marginal Cost (₹)
1	8	10
2	8	8
3	8	7
4	8	8
5	8	9

Sol.

Output (units)	**Marginal Revenue** (₹)	**Marginal Cost** (₹)
1	8	10
2	**8**	**8**
3	8	7
4	**8**	**8**
5	8	9

Producer is in equilibrium at 4th unit of output, because at an output level 2nd and 4th, the MR and MC are equal, i.e. profit maximisation.

But the producer is in equilibrium at 4th unit only where MR = MC, i.e. ₹ 8 and MC is rising (MC > MR) afterwards which means at 4th unit of output, both the conditions are satisfied.

Conditions of Producer's Equilibrium (When Price Falls with Rise in Level of Output)

When price is not fixed rather falls with rise in level of output, MR curve slopes downwards. Producer would like to produce that level of output at which MC should be equal to MR and MC curve cuts MR from below.

Explanation of Concept using following Schedule and Diagram

Producer's Equilibrium (When Price Falls)

Output	Price (₹)	TR (₹)	TC (₹)	MC (₹)	MR (₹)
1	16	16	12	12	16
2	14	28	22	10	12
3	12	36	30	**8**	**8**
4	10	40	40	10	4
5	8	40	52	12	0

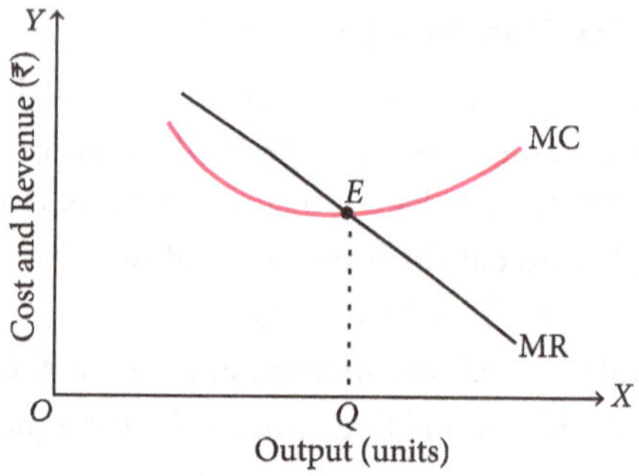

As per the above schedule, both the conditions of equilibrium are satisfied at 3 units of output. Also at this point, profit is maximum.

In the above figure, output is shown on the x-axis and revenue and cost are shown on the y-axis.

Producer's equilibrium will be determined at *OQ* level of output corresponding to point *E* because at this level, the conditions of equilibrium are met, i.e.

- MR = MC.
- MC is greater than MR post equality.

This implies that at equilibrium, producer produces *OQ* level of output and maximise his profits.

Relationship between MC and Price at Equilibrium

- When more output is sold only by reducing the prices, then price or AR becomes more than MR. As equilibrium is achieved when MR = MC, it means, price is more than MC at the equilibrium point.
- A producer may not always earn super normal profits. There may be situations of normal profit (break-even point) or losses (shut down point).

Break-even Point

A firm's break-even point occurs when AR equals AC (TR = TC). At this point, firm earns zero economic profit or normal profit. The market price passes through the minimum point of AC curve. At this point, a firm is able to cover its all costs of production.

Accordingly, break-even point is defined as a situation when AR = AC. Here, $P = AR$. The break-even point is graphically illustrated in the given diagram.

Break-even occurs at point S.

Here, AR = AC

The firm is just making normal profits at break-even point.

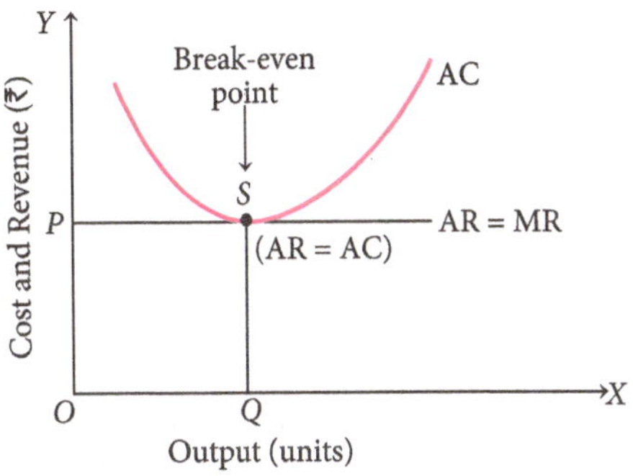

Break-even Point

A small bakery spends ₹ 50,000 per month on ingredients, wages and rent (its total costs). It sells cakes and pastries worth ₹ 50,000, meaning the bakery reaches its break-even point. While it covers all expenses, it doesn't make any extra profit.

Shut Down Point

Shut down point occurs when firm is just able to cover its variable costs, incurring the losses equal to fixed cost of production.

Accordingly, shut down point is defined as a situation when, TR = TVC *or* AR = AVC.

The shut down point is graphically illustrated in the following diagram

Shut down is struck at a point S.

Here, AR = AVC

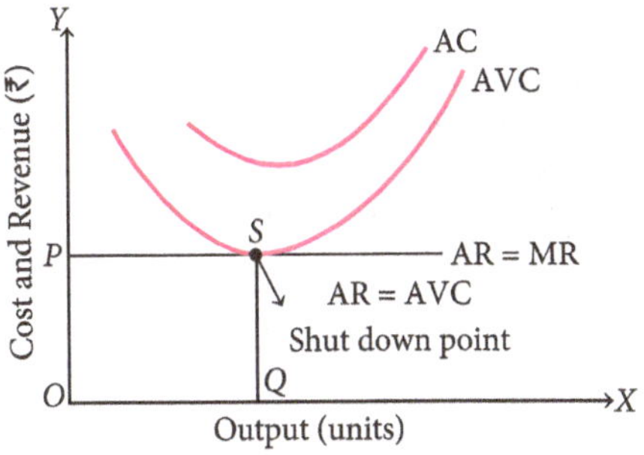

Shut down point

Mind Map

PRODUCER'S EQUILIBRIUM

1 Concept of Producer and Profit

- Producer is someone who converts input into output to earn profit.
- Profit is the difference between the revenue generated from selling goods and the cost incurred in producing them.
  Profit (π) = Total Revenue (TR) – Total Cost (TC)

Scenarios of Profitability

- Supernormal Profit (R > C) – Firm earns profit.
- Supernormal Loss (R < C) – Firm suffers loss.
- Normal Profit/Break-even (R = C) – No profit, no loss

2 Concept of Producer's Equilibrium

Producer's equilibrium is the point where profit is maximised or loss is minimised with the given input and producer has no tendency to change output level.

Assumptions

- Rational producer aims to maximise profit.
- Producer does not frequently change decisions.
- Only two factors (labour and capital) are considered.

3 Conditions for Producer's Equilibrium (MR-MC Approach, Perfect Competition)

Producer's equilibrium is determined using Marginal Revenue (MR) and Marginal Cost (MC) curves.
The conditions for equilibrium are as follows

- MR = MC or AR = MR = MC
- MC must exceed MR after the equality or MC should cut MR from below.

Implications

- At equilibrium, AR = MR = MC
- MC is greater than MR after MR = MC output level
- Ensures profit maximisation for the producer.

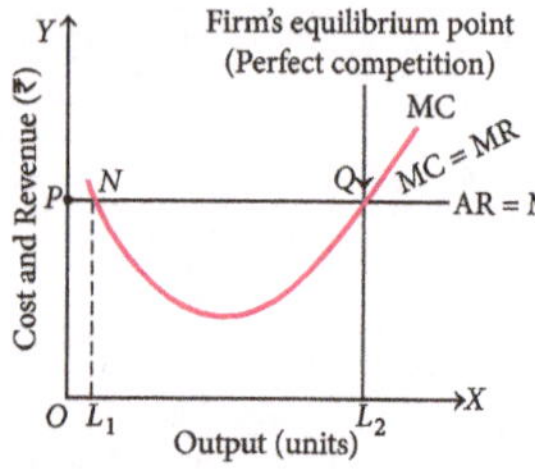

4 Conditions for Producer's Equilibrium (When Price Falls with Output Increase)

- In imperfect competition, price is not constant; instead, it falls with increase in output.
- When price falls with an increase in output, the MR curve slopes downward.
- Producer reaches equilibrium where MR = MC and MC curve cuts MR from below.

Conditions for Equilibrium

- MR = MC (Marginal Cost equals Marginal Revenue).
- MC is greater than MR after equality (MC must cut MR from below)

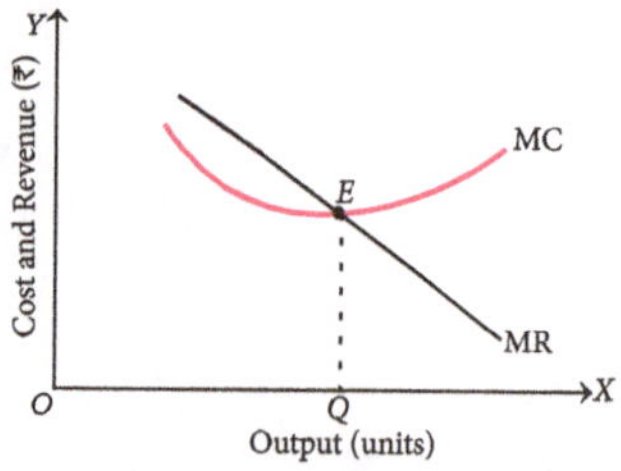

5 Break-even Point

- It is defined as a situation when AR = AC.
- At this point, firm earns zero economic profit or normal profit.
- A firm is able to cover its all costs of production and just makes normal profits.

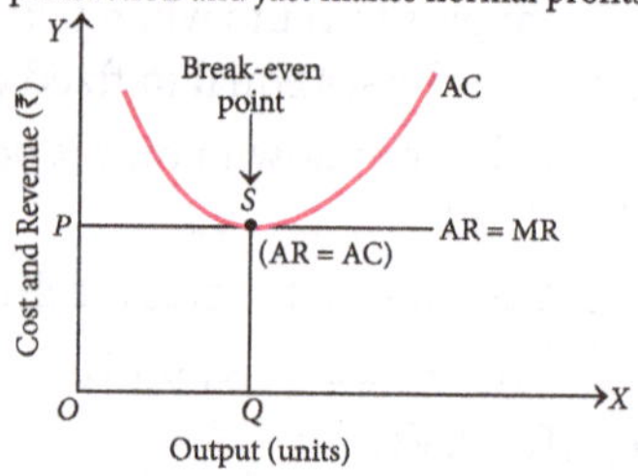

6 Shut Down Point

- It occurs when firm is just able to cover its variable costs, incuring the losses equal to fixed cost of production.
- It can be defined as a situation when, TR = TVC *or* AR = AVC.

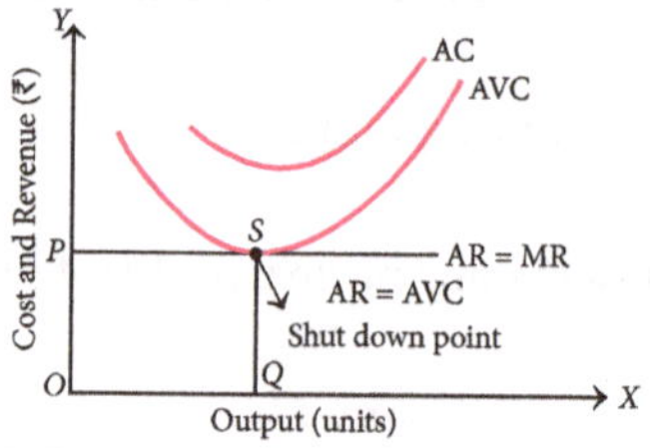

EXAM PATTERN QUESTIONS

Objective Type Questions

Multiple Choice Questions (MCQs)

1. Net profit is **NCERT (QR)**

(a) TR − MC (b) TR − TFC − TVC
(c) TR − TFC (d) TR − TVC

2. Sequence the following situations of a firm based on profitability. **Competency Based Que**

(i) Break-even point
(ii) Loss
(iii) Profit

Codes

(a) (iii) > (i) > (ii) (b) (iii) > (ii)> (i)
(c) (ii) > (i) > (iii) (d) (i)> (ii) > (iii)

3. Which of the following is incorrect about producer's equilibrium?

(a) It occurs when profit is maximised
(b) It happens when revenue equals cost
(c) It guides decisions on production levels
(d) It guarantees a firm will never experience loss

4. "Nestle India Q_3 Results: Profit surges 37% YoY to ₹ 908 crore, firm declares ₹ 140 per share interim dividend."

Source *https://economictimes.indiatimes.com/markets/stocks/earnings/nestle-india-q3-results-profit-surges-37-yoy-to-rs-908-crore-firm-declares-rs-140-per-share-interim-dividend/articleshow/104544457.cms?from=mdr*

Based on the headline, what can be inferred about Nestle India's financial performance in Q_3? **Competency Based Que**

(a) Nestle India is operating at a break-even point
(b) Nestle India is experiencing a super normal loss
(c) Nestle India's revenue equals its cost
(d) Nestle India is earning a super normal profit

5. "There are three possible scenarios: super normal profit, super normal loss and normal profit."
What is another term for normal profit? **Competency Based Que**

(a) Super normal profit (b) Break-even point
(c) Abnormal profit (d) Revenue maximisation

6. A tech company has been incurring losses for the last three quarters, where its cost exceeds revenue. The management is considering cutting back of production to reduce costs.

What outcome can they expect if they follow this plan? **Competency Based Que**

(a) Losses may be minimised, but not eliminated
(b) They will reach break-even instantly
(c) Production costs will increase further
(d) Profit will increase immediately

7. .... is a person who purchases factors of production (inputs) to convert them into outputs.

(a) Buyers (b) Consumer
(c) Producer (d) Government

8. If a firm's total revenue is ₹ 10,000 and total cost is ₹ 8,000, the profit will be ....

(a) ₹ 1,500 (b) ₹ 2,000
(c) ₹ 3,000 (d) ₹ 2,500

9. A firm incurs a cost of ₹ 12,000 and generates revenue of ₹ 9,000. The firm's loss is ....

(a) ₹ 2,000 (b) ₹ 1,000
(c) ₹ 3,000 (d) ₹ 500

10. When MC is greater than MR after producer equilibrium, it means

(a) profit of firm
(b) producing more will lead to decline in profit
(c) no profit no loss
(d) firm enjoys economic efficiency

11. The sufficient condition of producer's equilibrium under both perfect and imperfect competition is

(a) MR = MC (b) MR > MC
(c) MC > MR (d) None of these

12. Which concept is highlighted in the below image?

(a) Consumer satisfaction
(b) Break-even point
(c) Producer's equilibrium
(d) Producer's disequilibrium

13. Based upon the diagram given below, identify the point of producer's equilibrium.

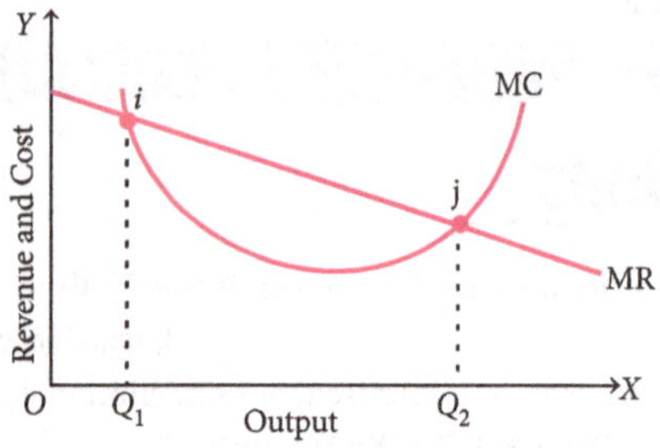

(a) Point *i* (b) Point *j*
(c) Both (a) and (b) (d) Neither (a) nor (b)

14. "The producer aims to make decisions that maximise profits."

Which assumption of producer's equilibrium is highlighted in the above statement? **Competency Based Que**

(a) Rational behaviour (b) Irrational behaviour
(c) Consistency (d) Competency

15. Which of the following are not the key assumptions of producer's equilibrium? **Competency Based Que**

I. The producer aims to minimise profits.
II. The producer makes irrational decisions.
III. The producer is consistent in behaviour.
IV. The producer constantly changes production decisions.

Codes
(a) I, III and IV (b) I and III
(c) I, II, III and IV (d) I, II and IV

16. Which of the following statements about producer's equilibrium is correct?

(a) Producer's equilibrium occurs when profits are minimised
(b) Producer's equilibrium occurs when production exceeds demand
(c) Producer's equilibrium is the point where profits are maximised
(d) Producer's equilibrium is irrelevant for cost management

17. Based upon the image given below, identify the situation at the point of equilibrium.

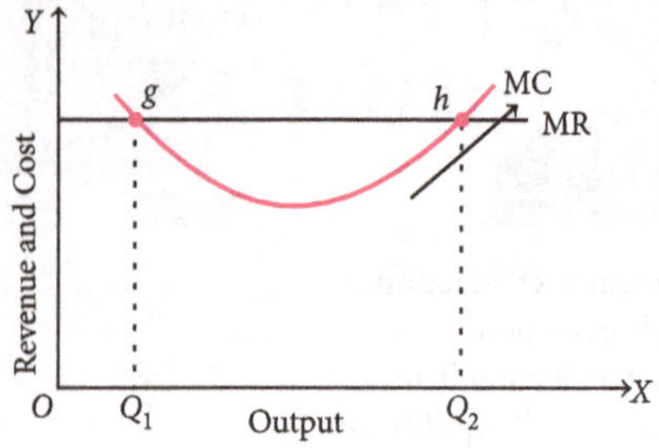

(a) Firm is earning super normal profits
(b) Firm is earning normal profits
(c) Firm is suffering losses
(d) State of profit or loss can't be predicted

18. What is the shape of MR curve in perfect competition market? **NCERT (QR)**

(a) Downward sloping from left to right
(b) Horizontal line parallel to x-axis
(c) Vertical line parallel to y-axis
(d) Upward sloping from left to right

19. "The announcement of cracker closures by two major European chemicals producers, ExxonMobil and Sabic, in April, 2024 brought into sharp relief the impact of overcapacity on the European chemical industry."

Source *https://www.icis.com/explore/resources/ cracker-closures-europe*

The news headline about ExxonMobil and Sabic's cracker closures in April 2024 reflects which economic concept related to a firm's decision-making? **Competency Based Que**

(a) Super normal profit
(b) Break-even point
(c) Shut down point
(d) Expansion of production

20. What are the two conditions required for producer's equilibrium? **Competency Based Que**

I. MR > MC II. MR = MC
III. MC cuts MR from below
IV. MR < MC

Codes
(a) I and II (b) I and IV
(c) III and IV (d) II and III

21. A firm produces 50 units and the total revenue is ₹ 2,000. What is the price per unit? **Competency Based Que**

(a) ₹ 50 (b) ₹ 40
(c) ₹ 30 (d) ₹ 20

22. The arrow in the diagram given below indicates which of the following situations?

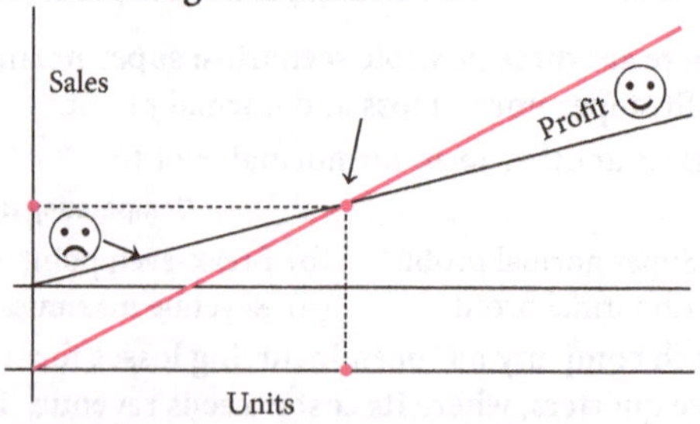

(a) Break-even point (b) Shut down point
(c) Maximum profit (d) Minimum loss

23. **What does the intersection of P_1 and Q_1 at AVC depict in the below image?**

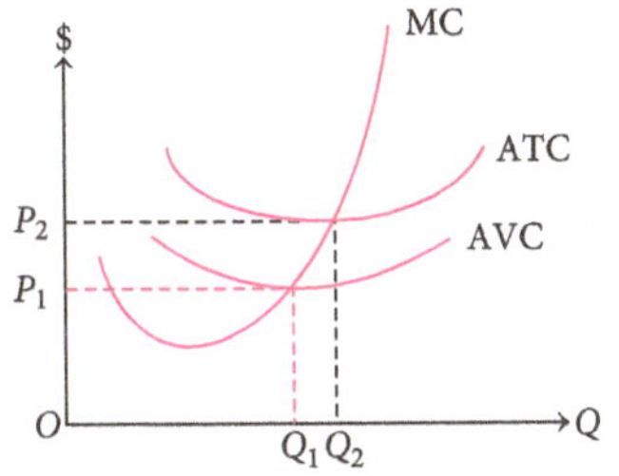

(a) Break-even point (b) Shut down point
(c) Loss (d) Profit

24. **A firm's Total Revenue (TR) and Total Cost (TC) at different levels of output are as follows**

Output (Q)	**Total Revenue** (TR)	**Total Cost** (TC)
1	₹ 100	₹ 120
2	₹ 200	₹ 180
3	₹ 300	₹ 300
4	₹ 400	₹ 350

At which level of output does the firm reach its break-even point? **Competency Based Que**

(a) Q = 1 (b) Q = 2
(c) Q = 3 (d) Q = 4

Direction *Read the case study and answer the questions 25 to 28 on the basis of the same*

A local bakery, Sweet Delights, has been operating for several years, providing freshly baked goods to the community. Due to increased competition from nearby bakeries and rising ingredient costs, Sweet Delights is facing challenges in maintaining profitability.

Sweet Delights incurs a total fixed cost of ₹ 20,000 per month, which includes rent, utilities and salaries. The bakery's Average Vvariable Cost (AVC) for producing pastries and bread is ₹ 30 per unit and it sells each unit for ₹ 50.

The bakery needs to determine how many units it must sell to cover its total costs (fixed and variable). The break-even point is critical for assessing whether the bakery can continue operations profitably. If the bakery's Total Revenue (TR) does not cover its variable costs, it may have to consider stopping production temporarily to prevent further losses.

25. **The break-even point for Sweet Delights is the output level where total revenue equals ....**

26. **What does the Average Variable Cost (AVC) represent in the context of Sweet Delights?**

(a) The total cost of production divided by the number of units produced
(b) The cost incurred for producing one additional unit of a good
(c) The fixed costs that do not change with production levels
(d) The cost of ingredients and labour for each unit produced

27. **Why is determining the break-even point crucial for Sweet Delights?**

(a) It helps in maximising revenue
(b) It allows the bakery to reduce fixed costs
(c) It indicates the level of sales needed to avoid losses
(d) It determines the selling price of each unit

28. **If the bakery's Total Revenue (TR) does not cover its variable costs, it may have to consider stopping production temporarily to prevent further losses. This points out to the .... point.**

Assertion-Reason

Direction (Q.No. 29 to 38) *Read the following Assertion (A) and Reason (R) and choose the correct alternative from the following*

Alternatives

(a) Both Assertion (A) and Reason (R) are true and Reason (R) is the correct explanation of Assertion (A)
(b) Both Assertion (A) and Reason (R) are true, but Reason (R) is not the correct explanation of Assertion (A)
(c) Assertion (A) is true, but Reason (R) is false
(d) Assertion (A) is false, but Reason (R) is true

29. **Assertion** (A) A producer is someone who creates goods and supplies them to the market with the goal of earning profit.

Reason (R) Producer earns profit which is the difference between the revenue generated from selling goods and the cost incurred in producing them.

30. **Assertion** (A) A firm can always earn profits.

Reason (R) At times, firms may suffer a loss, this is the case when cost exceeds revenue of a firm.

31. **Assertion** (A) Super normal profits occur when revenues are greater than costs.

Reason (R) Super normal profits are also called abnormal profits because it is a situation when revenue exceeds cost, resulting in excess profit.

32. **Assertion** (A) The goal of the producer is to find the output level where profit is maximised.

Reason (R) Normal profit is the shut down point for a firm.

33. **Assertion** (A) Producer's equilibrium is the state of profit maximisation or cost minimisation.

Reason (R) The concept of producer's equilibrium focuses on the point where a producer achieves maximum profit or minimises losses with the available resources.

34. Assertion (A) When a producer is in equilibrium, he/she depicts irrational behaviour.

Reason (R) The producer's behaviour remains stable and does not change frequently in equilibrium.

35. Assertion (A) A producer finds equilibrium by balancing production and costs.

Reason (R) At equilibrium point, the producer has no desire to change the output level because increasing or decreasing production would lead to lower profits.

36. Assertion (A) When a producer charges lesser price for additional units, marginal revenue falls.

Reason (R) Marginal revenue falls twice faster than average revenue.

37. Assertion (A) A producer minimises losses at the shut-down point.

Reason (R) The shut-down point is where average revenue equals average variable cost.

38. Assertion (A) Under perfect competition, a producer continues production as long as MR is greater than MC, even if MR is falling.

Reason (R) When MC is falling, producer earns more for each additional unit as compared to cost of each additional unit.

Two Statements Based MCQs

Direction (Q.No. 39 to 48) *Read the following statements carefully and choose the correct alternative*

Alternatives

(a) Statement I is correct and Statement II is incorrect
(b) Statement II is correct and Statement I is incorrect
(c) Both the statements are correct
(d) Both the statements are incorrect

39. Statement I A firm always earns profit at the equilibrium point.

Statement II Break-even points are always points of normal profits.

40. Statement I Normal profit occurs when revenue equals cost, indicating no profit or loss.

Statement II Super normal profit occurs when revenue exceeds cost, resulting in excess profit.

41. Statement I The concept of producer's equilibrium is irrelevant for decision-making in various market conditions.

Statement II At the break-even point, a firm is guaranteed to make a super normal profit.

42. Statement I The analysis of producer's equilibrium considers limited factors of production, primarily machine and labour.

Statement II A producer's behaviour changes frequently, reflecting instability in production decisions.

43. Statement I The producer can achieve equilibrium without considering the costs of production.

Statement II Rational behaviour is one of the key assumptions for producer's equilibrium.

44. Statement I There is stability in production decisions at the equilibrium point.

Statement II There is an importance of resource efficiency in achieving producer's equilibrium.

45. Statement I Equality of marginal cost and marginal revenue ensures equilibrium.

Statement II The vertical gap between total revenue and total cost is maximum when equilibrium conditions of MR – MC approach are satisfied.

46. Statement I In perfect competition, Marginal Revenue (MR) equals Average Revenue (AR), which is represented by a horizontal line.

Statement II Producer's equilibrium under perfect competition occurs when Marginal Revenue (MR) equals Marginal Cost (MC).

47. Statement I When the price falls as the level of output increases, the MR curve remains horizontal.

Statement II At equilibrium, the Average Revenue (AR) is always greater than Marginal Cost (MC).

48. Statement I The conditions for producer's equilibrium do not change when moving from perfect competition to monopolistic competition.

Statement II The shut down point occurs when a firm's Total Revenue (TR) only covers Total Variable Cost (TVC).

Matching

49. Match the following

Column I		Column II	
A.	Producer	(i)	A state where supply equals demand in a market.
B.	Profit	(ii)	A point where a producer maximises profit.
C.	Equilibrium	(iii)	An entity that creates goods or services for sale.
D.	Producer's equilibrium	(iv)	The financial gain when total revenue exceeds total cost.

Codes

	A	B	C	D		A	B	C	D
(a)	(iii)	(iv)	(i)	(ii)	(b)	(iv)	(i)	(ii)	(iii)
(c)	(ii)	(iii)	(iv)	(i)	(d)	(iii)	(ii)	(i)	(iv)

50. Match the following

Column I		Column II	
A.	Super normal profit	(i)	When cost exceeds revenue, leading to a loss.
B.	Supernormal loss	(ii)	When revenue equals cost, indicating no profit or loss, just covering the expenses.
C.	Normal profit	(iii)	When revenue exceeds cost, resulting in excess profit.

Codes

	A	B	C		A	B	C
(a)	(i)	(ii)	(iii)	(b)	(iii)	(i)	(ii)
(c)	(ii)	(iii)	(i)	(d)	(iii)	(ii)	(i)

51. Match the following

Column I		Column II	
A.	MC = MR	(i)	When the price falls as the level of output increases.
B.	MC exceeds MR	(ii)	This ensures the producer doesn't expand output, as it would reduce profit.
C.	Marginal Revenue (MR) curves slopes downward	(iii)	This is where profit is maximised.
D.	AR=AC	(iv)	Break-even point.

Codes

	A	B	C	D
(a)	(iii)	(iv)	(i)	(ii)
(b)	(iv)	(i)	(ii)	(iii)
(c)	(ii)	(iii)	(iv)	(i)
(d)	(iii)	(ii)	(i)	(iv)

52. Match the following

Column I		Column II	
A.	AR = AVC	(i)	Producer's equilibrium
B.	TR = TC	(ii)	Price falls without output
C.	MR = MC	(iii)	Shut down point
D.	MR >AR	(iv)	Break-even point

Codes

	A	B	C	D		A	B	C	D
(a)	(iii)	(iv)	(i)	(ii)	(b)	(iv)	(i)	(ii)	(iii)
(c)	(ii)	(iii)	(iv)	(i)	(d)	(iii)	(ii)	(i)	(iv)

53. Match the following

Column I		Column II	
A.	Profit	(i)	MR > MC
B.	Normal profit	(ii)	MR = MC
C.	Abnormal profit	(iii)	MR > MC and decreasing
D.	Abnormal loss	(iv)	MR < MC

Codes

	A	B	C	D		A	B	C	D
(a)	(iii)	(iv)	(i)	(ii)	(b)	(iv)	(i)	(ii)	(iii)
(c)	(i)	(ii)	(iii)	(iv)	(d)	(iii)	(ii)	(i)	(iv)

Concept Identification

54. It refers to profit exceeding normal profit in the short-run.

55. It is defined as the point where a producer maximises profit by equating marginal cost to marginal revenues.

56. It is a situation where a firm's total cost exceeds its total revenue, resulting in losses beyond the normal profit.

57. It describes the level of output where a firm should cease production due to losses.

58. It describes the state where total revenue equals total cost.

Answers

1. (b) TR – TFC – TVC
2. (a) (iii) > (i) > (ii)
3. (d) Producer's equilibrium focuses on maximising profit but does not eliminate the possibility of loss.
4. (d) A profit increase of 37% suggests that revenue significantly exceeds costs, leading to super normal profits.
5. (b) Break-even point
6. (a) Cutting back of production can help lower costs, but if revenue is still less than costs, losses will persist.
7. (c) Producer
8. (b) Profit = Total Revenue – Total Cost
   = 10,000 – 8,000 = ₹ 2,000
9. (c) Loss = Total Cost – Total Revenue
   = 12,000 – 9,000 = ₹ 3,000

10. (b) If MC > MR, this means that the firm is losing profit with each additional unit of output and it should produce less.
11. (c) MC > MR
12. (c) Producer's equilibrium
13. (b) Point *j*
14. (a) Rational behaviour
15. (d) I, II and IV
16. (c) Producer's equilibrium is the point where profits are maximised
17. (d) State of profit or loss can't be predicted
18. (b) Horizontal line parallel to x-axis
19. (c) The closures indicate that the firms are facing overcapacity issues, making it unfeasible to operate profitably.
20. (d) II and III
21. (b) Price per unit = 2,000/50 = ₹ 40
22. (a) Break-even point
23. (b) Shut down point
24. (c) At Q = 3, Total Revenue (TR) equals Total Cost (TC), making it the break-even point.
25. total cost
26. (d) AVC refers to the variable costs incurred in producing each unit of output, including ingredients and labour, which fluctuate with the level of production.
27. (c) It indicates the level of sales needed to avoid losses
28. shut down
29. (b) Both Assertion (A) and Reason (R) are true, but Reason (R) is not the correct explanation of Assertion (A)
30. (d) A firm may not always earn profit.
31. (a) Both Assertion (A) and Reason (R) are true and Reason (R) is the correct explanation of Assertion (A)
32. (c) Normal profit depicts the break-even point for a firm.
33. (a) Both Assertion (A) and Reason (R) are true and Reason (R) is the correct explanation of Assertion (A)
34. (d) In producer's equilibrium, a producer aims to maximise profit based on rational decision-making.
35. (a) Both Assertion (A) and Reason (R) are true and Reason (R) is the correct explanation of Assertion (A)
36. (b) Both Assertion (A) and Reason (R) are true, but Reason (R) is not the correct explanation of Assertion (A)
37. (a) Both Assertion (A) and Reason (R) are true and Reason (R) is the correct explanation of Assertion (A)
38. (a) Both Assertion (A) and Reason (R) are true and Reason (R) is the correct explanation of Assertion (A)
39. (b) A firm may suffer losses at the equilibrium level.
40. (c) Both the statements are correct
41. (d) Producer's equilibrium is crucial for guiding production decisions and understanding when to adjust output levels based on profitability. At the break-even point, a firm does not make any profit; it only covers its costs. Super normal profit occurs when revenue exceeds costs.
42. (a) The concept of producer's equilibrium assumes consistency in the producer's behaviour, indicating stability in production decisions rather than frequent changes.
43. (b) Costs are a crucial factor in determining producer's equilibrium. A producer must analyse costs to find the equilibrium point.
44. (c) Both the statements are correct
45. (b) Equality of MR and MC alone does not ensure equilibrium unless MC exceeds MR after MR = MC.
46. (c) Both the statements are correct
47. (d) When price falls, MR curve slopes downward. This reflects that each additional unit sold brings in less revenue. At equilibrium, when MR = MC, the price (AR) can be greater than or equal to MC, depending on the market structure.
48. (b) The conditions for producer's equilibrium change when moving from perfect competition to monopolistic competition. In perfect competition, equilibrium is determined where MR = MC and MR is constant. However, in monopolistic competition, MR slopes downward due to the price changes with output, leading to different conditions for equilibrium.
49. (a) (iii) (iv) (i) (ii)
50. (b) (iii) (i) (ii)
51. (d) (iii) (ii) (i) (iv)
52. (a) (iii) (iv) (i) (ii)
53. (c) (i) (ii) (iii) (iv)
54. Super normal profit (Abnormal profit)
55. Producer's equilibrium
56. Super normal loss
57. Shut down point
58. Break-even point

Subjective Questions

Short Answer Type Questions

1. Define profit in the context of production.

Ans. Profit is the financial gain a producer earns when total revenue from selling goods exceeds total costs incurred in their production. It can be calculated as the difference between Total Revenue (TR) and Total Costs (TC). Profit is essential for sustaining business operations, as it reflects the efficiency and effectiveness of a producer in the market.

2. "The goal of the producer is to find the output level where profit is maximised." What does this imply about producer's equilibrium? Competency Based Que

Ans. This statement highlights that producer's equilibrium is fundamentally about optimising production levels to achieve maximum profitability. Producers analyse costs and revenues to identify the output level where marginal revenue equals marginal cost, ensuring that they operate efficiently and avoid losses. This equilibrium is critical for informed decision-making in production strategies.

3. What strategies can producers implement to move from the break-even point to super normal profits?

Ans. To transition from the break-even point to super normal profits, producers can implement strategies such as enhancing product quality, investing in marketing, expanding distribution channels or optimising production processes to reduce costs. Additionally, conducting market research to identify consumer preferences can help producers tailor their offerings, attracting more customers and increasing sales.

4. Considering the image of the closed store, what might have led to the producer experiencing super normal loss? Discuss how awareness of profit and loss levels can guide a producer's operational decisions? Competency Based Que

Ans. The closed store, indicated by a 'Going out of business' sign, likely faced super normal loss due to several factors such as high fixed costs, low sales volume, increased competition or poor management decisions.

Awareness of profit and loss levels is essential for producers, as it informs their operational decisions. By understanding their financial situation, producers can adjust pricing strategies, control costs, evaluate product mixes and plan for market changes.

5. "It should be kept in mind that a firm may not always earn profit." Do you agree? Give reason. Competency Based Que

Ans. Yes, I agree that a firm may not always earn a profit. Various factors can lead to financial losses, such as increased production costs, decreased demand for products, intense competition or economic downturns. In some cases, businesses may struggle to cover their variable costs, leading to situations where they operate at a loss or even shut down. Understanding these dynamics is crucial for producers to make informed decisions and develop strategies to navigate challenging market conditions effectively.

6. Can there be a positive level of output that a profit maximising firm produces in a competitive market at which market price is not equal to marginal cost? Give an explanation. NCERT; Competency Based Que

Ans. No, because it is not possible as equality between market price and marginal cost is a necessary condition for perfectly competitive firm to be in equilibrium. Only when price remains constant at all output levels, the market price is equal to marginal revenue in case of perfect competition.

7. Is a producer in equilibrium under the following situations?

(i) When marginal revenue is greater than marginal cost.

(ii) When marginal revenue is equal to marginal cost.

Give reasons for your answer.

Ans. (i) No, if MR > MC, then it means that a producer is able to earn abnormal profits. This will motivate him to increase his production.

(ii) Yes, a producer will be in equilibrium where MR = MC and MC should be rising at this point. He will get maximum profit here.

8. Will a profit maximising firm in a competitive market produce a positive level of output in the short-run if the market price is less than the minimum of AVC? Give an explanation. NCERT

Ans. No, a profit maximising firm will not produce a level of output in the short-run when market price is less than the minimum of AVC.

It happens because equality between market price and minimum AVC indicates shut down point and a firm will never operate at a price less than the minimum AVC.

9. **"The shut down point occurs when a firm's total revenue only covers total variable cost."**
How does this affect a producer's decision to continue operating? **Competency Based Que**

Ans. When a firm's total revenue covers only its variable costs, it is better to cease operations to avoid incurring additional losses. The shut down point serves as a critical threshold for producers, guiding them to assess whether continued production is viable or if temporarily halting operations is more financially prudent.

10. **Why should MC be rising at the point of equilibrium?**
Or **"Equilibrium is never struck in a situation of falling MC." Why?**

Ans. Falling MC means that the cost of producing an additional unit of output tends to reduce. In a situation, when price is constant (as under perfect competition), this would mean a situation when the difference between the firm's TR (ΣMR) and TVC (ΣMC) tends to increase. This means a situation when firm's gross profit (TR – TVC) tends to rise. So, this will motivate the producer to produce more. Therefore, equilibrium is never struck in a situation of falling MC.

Long Answer Type Questions

11. **What conditions must hold if a profit maximising firm produces positive output in a competitive market?** **NCERT**

Ans. A firm produces that amount of output for which profit is maximised. If there is a positive level of output at which profit maximises, then the following conditions must be satisfied

(i) **Marginal Revenue (MR) = Marginal Cost (MC)**
The firm will produce where the addition to total revenue from selling one more unit of output is equal to the addition to total cost from producing that unit. This ensures that the firm is not overproducing or underproducing and is operating efficiently.

(ii) **Marginal Cost must be Rising after the Point where MR = MC**
If the MC curve is falling at the point where MR = MC, the firm can increase its profit by producing more units. Therefore, equilibrium is not achieved when the MC curve is still falling.
The equilibrium is achieved only when the MC curve is rising at the point where it equals MR, as this indicates that the firm is at the point where producing additional units would result in diminishing returns.

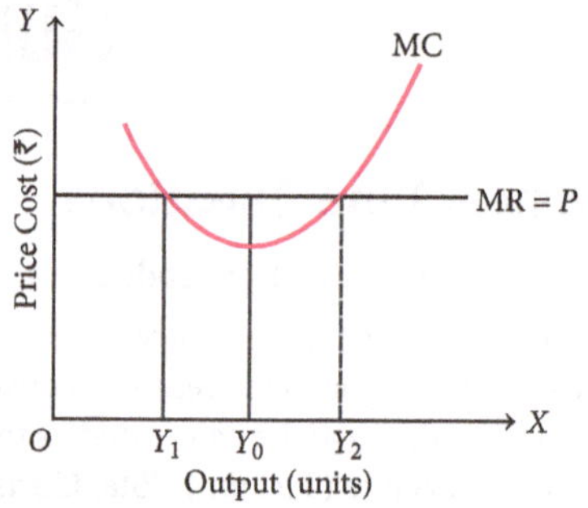

In the graph, the MR and MC curves intersect at point Y, where the firm is not in equilibrium because MC is still falling. At output levels beyond this point (at Y_1), MC starts rising. The firm reaches equilibrium at the point where MC intersects MR at point Y_2, where MC is rising, ensuring maximum profit.

12. **Explain the conditions of producer's equilibrium under perfect competition.**

Ans. Producer's equilibrium refers to a situation, where a producer is producing that level of output, at which its profits are maximum. In other words, it is a situation of profit maximisation or cost minimisation (under MR and MC approach).
Following schedule explain the producer's equilibrium

Units of Output (Q)	MR (₹)	MC (₹)
1	12	15
2	**12**	**12** MR = MC
3	12	10 MR > MC
4	12	9
5	12	8
6	12	7
7	12	8
8	12	9
9	12	10
10	**12**	**12** Producer's equilibrium MR = MC
11	12	15 MR < MC

Conditions of Producer's Equilibrium
Following are the two conditions of producer's equilibrium

(i) MR = MC (Marginal Revenue = Marginal Cost)
(ii) MC must be rising at the point of equilibrium or MC curve must cut MR curve from below.

In the given schedule MR = MC, both at 2 units and 10 units of output, but the second condition of rising MC is fulfilled only at 10th unit of output. So, the producer is in equilibrium when he is producing 10 units.

13. Explain the conditions of a producer's equilibrium in terms of marginal cost and marginal revenue. Use diagram.

Ans. According to this approach, the producer is in equilibrium when the Marginal Revenue (MR) is equal to the Marginal Cost (MC) and marginal cost curve cuts the marginal revenue curve from below. Two conditions under this approach are

(i) MC = MR

(ii) MC curve should cut the MR curve from below.

MR is the addition to total revenue from the sale of one more unit of output and MC is the addition to total cost for increasing the production by one unit. The basic aim of every producer is to maximise the profit. For this, a firm compares its MR with its MC.

As long as the addition to revenue is greater than the addition to cost, it is profitable for a firm to continue producing more units of output.

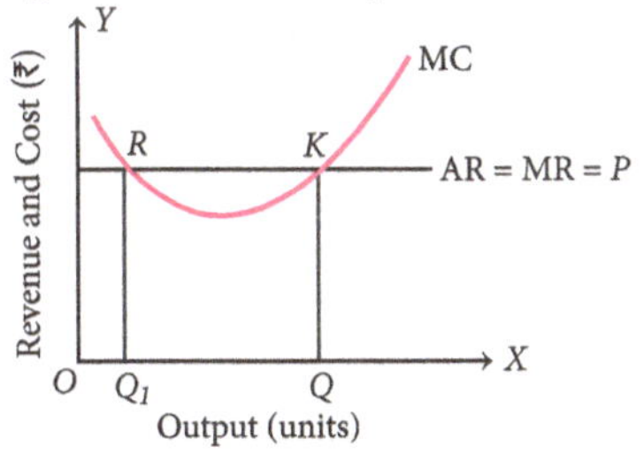

In the above diagram, output is shown on the x-axis, revenue and cost on the y-axis. The marginal cost curve is 'U' shaped and $P = \text{MR} = \text{AR}$.

MC = MR at two points, *R* and *K* in the diagram but profits are maximised at point *K*, corresponding to *OQ* level of output.

Between OQ_1 and *OQ* levels of output, MR exceeds MC.

Therefore, firm will not stop at point *R* but will continue to take advantage of additional profit. Thus, equilibrium will be at point *K* where both the conditions are satisfied.

Two other situations may also exist

(i) **MR > MC**

At output level less than *OQ*, MR > MC which implies that firm is earning profit on the last unit of output. The marginal profit provides an incentive to the firm to increase production and move towards *OQ* units of output. Therefore, when MR > MC, the firm increases output to maximise its profit.

(ii) **MR < MC**

At output level more than *OQ*, MR < MC which implies that firm is making a loss on its last unit of output. Hence, in order to maximise profit, a rational producer decreases output as long as MC > MR. Thus, the firm moves towards producing *OQ* units of output.

14. Briefly explain the break-even point and shut down point.

Ans. Break-even Point

The break-even point is a critical concept in economics, where a firm neither earns a profit nor incurs a loss. It occurs when Average Revenue (AR) equals Average Cost (AC), meaning Total Revenue (TR) is equal to Total Cost (TC).

At this point, the firm covers all its production costs and earns normal profit, but not more.

In simple terms, the break-even point is the level of output where the firm makes just enough revenue to cover its costs, without earning excess profit.

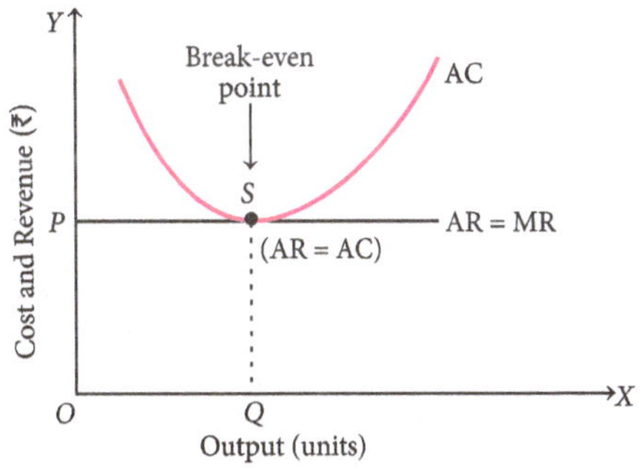

Break-even point

Break-even occurs at point *S*.

Here, AR = AC

The firm is just making normal profits at break-even point.

Shut Down Point

The shut down point occurs when a firm's Total Revenue (TR) only covers Total Variable Cost (TVC), meaning Average Revenue (AR) = Average Variable Cost (AVC). If the firm can't cover even its variable costs, it is better to stop production, as operating would result in more losses.

This is graphically illustrated where the AR curve meets the AVC curve.

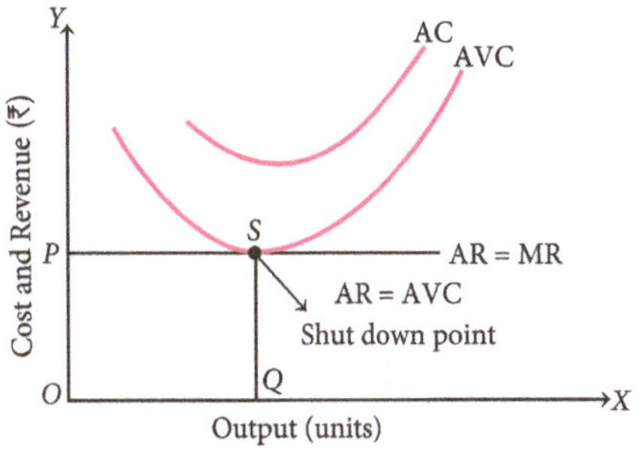

Shut down point

Shut down is struck at a point *S*.

Here, AR = AVC

15. Bakery Junction, a well-known chain of bakeries in India, has been in operation for over a decade. Owned by Mr. Sharma, the bakery offers a variety of products, including pastries, breads and cakes.

Recently, Mr. Sharma noticed a significant fluctuation in his profits during different seasons. During the festive season, sales surged, leading to super normal profits. However, during the monsoon months, the sales dropped considerably, often leading to situations where the bakery just covered its costs or even incurred losses.

To better manage production levels, Mr. Sharma began analysing the concept of producer's equilibrium, where Marginal Revenue (MR) equals Marginal Cost (MC). During the festive season, the revenue from selling each additional cake was greater than the cost of ingredients and labour, indicating that increasing production was advantageous.

In contrast, during the slower months, he realised that producing more pastries resulted in costs exceeding revenue, leading to losses. By understanding these dynamics, Mr. Sharma adjusted his production and marketing strategies, focusing on promotions during low seasons and optimising costs to maintain profitability. **Competency Based Que**

(i) What is meant by super normal profit in the context of Bakery Junction's operations?

(ii) Explain the significance of the break-even point for Bakery Junction.

(iii) How does the relationship between MR and MC influence Bakery Junction's decision-making?

Ans. (i) Super normal profit refers to the profit that exceeds the normal profit level, occurring when Bakery Junction's total revenue from sales surpasses its total production costs, indicating effective management and strong market demand during peak seasons.

(ii) The break-even point is significant for Bakery Junction as it represents the production level where total revenue equals total costs.

This understanding allows Mr. Sharma to make informed decisions about production levels, pricing and promotional strategies to ensure the bakery covers its expenses without incurring losses.

(iii) The relationship between Marginal Revenue (MR) and Marginal Cost (MC) is critical for Bakery Junction's decision-making.

Equilibrium is achieved when MR equals MC. When MR exceeds MC, it signals that increasing production will enhance profitability.

Conversely, if MC surpasses MR, it suggests that producing additional items will lead to decreased profits. By understanding this relationship, Mr. Sharma can effectively adjust output to maximise profits, ensuring that the bakery operates efficiently across different market conditions.

Numerical Questions

Numerical 1

XYZ Electronics manufactures gadgets. The Total Cost (TC) of producing 100 gadgets is ₹ 50,000 and the Total Revenue (TR) from selling them is ₹ 60,000. If the Average Cost (AC) per gadget is ₹ 500, calculate the profit per gadget and determine if XYZ Electronics is making a super normal profit, normal profit or a loss.

Sol. Profit = Total Revenue − Total Cost

Profit = 60,000 −50,000 = ₹ 10,000

$$\text{Average Revenue (AR)} = \frac{\text{TR}}{\text{Quantity}} = \frac{60{,}000}{100} = ₹\ 600$$

Profit per gadget = AR − AC = 600 − 500 = ₹ 100

Since the profit per gadget is positive, XYZ Electronics is making a super normal profit.

Numerical 2

A firm produces 200 units of a good with the following details

- **Total Revenue (TR) from selling 200 units = ₹ 30,000**
- **Average Cost (AC) = ₹ 120**
- **Fixed Costs (FC) = ₹ 6,000**

Calculate the profit and determine the type of profit (super normal, normal or loss) the firm is experiencing.

Sol. Total Cost (TC) = FC + (AC × Quantity)

TC = 6,000 + (120 × 200) = 6,000 + 24,000 = ₹ 30,000

Profit = TR − TC = 30,000 − 30,000 = ₹ 0

The firm is at the break-even point, earning normal profit.

Numerical 3

A manufacturer has fixed costs of ₹ 15,000 and produces 1,000 units of a product at a variable cost of ₹ 50 per unit. If the selling price is ₹ 90 per unit, determine the total profit or loss and analyse whether the producer is at a break-even point, experiencing super normal profit or facing a loss.

Sol. Total Revenue (TR) = Selling Price × Quantity

= 90 × 1,000 = ₹ 90,000

Total Variable Cost (TVC)

= Variable Cost per Unit × Quantity

= 50 × 1,000 = ₹ 50,000

Total Cost (TC) = Fixed Costs + Total Variable Cost

= 15,000 + 50,000

= ₹ 65,000

Profit = Total Revenue − Total Cost

= 90,000 − 65,000 = ₹ 25,000

The manufacturer earns a super normal profit of ₹ 25,000, indicating that the production level is sustainable and that the producer is well above the break-even point.

Numerical 4

The following table shows the total revenue and total cost schedules of a competitive firm.
Calculate the profit at each output level. Determine also the market price of the good. **NCERT**

Quantity Sold	0	1	2	3	4	5	6	7
TR (in ₹)	0	5	10	15	20	25	30	35
TC (in ₹)	5	7	10	12	15	23	33	40
Profit (in ₹)	—	—	—	—	—	—	—	—

Sol. Profit = TR − TC

Profit (₹)	−5	−2	0	3	5	2	−3	−5

Market price $= \frac{TR}{Q}$; i.e. $\Rightarrow \frac{5}{1} =$ ₹ 5 at II stage

$\Rightarrow \frac{10}{2} =$ ₹ 5 in III stage and so on.

Numerical 5

The following table shows the total cost schedule of a competitive firm. It is given that the price of the good is ₹ 10. Calculate the profit at each output level. Find the profit maximising level of output. **NCERT**

Output	0	1	2	3	4	5	6	7	8	9	10
TC (₹)	5	15	22	27	31	38	49	63	81	101	123

Sol.

Output	TC (₹)	Price (given)	TR = Q× P	Profit = (TR − TC)
0	5	10	0	−5
1	15	10	10	−5
2	22	10	20	−2
3	27	10	30	3
4	31	10	40	9
5	38	10	50	12
6	49	10	60	11
7	63	10	70	7
8	81	10	80	−1
9	101	10	90	−11
10	123	10	100	−23

The profit maximising level at 5 units sold where firm is earning profit of ₹ 12.

Numerical 6

From the following table, find out the level of output at which the producer is in equilibrium. Give reasons for your answer.

Output (units)	**Average Revenue** (₹)	**Total Cost** (₹)
1	12	14
2	12	26
3	12	35
4	12	52
5	12	64
6	12	70

Sol.

Output (Q) (units)	Average Revenue (AR) (₹)	Total Cost (TC) (₹)	Total Revenue (TR) (₹) (AR×Q)	Profit (₹) (TR−TC)
1	12	14	12	−2
2	12	26	24	−2
3	12	35	36	1
4	12	52	48	−4
5	12	64	60	−4
6	**12**	**70**	**72**	**2**

Producer is in equilibrium at 6th unit of output.

Reason Maximum profit, i.e. ₹ 2 (TR − TC).

Numerical 7

Given below is a cost and revenue schedule of a producer. At what level of output is the producer in equilibrium? Give reasons for your answer.

Output (units)	**Price** (₹)	**Total Cost** (₹)
1	10	13
2	10	22
3	10	30
4	10	38
5	10	47
6	10	57
7	10	71

Sol.

Output (Q) (units)	Price (P) (₹)	Total Cost (TC) (₹)	Total Revenue (TR) (₹) (P × Q)	MR (₹) ($TR_n - TR_{n-1}$)	MC (₹) ($TC_n - TC_{n-1}$)	Profit (₹) (TR − TC)
1	10	13	10	10	13	−3
2	10	22	20	10	9	−2
3	10	30	30	10	8	0
4	10	38	40	10	8	2
5	10	47	50	10	9	3
6	**10**	**57**	**60**	**10**	**10**	**3**
7	10	71	70	10	14	−1

Producer is in equilibrium at 6th unit of output.

Reason At output level of 5th and 6th units, the difference between total revenue and total cost (i.e. profit) is maximum which is equal to 3 in both the cases. But, producer is in equilibrium at 6th unit only where MR = MC, i.e. ₹ 10 as MC > MR afterwards.

Numerical 8

Observe the data given below

Output (units)	**Price** (₹)	**Total Cost** (TC in ₹)
1	24	26
2	24	50
3	24	72
4	24	92
5	24	115
6	24	139
7	24	165

(i) Find out profit and loss from the following data.

(ii) From the given schedule, find out the level of output, at which the producer is in equilibrium using MR-MC approach. Give reason for your answer.

Sol. (i)

Output (Q)	Price/ AR (₹)	Total Cost (TC in ₹)	Total Revenue (TR in ₹) (AR × Q)	Profit/Loss (TR − TC) (₹)
1	24	26	24	−2
2	24	50	48	−2
3	24	72	72	0
4	24	92	96	4
5	24	115	120	5
6	24	139	144	5
7	24	165	168	3

(ii)

Output (Q)	Price/AR (₹)	Total Cost (TC in ₹)	Total Revenue (TR in ₹) (AR × Q)	Marginal Revenue (MR in ₹) (P = MR)	Marginal Cost (MC in ₹) (MC = $TC_n - TC_{n-1}$)
1	24	26	24	24	26
2	24	50	48	24	24
3	24	72	72	24	22
4	24	92	96	24	20
5	24	115	120	24	23
6	24	139	144	24	24
7	24	165	168	24	26

Producer is in equilibrium at 6th unit of output. At an output level 2nd and 6th unit, marginal revenue is equal to marginal cost. But the producer is in equilibrium at 6th unit only, as at this point, MR = MC and MC is rising, thereafter, i.e. there is no further possibility of increasing profit after this level of output.

Numerical 9

From the following information about a firm, find the firm's equilibrium output in terms of marginal cost and marginal revenue. Give reasons. Also find profit at this output.

Output (units)	Total Revenue (₹)	Total Cost (₹)
1	6	7
2	12	13
3	18	17
4	24	23
5	30	31

Sol. **Determination of Firm's Equilibrium**

Output (units)	Total Revenue (TR) (₹)	Total Cost (TC) (₹)	Marginal Revenue (MR) (₹)	Marginal Cost (MC) (₹)	Profit (₹) (TR – TC)
1	6	7	6	7	– 1
2	12	13	6	6	– 1
3	18	17	6	4	1
4	24	23	6	6	1
5	30	31	6	8	– 1

$MR_n = TR_n - TR_{n-1}$, $MC_n = TC_n - TC_{n-1}$

According to the MR and MC approach, the firm attains its equilibrium, where the following two necessary and sufficient conditions are fulfilled

(i) MR = MC

(ii) MC must be rising after the equilibrium level of output.

Thus, by looking at the above table, we can say that the firm is in equilibrium at output equal to 4 units, because at 4th unit of output, MR = MC and MC increases after the 4th unit of output. Profit at 4th unit of output is ₹ 1.

Numerical 10

From the following information about a firm, find the firm's equilibrium output in terms of marginal cost and marginal revenue.

Give reasons. Also find profit at this output.

Output (units)	Total Revenue (₹)	Total Cost (₹)
1	7	8
2	14	15
3	21	21
4	28	28
5	35	36

Sol. **Determination of Firm's Equilibrium**

Output (units)	Total Revenue (TR) (₹)	Total Cost (TC) (₹)	Marginal Revenue (MR) (₹)	Marginal Cost (MC) (₹)	Profit (₹) (TR – TC)
1	7	8	7	8	– 1
2	14	15	7	7	– 1
3	21	21	7	6	0
4	28	28	7	7	0
5	35	36	7	8	– 1

$MR_n = TR_n - TR_{n-1}$, $MC_n = TC_n - TC_{n-1}$

Level of Output

Firm fulfilled the following two necessary conditions at 4th unit of output

(i) MR = MC

(ii) MC must be rising after the equilibrium output.

Reason

Firm is in equilibrium at 4th unit of output because at this unit MR = MC, i.e. ₹ 7 and MC is rising, thereafter. Profit at 4th unit of output is ₹ 0.

SELF ASSESSMENT TEST

Objective Type Questions

1. At what point is a producer said to achieve equilibrium?
   (a) When AR > MR
   (b) When MC = MR and MC is falling
   (c) When MC = MR and MC is rising
   (d) When AR = AC
2. What does the slope of the MC curve represent?
   (a) Revenue changes
   (b) Changes in cost with respect to output
   (c) Changes in TR
   (d) Price fluctuations
3. The point where AR equals AC is known as ....
   (a) shut down point (b) break-even point
   (c) profit maximising point (d) loss minimising point
4. A firm incurring abnormal losses is operating where ....
   (a) TR > TC (b) TR = TC
   (c) AR = AVC (d) TR < TC
5. .... is not a condition of producer's equilibrium in perfect competition.
   (a) MC = MR, where MC cuts MR from above
   (b) MC = MR, where MC cuts MR from below
   (c) AR = MR
   (d) AR = Price
6. Incremental revenue should be .... incremental cost for equilibrium.
   (a) equal to (b) more than
   (c) less than (d) None of these
7. Vertical gap between total cost and revenue represents ....
   (a) loss (b) profit
   (c) no profit no loss (d) None of these
8. Which of the following statements is/are correct?
   I. Incremental revenue is equal to price under both perfect and imperfect competition.
   II. Firm suffer losses when total cost exceeds total revenue at equilibrium level.

   Codes
   (a) Only I
   (b) Only II
   (c) Both I and II
   (d) None of the above

Answers 1. (c) 2. (b) 3. (b) 4. (d) 5. (a) 6. (a) 7. (b) 8. (b)

Short Answer Type Questions

9. What is profit? Give the three possible scenarios of profit for a producer.
10. "A producer is said to be in equilibrium when he produces the level of output at which his profits are maximum or losses are minimised, with the given input and has no tendency to change from that level of output." Do you agree? Give reasons.
11. Define the following
    (i) Break-even point (ii) Shut down point
12. Explain the conditions of producer's equilibrium when price falls with rise in level of output.

Long Answer Type Question

13. What are the conditions of producer's equilibrium when price remains constant? Explain with MC and MR curves.

Numerical Questions

14. Calculate MR and MC from the following schedule and find the equilibrium level.

Output (units)	Total Revenue (₹)	Total Cost (₹)
1	50	30
2	100	70
3	150	110
4	200	160
5	250	220

15. The following data represents a firm's cost and revenue structure

Output (units)	Total Revenue (₹)	Total Cost (₹)	Marginal Cost (₹)
1	100	80	80
2	200	150	70
3	300	230	80
4	400	330	100
5	500	460	130

(i) Calculate the Marginal Revenue (MR) for each level of output.
(ii) Identify the equilibrium output and explain your reasoning.

08

CHAPTER

Supply and Price Elasticity of Supply

The number of units of goods a supplier is willing and able to bring to the market for a specific price can be referred to as supply.

YOUR STUDY GOALS

8.1 Supply
8.2 Law of Supply
8.3 Movement Along the Supply Curve (Change in Quantity Supplied)
8.4 Shift in the Supply Curve (Change in Supply)
8.5 Price Elasticity of Supply

YOUR PRACTICE GOAL

- Objective Type Questions (63 Qs ; MCQs, A-R, Statements, Matching, Concept Identification)
- Subjective Questions (20 SAs, 10 LAs)
- 13 Numerical Questions
- Self Assessment Test (5 MCQs, 4 SAs, 1 LA, 8 Numerical)

8.1 Supply

Supply refers to the quantity of a commodity that a seller is willing and able to sell at a given price during a given period of time.
e.g. A seller is ready to sell 10 kg of wheat in a month at a price of ₹ 30 per kg.

Supply is a desired quantity, i.e. it is the quantity that producers are willing to sell rather than what is actually sold.

There are four **components** of supply

- Willingness of the producer to sell
- Ability of the producer to sell
- Price of the commodity
- Time period

Normally, 'supply' and 'stock' are used alternatively, but in economics, they are different.

Supply is a 'flow' concept, representing the quantity of commodity offered over time, while stock refers to the total quantity available with seller at a particular point, making it a 'stock' concept.

Supply for a commodity can be studied with respect to an individual or market as specified below

1. **Individual Supply** It refers to the quantity of a particular commodity that an individual firm is willing and able to sell at a given price during a given period of time.

2. **Market Supply** It means the total quantity of a commodity that all firms are willing and able to sell at a given price during a given period of time.

Quantity Supplied It refers to specific amount of commodity offered for sale against specific price at a given point of time.

Market Supply

All bakeries in a city, including 'Sweet Treats,' 'Bakewell' and 'Delicious Delights', collectively offer 1,000 cakes for sale at different prices, contributing to the total supply in the cake market.

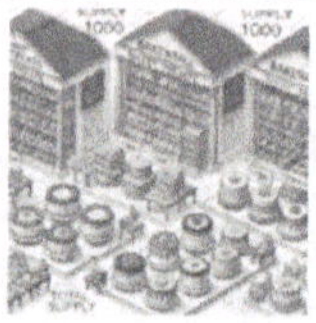

Determinants of Individual Supply

Determinants are also known as the factors which affect the supply of a commodity.

Determinant	Description	Example
Price of Given Commodity (P_X)	There is a direct relationship between price of commodity and quantity supplied. So, higher prices lead to higher quantity supplied and *vice-versa.*	A farmer increases the supply of apples when the price rises from ₹ 50 to ₹ 70 per kg.
Price of Related Goods (P_R)	The supply of a commodity is inversely related to the price of its substitutes. For complementary goods, an increase in one's price leads to a rise in the other's supply.	• **Substitute Goods** If the price of rice increases, a farmer may supply less wheat, focusing more on rice. • **Complementary Goods** With rise in petrol prices, supply of cars will rise.
Goal of the Firm (G)	A profit maximising firm increases supply only at higher prices, while a sales maximising firm supplies more even at same price or reduced price.	A profit maximising electronics company sells more smartphones only when prices rise, while a sales maximising company increases sales even during a discount period.
Price of Factors of Production (P_F)	Higher input costs raise production costs, resulting in decrease in supply due to lesser profit margin and *vice-versa.*	A bakery reduces the supply of cakes when the cost of flour rises, as profits decline.
State of Technology (T)	Technological advancements reduce production costs, encouraging increased supply and *vice-versa.*	A factory adopts automated machinery, reducing production costs and increasing the supply of shoes.

Determinants of Market Supply

Alongwith the determinants of individual supply, market supply is also influenced by following factors

Determinant	Description	Example
Number of Firms in the Industry (N_F)	More firms in the market increase market supply, while fewer firms reduce it.	When three new smartphone companies enter the market, the total supply of smartphones increases.
Expectation of Future Price (E_X)	If firms expect future price rises, they will reduce current supply to sell later at higher prices.	Oil companies hold back supply today, expecting prices to rise in next 2 days.
Government Policy (G_P)	Higher taxes decrease supply by reducing profit margins. Subsidies and tax concessions encourage increased supply by lowering costs.	A tax on plastic goods reduces their supply, while subsidies on solar panels lead to an increase in supply.

Supply Function

The supply function represents the functional relationship between the supply of a commodity and its determinants. The supply function can be further classified as

Individual Supply Function	Market Supply Function
This function explains the relationship between individual supply and its determinants. Mathematically, it can be expressed as $S_X = f(P_X, P_R, G, P_F, T)$ Here, S_X = Supply of commodity f = Functional relation P_X = Price of given commodity X P_R = Price of related goods G = Goal of the firm P_F = Price of factors of production T = State of technology	This function represents the relationship between market supply and its determinants. Mathematically, It can be expressed as $S_X = f(P_X, P_R, G, P_F, T, N_F, E_X, G_P)$ Here, S_X = Supply of commodity f = Functional relation ; P_X = Price of given commodity X P_R = Price of related goods ; G = Goal of the firm P_F = Price of factors of production ; T = State of technology N_F = Number of firms in the industry E_X = Business confidence/Expectation G_P = Government's policy

Supply Schedule

It is a tabular presentation that shows various quantities of a commodity a seller is willing to offer for sale at different prices, during a given time period. It shows the positive relationship between price and quantity supplied of a commodity.

It is of two types, which are as follows

1. Individual Supply Schedule

It refers to the supply schedule of an individual seller. It shows various quantities of a commodity that a seller is willing to sell at different possible prices of a commodity during given period of time.

Individual Supply Schedule

Price (₹)	**Quantity Supplied** (units)
1	100
2	200
3	300
4	400
5	500

From the above schedule, it is clear that as price rises, supply increases.

2. Market Supply Schedule

It refers to the supply schedule of all the producers/sellers in the market producing/selling a particular commodity. It shows various quantities of a commodity that all the sellers are willing to sell at different possible prices of a commodity during given period of time.

Market Supply Schedule

Price (₹)	Quantity Supplied of Firm A	Quantity Supplied of Firm B	Market Supply (A + B) (units)
1	10	5	10 + 5 = 15
2	20	10	20 + 10 = 30
3	30	15	30 + 15 = 45
4	40	20	40 + 20 = 60
5	50	25	50 + 25 = 75

Market supply schedule also shows the positive relationship between price and quantity supplied of a commodity.

Supply Curve

It is a graphical representation of the supply schedule, showing the positive relationship between the price of a commodity and the quantity supplied, while keeping other factors constant. It is an upward sloping curve. Like supply schedule, it is also of two types

1. Individual Supply Curve

This curve represents the relationship between the price and quantity supplied by an individual firm or seller or we can say, it is a graphical representation of the individual supply schedule.

Individual supply curve slopes upwards which shows that more of a commodity is supplied only at a higher price.

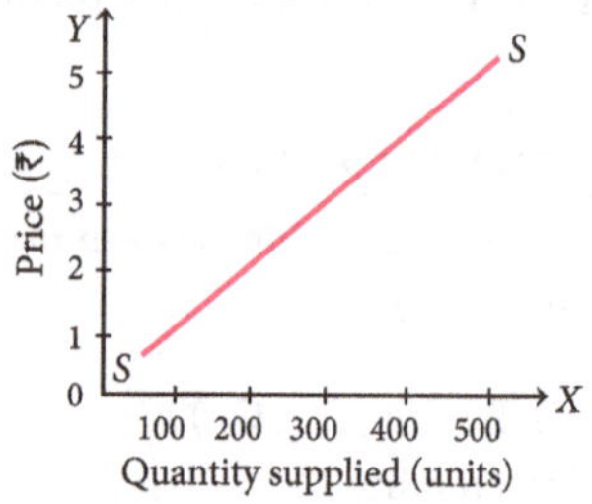

Individual supply curve

2. Market Supply Curve

It is a graphical representation of the relationship between price and supply of a commodity by all the firms in the market or we can say, it is a graphical representation of market supply schedule.

Market supply curve is a horizontal summation of individual supply curves.

It is also an upward sloping curve.

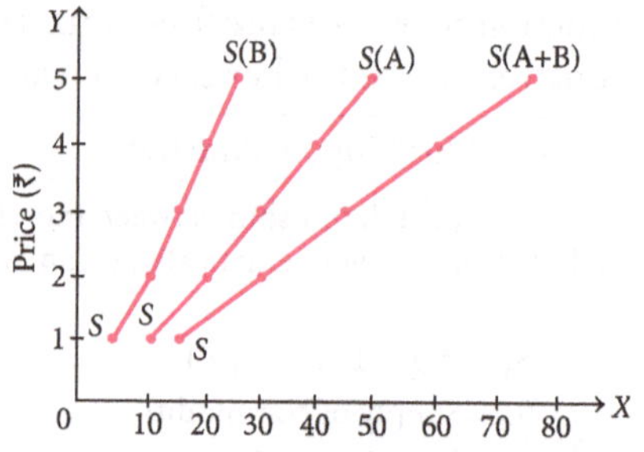

Market supply curve

Market supply curve is flatter while individual supply curves are steeper.

SS (*A*) is the individual supply curve of *A*.

SS (*B*) is the individual supply curve of *B*.

SS (*A*+*B*) is the market supply curve.

Slope of the Supply Curve

Slope of the supply curve is measured as the ratio of change in price with respect to change in quantity.

Mathematically, it is expressed as

$$\text{Slope of Supply Curve} = \frac{\Delta Y}{\Delta X} = \frac{\text{Change in Price } (\Delta P)}{\text{Change in Quantity } (\Delta Q)}$$

As the slope of supply curve is always positive, supply curve is upward sloping. The diagram given shows the slope of supply curve.

In the given graph, when price rises from ₹ 2 to ₹ 3, then quantity supplied rises from 3 units to 4 units.

In this situation, the slope of supply curve $= \frac{\Delta P}{\Delta Q} = \frac{3-2}{4-3} = 1$

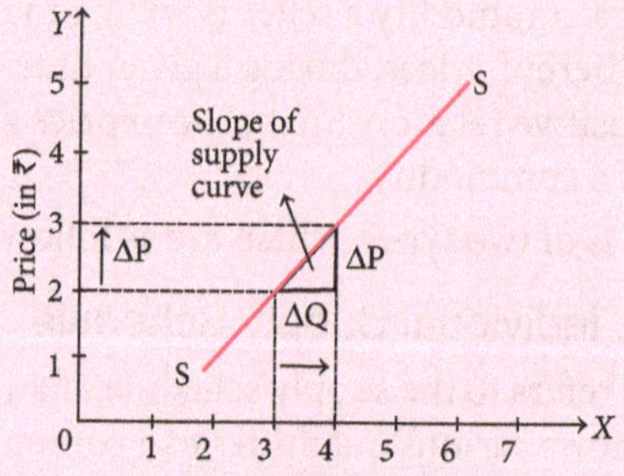

Slope of supply curve

8.2 Law of Supply

The law of supply states that keeping all other factors constant, the quantity supplied of a commodity increases with a rise in its price and decreases with a fall in its price. This indicates a direct relationship between price of given commodity and its quantity supplied. However, this law is qualitative approach as it only describes the direction of change in quantity due to change in own price and not the magnitude of shift.

Law of supply can be explained with the help of an imaginary schedule and the curve based on that data

Price (₹)	Quantity Supplied (units)
10	100
15	200
20	300

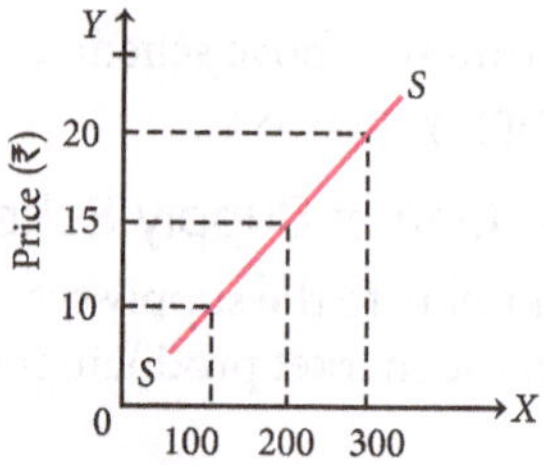

The schedule and graph given clearly depicts that supply of a commodity expands with rise in its price and contracts with fall in its price.

Assumptions of Law of Supply

Law of supply holds true when 'other factors remain constant'. Here 'other factors' is used to cover the following assumptions of law of supply

- There is no change in the price of the factors of production.
- There is no change in the goal of the firm.
- No change in government policy of taxes.
- There is no change in the techniques of production.
- There is no change in the price of related goods.

Causes for Operation of Law of Supply

Cause	Explanation
Profit Motive	Rise in prices leads to rise in profit margin for suppliers, which motivates them to increase supply and *vice-versa.*
Change in the Number of Firms	High margin of profit makes the particular business lucrative to new investors. As a result of this, the number of firms increases in the market, causing supply to rise simultaneously.
Reduction in Stock	As price rises, the producers supply more goods from their accumulated stocks, which causes stocks to deplete and supply to increase.

Exceptions to the Law of Supply

1. **Agricultural Goods** Law of supply does not apply to agricultural goods, as their supply depends on climatic conditions. If due to any natural calamity, production of agricultural product falls, then its supply will not increase, whatever may be the price.
2. **Perishable Goods** Suppliers are willing to sell perishable items like fruits or milk even when prices are falling because these goods cannot be stored for long.
3. **Antique Goods and Rare Articles** The supply of items like rare paintings or antiques remains limited, regardless of their price. e.g. The supply of Hussain's paintings cannot be increased even if buyers are willing to pay high price for it.
4. **Future Price Expectations** If sellers expect prices to rise further in future, then they would not increase their supply now even when prices are increasing.
5. **Lack of Resources** In underdeveloped or backward economies, production and supply may remain low due to the scarcity of resources.

8.3 Movement Along the Supply Curve (Change in Quantity Supplied)

Moving from one point to another on the same supply curve is called movement along supply curve. A movement along the supply curve is caused by change in quantity supplied of a good due to change in its own price, other factors remaining constant.

Movements along a supply curve can take the following forms

1. **Expansion** (Extension) **of Supply** When the price of a commodity rises, the quantity supplied expands, resulting in an upward movement on the same supply curve. It is explained with the help of an imaginary schedule and diagram

Price (₹)	**Quantity Supplied** (units)
1	10
2	20
3	30

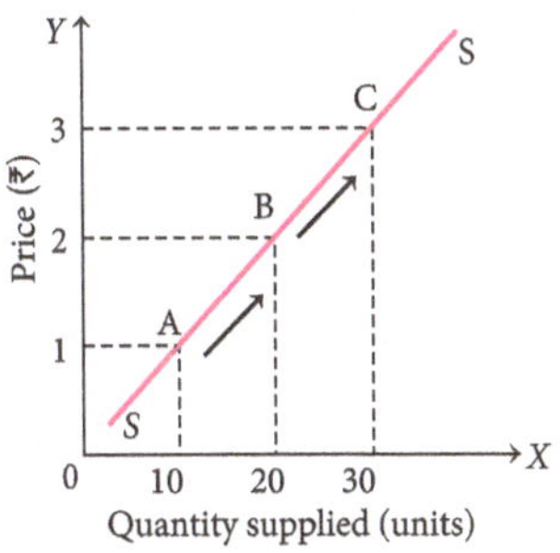

Extension of supply
(A→B→C)

Extension of supply is shown by a movement from point *A* to *B* to *C* on the same supply curve. More is supplied in response to increase in own price of the commodity. So, when price increases from ₹ 1 to ₹ 2, quantity supplied increases from 10 to 20 units and so on.

2. **Contraction of Supply** When the price of a commodity falls, the quantity supplied contracts, leading to a downward movement on the same supply curve. It is explained with the help of an imaginary schedule and diagram

Price (₹)	Quantity Supplied (units)
3	30
2	20
1	10

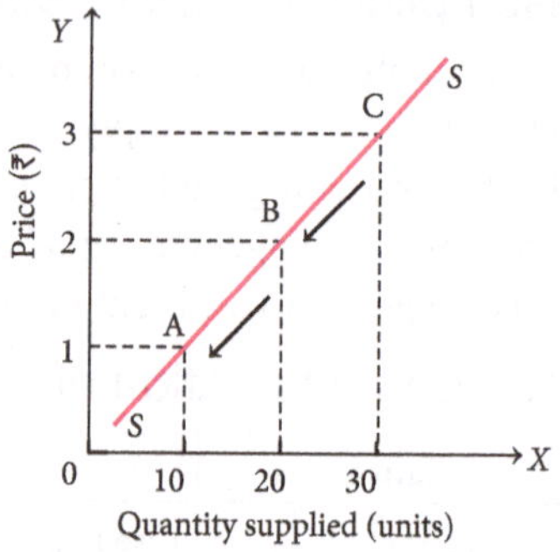

Contraction of supply
(C→ B→ A)

Contraction of supply is shown by a movement from point *C* to *B* to *A* on the same supply curve. Less is supplied in response to decrease in own price of the commodity. So, when price decreases from ₹ 3 to ₹ 2, quantity supplied falls to 20 units from 30 units.

8.4 Shift in the Supply Curve (Change in Supply)

Shift in the supply curve occurs when there are changes in factors other than the commodity's own price. Shift in supply curve can take the following forms

1. **Increase in Supply** When supply of a commodity increases due to favourable changes in factors other than its own price, it is called increase in supply.

   In this situation, supply curve shifts rightward (from *A* to *B* in graph).

   The following schedule and graph illustrates this situation

Price (₹)	Quantity Supplied (units)
10	100
10	200

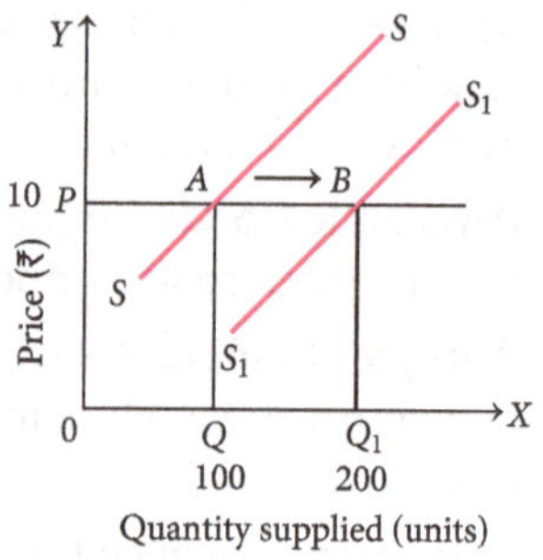

Increase in supply (A → B)

As is clear from the above schedule and graph, that at the same price, supply increases from 100 to 200 units.

Causes of Increase in Supply

- Fall in the price of substitute goods.
- Rise in the price of complementary goods.
- Fall in the price of factors of production.
- Improvements in technology.
- Increase in the number of firms in the market.
- Changes in government's policy, either by decreasing taxes or increasing subsidies.
- Changes in the goal of producers from profit maximisation to sales maximisation.

2. **Decrease in Supply** When supply of a commodity decreases due to unfavourable changes in factors other than its own price, it is called decrease in supply. In this situation, supply curve shifts leftward (from *B* to *A* in graph).

   The following schedule and graph illustrates this situation

Price (₹)	Quantity Supplied (units)
10	200
10	100

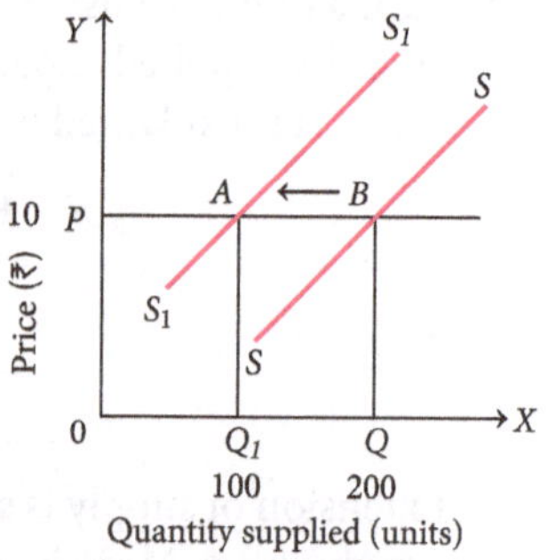

Decrease in supply (B ← A)

As is clear from the above schedule and graph, that at the same price, supply decreases from 200 to 100 units.

Causes of Decrease in Supply

- Rise in the price of substitute goods.
- Fall in the price of complementary goods.
- Changes in the goal of producers from sales maximisation to profit maximisation.
- Rise in the price of factors of production.
- Outdated technology.
- Decrease in the number of firms in the market.
- Changes in government policy, either by increasing taxes or decreasing subsidies.

Effect on Supply due to Change in its Determinants

Supply is influenced by various determinants beyond the price of the commodity itself. Changes in these determinants can cause shift or change in the supply curve, either increasing or decreasing supply.

These are discussed as follows

I. Change in the State of Technology

Technological changes affect the cost of production, directly influencing the supply of commodity. It includes

1. **Advancement of Technology** Improved technology lowers production costs, enabling producers to supply more at the same price. As a result, supply increases from OQ to OQ_2 at the same price OP. It leads to a rightward shift in the supply curve from SS to S_2S_2.

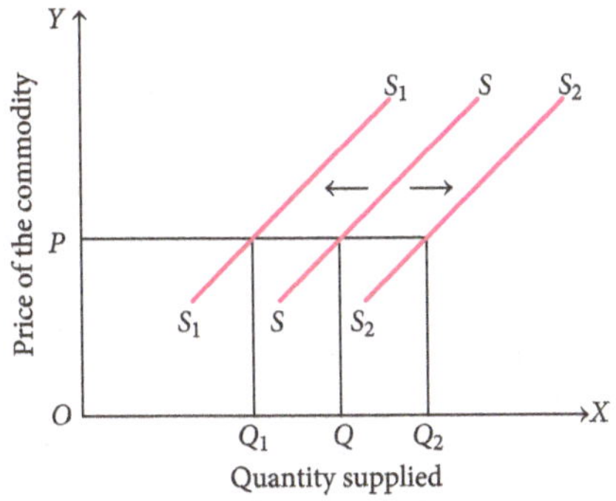

2. **Degradation of Technology** Outdated technology increases production costs, leading to reduced supply. As a result, supply decreases from OQ to OQ_1 at the same price OP. It leads to a leftward shift in the supply curve from SS to S_1S_1.

II. Change in Price of Related Goods

It includes

1. **Increase in Price of Related Goods** When the price of a related good (e.g. Tea) rises, producers may shift resources to produce more of that good instead of the given commodity (e.g. Coffee), decreasing its supply. As a result, supply (of coffee) falls from OQ to OQ_1, at the same price OP. It leads to a leftward shift in the supply curve from SS to S_1S_1.

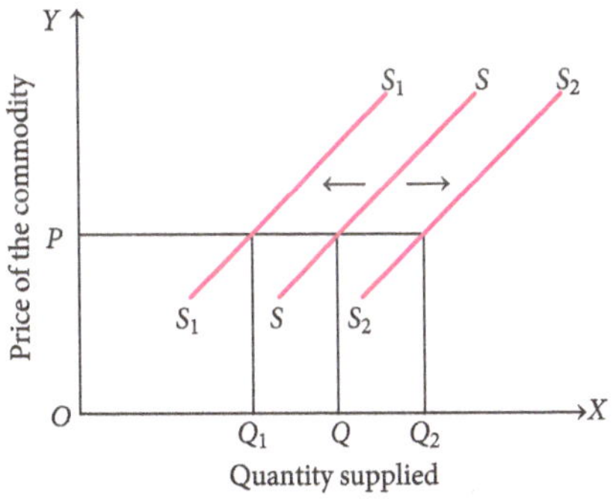

2. **Decrease in Price of Related Goods** Fall in prices of related goods (e.g. Tea) makes the given commodity (e.g. Coffee) more profitable to produce. As a result, supply (of coffee) increases from OQ to OQ_2, at the same price OP. It leads to a rightward shift in the supply curve from SS to S_2S_2.

III. Change in Price of Inputs (Factors of Production)

It includes

1. **Increase in Price of Inputs** Higher input costs raise production expenses and lead to fall in profit margin. As a result, supply falls from OQ to OQ_1 at the same price OP.

   It leads to a leftward shift in the supply curve from SS to S_1S_1.

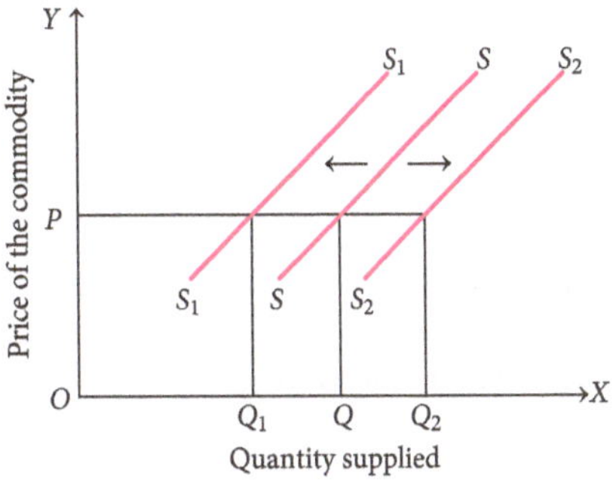

2. **Decrease in Price of Inputs** Fall in input costs reduces production expenses and leads to rise in profit margin.

   As a result, supply increases from *OQ* to OQ_2 at the same price *OP*. It leads to a rightward shift in the supply curve from *SS* to S_2S_2.

IV. Change in Taxation Policy

Taxes affect the cost of producing a commodity directly. It includes

1. **Increase in Taxes** Rising taxes increase production costs and reduce profit margin.

   As a result, supply falls from *OQ* to OQ_1 at the same price *OP*. It leads to a leftward shift in the supply curve from *SS* to S_1S_1.

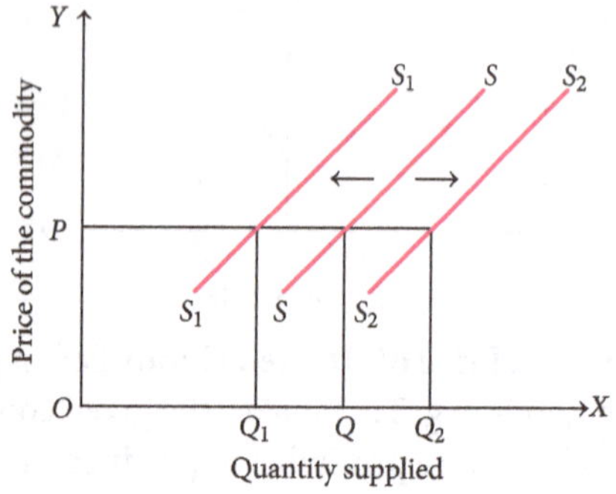

2. **Decrease in Taxes** Lower taxes reduces production costs and increase profit margin. As a result, supply increases from *OQ* to OQ_2 at the same price *OP*. It leads to a rightward shift in the supply curve from *SS* to S_2S_2.

8.5 Price Elasticity of Supply

It is defined as a measure of the responsiveness of quantity supplied of a commodity due to changes in its own price. It reflects relationship between price changes and the resulting changes in the quantity that producers are willing to supply.

Specifically, it is defined as the percentage change in the quantity supplied divided by the percentage change in price. It is a pure number, meaning it has no unit of measurement.

The value of price elasticity of supply is always positive, indicating a direct relationship between own price and quantity supplied of a commodity.

Measurement of Price Elasticity of Supply : Percentage Change Method

Price elasticity of supply can be calculated using percentage or proportionate method.

Under this method, elasticity of supply is measured by the ratio of proportionate change in quantity supplied to the proportionate change in own price of commodity.

$$\text{Price Elasticity of Supply } (E_s) = \frac{\text{Percentage Change in Quantity Supplied}}{\text{Percentage Change in Price}}$$

$$\text{Percentage Change in Quantity Supplied} = \frac{\Delta Q}{Q} \times 100$$

$$\text{Percentage Change in Price} = \frac{\Delta P}{P} \times 100$$

The formula of proportionate method can mathematically be presented as under

$$E_s = \frac{\Delta Q}{\Delta P} \times \frac{P}{Q}$$

where, Q = Initial or original quantity

ΔQ = Change in quantity supplied

P = Initial or original price; ΔP = Change in price

Solved Question 1 **The price elasticity of supply of commodities X and Y are equal. The price of X falls from ₹ 10 to ₹ 8 per unit and its quantity supplied falls by 16%. The price of Y rises by 10%. Calculate the percentage increase in its supply.**

Sol. Price Elasticity of Supply of Commodity X (E_s)

$$= \frac{\text{Percentage Change in Quantity Supplied of X}}{\text{Percentage Change in Price of X}}$$

Percentage Change in Price of X

$$= \frac{\Delta P}{P} \times 100 = \frac{2}{10} \times 100 = 20\%$$

$$\therefore \quad E_s \text{ of } X = \frac{16}{20} = 0.8$$

According to the question, E_s of X = E_s of Y

So, E_s of Y = 0.8

Now, Price Elasticity of Supply of Commodity Y

$$(E_s) = \frac{\text{Percentage Change in Quantity Supplied of Y}}{\text{Percentage Change in Price of Y}}$$

$$0.8 = \frac{\text{Percentage Change in Quantity Supplied of Y}}{10}$$

0.8×10 = Percentage change in quantity supplied of Y

$\therefore$ Percentage change in quantity supplied of Y = 8%

Solved Question 2 **A supplier supplies 1,000 units at a price of ₹ 10 per unit. When price goes up by ₹ 2 per unit, he sells 200 units more. Calculate price elasticity of supply by proportionate method.**

Sol. According to question

Initial price (P) = ₹ 10

New price (P) = 10 + 2 = ₹ 12

Change in price (ΔP) = ₹ 2

Initial quantity (Q) = 1,000

New quantity (Q_1) = 1,000 + 200 = 1,200

Change in quantity (ΔQ) = 200

$$E_s = \frac{\Delta Q}{\Delta P} \times \frac{P}{Q} = \frac{200}{2} \times \frac{10}{1{,}000} = 1 \text{ (Unit elastic supply)}$$

Degrees of Price Elasticity of Supply

There are five degrees of price elasticity of supply which are as follows

1. **Perfectly Inelastic Supply** ($E_S = 0$)
   In this, the quantity supplied remains constant regardless of any change in its price. In this case, supply curve will be a straight line parallel to y-axis.

Price (₹)	**Quantity Supplied** (units)
10	20
20	20
30	20

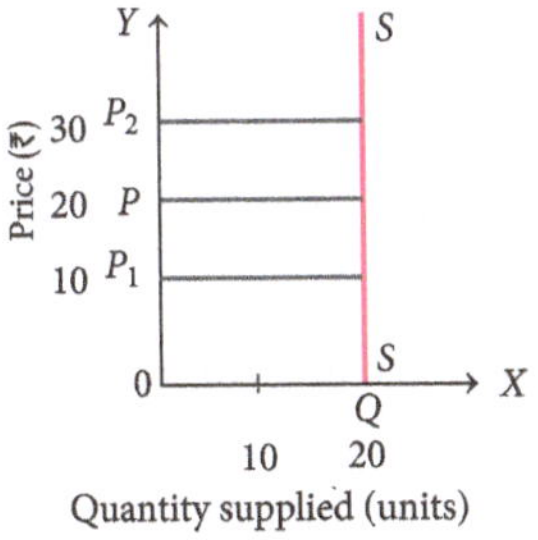

2. **Perfectly Elastic Supply** ($E_S = \infty$)
   Supply is said to be perfectly elastic when a small change in price leads to an infinite change in quantity supplied. In this case, supply curve is a horizontal straight line parallel to the x-axis.

Price (₹)	**Quantity Supplied** (units)
10	10
10	20
10	30

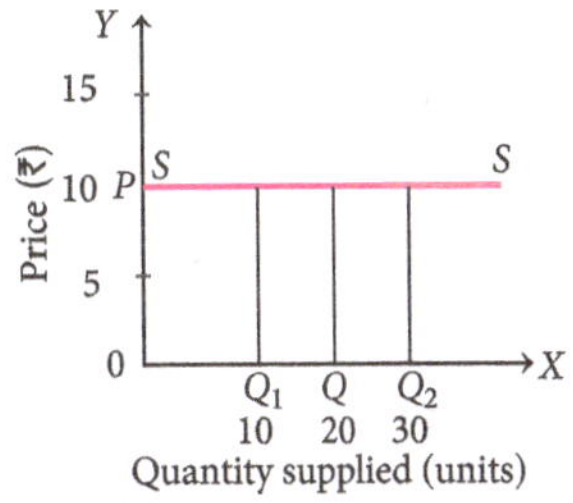

3. **Unit Elastic Supply** ($E_S = 1$)
   When the percentage change in quantity supplied is equal to the percentage change in price, the supply is said to be unit elastic.
   The supply curve, in this case, is a straight line passing through the origin, demonstrating a balanced relationship between price and quantity supplied.

Price (₹)	**Quantity Supplied** (units)
10	20
20	40

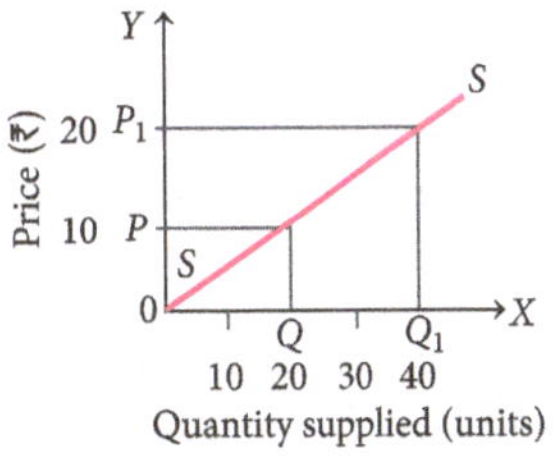

4. **Less than Unit Elastic Supply** ($E_S < 1$)
   This situation occurs when the percentage change in quantity supplied is less than the percentage change in price.
   The supply curve, in this case, intersects the x-axis in its positive range (or cuts the x-axis/quantity axis).

Price (₹)	**Quantity Supplied** (units)
10	20
20	25

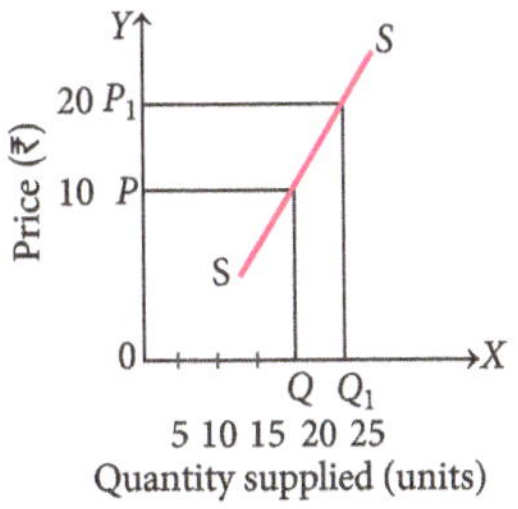

5. **More than Unit Elastic Supply** ($E_S > 1$)
When the percentage change in quantity supplied is more than the percentage change in price, it is called more than unit elastic supply.

In this case, the supply curve intersects the x-axis in its negative range (or cuts y-axis/price axis).

Price (₹)	Quantity Supplied (units)
10	20
11	40

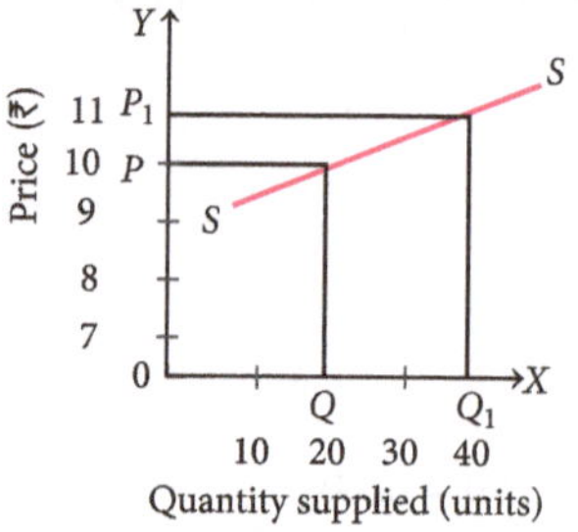

Relation between Slope of Supply Curve and Elasticity of Supply

We can establish the relation between slope of supply and elasticity from the equation given below

$$\text{Slope of Supply Curve} = \frac{\Delta P}{\Delta Q}$$

$$\text{Elasticity of Supply} = \frac{\Delta Q}{\Delta P} \times \frac{P}{Q} \quad or \quad = \frac{1}{\Delta P/\Delta Q} \times \frac{P}{Q} \quad or \quad = \frac{1}{\text{Slope of Supply Curve}} \times \frac{P}{Q}$$

Therefore, we can say that slope of supply curve is inversely related to elasticity of supply, i.e. with increase in slope, elasticity of supply falls and *vice-versa*.

Factors affecting Price Elasticity of Supply

1. **Nature of Inputs Used** Readily or commonly available inputs lead to more elastic supply, while scarce inputs will have inelastic supply.
2. **Risk Taking** Entrepreneurs willing to take risk typically have a more elastic supply, while entrepreneurs reluctant to take risk, will have inelastic supply.
3. **Nature of Commodity** Perishable goods have inelastic supply due to limited shelf-life, whereas durable goods tend to be more elastic.
4. **Time Factor** Longer time period allows producers to adjust more easily thereby increasing price elasticity of supply and *vice-versa*.
5. **Technique of Production** Complex and costly production methods or expensive technology will lead to less elastic supply, while simple techniques facilitate quicker adjustments.
6. **Cost of Production** Significant increase in production cost due to increase in production will reduce elasticity, while manageable cost increase allows for more elastic supply.

Mind Map

SUPPLY AND PRICE ELASTICITY OF SUPPLY

1 Supply

Supply is a desired quantity, i.e. it is the quantity that sellers are willing and able to sell at a given price during a given period of time.

Components of Supply

- Willingness of the producer to sell
- Ability of the producer to sell
- Price of the commodity
- Time period

2 Individual Supply

It is a quantity an individual firm is willing to sell at a given price.

Determinants of Individual Supply

- Price of given commodity
- Price of related goods
- Goal of the firm
- Price of factors of production
- State of technology

Individual Supply Function It is the functional relationship between individual supply and its determinants. $S_X = f(P_X, P_R, G, P_F, T)$

3 Market Supply

It is the total quantity that all firms are willing and able to sell at a given price.

Determinants of Market Supply

- Number of firms in the industry
- Expectation of future price
- Government policy

Market Supply Function It is the functional relationship between market supply and its determinants. $S_X = f(P_X, P_R, G, P_F, T, N_F, E_X, G_P)$

4 Supply Schedule and Curve

Supply Schedule It is a tabular representation showing different quantities of a commodity supplied at various prices over a given period.

It can be classified into individual supply schedule (showing supply by a single seller at different prices) and market supply schedule (showing total supply by all sellers in the market at different prices).

Supply Curve It is a graphical representation of the supply schedule, showing the positive relationship between the price of a commodity and its quantity supplied. It is classified into individual supply curve and market supply curve.

5 Law of Supply

It states that, keeping other factors constant, the quantity supplied of a commodity increases with a rise in its price and decreases with a fall in its price, showing a direct relationship between price and supply.

Exceptions to the Law of Supply

- **Agricultural Goods** Supply depends on climatic conditions, not price.
- **Perishable Goods** Sellers may supply even at lower prices to avoid spoilage.
- **Antique and Rare Items** Limited supply regardless of price (e.g. Rare paintings).
- **Future Price Expectations** Sellers may hold supply if they expect higher prices later.
- **Lack of Resources** In underdeveloped economies, supply remains low due to resource scarcity.

6 Movement and Shift in Supply Curve

Movement Along the Supply Curve

Change in quantity supplied or movement occurs when supply of a good changes due to a change in its own price, keeping other factors constant.

- **Extension** Supply rises as price increases.
- **Contraction** Supply falls as price decreases.

Shift in the Supply Curve

Change in supply or shift takes place when supply changes due to factors other than price, such as technology, input costs or government policies.

- **Increase in Supply** Rightward shift (e.g. Lower input costs, improved technology, increased subsidies)
- **Decrease in Supply** Leftward shift (e.g. Higher input costs, outdated technology, increased taxes)

7 Price Elasticity of Supply

It is a measure of the responsiveness of quantity supplied of a commodity due to changes in its own price. It reflects relationship between price changes and the resulting changes in the quantity that producers are willing to supply.

Key Features

- ***Always Positive*** Indicates a direct relationship between price and quantity supplied.
- ***Pure Number*** No unit of measurement.

Measurement of Price Elasticity of Supply:

Percentage Change Method Elasticity of supply is measured by the ratio of proportionate change in quantity supplied to the proportionate change in own price of commodity.

$$E_S = \frac{\Delta Q}{\Delta P} \times \frac{P}{Q}$$

8 Degrees of Price Elasticity of Supply

- **Perfectly Elastic Supply** ($E_S = \infty$) Quantity supplied changes infinitely with any price change (horizontal supply curve).
- **More than Unit Elastic Supply** ($E_S > 1$) Change in quantity supplied is more than a change in price.
- **Unitary Elastic Supply** ($E_S = 1$) Percentage change in quantity supplied is equal to percentage change in price.
- **Less Than Unit Elastic Supply** ($E_S < 1$) Percentage change in quantity supplied is less than the percentage change in price.
- **Perfectly Inelastic Supply** ($E_S = 0$) Quantity supplied remains constant regardless of any change in its price.

EXAM PATTERN QUESTIONS

Objective Type Questions

Multiple Choice Questions (MCQs)

1. The supply of a commodity implies

(a) actual product of a good
(b) stock available for sale
(c) total existing stock of the good
(d) the amount of goods offered for sale at a different prices over a given period of time

2. Supply of a commodity is ...... concept.

(a) stock (b) flow
(c) Both (a) and (b) (d) wholesale

3. The slope of the supply curve is typically

(a) downward (b) horizontal
(c) upward (d) vertical

4. Which determinant of market supply is given in the below image?

(a) Number of firms
(b) Goal of firm
(c) Price of related goods
(d) Government policies

5. The functional relationship between supply of a commodity and its various determinants is known as

(a) supply function (b) change in supply
(c) change in quantity supplied
(d) None of the above

6. Which of the following situations contradicts the law of supply?

(a) Farmers producing less wheat despite a rise in its price due to drought
(b) A rise in wages leads to higher employment in a factory
(c) An increase in price of smartphones results in increased production
(d) All of the above follow the law of supply

7. Which of the following statements is correct about the relationship between price and supply?

(a) A higher price leads to a lower quantity supplied
(b) A higher price reduces the supply in the long-run
(c) A higher price leads to more quantity supplied
(d) Supply is unrelated to price changes

8. Which of the following comes under the four components of supply? Competency Based Que

I. Time period
II. Willingness of the consumer
III. Stock
IV. Ability of the producer

Codes

(a) I and IV (b) I, II, III and IV
(c) I and III (d) I, III and IV

9. In the individual supply function, which of the following determinants explains the impact of input costs on supply?

(a) Price of factors of production
(b) Government policy
(c) Business expectations
(d) Price of related goods

10. "Crude oil shed three per cent today. OPEC+ cartel has been cutting oil output to support prices. However, prices are down nearly six per cent so far this year."

Source *https//www.livemint.com/market/commodities/oil-gives-up-us-fed-rate-cut-gains-sheds-3-on-opec-december-output-hike-bets-brent-drops-to-71bbl-11727370878332.html*

How does the OPEC+ cartel's decision to cut oil output relate to the supply of crude oil? Competency Based Que

(a) It increases the supply of crude oil
(b) It decreases the supply of crude oil
(c) It has no effect on the supply of crude oil
(d) It decreases both the supply and the price of crude oil

11. A firm producing handcrafted furniture is likely to have Competency Based Que

(a) perfectly elastic supply
(b) perfectly inelastic supply
(c) relative inelastic supply
(d) unitary elastic supply

12. What will be the impact of the following news on the supply curve of water?

REGULAR FEATURE EVERY SUMMER: LOCALS

TOI | APR 18, 2019

Water woes back in pockets of Salt Lake as mercury soars

Water filled from roadside taps are being supplied to houses in many Salt Lake blocks

There is supply shortage for some days now. Even a few weeks back, water used to overflow from underground reservoirs but that is not happening now

Sujit Chowdhury | AE BLOCK RESIDENT

We are not getting enough water in our locality. It seems the supply time has been reduced. Many are being forced to hire water tankers

Kavita Pal | HB BLOCK RESIDENT

(a) Supply curve shifts to the right
(b) Supply curve shifts to the left
(c) Upward movement along supply curve
(d) Downward movement along supply curve

13. "The law of supply explains the general behaviour of producers in response to price changes, but exceptions highlight circumstances where this behaviour does not hold true."

Based on this, what is one factor that can cause an exception to the law of supply? **Competency Based Que**

(a) Profit motive
(b) Future price expectations
(c) Increase in production resources
(d) Expansion of supply

14. The movement from point B to point A as shown in the diagram below is known as

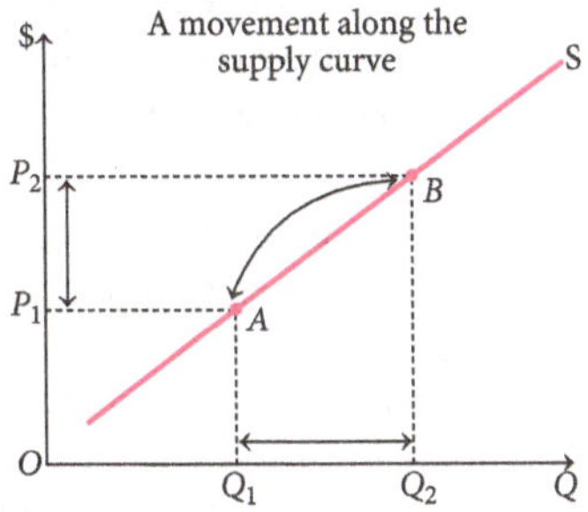

(a) increase in supply
(b) decrease in supply
(c) expansion in quantity supplied
(d) contraction in quantity supplied

15. Arrange the following events in the correct sequence that represents an expansion in supply. **Competency Based Que**

(i) Increase in the price of the commodity.
(ii) Upward movement along the supply curve.
(iii) Increase in quantity supplied.
(iv) Suppliers produce more goods.

Codes

(a) (i), (iii), (iv), (ii) (b) (i), (iv), (ii), (iii)
(c) (i), (iv), (iii), (ii) (d) (i), (ii), (iii), (iv)

16. Consider the following supply schedule.

Price (₹ per unit)	Quantity Supplied (in units)
10	200
10	100

It is called **Competency Based Que**

(a) decrease in supply
(b) decrease in quantity supplied
(c) decrease in demand
(d) All of the above

17. What happens to supply when the price of a complementary good rises?

(a) Supply increases
(b) Supply decreases
(c) Supply remains unchanged
(d) Supply is unaffected by complementary goods

18. Which change in supply is depicted in the below image?

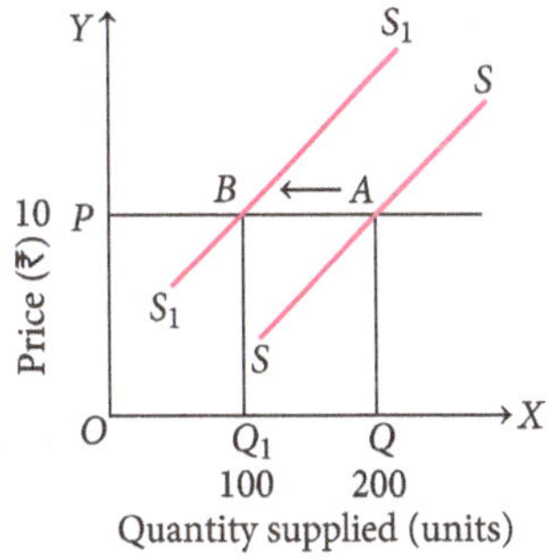

(a) Increase in supply (b) Expansion in supply
(c) Decrease in supply (d) None of the above

19. Which of the following statements about the law of supply are correct? **Competency Based Que**

I. The law of supply states that quantity supplied increases as the price increases.
II. The law of supply applies equally to all types of goods, including agricultural products.
III. Higher prices typically motivate suppliers to increase production and market entry.
IV. The law of supply indicates an inverse relationship between price and quantity supplied.

Codes

(a) I and III (b) I and IV
(c) II and IV (d) III and IV

20. Consider the following supply schedule.

Competency Based Que

Price (₹ per unit)	Quantity Supplied (in units)
25	50
35	70

This refers to

(a) expansion in supply
(b) contraction in supply
(c) increase in supply
(d) Both (b) and (c)

21. Which of the following best explains the concept of contraction of supply?

(a) Producers supply more at a higher price
(b) Producers supply less at a lower price
(c) Supply remains constant irrespective of price changes
(d) There is a shift in the supply curve

22. "Aldi pledges record investment to cut prices as sales soar."

Source *https://www.marketingweek.com/aldi-increase-store-numbers/*

What is likely to happen to the supply of products at Aldi in response to their record investment aimed at cutting prices? Competency Based Que

(a) Supply will decrease due to reduced profit margins
(b) Supply will increase as the investment allows for greater production efficiency
(c) Supply will remain unchanged since prices are being cut
(d) Supply will fluctuate based on market demand only

23. Identify the elastic supply from the given below.

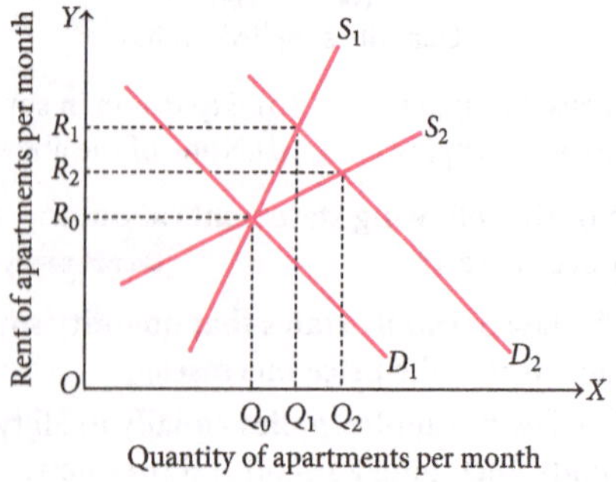

(a) S_1 (b) S_2
(c) D_1 (d) D_2

24. If the price of a commodity rises by 10% and the quantity supplied increases by 20%, what is the price elasticity of supply?

(a) 0.5 (b) 1
(c) 2 (d) 3

25. A smartphone's price increased from ₹ 30,000 to ₹ 36,000. What is the percentage change in price?

(a) 15% (b) 20%
(c) 25% (d) 30%

26. A product's price increases by 40% and the quantity supplied increases by 20%. What is the price elasticity of supply?

(a) 0.5 (b) 4
(c) 3 (d) 0.25

27. A firm increases its supply from 100 units to 150 units when the price rises from ₹ 10 to ₹ 15. Calculate the price elasticity of supply.

(a) 1 (b) 2 (c) 1.5 (d) 3

28. A dress is on sale for ₹ 3,600 after a price reduction from ₹ 4,800. What is the price elasticity of supply?

(a) 20% (b) 35% (c) 30% (d) 25%

29. "The price elasticity of supply is defined as the percentage change in the quantity supplied divided by the percentage change in price."

What does a price elasticity of supply greater than 1 indicate? Competency Based Que

(a) Perfectly inelastic supply
(b) Less than unit elastic supply
(c) More than unit elastic supply
(d) Unit elastic supply

Direction *Read the case study and answer the questions 30 to 33 on the basis of the same*

Fresh fields organic farm is a family owned farm that specialises in growing and selling organic vegetables in a local market. Over the past few years, the farm has seen a significant increase in demand for organic produce due to a growing awareness of health and environmental issues among consumers. This increase in demand has led the owner, Mr. Kumar, to consider various factors influencing his supply of vegetables.

In response to the rising prices of organic vegetables, which have jumped from ₹ 50 to ₹ 70 per kilogram, Mr. Kumar decided to expand his production. He invested in new irrigation technology to enhance yield and reduce water consumption. With these improvements, he could increase his supply significantly. However, he also faced challenges; the prices of fertilisers and organic seeds had risen, affecting his production costs. To maintain his profit margin, he had to decide how to balance the higher input costs with the increased prices for his vegetables.

To maximise his supply, Mr. Kumar evaluated the factors of production on his farm. He realised that the rise in the price of organic produce could motivate him to produce more, as outlined by the law of supply.

Additionally, Mr. Kumar started to consider the expectations of future prices. If he anticipated that prices would continue to rise, he might hold back some of his supply for sale later at higher prices.

30. What is the primary factor influencing Mr. Kumar's decision to increase the supply of organic vegetables?
(a) Increase in the number of farms
(b) Rising prices of organic vegetables
(c) Decrease in the cost of labour
(d) Availability of synthetic fertilisers

31. The law of supply states that as the price of a commodity increases, the .... also increases, assuming other factors remain constant.

32. Which of the following best describes the relationship between price and quantity supplied, as demonstrated by Mr. Kumar's situation?
(a) Inverse relationship (b) No relationship
(c) Direct relationship (d) Irregular relationship

33. Mr. Kumar's decision to invest in new irrigation technology is an example of how advancements in .... can influence supply by reducing production costs.

Assertion-Reason

Direction (Q.No. 34 to 43) *Read the following Assertion (A) and Reason (R) and choose the correct alternative from the following*

Alternatives
(a) Both Assertion (A) and Reason (R) are true and Reason (R) is the correct explanation of Assertion (A)
(b) Both Assertion (A) and Reason (R) are true, but Reason (R) is not the correct explanation of Assertion (A)
(c) Assertion (A) is true, but Reason (R) is false
(d) Assertion (A) is false, but Reason (R) is true

34. Assertion (A) Supply of a commodity is dynamic in nature as it keep on changing during a given period of time.
Reason (R) Supply is that part of stock which a seller is willing to sell at a given time.

35. Assertion (A) Higher input costs raise production costs, decreasing supply.
Reason (R) Technological advancements increase production costs, encouraging decreased supply.

36. Assertion (A) Market supply curve is the horizontal summation of individual supply curves at different possible prices in a particular market.
Reason (R) Market supply curve is flatter than individual supply curve as at each price, market supply represent greater quantity.

37. Assertion (A) Market supply schedule is a graphical representation of the supply schedule, showing the relationship between the price of a commodity and the quantity supplied.
Reason (R) The slope of the supply curve is positive, calculated by the ratio of the change in price to the change in quantity supplied.

38. Assertion (A) The law of supply states that, keeping all other factors constant, the quantity supplied of a commodity increases with a rise in its price and decreases with a fall in its price.
Reason (R) The law of supply indicates a direct relationship between price and quantity supplied.

39. Assertion (A) Movement along a supply curve occurs when the quantity supplied changes due to a change in the commodity's own price.
Reason (R) When the price of a commodity rises, the quantity supplied decreases, resulting in a downward movement along the supply curve.

40. Assertion (A) When supply of a commodity increases due to favourable changes in factors other than its own price, it is called increase in supply.
Reason (R) When supply of a commodity decreases due to unfavourable changes in factors other than its own price, it is called decrease in supply.

41. Assertion (A) Elasticity of supply is a quantitative measure of supply owing to change in price.
Reason (R) Elasticity measures the responsiveness of supply measured in proportion or percentage.

42. Assertion (A) Price elasticity of supply can be calculated using percentage or proportionate method.
Reason (R) The value of price elasticity of supply can be positive or negative.

43. Assertion (A) When quantity supplied changes by a larger percentage than the price, it is called more than unit elastic supply.
Reason (R) The supply curve for more than unit elastic supply cuts the price axis below zero.

Two Statements Based MCQs

Direction (Q.No. 44 to 53) *Read the following statements carefully and choose the correct alternative*

Alternatives
(a) Statement I is correct and Statement II is incorrect
(b) Statement II is correct and Statement I is incorrect
(c) Both the statements are correct
(d) Both the statements are incorrect

44. **Statement I** Supply refers to the quantity a supplier is willing to sell at different prices and time.

Statement II Large number of suppliers means greater elasticity of supply.

45. **Statement I** Supply is a 'flow' concept, representing the amount offered over time.

Statement II Stock refers to the total quantity available at a particular point, making it a 'stock' concept.

46. **Statement I** The supply function represents the mathematical relationship between the supply of a commodity and its determinants.

Statement II A market supply function explains the relationship between the supply of a single firm and its key determinants.

47. **Statement I** Greater slope of supply curve leads to higher elasticity of supply.

Statement II Law of supply does not gives any information regarding the magnitude of change in supply.

48. **Statement I** Higher taxes decrease supply by reducing profit margins.

Statement II If firms expect future price hikes, they may reduce current supply to sell later at higher prices.

49. **Statement I** The law of supply states that the quantity supplied of a commodity decreases as its price rises.

Statement II Technological advancements generally lead to a leftward shift in the supply curve.

50. **Statement I** The law of supply assumes that all non-price factors remain constant, so only price affects the quantity supplied.

Statement II Producers' expectations of future prices have no influence on their current supply decisions.

51. **Statement I** Movement along the supply curve occurs due to a change in the price of the commodity itself, while shifts in the supply curve occur due to changes in external factors.

Statement II An increase in the price of substitute goods can lead to a decrease in the supply of the given commodity.

52. **Statement I** Perfectly inelastic supply ($E_s = 0$) means that the quantity supplied remains constant regardless of price changes.

Statement II The supply curve for unit elastic supply is vertical.

53. **Statement I** Unit elastic supply ($E_s = 1$) occurs when the percentage change in quantity supplied is equal to the percentage change in price.

Statement II More than unit elastic supply ($E_s > 1$) indicates that the percentage change in quantity supplied exceeds the percentage change in price.

Matching

54. Match the following

Column I	Column II
A. Supply	(i) Total quantity from all producers.
B. Individual supply	(ii) Quantity from one producer.
C. Market supply	(iii) Total amount available at various prices.
D. Quantity supplied	(iv) Amount at a specific price.

Codes

	A	B	C	D		A	B	C	D
(a)	(iii)	(iv)	(i)	(ii)	(b)	(iv)	(i)	(ii)	(iii)
(c)	(ii)	(iii)	(iv)	(i)	(d)	(iii)	(ii)	(i)	(iv)

55. Match the following

Column I	Column II
A. T	(i) Supply of commodity
B. S_x	(ii) Functional relationship
C. f	(iii) Goal of the firm
D. G	(iv) State of technology

Codes

	A	B	C	D		A	B	C	D
(a)	(iii)	(iv)	(i)	(ii)	(b)	(iv)	(i)	(ii)	(iii)
(c)	(ii)	(iii)	(iv)	(i)	(d)	(iii)	(ii)	(i)	(iv)

56. Match the following

Column I	Column II
A. Expansion of supply	(i) Downward movement on the supply curve.
B. Increase in supply	(ii) Leftward shift of supply curve.
C. Contraction of supply	(iii) Upward movement on the supply curve.
D. Decrease in supply	(iv) Rightward shift of supply curve.

Codes

	A	B	C	D		A	B	C	D
(a)	(iii)	(iv)	(i)	(ii)	(b)	(iv)	(i)	(ii)	(iii)
(c)	(ii)	(iii)	(iv)	(i)	(d)	(iii)	(ii)	(i)	(iv)

57. Match the following

Column I	Column II
A. Advancement of technology	(i) Decrease in supply
B. Increased price of inputs	(ii) Increase in supply
C. Increase in price	(iii) Contraction in supply
D. Decrease in price	(iv) Expansion in supply

Codes

	A	B	C	D
(a)	(iii)	(iv)	(i)	(ii)
(b)	(iv)	(i)	(ii)	(iii)
(c)	(ii)	(i)	(iv)	(iii)
(d)	(iii)	(ii)	(i)	(iv)

58. Match the following

Column I	Column II
A. $E_s = 0$	(i) Less than unit elastic supply
B. $E_s = \infty$	(ii) More than unit elastic supply
C. $E_s < 1$	(iii) Perfectly inelastic supply
D. $E_s > 1$	(iv) Perfectly elastic supply

Codes

	A	B	C	D		A	B	C	D
(a)	(iii)	(iv)	(i)	(ii)	(b)	(iv)	(i)	(ii)	(iii)
(c)	(ii)	(iii)	(iv)	(i)	(d)	(iii)	(ii)	(i)	(iv)

Concept Identification

59. It describes the specific amount of goods producers are willing to sell at a particular price.

60. It states that as price increases, the quantity supplied also increases, ceteris paribus.

61. It measures how much the quantity supplied responds to a change in price.

62. It explains the combined supply of all producers of a particular commodity in the market.

63. It represents a mathematical relation showing how quantity supplied changes with price.

Answers

1. (d) the amount of goods offered for sale at a different prices, per unit of time
2. (b) flow
3. (c) upward
4. (d) Government policies
5. (a) supply function
6. (a) Farmers producing less wheat despite a rise in its price due to drought
7. (c) A higher price leads to more quantity supplied
8. (a) I and IV
9. (a) Price of factors of production
10. (b) It decreases the supply of crude oil
11. (c) relatively inelastic supply
12. (b) Supply curve shifts to the left
13. (b) Future price expectations
14. (d) contraction in quantity supplied
15. (c) (i), (iv), (iii), (ii)
16. (a) decrease in supply
17. (a) Supply increases
18. (c) Decrease in supply
19. (a) I and III
20. (a) Supply of a commodity expand only due to increase in price of the commodity and other factors remain constant.
    Quantity supplied increases from 50 units to 70 units of the commodity as a result of increase in its price from ₹ 25 to ₹ 35.
21. (b) Producers supply less at a lower price
22. (b) Supply will increase as the investment allows for greater production efficiency
23. (b) S_2
24. (c) Price Elasticity of Supply = % Change in Quantity Supplied/% Change in Price
    = 20%/10% = 2
25. (b) Change in price = 36,000 – 30,000 = ₹ 6,000
    Percentage change = 6,000/30,000 × 100 = 20%
26. (a) Price Elasticity of Supply = 20%/40% = 0.5
27. (a) Price Elasticity of Supply = % Change in Quantity Supplied/% Change in Price
    = [(150 – 100)/100]/[(15 – 10)/10] = 0.5/0.5 = 1
28. (d) Change in price = 4,800 – 3,600 = ₹ 1,200
    Percentage change = 1,200/4,800 ×100 = 25%
29. (c) More than unit elastic supply
30. (b) Rising prices of organic vegetables
31. quantity supplied
32. (c) Direct relationship
33. technology
34. (a) Both Assertion (A) and Reason (R) are true and Reason (R) is the correct explanation of Assertion (A)
35. (c) Technological advancements typically decrease production costs, which encourages an increase in supply, not a decrease.
36. (a) Both Assertion (A) and Reason (R) are true and Reason (R) is the correct explanation of Assertion (A)
37. (d) A market supply schedule is a tabular representation of the relationship between price and quantity supplied by all firms in the market.

38. (a) Both Assertion (A) and Reason (R) are true and Reason (R) is the correct explanation of Assertion (A)
39. (c) When the price of a commodity rises, the quantity supplied increases, resulting in an upward movement along the supply curve.
40. (b) Both Assertion (A) and Reason (R) are true, but Reason (R) is not the correct explanation of Assertion (A)
41. (a) Both Assertion (A) and Reason (R) are true and Reason (R) is the correct explanation of Assertion (A)
42. (c) The value of price elasticity of supply is always positive because price and quantity supplied move in the same direction.
43. (c) Assertion (A) is true, but Reason (R) is false
44. (b) Supply refers to the quantity that a supplier is willing and able to sell at a particular price.
45. (c) Both the statements are correct
46. (a) The individual supply function explains the relationship between the supply of a single firm and its key determinants.
47. (b) There exist inverse relation between elasticity of supply and slope of supply curve.
48. (c) Both the statements are correct
49. (d) The law of supply asserts that quantity supplied increases with a rise in price. Technological advancements typically reduce production costs, resulting in a rightward shift in the supply curve.
50. (a) Producers' expectations about future prices do influence their current supply decisions. If producers expect prices to rise in the future, they might reduce current supply to sell more at higher future prices.
51. (c) Both the statements are correct
52. (a) The supply curve for unit elastic supply is a straight line passing through the origin, representing a 1:1 relationship between price and quantity supplied.
53. (c) Both the statements are correct
54. (d) (iii) (ii) (i) (iv)
55. (b) (iv) (i) (ii) (iii)
56. (a) (iii) (iv) (i) (ii)
57. (c) (ii) (i) (iv) (iii)
58. (a) (iii) (iv) (i) (ii)
59. Quantity supplied
60. Law of supply
61. Price elasticity of supply
62. Market supply
63. Supply function

Subjective Questions

Short Answer Type Questions

1. What does supply indicate about a seller's willingness and ability to sell a commodity?

Ans. Supply indicates that a seller is prepared to offer a certain quantity of a commodity at specific prices over a defined time period. It reflects both the seller's readiness to provide the product and the capacity to do so.

This concept emphasises that supply is not just about the intention to sell, but also includes the actual capability to deliver the product in the market at various price levels.

2. How does technological progress affect the supply curve of a firm? NCERT; Competency Based Que

Ans. The technological progress will shift the supply curve of a firm to downward (to the right). Because a firm can produce same level of output using less of inputs with improved technology. It causes fall to the marginal cost.

3. How does an increase in the price of an input affect the supply curve of a firm? NCERT; Competency Based Que

Ans. An increase in the price of an input will affect marginal cost curve to move upward. So, supply curve shifts to the left. Therefore, an increase in the input price negatively affects the supply of the firm.

4. How does the market supply curve differ from the individual supply curve?

Ans. Difference between market supply curve and individual supply curve is as follows

Basis	Market Supply Curve	Individual Supply Curve
Definition	Represents the aggregate quantity of a commodity that all sellers in the market are willing to supply at different price levels.	Reflects the quantity a single seller is willing to supply at various prices.
Formation	Formed by horizontally summing the individual supply curves of all firms in the market.	Represents the supply decisions of a single seller.
Scope	Encompasses all sellers in the market.	Limited to a single seller.
Price Levels	Shows total quantity supplied by all sellers at each price level.	Shows quantity supplied by an individual seller at each price level.

5. **Look at the given image and identify which supply curve is given in the image.** **Competency Based Que**

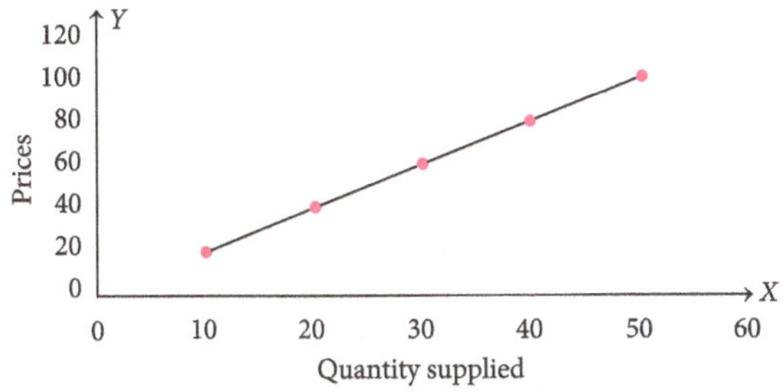

Ans. The image depicts an individual supply curve representing the relationship between the price of a specific commodity and the quantity that a single producer or firm is willing and able to supply at various price levels. It is a graphical depiction that illustrates how much of a good a particular seller will provide to the market as the price changes, while keeping other factors constant.

6. **"Developing countries have constraints." Do you agree? Give reason?** **Competency Based Que**

Ans. Yes, I agree. This is true that developing countries have supply constraints. Supply is limited due to underdeveloped technology, inadequate transportation and infrastructural facilities and scarce resources, etc. Producers are willing to increase supply but do not have the resources to do so.

7. **"Supply is a 'flow' concept, representing the amount offered over time, while stock refers to the total quantity available at a particular point." Do you agree? Give reason.** **Competency Based Que**

Ans. Yes, I agree. Supply is defined as a 'flow' concept because it measures the amount of a commodity offered for sale over a specific period, such as a day, week or month. In contrast, stock refers to the total quantity of a commodity available at a specific moment in time, like inventory at the end of a business day. This distinction is crucial for understanding market dynamics, as supply involves ongoing transactions and availability, while stock provides a snapshot of resources at a given moment.

8. **Using diagram and schedule, explain the law of supply.**

Ans. The law of supply states that other things remaining constant, quantity supplied increases with the increase in price and decreases with the decrease in price of a commodity. It can be explained with the help of following schedule and diagram

Price (₹)	**Quantity Supplied** (units)
10	100
20	200
30	300

The supply schedule shows the positive relationship between price and quantity supplied.

This is in accordance with the law of supply.

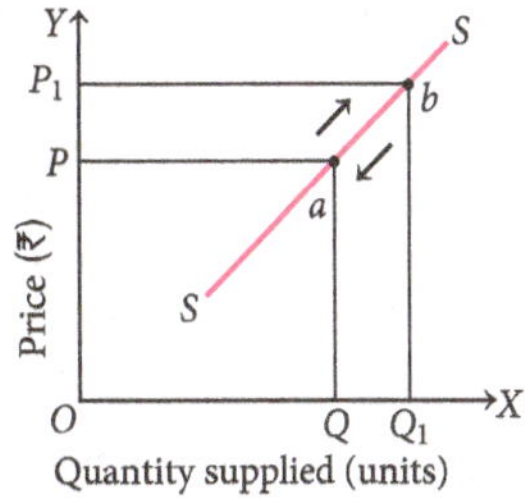

SS is the supply curve sloping upward. It shows a positive relationship between price and quantity supplied of a commodity. When price increases from ₹ 10 to ₹ 20, quantity supplied increases from 100 to 200 units.

9. **What are the two types of movements along the supply curve and what causes them?**

Ans. Types of movements are

(i) **Expansion of Supply**
When the price of a commodity rises, the quantity supplied increases, causing an upward movement along the supply curve.

(ii) **Contraction of Supply**
When the price of a commodity falls, the quantity supplied decreases, causing a downward movement along the supply curve.

Their Causes

(i) **Expansion of Supply**
Caused by an increase in the price of the commodity, which motivates sellers to supply more.

(ii) **Contraction of Supply**
Caused by a decrease in the price of the commodity, leading sellers to reduce the quantity supplied.

10. **Distinguish between change in supply and change in quantity supplied. Which of these causes a shift of supply curve?**

Ans. Difference between change in supply and change in quantity supplied

Basis	**Change in Supply**	**Change in Quantity Supplied**
Reason	It is caused by change in determinants other than own price of the commodity.	It is caused only by change in own price of the commodity, other determinants remaining constant.
Determinants	These include price of related goods, number of firms in the industry, goal of the firm, price of factors of production, state of technology, business confidence, government's policy.	Change in own price of the commodity is the only cause.

Basis	Change in Supply	Change in Quantity Supplied
Represen-tation	Diagrammatically, it is shown as a rightward and leftward shift in supply curve.	Diagrammatically, it is shown as a downward and upward movement on the same supply curve.

11. State any three causes of rightward shift in supply curve.

Ans. Three causes of rightward shift in supply curve are as follows

(i) Fall in the price of substitute goods.

(ii) Fall in the price of factors of production.

(iii) Improvement in technology.

12. What factors results in a decrease in supply?

Ans. Decrease in supply may occur on account of the following factors

(i) Rise in the price of substitute goods.

(ii) Fall in the price of complementary goods.

(iii) Changes in the goal of producers from sales maximisation to profit maximisation.

(iv) Rise in the price of factors of production.

(v) Outdated technology.

(vi) Decrease in the number of firms in the market.

(vii) Changes in government policy, either by increasing taxes or decreasing subsidies.

13. Distinguish between movement along the supply curve and shift in the supply curve with the help of a suitable diagram.

Ans. Difference between movement along the supply curve and shift in the supply curve

Basis	Movement along the Supply Curve	Shift in the Supply Curve
Movement	It represents expansion and contraction of supply due to change in the price of a concerned commodity.	It occurs due to factors other than price of a concerned commodity.
Effect	When price increases, there is an upward movement $(a \rightarrow b)$ along the supply curve showing increase in quantity supplied and when price decreases, there is a downward movement $(b \rightarrow a)$ along the supply curve showing decrease in quantity supplied as shown in figure A.	When other factors change in a positive direction, the supply curve shifts to the right, $(a \rightarrow b)$ showing increase in supply and when changes occur in the negative direction, the supply curve shifts to the left $(a \rightarrow c)$ showing a decrease in supply, as shown in figure B.
Graph	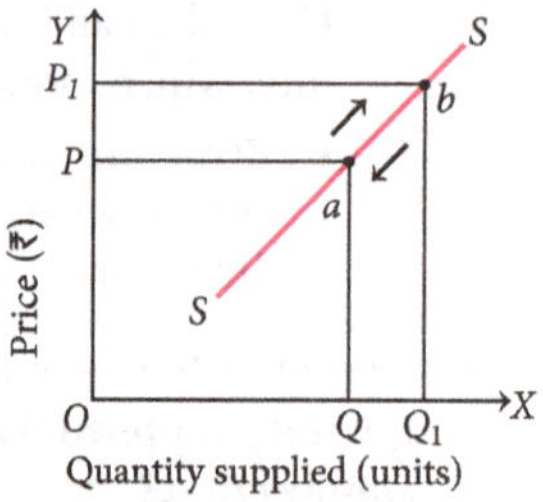	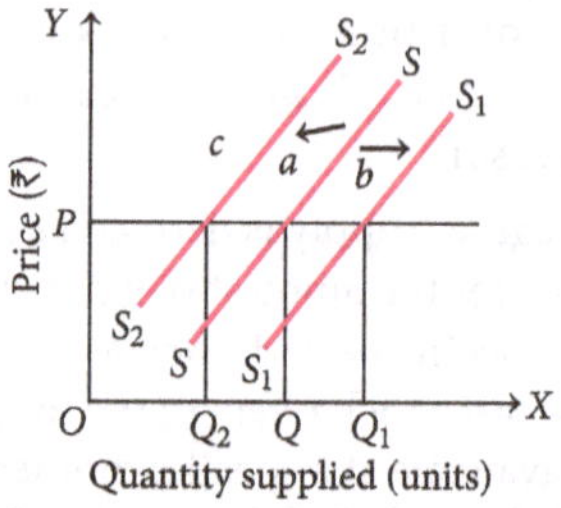

14. "Shifts in the supply curve occur when there are changes in factors other than the commodity's price." What does this shift in the supply curve indicate about market conditions? **Competency Based Que**

Ans. A shift in the supply curve indicates that there are changes in market conditions or external factors affecting supply. These shifts can result in an overall increase or decrease in supply, independent of price changes, due to influences such as changes in technology, production costs or government policies.

15. "A loss making firm has inelastic supply." Do you agree? If yes, why? **Competency Based Que**

Ans. Yes, I agree that a loss making firm has inelastic supply. This is mainly because the firm cannot adjust its production as quickly as the price increase. Such firm will not have enough money to invest in additional production. This will result in less percentage of increase in supply than the percentage of increase in price.

16. What does the price elasticity of supply mean? How do we measure it? **NCERT**

Ans. Price elasticity of supply is a percentage change in quantity supplied in response to percentage change in price of the commodity.

It can be measured as

$$E_s = \frac{\text{Percentage Change in Quantity Supplied}}{\text{Percentage Change in Price}}$$

$$or \quad = \frac{\Delta Q}{\Delta P} \times \frac{P}{Q}$$

Here, P = Initial price

ΔP = Change in price

Q = Initial quantity

ΔQ = Change in quantity supplied

17. "The value of price elasticity of supply is always positive."

In the light of this statement, what does a positive value for price elasticity of supply indicate? **Competency Based Que**

Ans. A positive value for price elasticity of supply indicates a direct relationship between price and quantity supplied, meaning that an increase in price typically leads to an increase in the quantity supplied and *vice-versa*.

18. Explain the situation of zero elasticity of supply with the help of a diagram.

Ans. It refers to a vertical straight line supply curve showing constant supply. In such a situation, it is assumed that supply is constant, whatever the changes in price.

It is shown in figure given below

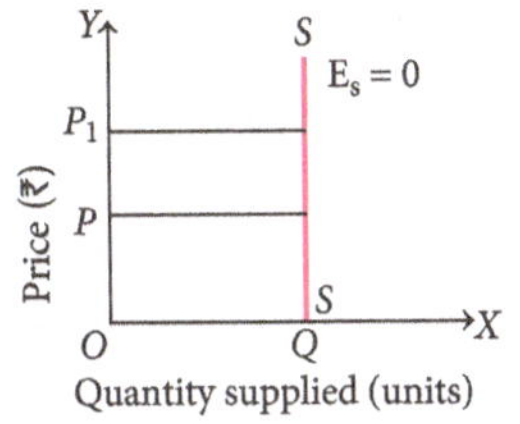

19. Which degree of price elasticity of supply is depicted in the below image? Explain. **Competency Based Que**

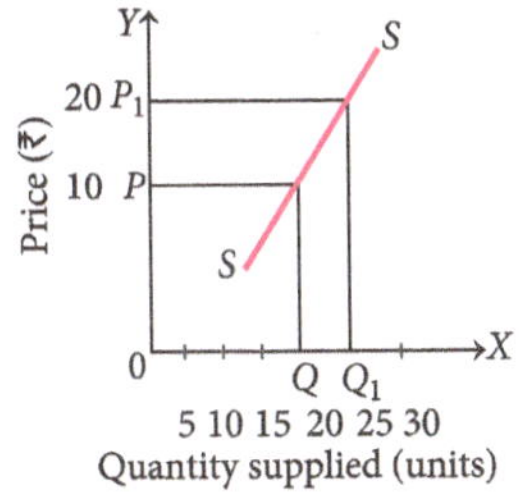

Ans. The degree of price elasticity of supply depicted in the image is more than unit elastic supply ($E_s > 1$). Unit elasticity occurs when a percentage change in price leads to an equal percentage change in quantity supplied.

In the given image, we see that a percentage increase in price (from P to P_1) leads to a proportionally larger percentage increase in quantity supplied (from Q to Q_1). This indicates that producers are highly responsive to changes in price and the supply curve is relatively flat. Therefore, the degree of price elasticity of supply is more than unit elastic.

20. "Supply is perfectly elastic when a small change in price leads to an infinite change in quantity supplied." Do you agree? Give reason. **Competency Based Que**

Ans. Yes, I agree. Perfectly elastic supply means that suppliers are extremely responsive to price changes. Specifically, even a tiny increase in price will result in an infinitely large quantity supplied, while any decrease in price would lead to no quantity being supplied at all.

This situation is often depicted with a horizontal supply curve, reflecting that suppliers are willing to supply any amount at a particular price but none at a lower price.

Long Answer Type Questions

21. What is individual and market supply? What are the determinants of individual and market supply?

Ans. Individual Supply

It refers to the quantity of a particular commodity that an individual firm is willing and able to sell at a given price during a given period of time.

Market Supply

Represents the total quantity all firms in the market are willing to sell.

Determinants of Individual Supply

(i) **Price of the Given Commodity** (P_x)
A direct relationship exists between price and quantity supplied. Higher prices lead to greater supply. e.g. A farmer increases the supply of apples when the price rises from ₹ 50 to ₹ 70 per kg.

(ii) **Price of Related Goods** (P_r)
Supply is inversely related to the price of substitutes and complementary goods. e.g. If rice prices increase, a farmer reduces wheat supply and focuses on rice.

(iii) **Goal of the Firm** (G)
Profit-maximising firms supply more at higher prices, while sales- maximising firms may supply more even at lower prices. e.g. A company increases smartphone supply during a discount period to boost sales.

(iv) **Price of Factors of Production** (P_f)
Higher input costs reduce supply as profit margins shrink and *vice-versa*. e.g. A bakery reduces cake supply when the cost of flour rises.

(v) **State of Technology** (T)
Advanced technology reduces production costs and increases supply. e.g. A factory adopts automation to increase shoe production.

Determinants of Market Supply

Alongwith the determinants of individual supply, market supply is also influenced by following factors

(i) **Number of Firms in the Industry** (N_i)
More firms increase total market supply, while fewer firms reduce it. e.g. Three new smartphone companies entering the market increase total supply.

(ii) **Expectation of Future Prices** (E_x)
If firms expect prices to rise in the future, they may hold back current supply. e.g. Oil companies reduce current supply, anticipating a price hike next month.

(iii) **Government Policy** (G_P)
Taxes reduce supply by lowering profits, while subsidies increase supply by lowering costs. e.g. A tax on plastic reduces supply, while subsidies on solar panels increase supply.

22. "Market supply schedule also shows the positive relationship between price and quantity supplied of a commodity."
In the light of the statement, explain how does the market supply schedule shows the positive relationship between price and quantity supplied and what factors can cause shifts in the supply curve?

Competency Based Que

Ans. The market supply schedule highlights the positive relationship between price and quantity supplied by showing that as the price of a commodity increases, producers are willing to supply more and as the price decreases, the quantity supplied reduces. This relationship is consistent with the law of supply, which states that higher prices incentivise producers to supply more due to the potential for greater profits.

This concept is visually represented through an upward sloping supply curve, which reflects how producers respond to price changes. The slope indicates that at higher prices, the willingness and ability of producers to offer goods in the market increase, and *vice-versa*.

However, the supply curve is not static. Factors such as changes in input costs, technological advancements, government policies and future price expectations can cause shifts in the supply curve.

For instance

(i) An increase in production costs (e.g. Raw materials or labour) shifts the supply curve to the left, reducing supply at each price level.

(ii) Technological improvements that lower production costs shift the curve to the right, increasing supply.

(iii) Government taxes can decrease supply, while subsidies may increase it.

Thus, the market supply schedule not only demonstrates the relationship between price and quantity supplied but also reflects how external factors can influence supply dynamics.

23. What is a supply curve? Explain the classification of supply curve with examples.

Ans. A supply curve is a graphical representation of the supply schedule, showing the relationship between the price of a commodity and the quantity supplied, while keeping other factors constant. It visually demonstrates the positive relationship between price and quantity supplied, represented as an upward sloping curve. As the price increases, sellers are willing to supply more of the commodity.

Supply curve can be further classified as

(i) **Individual Supply Curve**
This curve represents the relationship between the price and quantity supplied by a single firm or seller. It is the graphical version of the individual supply schedule. e.g. A farmer's individual supply curve shows that as the price of wheat rises, the farmer supplies more wheat.

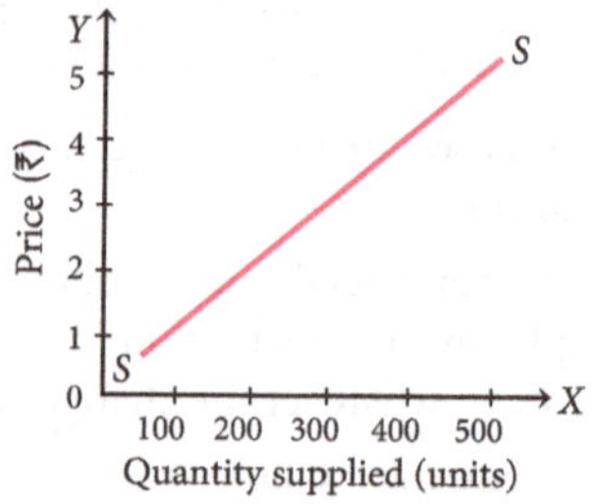

Individual supply curve

(ii) **Market Supply Curve**
This curve shows the total quantity supplied by all sellers in the market at various prices. It is the horizontal summation of all individual supply curves.
The market supply curve is usually flatter compared to individual supply curves, which are steeper. e.g. The market supply curve for wheat combines the supply curves of all wheat producers, showing the overall market supply.

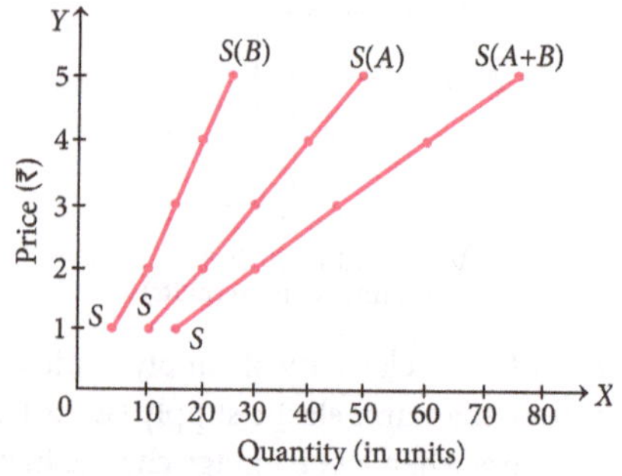

Market supply curve

SS (A) is the individual supply curve of A.
SS (B) is the individual supply curve of B.
SS (A + B) is the market supply curve.

24. Differentiate between expansion in supply and increase in supply.

Ans. Difference between expansion in quantity supply and increase in supply is as follows

Basis	Expansion in Quantity Supply	Increase in Supply
Meaning	When supply of a commodity expands due to increase in price keeping other factors constant.	When supply of a commodity increases due to favourable changes in other factors.
Cause	Increase in price.	(i) Decrease in input price. (ii) Improvement in technology etc.
Impact on Supply Curve	Upward movement along supply curve.	Rightward shift in supply curve.
Diagrammatic Presentation	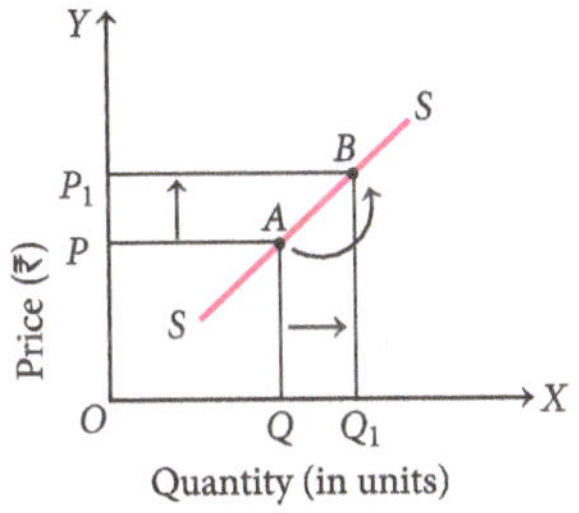	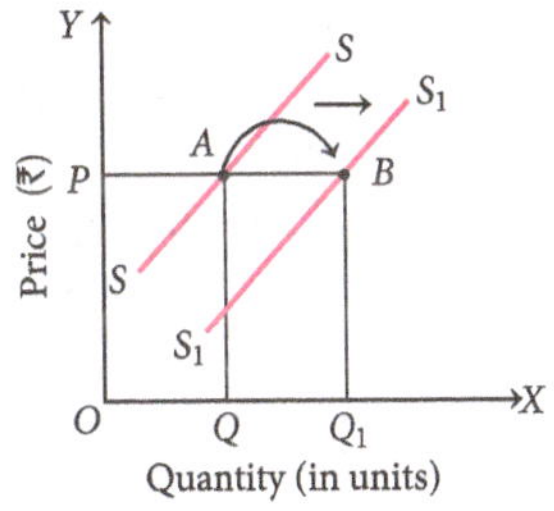

25. What are the causes of operation and exceptions of the law of supply?

Ans. Causes for Operation of Law of Supply

(i) **Profit Motive**
Rise in prices leads to rise in profit margin for suppliers, which motivates them to increase supply and *vice-versa*.

(ii) **Change in the Number of Firms**
High margin of profit makes the particular business lucrative to new investors.

As a result of this, the number of firms increases in the market, causing supply to rise simultaneously.

(iii) **Reduction in Stock**
As price rises, the producers supply more goods from their accumulated stocks, which causes stocks to deplete and supply to increase.

Exceptions to the Law of Supply

(i) **Agricultural Goods**
Law of supply does not apply to agricultural goods, as their supply depends on climatic conditions. If due to any natural calamity, production of agricultural product falls, then its supply will not increase, whatever may be the price.

(ii) **Perishable Goods**
Suppliers are willing to sell perishable items like fruits or milk even when prices are falling because these goods cannot be stored for long.

(iii) **Antique Goods and Rare Articles**
The supply of items like rare paintings or antiques remains limited, regardless of their price.

e.g. The supply of Hussain's paintings cannot be increased even if buyers are willing to pay high price for it.

(iv) **Future Price Expectations**
If sellers expect prices to rise further in future, then they would not increase there supply now even when prices are increasing.

(v) **Lack of Resources**
In underdeveloped or backward economies, production and supply may remain low due to the scarcity of resources.

26. How does outdated technology affect production costs and what is its impact on the supply of goods?

Competency Based Que

Ans. Outdated technology increases production costs because it often involves inefficient processes, higher labour usage and slower production rates compared to modern technology. When businesses rely on older technology, they face higher costs in terms of maintenance, energy and time, which reduces their ability to produce goods efficiently.

As a result, the cost per unit increases, reducing profit margins. The impact of outdated technology on supply is negative. Due to higher production costs, producers may not be able to supply as many goods at the same price. Consequently, the supply curve shifts to the left, indicating a reduction in the quantity supplied at every price level.

This decrease in supply can lead to higher market prices, shortages or both, as producers struggle to maintain profitability with outdated production methods.

27. List and explain any two determinants that results in the changes in supply with diagrams.

Ans. Supply is influenced by various determinants beyond the price of the commodity itself. Changes in these determinants can cause shift in the supply curve, either increasing or decreasing supply.

These are as follows

(i) **Change in the State of Technology**

- **Advancement of Technology**
  Improved technology lowers production costs, enabling producers to supply more at the same price. As a result, supply increases from OQ to OQ_2 at the same price OP. It leads to a rightward shift in the supply curve from SS to S_2S_2.
- **Degradation of Technology**
  Outdated technology increases production costs, leading to reduced supply. As a result, supply decreases from OQ to OQ_1 at the same price OP. It leads to a leftward shift in the supply curve from SS to S_1S_1.

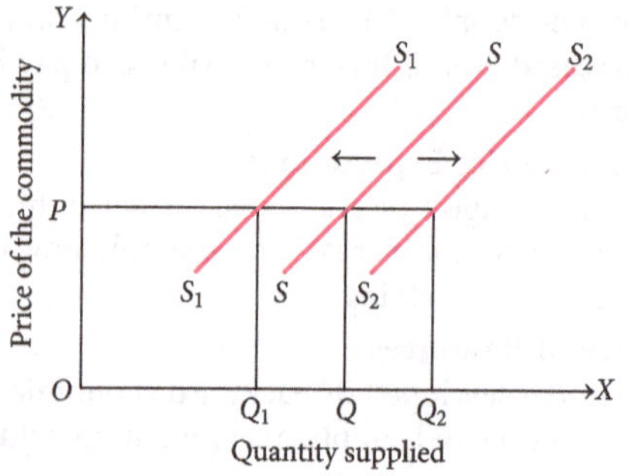

(ii) **Change in Price of Related Goods**

- **Increase in Price of Related Goods**
  When the price of a related good (e.g. Tea) rises, producers may shift resources to produce more of that good instead of the given commodity (e.g. Coffee), decreasing its supply. As a result, supply (of coffee) falls from OQ to OQ_1, at the same price OP. It leads to a leftward shift in the supply curve from SS to S_1S_1.
- **Decrease in Price of Related Goods**
  A drop in the price of related goods makes the given commodity (e.g. Coffee) more profitable to produce, resulting in an increase in supply. As a result, supply (of coffee) increases from OQ to OQ_2, at the same price OP. It leads to a rightward shift in the supply curve from SS to S_2S_2.

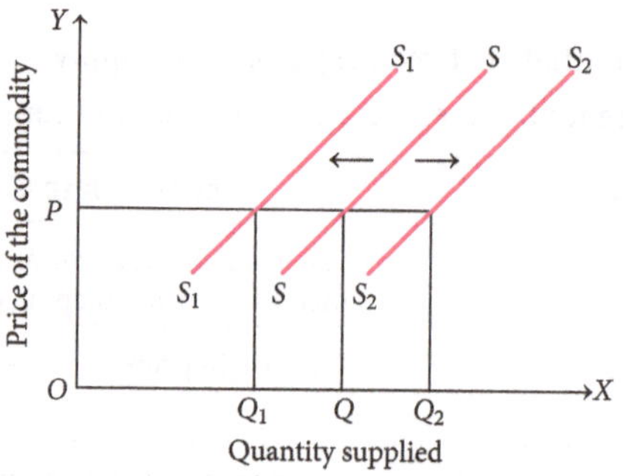

28. What does it mean when we say that price elasticity of supply is a pure number and why does it have no unit of measurement? **Competency Based Que**

Ans. Price elasticity of supply being referred to as a 'pure number' means that it is a ratio without any specific unit of measurement attached to it. Price elasticity of supply is calculated as the percentage change in the quantity supplied divided by the percentage change in price.

Since both the numerator (change in quantity supplied) and the denominator (change in price) are expressed as percentages, the units cancel each other out, resulting in a dimensionless or pure number.

The absence of units in price elasticity of supply makes it a versatile measure that can be applied across different markets and industries, regardless of the specific units used for quantity (such as kilograms, liters or units) or price (such as dollars, Euros, etc.) This allows for easy comparison of supply responsiveness across diverse goods and services.

Additionally, price elasticity of supply always has a positive value due to the direct relationship between price and quantity supplied, as higher prices typically lead to an increase in supply and *vice-versa*.

29. Using diagrams, explain various degrees of price elasticity of supply.

Ans. The various degrees of price elasticity of supply are given below

(i) **Perfectly Elastic Supply**
In this case, a slight change in price causes infinite change in quantity supplied. The supply curve SS is parallel to x-axis and $E_s = \infty$, as shown in the figure.

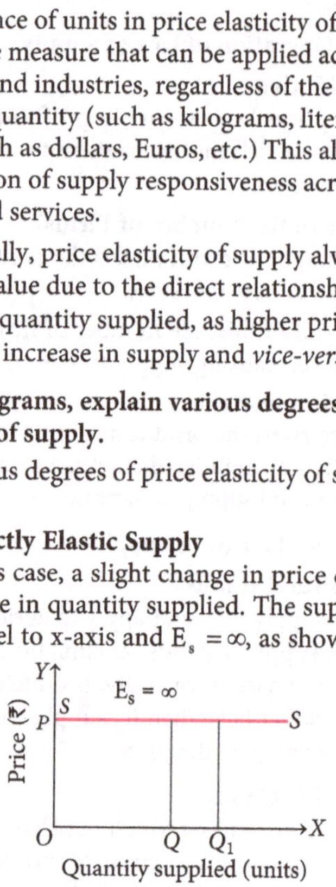

(ii) **Perfectly Inelastic Supply**

It is a situation where the quantity supplied remains unchanged, whatever be the changes in price. Hence, the supply curve is parallel to y-axis and $E_s = 0$, as shown in the figure.

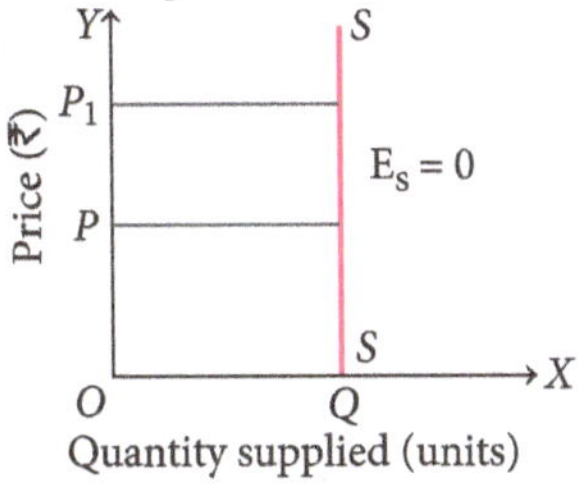

(iii) **Unitary Elastic Supply**

In this case, percentage change in quantity supplied is exactly equal to percentage change in price.

Hence, the supply curve is a straight line originating from the origin and sloping upward and $E_s = 1$, as shown in the figure.

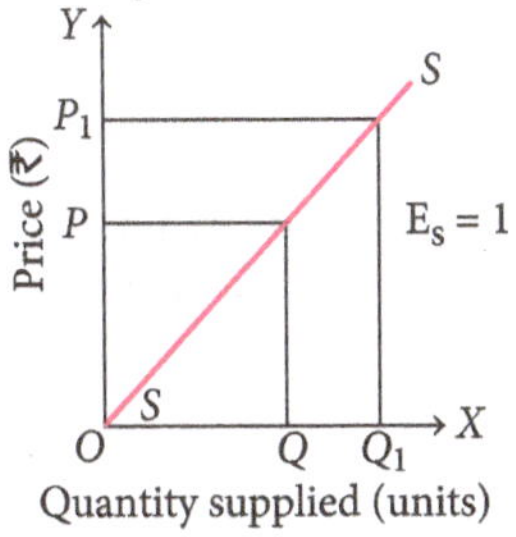

(iv) **More than Unitary Elastic Supply**

In this situation, percentage change in quantity supplied is greater than the percentage change in price. An upward sloping straight line supply curve originates from y-axis and $E_s > 1$, as shown in the figure.

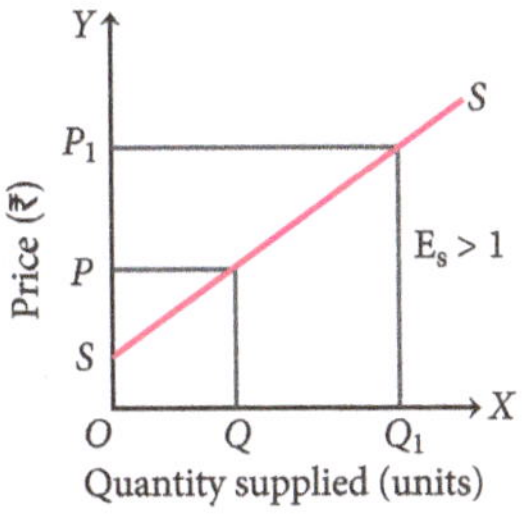

(v) **Less than Unitary Elastic Supply**

In this situation, percentage change in quantity supplied is less than percentage change in price.

An upward sloping straight line supply curve originates from x-axis and $E_s < 1$, as shown in the figure.

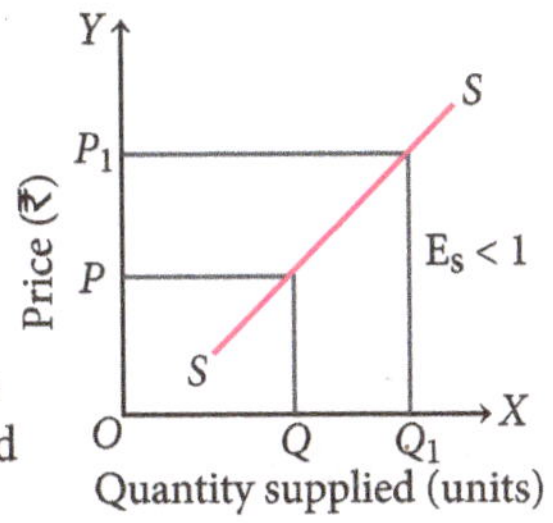

30. **In a bustling local market, several vendors sell fresh fruits. One vendor, Mrs. Rani, typically supplies 200 kg of apples each week at a price of ₹ 100 per kg.**

This year, due to a favourable growing season and increased harvest, Mrs. Rani decided to increase her supply to 300 kg per week, anticipating that this would lead to higher overall revenue.

However, as she increased her supply, she noticed that the market price for apples began to drop to ₹ 90 per kg due to an influx of competitors who also increased their supply. Mrs. Rani was initially concerned that the drop in price would reduce her profit margins, but she realised that the increase in quantity sold might off-set this loss. Mrs. Rani's decision to increase supply also took into account the rising costs of transportation and labour, which could potentially affect her profit. Despite these costs, she remained optimistic about the future demand for fresh fruits. Competency Based Que

(i) What factors can cause a shift in the supply curve for a product like apples in a competitive market?

(ii) How does the concept of elasticity of supply apply to the situation where Mrs. Rani increased her supply and the market price subsequently fell?

(iii) Explain the relationship between the quantity supplied and the price level in the context of the law of supply.

Ans. (i) A shift in the supply curve can be caused by changes in production costs, technological advancements and the number of suppliers, government policies and weather conditions. e.g. If production costs rise, the supply curve shifts left, indicating a decrease in supply.

(ii) Elasticity of supply measures how much the quantity supplied responds to price changes. If Mrs. Rani increased her supply despite a price drop, it suggests that she may expect future demand to rise or believes selling more at a lower price could increase overall revenue.

If the supply is elastic, a price decrease leads to a proportionately larger increase in quantity supplied, while inelastic supply indicates less responsiveness to price changes.

(iii) The law of supply states that there is a direct relationship between the quantity supplied and the price level, i.e. as the price increases, the quantity supplied also increases and *vice-versa*.

This relationship is driven by profit motives, i.e. suppliers like Mrs. Rani adjust their supply based on price changes to maximise profits. For instance, if the price of apples drops from ₹ 100 to ₹ 90 per kg, Mrs. Rani may reduce her supply since lower prices may not cover her costs, demonstrating the law of supply in action. Conversely, if prices rise, she would be incentivised to increase her supply to capitalise on higher potential revenues.

Numerical Questions

Numerical 1

Consider a market with two firms. The following table shows the supply schedules of the two firms. The SS_1 column gives the supply schedule of firm 1 and the SS_2 column gives the supply schedule of firm 2. Compute the market supply schedule. **NCERT**

Price (₹)	0	1	2	3	4	5	6
SS_1 (units)	0	0	0	1	2	3	4
SS_2 (units)	0	0	0	1	2	3	4

Sol. **Market Supply Schedule**

Price (₹)	SS_1 (units)	SS_2 (units)	Market Supply $= SS_1 + SS_2$ (units)
0	0	0	0
1	0	0	0
2	0	0	0
3	1	1	2
4	2	2	4
5	3	3	6
6	4	4	8

Numerical 2

Consider a market with two firms. In the following table, labelled as SS_1 and SS_2 give the supply schedules of firm 1 and firm 2, respectively. Compute the market supply schedule. **NCERT**

Price (₹)	SS_1 (kg)	SS_2 (kg)
0	0	0
1	0	0
2	0	0
3	1	0
4	2	0.5
5	3	1
6	4	1.5
7	5	2
8	6	2.5

Sol. **Market Supply Schedule**

Price (₹)	SS_1 (kg)	SS_2 (kg)	Market Supply $= SS_1 + SS_2$ (kg)
0	0	0	0
1	0	0	0
2	0	0	0
3	1	0	1
4	2	0.5	2.5
5	3	1	4
6	4	1.5	5.5
7	5	2	7
8	6	2.5	8.5

Numerical 3

There are three identical firms in a market. The following table shows the supply schedule of firm 1. Compute the market supply schedule. **NCERT**

Price (₹)	0	1	2	3	4	5	6	7	8
SS_1 (units)	0	0	2	4	6	8	10	12	14

Sol. **Market Supply Schedule**

Price (₹)	SS_1 (units)	SS_2 (units)	SS_3 (units)	Market Supply $= SS_1 + SS_2 + SS_3$ (units)
0	0	0	0	0
1	0	0	0	0
2	2	2	2	6
3	4	4	4	12
4	6	6	6	18
5	8	8	8	24
6	10	10	10	30
7	12	12	12	36
8	14	14	14	42

Numerical 4

A firm earns a revenue of ₹ 50 when the market price of a good is ₹ 10. The market price increases to ₹ 15 and the firm now earns a revenue of ₹ 150. What is the price elasticity of the firm's supply curve? **NCERT**

Sol. (i) When market price (P) = 10

Revenue = ₹ 50

$\therefore$ Quantity supplied (Q) $= \frac{50}{10} = 5$ units

(ii) When market price (P_1) = 15

Revenue = ₹ 150

$\therefore$ Quantity supplied $(Q_1) = \frac{150}{15} = 10$ units

Now given, $P = 10$; $P_1 = 15$

$Q = 5$ units; $Q_1 = 10$ units

Change in Price (ΔP) = 15 – 10 = ₹ 5

Change in Quantity (ΔQ) = 10 – 5 = 5 units

Price elasticity of supply $E_s = \frac{\Delta P}{\Delta Q} \times \frac{P}{Q} = \frac{5}{5} \times \frac{10}{5}$

$E_s = 2$ (elastic supply)

Numerical 5

The market price of a good changes from ₹ 5 to ₹ 20. As a result, the quantity supplied by a firm increases by 15 units. The price elasticity of the firm's supply curve is 0.5. Find the initial and final output levels of the firm. NCERT

Sol. Given, $P = 5$

New Price (P_1) = 20

ΔP = ₹ 15; ΔQ = 15 units

Elasticity of supply (E_s) = 0.5

Price elasticity of supply $(E_s) = \frac{\Delta Q}{\Delta P} \times \frac{P}{Q}$

$0.5 = \frac{15}{15} \times \frac{5}{Q}$

Initial Output (Q) = 10 units

Final Output = 10 + 15 = 25 units

Numerical 6

At the market price of ₹ 10, a firm supplies 4 units of output. The market price increases to ₹ 30. The price elasticity of the firm's supply is 1.25. What quantity will the firm supply at the new price? NCERT

Sol. Given, Q = 4 units; P = ₹ 10; P_1 = ₹ 30

Change in price (ΔP) = ₹ 20 $(P - P_1)$

$E_s = 1.25$

$E_s = \frac{\Delta Q}{\Delta P} \times \frac{P}{Q} = 1.25 = \frac{\Delta Q}{20} \times \frac{10}{4}$

$\Delta Q = 10$ units

$\therefore$ Quantity at new price = 10 + 4 = 14 units

Numerical 7

When the price of a good rises from ₹ 20 per unit to ₹ 30 per unit, the revenue of the firm producing this good rises from ₹ 100 to ₹ 300. Calculate price elasticity of supply.

Sol. Given,

Price (₹)	Total Revenue (TR) (₹)
20	100
30	300

Quantity Supplied (Q) $= \frac{TR}{P} = \frac{100}{20} = 5$

$Q_1 = \frac{300}{30} = 10$

So, $P = 20$; $Q = 5$; $P_1 = 30$; $Q_1 = 10$

$\Delta P = P_1 - P = 30 - 20 = 10$

$\Delta Q = Q - Q = 10 - 5 = 5$

Price Elasticity of Supply

$(E_s) = \frac{\Delta Q}{\Delta P} \times \frac{P}{Q} = \frac{5}{10} \times \frac{20}{5}$

$E_s = 2$ (more than unit elastic)

Numerical 8

A firm supplies 10 units of a good at a price of ₹ 5 per unit. Price elasticity of supply is 1.25.

What quantity will the firm supply at a price of ₹ 7 per unit?

Sol. Given, $E_s = 1.25$; P = ₹ 5; P_1 = ₹ 7; Q = 10

$Q_1 = ?$; $\Delta P = P_1 - P = 7 - 5 = 2$

Price Elasticity of Supply $(E_s) = \frac{\Delta Q}{\Delta P} \times \frac{P}{Q}$

$1.25 = \frac{\Delta Q}{2} \times \frac{5}{10}$; $\Delta Q = 1.25 \times 4 = 5$

Q_1 = Actual Quantity + Change in Quantity

$= Q + \Delta Q = 10 + 5$

$Q_1 = 15$ units

Numerical 9

Total revenue is ₹ 400 when the price of the commodity is ₹ 2 per unit. When price rises to ₹ 3 per unit, the quantity supplied is 300 units.

Calculate the price elasticity of supply.

Sol. When, Price (P) = ₹ 2; Total Revenue = ₹ 400

$\therefore$ Quantity supplied (Q) = 400 ÷ 2 = 200 units

Now, P = ₹ 2; P_1 = ₹ 3

$\Delta P = 3 - 2$ = ₹ 1

$Q = 200$; $Q_1 = 300$

$\Delta Q = 300 - 200 = 100$ units

Price Elasticity of Supply

$(E_s) = \frac{\Delta Q}{\Delta P} \times \frac{P}{Q} = \frac{100}{1} \times \frac{2}{200} = \frac{2}{2} = 1$

$\therefore$ Price Elasticity of Supply = 1 (unit elastic)

Numerical 10

A firm supplies 200 units of a good at a price of ₹ 5 per unit. When price changes, it supplies 100 units less. Price elasticity of supply is 2.5. Calculate price after change.

Sol. Given, $P = ₹\,5$; $\Delta Q = 100$ units ; $\Delta P = ?$

$Q = 200$ units ; $E_s = 2.5$

$$\text{Price Elasticity of Supply } (E_s) = \frac{\Delta Q}{\Delta P} \times \frac{P}{Q}$$

$$\Rightarrow \quad 2.5 = \frac{100}{\Delta P} \times \frac{5}{200} \Rightarrow \Delta P = \frac{5}{2.5 \times 2} = \frac{5}{5} = 1$$

$\therefore$ New price $(P_1) = P - \Delta P = 5 - 1 = ₹\,4$

Numerical 11

Commodities X and Y have equal price elasticity of supply. The supply of X rises from 400 units to 500 units due to a 20% rise in its price. Calculate the percentage fall in supply of Y if its price falls by 8%.

Sol. Given, E_s of X = E_s of Y

$Q_X = 400,\ Q'_X = 500$

Percentage change in price of $X = 20\%$

Percentage change in price of $Y = 8\%$

$\Delta Q_X = Q'_X - Q_X = 500 - 400 = 100$ units

Price Elasticity of Supply of X

$$(E_s) = \frac{\text{Percentage Change in Quantity Supplied}}{\text{Percentage Change in Price}}$$

$$= \frac{\frac{\Delta Q_X}{Q_X} \times 100}{20} = \frac{\frac{100}{400} \times 100}{20} = \frac{25}{20} = 1.25$$

Price Elasticity of Supply of Y

$$(E_s) = \frac{\text{Percentage Change in Quantity Supplied}}{\text{Percentage Change in Price}}$$

$$1.25 = \frac{\text{Percentage Change in Quantity Supplied}}{8}$$

[$\because E_s$ of X = E_s of Y]

$\therefore$ Percentage fall in quantity supplied of Y

$= 1.25 \times 8 = 10\%$

Numerical 12

The price elasticity of supply of a commodity is 2. When its price falls from ₹ 10 to ₹ 8 per unit, its quantity supplied falls by 500 units. Calculate the quantity supplied at the reduced price.

Sol. Given, $P = ₹\,10$; $P_1 = ₹\,8$; $\Delta P = 8 - 10 = (-)\,₹\,2$

$Q = ?$; $\Delta Q = -500$

$\Rightarrow \quad E_s = 2$; $Q_1 = ?$

$$\text{Price Elasticity of Supply } (E_s) = \frac{\Delta Q}{\Delta P} \times \frac{P}{Q}$$

$$2 = \frac{-500}{-2} \times \frac{10}{Q}$$

$$\Rightarrow \quad Q = \frac{-500 \times 10}{-2 \times 2} = 1{,}250$$

$\therefore$ Quantity supplied at the reduced price

$Q_1 = Q + \Delta Q = 1{,}250 + (-500) = 1{,}250 - 500$

$\therefore \quad Q_1 = 750$ units

Numerical 13

A firm supplies 500 units of a good at a price of ₹ 5 per unit. The price elasticity of supply of a good is 2. At what price will the firm supply 700 units?

Sol. Given, $P = ₹\,5$; $\Delta P = ?$; $Q = 500$ units ; $Q_1 = 700$ units

$\Delta Q = 700 - 500 = 200$ units

$E_s = 2$

$$\text{Price Elasticity of Supply } (E_s) = \frac{\Delta Q}{\Delta P} \times \frac{P}{Q}$$

$$\Rightarrow \quad 2 = \frac{200}{\Delta P} \times \frac{5}{500} \text{ or } \Delta P = \frac{200 \times 5}{500 \times 2} = 1$$

$\therefore$ New price $(P_1) = P + \Delta P = 5 + 1 = ₹\,6$

$\therefore$ The firm will supply 700 units at ₹ 6 per unit.

SELF ASSESSMENT TEST

Objective Type Questions

1. Which of the following shifts the supply curve to the right?
   (a) Increase in the price of factors of production
   (b) Decrease in government subsidies
   (c) Technological advancement
   (d) Increase in taxes
2. What happens when the price of a commodity rises and the supply of the commodity increases?
   (a) A movement along the supply curve occurs
   (b) The supply curve shifts to the right
   (c) The supply curve shifts to the left
   (d) There is no change in supply
3. The relationship between the quantity supplied of a commodity and its price is known as the ....
   (a) law of demand
   (b) law of supply
   (c) supply curve
   (d) elasticity of demand
4. In which case is the supply curve perfectly elastic?
   (a) When the price changes by a small amount and the quantity supplied changes infinitely
   (b) When the supply remains constant regardless of price
   (c) When the quantity supplied decreases as price increases
   (d) When the price and quantity supplied are not related
5. The supply curve for a good is upward sloping due to the .... relationship between price and quantity supplied.
   (a) negative (b) zero
   (c) indirect (d) positive

Answers 1. (c) 2. (a) 3. (b) 4. (a) 5. (d)

Short Answer Type Questions

6. What do you mean by the slope of supply curve? How is it calculated?
7. "Readily or commonly available inputs lead to more elastic supply, while scarce inputs will have inelastic supply." Do you agree? Give reasons.
8. Define the following
   (i) Movement along supply curve
   (ii) Shift in the supply curve
9. What are the assumptions of the law of supply?

Long Answer Type Question

10. How does an increase in the number of firms in a market affect the market supply curve?

Numerical Questions

11. The price of a commodity rises from ₹ 10 to ₹ 12 and as a result, the quantity supplied increases from 100 units to 150 units. Calculate the percentage change in quantity supplied.

Ans. 50%

12. If the price of a product increases by 10% and the quantity supplied increases by 15%, calculate the price elasticity of supply.

Ans. 1.5

13. A bakery's price increases from ₹ 50 to ₹ 60 per loaf of bread and the quantity supplied increases from 200 to 250 loaves. Calculate the price elasticity of supply.

Ans. 1.25

14. The price of smartphones increases from ₹ 20,000 to ₹ 22,000. As a result, the supply increases from 500 units to 600 units. Calculate the price elasticity of supply.

Ans. 2

15. A manufacturer of shoes is selling 1,000 pairs at ₹ 500 each. When the price increases to ₹ 600, the supplier is able to sell 1,200 pairs. Calculate the price elasticity of supply.

Ans. 1

16. The price of flour increases from ₹ 30 per kg to ₹ 35 per kg. The quantity of flour supplied increases from 500 kg to 600 kg. Calculate the price elasticity of supply.

Ans. 1.2

17. A supplier sells 2,000 units of a product at ₹ 100 each. When the price rises to ₹ 110, the quantity supplied increases to 2,400 units. Calculate the price elasticity of supply using the percentage change method.

Ans. 2

18. A supplier of handmade jewelry sells 1,000 pieces at ₹ 500 each. When the price rises to ₹ 550, the quantity supplied increases to 1,100 pieces. Calculate the price elasticity of supply. If the price rises further to ₹ 600 and the quantity supplied increases to 1,300 pieces, calculate the new price elasticity of supply and comment on the change.

Ans. 1, 2

09

CHAPTER

Market refers to a place where buyers and sellers of a particular commodity meet and exchange goods or services at a particular price, during a given time period.

Forms of Market and Price Determination

YOUR STUDY GOALS

9.1 Concept of Market
9.2 Perfect Competition
9.3 Market Equilibrium
9.4 Simple Applications of Tools of Demand and Supply

YOUR PRACTICE GOAL

- Objective Type Questions (63 Qs ; MCQs, A-R, Statements, Matching, Concept Identification)
- Subjective Questions (32 SAs, 17 LAs)
- 4 Numerical Questions
- Self Assessment Test (8 MCQs, 6 SAs, 2 LAs)

9.1 Concept of Market

Market may be defined as an arrangement where buyers and sellers come in contact with each other for sale and purchase of the commodities through any means of communication such as internet, telephones, etc.

It should be remembered that in economics, the term 'market' does not necessarily refers to a place, but always to a commodity. So, there exist a market for cars, a market for clothes, etc.

Forms of Market

Market may assume different forms depending on the factors like number of buyers and sellers, nature of the product, knowledge of market, degree of price control, etc.

On the basis of the given factors or competition level, there are two main forms of market

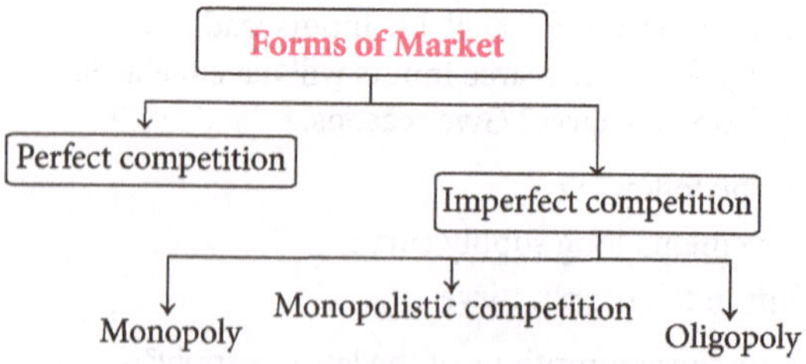

Note As per scope of syllabus, we will discuss only perfect competition in detail.

9.2 Perfect Competition

It is a form of market where there are very large number of buyers and sellers of a commodity, exchanging homogeneous products at a price determined by the market.

Pure Competition It is a market form in which there are very large number of buyers and sellers, presence of a homogeneous product and free entry or exit of firms, i.e. it follows some characteristics of perfect competition.
e.g. Local vegetable market where many sellers offer similar products.

Features of Perfect Competition

Perfectly competitive market exhibits the following features

Feature	Description	Example
Very Large Number of Buyers and Sellers	No individual buyer or seller can influence market price of commodity due to the large number of participants. Due to this reason, firm under perfect competition is said to be **price taker.**	Wheat farmers selling in a global market.
Homogeneous Product	All firms sell identical products, which are perfect substitutes for one another.	Fruits or vegetables in local markets.
Free Entry and Exit of Firms	There is no barrier to enter or exit of firms. They have freedom to move in and out of an industry without any government intervention.	Small shops entering or leaving a market.
Firms Earn Normal Profit	Firms earn only normal profit in the long-run. This is so because abnormal profits will attract new firms to enter the market while abnormal losses would force marginal firms to exit from market.	Small retailers making basic profits over time.
Perfect Knowledge	Buyers and sellers have complete knowledge about market prices, cost of inputs, commodity sold, etc.	Farmers knowing both input costs and market prices.
Perfect Mobility of Factors of Production	Resources like labour, capital, etc. can freely move to that industry which offers better returns.	Workers shifting from agriculture to manufacturing.
Absence of Transportation Costs	It is assumed that no additional transportation costs are incurred, ensuring uniform pricing.	Similar prices for basic goods like sugar across regions.

Demand Curve Under Perfect Competition

In a perfectly competitive market, a firm's demand curve is perfectly elastic ($E_d = \infty$), represented by a horizontal straight line parallel to x-axis. This means the firm can sell any quantity of goods at the prevailing market price, which is determined by the intersection of market demand and supply.

The given figure shows that at the given price *OP*, the firm can sell any quantity of the commodity it produces. Price remains constant which is determined by the market whether quantity demanded is *OA* or *OB* or even zero.

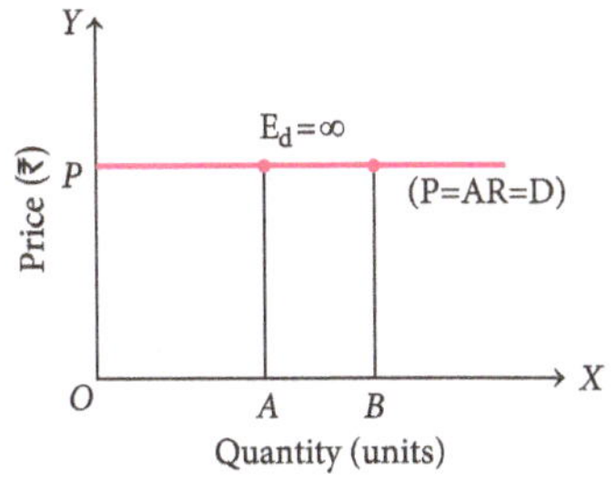

Firm is a Price Taker, Not a Price Maker

Perfect competition is comprised of very large number of sellers and each seller is very small hence an individual seller cannot fix the price on its own. Market price, under this market form, is determined at the equilibrium point, where market demand and market supply for industry as a whole are equal to each other. This equilibrium price applies to all individual firms.

At this point, AR curve becomes perfectly elastic and parallel to x-axis. This is why AR and MR curves of the firms coincide with each other as MR becomes equal to AR.

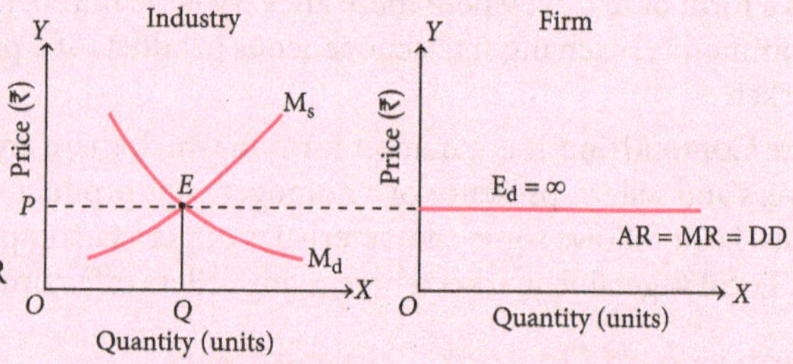

Demand curve and market price under perfect competition

Where,

M_S = Market supply ; E = Equilibrium point ; M_d = Market demand

P = Equilibrium price ; Q = Equilibrium quantity

Note In perfect competition, Price = Average Revenue = Marginal Revenue because of a constant price prevailing in the market.

Effect on Market Price Due to Change in Demand or Supply

Change in Demand	Change in Supply
If demand increases, the demand curve shifts to right, raising both equilibrium price and quantity. For instance, during a festival season, higher demand for goods like sugar may push prices up. Conversely, a decrease in demand causes a leftward shift, leading to fall in both equilibrium price and quantity. 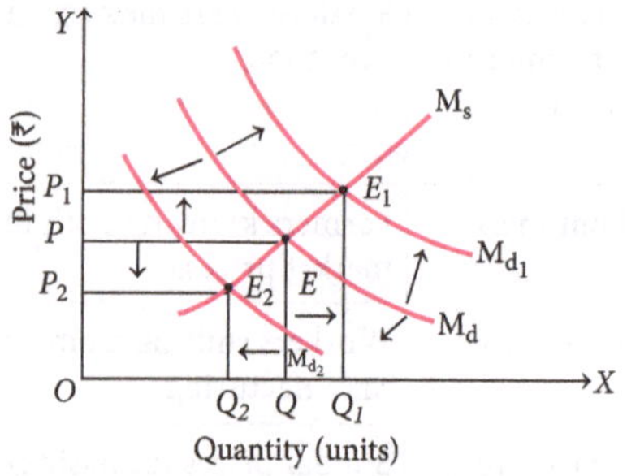 In short, • ↑ in Demand → Price and Quantity ↑ • ↓ in Demand → Price and Quantity ↓	When supply increases, the supply curve shifts to right, leading to fall in equilibrium price and rise in equilibrium quantity. e.g. A bumper crop of rice lowers market prices. Conversely, a decrease in supply shifts the curve to left, leading to rise in equilibrium price and fall in equilibrium quantity. 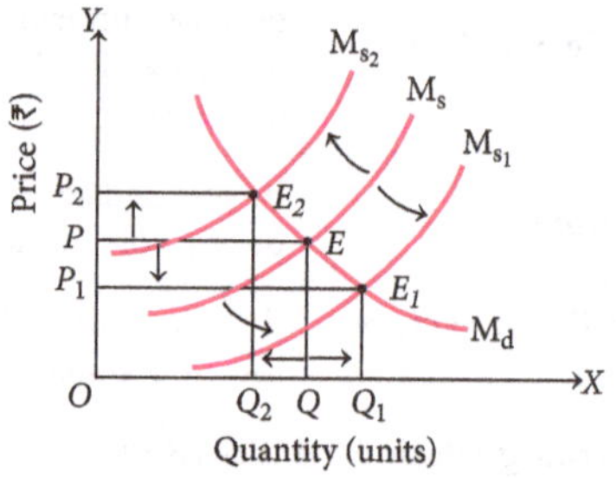 In short, • ↑ in Supply → Price ↓, Quantity ↑ • ↓ in Supply → Price ↑, Quantity ↓

Impact on Market Equilibrium of Free Entry and Exit of Firms

In the long-run, free entry and exit of firms takes place under perfect competition. Firms will earn only normal profit in the long-run. It is assumed that all firms in market are identical.

Given, diagram states that as there is short-run profit (equal to the shaded area of panel-B), new firm will enter the market hence market price fall as supply rises and profit will be wiped out in the long-run.

Similarly, loss in short-run will be wiped out by exit of some existing firms.

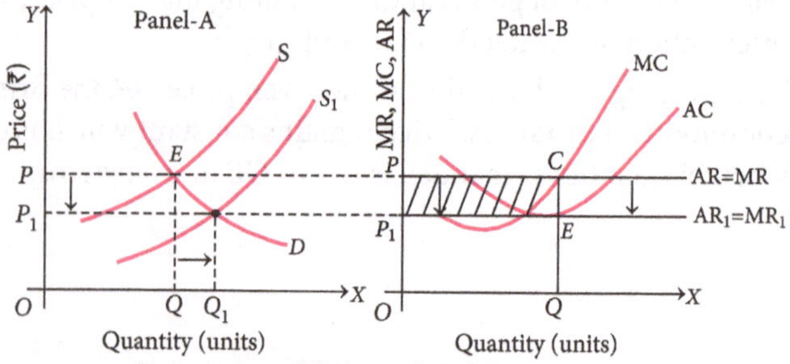

Long-run equilibrium of perfect competition

Let us understand this under different situations

- If the firm is earning supernormal profits in the short-run, it will attract new firms in the long-run till the super normal profits are wiped away (it occurs when P > AC).
- If the firms are incurring losses in the short-run, some of them will leave the industry in the long-run till normal profits are earned (it occurs when P < AC).
- If price is equal to the minimum AC of the firms, each firm will be earning normal profit (it occurs when P = AC).

Thus, with free entry and exit of firms, equilibrium is always there, where price is equal to minimum AC.

9.3 Market Equilibrium

Market equilibrium is the point where the quantity of a commodity demanded by consumers is exactly equal to the quantity supplied by producers at a specific price. At this equilibrium point, both the **equilibrium price** (the price at which quantity demanded and supplied are equal) and the **equilibrium quantity** (the quantity of the commodity demanded and supplied at equilibrium price) are determined.

Assumptions of Market Equilibrium

- The demand curve always has a negative slope, indicating that as prices decrease, the quantity demanded increases.
- The supply curve always has a positive slope, showing that as prices increase, the quantity supplied increases.

Determination of Market Equilibrium under Perfect Competition

Market equilibrium is influenced by two primary forces

1. **Market Demand** This is the total demand for a commodity by all buyers in the market.
2. **Market Supply** This refers to the total supply of the commodity by all firms in the market.

In a market, the equilibrium price and quantity are determined by the interaction of the demand and supply curves in the market. This has been explained with the help of an imaginary schedule and diagram

Price (₹)	**Demand** (units)	**Supply** (units)	
1	500	100	Excess demand
2	400	200	
3	300	300	[Equilibrium (D = S)]
4	200	400	Excess supply
5	100	500	

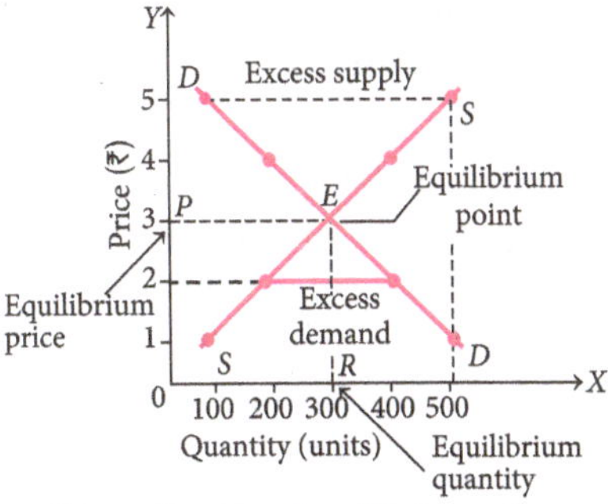

Determination of equilibrium price and quantity under perfect competition

Observation

In the above schedule and diagram, demand and supply are equal only at the price of ₹ 3, making it the equilibrium price. At this price, 300 units are demanded and supplied. So, equilibrium quantity is 300 units.

Also, it is clear from the diagram that equilibrium price is determined at the point, where demand and supply curves intersect each other. Also, except one equilibrium quantity, there will be either **excess demand** or **excess supply**.

Excess Demand

It means market demand exceeds market supply of a commodity at a given price. This situation arises at all prices below equilibrium price. The excess demand will lead to rise in market price due to the competition among buyers.

This situation will further lead to contraction in quantity demanded due to law of demand and expansion in quantity supplied due to law of supply till the equilibrium is attained.

Excess Supply

It means market supply of a commodity is more than the market demand for a commodity at a given price. This situation arises above equilibrium price. Here competition among sellers will lead to decrease the price. This situation will further lead to rise in market demand due to law of demand and fall in market supply due to law of supply till equilibrium is attained.

Change in Demand and its Effect on Equilibrium Price

1. **Increase in Demand**

Supply curve remaining unchanged, if there is increase in demand, demand curve and equilibrium point will shift to the right. As a result, equilibrium quantity and equilibrium price both will increase.

In the given diagram, actual demand curve *DD* and actual supply curve *SS* intersect at point *E* (i.e. equilibrium point). At this point, *OP* is equilibrium price and *OQ* is equilibrium quantity.

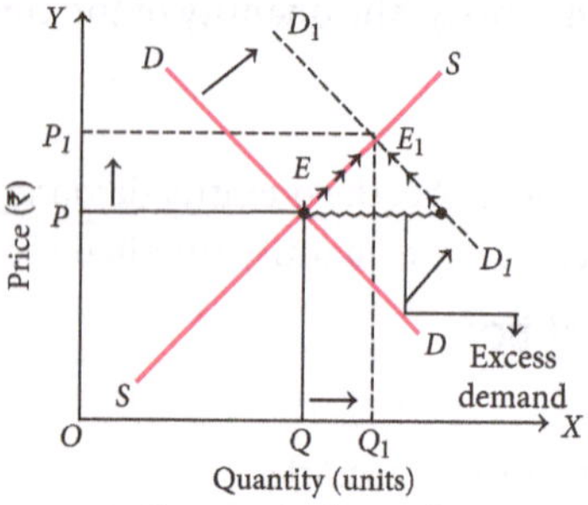

Increase in demand

Now, with the increase in demand, new demand curve becomes D_1D_1 implying a case of excess demand. So, equilibrium point shifts from *E* to E_1 and OP_1 is new equilibrium price and OQ_1 is the new equilibrium quantity.

2. **Decrease in Demand**

Supply curve remaining unchanged, if there is a decrease in demand, demand curve and equilibrium point will shift to the left.

As a result, equilibrium quantity and equilibrium price both will decrease.

In the given diagram, actual demand curve *DD* and actual supply curve *SS* intersect at point *E* (i.e. equilibrium point).

At this point, the equilibrium price is *OP* and equilibrium quantity is *OQ*.

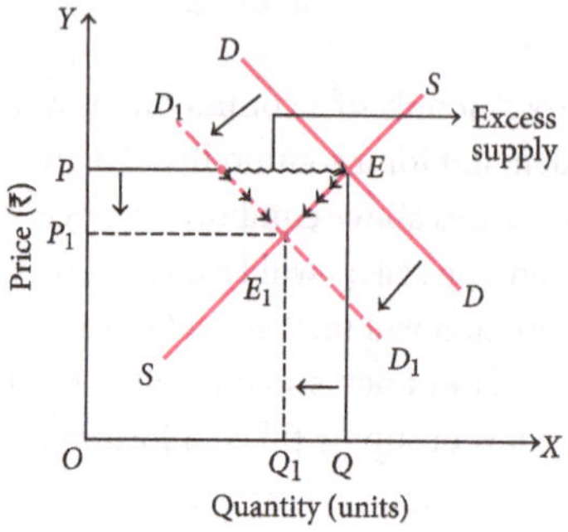

Decrease in demand

Now, due to decrease in demand, new demand curve is formed at D_1D_1, implying a case of excess supply. It shows that price declines from *OP* to OP_1 (new equilibrium price) because the demand has decreased from *OQ* to OQ_1 (new equilibrium quantity).

Change in Supply and its Effect on Equilibrium Price

1. **Increase in Supply**

If supply increases while the demand curve remains unchanged, the supply curve and equilibrium point will shift to the right. This will lead to decrease in equilibrium price and an increase in equilibrium quantity.

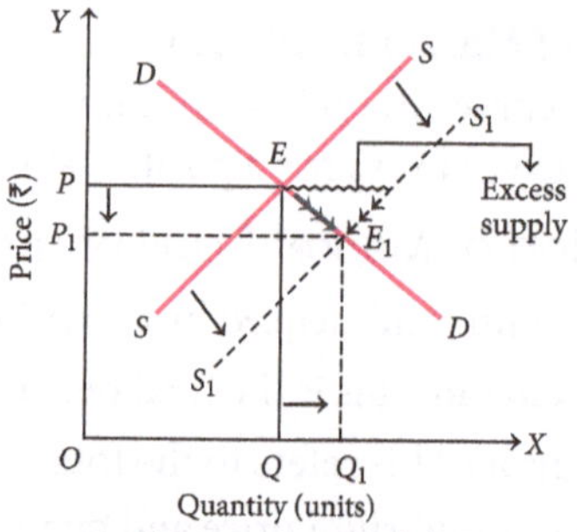

Increase in supply

In the given diagram, actual demand curve *DD* and actual supply curve *SS* intersect at point *E* (i.e. equilibrium point). At this point, the equilibrium price is *OP* and equilibrium quantity is *OQ*.

Now, due to increase in supply, new supply curve is formed at S_1S_1 implying a case of excess supply.

It shows that price declines from *OP* to OP_1 (new equilibrium price) and quantity increases from *OQ* to OQ_1 (new equilibrium quantity).

2. **Decrease in Supply**

When supply decreases while the demand curve remains unchanged, the supply curve and equilibrium point will shift to the left. This will lead to an increase in equilibrium price and decrease in equilibrium quantity.

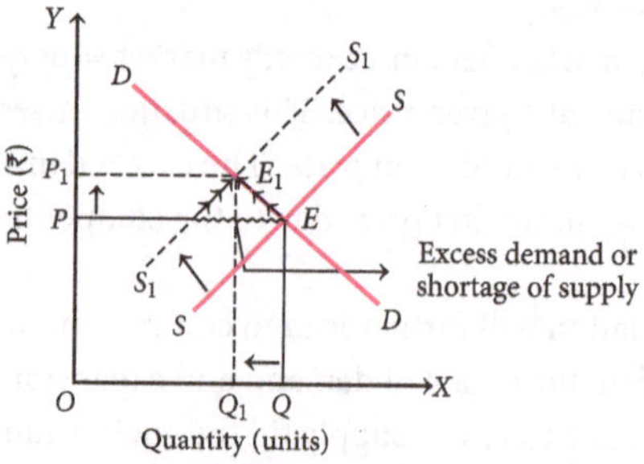

Decrease in supply

In the given diagram, actual demand curve DD and actual supply curve SS intersect at point E (i.e. equilibrium point).

At this point, OP is the equilibrium price and OQ is the equilibrium quantity.

Now, due to decrease in supply, new supply curve S_1S_1 is formed, implying a case of excess demand. It cuts demand curve at new equilibrium point E_1. At this point, new equilibrium price increases to OP_1 and the equilibrium quantity reduces to OQ_1.

Simultaneous Change in both Demand and Supply

There may be the cases when demand and supply change simultaneously. Different situations are discussed as under

1. **When both Demand and Supply Increase in the Same Proportion**

   In this case, price will remain the same, but equilibrium output will increase. In the given diagram, actual demand curve DD and actual supply curve SS intersect at point E, (i.e. equilibrium point). At this point, OP is the equilibrium price and OQ is equilibrium output.

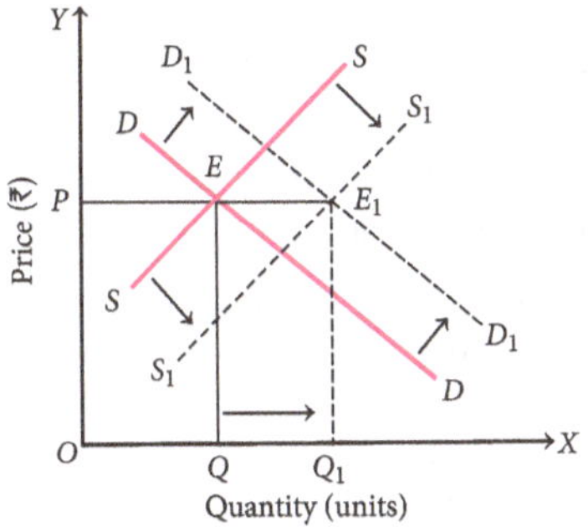

   Now, demand increases to D_1D_1 and supply increases to S_1S_1, such that both increases at equal level. The new curves intersect each other at point E_1.

   It shows that equilibrium price remains the same because increase in demand and supply are in the same proportion. However, equilibrium quantity increases from OQ to OQ_1.

2. **When Increase in Supply is Less than Increase in Demand**

   In this case, both equilibrium price and quantity will increase. In the given diagram, actual demand curve DD and actual supply curve SS intersect at point E, (i.e. equilibrium point).

   At this point, OP is the equilibrium price and OQ is equilibrium output.

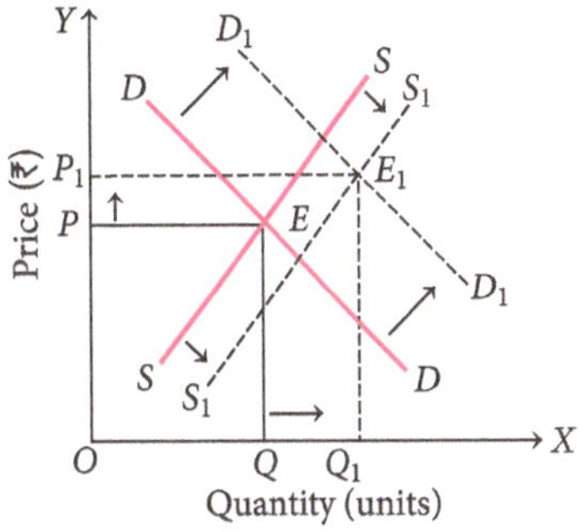

Increase in supply is less then increase in demand

   Now, demand increases to D_1D_1 and supply increases to S_1S_1, but the increase in demand is greater than the increase in supply. The new curves intersect each other at point E_1.

   It shows that equilibrium price has increased to OP_1 and equilibrium quantity has increased to OQ_1.

3. **When Increase in Supply is More than Increase in Demand**

   In this case, equilibrium price falls and equilibrium quantity goes up. In the given diagram, actual demand curve DD and actual supply curve SS intersect at point E (i.e. equilibrium point). At this point, OP is the equilibrium price and OQ is equilibrium quantity.

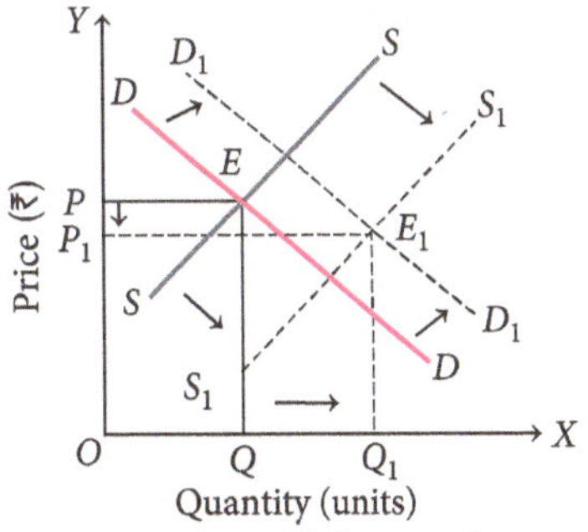

Increase in supply is more than increase in demand

   Now, demand increases to D_1D_1 and supply increases to S_1S_1, but the increase in supply is greater than the increase in demand. The new curves intersect each other at point E_1. It shows that equilibrium price has decreased to OP_1 and the equilibrium quantity has increased to OQ_1.

4. **When both Demand and Supply Decrease in the Same Proportion**

   In this case, equilibrium price will remain same, but equilibrium output will decrease.

In the given diagram, actual demand curve DD and actual supply curve SS intersect at point E (i.e. equilibrium point). At this point, OP is equilibrium price and OQ is equilibrium quantity.

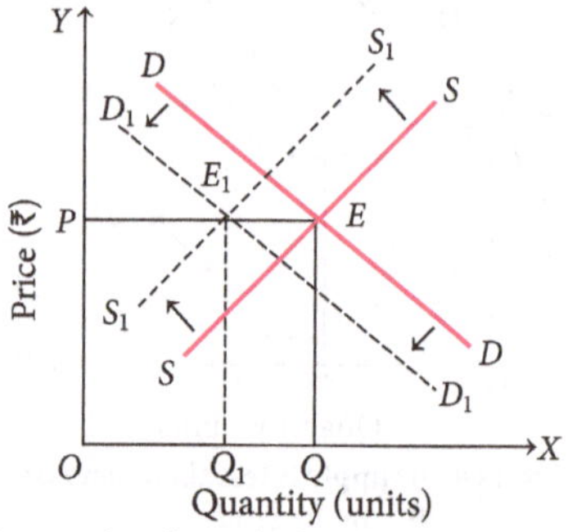

Demand and supply decrease in the same

Now, demand decreases to D_1D_1 and supply decreases to S_1S_1. The new curves intersect each other at point E_1. It shows that equilibrium price remains constant because both demand and supply have decreased in the same proportion. However, equilibrium quantity decreases to OQ_1.

5. **When Decrease in Demand is More than the Decrease in Supply**

In this case, both equilibrium price and output will fall. In the given diagram, actual demand curve DD and actual supply curve SS intersect at point E (i.e. equilibrium point). At this point, OP is equilibrium price and OQ is equilibrium quantity.

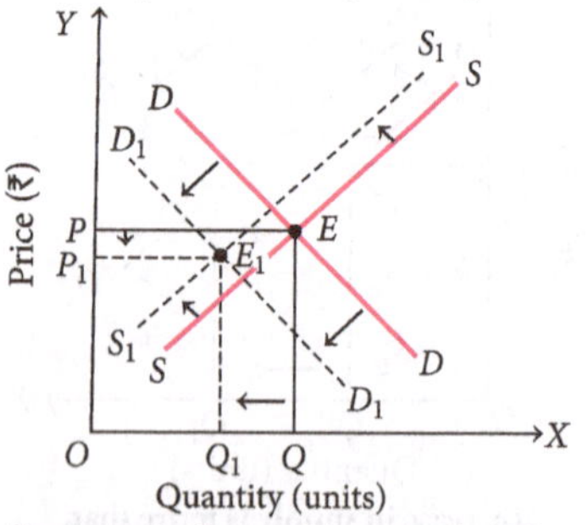

Decrease in demand is more than the decrease in supply

Now, demand decreases to D_1D_1 and supply decreases to S_1S_1, but decrease in demand is more than that of supply. The new curves intersect each other at point E_1, which is the new equilibrium point.

Thus, the equilibrium price reduces to OP_1 and equilibrium quantity will decrease to OQ_1.

6. **When Decrease in Demand is Less than the Decrease in Supply**

In this case, equilibrium price will rise and equilibrium quantity will fall.

In the given diagram, actual demand curve DD and actual supply curve SS intersect at point E (i.e. equilibrium point).

At this point, OP is equilibrium price and OQ is equilibrium quantity.

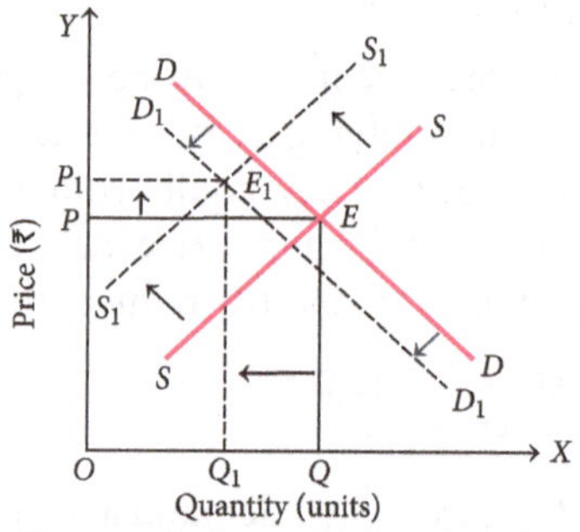

Decrease in demand is less than the decrease in supply

Now, demand decreases to D_1D_1 and supply decreases to S_1S_1, but decrease in demand is less than that of supply. The new curves intersect each other at point E_1, which is the new equilibrium point.

Thus, the equilibrium price increases from OP to OP_1 and equilibrium quantity will decrease from OQ to OQ_1.

7. **When Increase in Demand is Equal to Decrease in Supply**

In this case, equilibrium price will increase sharply, but equilibrium quantity will remain the same. In the given diagram, actual demand curve DD and actual supply curve SS intersect at point E (i.e. equilibrium point).

At this point, OP is equilibrium price and OQ is equilibrium quantity.

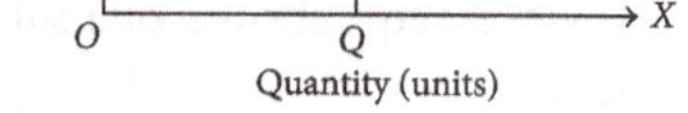

Now, demand increases to D_1D_1 and supply decreases to S_1S_1. New demand and supply curves intersect each other at point E_1.

The equilibrium price has risen from OP to OP_1 and equilibrium quantity remains the same at OQ units.

Thus, equilibrium price increases sharply when increase in demand is equal to decrease in supply.

8. **When Increase in Demand is More than Decrease in Supply**

In this case, both equilibrium price and quantity will increase. In the given diagram, actual demand *DD* and actual supply *SS* intersects at point *E* (i.e. equilibrium point). At this point, equilibrium price is *OP* and equilibrium quantity is *OQ*.

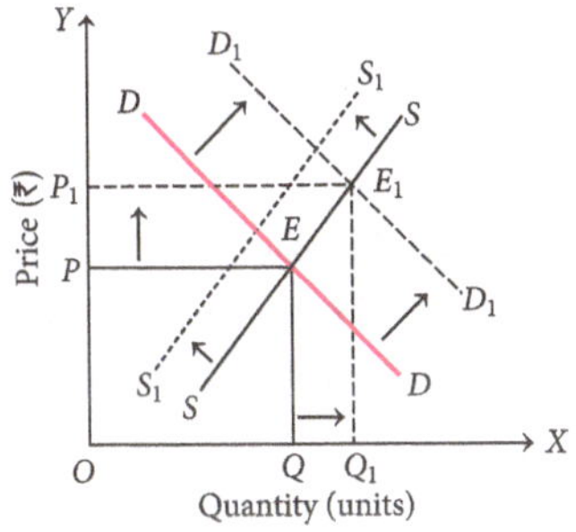

Now, when new demand increases to D_1D_1 and supply decreases to S_1S_1, new equilibrium shifts at point E_1.

Here, equilibrium price increases to OP_1 and equilibrium quantity increases to OQ_1.

9. **When Increase in Demand is Less than Decrease in Supply**

In this case, equilibrium price will increase, but equilibrium quantity will decrease. In the given diagram, actual demand *DD* and actual supply *SS* intersects at point *E* (i.e. equilibrium point). At this point, equilibrium price is *OP* and equilibrium quantity is *OQ*.

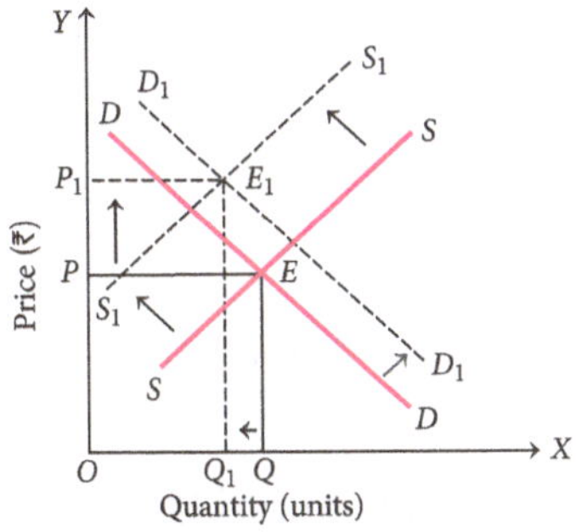

Now, when new demand increases to D_1D_1 and supply decreases to S_1S_1, new equilibrium shifts at point E_1. Here, equilibrium price increases to OP_1 and equilibrium quantity decreases to OQ_1.

10. **When Decrease in Demand is Equal to Increase in Supply**

In this case, equilibrium price will fall sharply, but equilibrium quantity will remain the same. In the given diagram, actual demand curve *DD* and actual supply curve *SS* intersect at point E (i.e. equilibrium point).

At this point, *OP* is equilibrium price and *OQ* is equilibrium quantity.

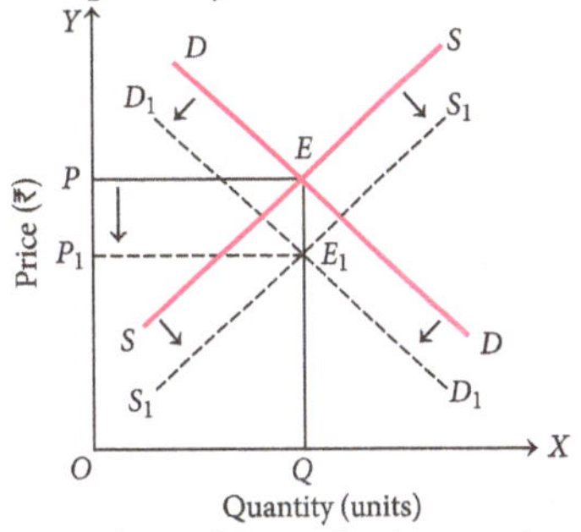

Decrease in demand is equal to increase in supply

Now, demand decreases to D_1D_1 and supply increases to S_1S_1. New demand and supply curves intersect each other at point E_1, which is the new equilibrium.

The equilibrium price falls from *OP* to OP_1 and equilibrium quantity remains the same at *OQ* units.

Thus, equilibrium price declines sharply when decrease in demand is equal to increase in supply.

11. **When Decrease in Demand is More than Increase in Supply**

In this case, both equilibrium price and quantity will decrease. In the given diagram, actual demand *DD* and actual supply *SS* intersects at point *E* (i.e. equilibrium point).

At this point, equilibrium price is *OP* and equilibrium quantity is *OQ*.

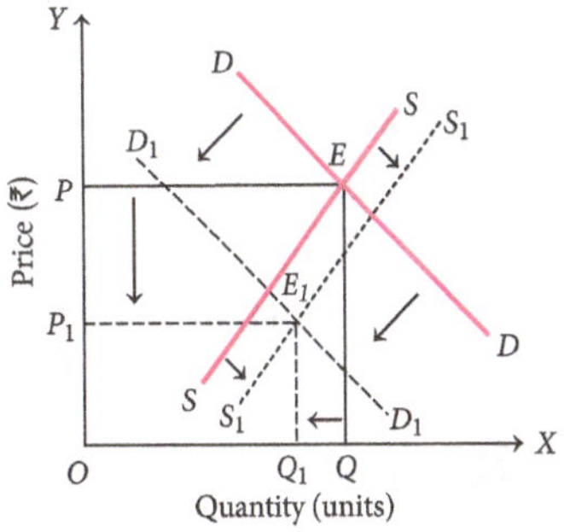

Now, when new demand decreases to D_1D_1 and supply increases to S_1S_1, new equilibrium shifts to E_1. Here, equilibrium price decreases to OP_1 and quantity decreases to OQ_1.

12. **When Decrease in Demand is Less than Increase in Supply**

In this case, equilibrium price decreases, but equilibrium quantity increases. In the given diagram, actual demand *DD* and actual supply *SS* interests at point *E* (i.e. equilibrium point).

At this point, equilibrium quantity is OQ and equilibrium price is OP.

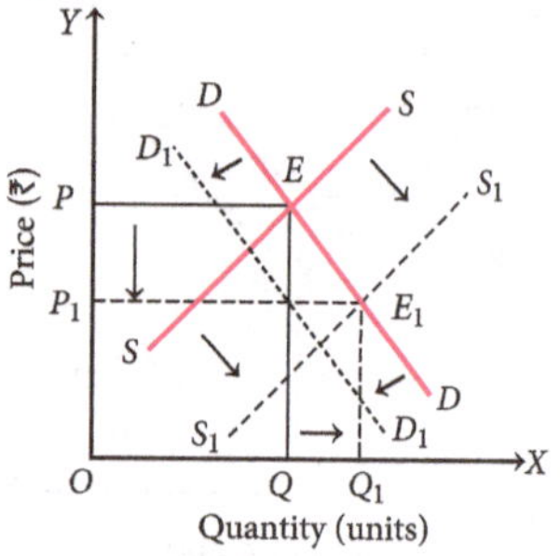

Now, when new demand decreases to D_1D_1 and supply increases to S_1S_1, new equilibrium shifts to E_1. Here, equilibrium price decreases to OP_1 and equilibrium quantity increases to OQ_1.

Special cases which Affect Equilibrium Price

These are as follows

1. **Change in Supply when Demand is Perfectly Elastic**

   In this case, price will remain constant, only quantity will increase with rise in supply and *vice-versa.*

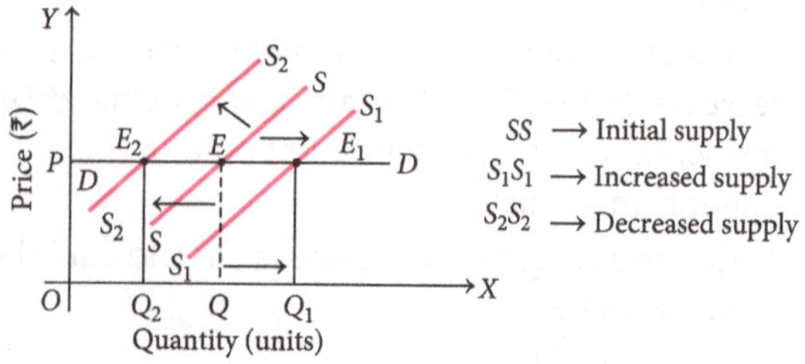

Change in supply when demand is perfectly elastic

2. **Change in Supply when Demand is Perfectly Inelastic**

   In this case, quantity will remain unchanged, only price will increase with fall in supply and *vice-versa.*

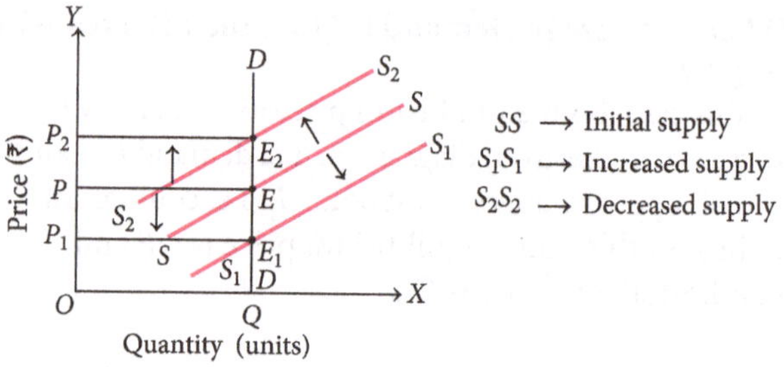

Change in supply when demand is perfectly inelastic

3. **Change in Demand when Supply is Perfectly Elastic**

   In this case, price will remain constant, quantity will increase with the increase in demand and *vice-versa.*

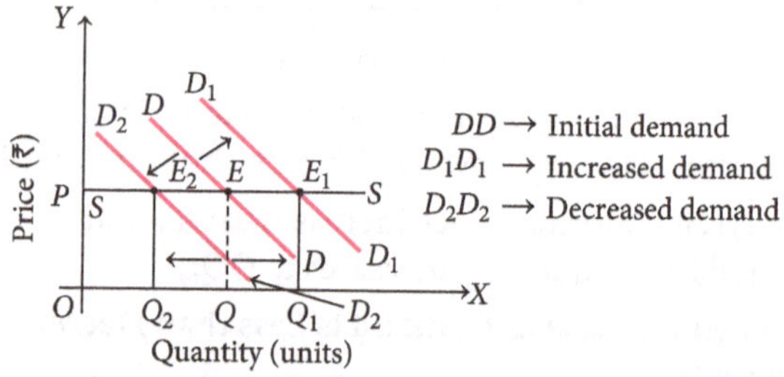

Change in demand when supply is perfectly elastic

4. **Change in Demand when Supply is Perfectly Inelastic**

   In this case, quantity will remain unchanged, only price will rise with rise in demand and *vice-versa.*

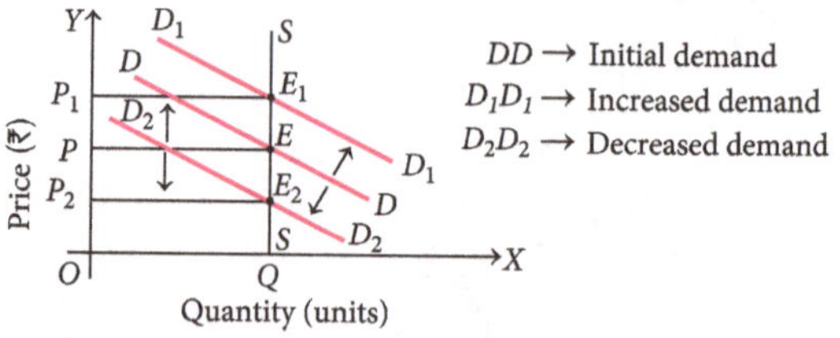

Change in demand when supply is perfectly inelastic

9.4 Simple Applications of Tools of Demand and Supply

Market equilibrium determines price and quantity through an automatic mechanism, but it may sometimes fail to give an efficient or fair price. In such cases, the government intervenes to correct the situation. This can be done through **direct actions** (like price ceiling and price floor) or **indirect actions** (like taxes or subsidies).

Let us discuss the direct actions now

1. Price Ceiling

A price ceiling means a maximum price that sellers can charge for a commodity, from the buyers, usually set below the equilibrium price. This helps make essential goods more affordable to poorer sections of society. e.g. Governments may set a price ceiling on essential commodities like wheat or rice to ensure the poor can access them.

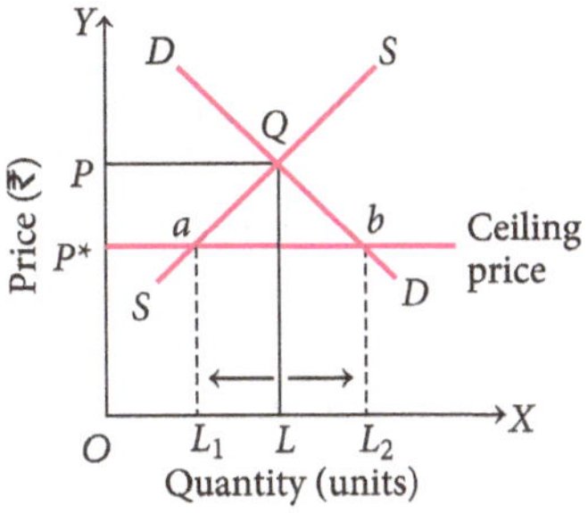

It is resorted to protect the interest of the consumer. It can be understood with the help of given diagram

Here,

Equilibrium price = OP; Equilibrium quantity = OL;

Ceiling price = OP^* Excess demand = ab = L_1L_2;

Excess demand may be fulfilled by

- Rationing
- First-cum-first serve basis

It leads to black marketing.

Black Marketing

It is a situation in which the controlled commodity is sold at a price higher than the price fixed by the government illegally under the desk. Black marketing can be termed as a direct consequence of price ceiling.

The reasons arising for this situation are

- Presence of such consumers who are willing to pay more than the ceiling price.
- Presence of excessive influential and wealthy consumers in large numbers.

Rationing

When demand exceeds supply, the government may introduce rationing to ensure fair distribution or control excess demand. Rationing limits the quantity each consumer can purchase, ensuring that even the weaker sections of the society get access to essential goods.

2. Price Floor

A price floor means the minimum price (above the equilibrium price) to protect producers, particularly in industries like agriculture. This is fixed by the government to ensure that producers earn a viable income, especially when market prices fall too low. e.g. In India, the government sets a Minimum Support Price (MSP) for crops like wheat and rice to protect farmers from market fluctuations.

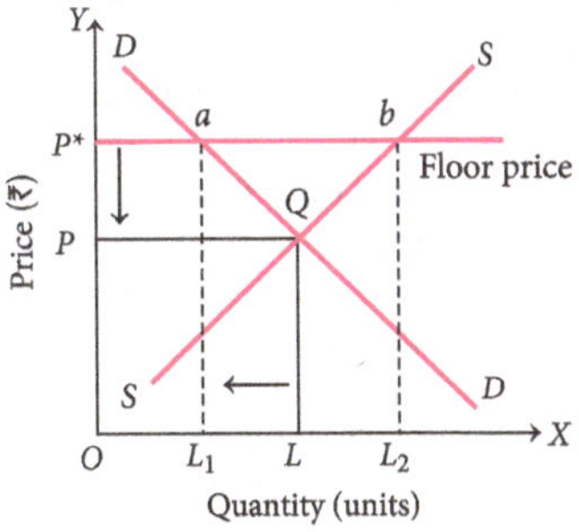

It can be understood with the help of the given diagram

Here,

Equilibrium price = OP; Equilibrium quantity = OL; Floor price = OP^*

Excess supply = $ab = L_1L_2$

Generally, government buys the excess supply at this price.

Viable Industry

An industry is said to be in viable condition, if corresponding to the minimum price, there is some demand in the market.

In such industries, demand and supply curves coincide in the positive quadrant.

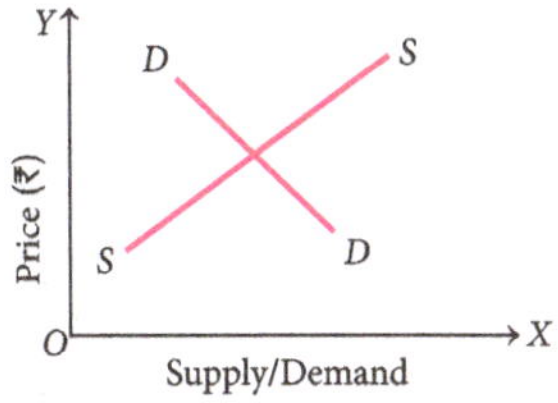

Non-viable Industry

A non-viable industry is one which will not produce the product in an economy.

It may be because cost of the product is too high and the consumers are not willing to pay a price that will cover the cost.

e.g. Commercial aircraft is a non-viable industry in India.

In this case, demand and supply curve will not intersect in the positive quadrant.

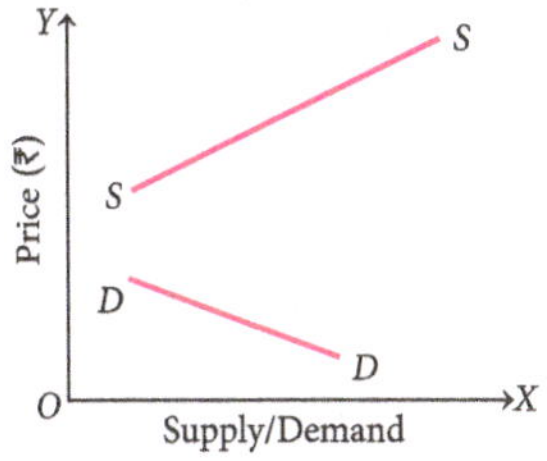

Mind Map

FORMS OF MARKET AND PRICE DETERMINATION

1 Concept of Market

Market is a mechanism or an arrangement that facilitates the sale and purchase of goods and services by bringing buyers and sellers in contact with each other.

Forms of Market

- Perfect competition
- Imperfect competition

2 Perfect Competition

It is a form of market where there are very large number of buyers and sellers of a commodity, exchanging homogeneous products at a price fixed by the market.

Features

- Homogeneous product
- Free entry and exit of firms
- Perfect knowledge
- No transportation cost
- Very large number of buyers or sellers
- Firms earn normal profit
- Perfect mobility of factors of production

3 Demand Curve under Perfect Competition

It is a horizontal straight line under perfect competition. It indicates that elasticity of demand $(E_d) = \infty$

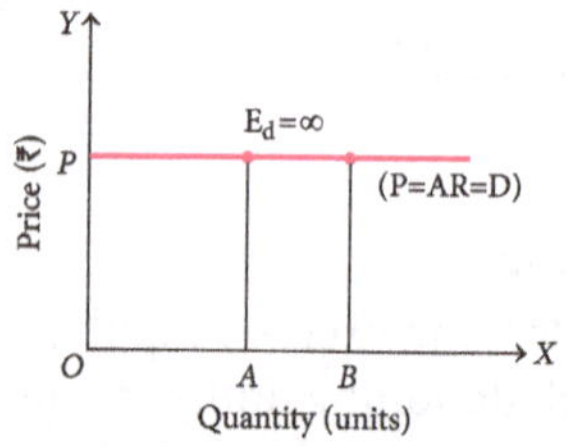

4 Effect of Demand and Supply Changes on Market Price

Change in Demand (Supply Constant)

- Increase in Demand – Higher price and quantity – Demand curve shifts right
- Decrease in Demand – Lower price and quantity – Demand curve shifts left

Change in Supply (Demand Constant)

- Increase in Supply – Lower price, higher quantity – Supply curve shifts right
- Decrease in Supply – Higher price, lower quantity – Supply curve shifts left

5 Market Equilibrium in Perfect Competition

- ***Market Equilibrium*** The point where market demand = market supply at a specific price.
- ***Equilibrium Price*** (P) Price at which quantity demanded = quantity supplied.
- ***Equilibrium Quantity*** (Q) Quantity exchanged at equilibrium price.

Assumptions of Market Equilibrium

- ***Demand Curve*** Negatively sloped – Lower price → Higher quantity demanded.
- ***Supply Curve*** Positively sloped – Higher price → Higher quantity supplied.

6 Simultaneous Change in Demand and Supply

Situation	Effect on Price	Effect on Quantity
Increase in Demand = Increase in Supply	No change	Quantity increases
Increase in Demand > Increase in Supply	Price increases	Quantity increases
Increase in Demand < Increase in Supply	Price decreases	Quantity increases
Decrease in Demand = Decrease in Supply	No change	Quantity decreases
Decrease in Demand > Decrease in Supply	Price decreases	Quantity decreases
Decrease in Demand < Decrease in Supply	Price increases	Quantity decreases
Increase in Demand = Decrease in Supply	Price increases sharply	Quantity remains the same
Increase in Demand > Decrease in Supply	Price increases	Quantity increases
Increase in Demand < Decrease in Supply	Price increases	Quantity decreases
Decrease in Demand = Increase in Supply	Price decreases sharply	Quantity remains the same
Decrease in Demand > Increase in Supply	Price decreases	Quantity decreases
Decrease in Demand < Increase in Supply	Price decreases	Quantity increases

7 Special Cases Affecting Equilibrium Price

- Change in Supply when Demand is Perfectly Elastic → Price Constant → Quantity Increases
- Change in Supply when Demand is Perfectly Inelastic → Price Increases → Quantity Constant
- Change in Demand when Supply is Perfectly Elastic → Price Constant → Quantity Increases
- Change in Demand when Supply is Perfectly Inelastic → Price Increases → Quantity Constant

8 Simple Applications of Tools of Demand and Supply

Price Ceiling (Maximum Price Limit)

Government sets a maximum price below equilibrium to make essential goods affordable.

Consequences

- Excess demand (Shortages)
- Black marketing (Illegal selling above price)
- Rationing (Limited quantity per consumer)

Solutions to Excess Demand

- Rationing → Limits quantity per consumer
- First-come-first-serve basis → Goods distributed fairly

Price Floor (Minimum Price Limit)

Government sets a minimum price above equilibrium to support producers.

Consequences

- Excess supply (surplus)
- Storage and disposal issues
- Government purchases excess stock

Industry Types

- Viable Industry → Demand exists at the minimum price.
- Non-viable Industry → No demand at the minimum price (e.g. Commercial Aircraft in India)

EXAM PATTERN QUESTIONS

Objective Type Questions

Multiple Choice Questions (MCQs)

1. What does the term 'market' refer to?

(a) A physical location where buyers and sellers meet
(b) A place where only goods are exchanged
(c) A system or arrangement through which buyers and sellers exchange commodities
(d) A government regulated space for transactions

2. **In perfect competition, as the firm is a price taker, the ...... curve is a horizontal straight line.**

(a) marginal cost (b) total cost
(c) total revenue (d) marginal revenue

3. **In perfect competition, firms earn which type of profit in the long-run?** **Competency Based Que**

I. Abnormal profit II. Super normal profit
III. Normal profit IV. Zero profit

Codes

(a) I and III (b) II and IV (c) Only III (d) Only I

4. **Which of the following features of perfect competition is highlighted in the below image?**

(a) Very large number of buyers and sellers
(b) Free entry and exit of firms
(c) Firms earn normal profit
(d) Perfect mobility of factors of production

5. **At a given price in a perfectly competitive market, the firm can sell**

(a) only a limited quantity of goods
(b) any quantity of goods at the prevailing market price
(c) goods at different prices based on demand
(d) None of the above

6. **Which of the following is not an essential condition of pure competition?**

(a) Large number of buyers and sellers
(b) Homogeneous product
(c) Freedom of entry and exit
(d) Absence of transport cost

7. How is AR and MR curves represented in the case of perfect competition? **NCERT (QR)**

(a) Right angled (b) Vertical straight line
(c) Both AR and MR curves slope downward
(d) Horizontal straight line

8. **Arrange the following in the correct sequence after a decrease in supply.** **Competency Basd Que**

(i) Equilibrium price rises
(ii) Supply curve shifts left
(iii) Equilibrium quantity falls

Codes

(a) (ii), (i), (iii) (b) (i), (ii), (iii)
(c) (ii), (iii) (i) (d) (i), (iii), (ii)

9. **"Food prices won't see festival season spike': Food secretary Sanjeev Chopra."**

Source *https//economictimes.indiatimes.com/news/economy/indicators/food-prices-wont-see-festival-season-spike-food-secretary-sanjeev-chopra/articleshow/113467185.cms?from=mdr*

Which of the following best explains why food prices may not spike during the festival season, according to the principles of market equilibrium in perfect competition? **Competency Based Que**

(a) Increase in supply to meet the demand
(b) Decrease in the number of sellers
(c) Firms earning supernormal profits indefinitely
(d) Price determination by individual firms

10. **If price is forced to stay below equilibrium price ....**

(a) excess supply exists (b) excess demand exists
(c) Either (a) or (b) (d) Neither (a) nor (b)

11. **Which of the following is a characteristic of pure competition?**

(a) Presence of differentiated products
(b) Few sellers controlling the market
(c) Free entry and exit of firms
(d) Limited number of buyers and sellers

12. **Identify the features of perfect competition from the following.** **Competency Based Que**

I. Perfect knowledge in the market
II. Absence of transportation costs
III. Imperfect mobility of factors of production
IV. Heterogeneous products present in the market

Codes

(a) I and II (b) II and IV
(c) I and III (d) I, II and IV

13. A new bakery chain enters a perfectly competitive market where several bakeries already exist. Due to its quality products, the bakery earns significant profits in the short-run. Over time, however, more bakeries enter the market and the price of baked goods starts falling. Eventually, the bakery notices that its profits are no longer increasing.

What will happen to the profits of the new bakery in the long-run? **Competency Based Que**

(a) It will continue earning supernormal profits
(b) It will incur continuous losses
(c) Its profits will fall to normal profits
(d) It will become a price setter in the market

14. "An increase in demand raises both the equilibrium price and quantity in perfect competition."

What happens to the market? **Competency Based Que**

(a) The demand curve shifts leftward, leading to a new lower equilibrium
(b) The demand curve shifts rightward, leading to a new higher equilibrium
(c) The supply curve shifts rightward, leading to lower prices
(d) The demand curve remains unchanged and prices stay constant

15. Based upon the image given below, identify the time period under perfectly competitive market.

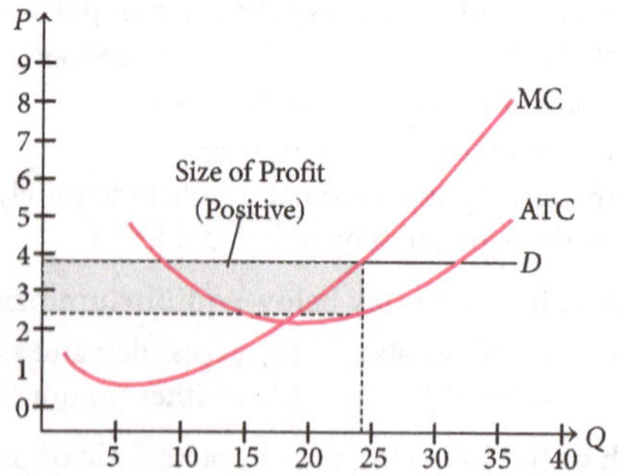

(a) Very short-run
(b) Short-run
(c) Medium-run (d) Long-run

16. If firms in a perfectly competitive market are making supernormal profits, what will happen in the long-run? **Competency Based Que**

(a) Existing firms will increase prices
(b) New firms will enter, driving prices down
(c) Firms will exit, leading to higher profits
(d) Firms will differentiate their products to maintain profits

17. Which of the following are the assumptions of market equilibrium? **Competency Based Que**

I. The demand curve always has a negative slope.
II. The demand curve always has a positive slope.
III. The supply curve always has a negative slope.
IV. The supply curve always has a positive slope.

Codes

(a) I and III (b) III and IV
(c) II and III (d) I and IV

18. Let us assume, the price of a textbook is ₹ 300. At this price, the publisher is expected to sell 1,000 copies of the textbook. If the price of the textbook is reduced to ₹ 250, then what quantity of textbooks should the publisher sell? **NCERT (QR); Competency Based Que**

(a) Less than 1,000 copies
(b) More than 1,000 copies
(c) There will be no change in the sale of text books
(d) Its sale will depend on the advertisement policy

19. Identify the nature of supply curve from the figure given below in the market.

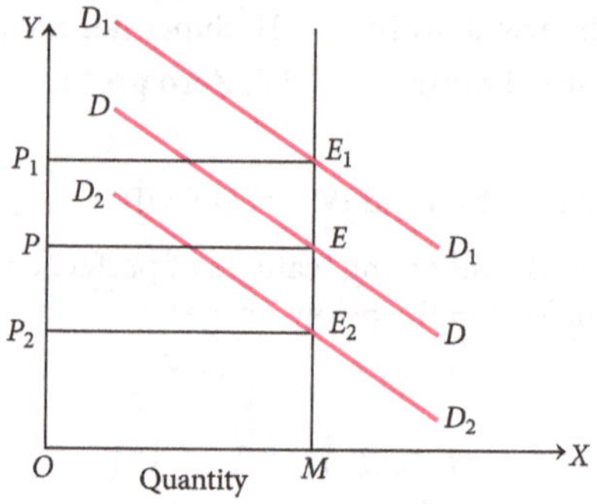

(a) Perfectly elastic supply curve
(b) Perfectly inelastic supply curve
(c) Elastic supply curve (d) Inelastic supply curve

20. Which of the following is true regarding an increase in demand?

(a) It causes the equilibrium price to decrease
(b) The supply curve shifts to the left
(c) It leads to excess supply
(d) It increases both equilibrium price and quantity

21. "Sri Lanka introduces fuel rationing for private vehicles amid severe shortage."

Source *https://www.business-standard.com/article/international/sri-lanka-introduces-fuel-rationing-for-pvt-vehicles-amid-severe-shortage-122062600788_1.html*

What economic situation does this headline represent? **Competency Based Que**

(a) Excess supply of fuel (b) Excess demand for fuel
(c) Price floor on fuel (d) Market equilibrium for fuel

22. **Under what condition, equilibrium price will increase and equilibrium quantity will decrease?**
(a) Increase in supply
(b) Decrease in supply
(c) Increase in demand
(d) Decrease in demand

23. **In the case where both demand and supply increase in the same proportion, what happens to the equilibrium quantity?**
(a) It decreases
(b) It remains unchanged
(c) It increases
(d) It fluctuates

24. **Which market phenomenon is highlighted in the below image?**

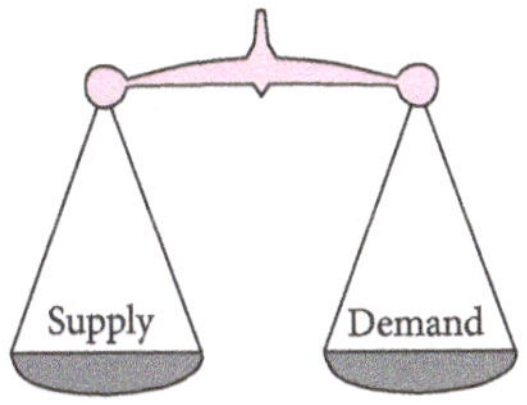

(a) Excess supply
(b) Excess demand
(c) Low demand
(d) Market equilibrium

25. **"Fuel for thought: oil market ponders price floor amid demand destruction."**
What is the likely impact of this news headline on the quantity supplied in the market? **Competency Based Que**
(a) Shortage of supply
(b) Surplus of supply
(c) No change in supply
(d) Either (a) or (b)

26. **Which of the following statements about the price floor is false?** **Competency Based Que**
I. **A price floor is set below the equilibrium price.**
II. **It helps protect producers.**
III. **It can lead to excess supply.**
IV. **The government often uses it in agriculture.**

Codes
(a) Only I
(b) I and IV
(c) Only III
(d) II and III

27. **Sequence of effects of a price floor being set above the equilibrium price will be** **Competency Based Que**
(i) **The supply exceeds demand**
(ii) **A surplus is created in the market**
(iii) **The price cannot fall below the price floor**

Codes
(a) (ii), (i) , (iii)
(b) (iii), (ii), (i)
(c) (iii), (i), (ii)
(d) (ii), (iii), (i)

28. **Identify the type of government action shown in the image below.**

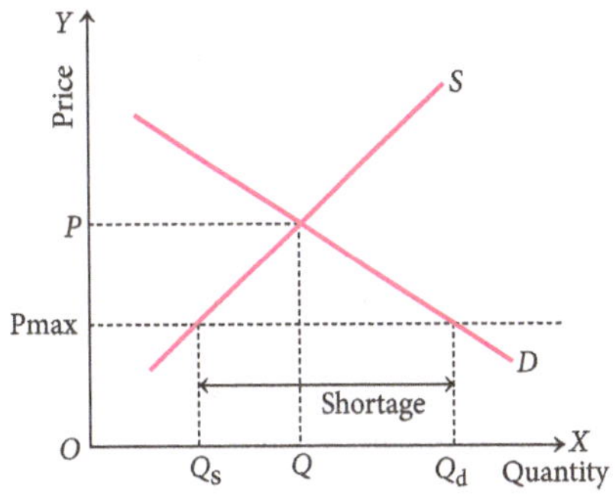

(a) Price ceiling
(b) Price flooring
(c) Price rigidity
(d) None of these

29. **If in an industry, demand and supply will not intersect in positive quadrant, then it is called**
(a) illegal industry
(b) viable industry
(c) non-viable industry
(d) sick industry

30. **If there is shortage of certain goods, the government introduces ...... for distribution of commodity to consumers.**
(a) planning
(b) marketing
(c) rationing
(d) financing

Direction *Read the case study and answer the questions 31 to 34 on the basis of the same*

In a small agricultural town, there are numerous wheat farmers who sell their crops in a perfectly competitive market. Each farmer produces a similar quality of wheat and the price of wheat is determined by the overall market demand and supply. The farmers are price takers; they cannot set their own prices and must accept the market price established by the equilibrium point of demand and supply.

During the harvesting season, the demand for wheat typically increases due to the demand for flour in local bakeries and increased consumption during festivals. As demand rises, the market price for wheat also increases. This encourages more farmers to enter the market, hoping to benefit from the higher prices. However, if an unexpected drought occurs, the wheat supply decreases significantly.

The remaining farmers struggle to meet the demand, leading to increased competition among buyers. The price of wheat rises further as consumers are willing to pay more for the limited supply. This situation creates an environment where only the most efficient farmers can thrive, while others may incur losses and exit the market.

31. **What characterises perfect competition in the wheat market in India?**

(a) A single seller controls the market price
(b) Homogeneous products that are perfect substitutes
(c) High barriers to entry for new firms
(d) Buyers have limited knowledge about prices

32. **How does the Minimum Support Price (MSP) affect the wheat market?**

(a) It ensures a fair price for farmers and stabilises the market
(b) It prevents farmers from exiting the market
(c) It increases competition among buyers
(d) It eliminates excess supply

33. **In a perfectly competitive market, the demand curve for individual firms is …………, indicating that firms are price takers and cannot influence market prices.**

34. **When there is an increase in demand for wheat due to a festival, the equilibrium price and quantity will ……………, reflecting the changes in market dynamics.**

Assertion-Reason

Direction (Q.No. 35 to 44) *Read the following Assertion (A) and Reason (R) and choose the correct alternative from the following*

Alternatives

(a) Both Assertion (A) and Reason (R) are true and Reason (R) is the correct explanation of Assertion (A)
(b) Both Assertion (A) and Reason (R) are true, but Reason (R) is not the correct explanation of Assertion (A)
(c) Assertion (A) is true, but Reason (R) is false
(d) Assertion (A) is false, but Reason (R) is true

35. **Assertion** (A) A firm under perfect competition can earn only normal profits in the short-run.

Reason (R) Individual firm under perfect competition is very small so there is no restriction of entry or exit of firms.

36. **Assertion** (A) Markets can take different forms depending on the number of buyers and sellers, product nature and competition level.

Reason (R) In a perfect competition market, numerous buyers and sellers trade homogeneous products at prices determined by the market forces of demand and supply.

37. **Assertion** (A) In a perfectly competitive market, a firm's demand curve is perfectly elastic.

Reason (R) Firms can sell any quantity of goods at the prevailing market price, which is determined by the intersection of market demand and supply.

38. **Assertion** (A) An increase in supply leads to a decrease in the equilibrium price.

Reason (R) When supply increases, the supply curve shifts to the right, resulting in a larger quantity being available at a lower price.

39. **Assertion** (A) Firms cannot earn super normal profits indefinitely.

Reason (R) New firms enter the market if there is profit potential.

40. **Assertion** (A) Price ceiling is a direct action by the government to protect the interest of the buyer.

Reason (R) Price ceiling leads to shortage in the market and increase competition among the buyers.

41. **Assertion** (A) A decrease in demand causes a rightward shift in the demand curve.

Reason (R) A decrease in demand results in a reduction in the quantity demanded at each price level, shifting the demand curve to the left.

42. **Assertion** (A) The demand curve faced by a perfectly competitive firm is downward sloping.

Reason (R) A firm in perfect competition cannot set its own price based on market demand.

43. **Assertion** (A) An increase in demand leads to an increase in both equilibrium price and equilibrium quantity.

Reason (R) When demand increases, the demand curve shifts to the right, leading to a higher equilibrium price and quantity.

44. **Assertion** (A) When demand exceeds supply, the government may introduce rationing to ensure fair distribution.

Reason (R) Rationing limits the quantity each consumer can purchase, ensuring that even the poorest consumers get access to essential goods.

Two Statements Based MCQs

Direction (Q.No. 45 to 54) *Read the following statements carefully and choose the correct alternative*

Alternatives

(a) Statement I is correct and Statement II is incorrect
(b) Statement II is correct and Statement I is incorrect
(c) Both the statements are correct
(d) Both the statements are incorrect

45. **Statement I** A pure competition market has characteristics like a large number of buyers and sellers, homogeneous products and free entry or exit of firms.

Statement II No individual buyer or seller can influence market price due to the large number of participants.

46. **Statement I** In a perfectly competitive market, a firm's demand curve is inelastic.

Statement II When supply increases, the supply curve shifts left, leading to a lower price and higher quantity.

47. **Statement I** Buyers and sellers do not have full knowledge of market prices and production costs in a perfectly competitive market.

Statement II It is assumed that no additional transportation costs are incurred, ensuring uniform pricing in perfectly competitive market.

48. **Statement I** Market equilibrium is the point where the quantity of a commodity demanded by consumers equals the quantity supplied by producers at a specific price.

Statement II Market equilibrium is influenced by two primary forces.

49. **Statement I** Market demand is the total demand for a commodity from all buyers in the market.

Statement II Market supply refers to the supply of the commodity from individual firms in the market.

50. **Statement I** Equilibrium price determined through the market mechanism always gives efficient output.

Statement II Price ceiling is imposed to protect the interest of the buyers in the market.

51. **Statement I** Excess demand occurs when the market demand for a commodity is less than its market supply at a given price.

Statement II In a market, the equilibrium price and quantity are determined by the interaction of the demand and supply curves in the market.

52. **Statement I** A price ceiling sets a minimum price that sellers can charge for a commodity, usually above the equilibrium price.

Statement II A price floor sets a maximum price below the equilibrium price to protect producers, particularly in industries like agriculture.

53. **Statement I** An industry is considered viable if there is enough demand for the product at the minimum price set by the government.

Statement II A non-viable industry is one where production costs are too high and consumers are unwilling to pay prices that cover those costs.

54. **Statement I** Price floor leads to shortage of demand in the market.

Statement II With increase in the number of suppliers in the market, equilibrium price increases.

Matching

55. Match the following

Column I	Column II
A. Market	(i) A firm that accepts the market price without influencing it.
B. Homogeneous product	(ii) Goods that are identical and cannot be differentiated by consumers.
C. Price taker	(iii) A place where buyers and sellers interact to exchange goods or services.
D. Price maker	(iv) A firm that has control over the price of its product due to lack of competition.

Codes

	A	B	C	D		A	B	C	D
(a)	(iii)	(iv)	(i)	(ii)	(b)	(iv)	(i)	(ii)	(iii)
(c)	(ii)	(iii)	(iv)	(i)	(d)	(iii)	(ii)	(i)	(iv)

56. Match the following

Column I	Column II
A. Market equilibrium	(i) Negative slope
B. Demand curve under equilibrium	(ii) Positive slope
C. Supply curve under equilibrium	(iii) Total demand for a commodity
D. Market demand	(iv) The commodity demanded by consumers equals the quantity supplied by producers

Codes

	A	B	C	D		A	B	C	D
(a)	(iii)	(iv)	(i)	(ii)	(b)	(iv)	(i)	(ii)	(iii)
(c)	(ii)	(iii)	(iv)	(i)	(d)	(iii)	(ii)	(i)	(iv)

57. Match the following

Column I	Column II
A. Demand curve shift right	(i) Increase in supply
B. Demand curve shift left	(ii) Decrease in supply
C. Supply curve shift right	(iii) Increase in demand
D. Supply curve shift left	(iv) Decrease in demand

Codes

	A	B	C	D		A	B	C	D
(a)	(iii)	(iv)	(i)	(ii)	(b)	(iv)	(i)	(ii)	(iii)
(c)	(ii)	(iii)	(iv)	(i)	(d)	(iii)	(ii)	(i)	(iv)

58. Match the following

Column I	Column II
A. When both demand and supply increase in the same proportion	(i) Price decreases, but equilibrium quantity increases.
B. When increase in supply is less than increase in demand	(ii) Price remains the same, but equilibrium output increases.
C. When decrease in demand is less than the decrease in supply	(iii) Both equilibrium price and quantity increase.
D. When decrease in demand is less than increase in supply	(iv) Equilibrium price rises, and equilibrium quantity decreases.

Codes

	A	B	C	D
(a)	(iii)	(iv)	(i)	(ii)
(b)	(iv)	(i)	(ii)	(iii)
(c)	(ii)	(iii)	(iv)	(i)
(d)	(iii)	(ii)	(i)	(iv)

59. Match the following

Column I	Column II
A. Price ceiling	(i) An industry that is unable to sustain profits and may not survive long-term.
B. Price floor	(ii) A maximum legal price set below the equilibrium price.
C. Viable industry	(iii) A minimum legal price set above the equilibrium price.
D. Non-viable industry	(iv) An industry that is profitable and sustainable in the long-run.

Codes

	A	B	C	D
(a)	(iii)	(iv)	(i)	(ii)
(b)	(iv)	(i)	(ii)	(iii)
(c)	(ii)	(iii)	(iv)	(i)
(d)	(iii)	(ii)	(i)	(iv)

Concept Identification

60. It describes a market structure where no single buyer or seller can influence the market price due to a very large number of participants.

61. It is represented by a horizontal line that reflects a firm's ability to sell any quantity at the prevailing market price in perfect competition.

62. It explains the point where the quantity demanded by consumers equals the quantity supplied by producers at a specific price.

63. It refers to the government imposed maximum price that sellers can charge for essential commodities to make them affordable.

Answers

1. (c) A system or arrangement through which buyers and sellers exchange commodities
2. (d) marginal revenue
3. (c) Only III
4. (b) Free entry and exit of firms
5. (b) any quantity of goods at the prevailing market price
6. (d) Absence of transport cost
7. (d) Horizontal straight line
8. (a) (ii), (i), (iii)
9. (a) Increase in supply to meet the demand
10. (b) excess demand exists
11. (c) Free entry and exit of firms
12. (a) I and II
13. (c) Its profits will fall to normal profits
14. (b) The demand curve shifts rightward, leading to a new higher equilibrium
15. (b) Short-run
16. (b) New firms will enter, driving prices down
17. (d) I and IV
18. (b) More than 1,000 copies as decrease in price leads to increase in market demand.
19. (b) Perfectly inelastic supply curve
20. (d) It increases both equilibrium price and quantity
21. (b) Excess demand for fuel
22. (b) Decrease in supply
23. (c) It increases
24. (d) Market equilibrium
25. (b) Surplus of supply
26. (a) Only I
27. (c) (iii), (i), (ii)
28. (a) Price ceiling
29. (c) non-viable industry
30. (c) rationing
31. (b) Homogeneous products that are perfect substitutes
32. (a) It ensures a fair price for farmers and stabilises the market
33. perfectly elastic
34. increase
35. (d) In the short-run, a firm under perfect competition can earn abnormal profits (supernormal profits), normal profits or even incur losses, depending on the market conditions.

While in the long-run, firms tend to earn only normal profits due to the entry and exit of firms, which drives economic profits to zero.

36. (b) Both Assertion (A) and Reason (R) are true, but Reason (R) is not the correct explanation of Assertion (A)
37. (a) Both Assertion (A) and Reason (R) are true and Reason (R) is the correct explanation of Assertion (A)
38. (a) Both Assertion (A) and Reason (R) are true and Reason (R) is the correct explanation of Assertion (A)
39. (a) Both Assertion (A) and Reason (R) are true and Reason (R) is the correct explanation of Assertion (A)
40. (b) Both Assertion (A) and Reason (R) are true, but Reason (R) is not the correct explanation of Assertion (A)
41. (d) A decrease in demand causes a leftward shift of the demand curve.
42. (d) The demand curve for an individual firm in perfect competition is perfectly elastic (horizontal) at the market price because firms cannot set their own price.
43. (a) Both Assertion (A) and Reason (R) are true and Reason (R) is the correct explanation of Assertion (A)
44. (a) Both Assertion (A) and Reason (R) are true and Reason (R) is the correct explanation of Assertion (A)
45. (c) Both the statements are correct
46. (d) In a perfectly competitive market, a firm's demand curve is perfectly elastic. When supply increases, the supply curve shifts right, leading to a lower price and higher quantity.
47. (b) Buyers and sellers have full knowledge of market prices and production costs in a perfectly competitive market.
48. (c) Both the statements are correct
49. (a) Market supply refers to the supply of the commodity from all firms in the market.
50. (b) Usually market mechanism gives efficient output. However, at times it fails and thus, government intervention becomes inevitable.
51. (b) Excess demand occurs when the market demand for a commodity is greater than its market supply at a given price.
52. (d) A price ceiling sets a maximum price that sellers can charge for a commodity, usually below the equilibrium price. A price floor sets a minimum price above the equilibrium price to protect producers, particularly in industries like agriculture.
53. (c) Both the statements are correct
54. (d) Price floor leads to surplus of supply in the market.
55. (d) (iii) (ii) (i) (iv)
56. (b) (iv) (i) (ii) (iii)
57. (a) (iii) (iv) (i) (ii)
58. (c) (ii) (iii) (iv) (i)
59. (c) (ii) (iii) (iv) (i)
60. Perfect competition
61. Perfectly elastic demand curve
62. Market equilibrium
63. Price ceiling

Subjective Questions

Short Answer Type Questions

1. Why cannot a firm earn abnormal profits under perfect competition in the long-run? Explain.

Ans. There is freedom of entry and exit of firms under perfect competition. In situations of abnormal profits, new firms will be induced to join the industry.

This increases market supply and lowers market price to finally wipe out abnormal profits. So, a firm cannot earn abnormal profits under perfect competition in the long-run.

2. "Perfectly competitive firms are considered as more efficient than monopolies." Do you agree?

Competency Based Que

Ans. Perfectly competitive firms are more efficient than monopolies because in a perfectly competitive market, firms have to accept the price prevailing in the market. So, they adjust their cost and revenue policy according to the prevailing price, thereby making them cost effective.

One the other hand, a monopolist is a price-maker. He can formulate his own cost and revenue policy. So, there is no compulsion to control cost. So, firms under perfect competition are more efficient than a monopoly firm.

3. "Markets can take different forms depending on the number of buyers and sellers, product nature and competition level."

How do the characteristics of a market change based on buyers, sellers and competition?

Competency Based Que

Ans. Market characteristics vary depending on the number of buyers and sellers, the nature of the products offered and the level of competition.

In a perfectly competitive market, many buyers and sellers exist, leading to homogeneous products and price taking behaviour, whereas monopolies or oligopolies involve fewer participants with more significant pricing power.

4. "Is a firm under perfect competiton, a price taker or a price maker?" Justify your answer. Competency Based Que

Ans. A firm under perfect competition is a price taker because of the following reasons

(i) A firm under perfect competition is contributing such a small fragment to the market supply that total supply schedule remains unaffected by any change in individual firm's supply.

(ii) All firms are selling homogeneous product. Accordingly, even partial control over price is not possible.

(iii) If any firm tries to fix its own price, it won't succeed. Higher price would drive the buyers to a large number of other sellers. Lower price would bring so many buyers to a firm that it cannot cope with the demand.

5. State three features of perfect competition.

Ans. Three features of perfect competition are as follows

(i) **Large Number of Buyers and Sellers**
Under perfect competition, market is dominated by a large number of buyers and sellers.

(ii) **Homogeneous Product**
Under this form, all sellers sell identical products. It implies that there is no product differentiation.

(iii) **Free Entry and Exit of Firms**
In perfect competition, there is no restriction on the entry and exit of the firms. Any firm can enter or leave the market at any time.

6. At what level of price do the firms in a perfectly competitive market supply when free entry and exit is allowed in the market? How is equilibrium quantity determined in such a market? NCERT

Ans. Equilibrium price will always be equal to minimum average cost in the long-run as due to the free entry and exit of the firms, all the firms earn zero economic profit.

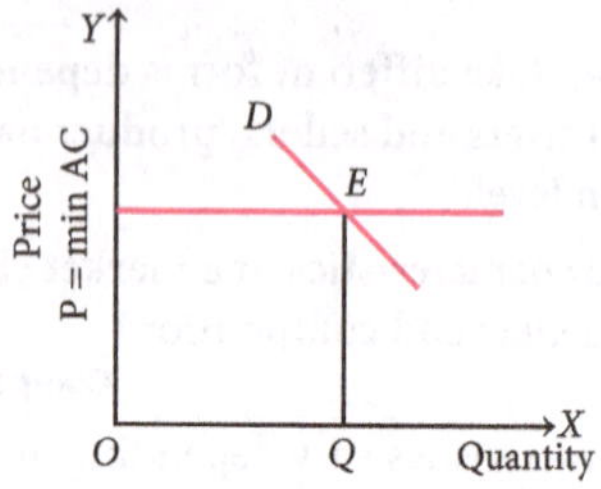

Equilibrium quantity is always determined by the equality of market demand and supply.

7. "In a perfectly competitive market, a firm's demand curve is perfectly elastic." Do you agree? Competency Based Que

Ans. Yes, I agree that in a perfectly competitive market, a firm's demand curve is perfectly elastic.

This is because firms are price takers, meaning they cannot influence the market price; they can sell any quantity of their product at the prevailing price but will lose all customers if they try to raise it. Since products are homogeneous and consumers can easily switch to competitors, the demand curve is represented as a horizontal line at the market price, indicating infinite demand at that price but none at a higher price.

8. Which feature of perfect competition is highlighted in the below image? Explain. Competency Based Que

Ans. The image highlights the large number of buyers and sellers feature of perfect competition. In a perfectly competitive market, there are numerous buyers and sellers, none of whom have a significant impact on the market price. This means that individual buyers and sellers are price takers, meaning they must accept the market price as given.

9. In what respect do the supply and demand curves in the labour market differ from those in the goods market? NCERT

Ans. They differ in following aspects

(i) Supply of labour is provided by households whereas demand for commodities is from the households.

(ii) The supply of commodities is by the firms, whereas demand for labour is by the firms.

10. Explain the implications of 'perfect knowledge about market' under perfect competition.

Ans. Perfect knowledge means that both buyers and sellers are fully informed about the market price. Therefore, no firm is in a position to charge a different price and no buyer will pay a higher price.

As a result, a uniform price prevails in the market. In case of perfect competition, buyers and sellers have perfect knowledge of the market.

11. "In a market characterised by perfect competition, many firms sell identical products and no single firm can influence the market price."

How does this statement reflect the nature of perfect competition? Competency Based Que

Ans. The statement highlights a key characteristic of perfect competition, where numerous firms operate in the market, each offering identical products.

This results in a situation where individual firms are price takers; they must accept the market price determined by overall supply and demand rather than having the power to set their own prices.

12. "If demand increases, the demand curve shifts right, raising both equilibrium price and quantity." Comment. Competency Based Que

Ans. When demand increases, it causes a rightward shift in the demand curve, indicating that consumers are willing to purchase more of the good at each price level.

This shift results in a higher equilibrium price, as sellers can charge more due to increased consumer interest.

Additionally, the equilibrium quantity also rises because producers respond to the higher price by supplying more of the product to meet the heightened demand. Consequently, both the equilibrium price and quantity are positively affected by an increase in demand.

13. Explain how, in the long-run, under equilibrium with free entry and exit, firms in perfect competition earn zero abnormal profits?

Ans. A perfectly competitive firm in the long-run can earn normal profits only. In case an industry is showing supernormal profits (TR>TC or AR>AC) in short-run, new firms will join the industry leading to increase in supply and will shift market supply curve to the right. Accordingly market price will be reduced and super-normal profits will be wiped out.

In case of negative abnormal profits (losses) in the short-run when (TR<TC or AR<AC) some of the existing firms will leave the industry.

Accordingly, supply will fall and market supply curve will shift to the left forcing the price to move up till the situation of zero normal profit is reached.

14. When do we say there is excess demand for a commodity in the market? NCERT

Ans. When the market demand exceeds market supply of a commodity at a given price then there is an excess demand for a commodity in the market.

15. What will happen if the price prevailing in the market is
(i) above the equilibrium price?
(ii) below the equilibrium price? NCERT

Ans. (i) If the price prevailing in the market is above equilibrium price, demand will be less than supply. It means a situation of excess supply in the market.

(ii) If the price prevailing in the market is below the equilibrium price, demand will be more than supply. It means a situation of excess demand.

16. How is the equilibrium number of firms determined in a market where entry and exit is permitted? NCERT

Ans. With the free entry and exit, the equilibrium number of firms determined in a market by equilibrium quantity supply per firm.

or Equilibrium Number of Firms

$$= \frac{\text{Equilibrium Quantity}}{\text{Supply of Each Firm}}$$

17. Can you think of any commodity on which price ceiling is imposed in India? What may be the consequence of price ceiling? NCERT; Competency Based Que

Ans. Price ceiling means the maximum price. In India, price ceilings are imposed on commodities like essential medicines, LPG and certain foodgrains (such as rice and wheat) under the public distribution system.

In this condition, the market price below the equilibrium price, consequences of price ceiling are

(i) Excess demand.
(ii) Emergence of black market.
(iii) Rationing due to shortage of supply of the commodity.

18. Explain how the demand curve in a perfectly competitive market behaves when there is a price change?

Ans. In a perfectly competitive market, the demand curve faced by an individual firm is perfectly elastic. If the market price increases, firms can sell more without affecting the price; if it decreases, they cannot sell at all, leading to a horizontal demand curve at the market price.

19. Explain market equilibrium. NCERT

Ans. Market equilibrium is a situation where the quantity demanded becomes equal to quantity supplied, corresponding to a particular price.

It means ⇒ Market demand = Market supply

20. Compare the effect of shift in demand curve on the equilibrium when the number of firms in the market is fixed with the situation when entry-exit is permitted. NCERT

Ans. If demand increase, then it creates excess demand for the goods.

It will lead to increase in price and in super normal profit. This will attract entry of new firms and it will lead to minimum AC.

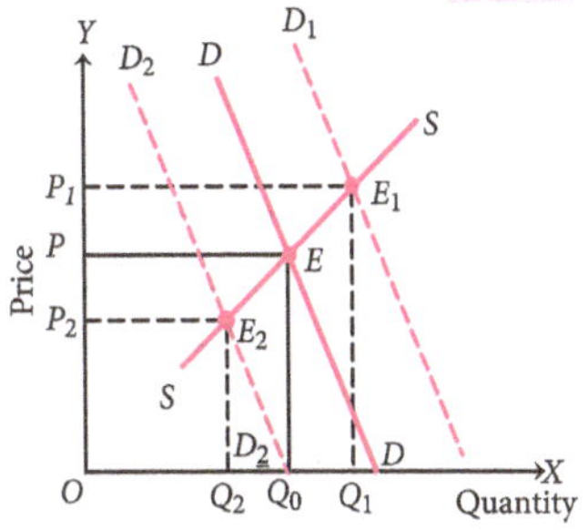

The effect of shift in demand curve when number of firms in the market is fixed

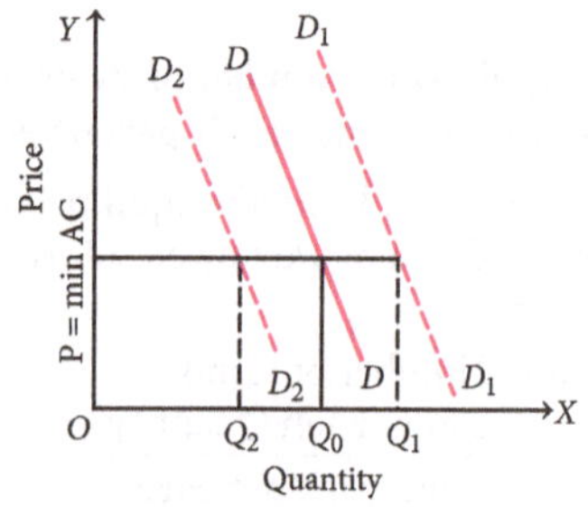

The effect of shift in demand curve when entry and exit remitted

21. Explain why the equilibrium price of a commodity is determined at that level of output at which its demand equals its supply?

Ans. Equilibrium is a point when at a given price, quantity demanded is equal to quantity supplied and equilibrium can be attained only at that point. If at a given price, supply is more, it will show excess supply and if demand is more, it will show excess demand.

In either case, there will be movement in price and hence quantities, i.e. these are not stable points. Only at equilibrium price, the quantity demanded is equal to quantity supplied and there is no tendency to change from this point.

22. "When supply increases, the supply curve shifts right, leading to a lower price and higher quantity." Do you agree? Give reasons. **Competency Based Que**

Ans. Yes, I agree. When supply increases, the supply curve shifts to the right, which means that more of the good or service is available at every price level. As a result, the equilibrium price tends to decrease because there is now more of the good available, creating a surplus at the previous price. To clear this excess supply, sellers are likely to lower the price, leading to a new equilibrium at a lower price and higher quantity. This is a typical outcome of an increase in supply in a competitive market.

23. How will a change in price of coffee affect the equilibrium price of tea? Explain the effect on equilibrium quantity also through a diagram. **NCERT**

Ans. Tea and coffee are substitute goods. A change in price of coffee will directly influence the equilibrium price and quantity of tea. As a result, the demand curve of tea will shift to the right (in case of an increase in the price of coffee).

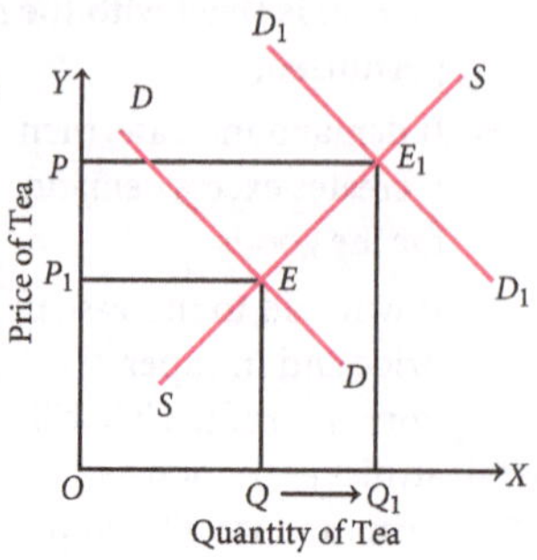

The supply curve of tea remain same, this will lead to an increase in price of tea (P_1) and increase in quantity (Q_1).

24. When do we say there is excess supply for a commodity in the market? **NCERT**

Ans. When the market supply of a commodity is greater than market demand, at a given price then there is an excess supply for a commodity in the market.

25. If the price of a substitute (Y) of good (X) increases, what impact does it have on the equilibrium price and quantity of good (X)? **NCERT**

Ans. An increase in price of a substitute (Y) of good (X) will directly affect the equilibrium price and quantity of good (X). Rise in price of (Y) will be relatively cheaper and demand for (X) will rise.

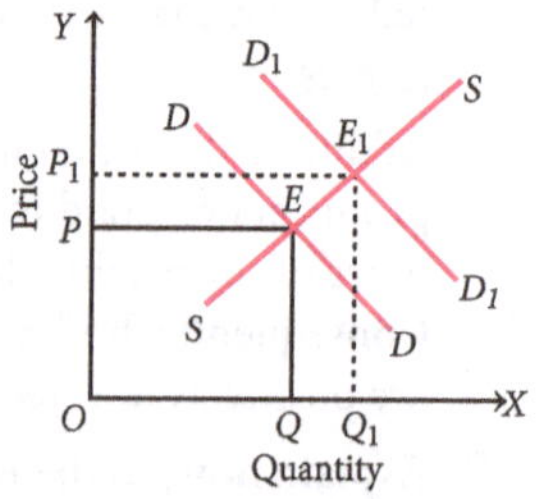

It will lead to excess demand which will lead to increase in both equilibrium price and equilibrium quantity.

26. How does rationing help in ensuring fair access to essential goods, especially for economically weaker sections of society? **Competency Based Que**

Ans. Rationing limits the quantity each consumer can purchase, ensuring that even those in economically weaker sections have access to essential goods.

This system helps prevent hoarding or monopolisation by wealthier individuals, promoting equitable distribution during times of scarcity or crisis.

27. "In the case of luxury items like diamond, decrease in demand decreases equilibrium price." Do you agree? **Competency Based Que**

Ans. No, this is not correct. The price of luxury items like diamond does not fall even if there is a decrease in demand. These items indicate social status of rich class due to which the price remains high, irrespective of change in demand.

28. Using supply and demand curves, show how an increase in the price of shoes affects the price of a pair of socks and the number of pairs of socks bought and sold. **NCERT; Competency Based Que**

Ans. Shoes and socks are complementary goods. An increase in the price of shoes will cause a decrease in demand of socks. It will lead to excess supply. This leads to competition among sellers, which reduces the price.

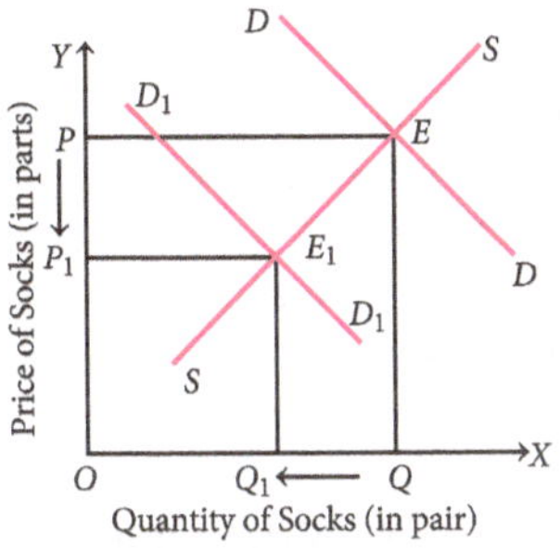

Fall in price leads to decrease in supply and rise in demand. These changes continue till supply and demand become equal at a new equilibrium price.

As a result, there is a decrease in demand of both shoes and socks.

29. How do the equilibrium price and quantity of a commodity change when price of input used in its production changes? **NCERT**

Ans. A change in price of inputs will directly affect the equilibrium price and quantity of goods. An increase in the price of an input, increase the unit cost of production of the commodity. This will cause a decrease in the supply of a commodity and leads to a leftward shift of supply curve.

But the demand curve will remain the same because market price of commodity will rise and quantity will fall.

As a result, supply will decrease and supply curve shift leftward as in figure.

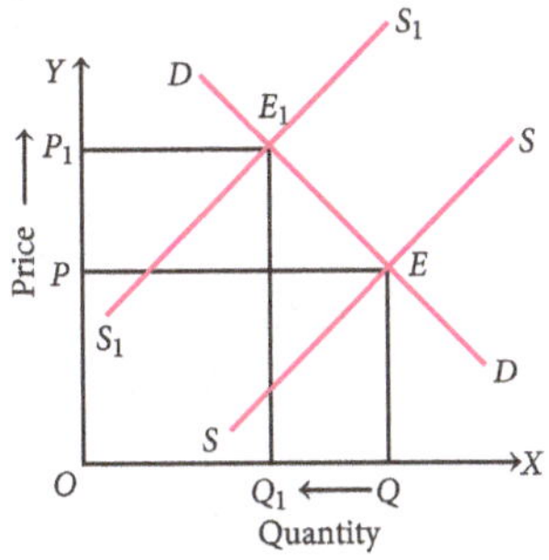

30. How is the optimal amount of labour determined in a perfectly competitive market? **NCERT**

Ans. The optimal amount of labour determined in a perfectly competitive market as

$$VMP_L = W$$

Where, W = Wage Rate

VMP_L = Value of Marginal Product of Labour

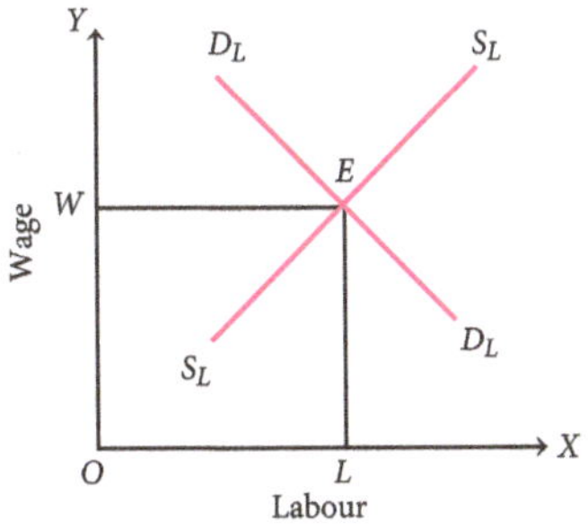

Here, $D_L = S_L$ (Demand and Supply of Labour) thus, the OL is the optimal amount of labour at equilibrium point E.

31. A shift in demand curve has a larger effect on price and smaller effect on quantity when the number of firms is fixed compared to the situation when free entry and exit is permitted. Explain. **NCERT; Competency Based Que**

Ans. Under the long-run, when free entry and exit is permitted, there is total change in quantity but no change in equilibrium price.

It happens when the demand curve intersects the supply curve at equilibrium point, then

Price = Minimum Average Cost.

As a result, demand curve shift upward, it effect, there is no change in price but quantity rises. When the number of firms is fixed, the supply curve is upward and demand curve is downward sloping. It results the demand effect more in price than quantity.

32. Identify the type of industrial structure shown in the image below and explain briefly about the same. Give one example such type of market in India. **Competency Based Que**

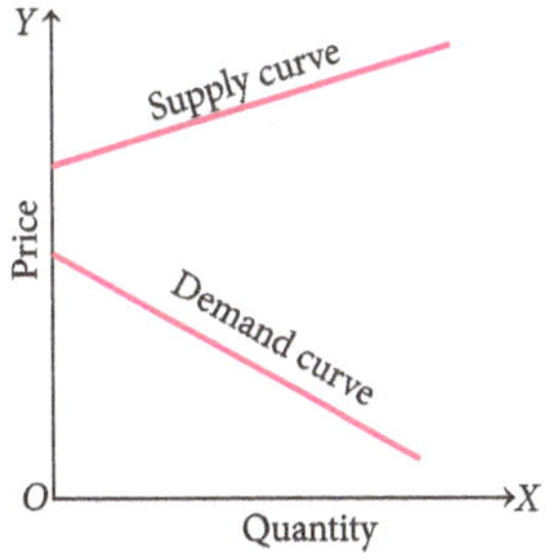

Demanded/Supplied

Ans. The image shown above indicates non-viable industry. Non-viable industry refers to an industry for which supply curve and demand curve never intersect each other in the positive axis. In India, commercial aircraft is an example of a non-viable industry.

Long Answer Type Questions

33. What is a market and how is it defined in economics?

Ans. A market is a system or an arrangement in which buyers and sellers come into contact to engage in the exchange of goods and services. It facilitates the transaction of commodities between individuals, firms or institutions. Markets can exist in physical locations like local markets, malls and stores or they can exist in virtual spaces like online platforms, where buyers and sellers interact digitally. The main objective of a market is to bring together buyers and sellers to agree on a price and quantity for goods and services.

In economics, the term market does not always refer to a physical location. Instead, it is defined more broadly as any mechanism or arrangement through which goods or services are exchanged. Markets are central to the functioning of an economy because they determine the prices of goods and services based on supply and demand. This interaction helps allocate resources efficiently across the economy.

Markets can take various forms depending on the structure

(i) **Perfect Competition**
A market structure where numerous small firms sell homogeneous products and no individual firm has the power to influence prices.

(ii) **Monopoly**
A market structures where there is only one seller who controls the entire supply of a product or service.

(iii) **Monopolistic Competition**
A market structure where many firms sell similar but not identical products, with some control over pricing.

(iv) **Oligopoly**
A market structure dominated by a small number of firms, which may set prices or restrict competition.

34. **"Loss in short-run will be wiped out by exit of existing firms." Do you agree? Give reasons.**
Competency Based Que

Ans. Yes, I agree that in the long-run, losses experienced by firms in a perfectly competitive market can lead to the exit of existing firms.

In the short-run, firms may incur losses due to various factors such as high costs or decreased demand. However, if they can cover their variable costs, they may continue to operate temporarily to minimise losses.

If losses persist, some firms will exit the market. This exit reduces the overall supply in the market, which can lead to higher prices.

As firms leave, the remaining firms begin to experience less competition, potentially leading to higher profits for them. Eventually, the market will reach a new equilibrium where supply and demand balances at a price that allows the remaining firms to cover their costs and earn normal profits.

In summary, while firms may endure short-run losses, the exit of firms ultimately contributes to a return to long-run equilibrium and profitability in a perfectly competitive market.

35. **What is perfect competition? Give its features.**

Ans. In a perfect competition market, numerous buyers and sellers trade homogeneous products at prices determined by the market forces of demand and supply.

For instance, farmers selling the same quality of grain cannot set their own prices; they must accept the market price.

Features of perfect competition are

(i) **Very Large Number of Buyers and Sellers**
In perfect competition, there are so many buyers and sellers that no individual buyer or seller can influence the market price.

(ii) **Homogeneous Product**
All firms sell identical products that are perfect substitutes for one another, meaning there is no differentiation between the goods offered by different sellers.

(iii) **Free Entry and Exit of Firms**
Firms can freely enter or exit the market without facing any barriers, ensuring that profits are kept at normal levels in the long-run.

(iv) **Firms Earn Normal Profit**
Firms earn just enough to cover their costs in the long-run, with no abnormal profits or losses, as competition drives any excess profits down.

(v) **Perfect Knowledge**
Buyers and sellers have complete knowledge of market prices, production costs and available products, ensuring no one can exploit the market.

(vi) **Perfect Mobility of Factors of Production**
Resources like labour and capital can freely move to industries offering better returns, ensuring that resources are allocated efficiently across the economy.

(vii) **Absence of Transportation Costs**
It is assumed that no additional transportation costs are incurred, which ensures uniform pricing for goods across different locations.

36. **Explain how price is determined in a perfectly competitive market with fixed number of firms?** **NCERT**

Ans. Equilibrium price is determined by the market forces of demand and supply in a perfectly competitive market. Where market equilibrium is determined when market demand is equal to market supply, under perfect competition.

Market demand is the sum total of demand for a commodity by all the

(i) buyers in the market. Its curve slopes downward due to law of demand.

(ii) Market supply is the sum total of supplies of a commodity by all the firms in the market. Its curve slopes upwards due to law of supply.

Considering market demand schedule on the one hand and market supply schedule on the other, identify equilibrium price on the one where

Market demand = Market supply.

It means market demand curve and market supply curve intersect each other.

Explanation by Table and Figure

Price of Commodity (₹)	Market Demand (Units)	Market Supply (Units)	
5	100	20	
7	80	40	
9	60	60	Equilibrium level (Demand = Supply)
11	40	80	
15	20	100	

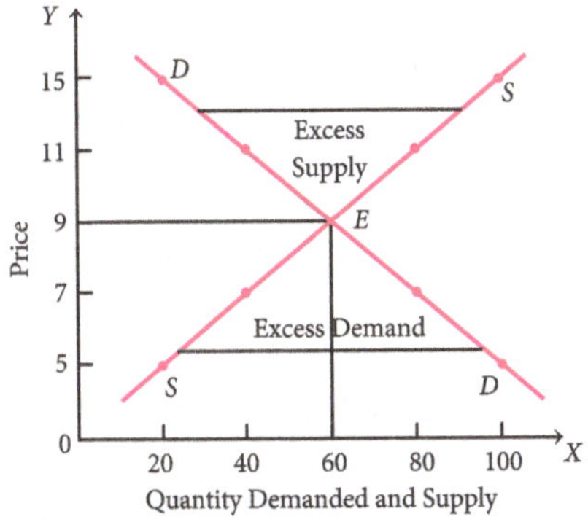

Note Market equilibrium is determined at point E, where price is ₹ 9. So, equilibrium price is determined at ₹ 9.

37. How is the demand curve represented under perfect competition? Explain with the help of a diagram.

Ans. In a perfectly competitive market, the firm's demand curve is perfectly elastic, meaning it is represented by a horizontal line at the prevailing market price. This characteristic indicates that the firm can sell any quantity of goods at the same price, which is determined by the market forces of supply and demand.

The horizontal demand curve reflects the fact that a perfectly competitive firm is a price taker. It cannot influence the price by changing the quantity of goods it sells, as the price is established by the overall market demand and supply. This is because the products offered by all firms in perfect competition are homogeneous and indistinguishable from one another.

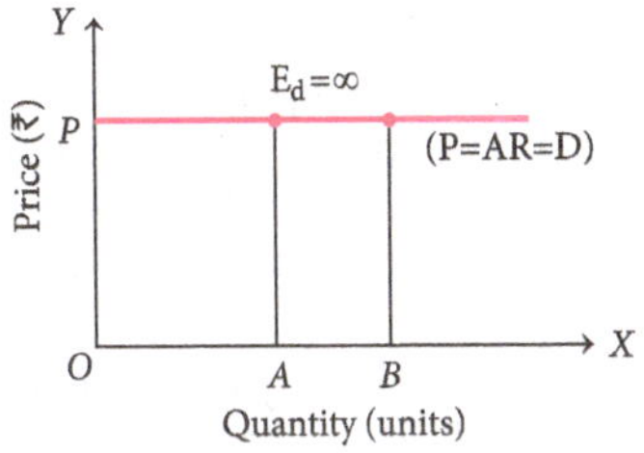

The diagram for the demand curves under perfect competition shows a horizontal line (the demand curve) at a price level where the firm can sell any amount of its product. The firm accepts the price set by the market and its demand curve is thus perfectly elastic.

In the diagram

(i) Price (*P*) remains constant, regardless of the quantity of goods sold.

(ii) The firm can sell any quantity, whether its quantity *OA* or *OB*, or even zero, at the same price *OP*.

(iii) The demand curve is horizontal because the firm cannot alter the price and the market dictates the price at which the goods are sold.

This behaviour illustrates that in a perfectly competitive market, the firm's output does not affect the market price, instead, the price is determined by the overall market supply and demand, and the firm simply adapts to this price.

This ensures that the firm can sell all its output at the same price, which is why its demand curve is horizontal at the market price.

38. "An increase in supply affects market equilibrium." Support or refute the statement with reasons.

Competency Based Que

Ans. I support this statement due to following reasons

(i) **Rightward Shift of the Supply Curve**

When supply increases, the supply curve shifts to the right.

This means that at every given price level, producers are willing to provide more of a good or service. e.g. If a farmer has a bumper crop of wheat, they are able to produce and offer more wheat at the same price.

(ii) **Price Adjustment**

As the supply increases and the quantity of goods available in the market rises, there is a surplus at the original equilibrium price. To clear this surplus, sellers will lower the price, which leads to a new equilibrium point where supply and demand are balanced again. Therefore, an increase in supply typically leads to a decrease in the equilibrium price.

(iii) **Increase in Equilibrium Quantity**

With the increase in supply, more goods are available at lower prices, which encourage consumers to buy more. The equilibrium quantity increases because more goods are being sold at the adjusted price.

For instance, the quantity of wheat demanded will increase at the lower price.

(iv) **Market Efficiency**

An increase in supply leads to a more efficient allocation of resources, as the market adjusts to meet the new supply-demand conditions.

This is beneficial for consumers, who enjoy lower prices and greater availability of goods.

A classic example of an increase in supply affecting market equilibrium is the agricultural market. If farmers have a good harvest, they will bring more produce to the market. This surplus lowers the price of fruits or vegetables, making them more affordable and increasing the quantity sold.

39. How does the availability of perfect knowledge affect the market?

Ans. In a perfectly competitive market, 'perfect knowledge' refers to the condition where all buyers and sellers have complete information about prices, product quality, and production costs.

This means that

(i) Buyers know the prices of the products sold by all sellers and are aware of the best deals available in the market.

(ii) Sellers know the prices being offered by competitors and are aware of the costs associated with production and distribution.

Perfect knowledge plays a significant role in ensuring efficiency in the market. Since buyers and sellers have full information, they can make decisions that maximise their utility and profits, respectively.

It leads to

(i) **Price Transparency**

No seller can charge excessively high prices because consumers are aware of all market prices and will buy from the cheapest seller.

(ii) **Product Standardisation**

Since products are homogeneous, consumers are willing to switch sellers if prices are lower, ensuring that firms maintain competitive prices.

(iii) **Efficient Resource Allocation**

Firms, knowing their cost structures and market prices, allocate resources efficiently, leading to the optimal production of goods.

The concept of perfect knowledge eliminates the possibility of price manipulation or exploitation, ensuring that the market operates efficiently and fairly.

40. Market of a commodity is in equilibrium, demand for the commodity increases. Explain the chain of effects of this change till the market again reaches equilibrium. Use diagram.

Ans. Effect of increase in demand of a commodity on equilibrium price and quantity is discussed below with reference to the given figure.

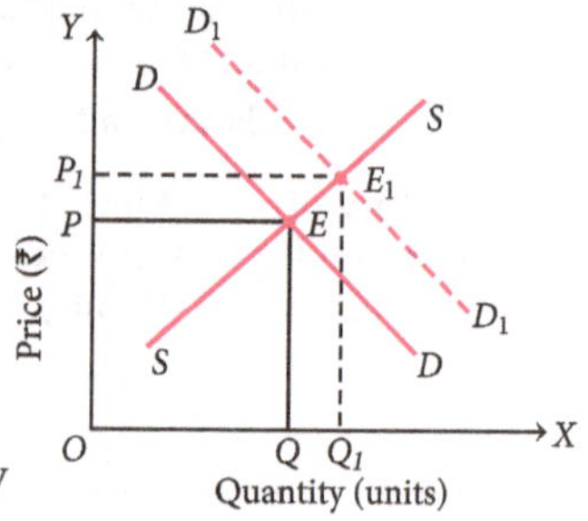

In the given figure, *DD* and *SS* are the initial demand curve and supply curve, respectively. *E* is the initial equilibrium point, *OQ* is the equilibrium quantity and *OP* is the equilibrium price.

Increase in demand implies a shift in demand curve to the right. It is indicated by D_1D_1. This sets in the following chain of effects.

Increase in demand implies that more is supplied at the existing price. Given supply, price of the commodity will tend to increase from *OP* to OP_1. Rise in price will cause contraction of demand and extension of supply. Hence, equilibrium quantity increases from *OQ* to OQ_1.

41. How are the equilibrium price and quantity affected when

(i) both demand and supply curves shift in the same direction?

(ii) demand and supply curves shift in opposite direction? NCERT

Ans. (i) When both demand and supply curves shift in same direction (shift to left) the equilibrium quantity will fall but equilibrium price may or may not be affected.

There may be three situations

- Equilibrium price will go up, when decrease in demand is less than decrease in supply.

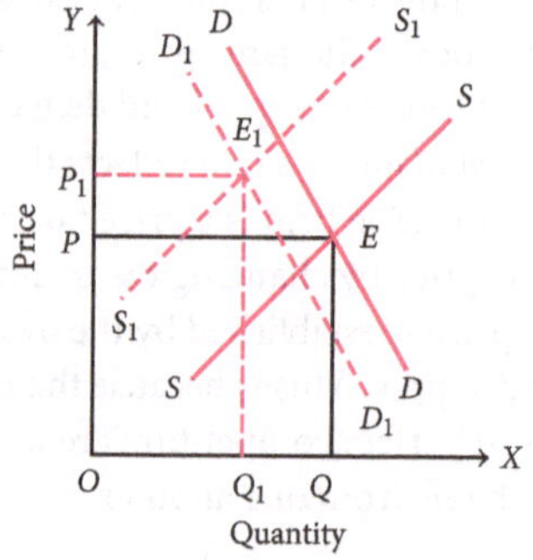

- Equilibrium price will fall, when decrease in demand is more than decrease in supply.

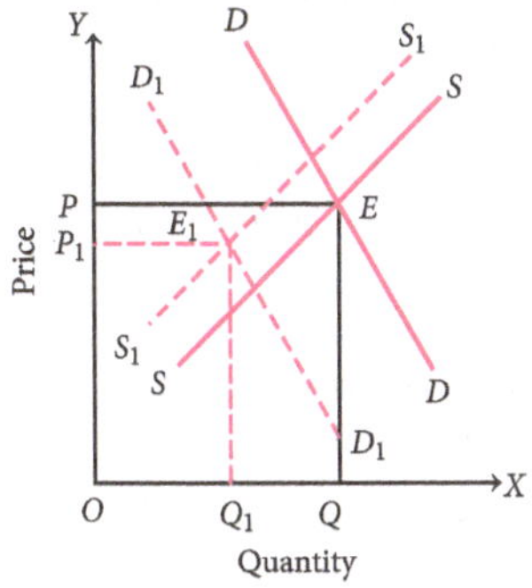

- No change in equilibrium price, when decrease in demand is equal to decrease in supply.

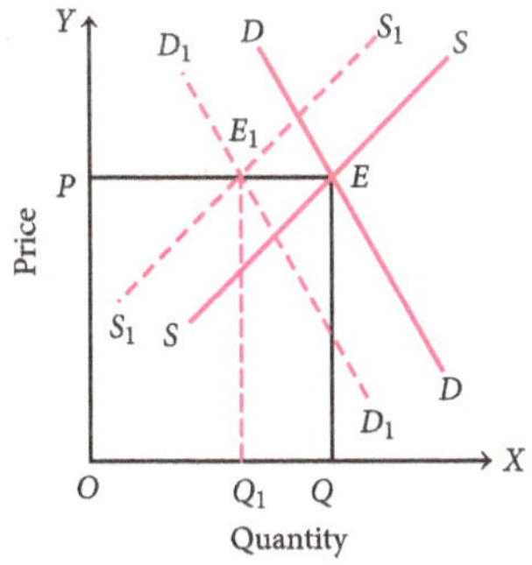

(ii) When demand and supply curves shift in opposite direction (demand curve shift to left and supply curve to the right), the equilibrium price will fall but the equilibrium quantity may or may not be affected.

There may be three situations

- The equilibrium quantity will rise, when decrease in demand is less than increase in supply.

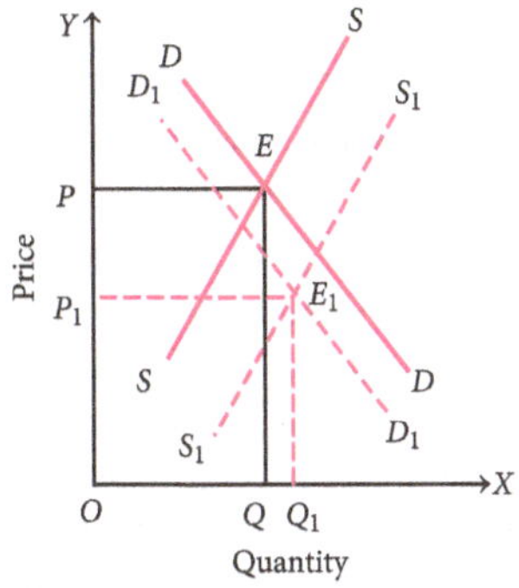

- The equilibrium quantity will fall, when decrease in demand is more than increase in supply.

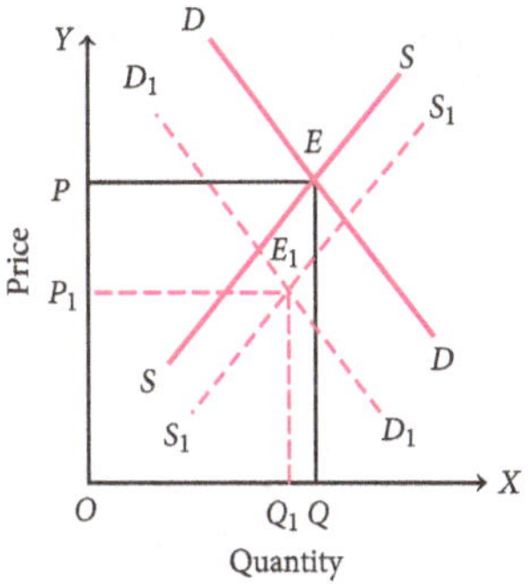

- No change in equilibrium quantity, when decrease in demand is equal to the increase in supply.

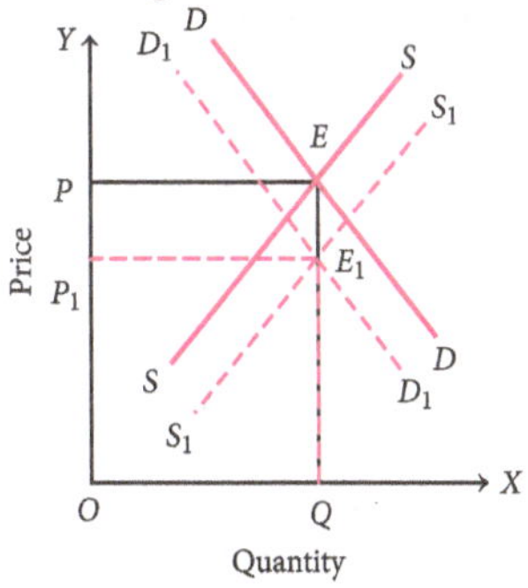

42. Market of a commodity is in equilibrium, demand for the commodity decreases. Explain the chain of effects of this change till the market again reaches equilibrium. Use diagram.

Ans. Effect of decrease in demand of a commodity on equilibrium price and quantity is discussed below with reference to the given figure.

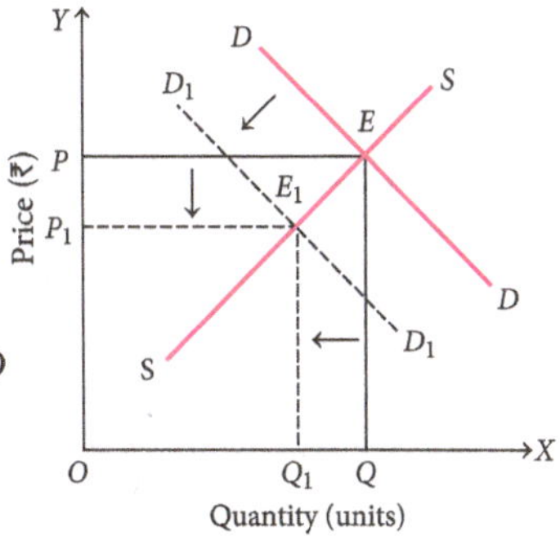

In the given figure, *DD* and *SS* are the initial demand curve and supply curve, respectively.

E is the initial equilibrium point, *OQ* is the equilibrium quantity and *OP* is the equilibrium price.

Decrease in demand implies a shift in demand curve to the left. It is indicated by D_1D_1. This sets in the following chain of effects. Decrease in demand implies that less is supplied at the existing price. Given the supply, price of the commodity will tend to decrease from *OP* to OP_1.

Fall in price will cause extension of demand and contraction of supply. Hence, equilibrium quantity decreases from *OQ* to OQ_1.

43. "A price ceiling is typically set by governments or regulatory authorities."

What is the purpose of implementing a price ceiling in the market? **Competency Based Que**

Ans. A price ceiling refers to the maximum price that sellers can charge for a commodity, set by the government or regulatory body, usually below the equilibrium price. This intervention is implemented to make essential goods more affordable to poorer sections of society, ensuring that even those with lower incomes can access basic necessities.

e.g. The government may set a price ceiling on essential commodities like wheat or rice during times of shortage or crisis to protect consumers from excessively high prices.

The primary goal of setting a price ceiling is to protect the interest of consumers by preventing exploitation and ensuring that essential goods remain affordable. The price ceiling creates a situation where the market price is restricted, which results in a lower price for consumers compared to what it would be in an unrestricted market. The equilibrium price is the price at which supply equals demand in a free market, but with a price ceiling, the price is set lower than this point.

In conclusion, a price ceiling is implemented to make goods more affordable and ensure accessibility for all consumers, particularly the economically disadvantaged. However, it can lead to a shortage, which requires regulatory measures like rationing to manage supply effectively.

44. "A price floor means the minimum price (above the equilibrium price) used particularly in industries like agriculture." How does a price floor benefit producers in the market? **Competency Based Que**

Ans. A price floor refers to the minimum price set by the government, which is above the equilibrium price. This price is implemented to protect producers, particularly in industries like agriculture.

The purpose of a price floor is to ensure that producers can earn a viable income, especially when market prices fall too low, causing producers to potentially suffer financial losses. For example, in India, the government sets a Minimum Support Price (MSP) for crops like wheat and rice to protect farmers from the fluctuations in market prices and ensure they receive a fair income for their products.

The price floor benefits producers in the market by guaranteeing them a minimum price for their goods, thus protecting them from volatile market conditions where prices could otherwise fall below their production costs.

The price floor ensures that producers can cover their costs and make a reasonable income, especially in times when there is a surplus in the market that would typically drive prices down.

In conclusion, a price floor benefits producers by guaranteeing them a minimum price for their products, thus ensuring they can sustain their livelihoods, even when market prices are low. The price floor also helps to prevent market fluctuations from negatively affecting producers' income, providing them with a more stable economic environment.

45. "Economists say inconsistent things, as price falls, demand rises, but as demand rises, price rises." Defend or refute. **Competency Based Que**

Ans. The statement that as price falls, demand rises, but as demand rises, price rises, can be defended. The first part of the statement, i.e. as price falls, demand rises shows the general behaviour of the consumer in the market. This is simply a forward movement along a demand curve.

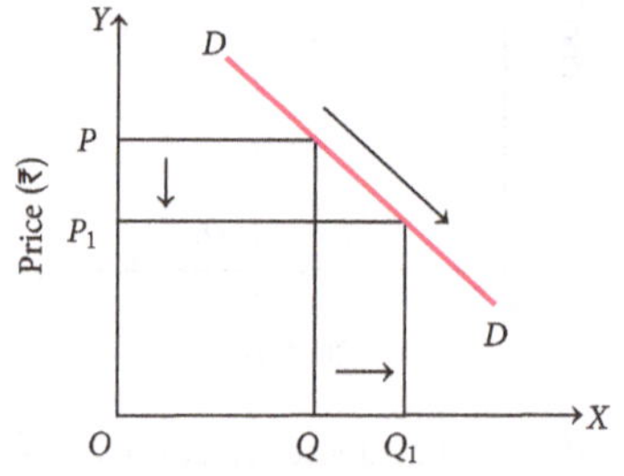

Figure A

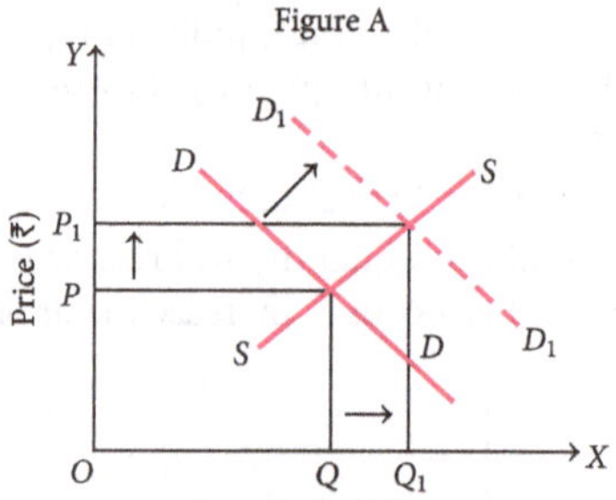

Figure B

But, there may also be a situation when increase in demand leads to increase in price.

When the supply of a commodity remains unchanged and demand increases due to factors other than price such as increase in income of the consumer or change in taste and preference of the consumer, the demand curve shifts upward and it raises the market price as shown in figure B.

Figure A shows when price falls from OP to OP_1, demand rises to OQ_1. This is extension of demand.

Figure B shows when there is increase in demand and demand curve shifts upward to D_1D_1, price rises to OP_1.

46. How is the equilibrium price and equilibrium quantity of a normal commodity affected by an increase in the income of the buyers? Explain with the help of a diagram.

Ans. When income of the consumer rises, demand curve will shift to the right, supply curve remains unaffected. However, when consumers are willing to pay higher price for the same quantity (because of increase in their income), price would tend to rise.

Consequently, quantity supplied by the producers would tend to rise.

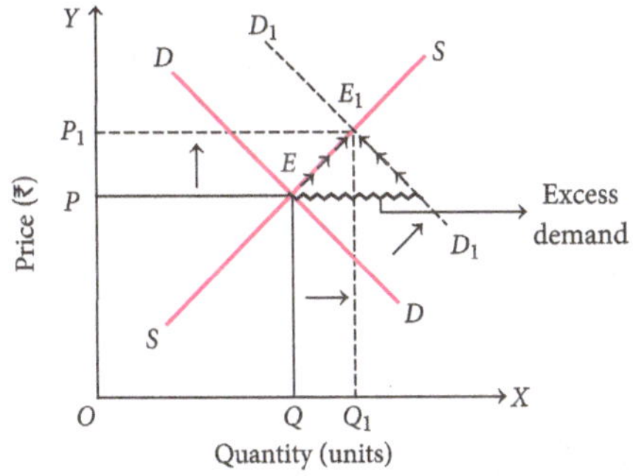

Thus, increase in demand and the consequent shift in demand curve to the right impacts producer's decisions by way of extension of supply in response to increase in price.

Finally, you would end up in a situation when equilibrium price as well as equilibrium quantity tends to rise, in response to increase in demand.

Here, OP = Initial equilibrium price

OQ = Initial equilibrium quantity

OP_1 = New equilibrium price

OQ_1 = New equilibrium quantity

47. At a given price of a commodity, there is excess demand. Is this price an equilibrium price? If not, how will the equilibrium price be reached?

Ans. By the definition, equilibrium price refers to the price at which market demand is equal to market supply (i.e. there is no excess demand or excess supply). So, the price with excess demand is not an equilibrium price.

This can be illustrated with the help of the given figure

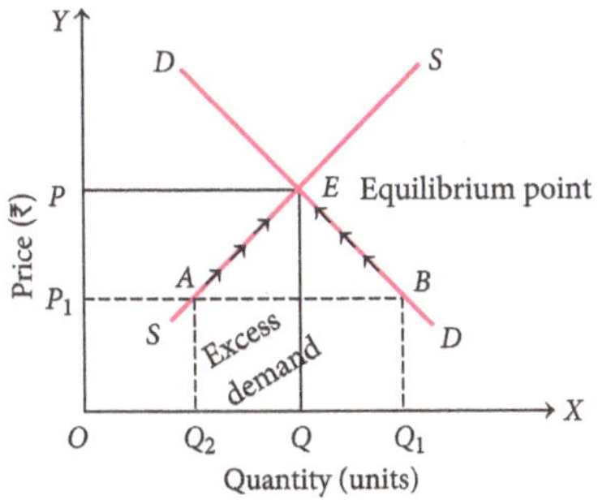

In this figure, at OP_1 level of price, AB is equal to Q_1Q_2 i.e. excess demand. With the market demand greater than market supply, the pressure exists to move the price upwards.

The quantity supplied tends to expand in correspondence with rising price because producers supply more at higher price and movement along the supply curve *SS* from point *A* to point E. At higher price *OP*, quantity supplied increases from OQ_2 to OQ.

Consumers react to rising price by reducing consumptions. Hence, movement is along demand curve *DD* from point *B* to point *E*. Thus, quantity demanded falls from OQ_1 to OQ.

The equilibrium is struck at point *E* with *OP* and *OQ* as the equilibrium price and equilibrium quantity, respectively. At *OP* price, there is no excess demand.

48. Give a brief explanation of viable and non-viable industry.

Ans. Viable Industry

An industry is considered viable if there is enough demand for the product at the minimum price set by the government. e.g. Agriculture is a viable industry in India due to strong demand for foodgrains.

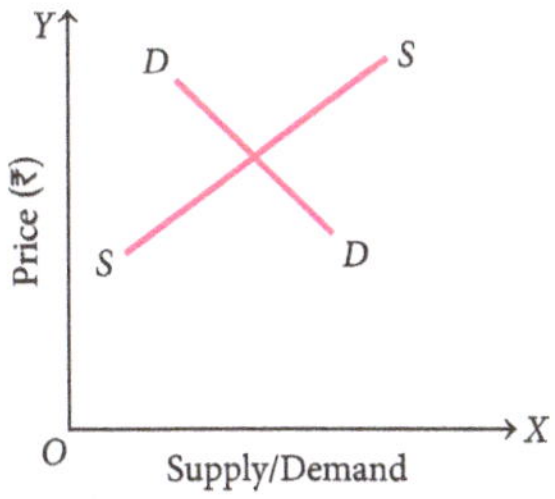

In such industries, demand and supply curves coincide in the positive quadrant.

Non-viable Industry

A non-viable industry is one where production costs are too high and consumers are unwilling to pay prices that cover those costs. For instance, commercial aircraft manufacturing in India is considered non-viable due to high costs and insufficient market demand.

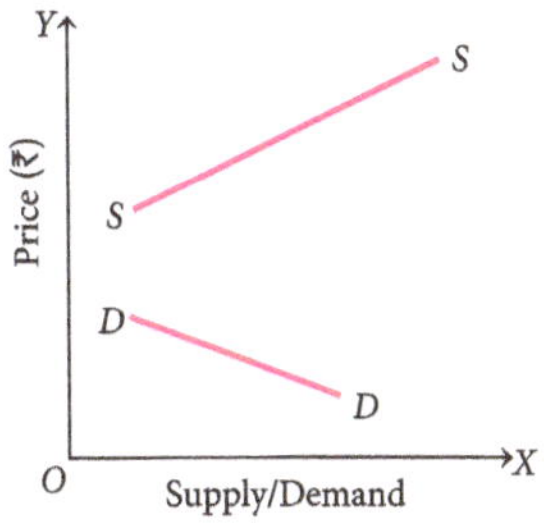

In this case, demand and supply curve will not intersect in the positive quadrant.

49. In a country facing rising food prices, the government decides to implement a price ceiling on essential commodities like wheat and rice. The price ceiling is set below the equilibrium price to make these staples more affordable for the low income population. As a result, the demand for these commodities increases, while the supply decreases due to reduced incentives for farmers to produce at the lower price.

To mitigate the effects of excess demand, the government introduces rationing, limiting the quantity each consumer can purchase.

Despite these measures, farmers express concerns about their income and the sustainability of their production levels, prompting the government to also establish a price floor for wheat and rice, ensuring farmers receive a minimum price above the equilibrium price. **Competency Based Que**

(i) What is a price ceiling and how does it affect the market for essential commodities?

(ii) Discuss the role of rationing in the context of a price ceiling. How does it help to address the issues arising from excess demand?

(iii) Explain the concept of a price floor and analyse its benefits and potential drawbacks in the agricultural sector, particularly for crops like wheat and rice.

Ans. (i) A price ceiling is a maximum price that sellers can charge for a commodity, typically set below the equilibrium price. It leads to increased demand and decreased supply, often resulting in shortages.

(ii) Rationing limits the quantity of goods that consumers can purchase, ensuring fair distribution when demand exceeds supply. It helps prevent shortages by managing the available supply and ensures that all consumers, especially the poorest, can access essential commodities.

(iii) A price floor is a minimum price set above the equilibrium price to protect producers from market fluctuations. Benefits include ensuring that farmers receive a viable income, which can lead to increased production and stability in the agricultural sector. However, drawbacks may include excess supply, as higher prices can discourage consumption, leading to surpluses. Additionally, if maintained long-term, it could result in inefficiencies in resource allocation and discourage market competition.

Numerical Questions

Numerical 1

Consider the following demand and supply functions for a good

Quantity demanded $= 160 - 2p$

Quantity supplied $= -40 + 2p$

(i) Calculate the equilibrium price and quantity.

(ii) Find out a price at which there is excess demand.

(iii) Find out a price at which there is excess supply.

Sol. (i) Quantity demanded $= 160 - 2p$

Quantity supplied $= -40 + 2p$

Equilibrium is attained at a point where market demand is equal to market supply, i.e.

Quantity demanded = Quantity supplied

Hence, $160 - 2p = -40 + 2p$

$160 + 40 = 2p + 2p$

$200 = 4p \Rightarrow p = \frac{200}{4} = 50$

Hence, equilibrium price = ₹ 50

Equilibrium quantity will be,

Quantity demanded = Quantity supplied

$= 160 - 2p = 160 - 2 \times 50$

$= 160 - 100 =$ ₹ 60

(ii) At any price below the equilibrium price there will be excess demand.

Let us take at price ₹ 20

At $p =$ ₹ 20

Quantity demanded $= 160 - 2p$

$= 160 - 2 \times 20 = 160 - 40 =$ ₹ 120

Quantity supplied $= -40 + 2p = -40 + 2 \times 20$

$= -40 + 40 = 0$

Quantity demanded > Quantity supplied

[excess demand]

Also, it can be concluded that at ₹ 20 there will be no supply of the commodity, hence between $20 < p < 50$, there will be excess demand.

(iii) At any price above equilibrium, there will be excess supply.

Let us take at price ₹ 80

Quantity demanded $= 160 - 2p = 160 - 2 \times 80$

$= 160 - 160 = 0$

Quantity supplied $= -40 + 2p = -40 + 2 \times 80$

$= -40 + 160 = 120$

Quantity demanded < Quantity supplied

[excess supply]

Also, it can be concluded that at $p =$ ₹ 80, demand will be zero, hence there will be excess supply between $50 < p < 80$.

Numerical 2

Suppose the demand and supply curve of commodity X in a perfectly competitive market are given by

$$q_d = 700 - p$$

$$q_s = 500 + 3p \text{ for } p \geq 15 = 0 \text{ for } 0 \leq p < 15$$

Assume that the market consists of identical firms. Identify the reason behind the market supply of commodity X being zero at any price less than ₹ 15. What will be the equilibrium price for this commodity? At equilibrium, what quantity of X will be produced? **NCERT**

Sol. From the given supply curve, it can be concluded that ₹ 15 must be the minimum Average Variable Cost (AVC) of producing commodity X. In a perfectly competitive market, firms do not produce positive level of output for any price less than AVC as they will be at loss, if they supply at a price less than AVC. Thus, firms will not produce commodity X at any price less than ₹ 15.

Calculation of Equilibrium Price and Equilibrium Quantity

At equilibrium, $q_d = q_s$

So, $700 - p = 500 + 3p \Rightarrow 4p = 200$

Thus, Equilibrium Price(p) = ₹ 50.

Putting the value of equilibrium price in the equation of demand curve

Equilibrium Quantity $(q_d) = 700 - 50 = 650$ units

Numerical 3

Considering the same demand curve as in numerical 2, now let us allow for free entry and exit of the firms producing commodity X. Also assume the market consists of identical firms producing commodity X. Let the supply curve of a single firm be explained as

$$q_f^s = 8 + 3p \text{ for } p \geq 20$$
$$= 0 \text{ for } 0 \leq p < 20$$

(i) What is the significance of p = 20?

(ii) At what price will the market for X be in equilibrium? State the reason for your answer.

(iii) Calculate the equilibrium quantity and number of firms. **NCERT**

Sol. $q_f^s = 8 + 3p$ for $p \geq$ ₹ $200 = 0$ for $0 \leq p <$ ₹ 20

$q_d = 700 - p$

(i) For the price between 0 to 20, no firm is going to produce anything as the price in this range is below the minimum of LAC. So, at the price of ₹ 20, the price line is equal to the minimum of LAC.

(ii) As there exists the freedom of entry and exit of firms, the minimum of AVC is at ₹ 20, also, the price of ₹ 20 is the equilibrium price. This is because in the long-run, all firms earn zero economic profit, which implies that the price of ₹ 20 is the equilibrium price and at any price lower than ₹ 20, the firm will move out of the market.

(iii) At equilibrium price of ₹ 20

Quantity supplied $= q_s = 8 + 3p = 8 + 3\,(20)$

$\Rightarrow \quad q_s = 68$ units

Quantity demanded $q_d = 700 - p = 700 - 20$

$\Rightarrow \quad q_d = 680$

Number of firms (n) $= \frac{q_d}{q_s}$; $n = \frac{680}{68} = 10$ firms

Therefore, the number of firms in the market is 10 and the equilibrium quantity in 680 units.

Numerical 4

Suppose the demand and supply curves of salt are given by

$$q_d = 1{,}000 - p;\ \ q_s = 700 + 2p$$

(i) Find the equilibrium price and quantity.

(ii) Now suppose that the price of an input used to produce salt has increased so that the new supply curve is $q_s = 400 + 2p$

How does the equilibrium price and quantity change? Does the change conform to your expectation?

(iii) Suppose the government has imposed a tax of ₹ 3 per unit of sale of salt. How does it affect the equilibrium price and quantity? **NCERT**

Sol. (i) At equilibrium price, $q_d = q_s$

$\therefore 1{,}000 - p = 700 + 2p \Rightarrow 3p = 300$

$\Rightarrow \quad p = 100$

Now, putting the value of equilibrium price into the demand curve equation, we get

$$q_d = 1{,}000 - p = 1{,}000 - 100 = 900$$

So, equilibrium quantity is 900 units.

(ii) If the price of input used increases, then the new supply curve becomes $q_s = 400 + 2p$

For equilibrium, $q_d = q_s$

$\therefore 1{,}000 - p = 400 + 2p \Rightarrow 3p = 600 \Rightarrow p = 200$

So, equilibrium price = ₹ 200

Substituting p = 200 into demand equation, we get

Equilibrium quantity $= 1{,}000 - p = 1{,}000 - 200 = 800$

So, equilibrium price increases and equilibrium quantity falls due to rise in the price of inputs.

(iii) If tax of ₹ 3 per unit of sale is imposed on the commodity, then the new supply curve becomes

$q_s = 700 + 2(p-3) \Rightarrow q_s = 700 + 2p - 6$

$q_s = 694 + 2p$

For equilibrium, $q_d = q_s$

$1{,}000 - p = 694 + 2p$

$1{,}000 - 694 = 3p$

$\Rightarrow \quad 3p = 306 \Rightarrow p = 102$

So, equilibrium price = ₹ 102

Substituting $p = 102$ to demand equation, we get

Equilibrium quantity $= 1{,}000 - 102 = 898$

Thus, the equilibrium price increases and equilibrium quantity decreases.

SELF ASSESSMENT TEST

Objective Type Questions

1. A price ceiling is set .... the equilibrium price.
   (a) above (b) below (c) at (d) far above
2. Which of the following is an example of a perfectly competitive market?
   (a) Automobile industry (b) Telecommunications (c) Fast food restaurants (d) Wheat market in a global market
3. If a firm in perfect competition increases its price above the market equilibrium price, it wills
   (a) lose some customers but retain others (b) increase its total revenue
   (c) lose all customers (d) reduce its production costs
4. The market supply curve in perfect competition is determined by the ....
   (a) government (b) consumers (c) firms (d) total production
5. When there is a price floor, the government typically .... the excess supply.
   (a) sells (b) controls (c) distributes (d) buys
6. What is the effect of a price floor set above the equilibrium price?
   (a) It creates a shortage (b) It creates a surplus
   (c) It leads to equilibrium (d) It lowers the price
7. What is the effect of an increase in supply in perfect competition?
   (a) Price rises and quantity remains the same (b) Both price and quantity increase
   (c) Price falls and quantity increases (d) Both price and quantity decrease
8. In a perfectly competitive market, firms earn .... profit in the long-run.
   (a) normal (b) supernormal (c) abnormal (d) negative

Answers 1. (b) 2. (d) 3. (c) 4. (c) 5. (d) 6. (b) 7. (c) 8. (a)

Short Answer Type Questions

9. "Perfect competition is comprised of very large number of sellers and each seller is very small." Do you agree? Give reasons.
10. What is the effect on market demand due to a change in supply?
11. What are the assumptions of market equilibrium?
12. Define the following
    (i) Excess demand (ii) Excess supply
13. "Supply curve remaining unchanged, if there is increase in demand, demand curve and equilibrium point will shift to the right." Support or refute the statement with valid reasons.
14. What is rationing? Explain.

Long Answer Type Questions

15. Explain the change in demand and its effect on equilibrium price with the help of appropriate diagrams.
16. Let the equation for the demand and supply curves of a particular commodity be $Q_d = 800 - 3{,}500\ P$ and $Q_s = 500 + 4{,}000\ P$. Solve the equations for the equilibrium price and quantity.

PROJECT WORK

Meaning of Project

The word project comes from the Latin word 'Projectum' which means 'before an action'. At school level, a project is a research assignment given to a student which generally requires a larger amount of effort and more independent work that is involved in a normal assignment.

It requires students to undertake their own fact finding endeavours, either from library, or from the internet or by means of primary data collection.

Utilities of Making a Project

Following points state the uses/utility of project work

(*i*) To provide information about the development and growth of institutions, business products and government activities.

(*ii*) To provide information to the consumers about the price of commodities, quality and uses, etc of a product as per their interest.

(*iii*) It is helpful in estimating the preference of consumers for petrol car or diesel car, telephone or mobile phone, etc.

(*iv*) Project report is helpful for the shareholders, who may be interested in knowing the earning of an enterprise and possibility of getting dividend.

(*v*) To help in the policy formulation about the economic and social development of any country.

Thus, we can say that project work may help marketers, shareholders, economists, consumers and government in effective and efficient decision-making.

Steps Towards Making a Project

The following steps are adviced to be taken while developing a project

1. *Identifying a Problem or an Area of Study*

At the outset, you should be clear about what you want to study. On the basis of your objective, you will proceed with the collection and processing of the data.

2. *Choice of Target Group*

The choice or identification of the target group is important for framing a project. This will also help in identifying those persons on whom you focus your attention.

3. *Collection of Data*

Data regarding project report should be collected using primary or secondary data or both the methods. Primary data can be collected by personal interviews or by mailing questionnaire. Secondary data are usually used when there is shortage of time, money and manpower resources and information is easily available.

4. *Organisation and Presentation of Data*

After collecting the data, project report can be presented using statistical tables, graphs or diagrams.

5. *Analysis and Interpretation*

Statistical measures like measures of central tendency, measures of disperson and correlation may be used as per the requirements of your analysis.

6. *Preparing a Project Report*

A project report is prepared for communicating the findings of the project.

Project Report

A project is represented with the help of a project report. The project report contains a detailed statement of the findings of the analyser. It should be prepared with great care and consideration. A project report should

- be handwritten
- be concise and clear
- have diagrammatic presentation
- have topics with suitable headings
- end up with conclusion

Elements of Project Report

A good project report should contain the following elements.

Title Page

This should include the project title, name of the company on which you are conducting your research and name of the student. You can also list the name of your school, class and subject teacher.

Acknowledgement

It is usual to thank those individuals, who have provided particularly useful assistance, technical or otherwise, during your project.

Content Page

This should list the main sections and sub-sections of your report. Choose self-explanatory titles with their respective pages and use double spacing for clarity.

Introduction

This is one of the most important component of the project report. It should begin with a clear statement of what the project is about, so that the nature and scope of the project can be understood by a reader. It should summarise everything which you set out to achieve and provide a clear summary of the project's background, relevance and main contributions. The introduction should set the context for the project and should provide the reader with a summary of the key things to look out for in, the remainder of the report.

Background

The background section of the report should set the project into action, it specifies the problem of the company, what remedial actions were taken by the company and what are its effects.

Body of Report

The central part of the report usually consists of three or four sections detailing the technical work undertaken during the project. The structure of these sections is highly project dependent. They can reflect the chronological development of the project. It includes the detailed description regarding the matter of the project.

Evaluation

This might involve quantitative and qualitative evaluation such as expressibility, functionality, ease-of-use, etc of a product. At some point, you should also evaluate the strengths and weaknesses of what you have done. It includes certain questionnaires, sampling test which help in evaluating the result on the basis of truths and facts.

Conclusion

The conclusion should list the things, which have been learnt as a result of the work you have done. It shows the ultimate response of the project undertaken by a student. It should be expressive and impressive so that a reader would clearly evaluate the result and rated you on the basis of your presentation.

Bibliography

In this section, you should mention the details of all the secondary sources, *i.e.*, magazines, newspapers, reports, internet links, etc. used for developing the project.

Sample Project

Changing Consumer Awareness among Households

Relation Between Level of Education and Consumer Awareness

Name : ....

Class : ....

Roll No. : ....

Subject : ....

School : ....

Submitted by .... Submitted to ....

Acknowledgement

I would like to extend my sincere and heartfelt obligation towards all those who have helped me in making this project. Without their active guidance, help, cooperation and encouragement, I would not have been able to present the project on time.

I am extremely thankful and pay my gratitude to my teacher Mr/Ms .... for his/her valuable guidance and support for completion of this project.

I extend my gratitude to my Principal Mr/Ms .... for the moral support extended during the tenure of the project.

I also acknowledge with a deep sense of reverence, my gratitude towards my parents, other faculty members of the school and friends for their valuable suggestions given to me in completing this project.

Date...........

....

Name of Student

Certificate

This is to Certify that the project work

.... is the bonafide work of

.... (Name of the student) who carried out the work under

my supervision ....

(Name and Signature of
Teacher/Supervisor)

Contents

Objectives of the Project

I choose the topic "Changing Consumer Awareness Among Households". This topic is quite relevant. The concept of consumer awareness has changed over the times. In the olden days the principle of 'Caveat Emptor' prevailed in the market which meant that a buyer should be beware while purchasing a good/service. In those days, buyers and sellers had a face-to-face interaction. The seller exhibited his goods and the buyer thoroughly examined them and then purchased them.

It was assumed that the buyer would use all care and skill while examining the good and would buy it only if he was completely satisfied.

This maxim relieved the seller of the obligation to make disclosure about the quality of the product. But, with the growth of trade and emergence of a global market, it is now impossible for the buyer to examine the goods before hand. In the age of information technology and the emergence of e-commerce, it is only the producer/seller who can assure the quality of goods services. As a result buyers are being misled, duped and deceived day in and day out.

Thus, consumers should be aware of their rights and be cautious while purchasing goods and services.

More specifically, the main objectives of this project are to know the following

- Are the consumers aware that the product they are using is a certified product? It should be certified as ISI, AGMARK, ISO–9002, etc.
- Are the consumers, aware of the statutory requirement that the product should show MRP, date of manufacture and the date showing 'best before use' or the expiry date of the product?
- Are the consumers aware that the product in question (like kerosene oil or sugar) may be available at the fair price shops regulated by the government?
- Are the consumers aware of the consumer courts which are meant to protect their interest against fraudulent practices by the shopkeepers?
- Are the consumers aware of the fact that if they buy goods against cash memo, they are ensuring purchase of genuine products as well as tax revenue to the government?
- Is there any relation between the level of education and consumer awareness in the country?

Introduction to Consumer Awareness

Nowadays, large number of goods and services are available in the market which make the consumer's choice difficult. Consumer awareness helps consumers to find the suitable goods and services available in the market.

Consumer awareness refers to the combination of the following

- The knowledge of the product purchased by the consumers in terms of its quality. **For example,** the consumer should know whether the product is good for health or not, whether the product is free of creating any environmental hazard or not, etc.
- The education about the various types of hazards and problems associated with marketing of a product. *For example*, one way of marketing a product is advertisement through newspapers, television, etc. Consumers should have proper education about the bad effects of advertisement. They must also verify the contents of the advertisement.
- The knowledge about 'consumer rights'. This means that the consumer should be aware about the various rights given to him under Consumer Protection Act, 1982.
- The knowledge about consumer's own responsibilities. This implies that consumers should not indulge in wasteful and unnecessary consumption.

Consumers' Rights

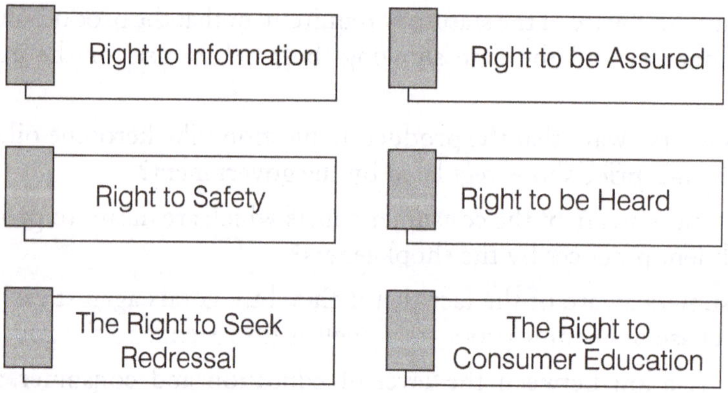

Need for Consumer Awareness

Mahatma Gandhi had also optly recognised the importance of consumer in the market mechanism. According to him, "A consumer is the most important visitor on our premises. He is not dependent on us, we are on him. He is not an interruption to our work; he is the purpose of it. We are not doing a favour to a consumer by giving him an opportunity. He is doing us a favour by giving an opportunity to serve him." However, inspite of this view of the father of nation, the consumer is constantly being exploited by the sellers and producers.

To overcome this problem, the consumer must be aware of his rights, raise voice against exploitation and seek redressal of his grievance. However in India, consumer awareness is low due to apathy and lack of education among the masses.

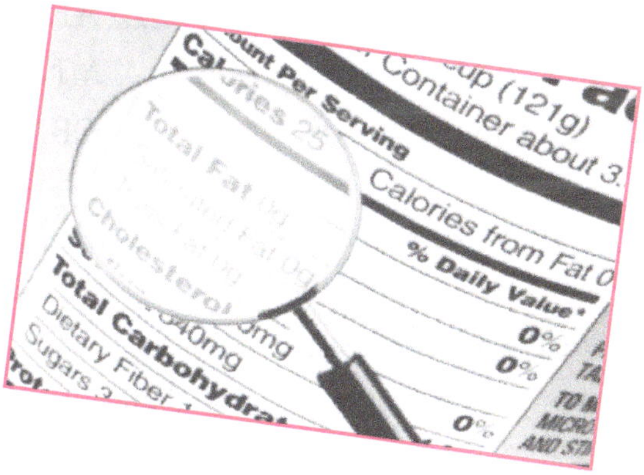

Assessing Consumer Awareness in Households

This project aims to assess the level of consumer awareness in literate and illiterate households by collecting primary data.

For this purpose the following steps have to taken.

- Collection of data
- Classification of data
- Presentation of data
- Interpretation of data.

Collection of Data

Data can be collected by various method such as direct personal investigation, indirect oral investigation, etc.

In this project, the data are collected through direct personal investigation method with the help of a questionnaire.

For the sake of convenience, there are 8 questions given in the questionnaire. The respondents are approached personally so that the results are accurate.

Questionnaire

Name	:	XYZ
Address	:	ABC
Age	:	MN
Occupation	:	CBN

Please tick (✔) in the squares as given against each question which is applicable in your case.

	Question	Yes	No
1.	Are you aware that the product purchased by you is certified like ISI, ISO 9002?	☑	☐
2.	Do you check Maximum Retail Price (MRP), manufacturing date and expiry date?	☑	☐
3.	Do you insist on bill at the time of purchase?	☐	☑
4.	Do you cross check the quantity of the product?	☑	☐
5.	Are you aware of taxes imposed on the goods?	☑	☐
6.	Do you check the warranty/guarantee of the product before purchasing it?	☑	☐
7.	Do you get influenced by the advertisements?	☐	☑
8.	Are you aware of consumer rights and consumer courts?	☑	☐

Data has been collected for a sample or 100 households; out of which 50 are literate and another 50 are illiterate.

Classification of Data

After collecting the data, this data is classified according to the characteristics for further analysis.

(A) Data Relating to 50 Literate Households

S.No.	Knowledge Features	Answer	Tally Bar	Frequency
1.	Awareness about certified product	Yes No	𝍸 𝍸 𝍸 𝍸 𝍸 𝍸 𝍸 𝍸 𝍸 𝍸	40 10
2.	Checking manufacturing date, MRP, expiry date	Yes No	𝍸 𝍸 𝍸 𝍸 𝍸 𝍸 𝍸 𝍸 𝍷𝍷𝍷𝍷 𝍸 𝍷	44 6
3.	Insist on bill	Yes No	𝍸 𝍸 𝍸 𝍸 𝍸 𝍸 𝍸 𝍷𝍷𝍷 𝍸 𝍸 𝍷𝍷	38 12
4.	Cross check of quantity	Yes No	𝍸 𝍸 𝍸 𝍸 𝍸 𝍸 𝍸 𝍸 𝍷𝍷𝍷𝍷 𝍸 𝍷	44 6
5.	Awareness about taxes	Yes No	𝍸 𝍸 𝍸 𝍸 𝍸 𝍸 𝍸 𝍸 𝍷𝍷𝍷𝍷 𝍸 𝍷	44 6
6.	Check of warranty or guarantee	Yes No	𝍸 𝍸 𝍸 𝍸 𝍸 𝍸 𝍸 𝍸 𝍷𝍷𝍷𝍷 𝍸 𝍷	44 6
7.	Influence of advertisements	Yes No	𝍸 𝍸 𝍸 𝍸 𝍸 𝍸 𝍸 𝍸 𝍸 𝍸	40 10
8.	Awareness about consumer rights and consumer courts	Yes No	𝍸 𝍸 𝍸 𝍸 𝍸 𝍸 𝍸 𝍸 𝍸 𝍸	40 10

(B) Data Relating to 50 Illiterate Households

S.No.	Knowledge Features	Answer	Tally Bar	Frequency
1.	Awareness about certified product	Yes No	卌 卌 卌 卌 卌 卌 卌 卌 卌 卌	20 30
2.	Check of Manufacturing date, MRP, expiry date	Yes No	卌 卌 卌 卌 卌 卌 卌 卌 II 卌 III	42 8
3.	Insist on bill	Yes No	卌 卌 卌 卌 卌 卌 卌 卌 卌 卌	20 30
4.	Cross check of quantity	Yes No	卌 卌 卌 卌 卌 卌 卌 I 卌 卌 IIII	36 14
5.	Awareness about taxes	Yes No	卌 卌 卌 卌 卌 卌 卌 卌 卌 卌	10 40
6.	Check of warranty or guarantee	Yes No	卌 卌 卌 卌 卌 卌 卌 卌 卌 卌	10 40
7.	Influence of advertisements	Yes No	卌 卌 卌 卌 IIII 卌 卌 卌 卌 卌 I	24 26
8.	Awareness about consumer rights and consumer courts	Yes No	 卌 卌 卌 卌 卌 卌 卌 卌 卌 卌	0 50

Presentation and Analysis of Data

The collected and classified data is presented in a tabular and diagrammatic form.

1. Tabular Presentation of Data

S.No.	Knowledge Features	Number of Household Showing Awareness (%)		Number of Household not showing Awareness (%)	
		Literate	Illiterate	Literate	Illiterate
1.	Awareness about certified product	80	40	20	60
2.	Check of MRP, manufacturing date, expiry date	88	84	12	16
3.	Insist on bill	76	40	24	60
4.	Cross check of quantity	88	72	12	28
5.	Awareness about taxes	88	20	12	80
6.	Check of warranty or guarantee	88	20	12	80
7.	Influence of advertisements	80	48	20	52
8.	Awareness about consumer rights and consumer courts	80	—	20	100

2. Diagrammatic Presentation of 'Consumer Awareness'

The summarised data of consumer awareness can be presented through following bar diagrams

(A) Literate Households

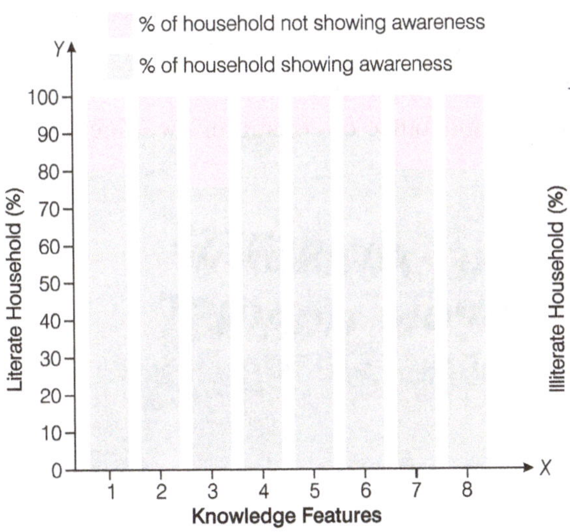

Note *Diagrammatic Presentation of Questionnaire are based upon Imaginary Data*

(B) Illiterate Households

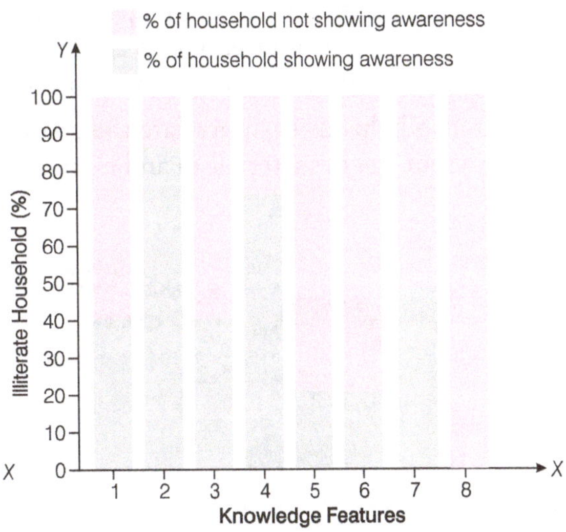

Note *Diagrammatic Presentation of Questionnaire are based upon Imaginary Data*

Project Work

Interpretation of Data

Interpretation of data gives us the conclusion of our study.

On the Basis of Study Conducted, We Conclude

- There is lack of consumer awareness among illiterate households whereas, literate consumers show a greater degree of consumer awareness. Lack of education is the obvious cause of lack of awareness among illiterate consumers.
- There are certain areas like cross checking the quantity and warranty of the products, where the illiterate consumers show relatively greater awareness. Reason being, they want to make rational use of their limited income.
- Illiterate consumers respond positively on the influence of advertisements.
- Literate and illiterate consumers both check MRP, manufacturing date and expiry date of the product.
- The illiterate consumers are not aware of taxes levied on goods. It may be because of the lack of education that they can't understand the system of taxation.
- 60% of the illiterate consumers do not insist on obtaining a bill of their purchases. This may be due to the fact that they either are not aware of the importance of a bill or they do not buy from the organised markets.
- The literate consumers are mostly aware of their rights whereas, illiterate ones are not. So, they are prone to exploitation by the shopkeepers.
- Illiterate consumers do not believe in going to consumer courts as compared to literate ones. This may be due to lack of awareness and also due to the fact that they do not have much time, money and efforts to spare.
- The above interpretations help us to reach the conclusion that consumer awareness is more in literate households as compared to illiterate households. This conveys the fact that the education is important for consumer awareness.
- It also helps us to appreciate the growing importance of consumer awareness in the present age of materialism and e-commerce.

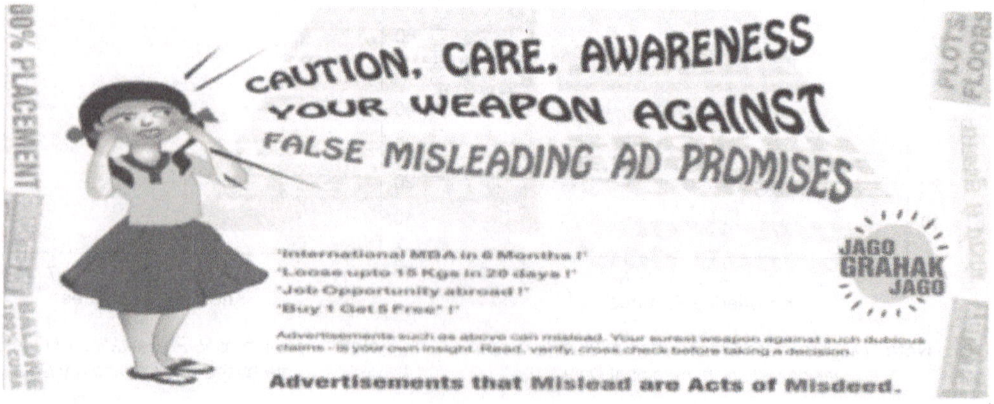

SUGGESTED PROJECTS

Some of the examples of the projects are as follows (they are not mandatory but suggestive)

(i) A report on demographic structure of your neighbourhood.

(ii) Dissemination of price information for growers and its impact on consumers.

(iii) Study of a cooperative institution: milk cooperatives, marketing cooperatives, etc.

(iv) Case studies on public private partnership, outsourcing and outward Foreign Direct Investment.

(v) Global warming.

(vi) Designing eco-friendly projects applicable in school such as paper and water recycle.

3 Sample Papers

SAMPLE QUESTION PAPER 1

A Highly Simulated Sample Question Paper for CBSE Class XI Examination

ECONOMICS

Time : 3 Hours **Max. Marks : 80**

General Instructions

1. This question paper contains two sections
   Section A – Statistics for Economics Section B – Introductory Microeconomics
2. This paper contains 20 Multiple Choice Questions of 1 mark each.
3. This paper contains 4 Short Answer Questions of 3 marks each to be answered in 60 to 80 words.
4. This paper contains 6 Short Answer Questions of 4 marks each to be answered in 80 to 100 words.
5. This paper contains 4 Long Answer Questions of 6 marks each to be answered in 100 to 150 words.

Section-A
(Statistics for Economics)

1. When the mean of series is a decimal number, then which method should be used for computing Karl Pearson's coefficient of correlation? (1)

(a) Direct method (b) Short-cut method
(c) Step deviation method (d) None of these

2. Which type of sampling is highlighted in the image? (1)

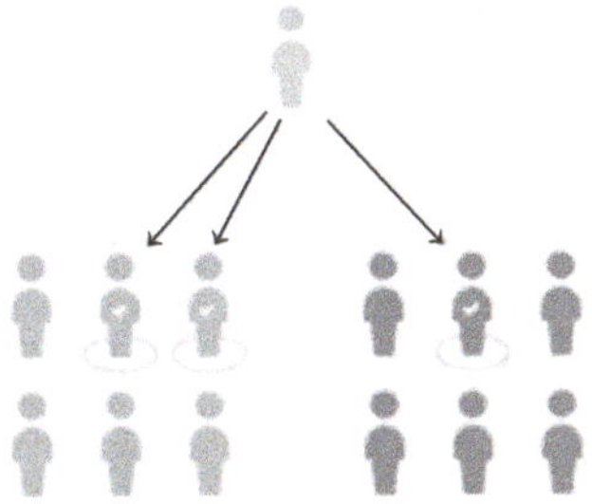

(a) Simple random sampling
(b) Stratified sampling
(c) Quota sampling (d) Cluster sampling

3. ...... method is suitable for small size of population. (1)

(a) Census (b) Sampling
(c) Both (a) and (b) (d) None of these

4. The class mid-point is equal to (1)

(a) the average of the upper class limit and the lower class limit
(b) the product of upper class limit and the lower class limit
(c) the ratio of the upper class limit and the lower class limit
(d) None of the above

5. Choose the correct pair from given below (1)

	Column I		Column II
A.	Primary data	(i)	Collected from recorded sources
B.	Secondary data	(ii)	Original data
C.	Enumerator	(iii)	Person who collects data from source
D.	Respondent	(iv)	The person who conducts survey

Codes

(a) A-(i) (b) B-(ii) (c) C-(iii) (d) D-(iv)

6. Tabulation is the process of presenting ...... in the form of table. (1)

(a) description (b) data (c) qualities (d) All of these

7. Identify the statistical measure used to measure the change shown in the image below. (1)

(a) Measure of central tendencies
(b) Measure of correlation
(c) Index numbers
(d) None of the above

8. **Statement I** Coefficient of correlation is zero when two variables are uncorrelated.

Statement II When two variables move in the same direction, there exists a positive correlation. (1)

Alternatives
(a) Statement I is correct and Statement II is incorrect
(b) Statement II is correct and Statement I is incorrect
(c) Both the statements are correct
(d) Both the statements are incorrect

9. **Assertion** (A) Index numbers are most appropriate to compare data based upon time period.

Reason (R) Index numbers are universal and always presented in percentage form. (1)

Alternatives
(a) Both Assertion (A) and Reason (R) are true and Reason (R) is the correct explanation of Assertion (A)
(b) Both Assertion (A) and Reason (R) are true, but Reason (R) is not the correct explanation of Assertion (A)
(c) Assertion (A) is true, but Reason (R) is false
(d) Assertion (A) is false, but Reason (R) is true

10. **Based on the study "Dietary water affects human skin hydration and biomechanics" from PubMed Central, what type of correlation exists between water intake and skin hydration?** (1)

Source *https://pmc.ncbi.nlm.nih.gov/articles/PMC4529263/*
(a) No correlation
(b) Positive correlation
(c) Negative correlation
(d) Inverse correlation

11. **The mean of 5 observations is 7. Later on it was found that two observations 4 and 8 were wrongly taken instead of 5 and 9. Find the corrected mean.** (3)

12. **Given below is the data of the ages of 15 children in a society. Find mean, median and mode.** (3)

5, 8, 7, 9, 4, 6 3, 9, 7, 7, 5, 8, 6, 3, 4.

Or **Find lower quartile and upper quartile from the following data.**

X	5	10	15	20	25	30	35	40	45
F	3	2	10	8	3	2	5	12	6

13. **Calculate index number by Laspeyre's method and Paasche's method from the following data** (2 + 2)

Commodity	Base Year		Current Year	
	Price (₹)	Quantity	Price (₹)	Quantity
Rice	10	6	15	8
Wheat	25	10	40	20
Oil	30	15	45	12
Pulses	15	20	30	15
Sugar	20	8	25	6

14. **The following table shows monthly pocket expenses of the students of a class. Find out the median from the following data** (4)

Pocket Expenses (₹)	20-29	30-39	40-49	50-59	60-69
No. of Students	10	8	6	4	2

Or (i) **A group of students in a class received marks in an exam with values: 30, 35, 40, 50, 60, 100. The teacher calculates the mean of these marks and finds it to be 52.5. Discuss how the presence of a single high score can affect the mean and whether the mean truly reflects the overall performance of the class.** (3)

(ii) **In another class, the marks are more evenly distributed without any very high or low scores. How would the mean in this case be different from the first class and why would it be a better representation of the class performance?** (1)

15. **Identify the type of correlation shown in the image below. Also explain other degrees of correlation and their significance.** (4)

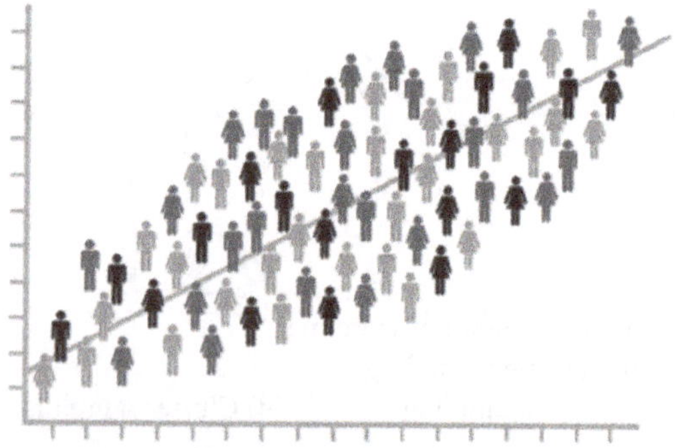

16. (i) **Examine whether there is any correlation between years of schooling of farmers and annual yield on the basis of following data, using Karl Pearson's method and interpret the result.** (4)

Years of Schooling	1	3	4	5	7	8
Annual Yield	2	6	8	10	14	16

(ii) Discuss the difference between correlation coefficient differ from Pearsonian correlation coefficient. (2)

Or Seven contestants in a poetry competition are judged by two judges in the following order

Judge 1	12	10	8	10	11	9	15
Judge 2	26	20	24	20	18	22	20

Calculate rank coefficient of correlation and also interpret the results. (6)

17. Read following case study carefully and answer the questions on the basis of the same

Suppose, you want to know about the popularity of a film star among school students. For this, you will have to enquire from a large number of school students, by asking questions from them to collect the desired information. Data you get, is an example of primary data.

If the data has been collected and processed (scrutinised and tabulated) by some other agency, they are called secondary data.

They can be obtained either from published sources or from any other source.

Thus, the data are primary to the source that collects and processes them for the first time and secondary for all sources that later use such data. Use of secondary data saves time and cost.
For example, after collecting the data on the popularity of the film star among students you can publish a report. If somebody uses that data collected by you for a similar study, it becomes secondary data.

(i) Differentiate between primary and secondary data. (3)

(ii) Which precautions should be kept in mind while collecting secondary data? (3)

Section-B

(Introductory Microeconomics)

18. Other things being constant, if prices of petrol go up, then demand for cars will .... . (1)

(a) decrease (b) increase
(c) remain constant (d) Can't be determined

19. The formula to calculate ATC is .... (1)

(a) ATC = TC/Q (b) ATC = AC/Q
(c) ATC = AVC/Q (d) None of these

20. "The Competition Commission of India (CCI) in October fined the Alphabet Inc unit with $161 million for exploiting its dominant position in the market for Android which powers 97% of smartphones in India, a key growth region for the US giant."

Which market form is indicated in the above situation? (1)

(a) Perfect competition (b) Imperfect competition
(c) Either (a) or (b) (d) Neither (a) nor (b)

21. In the context of revenue, choose the correct options from given below (1)

(i) Average revenue is always equals to price per unit of the commodity.

(ii) When price falls with rise in output, AR and MR coincides.

(iii) TR increases at a constant rate when price for additional unit remains constant.

Codes

(a) (i) and (ii) (b) (i) and (iii)
(c) (ii) and (iii) (d) (i), (ii) and (iii)

22. Total revenue of a firm is equal to .... (1)

(a) Cost − Profit (b) Cost + Profit
(c) Cost × Profit (d) Cost ÷ Profit

23. Complete the table given below

Quantity	TU	MU
1	10	...
2	...	8

Missing values of TU and MU will be (1)

(a) 10, 8 (b) 8, 10
(c) 10, 10 (d) 0, 18

24. Identify the market form from the image given below (1)

(a) Perfect competition (b) Imperfect competition
(c) Both (a) and (b) (d) Neither (a) nor (b)

25. Assertion (A) As the output increases, AFC decreases because the fixed cost is spread over more units of production.

Reason (R) AFC can be zero as it is derived from TFC. (1)

Alternatives
(a) Both Assertion (A) and Reason (R) are true and Reason (R) is the correct explanation of Assertion (A)
(b) Both Assertion (A) and Reason (R) are true, but Reason (R) is not the correct explanation of Assertion (A)
(c) Assertion (A) is true, but Reason (R) is false
(d) Assertion (A) is false, but Reason (R) is true

26. "The union government will not hesitate to import coal or impose Section 11 of the Electricity Act (Emergency Law), if needed, to meet the country's rising power demand, Power Minister RK Singh said on 1st February in an interaction with reporters in New Delhi."

How this move is expected to impact the demand for electricity in India? (1)
(a) Demand curve will shift to the right
(b) Demand curve will shift to the left
(c) Downward movement along demand curve
(d) Upward movement along demand curve

27. Statement I Every producer aims to maximise the total profits and profits increase as long as MR exceeds MC.

Statement II At producer's equilibrium, AR should be at least equal to AVC. (1)

Alternatives
(a) Statement I is correct and Statement II is incorrect
(b) Statement II is correct and Statement I is incorrect
(c) Both the statements are correct
(d) Both the statements are incorrect

28. "Governments often seek to assist farmers by setting price floors in agricultural markets. A minimum allowable price set above the equilibrium price is a price floor. With a price floor, the government forbids a price below the minimum."

Explain the consequences of the above situation. (3)

Or What is meant by average cost, marginal cost and total cost?

29. For a particular product, price was reduced from ₹ 50 per unit to ₹ 48 in order to attract more customers. It was observed that demand for the product subsequently increased from 100 to 110 units. Calculate the price elasticity of demand. (3)

30. Explain the concept of total fixed cost and average fixed cost with the help of a table and diagram. (4)

Or "A perfectly competitive firm's demand curve as a horizontal line under perfect competition shows that an individual producer has no control over price of his product." Is it true? Explain.

31. (i) Suppose the initial demand was 100 units. With the rise in price by ₹ 5, the quantity demanded decreases by 5 units. Price elasticity of demand is known to be 1.2. Find out the price before the change in demand. (2)

(ii) As a result of 10% fall in price of a good, its demand rises from 100 units to 120 units. Find out the price elasticity of demand. (2)

32. (i) Identify the type of goods shown in the image below. Show its impact on demand curve using suitable diagram. (3)

(ii) If the price of a good falls but its demand remains unchanged, what does it indicate about its nature? (1)

33. Following information is given about a firm

Quantity (Units)	0	1	2	3	4	5	6
Total Cost (₹)	150	300	420	600	790	1,000	1,260

Using this data, answer the following
(i) Find the Average Variable Cost (AVC) of producing 4 units. (3)
(ii) Calculate the Marginal Cost (MC) of producing the 5th unit. (2)
(iii) Identify the most economical AVC level. (1)

34. "Government of India has reduced the custom duty on the import of lithium, a vital component for batteries used for electronic vehicles."
(i) How does this effect the equilibrium price and quantity of the electronic vehicles in India? (2)
(ii) Explain the chain effect using suitable example. (4)

Or Giving suitable reason, state whether the following statements are true or false.
(i) Indifference curve to the right in indifference map always shows higher utility level. (3)
(ii) Marginal rate of substitution increases as we move downward along the indifference curve. (3)

Answers

1. (b) Short-cut method
2. (c) Quota sampling
3. (a) Census
4. (a) the average of the upper class limit and the lower class limit
5. (c) C-(iii)
6. (b) data
7. (c) Index numbers
8. (c) Both the statements are correct
9. (b) Both Assertion (A) and Reason (R) are true, but Reason (R) is not the correct explanation of Assertion (A)
10. (b) Positive correlation
11. 7.4
12. Mean = 6.06; Median = 6; Mode = 7

Or $Q_1 = 20$; $Q_3 = 40$

13. Laspayre's method = 161.06%

Paasche's method = 160.3 %

14. Median = 35.75
16. (i) $r = 1$ Perfect positive correlation

Or $r = -0.25$ Negative correlation

18. (a) decrease
19. (a) ATC = TC/Q
20. (b) Imperfect competition
21. (c) (ii) and (iii)
22. (b) Cost + Profit
23. (a) 10, 8
24. (b) Imperfect competition
25. (c) Assertion (A) is true, but Reason (R) is false
26. (b) Demand curve will shift to the left
27. (a) Statement I is correct and Statement II is incorrect
29. 2.5
31. (i) ₹ 120 (ii) 2
33. (i) ₹ 160 (ii) ₹ 210 (iii) ₹ 135 at 2 units

SAMPLE QUESTION PAPER 2

A Highly Simulated Sample Question Paper for CBSE Class XI Examination

ECONOMICS

Time : 3 Hours **Max. Marks : 80**

General Instructions

1. This question paper contains two sections
   Section A – Statistics for Economics Section B – Introductory Microeconomics
2. This paper contains 20 Multiple Choice Questions of 1 mark each.
3. This paper contains 4 Short Answer Questions of 3 marks each to be answered in 60 to 80 words.
4. This paper contains 6 Short Answer Questions of 4 marks each to be answered in 80 to 100 words.
5. This paper contains 4 Long Answer Questions of 6 marks each to be answered in 100 to 150 words.

Section-A
(Statistics for Economics)

1. Median of a given series is 'k'. If all the item values of series are increased by 'k', then what will be the new median? (1)

(a) $2k$ (b) k^2
(c) $k+2$ (d) Can't be determined

2. Index of industrial production is a ...... of quantitative relative. (1)

(a) simple average (b) weighted average
(c) Both (a) and (b) (d) None of these

3. In ...... method of primary data collection, the investigator can make necessary adjustment in his set of questions. (1)

(a) direct personal investigation
(b) indirect oral investigation
(c) telephone interviews (d) None of the above

4. Complete the following table (1)

Price (₹)	Quantity	Value
100	...	2,000
...	40	6,000

(a) 2,000, 300 (b) 200, 150
(c) 150, 200 (d) 300, 400

5. Assertion (A) The Sensex is a benchmark index of Bombay Stock Exchange (BSE).

Reason (R) The Sensex helps investors gauge the overall performance of the stock market and serves as a barometer for the Indian economy. (1)

Alternatives

(a) Both Assertion (A) and Reason (R) are true and Reason (R) is the correct explanation of Assertion (A)
(b) Both Assertion (A) and Reason (R) are true, but Reason (R) is not the correct explanation of Assertion (A)
(c) Assertion (A) is true, but Reason (R) is false
(d) Assertion (A) is false, but Reason (R) is true

6. Statement I Table based upon general characteristics is known as spatial table.

Statement II Chronological classification is arrangement of data on the basis of different time period. (1)

Alternatives

(a) Statement I is correct and Statement II is incorrect
(b) Statement II is correct and Statement I is incorrect
(c) Both the statements are correct
(d) Both the statements are incorrect

7. Identify the type of activity shown in the image below (1)

(a) Market economic activity
(b) Non-market economic activity
(c) Non-economic activity
(d) Both (b) and (c)

8. "Coastal inundation is increasing globally. Changes in tidal water levels contribute to flood risk alongside rain and sea storm events. Unlike the latter, temporal variations in tides may be predicted and their patterns analysed many years in advance."

In the light of the given statement, data that are grouped with reference to the attributes is known as .... (1)

(a) qualitative classification
(b) quantitative classification
(c) Both (a) and (b)
(d) Neither (a) nor (b)

9. The method in which the upper limit of a class interval is same as the lower limit of the next class interval is known as (1)

(a) cumulative method
(b) inclusive method
(c) exclusive method
(d) None of the above

10. Observe the given image and identify the correct sequence of economic activities depicted. (1)

(a) Mining, Distribution, Consumption
(b) Production, Distribution, Consumption
(c) Production, Exchange, Consumption
(d) Production, Distribution, Exchange

11. Categorise the following variables as discrete variables or continuous variables giving suitable reasons. (3)

(i) Height of students
(ii) Distance covered
(iii) Number of students in a class

Or

"All statistics are numerical facts but all numerical facts are not statistics." Comment.

12. Calculate coefficient of correlation from the following data and comment on the nature of correlation (3)

(i) Sum of squares of deviations of X values from its mean = 136
(ii) Sum of squares of deviations of Y values from its mean = 138
(iii) Sum of products of deviations of X and Y values from their respective means = 122

13. In a certain examination, there were 100 candidates of whom 21 failed, 6 secured distinctions, 12 were placed in the first division, 18 in the second division and 43 were placed in the third division.

It is known that at least 75 percent marks are required for distinction, 40 percent for passing, 50 percent for second division and 60 percent for first division.

(i) Convert the above data into frequency distribution with class intervals. (2)
(ii) Calculate the median of the distribution of marks. (2)

14. "A well-organised dataset allows for meaningful analysis and better decision-making. In statistics, classification and tabulation play a crucial role in simplifying complex data."

(i) Explain how classification and tabulation help in organising data for meaningful analysis. Support your answer with an example. (3)
(ii) List the different methods of classification used in organising data. (1)

15. Calculate the upper and lower quartiles for the following frequency distribution. (4)

Class Interval	Frequency (f)
13-25	6
25-37	11
37-49	23
49-61	7
61-73	3
Total	50

Or

Following table gives the distribution of companies according to the size of capital. Using step-deviation method, find out the mean size of the capital of a company.

Capital (₹ in lakhs)	Less than 5	Less than 10	Less than 15	Less than 20	Less than 25	Less than 30
Number of Companies	20	27	29	38	48	53

16. (i) Calculate CPI for 2011 using family budget method. (4)

Items	Price in 2000 (₹)	Price in 2011 (₹)	Weight
Food	100	140	30
Rent	50	100	20
Clothing	75	60	20
Fuel and Lighting	25	50	10
Miscellaneous	50	100	20

(ii) State any two important uses of the Consumer Price Index (CPI). (2)

17. A company plans to launch a new energy drink and decides to conduct a market survey using a questionnaire. The marketing team drafts a set of questions and distributes them among potential customers.

However, after analysing the responses, they realise that a significant number of answers seem inconsistent, some respondents skipped certain questions and others gave responses that seemed influenced by how the questions were framed.

Surprised by these issues, the team reviews the questionnaire and notices

- Some questions assume the respondent already has knowledge about energy drinks.
- A few questions subtly encourage positive responses about the product.
- Some questions require detailed financial data, making respondents hesitant to answer.

Based on the given case, answer the following

(i) What are the precautions needed to be taken while drafting a questionnaire to avoid such issues? (3)

(ii) If you were part of the marketing team, what decisions would you make regarding the types of questions to be incorporated in the questionnaire to ensure reliable data collection? (3)

Or

(i) Calculate Karl Pearson's coefficient of correlation from the following data (3)

X	20	25	30	35	40	45	50	55	60
Y	16	20	23	25	33	38	46	50	55

(ii) A researcher carefully computes the correlation coefficient between 2 variables and get $r = 1.13$. What does this value mean? (3)

Section-B
(Introductory Microeconomics)

18. "Utility analysis is criticised for one of its assumptions."

According to this, utility can be expressed in terms of (1)

(a) cardinal number (b) ordinal number
(c) Both (a) and (b) (d) None of these

19. Law of Variable Proportions is applicable in .... (1)

(a) short-run only (b) long-run only
(c) market period only (d) All of these

20. Identify the correct statement(s) from the given below (1)

(i) With increase in level of output, ATC and AVC comes closer.
(ii) MC is the rate of change in TC as well as TVC.
(iii) TVC varies indirectly with change in level of output.

Codes

(a) (i) and (ii) (b) (ii) and (iii)
(c) (i) and (iii) (d) (i), (ii) and (iii)

21. Assertion (A) Extension in supply is caused by change in factors other than own price. This leads to movement along the supply curve.

Reason (R) Change in quantity supplied is an impact of change in other factors leading to shift in supply curve to the right. (1)

Alternatives

(a) Both Assertion (A) and Reason (R) are true and Reason (R) is the correct explanation of Assertion (A)
(b) Both Assertion (A) and Reason (R) are true, but Reason (R) is not the correct explanation of Assertion (A)
(c) Assertion (A) is true, but Reason (R) is false
(d) Both are false

22. A .... economy allows individuals to own and operate businesses, but the government .... critical industries to ensure stability. (1)

(a) mixed, controls
(b) market, deregulates
(c) command, owns
(d) traditional, monitors

23. **Statement I** Demand curve of giffen goods is upward sloping.

Statement II Giffen goods are special type of inferior goods. (1)

Alternatives

(a) Statement I is correct and Statement II is incorrect
(b) Statement II is correct and Statement I is incorrect
(c) Both the statements are correct
(d) Both the statements are incorrect

24. **Identify the type of good shown in the image below** (1)

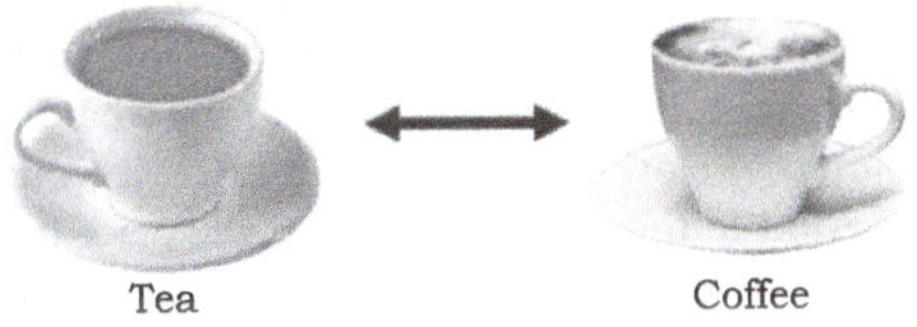

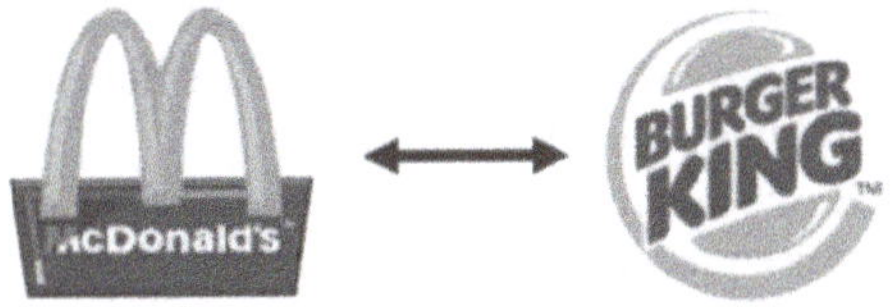

(a) Substitute goods
(b) Complementary goods
(c) Giffen goods
(d) Inferior goods

25. **A consumer consumes only two goods X and Y whose prices are ₹ 3 and ₹ 4 per unit respectively. If the consumer chooses a combination of the two goods with marginal utility of X equal to 4 and that of Y equal of 3, in this situation what will be the consumer's reaction?** (1)

(a) Buy more units of both X and Y
(b) Buy more units of Y and less of X
(c) Buy more units of X and less of Y
(d) Buy less units of both, X and Y

26. **...... is the slope of indifference curve** (1)

(a) MRT (b) MRS
(c) Price line (d) None of these

27. **Indifference curve doesn't touch ...... axis.** (1)

(a) X (b) Y
(c) Either (a) or (b) (d) Neither (a) nor (b)

28. **Complete the following table** (3)

Units of Labour	**Average Product** (AP)	**Marginal Product** (MP)	**Total Product** (TP)
1	8	...	...
2	10	...	...
3	...	10	...
4	9	...	...
5	...	4	...
6	7	...	...

Or **Complete the following table**

Output (Q) (Units)	**Price** (P) (₹)	**Total Revenue** (TR) (₹)	**Marginal Revenue** (MR) (₹)
4	9	36	...
5	...	...	4
6	...	42	...
7	6	...	...
8	...	40	...

29. **"Rationality of a producer is defined by his motive of profitability. Profit doesn't only depend upon the revenue but also cost.**

In economic sense, one of the important costs is additional cost of production. MC indicates the incremental cost of the producer."

In this context, why should MC be rising at the point of equilibrium? (3)

30. **(i) Based upon the image given below, identify the central problem and explain the same briefly.** (3)

(ii) How does scarcity lead to the existence of the central economic problems of an economy? (1)

31. (i) Why a higher indifference curve in an indifference map represents a higher level of satisfaction? (2)

(ii) Will a profit maximising firm in a competitive market produce a positive level of output in the short-run if the market price is less than the minimum of AC?

Give an explanation. (2)

Or

At the point of producer's equilibrium, a producer always maximises his profits. Defend or refute the statement with suitable reasons. (4)

32. Explain any four factors determining Price Elasticity of Demand (E_d). (4)

33. (i) Define Price Elasticity of Supply (E_s) and explain the methods of measuring it. (4)

(ii) Name and briefly describe the various degrees of Price Elasticity of Supply (E_s). (2)

Or

(i) Calculate total cost and average variable cost of a firm at each given level of output from its cost schedule given below (3)

Output (Units)	1	2	3	4	5	6
Average Fixed Cost (AFC) (₹)	60	30	20	15	12	10
Marginal Cost (MC) (₹)	32	30	28	30	35	43

(ii) Interpret the trend of the Marginal Cost (MC) at different output levels. What does it indicate about the firm's production process? (3)

34. Governments often seek to assist farmers by setting price floors in agricultural markets.

A minimum allowable price set above the equilibrium price is a price floor. With a price floor, the government forbids a price below the minimum. (Notice that, if the price floor were for whatever reason set below the equilibrium price, it would be irrelevant to the determination of the price in the market since nothing would prohibit the price from rising to equilibrium). A price floor that is set above the equilibrium price creates a surplus.

(i) Explain the consequences of price floor as a direct action by the government. (3)

(ii) How government should counter to deal with the consequences of price floor? (2)

(iii) What would be the impact of a price ceiling in agricultural markets? (1)

Answers

1. (c) $k+2$
2. (b) weighted average
3. (a) direct personal investigation
4. (b) 200, 150
5. (a) Both Assertion (A) and Reason (R) are true and Reason (R) is the correct explanation of Assertion (A)
6. (b) Statement II is correct and Statement I is incorrect
7. (c) Non-economic activity
8. (a) qualitative classification
9. (c) exclusive method
10. (b) Production, Distribution, Consumption
12. 0.89
13. (ii) Median $= 46.74$
15. $Q_1 = 32.09$, $Q_3 = 47.70$ *Or* ₹ 12.22 lakh
16. (i) 158
17. *Or* (i) $r = 0.99$
18. (a) cardinal number
19. (a) short-run only
20. (a) (i) and (ii)
21. (d) Both are false
22. (a) mixed, controls
23. (c) Both the statements are correct
24. (a) Substitute goods
25. (c) Buy more units of X and less of Y
26. (b) MRS
27. (d) Neither (a) nor (b)
28. AP = 10, 8; MP = –, 12, 6, 2

TP = 8, 20, 30, 36, 40, 42

Or Price = 8, 7, 5; TR = 40, 42; MR = –, 2, 0, – 2

33. *Or* (i) AVC = 32, 31, 30, 30, 31, 33

TC = 92, 122, 150, 180, 215, 258

SAMPLE QUESTION PAPER 3

A Highly Simulated Sample Question Paper for CBSE Class XI Examination

ECONOMICS

Time : 3 Hours **Max. Marks : 80**

General Instructions

1. This question paper contains two sections
   Section A – Statistics for Economics Section B – Introductory Microeconomics
2. This paper contains 20 Multiple Choice Questions of 1 mark each.
3. This paper contains 4 Short Answer Questions of 3 marks each to be answered in 60 to 80 words.
4. This paper contains 6 Short Answer Questions of 4 marks each to be answered in 80 to 100 words.
5. This paper contains 4 Long Answer Questions of 6 marks each to be answered in 100 to 150 words.

Section-A
(Statistics for Economics)

1. Statistical calculations classified data are based on ………… . (1)

(a) the actual values of observations
(b) the upper class limits
(c) the lower class limits
(d) the class mid-points

2. Complete the following table (1)

Sum of Items	Number of Items	Arithmetic Mean
100	…	5
…	20	25

(a) 20, 500 (b) 500, 20
(c) 25, 200 (d) 200, 25

3. For the given distribution, which of the following is the correct relationship among mean, median and mode? (1)

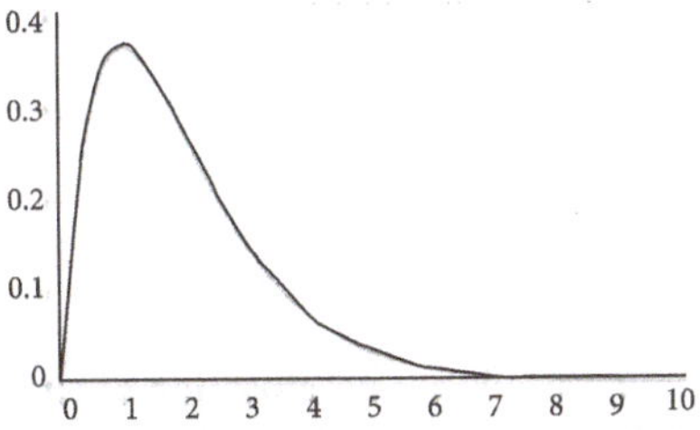

(a) Mean = Mode = Median (b) Mean > Median > Mode
(c) Mean < Median < Mode (d) Mode > Mean > Median

4. The mean of 40 numbers was found to be 38. Later on, it was detected that a number 56 was misread as 36. Find the correct mean of given numbers. (1)

(a) 38 (b) 38.5 (c) 40 (d) 42.5

5. Assertion (A) In a multi-modal series, each mode appears with equal frequency, which distinguisties it from other types of modal series.

Reason (R) A multi-modal series has more than two modes, with several values appearing with the highest frequency. (1)

Alternatives

(a) Both Assertion (A) and Reason (R) are true and Reason (R) is the correct explanation of Assertion (A)
(b) Both Assertion (A) and Reason (R) are true, but Reason (R) is not the correct explanation of Assertion (A)
(c) Assertion (A) is true, but Reason (R) is false
(d) Assertion (A) is false, but Reason (R) is true

6.

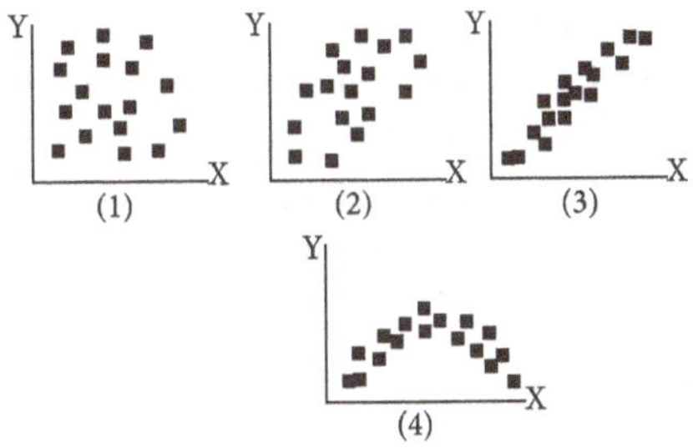

Which of the above figure shows no correlation between X and Y? (1)

(a) (1) and (2) (b) (1) and (4)
(c) (2) and (3) (d) (1), (2) and (4)

7. **Two variables are said to be positively correlated when with the ...... in the value of one variable the value of another ....** (1)

(a) rise, fall (b) rise, rise
(c) fall, rise (d) fall, fall

8. **Statement I** The second quartile (Q_2) is always equal to the fifth decile (D_5).

Statement II The sum of the first quartile (Q_1) and the third quartile (Q_3) is always twice the median (Q_2). (1)

Alternatives

(a) Statement I is correct and Statement II is incorrect
(b) Statement II is correct and Statement I is incorrect
(c) Both the statements are correct
(d) Both the statements are incorrect

9. **Multiple correlation refers to ....** (1)

(a) when the correlation is studied between three or more variables
(b) when the correlation is only studied between four variables
(c) when the correlation is only studied between two variables
(d) when the correlation is only studied between three variables

10. **Statement I** Scatter diagram method of correlation only indicates the degree of correlation.

Statement II Karl Person's method of correlation is based upon ranking method. (1)

Alternatives

(a) Statement I is correct and Statement II is incorrect
(b) Statement II is correct and Statement I is incorrect
(c) Both the statements are correct
(d) Both the statements are incorrect

11. **"Movements in prices will appear to be more or less significant, according to the year chosen for the prices of items selected. It is important, therefore, to select a year when prices were relatively stable and so years during periods either of severe inflation or deflation should be avoided."**
In this context, explain the importance of base year in the construction of index numbers. (3)

12. **Calculate the correlation coefficient between X and Y and comment on their relationship.** (3)

X	−3	−2	−1	1	2	3
Y	9	4	1	1	4	9

Or Draw three hypothetical scatter diagrams showing the following values of r.

(i) $r = -1$ (ii) $r = +1$
(iii) $r = 0$

13. **(i) Classification' and tabulation' are complementary to each other. Explain the given statement.** (3)

(ii) Identify the key advantage of tabulation over classification when it comes to presenting complex datasets. (1)

Or **"It is essential to assess various aspects when using secondary data in research. This includes evaluating the source for reliability, checking for potential biases and ensuring that the data is both current and relevant to the research objectives."**

(i) Explain how evaluating the source, checking for biases and ensuring relevance contribute to the overall quality of secondary data used in research. (2)

(ii) Discuss the potential impact of outdated or irrelevant secondary data on the conclusions of a research project. (2)

14. **In the following frequency distribution, if the arithmetic mean is 45.6, then find out missing frequency.** (4)

Class Interval	10–20	20–30	30–40	40–50	50–60	60–70	70–80
Frequency	5	6	7	?	4	3	9

15. **Two methods of statistical presentation are shown below. Briefly explain the difference between the same.** (4)

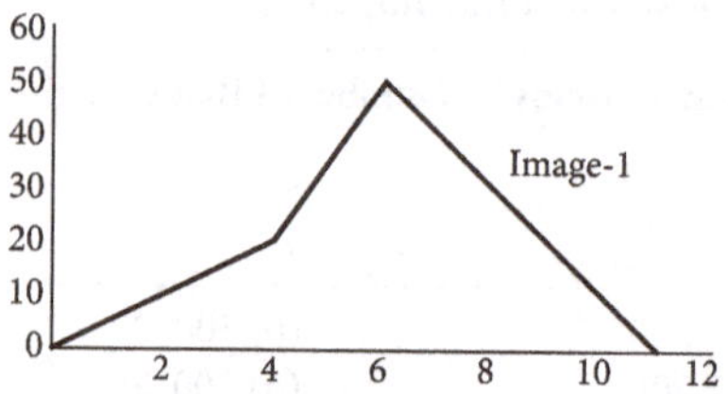

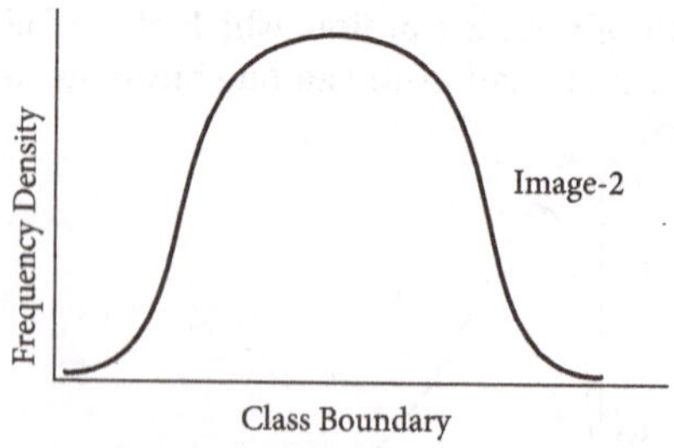

16. **"The main objective of organisation of data is to arrange the data in such a form that it becomes fairly easy to compare and analyse.**

Generally, we can do this by distributing data into various classes on the basis of some attributes or characteristics. This distribution of data into classes is the classification of data. Further each division of data is a class. All in all, through the process of classification we can group and divide data into classes according to general attribute, which facilitates comparison and analysis."

(i) Differentiate between classification of data and organisation of data. (2)

(ii) Briefly explain any four objectives of classification. (4)

17. Compute Paasche's and Laspeyre's index number from the following data. (3+3)

Commodity	Base Year		Current Year	
	Quantity	Price (₹)	Quantity	Price (₹)
A	40	4	35	3
B	15	3	20	4
C	20	6	15	5
D	30	5	25	2

Or An enquiry into the budgets of the middle-class families in a certain city gave the following information

Expenses on Items	Food (35%)	Fuel (10%)	Clothing (20%)	Rent (15%)	Miscell-aneous (20%)
Price in 2004 (in ₹)	1,500	250	750	300	400
Price in 1995 (in ₹)	1,400	200	500	200	250

What is the cost of living index of 2004 as compared with 1995? (6)

Section-B
(Introductory Microeconomics)

18. The sufficient condition of producer's equilibrium under both perfect and imperfect competition is .... (1)

(a) MR = MC (b) MR > MC
(c) MC > MR (d) None of these

19. Which of the following statements must be true for all indifference curves? (1)

(a) They can cross if consumer preferences change
(b) They always slope downward and are convex to the origin
(c) A lower indifference curve gives more satisfaction than a higher one
(d) The marginal rate of substitution remains constant along an indifference curve

20. Based upon the image given below, what is vertical distance between blue line and green line called? (1)

Fixed, Variable and Total Cost for a Hypothetical Firm

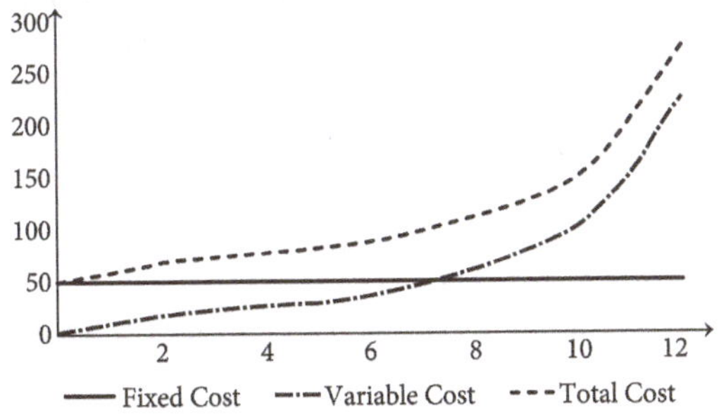

(a) Total cost
(b) Total fixed cost
(c) Total variable cost
(d) Marginal cost

21. Assertion (A) Two indifference curves cannot intersect each other as different IC represents different levels of satisfactions.

Reason (R) Indifference curve for substitute goods are downward sloping straight line. (1)

Alternatives

(a) Both Assertion (A) and Reason (R) are true and Reason (R) is the correct explanation of Assertion (A)
(b) Both Assertion (A) and Reason (R) are true, but Reason (R) is not the correct explanation of Assertion (A)
(c) Assertion (A) is true, but Reason (R) is false
(d) Assertion (A) is false, but Reason (R) is true

22. Elasticity of demand is affected by the availability of ...... and the proportion of ...... spent on the good. (1)

(a) necessities, supply (b) substitutes, income
(c) demand, cost (d) revenue, profit

23. **Statement I** Quantity demanded indicates specific quantity at specific price.

Statement II Inferior goods are an exception of law of demand. (1)

Alternatives

(a) Statement I is correct and Statement II is incorrect

(b) Statement II is correct and Statement I is incorrect

(c) Both the statements are correct

(d) Both the statements are incorrect

24. Choose the most appropriate statement from given below (1)

(i) Goods having no substitutes are elastic in nature.

(ii) Elasticity of demand is a quantitative measure of Law of demand.

(iii) Demand is said to be elastic when consumer spends more proportion of his/her income on a good.

Codes

(a) (i) and (ii) (b) (ii) and (iii)

(c) (i) and (iii) (d) (i), (ii) and (iii)

25. The market size of the toothpaste is estimated to be ₹ 10,000-₹ 12,000 cr. As of March 2020, Colgate Palmolive India Limited (CPIL) is the leader in the toothpaste market by value at 48.3%.

HUL is at a distant 16% and ranks 2nd. Dabur is catching up with HUL and has a 13.4% market share. Demand for toothpaste in Indian market is (1)

(a) elastic (b) inelastic

(c) unit elastic (d) None of these

26. If the percentage increase in the quantity of a commodity demanded is smaller than the percentage fall in its price, the coefficient of price elasticity of demand is (1)

(a) zero (b) 1

(c) more than 1 (d) less than 1

27. Statement I Marginal revenue is per unit revenue under perfect competition.

Statement II When price remains constant, average revenue and marginal revenue coincides with each other. (1)

Alternatives

(a) Statement I is correct and Statement II is incorrect

(b) Statement II is correct and Statement I is incorrect

(c) Both the statements are correct

(d) Both the statements are incorrect

28. Economists use the term demand to refer to the amount of some good or service consumers are willing and able to purchase at each price. Demand is based on needs and wants. A consumer may be able to differentiate between a need and a want, but from an economist's perspective they are the same thing. Demand is also based on ability to pay.

Based upon the above statement, differentiate between demand and quantity demanded. (3)

29. How is economics a positive science? (3)

Or Explain the major differences between the two branches of economics.

30. (i) Identify the approach of utility shown in the image below. Briefly explain any two characteristics of the same. (3)

(ii) If a product is free, will a rational consumer consume unlimited quantities? Why or why not? (1)

31. Draw Average Revenue (AR) and Marginal Revenue (MR) curves in a single diagram of a firm which can sell more units of a good only by lowering the price of that good. Explain. (4)

Or A manufacturing company produces 1,000 units and sells them at ₹ 5 each. Then the Total Revenue (TR) is ₹ 5,000. The Average Total Cost (AVC) is ₹ 7,000 with a fixed cost (FC) of ₹ 4,000 and a Variable Cost (VC) of ₹ 3,000 for all units. Evidently, this manufacturing company is operating at a loss of ₹ 2,000 (economic loss).

In economics, we assume that the fixed cost cannot be avoided. The company is obliged to pay it up regardless of whether it operates or not.

Based upon the above case, explain the difference between break-even point and shut down point.

32. (i) Briefly explain any two exceptions of law of demand. (2)

(ii) Briefly explain percentage change method of price elasticity of supply. (2)

33. (i) Establish the relationship between Marginal Cost (MC) and Average Variable Cost (AVC). (4)

(ii) Why is the Total Fixed Cost curve parallel to the horizontal axis (x-axis)? (2)

Or

State whether the following statements are true or false. Give reasons.

(i) As output increases, Average Cost (AC) tends to be closer to Average Variable Cost (AVC). (3)

(ii) When Marginal Revenue (MR) is zero, average revenue becomes maximum. (3)

34. Recent regulatory blowback against Uber, Lyft and other ridesharing services around the world have reignited the ongoing regulatory policy debate surrounding the ride service in India.

Most prominently, India's government recently enacted legislation that allows major cities to arbitrarily set limits on how much ride service companies such as Uber can charge riders during peak times.

As surge pricing often results in fares above the new price ceilings set by the Indian government resulting in supply-demand problems, a potential shortage of rides problem arises during times of peak demand.

Meanwhile, opponents against surge pricing in India argue that the fare price ceiling helps to maintain competitive fares for current cab drivers.

Source *https://www.forbes.com/sites/jonhartley/2016/05/31/indias-price-ceiling-on-uber-rides-hurts-riders-drivers-and-the-economy/?sh=134af1c32e0e*

(i) Identify the action mention in the above case. Use a well labelled diagram to explain the concept. (3)

(ii) Explain the implication of the above situation using examples taken from the case. (2)

(iii) In the case, who benefits from the price ceiling imposed on Uber rides? (1)

Answers

1. (d) the class mid-points
2. (a) 20, 500
3. (b) Mean > Median > Mode
4. (b) 38.5
5. (a) Both Assertion (A) and Reason (R) are true and (R) is the correct explanation of Assertion (A)
6. (b) (1) and (4)
7. (d) fall, fall
8. (a) Statement I is correct and Statement II is incorrect
9. (a) when the correlation is studied between three or more variables
10. (a) Statement I is correct and Statement II is incorrect
12. $r = 0$
14. 16
17. Paasche's index = 74.70; Laspeyre's index = 71.58
18. (c) MC > MR
19. (b) They always slope downward and are convex to the origin
20. (b) Total fixed cost
21. (b) Both Assertion (A) and Reason (R) are true, but Reason (R) is not the correct explanation of Assertion (A)
22. (b) substitutes, income
23. (a) Statement I is correct and Statement II is incorrect
24. (b) (ii) and (iii)
25. (a) elastic
26. (d) less than 1
27. (c) Both the statements are correct